MW01626898

The History of Men's Magazines

Volume 1: 1900 to Post-WWII

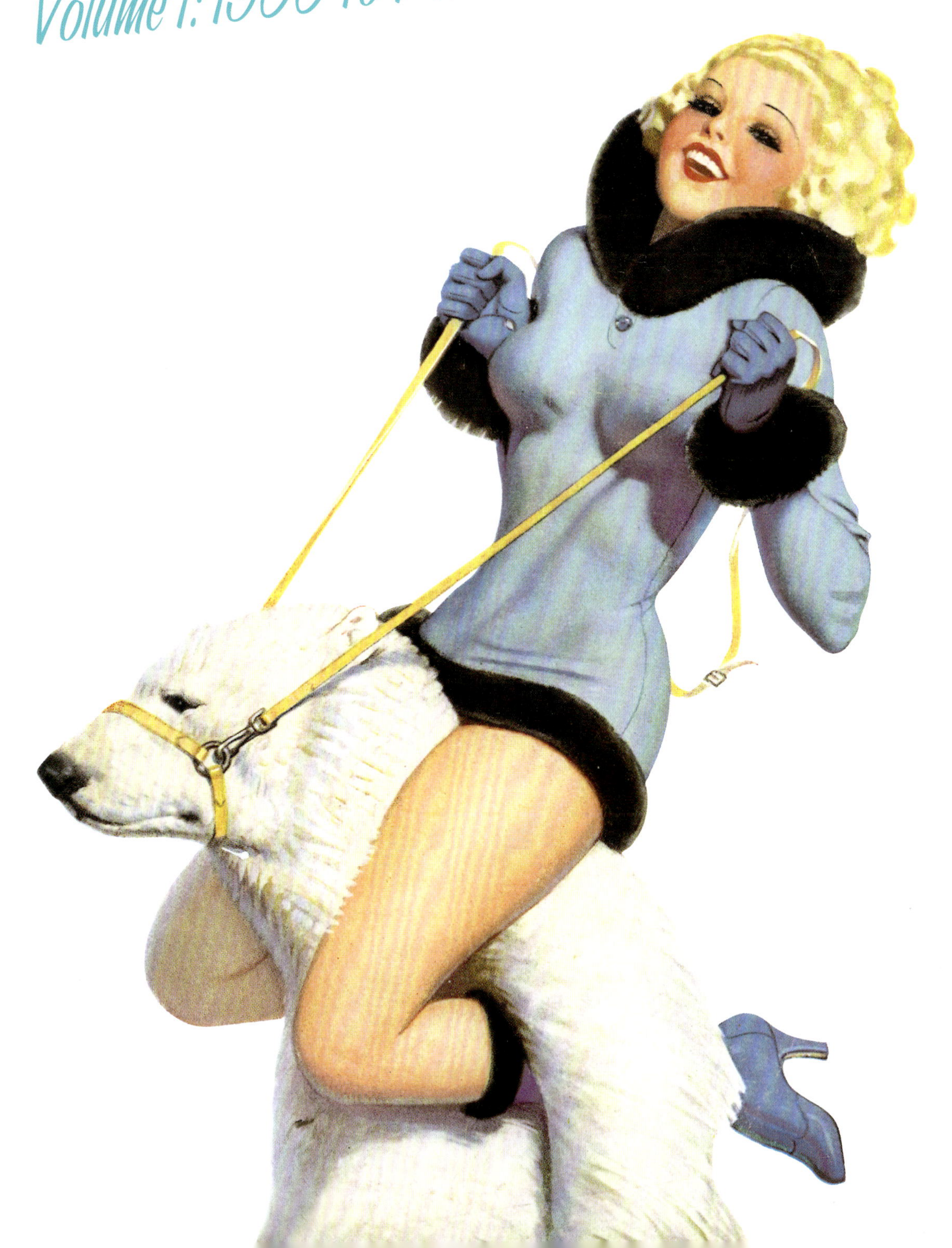

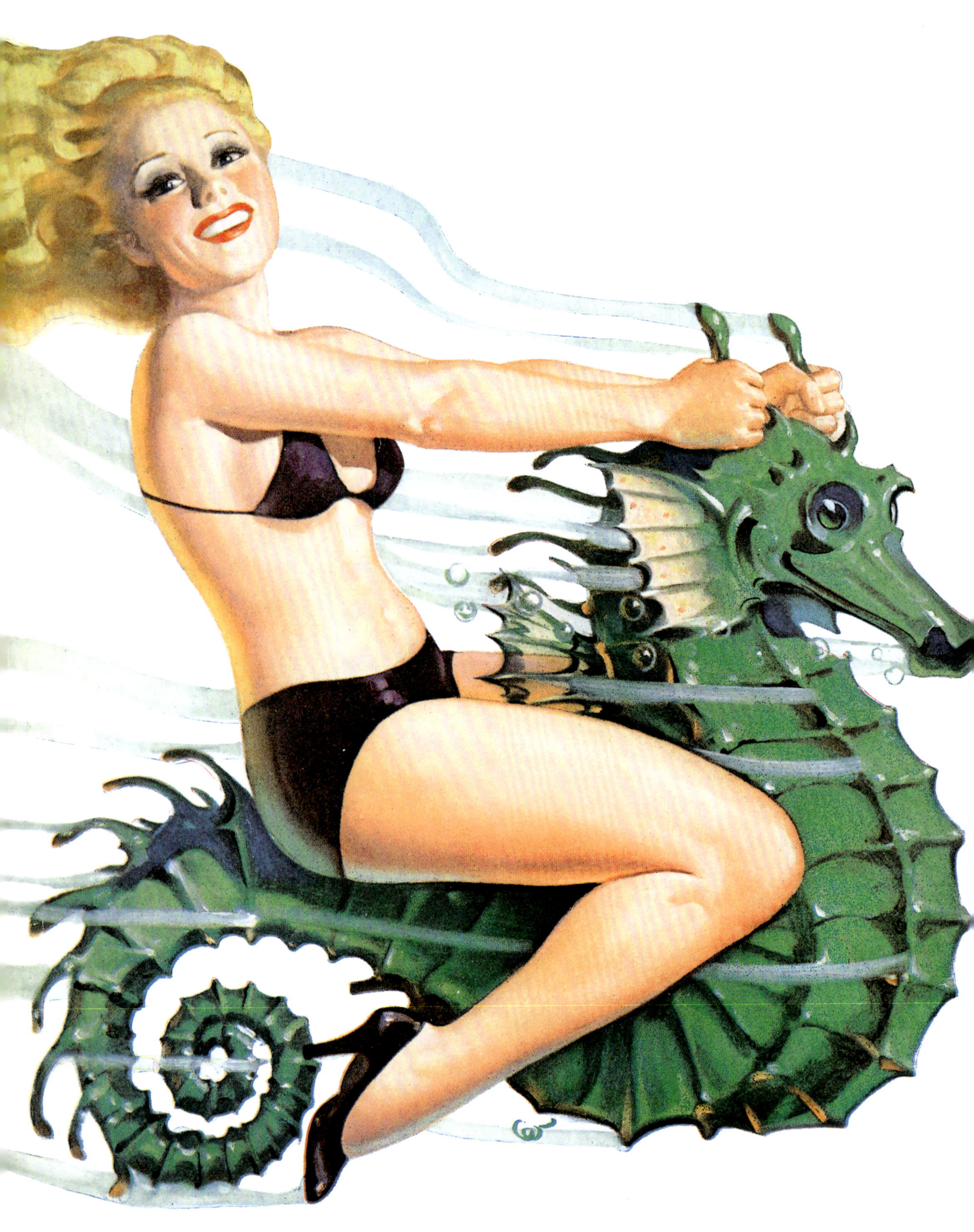

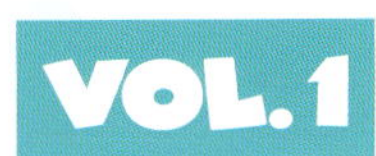

DIAN HANSON'S: THE HISTORY OF MEN'S MAGAZINES

Volume 1: 1900 to Post-WW II

TASCHEN

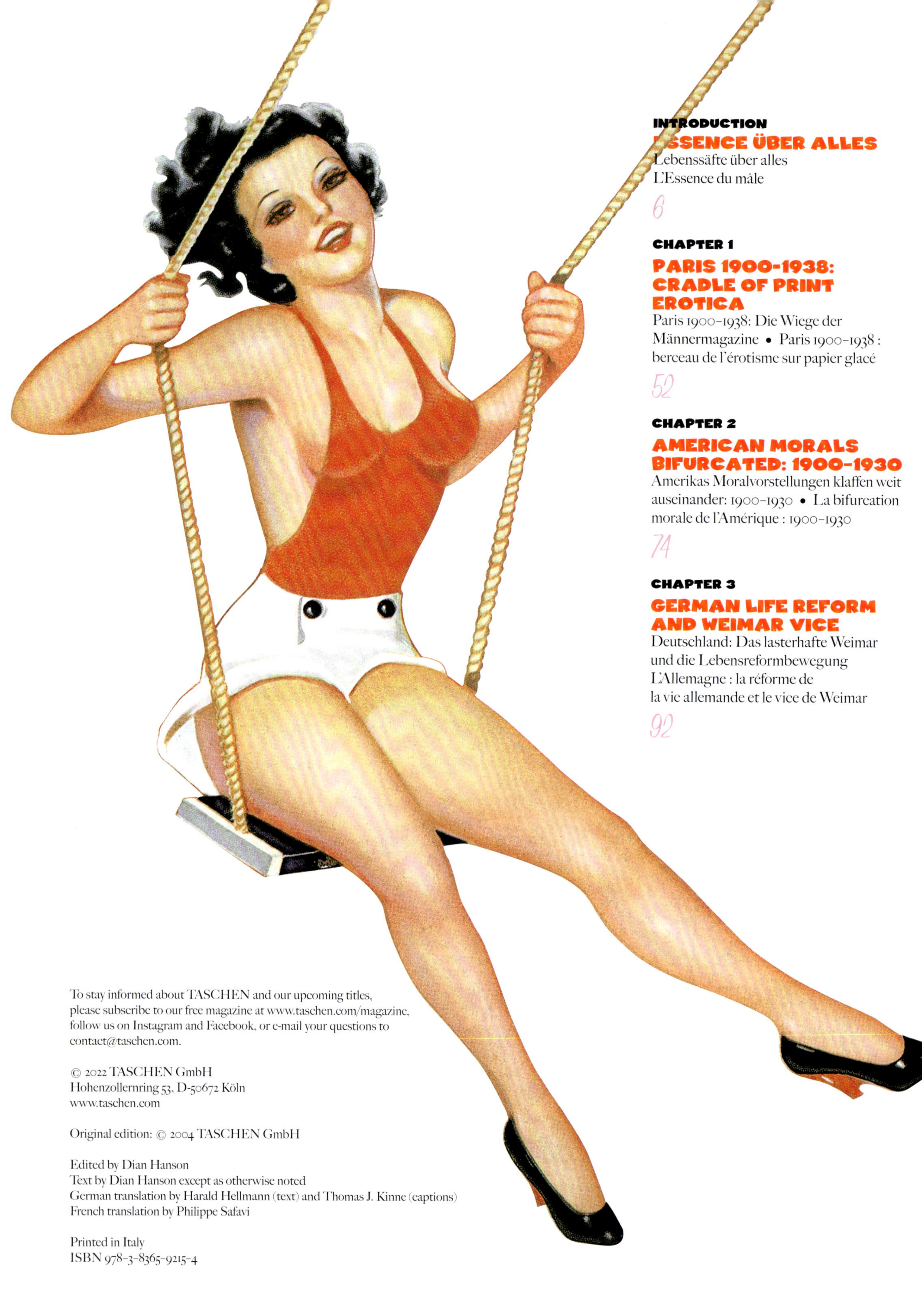

To stay informed about TASCHEN and our upcoming titles, please subscribe to our free magazine at www.taschen.com/magazine, follow us on Instagram and Facebook, or e-mail your questions to contact@taschen.com.

Hohenzollernring 53, D-50672 Köln
www.taschen.com

Edited by Dian Hanson
Text by Dian Hanson except as otherwise noted
German translation by Harald Hellmann (text) and Thomas J. Kinne (captions)
French translation by Philippe Safavi

Printed in Italy
ISBN 978-3-8365-9215-4

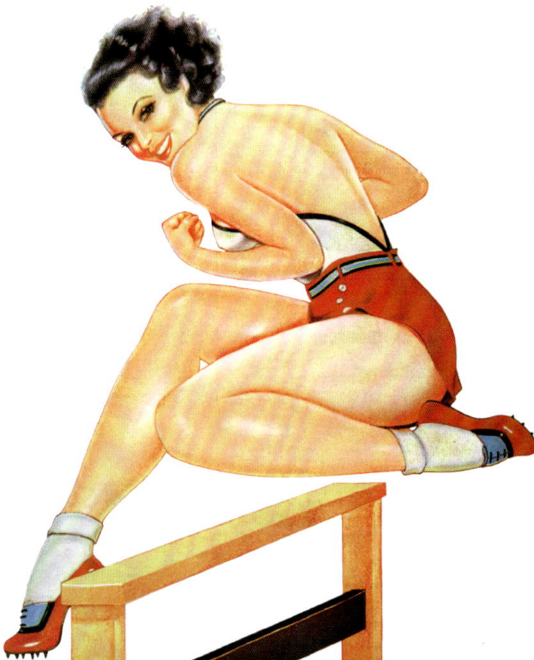

PAGE 1:
YEAR: **1933**. TITLE: **Film Fun**. COUNTRY: **USA**.
PAGE 2:
YEAR: **1936**. TITLE: **Real Screen Fun**. COUNTRY: **USA**.
PAGE 4:
YEAR: **1934**. TITLE: **Movie Humor**. ARTIST: **George Quintana**. COUNTRY: **USA**.

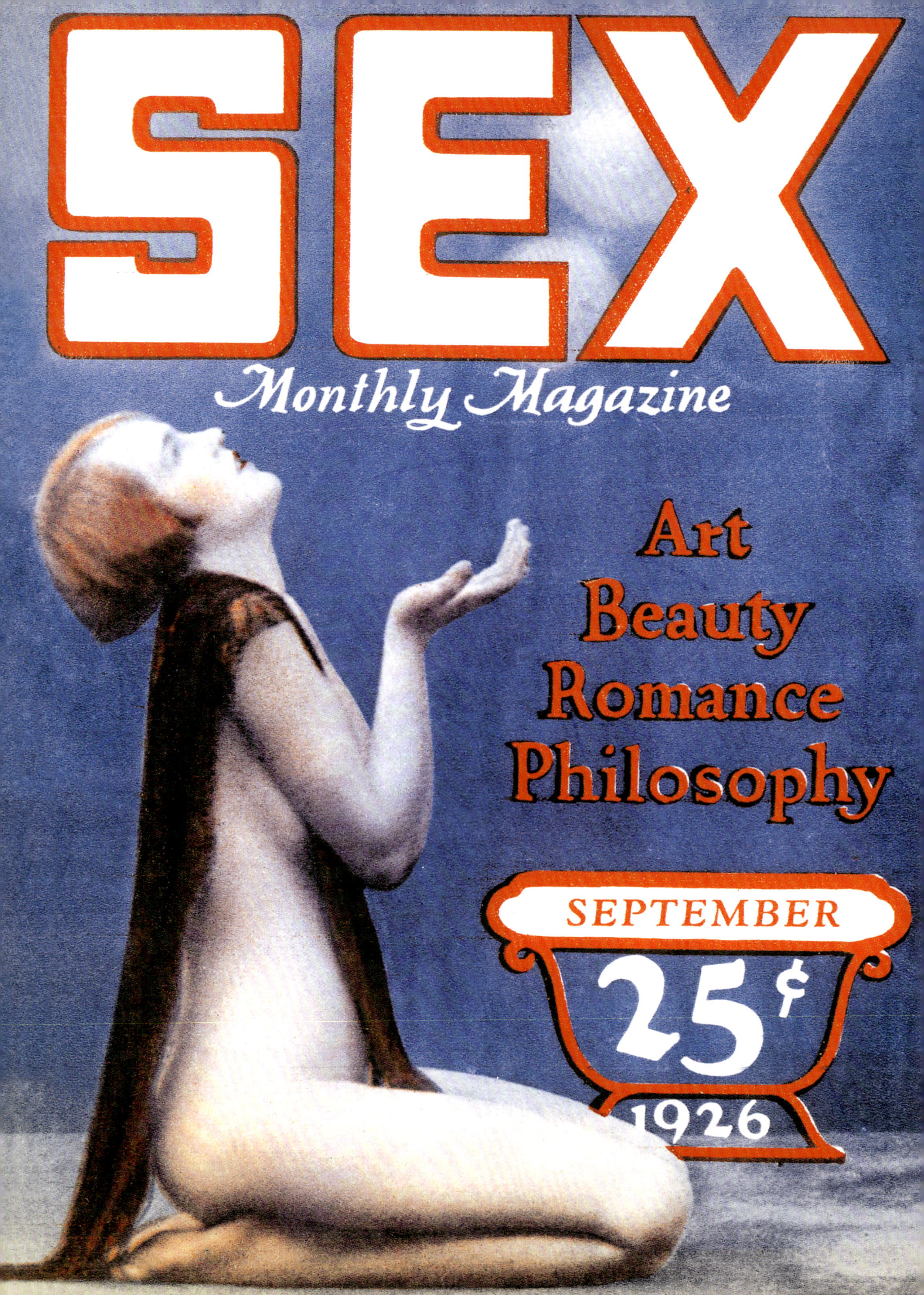
SEX
Monthly Magazine
Art
Beauty
Romance
Philosophy
SEPTEMBER
25¢
1926

Essence Über Alles

By Dian Hanson

"Sensational love stories, and even such warmly colored pictures as are presented in the *Arabian Nights* ... had better be tabooed ... All exciting literature must be renounced. Marriage need not be recommended to the confirmed masturbator in the hope of curing him of his vice. For natural intercourse he has little power or no desire; the indulgence of a depraved appetite has destroyed the natural appetite. And has a being so degraded any right to curse a child with the inheritance of such a wretched descent? Far better that the vice and its consequences die with him." *The Transmission of Life* by George H. Napheys, M.D., J.G. Fergus & Co, 1872.

Our Platform

Prevailing ignorance, prejudice, and hysteria concerning sex cause widespread misery, error and unhappiness.

We oppose the conspiracy of silence on the subject of sex because not ignorance but understanding will safeguard morals and happiness.

Likewise we oppose the conspiracy of shame whereby the beautiful and God-ordained fact of sex has been made to appear horrible and vile.

We oppose the conspiracy of repression because psychoanalysis has clearly shown that to repress an impulse does not kill it but produces nervousness, morbidness, depression, shame, a sense of inferiority, sickness and insanity.

When rationalized, frankly faced and understood, sex energy may be sublimated and used up in constructive activities leading to splendid achievement.

Conventions, customs and morals change from place to place and from time to time. Those who fail to accept any particular set of standards should not be condemned if they are sincere, considerate and constructive.

Marriage is the safest solution of the sex problem but now largely fails thru ignorance of sex laws and technique. The problem of happy marriage should be studied and discussed.

The human body is not immoral but beautiful and should be reverenced, appreciated and enjoyed. The nude in art may be beautifully and spiritually presented.

Promiscuous sex relationship leads to restless discontent, interferes with success, destroys happiness and endangers health and is not to be advocated as a solution.

Free love as generally conceived is virtually synonymous with promiscuity and hence will probably fail as a solution of the sex problem.

Yet love must be free and spontaneous—there is no worse immorality than to compel a man and woman to live together when they do not love each other.

We are in the midst of an almost universal revolt against the fading sex taboos and puritanic sex repression. This revolt needs to be guided in safe and sane channels. Excesses and extremes breed anarchy. Sex must be rationalized, studied, controlled and wisely directed.

This magazine proposes to supply sane, sound and clean discussion of this subject more important to human health, happiness and advancement than any other social problem.

Our program does not condone the salacious, suggestive, morbid sensationalism so current in certain contemporary magazines and daily papers. We propose to face the truth bravely, frankly, constructively, hoping to make a real contribution to social good.

YEAR: **1926**. TITLE: **Sex**. COUNTRY: **USA**.

Sex publishing has always been a battleground. On the one hand there were men, mentally and physically hardwired to respond to erotic images. On the other hand, other men, determined to deprive the first group of what they naturally desired. The first two volumes tracing the history of men's magazines are about the struggle between lust and taboo, beginning with the first bare French breasts in 1880 and ending with bare American breasts in 1958. It's amazing that it took 60 years to get photographs of topless women accepted on America's newsstands and on newsstands in most of the rest of the world, and that every step leading up to this small victory represented hundreds of obscenity arrests, years of collective court and prison time and millions of dollars and Deutschmarks and Kronen and Pesos, all spent in the futile attempt to keep men's eyes off the female body. When Dr. Napheys was writing about the effects of stimulating literature back in 1872 it was with the belief that men were born with all the "male essence" they would ever possess. Male essence wasn't just for procreation back then; a man who squandered his seed in self-abuse would soon waste his whole reserve, and with it would go his physical strength, his intellectual powers, his moral fortitude and his mind, in roughly that order. Dr. Napheys was one of the gentler doomsayers in his recommended treatment for this evil—he thought most men could be cured by simple blistering of the offending parts and that castration, recommended by many of his fellow physicians, was seldom necessary.

Most of the Victorian frenzy over sexy literature came from the degeneracy theories of Dr. Simon Tissot, a Swiss physician who studied the feminizing effects of castration on men in the mid-1700s and decided—incorrectly—that loss of semen was to blame. Compounding his error, he theorized that excessive masturbation would have the same effect on a man with a full testicular complement. This makes it particularly strange that castration became a treatment for intractable masturbation, but by then moralists all over Northern Europe and the US had lost sight of the point and were just bent on stamping out pleasure. In this crusade the camera and printing press were increasingly viewed as handmaids of Satan.

The camera was invented in the 1830s. In 1839 the first crude negative was invented, allowing multiple copies of a single image to be produced. By 1865

YEAR: **1926**. TITLE: **Sex**. COUNTRY: **USA**.

By 1865 camera and negative technology were sufficiently advanced that they could be mastered by ordinary men—who promptly began taking and distributing photos of naked women.

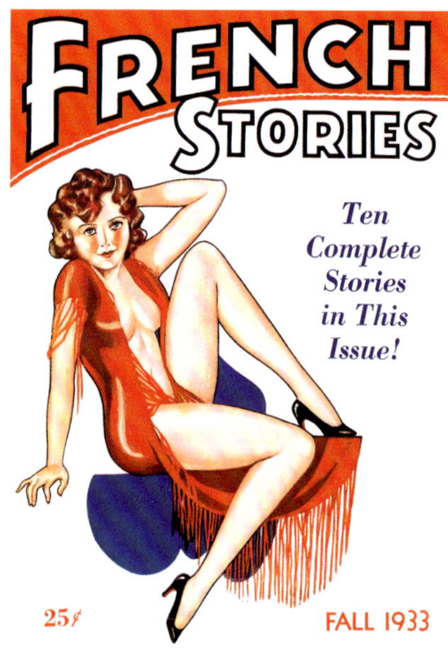

YEAR: **1933**. TITLE: **French Stories**. COUNTRY: **USA**.

camera and negative technology were sufficiently advanced that they could be mastered by ordinary men—who promptly began taking and distributing photos of naked women.

At the same time printing technology was improving, spurred by an increase in literacy. Prior to the Victorian era many people lived in the country, worked as farmers and were functionally illiterate. The Industrial Revolution brought the farmers, along with new immigrants, to the cities and into factories. The resulting working-class ghettos, with their crime, prostitution and high child mortality, eventually led to social reforms, including better education for all.

When only the upper classes read demand for print was limited, so books and magazines were made in small quantity, keeping them costly. With widespread literacy, reading for pleasure became a working-class fad. Publishers hastened to increase their output to meet the growing demand for a new kind of reading matter. Expensive hardbound books were beyond the average wage earner's means, but cheap magazines and magazine-like "dime novels" filled the bill. In America these publications focused on action stories of the Wild West, true crime and romance fiction. In England and France detective fiction was equally popular.

As early as 1860 more explicit "romance" publications appeared in New York. Sold clandestinely and in small quantity they were produced for years with no one taking much notice, until 1868, when they came to the attention of a young bookkeeper named Anthony Comstock. That Comstock had a special problem with what most men enjoy was clear from the start. A sample of his opinions on sexy literature:

"The effect of this cursed business on our youth and society, no pen can describe. It breeds lust. Lust defiles the body, debauches the imagination, corrupts the mind, deadens the will, destroys the memory, sears the conscience, hardens the heart and damns the soul. It unnerves the arm and steals away the elastic step. It robs the soul of manly virtues, and imprints upon the mind of the youth visions that throughout life curse the man or the woman. Like a panorama, the imagination seems to keep this hated thing before the mind, until it wears its way deeper and deeper, plunging the victim into practices that he loathes. This traffic has made rakes and libertines in society—skeletons in many a household. The family is polluted, the home desecrated, and each generation born into the world is more and more cursed by the inherited weakness, the harvest of this seed-sowing of the Evil One." Comstock wasted no time in smiting the Evil One in his own neighborhood; he rounded up a group of Irishmen he accused of producing pornography and demanded the police jail them. That started a life-long campaign against sexual literature that would lead to a pivotal law used to prosecute American publishers to this day. Comstock, with the backing of the Young Men's Christian Association (YMCA), lobbied the US government so long and hard that they finally gave this civilian bookkeeper power over the American postal service.

Why? Because along with the sin rampant in his Brooklyn neighborhood, Comstock had detected a flood of vile obscenity flowing into the US from across the sea, which was then being dispersed to vulnerable innocents via the US mail.

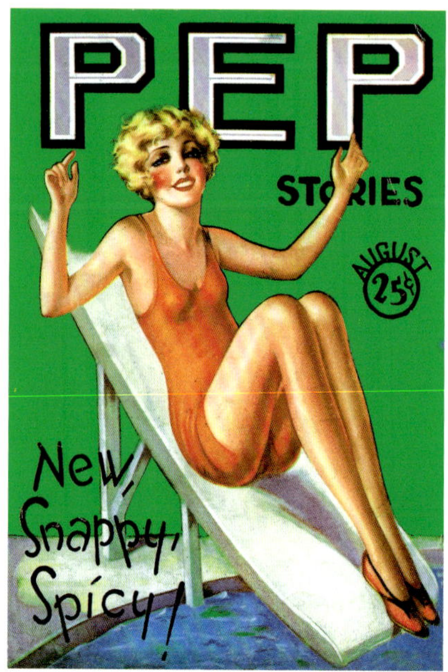

YEAR: **1928**. TITLE: **Pep Stories**. COUNTRY: **USA**.

YEAR: **1931**. TITLE: **La Paree**. ARTIST: **G. Greiner**. COUNTRY: **USA**.

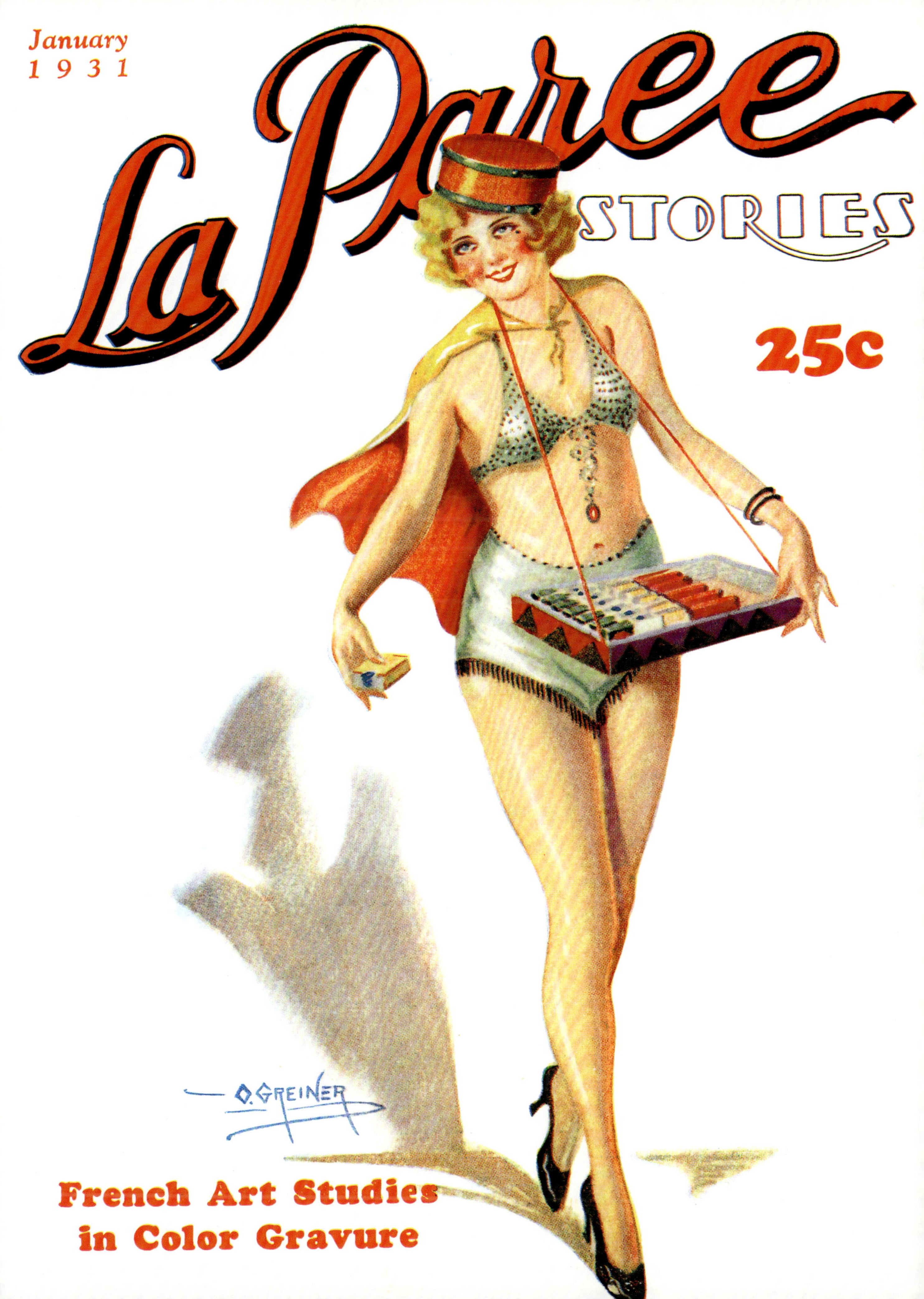
January
1931
La Paree
STORIES
25c
O. GREINER
French Art Studies
in Color Gravure

Year: **1931**. Title: **"Real Smart"**. Artist: **G. Greiner**. Country: **USA**.

Anthony Comstock convinced the US government that the new obscene literature from abroad put America's collective male essence in imminent peril.

He would not rest until he had taught the Europeans not to mess with America's male essence.

The French were leaders from the start in the photographic arts and by the late 1860s they were perfecting ways of printing naughty photographs. French postcards and playing cards were created at this time and were an immediate hit with men everywhere. Accordingly, in the 1870s the French produced the earliest men's magazines in the form of programs for Parisian cabarets that included photographs of bare-breasted dancers. When American men got wind of these advances they were understandably eager to augment their education with French studies. A few of the more enterprising entered the import trade.

With the support of experts like Dr. Napheys, Reverend Sylvester Graham of Graham cracker fame and John Harvey Kellogg, breakfast cereal inventor, enema enthusiast and rabid semen conservationist, Comstock convinced the US government that the new obscene literature from abroad put America's collective male essence in imminent peril. His passion for the suppression of passion was so convincing that in 1873 they adopted what has come to be called The Comstock Law. Its, ah, essence:

"That no obscene, lewd or lascivious book, pamphlet, picture, paper, print, or other publication of an indecent character, or any article or thing designed or intended for the prevention of contraception, or procuring of abortion, nor any article or thing intended or adapted for any indecent or immoral use or nature, nor any written or printed card, circular, book, pamphlet, advertisement or notice of any kind giving information directly or indirectly, where, or how, or of whom, or by what means either of the things before mentioned may be obtained or made, nor any letter upon the envelope of which, or postal-card upon which indecent or scurrilous epithets may be written or printed, shall be carried in the mail..." The Comstock Law put quite a crimp in the dissemination of early sexual materials in America, but the publicity surrounding its passage—contained in the newly available magazines and tabloid newspapers—also alerted the public to the existence of such literature. Most men hadn't even imagined that these things existed, but once they knew, and knew how much—Comstock claimed that literally tons

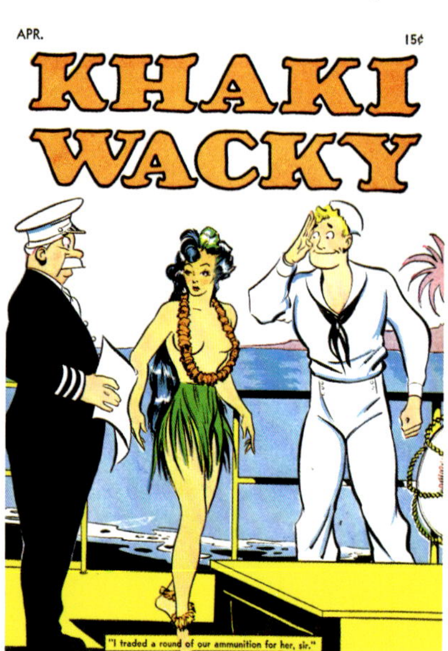

Year: **1942**. Title: **Khaki Wacky**. Country: **USA**.

were being shipped into the country—they wanted it.

There would still be no real men's magazines published in America until after World War I, but risqué tabloids began to appear in the 1880s and 90s, and books, photos and playing cards still managed to sneak through customs, despite the best efforts of Anthony Comstock and various newly formed citizens' vice committees. As the volume of "men's interest" literature grew, it became increasingly clear that a large segment of the public had viewed and was viewing this material without becoming physically wasted, imbecilic or insane. In *The Secret Museum* (University of California Press, 1987) Walter Kendrick notes that by the 1890s American courts were increasingly considering artistic merit when making obscenity determinations. Accordingly, in 1894 a case involving copies of *The Arabian Nights*, Ovid's *Art of Love* and Boccaccio's *Decameron* was thrown out because the Society for the Suppression of Vice found them to be "world renowned classics... unlikely to be sold or purchased, except by those who would desire them for their literary merit..."

This understanding was not extended to publishers catering to a less distinguished clientele: "In 1896, The United States Supreme Court reviewed two lower court convictions on obscenity charges. The first involved Lew Rosen, publisher of Broadway, an illustrated paper with no pretenses to classic stature. The special 'Tenderloin Issue' had contained patches of lampblack, which could be rubbed off with a piece of bread to reveal 'females in different attitudes of indecency'... The Supreme Court upheld this conviction..."

I tried hard to find this choice example of early American erotica, without luck; but I imagine even when it does show up, finding a copy that hasn't been

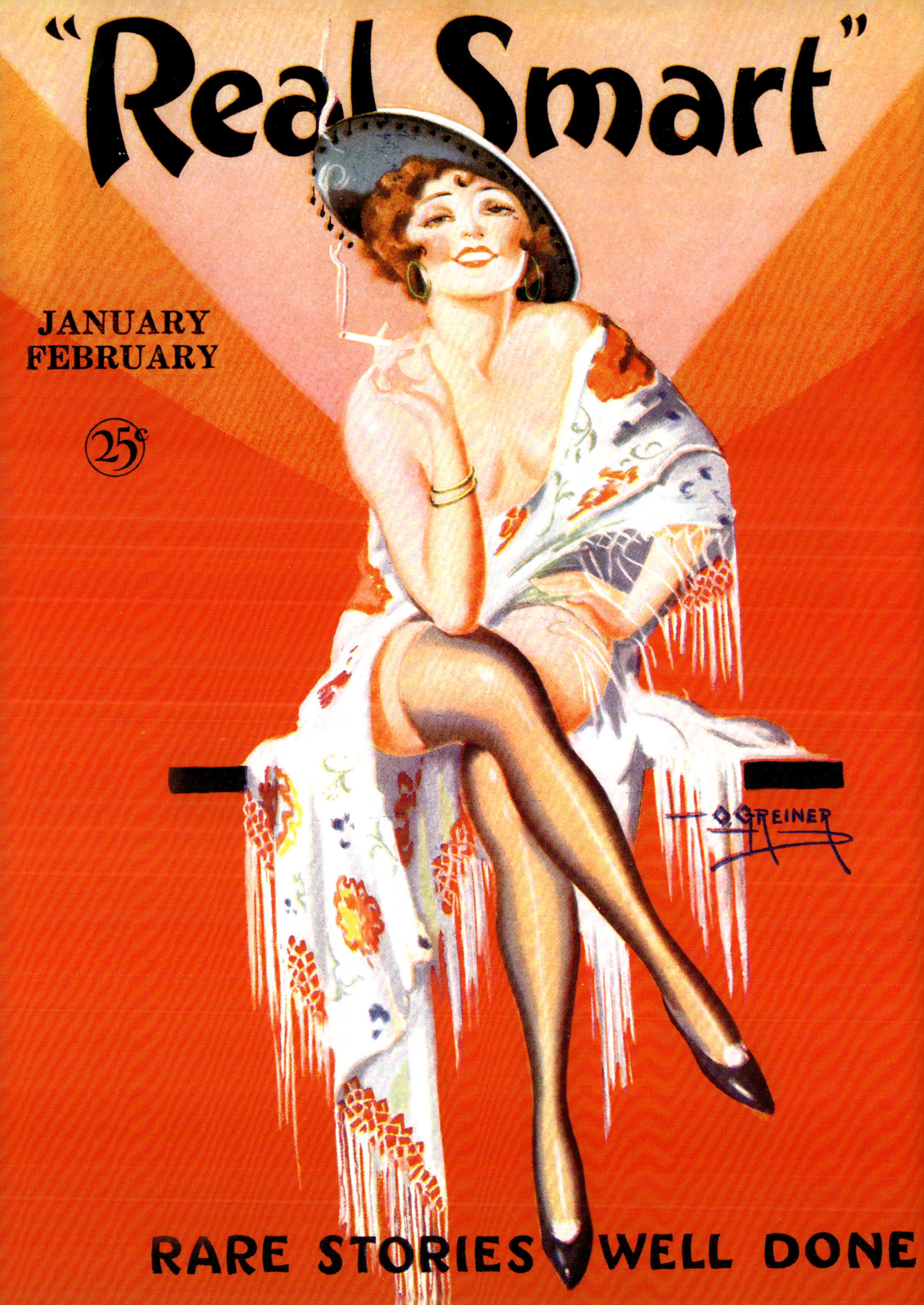
"Real Smart"
JANUARY
FEBRUARY
25¢
O. GREINER
RARE STORIES WELL DONE

YEAR: **1934**. TITLE: **Screen Humor**. ARTIST: **Cardwell Higgins**. COUNTRY: **USA**.

By the time the Weimar Republic fell in 1933 there were hundreds of magazine titles in Germany that included nudity as part of dozens of philosophical packages, none of which admitted (they were for) sexual titillation.

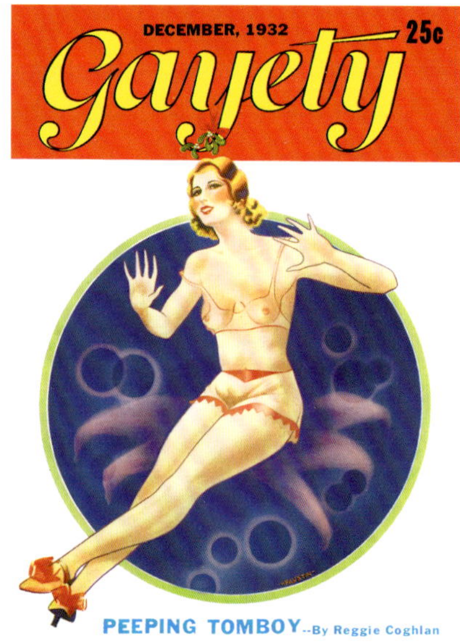

YEAR: **1932**. TITLE: **Gayety**. COUNTRY: **USA**.

"breaded" is pretty much impossible. Publisher Rosen was one of the first of what would become an American cliché: the urban Jewish pornographer. Most of these early erotic entrepreneurs were immigrants from Eastern Europe with strong literary backgrounds, limited means of making a living in the new world and none of the dreary Christian anhedonia that dogged men like Comstock. In time the American men's magazine industry would be nicknamed "The Jewish Mafia," but in 1900 it was just a handful of New York ghetto dwellers, often helped by their wives and children, making porn to make ends meet.

It was around this time, the late 1890s, that pulp paper was introduced. This would soon become a great boon to the budding men's magazine industry and to the print-hungry public. Prior to pulp, all paper was made of rag—often literally recycled cotton clothing—whitened with clay. Paper such as this provides beautiful reproduction and is extremely durable; books printed on it can last hundreds of years. It is also comparatively expensive to produce and makes little sense for printing cheap, disposable magazines upon. Still, until 1890, this is what most magazines were printed on, while newspapers were on thin, so-called newsprint. Pulp paper came out of the new western timber industry. Made of wood fiber softened with acid, it was sturdier than newsprint, far cheaper to make than rag, and essentially self-destructing, as the acids used in its production quickly consumed it. Pulp was too coarse for good image reproduction, but just perfect for the kind of cheap fiction much in demand at the turn of the century. From 1900 through the 1950s hundreds of millions of lurid and sensational novels and fiction magazines on subjects including detectives, western adventure, romance, science fiction and sex, would be affordably delivered to the public on cheap pulp paper. To give the titles newsstand appeal the inferior internal pages were wrapped in a glossy, vividly painted cover, usually featuring a voluptuous woman in skimpy clothing, even when the subject was sci-fi or romance. "Pulps," as the whole genre came to be called, catered to thrill-seekers of both sexes, at a time when photographic thrills were heavily censored.

Meanwhile, in turn-of-the-century France, words were more likely to be prosecuted than photos, if those photos pretended to be art. The French had historically held art in higher regard than the Americans and were above being alarmed by a bit of bosom. They pioneered the "nude study" art magazine, which showed completely naked women, when America was still scrubbing lampblack with bread for a peek at a stocking top. There was considerably more censorship of magazines that admitted their purpose was titillation, but *La Vie Parisienne*, founded in 1863 and relaunched just before World War I, managed to mix discreet nudes with spicy fiction and humor and still gain wide spread acceptance because it was reasonably sophisticated, a quality nearly as respected in France as art.

Germany was the third country preparing for a rich erotic future in 1900, while struggling with its own peculiar moral issues. The degenerative effects of recreational masturbation were widely publicized there as in America, but Germany had the counter-force of Sigmund Freud warning that sexual repression was just as dangerous. There was also the issue of Germany's Industrial Revolution, which brought undesirables into the country and ill health upon its citizens. This inspired a fast-growing eugenics cult and the rise of early socialism. Out of this stew came the Beauty Movement and its magazines, worshipping all that was lovely, but particularly young, naked female Aryan bodies. As in France, it was all in the context; nudity was accepted when presented asexually. Of course, as any boy will tell you who's ever taken pleasure from the underwear ads in the catalogue for Victoria's Secret or in fact, that of Sears, context is crap; but if we assume many censors through the ages have been consciously or unconsciously in on the game—that they, in fact, want to see nudes as much as any man but can't admit it—then we see what an ally context has been for all

SCREEN HUMOR

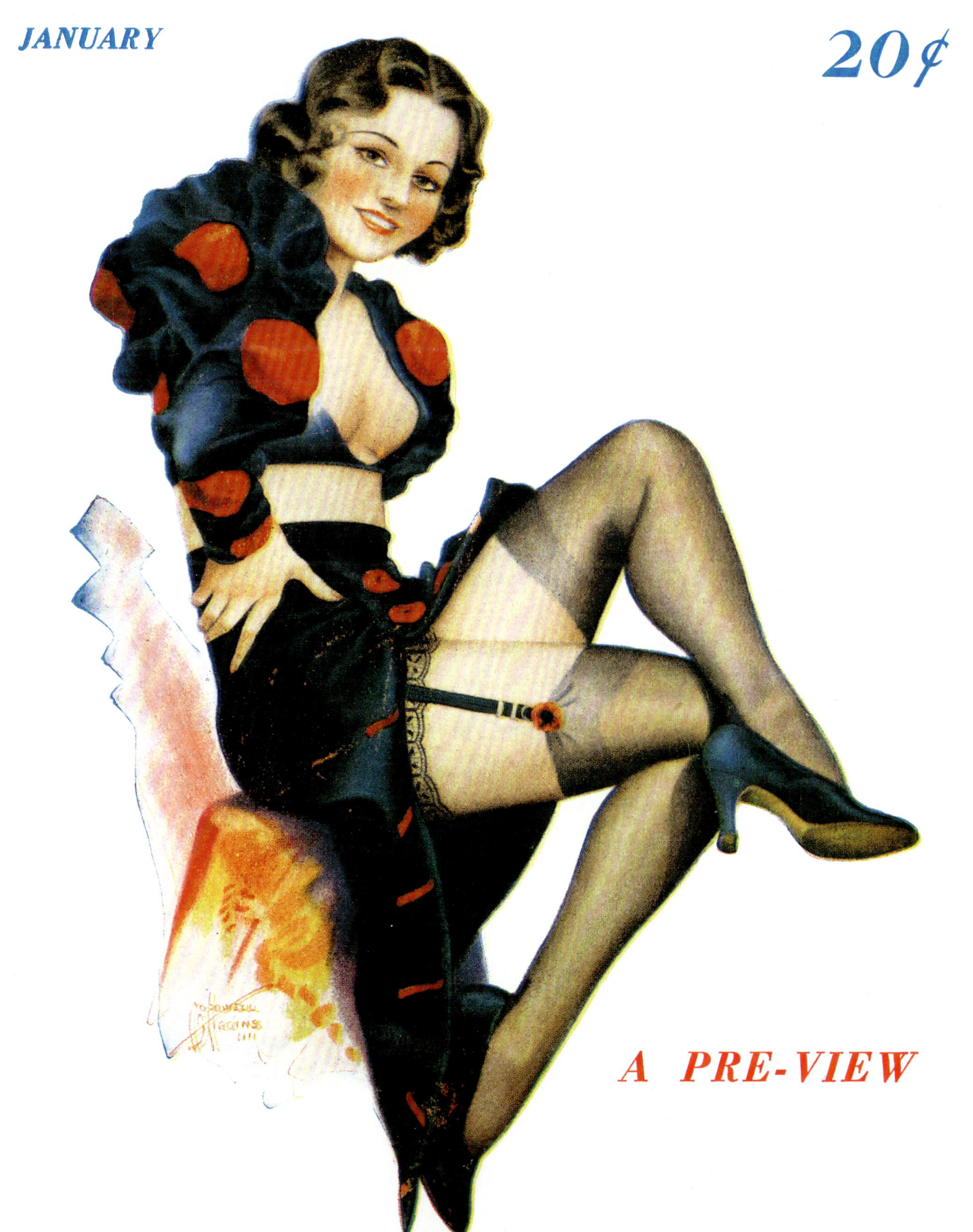

Year: **1944**. Title: **Gay Book**. Country: **USA**.

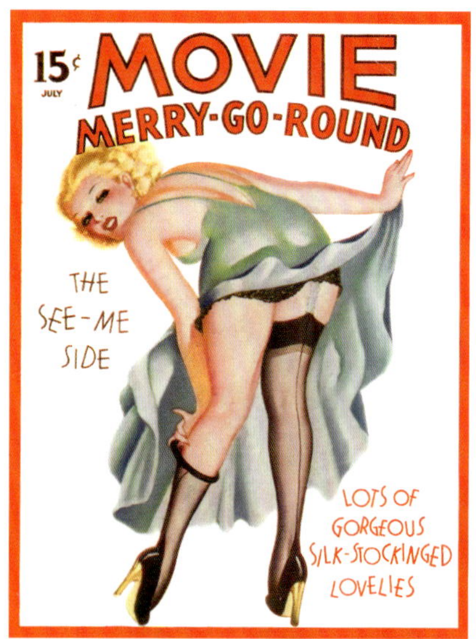

Year: **1937**. Title: **Movie Merry-Go-Round**. Country: **USA**.

concerned. In Germany the concept of context vis-à-vis nudity would be tested as nowhere else in the first three decades of the 20th century. When the Weimar Republic fell in 1933, there were hundreds of magazine titles in Germany that included nudity as part of dozens of philosophical packages, none of which admitted sexual titillation as any part of their purpose.

As the century progressed publishers in England, Sweden, Argentina, Japan, Mexico, Denmark and other nations would join the assault on male essence—and male essence would prove itself equal to it all. In rigorous and often vigorous self-testing men made it clear that no number of sensational love stories or warmly colored pictures could make the male well run dry. This did take many more years than most would imagine; eugenics, the 20th century's answer to Tissot's degeneracy theories, found adherents in many countries and would not fall into disgrace until The Third Reich twisted it to their purposes in the early 1940s. In 1928, Safe Council or Practical Eugenics by Dr. B.G. Jefferis still cautioned: "Boys are sometimes strongly tempted to buy and to pass around among themselves pictures representing the body without proper clothing or even the relations of sex. You simply cannot afford to let the unclean picture get itself stamped upon your mind. It does not fade away. Long years after you saw it, and probably long after sentences that you have heard on the subject are quite forgotten, you will remember the picture. I have heard men say that they would give any sum of money that they could command if they might wipe off their memory some foul picture that they saw and brooded upon when they were boys."

I wasn't there, so I can't argue with the good doctor, but during the more than two years collecting the material for this book I have also spent a few (dozen) days in the Mature Audiences section of the Ebay Internet auction site. With the dubious authority that confers, I can attest that many men will give any sum of money they can command to buy that picture they brooded upon as boys.

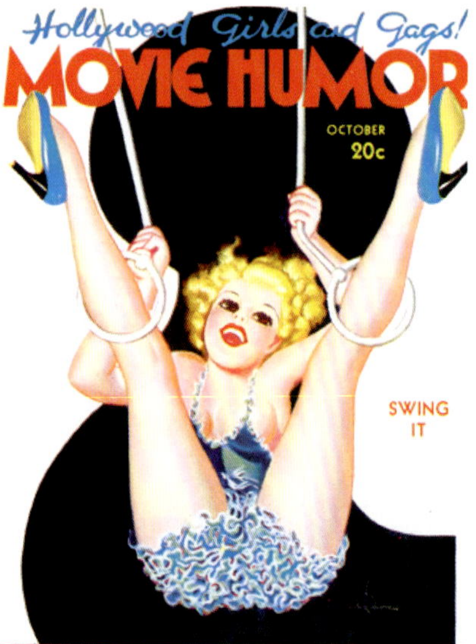

Year: **1935**. Title: **Movie Humor**. Country: **USA**.

If you're old enough you may find some of your own cherished memories in these books, but no matter what your age, you'll find things that amuse, amaze, inform and yes, stir the essence from the early days of men's magazines. In the beginning this was supposed to be a two-book project, starting in 1945 and ending in 1980. As I began prowling used magazine stores, talking to collectors and spending the first of many 12-hour days on Ebay, I saw the start date had to be pushed back. I finally settled on 1900, then came upon the French "folies" program from the 1880s. The project grew from two to three volumes and finally to six, and yet there were always more titles than could ever be accommodated. I've done what I could to get correct information on the magazines and those who made them in the short year I worked on this, but inevitably, given the secrecy with which much of these were produced, some of my facts will prove false; let me apologize up front. No apologies are needed for the magazines. The creativity lavished on these early men's titles puts everything made now to shame. But then I imagine you've already noticed that, as not even Anthony Comstock could have mustered the willpower to read this long-winded introduction before enjoying the photos that follow.

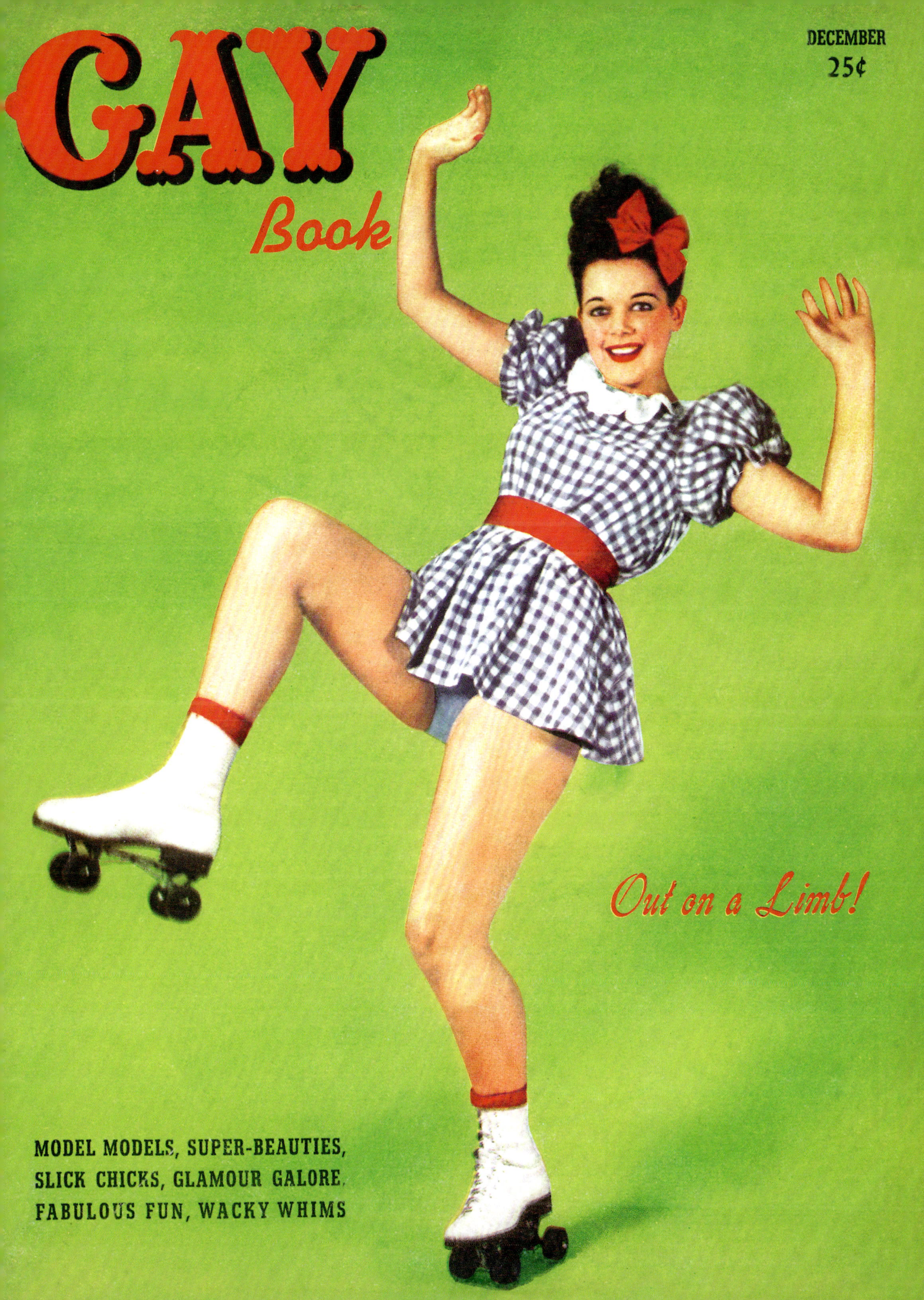
GAY
Book
DECEMBER
25¢
Out on a Limb!
MODEL MODELS, SUPER-BEAUTIES,
SLICK CHICKS, GLAMOUR GALORE,
FABULOUS FUN, WACKY WHIMS

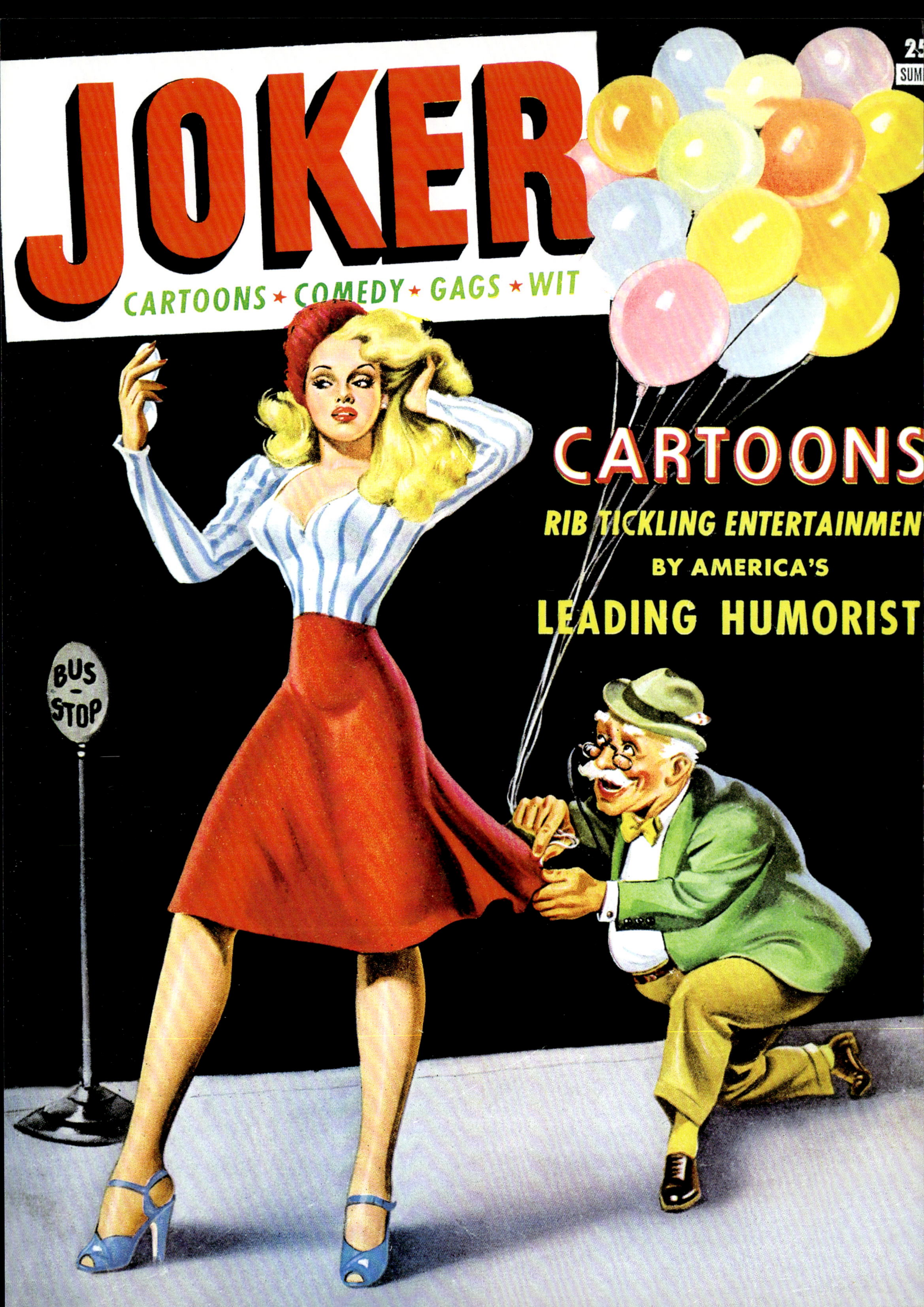

JOKER
CARTOONS ★ COMEDY ★ GAGS ★ WIT
CARTOONS
RIB TICKLING ENTERTAINMEN
BY AMERICA'S
LEADING HUMORIST
BUS - STOP

DISTRIBUTION:

How Men's Magazines Got to the Masses

By Michael Feldman

When we confront a rack bulging with the seemingly endless product variations with which publishers compete for our attention, a question that is rarely asked is: How do these magazines get here? And the corollary: Who put them there?

In 1864, a consolidation of New York City's two largest distributors formed the American News Company. The first continental distribution system, American News, maintained a powerful monopoly on what periodicals were made available. They established thousands of outlets at high traffic junctures, railroad stations and, later, bus terminals, plus hundreds of warehouses in key locations.

Expediting nationwide availability, the US Federal Government, initially to ensure freedom of the press, allowed newspapers and anything else that qualified as a periodical to obtain a subsidized rate to travel on the rapidly expanding railway system. This made transporting a magazine or newspaper, sometimes as far as 3,200 miles, economically viable. Enterprising publishers of less than pure news were immediately apprised of this enormous advantage and one of the US Post Office's earliest Second Class Mailing Permits was issued in 1879 to The Police Gazette.

This so-called newspaper became late 19th-century America's number one source of information on the seamy side of life, graphically enriched by risqué photographs of semi-clothed ladies.

The first challenge to ANC's stranglehold came when Frank Munsey, the progenitor of the American pulp magazine, decided he wanted his mass-audience fiction magazines available on newsstands.

Munsey's competitive cover price, a mere $.10 compared to the $.25 to $.50 norm, was considered too low for American News, and they rejected him. Undaunted, he set up *Red Star News*, America's first completely independent magazine distribution company. Success was almost immediate.

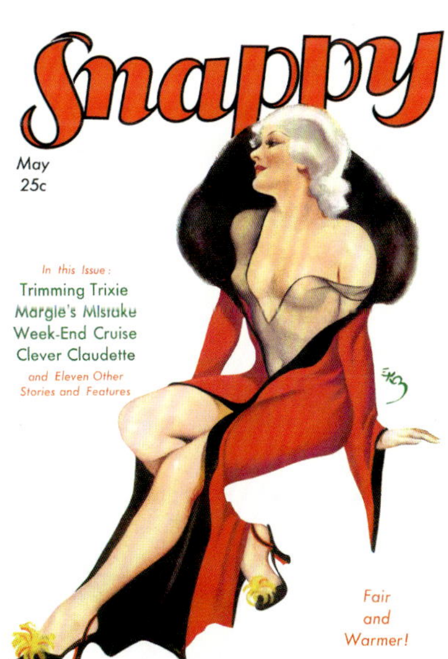

Year: **1935**. Title: **Snappy**. Country: **USA**.

Other print purveyors followed suit. Newspaper magnate William Randolph Hearst established a distribution system for his papers and for a growing magazine line. A series of big city newspaper circulation wars ensued in the 1920s, with delivery truck drivers carrying shotguns. In this volatile period, archetypal mobster-distributor and strong-arm circulation director for Hearst, M.L. Annenberg, created an efficient continental infrastructure just for the dissemination of his own specialized product—the daily horse racing forms. Speed and timeliness were introduced as necessary components of regular and reliable magazine availability.

A flood of other independent publisher-distributors had arrived in the 20s with new product lines, many too hot for conservative ANC to handle. One was Wilford Fawcett's *Capt. Billy's Whiz Bang*—originally a single sheet of dirty military jokes that quickly evolved into America's first risqué humor magazine. Fawcett developed a strong line of new magazines and a parallel distribution arm.

The Independent Distributors, or IDs, grew in size and number through the 1920s, fueled by circulation-hungry publishers wanting to circumvent the complacent *American News*.

Year: **1943**. Title: **Joker**. Country: **USA**.

Year: **1941**. Title: **Squads Riot**. Country: **USA**.

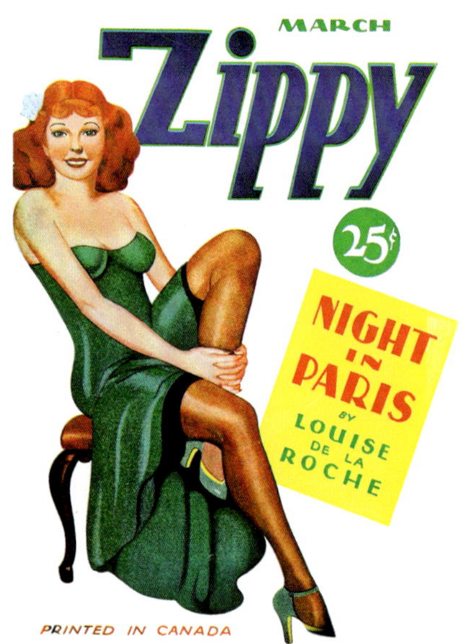

Year: **1939**. Title: **Zippy**. Country: **USA**.

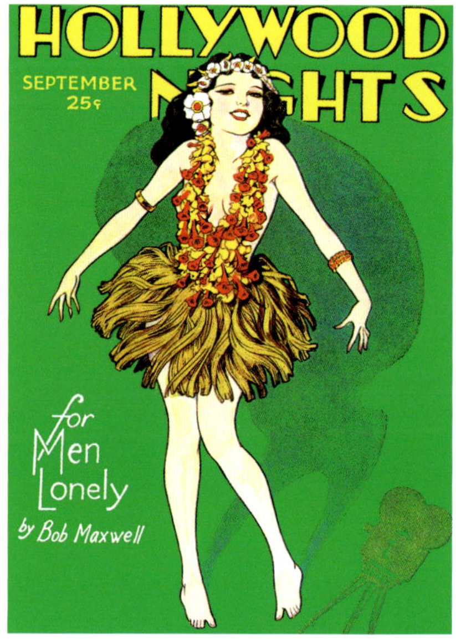

Year:**1931**. Title: **Hollywood Nights**.Country: **USA**.

In Europe the more liberal publishing climate and smaller markets created different situations. In France, the government felt that magazine publishers had enforceable civil rights, and distributors were actually required to give fair distribution to all publications. The French used their greater freedom of lifestyle expression to establish avant-garde visual experiments like the "folies" nude photography magazines of the 20s and 30s, while Germany specialized in more sober "health, art, beauty and esthetics" variations.

Boatloads of these European magazines found their way into the American markets through the new Independent Distribution system in the 1920s, influencing American publishers to make racier products themselves.

In 1932, Harry Donenfeld, a printer specializing in mildly prurient magazine covers, found himself in reluctant possession of the pseudo-art nudie mags of King Publishing when they defaulted on their print bill. Now a fledgling publisher, Donenfeld spearheaded a new and highly dedicated distribution company, Independent News, which was the sole distributor for his own innovative integration of fiction and sex—the *Spicy* pulp line, along with *Ginger Stories* and *Broadway Nights*.

World War II was a boom time, but the decade after the war saw tastes in consumer entertainment rapidly changing. Magazine sales were up worldwide, but Americans were quickly embracing the new television medium—delivering entertainment free into their own homes.

Meanwhile, limping American News was becoming infiltrated by the Mob.

A series of big city newspaper circulation wars ensued in the 1920s, with delivery truck drivers carrying shotguns.

There were Senate investigations on organized crime throughout the 50s, and American News did not escape scrutiny.

In early 1957 out-of-step and already forced by government decree to abandon its monopolistic tactics, American News closed down its periodical distribution arm. With family-oriented television reluctant to deal with anything resembling sexual content, a second wave of men's magazines and sexually overt paperbacks hit the market in the late 50s. American publishers and distributors began to demand the same level of tolerance and acceptance enjoyed in other world markets for so many years.

The 1950s ended on an up note with the newly emerged original paperback novel, cultivated by the Independent Distributors, assuming the role of the dominant reading form in North America. In this newly liberal atmosphere Mickey Spillane, with his heady mixture of sex and violence, became the best-selling author in US history; the publishing industry successfully penetrated every corner of the continent; and men's magazines were at last openly displayed and readily available on America's newsstands.

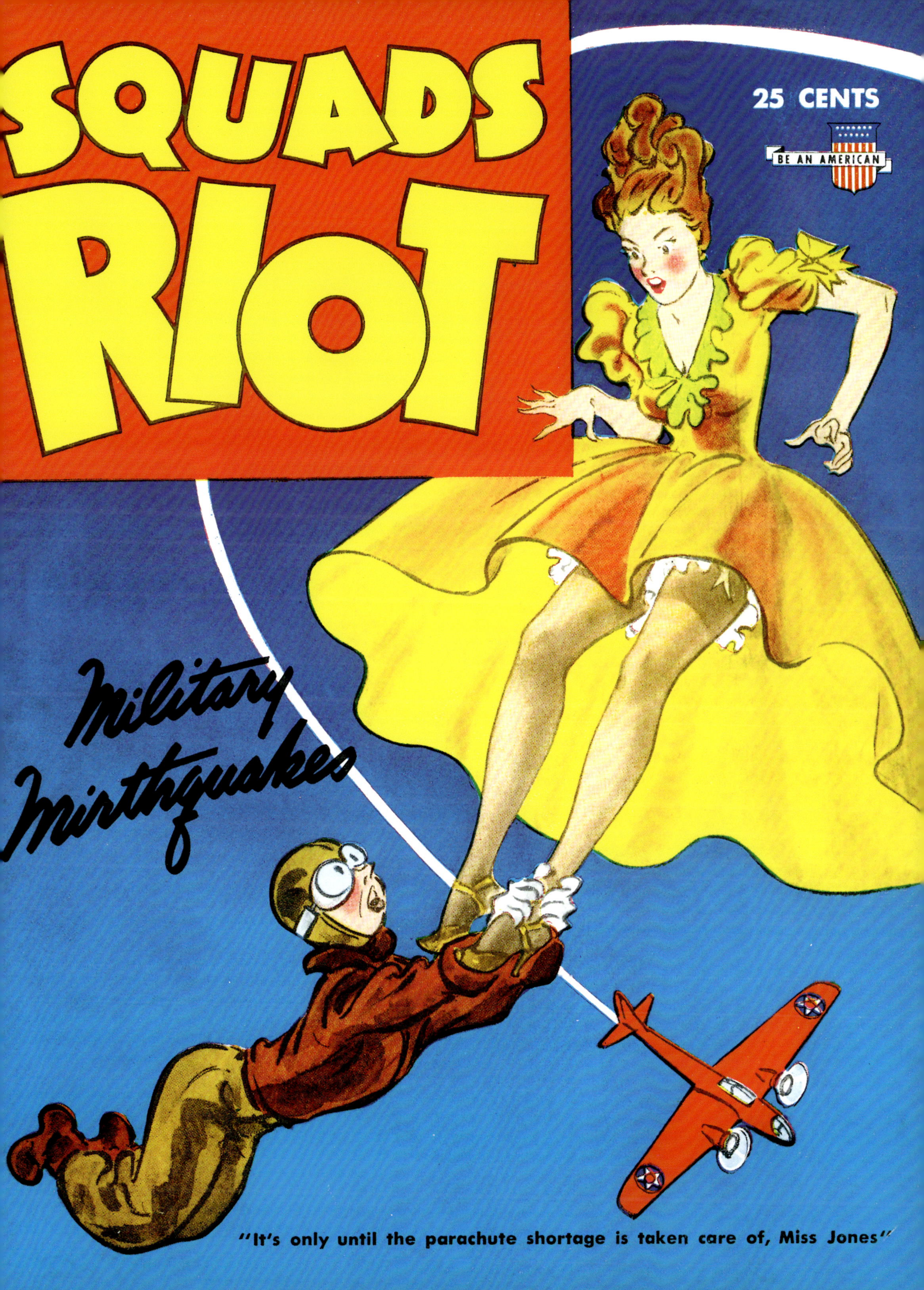
SQUADS RIOT
25 CENTS
BE AN AMERICAN
Military Mirthquakes
"It's only until the parachute shortage is taken care of, Miss Jones"

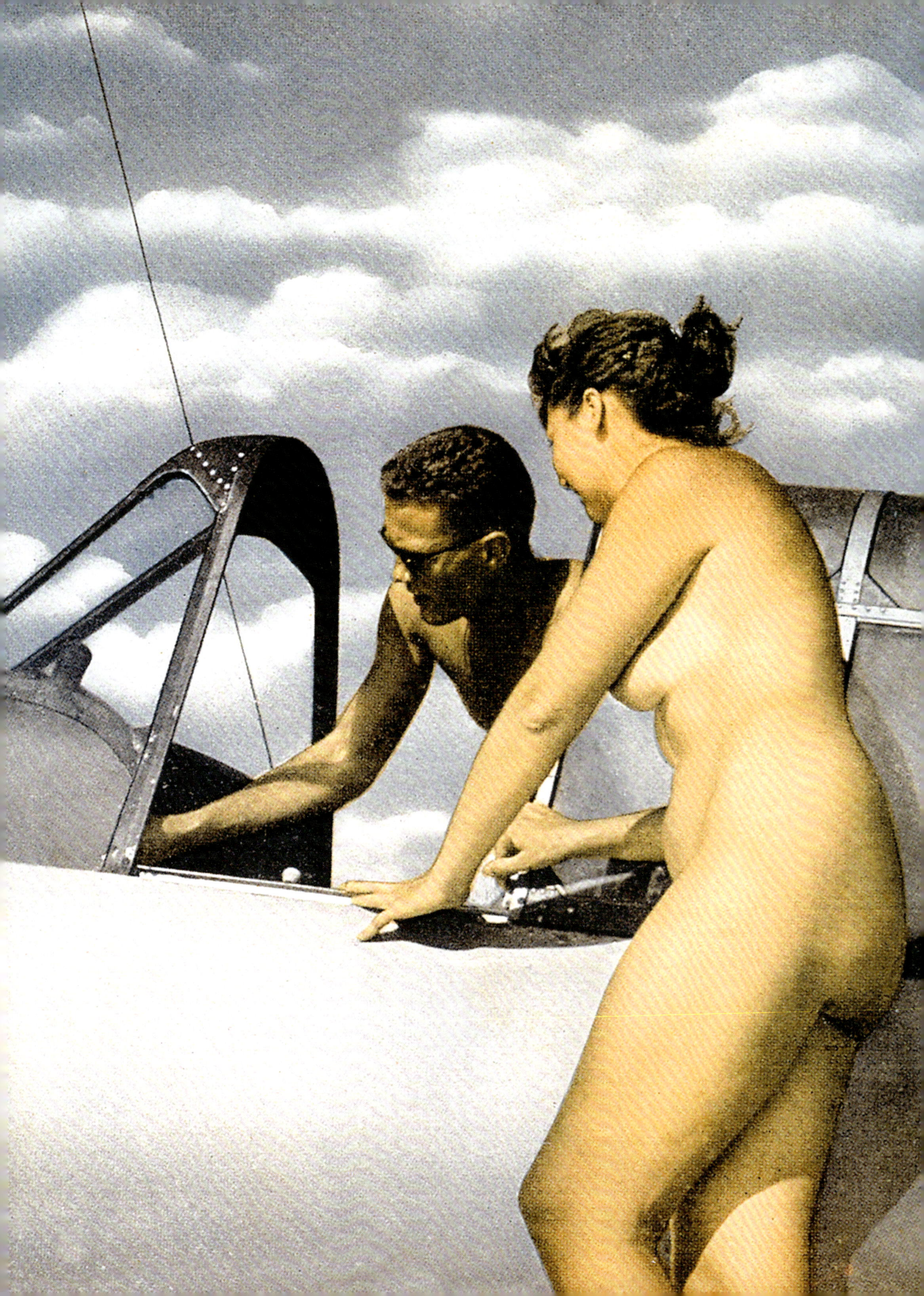

Lebenssäfte über alles

Von Dian Hanson

„Die Sinne ansprechende Liebesgeschichten, selbst in so warmen Farben geschilderte wie die aus *1001 Nacht* ... sollten besser vermieden werden ... auf jedwede aufreizende Literatur muss verzichtet werden. Dem überführten Onanisten darf nicht zur Ehe geraten werden, in der Hoffnung, ihn dergestalt von seinem Laster zu heilen. Zu dem natürlichen Beischlaf mangelt es ihm an Vermögen oder Begehren; die Hingabe an ein unnatürliches Verlangen hat das natürliche Verlangen abgetötet. Hat nun ein derart herabgewürdigtes Geschöpf das Recht, ein Kind zum Makel einer so elenden Herkunft zu verdammen? Besser wäre es, wenn sein Laster und dessen Konsequenzen mit ihm stürben."
– George H. Napheys, M.D.: *The Transmission of Life*. J. G.Fergus & Co, 1872.

Um erotische Publikationen wurde von jeher erbittert gestritten. Auf der einen Seite standen Männer, die von ihrer mentalen und physischen Disposition dazu neigten, auf erotische Bilder anzusprechen, auf der anderen Männer, die sich ihnen vorenthalten wollten. Die ersten zwei Bände der Geschichte der Männermagazine verfolgen die Entwicklung von entblößten Brüsten im Frankreich des Jahres 1880 bis zu den nackten amerikanischen Busen des Jahres 1958. Man mag heute kaum glauben, dass es 60 Jahre dauerte, bis Bilder barbusiger

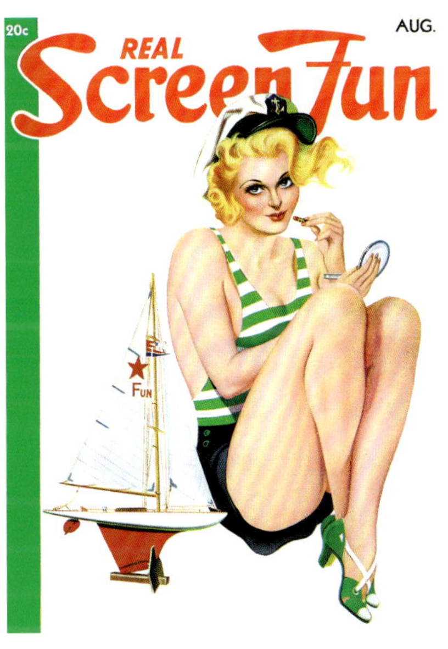

Year: **1938**. Title: **Real Screen Fun**. Country: **USA**.

Frauen an amerikanischen Zeitungsständen und an Zeitungsständen fast überall sonst auf der Welt akzeptiert waren. Jeder Schritt hin zu diesem bescheidenen Erfolg war gleichbedeutend mit hunderten von Festnahmen wegen Erregung öffentlichen Ärgernisses, endlosen Gerichtsverfahren, insgesamt ein paar Hundert Jahren Gefängnis und Millionen von Dollars, D-Mark, Kronen und Pesos, die der fruchtloseVersuch verschlang, nackte Frauenkörper dem männlichen Blick vorzuenthalten. Als Dr. Napheys 1872 über die Auswirkungen erotisch stimulierender Literatur schrieb, geschah das in dem Glauben, Männer kämen mit einem begrenzten Vorrat an „männlichen Säften" zur Welt, der ein Leben lang vorhalten müsse. Diese männlichen Säfte waren nicht allein zur Fortpflanzung nötig; ein Mann, der seinen Samen in Selbstbefleckung vergeudete, verschwendete angeblich in kürzester Zeit seine gesamten Reserven, was zu Lasten seiner physischen Kraft, seiner intellektuellen Fähigkeiten,seiner moralischen Stärke und seines Verstandes ginge, in ungefähr dieser Reihenfolge.

Dr. Napheys war mit seinem Behandlungsvorschlag für dieses Übel noch einer der zart besaiteteren Schwarzmaler – er meinte, die meisten Männer wären zu heilen, indem man die anstößigen Teile verätzte, und die Kastration, zu der viele seiner Kollegen geraten hätten, müsse nur in Ausnahmefällen sein.

Ein Großteil der viktorianischen Hysterie um erotische Literatur fußt auf der Degenerationstheorie des Schweizer Arztes Dr. Simon Tissot, der in der Mitte des 18. Jahrhunderts die verweiblichende Wirkung der Kastration am Mann untersucht hatte und zu dem – irrigen – Schluss gekommen war, deren Ursache wäre der Verlust des Samens. Um seinen Irrtum noch zu verschlimmern, stellte er die Theorie auf, exzessives Masturbieren

Year: **1952**. Title: **Sun Tan**. Country: **USA**.

Year: **1930**. Title: **Nifty Stories**. Artist: **G. Greiner**. Country: **USA**.

1865 war die Fototechnik so weit fortgeschritten, dass auch der Mann von der Straße sie benutzen konnte – und prompt anfing, Fotos nackter Frauen zu machen und zu verkaufen.

habe den gleichen Effekt auf einen mit vollständigen Hoden bestückten Mann. Um so unverständlicher ist es, dass Kastration als probates Mittel gegen hartnäckiges Masturbieren empfohlen wurde, doch da hatten die Moralapostel in Europa und den USA den ursprünglichen Sinn und Zweck längst aus den Augen verloren und waren nur noch darauf aus, jedes Vergnügen auszurotten. In diesem Kreuzzug wurden Kamera und Druckerpresse zunehmend als Werkzeuge Satans verteufelt.

Die Fotokamera wurde in den dreißiger Jahren des 19. Jahrhunderts entwickelt. 1839 wurde das erste primitive Negativ erfunden, das es ermöglichte, von einer einzelnen Aufnahme zahlreiche Abzüge zu machen. 1865 war die Fototechnik so weit fortgeschritten, dass auch der Mann von der Straße sie benutzen konnte – und prompt anfing, Fotos nackter Frauen zu machen und zu verkaufen.

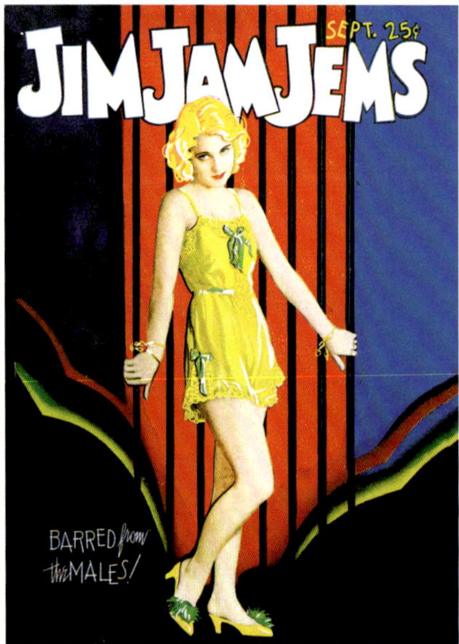

Year: **1930**. Title: **Jim Jam Jems**. Country: **USA**.

Gleichzeitig verbesserte sich auch die Drucktechnik, beflügelt durch die zunehmende Alphabetisierung. Vor der viktorianischen Ära lebten viele Menschen auf dem Land und waren zumeist Analphabeten. Die industrielle Revolution lockte viele Landbewohner und Einwanderer in die Städte und Fabriken. Die dadurch entstehenden Arbeiterghettos mit ihrer Kriminalität, Prostitution und hohen Kindersterblichkeit führten schließlich zu sozialen Reformen, wie beispielsweise einer besseren Schulbildung für alle.

Als nur die Oberschicht des Lesens mächtig war, bestand eine relativ geringe Nachfrage nach Gedrucktem, daher erschienen Bücher und Zeitschriften in sehr begrenzter Auflage, was sie teuer machte. Als die Alphabetisierung fortschritt, wurde es auch in der Arbeiterschaft populär, zum Vergnügen zu lesen. Die Verleger beeilten sich, ihre Produktion der gewachsenen Nachfrage nach einer neuen Art von Lesestoff anzupassen. Teure gebundene Bücher waren für den Durchschnittsverdiener unerschwinglich, aber preiswerte Magazine und Groschenhefte waren genau das Richtige. In den USA schilderten diese Publikationen vornehmlich Geschichten aus dem Wilden Westen, wahre Verbrechen und romantische Liebesabenteuer. In England waren Detektivgeschichten ebenso populär.

Schon um 1860 erschienen in New York explizitere „Liebesgeschichten". Insgeheim und in kleinen Mengen verkauft, nahm jahrelang kaum jemand Notiz von ihnen, bis sie 1868 die Aufmerksamkeit eines jungen Buchhalters

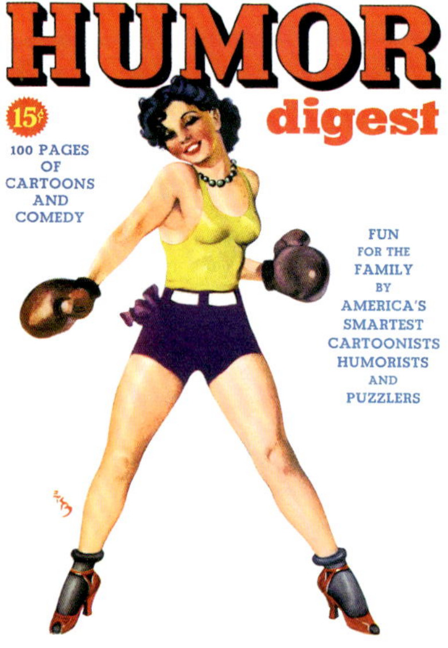

Year: **1939**. Title: **Humor Digest**. Country: **USA**.

namens Anthony Comstock erregten. Dass Comstock mit dem, was den meisten Männern Spaß machte, ein schweres Problem hatte, war von Anfang an unübersehbar. Ein Beispiel seiner Ausführungen zur erotischen Literatur:

„Die Wirkung dieses verfluchten Geschäftes auf unsere Jugend und Gesellschaft lässt sich nicht in Worte fassen. Es verursacht geschlechtliche Lust. Lust besudelt den Körper, verdirbt die Vorstellungskraft, korrumpiert den Geist, stumpft den Willen ab, zerstört das Gedächtnis, lähmt das Gewissen, verhärtet das Herz und verdammt die Seele.

Anthony verschwendete keine Zeit, den Satan in seiner eigenen Nachbarschaft zu ergreifen; er nahm eine Gruppe von Iren hoch, die er der Produktion von Pornografie bezichtigte, und verlangte von der Polizei, sie einzusperren. So

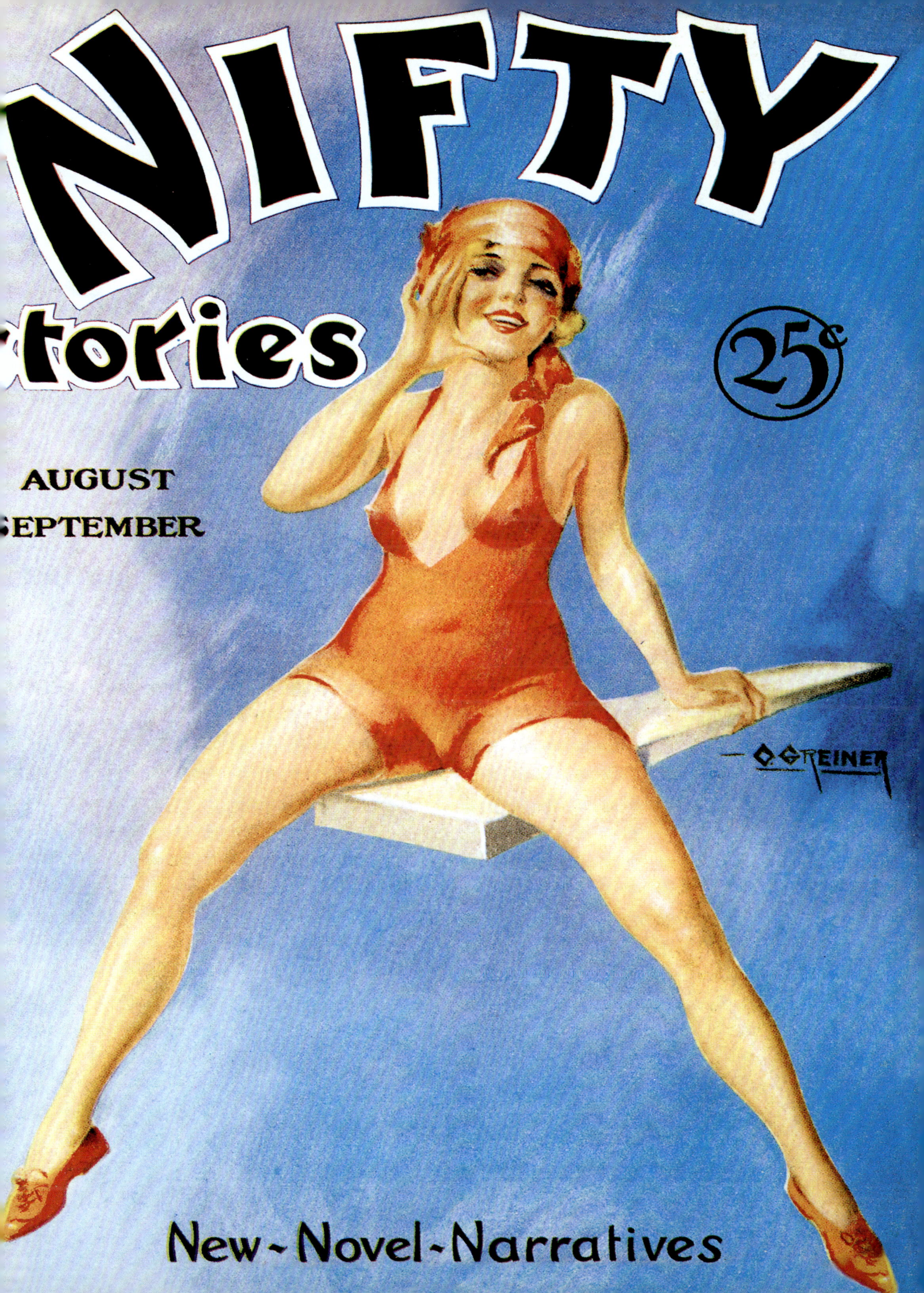
NIFTY
Stories
25¢
AUGUST
SEPTEMBER
O. GREINER
New-Novel-Narratives

Anthony Comstock überzeugte die US-Regierung, dass die neue obszöne Literatur aus dem Ausland eine drohende Gefahr für Amerikas gesamte männliche Lebenssäfte darstellte.

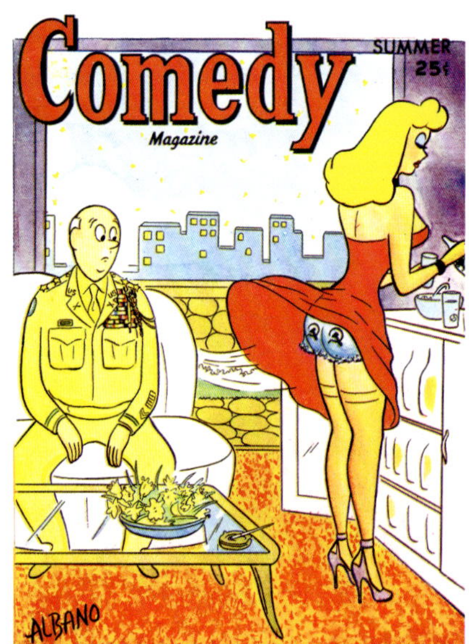

Year: **1951**. Title: **Comedy**. Country: **USA**.

begann eine lebenslange Hatz auf erotische Literatur, die schließlich zu einem folgenreichen Gesetz führte, das bis heute dazu dient, amerikanische Verleger strafrechtlich zu verfolgen. Mit dem „Christlichen Verein Junger Männer" (YMCA) im Rücken bearbeitete Comstock die amerikanische Regierung so lange und intensiv, dass diese schließlich kapitulierte und dem juristischen Laien die Verfügungsgewalt über das amerikanische Postwesen gab.

Warum? Weil er neben dem Sündenpfuhl gleich um die Ecke in Brooklyn auch eine Flut von Obszönitäten entdeckt hatte, die von jenseits des Ozeans in die USA strömten und dann durch die Post an wehrlose Unschuldige verteilt wurden. Er wollte nicht ruhen, bis er den Europäern beigebracht hatte, nicht leichtfertig mit den Lebenssäften amerikanischer Männer umzugehen.

Frankreich war auf dem Gebiet der Fotografie führend und perfektionierte Ende der sechziger Jahre des 19. Jahrhunderts den Druck schlüpfriger Fotografien. Zu dieser Zeit entstanden die berühmten „French postcards" und erotischen Spielkarten und fanden allerorten ein dankbares männliches Publikum. In dem darauf folgenden Jahrzehnt entstanden in Paris die frühesten Männermagazine in Form von Kabarettprogrammen, die Oben-ohne-Fotos der Tänzerinnen zeigten. Als die amerikanischen Männer Wind von diesen Fortschritten bekamen, waren sie verständlicherweise bestrebt, ihre Bildung durch französische Studien zu vertiefen. Ein paar unternehmerisch Veranlagte gingen ins Importgewerbe.

Mit Hilfe solcher Experten wie Dr. Napheys, Reverend Sylvester Graham von den berühmten Graham-Cräckern und John Harvey Kellog, dem Erfinder der Frühstücksflocken, Einlauffan und fanatischen Samenbewahrer, überzeugte Anthony Comstock die US-Regierung, dass die neue obszöne Literatur aus dem Ausland eine drohende Gefahr für Amerikas gesamte männliche Lebenssäfte darstellte. Seine Leidenschaft für die Unterdrückung der Leidenschaft war so überzeugend, dass 1873 ein Gesetz verabschiedet wurde, das als Comstock Law bekannt wurde und das im Wesentlichen darauf hinausläuft, „dass kein obszönes, anstößiges oder lüsternes Buch, Pamphlet, Bild und keine obszöne, anstößige oder lüsterne Zeitschrift, Schrift oder anderes Druckwerk von anstößigem Charakter, oder irgendein Artikel oder Ding, das zur Empfängnisverhütung entwickelt oder vorgesehen ist oder einen Schwangerschaftsabbruch herbeiführt, oder irgendein anderer Gegenstand, der zu anstößigem oder unmoralischem Gebrauch verwendbar ist, noch irgendeine handschriftliche oder gedruckte Karte, irgendein Rundschreiben, Buch, Pamphlet, irgendeine Anzeige oder Nachricht, die direkt oder indirekt Informationen darüber verbreitet, wo, wie, von wem oder auf welche Weise, oben erwähnte Dinge hergestellt werden oder zu beziehen sind, noch irgendein Brief, auf dessen Umschlag, oder eine Postkarte, auf die anstößige oder zotige Beinamen geschrieben oder gedruckt sind, mit der Post befördert werden dürfen …"

Das Comstock Law wirkte sich zwar nachteilig auf die Verbreitung früher Erotika in den Vereinigten Staaten aus, aber das öffentliche Aufsehen, das seine Ratifizierung begleitete und über das in den neuen Zeitschriften und Boulevardblättern berichtet wurde, wies eine hellhörige Öffentlichkeit auch auf die Existenz solcher Druckwerke hin. Die meisten Männer hatten gar nicht gewusst, dass solche Dinge existierten, aber sobald sie davon erfahren hatten und wussten, in welchen Mengen sie ins Land kamen – Comstock hatte von „Tonnen" von Druckerzeugnissen gesprochen – wollten sie sie haben.

Erst nach dem Ersten Weltkrieg sollten in den USA echte Männermagazine verlegt werden, doch bereits Ende des 19. Jahrhunderts erschienen pikante Boulevardzeitungen, und allen Anstrengungen von Anthony Comstock und der zahlreichen neu gegründeten Sittlichkeitsvereine zum Trotz gelangten weiterhin erotische Bücher, Fotos und Spielkarten durch den Zoll. Als der Umfang „männerspezifischer" Literatur wuchs, wurde

Year: **1956**. Title: **Girlie Gags**. Country: **USA**.

CHUCKLE AND ROAR 25¢

GIRLIE GAGS

WITTY AND SPICY JOKES GALORE

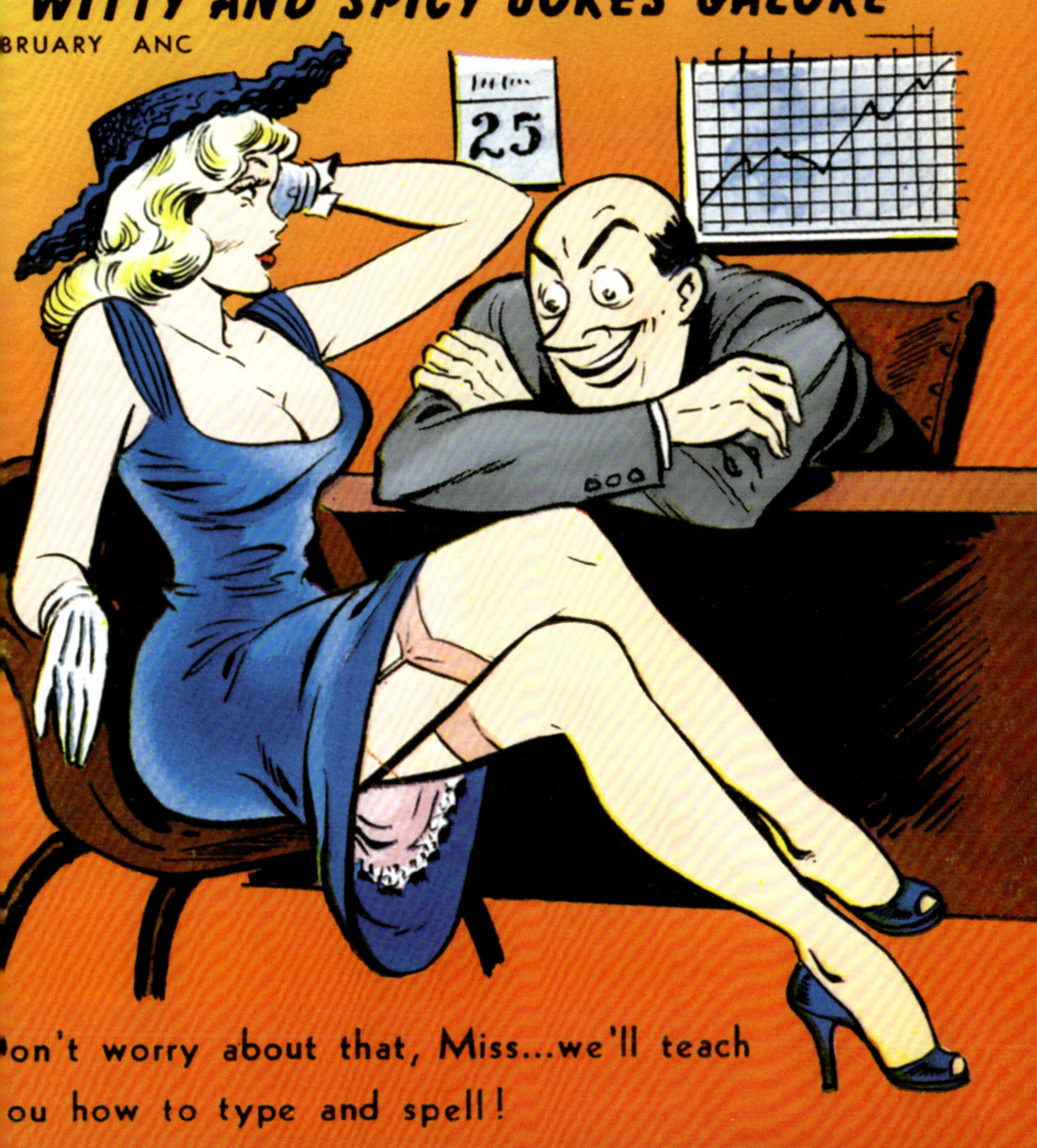

YEAR: **1949**. TITLE: **Schönheit**.
COUNTRY: **Germany**.

auch zunehmend deutlich, dass ein Großteil der Menschen sie konsumiert hatte und weiterhin konsumierte, ohne körperlich ruiniert, schwachsinnig oder irre geworden zu sein. In seinem Buch *The Secret Museum* (University of California Press, 1987) weist Walter Kendrick darauf hin, dass amerikanische Gerichte im letzten Jahrzehnt des 19. Jahrhunderts bei der Feststellung Bestimmung von Obszönität zunehmend auch künstlerische Qualitäten in Erwägung zogen. Dementsprechend wurde 1894 eine Klage abgewiesen, in der es um 1001 Nacht, Ovids *Liebeskunst* und Boccacios *Dekameron* ging, weil die „Gesellschaft zur Unterdrückung des Lasters" befand, es handle sich dabei um „weltberühmte Klassiker ... die kaum verkauft oder erworben werden, es sei denn von denen, die sie wegen ihrer literarischen Qualitäten schätzen ..."

Verleger, die sich an ein weniger kultiviertes Publikum richteten, konnten allerdings nicht so viel Verständnis erwarten: „1896 unterzog der amerikanische Supreme Court zwei Verurteilungen wegen Obszönität durch untergeordnete Gerichte der Revision. Die erste betraf Lew Rosen, den Verleger von Broadway, einer Illustrierten, die keinen Anspruch auf literarische Größe erhob. In deren ‚Tenderloin'-Sondernummer waren mit Lampenruß geschwärzte Stellen gewesen, die man mit einem Stück Brot hatte abrubbeln können, um ‚Frauen in verschiedenen schamlosen Posen' zu enthüllen ... Der Supreme Court bestätigte dieses Urteil ..."

Ich habe mich vergebens gemüht, dieses erlesene Beispiel für frühe amerikanische Erotika aufzuspüren, aber selbst wenn ich erfolgreich gewesen wäre, hätte

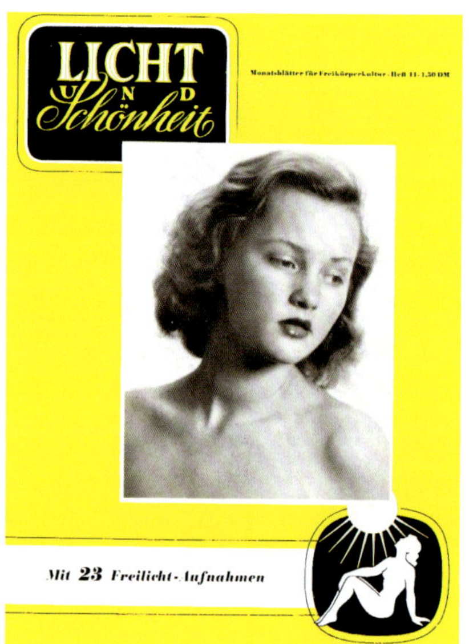

YEAR: **1952**. TITLE: **Licht Und Schönheit**.
COUNTRY: **Germany**.

ich wohl kaum ein Exemplar gefunden, das keine Abreibung mit der Stulle bekommen hatte. Der Verleger Rosen war einer der ersten Vertreter eines amerikanischen Klischees: der urbane jüdische Pornoverleger. Die meisten frühen Unternehmer auf diesem Gebiet waren Immigranten aus Osteuropa, die über literarische Vorbildung verfügten, über begrenzte Mittel, um in der Neuen Welt ihren Lebensunterhalt zu verdienen, und über gar nichts von der tristen christlichen Sinnenfeindlichkeit, die Leute wie Comstock umtrieb. Mit der Zeit sollte die amerikanische Männermagazin-Industrie sich den Spitznamen „jüdische Mafia" einhandeln, aber um 1900 bestand sie nur aus ein paar Ghettobewohner aus New York, oft unterstützt von ihren Frauen und Kindern, die Pornos machten, um sich über Wasser zu halten.

Etwa um diese Zeit kam Papier aus Zellstoff auf, das sich bald als Segen für die sich entwickelnde Männermagazin-Industrie erweisen sollte. Vorher wurde Papier ausschließlich aus Lumpen hergestellt – häufig recycelte Baumwollkleidung – und mit Ton weiß gebleicht. Dieses Papier erlaubt eine wunderbare Druckqualität und ist extrem haltbar; Bücher aus diesem Material können hunderte Jahre überdauern. Die Herstellung ist relativ teuer, und es macht wenig Sinn, es zur Herstellung billiger Wegwerfartikel wie Zeitschriften zu benutzen. Dennoch wurden die meisten Magazine bis gegen Ende des 19. Jahrhunderts darauf gedruckt, während Zeitungen auf extra dünnem Zeitungspapier, dem so genannten „Newsprint", gedruckt wurden. Pulp-Papier stammte aus der neuen Holzindustrie im Westen. Hergestellt aus Holzfasern, die durch Säure (Sulfit) aufgebrochen wurden, war es fester als Zeitungspapier, wesentlich billiger herzustellen als Papier aus Lumpen und von der Beschaffenheit her wenig haltbar, denn die Säuren, die zu seiner Herstellung benötigt wurden, zersetzten es auch schnell wieder. Es war zu grob, um die gute Wiedergabe von Bildern zu erlauben, aber genau richtig für die zur Jahrhundertwende so begehrten Groschenhefte. In der ersten Hälfte des 20. Jahrhunderts wurden Millionen von reißerischen Detektiv-, Western-, Abenteuer- und Liebesgeschichten, Science Fiction und Sexgeschichten auf billigem Papier zu erschwinglichen Preisen verkauft. Um am Kiosk aufzufallen, hüllte man das minderwertige Innere in schreiend bunte Hochglanzcover, auf denen in der Regel eine knapp bekleidete Sexbombe zu sehen war, selbst

SCHÖNHEIT

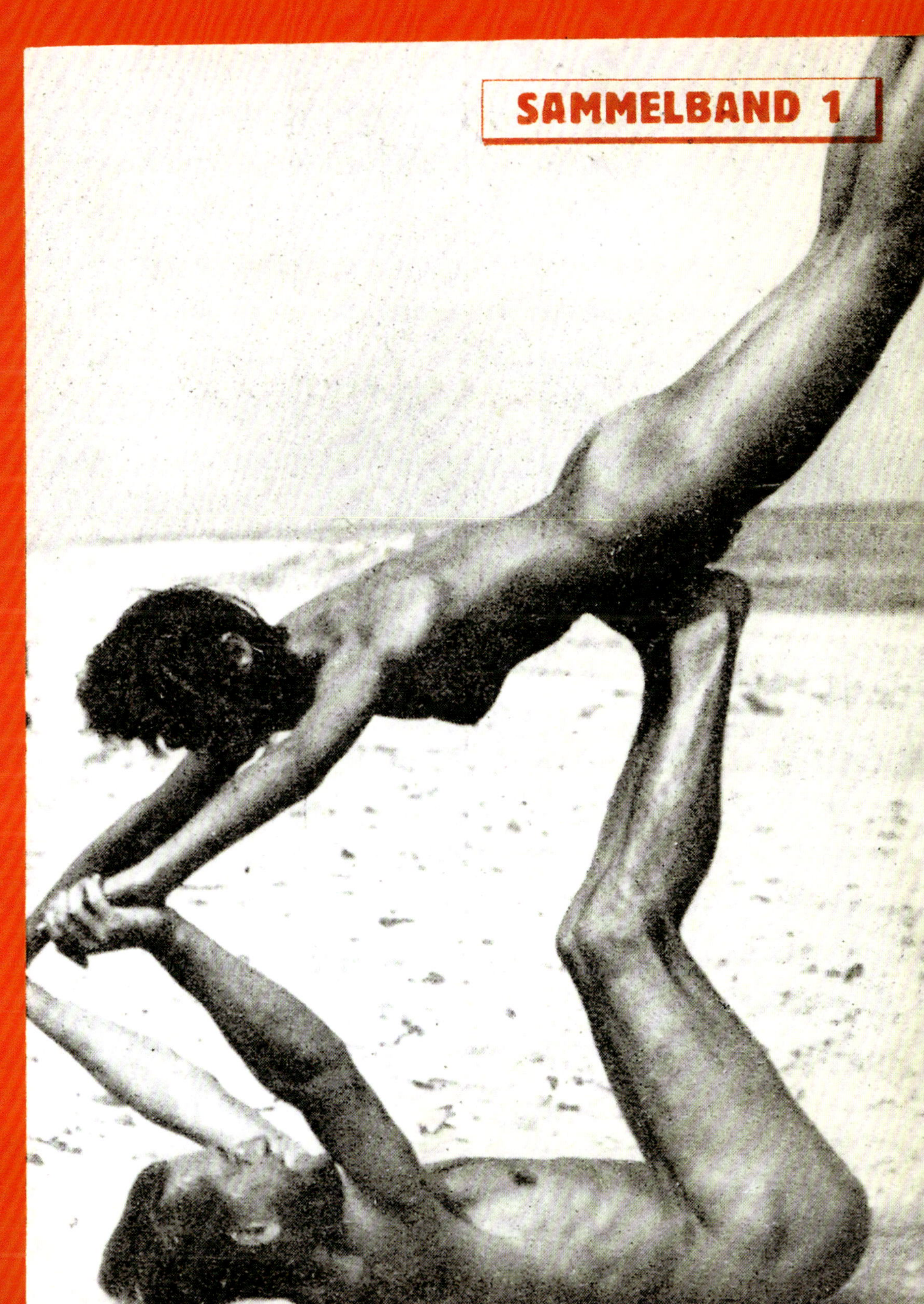

Statt
DM 3.50
nur
DM 2.-

SCHRIFTENREIHE FÜR SCHÖNHEIT UND KÖRPERKULTUR

wenn es um Weltraumabenteuer oder eine romantische Liebesgeschichte ging. Zu einer Zeit, in der aufreizende Fotos noch heftig zensiert wurden, bedienten „Pulps", wie das ganze Genre genannt wurde, die Sensationslüsternen beiderlei Geschlechts.

Im Frankreich der Jahrhundertwende wurden derweil eher Worte als Fotos zensiert, solange die Fotos einen Kunstanspruch für sich reklamierten. Die Franzosen waren in Sachen Kunst schon immer aufgeschlossener als die Amerikaner und ließen sich durch ein bisschen Busen nicht aus der Ruhe bringen. Sie brachten als Erste Magazine mit „Aktstudien" heraus, die bereits völlig nackte Frauen zeigten, während man in den USA noch Ruß wegrubbelte, um einen Blick auf ein Strumpfband zu erhaschen. Magazine, die sich dazu bekannten, dass es ihnen in erster Linie um Frivolitäten ging, wurden heftiger zensiert, aber *La Vie Parisienne*, das 1863 gegründet wurde und kurz vor dem Ersten Weltkrieg erneut auf den Markt kam, gelang es, geschmackvolle Nackte mit pikanten Geschichten und Humor zu verquicken und trotzdem sehr populär zu werden, weil es Raffinesse bewies, was in Frankreich fast ebenso geschätzt wird wie der Kunstcharakter.

Deutschland war das dritte Land, das sich um 1900 auf eine erotisch mannigfaltige Zukunft einstellte, sich jedoch zugleich mit seinen eigenen moralischen Problemen herumschlug. Über die degenerierende Wirkung der Masturbation wurde ebenso viel veröffentlicht wie in den Staaten, doch in Europa hielt Sigmund Freud dagegen, die Unterdrückung der Sexualität sei ebenso schädlich. Darüber hinaus sah sich Deutschland im

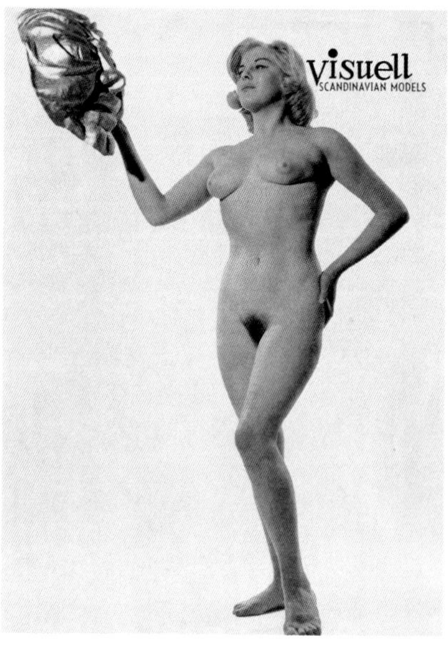

Year: **1950s**. Title: **Visuell**. Country: **Sweden**.

Laufe der industriellen Revolution mit einem Zuzug unerwünschter Ausländer und einer kränkelnden Volksgesundheit konfrontiert. Dies gab den Anstoß zu einer schnell Zulauf findenden Eugenik-Bewegung und dem Aufkeimen sozialistischer Ideen. Aus diesem Gebräu entstand die Schönheitsbewegung, deren Publikationen alles Schöne, doch vor allem junge, nackte, arische Körper priesen. Wie in Frankreich hing alles am Kontext: Nacktheit wurde toleriert, wenn sie asexuell dargeboten wurde. In Deutschland wurde die Frage des Kontexts in Bezug auf Nacktheit in den ersten drei Jahrzehnten des 20. Jahrhunderts stärker ausgereizt als sonst irgendwo auf der Welt. Als 1933 die Zeit der Weimarer Republik zu Ende ging, gab es hunderte von Zeitschriften in Deutschland, die im Kontext dutzender unterschiedlicher Weltanschauungen Nacktheit abbildeten, ohne dass eine einzige davon einräumte, dass sie auch sexuelle Stimulation im Sinn hätte.

Im Laufe des 20. Jahrhunderts bliesen auch Verleger in England, Schweden, Argentinien, Japan, Mexiko, Dänemark und anderen Ländern zum Großangriff auf die männlichen Säfte – und die männlichen Säfte sollten sich dem durchaus gewachsen zeigen. In gründlichen und oft feurigen Selbstversuchen bewiesen die Männer, dass die Quelle der männlichen Säfte durch noch so viele die Sinne ansprechende Geschichten oder Schilderungen in warmen Farben nicht zum Versiegen gebracht wurde. Das alles hielt sich länger, als mancher glaubt; Eugenik, die Antwort des 20. Jahrhunderts auf Tissots Degenerationstheorien, fand in vielen Ländern Anhänger und wurde erst unpopulär, als das Dritte Reich sie sich nach den eigenen Vorstellungen zurechtbog. 1928 warnte Dr. B. G. Jeffries in seinem Buch *Safe Council or Practical Eugenics* noch: „... Knaben sind mitunter in großer Versuchung, Bilder zu erwerben und herumzureichen, die den Körper ohne schickliche Bekleidung oder gar geschlechtliche Beziehungen zeigen. Man darf nicht zulassen, dass sich ein schmutziges Bild ins Gedächtnis einbrennt. Es wird nie verlöschen. Noch viele Jahre nachdem man es gesehen hat, und höchstwahrscheinlich lange, nachdem man alle Bemerkungen zu diesem Thema vergessen hat, wird man sich an dieses Bild erinnern. Ich habe erwachsene Männer sagen hören, dass sie alles Geld der Welt hergeben würden, könnten sie nur die Erinnerung an ein verdorbenes Bild löschen, das sie als Knabe gesehen und über das sie damals gebrütet haben."

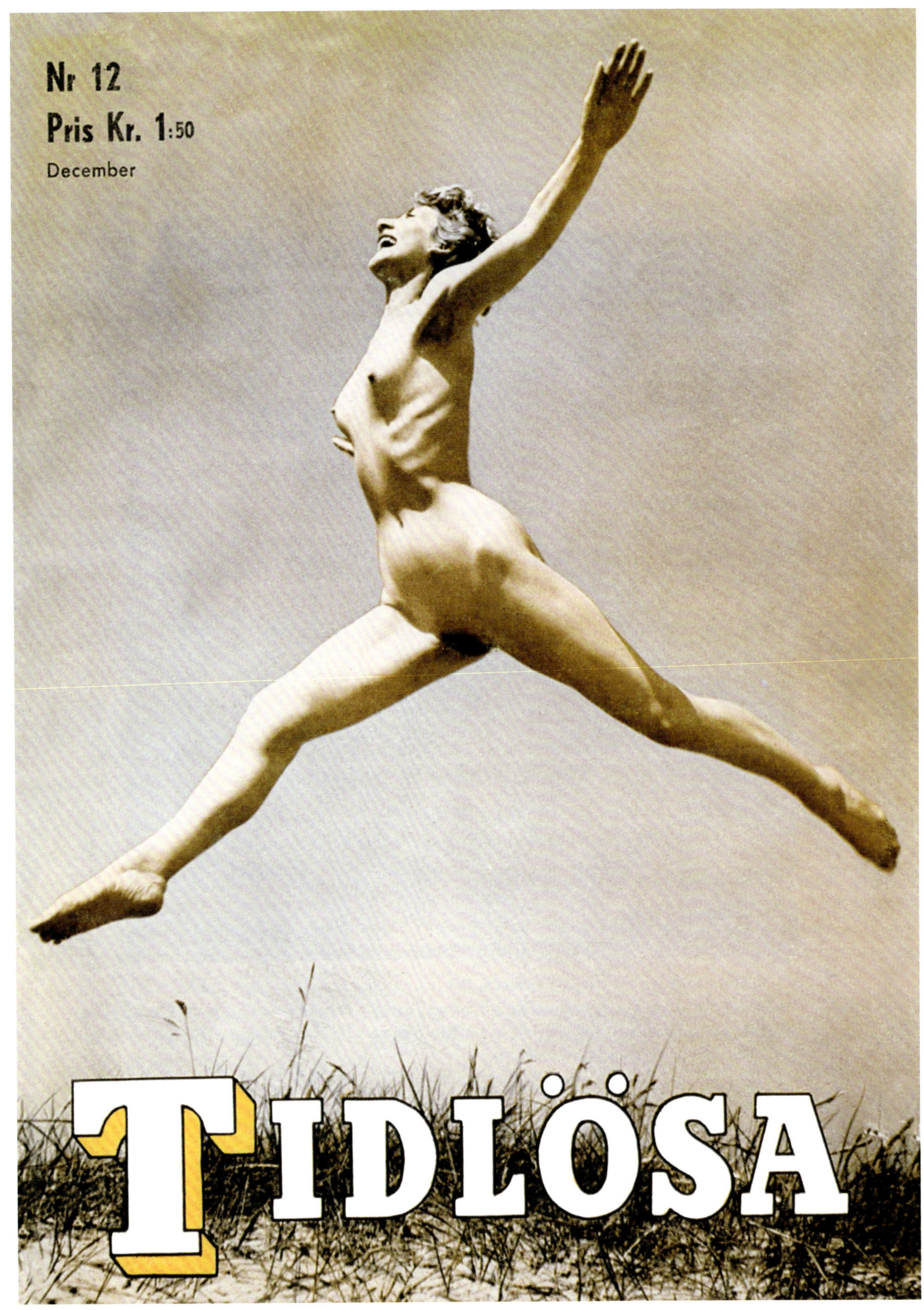

Year: **1956**. Title: **Tidlösa**. Country: **Sweden**.

Year: **1951**. Title: **L'Amour en Poche**. Country: **France**.

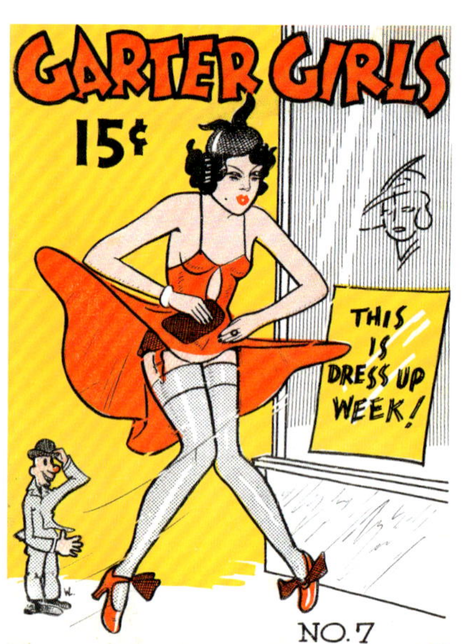

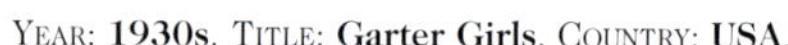

Year: **1930s**. Title: **Garter Girls**. Country: **USA**.

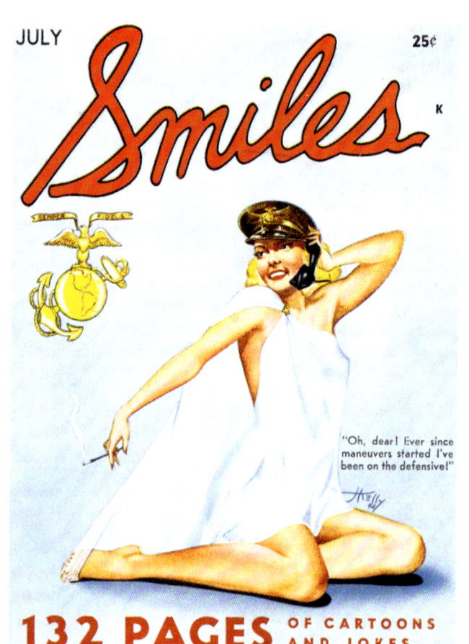

Year: **1942**. Title: **Smiles**. Country: **USA**.

French photographer Lerebours photographed some nudes as early as 1840, only one year after the historic introduction of Daguerre's process.

—*Simon's Book of World Sexual Records*, G. L. Simons, 1975

Ich war nicht dabei, daher kann ich mit dem guten Doktor nicht streiten, doch in den mehr als zwei Jahren, in denen ich das Material für diese Bücher zusammengesucht habe, habe ich auch viel Zeit in den nicht jugendfreien Seiten des Internet-Auktionshauses Ebay verbracht. Mit der zweifelhaften Autorität, die sich daraus ergibt, kann ich bestätigen, dass mancher erwachsene Mann alles Geld der Welt hergeben würde, um das Bild zu kaufen, über das er als Knabe gebrütet hat.

Ursprünglich sollte dieses Projekt zwei Bände umfassen und die Jahre von 1945 bis 1980 abdecken. Doch als ich begann, mich umzusehen, erkannte ich, dass man viel früher ansetzen musste. Zuerst legte ich mich auf das Jahr 1900 fest, doch dann stieß ich auf die französischen Kabarettprogramme aus den achtziger Jahren des 19. Jahrhunderts. Das Projekt wuchs von zwei auf drei Bände, schließlich auf sechs, und doch gab es immer sehr viel mehr Titel, als jemals hätten untergebracht werden können. Ich habe mein Bestes getan, in dem knappen Jahr, das mir zur Verfügung stand, die korrekten Informationen über die Magazine und die Menschen, die sie hergestellt haben, aufzuspüren, doch wenn man bedenkt, dass viele dieser Hefte im Verborgenen produziert wurden, werden sich manche meiner Informationen wohl als falsch erweisen. Dafür möchte ich mich jetzt schon entschuldigen. Die Magazine jedoch müssen sich für nichts entschuldigen. Die Kreativität, die in diese frühen Männermagazine einfloss, lässt alles, was heute produziert wird, blass aussehen. Aber ich denke, das haben Sie bereits bemerkt, denn nicht einmal Anthony Comstock hätte die Geduld aufgebracht, sich erst durch diese langatmige Einleitung zu lesen, ehe er sich den Fotos zuwandte.

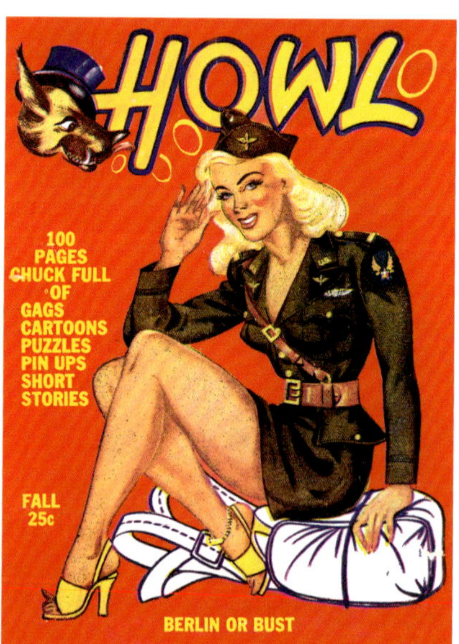

Year: **1944**. Title: **Howl**. Country: **USA**.

amour en poche

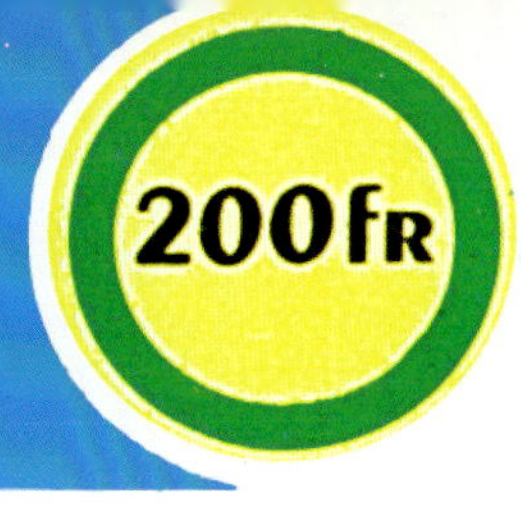

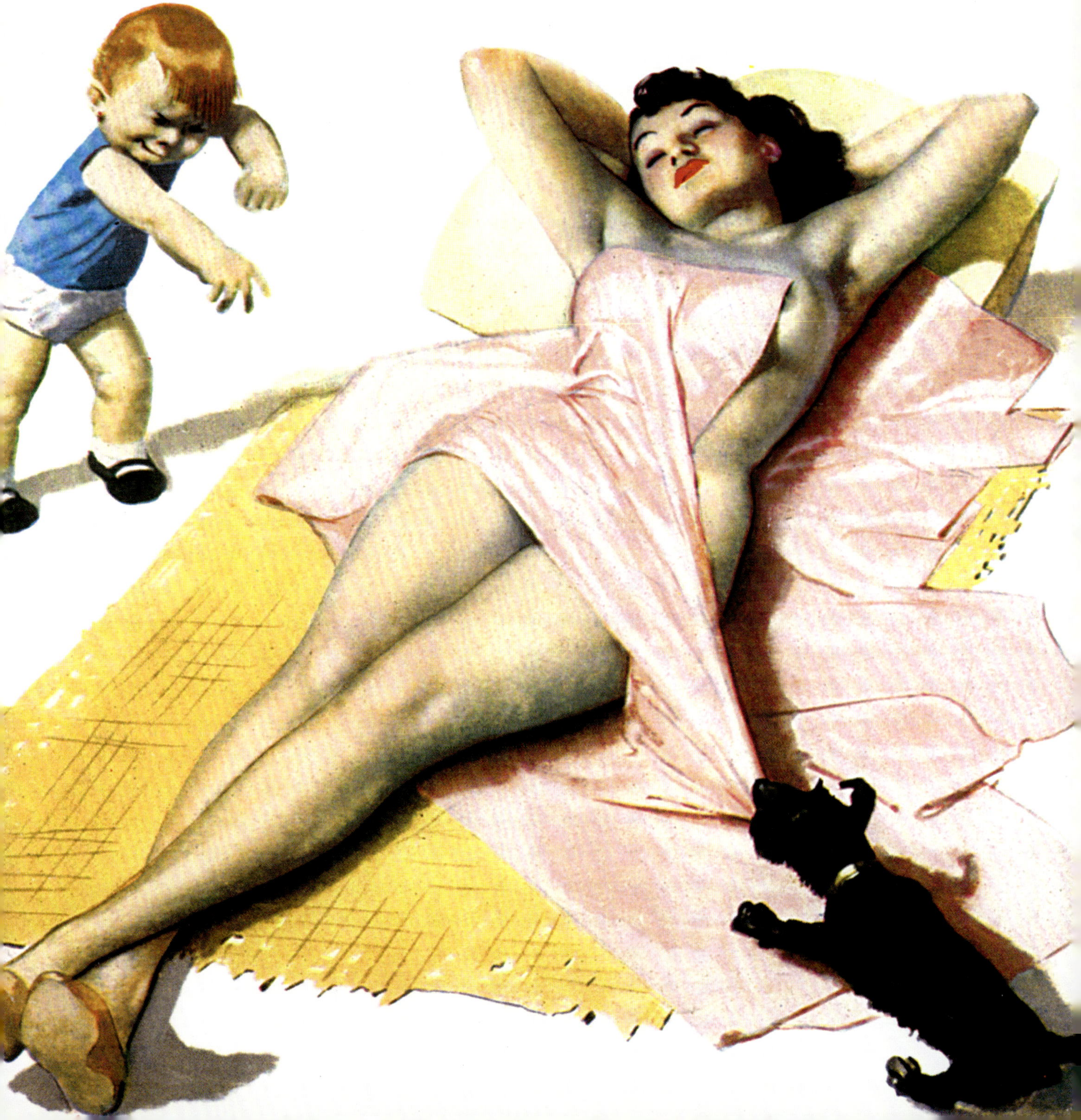

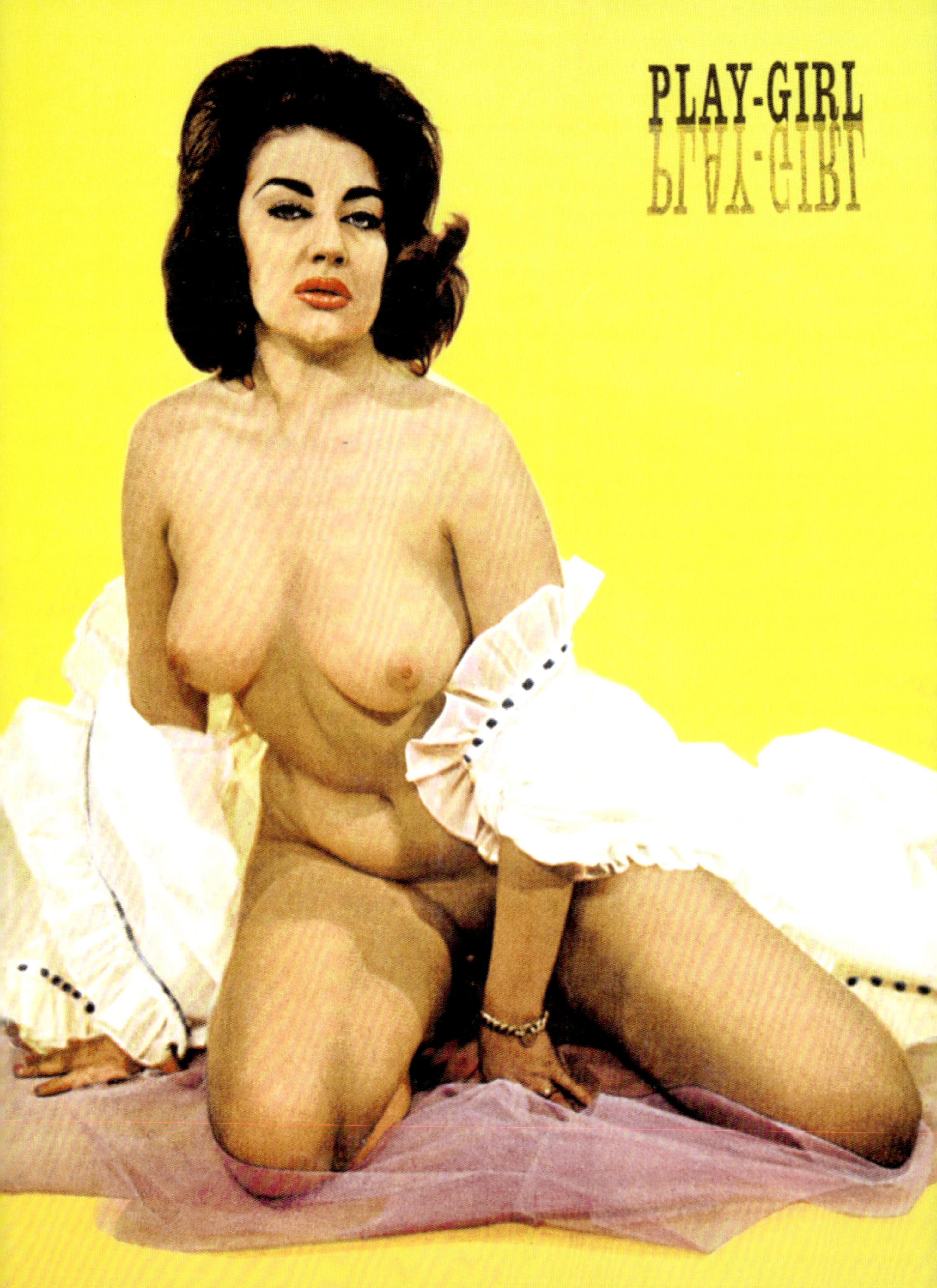
PLAY-GIRL
PLAY-GIRL

VERTRIEB:

Wie man Männermagazine an den Mann bringt

Von Michael Feldman

Wenn man vor einem Regal steht, das von Titeln überquillt, die unser Interesse zu fesseln versuchen, stellt man sich nur selten die Frage: Wie kommen diese Zeitschriften hierhin? Und wer hat sie hierhin gebracht? 1864 schlossen sich in New York zwei der größten Grossisten zur American News Company zusammen. Als erster landesweiter Grossist hatte American News das Monopol darauf, welche Zeitschriften in Umlauf kamen. Die Firma richtete tausende von Verkaufsstellen an Verkehrsknotenpunkten, Bahnhöfen und später Busbahnhöfen und hunderte von zentral gelegenen Auslieferungslagern ein.

Die amerikanische Regierung hatte, ursprünglich um die Pressefreiheit zu gewährleisten, den Transport von Zeitungen und allem anderen, was sich irgendwie als Zeitschrift qualifizierte, über das rasch expandierende Eisenbahnnetz subventioniert, was die landesweite Verbreitung begünstigte. Es wurde dadurch wirtschaftlich rentabel, Illustrierte oder Zeitungen über Entfernungen von manchmal bis zu 5000 Kilometern zu verschicken. Geschäftstüchtige Verleger alles andere als seriöser Blätter erkannten sofort, welche Möglichkeiten sich damit eröffneten, und eine der ersten Second Class Mailing Permits des US Post Office wurde 1879 der Police Gazette erteilt. Dieses sogenannte

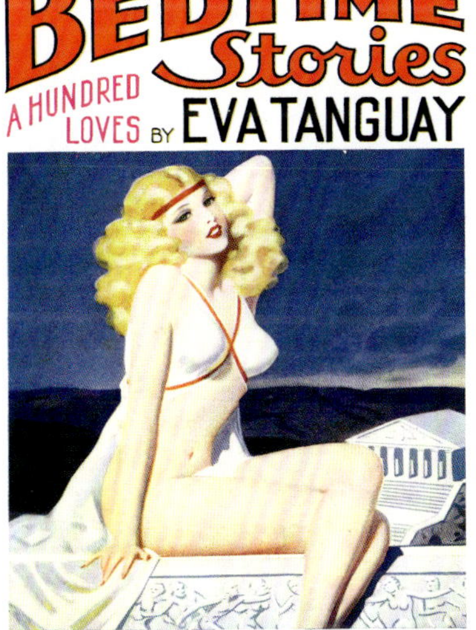

YEAR: **1933**. TITLE: **Bedtime Stories**.
COUNTRY: **USA**.

Nachrichtenblatt war im späten 19. Jahrhundert in den USA die wichtigste Quelle für Informationen von der Schattenseite des Lebens, optisch angereichert mit Fotografien halbnackter Frauen.

Die erste Konkurrenz erwuchs ANC, als Frank Munsey, der Pionier der amerikanischen Pulp-Magazine, auf die Idee kam, dass seine populären Unterhaltungsmagazine an den Zeitungsständen erhältlich sein sollten.

Munseys Kampfpreis von gerade einmal zehn Cent im Vergleich zu den üblichen fünfundzwanzig bis fünfzig Cent war American News zu wenig, und sie wiesen ihn ab. Ungerührt gründete er *Red Star News*, den ersten völlig unabhängigen Zeitschriftenvertrieb in den Staaten. Der Erfolg ließ nicht lange auf sich warten.

In den Zwanzigern des 20. Jahrhunderts kam es in den Großstädten zu echten Kriegen zwischen den Vertrieben, und so mancher Auslieferungsfahrer führte eine Schrotflinte mit sich. In dieser brisanten Phase etablierte Hearst archetypischer Gangster-Grossist und Brutalo-Vertriebschef M.L. Annenberg eine effiziente landesweite Infrastruktur für den Vertrieb seines eigenen speziellen Produktes: den täglichen Renntabellen für Pferdewetten. Geschwindigkeit und Pünktlichkeit wurden damit zur elementaren Voraussetzung eines regelmäßigen und zuverlässigen Zeitschriftenvertriebs.

In den Zwanzigern tauchten zahllose unabhängige Verleger-Grossisten mit neuen Titeln auf, die der konservativen ANC zu anstößig waren. Einer dieser Titel war Wilford Fawcetts *Capt. Billy's Whiz Bang* – ursprünglich nur ein Faltblatt mit derben Soldatenwitzen, das sich schnell zum auflagenstärksten Magazin für schlüpfrigen Humor in den Staaten mauserte. Fawcett baute eine starke Reihe neuer Zeitschriften und parallel dazu einen eigenen Vertriebszweig aus. Dank der absatzhungrigen

YEAR: **1950s**. TITLE: **Play-Girl**.
COUNTRY: **Denmark**.

Year: **1950s**. Title: **Natura**. Country: **Peru**.

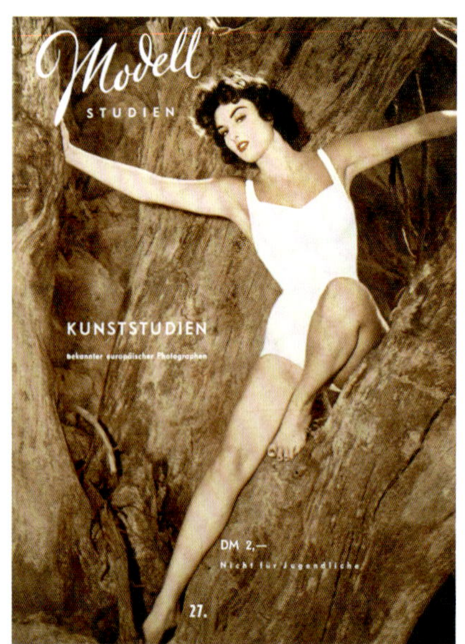

Year: **1950s**. Title: **Modellstudien**.
Country: **Germany**.

Verleger, die die selbstgefälligen *American News* umgehen wollten, gewannen die Independent Distributors, kurz IDs genannt, in den Zwanzigern an Zahl und Bedeutung.

In Europa mit seinen liberaleren Pressegesetzen und kleineren Märkten stellte sich die Situation anders dar. In Frankreich war die Regierung der Ansicht, dass Verleger durchsetzbare Bürgerrechte hätten, und die Grossisten wurden geradezu aufgefordert, alle Publikationen gleichwertig zu behandeln. Die Franzosen nutzten ihr größere Meinungsfreiheit, um zukunftsweisende visuelle Experimente wie die Folies-Aktfotoillustrierten der Zwanziger und Dreißiger zu etablieren, während man sich in Deutschland auf eher gesetztere Hefte spezialisierte, die sich mit diversen Gesundheits-, Kunst-, Schönheits- und Ästhetikaspekten befassten.

Ganze Schiffsladungen dieser europäischen Zeitschriften fanden durch das neue unabhängige Vertriebssystem der Zwanziger ihren Weg auf die amerikanischen Märkte und bewegten die amerikanischen Verleger, selbst ebenfalls schärfere Produkte anzubieten.

1932 gelangte Harry Donenfeld, ein Drucker, der sich auf moderat frivole Illustriertencover spezialisiert hatte, unfreiwillig in den Besitz einiger Pseudo-Aktkunstmagazine der Firma King Publishing, die ihre Druckrechnung nicht begleichen konnte. Plötzlich zum Verleger geworden, gründete Donenfeld eine neue und engagierte Vertriebsfirma namens Independent News. Sie wurde der Alleinvertreiber einer eigenen innovativen Mixtur von Trivialgeschichten und Sex-, der *Spicy*-Pulp-Reihe und der Titel *Ginger Stories* und *Broadway Nights*.

Der Zweite Weltkrieg war eine Boomzeit, aber in dem Jahrzehnt nach dem Krieg änderte sich das Unterhaltungsangebot dramatisch. Zeitschriften verkauften weltweit hohe Auflagen, doch die Amerikaner fanden schnell Gefallen an dem neuen Medium Fernsehen.

Die schwächelnde American News Company wurde derweil vom organisierten Verbrechen infiltriert. Während der gesamten fünfziger Jahre gab es Senatsuntersuchungen über das organisierte Verbrechen, bei denen auch *American News* unter die Lupe genommen wurde.

Anfang 1957 zog sich American News, angeschlagen und per Regierungsbeschluss gezwungen, ihre monopolistischen Praktiken aufzugeben, ganz aus dem Zeitschriftenmarkt zurück.

Da das familienfreundliche Fernsehen allem skeptisch gegenüberstand, das irgendetwas mit Sex zu tun hatte, kam in den späten Fünfzigern eine zweite Welle von Männermagazinen und unverhohlen sexorientierten Taschenbüchern auf den Markt. Amerikanische Verleger und Händler klagten die gleiche Toleranz und Akzeptanz ein, die für andere Märkte schon lange galten. Mit den neuen, von den unabhängigen Verlagen aufgebauten Originalausgaben im Taschenbuchformat, die bald zur vorherrschenden Lektüreform in den USA wurden, endeten die Fünfziger mit optimistischem Ausblick.

In dieser neuen liberalen Atmosphäre wurde Mickey Spillane mit seiner mitreißenden Mischung aus Sex und Gewalt zum meistverkauften Autor in der Geschichte der USA; die Printmedien eroberten auch die entlegensten Plätze des Kontinents, und Männermagazine wurden endlich offen an amerikanischen Zeitungsständen angeboten.

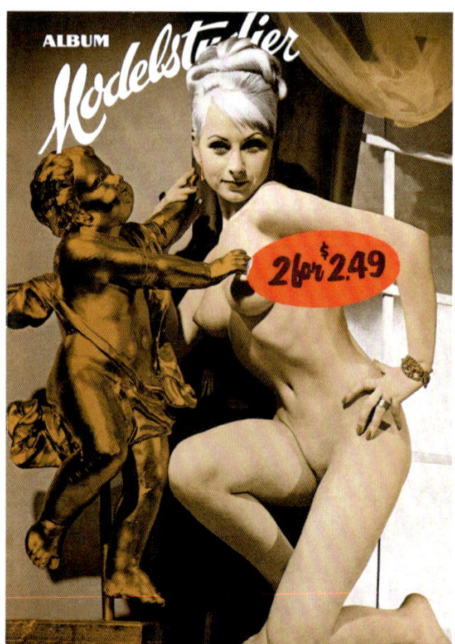

Year: **1950s**. Title: **Modellstudier**.
Country: **Denmark**.

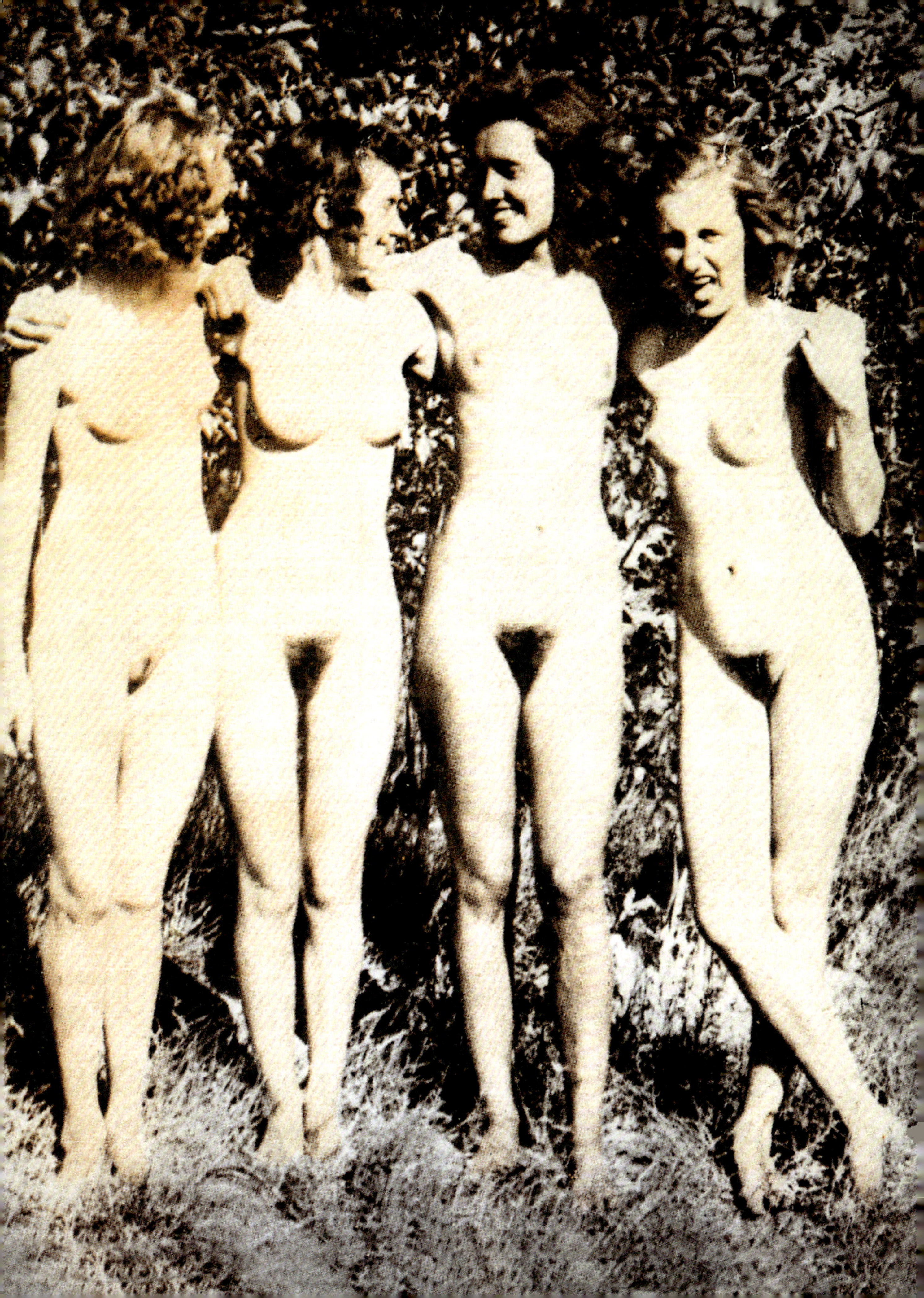

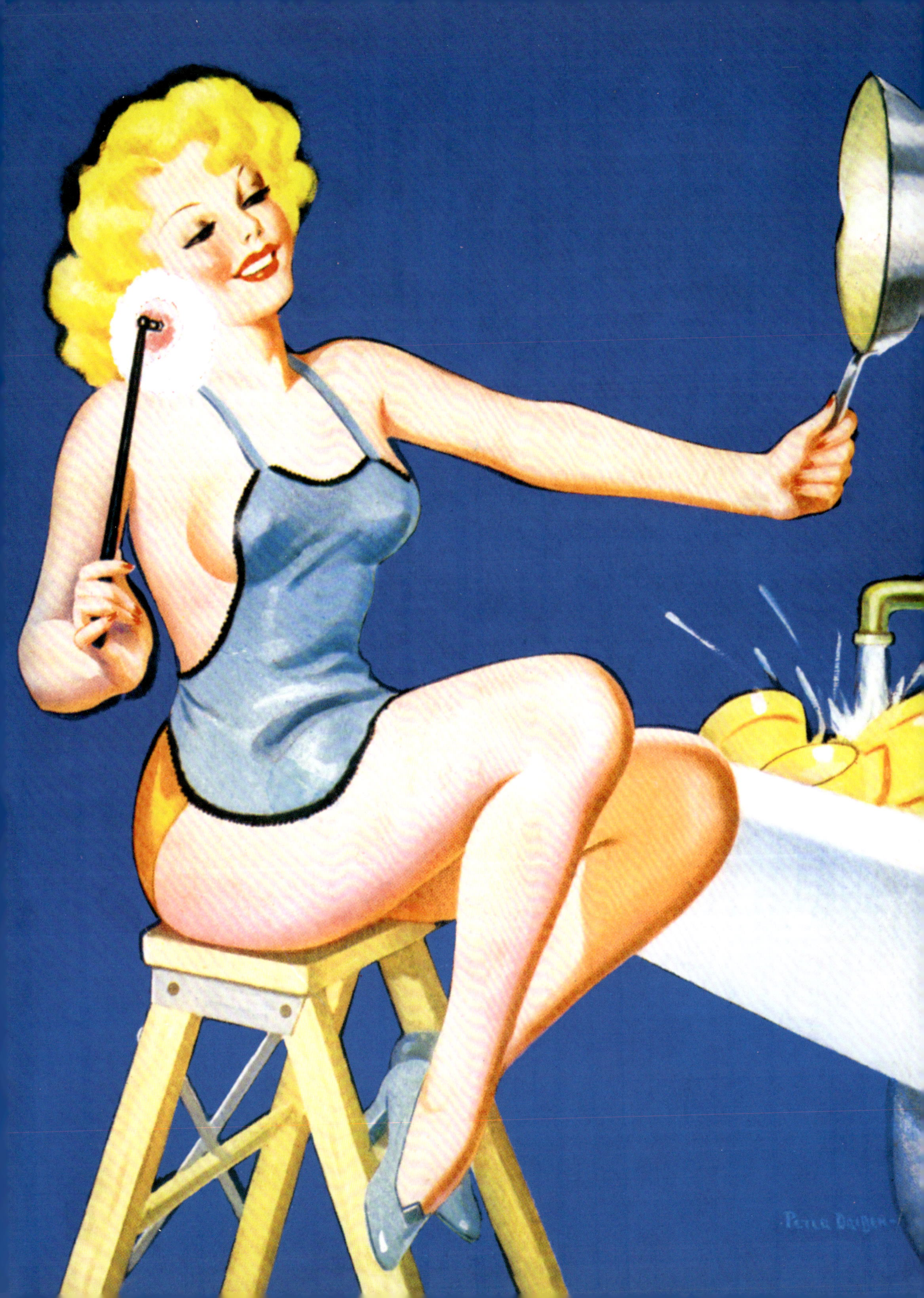

L'Essence du mâle

Par Dian Hanson

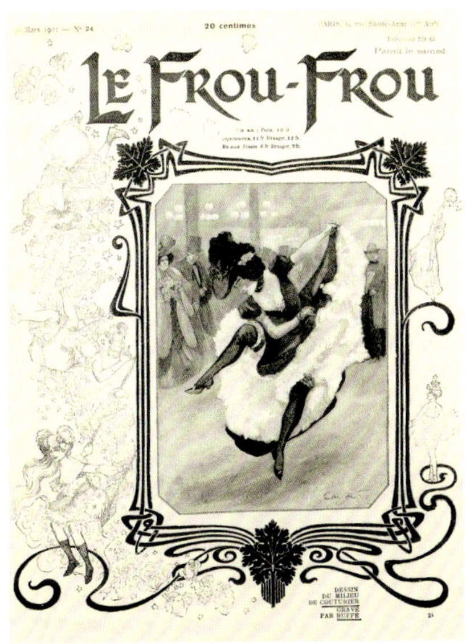

Year: **1901**. Title: **Le Frou-Frou**.
Country: **France**.

« Les histoires d'amour sensationnelles, et même les illustrations colorées de tons chauds telles que celles des Mille et une nuits (...) devraient être bannies (...) Renonçons à toute littérature excitante. Inutile de recommander le mariage au masturbateur impénitent dans l'espoir de le guérir de son vice. Celuici n'a plus ni le pouvoir ni le désir d'avoir des rapports naturels. En laissant libre cours à ses penchants dépravés, il a détruit en lui l'appétit naturel. Un être aussi dégénéré at-il le droit d'affliger sa descendance d'un héritage aussi pitoyable ? Il vaut mieux pour tous qu'il emporte dans sa tombe son vice et ses conséquences ». La Transmission de la vie, par le docteur George H. Napheys, J.G. Fergus & Co, 1872

Les publications sur la sexualité ont toujours été un champ de bataille. Dans un camp se trouvaient des hommes programmés mentalement et physiquement pour réagir à des images érotiques ; dans l'autre, d'autres hommes résolus à empêcher les premiers d'obtenir de ce qu'ils désiraient naturellement. Les deux premiers volumes retraçant l'histoire des magazines pour hommes traitent du combat entre la luxure et les tabous, débutant avec les premiers seins nus français en 1880 et s'achevant sur les seins nus américains en 1958. On peine à croire qu'il fallut soixante ans pour faire accepter les photos topless dans les kiosques à journaux des États-Unis et dans ceux de la plupart des autres pays du monde, et que chaque étape menant à cette petite victoire a représenté des centaines d'arrestations pour obscénité, des années de procès collectifs et d'emprisonnements, des millions de dollars, de marks, de couronnes et de pesos dépensés vainement pour tenter de soustraire le corps de la femme aux regards des hommes. En 1872, lorsque le docteur Napheys écrivait sur les effets de la littérature stimulante, on croyait que les

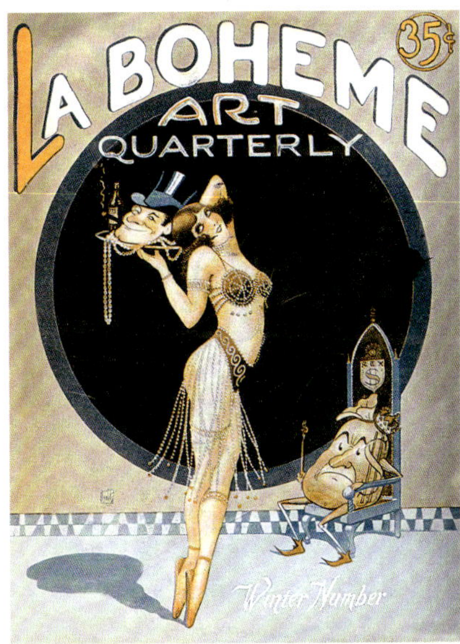

Year: **1925**. Title: **La Boheme Art Quarterly**.
Country: **USA**.

hommes naissaient avec un stock définitif « d'essence mâle ». Celle-ci ne servait pas uniquement à la procréation. Celui qui la gaspillait en se masturbant épuisait rapidement ses réserves, minant ainsi sa force physique, ses facultés intellectuelles, sa force morale et son courage, plus ou moins dans cet ordre. Et encore, le docteur Napheys comptait parmi les prophètes de malheur les plus mesurés. En guise de traitement contre le mal, il préconisait l'application d'un fer rouge sur les parties offensantes, et estimait, contrairement à bon nombre de

Year: **1937**. Title: **Pep Stories**.
Country: **USA**.

Year: **1925**. Title: **Paris Plaisirs**.
Country: **France**.

En 1865, l'appareil photo et la technologie du négatif s'étaient suffisamment développés pour pouvoir être utilisés par le tout-venant, qui s'empressa de prendre et de distribuer des photos de femmes nues.

ses collègues, que la castration était rarement nécessaire.

Cette hargne victorienne à l'encontre de la littérature érotique puisait en grande partie ses origines dans les théories de la dégénérescence du docteur Simon Tissot. Ce médecin suisse étudiait les effets féminisants de la castration au milieu des années 1700 et avait conclu – à tort – qu'ils étaient la conséquence directe de l'absence de sperme. Aggravant encore son erreur, il décréta que la masturbation excessive avait le même effet sur un homme aux testicules intègres. On peut s'étonner alors que la castration ait été envisagée comme traitement à la masturbation réfractaire mais, avec le temps, les moralistes du nord de l'Europe et des États-Unis avaient oublié l'idée de base et s'attelaient surtout à éradiquer le plaisir. Dans cette croisade, l'appareil photo et la presse écrite étaient considérés de plus en plus comme les suppôts de Satan.

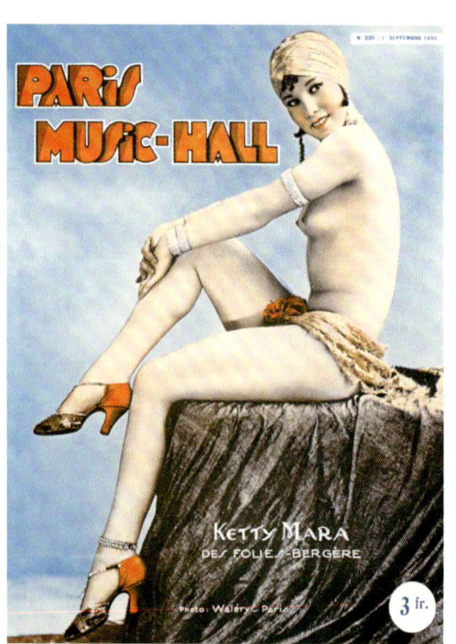

Year: **1930**. Title: **Paris Music-Hall**.
Country: **France**.

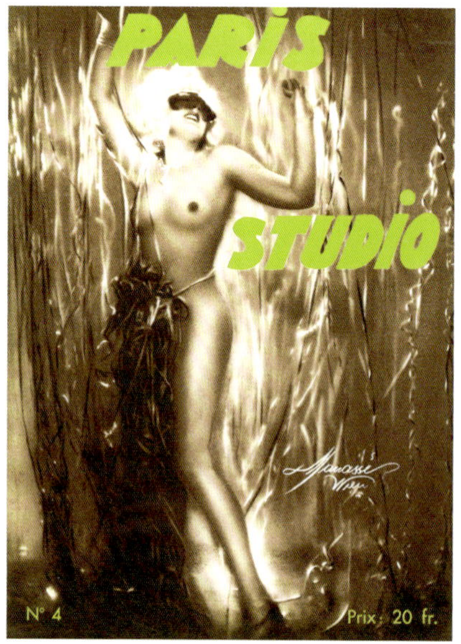

Year: **1920s**. Title: **Paris Studio**.
Artist: **Manassé**. Country: **France**.

L'appareil photo fut inventé dans les années 1830. En 1839, on parvint à obtenir un négatif rudimentaire permettant de produire plusieurs copies d'une même image. En 1865, l'appareil photo et la technologie du négatif s'étaient suffisamment développés pour pouvoir être utilisés par le tout-venant, qui s'empressa de prendre et de distribuer des photos de femmes nues.

Parallèlement, la technologie de l'imprimerie se perfectionnait, stimulée par l'augmentation du taux d'alphabétisation de la population. Avant la période victorienne, celle-ci était pratiquement illettrée, vivant en grande partie dans les campagnes, travaillant la terre. La révolution industrielle conduisit les paysans, ainsi que de nouveaux immigrants, dans les villes et les usines. Les ghettos de la classe ouvrière qui furent ainsi créés, avec leur criminalité, leur prostitution et leurs forts taux de mortalité infantile, entraînèrent des réformes sociales, dont une meilleure éducation pour tous.

Tant que la lecture restait l'apanage des classes supérieures, la demande en textes imprimés demeura limitée. Produits à petite échelle, les livres et les revues étaient chers. Avec l'alphabétisation, les classes ouvrières découvrirent le plaisir de lire. Les éditeurs s'empressèrent d'augmenter leurs productions pour satisfaire la demande toujours croissante en textes. Les bourses moyennes ne pouvaient s'offrir les livres luxueux à couverture dure, mais on s'arrachait les magazines bon marché et les romans de quatre sous proches des magazines. En Amérique, ces publications se concentraient sur des récits d'aventures dans le Far West, des faits divers sanglants et les romans sentimentaux. En Grande-Bretagne et en France, les histoires policières étaient également très prisées.

Dès 1860, des « romans sentimentaux » plus explicites firent leur apparition à New York. Vendus en petits nombres sous le manteau, ils furent produits pendant des années sans trop se faire remarquer jusqu'à 1868, lorsqu'ils attirèrent l'attention d'un jeune comptable nommé Anthony Comstock. Il est clair que Comstock avait toujours eu un problème avec ce qui procurait du plaisir à la plupart des hommes. Voici un échantillon de ses opinions sur la littérature érotique :

« Aucune plume ne saurait décrire les effets de cette malédiction sur nos jeunes et la société. Elle engendre le

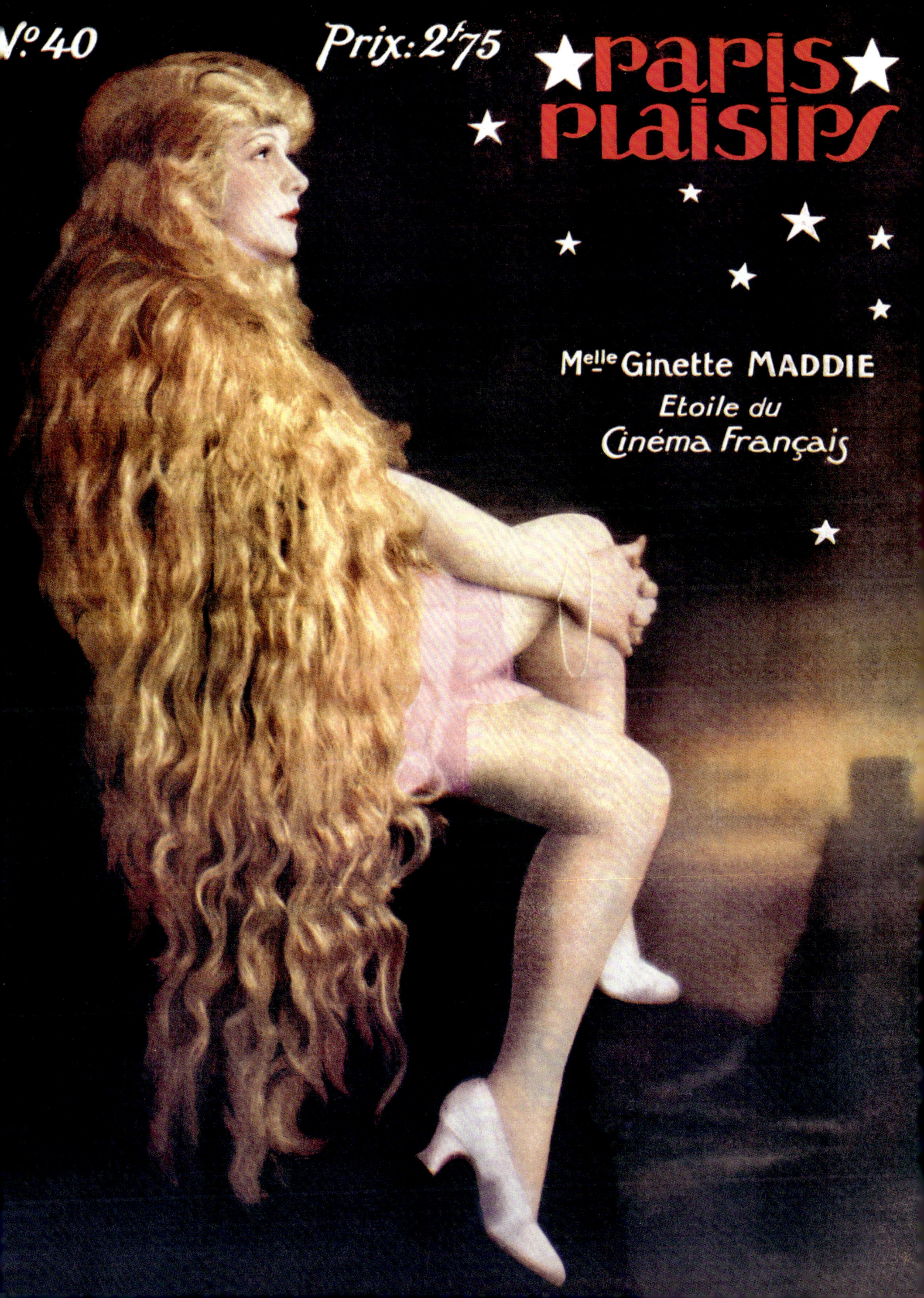

N°40
Prix: 2f75
PARIS PLAISIRS
Melle Ginette MADDIE
Etoile du
Cinéma Français

Au moment de la chute de la République de Weimar en 1933, des centaines de revues allemandes montraient du nu drapé dans des dizaines de prétextes philosophiques différents, sans qu'aucune n'admette chercher à titiller le lecteur.

stupre. La luxure souille le corps, dévergonde l'imagination, corrompt l'esprit, étouffe la volonté, détruit la mémoire, flétrit la conscience, endurcit le cœur et damne l'âme. Elle affaiblit le bras et rend le pas traînant. Elle dépouille l'âme de ses vertus viriles et imprime dans l'esprit des jeunes hommes et femmes des visions qui les hanteront pour le restant de leurs jours. Telle un panorama, l'imagination ramène toujours l'objet détestable devant l'esprit, s'imprégnant chaque fois un peu plus profondément en lui, plongeant la victime dans des pratiques qu'elle abhorre. Ce trafic multiplie les débauchés et les libertins dans notre société, les squelettes qui hantent bien des maisons. La famille est souillée, le foyer profané, et chaque nouvelle génération qui vient au monde est encore un peu plus affligée par cette faiblesse congénitale, fruit des graines semées par le Malin ».

Anthony Comstock ne perdit pas de temps pour se lancer à l'assaut des forces du mal dans son quartier. Il s'en prit à une poignée d'Irlandais qu'il accusa de produire de la pornographie et exigea de la police qu'elle les emprisonne. Cela devait marquer le début d'une longue campagne contre la littérature érotique qui déboucherait sur une loi fondamentale encore utilisée à ce jour pour poursuivre les éditeurs américains. Avec le soutien de la Young Men's Christian Association (YMCA), Comstock exerça sur le gouvernement des pressions si fortes et si longues que, de simple comptable qu'il était, il finit par tenir les rênes des services postaux des États-Unis.

Pourquoi ? Parce qu'outre le péché galopant dans les rues de son quartier de Brooklyn, Comstock s'était rendu

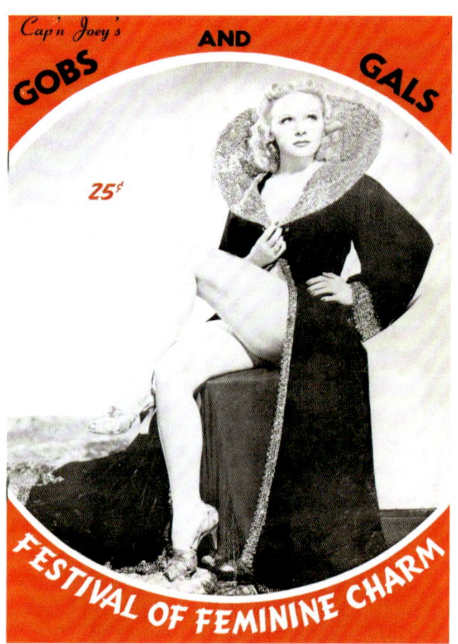

YEAR: **1940s.** TITLE: **Cap'n Joey's Gobs and Gals.** COUNTRY: **USA.**

compte qu'un flot d'obscénités abominables déferlait sur les États-Unis depuis le Vieux Continent, avant d'être acheminé par la poste jusqu'entre des mains innocentes. Il s'était juré de combattre les Européens jusqu'à ce qu'ils cessent de contaminer l'essence des mâles américains.

Dès le début, les Français furent des pionniers de l'art photographique. Vers la fin des années 1860, ils perfectionnaient déjà les techniques d'impression de clichés licencieux. Leurs cartes postales et leurs jeux de cartes, créés à cette époque, conquirent immédiatement le public masculin aux quatre coins du monde. Dans la foulée, ils réalisèrent dans les années 1870 les premiers magazines de charme sous forme de programmes de cabarets parisiens, incluant des photos de danseuses légères. Lorsque les mâles américains eurent vent de ces progrès, ils se montrèrent tout naturellement impatients d'enrichir leur éducation par des études françaises. Les plus entreprenants d'entre eux se lancèrent dans l'importation.

Avec le soutien d'experts tels que le docteur Napheys, le révérend Sylvester Graham (des fameux crackers Graham) et John Harvey Kellogg, (inventeur des cornflakes, protecteur acharné de l'intégrité du sperme et grand adepte du lavement), Anthony Comstock persuada le gouvernement que la nouvelle littérature obscène provenant de l'étranger faisait courir à l'essence mâle américaine un péril collectif imminent. Sa passion pour la suppression de la passion était si convaincante qu'en 1873 fut adoptée ce qu'on a baptisé la « Loi Comstock ». Son… euh… « essence » était la suivante :

« Aucun livre, pamphlet, image, essai, impression à caractère obscène, lubrique ou lascif ; aucune publication de nature indécente ; aucun article ou objet conçu pour ou destiné à la prévention de la contraception ou susceptible de provoquer un avortement ; aucun article ou objet visant ou adapté à tout usage indécent ou immoral ; aucun livre, pamphlet, carte, circulaire, publicité ou annonce, imprimé ou manuscrit, donnant directement ou indirectement des informations permettant de se procurer ou de fabriquer les éléments susmentionnés ; aucune carte postale ou lettre sur l'enveloppe de laquelle des épithètes indécents ou obscènes seraient écrits ou imprimés, ne seront acheminés par voie postale… »

La loi Comstock mit effectivement un sérieux frein à la propagation des premiers documents érotiques aux États-Unis, mais la couverture médiatique suscitée par son adoption dans les

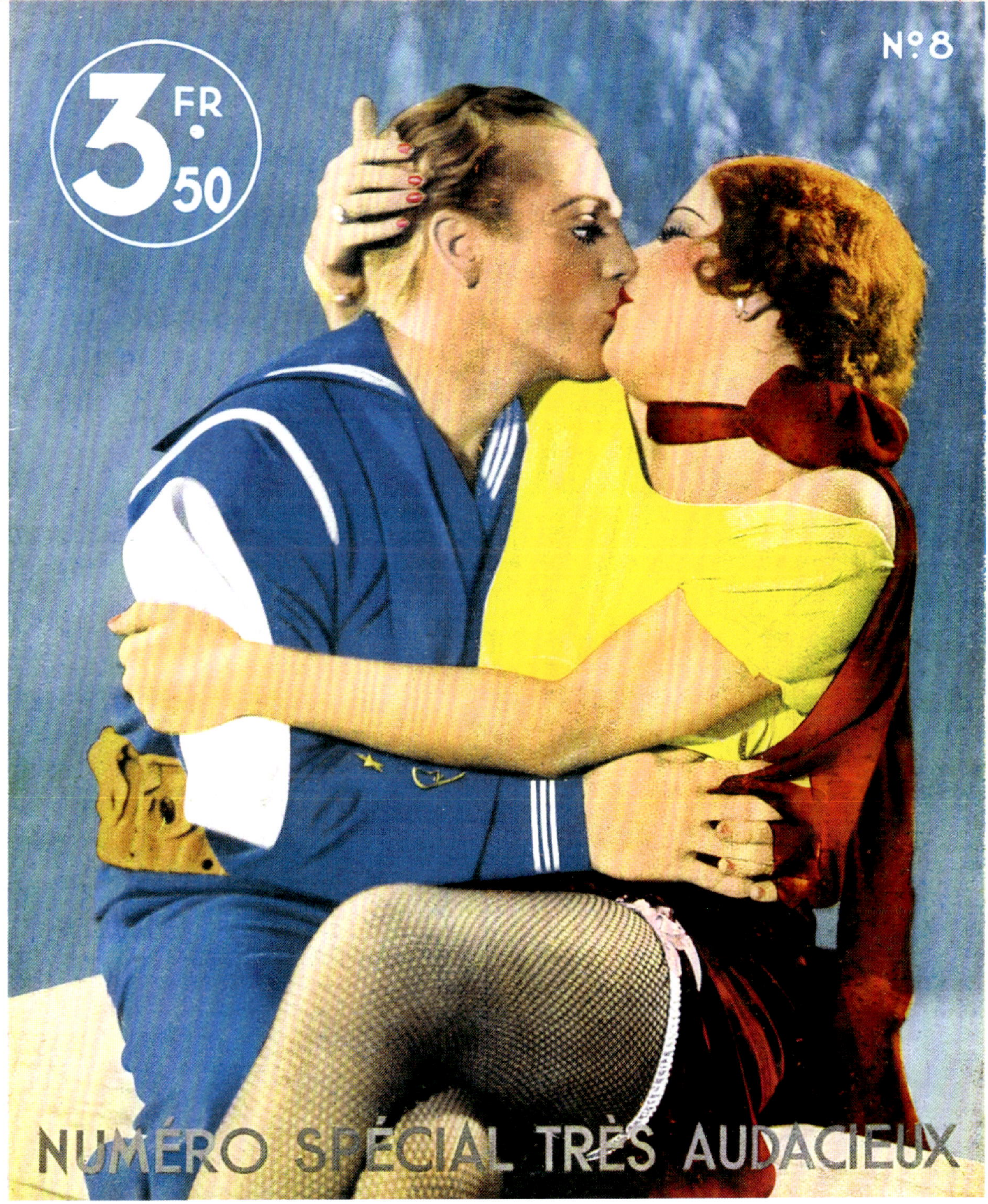

YEAR: **1935**. TITLE: **Pour Lire a Deux**. COUNTRY: **France**.

YEAR: **1950s**. TITLE: **Nouvelle Studio**. COUNTRY: **Denmark**.

Anthony Comstock persuada le gouvernement que la nouvelle littérature obscène provenant de l'étranger faisait courir à l'essence mâle américaine un péril collectif imminent.

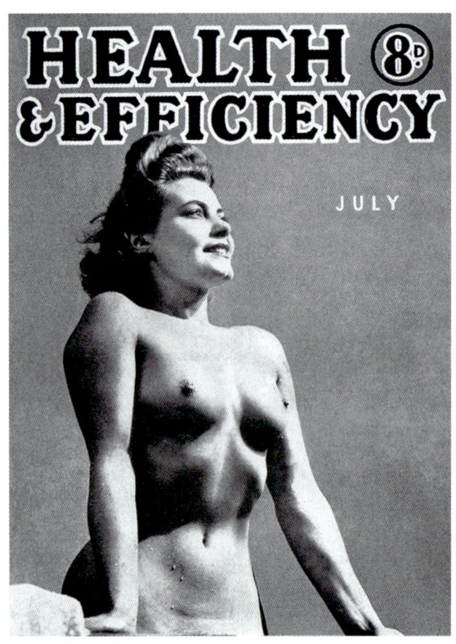

YEAR: **1945**. TITLE: **Health & Efficiency**. COUNTRY: **England**.

nouveaux magazines et tabloïdes alerta également le public sur la disponibilité d'une telle littérature. La plupart des hommes ne soupçonnaient même pas son existence. Une fois informés, et sachant dans quelles quantités (Comstock affirmait qu'il en arrivait des tonnes entières dans le pays), ils en voulurent.

Il faudrait attendre la fin de la Grande Guerre pour que de vrais magazines pour hommes soient publiés aux États-Unis mais des tabloïdes osés commencèrent à apparaître dès les années 1880 et 90. En outre, des livres, des photos et des jeux de cartes parvenaient à se faufiler entre les mailles des douanes, en dépit des efforts zélés d'Anthony Comstock et de divers « comités citoyens contre le vice » nouvellement créés. À mesure que le volume de littérature « intéressant les hommes » augmentait, il apparut de plus en plus évident qu'une grande partie du public avait consulté ou consultait ce genre de matériel sans en avoir été physiquement diminué, être devenu abruti ou avoir sombré dans la folie. Dans *The Secret Museum* (University of California Press, 1987), Walter Kendrick observe qu'à partir des années 1890, les tribunaux américains prirent de plus en plus en compte la qualité artistique dans leur définition de ce qui était obscène ou pas. Par exemple, une affaire jugée en 1894 concernant des exemplaires des Mille et une nuits, de l'Art de l'amour d'Ovide et du Décaméron de Boccace fut rejetée car l'Association pour la suppression du vice estima qu'il s'agissait de « classiques de réputation internationale… ne risquant guère d'être achetés ou vendus hormis par ceux qui s'intéressent à leurs qualités purement littéraires ».

Cette clémence ne s'étendait pas aux éditeurs qui s'adressaient à une clientèle moins raffinée.

« En 1896, la Cour suprême des États-Unis réexamina deux condamnations pour obscénité émises par des tribunaux d'instance inférieure. La première concernait Lew Rosen, éditeur de Broadway, un journal illustré sans aucune prétention au classicisme. Son numéro spécial ‹canaille› contenait des parties noircies au charbon que l'on pouvait frotter avec de la mie de pain pour révéler des femmes dans ‹différentes attitudes impudiques›. La Cour suprême confirma la sentence… »

J'ai longtemps cherché en vain un exemple de cette première tentative d'érotisme à l'américaine, mais je devine que, même si je parviens un jour à mettre la main sur un exemplaire, il doit être pratiquement impossible d'en retrouver un qui n'ait pas été « gratté ». L'éditeur Rosen inaugurait ce qui allait devenir un cliché américain : le pornographe juif des villes. La plupart de ces premiers entrepreneurs du secteur de l'érotisme étaient des immigrants d'Europe de l'Est possédant une grande culture littéraire, des moyens limités pour assurer leur subsistance dans le Nouveau Monde et aucun des sinistres préjugés chrétiens qui hantaient des hommes comme Comstock. Plus tard, l'industrie américaine des revues de charme serait surnommée « la mafia juive » mais, en 1900, ils n'étaient qu'une poignée vivant dans les ghettos de New York à faire du porno pour joindre les deux bouts, souvent aidés par leurs femmes et leurs enfants.

La pâte à papier fit son apparition vers la même époque, à la fin des années 1890. Ce fut vite une véritable aubaine pour l'industrie naissante de la revue pour hommes comme pour le public en mal de publications. Auparavant, on connaissait surtout le « papier chiffon », littéralement fabriqué avec des chiffons (le plus souvent des vêtements en coton recyclés puis blanchis à l'argile). Cela donnait un support extrêmement durable aux excellentes qualités de reproduction. Les livres imprimés sur ce genre de papier peuvent survivre des siècles. Toutefois, le procédé était comparativement coûteux et ne convenait pas à la production de magazines bon marché jetés, sitôt lus. Néanmoins, jusqu'en 1890, la plupart des revues étaient imprimées sur ce genre de papier alors que les quotidiens recouraient au fin papier journal. La pâte ou pulpe à papier était un produit de la nouvelle industrie du bois de l'Ouest. Fabriquée avec de la fibre de bois ramollie à l'acide, elle était plus robuste que le papier journal,

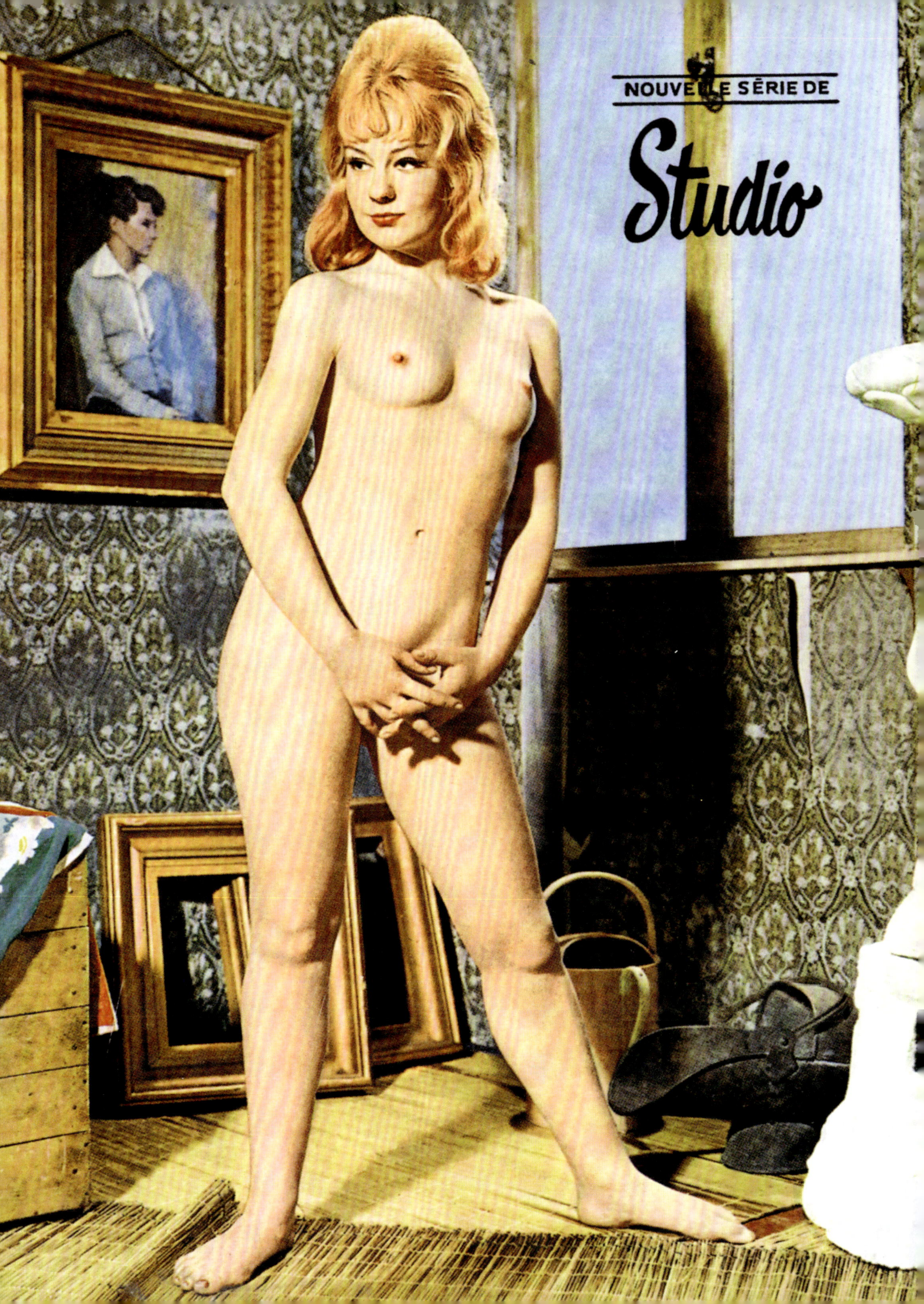
NOUVELLE SÉRIE DE
Studio

Year: **1937**. Title: **Stocking Parade**. Country: **USA**.

beaucoup moins coûteuse à produire que le papier chiffon. En outre, elle s'autodétruisait au bout d'un moment, les acides utilisés dans sa fabrication la rongeant rapidement. La pulpe de papier était trop rêche pour obtenir une bonne qualité de reproduction mais assez bonne pour le genre de fiction bon marché très prisé au début du siècle. De 1900 aux années 1950, des centaines de millions de romans et de magazines de fiction à sensation abordant des domaines aussi divers que les enquêtes policières, la conquête de l'Ouest, les histoires d'amour, la science-fiction et l'érotisme, seraient proposés au public à des prix abordables sur du papier « pulp » bon marché. Pour accrocher le client dans les kiosques, les pages intérieures, de qualité inférieure, étaient prises en sandwich entre des couvertures en papier glacé et aux couleurs vives, arborant le plus souvent une femme voluptueuse chichement vêtue, même s'il s'agissait de science-fiction ou d'une histoire fleur bleue. Les « pulps » comme on finit par appeler l'ensemble du genre, s'adressaient à un public des deux sexes, avide de sensations, à une époque où les photos coquines étaient lourdement censurées.

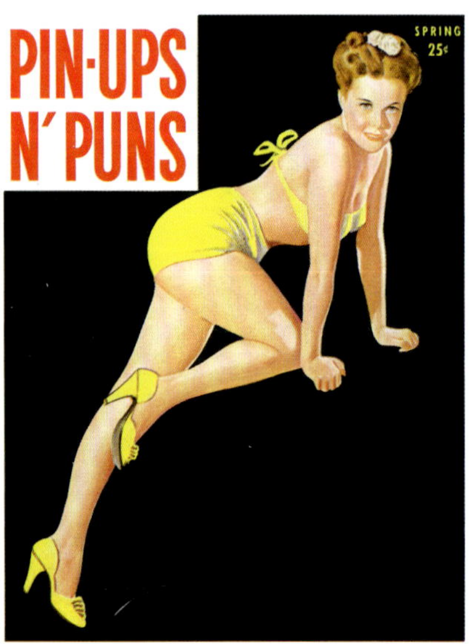

Year: **1944**. Title: **Pin-ups n' Puns**. Country: **USA**.

Pendant ce temps, dans la France du début du siècle, les paroles étaient plus sujettes à la censure que les photos… tant que ces photos affirmaient être de l'art. Les Français avaient, traditionnellement, une bien plus haute estime pour l'art que les Américains et n'étaient pas du genre à s'effaroucher pour un petit bout de sein. Ils connaissaient les magazines d'art contenant des « études » (où l'on montrait des femmes intégralement nues), à un âge où l'Amérique en était encore à frotter du noir de charbon avec un bout de pain pour apercevoir une vague jarretelle. La censure était nettement plus sévère avec les revues qui admettaient ne chercher qu'à émoustiller leurs lecteurs mais *La Vie Parisienne*, fondée en 1863 et relancée juste avant la Première Guerre mondiale, parvenait à mêler nus discrets, nouvelles osées et humour tout en était largement acceptée en raison du fait qu'elle était raisonnablement sophistiquée, une qualité aussi respectée en France que l'art.

En 1900, l'Allemagne était le troisième pays à se préparer un riche avenir érotique tout se débattant avec ses propres conflits moraux. Les effets dégénérescents de la masturbation récréative étaient dénoncés avec autant de vigueur qu'aux États-Unis mais l'Allemagne avait le contrepoids de Sigmund Freud, qui mettait en garde contre un refoulement sexuel tout aussi néfaste. En outre, l'Allemagne était également confrontée aux effets de la révolution industrielle, qui amenait des indésirables dans le pays et minait la santé de ses citoyens. Cela inspira un culte de l'eugénisme qui prit rapidement de l'ampleur et favorisa l'essor du socialisme. Ce mélange donna naissance au « mouvement de la beauté » et à ses magazines. On y vénérait tout ce qui était charmant, mais particulièrement les corps nus des jeunes aryennes. Comme en France, tout était une question de contexte : la nudité était acceptée tant qu'elle était présentée de manière asexuelle. Naturellement, n'importe quel adolescent ayant fantasmé en regardant un catalogue de lingerie fine (ou même les pages de sous-vêtements du catalogue de La Redoute) vous dira qu'il se fiche pas mal du contexte. Mais en présumant qu'à toute époque, bon nombre de censeurs étaient dans le coup, à savoir qu'ils avaient autant envie de voir des nus que n'importe quel autre homme mais ne pouvaient l'admettre, nous comprenons que cette histoire de contexte arrangeait tout le monde. En Allemagne, au cours des trois premières décennies du 20e siècle, ce concept du contexte de la nudité serait poussé plus loin que nulle part ailleurs. Au moment de la chute de la République de Weimar en 1933, des centaines de revues allemandes montraient du nu drapé dans des dizaines de prétextes philosophiques différents, sans qu'aucune n'admette chercher à titiller le lecteur.

Au fil du siècle, des éditeurs en Angleterre, en Suède, en Argentine, au Japon, aux Mexique, au Danemark et ailleurs allaient se lancer à leur tour à l'assaut de l'essence mâle… et celle-ci s'avérer inépuisable. Allant au bout de leurs forces

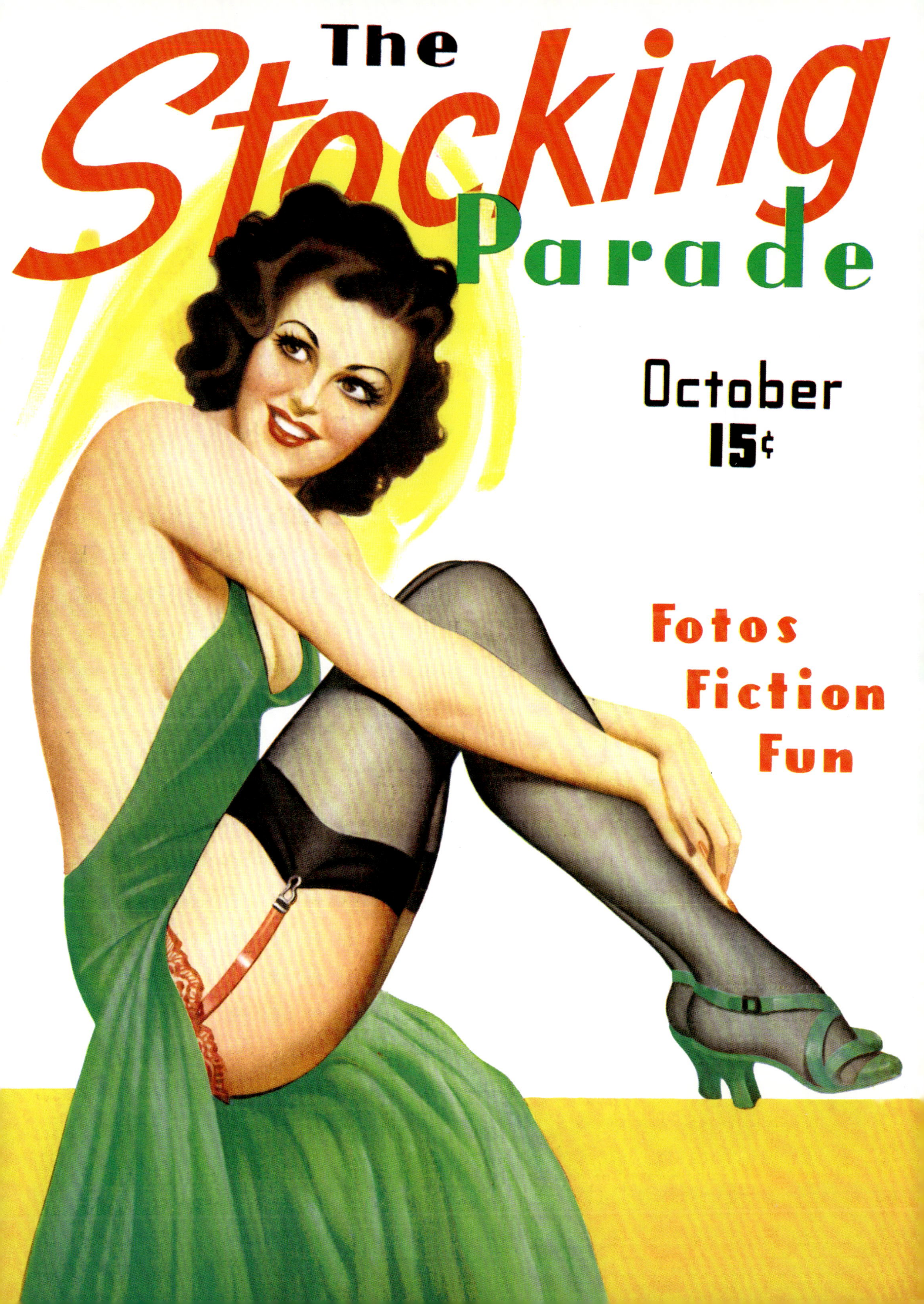
The
Stocking
Parade
October
15¢
Fotos
Fiction
Fun

Year: **1957**. Title: **Showgirls**.
Artist: **McCartney**. Country: **USA**.

avec rigueur et souvent vigueur, les hommes démontrèrent qu'aucune quantité d'histoires d'amour sensationnelles ou d'images vivement colorées ne pouvait tarir leur source de virilité. Toutefois, cela prit beaucoup plus de temps qu'on aurait pu le croire. L'eugénisme, la réponse du vingtième siècle aux théories de la dégénérescence du docteur Tissot, fit des adeptes dans de nombreux pays et ne tomba en disgrâce qu'après que le Troisième Reich l'eut détourné de sa fonction première au début des années 1940. En 1928, dans Safe Council or Practical Eugenics, le docteur B.G. Jefferis mettait encore en garde :

« ...Les garçons sont parfois fortement tentés d'acheter et de faire circuler entre eux des images représentant le corps sans vêtements décents, voire même des rapports charnels. On ne peut tout simplement pas se permettre de laisser des images impures s'imprimer dans nos esprits. Elles ne s'effacent plus. Des années après les avoir vues, et probablement longtemps après que ce qu'on vous en a dit a été oublié, vous vous en souvenez encore. (...) J'ai entendu des hommes dire qu'ils donneraient n'importe quelle somme d'argent pour pouvoir débarrasser leur mémoire de quelque image abjecte sur laquelle ils s'étaient trop épanchés dans leur jeunesse. »

Je n'étais pas là et ne peux donc pas en débattre avec le bon docteur Jefferis mais, pour préparer cet ouvrage, j'ai passé quelques jours (une dizaine) connectée au site Internet de vente aux enchères Ebay, section « public averti ». Forte de l'autorité discutable que cela me confère, je peux témoigner que de nombreux hommes sont prêts à se départir de n'importe quelle somme d'argent

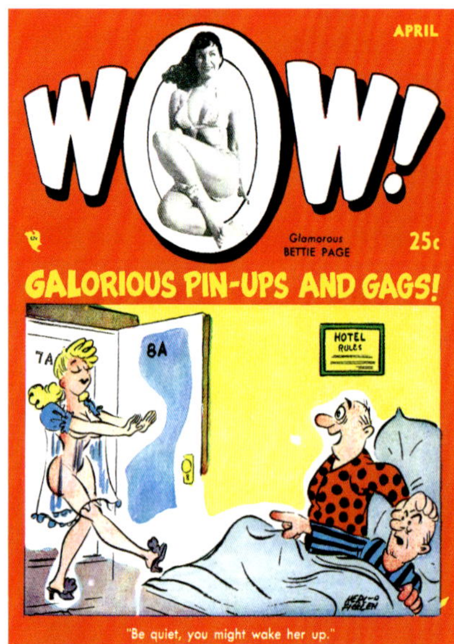

Year: **1956**. Title: **Wow**. Country: **USA**.

pour racheter cette image sur laquelle ils s'épanchaient adolescents.

Si vous avez vécu assez longtemps, vous retrouverez sans doute entre ces pages quelques bons souvenirs, mais, quel que soit votre âge, vous y découvrirez des choses qui vous feront sourire, vous stupéfieront, vous en apprendront, et qui, disons-le, réveilleront votre essence. À l'origine, ce projet devait comporter deux volumes couvrant la période de 1945 aux années 1980. Quand je me suis mise à chiner chez les bouquinistes spécialisés dans les vieux journaux, à parler à des collectionneurs et après avoir passé mes premières douze heures d'affilée sur Ebay, je me suis rendue compte qu'il fallait commencer plus tôt. Je venais de décider de démarrer en 1900 quand je suis tombée sur les programmes des Folies françaises datant des années 1880. Le projet est passé de deux à trois volumes, puis à six, et pourtant il y avait toujours plus de titres qu'on ne pouvait en loger. Au cours de la brève année pendant laquelle j'ai travaillé à ce projet, j'ai fait mon possible pour obtenir les informations correctes sur les publications et ceux qui les ont réalisées mais, inévitablement, compte tenu du fait que la plupart travaillaient dans le plus grand secret, certains faits s'avéreront inexacts. D'emblée, je m'en excuse. En revanche, les magazines n'ont pas à rougir de quoi que ce soit. La créativité avec laquelle ces premiers titres de charme furent réalisés a de quoi faire honte à tout ce qui se fait aujourd'hui. Mais je suppose que vous vous en êtes déjà aperçu car même Anthony Comstock n'aurait eu la force de caractère de lire cette introduction interminable avant d'avoir admiré les photos qui suivent.

GAGS...GALS AND LAUGHS GALORE ★ ★ 25¢ ANC

SHOWGIRLS

LY

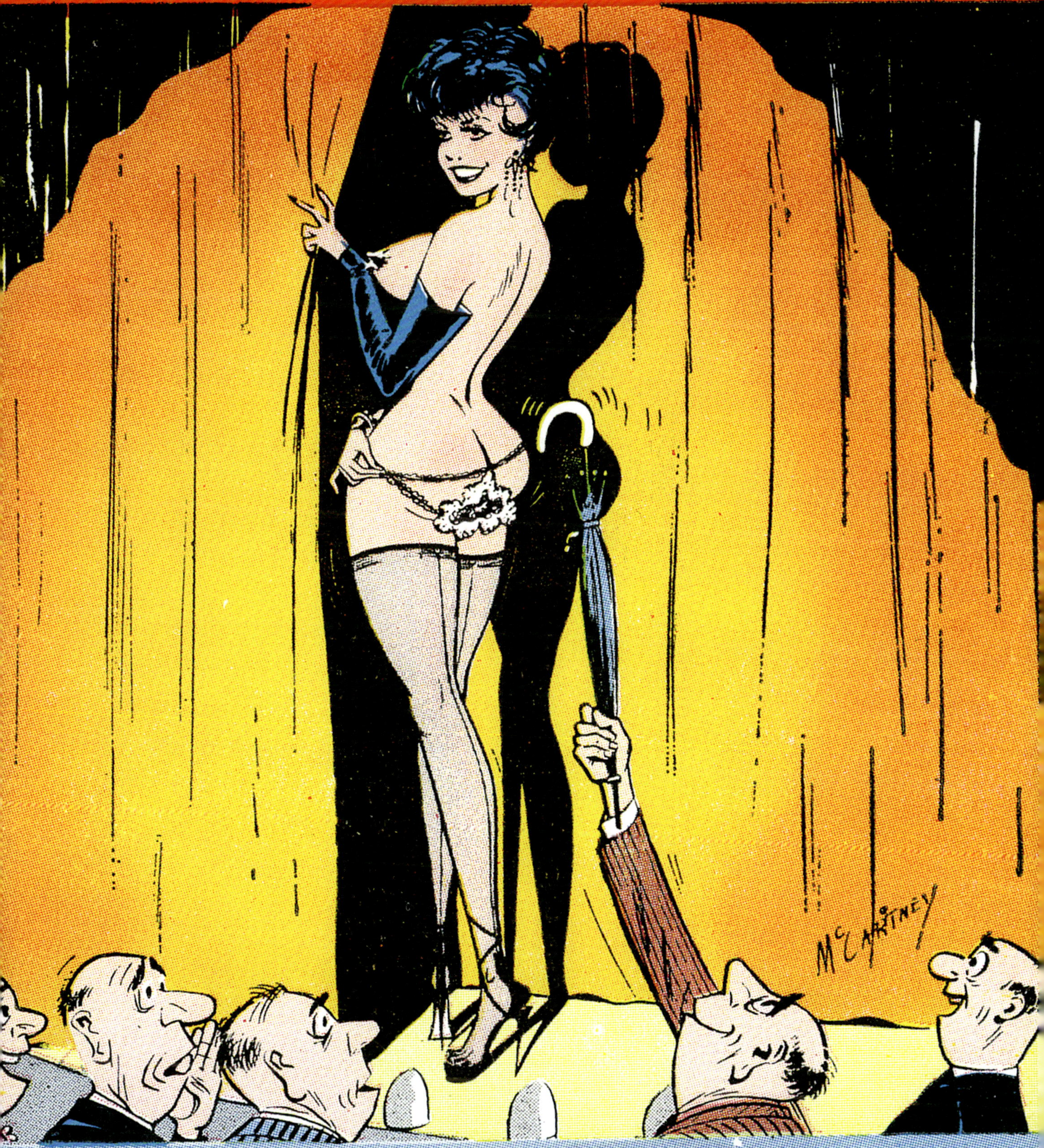

HE'S A DO-IT-YOURSELF FANATIC!

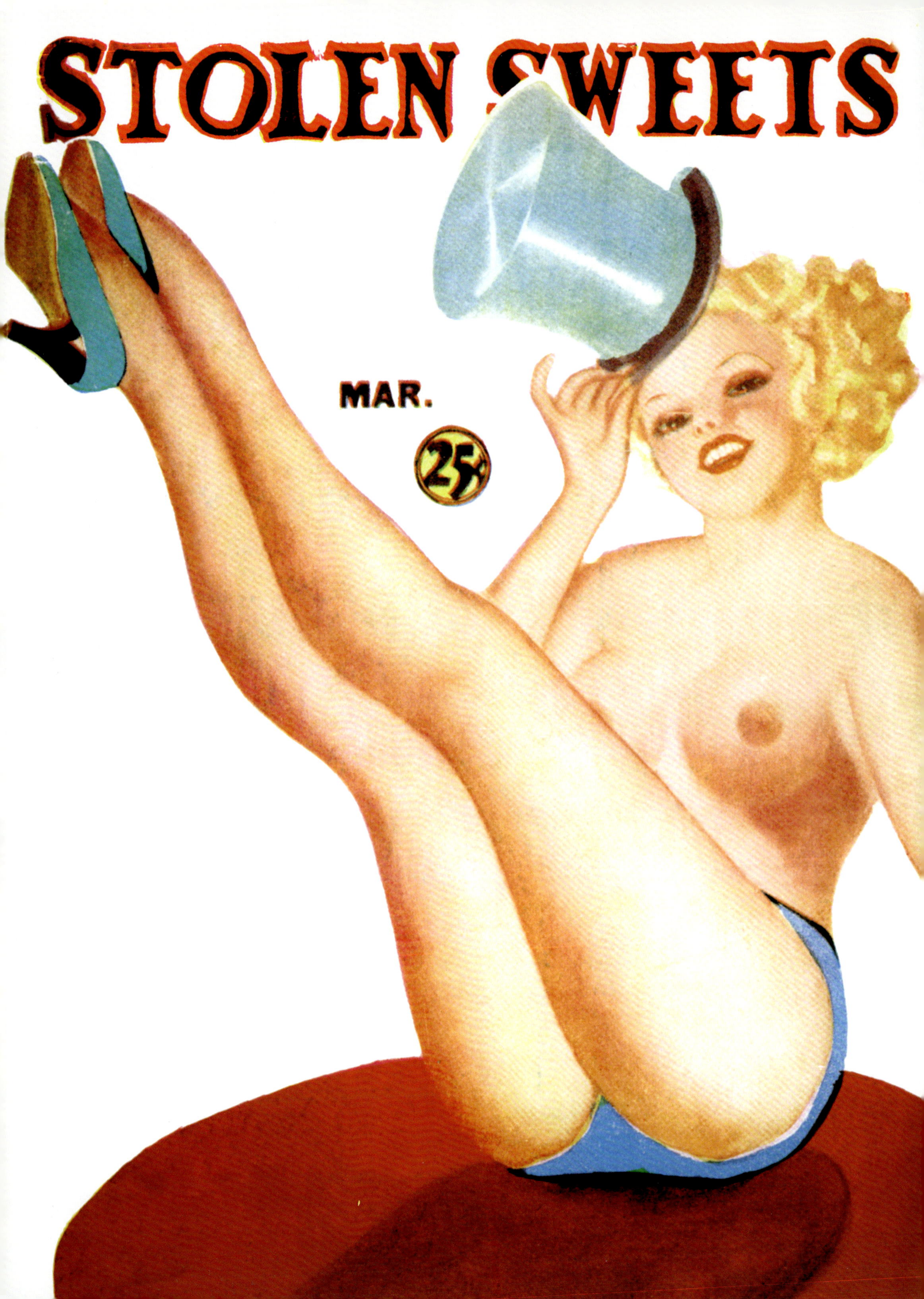
STOLEN SWEETS
MAR.
25¢

La distribution pour les masses

Par Michael Feldman

Face à un rayon croulant sous un éventail apparemment infini de produits avec lesquels les éditeurs rivalisent pour attirer notre attention, on se pose rarement la question : comment ces magazines sontils arrivés jusqu'ici ? Et sa corollaire : qui les y a mis ?

En 1864, les deux plus gros distributeurs des États-Unis fusionnèrent pour créer l'American News Company (l'ANC). Premier système de distribution couvrant tout le continent, l'ANC établit un puissant monopole sur tous les périodiques existants. Il créa des milliers de points de vente situés à proximité des grands carrefours, dans les gares ferroviaires puis, plus tard, les gares routières, et construisit des centaines d'entrepôts dans des lieux stratégiques.

Accélérant leur diffusion à l'échelle nationale, le gouvernement fédéral des États-Unis, initialement pour assurer la liberté de la presse, accorda aux journaux et à tout ce qui pouvait passer pour des périodiques des tarifs subventionnés leur permettant d'être acheminés à moindre frais par le réseau ferroviaire, alors pleine expansion. De la sorte, envoyer un magazine ou un quotidien à 5000 km devenait économiquement rentable. Les éditeurs entreprenants sautèrent immédiatement sur cette occasion en or. L'une des premières « autorisation d'acheminement à tarif réduit »

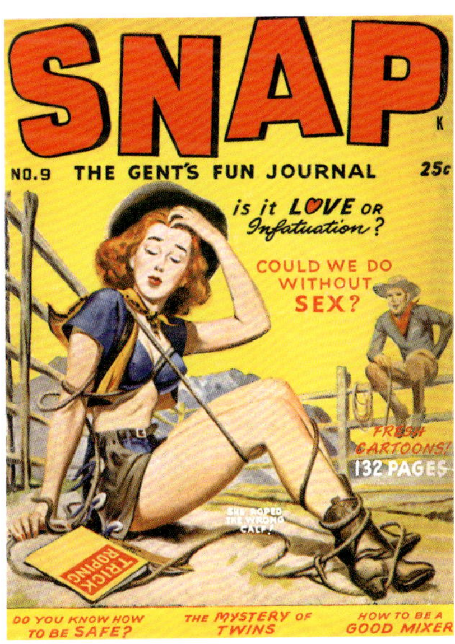

Year: **1949**. Title: **Snap**. Country: **USA**.

fut accordée par les services postaux américains en 1879 à *The Police Gazette*. À la fin du 19e siècle, ce « journal » devint le premier pourvoyeur de faits divers sordides, généreusement illustrés de photos osées de dames en petites tenues.

Frank Munsey, père de la revue « pulp » américaine, fut le premier à desserrer l'étau de l'ANC en décidant que ses magazines de fiction grand public devaient être disponibles dans des kiosques.

Le prix au numéro des revues de Munsey, à peine 0,10$ alors que la norme oscillait entre 0,25 et 0,50$, était considéré trop bas par l'ANC, qui le rejeta. Ne se laissant pas abattre, il fonda alors *Red Star News*, le premier distributeur de journaux totalement indépendant des États-Unis. Le succès fut pratiquement instantané.

D'autres éditeurs lui emboîtèrent le pas. Le magnat de la presse William Randolph Hearst créa un système de distribution pour ses journaux et sa collection croissante de magazines. Dans les années vingt, une série de réseaux de distribution des quotidiens furent installés dans les grandes villes, avec des chauffeurs des camions de livraison armés. Au cours de cette période explosive, M. L. Annenberg, archétype du gangster distributeur, directeur de la diffusion et gros bras de Hearst, créa une infrastructure efficace pour la diffusion dans tout le pays de son propre produit spécialisé, les rapports quotidiens des courses de chevaux. La vitesse et la ponctualité devinrent les éléments fondamentaux de messageries de presse régulières et fiables.

Une nuée d'autres éditeurs/distributeurs indépendants inaugurèrent les années vingt avec de nouvelles gammes de produits, dont bon nombre trop corsés pour la prude ANC. Parmi eux, Wilford Fawcett et son *Capt. Billy's Whiz Bang*, initialement une simple feuille de plaisanteries de corps de garde qui évolua

Year: **1936**. Title: **Stolen Sweets**.
Country: **USA**.

Year: **1956**. Title: **Mirth**. Country: **USA**.

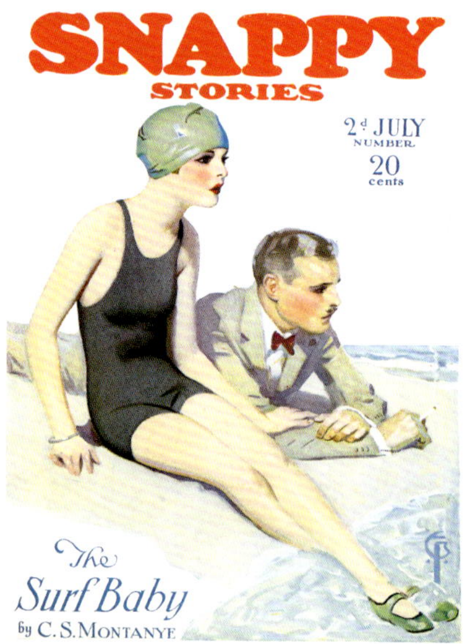

Year: **1936**. Title: **Snappy Stories**.
Country: **USA**.

rapidement en premier magazine américain d'humour salace. Fawcett mit sur pied une solide collection de nouveaux magazines et une branche de distribution parallèle.

Au cours des années vingt, les Distributeurs Indépendants (I. D.), augmentèrent en nombre et en taille, alimentés par des éditeurs pressés d'acheminer leurs publications et souhaitant contourner l'ANC jugée trop arrogante.

La situation en Europe était différente, grâce à un climat éditorial plus libéral et des marchés plus réduits. En France, le gouvernement estimait que les éditeurs de journaux jouissaient de droits civils devant être respectés et que les distributeurs avaient donc l'obligation de distribuer équitablement toutes les publications. Dans les années 1920 et 30, grâce à une plus grande liberté dans l'expression de leurs modes de vie, les Français purent réaliser des expériences visuelles avant-gardistes tels que les « folies », ou magazines de photos de nu, tandis que l'Allemagne se spécialisait dans des variantes plus centrées sur « la santé, l'art, la beauté et l'esthétique ».

Dans les années vingt, ces magazines européens débarquaient sur les marchés américains par bateaux entiers, acheminés par le nouveau système de Distribution Indépendante, incitant les éditeurs américains à produire à leur tour des revues plus osées.

En 1932, Harry Donenfeld, un imprimeur spécialisé dans les couvertures de magazine vaguement suggestives, se retrouva malgré lui propriétaire de revues de nus pseudoartistiques dont l'éditeur, King Publishing, était en cessation de paiement. Reconverti en éditeur, il devint le fer de lance d'une nouvelle société de distribution énergique et très efficace, Independent News, qui était l'unique distributeur de sa nouvelle ligne de magazines « pulp » *Spicy*, mélange innovateur de fiction et d'érotisme, ainsi que de *Ginger Stories* et de *Broadway Nights*.

La Seconde Guerre mondiale fut une période prospère mais au cours de la décennie qui suivit la guerre, les goûts des consommateurs évoluèrent rapidement. Les ventes de magazines étaient en augmentation partout dans le monde mais les Américains furent vite séduits par le nouveau média télévisuel qui amenait les divertissements gratuitement et directement dans leurs foyers.

Entretemps, l'ANC déjà boiteuse était de plus en plus infiltrée par la mafia. Tout au long des années cinquante, le Sénat ordonna des enquêtes sur le crime organisé et l'ANC fut surveillée de près.

Au début de 1957, l'ANC, désormais dépassée et contrainte par un décret gouvernemental d'abandonner ses tactiques monopolistiques, ferma sa branche de distribution de périodiques.

La télévision, à vocation familiale, rechignait à traiter quoi que ce soit ayant trait de près ou de loin à la sexualité, ce qui favorisa une seconde vague de revues pour hommes et de romans érotiques explicites qui déferla sur le marché à la fin des années cinquante. Les éditeurs et les distributeurs américains commencèrent à exiger le même degré de tolérance et d'acceptation que celui dont bénéficiaient d'autres marchés mondiaux depuis tant d'années.

Les années 1950 s'achevèrent sur une note encourageante : le roman à couverture souple, soutenu par I.D., devint la forme de lecture dominante en Amérique du Nord. Dans cette nouvelle atmosphère libérale, les romans de Mickey Spillane, avec leur mélange capiteux de sexe et de violence, devinrent des bestsellers, battant tous les records de vente aux États-Unis. La presse s'immisça avec succès dans les moindres recoins du continent et les revues pour hommes purent enfin être présentées ouvertement et librement dans les kiosques à journaux américains.

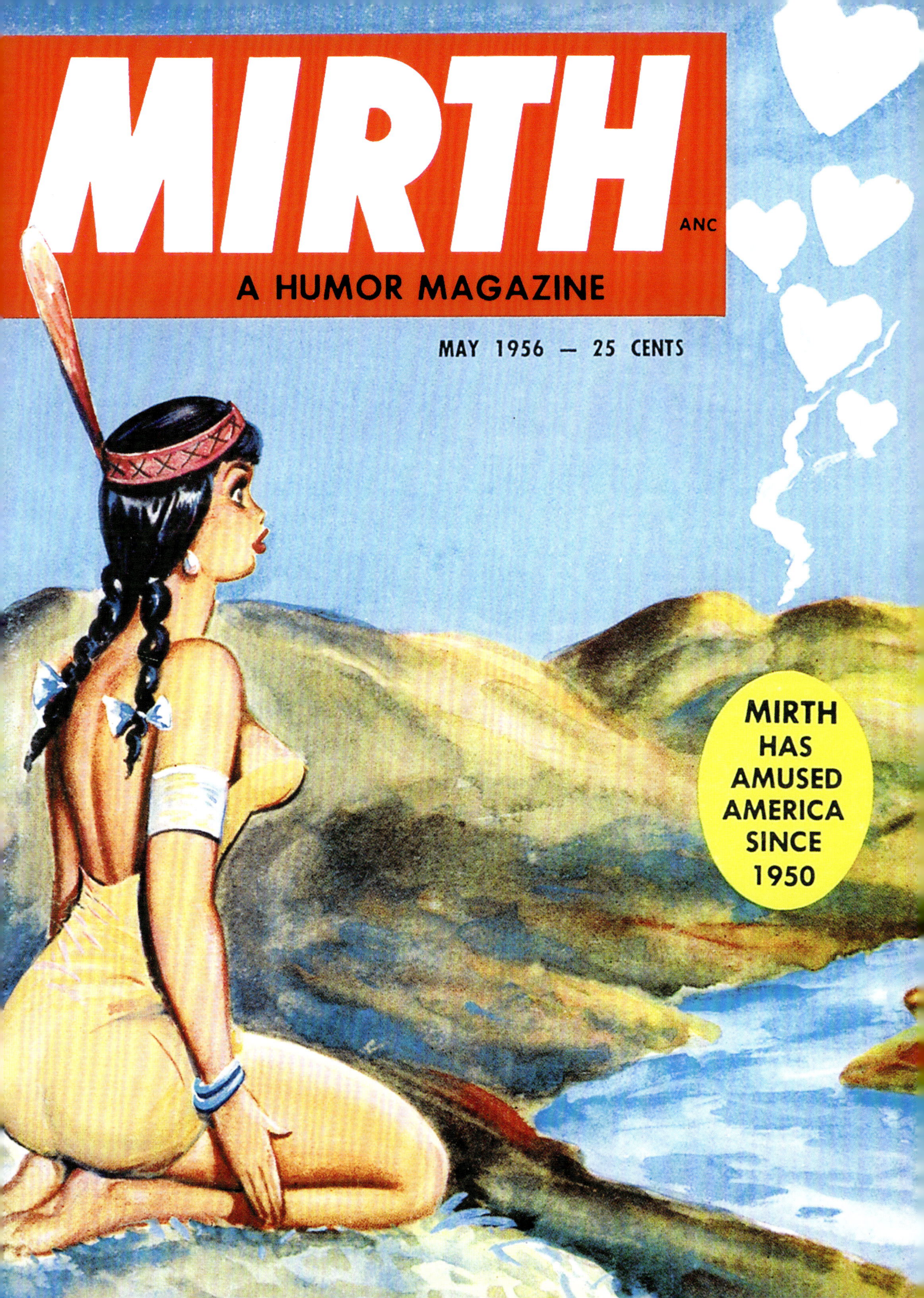
MIRTH
ANC
A HUMOR MAGAZINE
MAY 1956 — 25 CENTS
MIRTH
HAS
AMUSED
AMERICA
SINCE
1950

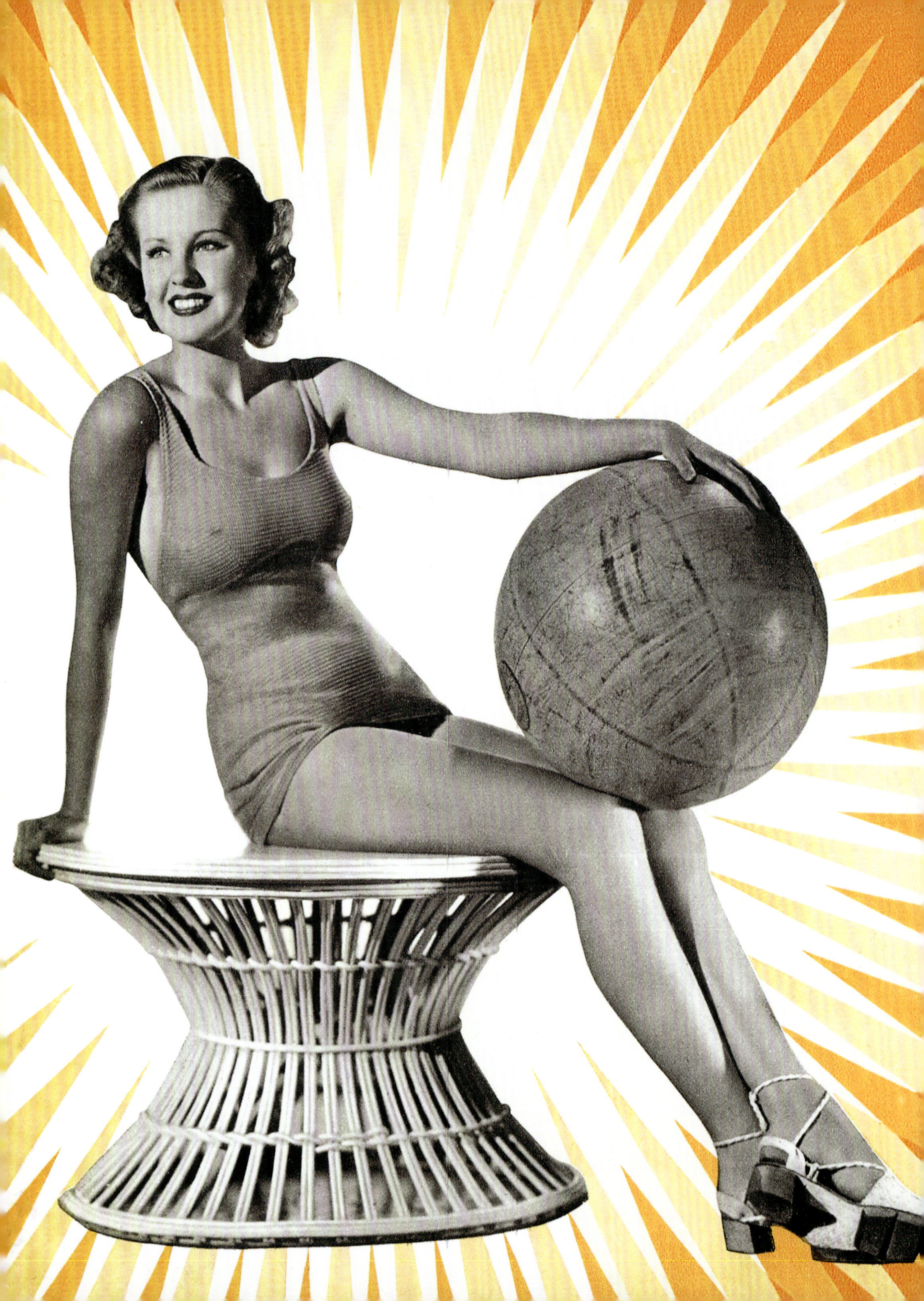

PARIS 1900–1938:

Cradle of Print Erotica

Paris 1900–1938: Die Wiege der Männermagazine
Paris 1900–1938 : berceau de l'érotisme sur papier glacé

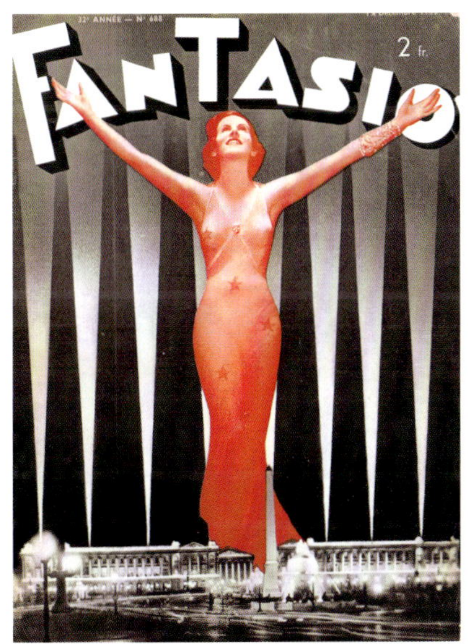

YEAR: **1935**. TITLE: **Fantasio**. COUNTRY: **France**.

According to art historian Gilles Néret it was armor-plated underwear that triggered the flood of erotica in early 20th-century Paris. The corset came into fashion in the 1880s, followed by the bustle and the petticoat, and by 1900 women were so perversely trapped in their armpit-to-thigh cinchers, their underbodices and overbodices, their knickers and chemises and multiple petticoats, that no hint of the real female figure remained. It was in this time that the chaise longue was nicknamed "the fainting couch," so often

Folgen wir dem Kunsthistoriker Gilles Néret, war es der durch Unterwäsche gepanzerte Frauenkörper zu Beginn des 20. Jahrhunderts, der in Paris eine wahre Flut erotischer Printerzeugnisse auslöste. Das Korsett kam in den achtziger Jahren des 19. Jahrhunderts in Mode, gefolgt von der Turnüre beziehungsweise diversen Unterröcken. Um die Jahrhundertwende waren die Frauen so widernatürlich in ein von der Achsel bis zu den Oberschenkeln reichendes Korsett verschnürt, in Mieder, Untertaillen und mehrlagige Unterröcke verpackt, dass nichts mehr an den eigentlichen weiblichen Körperbau erinnerte. Damals wurde die Chaiselongue oft von Damen beansprucht, denen das Übermaß an Unterwäsche den Atem nahm, was diesem Möbel den Spitznamen „fainting couch" einbrachte. Männer erhoben diesen spitzenbesetzten Panzer, eigentlich dazu gedacht, die Tugend der Frau zu bewahren, zum erotischen Kult. Die einen hielten sich an die Wäsche selbst anstelle des darunter verborgenen Körpers. Andere fetischisierten die winzigen Hautpartien, die unter den vielen Kleidungsschichten hervorlugten, und maßen Händen und Knöcheln erotischen Status bei. Vielen anderen wurde es zur Obsession, in privaten Hinterzimmern zuzusehen, wie sich Frauen Schicht für Schicht entblättern. Die Prozedur war so langwierig, dass

Selon l'historien d'art Gilles Néret, ce sont les dessous cuirassés qui déclenchèrent le déferlement d'art érotique que connut Paris au début du 20e siècle. Le corset devint à la mode dans les années 1880, suivi par le faux cul et les jupons. Vers 1900, les femmes étaient sanglées de manière si perverse des aisselles aux mollets dans des jarretières, des sous-corsets, des cache corsets, des pantalons bouffants, des chemises longues et d'innombrables jupons qu'il ne restait plus aucune trace de la véritable silhouette féminine. Ce fut à cette époque que les chaises longues furent surnom-

> Only the French dared bring the striptease out of the bedroom and put it on stage.

mées « canapés à évanouissement » car elles étaient régulièrement réquisitionnées par les femmes qui tournaient de l'œil, étouffées par l'excès de sous-vêtements. Naturellement, alors que cette armure de dentelle était censée protéger la vertu féminine, les hommes étant ce qu'ils sont, ils l'érotisèrent. Certains s'entichèrent du vêtement en

YEAR: **1935**. TITLE: **Fantasio**. COUNTRY: **France**.

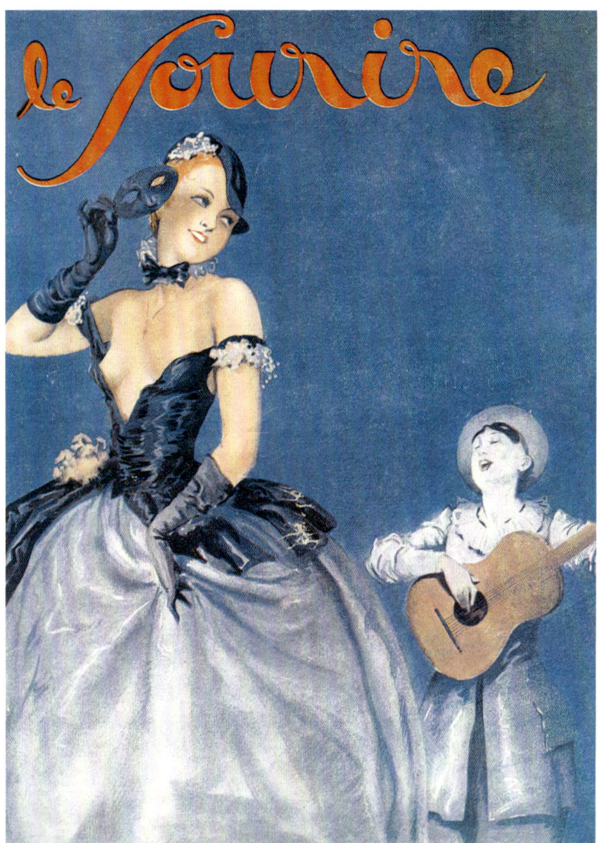
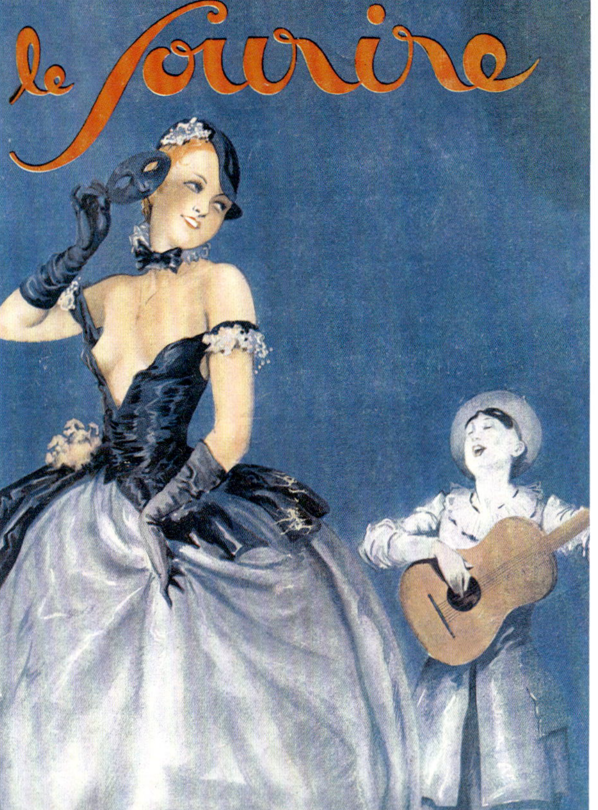

YEAR: **1932**. TITLE: **Le Sourire**. COUNTRY: **France**.

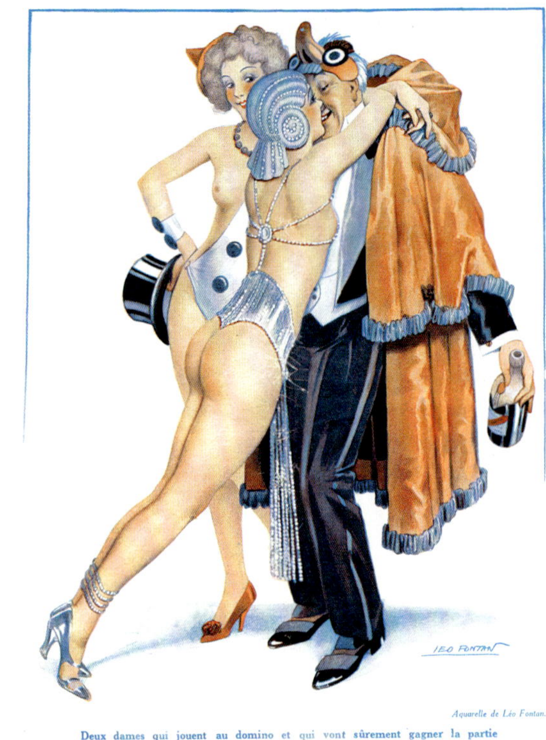

YEAR: **1927**. TITLE: **Le Sourire**. ARTIST: **Leo Fontan**. COUNTRY: **France**.

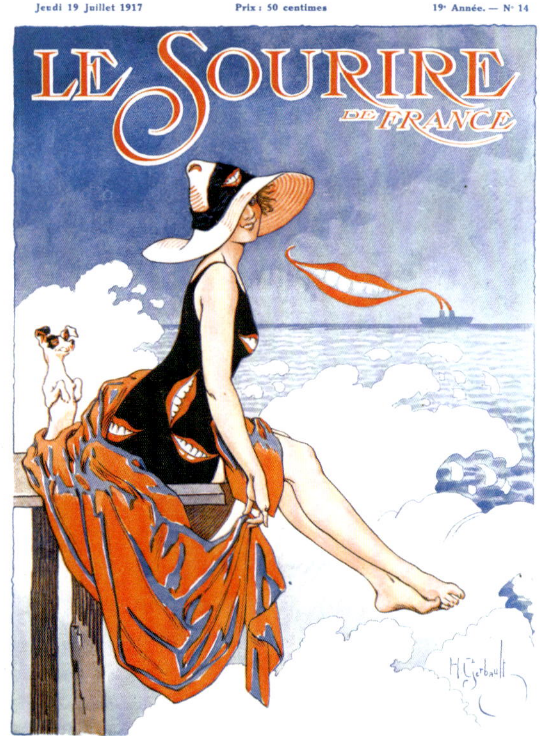

YEAR: **1917**. TITLE: **Le Sourire**. ARTIST: **H. Gerbault**. COUNTRY: **France**.

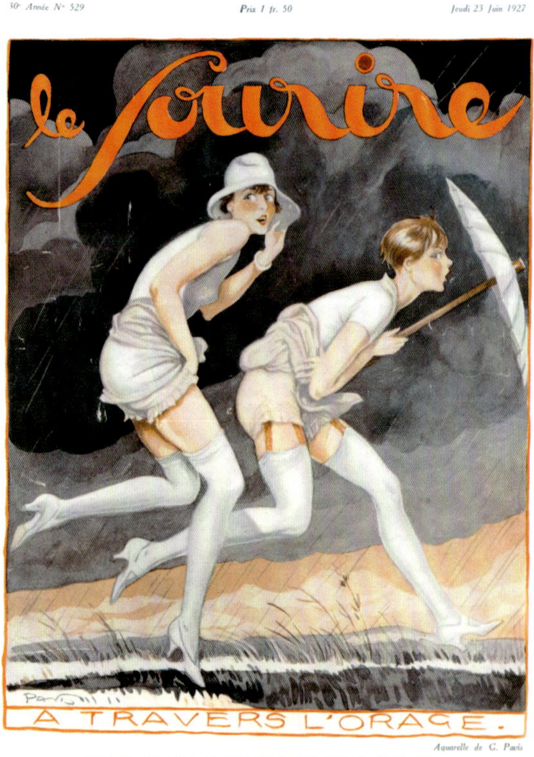

YEAR: **1927**. TITLE: **Le Sourire**. ARTIST: **G. Pavis**. COUNTRY: **France**.

YEAR: **1926**. TITLE: **Le Sourire**.
ARTIST: **M. Millière**. COUNTRY: **France**.

29e Année N° 484 Prix 1 fr. 50 Jeudi 12 août 1926

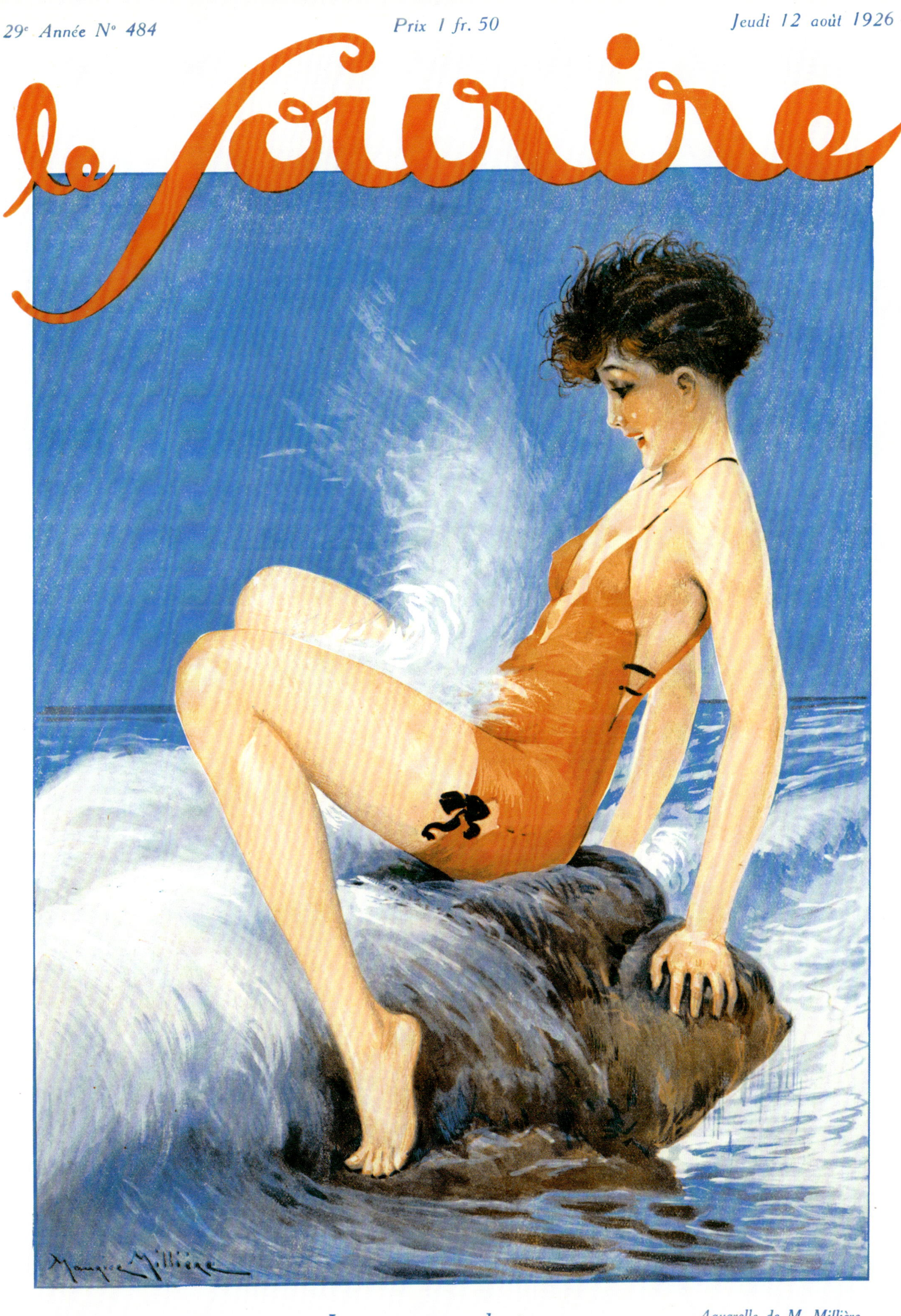

La vague audacieuse

Aquarelle de M. Millière

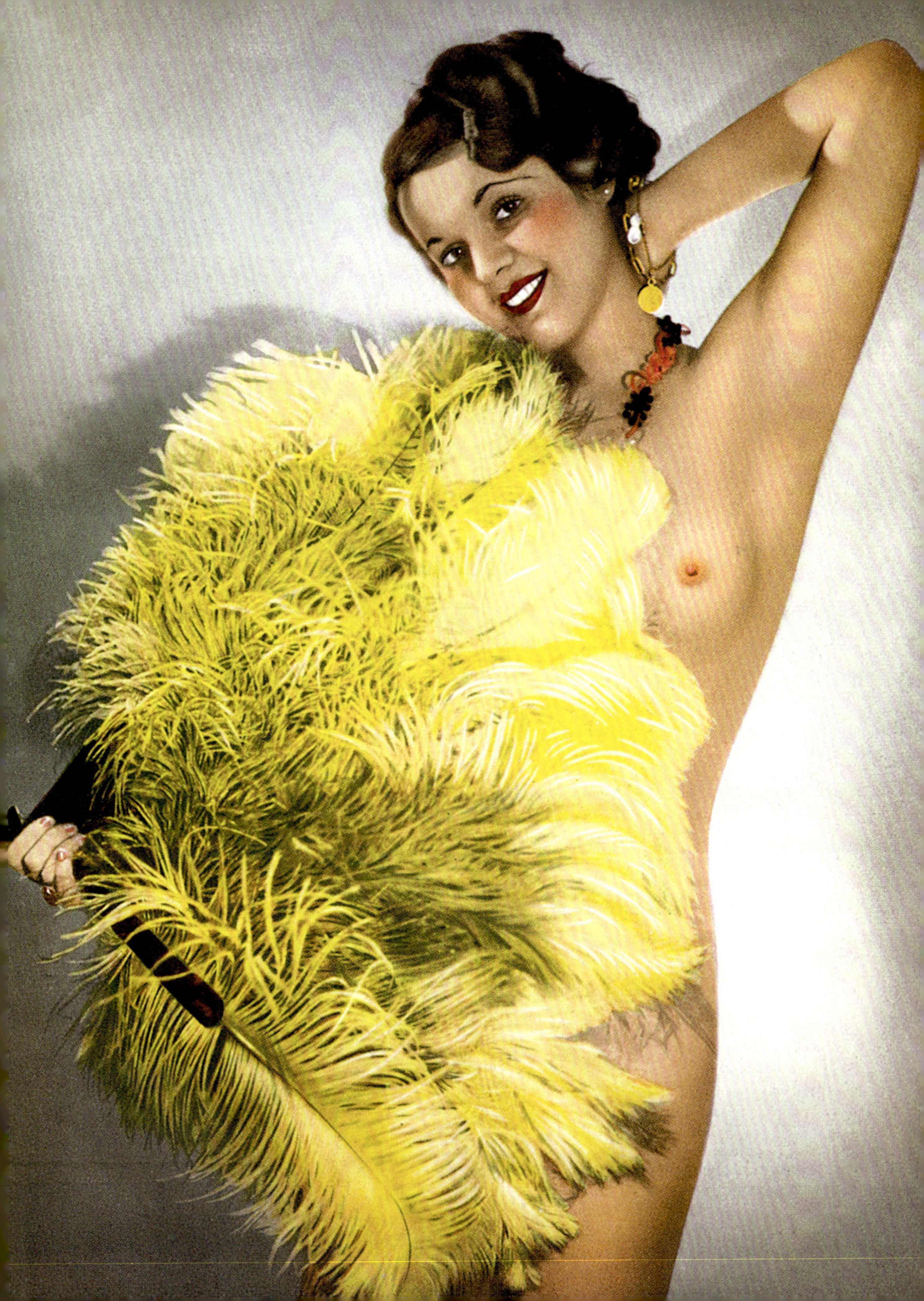

Year: **1934**. Title: **Pages Folles**. Country: **France**.

Pages 58 & 59:
Year: **1920**. Title: **Petites Amies**.
Country: **France**.

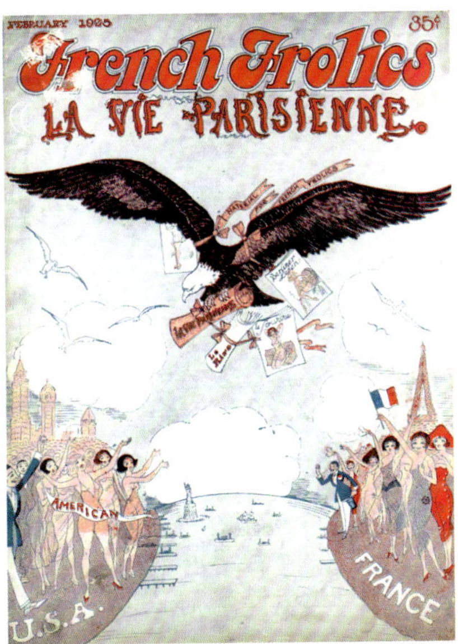

Year: **1925**. Title: **French Frolics, La Vie Parisienne**. Country: **France**.

was it commandeered by women rendered breathless from excess of underwear. And while all this lacy armor was supposed to guard feminine virtue, men, being men, eroticized it. Some went for the clothing itself, substituting what was visible for the well-concealed body. Others fetishized the slivers of flesh that peeked from beneath and between the layers, bestowing erogenous status on hands and ankles. Many more became obsessed with watching the layers peel off in private boudoir strip shows that took so long they were termed striptease to describe the combination of frustration and arousal resulting in the viewer.

Dr. Freud, near the height of his popularity, took notice of all this and began publicizing the perversion of natural sexuality brought about by clothing fetishism. The medical establishment joined him in condemning the corset, not because it encouraged perversion,

man diese Veranstaltungen „Striptease" taufte, um die Kombination aus Frustration und Erregung zu bezeichnen, die sie beim Betrachter hervorrief. In Wien befasste sich Dr. Freud mit diesen Entwicklungen und schrieb Abhandlungen über die Pervertierung der natürlichen Sexualität durch Fetischisierung der Kleidung. Die Medizin teilte seine Ablehnung des Korsetts, allerdings nicht, weil es Perversionen Vorschub leistete, sondern weil es die inneren Organe einquetschte und negativen Einfluss auf die Gebärfähigkeit hatte.

In England, Deutschland und den Vereinigten Staaten kleideten die Frauen sich nicht anders als in Frankreich, und die Obsessionen waren die gleichen, doch fehlte diesen Ländern Frankreichs mediterrane Leichtigkeit und lange Tradition sexueller und künstlerischer Toleranz. Daher waren es nur die Franzosen, die mit dem Cancan den Wust von Unterröcken zur Volksbelustigung machten und es wagten, den Striptease aus den Schlafzimmern auf öffentliche Bühnen zu bringen. Selbstverständlich schritten häufig die Behörden ein, und auch die Kirche wollte ein Wörtchen mitreden, doch die Franzosen waren nie besonders obrigkeitshörig, und der Zensur war kein großer Erfolg beschieden. In diesem toleranten Klima erschienen in Paris die ersten Vorläufer der Männermagazine. Die frühesten wurden in den achtziger Jahren des 19. Jahrhunderts für die Kunden der diversen Pariser „Folies" produziert. *Le Frou-Frou* feierte 1901 den Cancan. *L'Étude Académique* präsentierte völlig unbekleidete Damen, dies jedoch nur als Service für ernsthafte Künstler, die sich keine Aktmodelle in Fleisch und Blut leisten konnten, ein Kniff, dessen man

soi, remplaçant le corps dissimulé par ce qui était visible. D'autres fétichisèrent les fragments de chair qui apparaissaient sous et entre les couches de tissu, accordant un statut érogène aux mains et aux chevilles. D'autres encore, les plus nombreux, devinrent obsédés par le spectacle du lent effeuillage des vêtements, couche après couche, dans des boudoirs privés, une opération qui prenait tant de temps qu'on en vint à le baptiser « striptease » (de l'anglais strip « déshabiller » et tease « taquiner »), pour décrire le mélange de frustration et d'excitation ressenti par le spectateur. Sigmund Freud, alors presque au sommet de sa popularité, le remarqua et rendit publique la perversion sexuelle suscitée par le fétichisme vestimentaire. Le corps médical se joignit à sa condamnation du corset, non pas parce qu'il encourageait la perversion mais parce qu'il

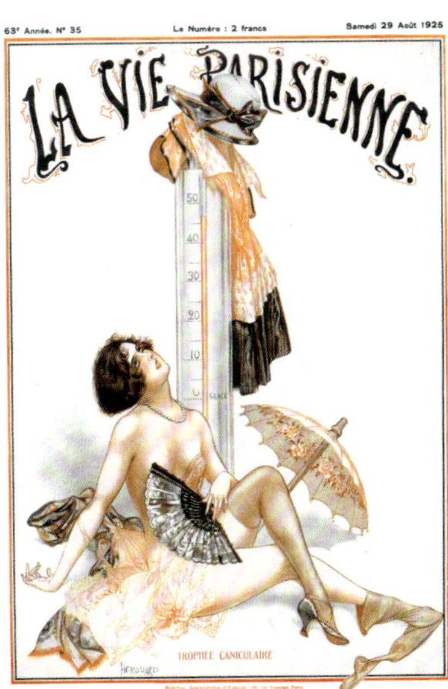

Year: **1925**. Title: **La Vie Parisienne**.
Artist: **Herouard**. Country: **France**.

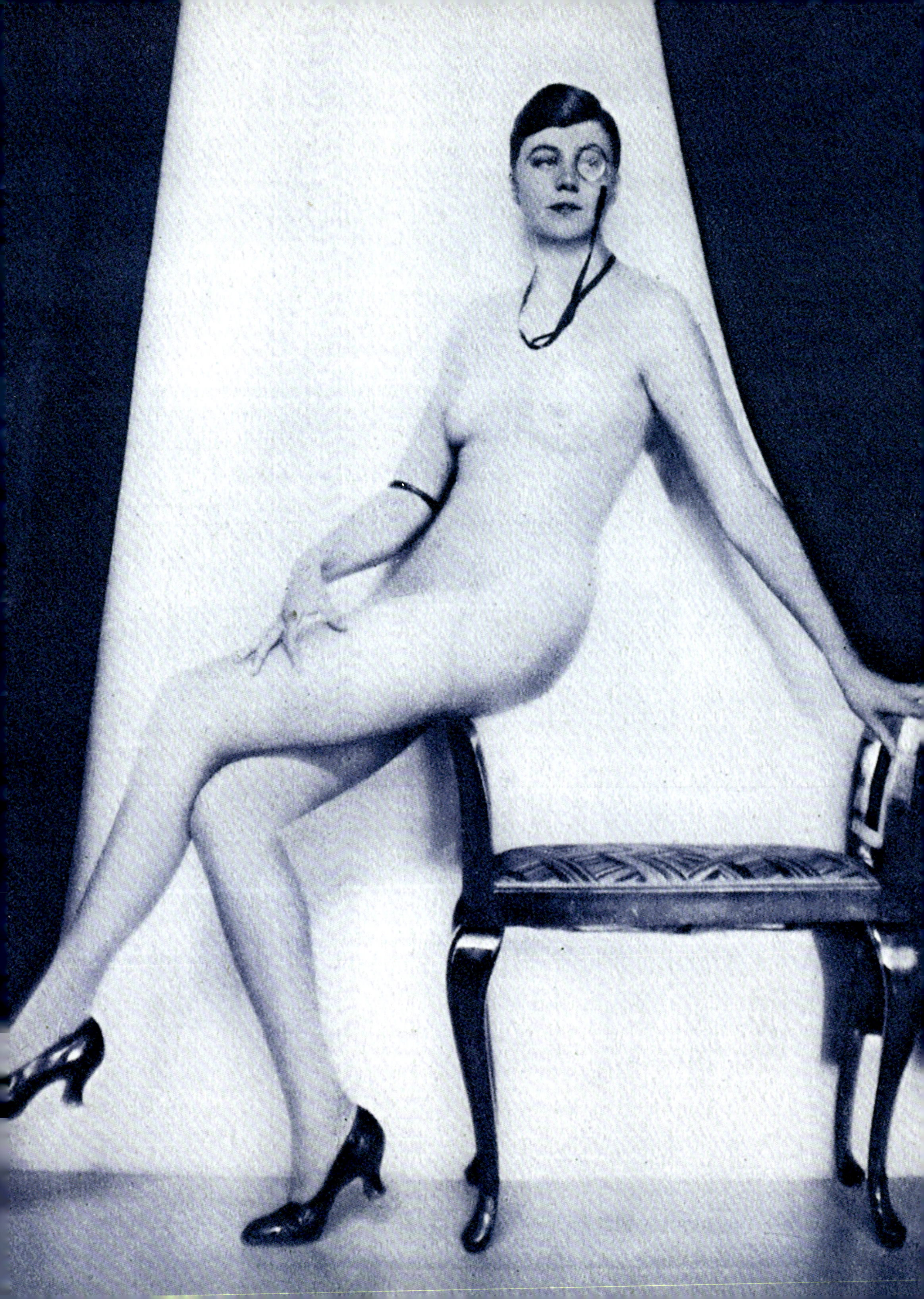

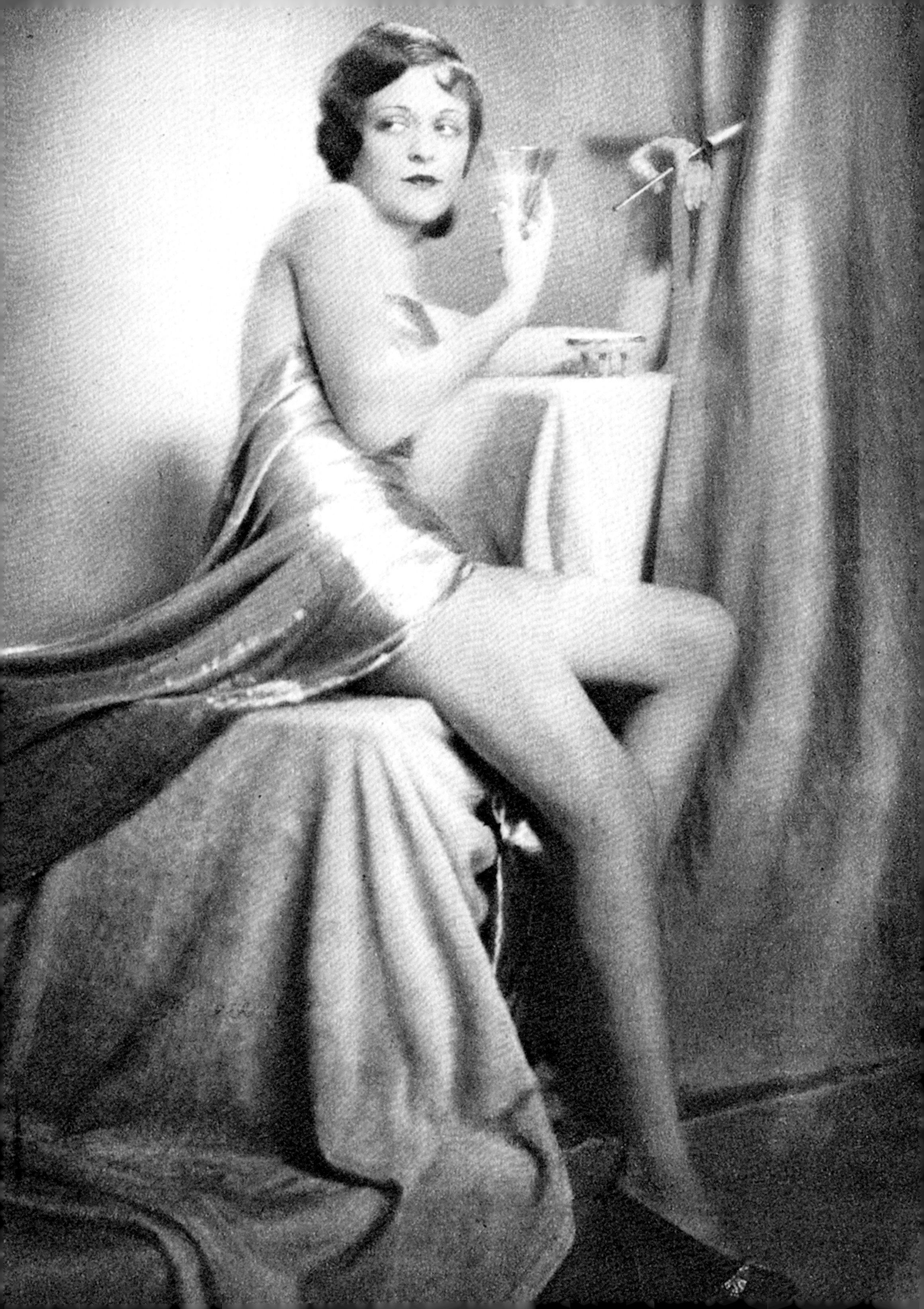

YEAR: **1936**. TITLE: **Fantasio**. COUNTRY: **France**.

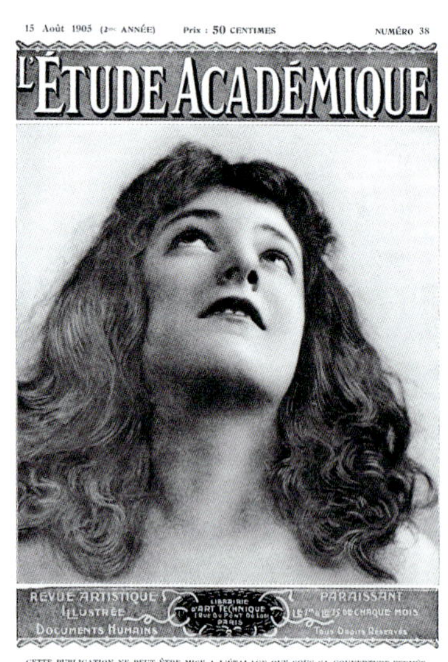

YEAR: **1905**. TITLE: **L'Étude Académique**.
COUNTRY: **France**.

but because it displaced organs and hindered childbearing.

In England, Germany and America the same clothes were worn and the same perversions were at work, but these countries lacked France's Latin culture and long history of sensual and artistic tolerance. Thus only the French turned the layers of underwear into entertainment with the cancan, or dared bring the striptease out of the bedroom and put it on stage. And yes, the government stepped in every so often, and the Church had its opinions, but the French have never paid more attention than is necessary to their institutions, and their institutions have thus never been totally effective. So it was in this atmosphere that magazines were added to the sexual entertainments of Paris. The earliest were produced in the 1880s as souvenirs for patrons of the various Parisian 'Folies.' *Le Frou-Frou* celebrated the

sich auch Jahrzehnte später noch auf der ganzen Welt bediente. *La Vie Parisienne* begann 1914 als elegante, großformatige Zeitschrift, die sich an Männer wie Frauen richtete und schlüpfrige Geschichten, subtilen Humor und Damen in verführerischer Unterwäsche bot.

Der Erste Weltkrieg brachte einen drastischen Einbruch, nur *La Vie Parisienne* erschien weiterhin. Nach dem Krieg erschienen auch die anderen Zeitschriften wieder mit neuem Schwung und in besserer Qualität. Während Deutschland die Wirren der Weimarer Republik durchlebte und die Vereinigten Staaten mit dem künstlerischen Akt und Eugenik experimentierten, blieb Frankreich konsequent auf hedonistischem Kurs. In diesen Jahren erschienen die besten Ausgaben von *La Vie Parisienne,* und *Paris Plaisirs* definierte die kontinentaleuropäische Kultiviertheit/Raffinesse. In den

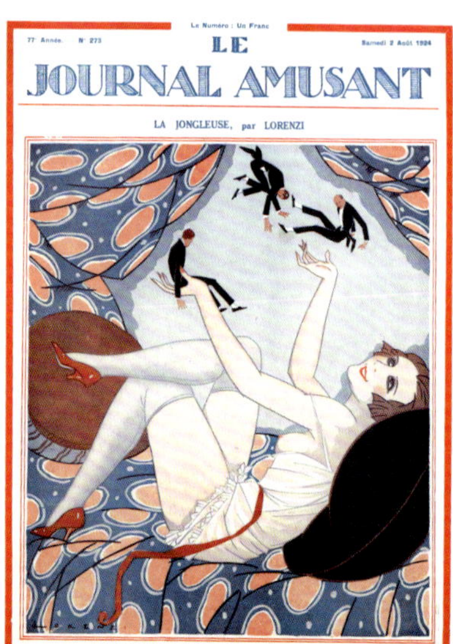

YEAR: **1924**. TITLE: **Le Journal Amusant**.
COUNTRY: **France**.

provoquait des déplacements d'organes et entravait la grossesse.

Les Anglais, les Allemands et les Américains portaient les mêmes tenues et nourrissaient les mêmes perversions, mais ces sociétés n'avaient pas la culture latine de la France, ni sa longue histoire de tolérance sensuelle et artistique. Les Français furent les seuls à transformer les couches de vêtements en divertissement avec le cancan et à oser faire sortir le striptease du boudoir pour le faire monter sur scène. Certes, le gouvernement intervenait de temps à autre et l'Église avait son opinion, mais les Français n'ont jamais accordé plus d'attention que nécessaire à leurs institutions. C'est dans ce contexte que des magazines vinrent enrichir l'éventail parisien des plaisirs sexuels. Les premiers furent réalisés dans les années 1880 pour les clients des diverses revues de variétés. En 1901, *Le Frou-Frou* se concentra sur le cancan. *L'Étude Académique* présentait des photos de nu intégral, mais uniquement pour rendre service aux artistes sérieux n'ayant pas accès à des modèles vivants, un prétexte qui serait repris par des magazines dans le monde entier au cours des décennies à venir. *La Vie Parisienne* fut lancée en 1914 comme une revue chic de format géant pour hommes et femmes. Elle contenait de la fiction coquine, de l'humour raffiné et des images de dames aux dessous charmants.

La Première Guerre mondiale porta un coup sérieux aux revues françaises. Seule *La Vie Parisienne* continua de paraître. Après la guerre, les magazines refleurirent avec une vigueur et une qualité accrues. Tout au long des années 1920, tandis que l'Allemagne pataugeait dans l'étrangeté de Weimar et que les

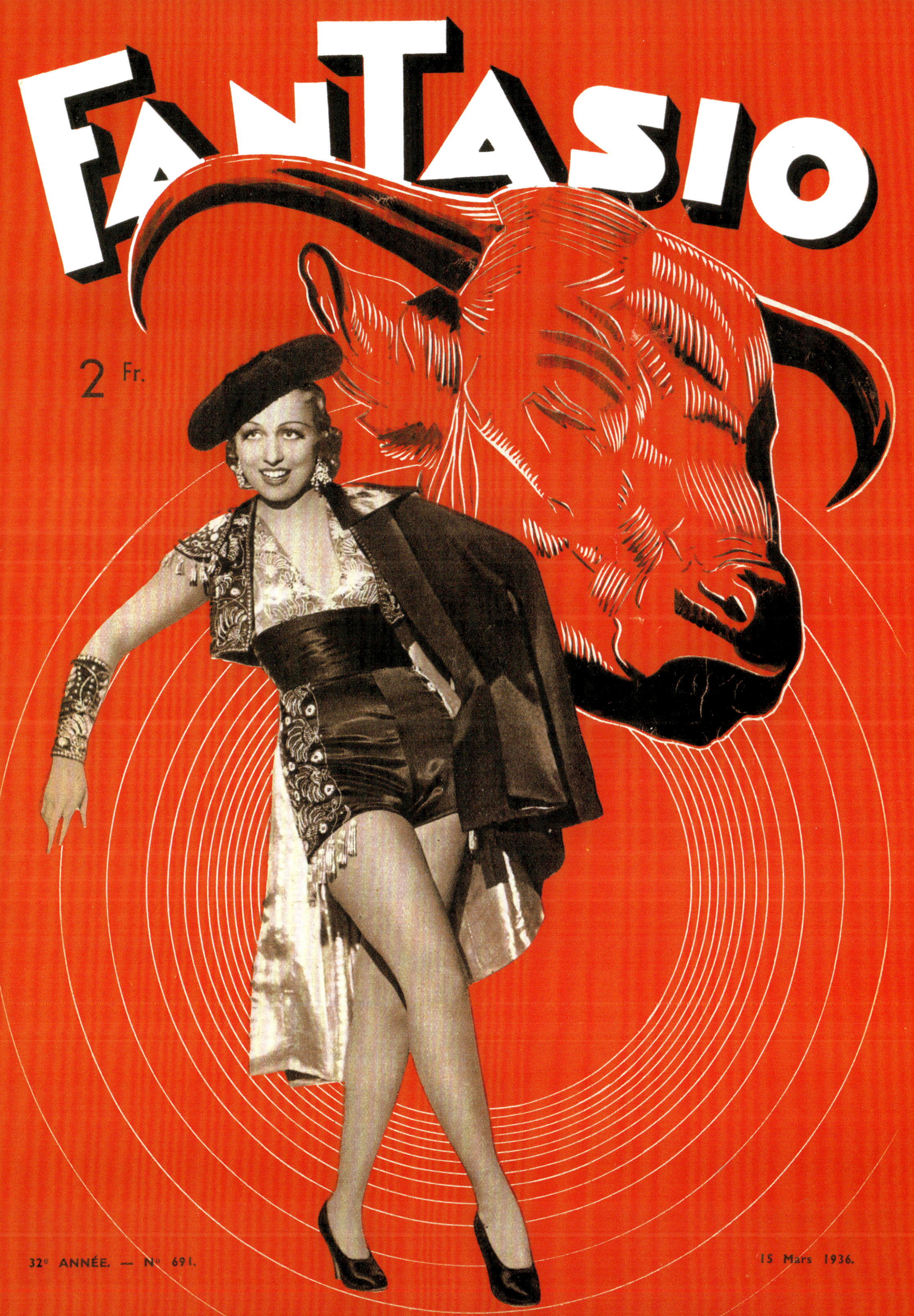
FANTASIO
2 Fr.
32e ANNÉE. — No 691.
15 Mars 1936.

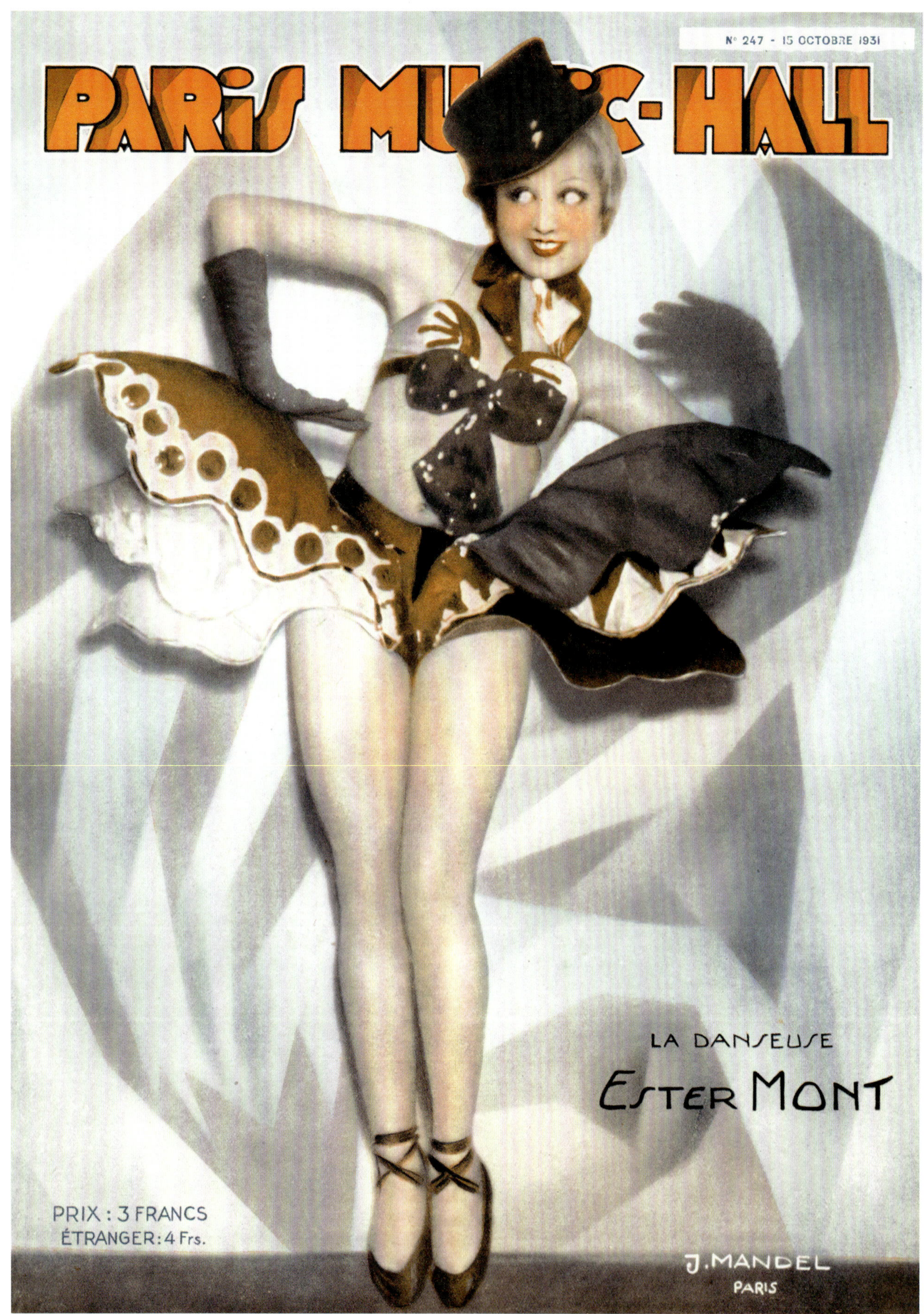

YEAR: **1930**. TITLE: **Paris Music-Hall**. ARTIST: **J. Mandel**. COUNTRY: **France**.

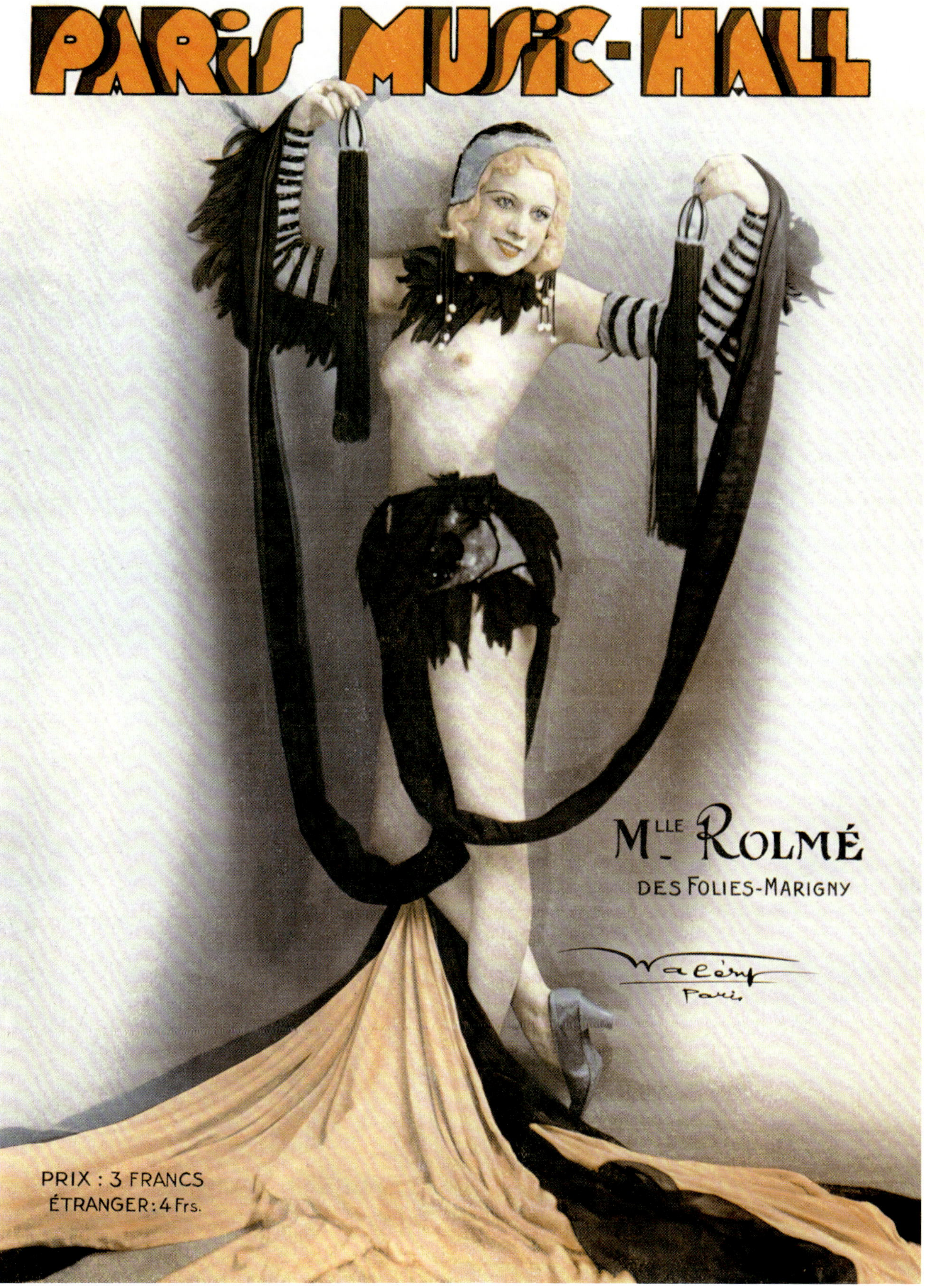

YEAR: **1931**. TITLE: **Paris Music-Hall**. COUNTRY: **France**.

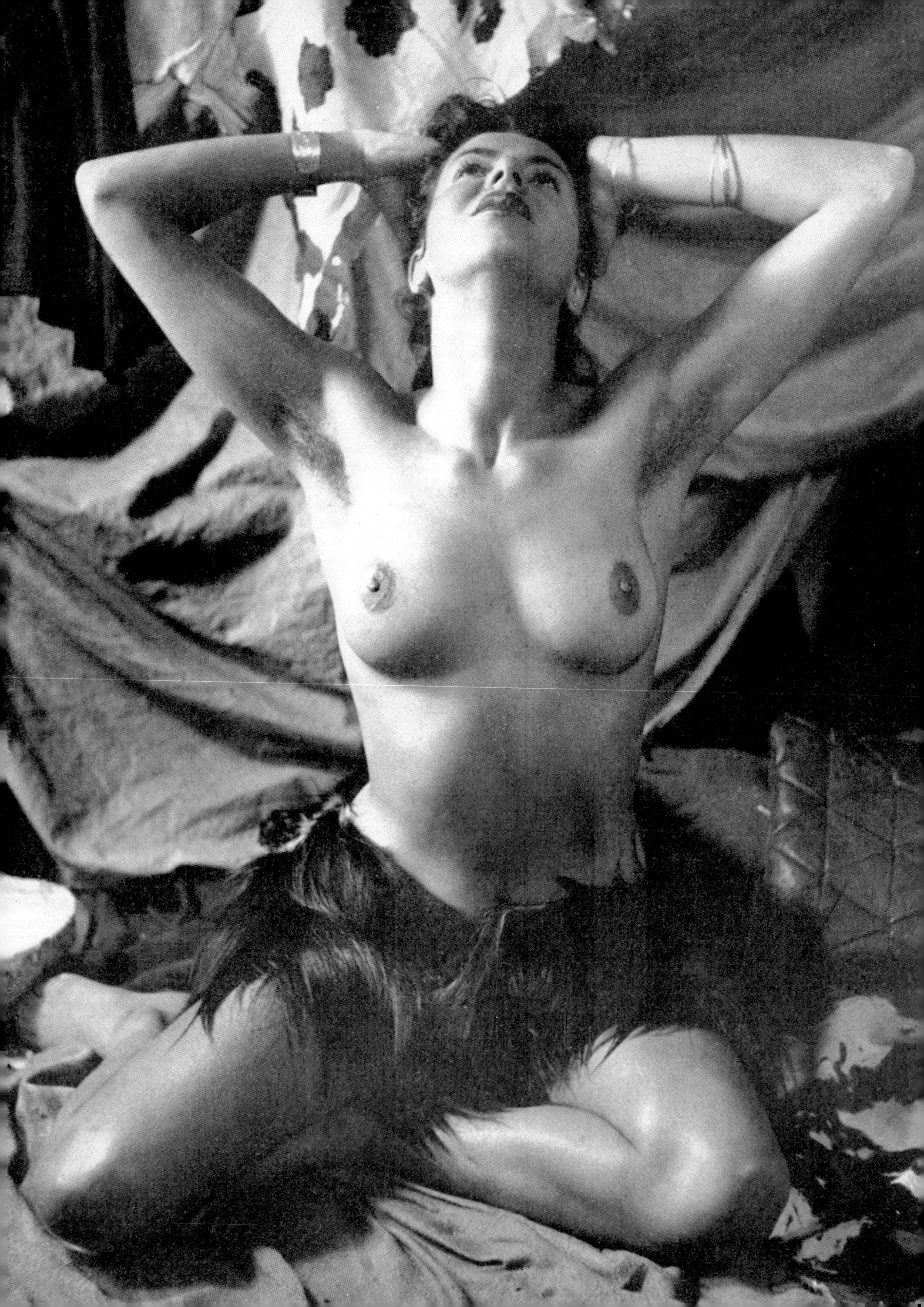

Year: **1936**. Title: **Paris Sex-Appeal**. Country: **France**.

cancan in 1901. *L'Étude Académique* offered completely nude photos, but only as a public service to serious artists without access to life study models, a ploy that would be repeated in magazines the world over in the decades to follow. *La Vie Parisienne* (Paris Life) began in 1914 as an upscale, oversized magazine for both men and women concentrating on sexy fiction, sophisticated humor and ladies in alluring lingerie.

World War I put a serious crimp in French publishing; only *La Vie Parisienne* maintained production. Post-war the magazines came back with renewed vigor and higher quality. Through the 1920s, when Germany wallowed in Weimar weirdness and America experimented with art nudes and eugenics, France stuck to its clear hedonistic path. *La Vie Parisienne* produced its best issues during this decade while Paris Plaisirs defined continental sophistication. In the 1930s Hitler purged the decadence from Berlin while Parisian publishing was reaching its zenith. Gorgeously printed magazines on top quality paper displayed the erotic riches of the Paris dance halls. *Beauté* was perhaps the best, but *Paris Sex-Appeal* and *Pages Folles* were also impressive. Into the late 1930s, with Berlin neutered and America experimenting with censorship, France was truly top of the erotic heap. Then World War II blew it all away.

Year: **1927**. Title: **Le Sourire**. Artist: **Leo Fontan**. Country: **France**.

Dreißigern, als Hitler der Dekadenz Berlins ein Ende machte, erlebte das Verlagswesen für Erotisches in Paris seinen Höhepunkt. Farbenfrohe Magazine auf erstklassigem Papier präsentierten die erotische Vielfalt der Pariser Cabarets. Das beste Magazin war vielleicht *Beauté*, doch auch *Paris Sex-Appeal* und *Pages Folles* waren nicht ohne. Als Ende der Dreißiger Berlin gleichgeschaltet war und Amerika in Puritanismus zurückfiel, war Frankreich die Nummer eins, was erotische Druckerzeugnisse betraf. Doch der Zweite Weltkrieg sollte dies bald ändern.

Américains expérimentaient avec les nus artistiques et l'eugénisme, la France poursuivit son chemin résolument hédoniste. Pendant cette décennie, *La Vie Parisienne* publia ses meilleurs numéros tandis que *Paris Plaisirs* incarnait la sophistication du Vieux Continent. Dans les années 30, Hitler purgea Berlin de sa décadence alors que les publications parisiennes atteignaient leur zénith. Des revues présentaient les fastes érotiques des dancings de la capitale. *Beauté* était sans doute la meilleure d'entre toutes mais *Paris Sex-Appeal* et *Pages Folles* n'étaient pas en reste. Vers la fin de la décennie, alors que Berlin se retrouvait châtrée et que l'Amérique jouait avec la censure, Paris atteignit des sommets de sensualité. Puis la Seconde Guerre mondiale vint tout remettre en question.

Through the 1920s, France stuck to its clear hedonistic path.

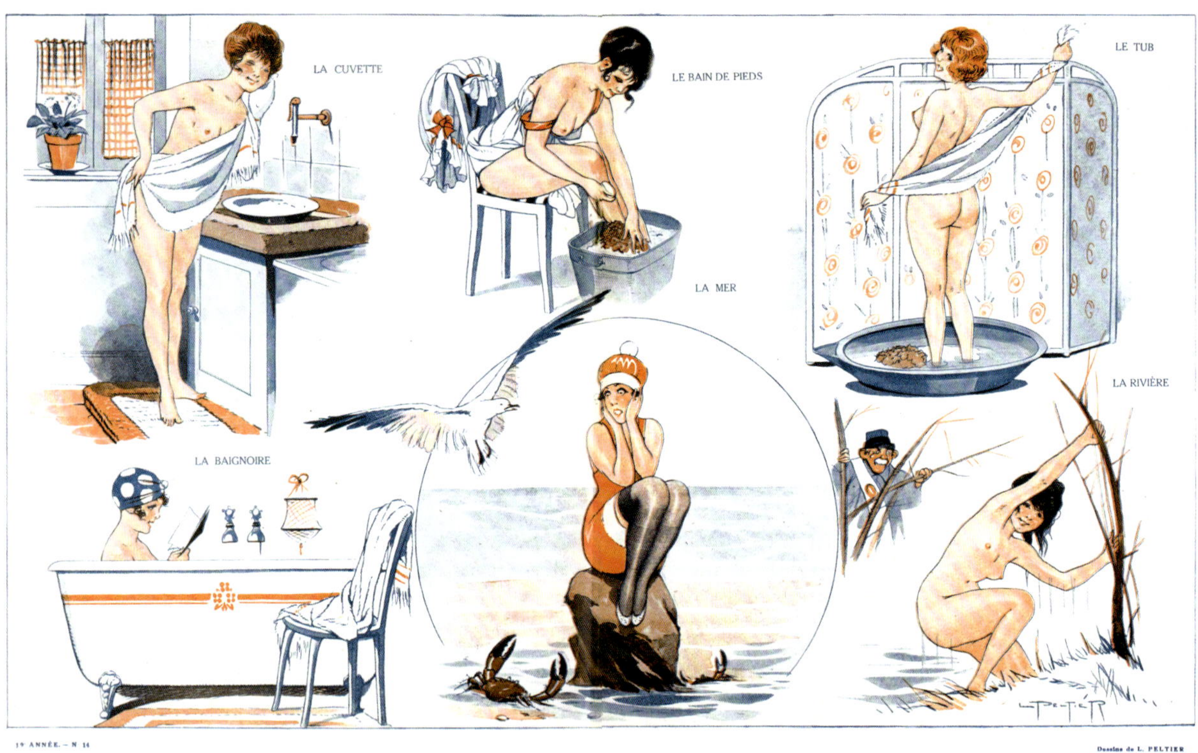

YEAR: **1917**. TITLE: **Le Sourire**. ARTIST: **L. Peltier**. COUNTRY: **France**.

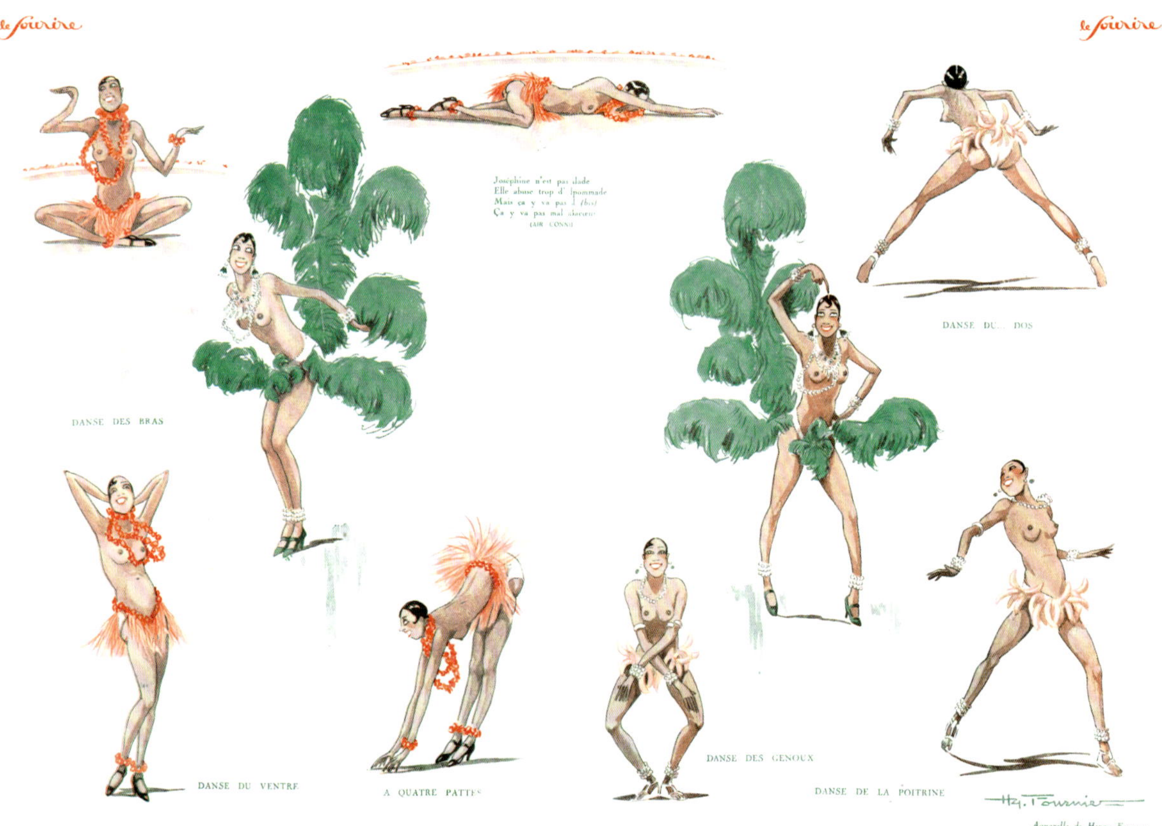

YEAR: **1926**. TITLE: **Le Sourire**. COUNTRY: **France**.

RIGHT: YEAR: **1925**. TITLE: **La Vie Parisienne**. COUNTRY: **France**.
PAGES 68 & 69: YEAR: **1933**. TITLE: **Beauté**. COUNTRY: **France**.

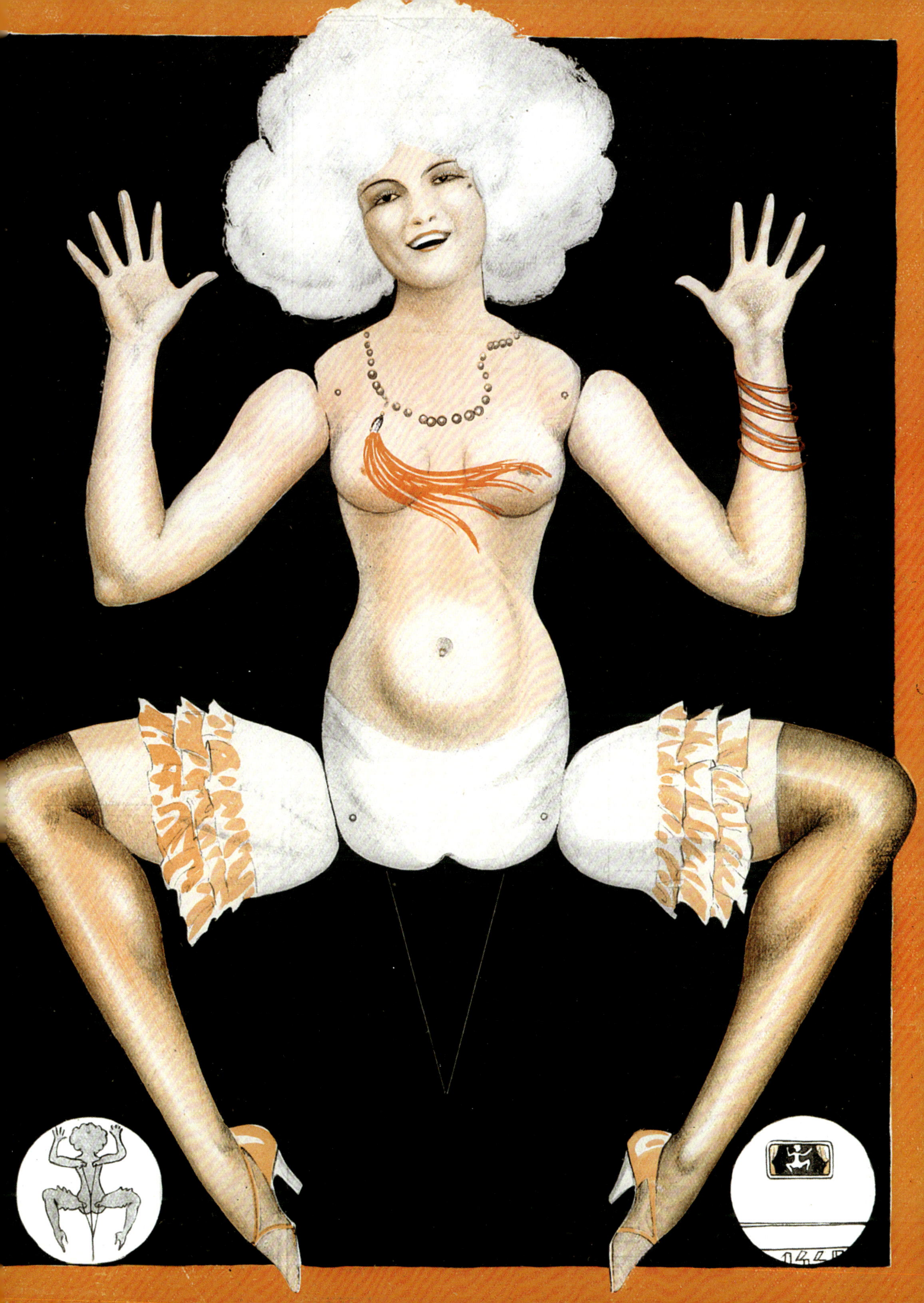

5 fr

N° 25 – FEV 33

beauté

MAGAZINE

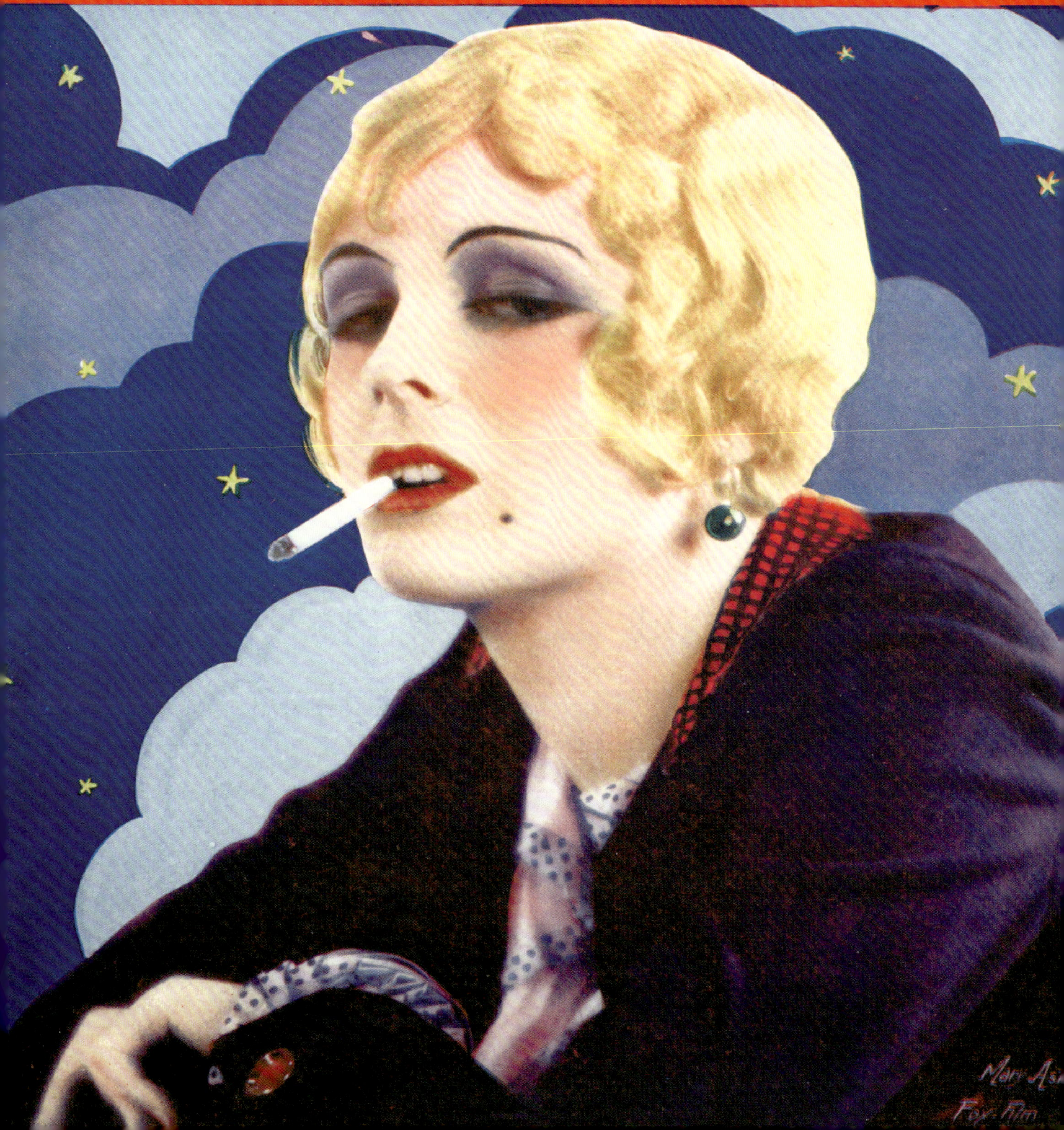

Mary As

Fox-Film

5 frs

N° 33 OCTOBRE 33

beauté

MAGAZINE

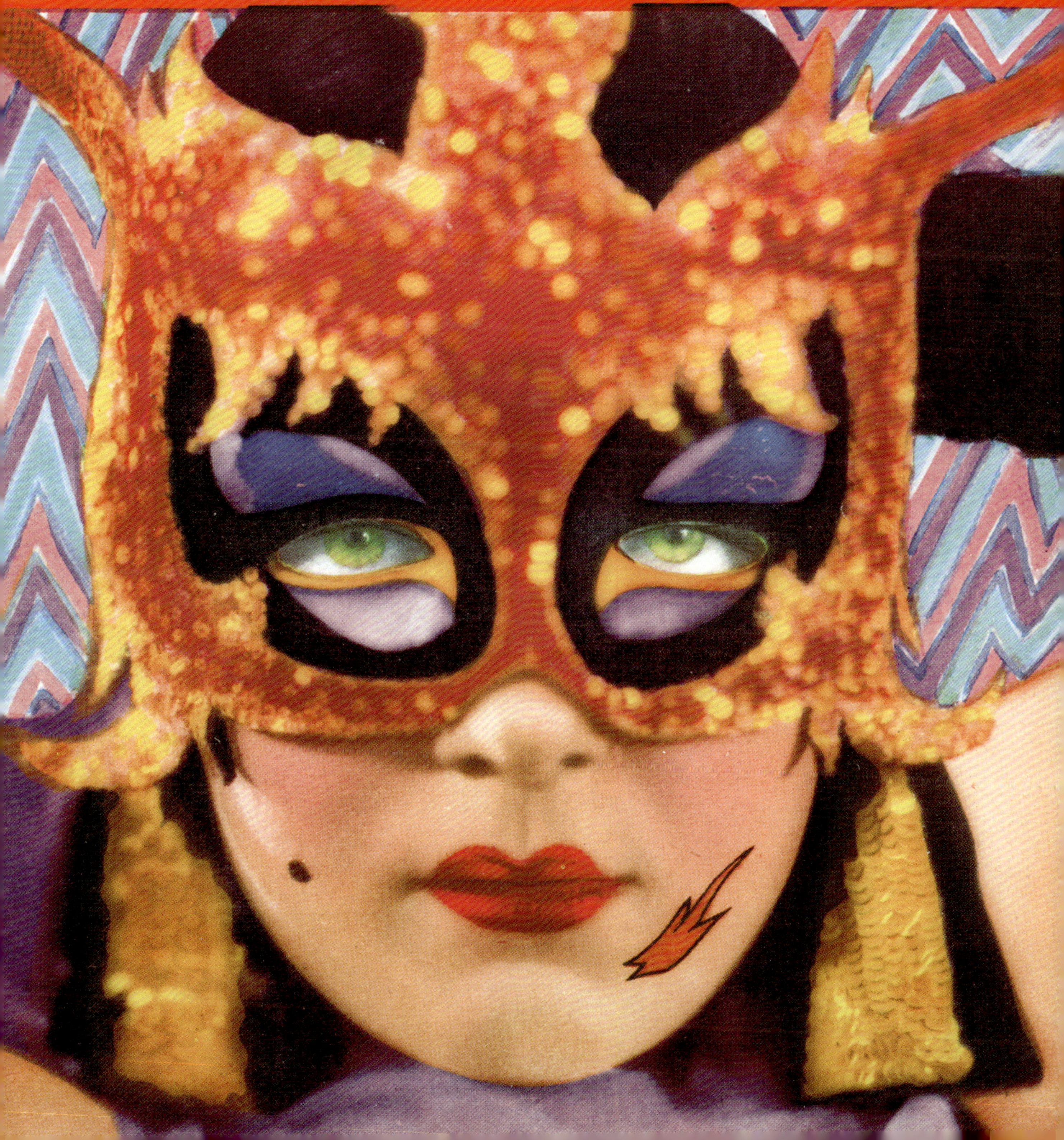

PAGES folles

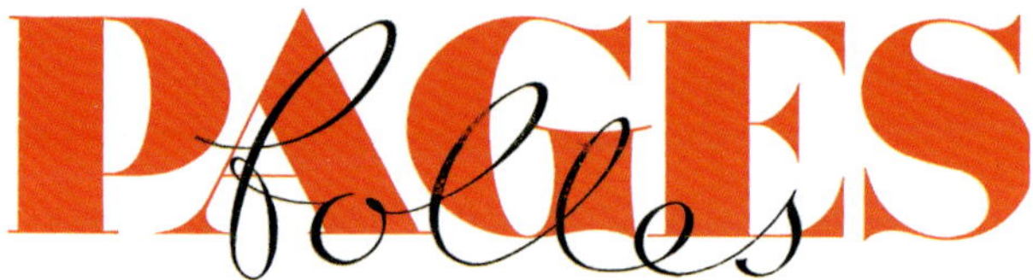

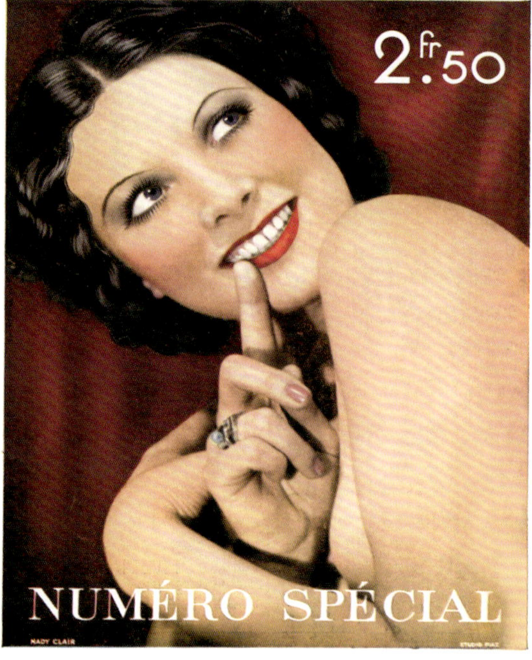

Year: **1934**. Title: **Pages Folles**. Country: **France**.

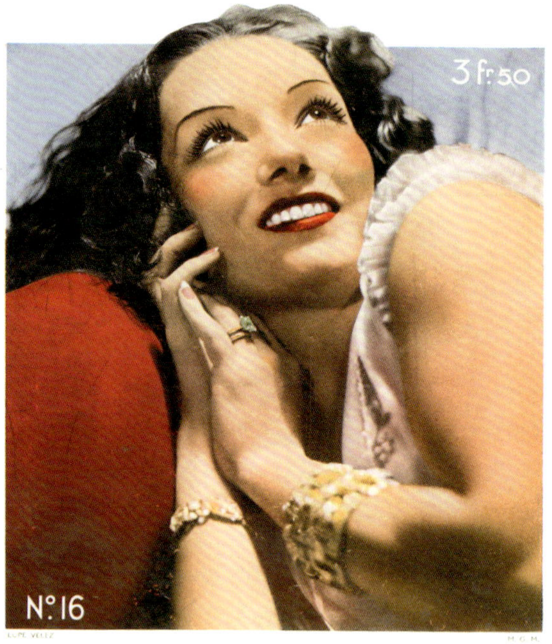

Year: **1935**. Title: **Pages Folles**. Country: **France**.

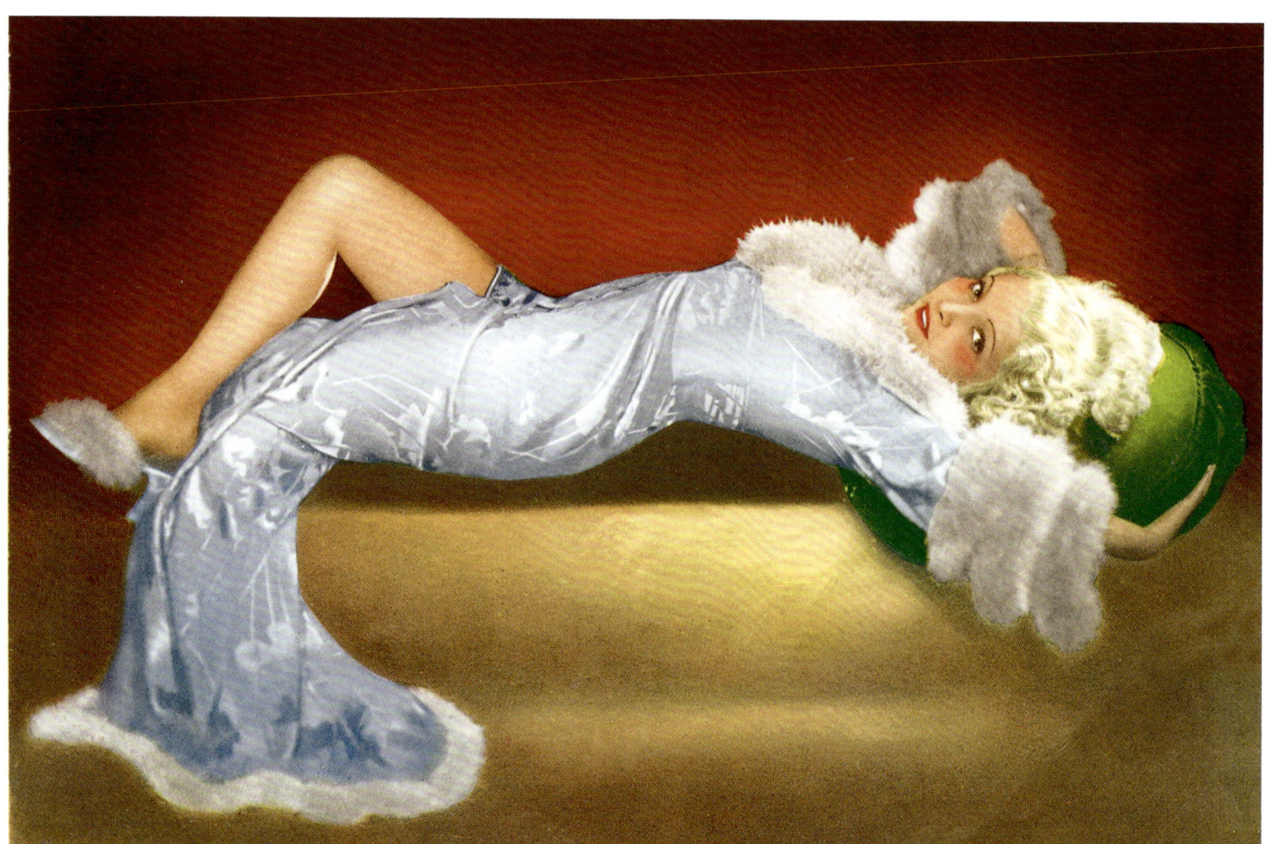

Year: **1935**. Title: **Pages Folles**. Country: **France**.

Year: **1936**. Title: **Paris Sex-Appeal**. Country: **France**.

RIS PARIS PARIS PARIS PARIS PARIS PARIS PARIS

SEX·APPEAL

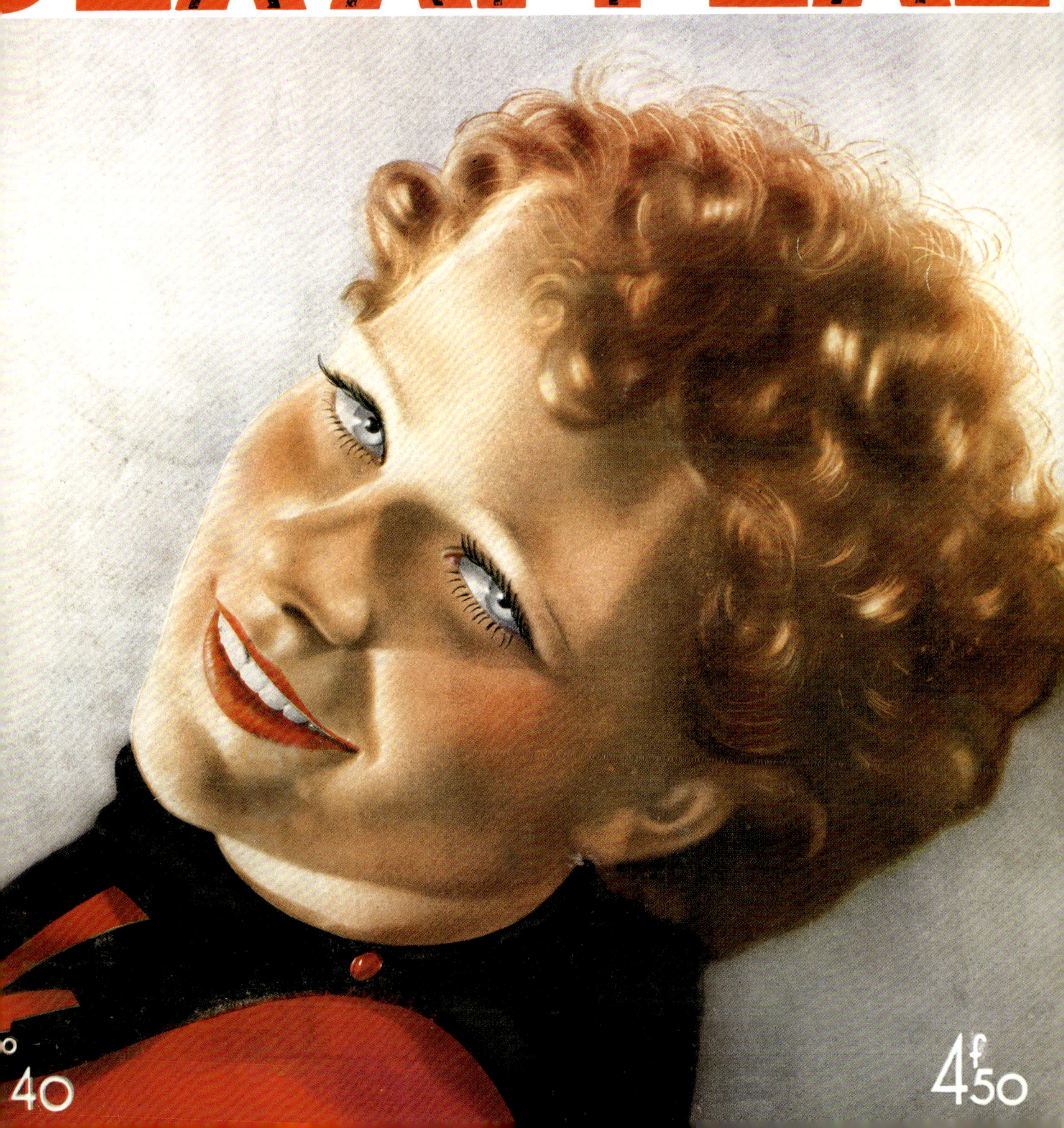

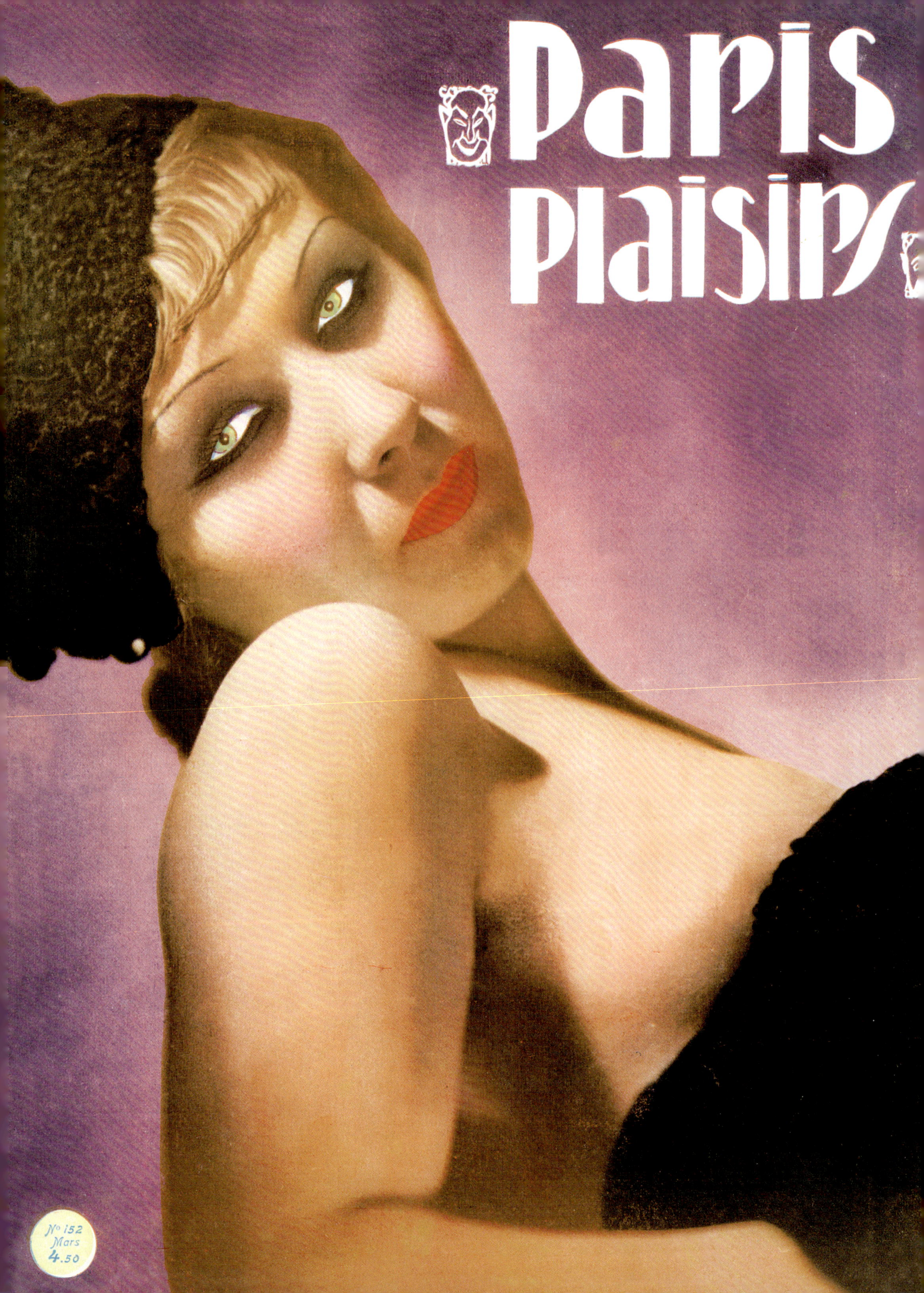
Paris Plaisirs
No 152
Mars
4.50

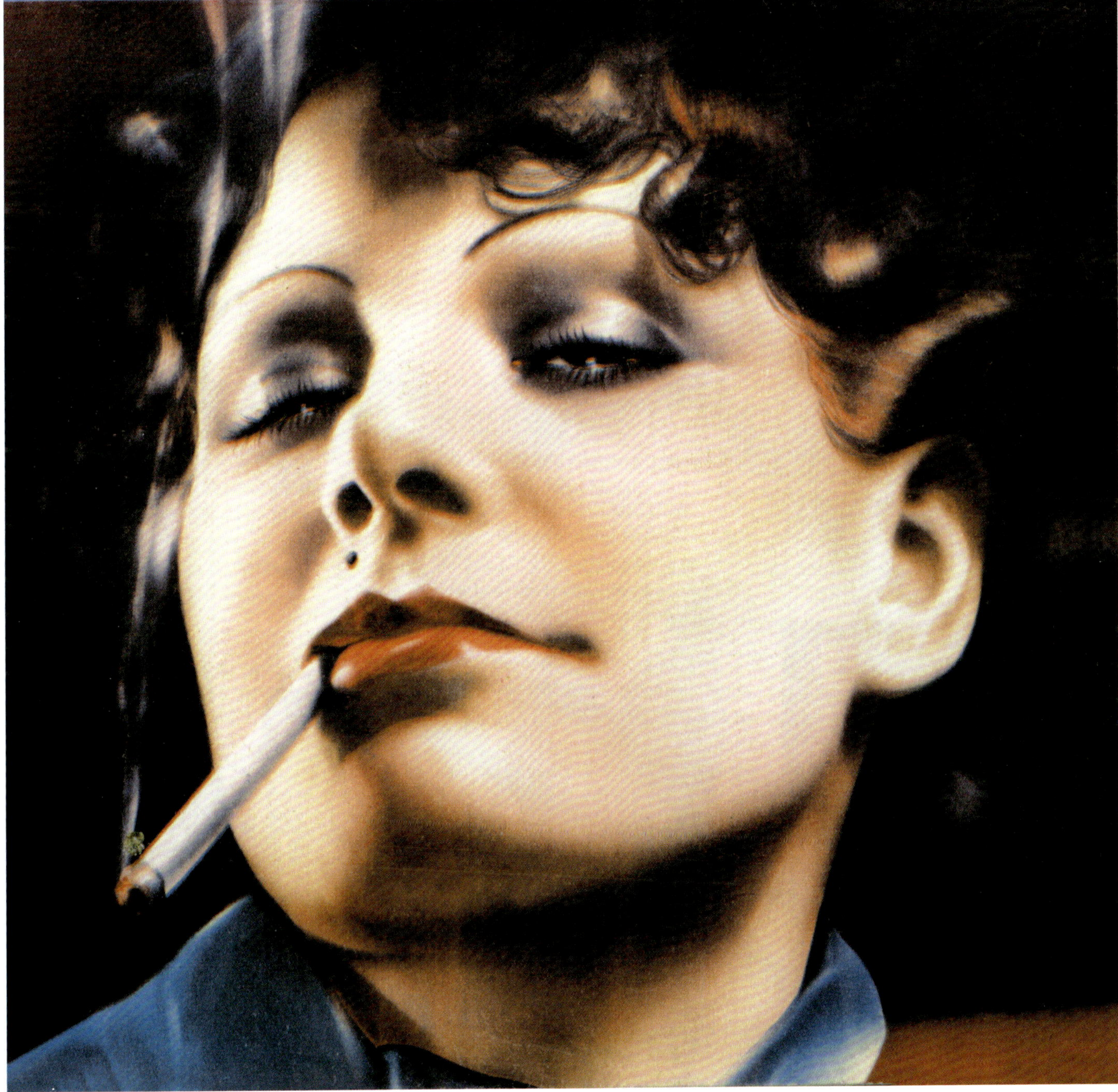

YEAR: **1937**. TITLE: **Paris Sex-Appeal**. COUNTRY: **France**.

YEAR: **1930s**. TITLE: **Paris Plaisirs**. COUNTRY: **France**.

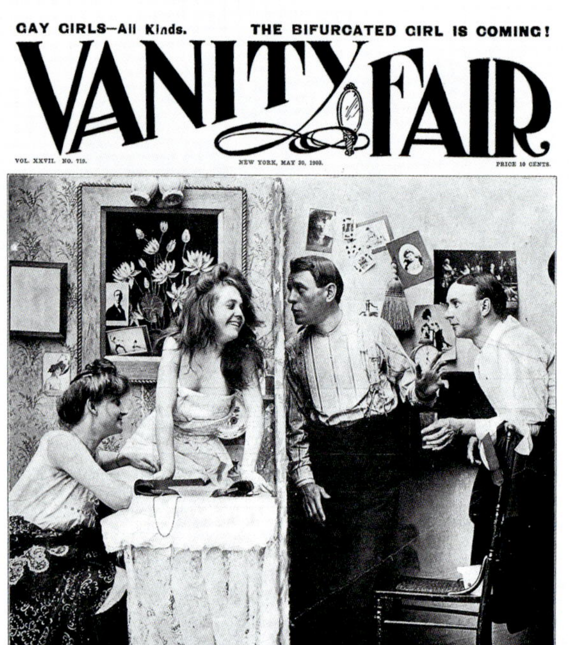

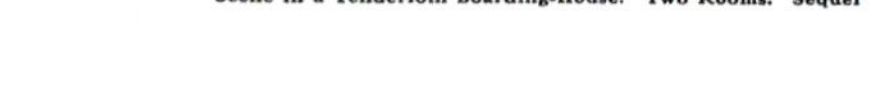

YEAR: **1903**. TITLE: **Vanity Fair**. COUNTRY: **USA**.

VANITY FAIR. 15

A Baseball Game—The Girl Who Went on a "Bat," Being "Fly," Was Struck Out.

A.
She thinks it over and decides to——

B.
Strike out for the home of a certain lovely lady she knows. But before reaching the apartments of that friend she imbibes freely along the way and thinks a pail should be her calling card. The friend chides her.

C.
After the chiding the friend gives her a little fatherly advice and advises her to make a home run.

D.
Now she has reached the plate and is being scored by her wife. The fact that the wife is smiling will be explained in *four pictures in the big* **BIFURCATED GIRL NUMBER** of **VANITY FAIR**, *to be published next week.*

A SCENE IN A SOUBRETTE'S FLAT.
Two girls shaking dice to see who will wear the trousers during the day.

A NATURAL-BORN ARTIST'S MODEL.
Her own pose; her own smile; everything about her is her own.

HIS EARNEST DESIRE.

LITTLE THEODORE—Shall I take your hat, Miss Peake?

MISS PEAKE—No, thank you; but you're a polite little man, all the same.

LITTLE THEODORE—No; 'tain't that. I just wanted to get the hatpin to stick into Tommy. Me an' him's goin' to have a fight in the hall.

HER SCHEME.

"There is one thing I like about your husband; he never hurries you when getting ready for a walk."

"Very little credit is due to him for that, my dear. Whenever I see that I am not likely to be ready in time, I simply hide his hat or his gloves and let him hunt for them up and down until I have finished dressing."

DISCARDED LOCOMOTIVES OF THE MANHATTAN "L" ROAD.
These engines—to the number of several thousand—are being sold out at rapidly as possible. The company is gradually installing electricity as the motive power on their lines. The scene shows the terminal at One Hundred and Fifty-fifth Street.

A SPITEFUL GIRL AND AN ENDURING FRIEND.
The spiteful girl heard that her friend had said certain things about her to the stage manager. Here she is seen in a ferocious pose, scratching the shoulder of the girl who laughs.

YEAR: **1903**. TITLE: **Vanity Fair**. COUNTRY: **USA**.

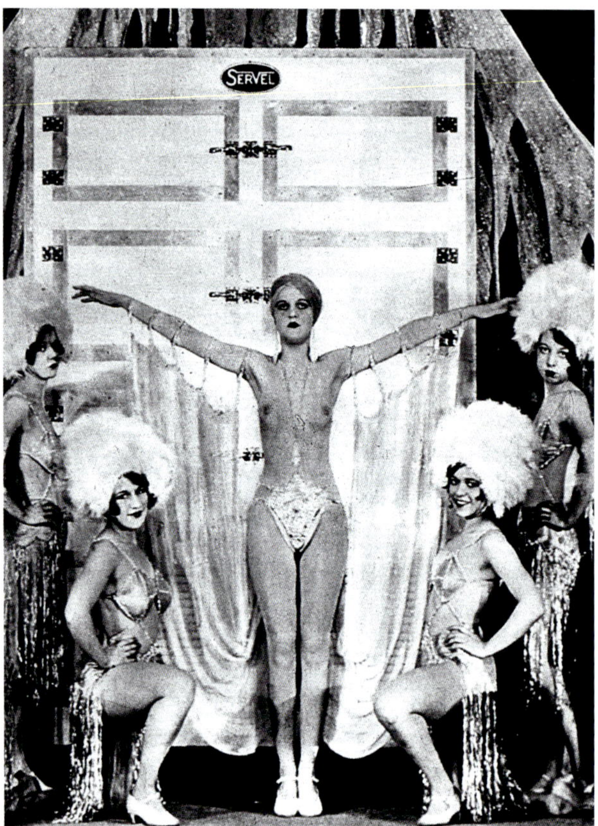

YEAR: **1922**. TITLE: **Shadowland**. COUNTRY: **USA**.

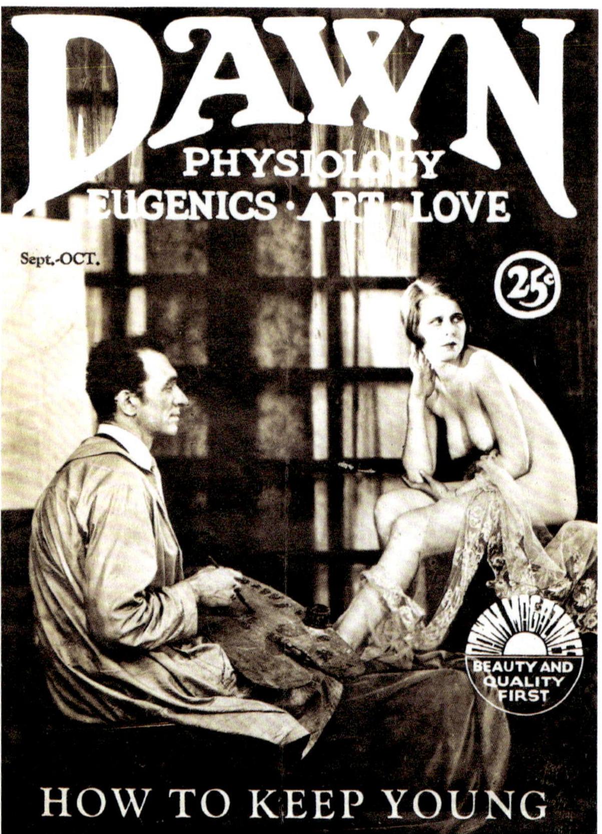

YEAR: **1920s**. TITLE: **Dawn**. COUNTRY: **USA**.

YEAR: **1903**. TITLE: **Vanity Fair's Bifurcated Girls**. COUNTRY: **USA**.

PAGES | 100 Stunts in "Pants." | 25 CENTS.

VANITY FAIR'S
BIFURCATED GIRLS

VOL. XXVII. NO. 720. NEW YORK, JUNE 6, 1903.

GAY GIRLS IN TROUSERS

LEADING ACTRESSES–MENS TOGS

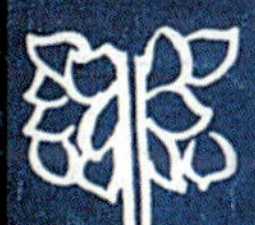

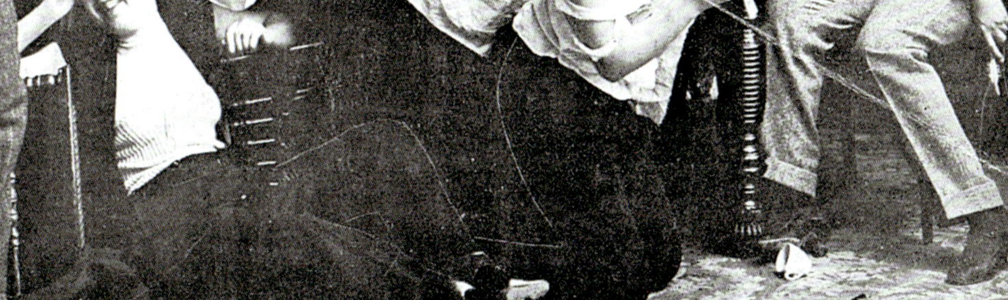

"HURRAH! MAMA'S AT THE SEASHORE AND PAPA'S IN HEAVEN!"

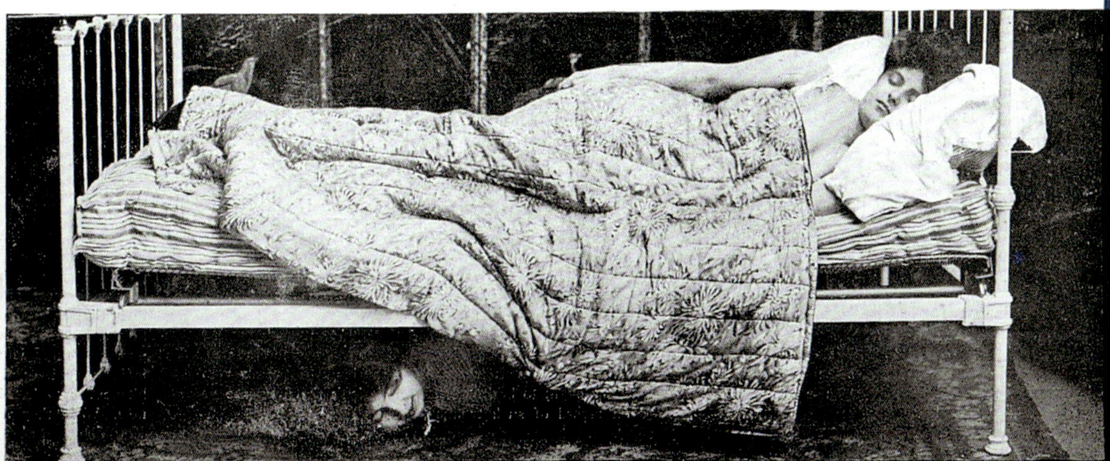

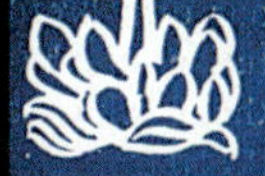

Year: **1930**. Title: **Jim Jam Jems**. Country: **USA**.

Bloomers, an invention of the 1880s, designed to allow women to bicycle modestly, were declared indecently masculine.

Women's legs were objects of great mystery and by extension desire in the age of floor-sweeping skirts. Even if a man burrowed under the skirts, there were loose leggings from waist to ankle to conceal the limbs' contours. Bloomers, an invention of the 1880s, designed to allow women to bicycle modestly (traditional leggings were open at the crotch for toilet functions), backfired when they were declared indecently masculine. The transgression of a woman who dared to adopt male clothing had as many layers as her skirts in 1903. First, it suggested she was stepping outside her Heaven-ordained role as hand-maiden to man; second, it hinted at Sapphic perversion; third, it revealed she had legs, which if followed upward from the ankle could lead a good man straight to Hell. So the June 6th 1903 *Bifurcated Girls* issue of *Vanity Fair* was really very naughty indeed, even if unrecognizable as a men's magazine today. And in the years immediately following there was little to top it, though French magazines occasionally filtered into the country, to the great delight of those lucky enough to find them. The next step forward wouldn't be until 1919 when *Capt. Billy's Whiz Bang*, a crude humor magazine, appeared from

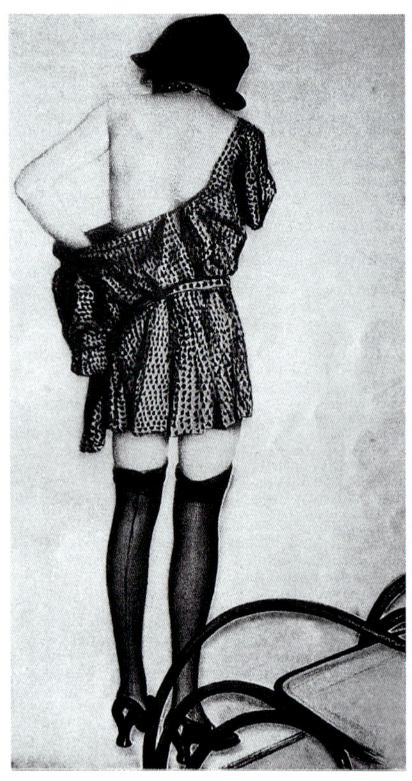

Year: **1925**. Title: **10 Story Book**. Country: **USA**.

die Röcke gearbeitet hatte, trug die Frau darunter noch bis auf die Knöchel fallende, weite Unterhosen, um die Kontur ihrer Beine zu verbergen. Mit den Bloomers, einer Erfindung aus den achtziger Jahren des 19. Jahrhunderts, die den Frauen das Radfahren erleichtern sollte (traditionelle Unterhosen waren aus hygienischen Gründen im Schritt offen), war es vorbei, nachdem man sie als unzüchtig maskulin gebrandmarkt hatte.

Die Vorwürfe, denen sich eine Frau aussetzte, die männliche Kleidung anzulegen wagte, waren 1903 noch so mannigfach wie ihre Röcke. Zum einem verstieß sie damit gegen die gottgewollte Rolle als Dienerin des Mannes, des weiteren ließ

de parfaits modèles pour ce genre de galipettes. Mais le summum de l'érotisme était la bifurcation. « La quoi ? » demanderez-vous. La bifurcation, à savoir « la division en deux branches », faisait référence à la silhouette de jambes féminines révélée par le port d'un pantalon d'homme. C'était l'un des traits récurrents les plus prisés de *Vanity Fair*, sa popularité menant aux *Vanity Fair's Bifurcated Girls* présentées ici.

À une époque où les jupes balayaient encore le plancher, les jambes de femmes étaient un vrai mystère et, par extension, un objet de désir. Même lorsqu'un homme parvenait à s'immiscer sous une jupe, des pantalons tombant jusqu'aux chevilles dissimulaient encore le contour de la jambe. Les culottes bouffantes, une invention des années 1880 pour permettre aux femmes de faire de la bicyclette en toute modestie (les caleçons longs traditionnels étaient ouverts à l'entrejambe pour des raisons hygiéniques) connurent un revers brutal quand elles furent soudain déclarées indécentes. En 1903, une femme qui osait adopter une tenue masculine commettait une série de transgressions aussi nombreuses que ses jupons. Primo, elle sortait de son rôle de servante de l'homme que lui avaient attribué les cieux. Secundo, cela laissait supposer une perversion saphique. Tertio, cela révélait qu'elle avait des jambes qui, s'il les remontait à partir de la cheville, pouvaient mener un homme honnête tout droit aux enfers. Aussi le numéro du 6 juin 1903 de *Vanity Fair*, un spécial *Bifurcated Girls*, était particulièrement osé, même si on peine aujourd'hui à l'identifier comme une revue de charme. Il ne connut pratiquement pas d'équivalent au cours des années qui suivirent, même si quelques

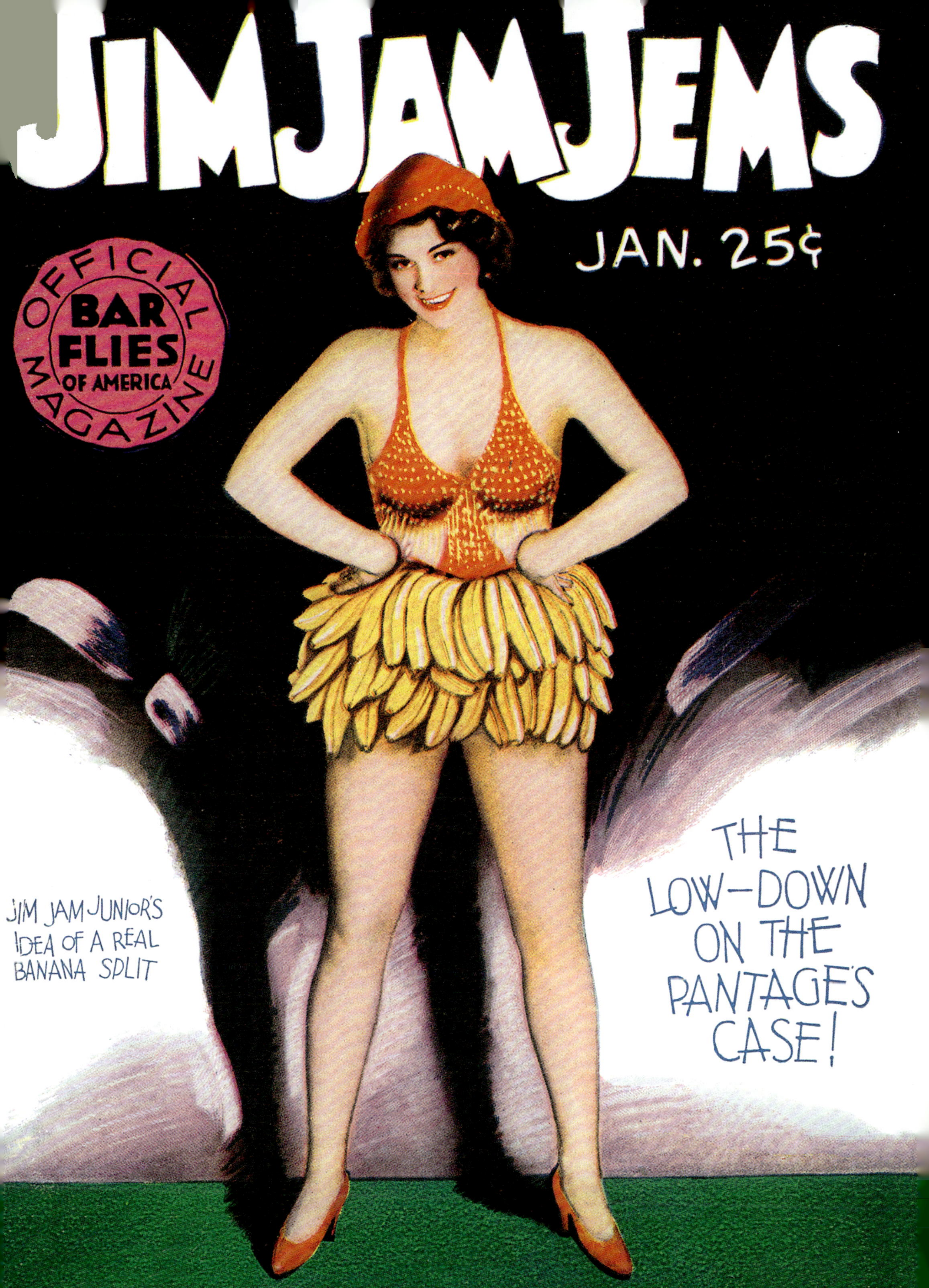
JIM JAM JEMS
JAN. 25¢
OFFICIAL BAR FLIES OF AMERICA MAGAZINE
JIM JAM JUNIOR'S
IDEA OF A REAL
BANANA SPLIT
THE
LOW-DOWN
ON THE
PANTAGES
CASE!

Year: **1930**. Title: **Calgary Eyeopener**.
Country: **Canada**.

Fawcett Publishing (see Humor Magazines). Then in the early 20s, in the giddy hedonistic grip of post-war prosperity, America discovered nudity. Call it America's first sexual revolution. Women abandoned their corsets, bobbed their hair and took up smoking, drinking and dancing. Ford's affordable automobiles gave young people mobility, and a place to be alone, while the new latex condom offered reliable birth control for those private moments. In the big cities burlesque theaters introduced striptease; sexy magazines came along as an extension of the general good time.

The first magazines used the time-honored nude-studies-for-art-students ploy, often featuring Hollywood starlets as models. As the decade progressed the ploy was dropped. *Shadowland*, the most elegant thing ever conceived in Queens, New York, was a sophisticated film and literary review with "continental" photos

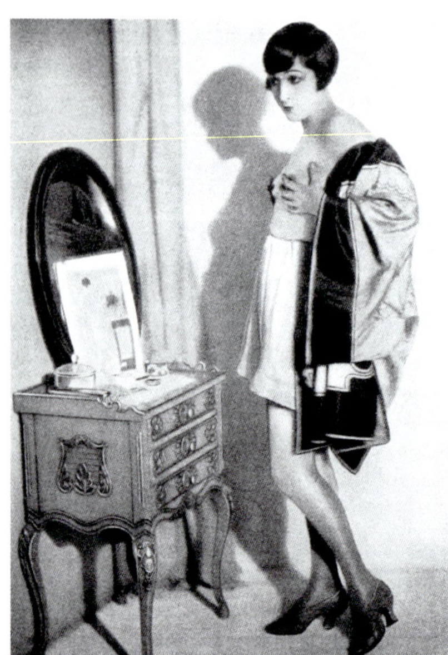

Year: **1925**. Title: **10 Story Book**.
Country: **USA**.

es auf eine lesbische Verirrung schließen, und drittens verriet es, dass sie Beine besaß. Und für einen braven Mann war es womöglich die Fahrkarte in die Hölle, wenn er den Blick von den Fesseln an aufwärts wandern lassen konnte.

Daher war die *Bifurcated Girls*-Ausgabe von *Vanity Fair* vom 6. Juni 1903 in der Tat äußerst verdorben, auch wenn man so etwas heute kaum noch als Männermagazin beschreiben würde. Und die folgenden Jahren brachten nur wenig, was darüber hinaus ging, auch wenn zur Begeisterung weniger Glücklicher gelegentlich französische Magazine ins Land gelangten.

Der nächste große Schritt wurde erst 1919 mit *Capt. Billy's Whiz Bang* getan, einer derben humoristischen Zeitschrift, die von Fawcett Publishing herausgegeben wurde (siehe unter Humour Magazines). Doch in den frühen Zwanzigern, im lebenslustigen, hedonistischen Griff des Nachkriegswohlstands, entdeckte Amerika die Nacktheit, sozusagen die erste sexuelle Revolution in den Vereinigten Staaten.

Die Frauen legten ihre Korsetts ab, ließen sich einen Bubikopf schneiden, begannen zu rauchen, zu trinken und zu tanzen. Die preiswerten Automobile von Ford gewährten der Jugend Mobilität und einen Ort, an dem man ungestört war, und mit den neuen Latexkondomen gab es auch eine verlässliche Verhütungsmethode für diese intimen Momente. Die Varietés in den Großstädten zeigten Striptease-Shows, und frivole Magazine spiegelten den Zeitgeist wieder.

Die ersten dieser Zeitschriften bemühten noch den Trick mit den „Künstlermodellen" und präsentierten häufig Starlets aus Hollywood. Im Laufe des Jahrzehnts

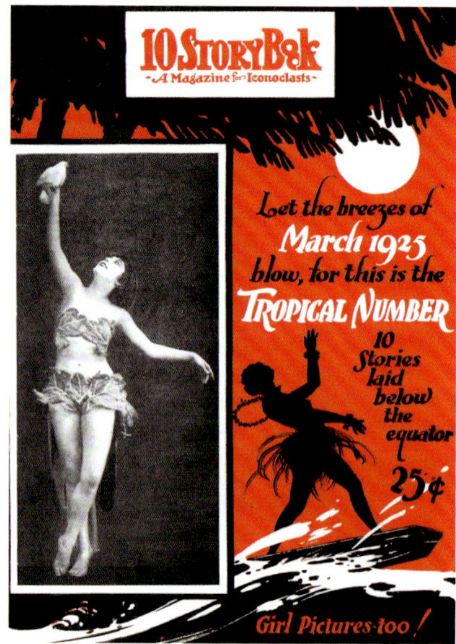

Year: **1925**. Title: **10 Story Book**. Country: **USA**.

magazines français circulaient parfois dans le pays, pour le plus grand plaisir des rares heureux à mettre la main dessus. Il fallut attendre 1919 pour franchir l'étape suivante, avec la publication par Fawcett Publishing de *Capt. Billy's Whiz Bang*, un magazine à l'humour cru (voir le chapitre sur les magazines d'humour). Puis, au début des années 20, dans l'élan hédoniste grisant de la prospérité d'après-guerre, l'Amérique découvrit la nudité. On peut même parler de première révolution sexuelle. Les femmes abandonnèrent leurs corsets, coupèrent leurs cheveux au carré, se mirent à fumer, à boire et à danser. Les automobiles Ford, plus accessibles, offrirent aux jeunes une plus grande mobilité et des lieux où s'isoler, tandis que les nouveaux préservatifs en latex rendaient la contraception plus fiable lors de ces moments d'intimité. Dans les grandes villes, les vaudevilles se mirent au striptease. Les revues légères

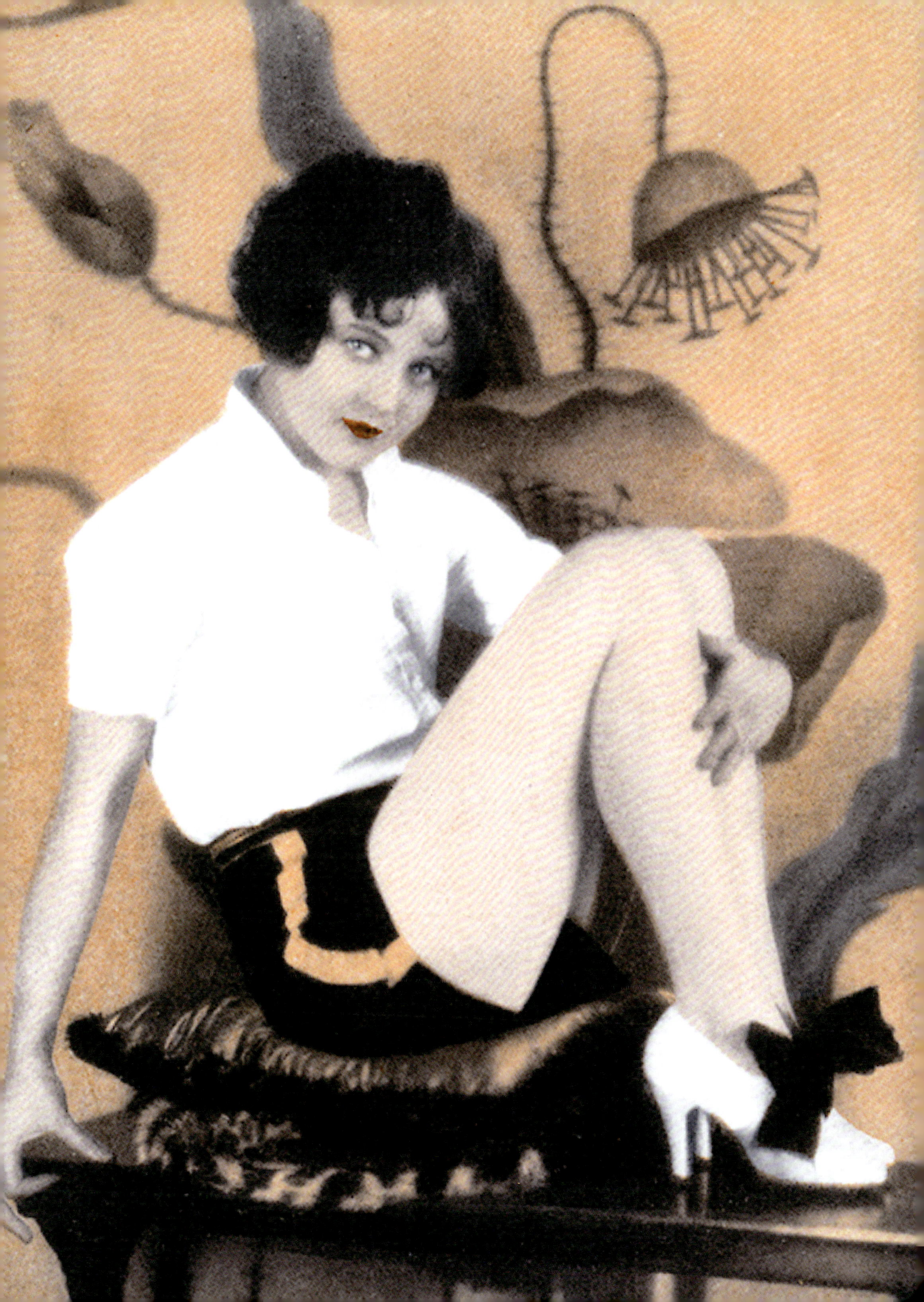

Below: This 1922 title was based on sophisticated European lifestyle magazines like La Vie Parisienne *and* Berliner Leben*, but originated from humble Queens, New York.*

Unten: Dieser Titel von 1922 war den anspruchsvollen europäischen Lifestyle-Magazinen wie La Vie Parisienne *und* Berliner Leben *nachempfunden, stammte aber aus dem eher ärmlichen New Yorker Stadtteil Queens.*

En bas : Ce titre de 1922 s'inspirait des magazines sophistiqués européens comme La Vie Parisienne *et* Berliner Leben*, mais était réalisé dans l'humble quartier de Queens, à New York.*

YEAR: **1926**. TITLE: **Sex**. ARTIST: **M. Desabtis**. COUNTRY: **USA**.

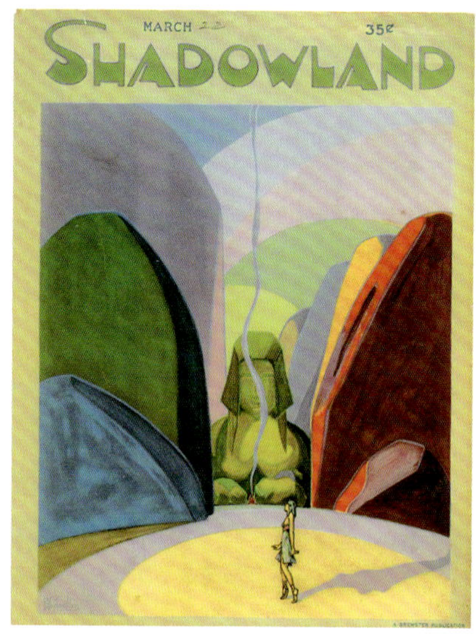

YEAR: **1922**. TITLE: **Shadowland**. COUNTRY: **USA**.

and illustrations. *10 Story Book*, "A Magazine for Iconoclasts," had been around since 1901, but not until the 20s did it fulfill its promise to be "Smarter, Snappier, Breezier, Livelier, and Saucier Than All The Rest," Even if the stories stopped short of explicit sexual description the photos were indeed snappy, and in the back were ads offering even snappier photo packs from France.

America enjoyed a eugenics craze in the 20s that required magazines to demonstrate the ideal physical form. Make that the ideal *female* physical form. The leader in this area was the somewhat sinister Dawn Press in New York, whose flagship, *Dawn Magazine*, specialized in "eugenics, nudism and figure studies." *Dawn* presented only genetically superior art nudes for American Beauty Cultists and there were rumors that birth control reformer Margaret Sanger had a hand in its production. Apparently she saw masturbation

kam man von dieser Masche ab. *Shadowland*, das Eleganteste, was jemals in dem New Yorker Stadtteil Queens ersonnen wurde, war ein anspruchsvolles Blatt mit Film- und Buchrezensionen und zeigte Fotos und Illustrationen im „kontinentaleuropäischen Stil". *10 Story Book*, das „Magazin für Ikonoklasten" existierte bereits seit 1901, aber erst in den Zwanzigern löste es sein Versprechen ein, „smarter, gewagter, forscher, lebendiger und frecher als der Rest" zu sein. Die Texte mogelten sich zwar an eindeutigen sexuellen Schilderungen haarscharf vorbei, aber die Fotos waren in der Tat gewagt, und hinten im Anzeigenteil wurden noch gewagtere Fotos aus Frankreich zum Kauf angeboten.

Während der zwanziger Jahre erlebten die Vereinigten Staaten einen Eugenik-Boom, der Zeitschriften brauchte, um den idealen Körperbau vorzuführen – den idealen *weiblichen* Körperbau, genau gesagt. Führend auf diesem Gebiet war die obskure Dawn Press aus New York, deren Flagschiff, das *Dawn Magazine*, sich auf „Eugenik, Freikörperkultur und Körperstudien" spezialisiert hatte. *Dawn* ließ nur genetisch einwandfreie Aktmodelle für American Beauty Cultists ins Heft, und es gab Gerüchte, dass

suivirent, comme une extension à l'atmosphère de liesse générale.

Les premiers magazines exploitaient une formule qui avait fait ses preuves : les études de nus pour étudiants d'art, prenant souvent des starlettes d'Hollywood comme modèles. Au fil de la décennie, le prétexte disparut. *Shadowland*, ce qu'on a conçu de plus élégant dans le Queens (New York), était un film sophistiqué et un revue littéraire contenant des photos et des illustrations « européennes ». *10 Story Book*, « un magazine pour iconoclastes », existait depuis 1901 mais attendit les années 20 pour tenir sa promesse d'être plus « malin, chic, pétillant et impertinent que les autres ». Même si les histoires n'allaient pas jusqu'aux descriptions sexuelles explicites, les photos étaient effectivement très coquines. En outre, les dernières pages contenaient des publicités pour des portfolios encore plus salaces provenant de France.

Dans les années 1920, l'Amérique connut un fort engouement pour l'eugénisme, imposant aux revues de représenter la forme physique idéale, ou plutôt, la forme féminine idéale. Dans ce domaine, le leader était la sinistre maison newyorkaise Dawn Press dont la publication phare, *Dawn Magazine*, se spécialisait

> Sex began to rear its head when four million men were called to the colours in the First World War. The war showed Americans that there were other husbands and other wives besides their own, and ended with 300,000 divorces.
>
> —*A History of Sexual Customs*, Richard Lewinsohn

Are you your wife's lover?

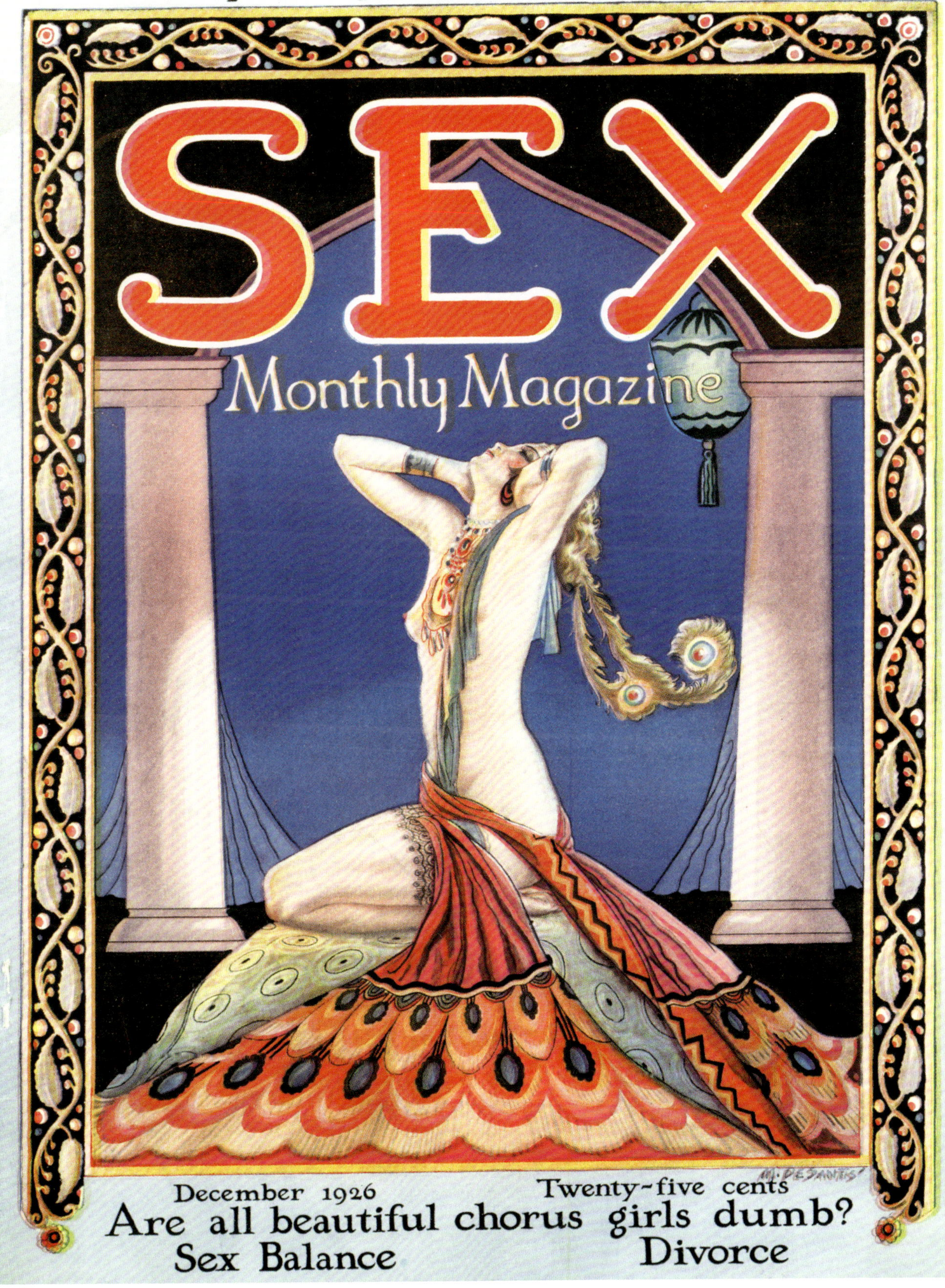

Yes, Virginia, there really was a Sex *magazine published in America in 1926. This art deco masterpiece was from Dawn Publishing, and rumored to be the work of Margaret Sanger and her league of birth control activists.*

Ja, Virginia, es gab 1926 ein Magazin mit dem Titel Sex *in Amerika. Dieses Meisterwerk des Art deco stammte aus dem Hause Dawn und war, Gerüchten zufolge, das Werk von Margaret Sanger und ihrer Liga für Geburtenkontrolle.*

Oui, il existait vraiment un magazine américain intitulé Sex *en 1926. Ce chef d'œuvre Art déco, publié par Dawn Publishing, aurait été réalisé par Margaret Sanger et ses militants pour le contrôle des naissances.*

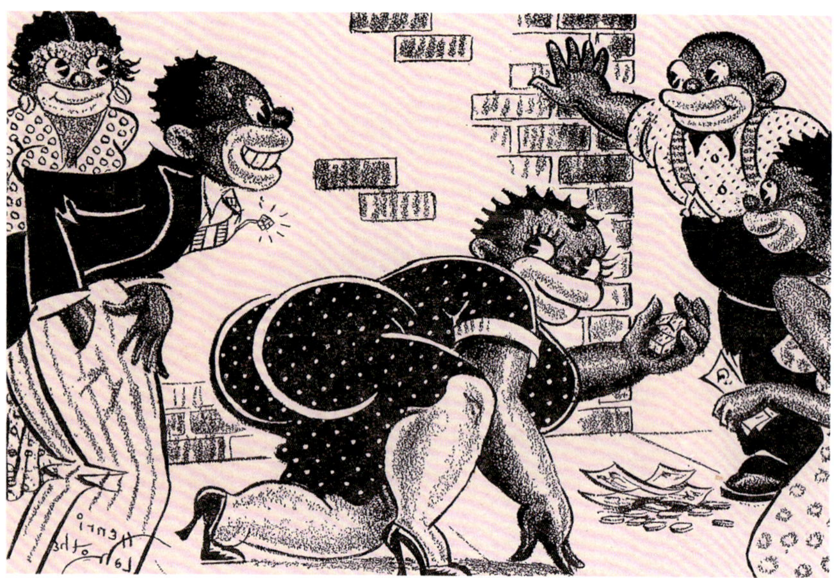

Helen Brown: **"Man, if you've got 2 bucks, you can get into this!"**
Year: **1932**. Title: **Brevities**. Country: **USA**.

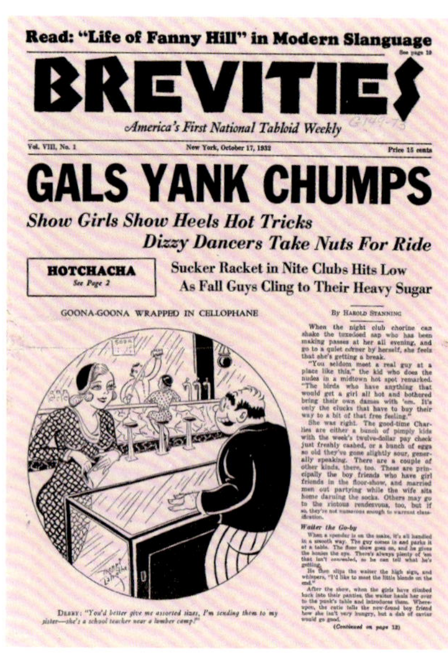

Read: "Life of Fanny Hill" in Modern Slanguage
See page 10

BREVITIES

America's First National Tabloid Weekly

Vol. VIII, No. 1 — New York, October 17, 1932 — Price 15 cents

GALS YANK CHUMPS

Show Girls Show Heels Hot Tricks
Dizzy Dancers Take Nuts For Ride

HOTCHACHA
See Page 2

Sucker Racket in Nite Clubs Hits Low
As Fall Guys Cling to Their Heavy Sugar

GOONA-GOONA WRAPPED IN CELLOPHANE

Derby: *"You'd better give me assorted sizes, I'm sending them to my sister—she's a school teacher near a lumber camp!"*

By Harold Stanning

When the night club chorine can shake the tuxedoed sap who has been making passes at her all evening, and go to a quiet corner by herself, she feels that she's getting a break.

"You seldom meet a real guy at a place like this," the kid who does the nudes in a midtown hot spot remarked. "The birds who have anything that would get a girl all hot and bothered bring their own dames with 'em. It's only the clucks that have to buy their way to a bit of that free feeling."

She was right. The good-time Charlies are either a bunch of pimply kids with the week's twelve-dollar pay check just freshly cashed, or a bunch of eggs so old they've gone slightly sour, generally speaking. There are a couple of other kinds, there, too. These are principally the boy friends who have girl friends in the floor-show, and married men out partying while the wife sits home darning the socks. Others may go to the riotous rendezvous, too, but if so, they're not numerous enough to warrant classification.

Waiter the Go-by

When a spender is on the make, it's all handled in a smooth way. The guy comes in and parks it at a table. The floor show goes on, and he gives the honies the eye. There's always plenty of 'em that isn't concealed, so he can tell what he's getting.

He then slips the waiter the high sign, and whispers, "I'd like to meet the little blonde on the end."

After the show, when the girls have climbed back into their panties, the waiter hauls her over to the punk's table and introduces them. Whereupon, the cutie tells the new-found boy friend how she isn't very hungry, but a dab of caviar would go good.

(Continued on page 12)

Year: **1932**. Title: **Brevities**. Country: **USA**.

as a deterrent to inferior males breeding. Whatever the motives, in 1929 Dawn published the very progressive *Sex* magazine. *Sex* was snappy as snappy could be, and if it hadn't been hit squarely by the crashing stock market who knows just how snappy it might have become?

In the 1930s, in the grip of The Great Depression, *Sex* and the rest of the 20s indulgence slipped away. The new decade called for a new kind of men's magazine, one admittedly less snappy, but with a spiciness all its own.

Margaret Sanger, die amerikanische Vorkämpferin für Geburtenkontrolle, bei dem Magazin ihre Hand im Spiel hätte. Angeblich betrachtete Margaret Sanger Masturbation als probates Mittel gegen die unkontrollierte Fortpflanzung minderwertiger Männer.

1929 erschien bei Dawn Press, aus welchen Motiven auch immer, das sehr fortschrittliche Magazin *Sex*. *Sex* war so gewagt wie man es sich nur wünschen konnte, und wäre der Börsenkrach nicht dazwischen gekommen, wer weiß, wie gewagt es noch geworden wäre.

In den von der großen Depression geschüttelten Dreißigern verschwanden *Sex* und die anderen Frivolitäten der Zwanziger. Das neue Jahrzehnt brachte eine neue Generation von Männermagazinen hervor; zugegebenermaßen weniger gewagt, aber mit einer ganz eigenen Art von Schlüpfrigkeit.

dans « l'eugénisme, le nudisme et les études académiques ». Dawn s'adressait aux adeptes du culte de la beauté américaine et ne montrait que des nus artistiques génétiquement supérieurs. Le bruit courait que Margaret Sanger, la réformatrice du contrôle des naissances, n'était pas étrangère à sa réalisation. Apparemment, elle pensait que la masturbation dissuaderait les mâles inférieurs de se reproduire. Quels que soient ses motifs, en 1929 Dawn Press lança le très progressiste *Sex*. Ce magazine était on ne peut plus insolent, et si le krach de Wall Street ne lui avait pas coupé les ailes en plein vol, on se demande jusqu'où il aurait pu aller.

Dans les années 1930, étranglés par la Grande Dépression, *Sex* et les autres petites gâteries des années folles disparurent. La nouvelle décennie appelait à un nouveau genre de magazines pour hommes, pourvus d'un charme bien particulier.

NIGHT LIFE

Vol. 2
No. 4
STORIES
25¢
on't Miss !!!
AUGHT IN
THE ACT
by
Herbert
French

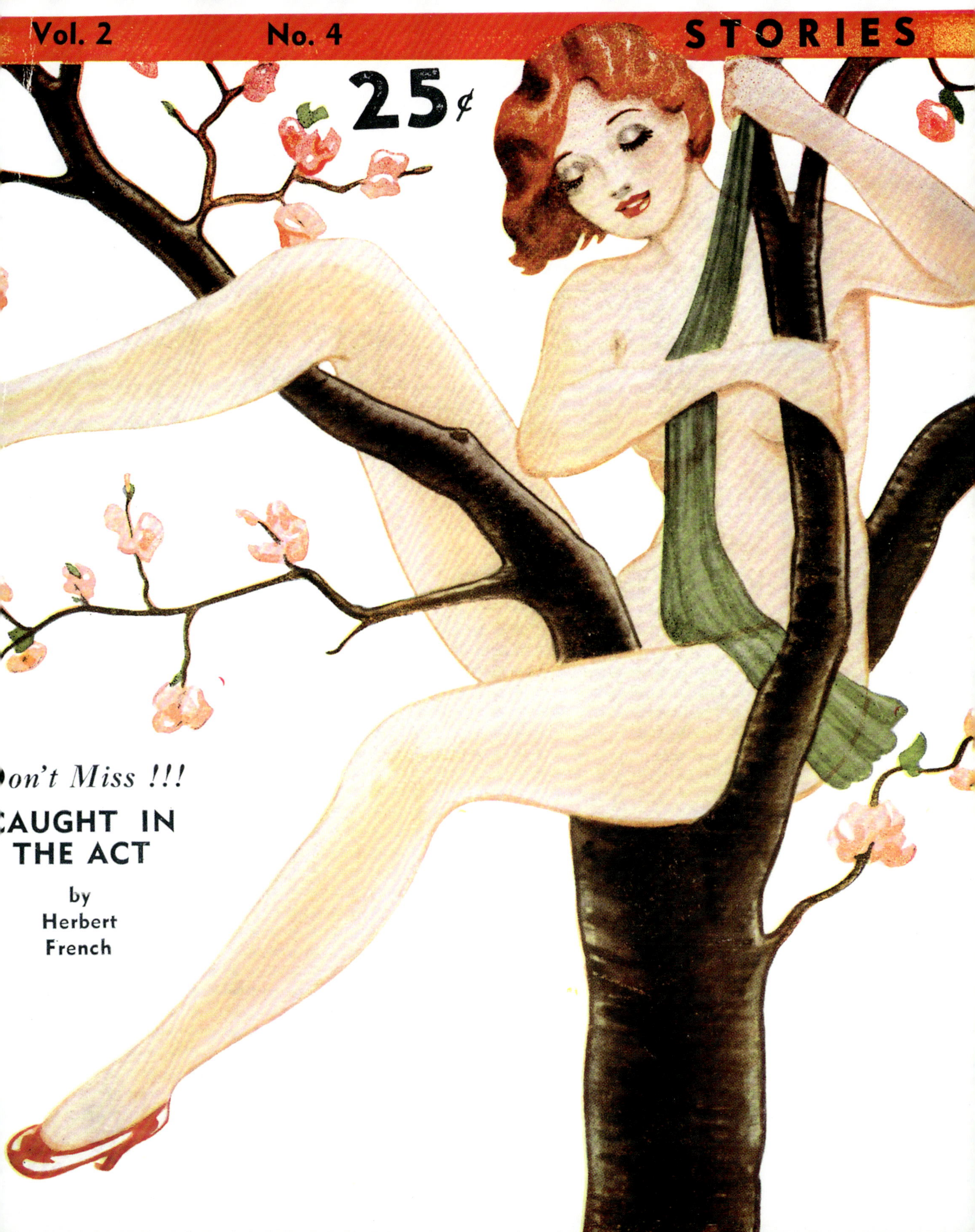

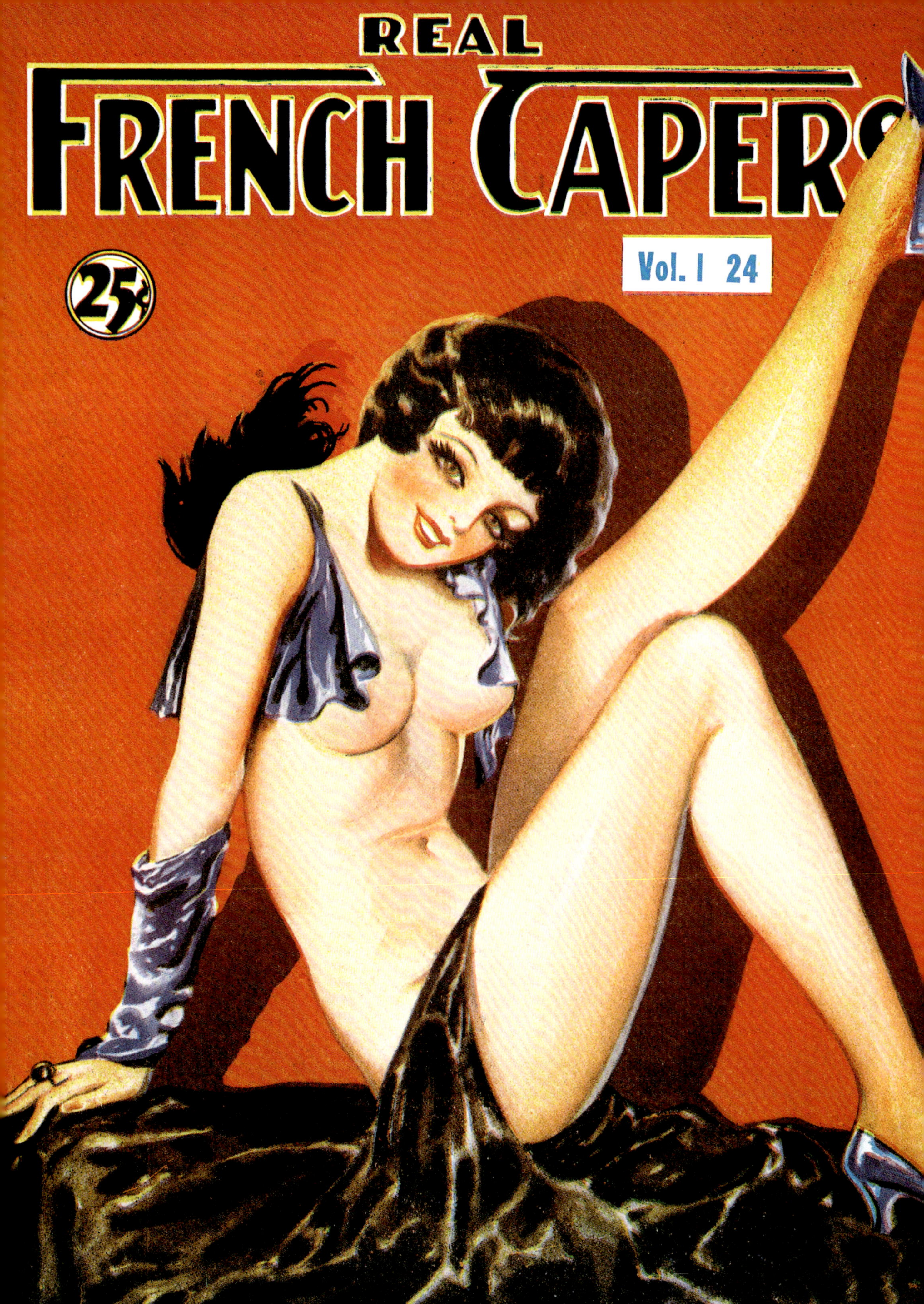
REAL
FRENCH CAPERS
25¢
Vol. I 24

YEAR: **1920s**. TITLE: **Parisienne Revue**. COUNTRY: **USA**.

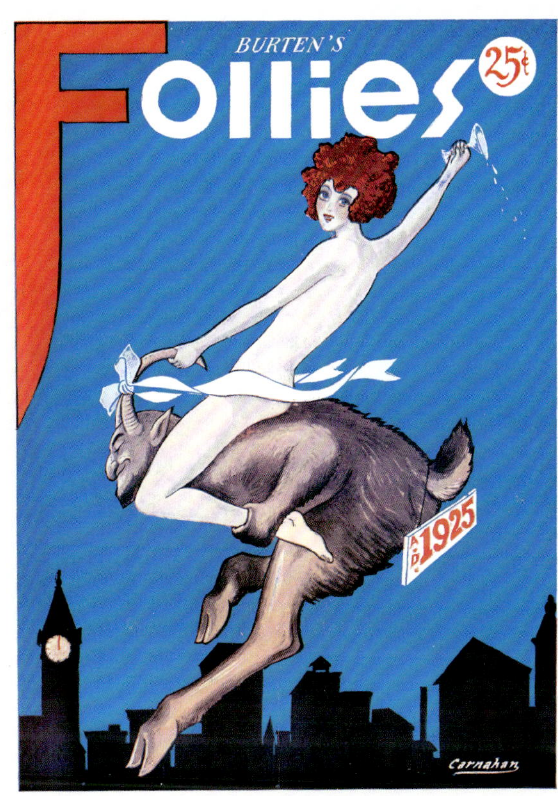

YEAR: **1925**. TITLE: **Burten's Follies**. ARTIST: **Carnahan**. COUNTRY: **USA**.

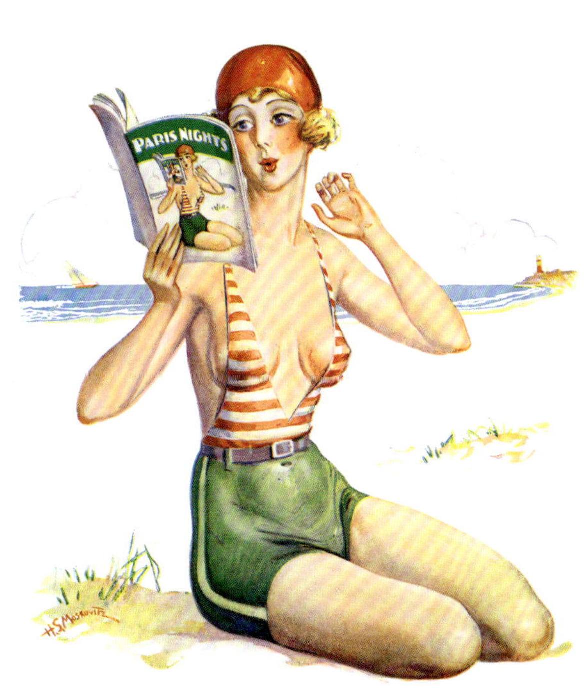

YEAR: **1929**. TITLE: **Paris Nights**. ARTIST: **H. S. Moscovitz**. COUNTRY: **USA**.

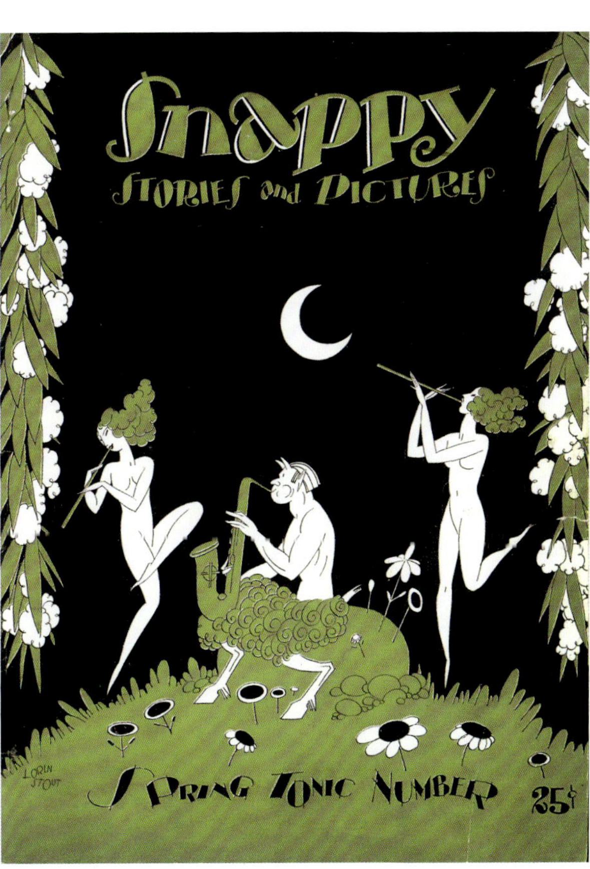

YEAR: **1928**. TITLE: **Snappy Stories and Pictures**. ARTIST: **Lorin Stout**. COUNTRY: **USA**.

YEAR: **1920s**. TITLE: **Real French Capers**. OUNTRY: **USA**.

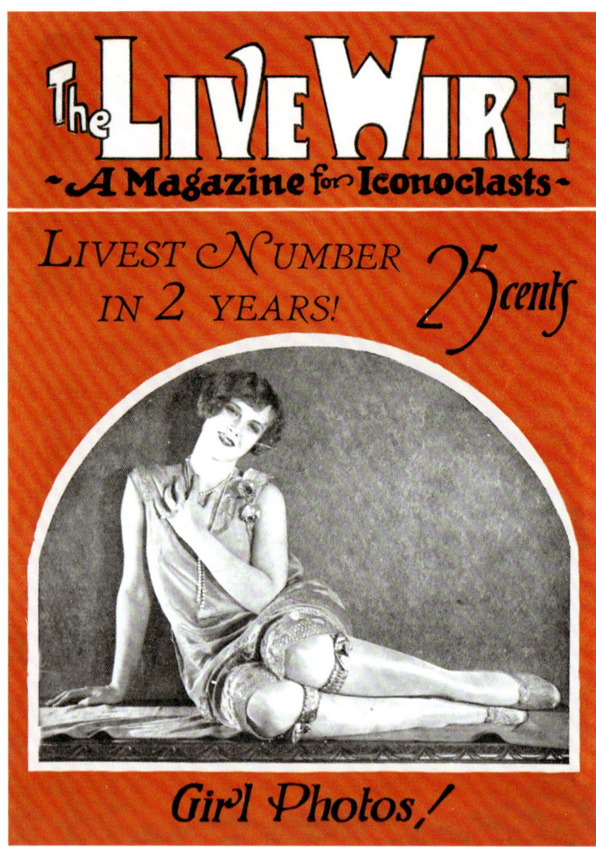

Year: **1926**. Title: **The Live Wire**. Country: **USA**.

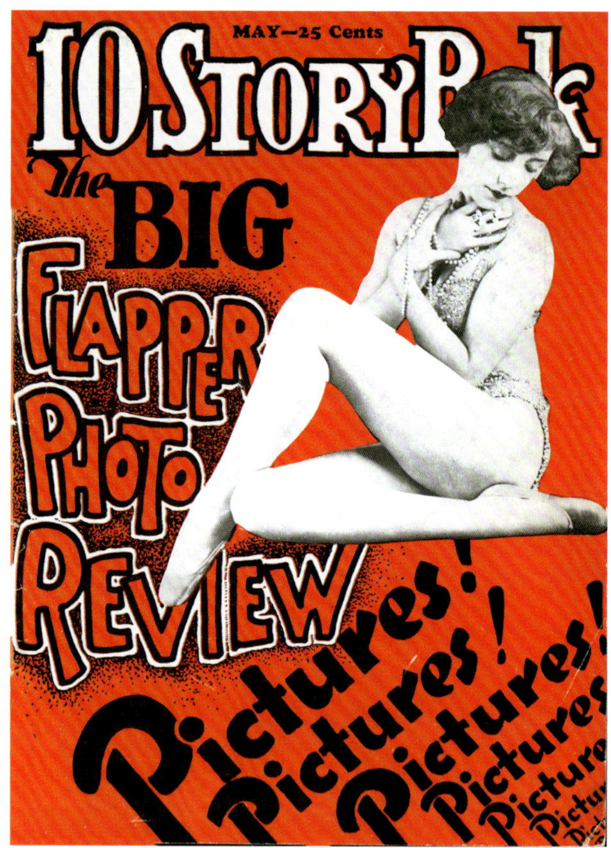

Year: **1928**. Title: **10 Story Book**. Country: **USA**.

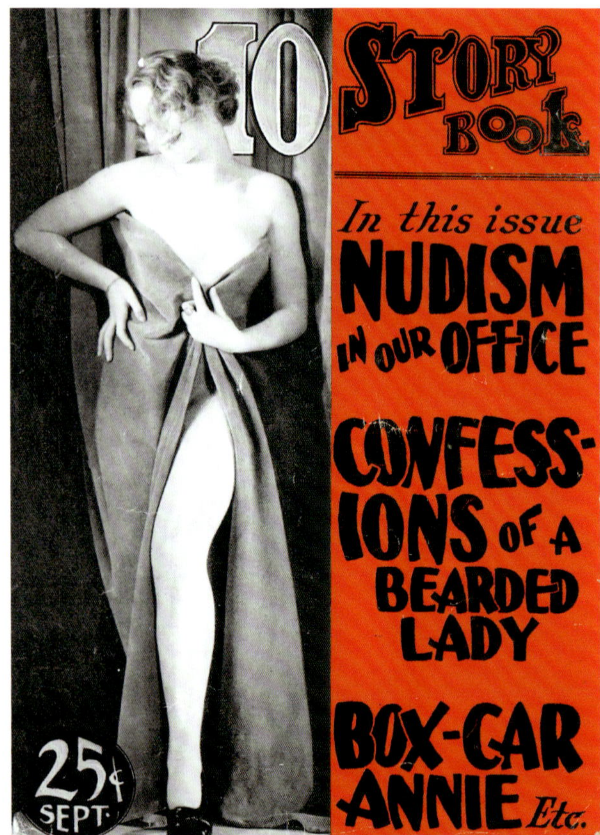

Year: **1935**. Title: **10 Story Book**. Country: **USA**.

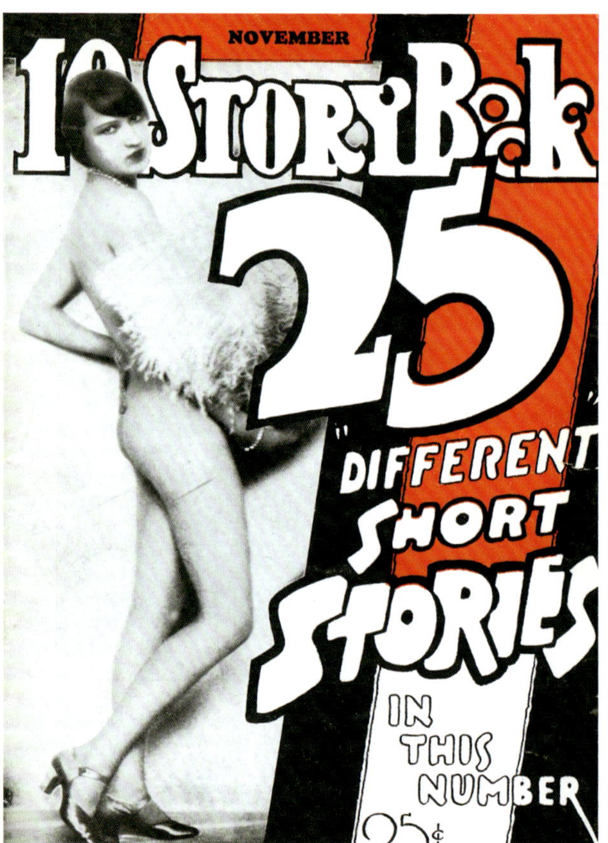

Year: **1930**. Title: **10 Story Book**. Country: **USA**.

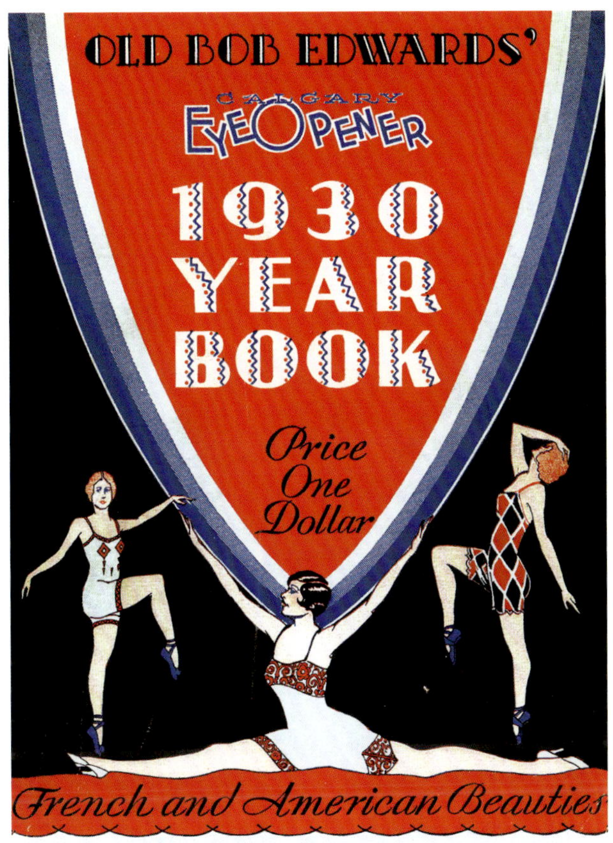

YEAR: **1930**. TITLE: **Calgary Eyeopener**. COUNTRY: **Canada**.

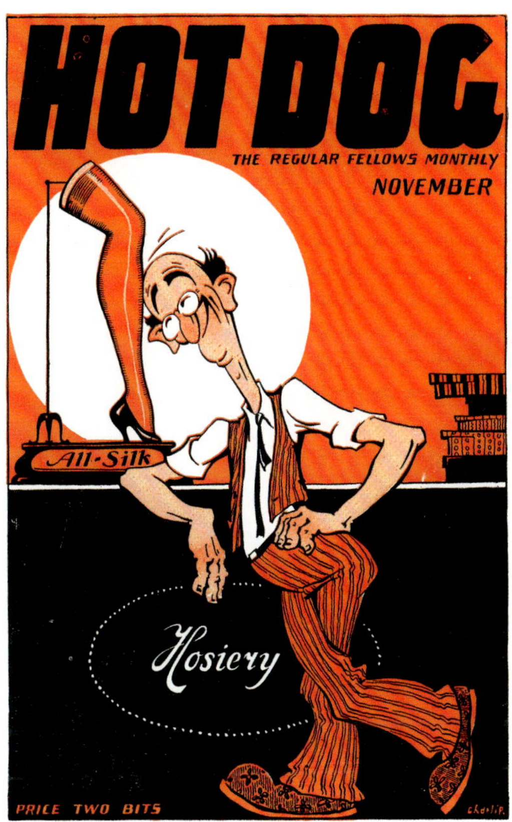

YEAR: **1925**. TITLE: **Hot Dog**. ARTIST: **Charlie**. COUNTRY: **USA**.

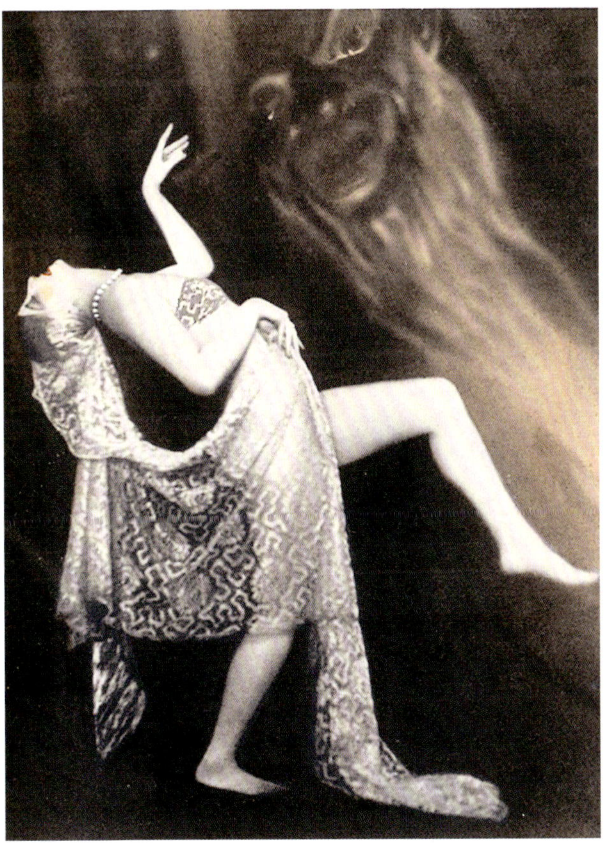

YEAR: **1930**. TITLE: **Calgary Eyeopener**. COUNTRY: **Canada**.

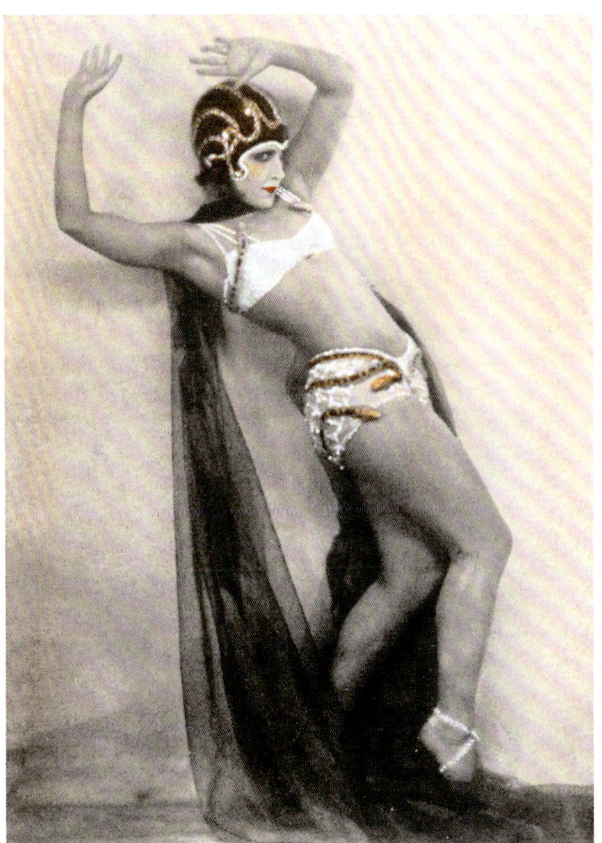

YEAR: **1930**. TITLE: **Calgary Eyeopener**. COUNTRY: **Canada**.

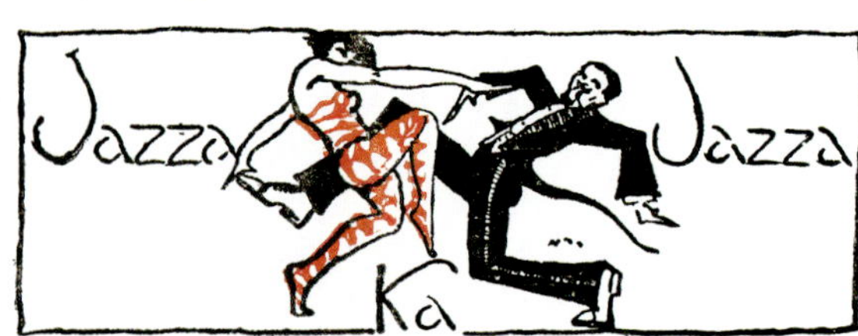

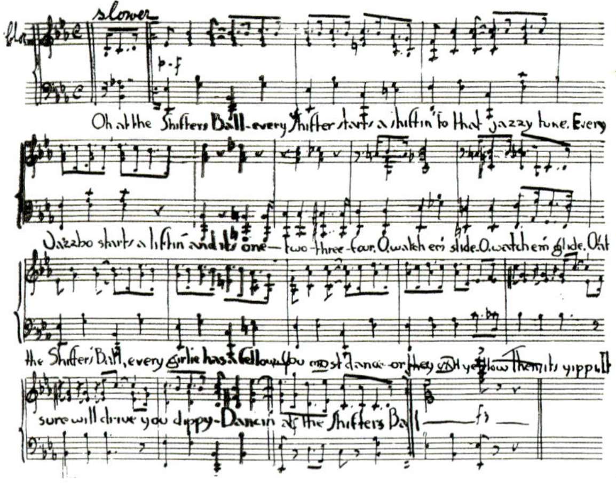

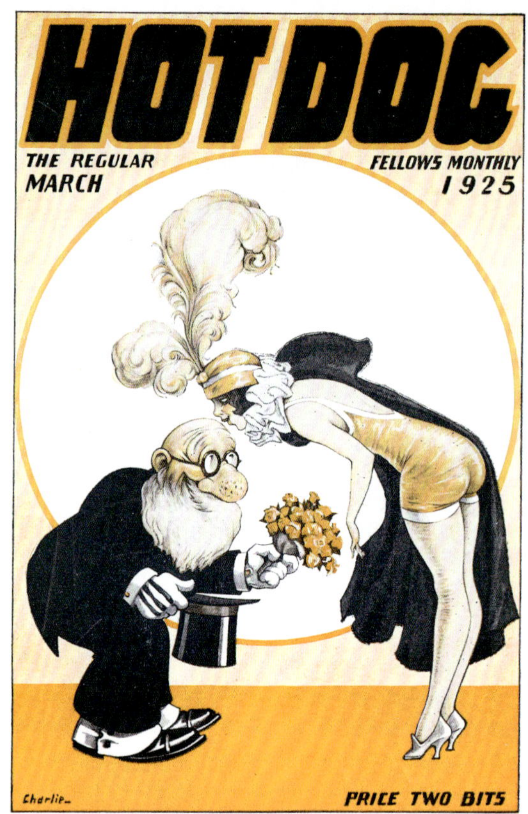

YEAR: **1922**. TITLE: **Cap'n Joey's Jazza-Ka-Jazza**. COUNTRY: **USA**.

YEAR: **1925**. TITLE: **Hot Dog**. ARTIST: **Charlie**. COUNTRY: **USA**.

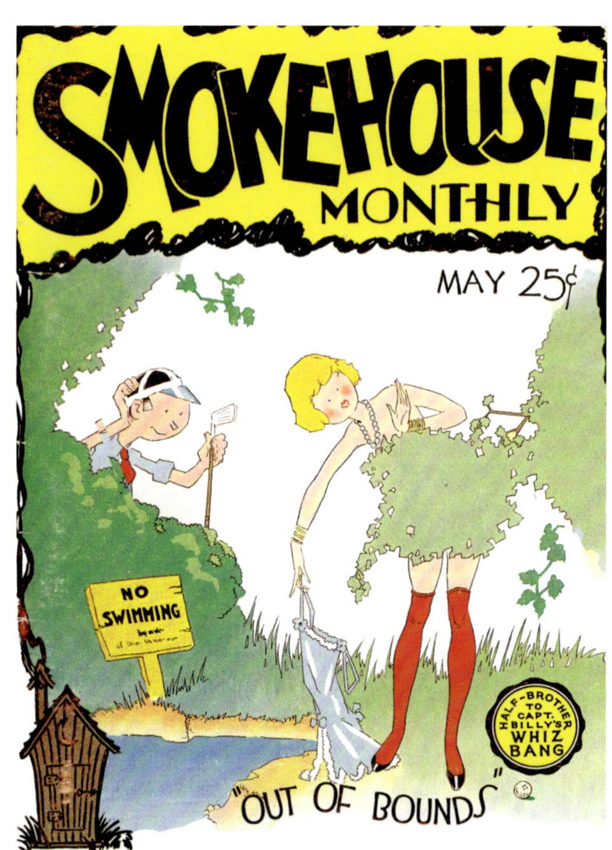

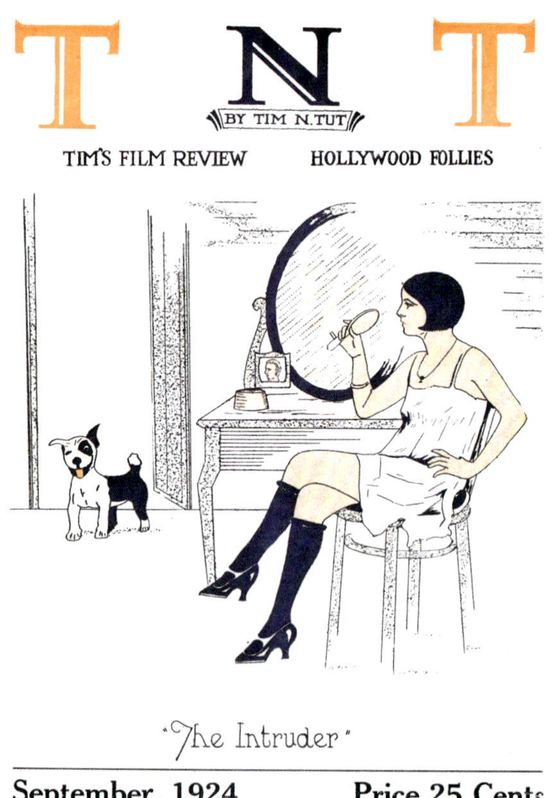

YEAR: **1929**. TITLE: **Smokehouse Monthly**. COUNTRY: **USA**.

YEAR: **1924**. TITLE: **TNT**. COUNTRY: **USA**.

YEAR: **1922**. TITLE: **Cap'n Joey's Jazza-Ka-Jazza**.
ARTIST: **Walter Dean Slager**. COUNTRY: **USA**.

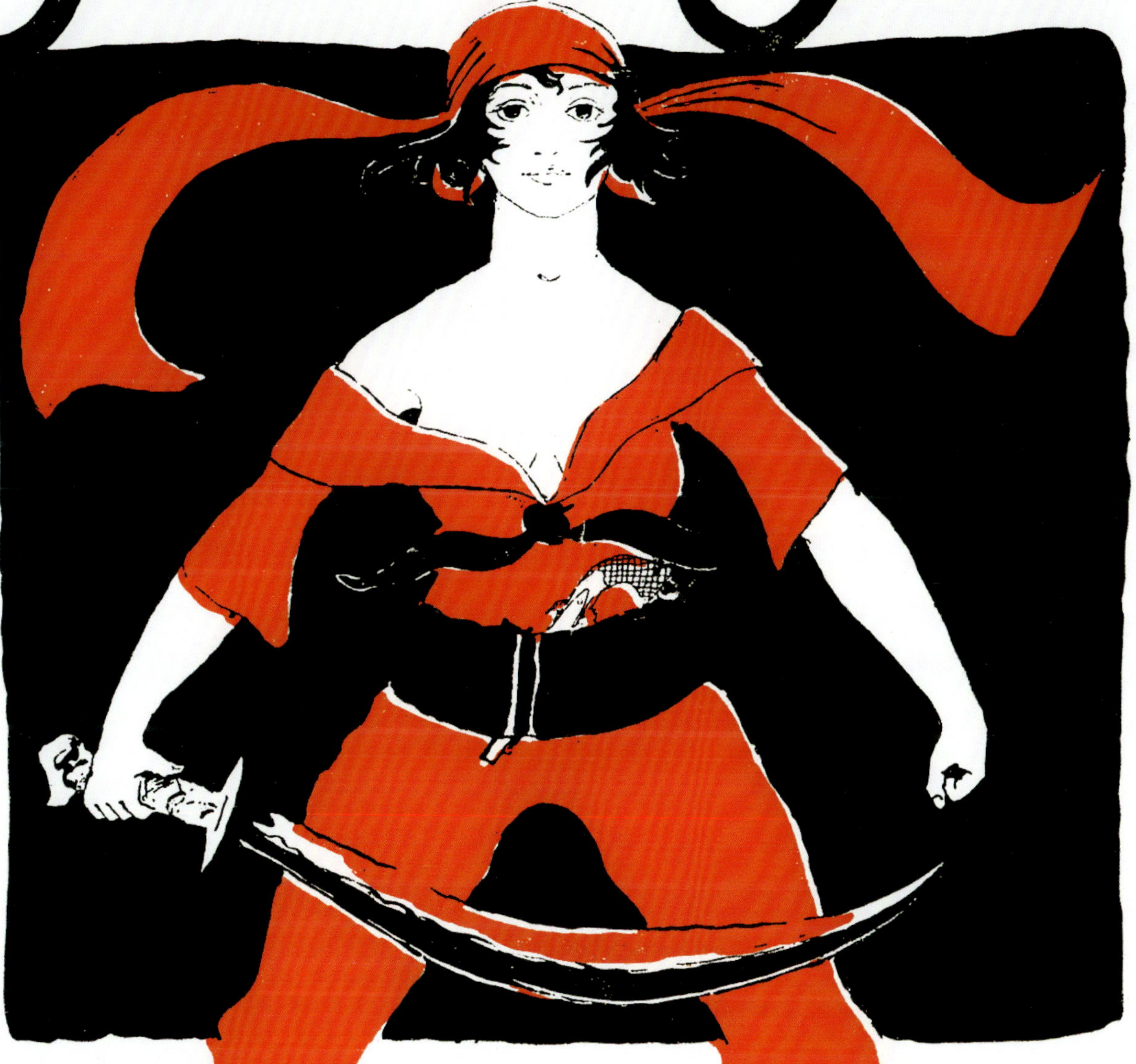
CAP'N JOEY'S
JAZZA KA JAZZA
SUMMERTIME
20c.
BURLESQUE OF "MONTMARTRE"
WALTER DEAN SLAGER '22'

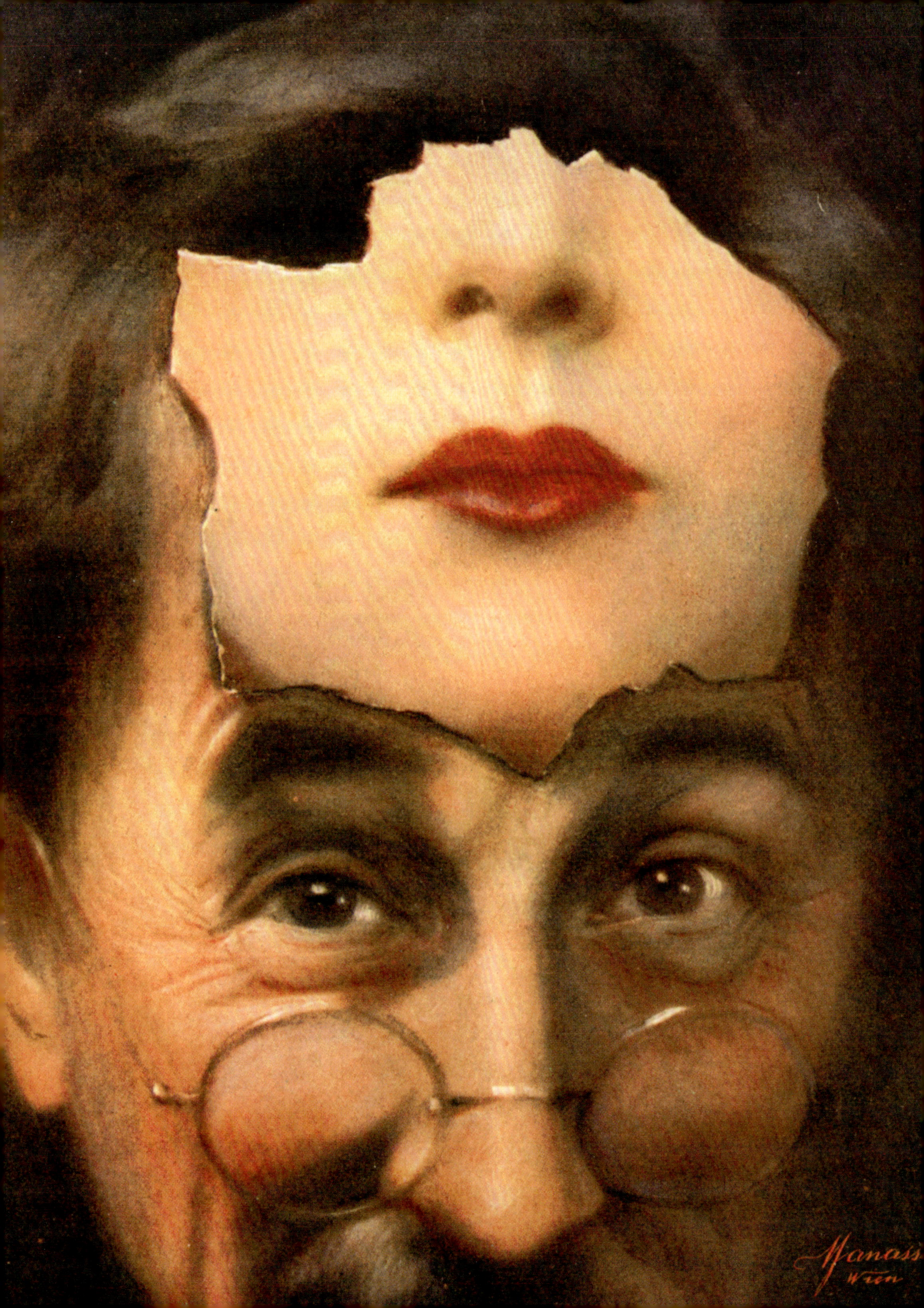
Manass
Wien

German Life Reform and Weimar Vice

Deutschland: Das lasterhafte Weimar und die Lebensreformbewegung
L'Allemagne : la réforme de la vie allemande et le vice de Weimar

By Mel Gordon

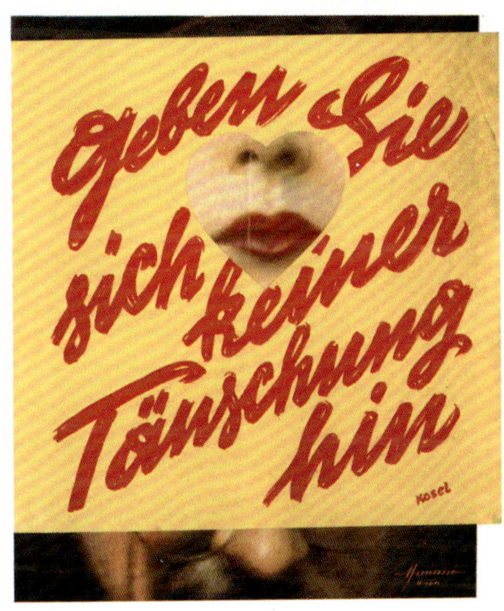

YEAR: **1930**. TITLE: **Wiener Magazin**.
COUNTRY: **Germany**.

Wiener Magazin *1930:*
"Don't fall for any deception"

The modern nudist movement began in Central Europe around 1900 as an organized response to the visible decline in the health of the German nation, brought about by rapid industrialization and by the stupefying bourgeois mores of the Kaiser Wilhelm era. "Body Culture" societies and nudist communities sprung up in other European countries, like France, Sweden, and Austro-Hungary in the first part of the 20th century, but only in Germany did the Adamite philosophy attract hundreds of thousands of devoted participants and absolute

Berlin, with its prostitutes, homosexuals and cabarets, came to represent all that was decadent in Germany.

Die moderne Nudistenbewegung entstand in Deutschland um 1900 als Antwort auf den unübersehbaren Schaden, den die Volksgesundheit in Folge der Industrialisierung genommen hatte, und den lähmenden Sittenkodex des Bürgertums der Wilhelminischen Ära. Auch in anderen europäischen Ländern wie Frankreich, Schweden oder Österreich-Ungarn entstanden Körperkulturbewegungen und Nudistengemeinden, doch nur in Deutschland gewann die adamitische Philosophie tausende von begeisterten und auch fanatischen Anhängern aus allen Klassen, Religionen, Berufsständen, sexuellen und politischen Lagern. Und nur im deutschsprachigen Raum stellten Zeitschriften der Nudisten- und Lebensreformbewegung den sozialen und religiösen status quo in Frage und griffen in die gesellschaftlichen Kämpfe dieser

Wiener Magazin *1930:*
« Ne soyez pas dupe ! »

Le mouvement nudiste moderne vit le jour en Europe centrale autour de 1900. C'était une réaction organisée au déclin visible de la santé de la nation allemande, conséquence de l'industrialisation rapide, et aux mœurs bourgeoises bêtifiantes de l'ère du Kaiser. Au cours de la première moitié du 20e siècle, des associations de « culture physique » et des communautés nudistes fleurirent dans d'autres pays d'Europe, comme la France, la Suède et l'Autriche-Hongrie, mais ce ne fut qu'en Allemagne que l'adamisme attira des centaines de

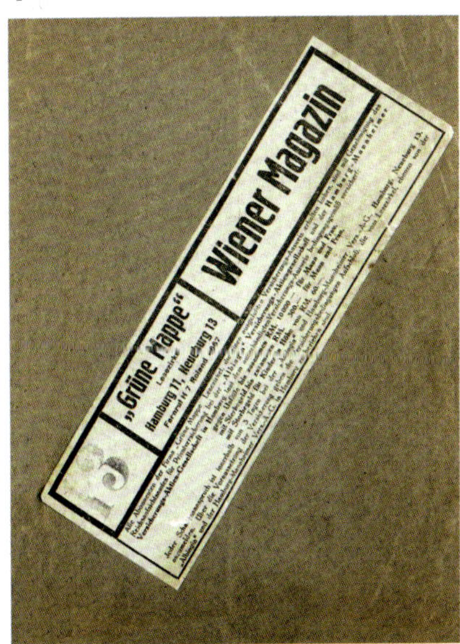

YEAR: **1930**. TITLE: **Wiener Magazin**.
COUNTRY: **Germany**.

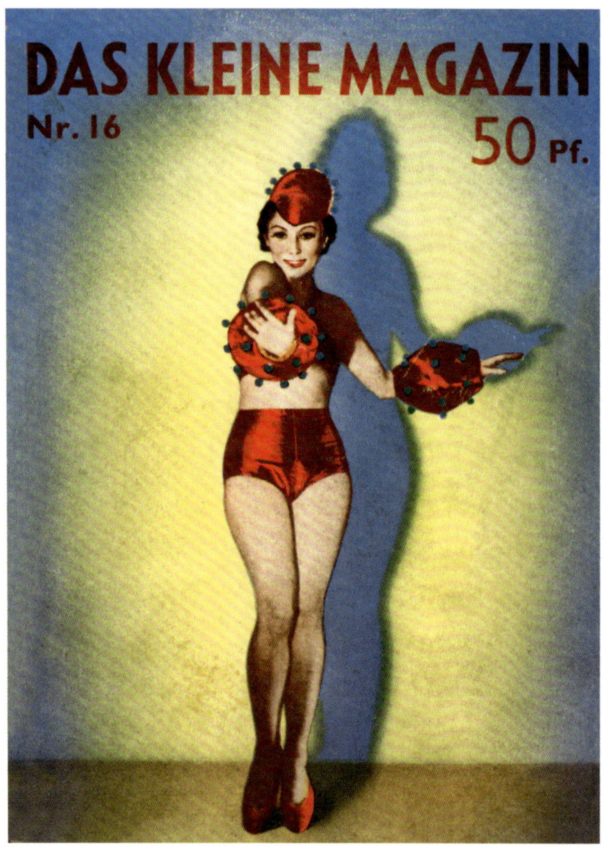

YEAR: **1938**. TITLE: **Das kleine Magazin**. COUNTRY: **Germany**.

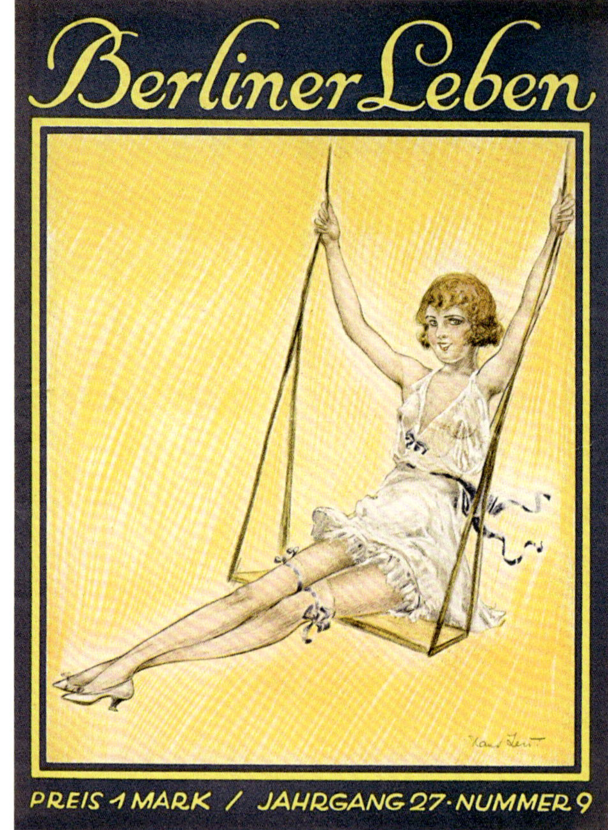

YEAR: **1924**. TITLE: **Berliner Leben**. COUNTRY: **Germany**.

RIGHT: YEAR: **1923**. TITLE: **Reigen**.
ARTIST: **Hahn**. COUNTRY: **Germany**.

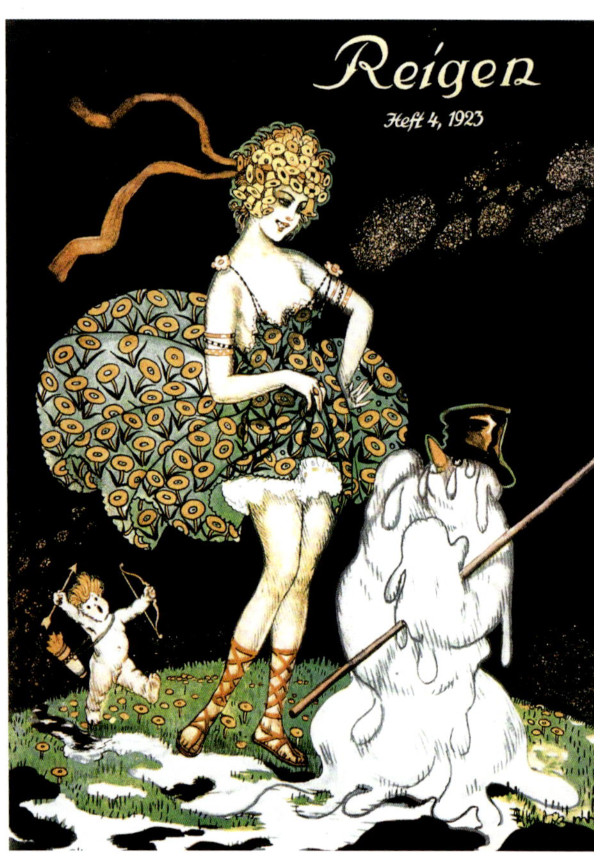

YEAR: **1923**. TITLE: **Reigen**. COUNTRY: **Germany**.

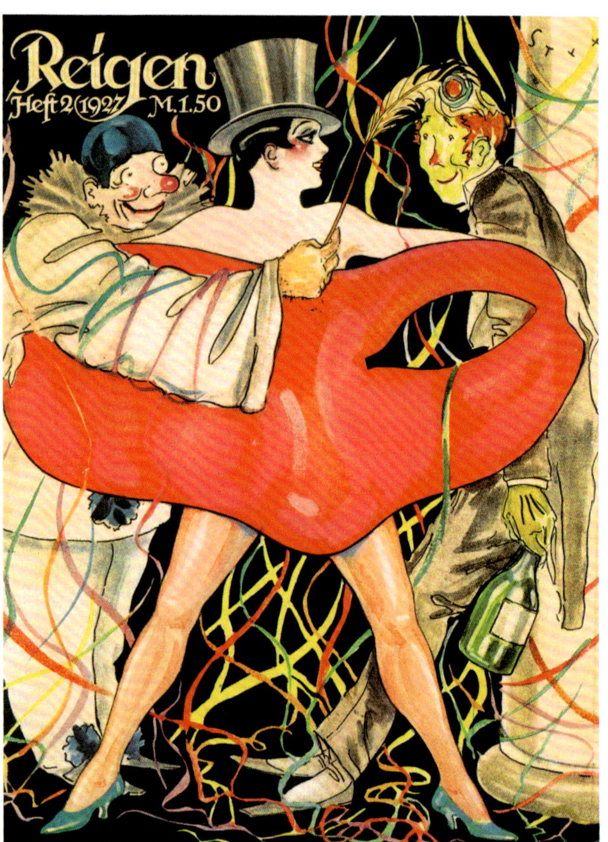

YEAR: **1927**. TITLE: **Reigen**. COUNTRY: **Germany**.

PAGE 92:
YEAR: **1930**. TITLE: **Wiener Magazin**.
ARTIST: **Manassé**. COUNTRY: **Germany**.

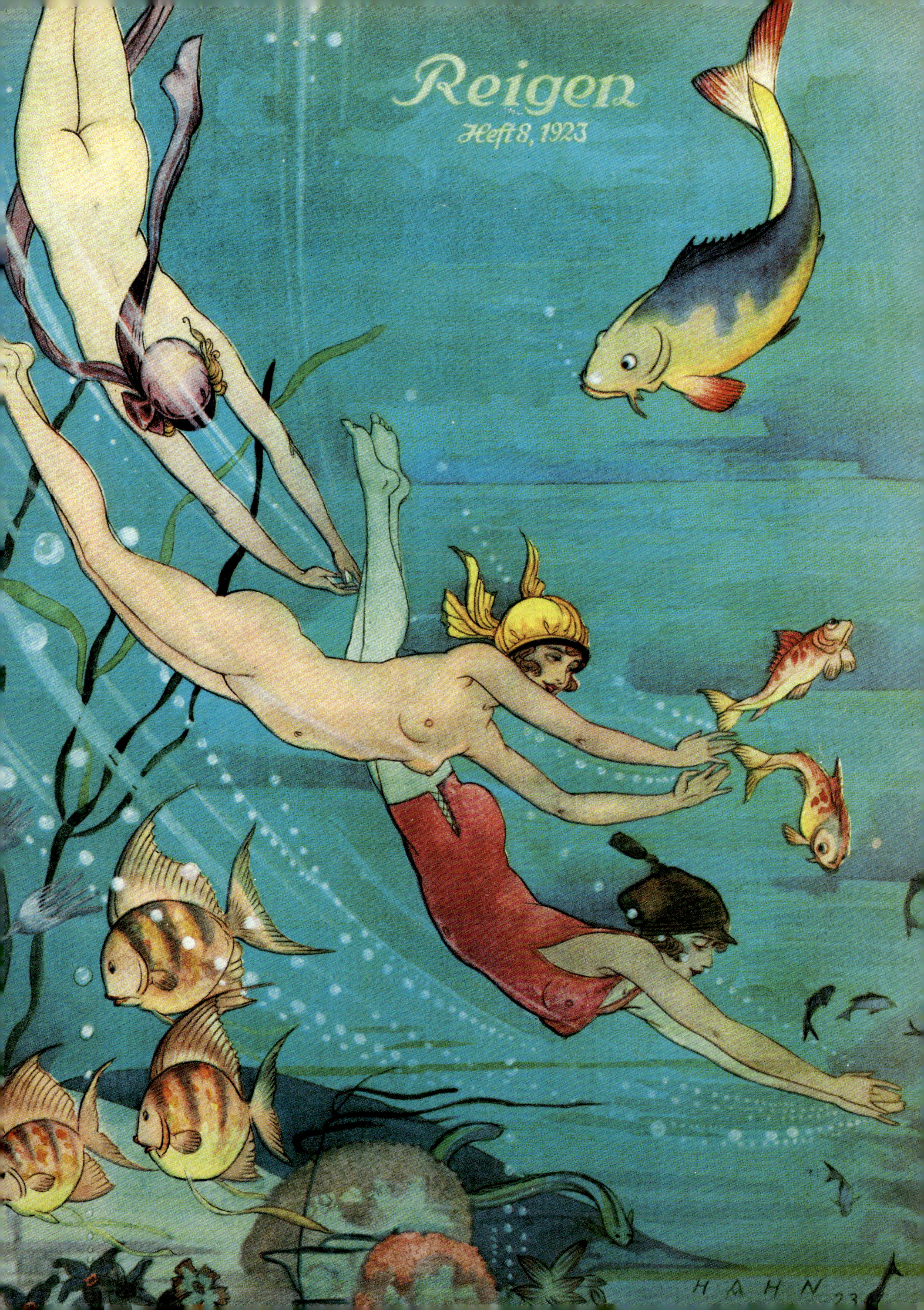
Reigen
Heft 8, 1923
HAHN 23

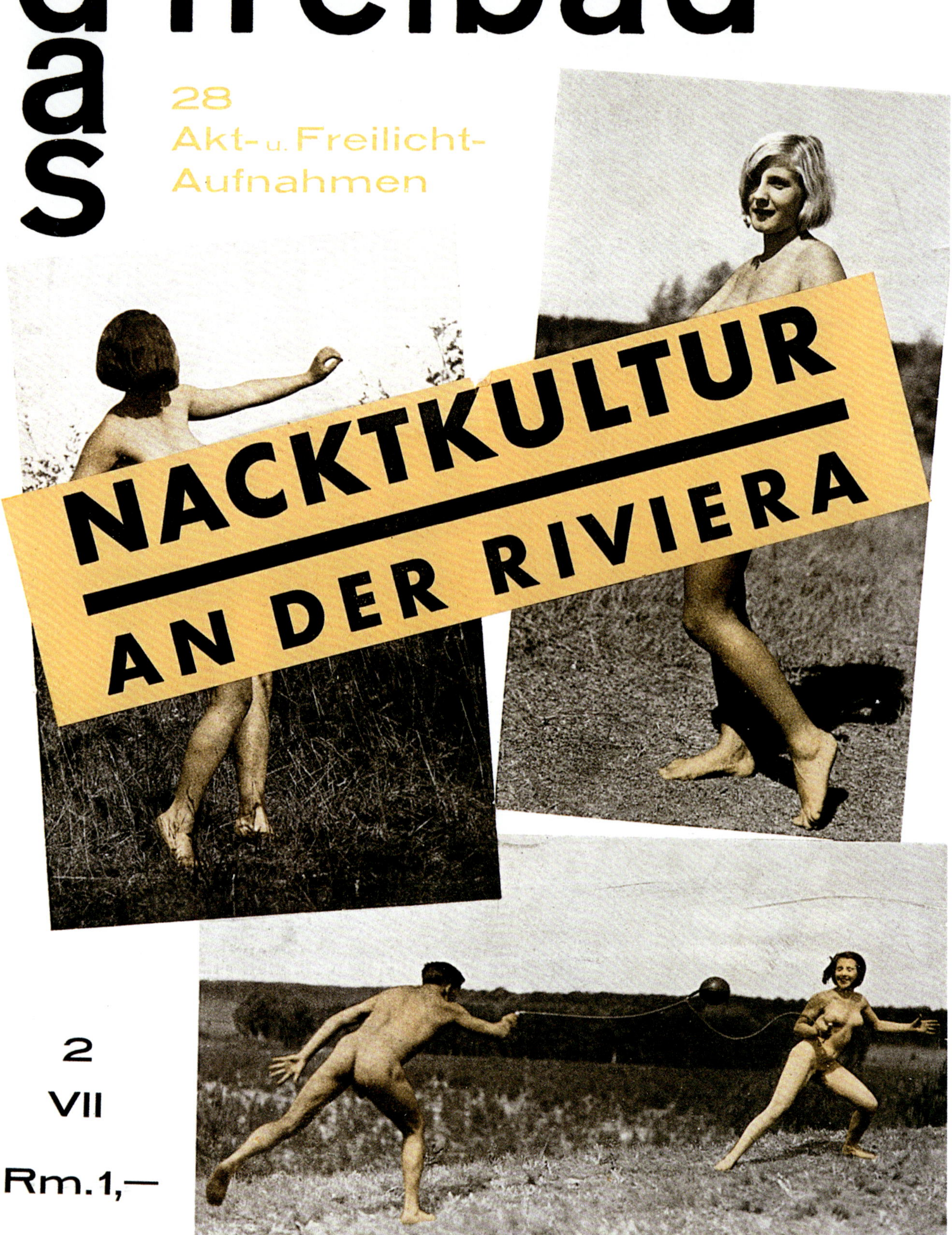

YEAR: **1933**. TITLE: **Das Freibad**. COUNTRY: **Germany**.

The international image of the naked body before 1940 was that of blue-eyed Nordic gods and goddesses.

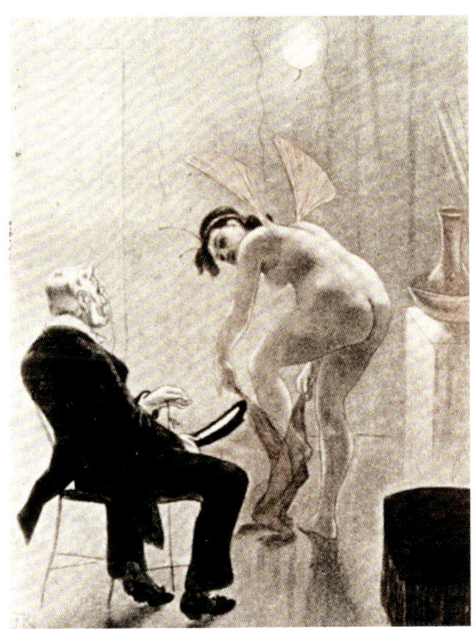

YEAR: **1923**. TITLE: **Reigen**. COUNTRY: **Germany**.

fanatics from all classes, regions, professions, sexual orientations, religions, and political philosophies. And only in the German-speaking world did nudist and "Life Reform" magazines challenge the social and religious *status quo* and enter into the charged civic arena. To a large degree, the international image of the naked body before 1940 was that of blue-eyed Nordic gods and goddesses with their slim blonde offspring in tow, frolicking contentedly under German skies in the health-giving environs of German fields, streams, and shores.

The first nudist journals, *Kraft und Schönheit* (Strength and Beauty) and *Die Schönheit* (Beauty) were issued in 1901 and 1902, respectively, by ideologues who called for the elimination of bathing suits (the shameful marks of Cain) and the Aryan regeneration of Germany through open-air sunbathing. Both the magazines and the naturist parks that were inspired by them, how-

Zeit ein. Das internationale Bild vom nackten Körper war vor 1940 zu einem großen Teil vom Typ des blauäugigen nordischen Übermenschen bestimmt, der mit seinem ranken, schlanken, blonden Nachwuchs im Gefolge zufrieden in der gesundheitsfördernden Natur unter deutschem Himmel herumtollte.

Die ersten Nudistenzeitschriften *Kraft und Schönheit* und *Die Schönheit* wurden 1901 respektive 1902 von Ideologen herausgegeben, die den Badeanzug (dieses schändliche Kainsmal) verdammten und die arische Regeneration Deutschlands durch Lichtbäder unter freiem Himmel einklagten. Sowohl ihre Zeitschriften wie die nach ihren Vorstellungen eingerichteten Naturistencamps hatten massive Probleme mit den zuständigen Behörden. Im wilhelminischen Deutschland durfte man zwar nackt aus dem

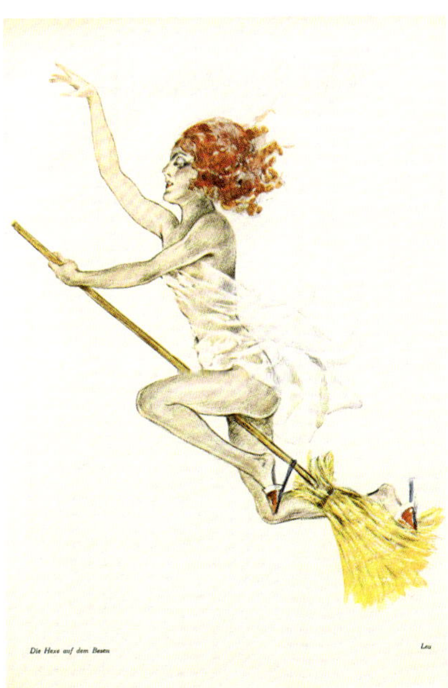

YEAR: **1926**. TITLE: **Berliner Leben**. COUNTRY: **Germany**.

milliers d'adeptes et de fanatiques absolus de toutes classes, régions, professions, orientations sexuelles, religions et philosophies politiques. Ce n'est également que dans le monde germanophone que les magazines nudistes et « de la réforme de la vie » défièrent le statu quo social et religieux, s'imposant dans une sphère civique survoltée. Dans une large mesure, avant 1940, l'image internationale du corps nu était celle des dieux et déesses nordiques aux yeux bleus traînant derrière eux une progéniture blonde et svelte, batifolant béatement dans un air pur et un décor sain de champs, de ruisseaux et de rivages teutons.

Les premiers journaux nudistes, *Kraft und Schönheit* (« Force et beauté ») et *Die Schönheit* (« La beauté ») parurent respectivement en 1901 et 1902, publiés par des idéologues qui prônaient l'élimination du costume de bain (les marques honteuses de Caïn) et la régénération aryenne de l'Allemagne par des bains de soleil en plein air. Toutefois, ces magazines et les parcs naturistes qu'ils inspirèrent furent lourdement réprimés par les autorités locales.

Dans l'Allemagne du Kaiser on pouvait se réveiller nu, se promener dans sa maison et son jardin dans le plus simple appareil et même photographier une paire de fesses à l'air, mais la publication de ce genre d'activité était, plus ou moins, *verboten*. La Grande Guerre, l'abdication du Kaiser et le déshonneur de l'armistice changèrent définitivement l'Allemagne. Avec la création de la république de Weimar, Berlin, avec ses prostituées, ses homosexuels et ses cabarets, devint l'incarnation même de la décadence.

Par réaction, les vieux pionniers du nudisme, à présent rebaptisé *Freikörper-*

Das Freibad *(The Open-Air Bath) 1936: "Naturism on the Riviera"*

Das Freibad *(Le bain de grand air) 1936: « Le nudisme sur la Riviera »*

Year: **1923**. Title: **Reigen**. Country: **Germany**.

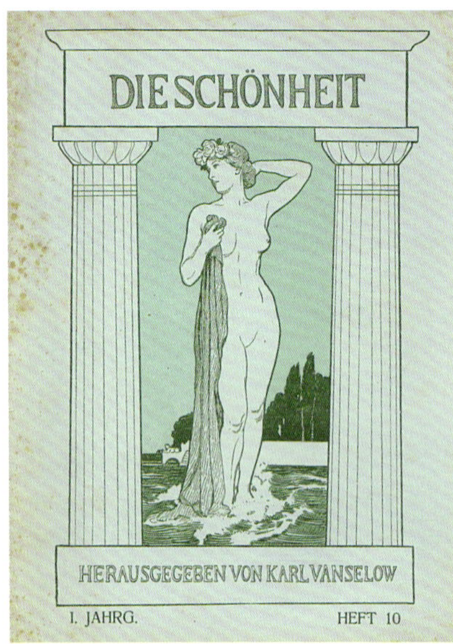

Year: **1903**. Title: **Die Schönheit**.
Country: **Germany**.

ever, were heavily suppressed by local authorities. In the Kaiser's Germany, one could wake up naked, walk around one's house and yard without a stitch of clothing, even photograph a bare buttock or two, but publication of such activities was more or less verboten. The World War, the abdication of the Kaiser and the dishonorable Armistice that followed changed Germany forever. With the founding of the Weimar Republic, Berlin, with its prostitutes, homosexuals and cabarets, came to represent all that was decadent in Germany. In reaction, the stodgy pioneers of nudism, now called "Freikörperkultur" (Free Body Culture, or FKK), were joined by disaffected soldiers and their families, hirsute revolutionaries, Primitive Christians, Hollow-Earth mystics, middle-of-the-road Socialists, free-thinkers, Nationalist academics, health fanatics, eye-fluttering gurus, unrepentant feminists, pseudo-Buddhists, and flat-out

Bett steigen, ohne einen Fetzen Kleidung am Leib in seinem Haus und Hof herumlaufen und sogar blanke Hintern fotografieren, aber die Publikation solcher Aktivitäten war größtenteils verboten. Der Erste Weltkrieg, die Abdankung des Kaisers und der unrühmliche Frieden von Versailles veränderten Deutschland radikal. In der neuen Weimarer Republik stand Berlin mit seinen Prostituierten, Homosexuellen und Kabaretts für alles Dekadente. Als Reaktion darauf schlossen sich desillusionierte Soldaten mit ihren Familien, ungekämmte Revolutionäre, Urchristen, Hohlwelt-Gläubige, gemäßigte Sozialisten, Freidenker, konservative Bildungsbürger, Gesundheitsfanatiker, Gurus mit flackerndem Blick, unbekehrbare Feministinnen, Pseudo-Buddhisten und schamlose Hedonisten den spießigen Vordenkern des Nudismus an, der nun Freikörperkultur hieß, um den unbekleideten Körper als gesunde Alternative zu propagieren.

Ab 1919 hoben illustrierte Zeitschriften und Vierteljahresschriften der FKK-Bewegung wie die völkisch geprägte Zeitschrift *Nacktsport*, die „Illustrierte Zeitschrift für Theorie und Praxis des gesundheitsfördernden Nacktsportes", oder *Der Leib* („Ein Bilderbuch idealer Nacktheit"), immer wieder den Gegensatz ihres gesunden und robusten Lebens stils zum dekadenten Berlin hervor. Ein Fotomotiv erfreute sich besonderer Beliebtheit: die Gegenüberstellung von jungen Anhängerinnen des Naturalismus und Mädchen, die auf die schiefe Bahn geraten waren. Auf der einen Seite sah man da vergnügte nackte Frauen, die sich Medizinbälle zuwarfen, auf der anderen verworfen grinsende Prostituierte, die nachts vor den Schaufenstern

kultur (« Culture du corps libre », ou FKK), furent rejoints par les soldats aigris et leurs familles, les révolutionnaires chevelus, les chrétiens « primitivistes », les mystiques de la « terre creuse », les socialistes modérés, les libres penseurs, les universitaires nationalistes, les fanatiques de la santé, les gourous aux yeux révulsés, les féministes impénitentes, les pseudobouddhistes et les hédonistes purs et durs, tous unis pour promouvoir le culte du corps sans fard comme une saine alternative.

À partir de 1919, des périodiques illustrés et des gazettes trimestrielles du FKK, tels que le protonazi *Nacktsport* (« Sport nu »), le « journal illustré de la théorie et de la praxis d'un développement sain au travers du sport », ou *Der Leib* (« Le corps »), « la publication photographique de la nudité idéale », se

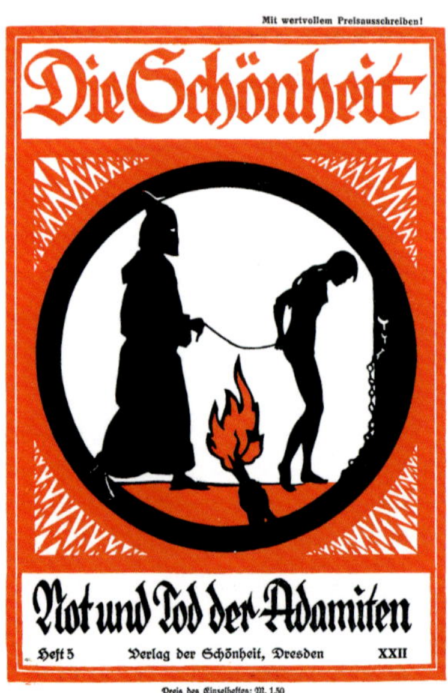

Year: **1926**. Title: **Die Schönheit**.
Country: **Germany**.

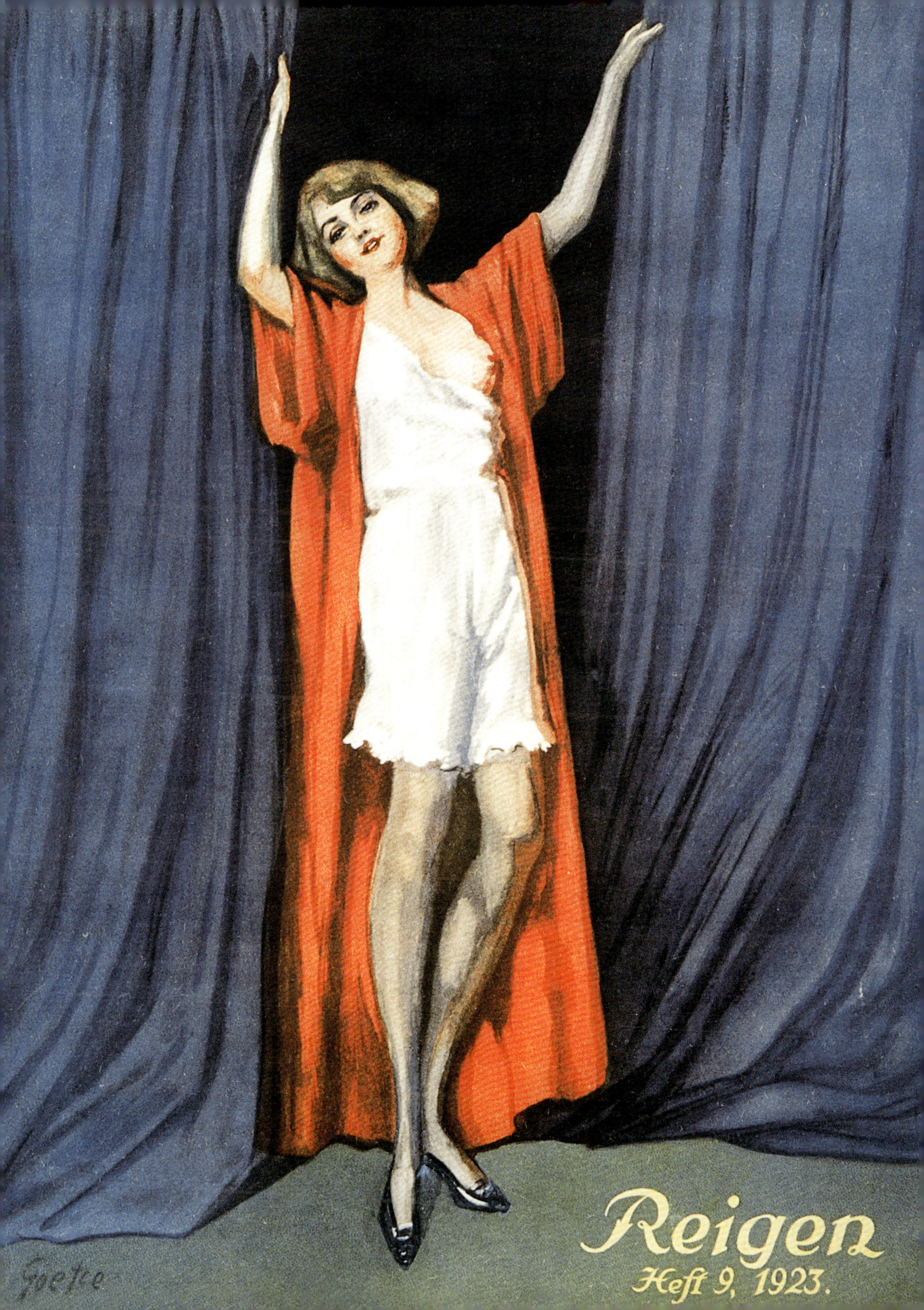
Goetze
Reigen
Heft 9, 1923.

YEAR: **1930**. TITLE: **Wiener Magazin**.
ARTIST: **Manassé**. COUNTRY: **Germany**.

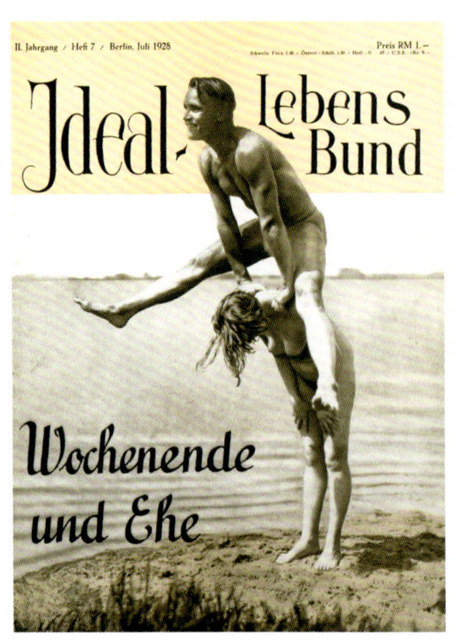

YEAR: **1928**. TITLE: **Ideal-Lebensbund**.
COUNTRY: **Germany**.

hedonists, who all linked arms to promote the cult of the unadorned human body as a healthy alternative.

Starting in 1919, illustrated periodicals and quarterlies of the FKK, like the proto-Nazi *Nacktsport* (Naked Sport), the "Pictorial Journal for the Theory and Praxis of Healthful Development Through Sports" or *Der Leib* (The Body), the "Photographic Publication of Ideal Nudity," harped on the contrasts between their hale and robust lifestyles and those of decadent Berlin. One pictorial theme appeared repeatedly: the Naturalist Girl and the Bad Girl. Typically, a photomontage spread would juxtapose a series of carefree women in the nude tossing medicine balls with nighttime shots of smirking prostitutes posed before the display windows of American-looking department stores. The disparities, for the Life Reformers, could not be presented more

amerikanisch anmutender Kaufhäuser auf Freier warteten. Für die Lebensreformer konnte es nichts Unvereinbareres geben. Die meisten Nudistenmagazine der Weimarer Zeit bezogen eindeutig politisch Stellung. Sprachrohr der eher linksorientierten Nudistenorganisationen waren auflagenstarke Blätter wie *Leben und Sonne* („Die Zeitschrift der Freien Körperkultur"), Adolf Kochs *Körperbildung – Nacktkultur*, die *Blätter freier Menschen*, und *Freikörperkultur und Lebensreform*. Andere Blätter wie etwa *Licht-Luft-Leben* („Monatsschrift für Schönheit, Gesundheit, Geist, Körperbildung"), und *Die Freude*, die über dreißig unterschiedliche FKK-Gruppen vertraten, machten sich für nationalistische wie liberale Interessen stark. Aus heutiger Sicht erscheint es seltsam, dass der nackte Körper das verbindende Element in diesen politischen Debatten war, aber schon damals wollten die meisten Leser der Nudisten-Zeitschriften wohl in erster Linie attraktive nackte Frauen und Männer sehen. Die mit Abstand erfolgreichsten Nudisten-Magazine der Weimarer Zeit waren jene Hochglanzillustrierten, die dem Streit zwischen den politischen Lagern ganz

Only in the German-speaking world did nudist magazines challenge the social and religious status quo.

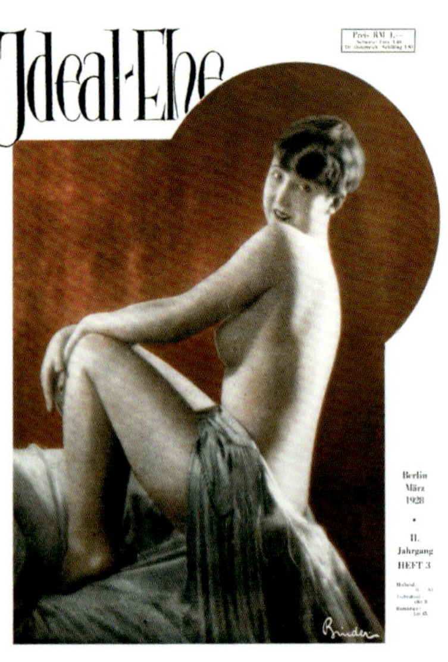

YEAR: **1928**. TITLE: **Ideal-Ehe**.
COUNTRY: **Germany**.

mirent rabâcher tout ce qui opposait leurs modes de vie sains et vigoureux à ceux de Berlin la décadente.

Parmi les illustrations, un thème revenait sans cesse : la fille naturiste opposée à la mauvaise fille. Le plus souvent, un photomontage juxtaposait une série de femmes insouciantes se lançant des médecine-balls dans le plus simple appareil à des prostituées photographiées la nuit, le visage ricanant, posant devant les vitrines de grands magasins à l'américaine. Pour les « réformateurs de vie », le contraste ne pouvait s'exprimer de manière plus crue.

La plupart des magazines nudistes de la république de Weimar adoptaient des positions politiques très tranchées. Les organisations socialistes et gauchistes avaient leurs propres revues illustrées destinées au marché de masse dont *Leben und Sonne* (« Vie et soleil »),

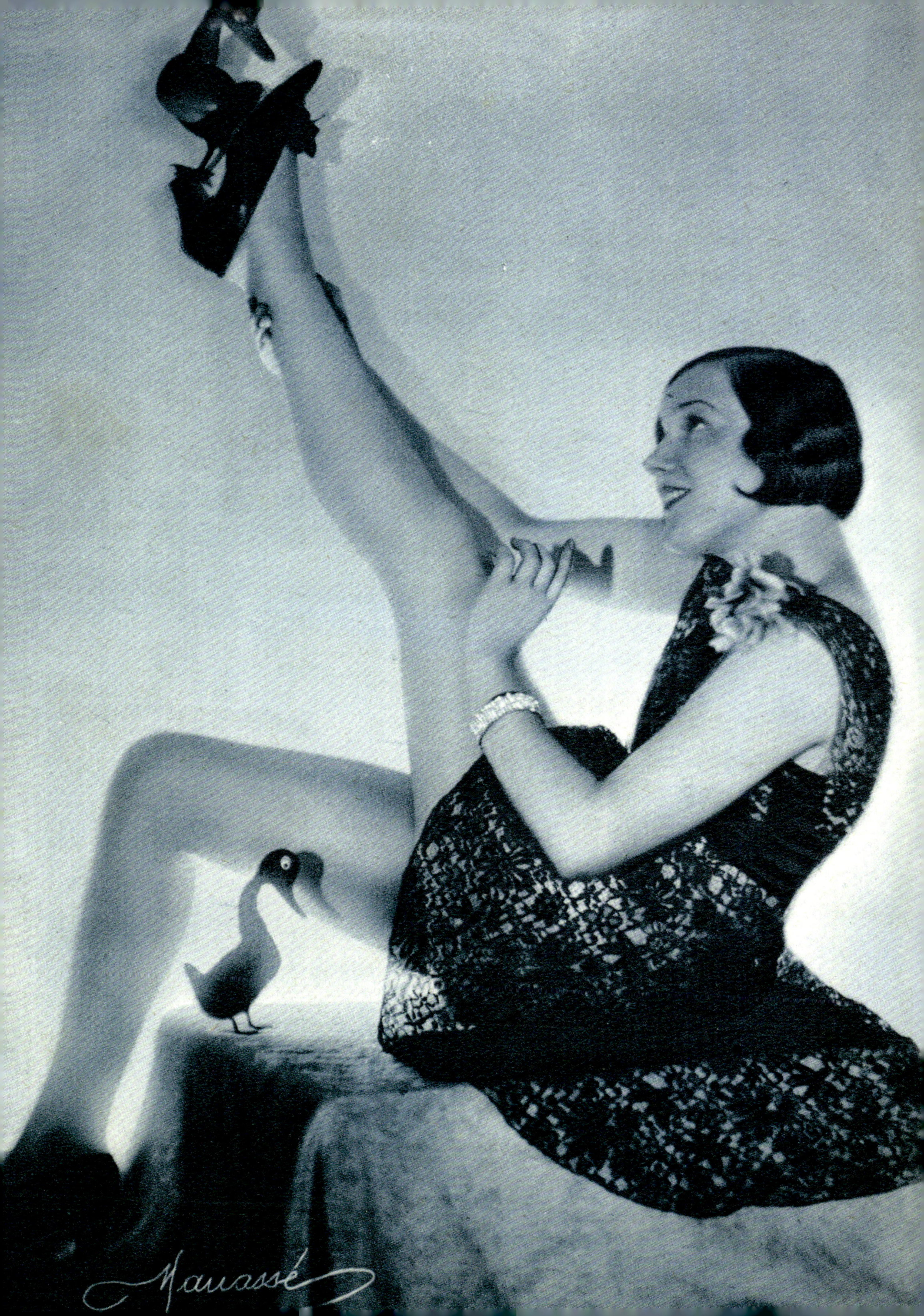
Manassé

Die Ehe *(Marriage) was tamed in 1933 following Hitler's rise to power.*

Nach Hitlers Machtübernahme 1933 wurde Die Ehe *deutlich gezähmt.*

Die Ehe *(le mariage) devint plus prude à partir de 1933 à la suite de la montée au pouvoir d'Hitler.*

In the middle of March 1933, the Weimar Republic ended with the imposition of Adolf Hitler's Third Reich.

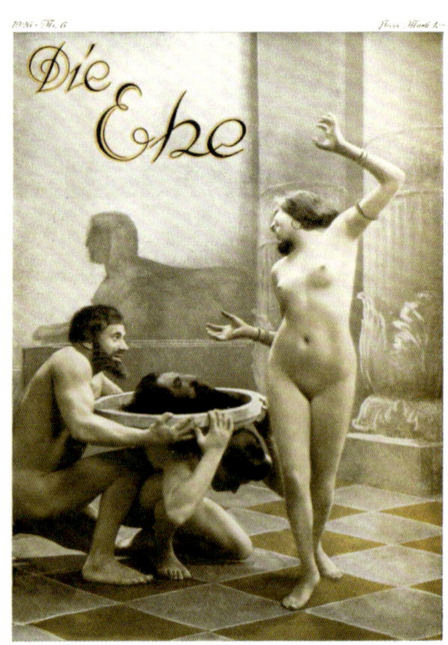

YEAR: **1926**. TITLE: **Die Ehe**. COUNTRY: **Germany**.

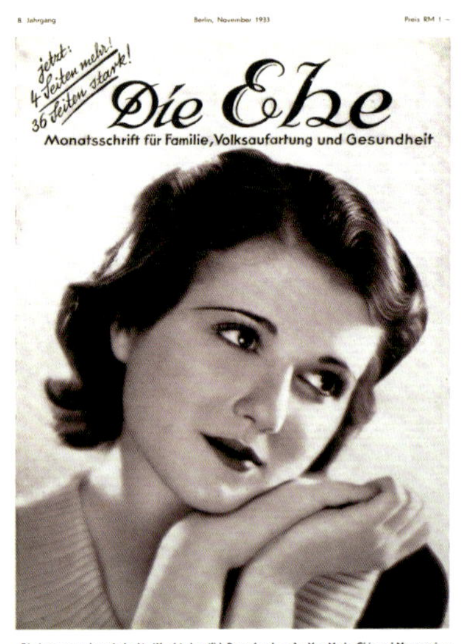

YEAR: **1933**. TITLE: **Die Ehe**. COUNTRY: **Germany**.

starkly. Most of the Weimar nudist magazines took a strong political stance. Socialist and left-leaning nudist organizations had their own mass-market illustrated magazines: *Leben und Sonne* (Life and Sun), the "Monthly of the FKK"; Adolf Koch's *Körperbildung/Nacktkultur* (Body Development/Naked Culture), the "Organ of Free Men"; and *Freikörperkultur und Lebensreform* (FKK and Life Reform). Other nudies, like *Licht-Luft-Leben* (Light-Air-Life), the "Monthly Journal for Beauty, Health, Spirit, Body Development," and *Die Freude* (Joy) championed the activities of thirty-odd separate FKK groups, embracing both Nationalist and liberal points of view. It seems odd today that the naked body should be the common element in these political debates; but even then most fans of the nudist magazines simply wanted to see attractive nude women and men. The most successful of the Weimar nudist

aus dem Weg gingen; sie präsentierten lieber optimistische Bildgeschichten über die individuelle Befreiung und andere freche Bilder. Zu ihnen zählten *Figaro*, *Lachendes Leben* („Zeitschrift für gesunde Weltanschauung"), *Das Freibad* („Monatsschrift zur Förderung des Nacktbadens"), *Sonniges Land*, die in der Schweiz verlegte *Neue Zeit*, *Sonnenland* und *Pelagius*.

Als die FKK-Bewegung in den späten Zwanzigern rapiden Zuwachs bekam, erschienen plötzlich auch Nudisten-Zeit schriften anderer Coleur, Blätter, die sich an sexuelle Randgruppen wandten und Bilder nackter Körper mit Bekehrungstraktaten vermählte. Die Anhänger der Sexualmagie lasen die Monatsblätter *ASA* und *Soma*, die deutschen Buddhisten *Urania*, die Feministinnen die *Ideal-Ehe* („Monatsschrift für Geistes- und Körper-Erziehung zur Ehe"), und den *Ehe-Berater*, Sexualwissenschaftler und

le mensuel du FKK, *Körperbildung/Nacktkultur* d'Adolf Koch (« Développement corporel /culture nue »), « l'organe des hommes libres », et *Freikörperkultur und Lebensreform* (« FKK et réforme de la vie »). D'autres revues nudistes comme *Licht-Luft-Leben* (« Lumière-air-vie »), le « mensuel de la beauté, de la santé, de la spiritualité et du développement physique », ou *Die Freude* (« Joie ») défendaient les activités d'une trentaine de groupes FKK séparés, épousant à la fois des points de vue nationalistes et libéraux.

On peut trouver étrange aujourd'hui que le point commun de ces débats politiques soit le corps nu mais, même alors, la plupart des amateurs de revues nudistes voulaient simplement voir de beaux corps nus de femmes et d'hommes. Les publications nudistes de Weimar les plus prisées étaient de loin les magazines

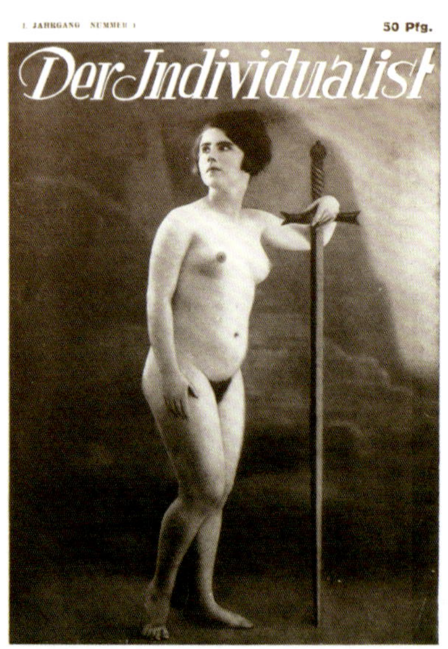

YEAR: **1928**. TITLE: **Der Individualist**. COUNTRY: **Germany**.

YEAR: **1923**. TITLE: **Die Ehe**. COUNTRY: **Germany**.

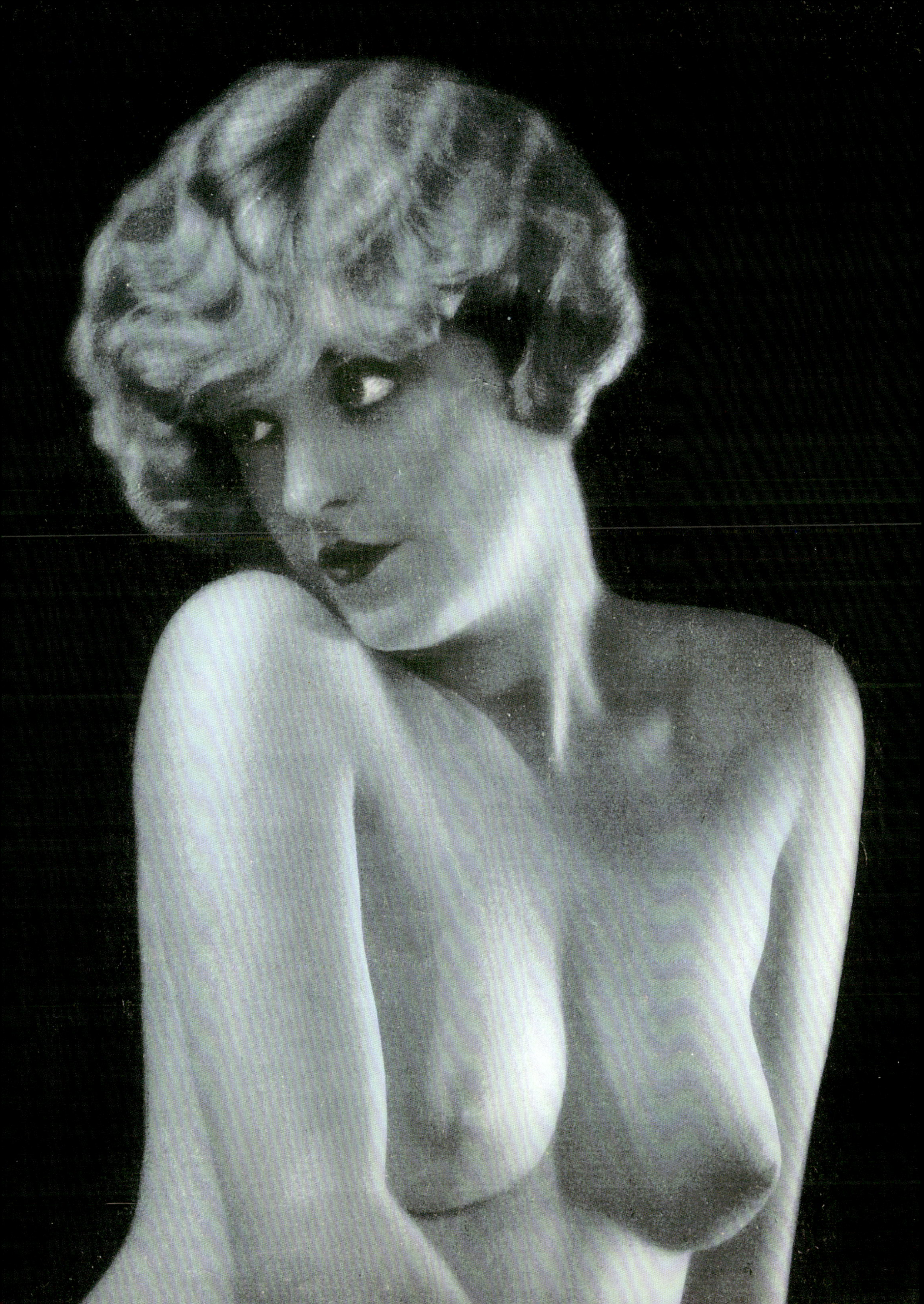

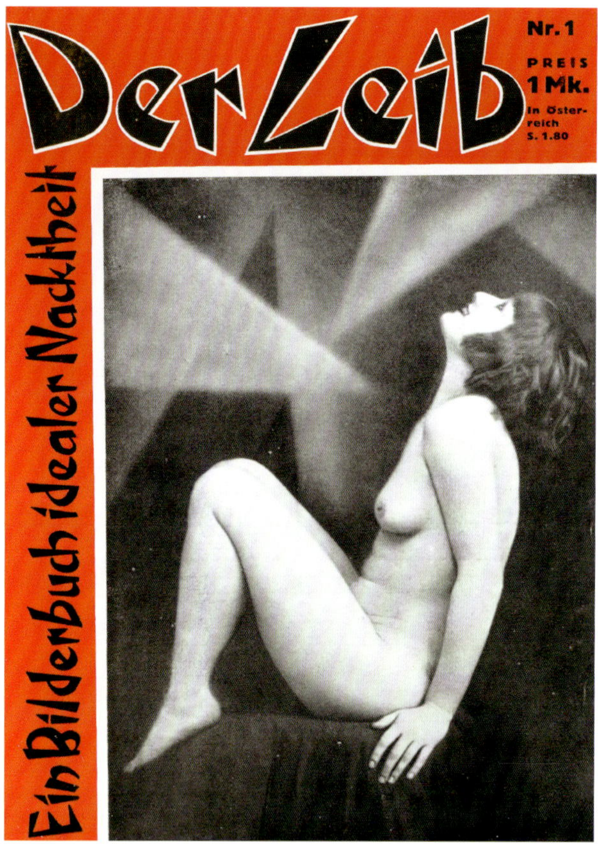

YEAR: **1920s**. TITLE: **Der Leib**. COUNTRY: **Germany**.

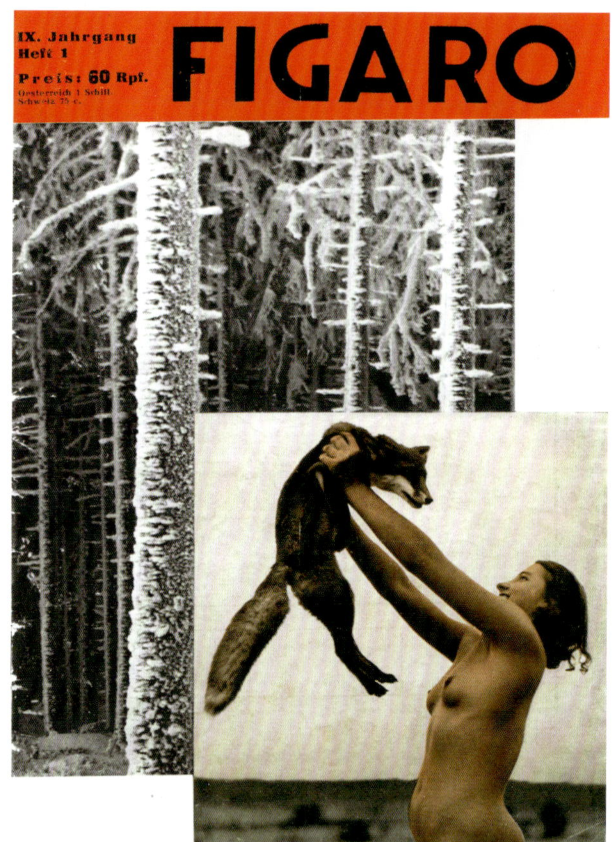

YEAR: **1932**. TITLE: **Figaro**. COUNTRY: **Germany**.

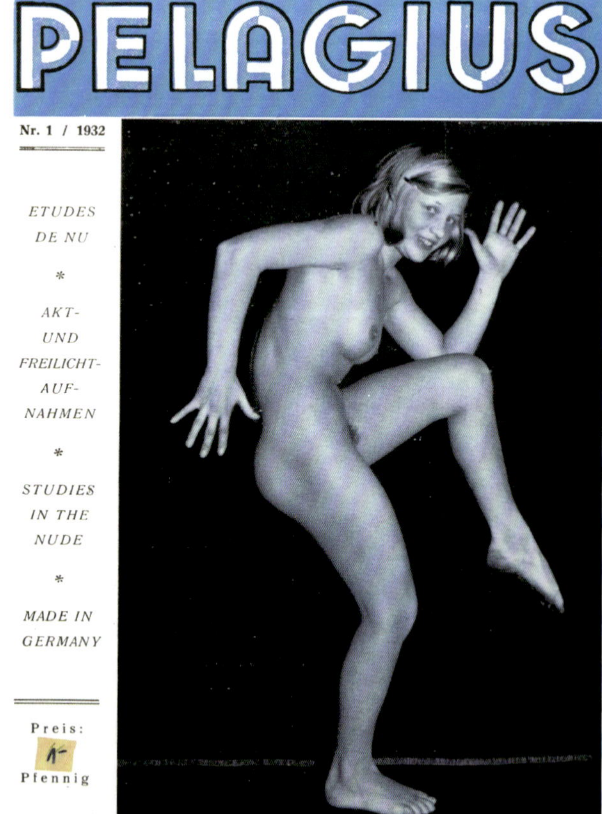

YEAR: **1932**. TITLE: **Pelagius**. COUNTRY: **Germany**.

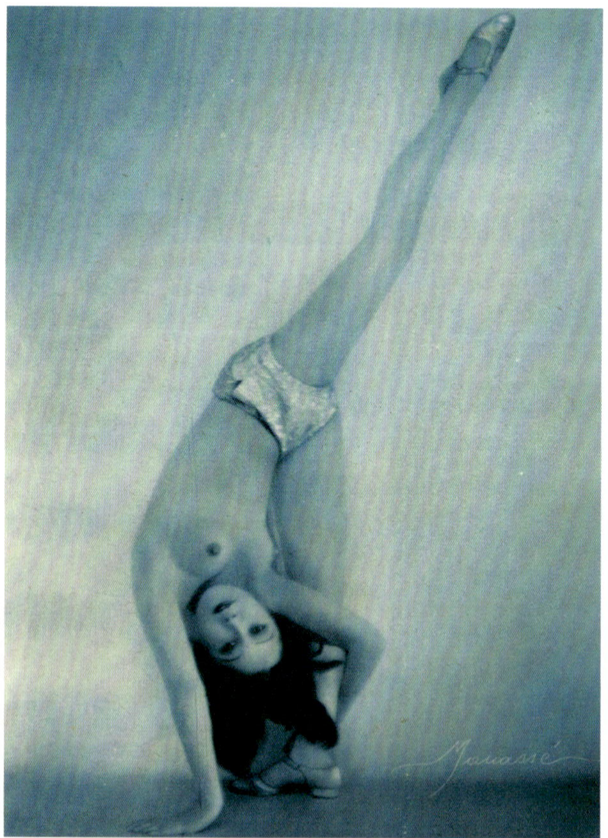

YEAR: **1930**. TITLE: **Wiener Magazin**. ARTIST: **Manassé**. COUNTRY: **Germany**.

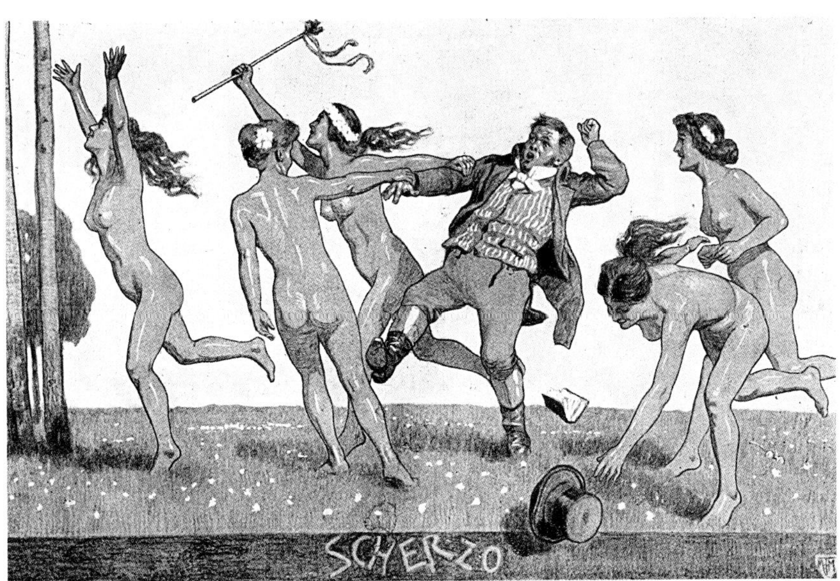

Year: **1923**. Title: **Die Schönheit**. Country: **Germany**.

journals were the glossy pictorial magazines that eschewed the entire left-right political debate; they offered in its place upbeat illustrated stories of personal liberation and titillating pictures. These included *Figaro*, "The Bi-Monthly Journal That Fights in Word and Picture for Cultural Freedom," *Lachendes Leben* (Laughing Life), "The Magazine for a Healthy World-Philosophy", *Das Freibad* (The Open-Air Bath), "The Journal for the Promotion of Naked Bathing," *Sonniges Land* (Sunny Land), the Swiss-based *Die Neue Zeit* (The New Era), *Sonnenland* (Sun Land), and *Pelagius*, "The Monthly with Beautiful Photographs from the Naked and Free Air Movement." As the FKK movement grew exponentially in the late 20s, another type of nudist journal suddenly appeared: periodicals that were targeted toward fringe erotic communities, where images of the naked body were wedded to specific proselytizing

Progressive den *Ideal-Lebensbund*, *Die Ehe*, die „Monatsschrift für Familie, Volksaufartung und Gesundheit", und *Die Aufklärung*, die „Monatsschrift für Sexual- und Lebensreform", von Dr. Magnus Hirschfeld. Diese Magazine erinnerten eher an die Dekadenz Berlins denn an den gesunden Lebensstil der Nudisten, und tatsächlich wurde ein Großteil davon in diesem Sündenbabel der Weimarer Republik verlegt. Während die frühen Nudisten-Blätter von und für den arischen Deutschen gemacht wurden, wurden die sexuell unverblümteren der späten zwanziger und frühen dreißiger Jahre größtenteils von deutschen Juden verlegt. Berlin war für den Durchschnittsdeutschen eine fremde Welt, der er ablehnend gegenüber stand. Als Hitler 1933 zum Reichskanzler gemacht wurde, kündigte sich das Ende der Weimarer Republik an. Schon im Sommer '33 wurden die Nudistenorganisationen

illustrés sur papier glacé qui évitaient complètement le débat politique gauche/droite. À sa place, ils proposaient des histoires enjouées de libération personnelle et des images aguichantes. Parmi eux, *Figaro* « le bimensuel qui lutte pour la liberté culturelle avec des mots et des images », *Lachendes Leben* (« la vie rieuse ») « le magazine pour une philosophie saine du monde », *Das Freibad* (« Le bain de grand air ») « le journal pour la promotion des bains nus », *Sonniges Land* (« Terre ensoleillée »), *Die Neue Zeit* (« La nouvelle ère », basée en Suisse), *Sonnenland* (« Terre de soleil »), et *Pelagius*, « le mensuel aux belles photographies du mouvement de la nudité et de l'air libre ».

À la fin des années vingt, alors que le mouvement FKK prenait de plus en plus d'importance, un nouveau type de magazine nudiste apparut. Ces périodiques s'adressaient à des communautés

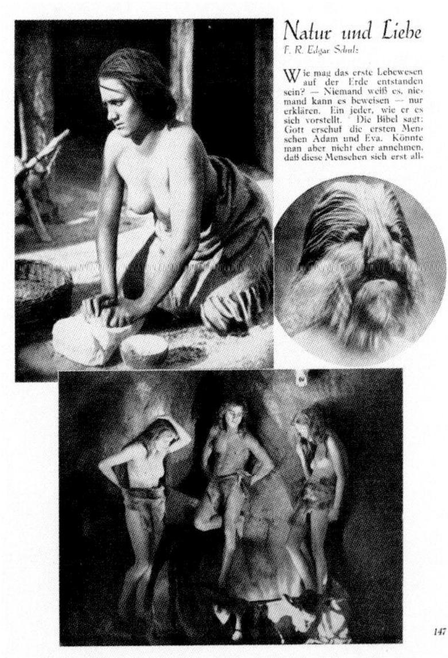

Natur und Liebe

F. R. Edgar Schulz

Wie mag das erste Lebewesen auf der Erde entstanden sein? — Niemand weiß es, niemand kann es beweisen — nur erklären. Ein jeder, wie er es sich vorstellt. Die Bibel sagt: Gott erschuf die ersten Menschen Adam und Eva. Könnte man aber nicht eher annehmen, daß diese Menschen sich erst all-

147

Year: **1928**. Title: **Ideal-Ehe**. Country: **Germany**.

Year: **1929**. Title: **Die Aufklärung**.
Country: **Germany**.

screeds. The devotees of sex magic had their monthlies, *ASA* and *Soma*; German Buddhists, Urania, the mystic "Monthly for Nature-Consciousness and Social Learning"; feminists, *Ideal-Ehe* (Ideal Marriage), the "Textbook for Spiritual and Corporal Education in Marriage," and *Der Eheberater* (The Marriage Counselor); sexologists and progressives had *Ideal-Lebensbund* (The Ideal Life League), *Die Ehe* (Marriage), and Dr. Magnus Hirschfeld's *Die Aufklärung* (The Enlightenment), "The Monthly Journal for Sex and Life Reform." The content of these magazines bore more resemblance to the decadence of Berlin than to the healthy nudist lifestyle, and in fact, many of them were published in Weimar's Sin City. And while the early naturist magazines were made by and for ethnically Nordic Germans, the more sexually blatant late 20s and early 30s magazines were overwhelmingly published by German Jews.

The students demanded admittance to every room, and broke in the doors of those which were closed... they emptied the ink bottles over manuscripts and carpets and then made for the book-cases.

On the destruction of M. Hirschfeld's Sexual Science Institute by young Nazis, May 6th, 1933

DAS HERRENJOURNAL

Year: **1941**. Title: **Das Herrenjournal**.
Country: **Germany**.

und ihre Printmedien arisiert. Verleger und Chefredakteure, die man als Gegner des Dritten Reiches einschätzte, wurden durch linientreue Mitarbeiter ersetzt. Manchmal bedeutete das, dass Sekretäre oder Lagerarbeiter in Spitzenpositionen gelangten. Aus Adolf Kochs militant sozialistischem Monatsblatt wurden flugs die apolitischen *Adolf-Koch-Blätter*. Andere Zeitschriften gingen in nationalsozialistischen Nudistenbulletins wie *Gesetz und Freiheit* auf, in denen der Führer als Förderer der Lebensreform gepriesen wurde (sein Vegetarismus wurde als Nudismus des Gaumens gedeutet), oder *Deutsche Leibeszucht*. Viele Zeitschriften, vor allem die am eindeutigsten sexuell orientierten, verschwanden ganz. Ab Mitte der Dreißiger

érotiques marginales et associaient les images du corps nus à des verbiages prosélytes spécifiques. Les adeptes de la magie sexuelle avaient leurs mensuels, *ASA* et *Soma* ; les bouddhistes allemands, *Urania*, le mensuel mystique « pour la conscience de la nature et l'apprentissage social » ; les féministes, *Ideal-Ehe* (« Mariage idéal »), le « manuel pour une éducation de l'esprit et du corps au sein du mariage », et *Der Eheberater* (« le conseiller matrimonial ») ; les sexologues et les progressistes *Ideal-Lebensbund* (« La ligue pour la vie idéale »), *Die Ehe* (« Mariage ») et la revue du docteur Magnus Hirschfeld *Die Aufklärung* (« La lumière »), le « mensuel pour la réforme de la sexualité et de la vie ».

Le contenu de ces publications se rapprochait plus de la décadence berlinoise que du mode de vie sain des nudistes et, d'ailleurs, bon nombre d'entre eux étaient publiés dans la « ville du pêché ». En outre, alors que les premiers magazines naturistes étaient réalisés par et pour des Allemands d'ethnie nordique, les revues plus ouvertement érotiques de la fin des années vingt et des années trente étaient en grande majorité publiées par des Juifs allemands. Berlin était de plus en plus isolée et méprisée par le citoyen allemand moyen.

À la mi-mars 1933, la République de Weimar céda la place au Troisième Reich d'Adolph Hitler. En un premier temps, la plupart des associations de nudistes et leurs publications ne furent pas inquiétées, puis, au cours de l'été de la même année, ils furent « aryanisés ». Les éditeurs et les rédacteurs considérés ennemis du Reich furent remplacés par un personnel homologué. Cela

DIE AUFKLÄRUNG

HERAUSGEGEBEN VON
MAGNUS HIRSCHFELD
UND MARIA KRISCHE

MONATSSCHRIFT FÜR SEXUAL- UND LEBENSREFORM • PREIS EINE MARK

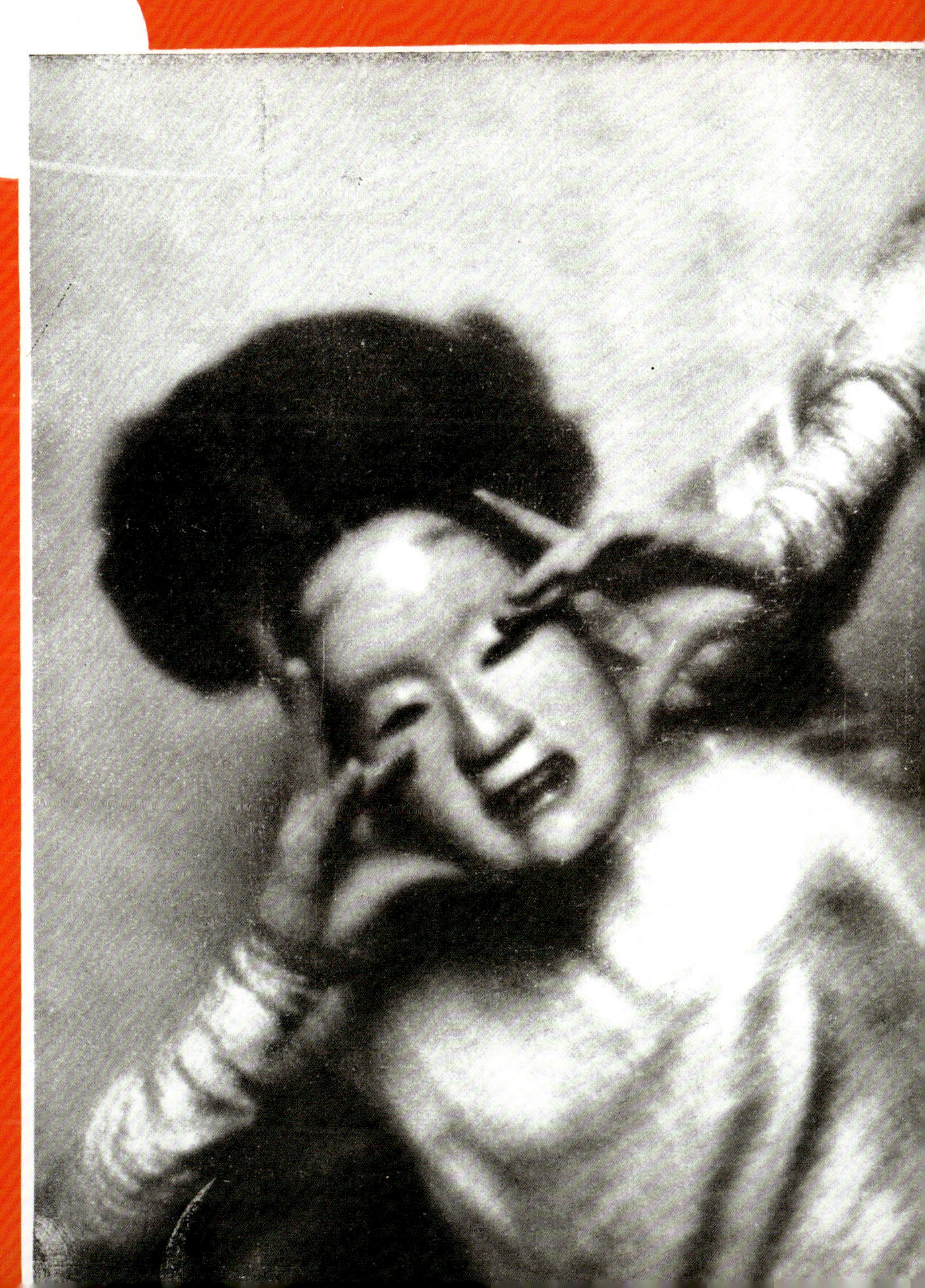

3 BERLIN
April 1929

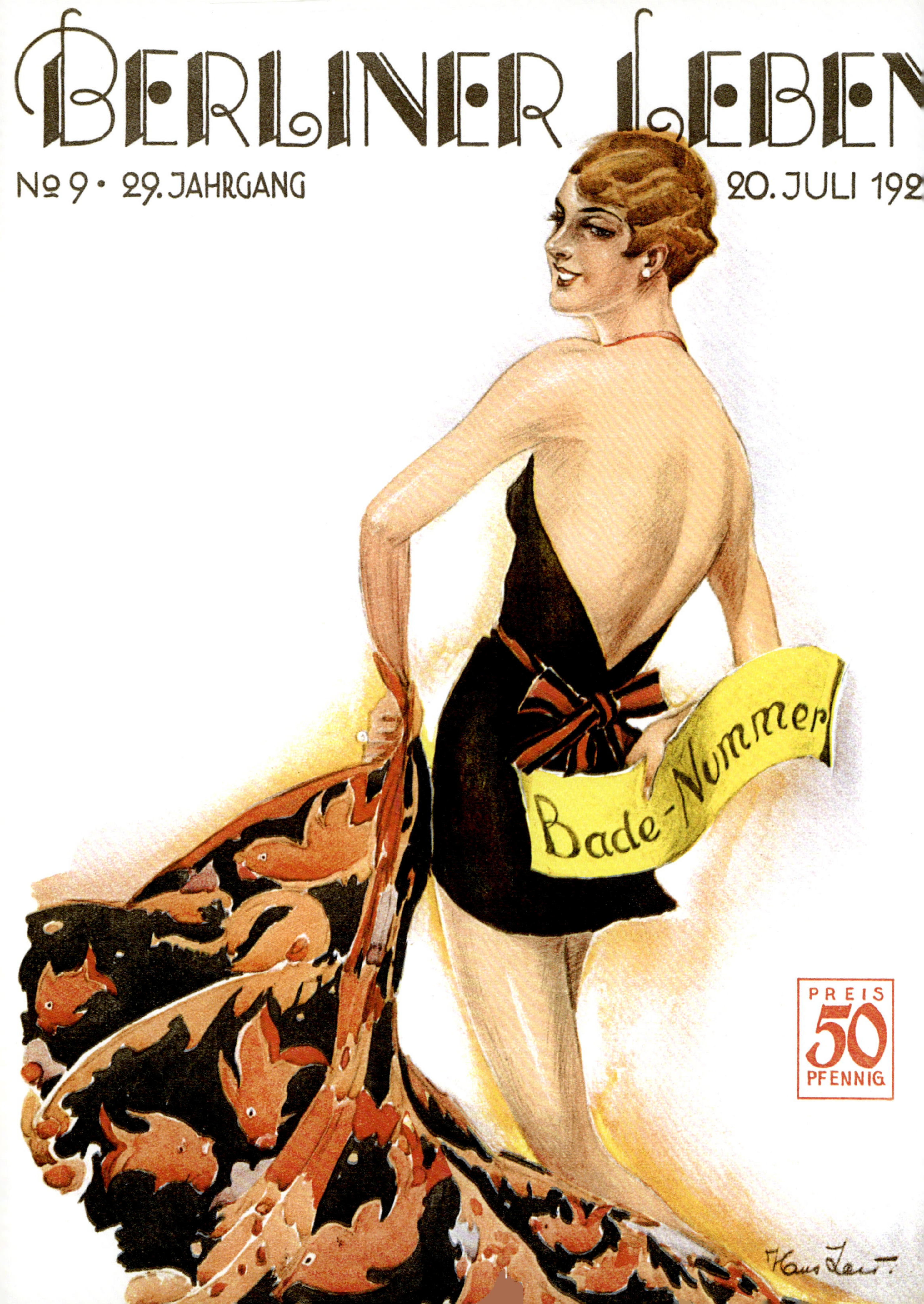
BERLINER LEBEN
Nº 9 • 29. JAHRGANG
20. JULI 192
Bade-Nummer
PREIS
50
PFENNIG

Year: **1926**. Title: **Berliner Leben**. Country: **Germany**.

Berlin grew increasingly detached from and despised by the average German citizen. In the middle of March 1933, the Weimar Republic ended with the imposition of Adolf Hitler's Third Reich. Most of the German nudist societies and their print organs remained untouched initially, then over the summer of 1933, they became Aryanized. Publishers and editors, deemed enemies of the Reich, were replaced by approved staff members. Sometimes this meant secretaries and stockroom clerks receiving promotions to top positions. Adolf Koch's militant Socialist monthly quietly transformed into the apolitical *Adolf-Koch-Blätter* (Adolf Koch Journal). Other magazines coalesced into one of the Nazi nudist bulletins like *Gesetz und Freiheit* (Law and Freedom), where the Führer was praised as a Life Reform advocate (his vegetarianism being a form of nudism of the palate), or *Deutsche Leibeszucht* (German Physical Training). And many magazines, especially the most sexually oriented, simply ceased to exist. From the mid-30s on, the Aryanized journals and their companion color photo books (many with obvious homoerotic appeal) popularized nudism as a special health regimen of the Reich. In this mode most of them continued to publish until 1943 and 1944, when the health of The Third Reich took a sharp downward turn.

After the war and the rebuilding of Germany nudist magazines reappeared. Some pre-war titles, like *Sonnenland* and *Die Neue Zeit*, even survived, but now the emphasis was purely on the health-giving qualities of nude sunbathing. Politics and prurience alike were purged, and in a nation weary of war and scandal, this suited most just fine.

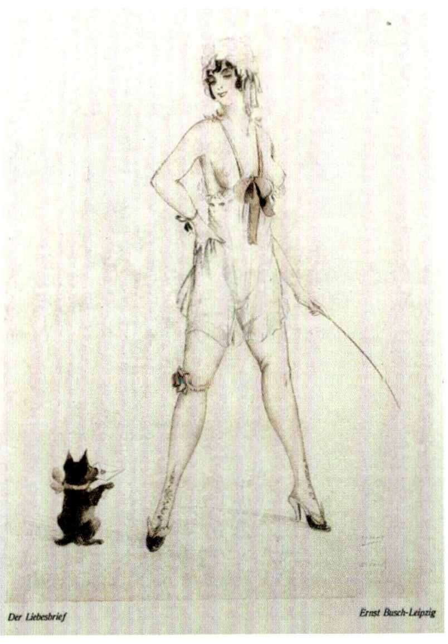

Year: **1923**. Title: **Reigen**. Country: **Germany**.

propagierten diese gleichgeschalteten Zeitschriften und begleitende Farbfotobücher (viele mit unverkennbar homoerotischem Anstrich) den Nudismus als spezielle Gesundungskur für das Reich. Dies ging so bis 1943 und 1944, als es mit der Gesundheit des Reiches steil bergab ging.

Nach dem Krieg und Wiederaufbau erschienen auch die Nudisten-Zeitschriften wieder. Einige Vorkriegstitel wie *Sonnenland* und *Die Neue Zeit* hatten gar den Krieg überdauert, aber nun betonte man ausschließlich den Gesundheitsaspekt des nackten Sonnenbadens. Politik und Anzüglichkeiten waren ersatzlos gestrichen, was einer kriegs- und skandalmüden Nation gerade recht kam.

signifiait parfois que des secrétaires et des manutentionnaires étaient promus à des postes décisionnels. Le mensuel socialiste militant d'Adolph Koch se transforma discrètement en l'apolitique *Adolf-Koch-Blätter* (« Journal d'Adolf Koch »). D'autres revues se fondirent en un des bulletins nudistes nazis tels que *Gesetz und Freiheit* (« Droit et liberté »), où le Führer était loué en tant que défenseur de la réforme de la vie (son végétarisme étant considéré comme une forme de nudisme du palais), ou *Deutsche Leibeszucht* (« Entraînement physique allemand »). De nombreux magazines, surtout les plus orientés sur la sexualité, disparurent purement et simplement.

À partir du milieu des années trente, les journaux « aryanisés » et les albums photos en couleurs qui les accompagnaient (dont bon nombre présentaient un caractère homoérotique) popularisèrent le nudisme en tant que régime spécial de santé du Reich. La plupart continuèrent à paraître sous cette forme jusqu'en 1943, lorsque la santé du Troisième Reich périclita soudainement. Après la guerre et au cours de la reconstruction de l'Allemagne, les magazines nudistes réapparurent. Certains titres d'avant-guerre, tels que *Sonnenland* et *Die Neue Zeit*, survécurent mais désormais l'accent portait exclusivement sur les qualités salutaires des bains de soleil. La politique et la luxure avaient été expurgées. Dans une nation éreintée par la guerre et les scandales, personne ne s'en plaignait.

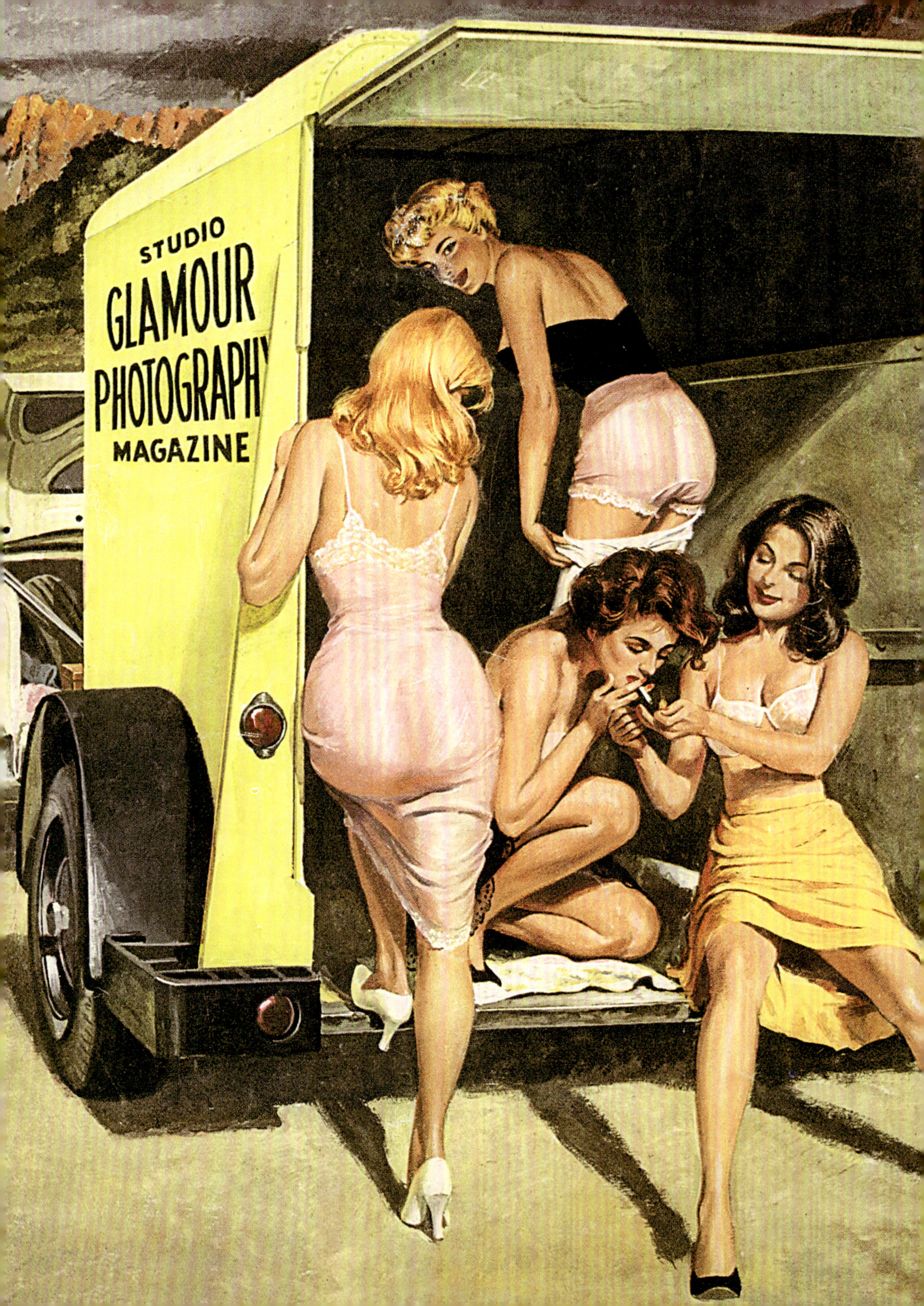
STUDIO
GLAMOUR
PHOTOGRAPHY
MAGAZINE

FOR SERIOUS ART STUDENTS ONLY:

The Rise and Fall of "Model Study" Magazines

Nur für ernsthafte Jünger der Kunst: Aufstieg und Fall der „Künstlerischen Aktstudien"

Réservé aux étudiants en art sérieux : grandeur et décadence des magazines « de modèles académiques »

The three devices employed by magazine publishers to evade censorship of nude images in the first half of the 20th century were nudism, film review and art. Of these art was the first and, I'm certain to no one's surprise, it was a French invention. *L'Étude Académique* appeared before 1900, showing fully nude, uncensored studies of probable prostitutes "for serious art students only." For cultural contrast, that same year an "art" magazine was produced in England called *Tidbits of Beauty*. It too was for serious art students only, though limited to students of silhouette technique since that's all it showed of its beauties, whose virtue was further protected by knee-length bathing costumes. America began printing art magazines around 1920. The most prolific publishers were the Educational Art Press in Wilmington, Delaware, and Independent News in New York. Dawn Publishing also offered "art studies," but as a minor part of its general eugenics campaign. Overall, Educational Art Press

Die drei Dinge, die Verleger von Männermagazinen in der ersten Hälfte des 20. Jahrhunderts vorschoben, um die Zensur zu umgehen, waren Nudismus, Filmrezensionen und Kunst. Auf die Kunst berief man sich zuerst – wen überrascht es – in Frankreich. Vor 1900 erschien bereits *L'Étude Académique* und zeigte für die „ernsthaften Jünger der Kunst" weibliche Ganzkörperakte; die Models waren höchstwahrscheinlich Prostituierte. Um kulturelle Gegensätze deutlich zu machen, sei auf ein „Kunst"-Magazin mit dem Titel *Tidbits of Beauty* verwiesen, das zur gleichen Zeit in England erschien. Auch dieses Blatt richtete sich an Kunststudenten, doch anscheinend ausschließlich an solche, die sich mit der Kunst des Scherenschnitts befassten, denn mehr als die Silhouette sah man von den Damen nicht, deren Tugend zudem noch von knielangen Badeanzügen geschützt wurde. In den USA erschienen die ersten dieser Magazine um 1920. Die rührigsten Verlage

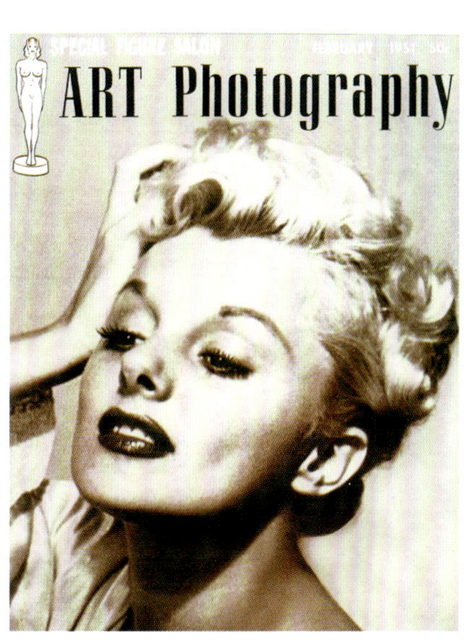

Year: **1951**. Title: **Art Photography**. Country: **USA**.

Many men preferred the subterfuge that they weren't just gawking at smut but appreciating nudity on a higher plane.

Au cours de la première moitié du 20e siècle, les éditeurs de magazines disposaient de trois stratagèmes pour échapper à la censure : le nudisme, la critique cinématographique et l'art. De ces trois outils, l'art fut le premier et, cela ne surprendra probablement personne, il fut inventé par les Français. *L'Étude Académique* commença à paraître avant 1900. Elle présentait des nus intégraux, probablement des prostituées, servant de modèles « uniquement aux étudiants en art sérieux ». À titre de comparaison, la même année en Angleterre parut un

Year: **1957**. Title: **Glamour Photography**. Country: **USA**.

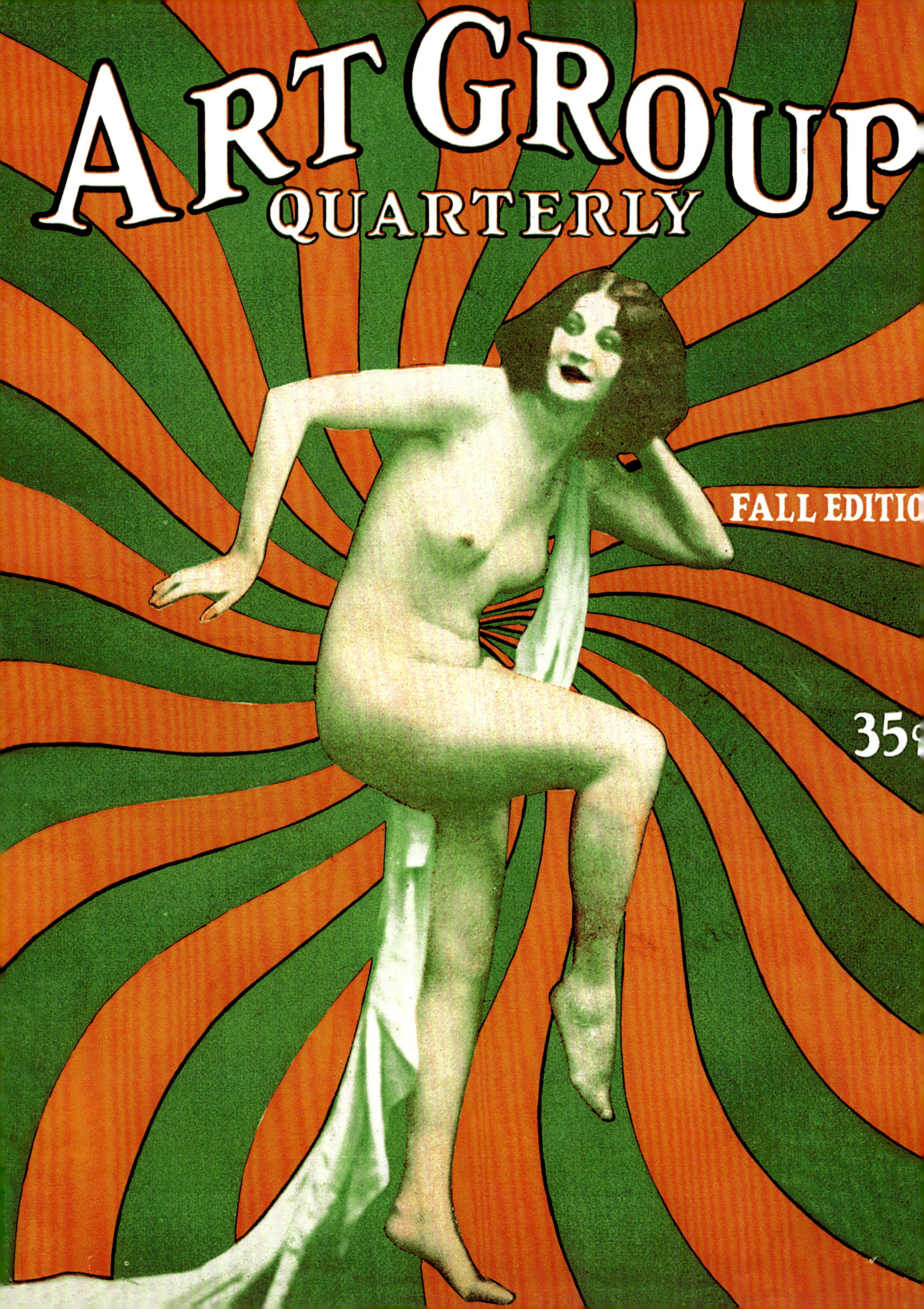
ART GROUP
QUARTERLY
FALL EDITIO
35¢

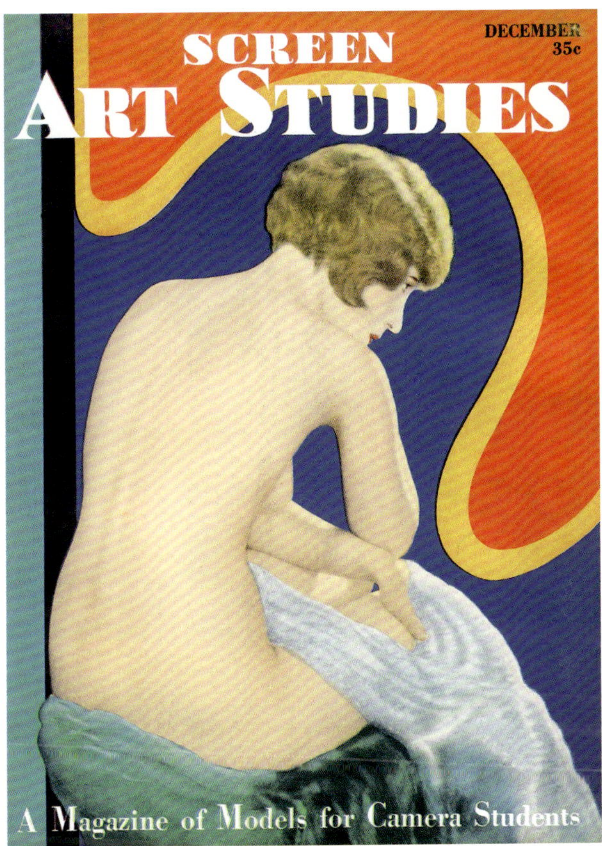

YEAR: 1929. TITLE: Screen Art Studies. COUNTRY: USA.

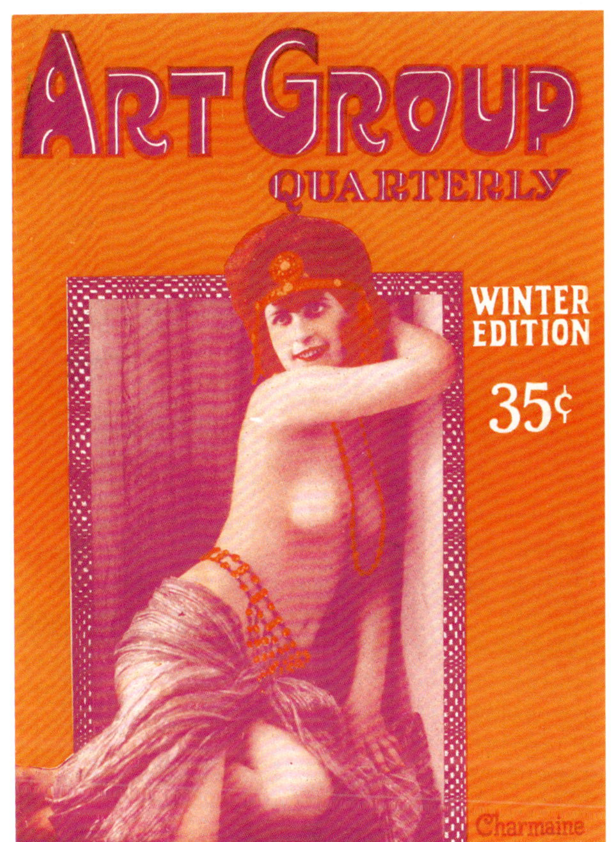

YEAR: 1920s. TITLE: Art Group Quarterly. COUNTRY: USA.

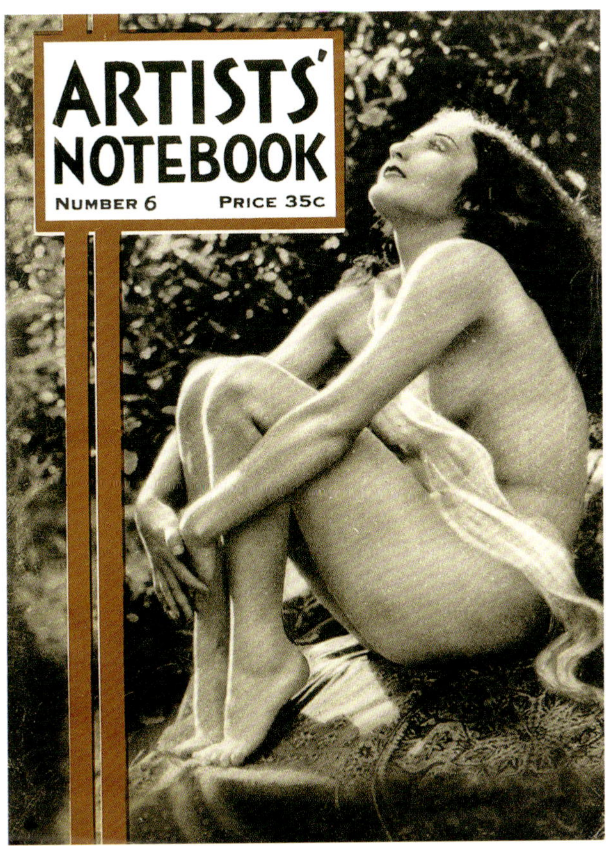

YEAR: 1930. TITLE: Artists' Notebook. COUNTRY: USA.

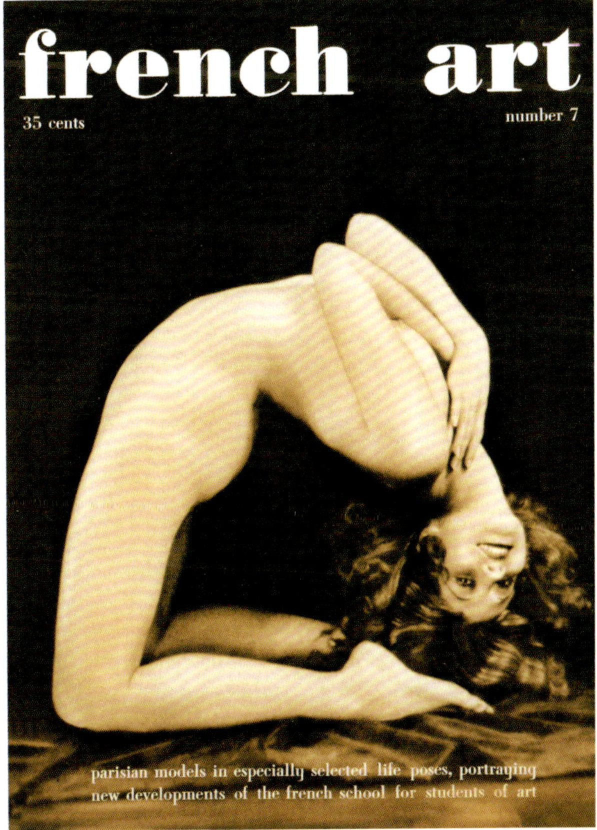

YEAR: 1920s. TITLE: French Art. COUNTRY: USA.

YEAR: 1920s. TITLE: Art Group Quarterly. COUNTRY: USA.

Year: **1950s**. Title: **The New Models Beautiful**. Country: **USA**

in Wilmington was the nude leader, and its premier talent was a now-forgotten photographer named Edwin Bower Hesser.

Information about Hesser is scarce, but it seems his primary occupation was advertising and portrait photography. Sometime in the mid-20s he became fledgling Hollywood's first glamour photographer. This was a time when actresses were no more than whores in the minds of many Americans, and the studios seemed bent on bolstering that perception by turning young starlets over to Hesser for art studies. He photographed Jean Harlow and Louise Brooks for *Art Quarterly*, along with dozens of other contract players from Universal, Mack Sennett and Fox Films. It's possible the infamous Joan Crawford nude was Hesser's, but there's no notation on my print.

The American art magazines declined in the 40s, with the exception of the distinctive *Girl Pageant*, and rebounded strongly in the 50s. Even though men's magazines were starting to show bare breasts in an admittedly sexual context, many men still preferred the subterfuge of the art magazines, the sense that they weren't just gawking at smut but appreciating nudity on a higher plane.

This was a time when actresses were no more than whores in the minds of many Americans.

waren die Educational Art Press aus Wilmington, Delaware und die Independent News aus New York. Auch Dawn Publishing bot „art studies" an, doch dies nur als Nebenprodukt seiner Eugenik-Kampagne. Educational Press war der Marktführer in Sachen nackter Haut, und ihr wichtigster Künstler war ein heute vergessener Fotograf namens Edwin Bower Hesser.

Über Hesser ist wenig überliefert, aber anscheinend beschäftigte er sich vorwiegend mit Werbe- und Porträtfotografie. Irgendwann Mitte der Zwanziger wurde er Hollywoods erster Glamourfotograf. Zu dieser Zeit waren Schauspielerinnen in den Augen vieler Amerikaner nicht mehr als Prostituierte, und die Studios schienen entschlossen zu sein, diese Auffassung noch zu unterstützen, indem sie junge Starlets für künstlerische Akte zu Hesser schickten. Er fotografierte Jean Harlow und Louise Brooks für *Art Quarterly* und Dutzende anderer Schauspielerinnen von Universal, Mack Sennett und Fox Films. Möglicherweise stammt auch das berüchtigte Nacktfoto von Joan Crawford von Hesser, doch mein Abzug trägt keinen Stempel.

Mit Ausnahme des unverwechselbaren *Girl Pageant* ließ das Interesse an diesen Magazinen in den Staaten in den Vierzigern nach, erlebte aber in den Fünfzigern wieder einen Aufschwung. Obwohl Männermagazine nun auch blanke Busen in einem offen sexuellen Kontext zu zeigen begannen, bevorzugten viele Männer weiterhin den Kunstkontext, die Illusion, nicht nur unanständige Bilder anzustarren, sondern Nacktheit auf höherer Ebene zu goutieren.

Zu den Fotografen in den USA, die Bilder in diesem Sinne produzierten,

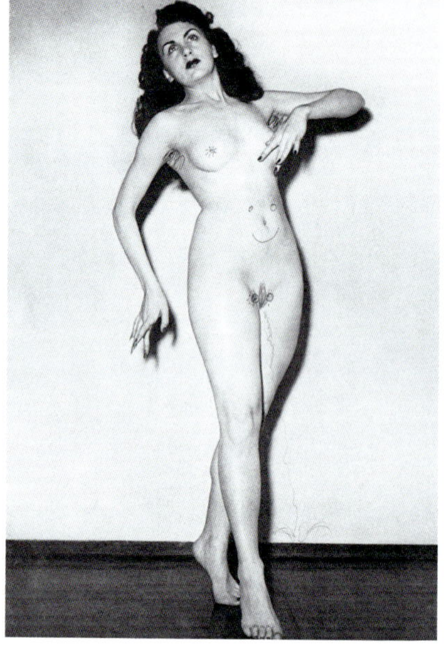

Year: **1950s**. Title: **The New Models Beautiful**. Country: **USA**.

autre magazine « d'art » intitulé *Tidbits of Beauty* (« fragments de beauté »). Il s'adressait lui aussi aux étudiants en art sérieux mais uniquement à ceux s'intéressant à la technique de la silhouette, car c'est tout ce qu'on y voyait de ces beautés, dont la vertu était en outre protégée par le port d'un costume de bain descendant jusqu'aux genoux. Aux États-Unis, on commença à publier des magazines d'art vers 1920. Les éditeurs les plus prolifiques étaient l'Educational Art Press basé à Wilmington dans le Delaware, et Independant News, à New York. Dawn Publishing proposait également des « études artistiques » mais celles-ci ne constituaient qu'une part mineure de sa campagne pour l'eugénisme. Educational Art Press était le leader en matière de nudité et faisait appel à un photographe de talent du nom d'Edwin Bower Hesser aujourd'hui oublié.

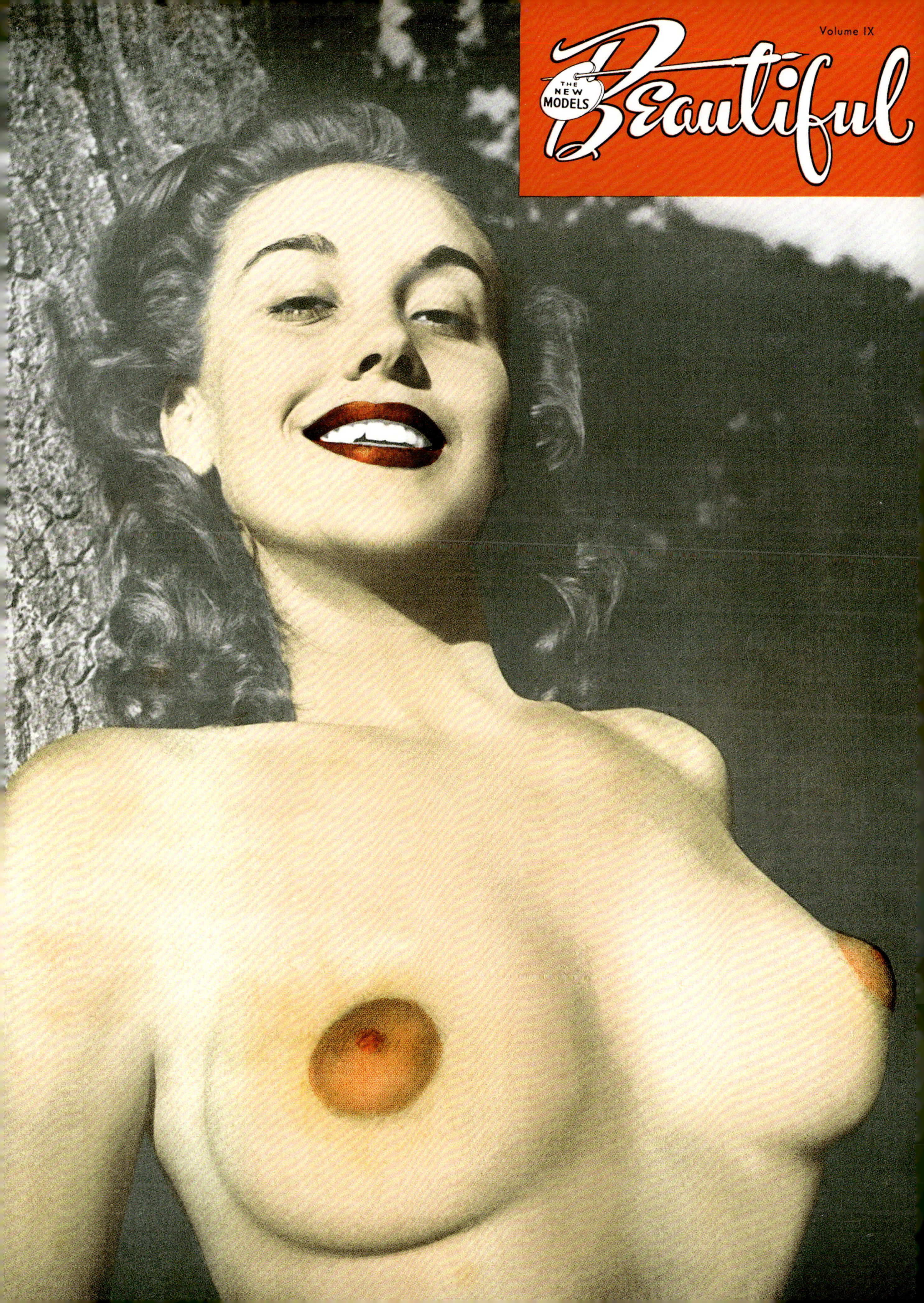
Volume IX
THE NEW MODELS
Beautiful

Year: **1957**. Title: **Glamour Photography**. Country: **USA**.

The magazines considered eye contact seductive, so if the girls looked away it became art.

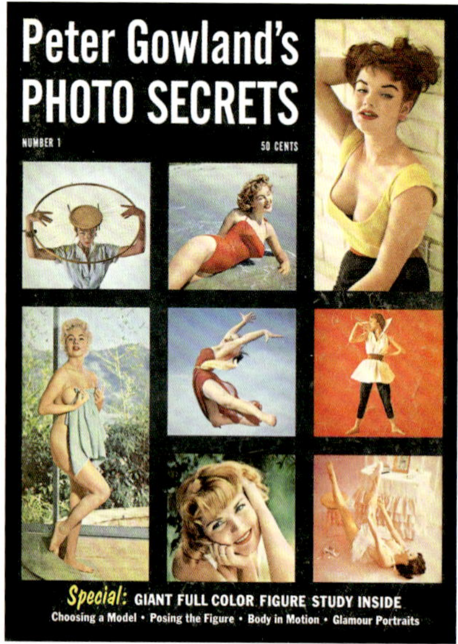

Year: **1958**. Title: **Peter Gowland's Photo Secrets**. Country: **USA**.

The American photographers who delivered this sense of superiority were Peter Gowland, André de Dienes, Peter Basch, Philip O. Stearns and even Bunny Yeager. Edmund Leja, a lesser star who shot for *Art and Camera* in the 50s, as well as for nudist and girlie magazines, explained: "For the girlie magazines we had the models look into the camera and for the art magazines we had them look away from the camera. The magazines considered eye contact seductive, so if the girls looked away it became art." In the art magazines models were totally nude, but always with airbrushed crotches, while for the girlie magazines lingerie covered the crotch, and for the nudist magazines, says Leja, "They told us to make it look natural, but raise the leg to hide the crotch, don't let the sun shine on it." He admits the rules could get confusing, especially since Camerarts Publishing of Chicago made not only the art nude

zählten Peter Gowland, André de Dienes, Peter Basch, Philip O. Stearns und selbst Bunny Yeager. Edmund Leja, ein weniger bekannter Fotograf, der in den Fünfzigern für *Art and Camera* ebenso wie für Nudisten- und Girlie-Magazine fotografierte, erinnert sich: „Für die Girlie-Magazine ließen wir die Models in die Kamera blicken und für die Kunstmagazine von der Kamera weg. Beiden Magazinen galt Blickkontakt als verführerisch, guckten die Models weg, war es Kunst."

In den Kunstmagazinen waren die Models völlig nackt, doch die Scham war stets retuschiert, während in den Girlie-Magazinen Unterwäsche die Schamgegend bedeckte. Anders in den Nudistenzeitschriften: „Wir sollten es natürlich aussehen lassen", so Leja, „das Model sollte jedoch ein Bein anwinkeln, um die Scham zu verbergen, anstatt sie allzu augenfällig in die Sonne zu halten". Da konnte man manchmal den Überblick verlieren, wie er einräumte, vor allem, da Camerarts Publishing aus Chicago nicht nur Aktmagazine, sondern auch Nudisten- und mehrere Girlie-Magazine verlegte.

In Europa funktionierten die Nacktmagazine nach denselben Regeln, auch hier war man um den ernsthaften Kunststudenten besorgt, der sich kein lebendes Model leisten konnte, aber erst nach dem Zweiten Weltkrieg schlossen sich auch Dänemark, Schweden und England auf diesem Gebiet Frankreich und Deutschland an. Bestimmte Floskeln, um die Magazine von minderwertigen Sexheften zu unterscheiden, waren in all diesen Ländern identisch.

In England fand man *Line and Form*, in Deutschland *Formen + Linien*, in Dänemark *Forms in Color*. Schweden

On ne sait pas grand-chose sur Hesser mais il semble que son activité principale ait été la photographie publicitaire et le portrait. Vers le milieu des années 1920, il devint l'un des premiers photographes glamour de l'industrie naissante d'Hollywood. À cette époque, beaucoup d'Américains considéraient qu'une actrice n'était guère plus qu'une prostituée. Les studios semblaient déterminés à encourager cette vision en envoyant leurs jeunes starlettes chez Hesser pour poser pour des études artistiques. Il photographia Jean Harlow et Louise Brooks pour *Art Quarterly*, ainsi que des dizaines d'autres acteurs sous contrat chez Universal, Mack Sennett et Fox Films. Il est possible que le célèbre nu de Joan Crawford soit de lui mais je n'en ai pas la preuve.

Les magazines d'art américains périclitèrent dans les années 1940, à l'exception

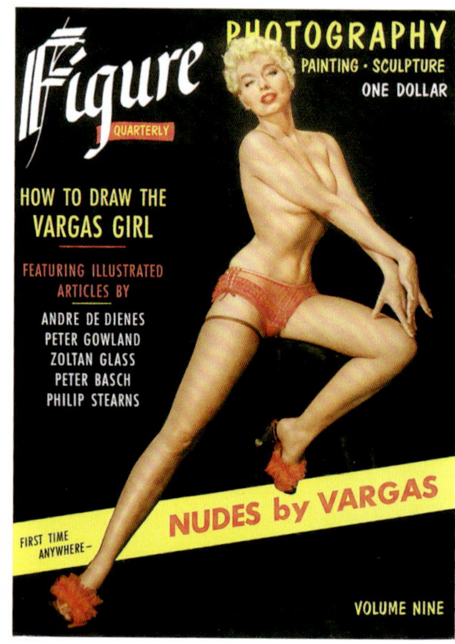

Year: **1950s**. Title: **Figure Quarterly**. Country: **USA**.

Glamour Photography

TRADEMARK REGISTERED, U. S. PATENT OFFICE

PRICE 50c

SUMMER 1957

THE GLAMOUR STUDIO ON WHEELS

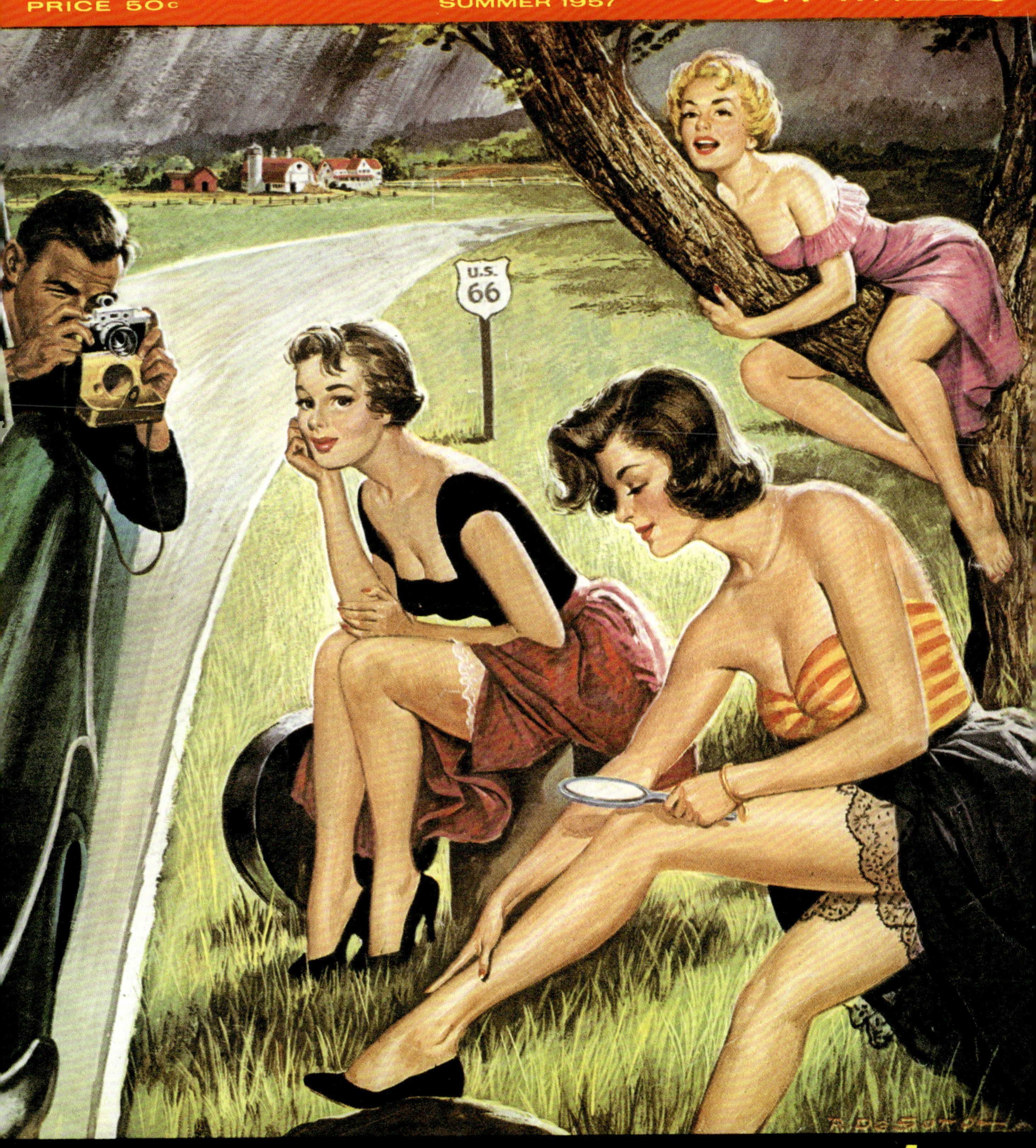

the great cross-country

GIRL HUNT

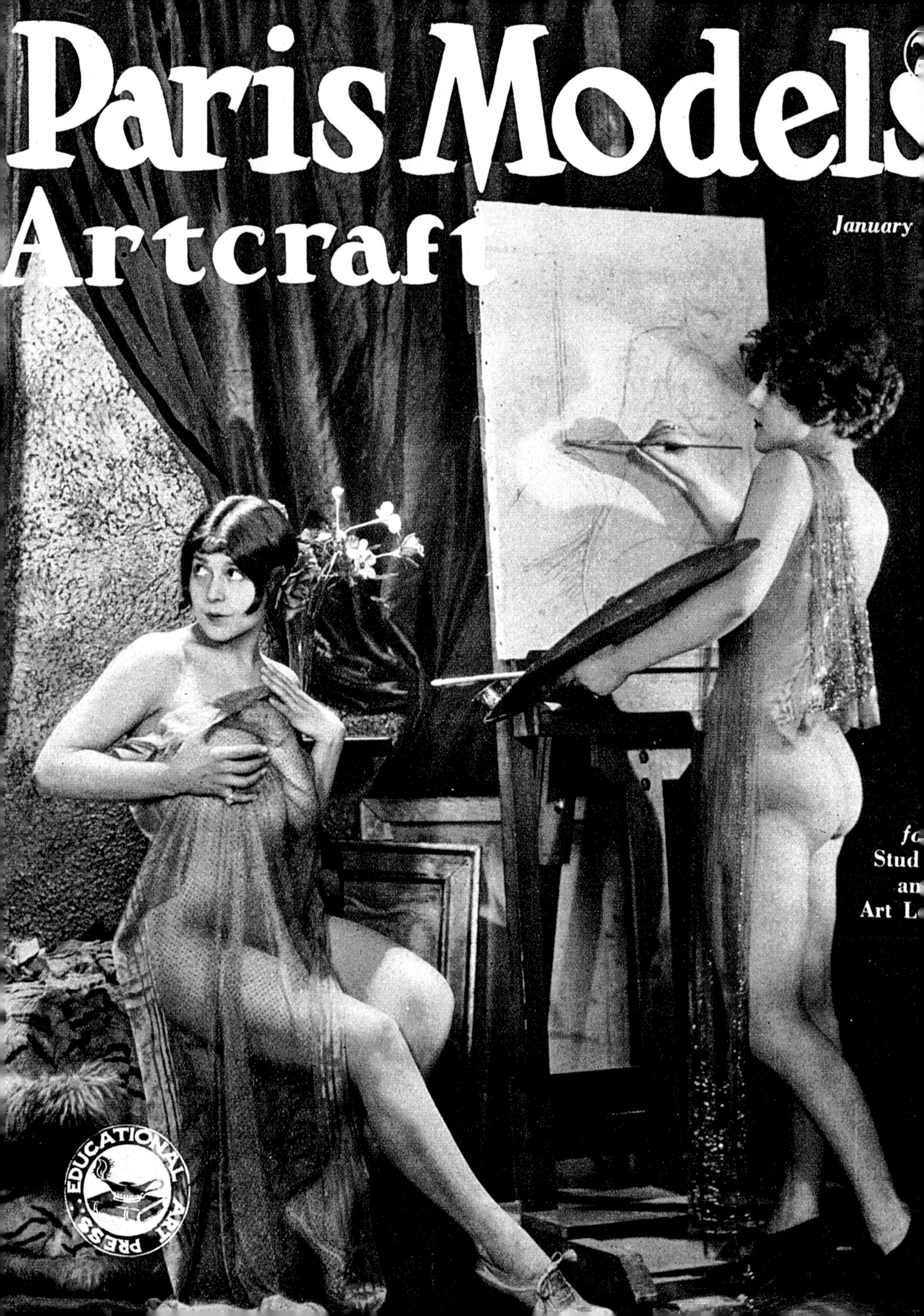
Paris Models
Artcraft
January
Stud
Art L
EDUCATIONAL ART PRESS

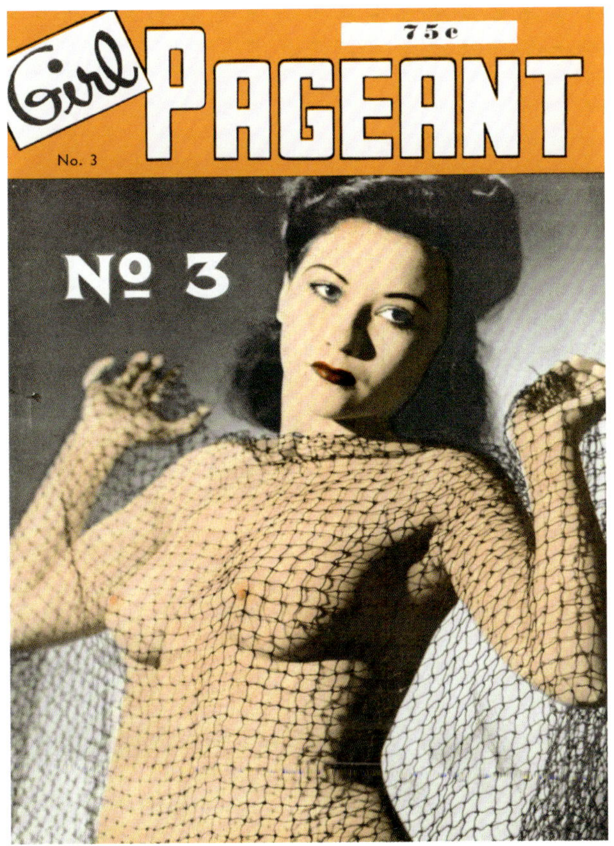

YEAR: **1940s**. TITLE: **Girl Pageant**. COUNTRY: **USA**.

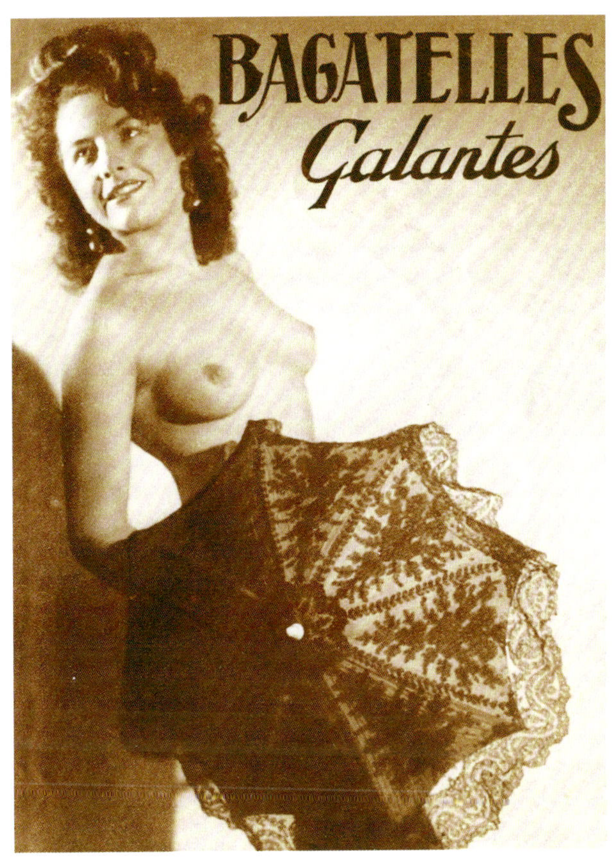

YEAR: **1940s**. TITLE: **Bagatelles Gallantes**. COUNTRY: **France**.

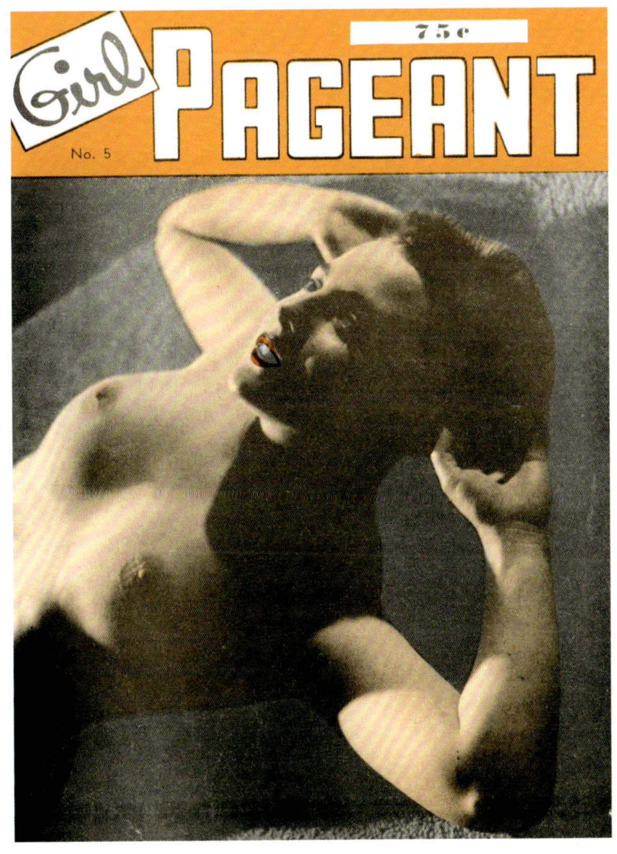

YEAR: **1940s**. TITLE: **Girl Pageant**. COUNTRY: **USA**.

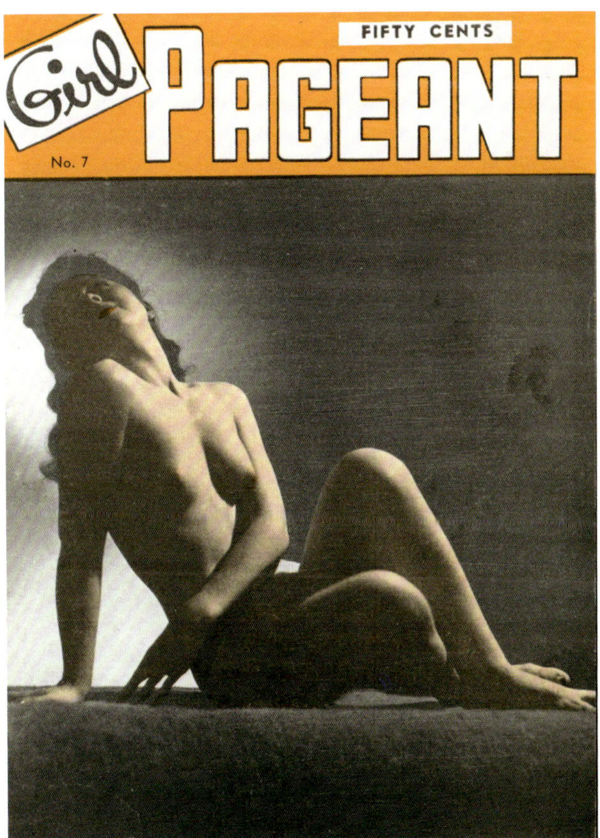

YEAR: **1940s**. TITLE: **Girl Pageant**. COUNTRY: **USA**.

YEAR: **1920s**. TITLE: **Paris Models Artcraft**. COUNTRY: **USA**.

The first nude photography magazine was *Camera Work*, founded in 1903 by Alfred Stieglitz.

—*Simon's Book of World Sexual Records*, G.L. Simons, 1975

and nudist magazines he shot for, but several girlie titles.

The Northern European art nude magazines worked by the same rules as the American ones, sharing their concern for the serious art student and his lack of life models, but it wasn't until after World War II that Denmark, Sweden and England joined France and Germany in the game. Certain buzzwords were common to all these countries in elevating their serious art magazines above the lowbrow journals of mere titillation. In England you found the title *Line and*

präsentierte *Foto-Studier*, Dänemark *Model-Studier* und Deutschland *Modell-Studien*. *Nus*, ein französisches Magazin aus den Fünfzigern, war das aufwendigste und zeigte Schwarzweiß-Studien im Großformat und auf dickem „Kunst"-Papier. Das deutsche *Atelier* war dünner und kleiner, aber sehr viel hübscher: die liebevoll handkolorierten Titelbilder belegen den erneuten Aufschwung bei den deutschen Printmedien nach dem Krieg.

Um das Jahr 1960 ging es aufgrund der zunehmenden Akzeptanz unverholen

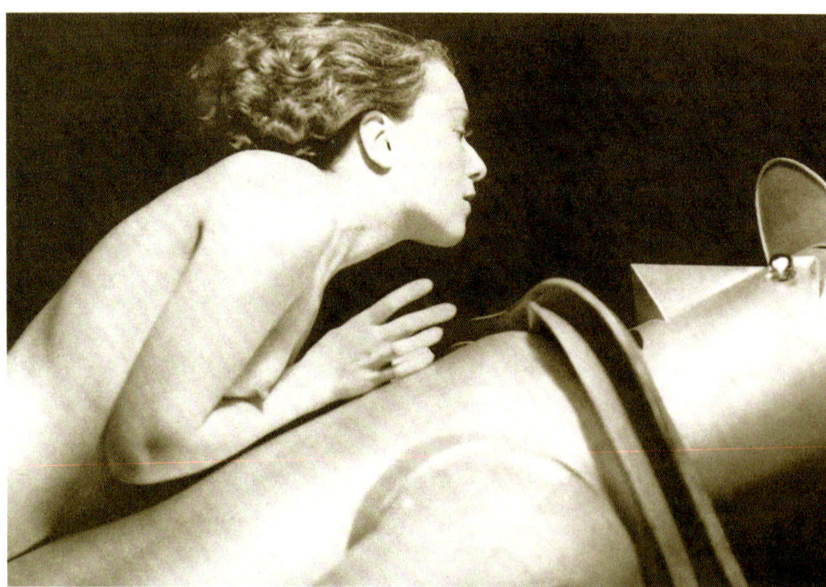

Year: **1940s**. Title: **Bagatelles Gallantes**. Artist: **Manassé**. Country: **France**.

de *Girl Pageant*, d'un genre à part, pour connaître un net regain d'intérêt dans les années 1950. Même si les magazines pour hommes commençaient à montrer des seins nus dans un contexte ouvertement érotique, de nombreux lecteurs continuaient à préférer le prétexte de l'art et l'impression qu'ils ne lorgnaient pas sur des images salaces mais appréciaient la nudité à un niveau plus noble. Les photographes américains qui leur offraient ce sentiment d'élévation se nommaient Peter Gowland, André de Dienes, Peter Basch, Philip O. Stearns et même Bunny Yeager. Edmund Leja, photographe vedette moins connu qui travaillait pour *Art and Camera* dans les années 1950 ainsi que pour des revues nudistes et de charme, explique : « Pour les magazines de charme, on demandait aux filles de regarder directement dans l'objectif et pour les revues d'art, de détourner les yeux. Les magazines considéraient qu'un regard direct était séducteur, mais à partir du moment où le modèle regardait ailleurs, c'était de l'art ». Dans les magazines d'art, les modèles étaient entièrement nus mais leurs entrejambes étaient systématiquement retouchés à l'aérographe ; dans les revues de charme, le pubis était caché par de la lingerie fine tandis que dans les publications nudistes, Leja confie : « On nous demandait que ça ait l'air naturel, que le modèle lève la jambe pour cacher son sexe, que celui-ci ne soit pas directement éclairé par un rayon de soleil ». Il reconnaît qu'il y avait parfois de quoi s'embrouiller, notamment dans le cas de Camerarts Publishing, basé à Chicago, qui publiait, outre des magazines d'art et de nudisme, plusieurs titres de charme.

Les magazines de nus artistiques d'Europe du Nord fonctionnaient avec les

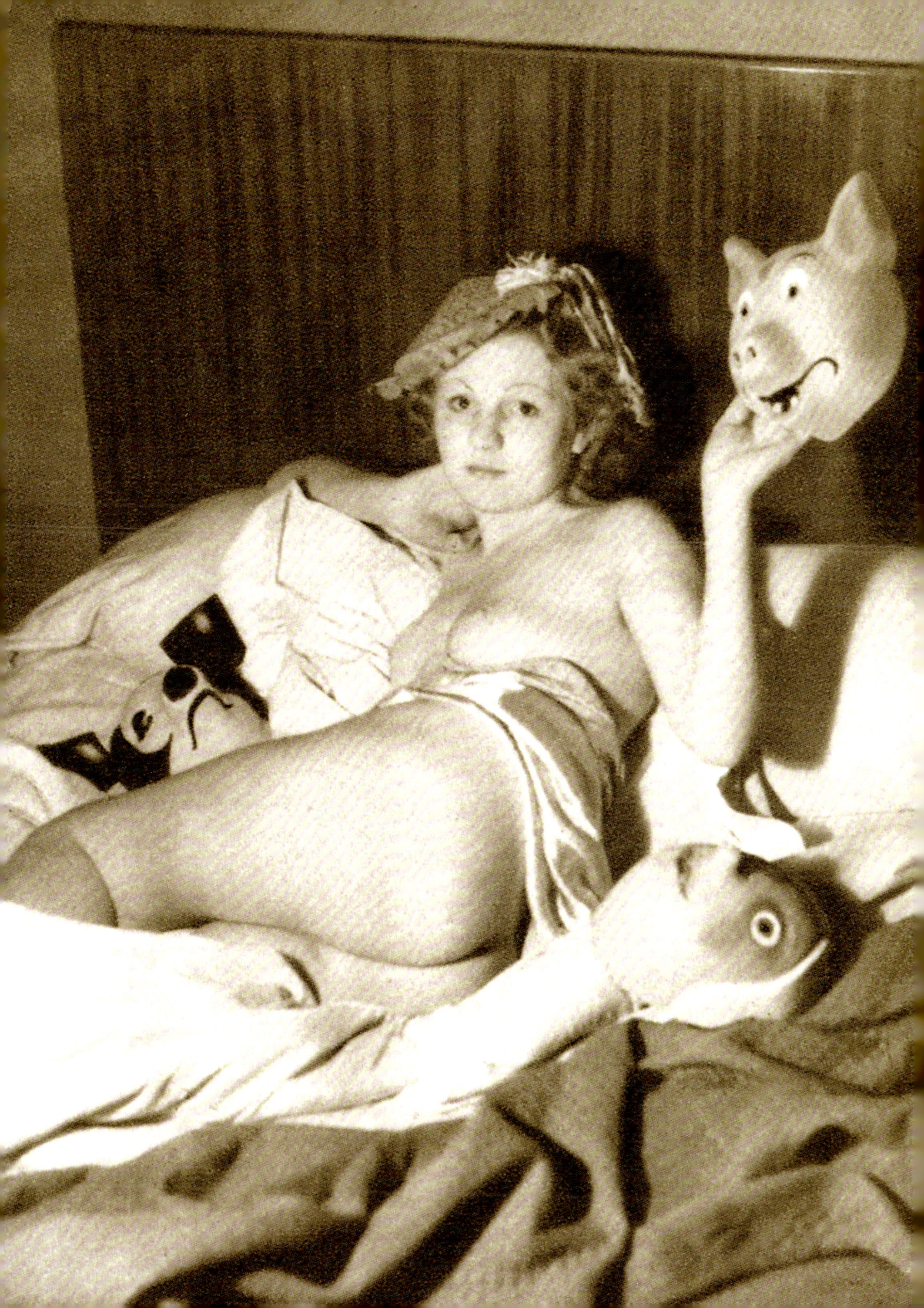

YEAR: **1964**. TITLE: **Foto-Studier**.
COUNTRY: **Sweden**.

PAGES 124 & 125:
YEAR: **1950s**. TITLE: **Paris Models**.
COUNTRY: **Denmark**.
YEAR: **1952**. TITLE: **L'art et le Nu**.
COUNTRY: **France**.

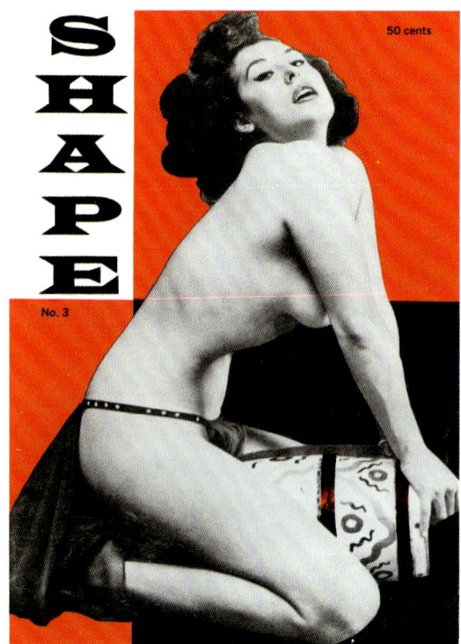

YEAR: **1950s**. TITLE: **Shape**.
COUNTRY: **USA**.

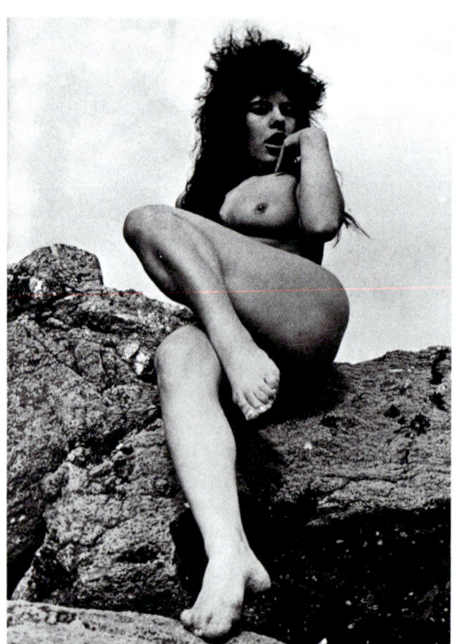

YEAR: **1964**. TITLE: **Foto-Studier**.
COUNTRY: **Sweden**.

Form; in Germany *Formen + Linien*; in Denmark *Forms in Color*. Sweden offered *Foto-Studier*; Denmark *Model-Studier*; Germany *Modell-Studien*. *Nus*, a French magazine of the 50s, was the most lavish, offering a full-size format and black and white model studies printed on thick "art" paper. Germany's *Atelier* was smaller and slimmer but more strikingly beautiful, its delicate hand tinted covers a sign of the country's post-war publishing recovery. By 1960 art nude magazines were in serious decline the world over due to increased acceptance of frankly sexual publications. When you picked up an art magazine in 1965, be it in Sweden or France or Denmark or the US, you could be reasonably sure it would contain only actual art. Which must have been a terrible blow to serious art students without access to life models.

erotischer Publikationen weltweit mit den Aktstudienmagazinen bergab. Wenn man sich 1965 in Schweden, Frankreich, Dänemark oder den USA eine Kunstzeitschrift kaufte, konnte man relativ sicher sein, dass tatsächlich Kunst darin war. Was ein schwerer Schlag für die ernsthaften Kunststudenten gewesen sein muss, die sich keine echten Models leisten konnten.

Sweden offered *Foto-Studier*, Denmark *Model-Studier*, Germany *Modell Studien*.

mêmes règles que les américains, partageant la même sollicitude pour l'étudiant en art sérieux et son manque de modèles vivants. Ce ne fut qu'après la Seconde Guerre mondiale que le Danemark, la Suède et la Grande-Bretagne rejoignirent la France et l'Allemagne sur le terrain de jeu. Pour s'élever au dessus des vulgaires torchons s'abaissant à la simple titillation, ces magazines d'art sérieux avaient en commun certains mots clefs. En Angleterre, on trouvait le titre *Line and Form* (« la ligne et la forme ») ; en Allemagne *Formen + Linien* ; au Danemark, *Forms in Color*. La Suède avait son *Foto-Studier*, le Danemark son *Model-Studier* ; l'Allemagne son *Modell-Studien*. *Nus*, un magazine français des années cinquante, était le plus luxueux de tous, offrant un format pleine page et des études en noir et blanc imprimés sur un épais papier « d'art ». *L'Atelier* allemand était plus petit et plus mince, mais d'une beauté plus frappante, ses couvertures délicates teintes à la main étant un signe du rétablissement du secteur de l'édition dans l'après-guerre. Dans les années soixante, l'acceptation croissante des publications à caractère ouvertement érotique marqua le déclin des magazines de nus artistiques. À partir de 1965, lorsque vous ouvriez un magazine d'art en Suède, en France, au Danemark ou aux États-Unis, vous pouviez être pratiquement sûr qu'il ne contenait que de l'art. Ce qui dut poser de graves problèmes à tous ces étudiants en art sérieux qui n'avaient pas accès à des modèles vivants.

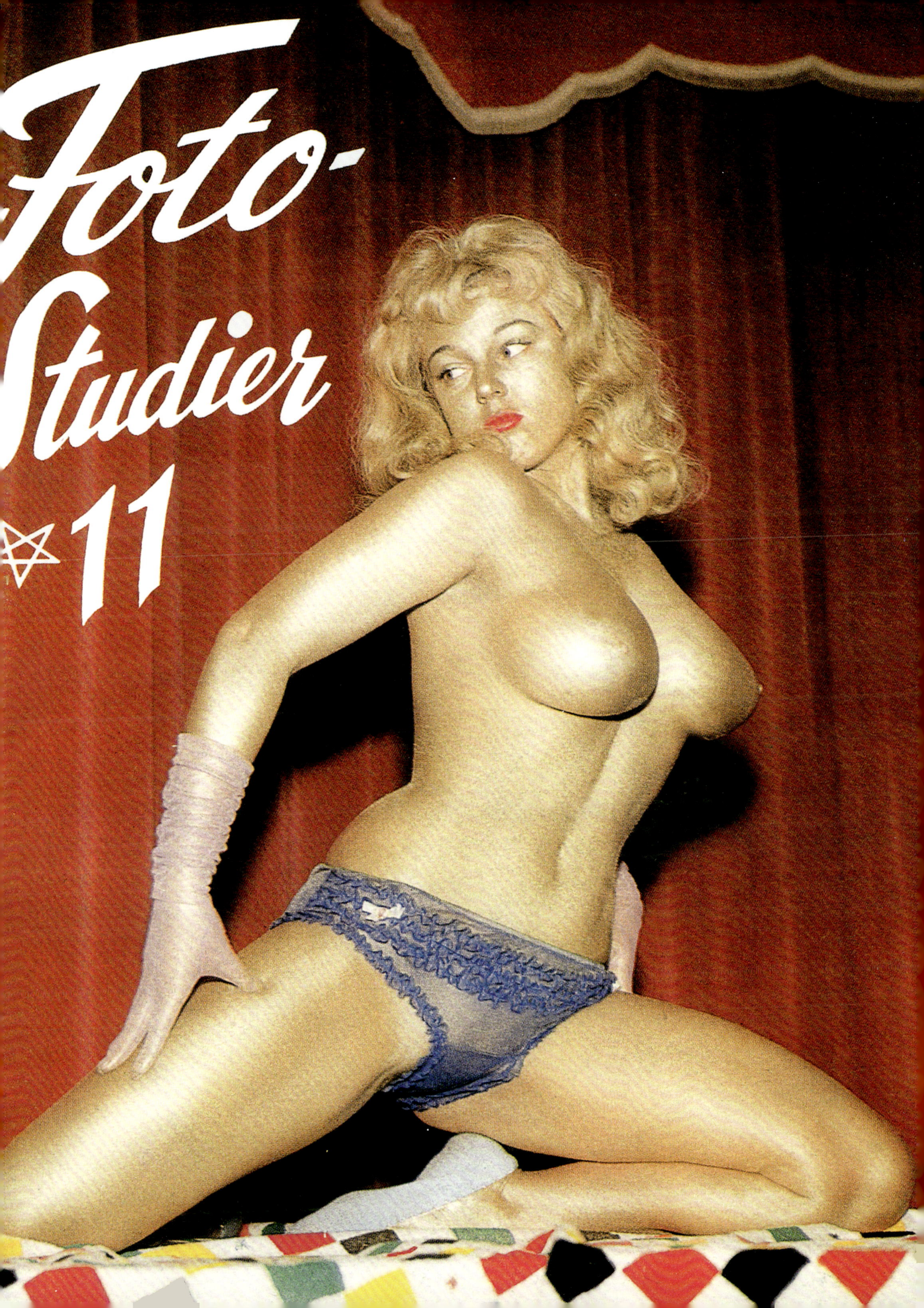

Foto-
Studier
11

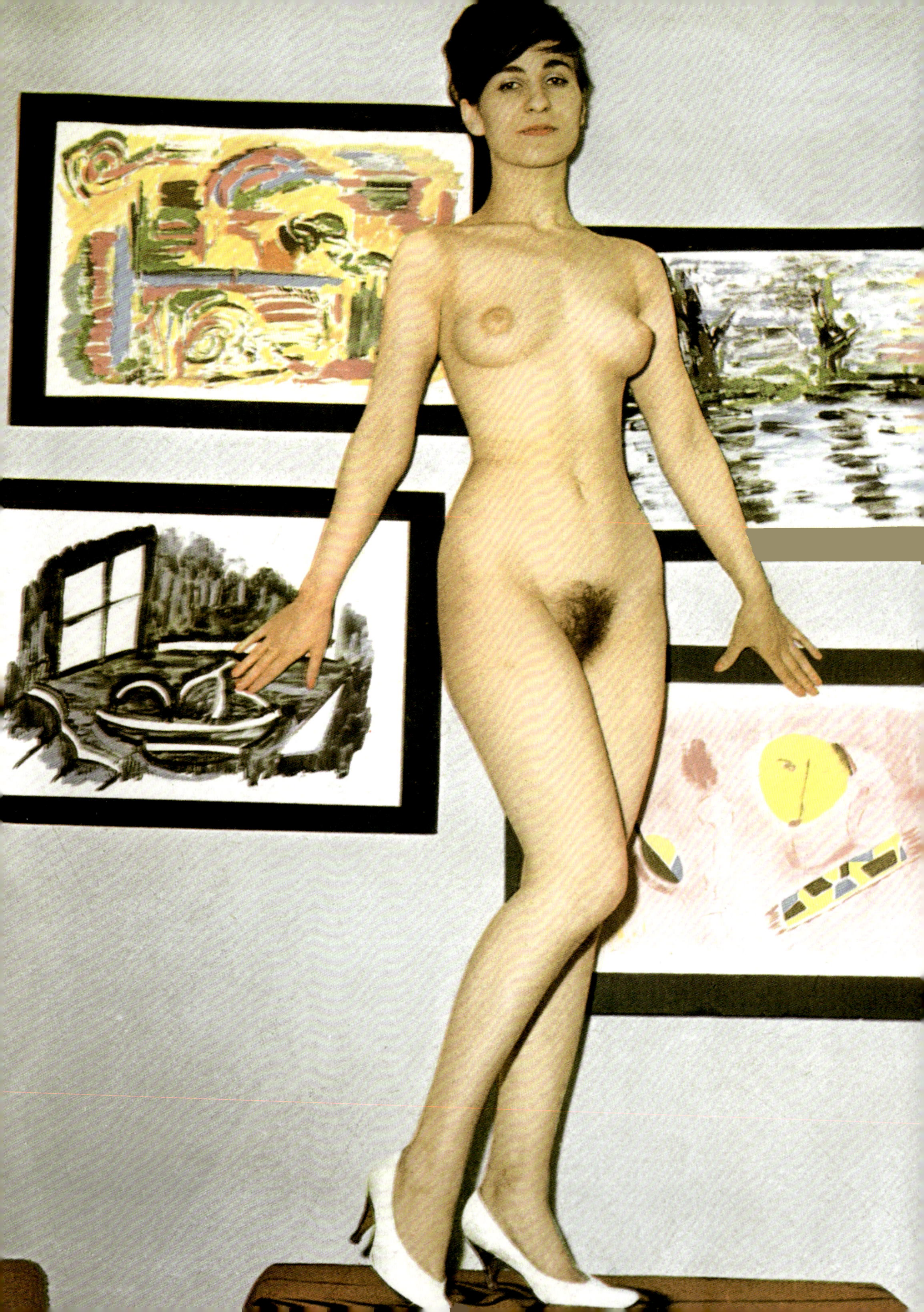

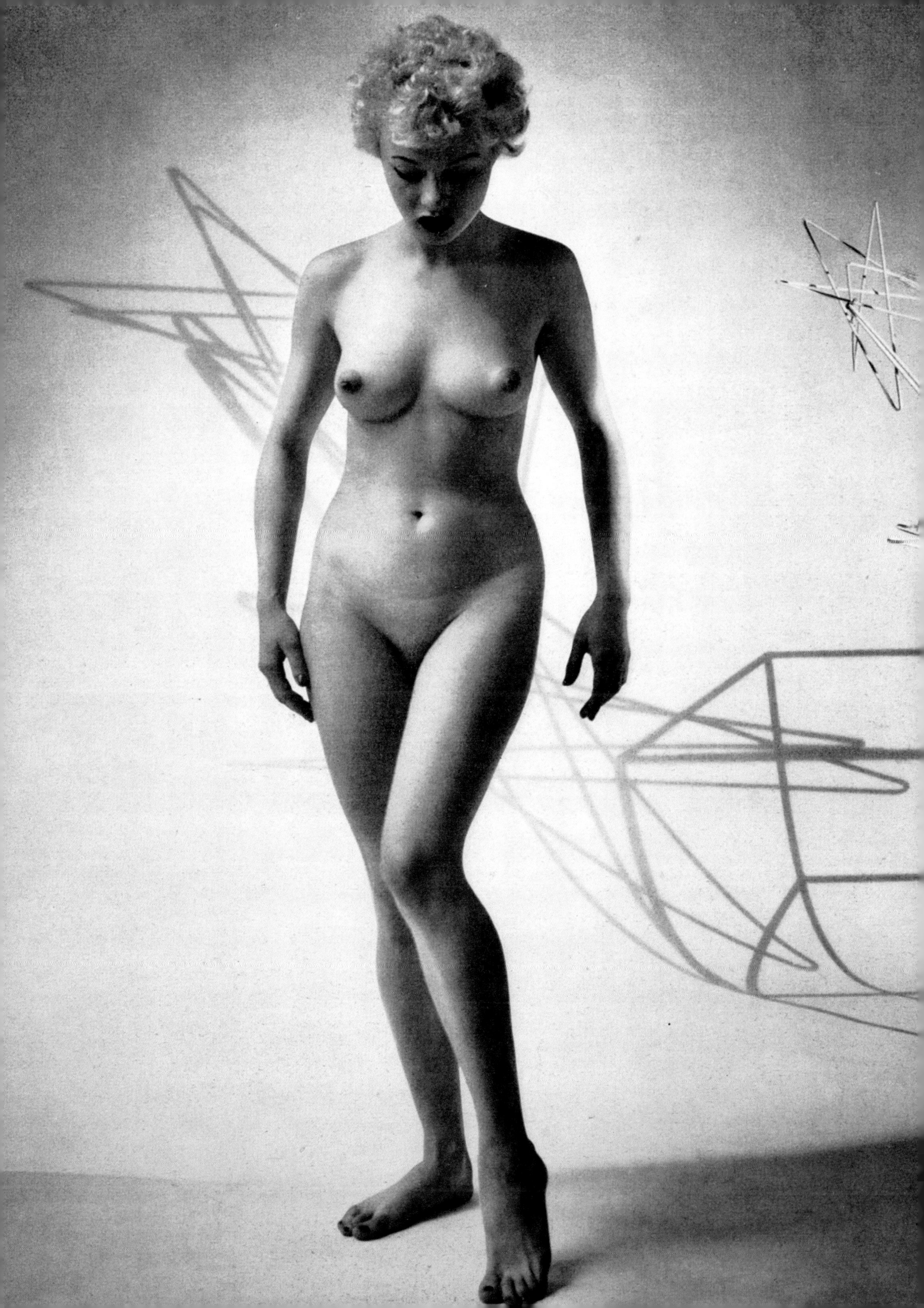

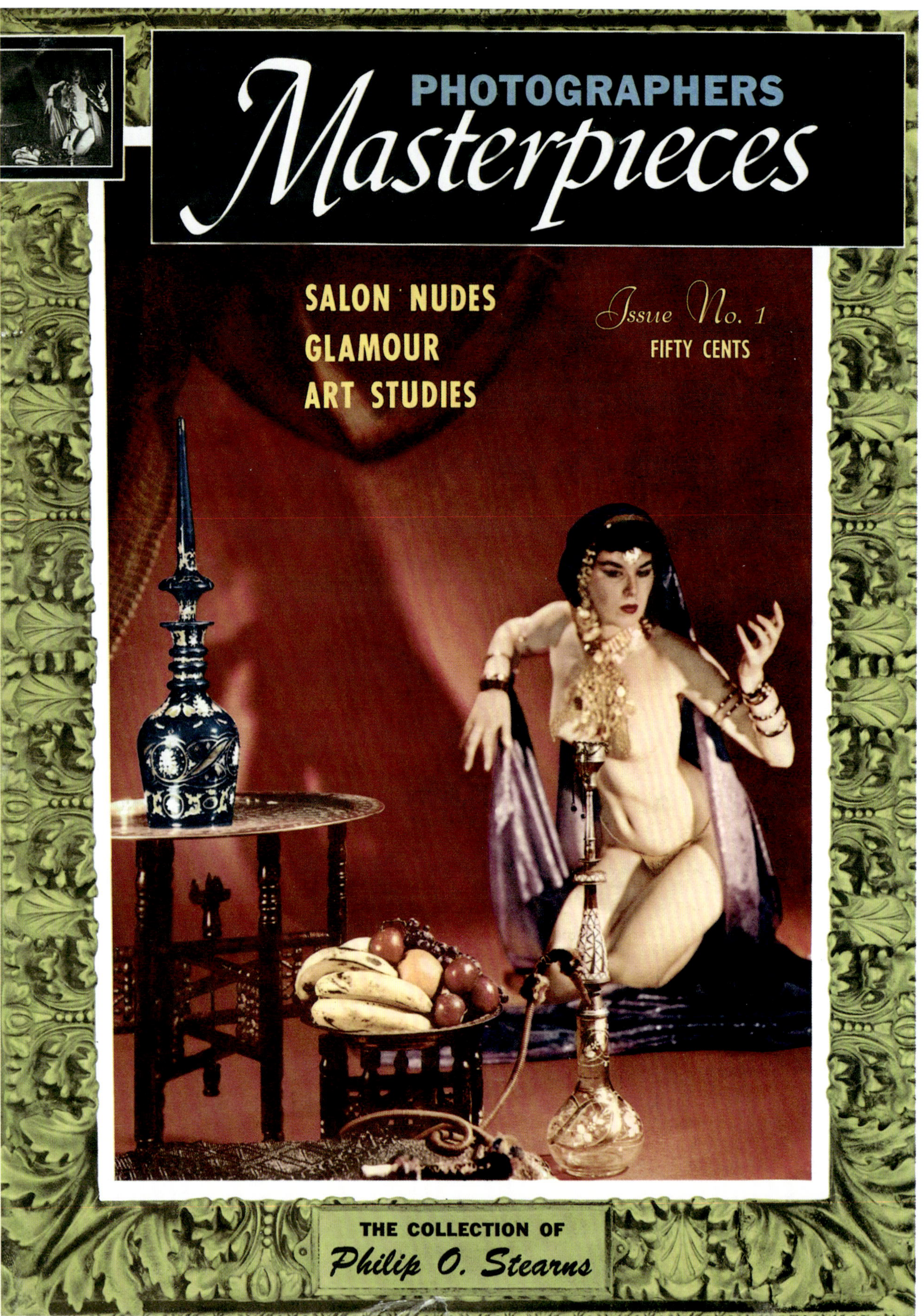

YEAR: **1957**. TITLE: **Photographers Masterpieces**. COUNTRY: **USA**.

YEAR: **1951**. TITLE: **Art and Camera**. COUNTRY: **USA**.

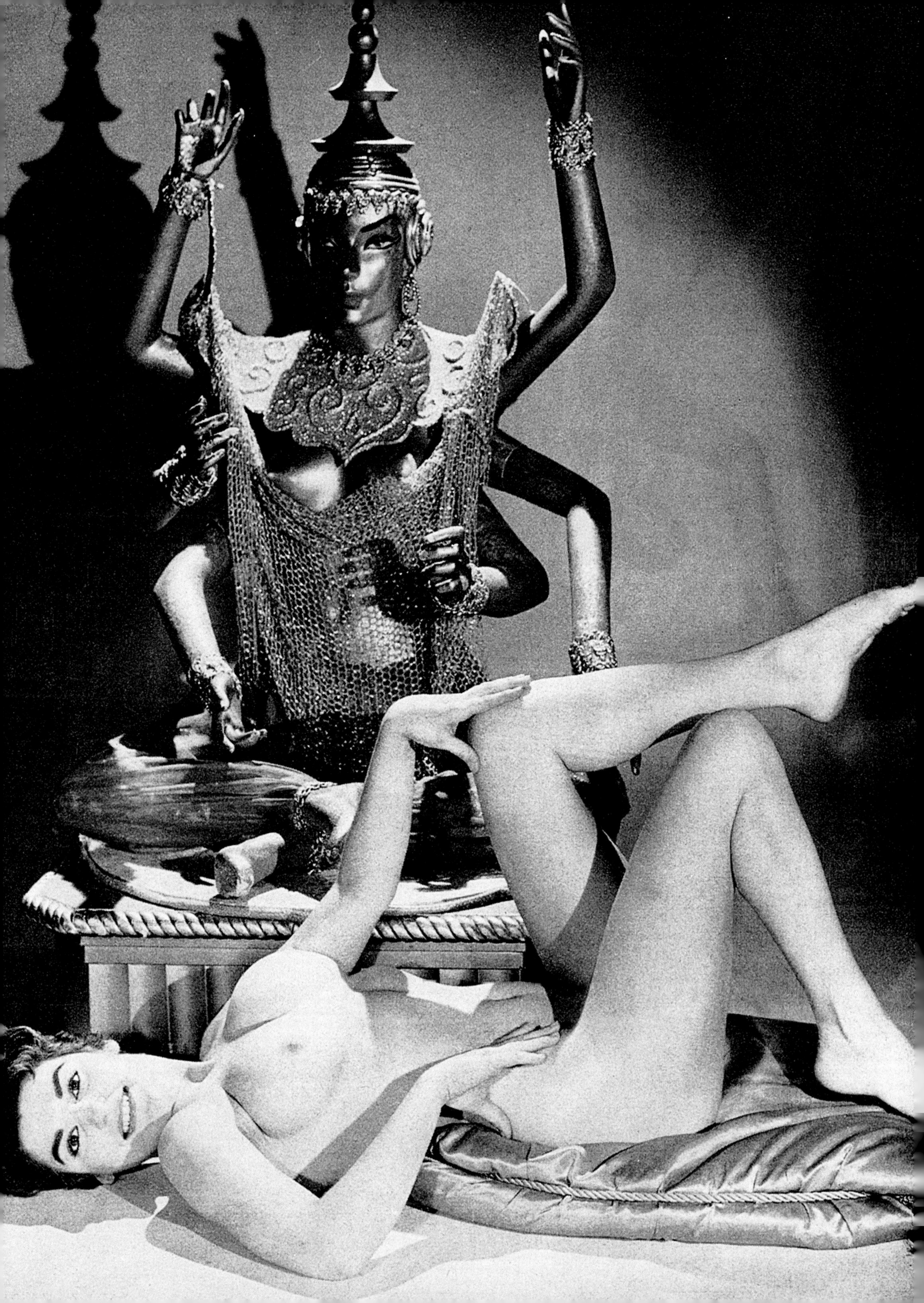

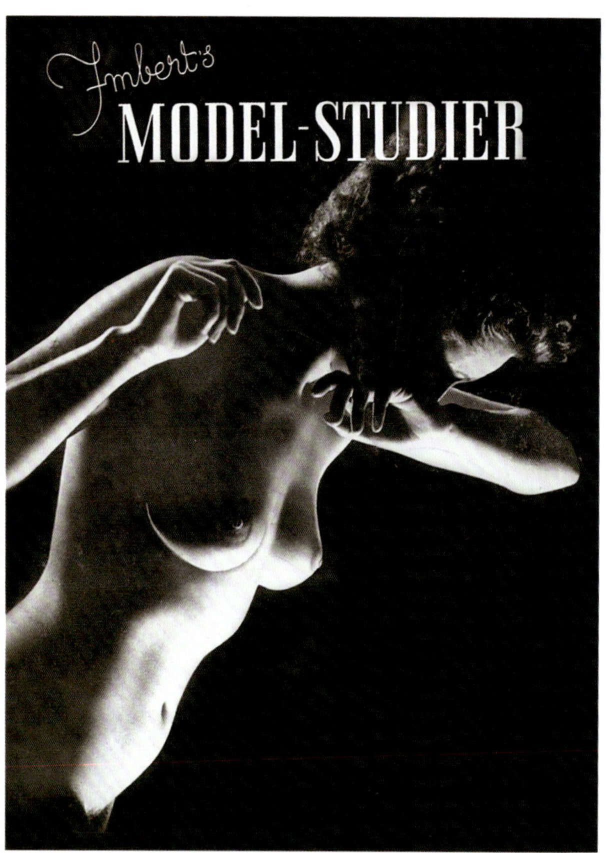

YEAR: **1950s**. TITLE: **Model Studier**. COUNTRY: **Denmark**.

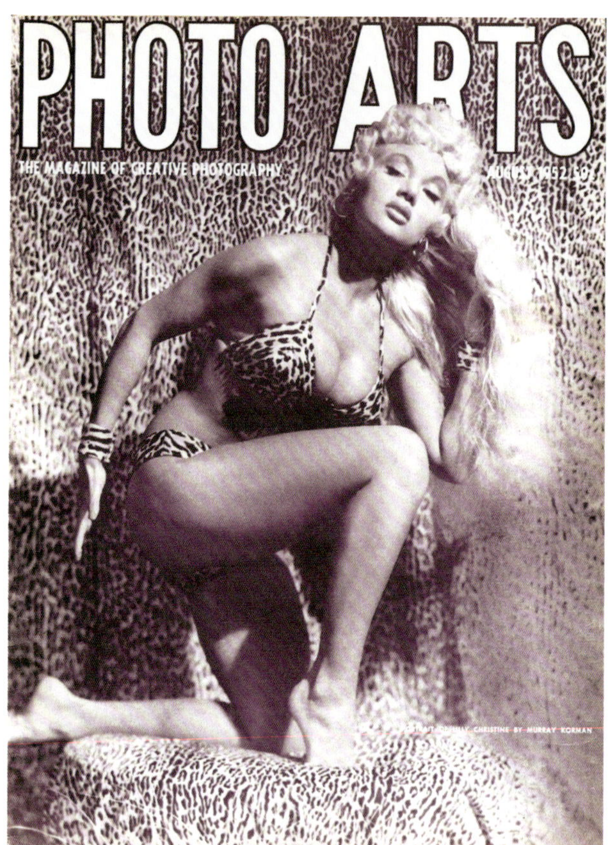

YEAR: **1952**. TITLE: **Photo Arts**. COUNTRY: **USA**.

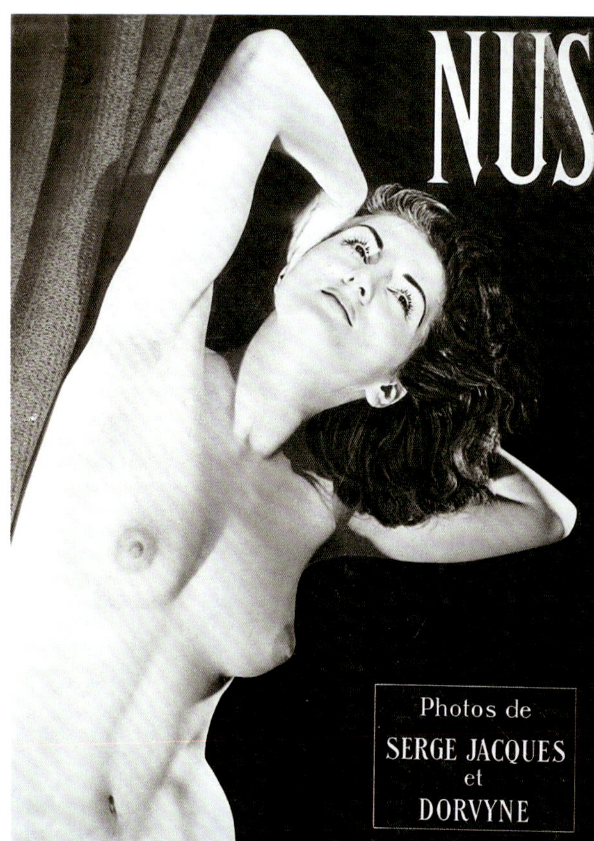

YEAR: **1950s**. TITLE: **Nus**. COUNTRY: **France**.

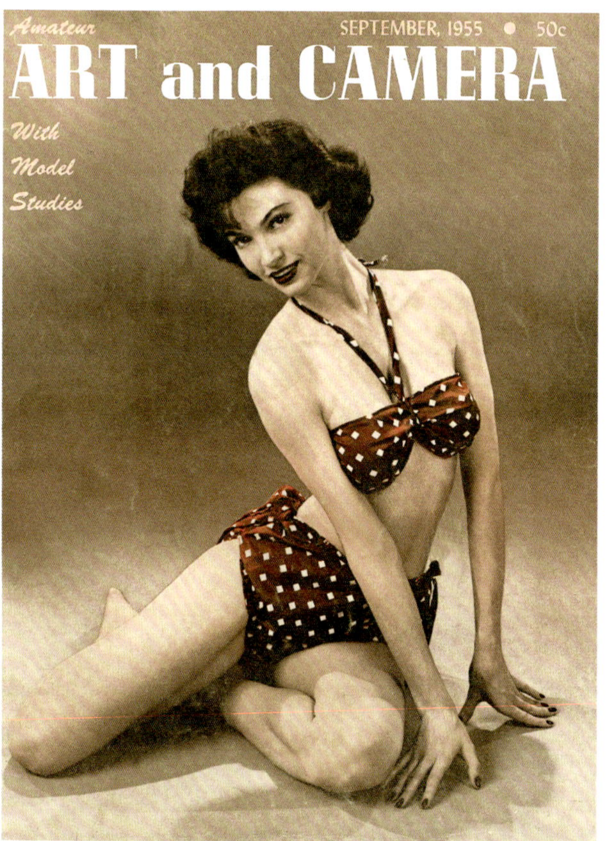

YEAR: **1955**. TITLE: **Art and Camera**. COUNTRY: **USA**.

YEAR: **1955**. TITLE: **Art and Camera**.
COUNTRY: **USA**.

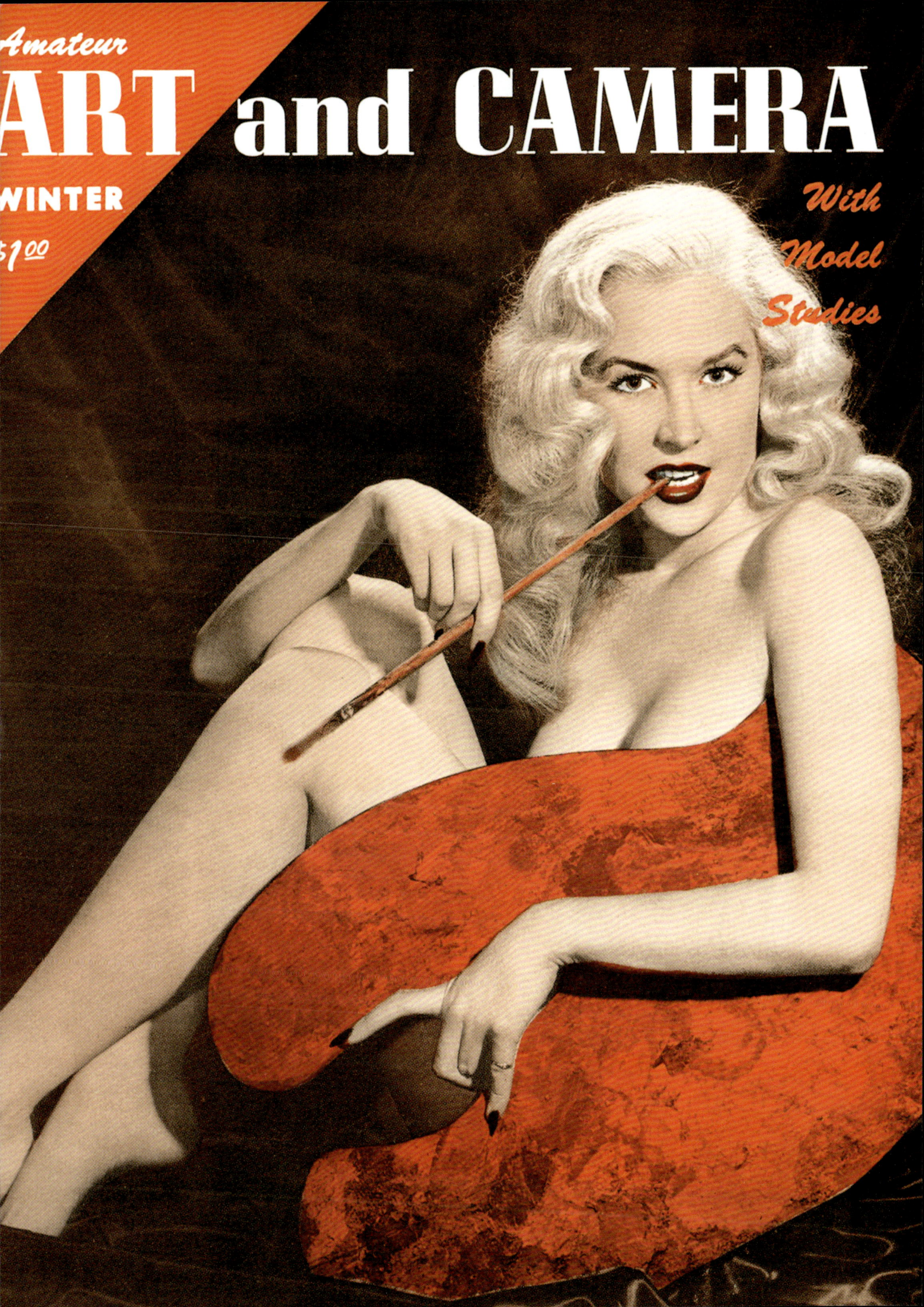
Amateur
ART and CAMERA
WINTER
$1.00
With Model Studies

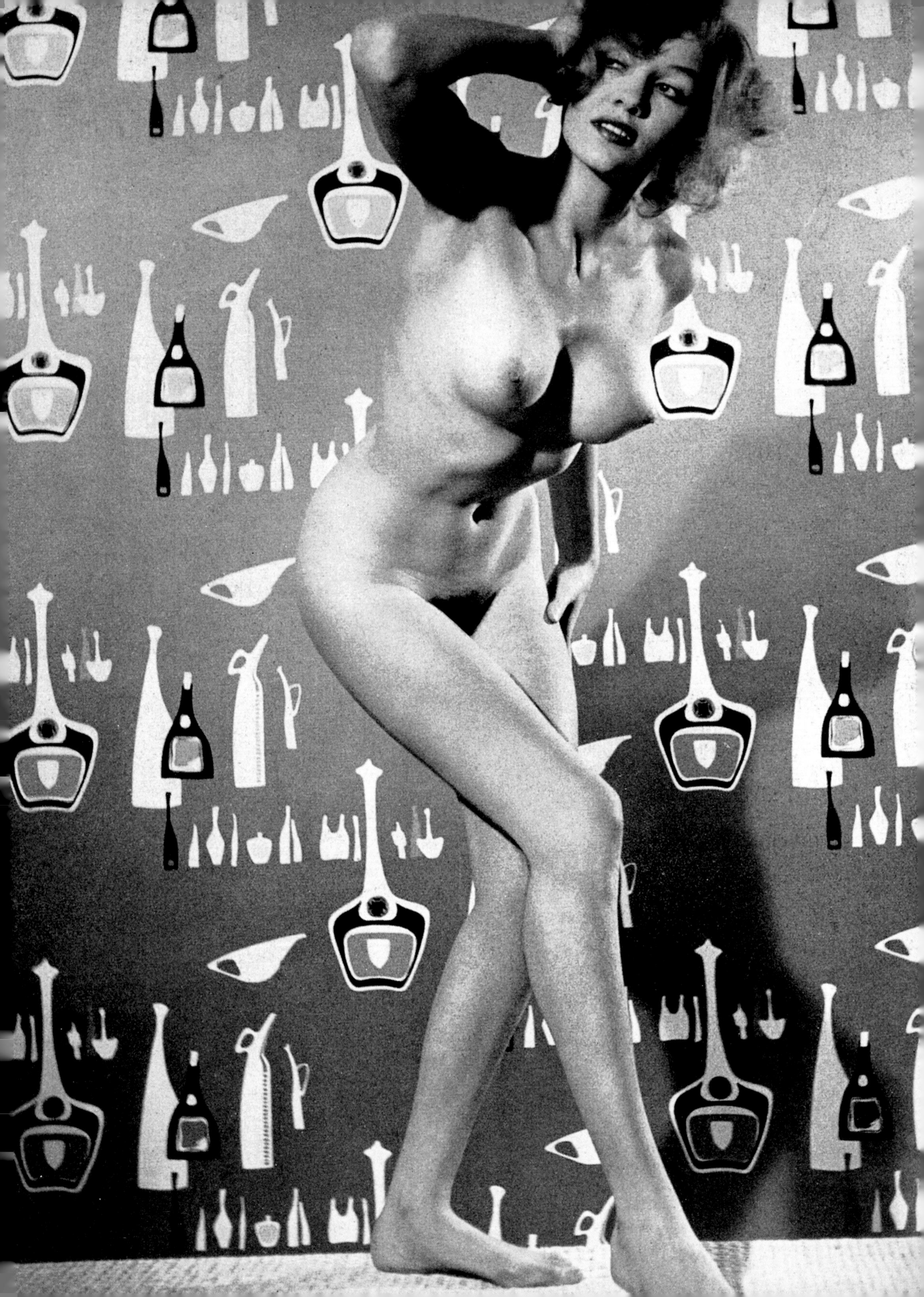

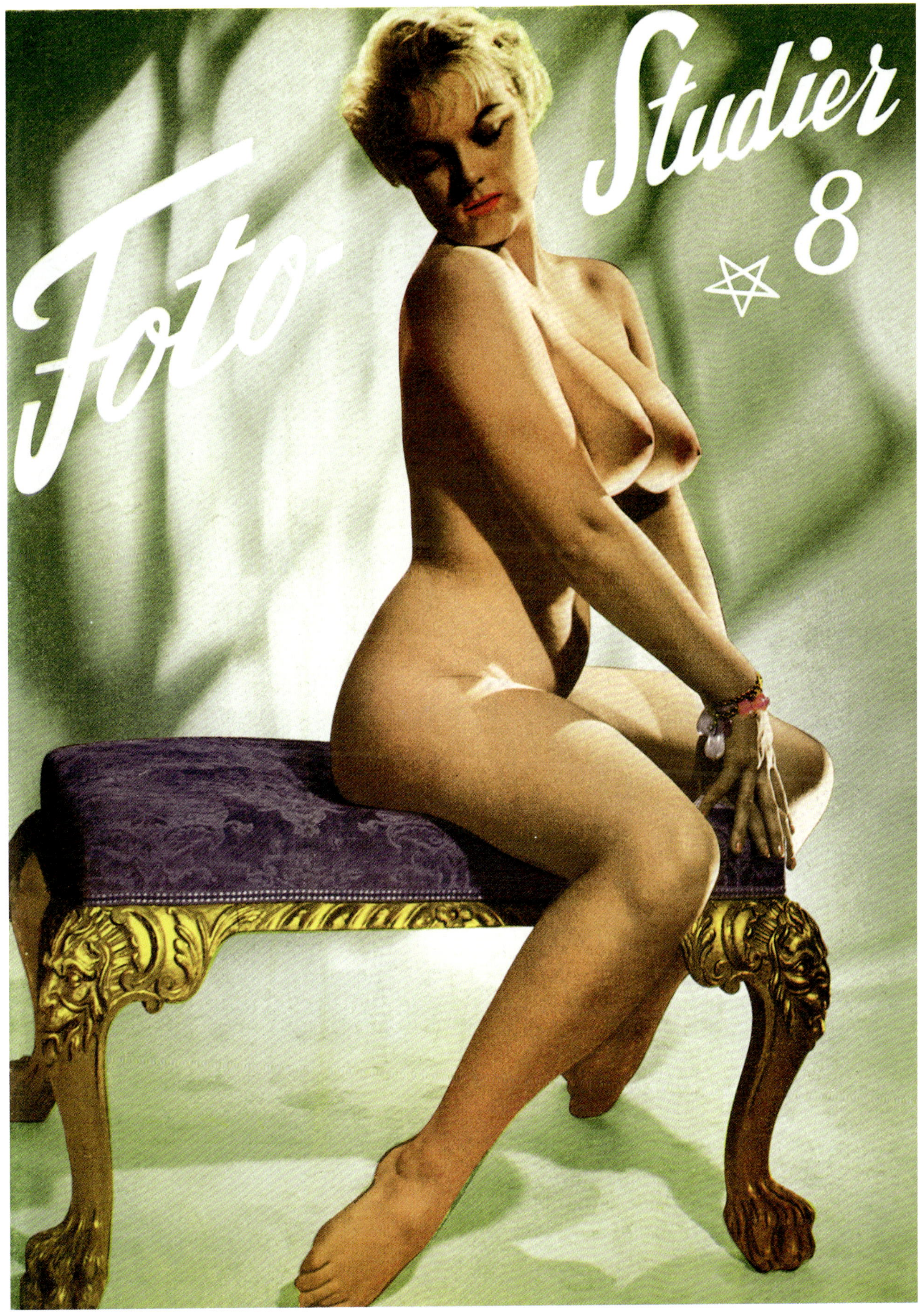

Year: **1964**. Title: **Foto-Studier**. Country: **Sweden**.

Year: **1964**. Title: **Foto-Studier**. Country: **Sweden**.

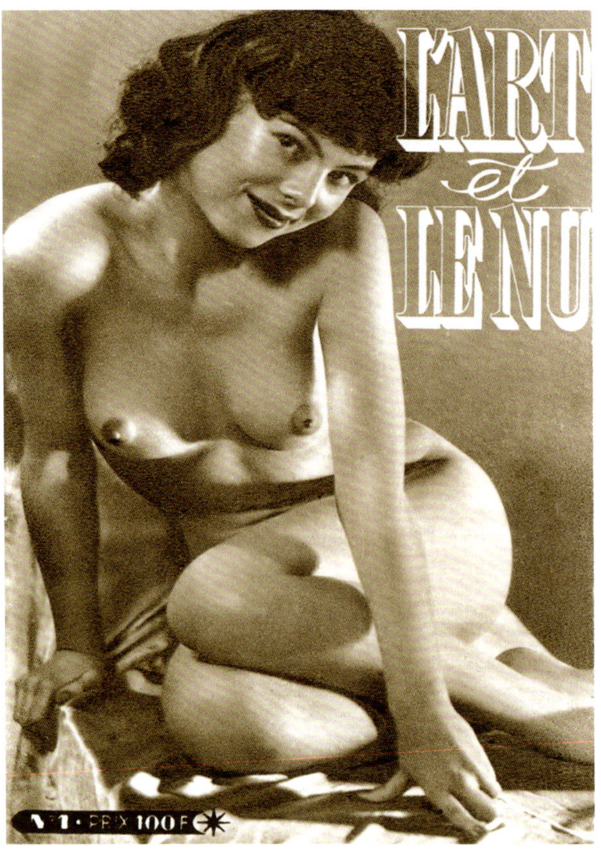

YEAR: **1952**. TITLE: **L'art et le nu**. COUNTRY: **Germany**.

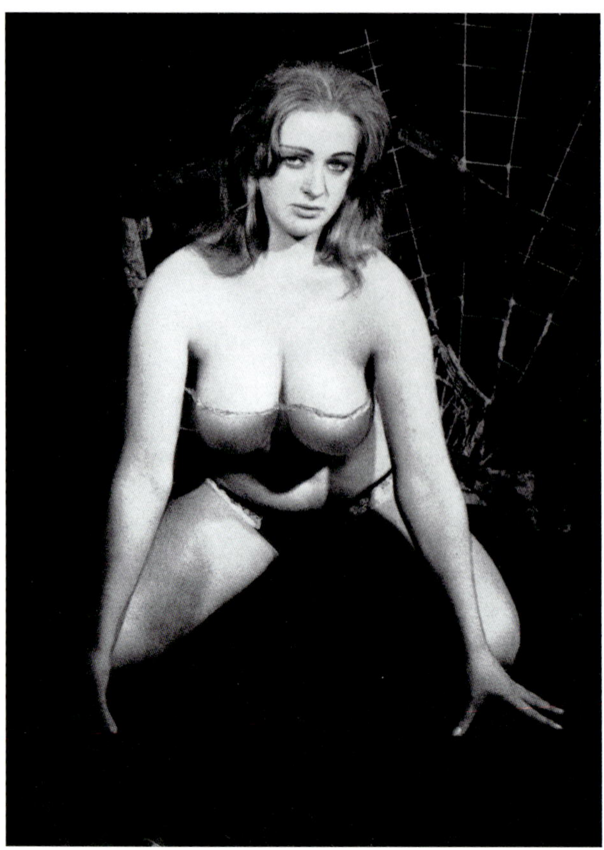

YEAR: **1960s**. TITLE: **The Fiery Flesh of Francine**. COUNTRY: **USA**.

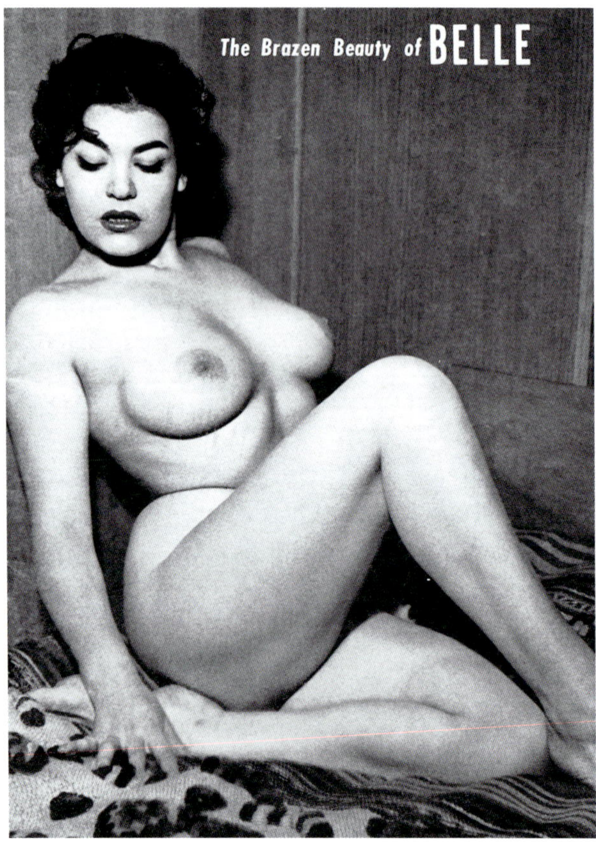

YEAR: **1950s**. TITLE: **The Brazen Beauty of Belle**. COUNTRY: **USA**.

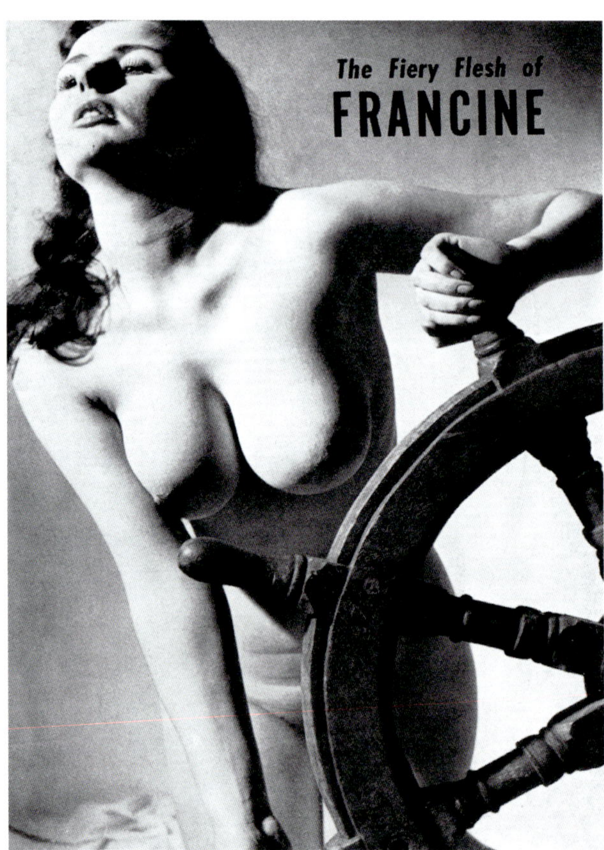

YEAR: **1950s**. TITLE: **The Fiery Flesh of Francine**. COUNTRY: **USA**.

YEAR: **1960s**. TITLE: **Model Studies Annual**. COUNTRY: **USA**.

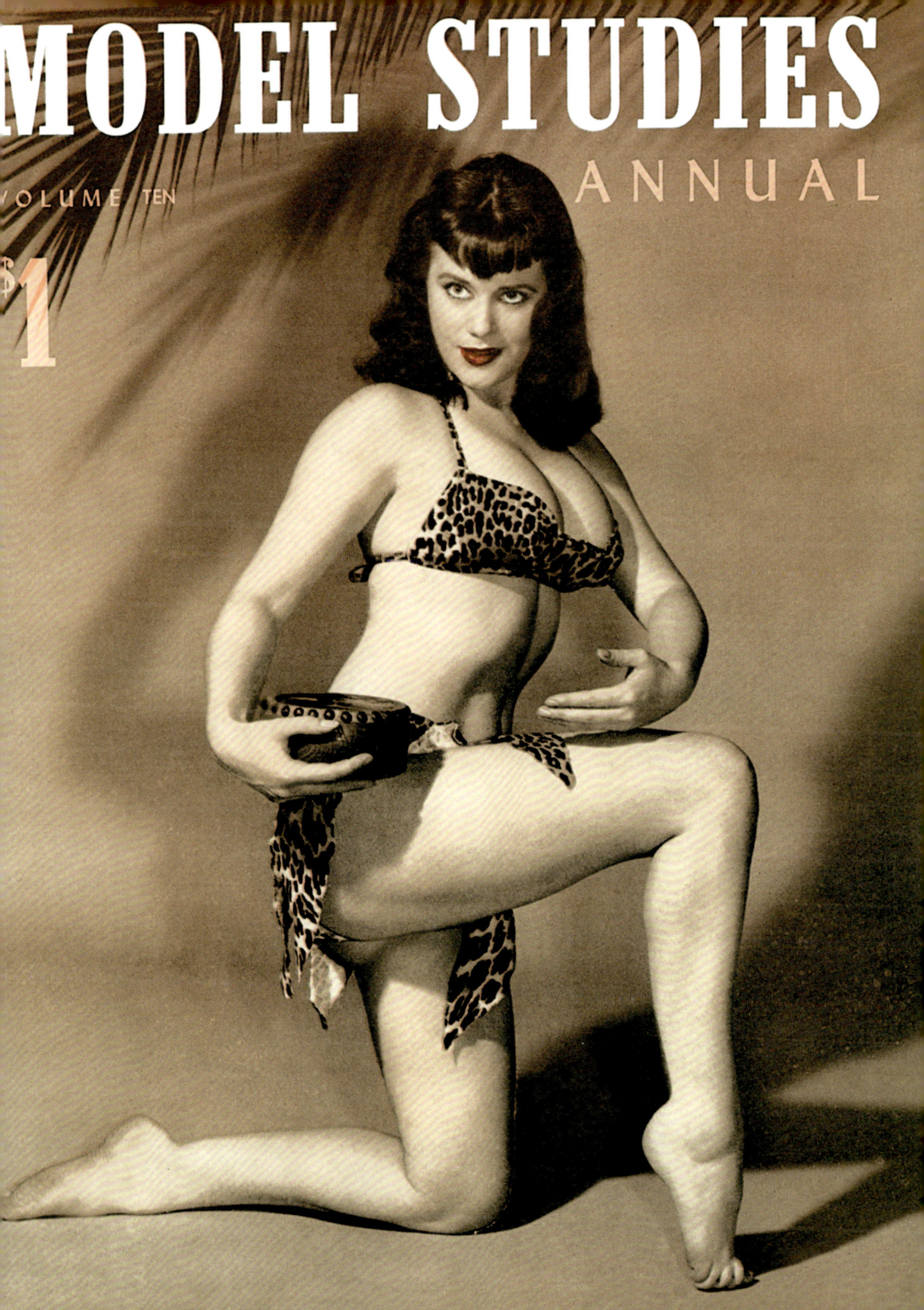
MODEL STUDIES
ANNUAL
VOLUME TEN
$1

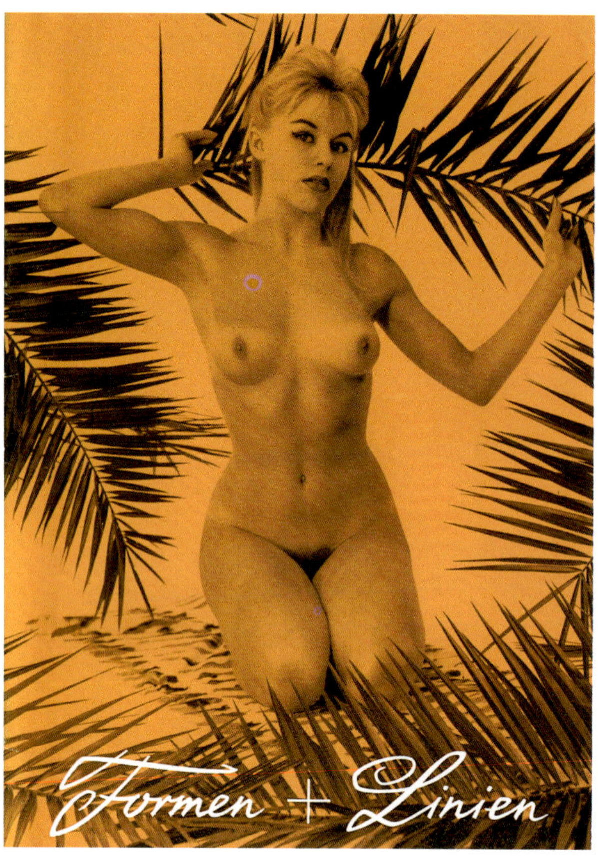

YEAR: **1963**. TITLE: **Formen + Linien**. COUNTRY: **Germany**.

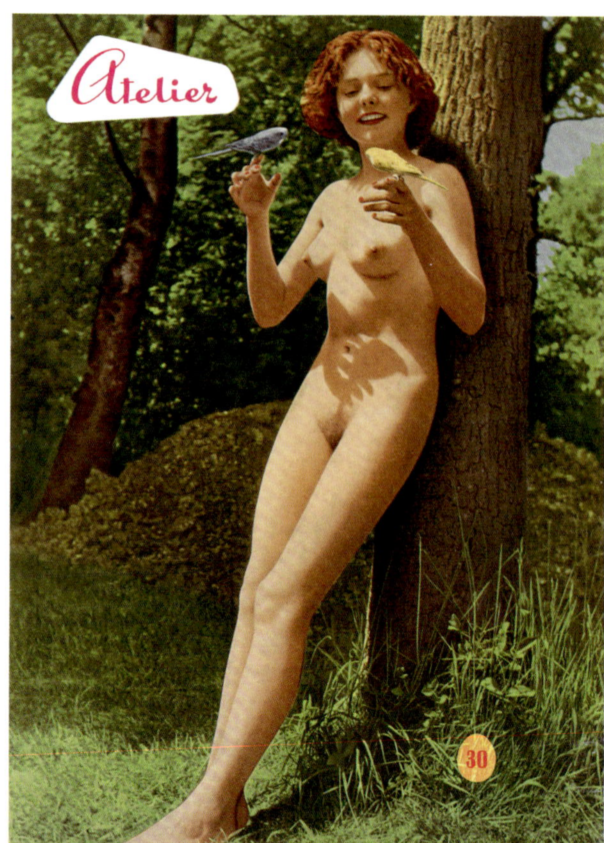

YEAR: **1958**. TITLE: **Atelier**. COUNTRY: **Germany**.

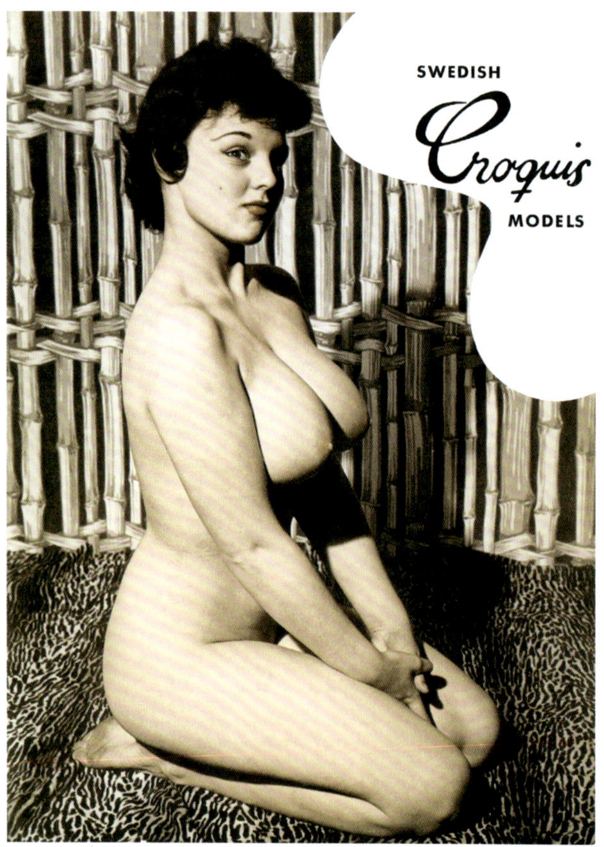

YEAR: **1950s**. TITLE: **Swedish Croquis Models**. COUNTRY: **Sweden**.

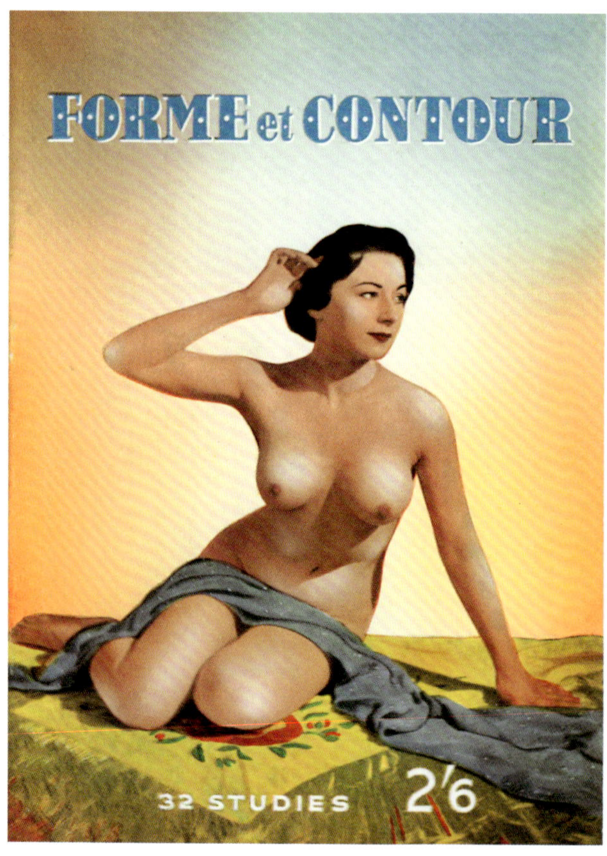

YEAR: **1950**. TITLE: **Forme et contour**. COUNTRY: **England**.

YEAR: **1958**. TITLE: **Atelier**.
COUNTRY: **Germany**.

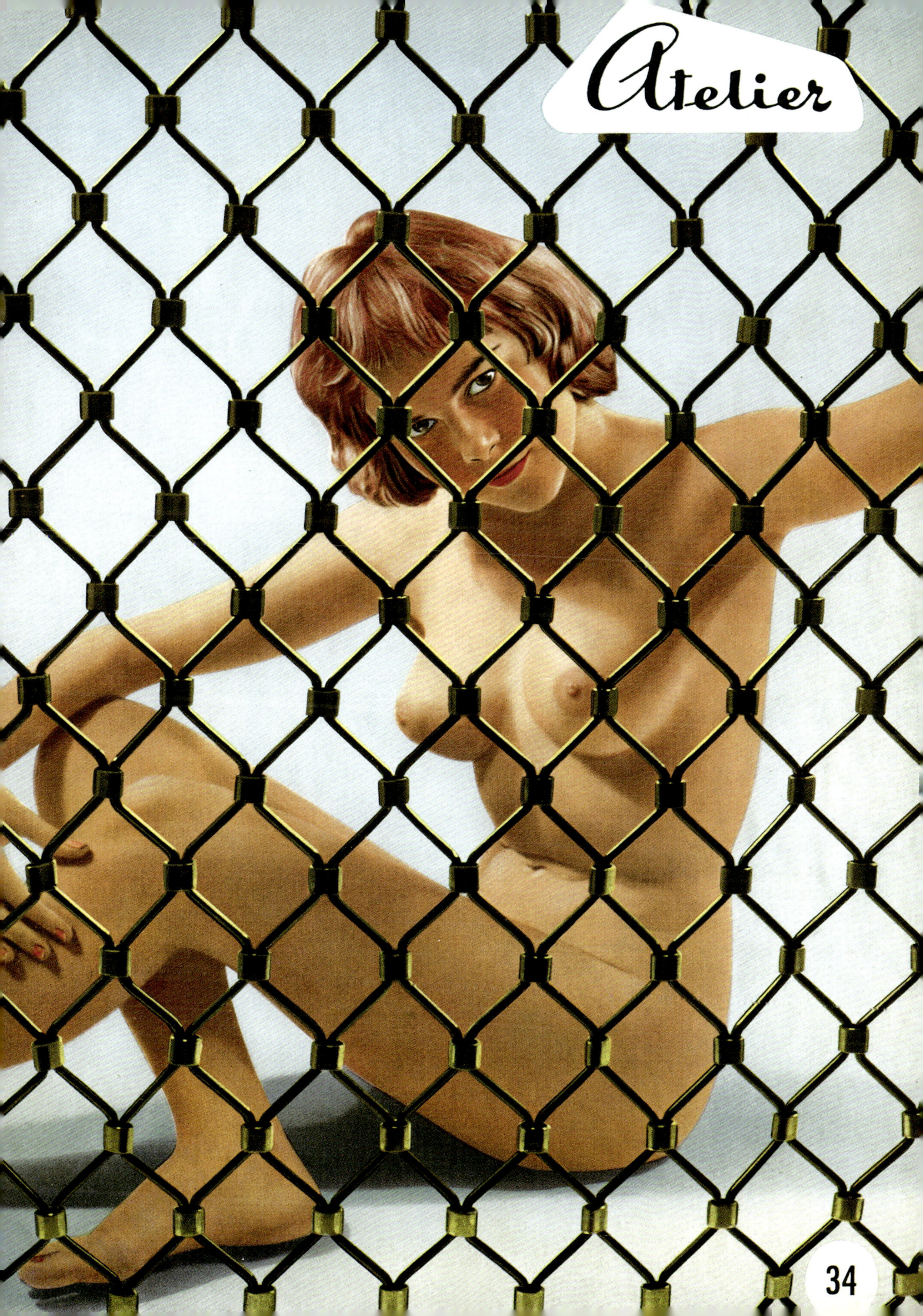
Atelier
34

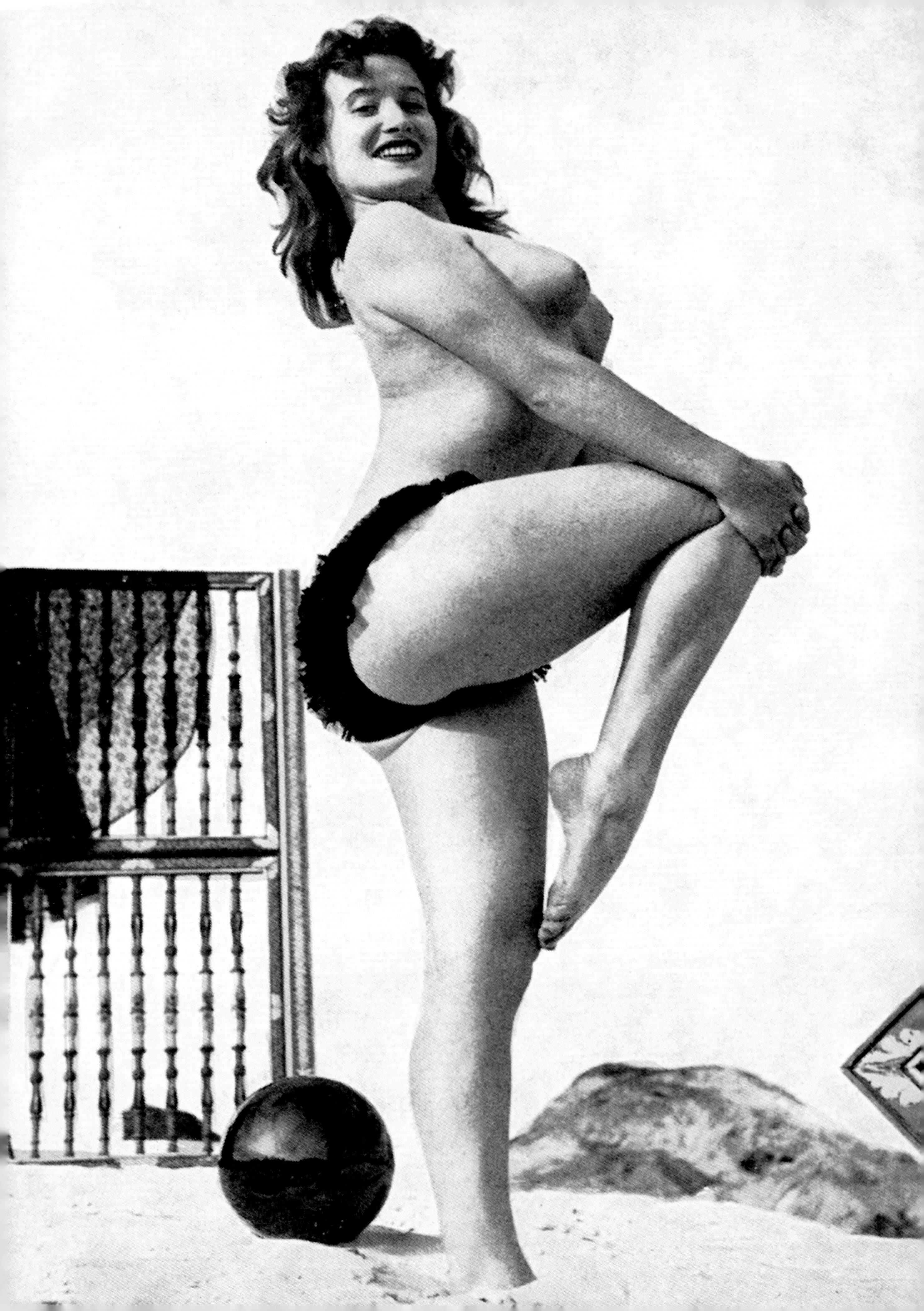

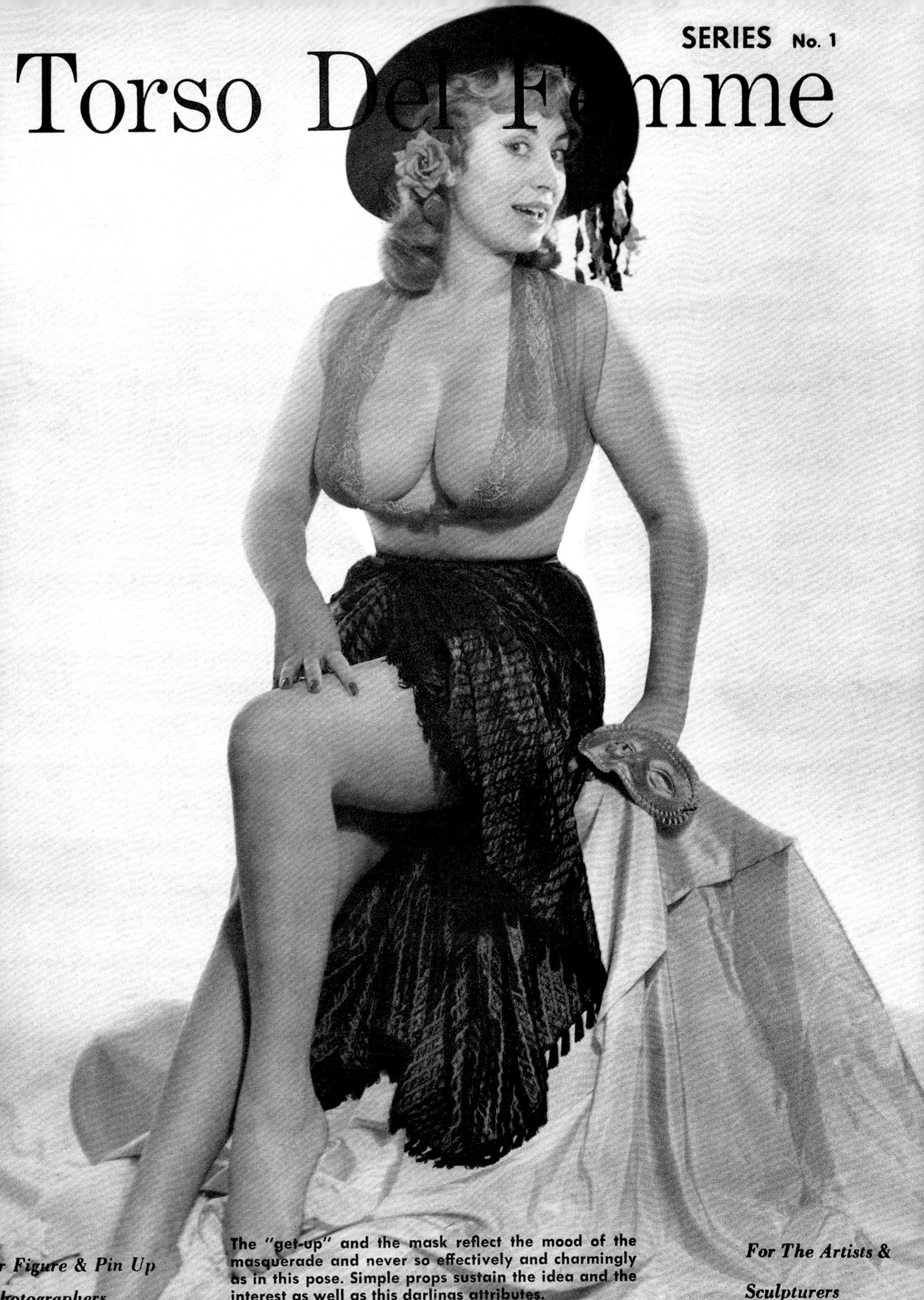

SERIES No. 1
Torso Del Femme
r Figure & Pin Up
hotographers
The "get-up" and the mask reflect the mood of the masquerade and never so effectively and charmingly as in this pose. Simple props sustain the idea and the interest as well as this darlings attributes.
For The Artists &
Sculpturers

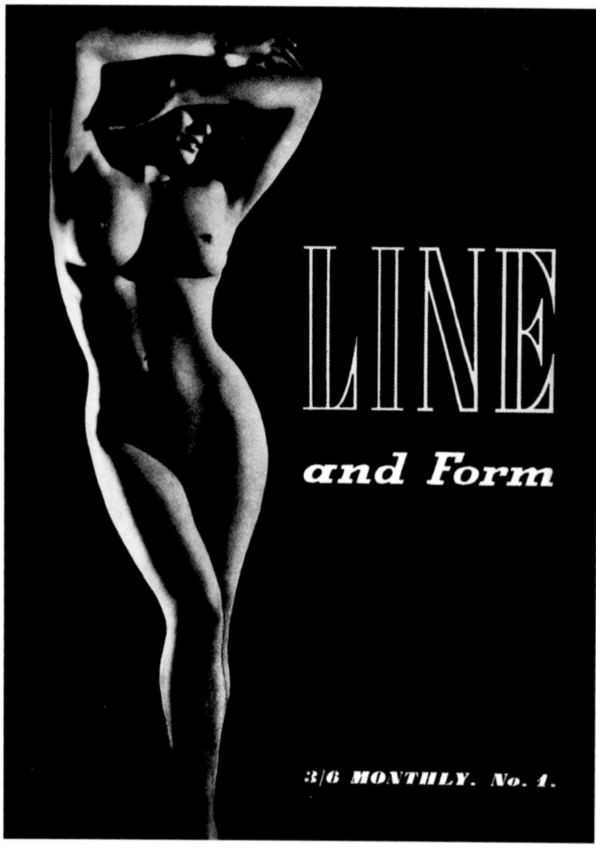

Year: **1950s**. Title: **Line and Form**. Country: **England**.

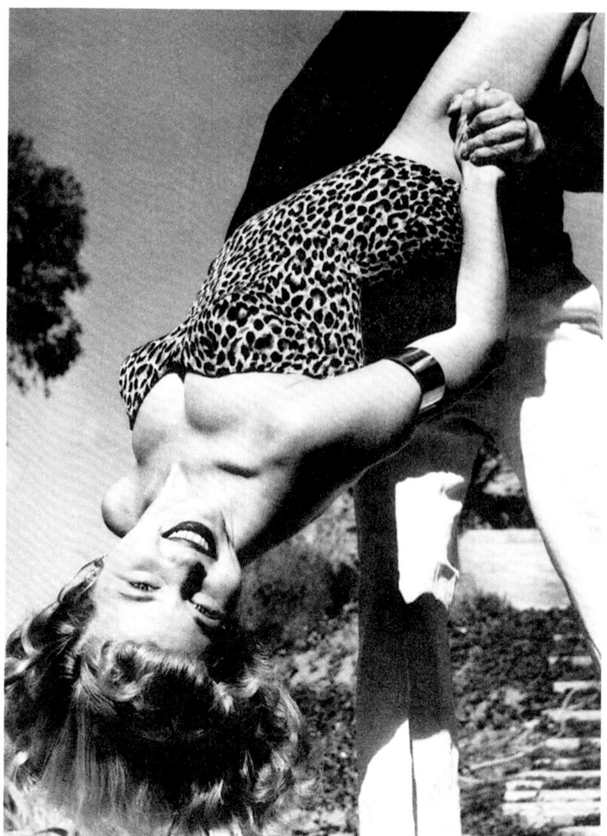

Year: **1963**. Title: **Formen + Linien**. Country: **Germany**.

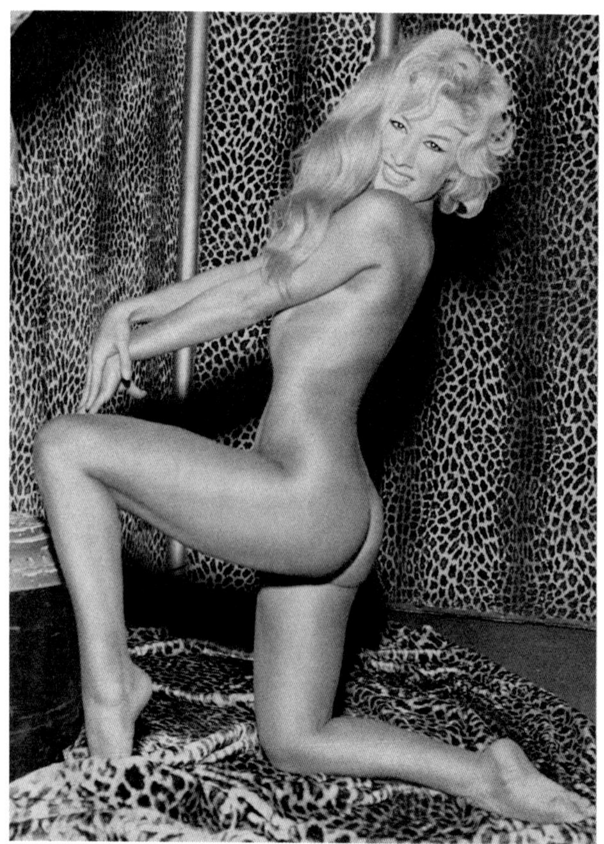

Year: **1963**. Title: **Formen + Linien**. Country: **Germany**.

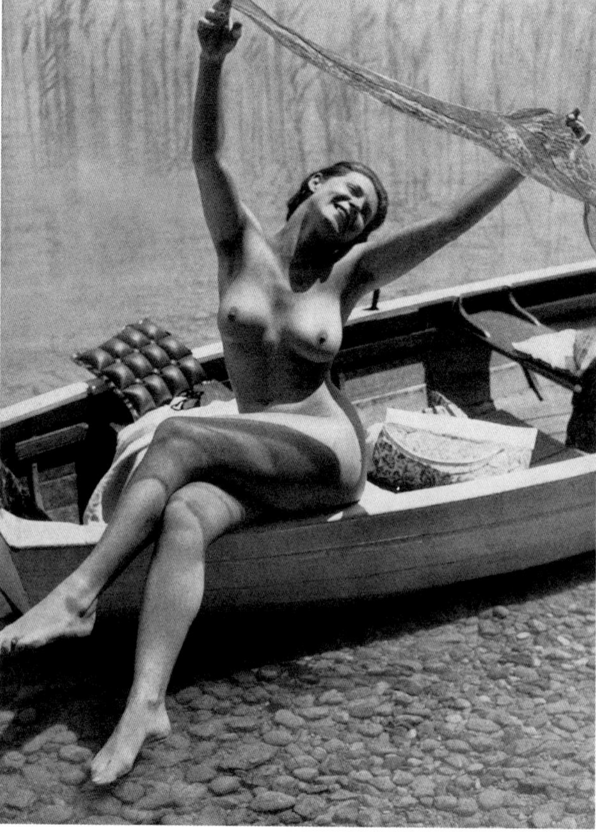

Year: **1958**. Title: **Atelier**. Country: **Germany**.

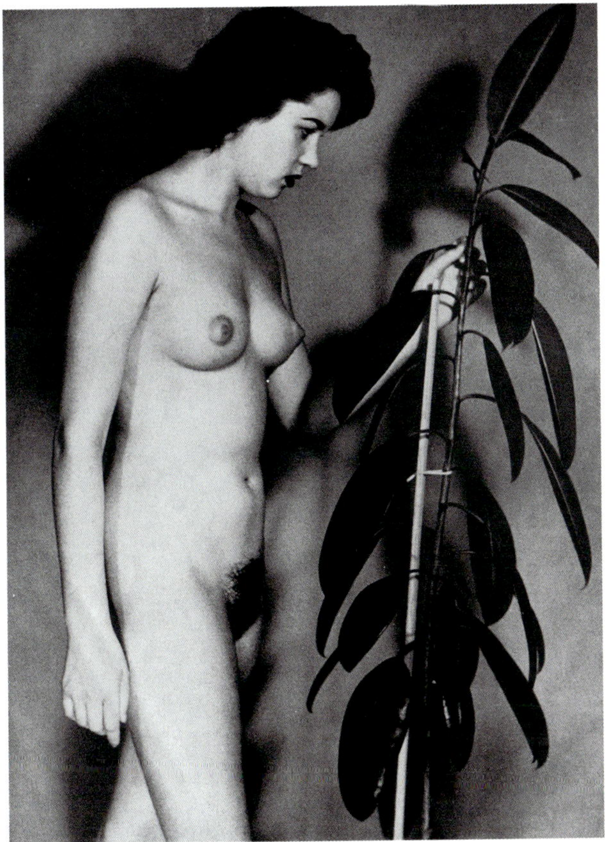

Year: **1950s**. Title: **Visuell**. Country: **Sweden**.

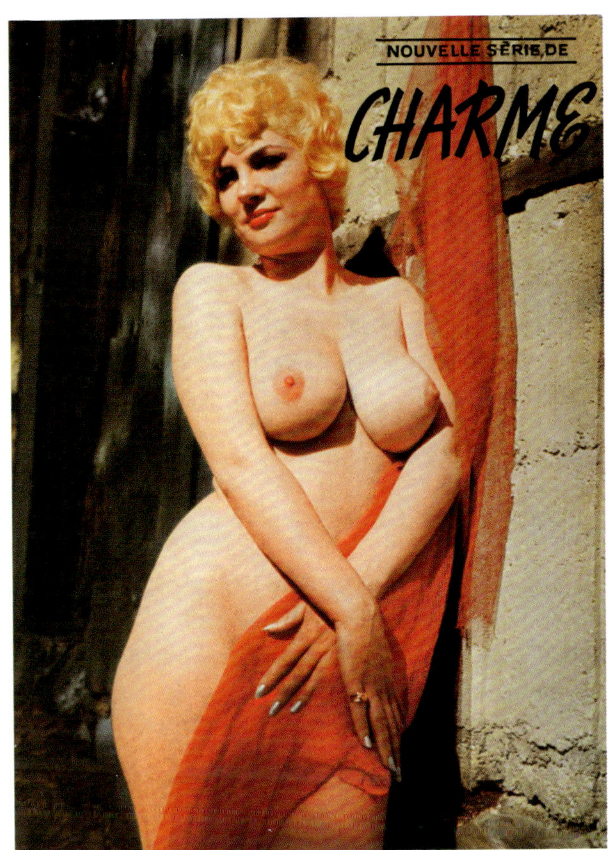

Year: **1950s**. Title: **Charme**. Country: **Denmark**.

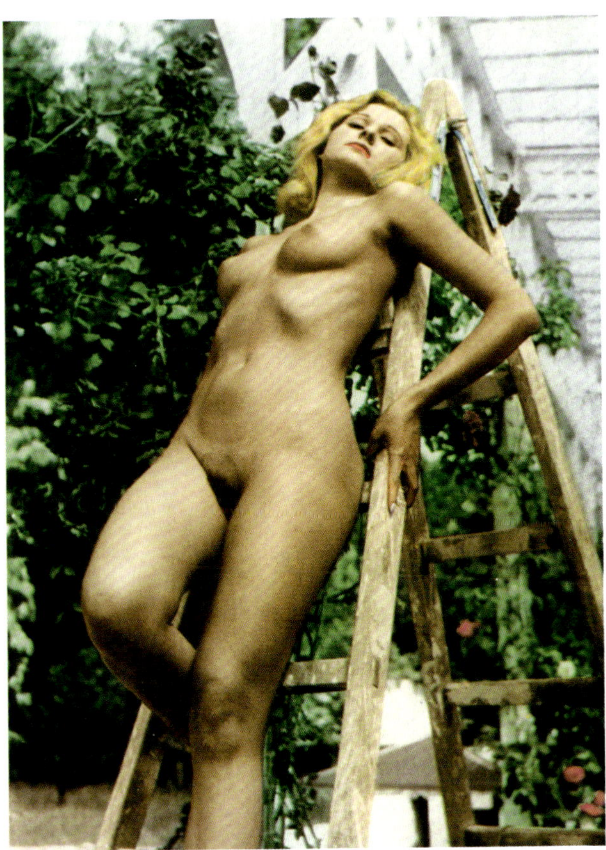

Year: **1950s**. Title: **Beaute**. Country: **Denmark**.

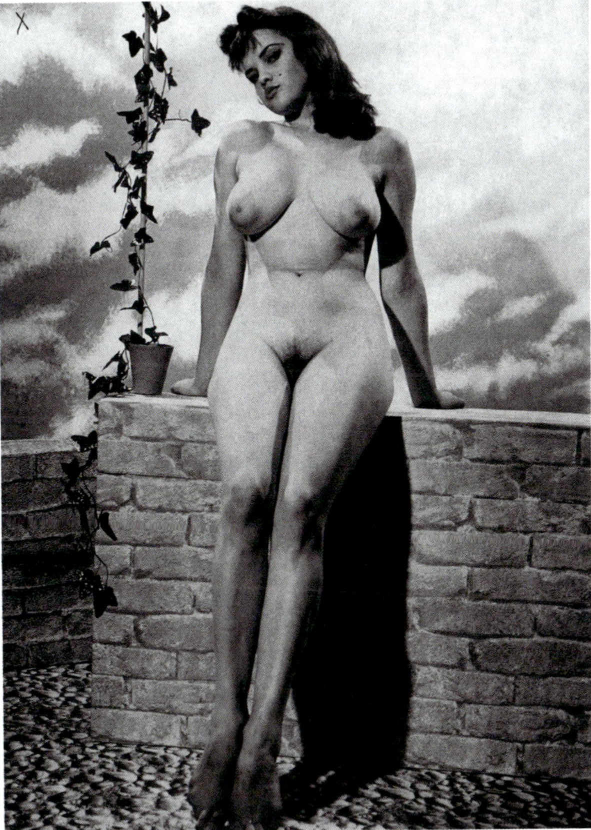

Year: **1950s**. Title: **Swedish Croquis Models**. Country: **Sweden**.

C

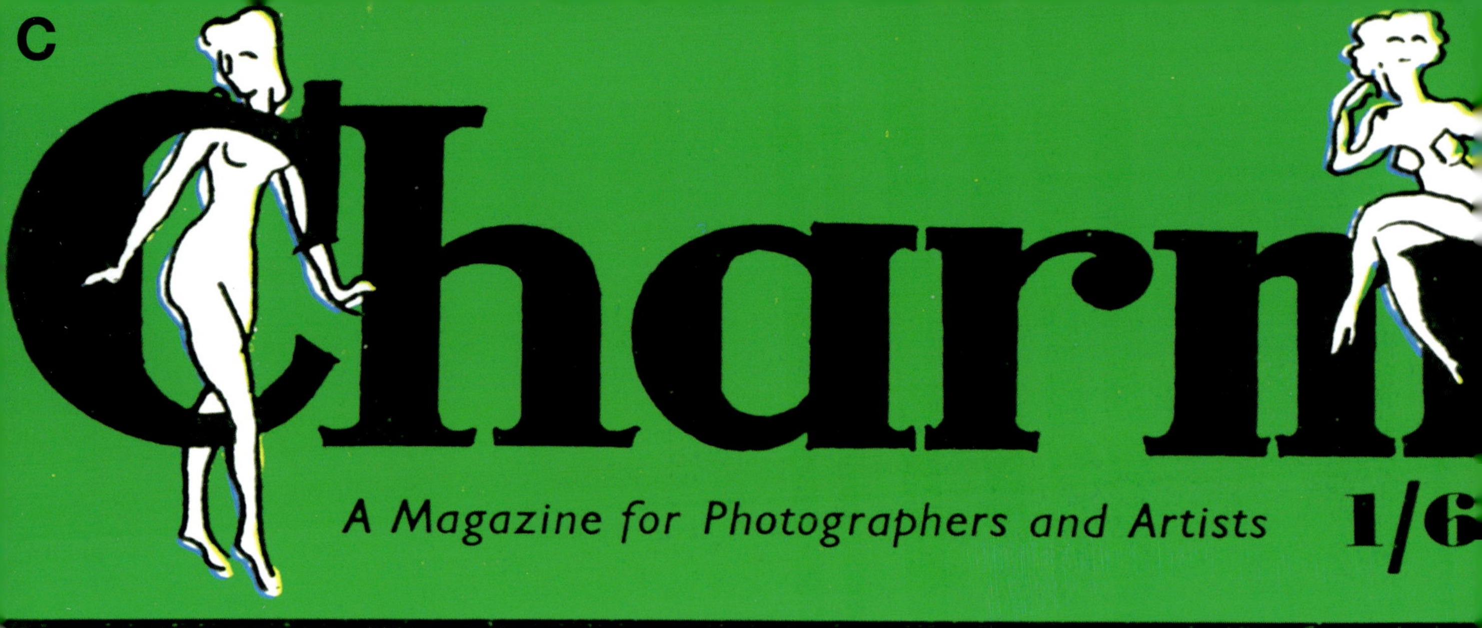

FOCUS ON BEAUTY

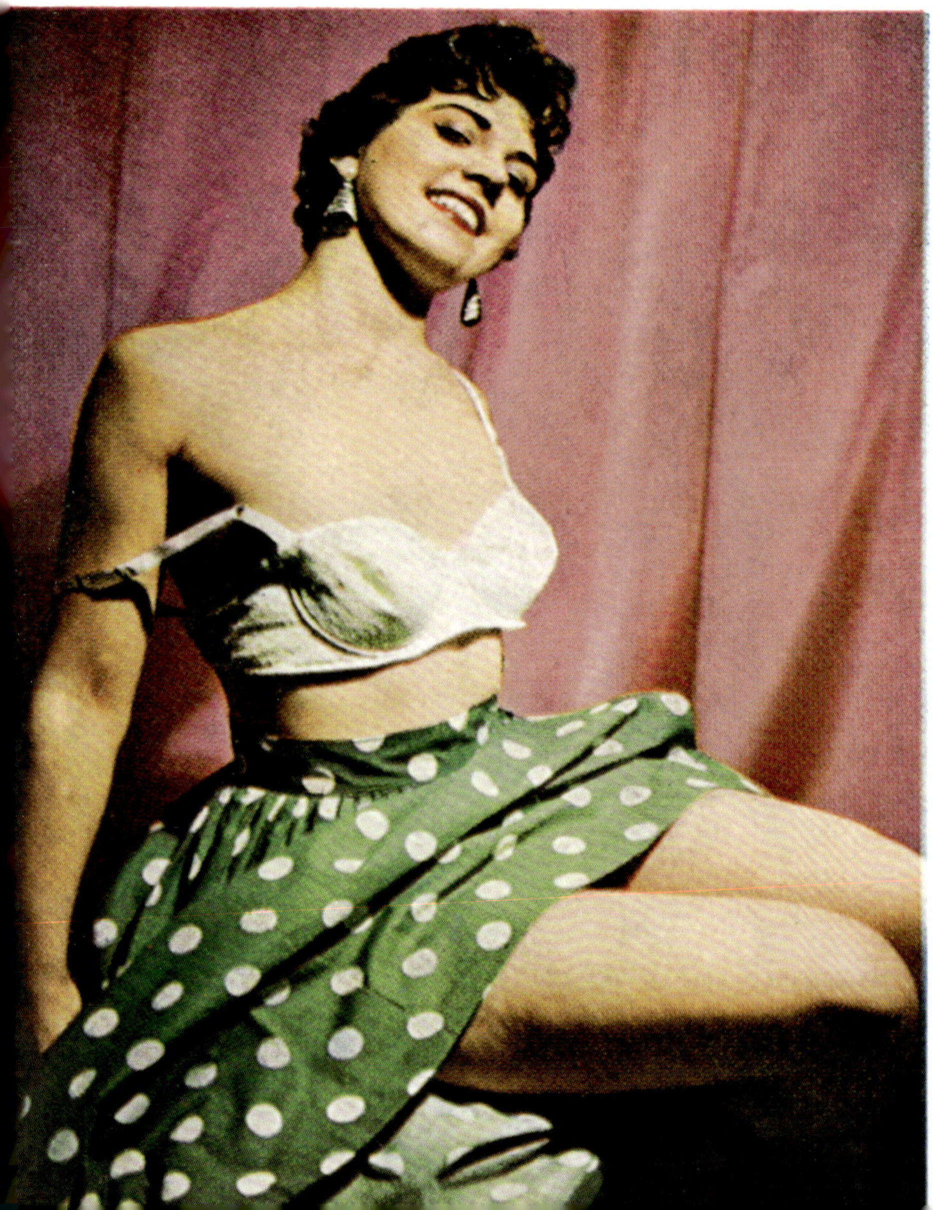

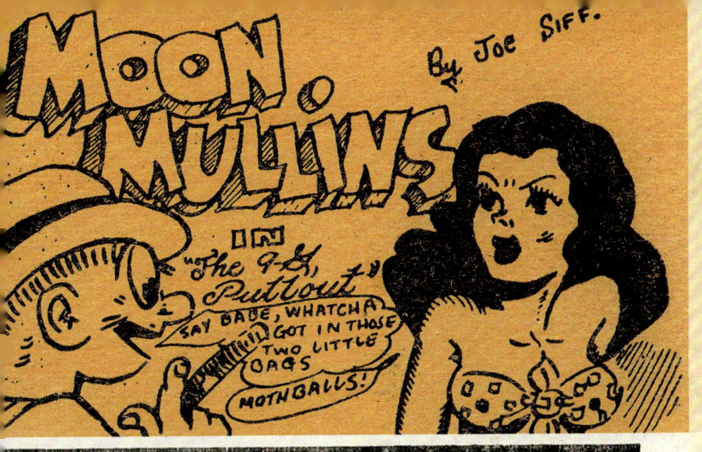
MOON MULLINS
By Joe Siff.
in
SAY BABE, WHATCHA GOT IN THOSE TWO LITTLE BAGS
MOTHBALLS!

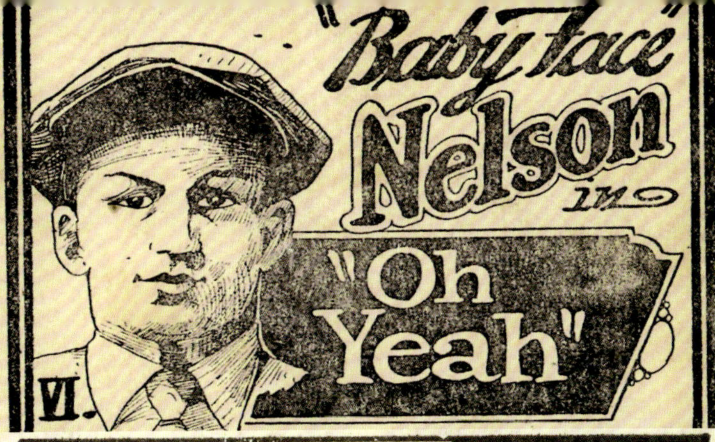
"Baby Face" Nelson in
"Oh Yeah"
VI.

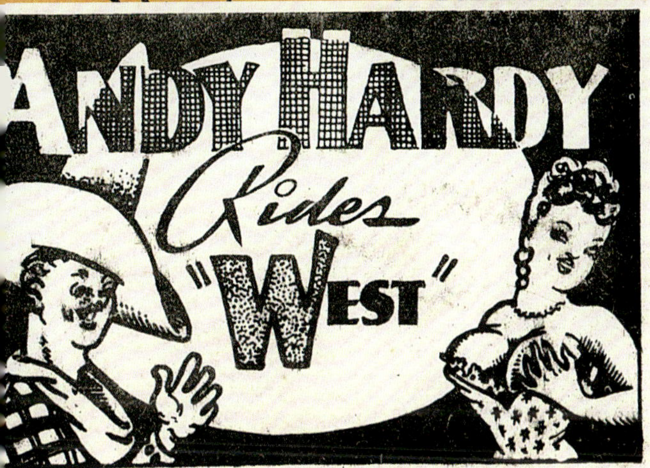
ANDY HARDY
Rides
"WEST"

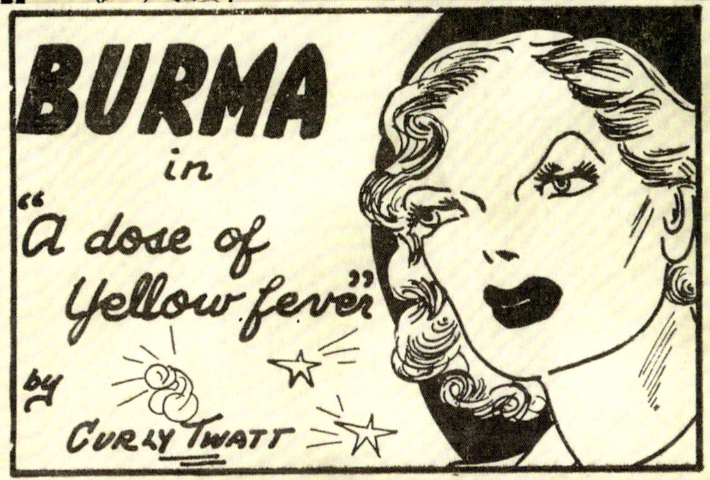
BURMA
in
"A dose of yellow fever"
by
CURLY TWATT

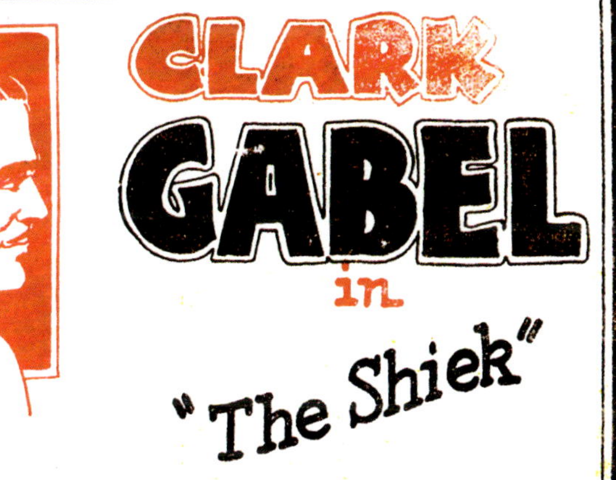
CLARK
GABEL
in
"The Shiek"

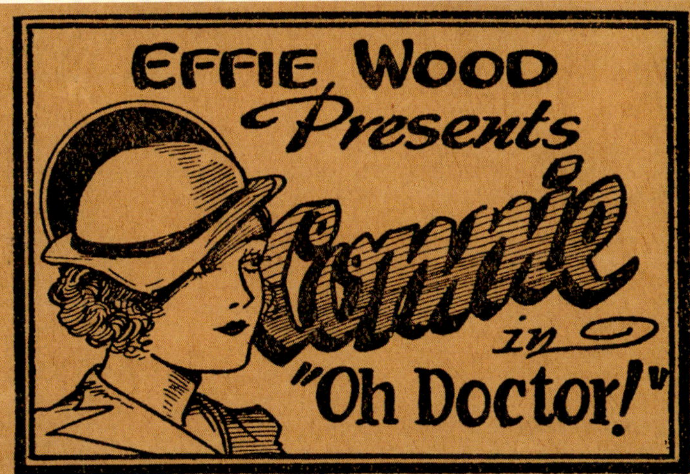
EFFIE WOOD
Presents
Connie
in
"Oh Doctor!"

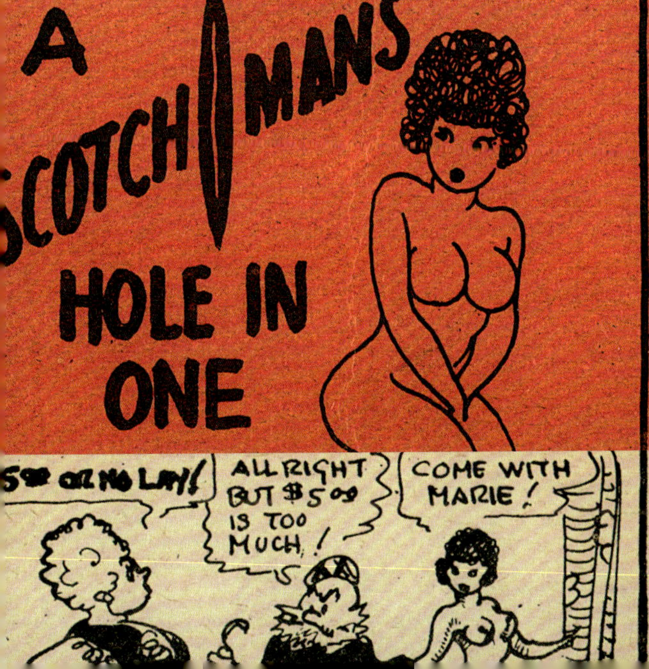
A SCOTCHMANS HOLE IN ONE
5.00 OR NO LAY!
ALLRIGHT BUT $5.00 IS TOO MUCH!
COME WITH MARIE!

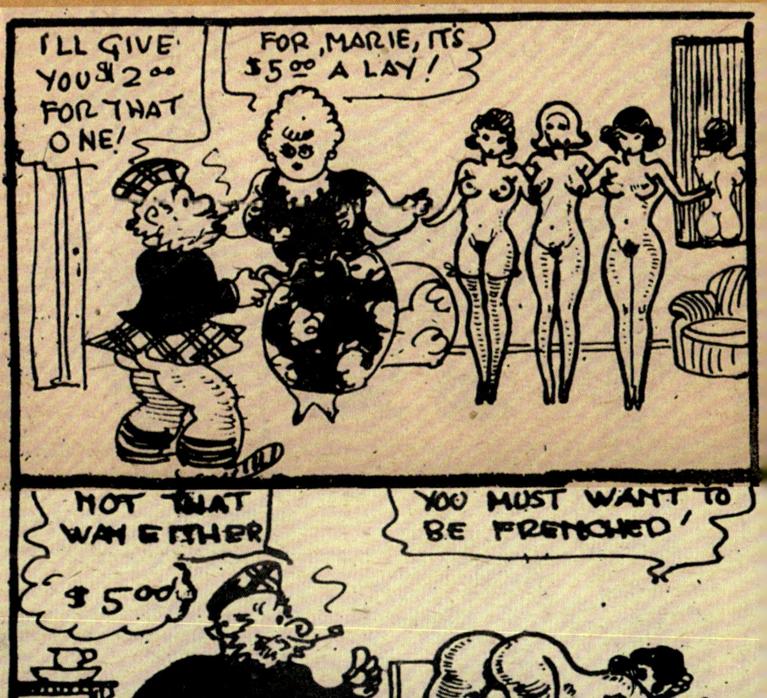
I'LL GIVE YOU $2.00 FOR THAT ONE!
FOR MARIE, IT'S $5.00 A LAY!
NOT THAT WAY EITHER
$5.00
YOU MUST WANT TO BE FRENCHED!

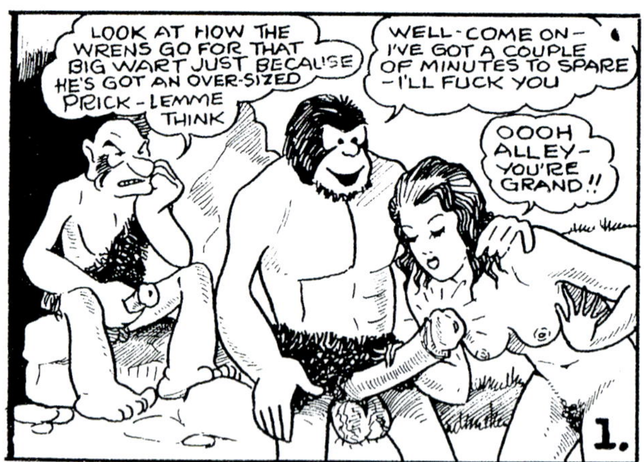

YEAR: **1930s**. TITLE: **Foozy Decoy**. COUNTRY: **USA**.

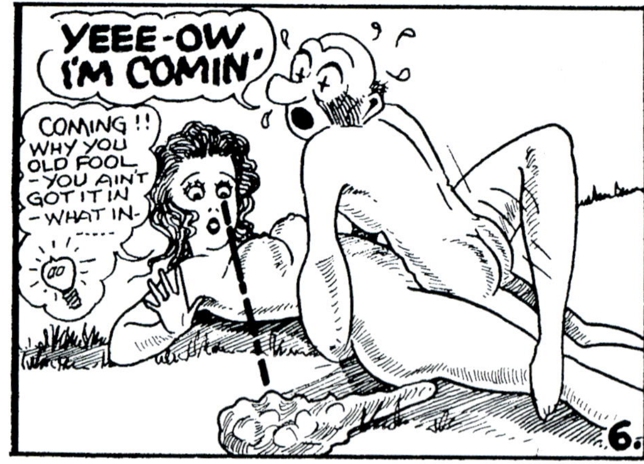

YEAR: **1930s**. TITLE: **Foozy Decoy**. COUNTRY: **USA**.

most widely published artist was Doc Rankin, who did many of the most popular Bibles of the early 1930s.

For those who knew where to look the little comics could be found in most towns and cities throughout the country. Newsstands, cigar stores, second-hand bookstores, bars, and burlesque houses were likely sources. The traveling salesmen of dirty joke fame were also purveyors of the cartoon books that featured them. Like a dirty joke, comics were passed along. Half the readers didn't know where to buy them—they were found in "your father's sock drawer" or passed along by "a friend of a friend."

The Bibles weren't just about sex and jokes. They were a form of rebellion.

One reason they're so rare today is that many were literally read to pieces.

The publishers of erotic books and playing cards also published the sex

Comiczeichner der Zeitung auch dieses Heftchen produziert hätte. Sie erlaubten dem Leser auch die Fantasien verwirklicht zu sehen, die von den Originalcomics inspiriert waren, aber sonst nie gezeigt wurden. Eine Datierungshilfe für Tijuana Bibles bieten auch die Anzeigen in den Spicy-Pulps, mit denen sie bereits ab 1929 beworben wurden. Auch wenn die Kunden selten das bekamen, wofür sie bezahlt hatten, zeigte doch ihre Vertrautheit mit den Titeln, dass sie wussten, was sie erwartete.

Ein Vorläufer der Bibles waren die *Broadway Brevities* des Witzblattverlegers Louis Shomer. Die Zeichner dieser Witzhefte waren vermutlich die ersten Zeichner von Tijuana Bibles.

Der bekannteste dieser Künstler ist heute Wesley Morse, berühmt durch

bien rire de voir les personnages des bandes dessinées de leurs quotidiens habituels s'adonner à toutes sortes d'ébats, prenant soudain une vie propre. Beaucoup devaient d'ailleurs penser que ces grivoiseries étaient dessinées par les vrais créateurs des personnages. Elles permettaient de poursuivre les fantasmes inspirés par la presse populaire, mais jamais montrés.

On peut également dater ces bibles grâce à leurs publicités placées dans les magazines pulp de la série des Spicys, qui commencèrent à paraître dès 1929. Bien que les acheteurs potentiels aient rarement obtenu les numéros qu'ils avaient commandés, leur familiarité avec leurs titres indiquent qu'ils savaient à quoi s'attendre.

Les bibles eurent, entre autres précurseurs, les *Broadway Brevities* (« Brèves de Broadway ») de l'éditeur de livres de blagues Louis Shomer. Les premiers auteurs de ces bandes dessinées pornographiques étaient probablement des illustrateurs de magazines humoristiques.

Aujourd'hui, l'auteur de ces bibles le plus célèbre est Wesley Morse, plus connu

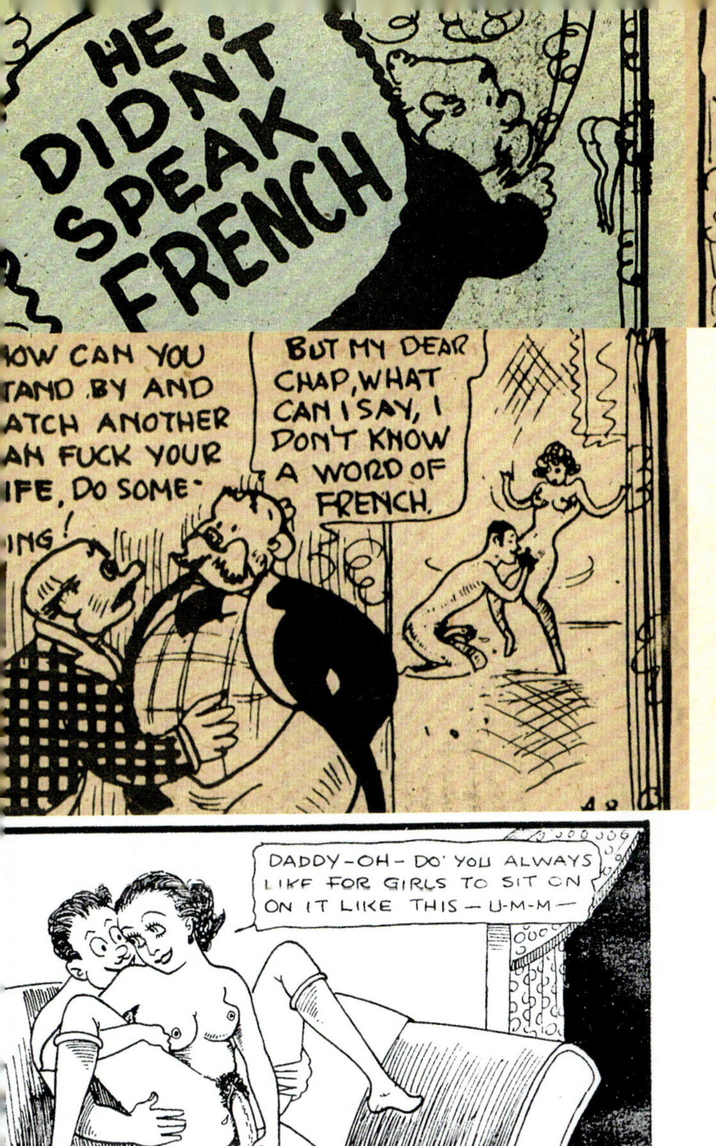

HE DIDN'T SPEAK FRENCH
OW CAN YOU TAND BY AND ATCH ANOTHER AN FUCK YOUR IFE, DO SOME- ING!
BUT MY DEAR CHAP, WHAT CAN I SAY, I DON'T KNOW A WORD OF FRENCH.

AH, A BALLY FRENCHMEN
ZE PUSSY IS SWEET MADAME

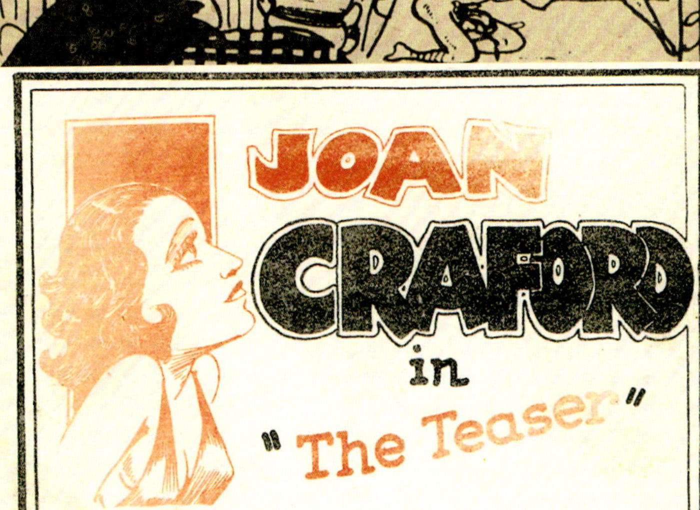

JOAN CRAFORD
in
"The Teaser"

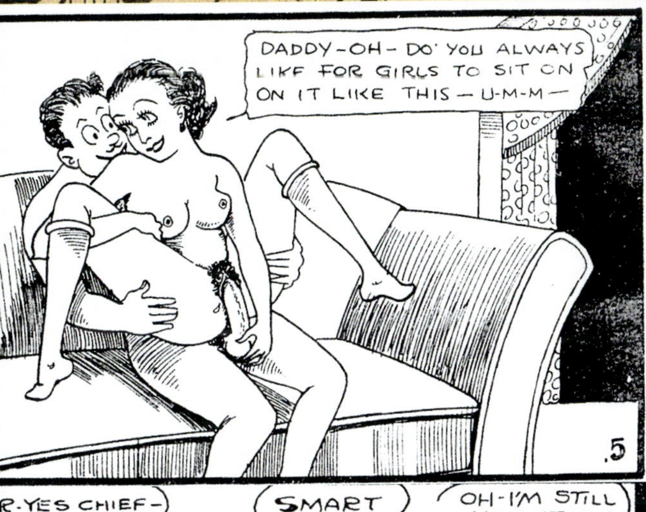

DADDY-OH- DO YOU ALWAYS LIKE FOR GIRLS TO SIT ON ON IT LIKE THIS— U-M-M—
5

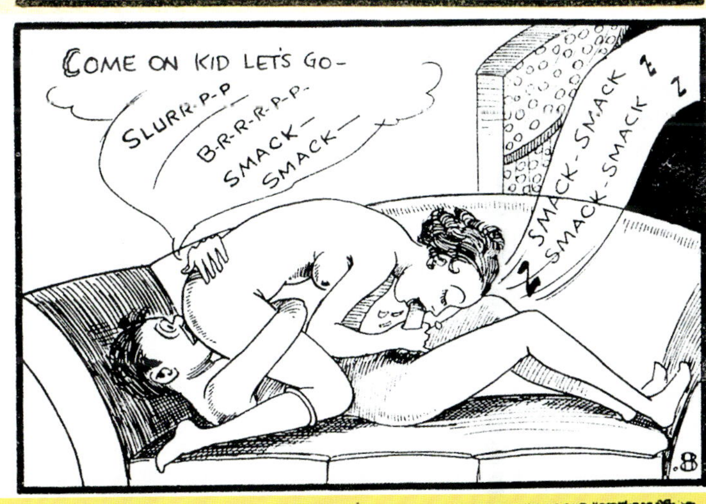

COME ON KID LET'S GO-
SLURR-P-P
B-R-R-R-P-P-
SMACK—
SMACK—
SMACK-SMACK
SMACK-SMACK
8

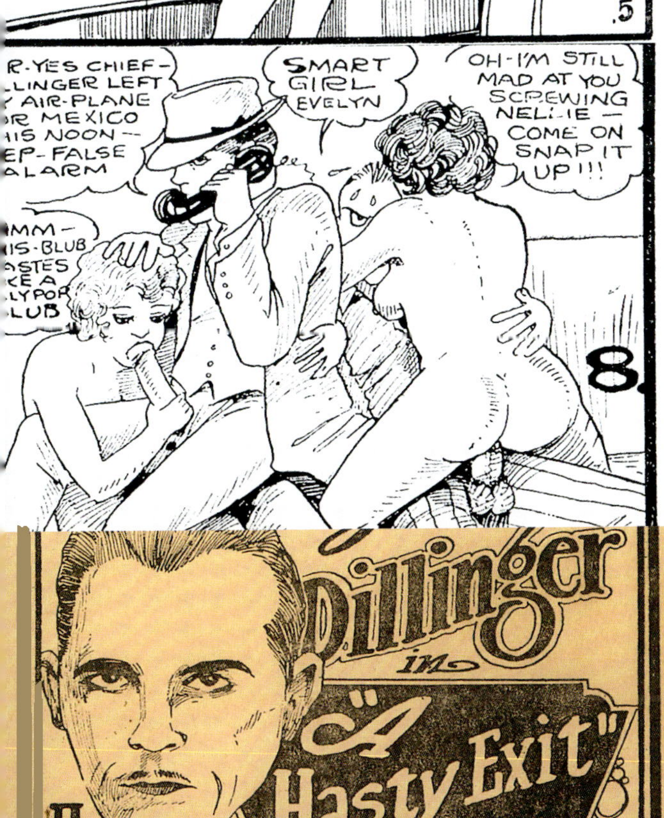

R-YES CHIEF- LINGER LEFT AIR-PLANE R MEXICO HIS NOON-- EP-FALSE ALARM
SMART GIRL EVELYN
OH-I'M STILL MAD AT YOU SCREWING NELLIE — COME ON SNAP IT UP!!!
MM- IS-BLUB OSTES KE A LYPOP LUB
8.
Dillinger
in
"A Hasty Exit"
II.

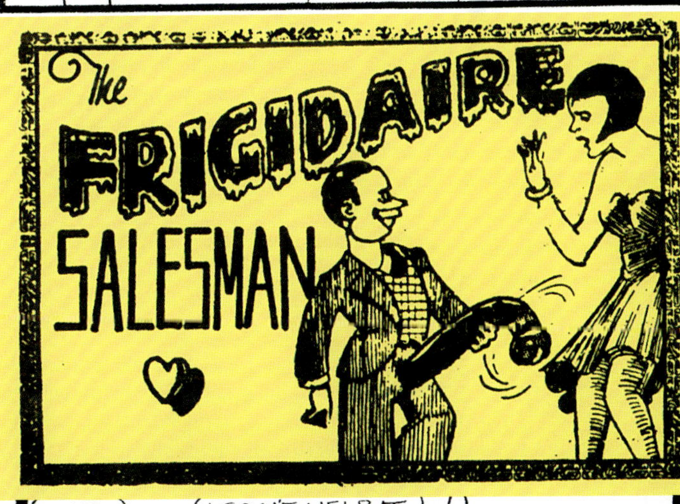

The FRIGIDAIRE SALESMAN

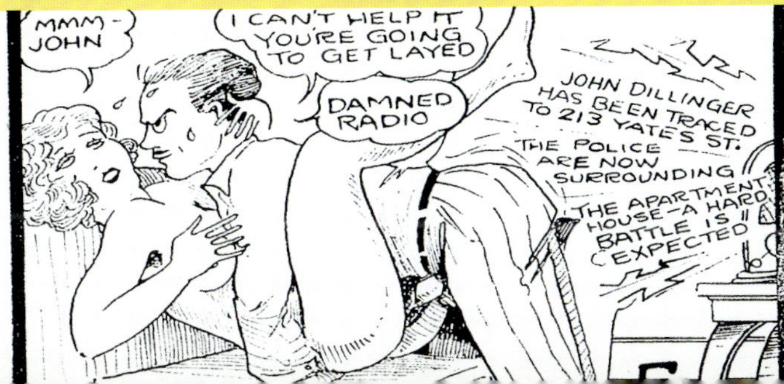

MMM- JOHN
I CAN'T HELP IT YOU'RE GOING TO GET LAYED
DAMNED RADIO
JOHN DILLINGER HAS BEEN TRACED TO 213 YATES ST. THE POLICE ARE NOW SURROUNDING THE APARTMENT HOUSE—A HARD BATTLE IS EXPECTED

Year: **1930s**. Title: **Phil Fumble**. Country: **USA**.

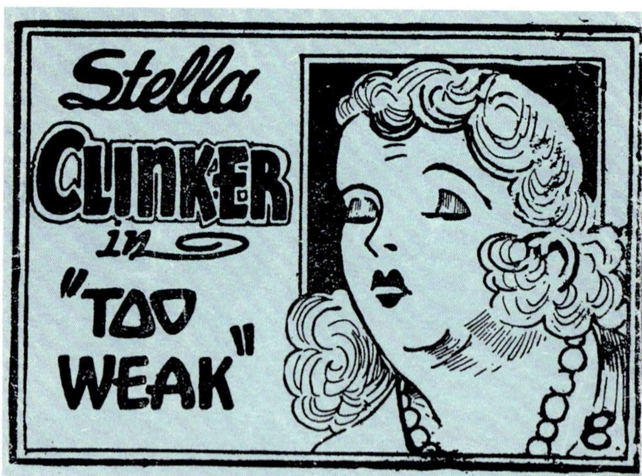

Year: **1930s**. Title: **Stella Clinker**. Country: **USA**.

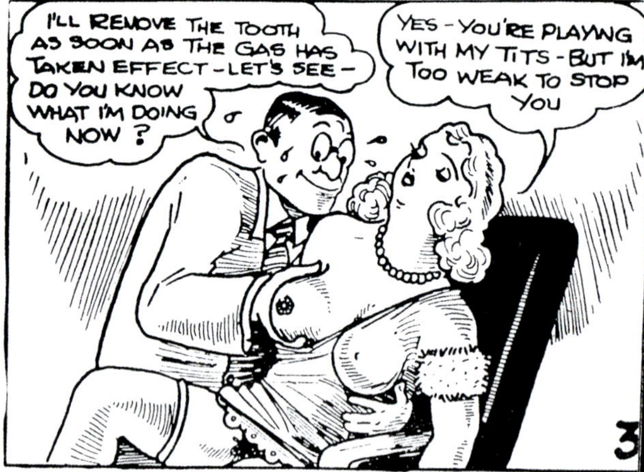

Year: **1930s**. Title: **Stella Clinker**. Country: **USA**.

comics: David and Jacob Brotman, Jacob and I. R. Brussel, Alex Field, and Samuel and Max Roth—all printed and sold them to individual store owners and peddlers.

There were about 800 different original comics produced over thirty years, and at least as many reprints.

Some recall that organized crime was involved, but because they were easily pirated, there could be many sources for the same comic. There were about 800 different original comics produced over thirty years, and at least as many reprints. The desire for a quick buck led to many means of reproduction, from

seine Arbeit an dem äußerst populären Comic *Bazooka Joe*, in den Fünzigern. Der meistgedruckte Künstler war Doc Rankin, der zahlreiche der populärsten Bibles der Dreißiger gezeichnet hat.

Für Eingeweihte waren diese kleinen Comics in den meisten Städten des Landes leicht zu finden. Es gab sie an Zeitungsständen, in Tabakgeschäften, Second-Hand-Läden, Bars und Varieté-Theatern. Die für ihre schmutzigen Witze bekannten Handlungsreisenden lieferten auch die Comichefte, in denen sie nachzulesen waren. Wie ein schmutziger Witz wurden auch diese Heftchen weitergegeben. Gut die Hälfte der Leser wusste gar nicht, wo man sie zu kaufen bekam – sie fanden sie "zwischen Vaters Socken" oder bekamen sie vom "Freund eines Freundes." Dass sie buchstäblich zerlesen wurden, ist einer der Gründe, warum sie heute so selten sind.

Auch Verleger erotischer Bücher und Spielkarten veröffentlichten Sex-Comics: David und Jacob Brotman, Jacob und I. R. Brussel, Alex Field und

pour son travail dans les années cinquante sur le « comics » le plus populaire de tous les temps *Bazooka Joe*. L'artiste le plus publié était Doc Ranklin, qui réalisa un grand nombre des bibles les plus prisées au début des années trente.

Ceux qui savaient où chercher ces petites bandes dessinées les dénichaient dans la plupart des villes des États-Unis. Les kiosques à journaux, les marchands de cigares, les librairies d'occasion, les bars et les cabarets étaient des sources probables. Les voyageurs de commerce, eux-mêmes objet de nombreuses plaisanteries salaces, vendaient également les bandes dessinées qui les montraient à l'œuvre.

Comme les blagues grivoises, les bibles se transmettaient. La moitié de leurs lecteurs ne savaient pas où les acheter. Ils les trouvaient dans le « tiroir à chaussettes de leur père », les obtenaient d'un ami d'un ami. Une des raisons pour lesquelles elles sont si rares est que la plupart ont été lues jusqu'à la dislocation complète.

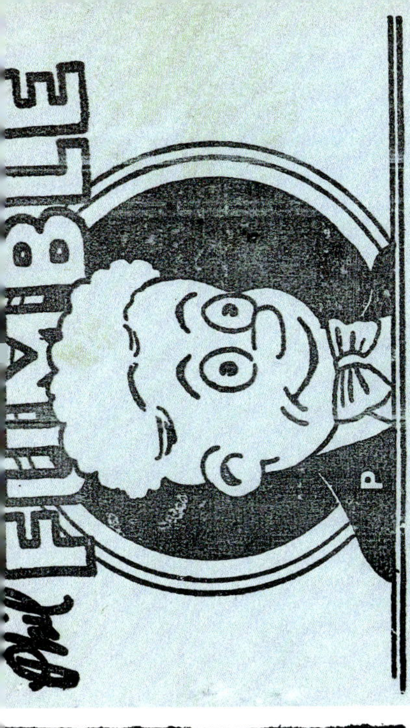
Phil FUMBLE

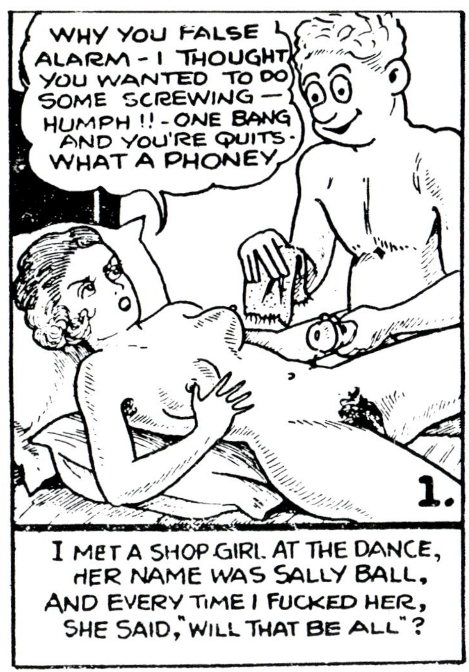
WHY YOU FALSE ALARM - I THOUGHT YOU WANTED TO DO SOME SCREWING — HUMPH !! - ONE BANG AND YOU'RE QUITS - WHAT A PHONEY
1.
I MET A SHOP GIRL AT THE DANCE,
HER NAME WAS SALLY BALL,
AND EVERY TIME I FUCKED HER,
SHE SAID, "WILL THAT BE ALL"?

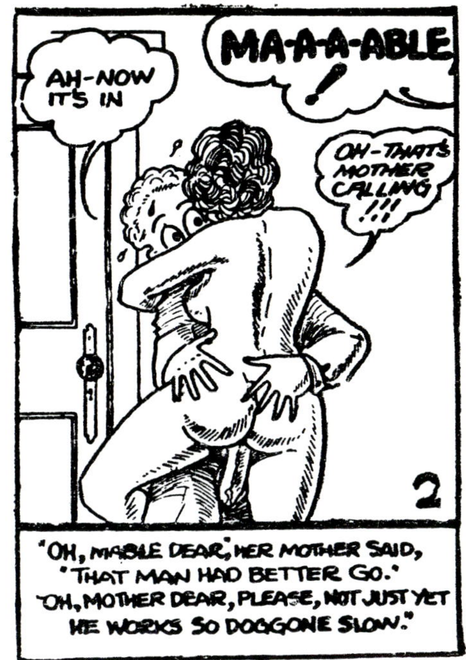
MA-A-A-ABLE !
AH-NOW IT'S IN
OH-THAT'S MOTHER CALLING !!!
2
"OH, MABLE DEAR," HER MOTHER SAID,
"THAT MAN HAD BETTER GO."
"OH, MOTHER DEAR, PLEASE, NOT JUST YET
HE WORKS SO DOGGONE SLOW."

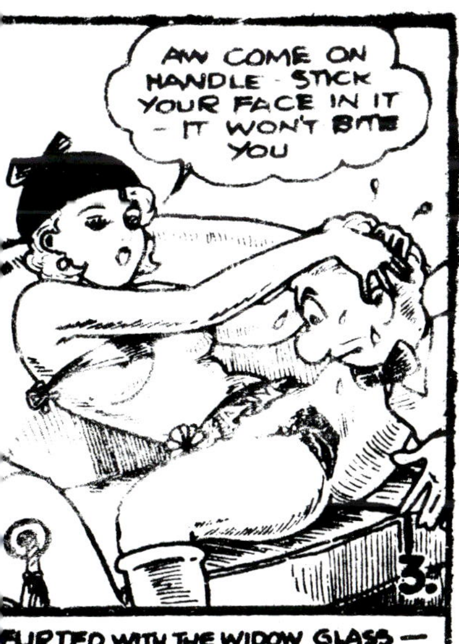
AW COME ON HANDLE - STICK YOUR FACE IN IT - IT WON'T BITE YOU
3.
FLIRTED WITH THE WIDOW GLASS —
BY GOSH, I LIVED TO RUE IT !
HE TRIED TO MAKE ME KISS HER AS
HER HUSBAND USED TO DO IT.

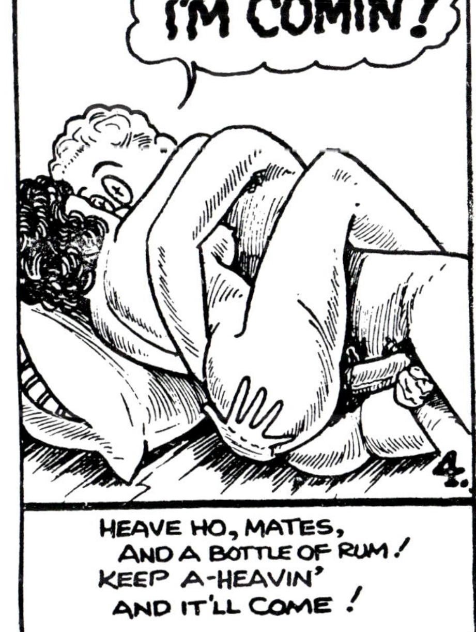
I'M COMIN'!
4.
HEAVE HO, MATES,
AND A BOTTLE OF RUM !
KEEP A-HEAVIN'
AND IT'LL COME !

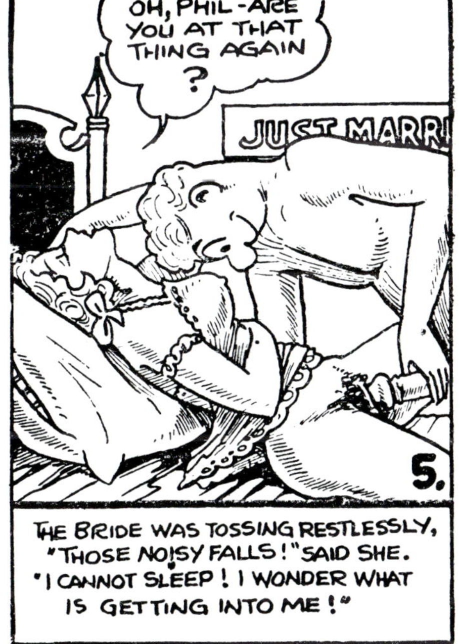
OH, PHIL - ARE YOU AT THAT THING AGAIN ?
JUST MARRI
5.
THE BRIDE WAS TOSSING RESTLESSLY,
"THOSE NOISY FALLS!" SAID SHE.
"I CANNOT SLEEP! I WONDER WHAT
IS GETTING INTO ME!"

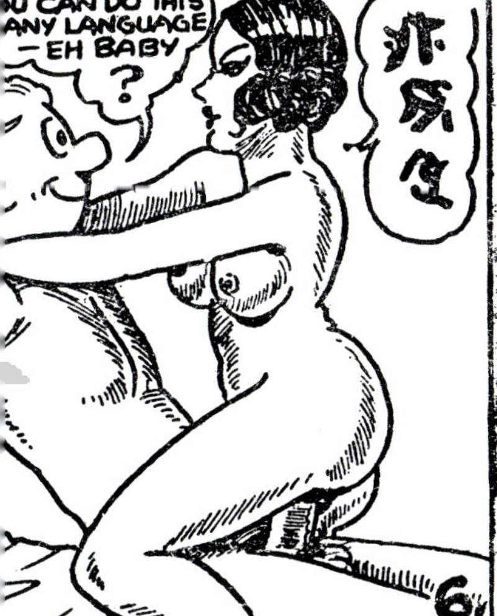
U CAN DO THIS ANY LANGUAGE - EH BABY ?
6.
DRINK A TOAST TO
CHINESE MAMIE —
OLIVE-SKINNED, BUT
ALLEE SAMEE.

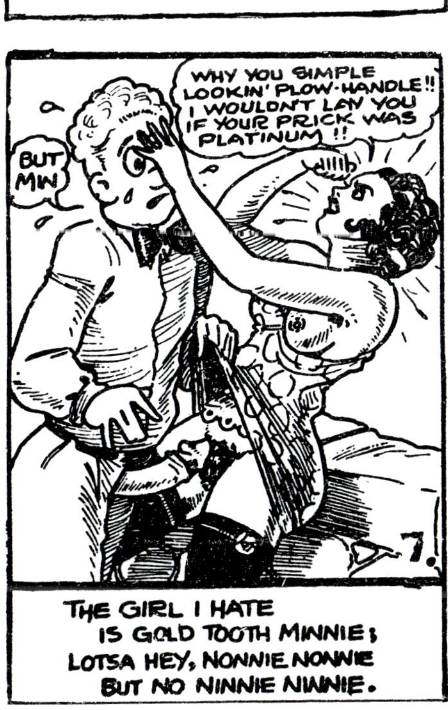
WHY YOU SIMPLE LOOKIN' PLOW-HANDLE!! I WOULDN'T LAY YOU IF YOUR PRICK WAS PLATINUM !!
BUT MIN
7.
THE GIRL I HATE
IS GOLD TOOTH MINNIE;
LOTSA HEY, NONNIE NONNIE
BUT NO NINNIE NINNIE.

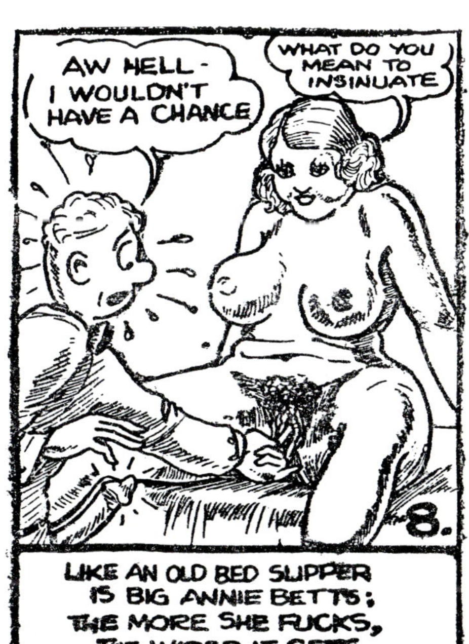
AW HELL - I WOULDN'T HAVE A CHANCE
WHAT DO YOU MEAN TO INSINUATE
8.
LIKE AN OLD BED SLIPPER
IS BIG ANNIE BETTS;
THE MORE SHE FUCKS,
THE WIDER IT GETS.

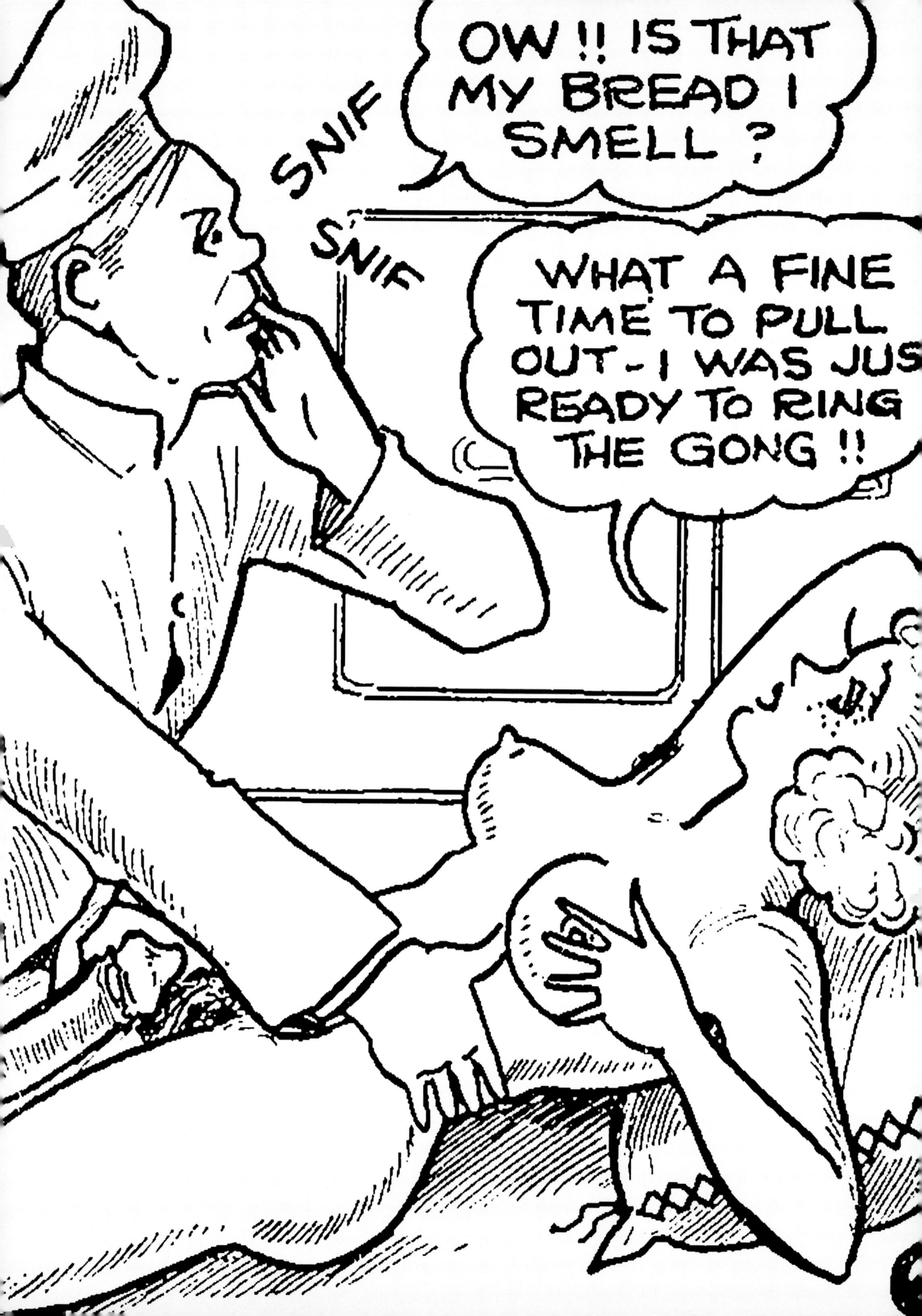

SNIF
SNIF
OW !! IS THAT MY BREAD I SMELL ?
WHAT A FINE TIME TO PULL OUT - I WAS JUS READY TO RING THE GONG !!

Year: **1930s**. Title: **Maggie**. Country: **USA**.

Pornography is one of the most restricted of the literary arts, I was even about to say one of the purest.

—Clifton Fadiman, Editor-in-Chief, Simon & Schuster, 1930s

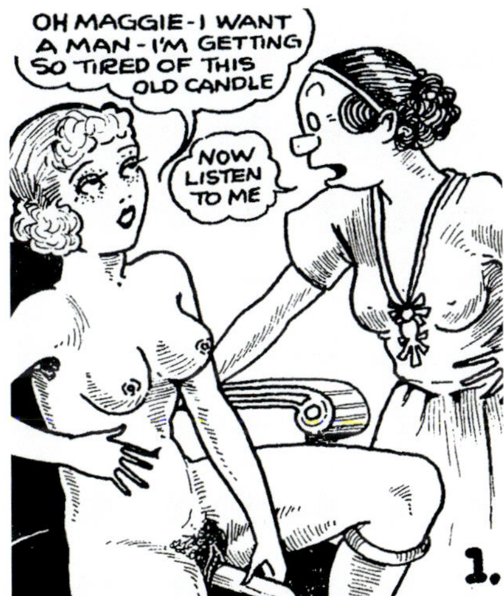

OUR OLD FRIEND MAGGIE,
WHO'S SCREWED A GREAT MANY,
WAS ADVISING A MAIDEN
WHO HADN'T HAD ANY:

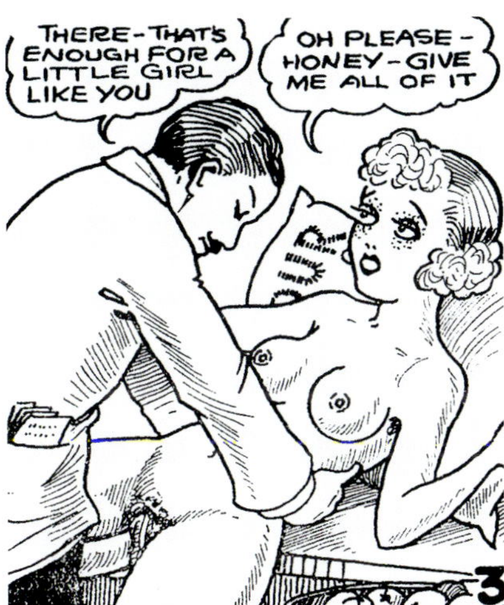

DON'T FUCK A GROCER;
HIS LOVE IS NO PLEASURE
HE DOESN'T BELIEVE IN
GIVING FULL MEASURE.

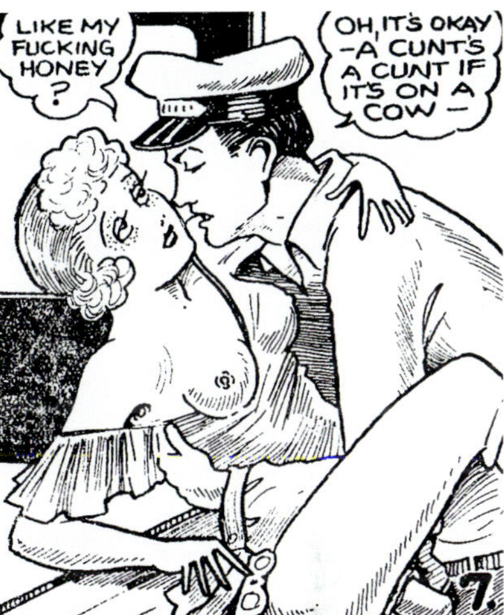

DON'T SCREW A TRUCKMAN,
OR YOU'LL BE SORE;
FOR HE'S HAD TRUCK WITH
A HUNDRED OR MORE.

Year: **1930s**. Title: **Maggie**. Country: **USA**.

professional photo-offset to mimeograph down to rubber stamps!

Along with the eight-pagers, a discerning book-lover could also find "Readers." They were available from the same sources as the comics and were approximately the same size (an ordinary typewriter sheet folded in fourths or fifths). But the Readers were text stories, variations on the carbon, mimeographed, or typescript erotic literature that passed hand-to-hand. The stories were illustrated by photographs of prostitutes in action that had no connection with the story other than their depiction of explicit sexual activity.

The Bibles, and to a lesser extent the Readers, weren't just about sex and jokes. They were a form of rebellion. They poked fun at modern times and challenged established values. Bible readers were automatically giving the finger to authority.

auch Samuel und Max Roth druckten und verkauften sie an einzelne Ladenbesitzer oder Hausierer. Das organisierte Verbrechen soll ebenfalls mitgemischt haben, doch da sie so leicht zu kopieren waren, konnte es etliche Bezugsquellen für denselben Comic geben.

Im Verlauf von dreißig Jahren wurden 800 verschiedene Originalcomics und mindestens ebensoviele Reprints produziert. Die Gier nach schnellem Geld brachte die unterschiedlichsten Reproduktionstechniken hervor, vom professionellen Offset-Druck über den Mimeographen bis zum einfachen Stempeldruck!

Neben den Eight-Pagers konnte der anspruchsvolle Bücherfreund auch so genannte „Readers" bekommen. Sie waren an denselben Orten zu bekommen wie die Comics und hatten in etwa auch deren Format (eine normale

Les éditeurs de livres et de cartes à jouer érotiques en publiaient également : David et Jacob Brotman, Jacob et I. R. Russell, Alex Field, Samuel et Max Roth en imprimaient tous et les vendaient à des propriétaires de boutiques et des colporteurs. Certains se souviennent que la mafia était également impliquée dans ce trafic, mais ces plaquettes étaient si faciles à pirater qu'une même bande dessinée pouvait avoir de nombreuses sources différentes.

Environ 800 bandes dessinées originales furent réalisées en trente ans, et on compte presque autant de rééditions. L'attrait d'un dollar vite gagné donna lieu à de nombreuses techniques de reproduction, de l'impression offset professionnelle à la polycopie en passant par les tampons en caoutchouc !

Outre les plaquettes de huit pages, le bibliophile averti pouvait également

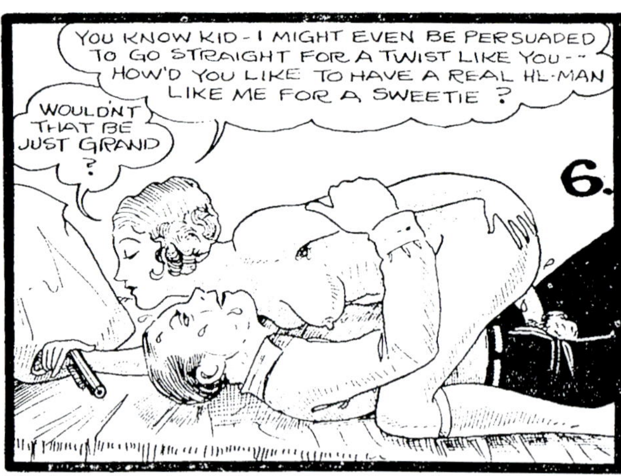

YEAR: **1930s**. TITLE: **Machine Gun Kelly**. COUNTRY: **USA**.

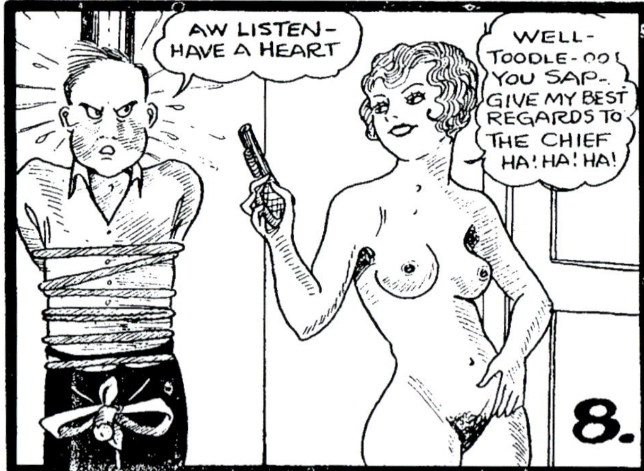

YEAR: **1930s**. TITLE: **Machine Gun Kelly**. COUNTRY: **USA**.

The best known of the Bible artists today is Wesley Morse, better known for his work on the comic strip *Bazooka Joe.*

The sex comics illustrated Depression realities that were often ignored in the newspapers. When country girls looked for work in the big city they found that a secretary might have to do more than type to get a job. To land a job in Hollywood required a session on the casting couch. The sympathy of comic writers was often with the suppressed; when a broke renter agreed to trade sex for rent, landlord Judge Piffle turned out to be impotent.

Schreibmaschinenseite vier- oder fünfmal gefaltet). Die Reader enthielten allerdings richtige Texte, Variationen der durchgepausten, mimeografierten oder abgetippten erotischen Literatur, die von Hand zu Hand weitergegeben wurde. Die Geschichten wurden mit Fotos von Prostituierten im Nahkampf illustriert, die – abgesehen von der krassen Darstellung sexueller Aktivitäten – keinerlei Zusammenhang mit den Geschichten hatten. Bei den Bibles und im geringeren Maße auch bei den Readers ging es nicht nur um Sex und schmutzige Witze. Sie waren eine Form der Rebellion. Sie machten sich über Zeitgeist und herrschende Moralvorstellungen lustig. Diese Hefte zu lesen, hieß zugleich, den Behörden den Stinkefinger zu zeigen.

Die Sexcomics illustrierten häufig Aspekte der Depressionsjahre, die von den Zeitungen gerne ignoriert wurden. Wenn Mädchen vom Lande in die Stadt kamen, stellten sie oft fest, dass von einer Sekretärin mehr als nur gute Schreibmaschinenkenntnisse erwartet wurden. Wenn man in Hollywood einen Job wollte,

trouver des « readers ». Ils provenaient des mêmes sources et avaient plus ou plus la même taille (une feuille de format A4 pliée en quatre ou en cinq). Toutefois, ces readers contenaient des histoires écrites, variations sur la littérature polycopiée, passée au papier carbone, ou dactylographiée qu'on se passait de la main à la main. Les histoires étaient illustrées avec des photos de prostituées en pleine action sans aucun lien avec les histoires si ce n'était par leur représentation explicite du sexe. Les bibles, et dans une moindre mesure les readers, n'était pas que sexe et blagues grivoises. Elles exprimaient une forme de rébellion. Elles tournaient en dérision les temps modernes et défiaient les valeurs établies. En lisant une de ces bibles, on faisait un bras d'honneur aux autorités.

Les bandes dessinées érotiques illustraient des réalités de la dépression souvent tues par la presse. Lorsque les filles de la campagne arrivaient en ville, elles s'apercevaient vite que, pour obtenir un poste de secrétaire, savoir taper à la machine ne suffisait pas. Pour décrocher

Prick Has No Conscience

Illustrated
By
Life

Price 5 Lire

Privately Printed
For Adults
by
All Sport Fornications Press

Through a Door

BY
FRANK NOONY

ILLUSTRATED FROM LIFE

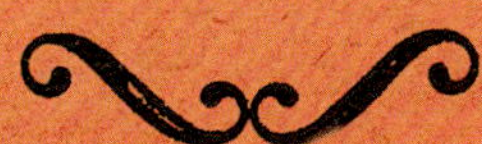

PUBLISHED BY
EMOTION PUBLISHING CO.
LONDON :•: PARIS

THIS WAS THEIR LOVE

PRICE 500 FRANCS

PARIS
BIBLIOTHEQUE ST. GERMAINE

A FATHER ELUDED

ILLUSTRATED
FROM LIFE

Price $2.50

CUNTIOUR PUBLISHING
Paris France

1935

CORA AND HER WANTS

★

Illustrated from Life

PRICE $5.00

★

Privately Printed

Published by M. SEUFERIN, Nice, France

Second Book

TANTALIZING TALES

Requoit Publishing Co.
Paris, France

Price: ONE HUNDRED FRANC

The Mad Fuckers

Illustrated
By
Life

Ten Lire

Privately Printed For Adults
by
Mod Mod Fornications Press

Seven Whores

ILLUSTRATED

☆

PRICE $5.00

☆

PARIS, FRANCE

What A Wonderful Fucking World

Illustrated
By
Life

Ten Lire

Privately Printed For Adults
by
Mod Mod Fornications Press

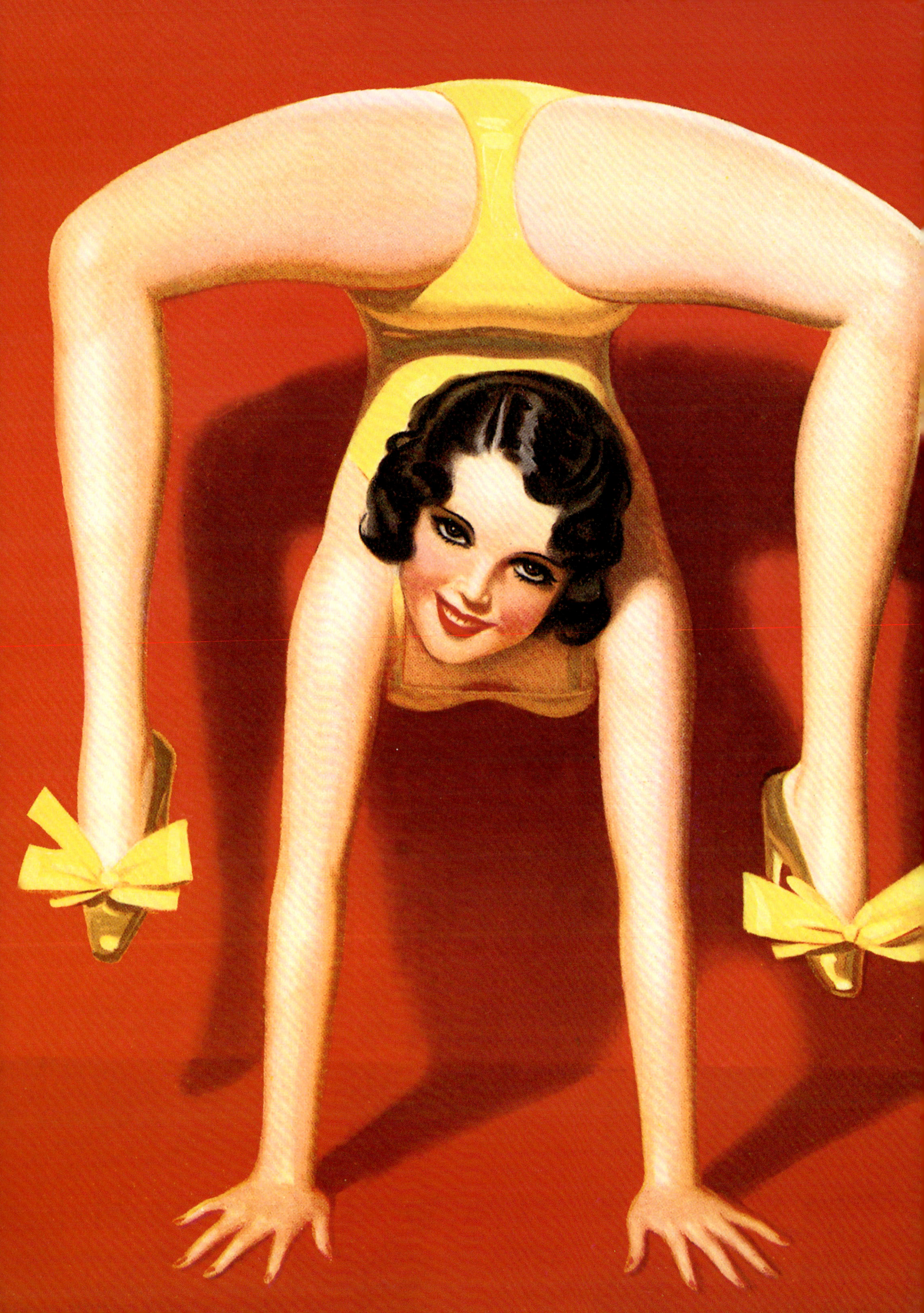

SPICY PULPS OF THE 1930s:

Hot Words under Glossy Covers

„Spicy Pulps“ der Dreißiger: Starker Tobak unter Hochglanzcover

Les pulps *Spicy* des années trente : des mots brûlants sous des couvertures en papier glacé

By Robert Gluckson

If you were looking for "hot stuff" to read in the 1920s, the newsstands offered erotic fiction and pin-up style magazines; if you asked at many of the same newsstands, you could buy under-the-counter nudie mags; and if you knew just where to go, you could find hardcore pornographic photos, stories, or comic books (Tijuana Bibles). There was plenty of money in under-the-counter porno magazines, but there were problems, too: like cops, vice-societies, and the impediment of not being able to take advantage of subsidized postal rates to distribute your magazines. Still, there was a constant demand for the stronger stuff, with a fairly equal counter-demand from the legal and religious community to censor sexual content. Cheap, legal popular fiction magazines, called pulps, were new moneymakers in the 20s, but they didn't deliver much erotic stimulation—until the Spicy pulps.

Spicy meant "sexy," and the idea was to sell sex without getting busted.

Spicy meant "sexy," and the idea was to sell sex without getting busted. Naked breasts were like a red flag to the censors.

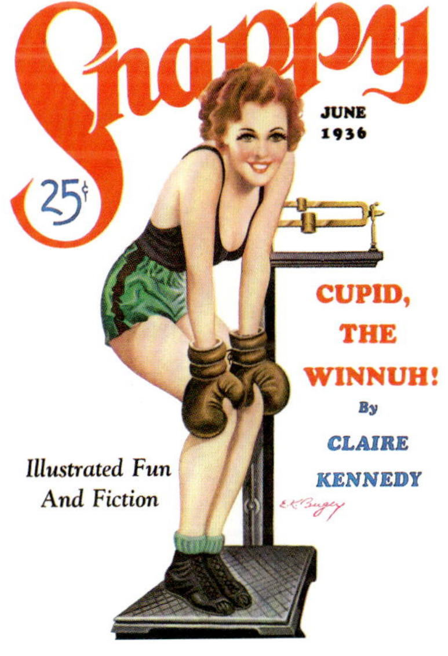

Year: **1936**. Title: **Snappy**. Artist: **Earle Bergey**. Country: **USA**.

Wenn man sich in den Zwanzigern etwas „Verbotenes“ am Zeitungskiosk kaufen wollte, wurden einem erotische Liebesromane und Pin-up-Magazine angeboten; wenn man hartnäckig blieb, konnte man an demselben Zeitungsstand echte Sexhefte kaufen, die unter der Theke gehandelt wurden, und wenn man wusste, an wen man sich zu wenden hatte, fand man auch pornografische Fotos, Stories oder Comicbücher (so genannte „Tijuana Bibles“). Mit der Pornografie unter der Ladentheke ließ sich viel Geld

À ceux qui cherchaient quelque chose de « chaud » à lire dans les années vingt, les kiosques proposaient un choix de fiction érotique et de magazines de pin-up. Dans bon nombre de ces kiosques, si vous le demandiez au marchand, il vous sortait de sous le comptoir des magazines de nus. Et si vous saviez à qui vous adresser, vous trouviez même de vraies photos, histoires et bandes dessinées pornographiques (les fameuses « bibles de Tijuana »). Il y avait beaucoup d'argent à se faire avec la vente sous le manteau de revues porno mais ce n'était pas sans risques : il fallait compter avec la police et les associations de lutte contre le vice. En outre, on ne pouvait bénéficier des tarifs postaux avantageux pour distribuer ses magazines. Toutefois, il y avait une demande constante de matériel plus corsé, à laquelle les communautés juridiques et religieuses ripostaient par une demande plus ou moins équivalente de censure. Les magazines légaux de fiction populaire et bon marché, baptisés « pulps », rapportaient beaucoup d'argent mais n'étaient pas très érotiques. Jusqu'à l'apparition des pulps *Spicy*.

Par *spicy* (ou « épicé »), il fallait comprendre sexy. L'idée était de vendre du sexe sans se faire arrêter. Montrer des seins nus revenait à agiter un drapeau rouge sous le nez des censeurs. Le mot « Spicy » sur une couverture alertait

An incredibly provocative contortionist cover from 1930.

Ein unglaublich provokatives Kontortionisten-Cover aus dem Jahre 1930.

Une couverture de 1930 avec une contorsionniste incroyablement provocatrice.

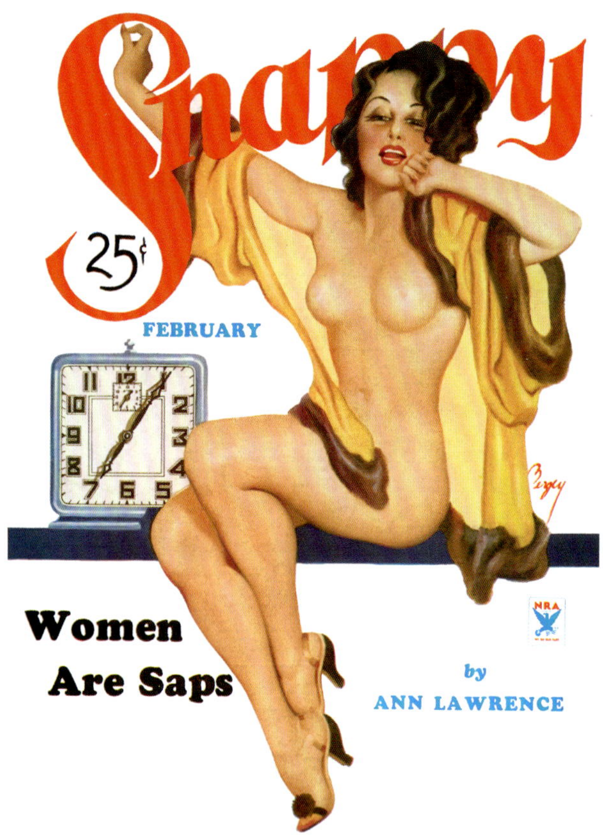

Year: **1934**. Title: **Snappy**. Country: **USA**.

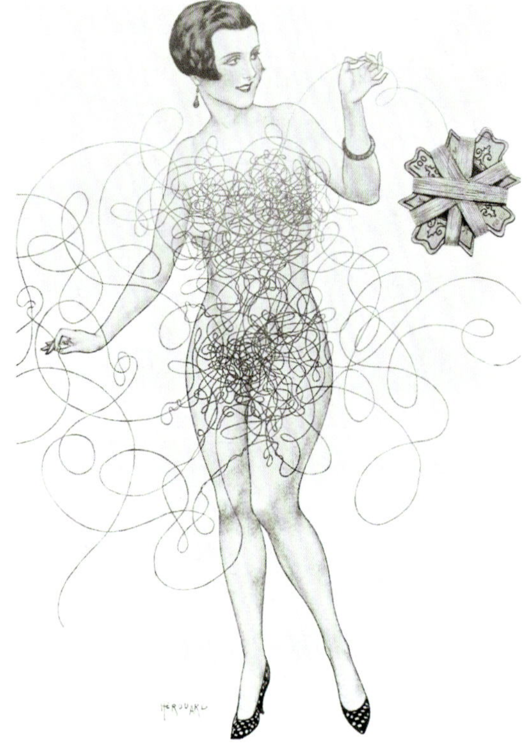

Year: **1936**. Title: **Spicy Stories**. Country: **USA**.

Right: Year: **1930**. Title: **French Follies**.
Artist: **Bakos**. Country: **USA**.

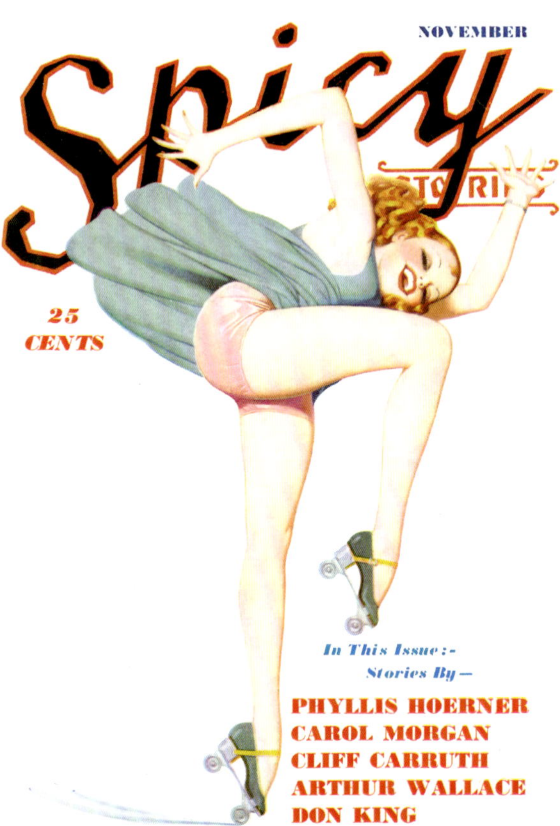

Year: **1936**. Title: **Spicy Stories**. Country: **USA**.

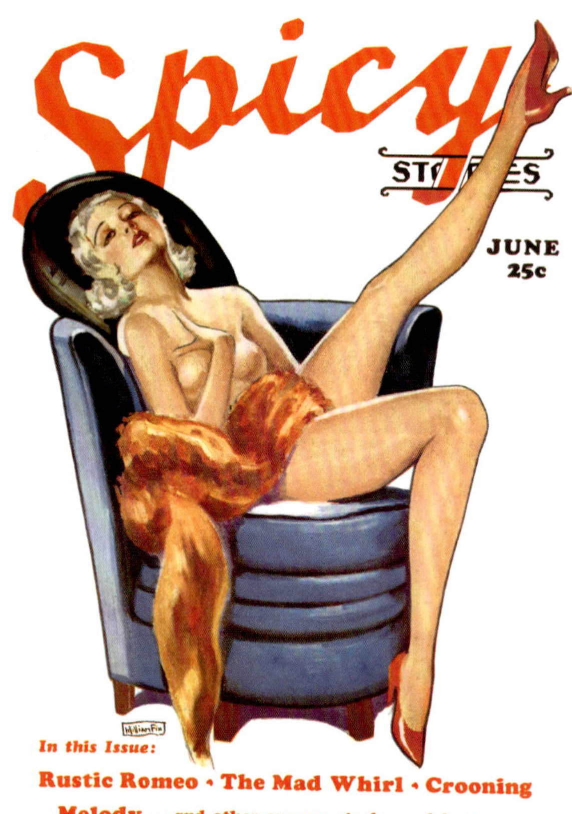

Year: **1932**. Title: **Spicy Stories**. Country: **USA**.

Page 158:
Year: **1930s**. Title: **Cupid's Capers**.
Country: **USA**.

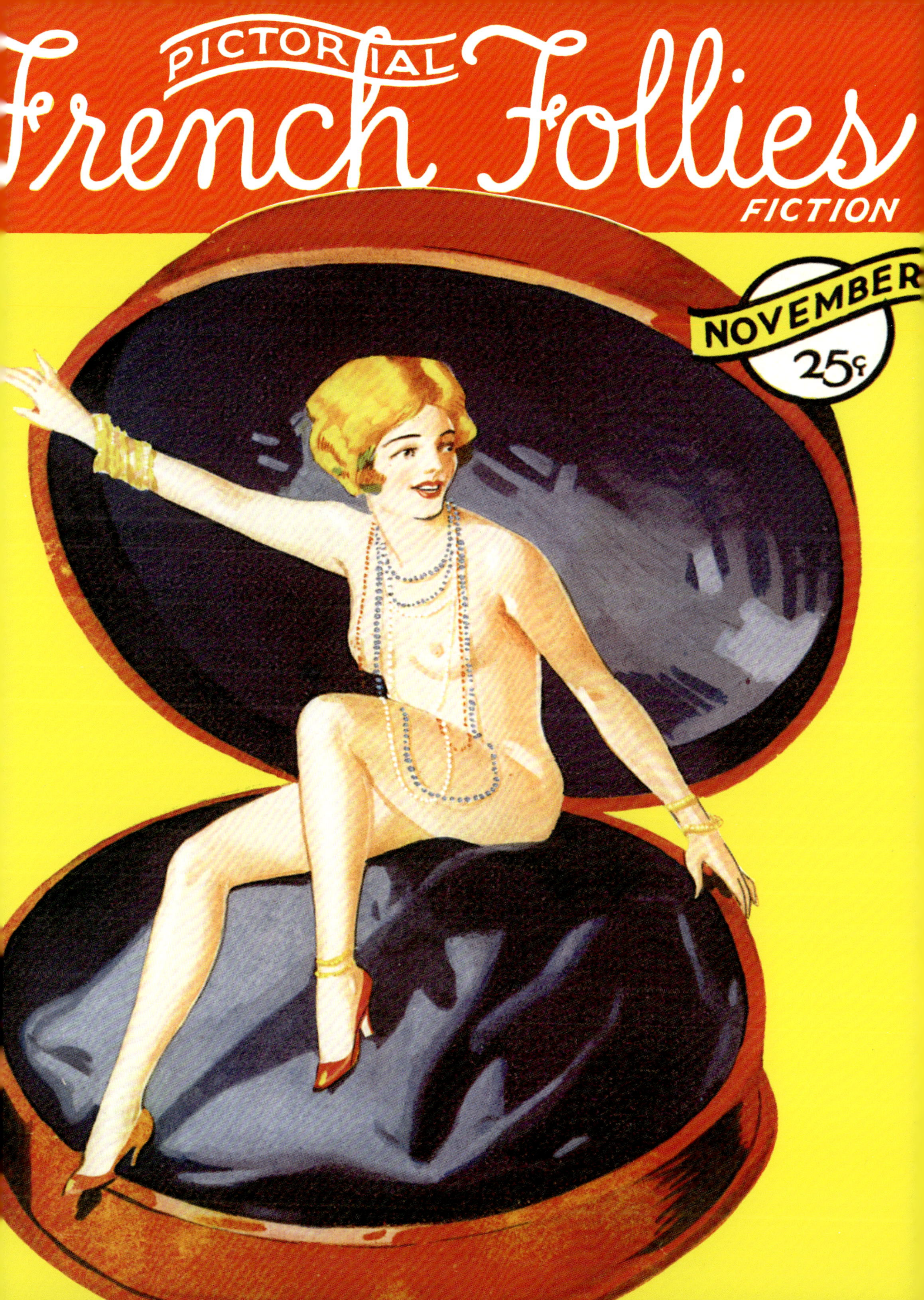
PICTORIAL
French Follies
FICTION
NOVEMBER
25¢

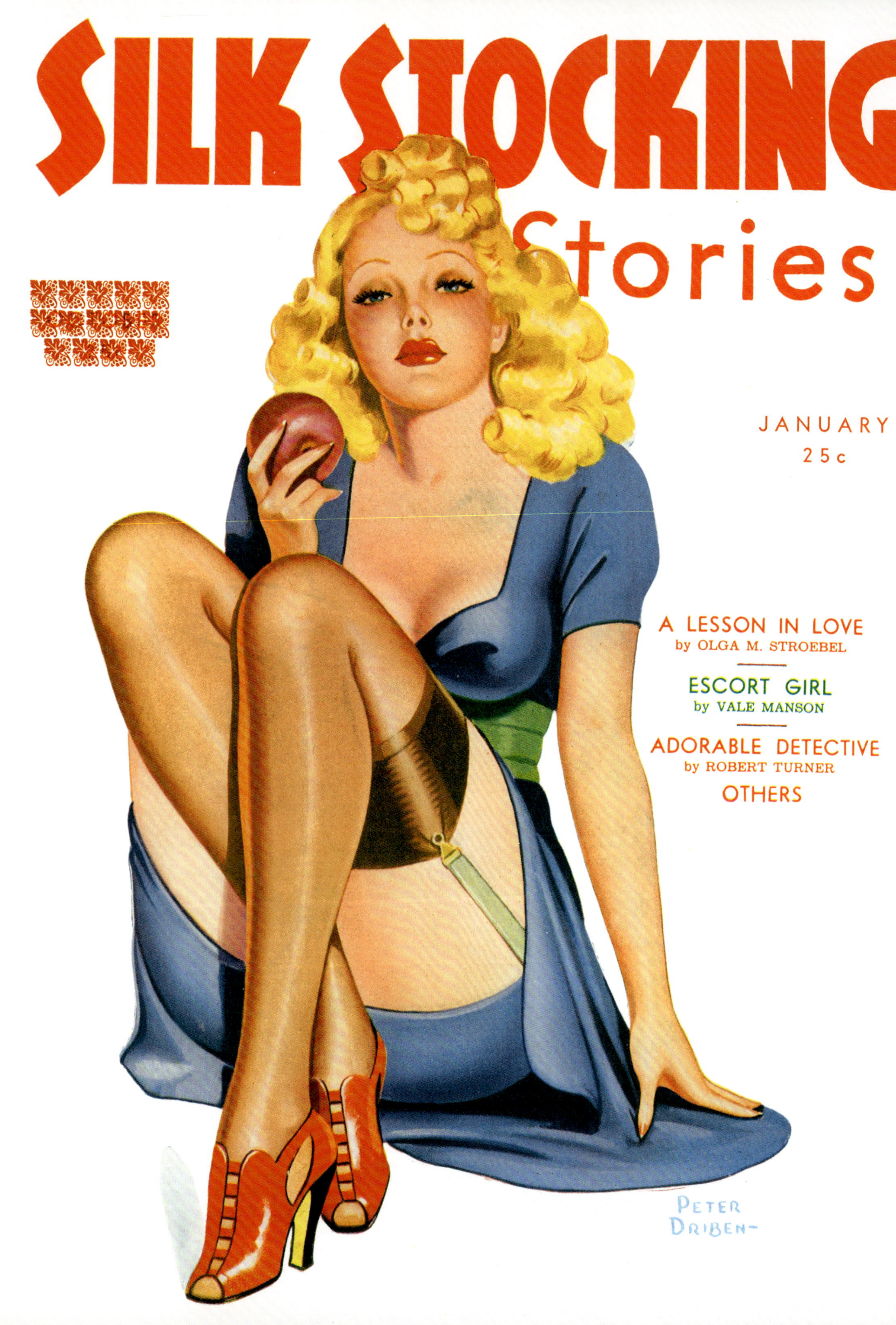
SILK STOCKING
Stories
JANUARY
25c
A LESSON IN LOVE
by OLGA M. STROEBEL
ESCORT GIRL
by VALE MANSON
ADORABLE DETECTIVE
by ROBERT TURNER
OTHERS
PETER
DRIBEN-

YEAR: **1939**. TITLE: **Silk Stocking Stories**.
ARTIST: **Peter Driben**. COUNTRY: **USA**.

For those who could not actually consort with gangsters, prostitutes, con men, and gigolos, a vicarious participation was provided through the printed word, the retouched photo, and the off-color novelty item.

—*Bootleggers and Smuthounds*, Jay A. Gertzman, 1999

The word "spicy" on the cover alerted the sex-hungry audience without resorting to nudity, and sexy stories instead of photos meant that these pulps could be displayed on a newsstand. The first *Spicy* fiction combined sex and romance and may have begun with the French magazine *La Vie Parisienne* in 1914. Many returning servicemen had become familiar with the more liberal sexual standards in France. *La Vie Parisienne* dealt with women's flirtation, adultery, or involvement with underworld figures. While sold under-the-counter, the sexual activity was only implied; but the drama of intimate involvement was an important step leading to the romance pulp *Love Story* in the 1920s. The sex fiction pulps actually developed from these magazines for women into titles like *Zest*, *Pep*, and *Droll Stories*, featuring "Lively Stories Sizzling with

YEAR: **1935**. TITLE: **Stolen Sweets**.
ARTIST: **George Quintana**. COUNTRY: **USA**.

machen, aber man hatte auch mit Problemen zu kämpfen: der Polizei, Tugend-Gesellschaften und der missliche Umstand, dass man keinen ermäßigten Tarif beanspruchen konnte, wenn man seine Magazine mit der Post befördern wollte. Dennoch blieb die Nachfrage nach noch härteren Sachen ebenso rege, wie der Ruf nach Zensur seitens der Justiz und Kirche. Preiswerte, legale Unterhaltungsmagazine, die so genannten Pulps, waren in den Zwanzigern ein neuer Geschäftszweig, boten jedoch kaum erotische Stimulation. Das änderte sich mit den „Spicy Pulps."

„Spicy" bedeutete sexy, und der Plan war, Sex zu verkaufen, ohne deswegen Besuch von der Polizei zu bekommen. Ein nackter Busen wirkte auf Zensoren wie ein rotes Tuch. Das Wort „spicy" auf dem Cover mobilisierte ein sexhungriges Publikum, ohne auf Nacktheit zurückgreifen zu müssen, und erregende Stories anstelle von Fotos bedeutete, dass man diese Pulps offen an Kiosken anbieten konnte. Wahrscheinlich markiert *La Vie Parisienne*, 1914 in Paris erschienen, den Anfang dieser pikanten Geschichten von Sex und Liebe. Viele heimkehrende US-Soldaten brachten die liberaleren Moralvorstellungen, die sie in Frankreich kennengelernt hatten, mit nach Hause. *La Vie Parisienne* erzählte von Liebesaffären, Ehebruch und Halbweltumgang französischer Frauen. Obwohl unter der Ladentheke verkauft, waren die sexuellen Aktivitäten nur angedeutet, aber das Drama der intimen Beziehungen war ein wichtiger Schritt auf dem Weg zu den Liebesgeschichten in *Love Story* in den Zwanzigern. Aus diese Magazinen für Frauen gingen später die Pulps mit Sexgeschichten, Titel

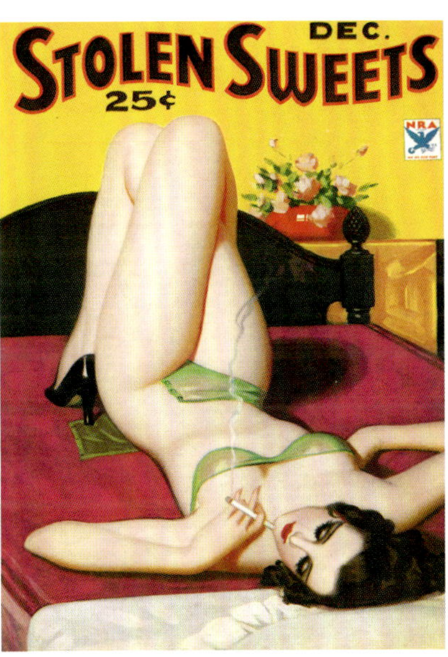

YEAR: **1935**. TITLE: **Stolen Sweets**.
ARTIST: **Enoch Bolles**. COUNTRY: **USA**.

l'amateur d'érotisme sans avoir à recourir à la nudité et, en publiant des histoires coquines plutôt que des photos, ces pulps pouvaient être exposés sur les rayons. Les premiers textes associaient érotisme et histoires d'amour, puisant peut-être leurs racines dans la revue française *La Vie Parisienne*, lancée en 1914. De nombreux soldats américains revenant de la Grande Guerre s'étaient familiarisés avec les mœurs plus libres de la France. Dans *La Vie Parisienne*, on lisait des histoires de femmes légères, d'adultère et de pègre. La revue se vendait clandestinement même si, dans les textes, l'activité sexuelle n'était que suggérée. Toutefois, la mise en scène des rapports intimes marqua une étape importante menant au pulp sentimental *Love Story* dans les années vingt. Les pulps de fiction érotique se développèrent à partir de ces magazines féminins pour donner des titres tels que *Zest*, *Pep* et *Droll*

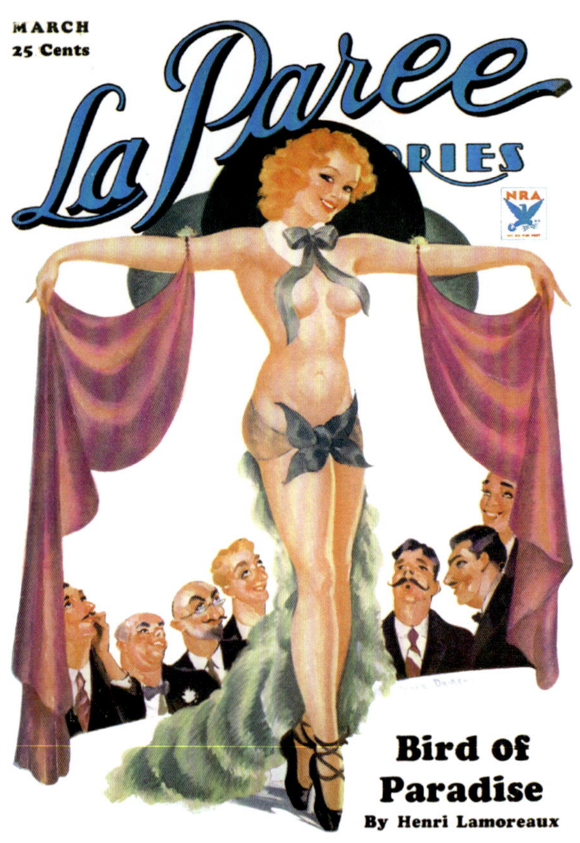

Year: 1934. Title: La Paree. Artist: Peter Driben. Country: USA.

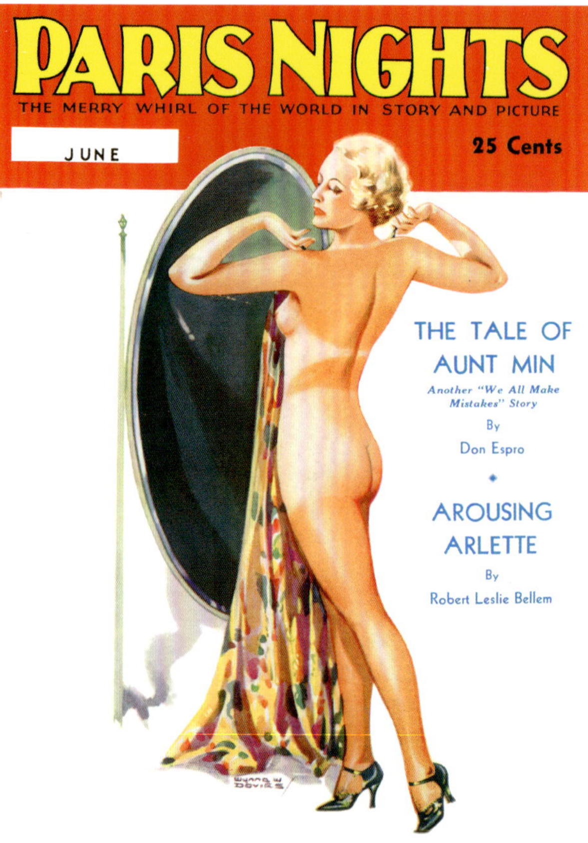

Year: 1930. Title: Paris Nights. Country: USA.

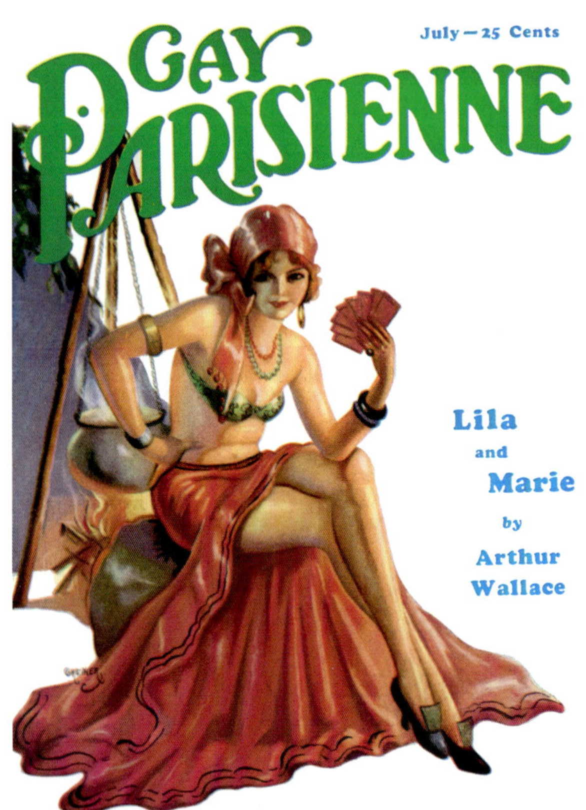

Year: 1933. Title: Gay Parisienne. Artist: O. Greiner. Country: USA.

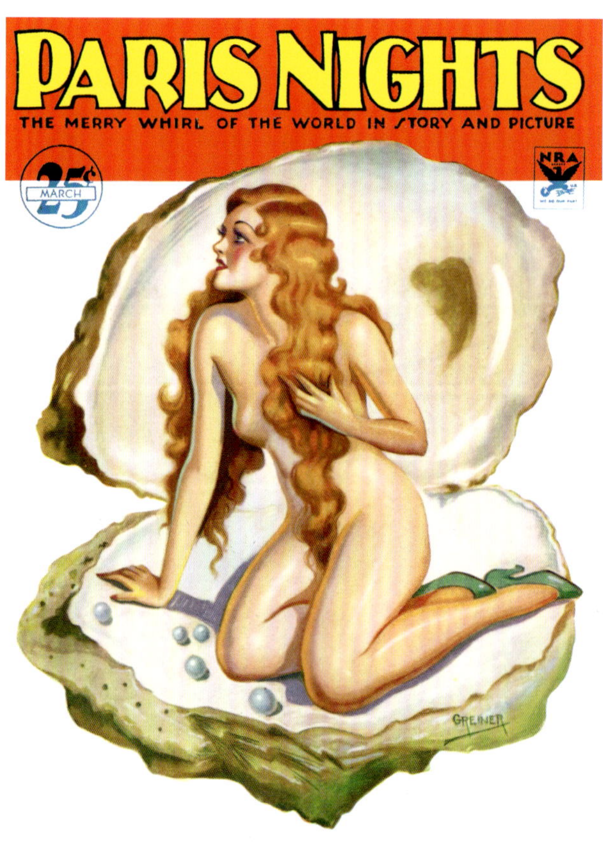

Year: 1930. Title: Paris Nights. Artist: O. Greiner. Country: USA.

Year: 1931. Title: Broadway Nights. Country: USA.

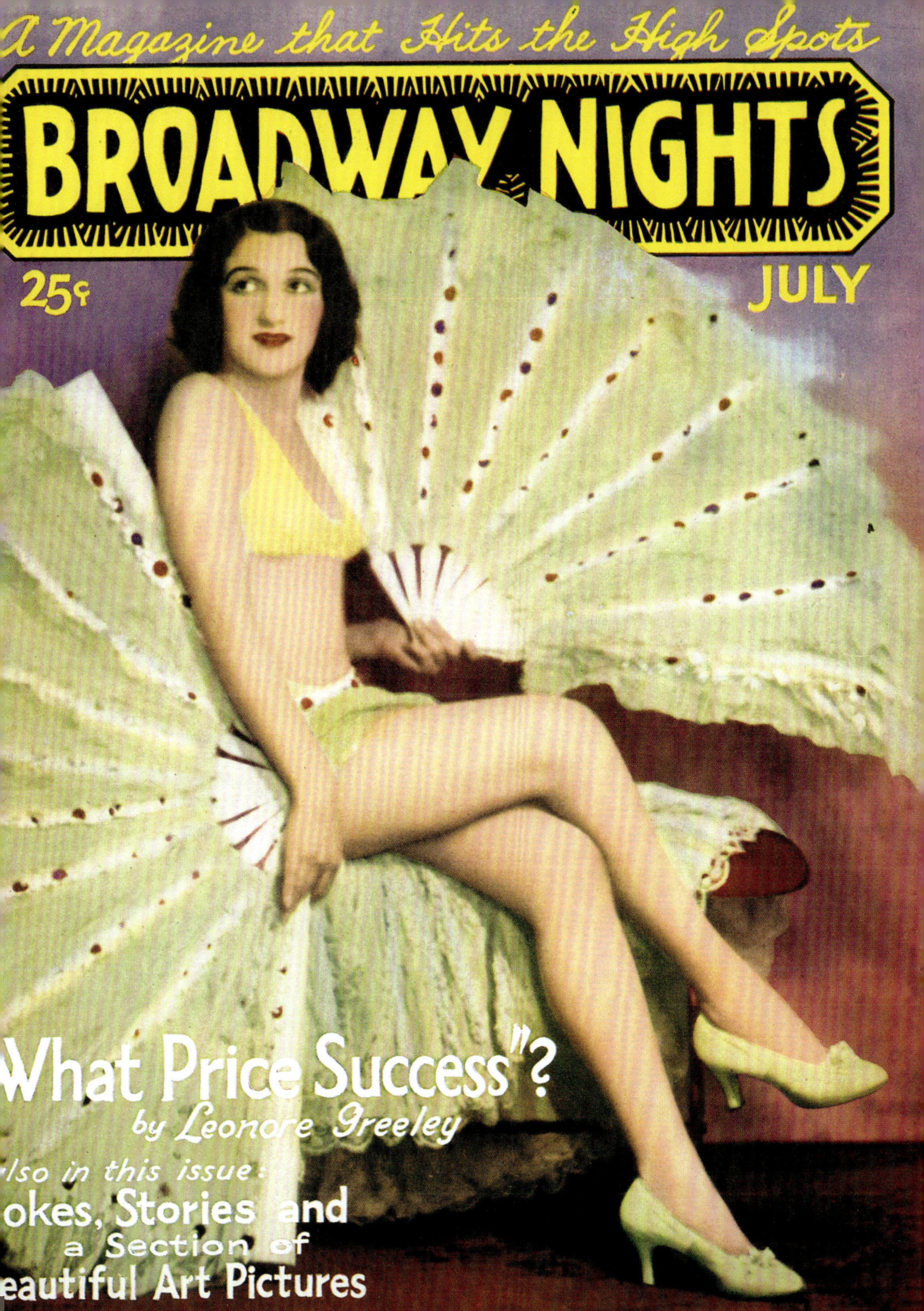

A Magazine that Hits the High Spots
BROADWAY NIGHTS
25¢
JULY
"What Price Success"?
by Leonore Greeley
lso in this issue:
okes, Stories and
a Section of
eautiful Art Pictures

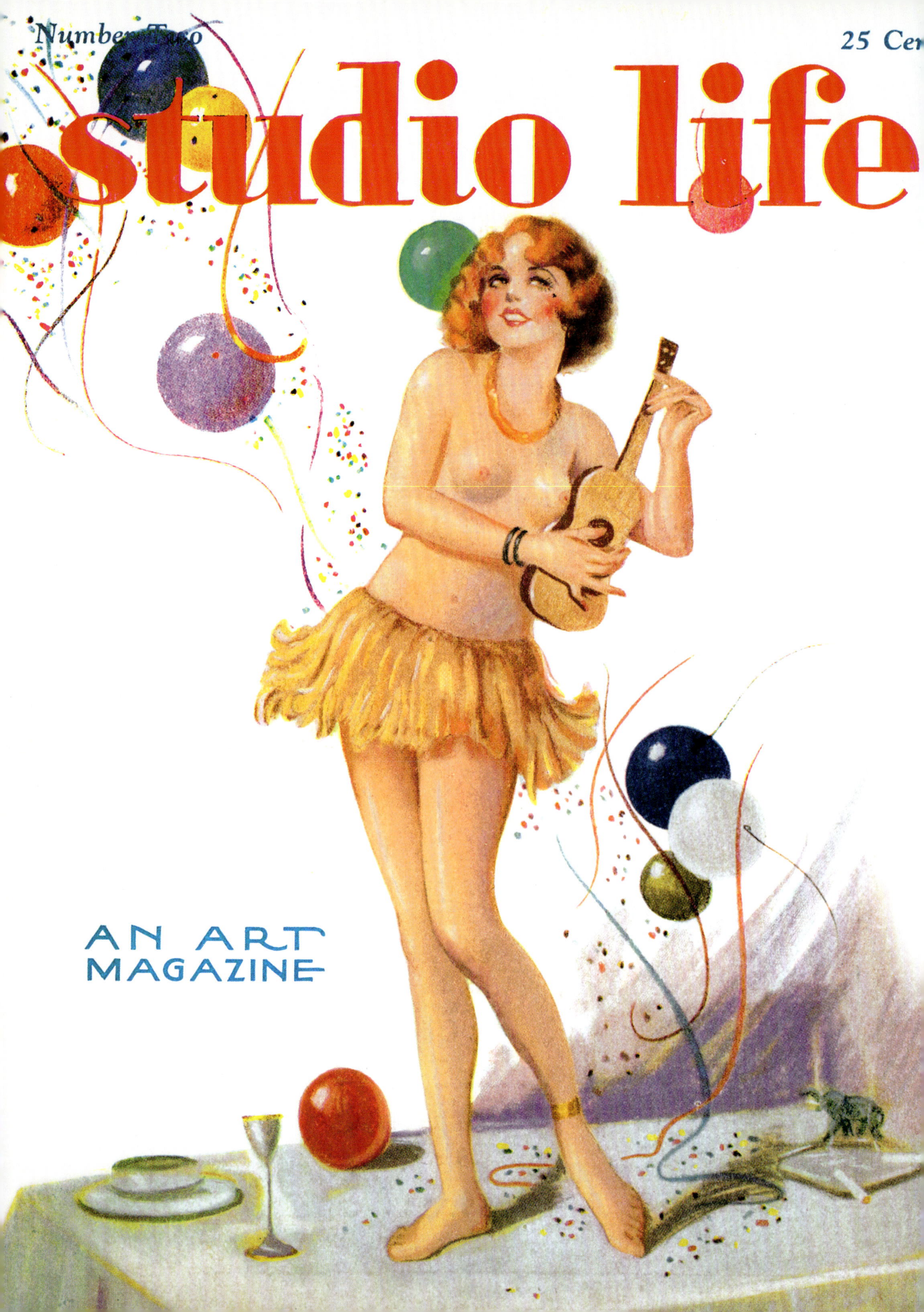
Number Two
25 Cen
studio life
AN ART
MAGAZINE

Year: **1930s**. Title: **Studio Life**.
Country: **USA**.

In 1928 King Publishing added photo inserts to fiction titles *Broadway Nights, Ginger, Pep, Real Story Book Frolics/Folies.*

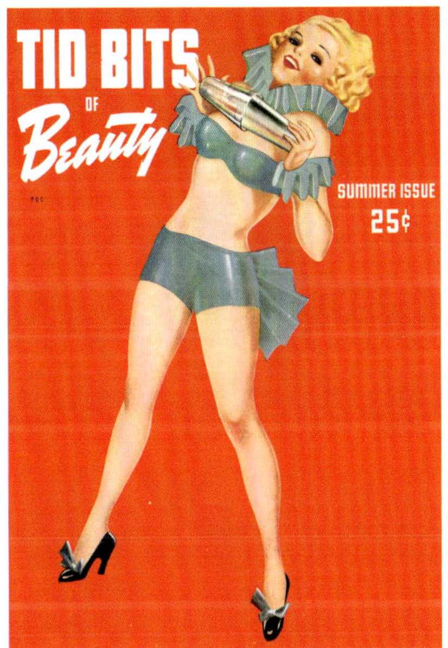

Year: **1943**. Title: **Tidbits of Beauty**.
Country: **USA**.

Speed-Spice-Sparkle." Publishers kept new products coming, searching for the right formula. In 1928 King Publishing Company's Frank Armer added photo inserts to his fiction titles *Broadway Nights*, *Ginger*, *Pep*, *Real Story Book Frolics/Folies*, and an early version of *Spicy Stories*. Competitor Harry Donenfeld and his brother Irwin put out some similar short-lived titles like *Hot Stories*, *Juicy Tales*, and *Joy Stories* in late 1929, under the company names Irwin and Merwil. In 1932 Armer and Donenfeld joined forces. The *Spicy* pulps, those most famous 30s sex pulps with "Spicy" in the title, soon followed. Donenfeld was a printer and fledgling distributor. Armer was likely the genius behind the *Spicy* concept, but Donenfeld made it work. Their company was called Culture Publications.

wie *Zest*, *Pep* und *Droll Stories* („Lively Stories Sizzling with Speed-Spice-Crackle") hervor. Die Verleger brachten immer neue Titel auf den Markt und suchten nach dem richtigen Erfolgsrezept. Frank Armer von King Publishing fügte 1928 seinen Pulps wie *Broadway Nights*, *Ginger*, *Pep*, *Real Story Book Frolics/Folies* und einer frühen Version von *Spicy Stories* auch Fotos bei. Sein Konkurrent Harry Donenfeld und dessen Bruder Irwin brachten Ende 1929 unter dem Namen Irwin and Merwil ähnliche kurzlebige Titel heraus, Magazine wie *Hot Stories, Juicy Tales* und *Joy Stories*. 1932 taten sich Armer und Donenfeld zusammen. Bald darauf erschienen die ersten *Spicy*-Pulps, die berühmtesten Sexhefte der Dreißiger, die alle das Wort „spicy" im Titel trugen. Donenfeld war Drucker und besaß einen expandierenden Vertrieb. Armer war wahrscheinlich der schlaue Kopf hinter dem *Spicy*-Konzept, aber Donenfeld war der Mann fürs Praktische. Ihre Firma nannten sie Culture Publications.

Die Groschenhefte von Culture Publication waren die sexuell provokantesten der legalen Hefte, die in den Dreißigern zu kaufen waren. Diese Magazine, die Fans von Action- und Detektivgeschichten gleichermaßen ansprachen, wie diejenigen, die einfach Sex wollten, setzten einen neuen Maßstab für Erotika. Sie lieferten die heißesten Titel und die besten Sexstorys der Pulp-Ära. 1934 wurden *Spicy Mystery*, *Spicy Detective* und *Spicy Adventure* vorgestellt. Bald darauf folgte *Spicy Western*. Es waren vor allem die Titelbilder von H. J. Ward und H. L. Parkhurst, an denen sich die Fantasie entzünden konnte. Der Star-Autor der *Spicy*-Titel

Stories, présentant « des histoires palpitantes, lestes, épicées et pétillantes ». Les éditeurs lançaient sans cesse de nouveaux titres, cherchant la bonne formule. En 1928, la maison d'édition de Frank Armer, King Publishing, ajouta des photos dans ses magazines de fiction *Broadway Nights*, *Ginger*, *Pep*, *Real Story Book Frolics/Folies* et une première mouture de *Spicy Stories*. À la fin de 1929, son concurrent Harry Donenfeld monta une société avec son frère Irwin, « Irwin & Merwil », pour éditer des titres similaires et éphémères tels que *Hot Stories*, *Juicy Tales* et *Joy Stories*. En 1932, Armer et Donenfeld unirent leurs efforts. Les magazines *Spicy*, ces célèbres pulps érotiques des années trente contenant tous le mot *spicy* dans leur titre, virent le jour peu après. Armer était probablement le cerveau derrière le concept *Spicy*, mais

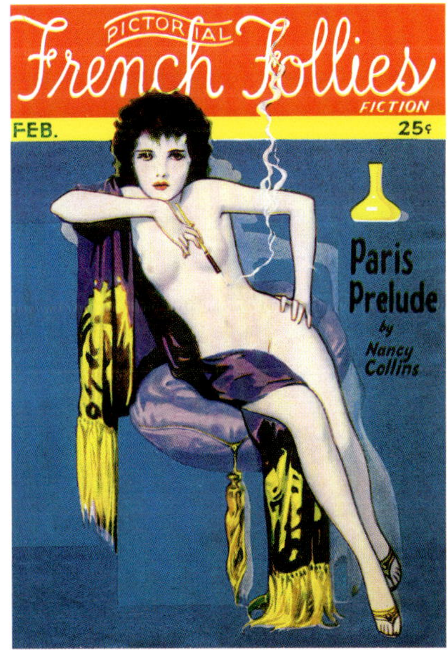

Year: **1930s**. Title: **French Follies**.
Country: **USA**.

Modern Girl Book *debuted late in the spicy era (1939) from new player Lex Publications of New York. The content was more good girl than vamp.*

Modern Girl Book *kam spät in der Ära der* Spicys *(1939) bei Lex Publications in New York heraus, die neu im Geschäft waren. Der Inhalt bestand eher aus braven Mädchen denn aus Vamps.*

Modern Girl Book *parut à la fin de « l'ère piquante » (1939) chez Lex Publications de New York. Le contenu révélait plutôt des braves filles que des vamps.*

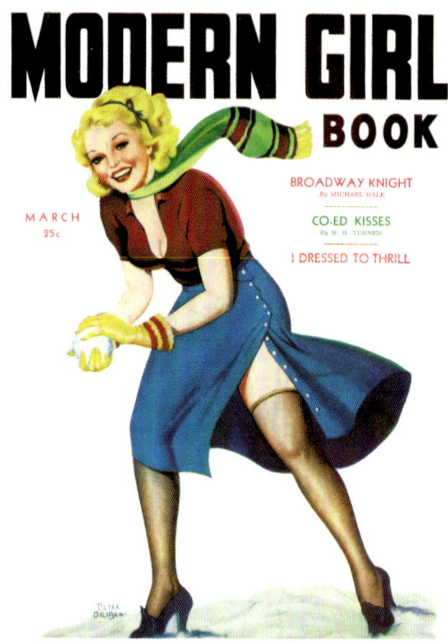

Year: **1939**. Title: **Modern Girl Book**.
Country: **USA**.

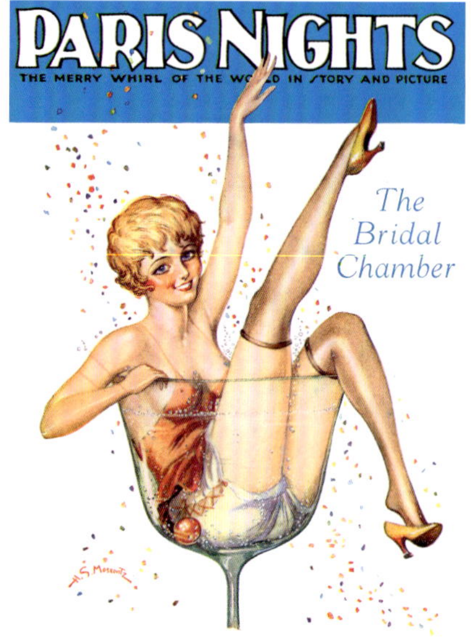

Year: **1930**. Title: **Paris Nights**.
Country: **USA**.

Culture Publications' pulps were the most sexually provocative legal fiction that could be purchased in the 1930s. Appealing to fans of adventure and detective stories as well as those after straight sex, these magazines set a new standard for erotic art. They featured the most graphic covers and the best-known sex fiction of the pulp era. *Spicy Mystery*, *Spicy Detective*, and *Spicy Adventure* were introduced in 1934. *Spicy Western* soon followed.

It was the covers that fired the imagination, featuring the art of H. J. Ward and H. L. Parkhurst. The star writer of the Spicy line was Robert Bellem, best known for his "Dan Turner, Hollywood Detective" character. Among the competitors Enoch Bolles was the top cover artist.

A slew of imitators joined the *Spicys* on the magazine racks. First came Hubbard publications, veterans of the nudie magazine wars, with their line of *Saucy* pulps: *Saucy Stories*, *Saucy Romantic Adventures*, and *Saucy Detective*. From other publishers came *Broadway Nights*, *French Follies*, *Gay Parisienne*, *Ginger Stories*, *High Heel Magazine*, *Hollywood Nights*, *La Paree*, *Silk Stocking Stories*, *Snappy*, *Stolen Sweets*, *Breezy Stories*, and *Cupid's Capers*. Armer and Donenfeld fought off the competition by filling the stands with their own one-shot knockoffs, first *Snappy Mystery*, *Snappy Detective*, and *Snappy*; then *Sizzling Romance*

The *Spicy* pulps were where the social mores of the era collided.

war Robert Bellem, bekannt durch seinen Helden Dan Turner, den Hollywood-Detektiv. Bei den Konkurrenzheften war Enoch Bolles der beste Cover-Künstler. Eine Menge Imitatoren gesellte sich an den Zeitungsständen zu den *Spicys*. Als erste Hubbard Publications, ein Veteran der großen Nudie-Magazine-Kriege, mit der *Saucy*-Reihe: *Saucy Stories*, *Saucy Romantic Adventures* und *Saucy Detective*. Andere Verlage brachten Titel wie *Broadway Nights*, *French Follies*, *Gay Parisienne*, *Ginger Stories*, *High Heel Magazine*, *Hollywood Nights*, *La Paree*, *Silk Stocking Stories*, *Snappy*, *Stolen Sweets*, *Breezy Stories* und *Cupid's Capers*. Armer und Donenfeld boten

celui-ci fonctionnait grâce à Donenfeld, également imprimeur et distributeur débutant. Leur société s'appelait Culture Publications.

Les pulps de Culture Publications proposait les nouvelles les plus émoustillantes que l'on pouvait acheter légalement dans les années trente. Établissant de nouvelles normes en matière d'art érotique, ils séduisaient autant les amateurs d'aventures et d'histoires policières que ceux qui recherchaient avant tout du sexe. Ils offrirent les couvertures les plus provocantes et les textes érotiques les plus connus de toute l'ère du pulp. *Spicy Mystery, Spicy Detective* et *Spicy Adventure* furent lancés en 1934. *Spicy Western* suivit peu après. Leurs couvertures, peintes par des artistes tels que H. J. Ward et H. L. Parkhurst, enflammaient l'imagination. L'auteur vedette de la collection était Robert Bellem, surtout connu pour son personnage de

Year: **1939**. Title: **Gay French Life**.
Artist: **George Quintana**. Country: **USA**.

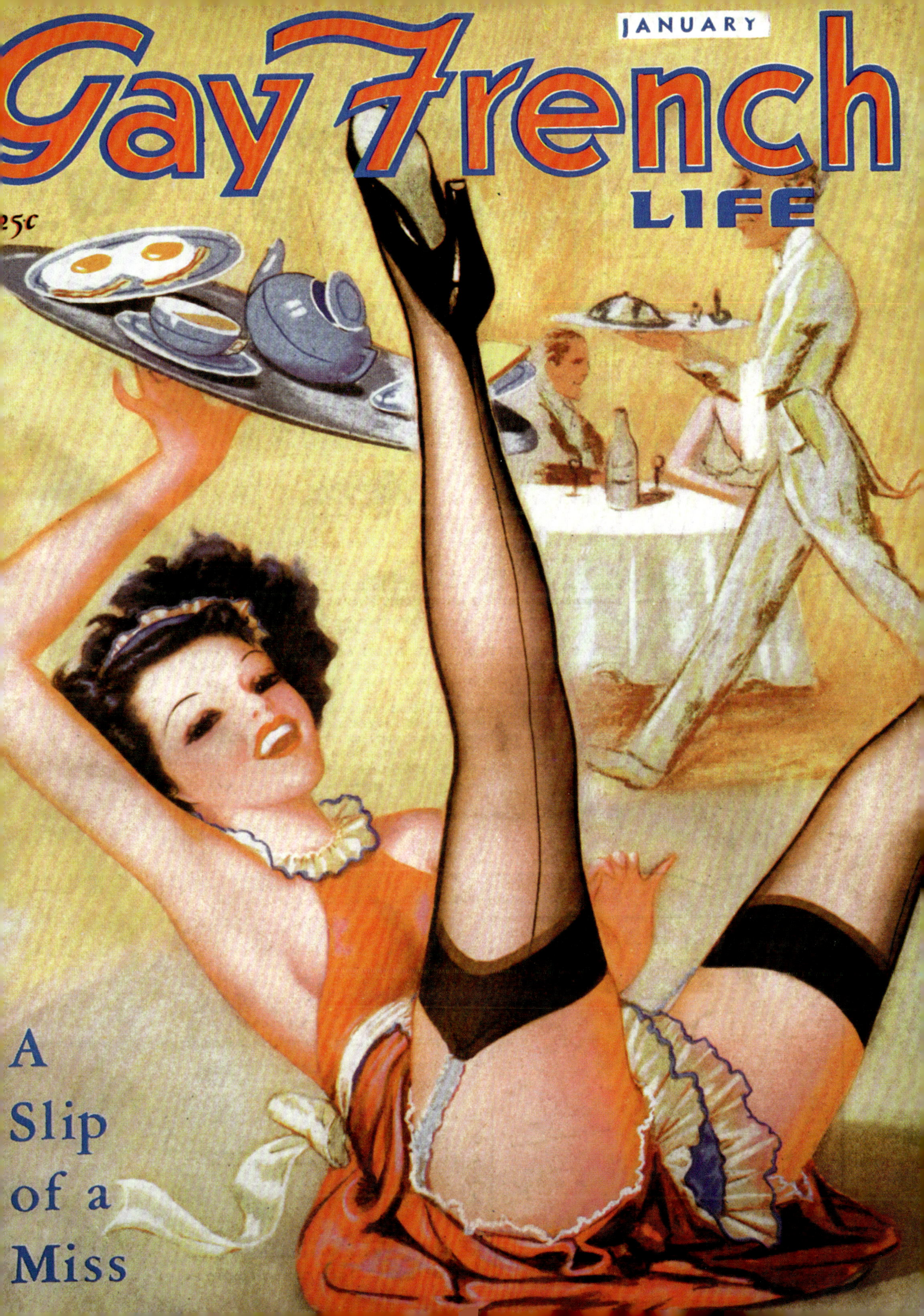
JANUARY
Gay French
LIFE
25¢
A
Slip
of a
Miss

Spicy Beauty Parade *would be taken over by legendary publisher Robert Harrison a year after its introduction in 1941 and revamped as a burlesque title.*

Beauty Parade *wurde vom legendären Verleger Robert Harrison ein Jahr nach seinem ersten Erscheinen 1941 übernommen und in einen Varietétitel umfunktioniert.*

Beauty Parade, *de la série des Spicy, fut repris par l'éditeur légendaire Robert Harrison un an après sa parution en 1941 et relancé comme un titre de burlesque.*

There was a constant demand for the stronger tuff, with a fairly equal counter-demand to censor sexual content.

and *Sizzling Detective*. The popularity of these magazines can be measured in their prices. In the wake of the Depression all other publishers were lowering their prices from $.25 to $.15, or even down to a dime, for 128 pages of rough paper featuring rough artwork and rougher stories; the *Spicys* continued to sell well for a quarter.

The *Spicy* pulps were published in a battleground of censor vs. booklegger; their pages were where the social mores of the era collided. In the ongoing cops-and-robbers game Donenfeld printed many different addresses in his magazines, ranging from multiple "fronts" in a single building (the Grand Central Palace, between 46th and 47th streets in Manhattan, and 1790 Broadway, the address of his bindery) to false addresses in Delaware, a state that was more interested in protecting corporations than

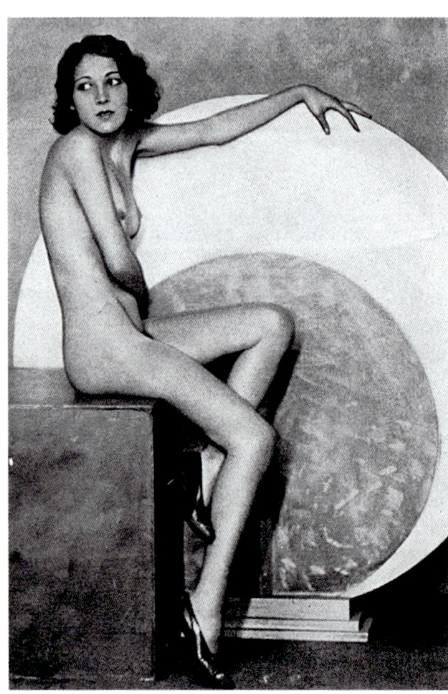

YEAR: **1930s**. TITLE: **Nifty Stories**. COUNTRY: **USA**.

der Konkurrenz Paroli, indem sie mit immer neuen kurzfristig produzierten Titeln die Kioske bepflasterten, zuerst *Snappy Mystery, Snappy Detective* und *Snappy*, später *Sizzling Romance* und *Sizzling Detective.*

Die Beliebtheit dieser Magazine lässt sich an der Preisentwicklung ablesen. Im Gefolge der Depression senkten alle anderen Verleger ihre Preise von 25 auf 15 Cent, manchmal sogar unter zehn Cent für 128 Seiten mit rauhen Illustrationen und noch rauheren Geschichten auf rauhem Papier, nur die *Spicy*-Titel verkauften sich weiterhin gut für einen Vierteldollar. Die *Spicy*-Pulps erschienen vor dem Hintergrund des Kleinkriegs zwischen der Zensur und den Schundverlegern, auf ihren Seiten wurden die Schlachten um die Moralvorstellungen der Ära geschlagen. In einem fortwährenden Räuber-und-Gendarm-Spiel druckte

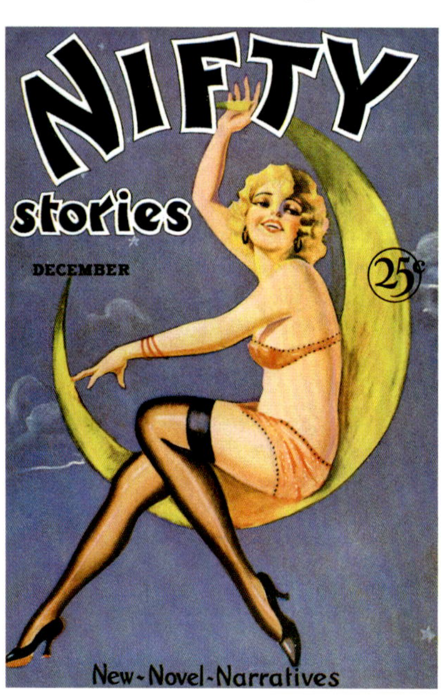

YEAR: **1930s**. TITLE: **Nifty Stories**. COUNTRY: **USA**.

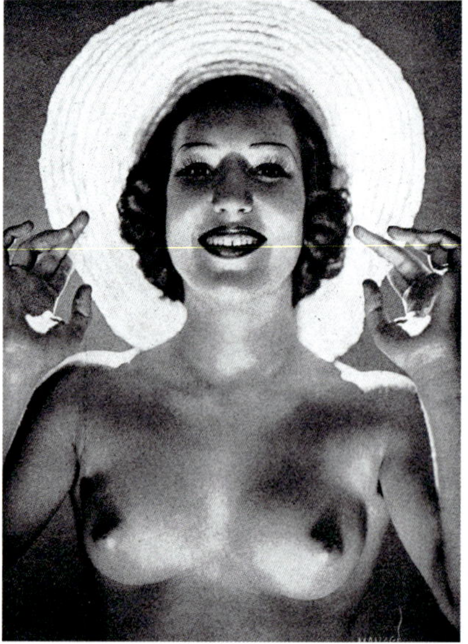

YEAR: **1936**. TITLE: **Spicy**. COUNTRY: **USA**.

« Dan Turner, détective à Hollywood ». Chez la concurrence, le meilleur illustrateur de couvertures était Enoch Bolles. Une vague d'imitateurs ne tarda pas à apparaître sur les rayons. Les publications Hubbard, vétérans des luttes pour les magazines de nus, furent les premiers avec leur collection de pulps « Saucy » (« impertinent ») : *Saucy Stories, Saucy Romantic Adventures* et *Saucy Detective*. Parmi les titres d'autres d'éditeurs, on compte *Broadway Nights, French Follies, Gay Parisienne, Ginger Stories, High Heel Magazine, Hollywood Nights, La Paree, Silk Stocking Stories, Snappy, Stolen Sweets, Breezy Stories* et *Cupid's Capers*. Armer et Donenfeld contre-attaquèrent en inondant les kiosques de numéros uniques imitant leurs propres publications, d'abord *Snappy Mystery, Snappy Detective* et *Snappy* ; puis *Sizzling Romance* et *Sizzling Detective*. On peut évaluer la

YEAR: **1941**. TITLE: **Beauty Parade**. ARTIST: **Earl Moran**. COUNTRY: **USA**.

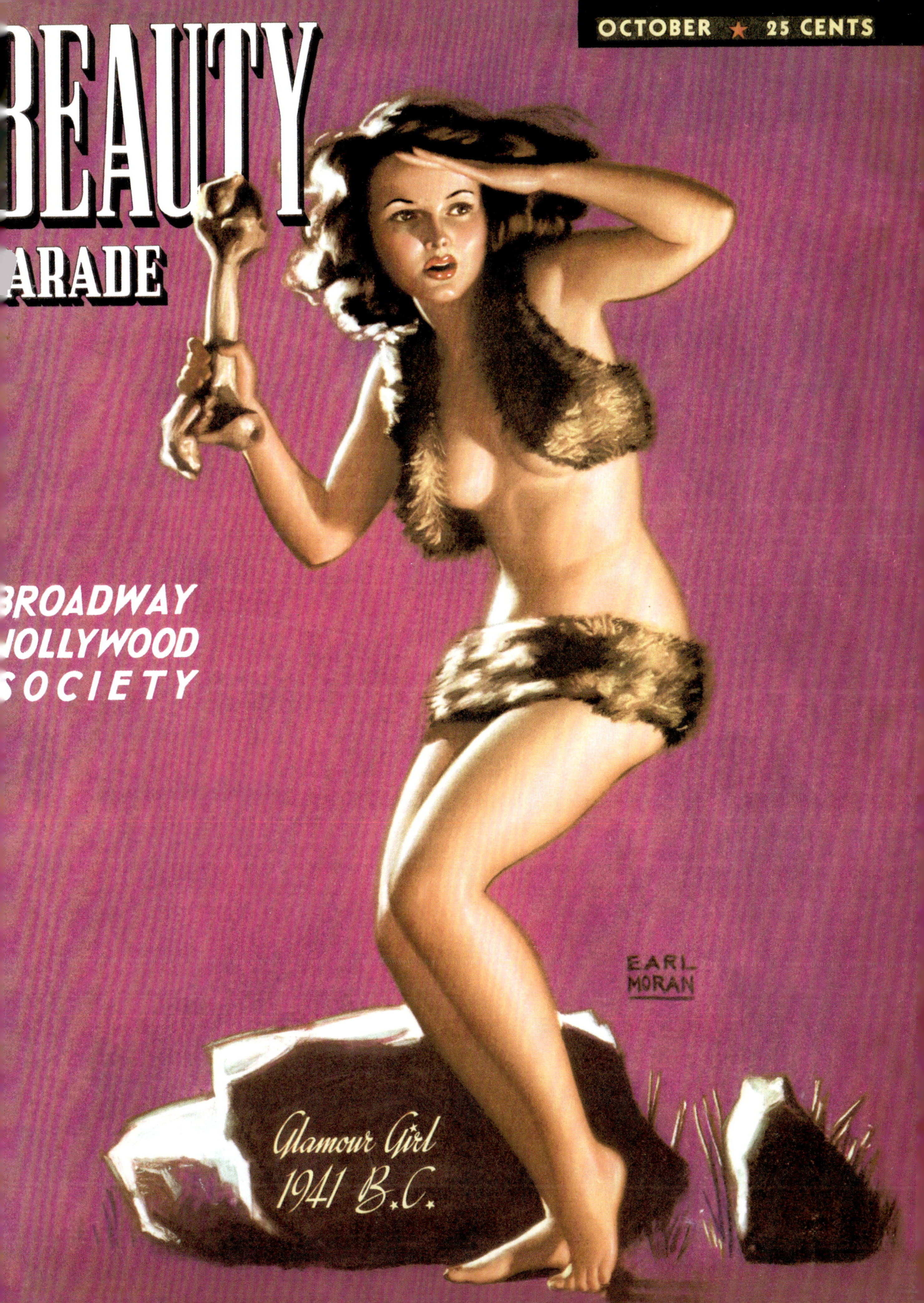
OCTOBER ★ 25 CENTS
BEAUTY
ARADE
ROADWAY
OLLYWOOD
OCIETY
EARL MORAN
Glamour Girl
1941 B.C.

Year: **1937**. Title: **High Heel Magazine**. Artist: **Cardwell Higgins**. Country: **USA**.

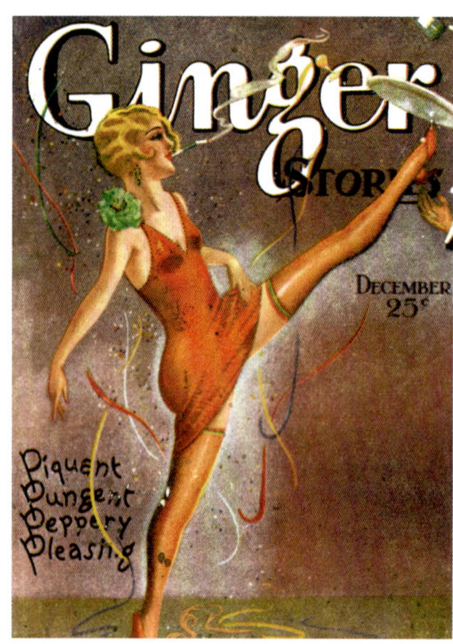

Year: **1928**. Title: **Ginger Stories**. Country: **USA**.

helping the cops or bankruptcy courts. Another tactic was to publish under many corporate names: Donenfeld used Irwin Publishing (after his son and brother), Culture, DM, King and Elmo Press. By the early 1940s America's need for purity to fight the war resulted in a society-wide tightening of sexual content. All the pulps had to tone down their sexual content. December 1942 saw the last of the *Spicy* name titles. Paper restrictions meant that established publishers could continue publishing, but new competitors couldn't join the game. Donenfeld and Armer managed to squeeze out one last line of magazines, the *Speed* titles, before all disappeared post-war.

Spicy today: *Spicys* are among the most alluring publications of all time, though their actual sexual content would compare today to the more graphic *Harlequin Romances*. Their reputation has meant that carefully hoarded

Donenfeld viele unterschiedliche Adressen ins Impressum seiner Magazine, entweder eine von mehreren Scheinfirmen in einem einzigen Gebäude (dem Grand Central Palace zwischen der 46th und 47th Straße in Manhatten und 1790 Broadway, wo sich seine Buchbinderei befand) oder eine seiner falschen Adressen in Delaware, einem Staat, dem mehr daran lag, Firmen zu decken, als der Polizei oder den Konkursgerichten zu helfen. Eine andere Taktik bestand darin, unter vielen verschiedenen Firmennamen zu publizieren, bei Donenfeld waren das Irwing Publishing (nach seinem Sohn und seinem Bruder benannt), Culture, DM, King und Elmo Press. Als man in den frühen Vierzigern für den Krieg alle Moral zusammennehmen musste, wurde die Gesellschaft insgesamt wieder prüder. Alle Pulp-Magazine sahen sich gezwungen, ihren Inhalt zu entschärfen.

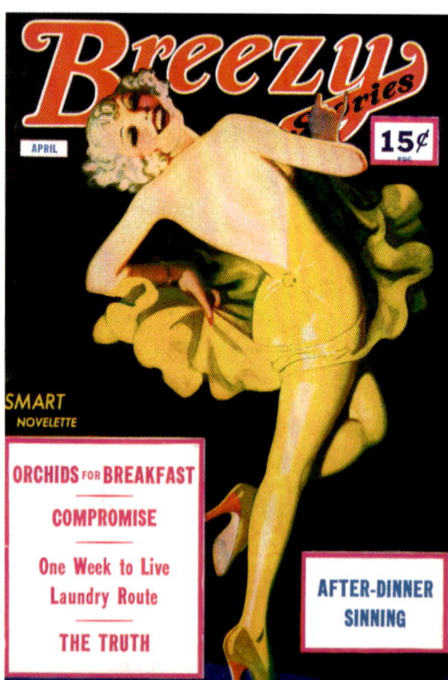

Year: **1937**. Title: **Breezy Stories**. Country: **USA**.

popularité de ces magazines à leurs prix. En pleine dépression, alors que tous les autres éditeurs baissaient leurs prix de 25 à 15 cents, voire 10, pour 128 pages d'illustrations frustes et d'histoires encore plus sommaires sur du papier bon marché, les *Spicys* conservèrent leur prix de 25 cents.

À travers les pulps *Spicy* s'exprimait la collision entre les différentes mœurs de l'époque, ce qui les plaça au cœur de la bataille entre les censeurs et les marchands de publications interdites. Dans

While sold under-the-counter, the sexual activity was only implied.

ce jeu permanent de gendarmes et de voleurs, Donenfeld changeait régulièrement d'adresse dans ses magazines, allant de divers « bureaux de façades » dans un même immeuble (le Grand Central Palace, entre les 46e et 47e Rues, et le n°1790 à Broadway, l'adresse de son relieur) à de fausses adresses dans le Delaware, un État qui préférait aider ses entreprises que la police ou les tribunaux de commerce. L'autre tactique consistait à publier sous différents noms de société : Donenfeld utilisa Irwin Publishing (du prénom de son fils et de son frère), Culture, DM, King et Elmo Press. Au début des années quarante, l'Amérique ressentit un besoin de se purifier pour partir à la guerre, ce qui entraîna un resserrement des mœurs dans l'ensemble de la société. Tous les pulps durent édulcorer leurs contenus. En décembre 1942

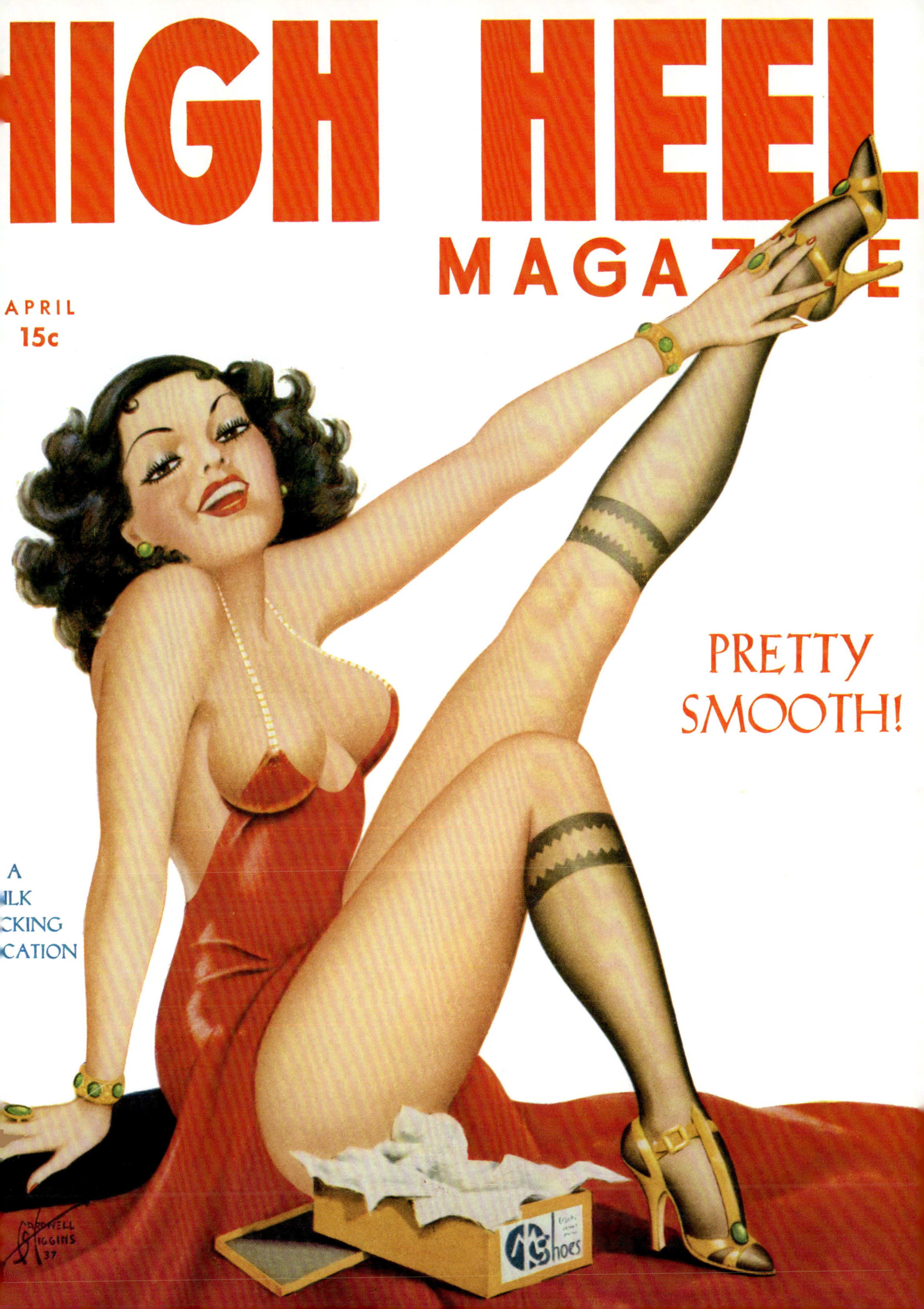
HIGH HEEL
MAGAZ E
APRIL
15c
PRETTY
SMOOTH!
A
ILK
CKING
CATION
Shoes

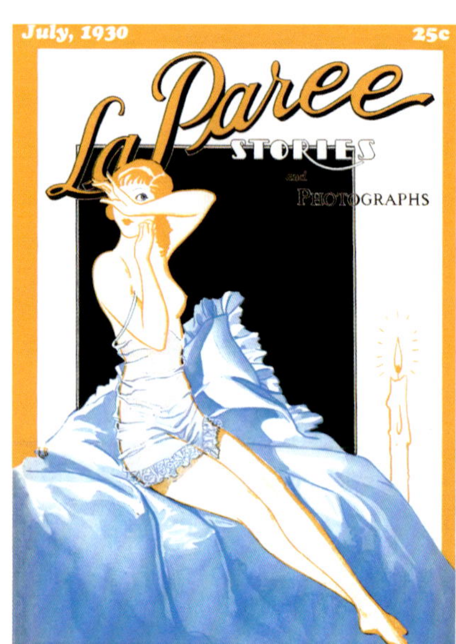

Year: **1930**. Title: **La Paree**. Country: **USA**.

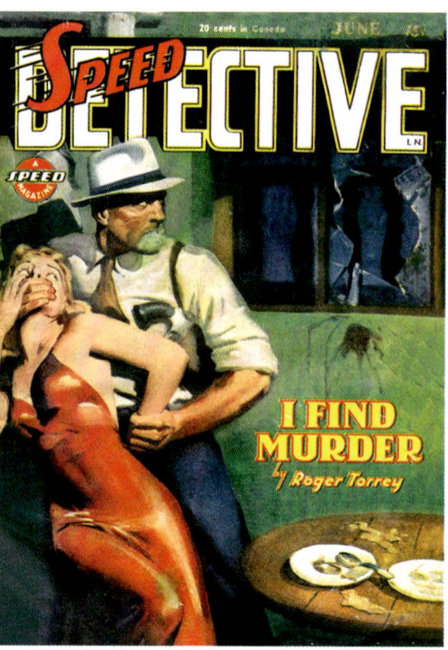

Year: **1945**. Title: **Speed Detective**. Country: **USA**.

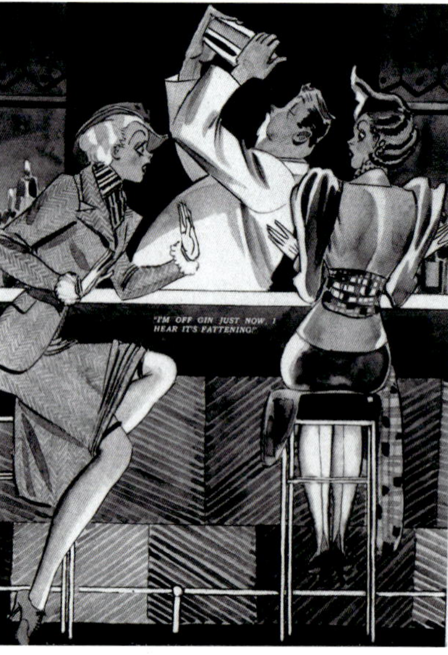

Year: **1939**. Title: **Modern Girl**. Country: **USA**.

copies are among the most valued of all pulps. Collectors will pay premium prices, often two to ten times the amount of a similar "hot" title of the same age. The cover artists are revered, and the covers themselves have appeared on a host of products.

Culture Publications' pulps were the most sexually provocative legal fiction that could be purchased in the 1930s.

Im Dezember 1942 erschien der letzte der *Spicy*-Titel. Die Papierrationierung erlaubte es nur etablierten Verlegern weiterzumachen, Neulinge blieben außen vor. Donenfeld und Armer schafften es gerade noch, eine letzte Reihe von Magazinen, die *Speed*-Titel, auf den Markt zu bringen, bevor sie in der Nachkriegszeit vollends verschwanden.

Spicy heute: *Spicys* zählen zu den reizvollsten Veröffentlichungen überhaupt, auch wenn darin im Grunde nicht mehr Sex vorkam als bei den etwas expliziteren der heute am Kiosk erhältlichen Liebesromane. Sorgsam gehütete Hefte zählen heute zu den begehrtesten unter den Pulp-Magazinen. Sammler zahlen Spitzenpreise, oft das Zwei- bis Zehnfache wie für ähnliche „scharfe" Titel gleichen Alters. Die Coverillustratoren sind heute Berühmtheiten, und die Titel selbst sind auf einer Vielzahl von Produkten wieder aufgetaucht.

parut le dernier titre *Spicy*. Avec les restrictions sur le papier, les éditeurs établis pouvaient continuer à publier, mais les nouveaux concurrents ne tenaient plus la route. Donenfeld et Armer parvinrent à éditer tant bien que mal une nouvelle série de magazines, les titres *Speed,* qui disparurent tous après la guerre.

Les *Spicy* aujourd'hui : Les *Spicy* comptent parmi les publications les plus séduisantes de tous les temps, même si leur teneur érotique serait comparable aujourd'hui aux romans *Harlequin* les plus osés. Du fait de leur réputation, leurs exemplaires soigneusement conservés en font les pulps les plus recherchés. Les collectionneurs les achètent au prix fort, souvent deux à dix fois le montant d'un titre « chaud » similaire de la même époque. Les illustrateurs de leurs couvertures sont vénérés et leurs couvertures elles-mêmes ont été reproduites sur une large éventail de produits.

Year: **1930**. Title: **"Real Smart"**. Artist: **O. Greiner**. Country: **USA**.

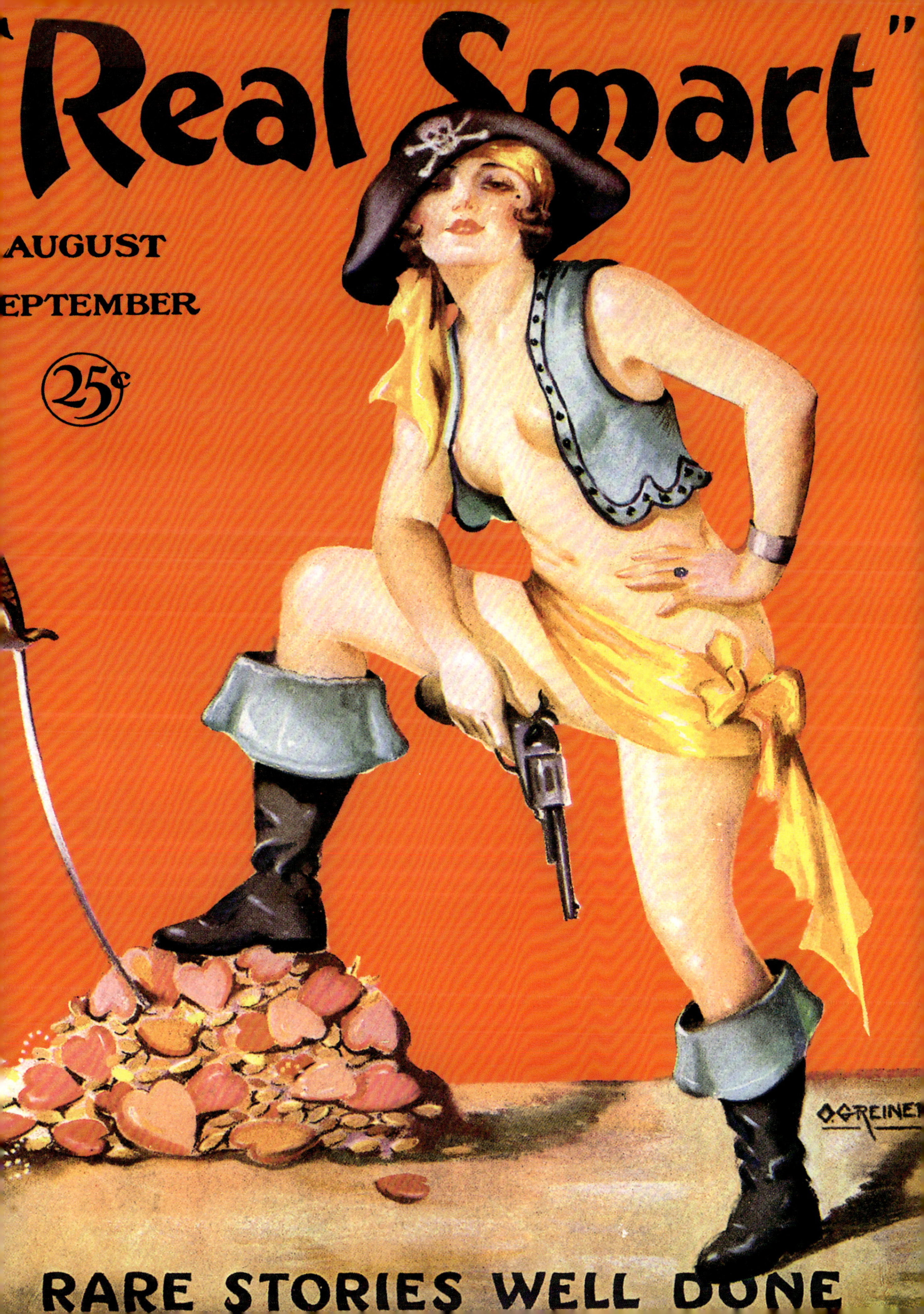
"Real Smart"
AUGUST
EPTEMBER
25¢
O.GREINE
RARE STORIES WELL DONE

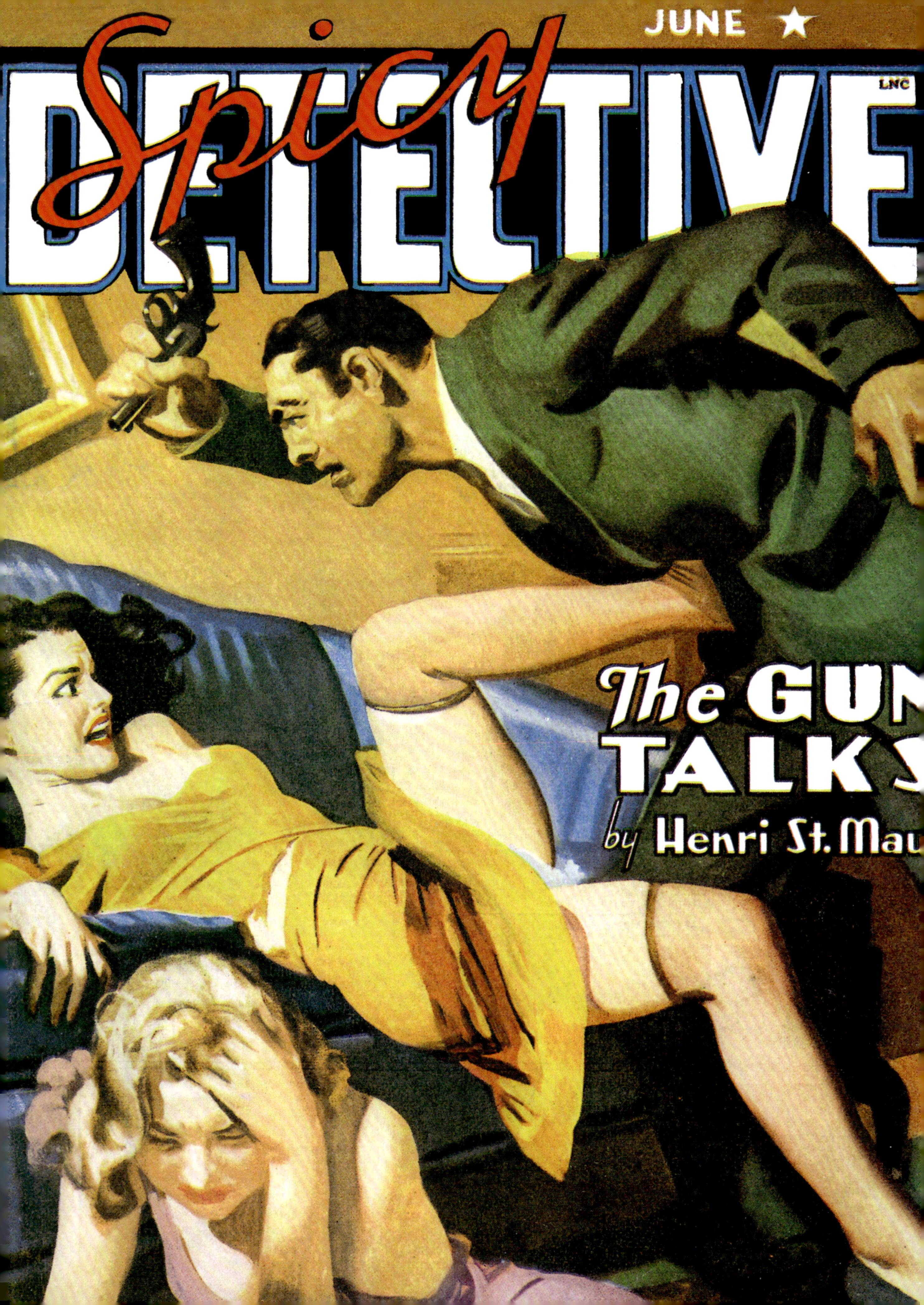
JUNE
Spicy
DETECTIVE
INC
The GUN
TALKS
by Henri St. Mau

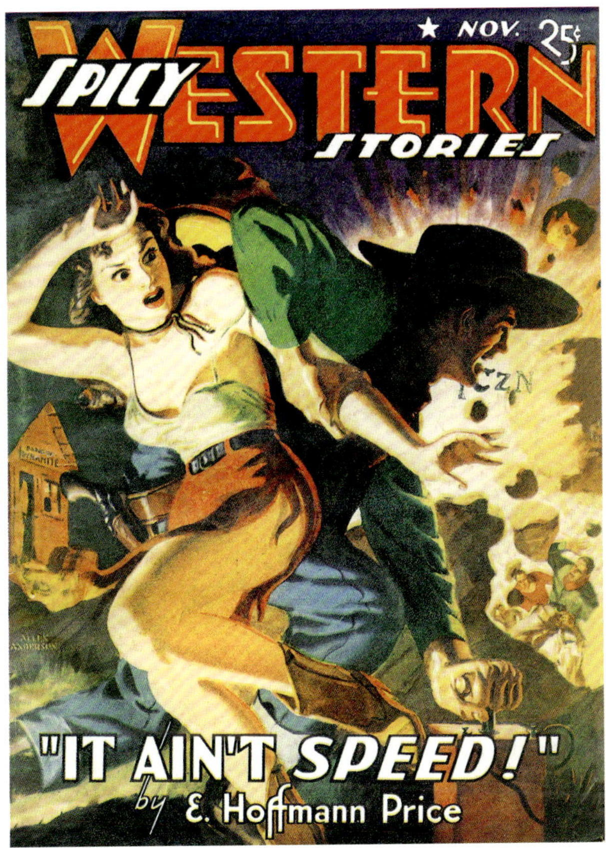

YEAR: **1941**. TITLE: **Spicy Western Stories**. COUNTRY: **USA**.

LEFT: YEAR: **1941**. TITLE: **Spicy Detective**. COUNTRY: **USA**.
BELOW: YEAR: **1943**. TITLE: **Speed Mystery**. COUNTRY: **USA**.

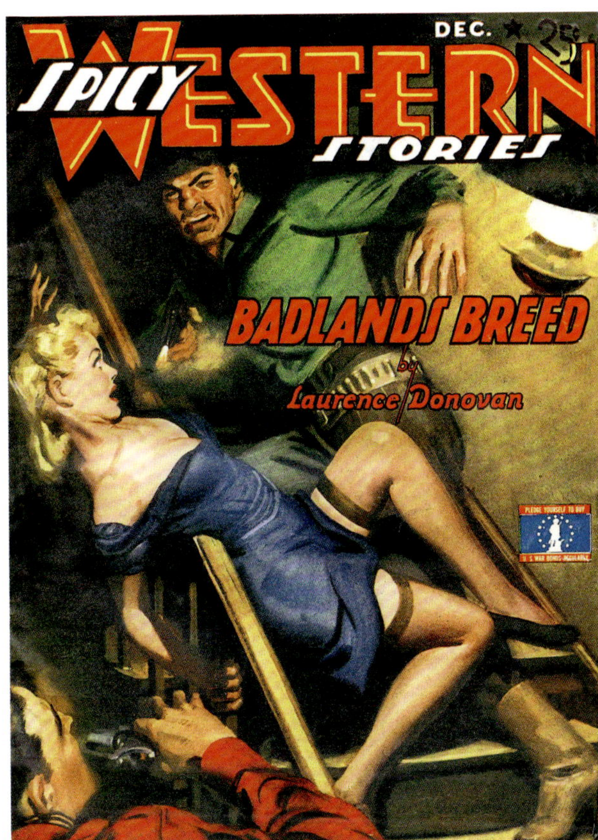

YEAR: **1942**. TITLE: **Spicy Western Stories**. COUNTRY: **USA**.

BELOW: YEAR: **1941**. TITLE: **Spicy Detective**. COUNTRY: **USA**.

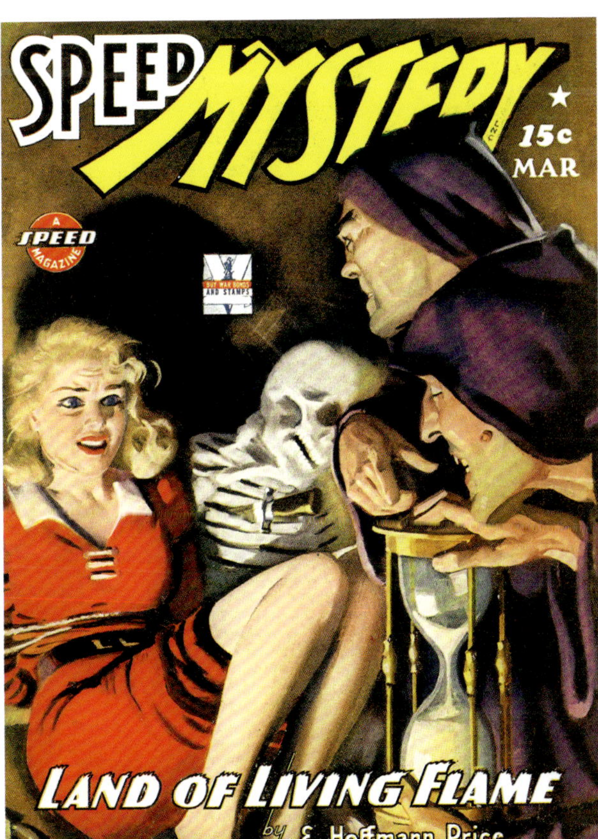

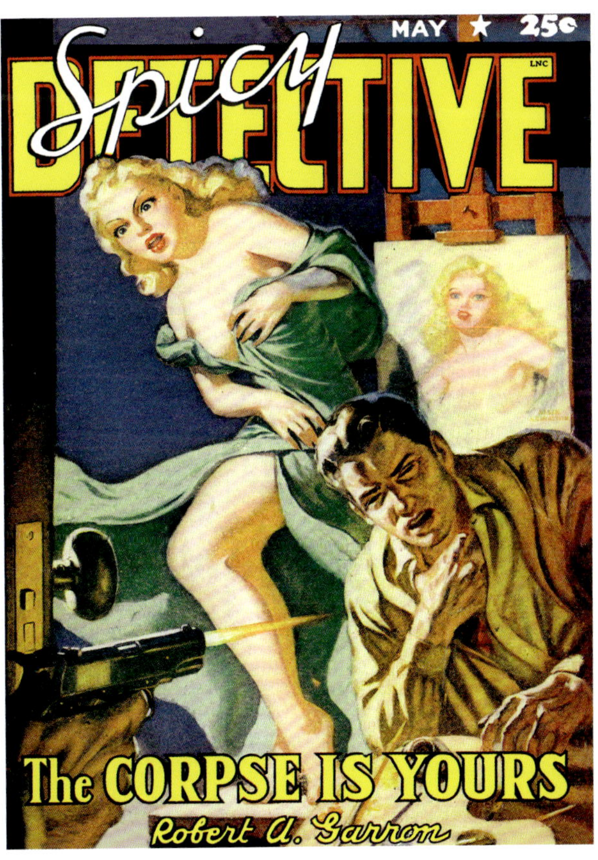

The Speed series was the last from Spicy's publisher Culture Publications, following Saucy, Snappy *and* Sizzling *fiction series.*

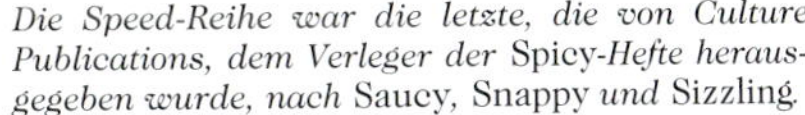

Die Speed-Reihe war die letzte, die von Culture Publications, dem Verleger der Spicy-Hefte herausgegeben wurde, nach Saucy, Snappy *und* Sizzling*.*

La série des Speed fut la dernière de Culture Publications, les éditeurs des Spicy, à la suite des autres séries de fiction Saucy, Snappy *et* Sizzling*.*

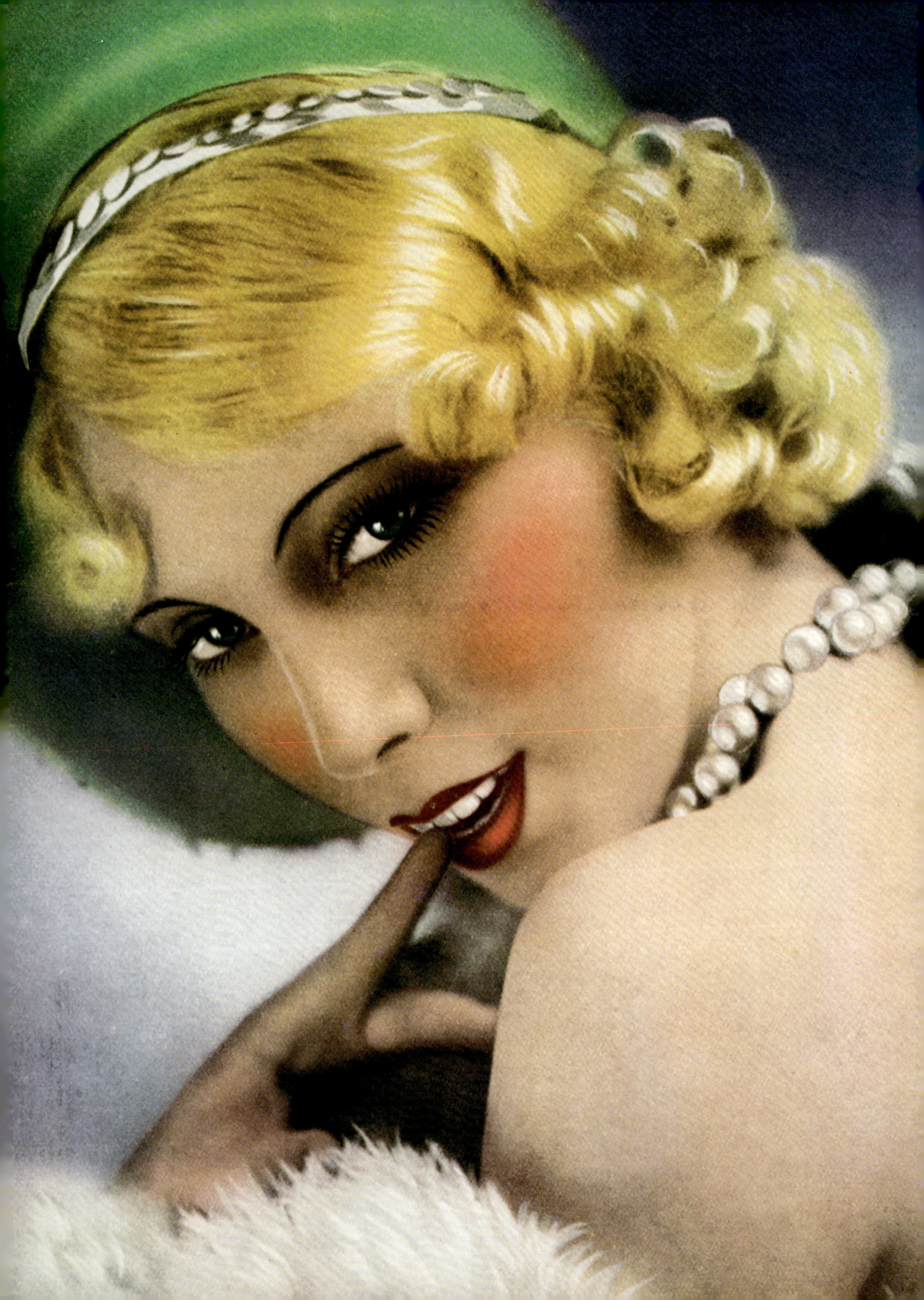

Naughty Magazines about Naughty Films

Unziemliche Hefte über unziemliche Filme

Magazines coquins sur des films coquins

Sexy film magazines are as old as sexy films, meaning they debuted in the mid-20s. The early American art nude magazines relied heavily on Hollywood starlets, at first just as models, then with an increasing emphasis on cinema itself. The studios presumably provided the racy stills. It was perfect symbiosis, the studios trading magazine content for free publicity, with both sides benefiting more or less equally. It's doubtful the actresses even had to be paid for these photos; under contract they were obliged to make themselves available for publicity as their studios saw fit. In Germany, where film production was almost apace with Hollywood, publishers discovered this popular formula at about the same time. *Film, Tanz, Exotik* exposed the slinky, vampiric heroines of Fritz Lang and Ernst Lubitsch in even more exotic vignettes than their American counterparts (note the stuffed ape). With a less significant film industry France relied more on its cabarets to fill magazines in the 20s, but by the 30s *Paris Magazine*, *Pages Folles*, and *Beauté* were increasing sales with topless photos of European and American stars.

In 1930s Hollywood the new moral code discouraged nude scenes but actresses could still be convinced to pose in provocative lingerie. *Film Fun*, *Movie Humor* and *Real Screen* offered their

Year: **1933**. Title: **Paris Magazine**.
Country: **France**.

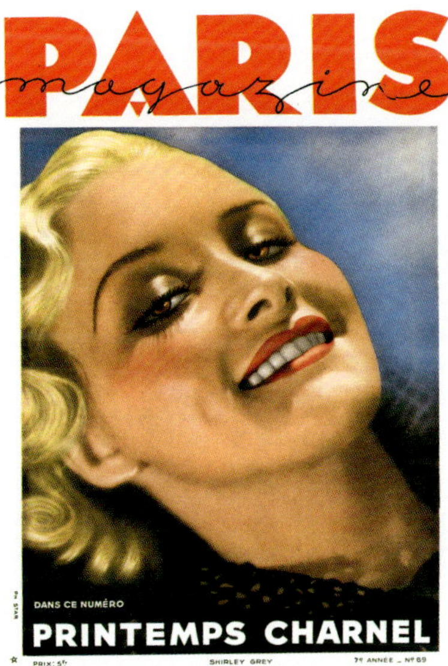

Year: **1937**. Title: **Paris Magazine**.
Country: **France**.

Filmmagazine mit der Betonung auf Sex gibt es, seit es Filme mit der Betonung auf Sex gibt, also seit den Zwanzigern. Die frühen Magazine mit „Künstlerakten" setzten stark auf Hollywood-Starlets, zuerst lediglich als Models, dann verlegten sie ihr Interesse zunehmend auf die Filme selbst. Vermutlich lieferten die Studios die gewagten Standfotos. Es war die perfekte Symbiose – die Studios lieferten den Magazinen das Material und machten dadurch kostenlose Reklame für ihre Filme. Man darf

Les magazines sexy de cinéma sont aussi vieux que les films sexy, ce qui signifie qu'ils sont apparus vers le milieu des années vingt. Les premiers magazines de nus artistiques dépendaient en grande partie des starlettes d'Hollywood, tout d'abord en tant que modèles, puis parce qu'ils mettaient de plus en plus l'accent sur le cinéma. Les studios fournissaient

> It was perfect symbiosis, the movie studios trading magazine content for free publicity.

vraisemblablement les images osées. C'était une symbiose parfaite, les studios assurant le contenu des magazines en échange de la publicité gratuite, les deux parties y trouvant un profit plus ou moins équivalent.

Il est probable que les actrices n'étaient même pas payées pour ces photos. Elles étaient obligées par contrat de se prêter à tout forme de promotion jugée utile par les studios. En Allemagne, où la production cinematographique était aussi intense qu'à Hollywood, les éditeurs découvrirent cette formule populaire vers

Year: **1934**. Title: **Movie Humor**.
Artist: **George Quintana**. Country: **USA**.

Those who sit in the State Film Bureau pay homage to the dogma that young people suffer damage if they see sex acts in the movies. Violence, however, does them no harm at all.

—*The Erotic Minorities*, Lars Ullerstam

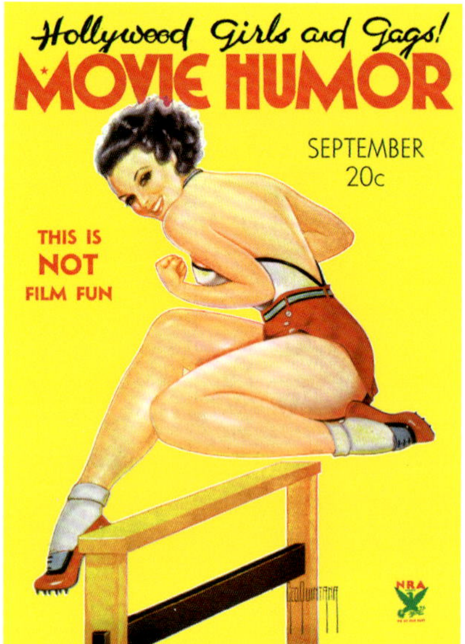

Year: **1934**. Title: **Movie Humor**.
Artist: **George Quintana**. Country: **USA**.

readers breathtaking photos of leggy young actresses by the best glamour photographers of the day. The fine rag paper and superb printing in these magazines speak for their immense popularity.

In Germany all the fine magazines were gone; when Hitler took power in 1933 he turned the film studios into propaganda mills with no time or place for slinky starlets. During and immediately after the war neither France nor Germany had the resources for film production. In Hollywood all was perky patriotism, a sexual void. Even when America emerged from the war its films extolled sappy domestic bliss, driving its men's magazines to burlesque for content. *French Peep Show* was a rare one shot from 1952 that documented the making of Russ Meyer's first commercial film. Appropriately it was a documentary about a burlesque show. In

bezweifeln, dass die Schauspielerinnen für diese Aufnahmen ein Honorar erwarten konnten; vertraglich an die Studios gebunden, mussten sie nach deren Gutdünken für Publicity zur Verfügung stehen. In Deutschland, wo die Filmindustrie fast auf einer Höhe mit Hollywood war, entdeckten Verleger diese Erfolgsformel praktisch zur gleichen Zeit. *Film, Tanz, Exotik* zeigte die aufreizenden, vampirhaften Heldinnen von Fritz Lang und Ernst Lubitsch in noch exotischeren Vignetten als ihre amerikanischen Pendants (man beachte den ausgestopften Affen). Frankreich mit seiner nicht ganz so bedeutenden Filmindustrie fand in den Zwanzigern das Material für seine Magazine eher in den Cabarets, aber in den Dreißigern steigerten Blätter wie *Paris Magazine*, *Pages Folles* oder *Beauté* ihre Auflagen auch mit Obenohne-Fotos europäischer und amerikanischer Filmschauspielerinnen.

In den Dreißigern verhinderte der neue Moralkodex Nacktszenen in Hollywoodfilmen, doch man konnte die Schauspielerinnen immer noch bewegen, in provozierenden Dessous zu posieren. *Film Fun*, *Movie Humor* und *Real*

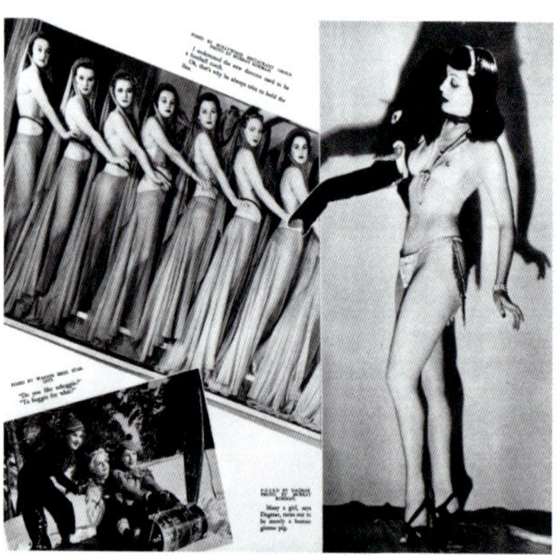

Year: **1938**. Title: **Reel Humor**. Country: **USA**.

la même époque. *Film, Tanz, Exotik* publiait des portraits des voluptueuses héroïnes vampiriques de Fritz Lang et d'Ernst Lubitsch, encore plus exotiques que ceux de ses concurrents américains (on remarquera le singe empaillé).

Dans les années vingt, la France possédait une industrie cinématographique moins prolifique et se reposait davantage sur ses cabarets pour remplir les pages des magazines mais, dès les années trente, *Paris Magazine*, *Pages Folles* et *Beauté* augmentèrent leurs ventes grâce aux photos de vedettes américaines et européennes les seins nus.

Dans le Hollywood des années trente, le nouveau code moral décourageait la nudité à l'écran mais on pouvait encore convaincre les actrices de prendre des poses aguicheuses de la lingerie fine. *Film Fun*, *Movie Humor* et *Real Screen* offraient à leurs lecteurs des photos étourdissantes de jeunes actrices toutes en jambes réalisées par les meilleurs photographes glamour de l'époque. Le beau papier chiffon et la superbe impression de ces magazines témoignent de leur immense popularité.

En Allemagne, toutes les belles revues disparurent. Lorsqu'Hitler prit le pouvoir en 1933, il transforma les studios de cinéma en usines de propagande où il n'y avait ni place ni temps pour de langoureuses starlettes. Pendant et immédiatement après la guerre, la France et l'Allemagne n'avaient plus les ressources pour produire des films. Hollywood était en proie à un patriotisme guilleret où le sexe aurait été déplacé. Même lorsque l'Amérique émergea de la guerre, ses films exaltaient une béatitude conjugale nunuche, obligeant les magazines pour hommes à se rabattre sur les cabarets

"This is not Film Fun!"

„Das ist kein Filmspaß!"

« Ce n'est pas du divertissement cinématographique ! »

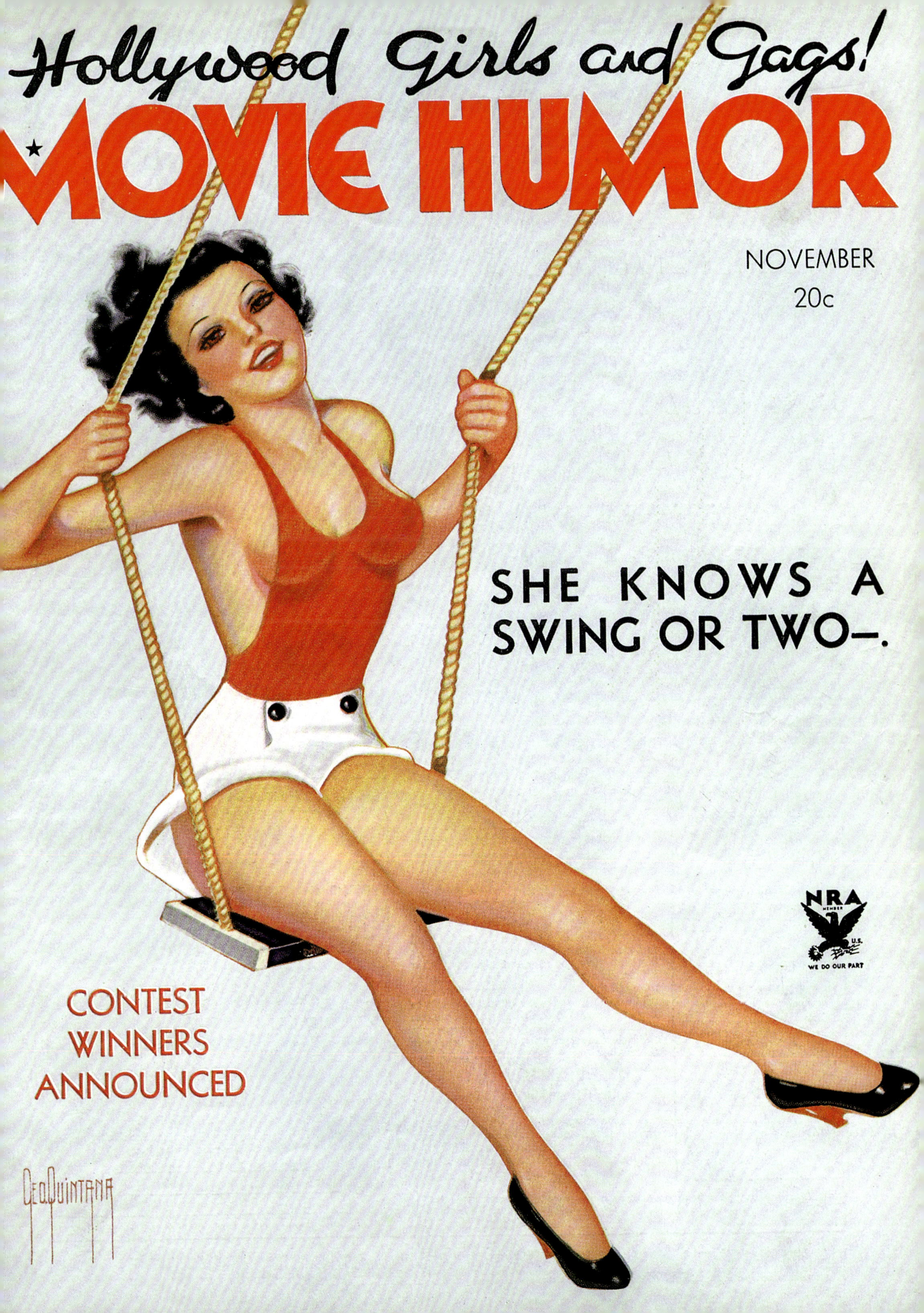
Hollywood Girls and Gags!
MOVIE HUMOR
NOVEMBER
20c
SHE KNOWS A
SWING OR TWO–.
NRA
WE DO OUR PART
CONTEST
WINNERS
ANNOUNCED
GEO QUINTANA

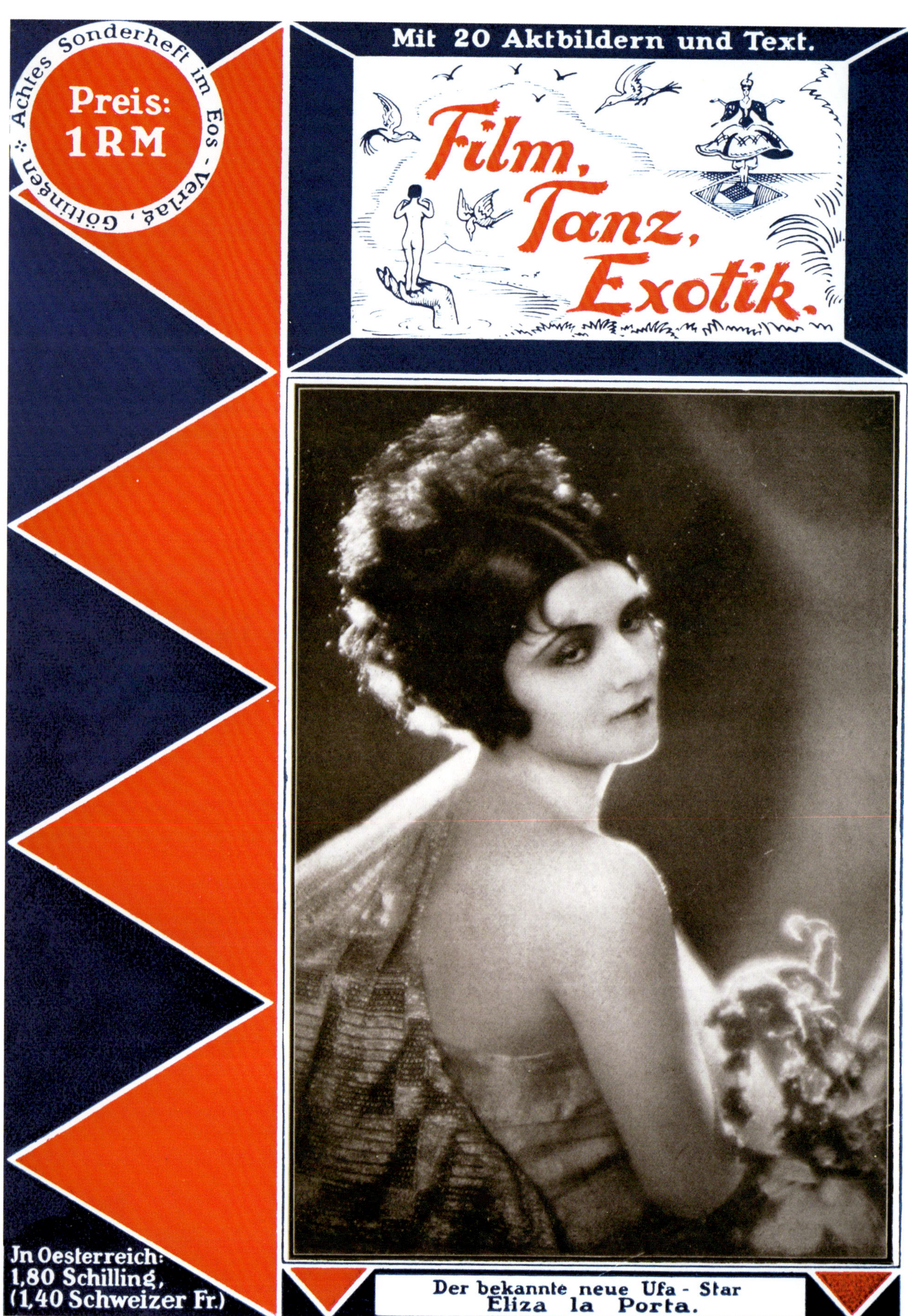

YEAR: **1928**. TITLE: **Film, Tanz, Exotik**. COUNTRY: **Germany**.

YEAR: **1928**. TITLE: **Film, Tanz, Exotik**.
COUNTRY: **Germany**.

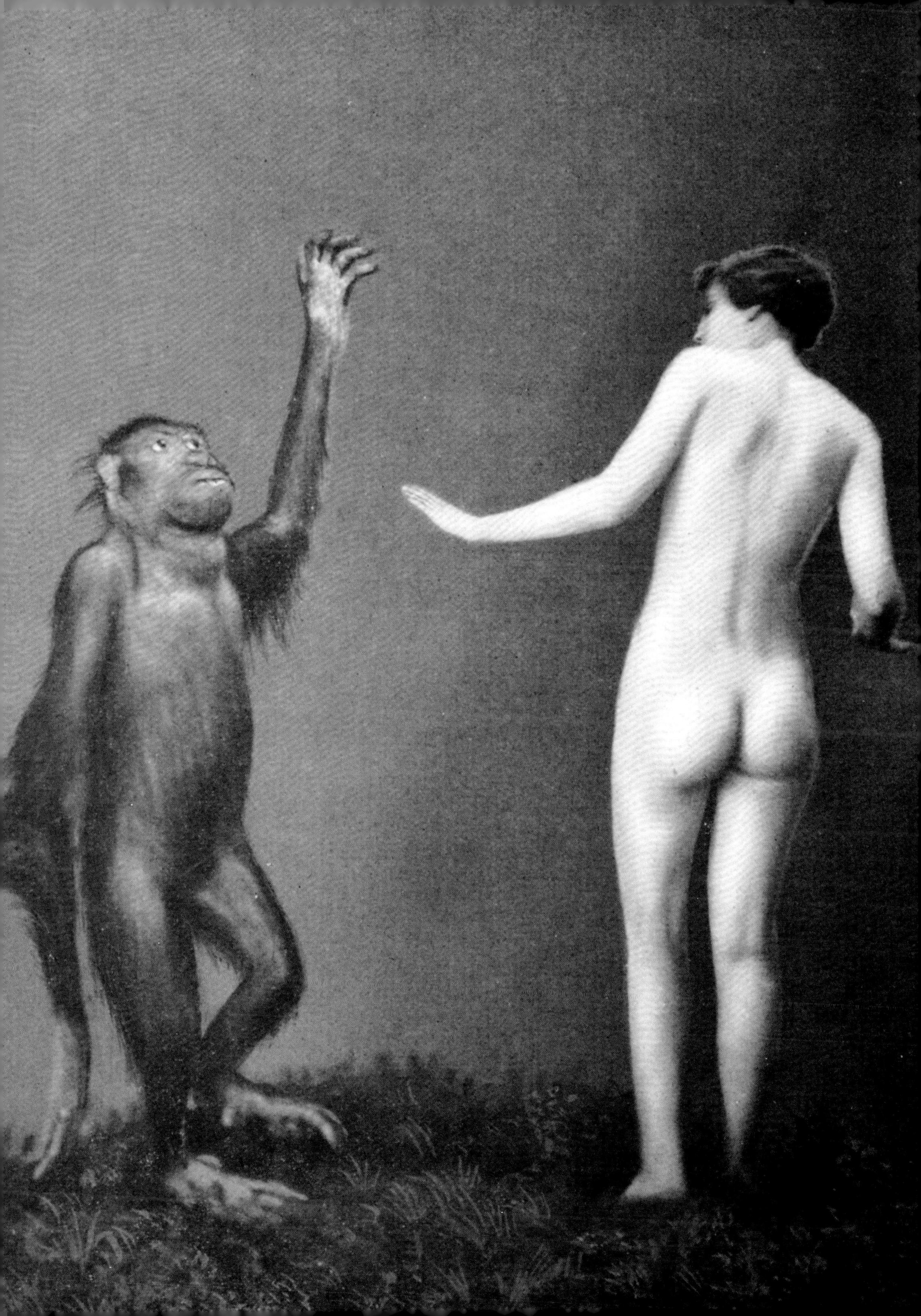

YEAR: **1952**. TITLE: **French Peep Show**. COUNTRY: **USA**.

French Peep Show was a rare one shot from 1952 that documented the making of Russ Meyer's first commercial film.

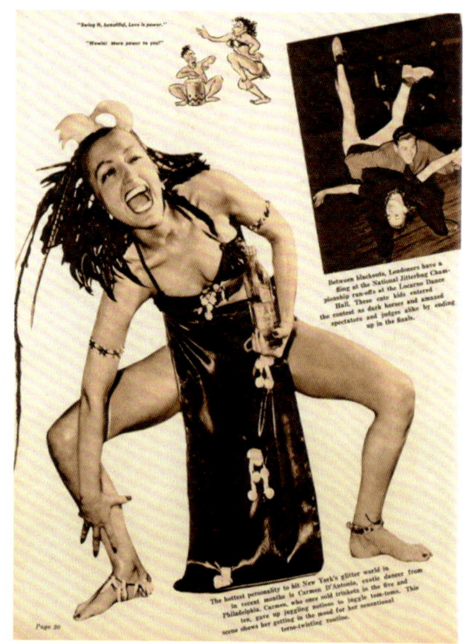
"Swing it, beautiful. Love is power."

"Wowie! More power to you!"

Between blackouts, Londoners have a fling at the National Jitterbug Championship run-offs at the Locarno Dance Hall. These cute kids entered the contest as dark horses and amazed spectators and judges alike by ending up in the finals.

The hottest personality to hit New York's glitter world in recent months is Carmen D'Antonio, exotic dancer from Philadelphia. Carmen, who once sold trinkets in the five and ten, gave up juggling notions to juggle tom-toms. This scene shows her getting in the mood for her sensational torso-twisting routine.

Page 20

YEAR: **1941**. TITLE: **Film Fun**. COUNTRY: **USA**.

Germany *Gondel* magazine mixed Hollywood publicity stills with pin-ups, but it was no *Film, Tanz, Exotik*. France alone picked up the pre-war thread with *Paris-Hollywood*, blending sexy American actresses with topless Parisian cabaret stars. Not until the late 60s would American sexy film magazines return, and the new magazines would bear no resemblance to their predecessors.

Screen boten ihren Lesern atemberaubende Aufnahmen langbeiniger junger Schauspielerinnen, aufgenommen von den besten Glamourfotografen der Zeit. Das edle Hadernpapier und die erstklassige Druckqualität dieser Magazine verraten ihre immense Popularität.

In Deutschland verschwanden die pikanten Magazine, als Hitler 1933 an die Macht kam und die Filmstudios in Propagandamühlen verwandelte, in denen aufreizende Starlets keinen Platz mehr hatten. Unmittelbar nach dem Krieg hatten weder Deutschland noch Frankreich die Ressourcen für eine Filmindustrie. In Hollywood regierte blitzsauberer Patriotismus, eine sexuelle Leerstelle. Selbst nach dem Krieg zeigten die Filme in den Staaten noch öde häusliche Glückseligkeit und zwangen die Magazine, sich beim Varieté umzusehen. *French Peep Show* war ein heute seltenes Sonderheft, das 1952 die Dreharbeiten zu Russ Meyers erstem kommerziellen Film dokumentierte, der wiederum passenderweise eine Dokumentation über eine Varietéshow war. In Deutschland zeigte das Magazin *Gondel* Werbefotos aus Hollywood und Pin-ups, und in Frankreich nahm *Paris-Hollywood* die Tradition der Vorkriegszeit wieder auf und präsentierte amerikanische Schauspielerinnen mit Sexappeal und barbusige Stars aus den Pariser Varietés. In den USA sollten erst in den späten Sechzigern wieder sexy Filmmagazine erscheinen, und diese erinnerten in nichts mehr an ihre Vorläufer.

pour remplir leurs pages. *French Peep Show* fit une tentative unique en 1952, documentant le tournage du premier film de commande de Russ Meyer. Comme par hasard, il s'agissait d'un documentaire sur un spectacle de strip-tease.

En Allemagne, le magazine *Gondel* mélangeait les images promotionnelles de films d'Hollywood et les pin-up, mais on était loin de *Film, Tanz, Exotik*. Seule la France reprit son élan d'avant-guerre avec *Paris-Hollywood*, faisant se côtoyer les actrices américaines sexy et les vedettes des cabarets topless parisiens. Il faudrait attendre la fin des années soixante pour voir le retour aux États-Unis des magazines érotiques de cinéma, mais les nouveaux venus n'auraient plus rien à voir avec leurs prédécesseurs.

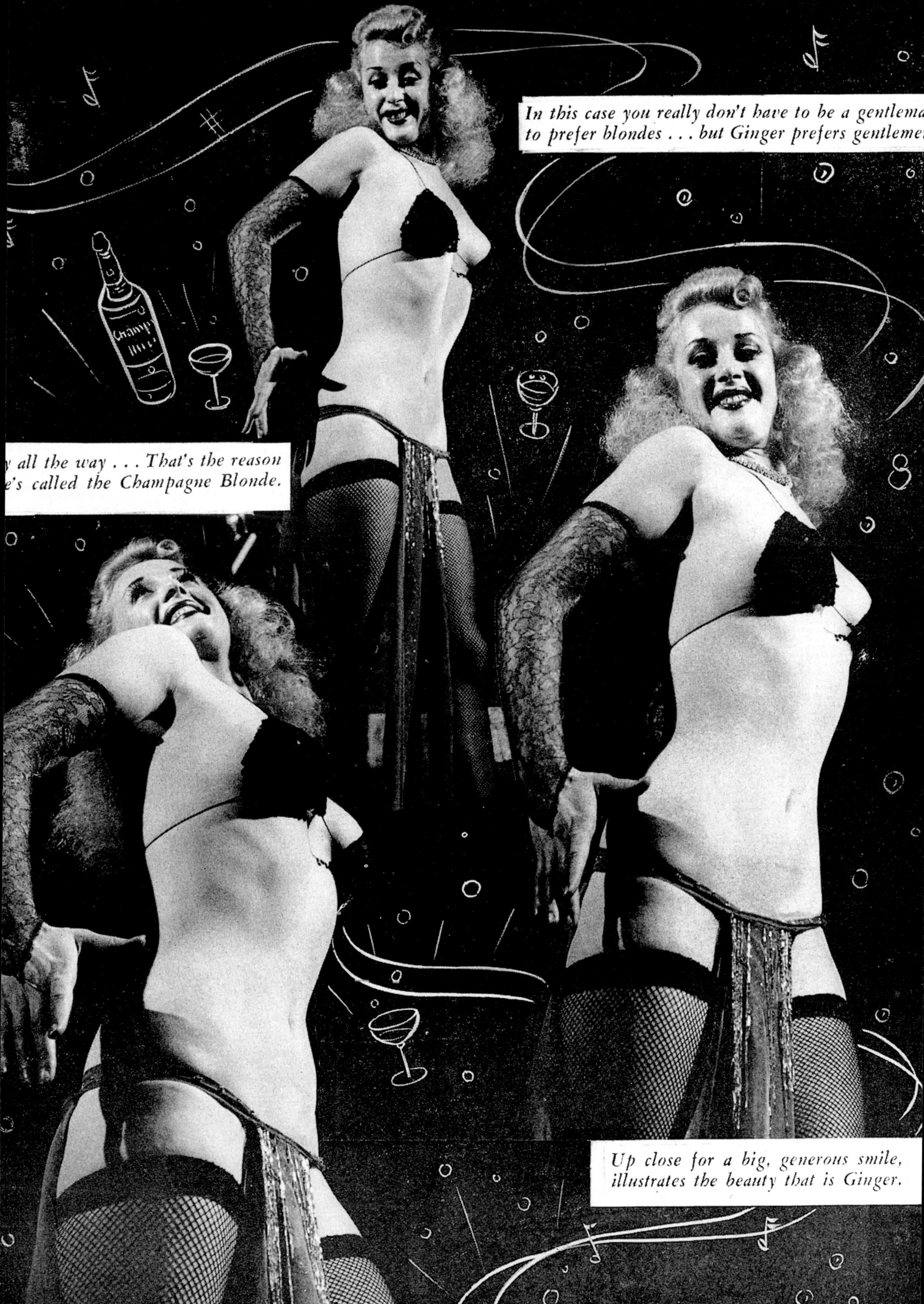

In this case you really don't have to be a gentlema to prefer blondes . . . but Ginger prefers gentlemen

y all the way . . . That's the reason e's called the Champagne Blonde.

Up close for a big, generous smile, illustrates the beauty that is Ginger.

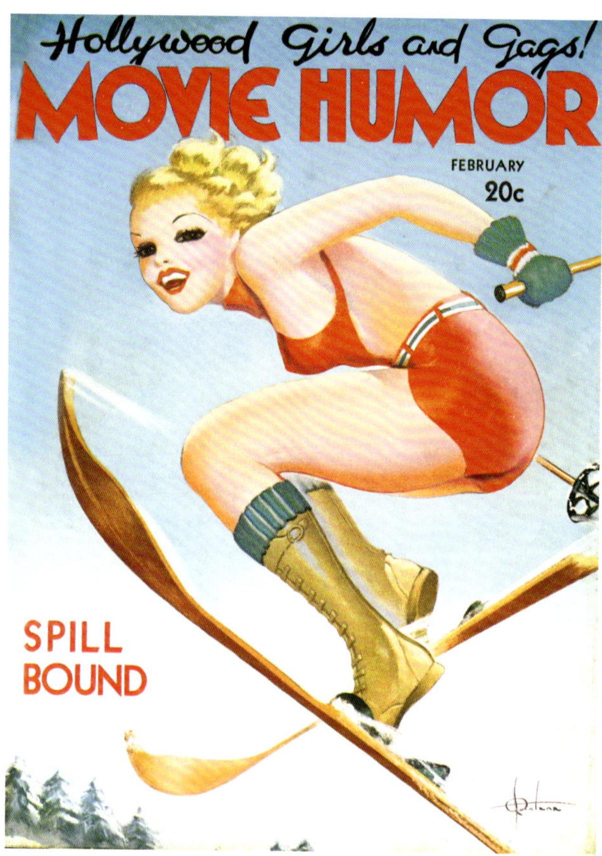

Year: **1937**. Title: **Movie Humor**. Artist: **George Quintana**. Country: **USA**.

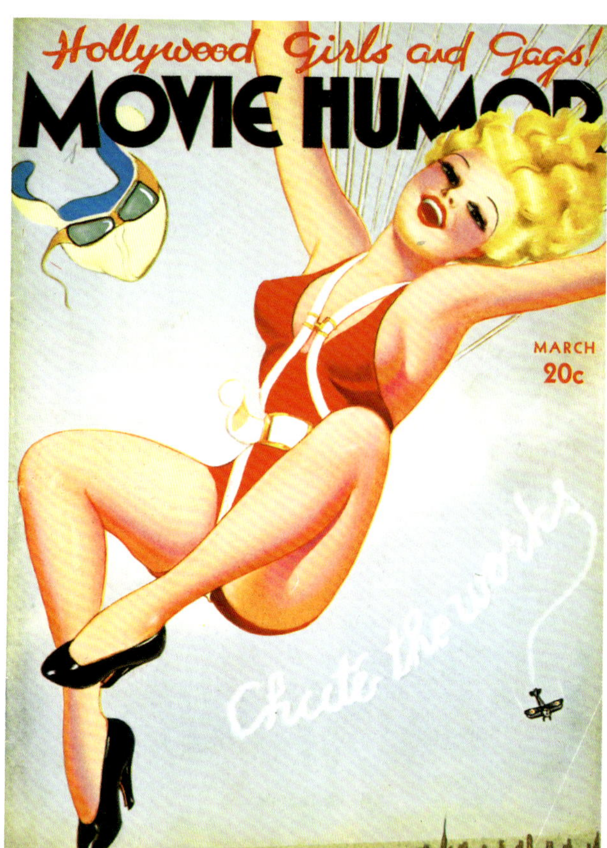

Year: **1936**. Title: **Movie Humor**. Artist: **George Quintana**. Country: **USA**.

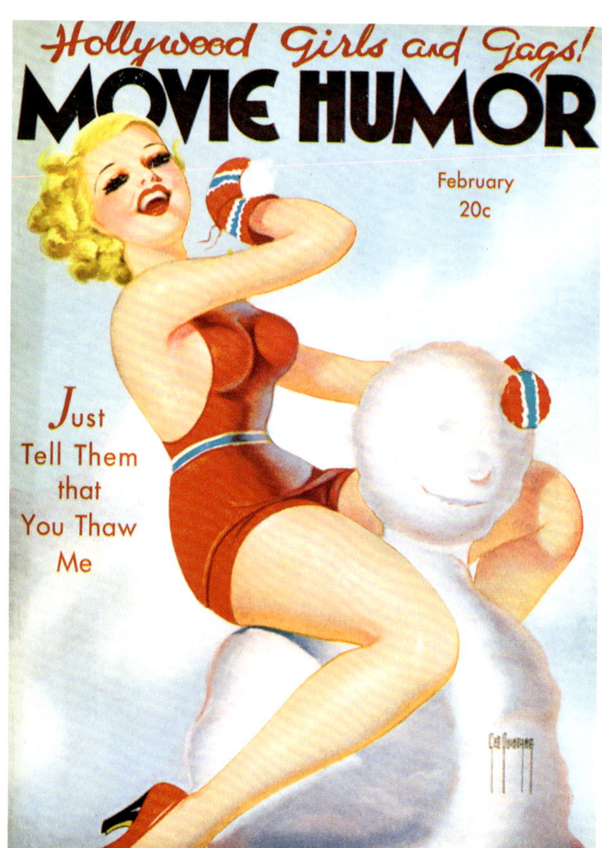

Year: **1936**. Title: **Movie Humor**. Artist: **George Quintana**. Country: **USA**.

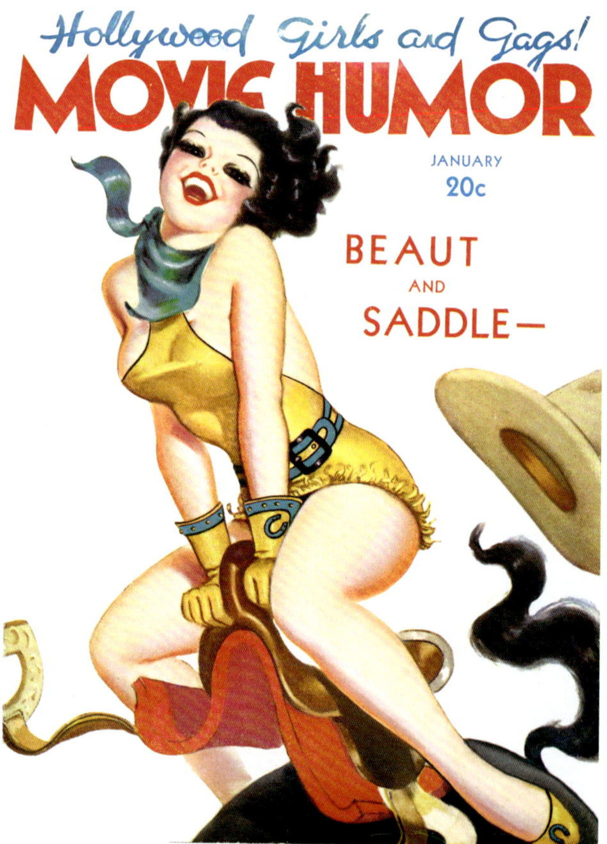

Year: **1937**. Title: **Movie Humor**. Artist: **George Quintana**. Country: **USA**.

Year: **1936**. Title: **Movie Humor**. Artist: **George Quintana**. Country: **USA**.

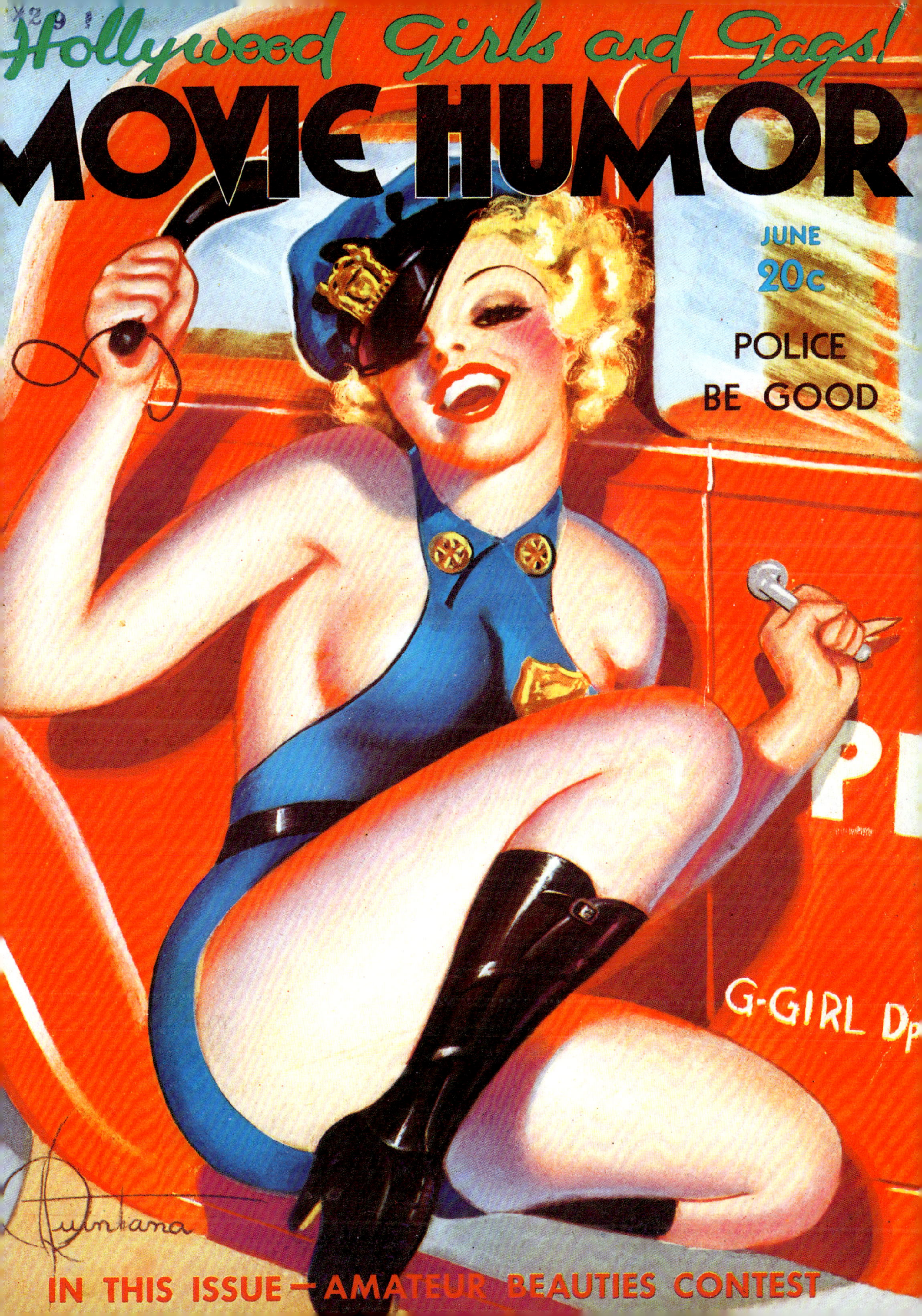

Hollywood Girls and Gags!
MOVIE HUMOR
JUNE
20c
POLICE
BE GOOD
PI
G-GIRL Dp
Quintana
IN THIS ISSUE—AMATEUR BEAUTIES CONTEST

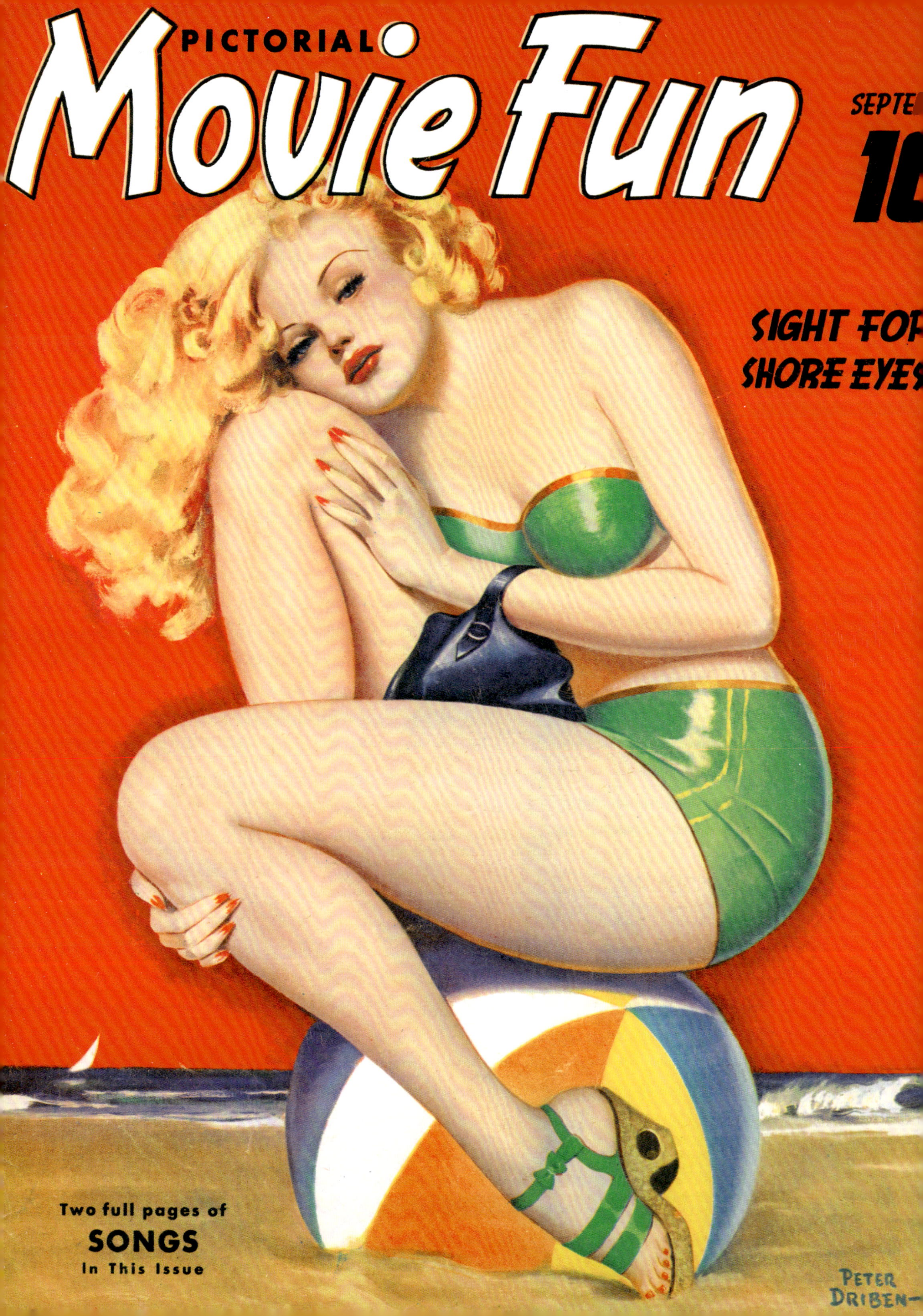
PICTORIAL
Movie Fun
SEPTE
10
SIGHT FOR
SHORE EYES
Two full pages of
SONGS
In This Issue
PETER
DRIBEN

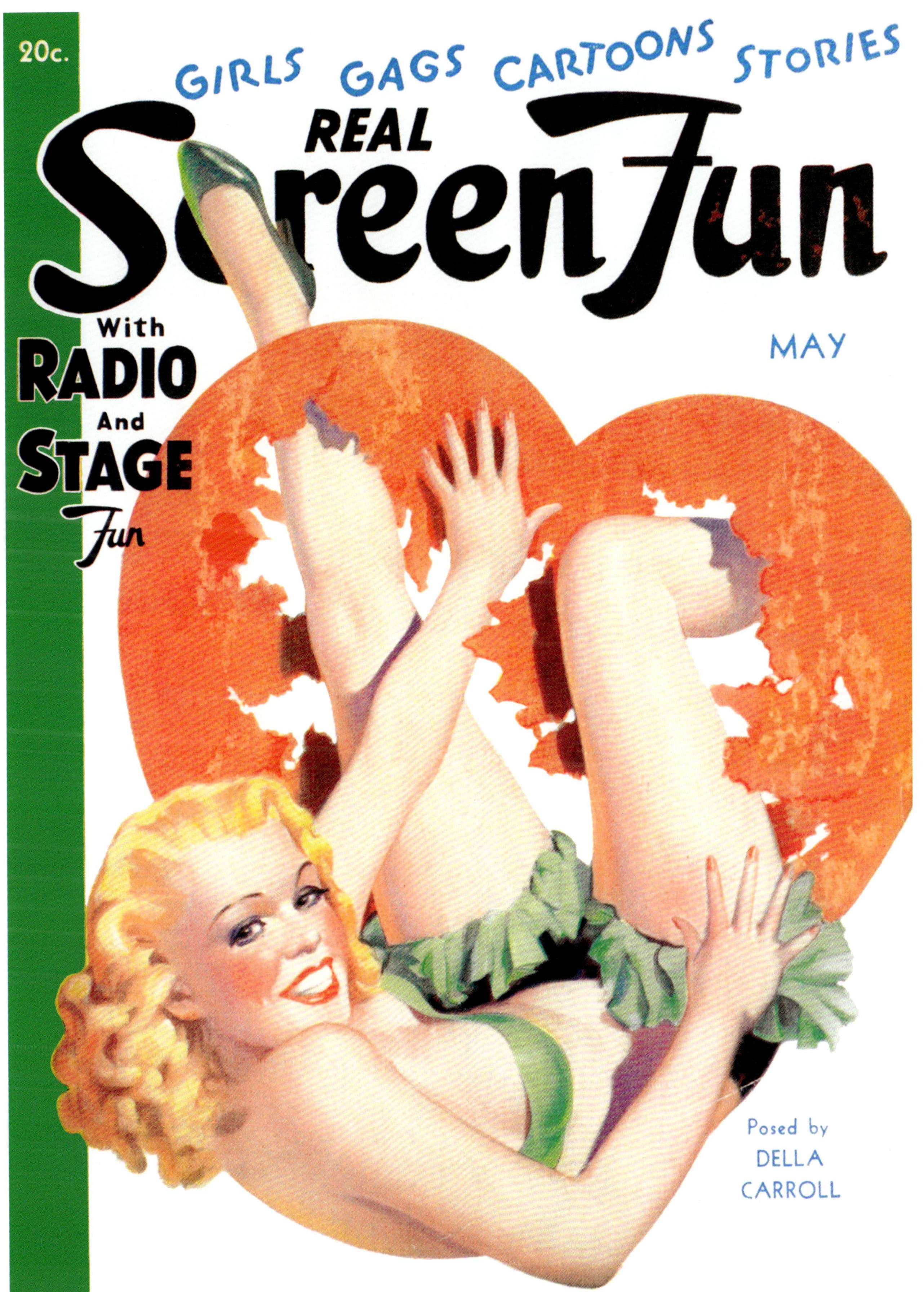

Year: **1936**. Title: **Real Screen Fun**. Country: **USA**.

Year: **1940**. Title: **Movie Fun**. Artist: **Peter Driben**. Country: **USA**.

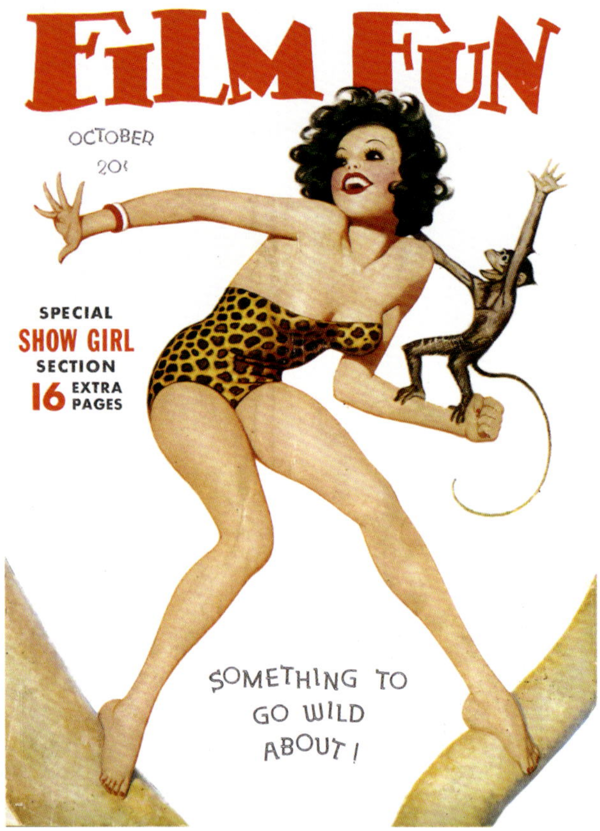

Year: **1936**. Title: **Film Fun**. Artist: **George Quintana**. Country: **USA**.

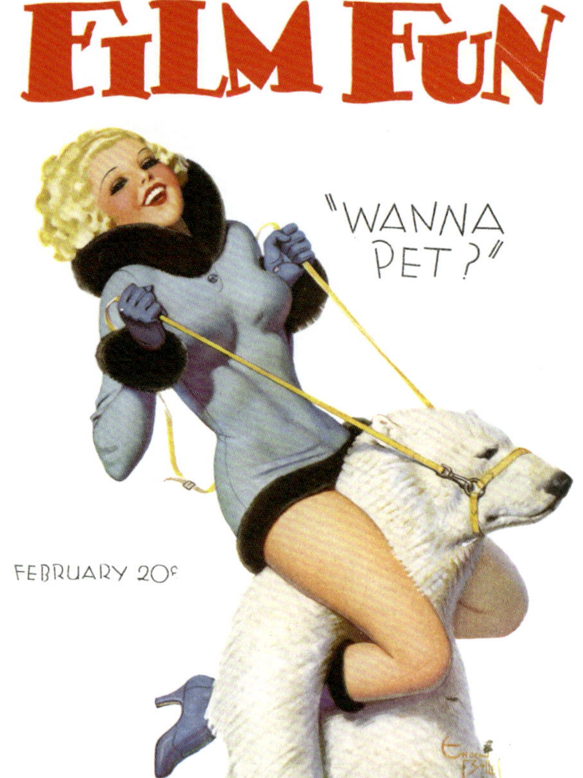

Year: **1933**. Title: **Film Fun**. Artist: **George Quintana**. Country: **USA**.

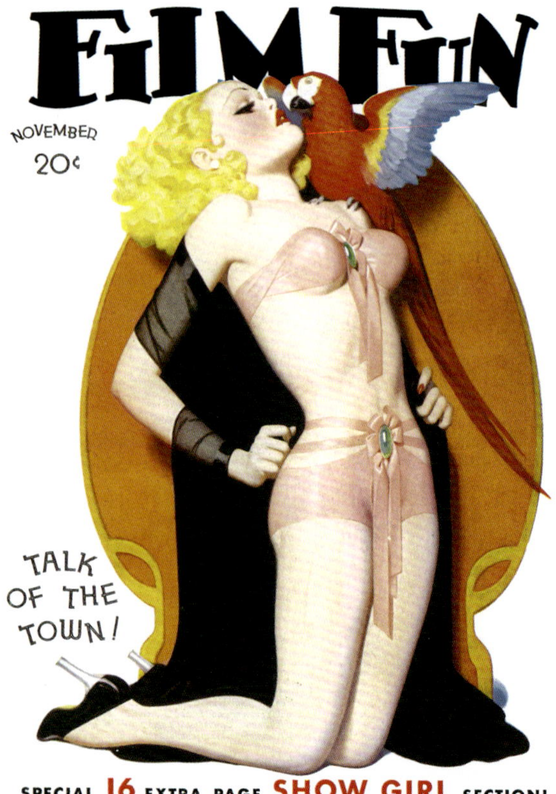

Year: **1936**. Title: **Film Fun**. Artist: **Enoch Bolles**. Country: **USA**.

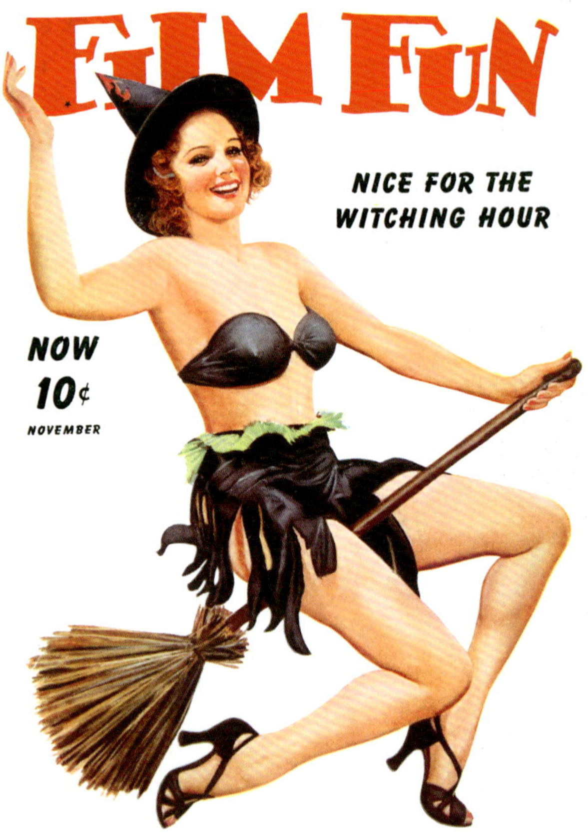

Year: **1939**. Title: **Film Fun**. Country: **USA**.

Year: **1936**. Title: **Real Screen Fun**. Country: **USA**.

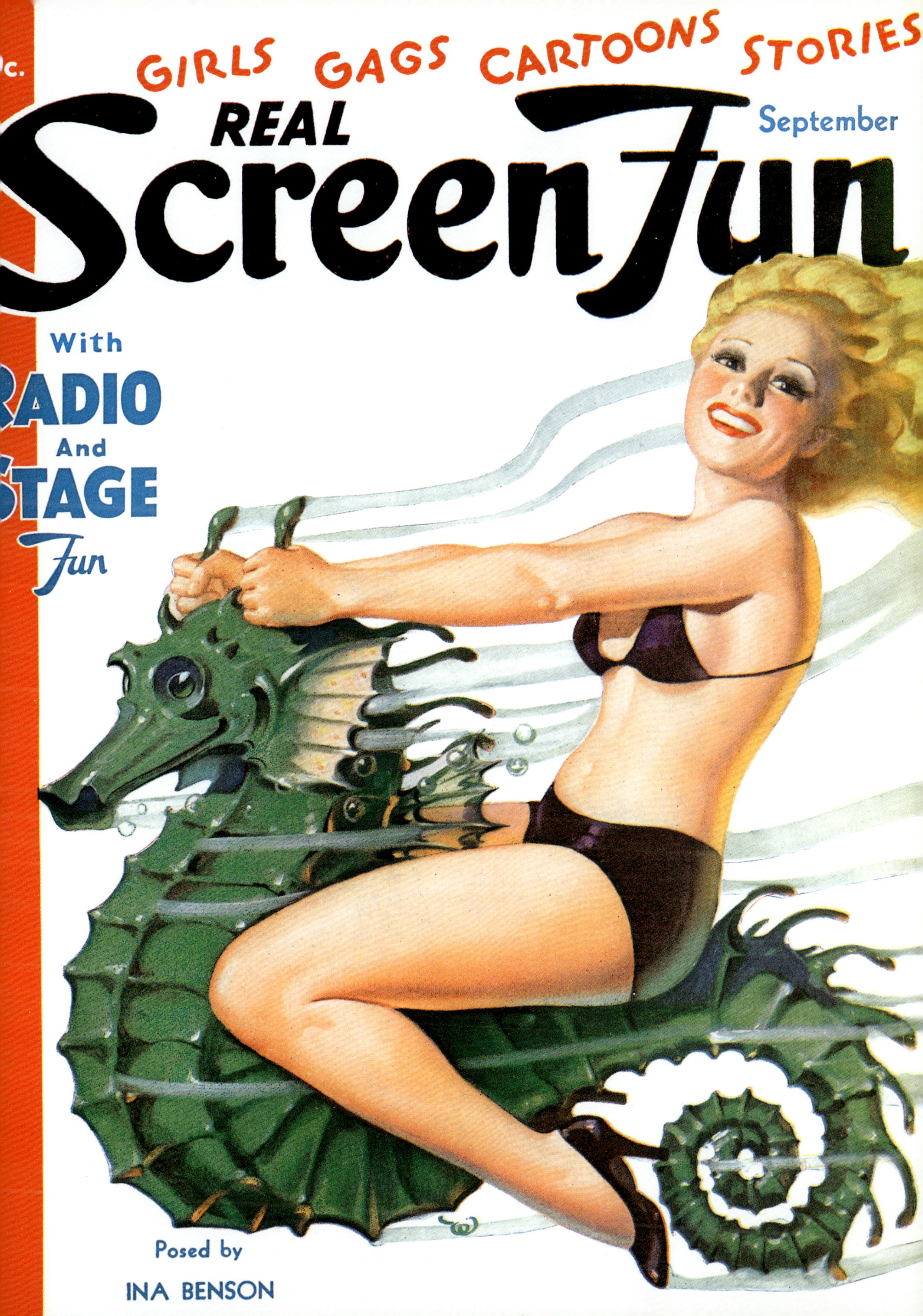

GIRLS GAGS CARTOONS STORIES
REAL
Screen Fun
September
With
RADIO
And
STAGE
Fun
Posed by
INA BENSON

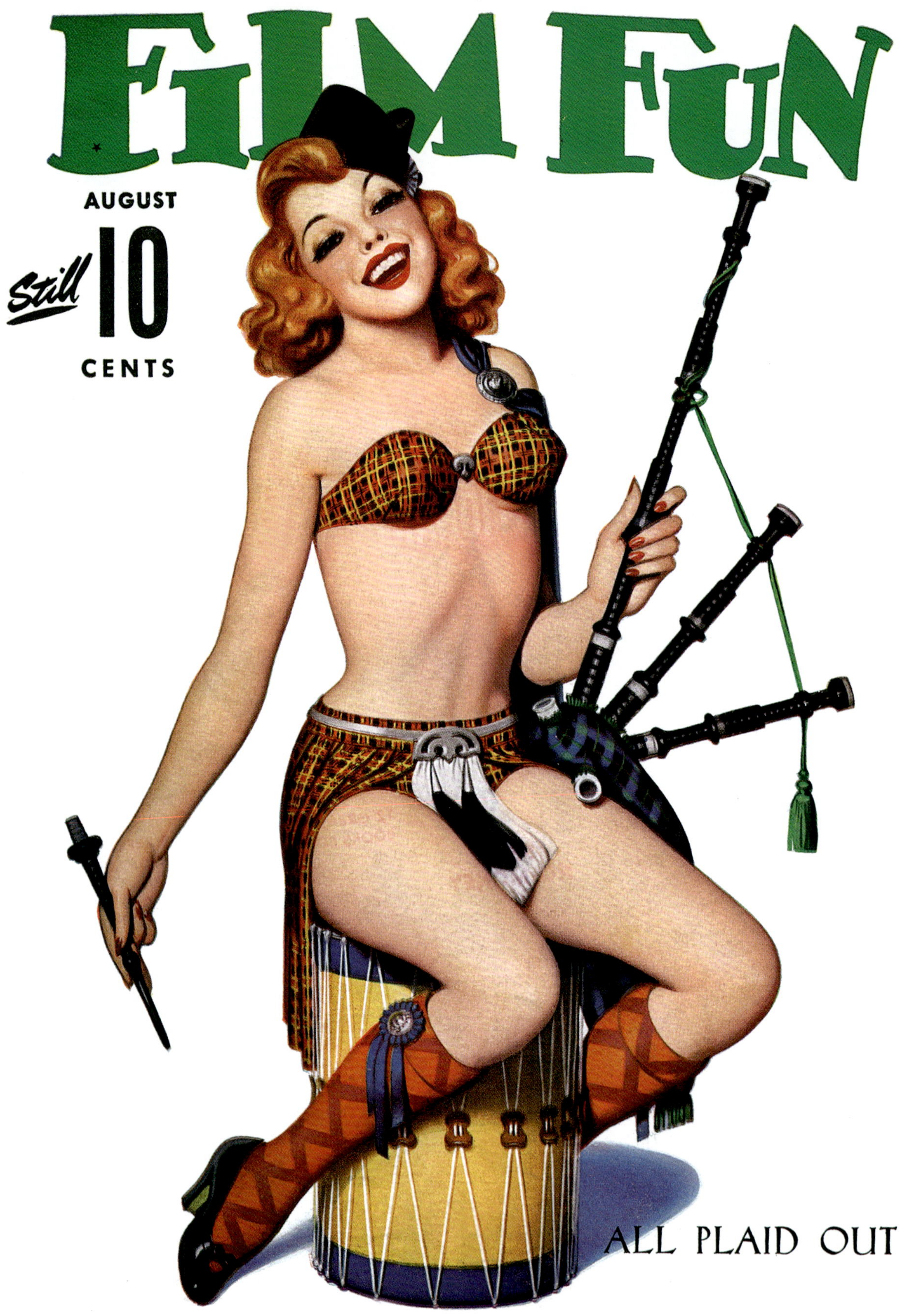

YEAR: **1942**. TITLE: **Film Fun**. COUNTRY: **USA**.

YEAR: **1934**. TITLE: **Film Fun**. COUNTRY: **USA**.

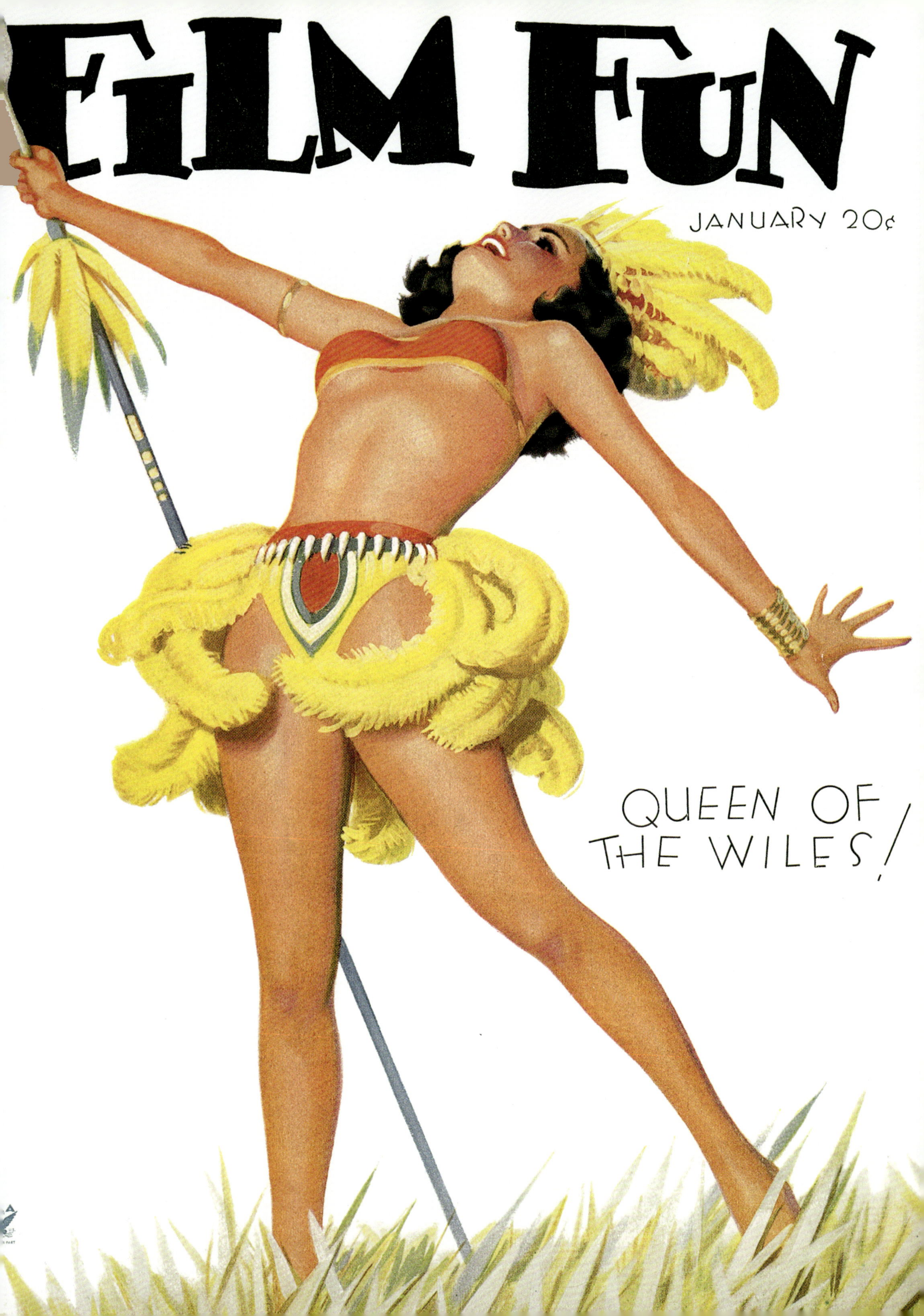
FILM FUN
JANUARY 20¢
QUEEN OF
THE WILES!

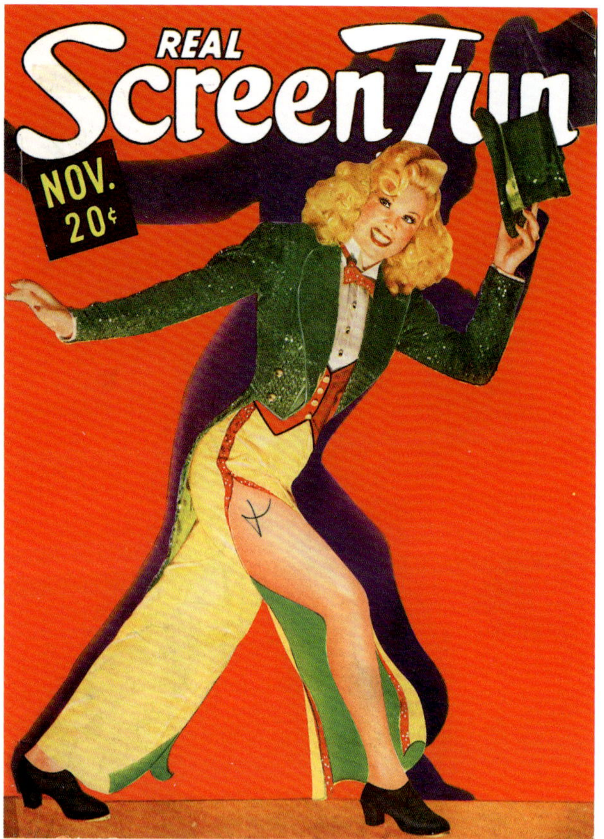

Year: **1938**. Title: **Real Screen Fun**. Country: **USA**.

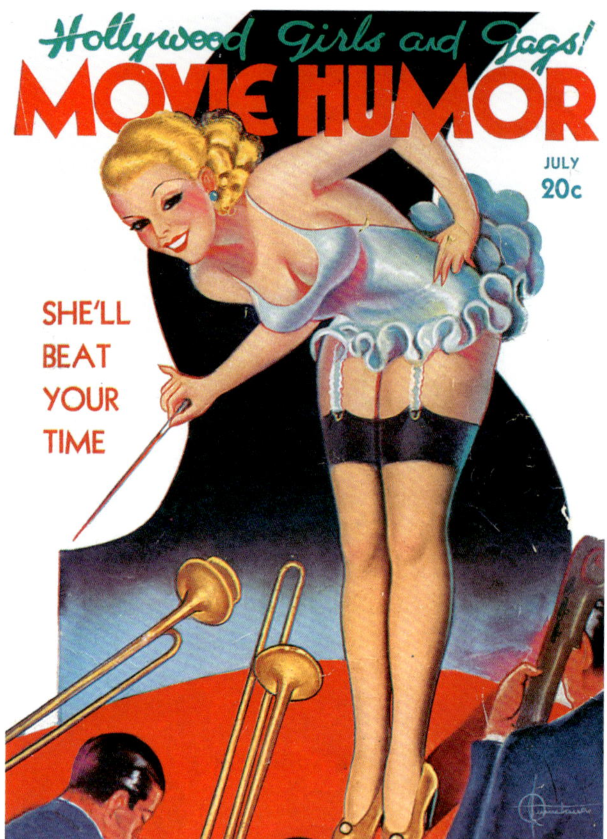

Year: **1936**. Title: **Movie Humor**. Artist: **George Quintana**. Country: **USA**.

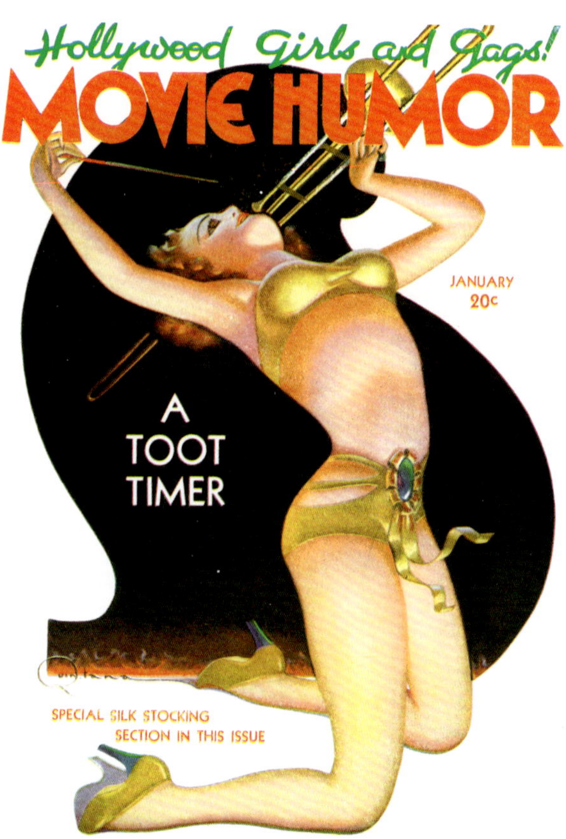

Year: **1935**. Title: **Movie Humor**. Artist: **George Quintana**. Country: **USA**.

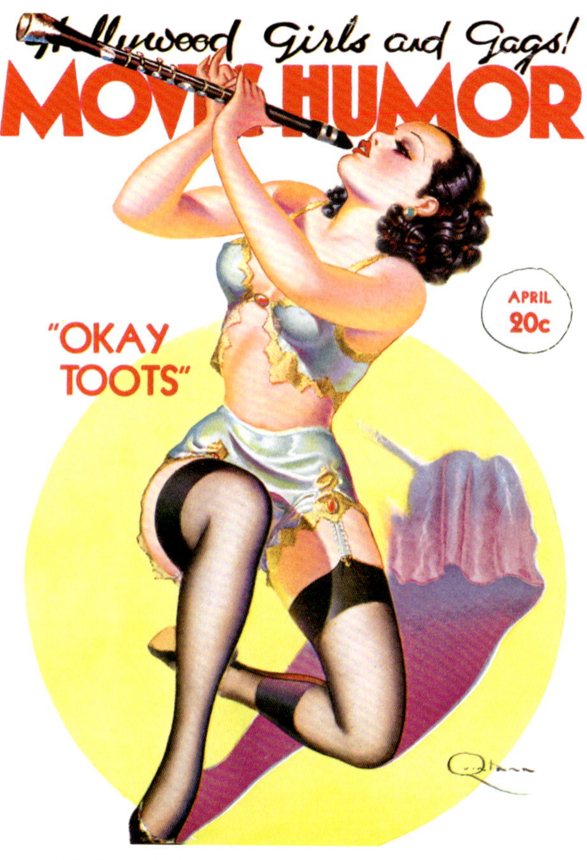

Year: **1937**. Title: **Movie Humor**. Artist: **George Quintana**. Country: **USA**.

Year: **1936**. Title: **Movie Humor**. Artist: **George Quintana**. Country: **USA**.

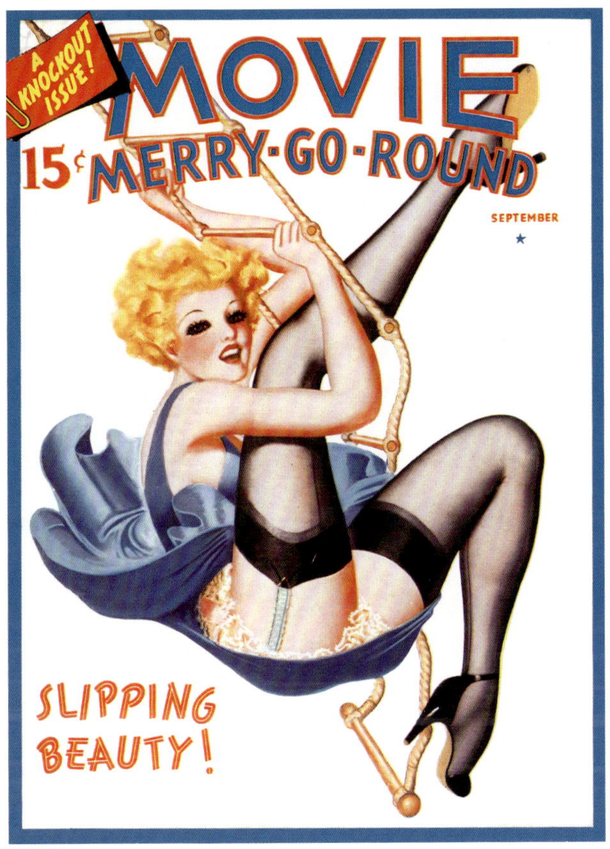

Year: **1937**. Title: **Movie Merry-go-round**. Artist: **George Quintana**. Country: **USA**.

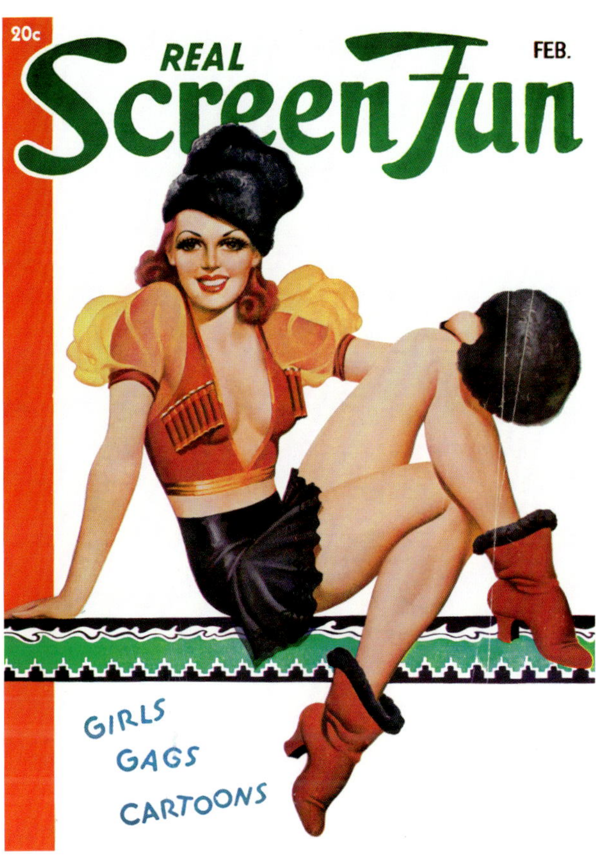

Year: **1938**. Title: **Real Screen Fun**. Country: **USA**.

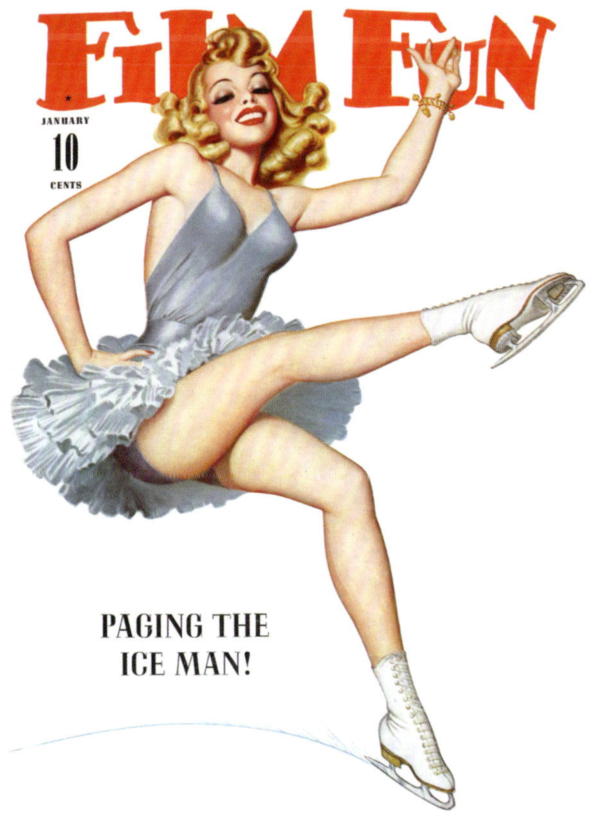

Year: **1942**. Title: **Film Fun**. Country: **USA**.

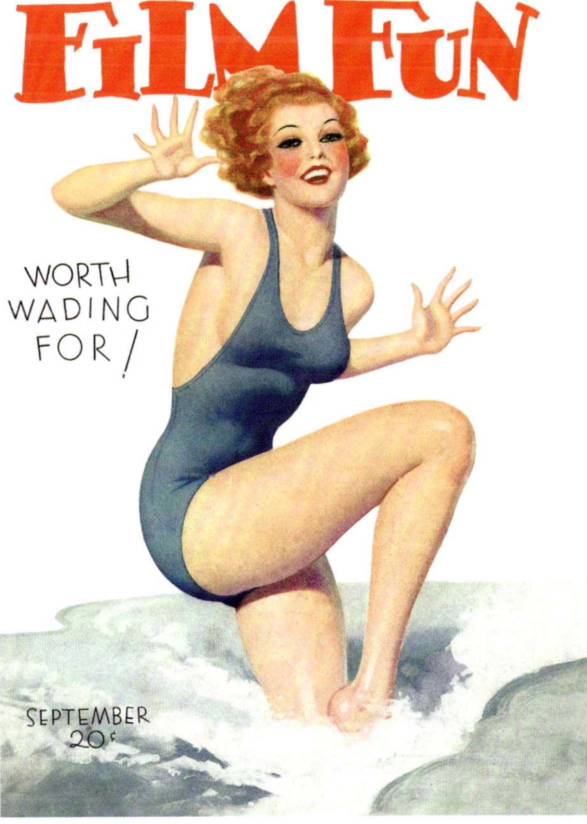

Year: **1933**. Title: **Film Fun**. Country: **USA**.

Pages 198 & 199: Year: **1941**. Title: **Real Screen Fun**. Country: **USA**.
Year: **1941**. Title: **Film Fun**. Country: **USA**.

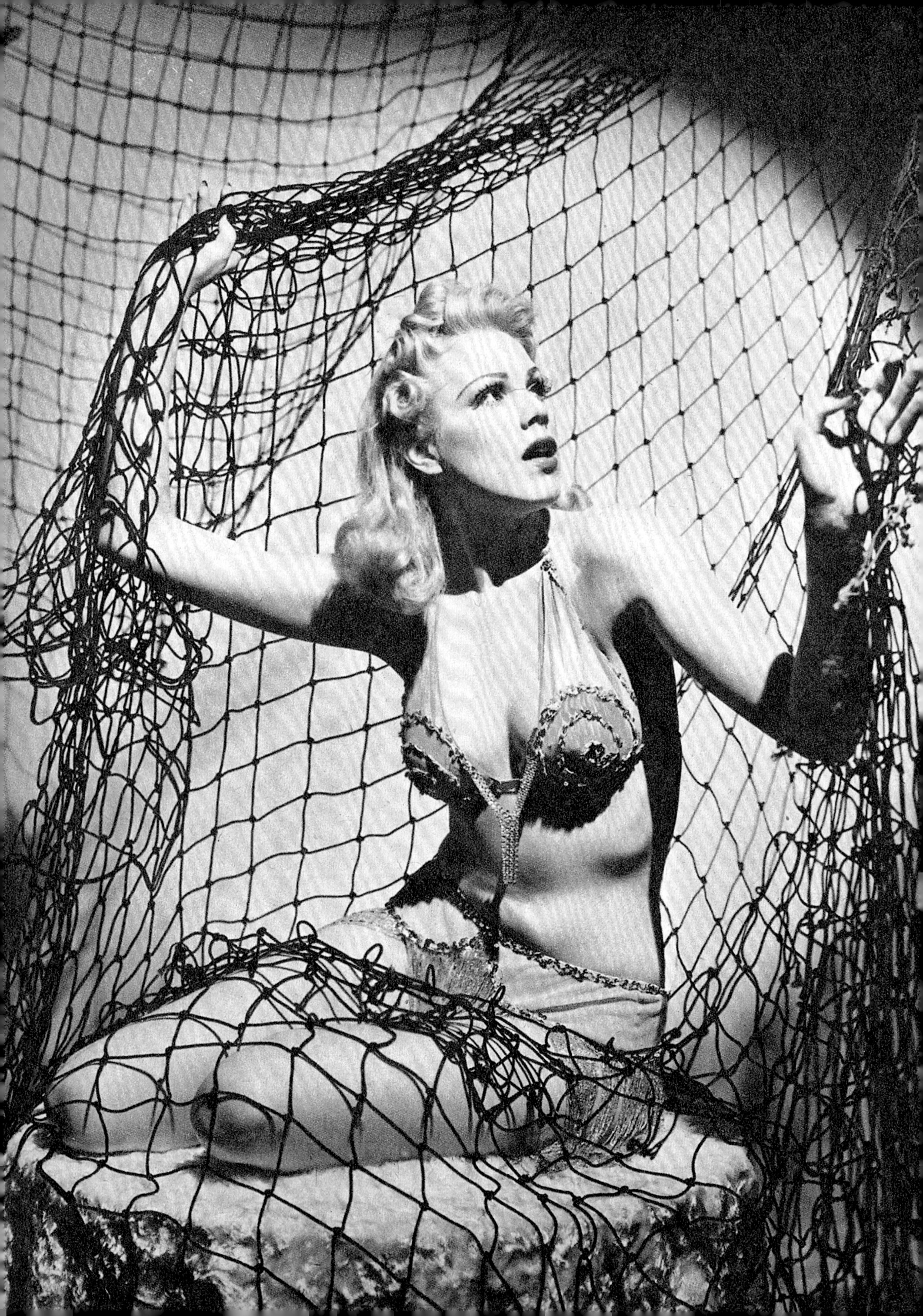

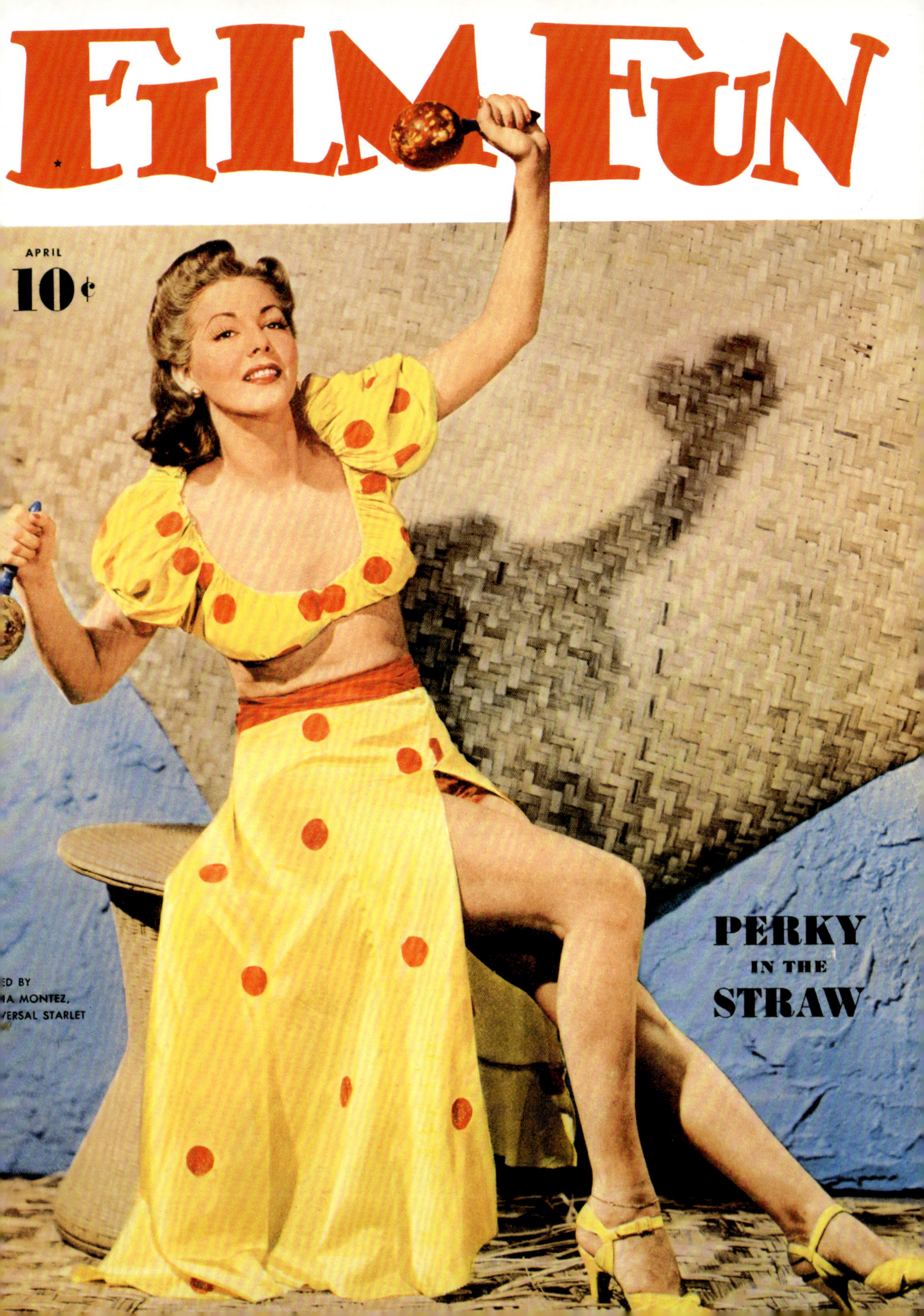
FILM FUN
APRIL
10¢
ED BY
IA MONTEZ,
VERSAL STARLET
PERKY
IN THE
STRAW

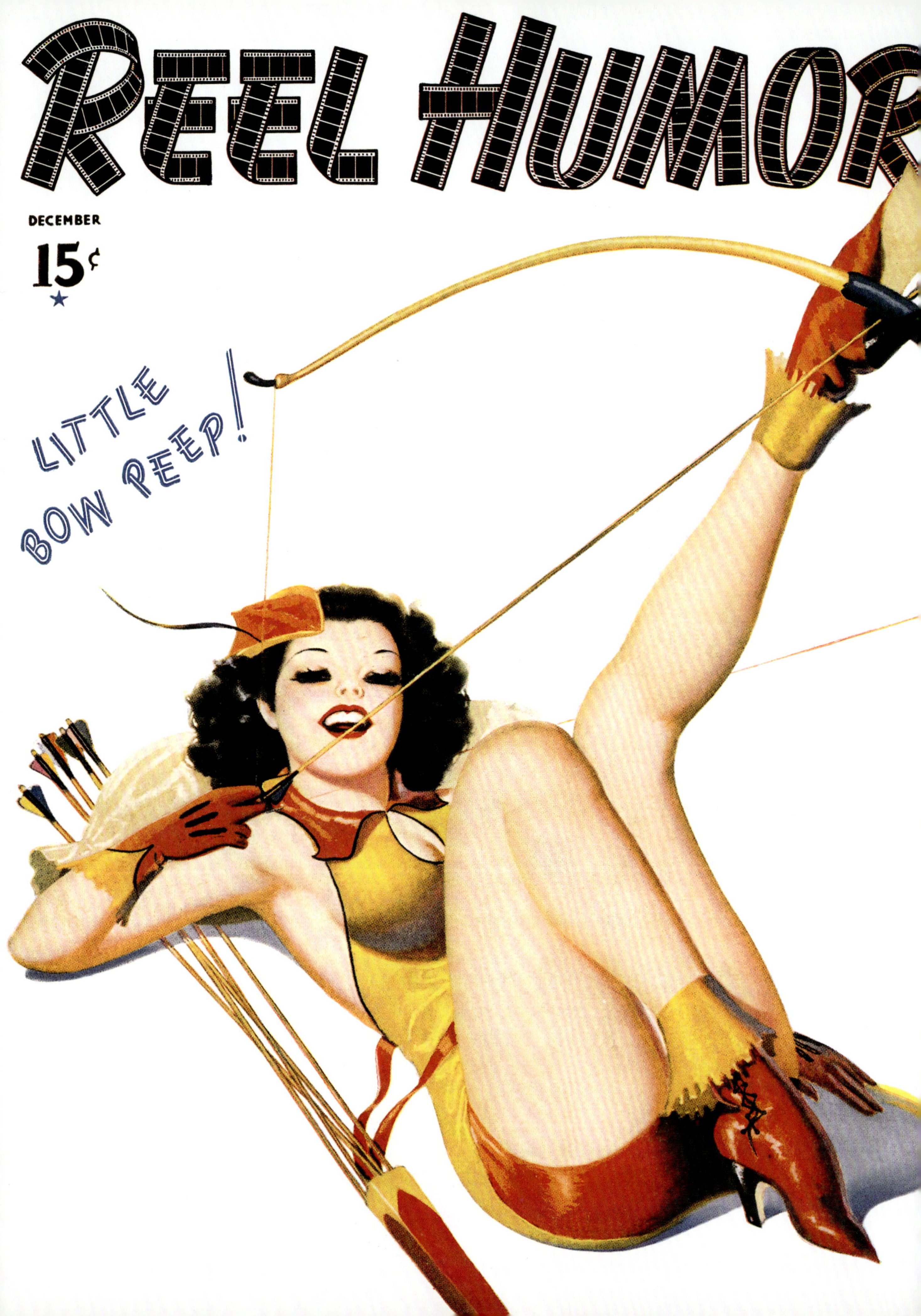
REEL HUMOR
DECEMBER
15¢
LITTLE BOW PEEP!

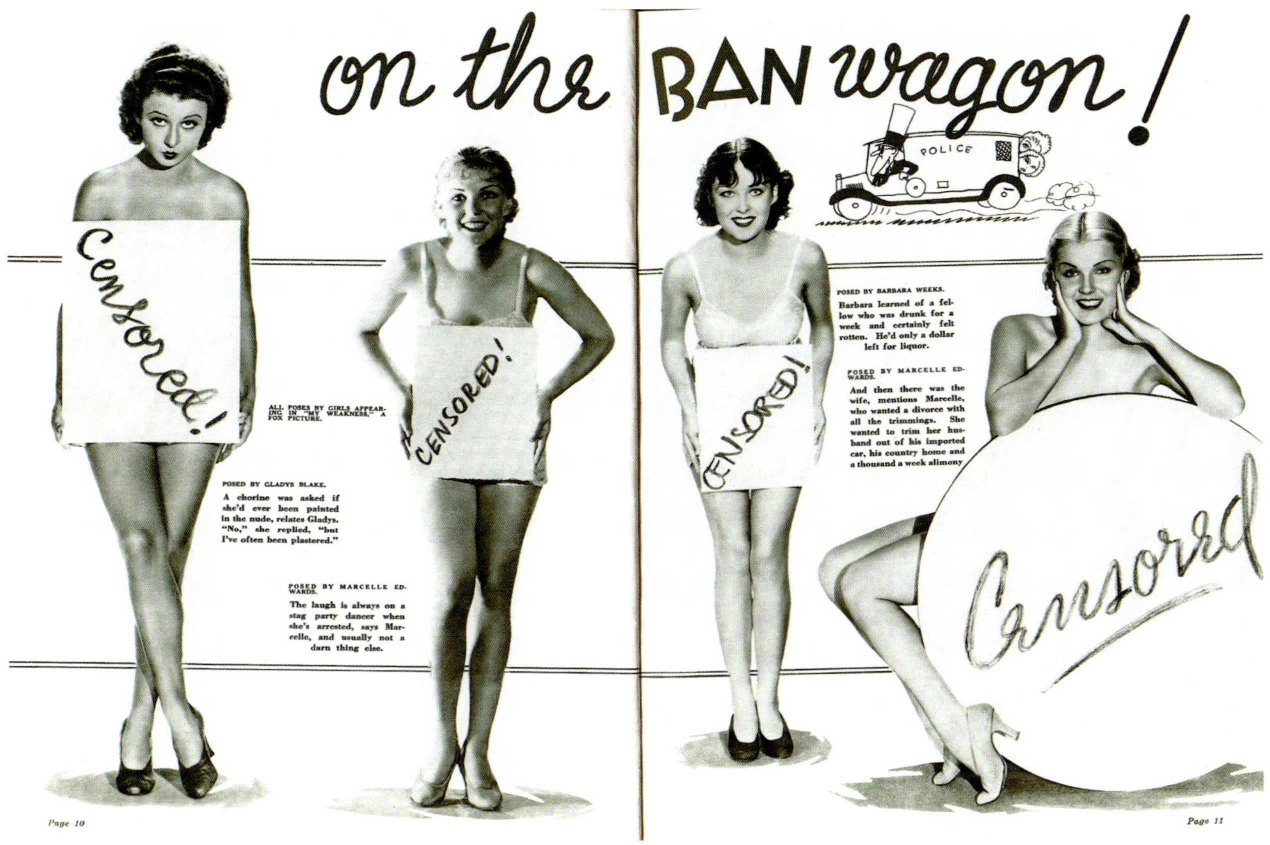

on the BAN wagon!

ALL POSES BY GIRLS APPEARING IN "MY WEAKNESS," A FOX PICTURE.

POSED BY GLADYS BLAKE.

A chorine was asked if she'd ever been painted in the nude, relates Gladys. "No," she replied, "but I've often been plastered."

POSED BY MARCELLE EDWARDS.

The laugh is always on a stag party dancer when she's arrested, says Marcelle, and usually not a darn thing else.

POSED BY BARBARA WEEKS.

Barbara learned of a fellow who was drunk for a week and certainly felt rotten. He'd only a dollar left for liquor.

POSED BY MARCELLE EDWARDS.

And then there was the wife, mentions Marcelle, who wanted a divorce with all the trimmings. She wanted to trim her husband out of his imported car, his country home and a thousand a week alimony

Page 10

Page 11

YEAR: **1934**. TITLE: **Film Fun**. COUNTRY: **USA**.

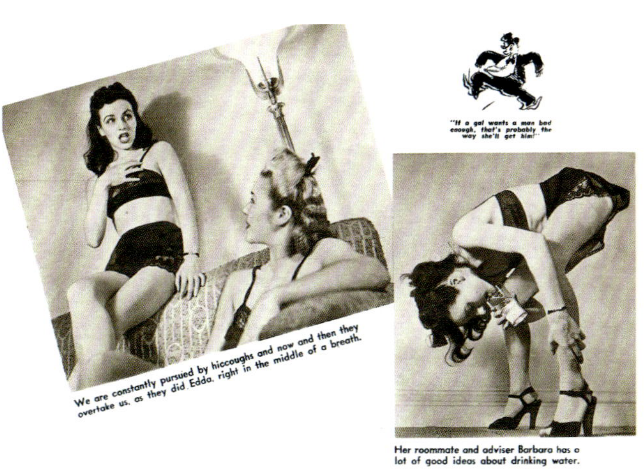

We are constantly pursued by hiccoughs and now and then they overtake us, as they did Edda, right in the middle of a breath.

"If a gal wants a man bad enough, that's probably the way she'll get him!"

Her roommate and adviser Barbara has a lot of good ideas about drinking water.

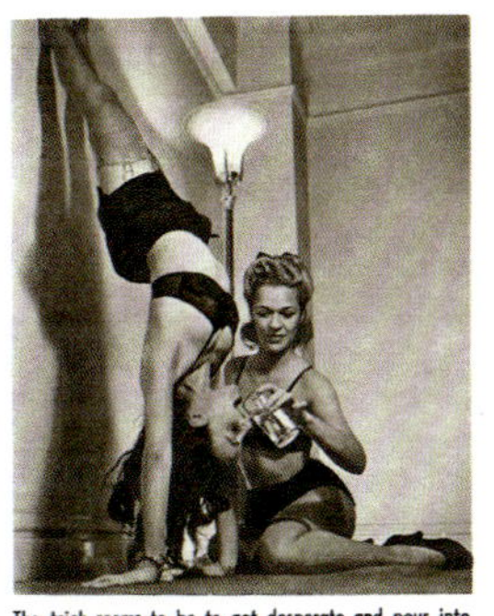

The trick seems to be to get desperate and pour into your nose and mouth enuff water to drown the noises!

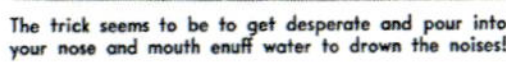

the bottom of my foot."
Drip: "You're lucky. Nobody but you can step on it."

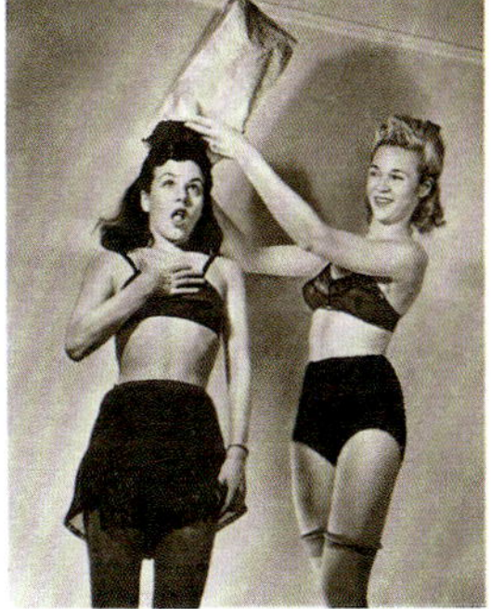

Nothing has worked and it's—hic—hard to say what the bag will do over the head except hide Edda's trouble.

WHAT TO DO WITH HICCOUGHS

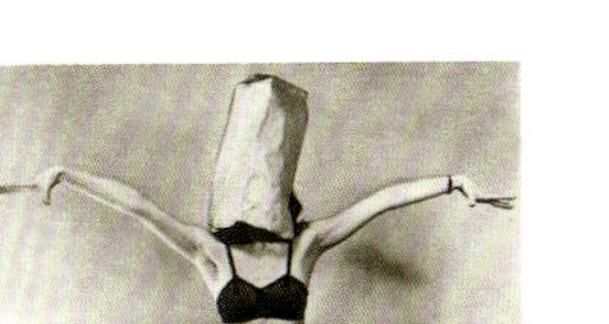

Just what knee bending has to do with the windpipe is a secret. But it's an old act in Barbara's confidential tips.

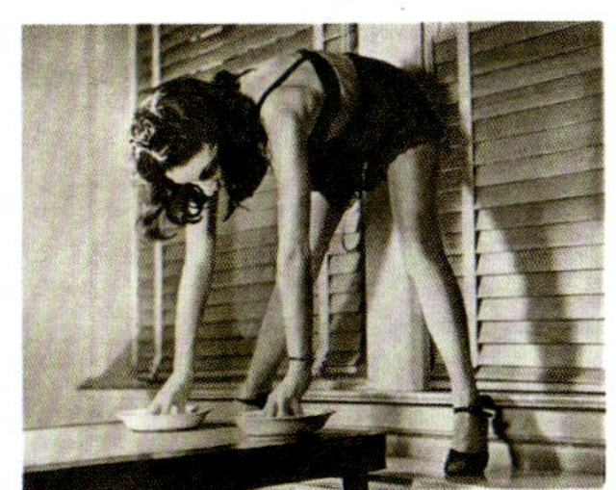

Dipping the fingers in hot and cold water live and learn, we say, Edda.

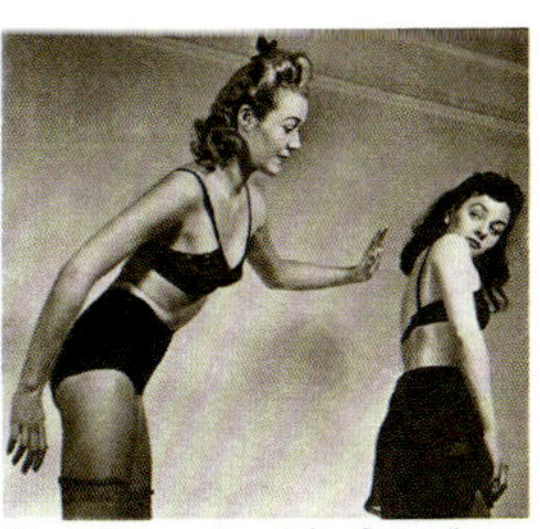

"I'm going to scare you", says Barbara, "you see these are things to do *with* hiccoughs not *for* them! Oh, Doctor!"

Page 12

Page 13

YEAR: **1942**. TITLE: **Film Fun**. COUNTRY: **USA**.

YEAR: **1938**. TITLE: **Reel Humor**.
ARTIST: **George Quintana**. COUNTRY: **USA**.

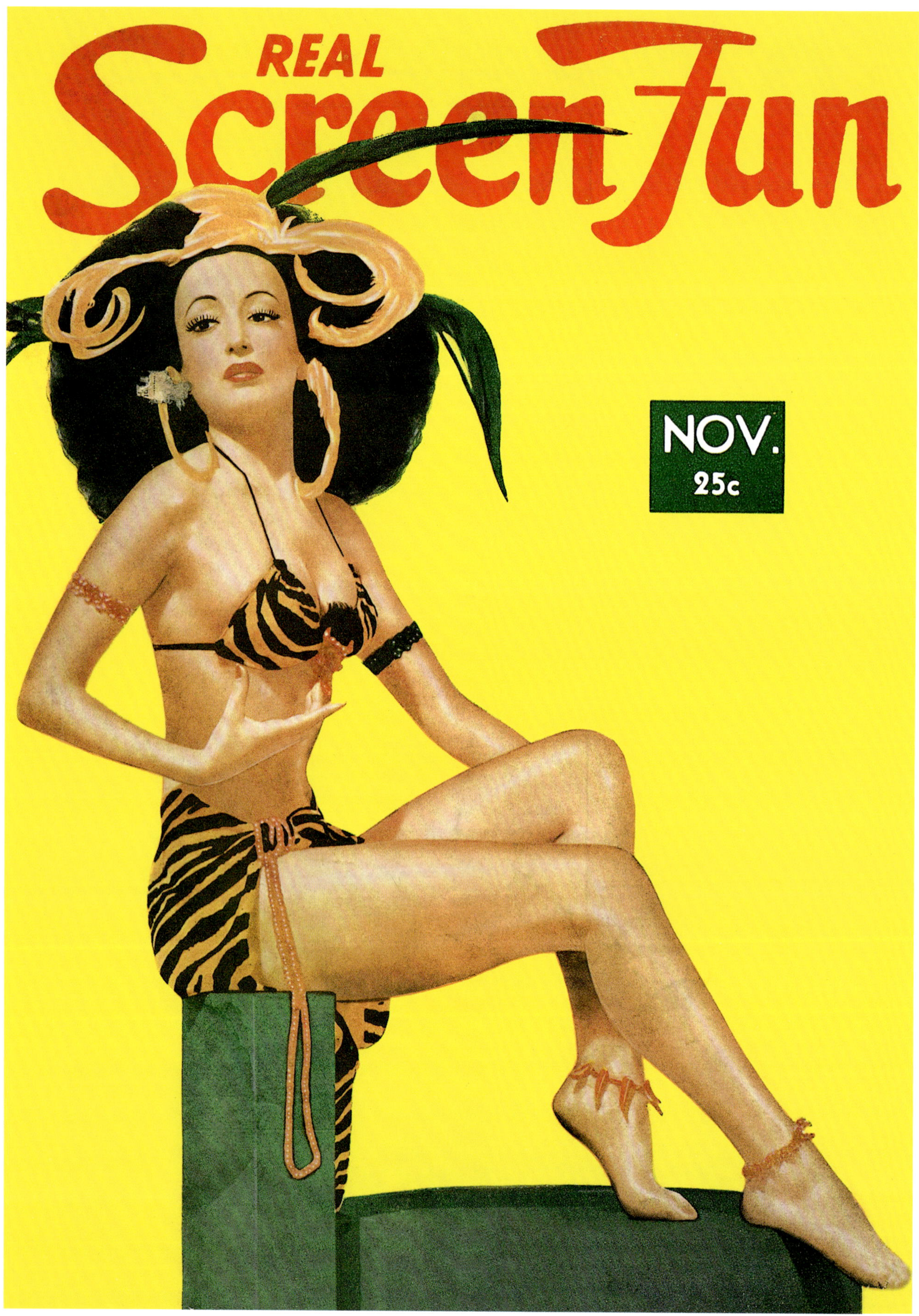

YEAR: **1941**. TITLE: **Real Screen Fun**. COUNTRY: **USA**.

RIGHT:
YEAR: **1941**. TITLE: **Real Screen Fun**. COUNTRY: **USA**.

PAGES 204 & 205:
YEAR: **1952**. TITLE: **French Peep Show**. COUNTRY: **USA**.

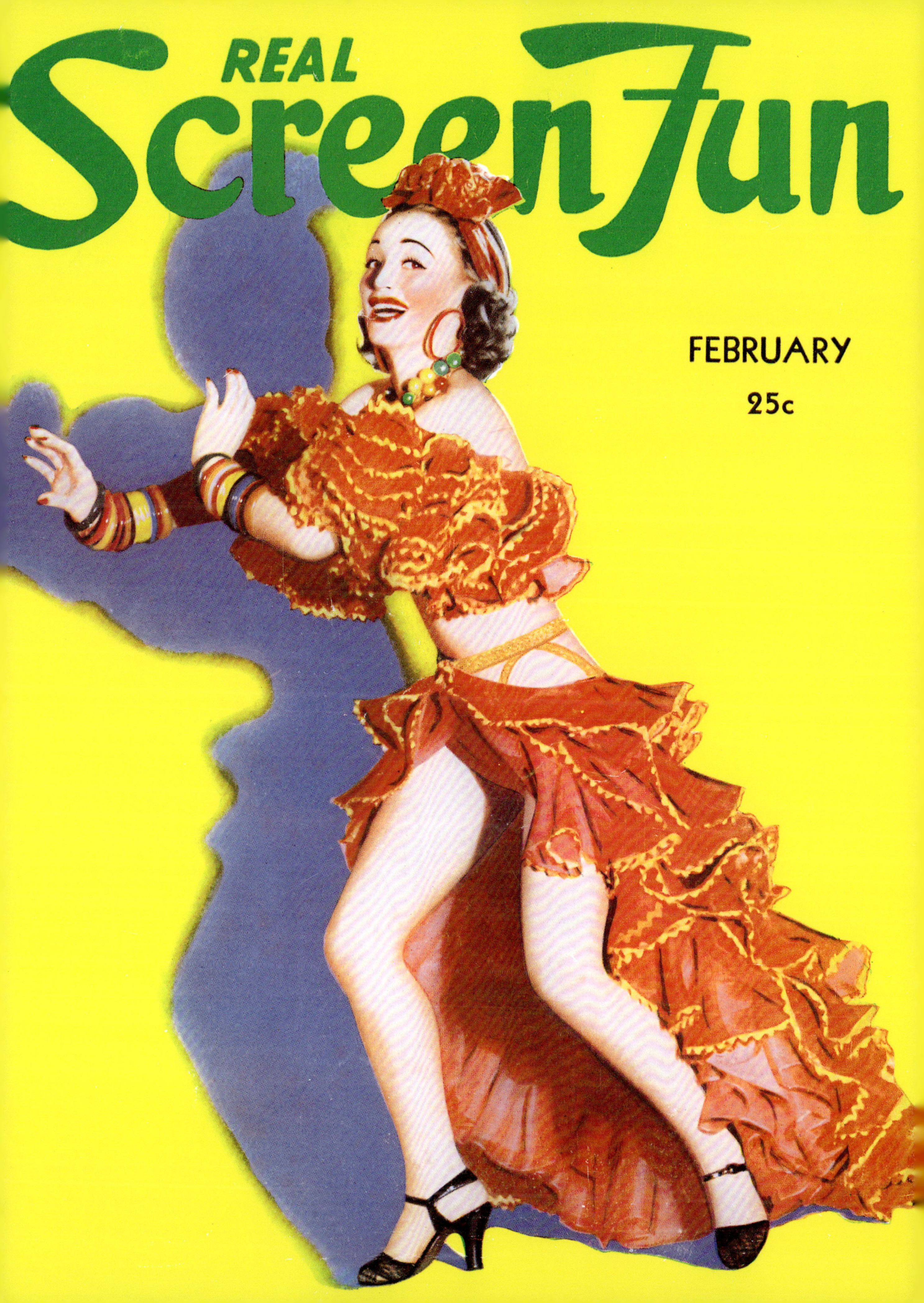
REAL
Screen Fun
FEBRUARY
25c

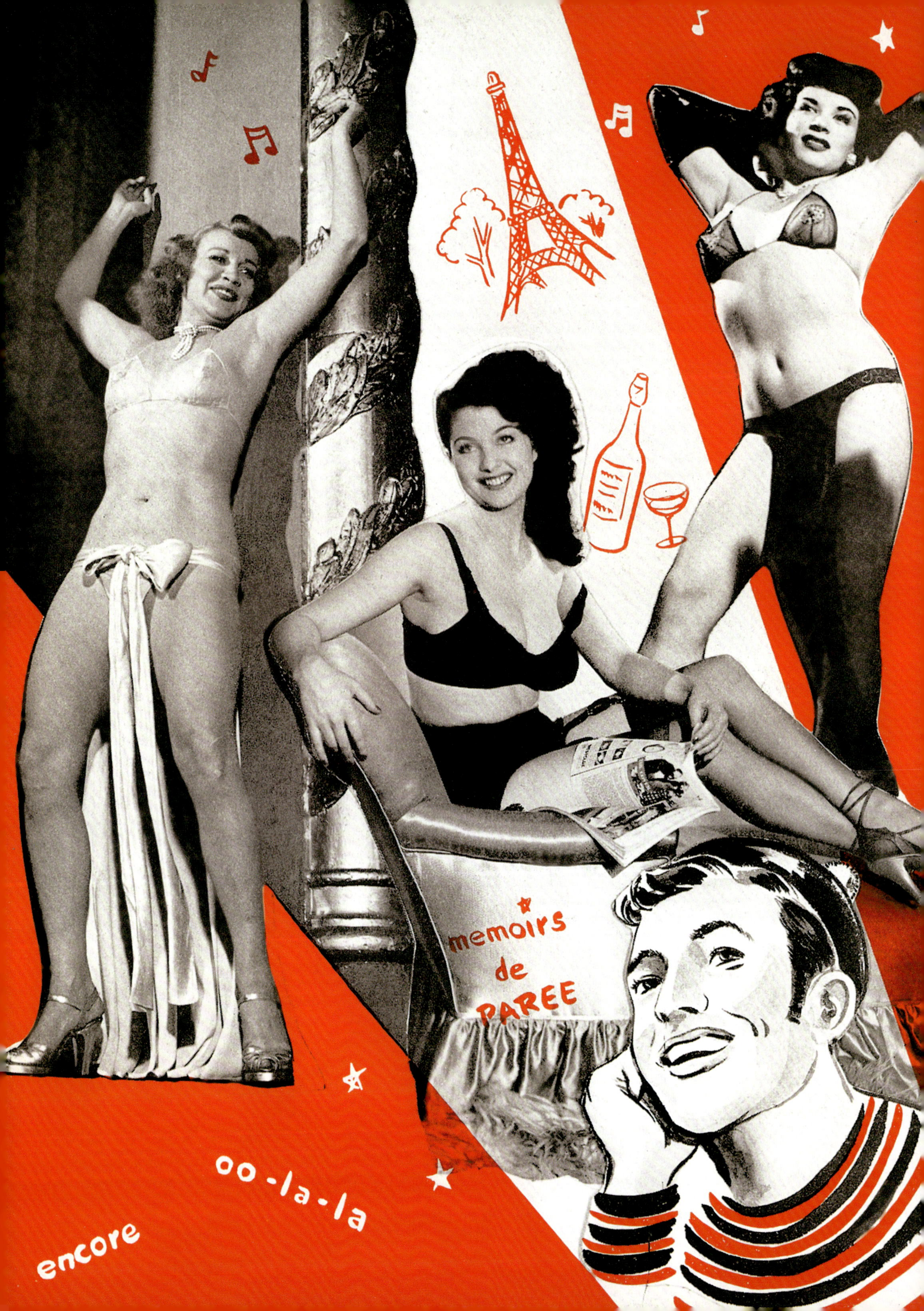
memoirs
de
PAREE
oo-la-la
encore

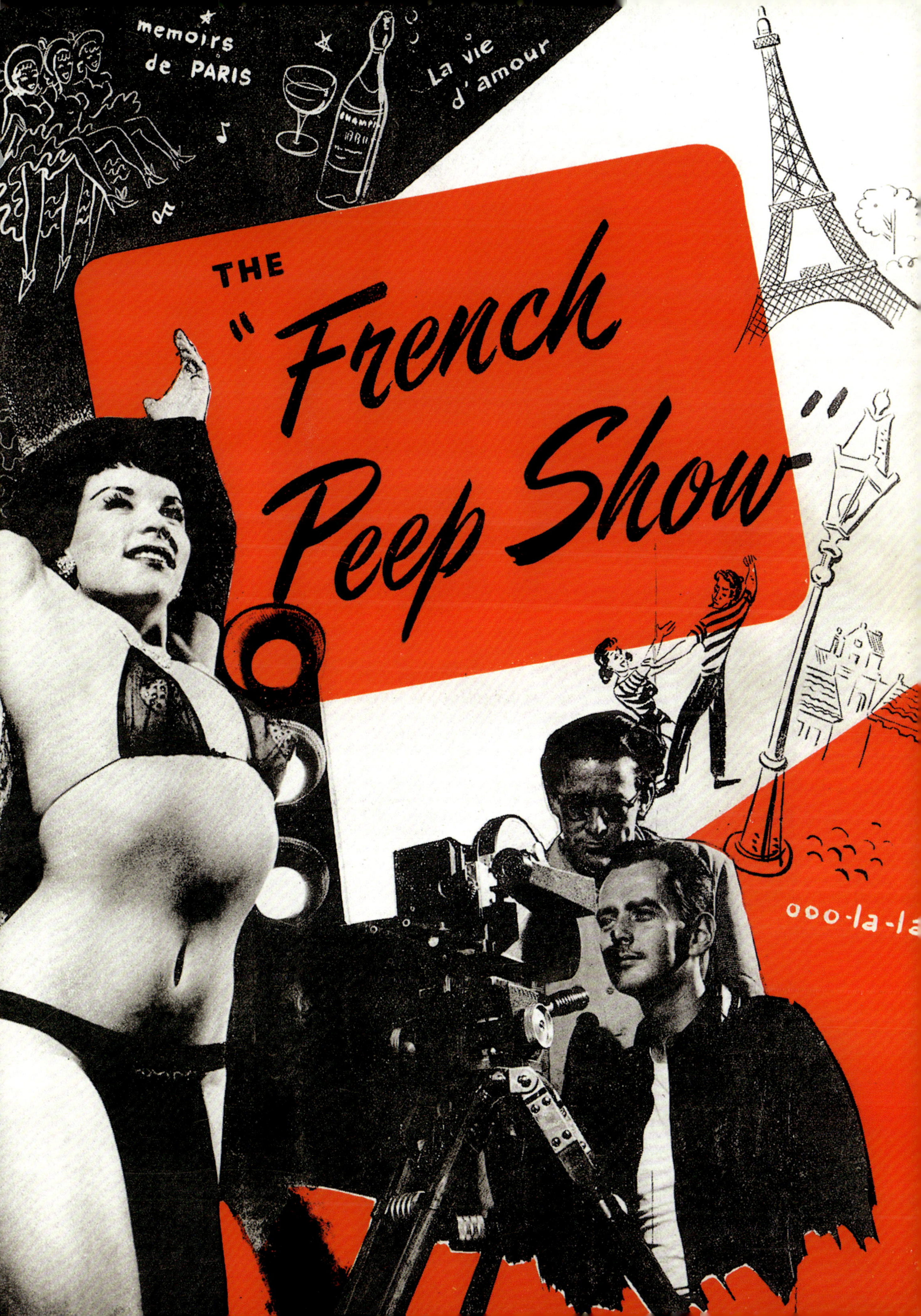
memoirs de PARIS
La vie d'amour
THE
"French Peep Show"
ooo-la-la

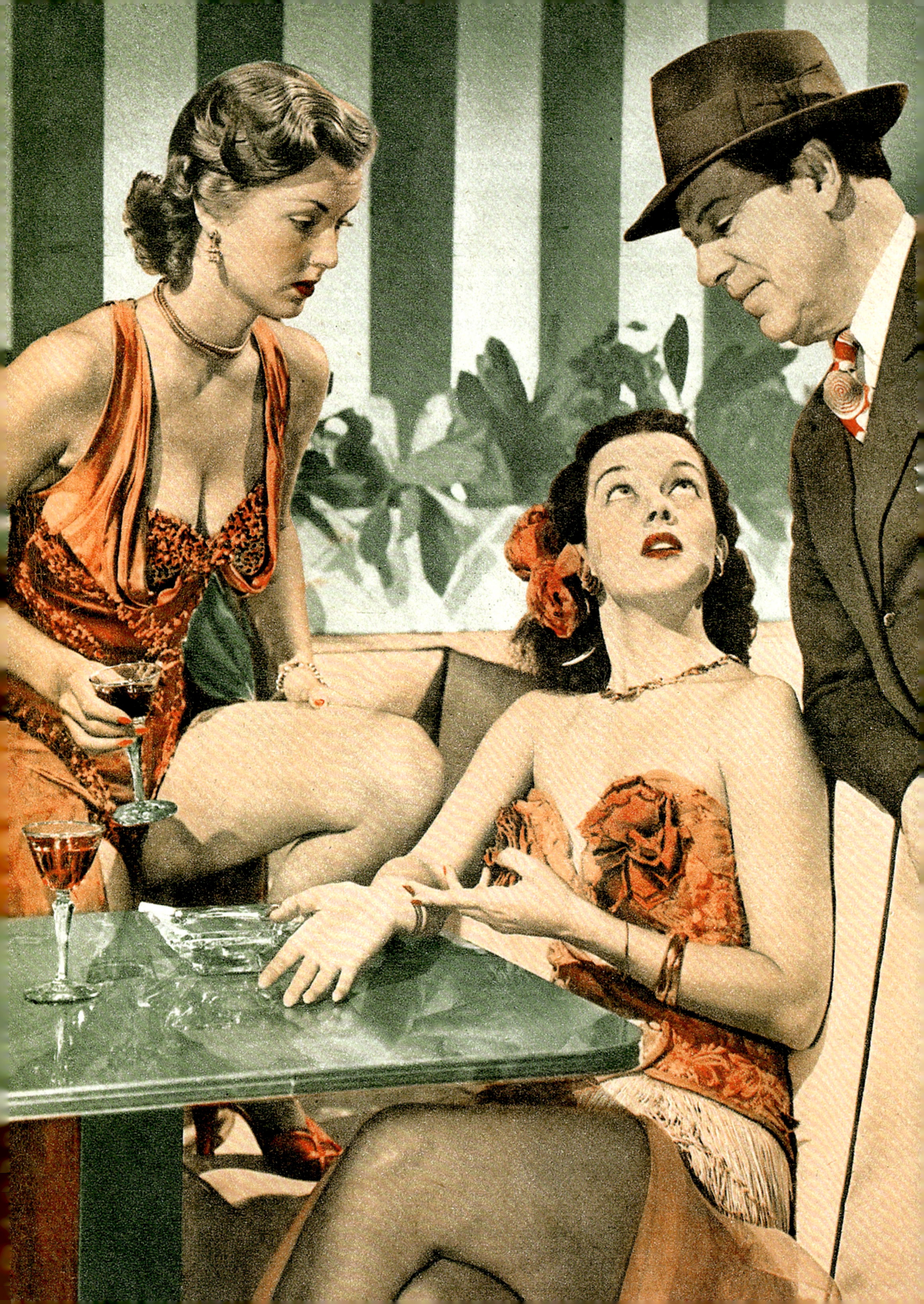

FROM AMERICAN HERO TO AMERICAN PSYCHO:

80 Years of Detective Magazines

Vom amerikanischen Helden zum American Psycho: 80 Jahre Detektivmagazine

Du héros au psycho : 80 ans de magazines policiers américains

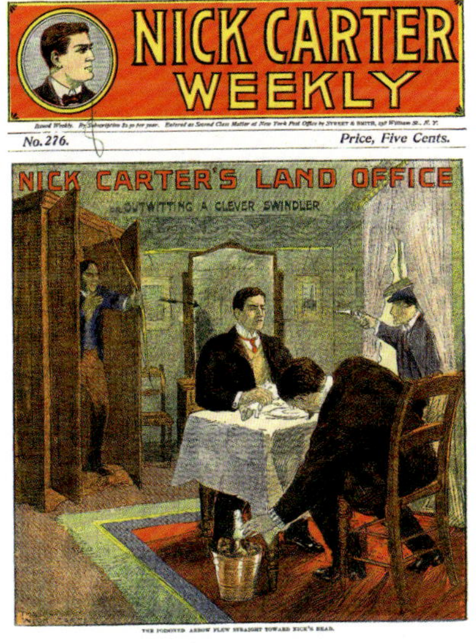

Year: **1902**. Title: **Nick Carter Weekly**. Country: **USA**.

Some would debate the inclusion of detective magazines in this book, but I respect the authority of medical examiner Park Dietz. In an article for the *Journal of Forensic Sciences* published in 1986, Dietz, writing with Harry Hazelwood, made a convincing case that detective magazines were the preferred pornography for sexual sadists, were in fact training manuals for them and should be regulated like the hardest pornography. Certainly by the 70s the genre had grown intensely misogynistic, with cover models cowering in terror, guns in

Year: **1949**. Title: **Front Page Detective**. Country: **USA**.

Der ein oder andere mag sich fragen, was Detektivmagazine in diesem Buch zu suchen haben, aber ich halte mich da ganz an den Pathologen Park Dietz. In einem gemeinsam mit Harry Hazelwood verfassten Artikel im *Journal of Forensic Sciences* legte Dietz 1986 überzeugend dar, Detektivmagazine seien die bevorzugte Lektüre sexueller Sadisten, ja, dienten ihnen geradezu als Gebrauchsanweisung, darum müssten für sie ebenso strenge Auflagen gelten wie für härteste Pornografie. Das Genre war tatsächlich in den Siebzigern extrem frauenfeindlich geworden, und die Titel zeigten vor Entsetzen gelähmte Models mit Pistolenläufen im Mund, Messern im blutbesudelten Bauch oder wie tot daliegend, während die Schlagzeilen marktschreierisch Vergewaltigung, Folter und Lustmord versprachen.

Das war jedoch zunächst nicht so, nicht in den ersten siebzig Jahren der Existenz solcher Hefte. Detektivmagazine zählen zu den frühesten amerikanischen Publikationsformen, ihre Geschichten vom Kampf des einsamen Helden gegen das Böse passten perfekt zum nationalen Selbstverständnis. Allerdings sind sie keine rein amerikanische Erfindung. Ihr verschlungener Weg nahm seinen Anfang im England des 18. Jahrhunderts, wo auf Flugblättern die Geschichten wahrer Verbrechen

L'inclusion des magazines policiers dans cet ouvrage peut paraître discutable mais je m'en remets à l'autorité du médecin légiste Park Dietz. Dans un article parut en 1986 dans le *Journal of Forensic Sciences* (« Journal médico-légal »), Dietz et son collaborateur Harry Hazelwood expliquèrent de manière convaincante que les magazines policiers étaient la pornographie de prédilection des sadiques sexuels, qu'ils leur servaient de manuels d'instruction et devaient être réglementés comme la pornographie la plus hard. Le fait est que, dans les années soixante-dix, le genre était devenu profondément misogyne, les couvertures montrant des jeunes femmes pétrifiées de terreur, avec des canons de revolver dans la bouche, des couteaux plantés dans leur ventre sanglant, parfois même apparemment mortes. Les

In 1986 Park Dietz made a convincing case that detective magazines were the preferred pornography for sexual sadists.

Year: **1956**. Title: **True Police**. Country: **USA**.

Headquarters Detective, Line-up Detective Crime and many, many others featured bad women doing bad things and paying dearly for it.

mouths, knives protruding from bleeding bellies, sometimes even appearing to be dead, while coverlines cried rape, torture and lust murder.

That's not how it started or how the magazines existed in America for their first 70 years. Detective magazines were among the earliest American publications, their "one man against evil" device perfectly suited to our peculiar national identity. They're not strictly an American invention, though. The winding path started in England with the true-crime broadsheets of the 18th century and moved on to France and François Eugène Vidocq, an adventurer who ran a private security service in Paris in the early 1800s. His memoirs, published in 1828, inspired Honoré de Balzac, Charles Dickens and Edgar Allan Poe to include detectives in their writing.

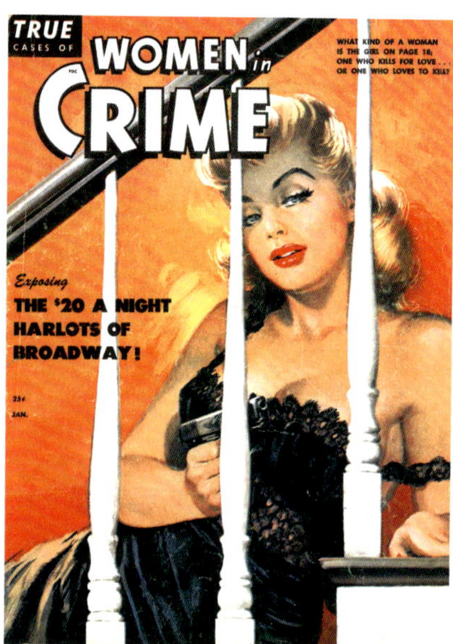

Year: **1950**. Title: **Women in Crime**.
Country: **USA**.

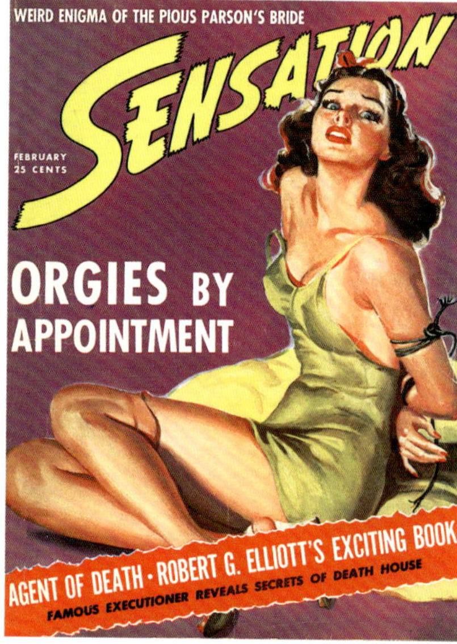

Year: **1942**. Title: **Sensation**.
Country: **USA**.

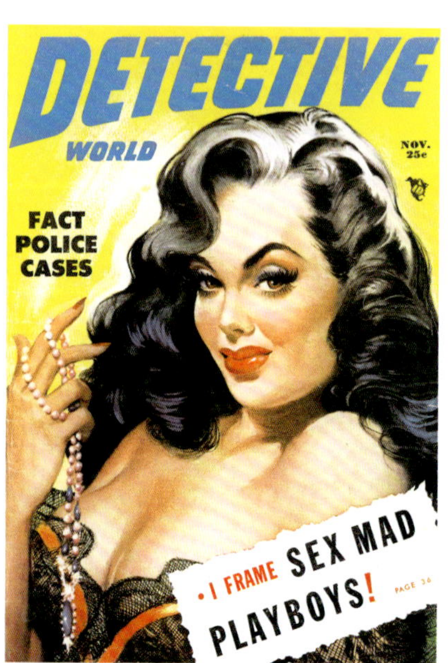

Year: **1948**. Title: **Detective World**.
Country: **USA**.

geschildert wurden, und führte dann nach Frankreich und zu François Eugène Vidocq, einem Abenteurer, der im Paris des frühen 19. Jahrhunderts einen privaten Sicherheitsdienst unterhielt. Seine 1828 erschienenen Memoiren inspirierten Honoré de Balzac, Charles Dickens und Edgar Allan Poe, die Figur des Detektivs zum Thema zu machen. Zur Zeit des Bürgerkriegs erschienen in den USA die so genannten „Dime Novels", Groschenhefte mit Westernabenteuern, die jedoch bald auch den Verbrecherjäger in der Großstadt für sich entdeckten, um ein breiteres Publikum anzusprechen. 1875 veröffentlichte Allen Pinkerton das erste True-Crime-Buch, in dem er seine Abenteuer als Privatdetektiv, als „Private Eye" schilderte, eine Anspielung auf sein Markenzeichen, das Argusauge auf der Visitenkarte. Es sollte noch mehr als zehn Jahre dauern, bis

titres hurlaient au viol, à la torture et aux meurtres sexuels. Mais il n'en fut pas toujours ainsi, ces magazines existant déjà aux États-Unis depuis soixante-dix ans. Ils furent même parmi les premières publications américaines, leur principe – « un homme seul contre le mal » – convenant parfaitement à notre singulière identité nationale. Toutefois, ils ne sont pas à proprement parler une invention américaine. Ils puisaient leurs racines dans les placards de faits divers de l'Angleterre du 18e siècle puis, en France, dans les aventures de François Eugène Vidocq, aventurier devenu chef d'une brigade de sûreté privée au début du 19e siècle. Ses *Mémoires*, publiées en 1928, inspirèrent Honoré de Balzac, Charles Dickens et Edgar Allan Poe, qui introduisirent des inspecteurs de police dans leurs récits. Aux États-Unis, les romans à deux sous publiés à l'époque de

Rape on the Highway

BY LEE TRAVIS

The sex prowler used his car to run down and daze his victims.

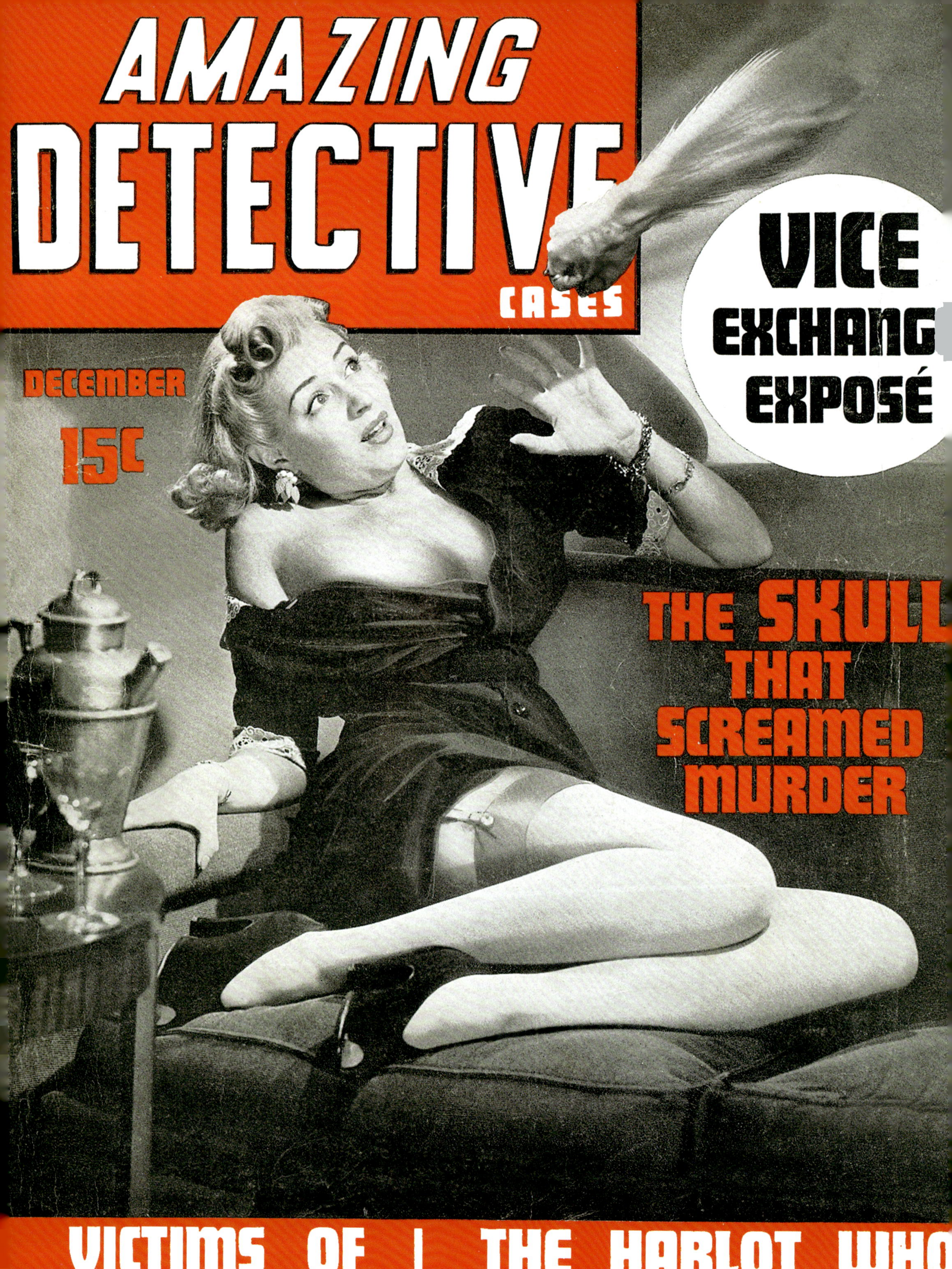

VICTIMS OF FREE LOVE | THE HARLOT WHO ATE LIKE A HORSE

Year: **1940**. Title: **Amazing Detective**.
Country: **USA**.

We could point out literature so inconceivably devilish as to advocate and extol utter depravity. But it is enough for us to hint at these abysses of iniquity.

—*The Transmission of Life*, George H. Napheys, 1872

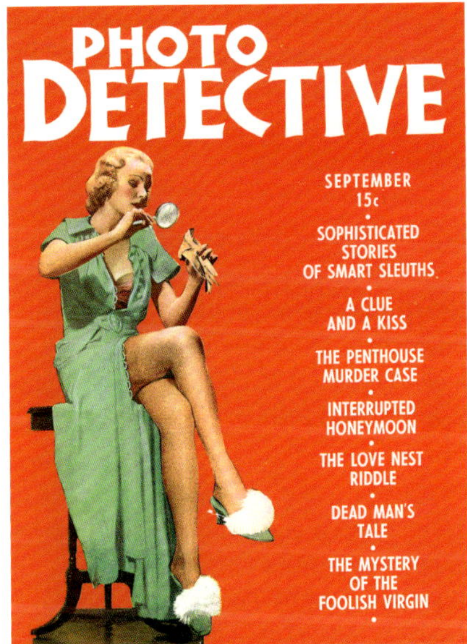

Year: **1937**. Title: **Photo Detective**.
Country: **USA**.

In the US the Civil War-era dime novels started with western adventure but soon added urban crime-fighters to broaden their fan base. Allen Pinkerton published America's first true detective book in 1875, detailing his adventures as a "private eye," a reference to the drawing of an all-seeing eye on his business card. It would be ten years before Arthur Conan Doyle's elegant Sherlock Holmes first solved crime with intelligence and wit, sparking England's love of detective stories. America, being America, preferred guns and muscle for their crime fighting, with any amount of mayhem acceptable (and desirable) so long as the good guy won. Scholar Leslie Fiedler called the detective in this context "a cowboy adapted to life on the city streets, the embodiment of innocence moving untouched through universal guilt." *Nick Carter Weekly*, the first American detective magazine, started around 1900

Arthur Conan Doyles eleganter Held Sherlock Holmes seinen ersten Fall mit Intelligenz und Witz löste und so Englands Liebe zu Detektivgeschichten weckte. Typisch amerikanisch, bevorzugte man hier Waffen und Muskeln zur Verbrechensbekämpfung und erlaubte (und wünschte) so viel Gewalt wie möglich, wenn nur der Gute gewann. Leslie Fiedler bezeichnete den Detektiv in diesem Kontext einmal als „einen Cowboy, der an das Leben auf den Großstadtstraßen angepasst war, die Verkörperung der Reinheit, unberührt von der universellen Schuld". Das erste amerikanische Detektivmagazin *Nick Carter Weekly* erschien erstmals Ende des 19. Jahrhunderts und entsprach ganz dieser Beschreibung. Der Titelheld schlug sich im wahrsten Sinne des Wortes durch, löste Verbrechen und vertrimmte die Schurken. Kurz später

la guerre de Sécession se concentrèrent d'abord sur la conquête de l'Ouest mais ne tardèrent pas à recruter en ville des défenseurs de la veuve et des orphelins pour élargir leur lectorat. Allen Pinkerton publia le premier vrai polard américain en 1875, détaillant ses aventures de « private eye » (jeu de mots entre « œil privé » et P. I., *private investigator*, « détective privé »), référence à l'œil dessiné sur sa carte de visite. Il faudrait encore attendre dix ans avant que l'élégant Sherlock Holmes d'Arthur Conan Doyle ne résolve sa première affaire criminelle avec intelligence et humour, déclenchant l'engouement des Anglais pour les énigmes policières. L'Amérique étant ce qu'elle est, on y préférait les justiciers musclés et armés, et toute forme de baston était acceptable (et bienvenue) à condition que le bon l'emporte

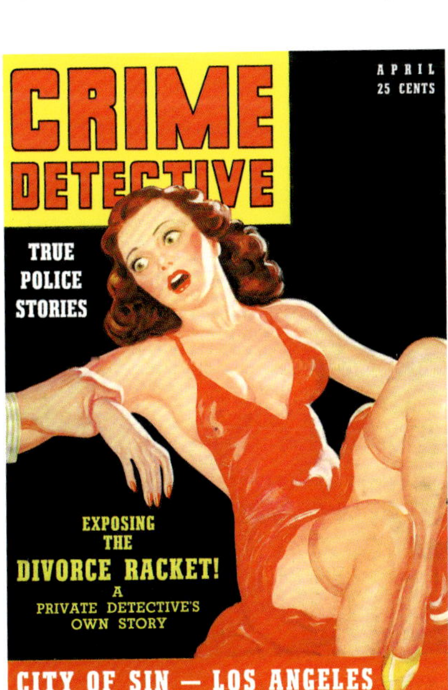

Year: **1939**. Title: **Crime Detective**.
Country: **USA**.

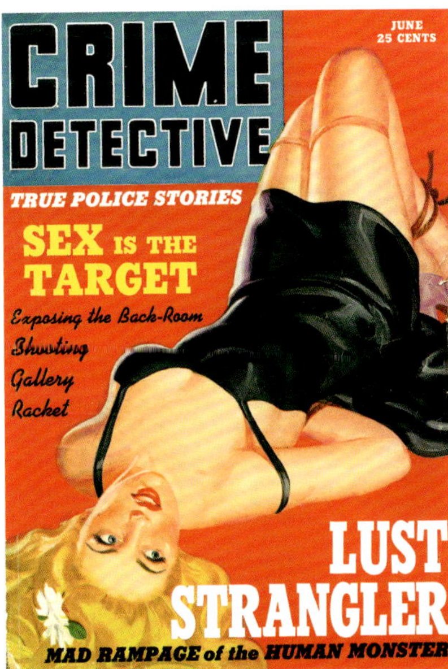

Year: **1941**. Title: **Crime Detective**.
Country: **USA**.

Year: **1959**. Title: **Special Detective**.
Country: **USA**.

What's amazing is that the magazines managed to continue into the mid-80s in this politically explosive form.

and was very much in this mode. Its title character brawled his way around the world, solving crimes and bashing bad guys. *Detective Story Magazine* appeared shortly after, also full of two-fisted man-to-man action. By the 1920s a subtle shift had begun. Better writers, notably Raymond Chandler, were producing a more complex fiction with a sexy slant. By the 30s the urban cowboy was replaced by the hard-boiled guy with a doll on his arm, and what dolls they were! *Spicy Detective*, *Private Detective Stories* and others commissioned exquisite cover art of bosomy women in torn clothing, often tied up, tortured or generally menaced. Alternately women played the criminals, still scantily clad, but cigarette smoking, gun toting and just begging to be slapped around for their sins.

The trend continued in the 40s with *Big Detective Cases*, *Real Detective*, *Headquarters Detective*, *Line-up Detective*

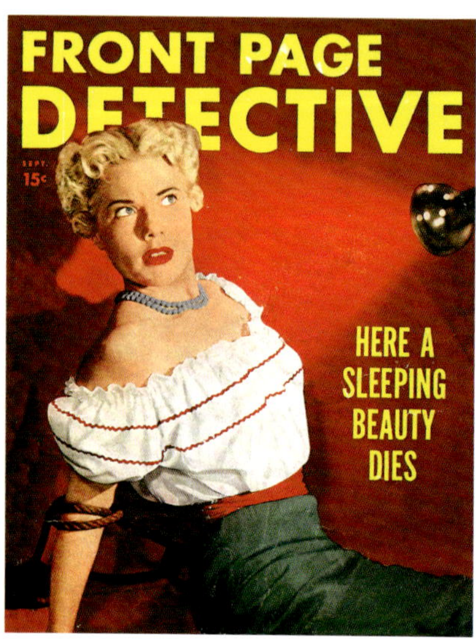

Year: **1949**. Title: **Front Page Detective**.
Country: **USA**.

erschien *Detective Story Monthly*, ebenfalls ein Loblied auf schlagkräftige Helden. In den Zwanzigern vollzog sich ein subtiler Wandel. Bessere Autoren, vor allem Raymond Chandler, schufen komplexere Geschichten mit einem gewissen Sexappeal. In den Dreißigern wurde der Cowboy endgültig vom Hardboiled-Helden mit einer kessen Biene im Arm abgelöst. *Spicy Detective*, *Private Detective Stories* und andere Hefte zeigten erstklassige Coverillustrationen mit tief dekolletierten Frauen in zerfetzter Kleidung, die häufig auch noch gefesselt waren und gefoltert oder anderweitig bedroht wurden. Natürlich gab es auch die Gangsterbraut, ebenfalls spärlich bekleidet, aber mit Kippe im Mundwinkel und Revolver in der Hand, die es geradezu darauf anlegte, für ihre Verworfenheit eine Tracht Prügel zu kassieren.

Dieser Trend setzte sich in den Vierzigern bei *Big Detective Cases*, *Real Detective*, *Headquarters Detective*, *Line-up Detective Crime* und zahllosen anderen fort, die schlimme Frauen zeigten, die schlimme Sachen machten und dafür teuer bezahlten. In dieser Zeit erschienen auch die ersten Fototitel, die sich aber erst in den Sechzigern durchsetzten. Die große Neuerung in den Fünfzigern waren Sadismus versprechende Coverzeilen und Covergirls, die ausschließlich auf der Opferseite waren. In den Vierzigern konnte eine Titelzeile „Die Spur des roten Lippenstifts" (*Big Detective Cases*, 1944) oder schlimmstenfalls „Weiße Sklavinnen in Harlem" (*Real Detective*, 1942) lauten. In den Fünfzigern dagegen: „Gequälte Sexsklavin von vagabundierendem Sexkiller vergewaltigt" (*True Police Yearbook*, 1952) oder „Ich musste sie schnell

à la fin. L'universitaire Leslie Fiedler a qualifié ce type de détective de « cowboy adapté à la vie dans les rues de la grande ville, incarnation de l'innocence avançant intacte à travers la culpabilité universelle ». *Nick Carter Weekly*, premier magazine policier américain lancé vers 1900, fonctionnait presque entièrement sur ce modèle. Son personnage titre déambulait dans le monde à grand renfort d'uppercuts, résolvant des enquêtes criminelles tout en tabassant les méchants. *Detective Story Magazine* parut peu après et abondait également en corps à corps musclés. À partir des années vingt, on observa un glissement subtil. De meilleurs auteurs, dont Raymond Chandler, écrivaient des textes plus complexes avec une touche érotique. Dans les années trente, le cowboy urbain avait définitivement cédé le pas au dur à cuire avec une poule à son bras, et quelle poule ! *Spicy Detective*, *Private Detective Stories* et d'autres affichaient des couvertures affolantes avec de belles plantureuses aux vêtements en lambeaux, souvent ligotées, torturées, ou généralement sous une menace quelconque. Il arrivait également que la femme joue le rôle de la méchante mais elle n'en était pas moins déshabillée, fumant la cigarette, brandissant un flingue et n'attendant qu'à être punie.

Cette tendance se poursuivit dans les années quarante avec *Big Detective Cases*, *Real Detective*, *Headquarters Detective*, *Line-up Detective Crime* et de très nombreux autres titres où de vilaines filles faisaient de vilaines choses et le payaient cher. Les photos en couverture firent également leur apparition à cette époque mais ne prédomineraient

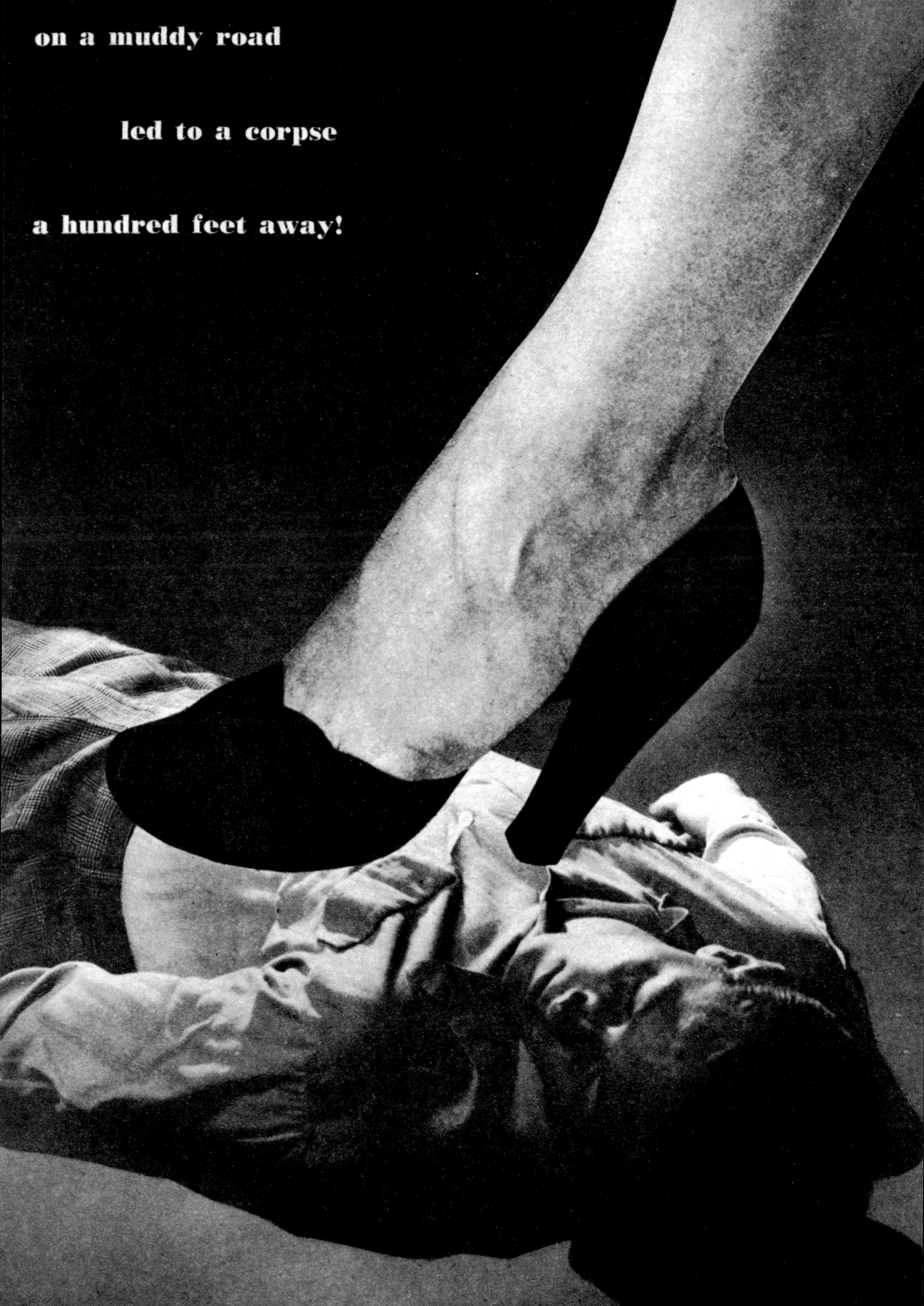
on a muddy road
led to a corpse
a hundred feet away!

YEAR: **1951**. TITLE: **True Cases of Women in Crime**. COUNTRY: **USA**.

Crime and many, many others featuring bad women doing bad things and paying dearly for it. Photo covers were also introduced at this time, but they would not predominate until the 60s. The big change in the 50s was the addition of sadistic coverlines and covergirls moving exclusively toward the victim end of the spectrum. In the 40s a line might read "Clue of the Coral Kiss" (*Big Detective Cases*, 1944), or at most "White Slaves of Black Harlem" (*Real Detective*, 1942). In the 50s: "Tortured Sex Captive and the Roving Rapist Killer" (*True Police Yearbook*, 1952) and "I Had to Kill Her Fast" (*Master Detective*, 1958). Photo bondage covers were a standard by the late 50s, and while some magazines used the provocative covers to sell tame interiors, others embraced misogyny throughout, running only stories about rape and lust murder, with interior photos posed by professional models to accompany the gory stories.

By the 60s detective magazines had slumped into decline. Sex magazines were stealing their readers and a drastic make-over was needed if they were to survive. That make-over would be the end of the magazines instead of their salvation, but for that story you'll have to read one of the later volumes in this series.

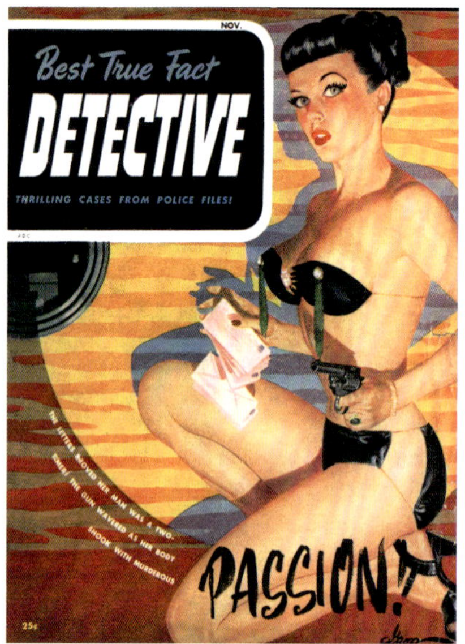

YEAR: **1946**. TITLE: **Best True Fact Detective**. COUNTRY: **USA**.

kaltmachen" (*Master Detective*, 1958). Bondage-Fotocover waren in den späten Fünfzigern der Standard, und während die einen Zeitschriften über die reißerischen Cover nur einen zahmen Inhalt an den Mann bringen wollten, waren andere durch und durch frauenfeindlich und brachten nur noch blutrünstige Storys über Vergewaltigung und Lustmord, die auf den Fotos zur Geschichte von professionellen Models nachgestellt wurden.

In den Sechzigern ging es mit den Detektivmagazinen bergab. Sexmagazine machten ihnen die Leser abspenstig, und es musste eine radikale Neuorientierung her, wenn das Genre überleben wollte. Warum aber dieses Facelifting den Detektivmagazinen statt der erhofften Rettung das endgültige Aus bescherte, können Sie in einem der späteren Bände nachlesen.

pas avant les années soixante. Le grand changement des années cinquante fut l'ajout de manchettes sadiques et de couvertures montrant des filles qui se situaient nettement dans le camp des victimes. Dans les années quarante, les titres étaient du genre « L'indice du baiser de corail » (*Big Detective Cases*, 1944) ou, au pire, « Esclaves blanches du Harlem noir » (*Real Detective*, 1942). Dans les années cinquante, on était passé à : « Séquestrée et torturée par un vagabond violeur et tueur » (*True Police Yearbook*, 1952) ou « J'ai dû la buter fissa » (*Master Detective*, 1958). À la fin des années cinquante, les couvertures arborant des photos de bondage étaient monnaie courante et, si certains magazines utilisaient des couvertures provocantes pour vendre un contenu plus sage, d'autres vouaient un culte à la misogynie, ne publiant que des récits sanglants de viols et de meurtres sexuels illustrées par des photos montrant des modèles professionnels.

Dans les années soixante, les magazines policiers connurent un grave déclin, leur lectorat se détournant au profit des revues de charme. Pour survivre, un sérieux remaniement s'imposait. Loin de les sauver, les mesures prises par les éditeurs allaient signer leur arrêt de mort mais, pour en savoir plus à ce sujet, il faudra vous reporter à l'un des volumes ultérieurs de cette collection.

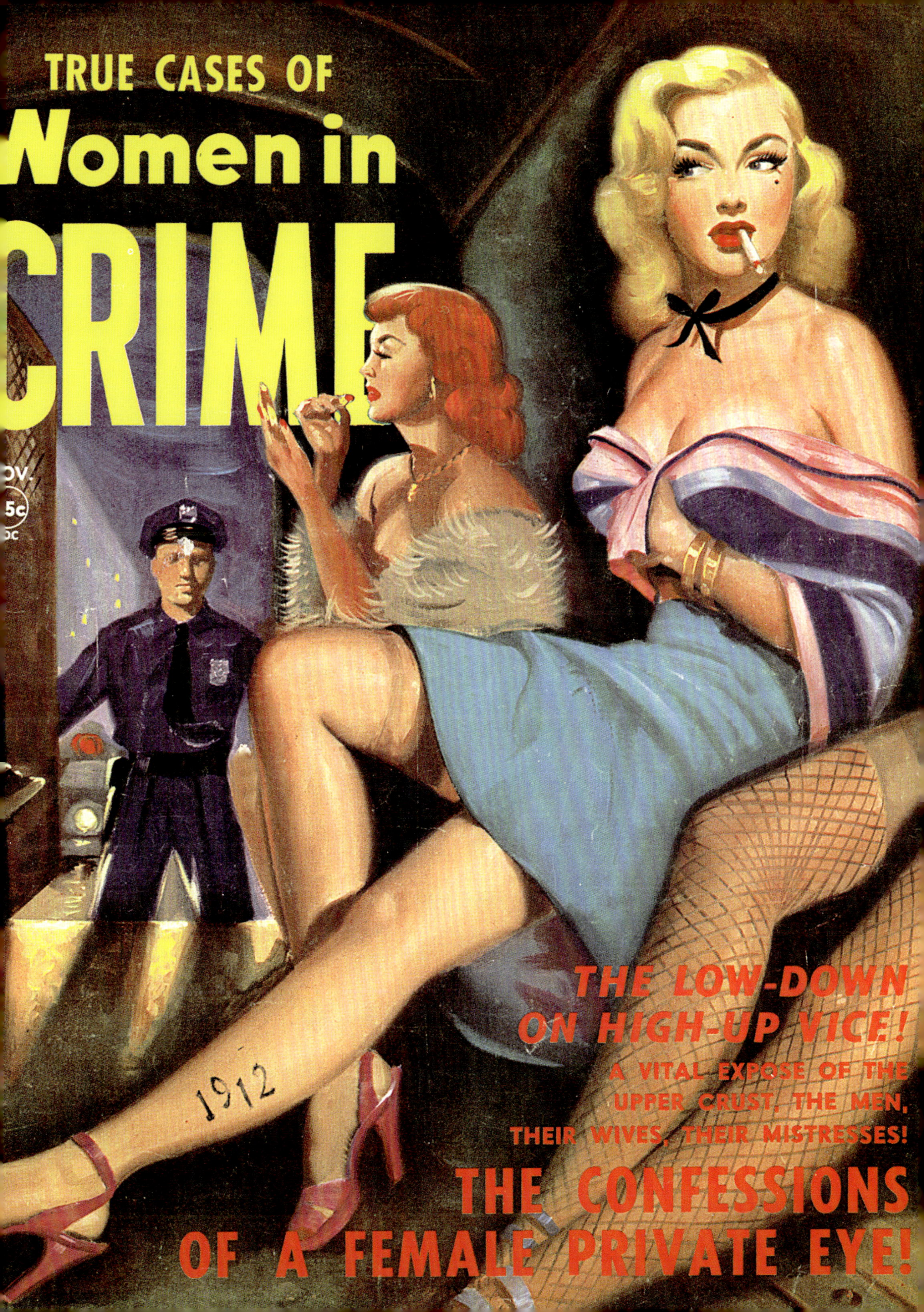
TRUE CASES OF
Women in
CRIME
OV.
5c
THE LOW-DOWN
ON HIGH-UP VICE!
A VITAL EXPOSE OF THE
UPPER CRUST, THE MEN,
THEIR WIVES, THEIR MISTRESSES!
THE CONFESSIONS
OF A FEMALE PRIVATE EYE!
1912

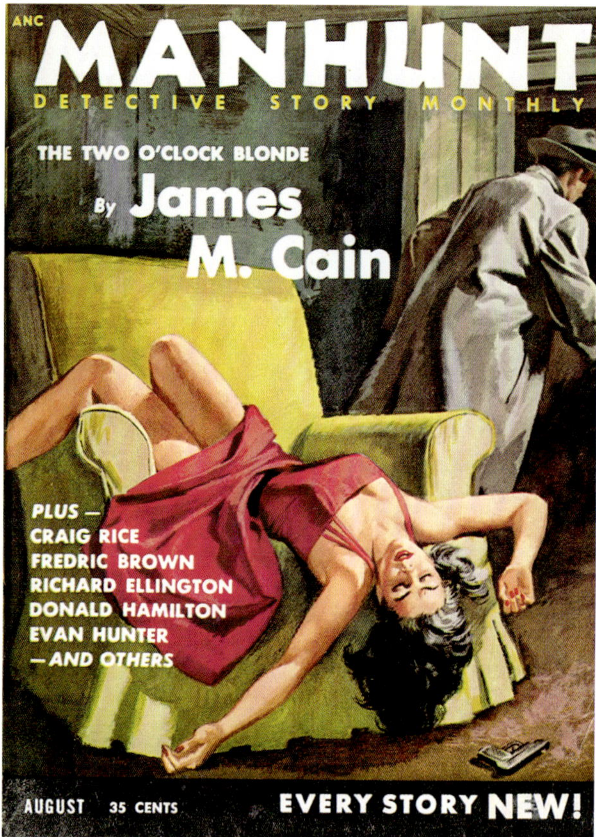

YEAR: **1953**. TITLE: **Manhunt**. COUNTRY: **USA**.

YEAR: **1953**. TITLE: **Manhunt**. COUNTRY: **USA**.

RIGHT: YEAR: **1954**. TITLE: **Special Detective**. COUNTRY: **USA**.

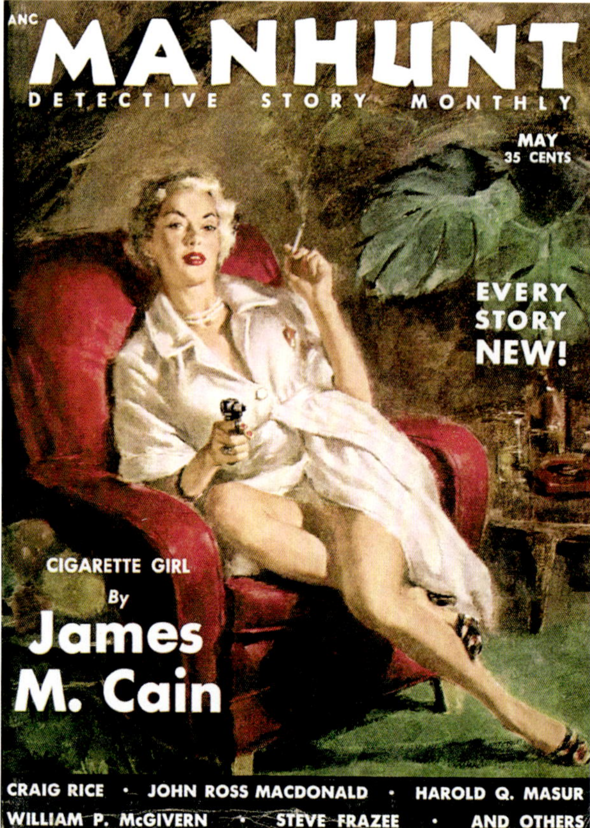

YEAR: **1953**. TITLE: **Manhunt**. COUNTRY: **USA**.

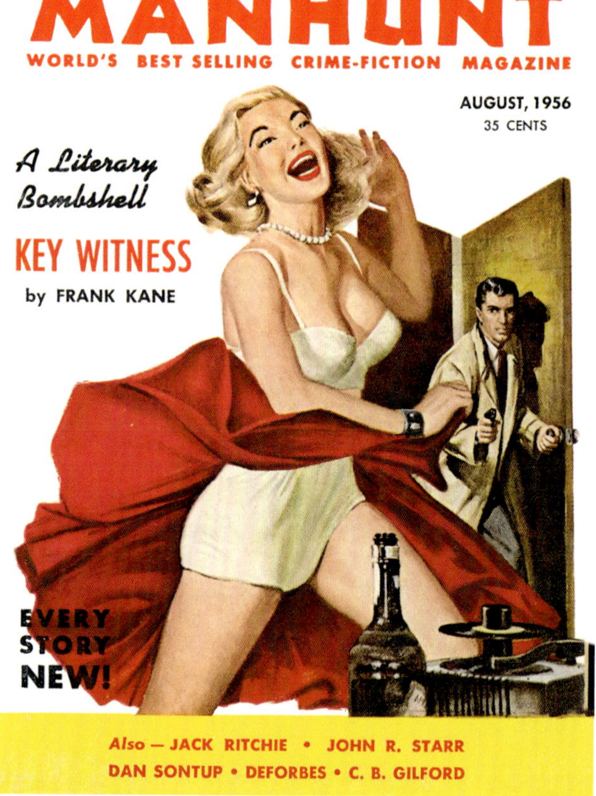

YEAR: **1956**. TITLE: **Manhunt**. COUNTRY: **USA**.

Manhunt, *this from 1953, was a classic example of the detective fiction digests prevalent in the 1950s.*

Manhunt, *hier Hefte von 1953, war ein klassisches Beispiel für die Krimihefte, die in den fünfziger Jahren weitverbreitet waren.*

Manhunt, *ici des numéros de 1953, est un exemple classique des digests de nouvelles policières très prisés dans les années 50.*

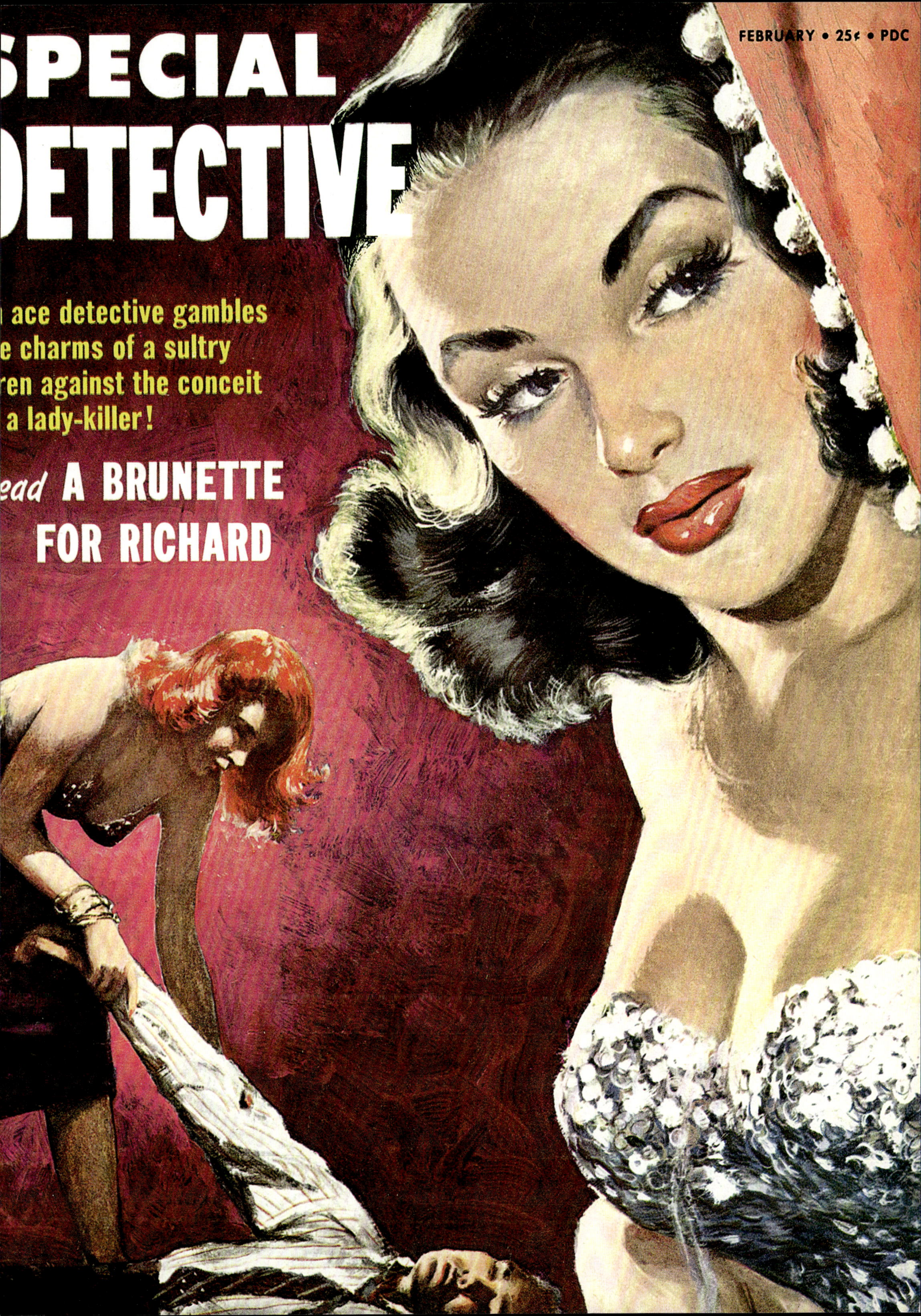

FEBRUARY • 25¢ • PDC
SPECIAL
DETECTIVE
n ace detective gambles
e charms of a sultry
ren against the conceit
a lady-killer!
ead A BRUNETTE
FOR RICHARD

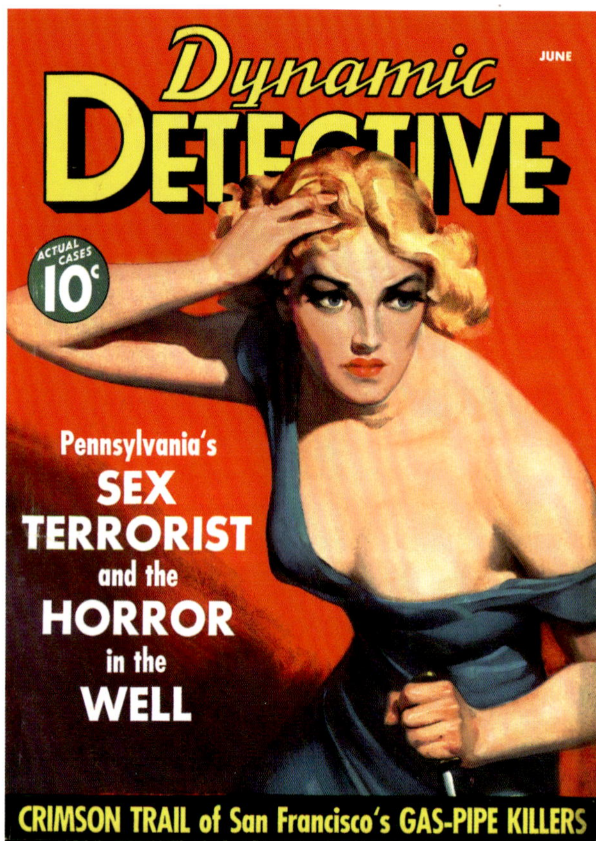

YEAR: **1937**. TITLE: **Dynamic Detective**. COUNTRY: **USA**.

Daring
Detective
JANUARY
FACT STORIES
15¢
Mountain
LOVE NEST
and the
AVENGING
HUSBAND

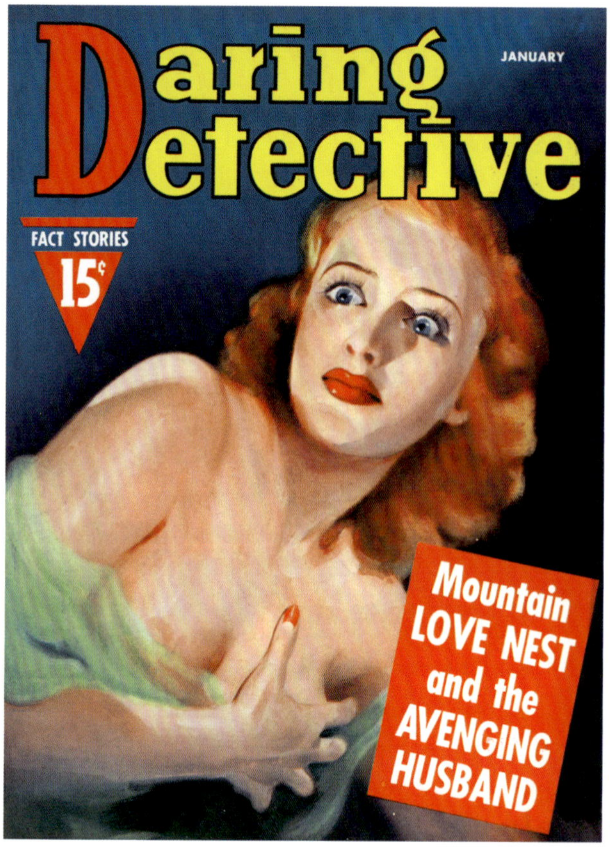

YEAR: **1938**. TITLE: **Daring Detective**. COUNTRY: **USA**.

RIGHT: YEAR: **1942**. TITLE: **Real Detective**. COUNTRY: **USA**.

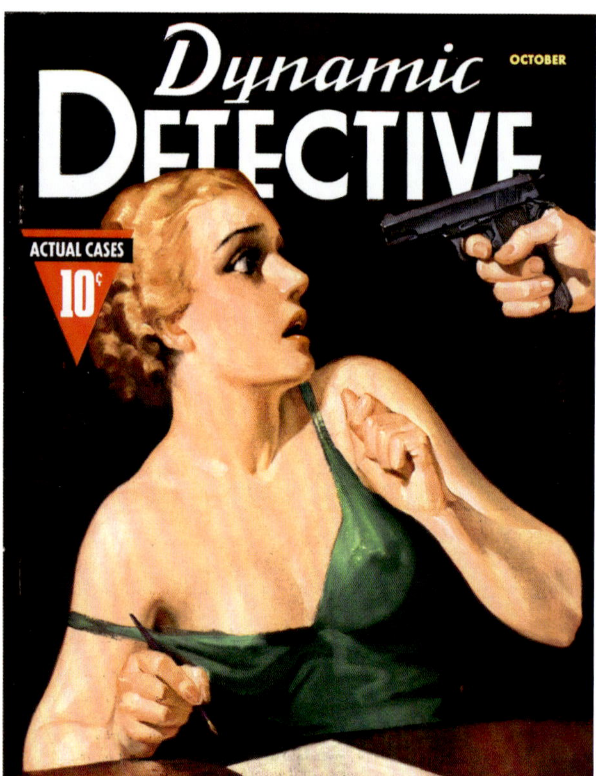

YEAR: **1938**. TITLE: **Dynamic Detective**. COUNTRY: **USA**.

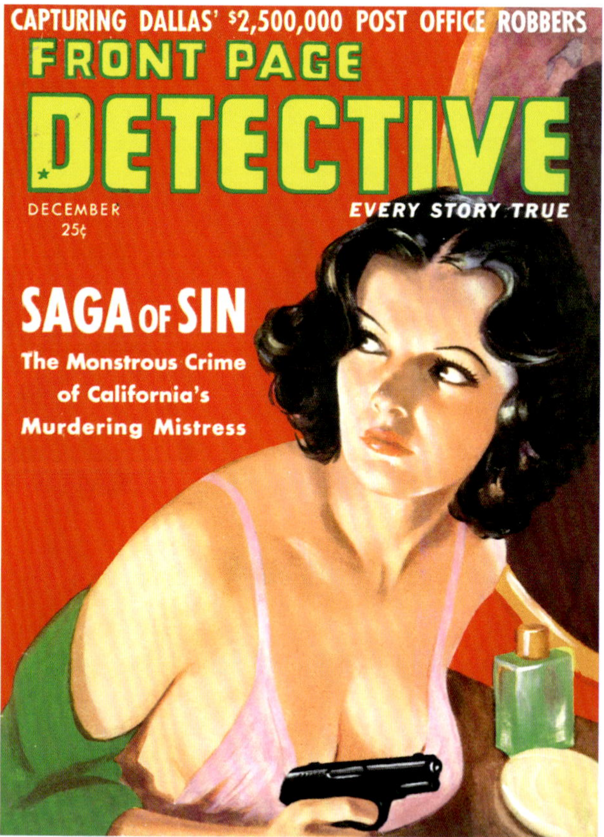

YEAR: **1937**. TITLE: **Front Page Detective**. COUNTRY: **USA**.

Opposite page: In the 1940s women were perpetrators as often as victims, though hand tinted photo covers like this were a rarity.

Rechte Seite: In den vierziger Jahren waren Frauen ebenso häufig Täter wie Opfer, aber handkolorierte Fototitelbilder wie dieses waren eher die Ausnahme.

Page de droite : Dans les années 40, les femmes étaient aussi souvent criminelles que victimes. Les couvertures avec des photos teintes à la main comme celle-ci étaient rares.

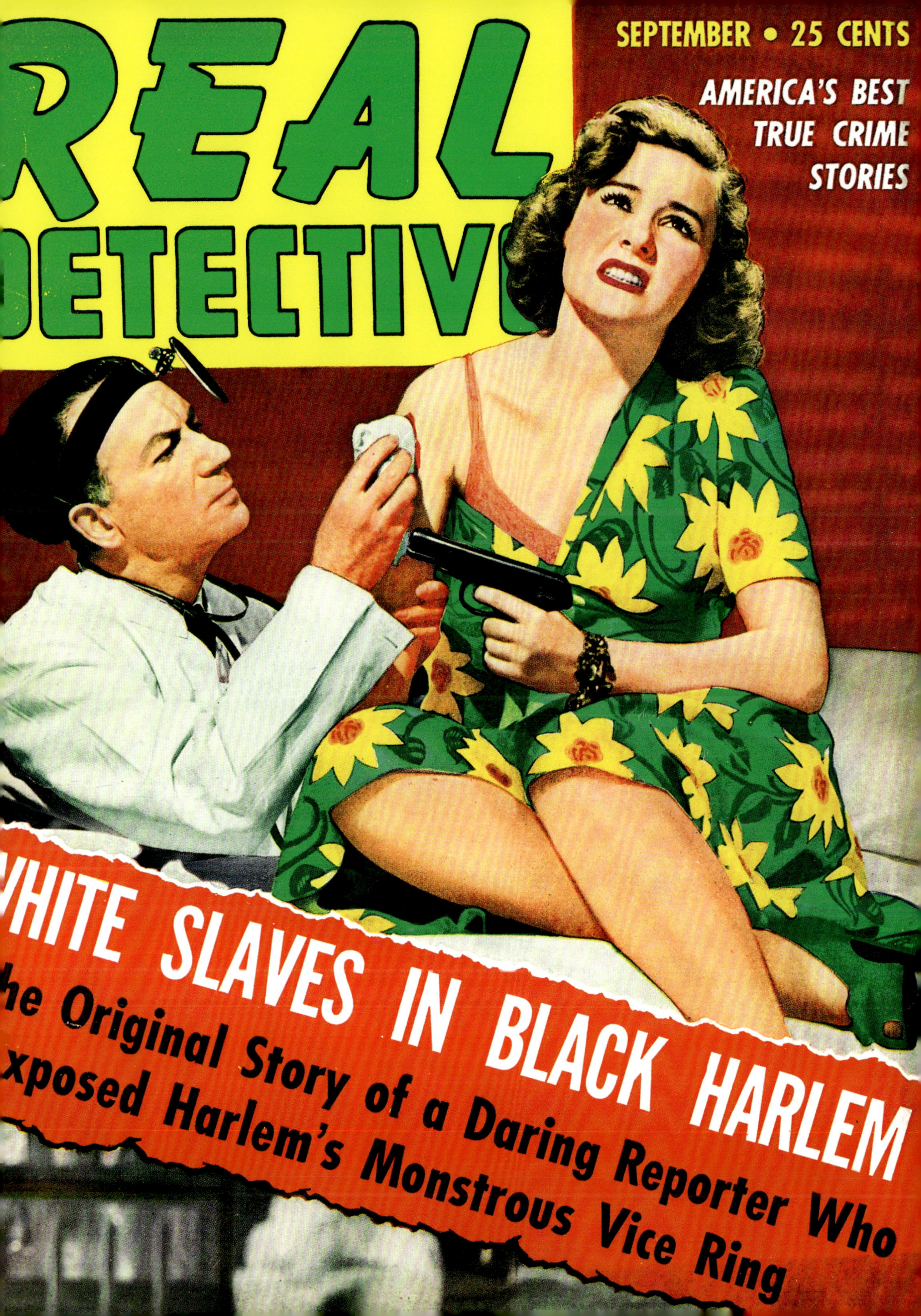
REAL
DETECTIVE
SEPTEMBER • 25 CENTS
AMERICA'S BEST
TRUE CRIME
STORIES
WHITE SLAVES IN BLACK HARLEM
The Original Story of a Daring Reporter Who
Exposed Harlem's Monstrous Vice Ring

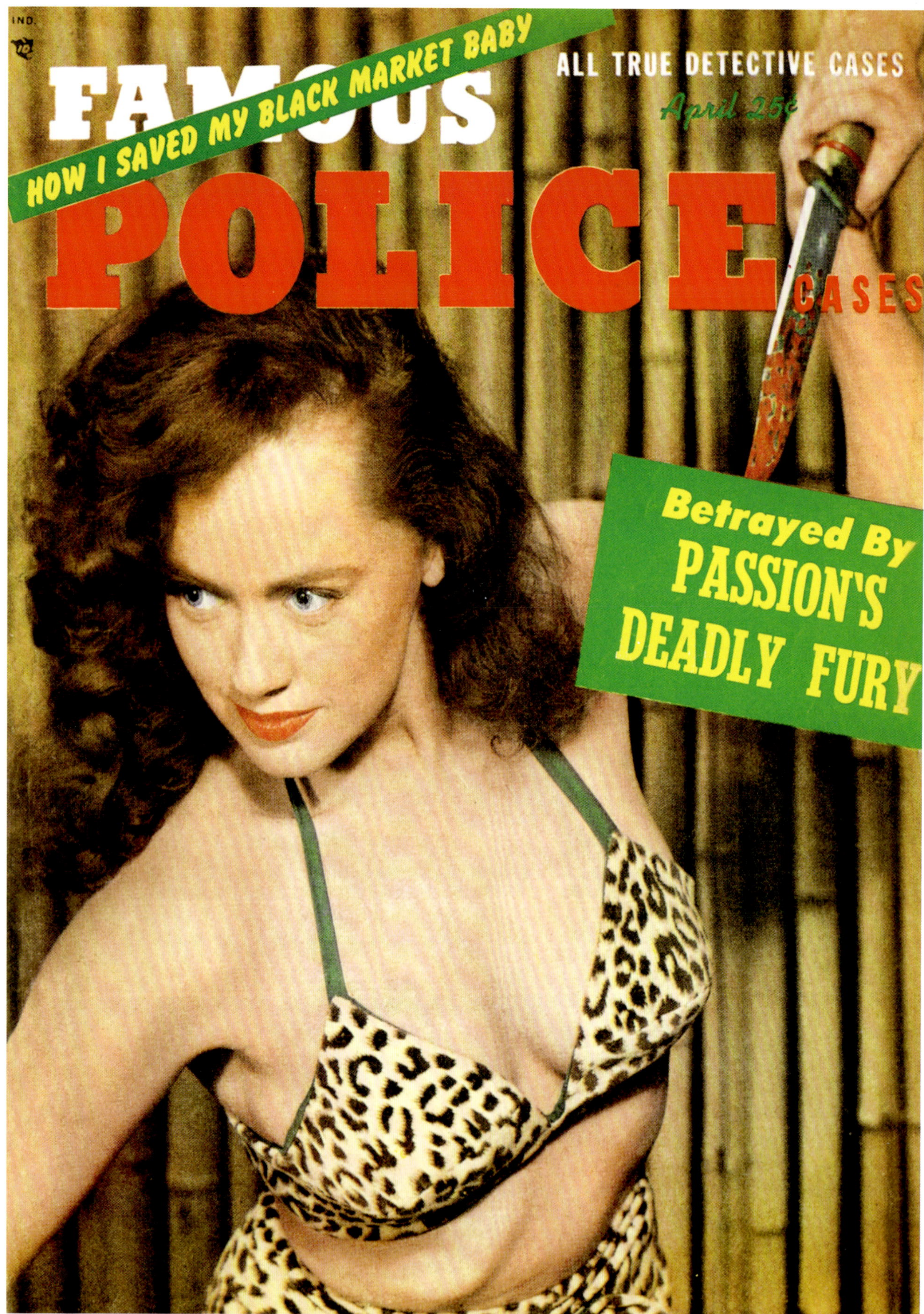

Year: **1953**. Title: **Famous Police Cases**. Country: **USA**.

Year: **1952**. Title: **Uncensored Detective**.
Country: **USA**.

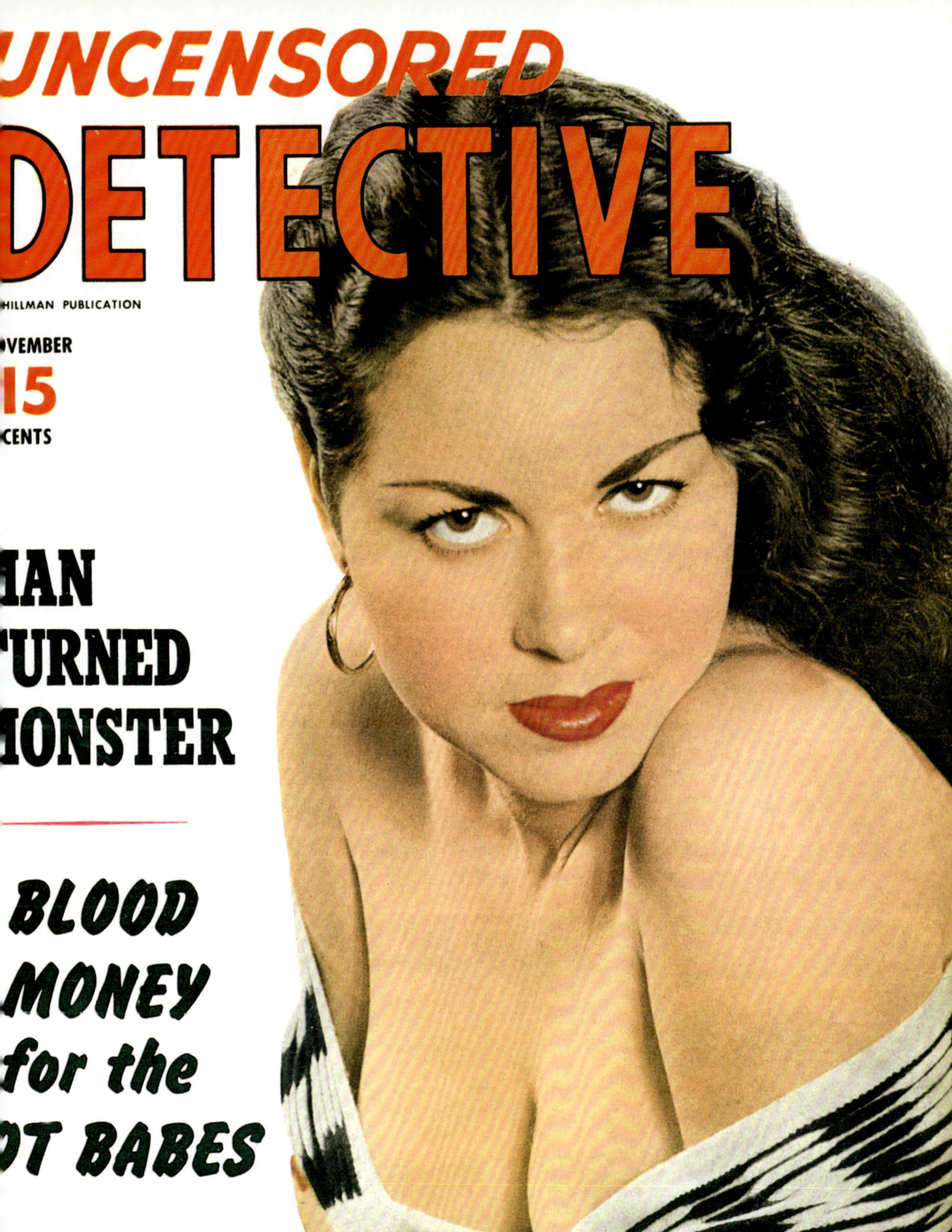
UNCENSORED
DETECTIVE
HILLMAN PUBLICATION
VEMBER
15
CENTS
IAN
URNED
IONSTER
BLOOD
MONEY
for the
OT BABES

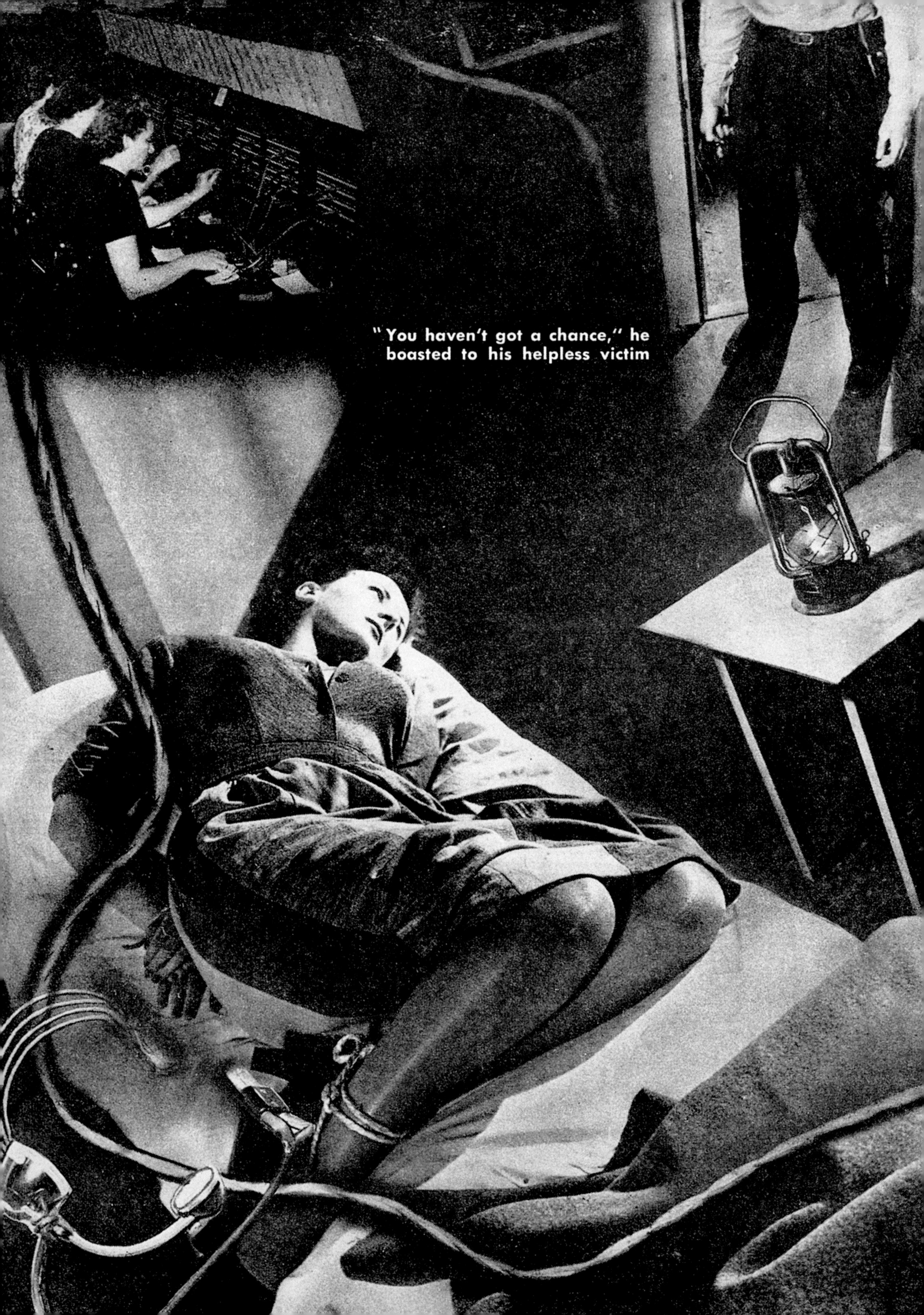

"You haven't got a chance," he boasted to his helpless victim

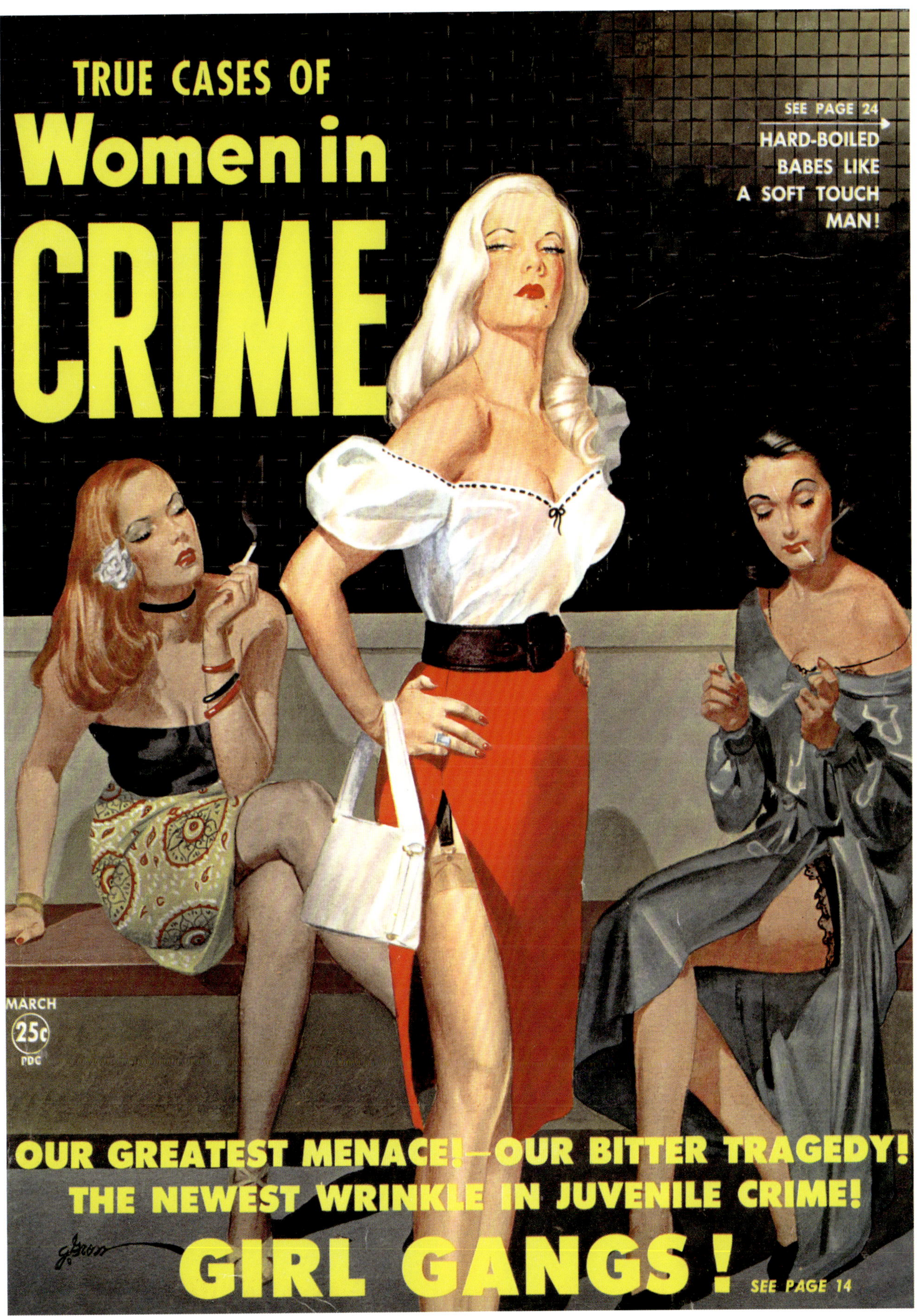

YEAR: **1950**. TITLE: **True Cases of Women in Crime**. ARTIST: **George Gross**. COUNTRY: **USA**.

YEAR: **1949**. TITLE: **Master Detective**. COUNTRY: **USA**.

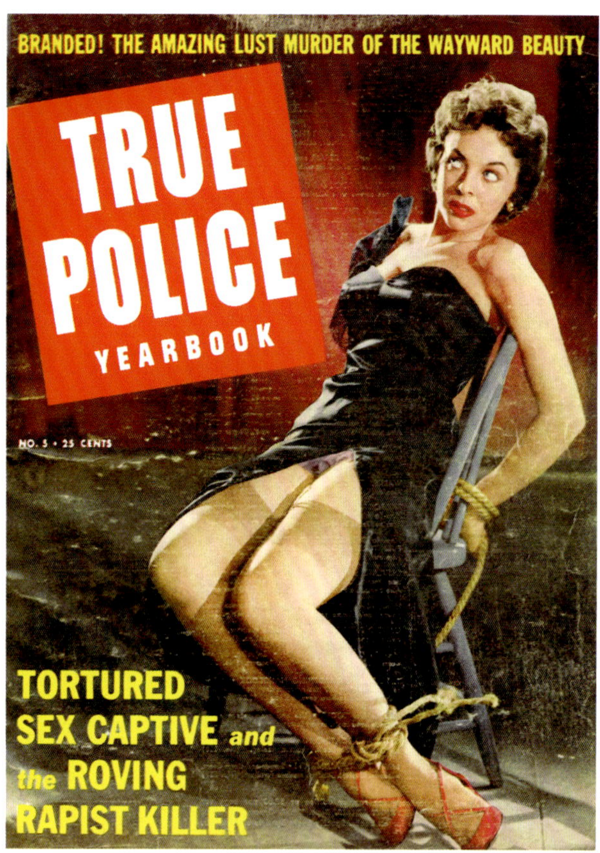

YEAR: **1956**. TITLE: **True Police Yearbook**. COUNTRY: **USA**.

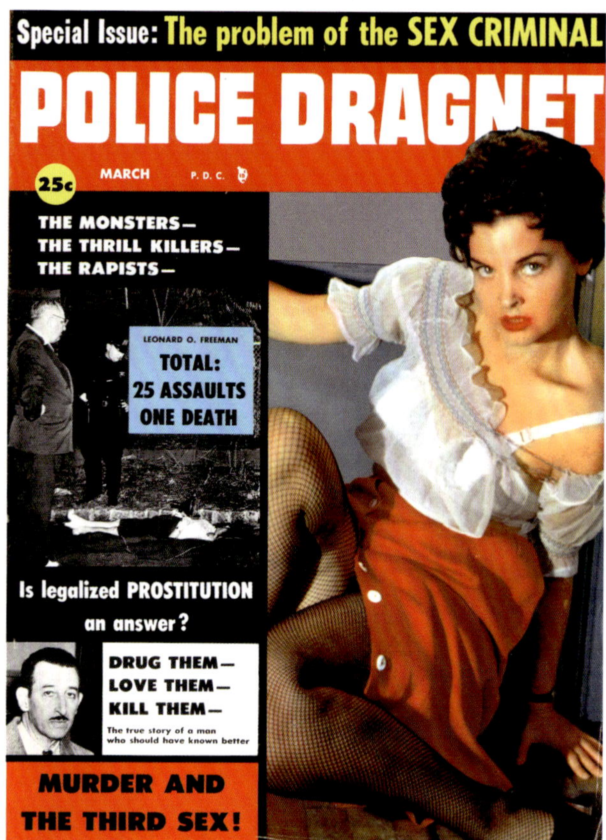

YEAR: **1956**. TITLE: **Police Dragnet**. COUNTRY: **USA**.

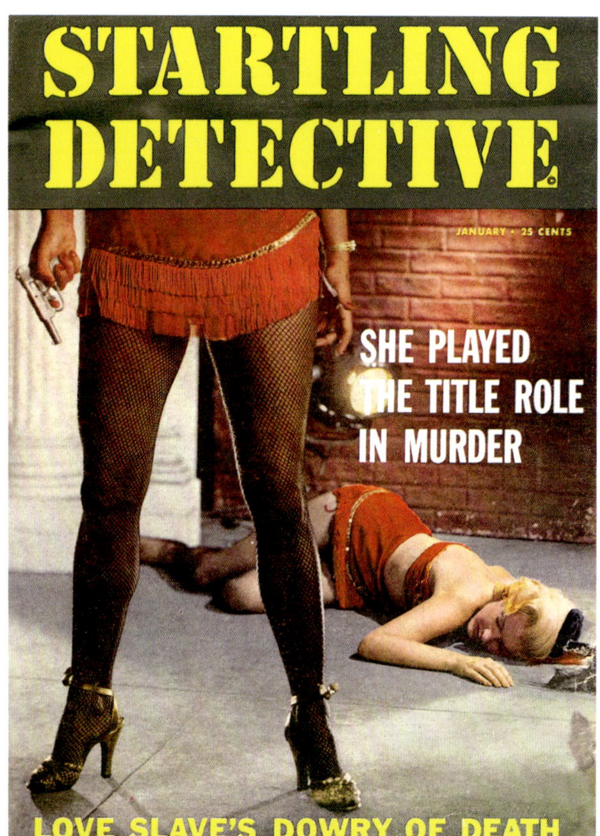

YEAR: **1955**. TITLE: **Startling Detective**. COUNTRY: **USA**.

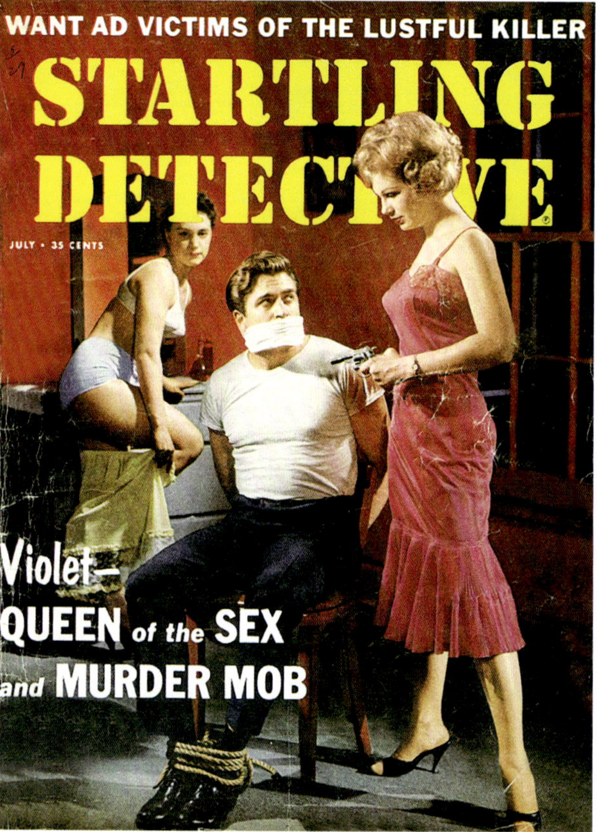

YEAR: **1958**. TITLE: **Startling Detective**. COUNTRY: **USA**.

YEAR: **1956**. TITLE: **Expose Detective**. COUNTRY: **USA**.

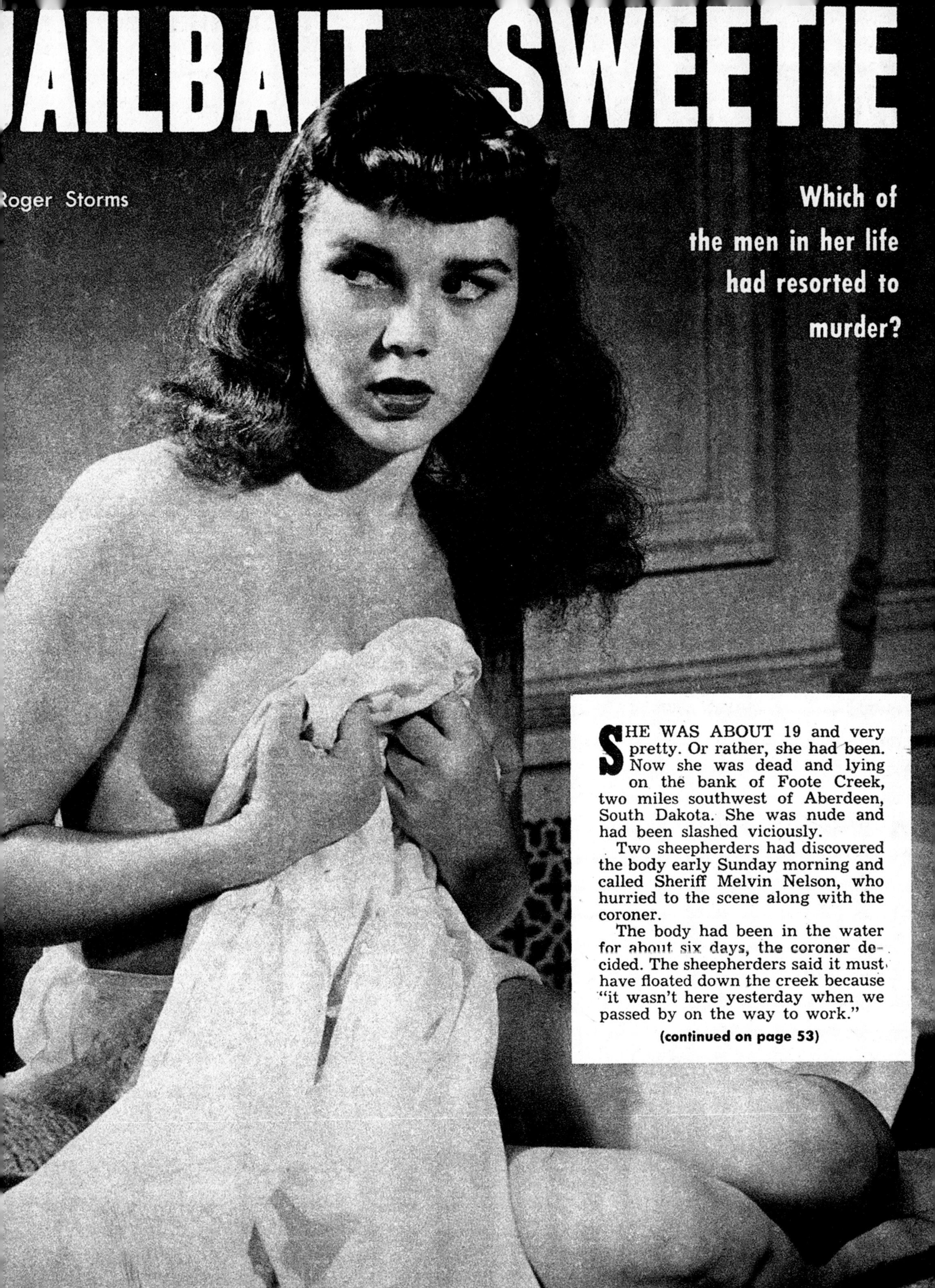

JAILBAIT SWEETIE

Roger Storms

Which of the men in her life had resorted to murder?

SHE WAS ABOUT 19 and very pretty. Or rather, she had been. Now she was dead and lying on the bank of Foote Creek, two miles southwest of Aberdeen, South Dakota. She was nude and had been slashed viciously.

Two sheepherders had discovered the body early Sunday morning and called Sheriff Melvin Nelson, who hurried to the scene along with the coroner.

The body had been in the water for about six days, the coroner decided. The sheepherders said it must have floated down the creek because "it wasn't here yesterday when we passed by on the way to work."

(continued on page 53)

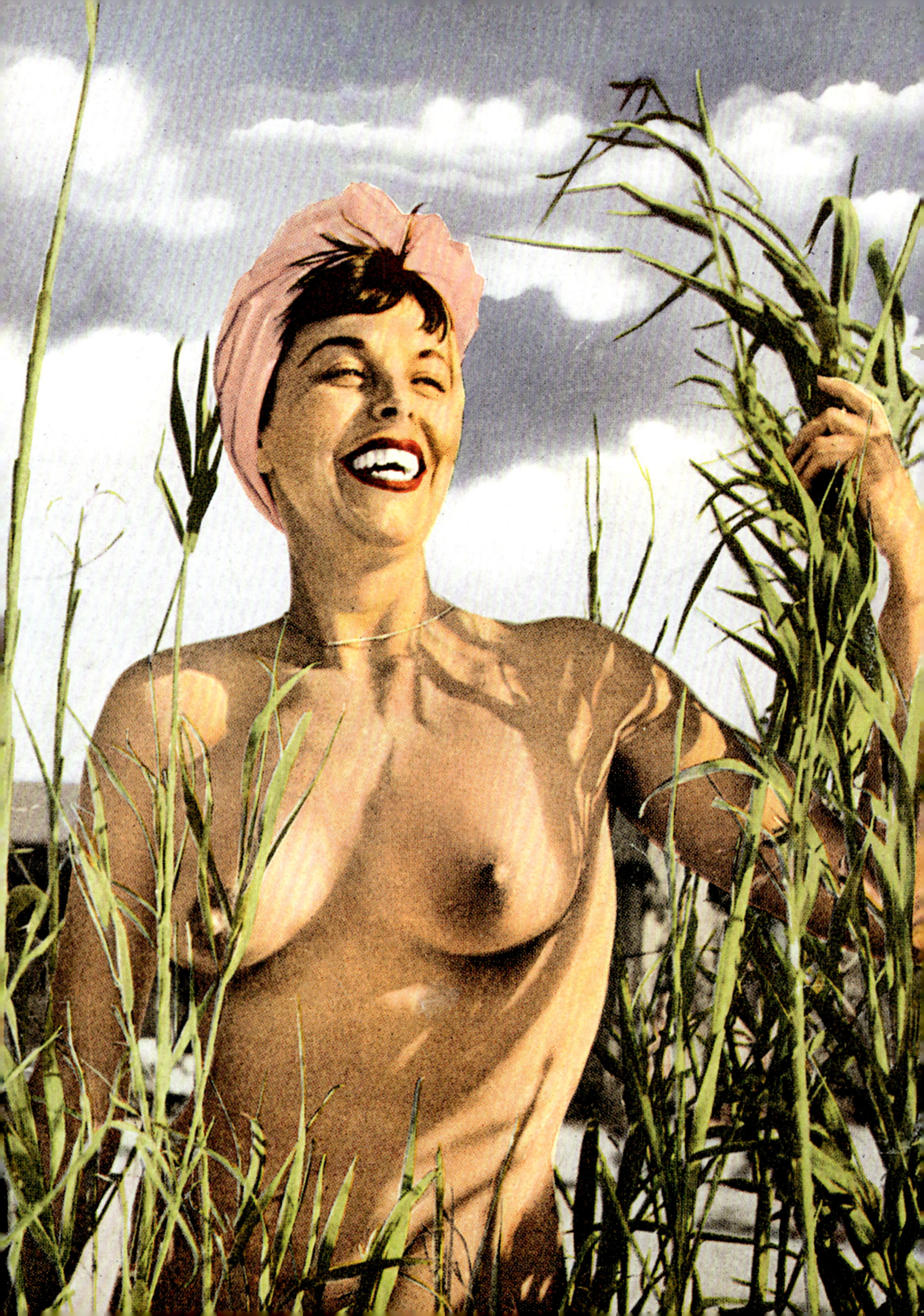

NAKED VS. NUDE:

American Naturist Magazines 1933 to 1958

Wie Gott sie schuf: Die amerikanischen Naturalistenmagazine zwischen 1933 und 1958

Nu mais pur : les magazines naturistes américains de 1933 à 1958

America's first nudist park opened in upstate New York in 1932, and since nudists are by nature proselytizers, it took less than a year for the first magazine to follow. It was published by the Reverend Ilsley "Uncle Danny" Boone, a Baptist zealot who would push his new religion with the same single-minded conviction he once applied to the gospel. His magazine was called, simply, *The Nudist*. Its (censored) photos of happy naked families were mixed with inspirational text on the physical, mental and spiritual benefits of what was popularly called "air bathing." That there could be a sexual element to public nakedness was always vigorously denied. Nonetheless nudism was outlawed in New York in 1935, due almost entirely to Boone's high profile. Even when *The Nudist* changed its title to the less confrontational *Sunshine & Health* Boone remained a controversial character because he kept challenging the government over the censorship of his photos. He was adamant that nudism had nothing to do with sexuality, and therefore he should be able to print photos that showed pubic hair and both

Amerikas erstes Nudistencamp öffnete seine Pforten 1932 in New York, und da Nudisten mit Sendungsbewusstsein reich beschenkt sind, dauerte es kein Jahr, bis die erste Nudistenzeitschrift erschien. Sie wurde von Reverend Ilsley „Uncle Danny" Boone herausgegeben, einem baptistischen Eiferer, der seine neue Religion mit der gleichen unbeirrbaren Überzeugung vertreten sollte, wie zuvor das Evangelium. Seine Zeitschrift hieß schlicht *The Nudist*. Ihre (zensierten) Fotos von glücklichen nackten Familien waren vermischt mit beseelten Artikeln, die die physischen, mentalen und spirituellen Vorteile dessen priesen, was man volkstümlich „Luftbaden" nannte. Dass es bei der öffentlichen Nacktheit auch eine sexuelle Komponente geben könnte, wurde stets vehement abgestritten. Trotzdem wurde der Nudismus 1935 in New York für ungesetzlich erklärt, was nahezu ausschließlich auf Boones lautstarkes Auftreten zurückzuführen war. Selbst nachdem die Zeitschrift sich von *The Nudist* in (etwas unverfänglicher) *Sunshine & Health* umbenannte, blieb Boone ein streitbarer Charakter und

That there could be a sexual element to public nakedness was always vigorously denied.

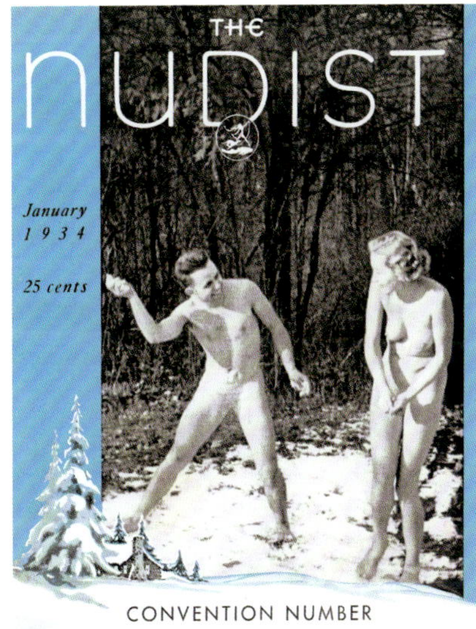

Year: **1934**. Title: **The Nudist**. Country: **USA**.

Le premier camp nudiste des États-Unis ouvrit ses portes en 1932 dans le nord de l'État de New York et, les nudistes étant par nature enclins au prosélytisme, le premier magazine parut moins d'un an plus tard. Il était publié par le révérend Ilsley « Uncle Danny » Boone, un fervent baptiste qui devait promouvoir sa nouvelle religion avec la même conviction fanatique qu'il avait autrefois appliquée aux évangiles. Il s'intitulait tout simplement *The Nudist*. Des photos (censurées) de familles nues et heureuses y cohabitaient avec des textes édifiants

Year: **1951**. Title: **Sunshine & Health**.
Country: **USA**.

YEAR: **1950s**. TITLE: **Sunbathing for Health Magazine**. COUNTRY: **USA**.

I rise almost every morning, and sit in my chamber without any clothes whatever... either reading or writing. This practice is not in the least painful, but, on the contrary, agreeable.

—Benjamin Franklin, 1760

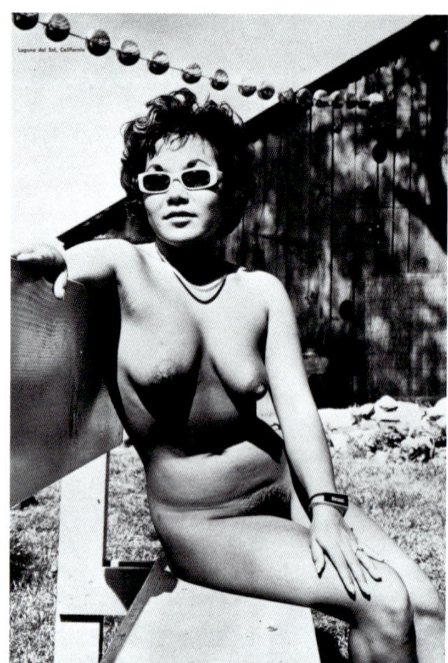

YEAR: **1955**. TITLE: **Sun and Health**. COUNTRY: **USA**.

female and male genitalia. One of the problems with this argument was that his magazine featured a disproportionate number of photos of attractive young women, an issue that undermined the credibility of nudist magazines from their inception. And his cause wasn't helped when, in the late 40s, GIs returning from European reconstruction brought home French, Danish and Austrian nudist magazines. The post-war European digests looked more like figure model magazines than anything being published by American nudists. Boone couldn't resist trying to match their sensual style, introducing his own Euro knock-off *Sun* in 1950. Meanwhile he continued battling the government, with the post office regularly snatching his magazines as obscene. Competing magazines *Sun Lore*, *American Sunbather* and *Modern Sunbathing and Hygiene*, each representing

schlug sich beharrlich mit den Behörden herum, weil sie seine Fotos zensierten. Er beharrte darauf, dass Nudismus nichts mit Sexualität zu tun habe und man ihm folglich nicht verbieten könne, Fotos abzudrucken, die Schambehaarung und weibliche wie männliche Genitalien zeigten. Es stärkte Boones Position nicht unbedingt, dass sein Blatt unverhältnismäßig viele Fotos attraktiver junger Frauen abdruckte, ein Sachverhalt, der die Glaubwürdigkeit der Nudistenzeitschriften von Anfang an untergraben hatte. Und es war der Sache auch nicht dienlich, als in den späten Vierzigern amerikanische Soldaten französische, dänische und österreichische Nudistenzeitschriften mit in die Heimat brachten. Die europäischen Nachkriegshefte erinnerten wesentlich mehr an Aktmodell-Magazine als irgendeine Publikation amerikanischer Nudisten. Boone konnte nicht widerstehen, ihren Stil zu kopieren, und brachte 1950 *Sun* auf den Markt, ein Magazin im europäischen Stil.

Die ganze Zeit stritt er sich weiterhin mit den Behörden, da das Post Office seine Zeitschriften mit schöner Regelmäßigkeit wegen Obszönität einkassierte. Während Konkurrenzblätter wie *Sun Lore*, *American Sunbather* und *Modern Sunbathing and Hygiene*, die jeweils eine rivalisierende Nudistenorganisation repräsentierten, es vorzogen, sich den Zensurmaßnahmen zu fügen, kämpfte „Uncle Danny" hartnäckig weiter.

1958 kapitulierte die Staatsgewalt. Die Sitten änderten sich, und ein bisschen Nudistenschamhaar lohnte die Aufregung nicht mehr. Obschon die FKK-Zeitschriften Nicht-Nudisten immer schon als Masturbationsvorlage gedient hatten,

sur les bienfaits physiques, mentaux et spirituels de ce qu'on appelait alors les « bains d'air ». Qu'il put y avoir un élément sexuel dans la nudité publique était farouchement nié. Cela n'empêcha pas le nudisme d'être interdit dans l'État de New York en 1935, une interdiction largement due à la personnalité haute en couleurs de Boone.

Même après avoir rebaptisé son magazine du titre moins compromettant *Sunshine & Health* (« Soleil et santé »), Boone resta un personnage à controverses, ne cessant de défier le gouvernement sur la question de la censure de ses images. Soutenant catégoriquement que le nudisme n'avait rien à voir avec la sexualité, il revendiquait le droit publier des photos montrant les poils pubiens et les organes génitaux des hommes et des femmes. L'un des hics de cette ligne de défense était que sa revue présentait un nombre disproportionné de photos de jeunes et jolies femmes, détail qui mina sérieusement la crédibilité des magazines nudistes dès leur apparition. Sa cause ne fut guère arrangée lorsque, à la fin des années quarante, les G.I.s rentrèrent d'Europe en pleine reconstruction avec des magazines nudistes français, danois et autrichiens. Les publications européennes de l'après-guerre ressemblaient

In 1958 the only place pubic hair could be legally viewed in America was in nudist magazines.

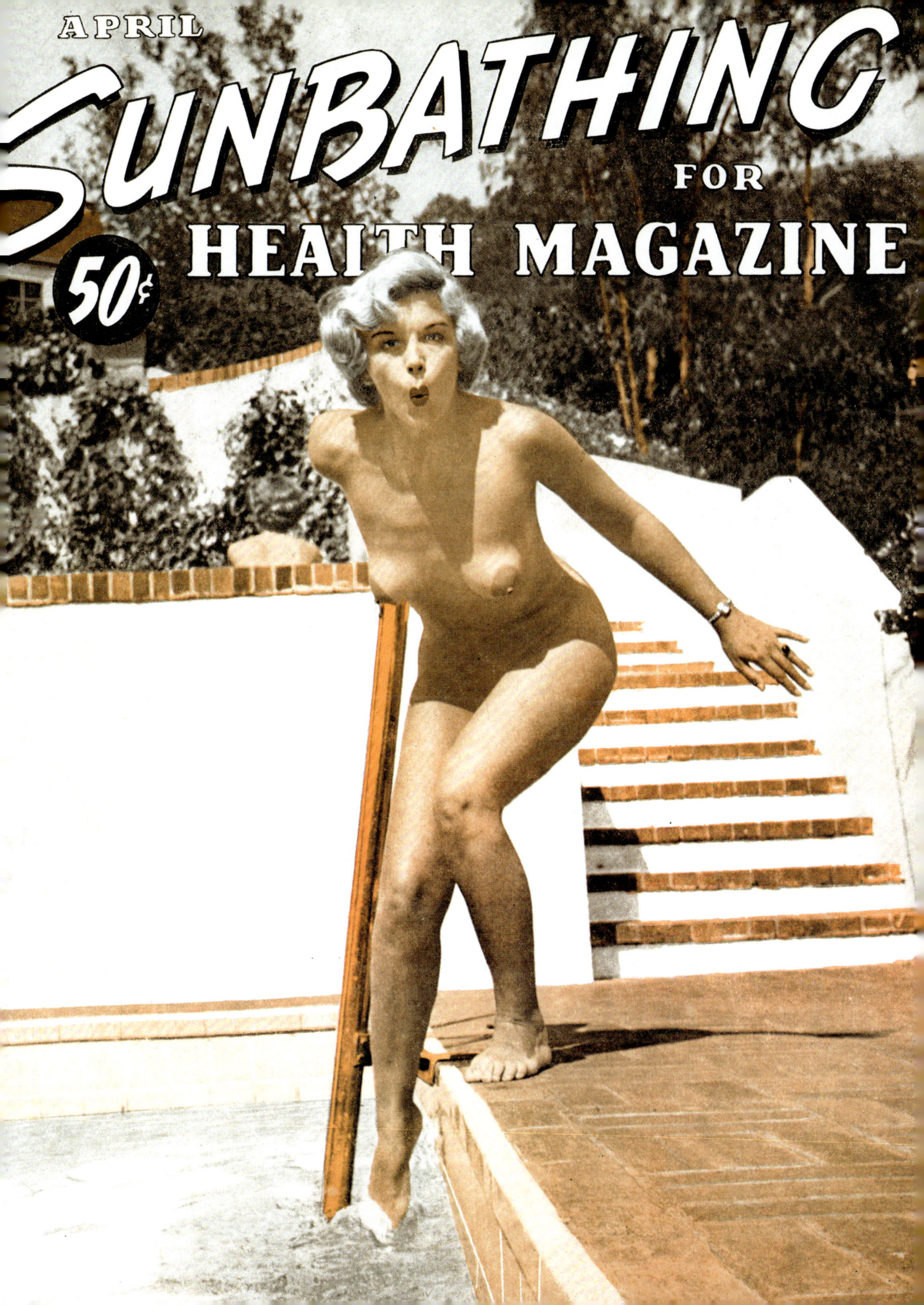
APRIL
SUNBATHING
FOR
HEALTH MAGAZINE
50¢

"Uncle Danny's" magazine featured a disproportionate number of photos of attractive young women.

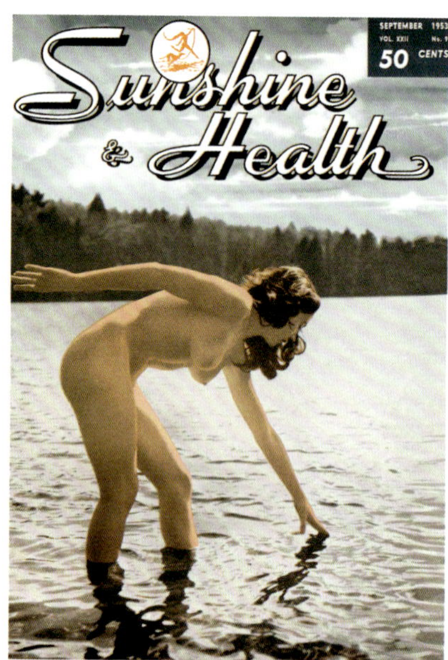

Year: **1953**. Title: **Sunshine & Health**. Country: **USA**.

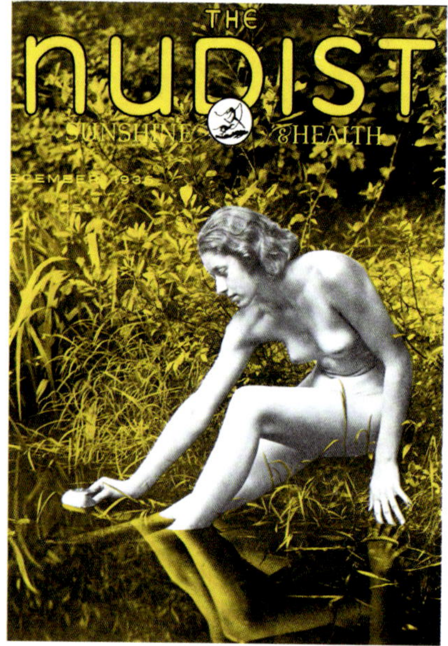

Year: **1936**. Title: **The Nudist**. Country: **USA**.

a rival nudist organization, chose to accept censorship while "Uncle Danny" fought on.

In 1958 the government gave up. Mores were changing and a little nudist fuzz didn't seem such a big deal anymore. Though non-nudists had been using the magazines as masturbatory material all along, the courts finally accepted Boone's argument that they weren't sexual and were therefore exempt from obscenity laws and could have their hair. For the next ten years the only place pubic hair could be legally viewed in America was in nudist magazines, which made them popular beyond "Uncle Danny's" wildest dreams.

schlossen sich die Gerichte letztendlich Boones Argumentation an, dass sie nicht obszön seien und somit nicht unters Obszönitäts-Gesetz fielen, und gaben dem Schamhaar ihren Segen. Für die nächsten zehn Jahre waren die Nudistenblätter die einzige Stelle, an der man in den Staaten Schamhaar betrachten durfte, ohne sich strafbar zu machen, und das machte sie populärer, als es sich „Uncle Danny" je hätte träumen lassen.

plus à des revues de modèles professionnels que tout ce qu'avaient publié les nudistes américains. Boone ne résista pas à l'envie d'égaler leur sensualité, lançant sa propre imitation européenne *Sun* en 1950.

Pendant ce temps, il continua de batailler contre les autorités, le service des postes confisquant régulièrement ses magazines pour cause d'obscénité. Les revues concurrentes, *Sun Lore*, *American Sunbather* et *Modern Sunbathing and Hygiene*, chacune représentant une organisation nudiste rivale, acceptaient de se plier à la censure tandis que « Uncle Danny » poursuivait la lutte.

En 1958, le gouvernement céda. Les mœurs évoluaient et la vue de quelques poils pubiens ne semblait plus choquer grand monde. Bien que les non nudistes aient utilisé ces magazines comme support masturbatoire depuis le début, les tribunaux validèrent finalement l'argument de Boone selon lequel ils n'étaient pas sexuels et donc exemptés des lois sur l'obscénité. Les toisons pouvaient rester. Au cours de la décennie suivante, les seuls poils pubiens que l'ont pouvait voir légalement aux États-Unis se trouvaient dans les magazines nudistes, ce qui les rendit populaires bien au-delà des rêves les plus fous d' « Uncle Danny ».

Right:
Year: **1956**. Title: **Modern Sunbathing and Hygiene**. Country: **USA**.

Pages 232 & 233:
Year: **1945**. Title: **Sunshine & Health**. Country: **USA**.
Year: **1945**. Title: **Sunshine & Health**. Country: **USA**.

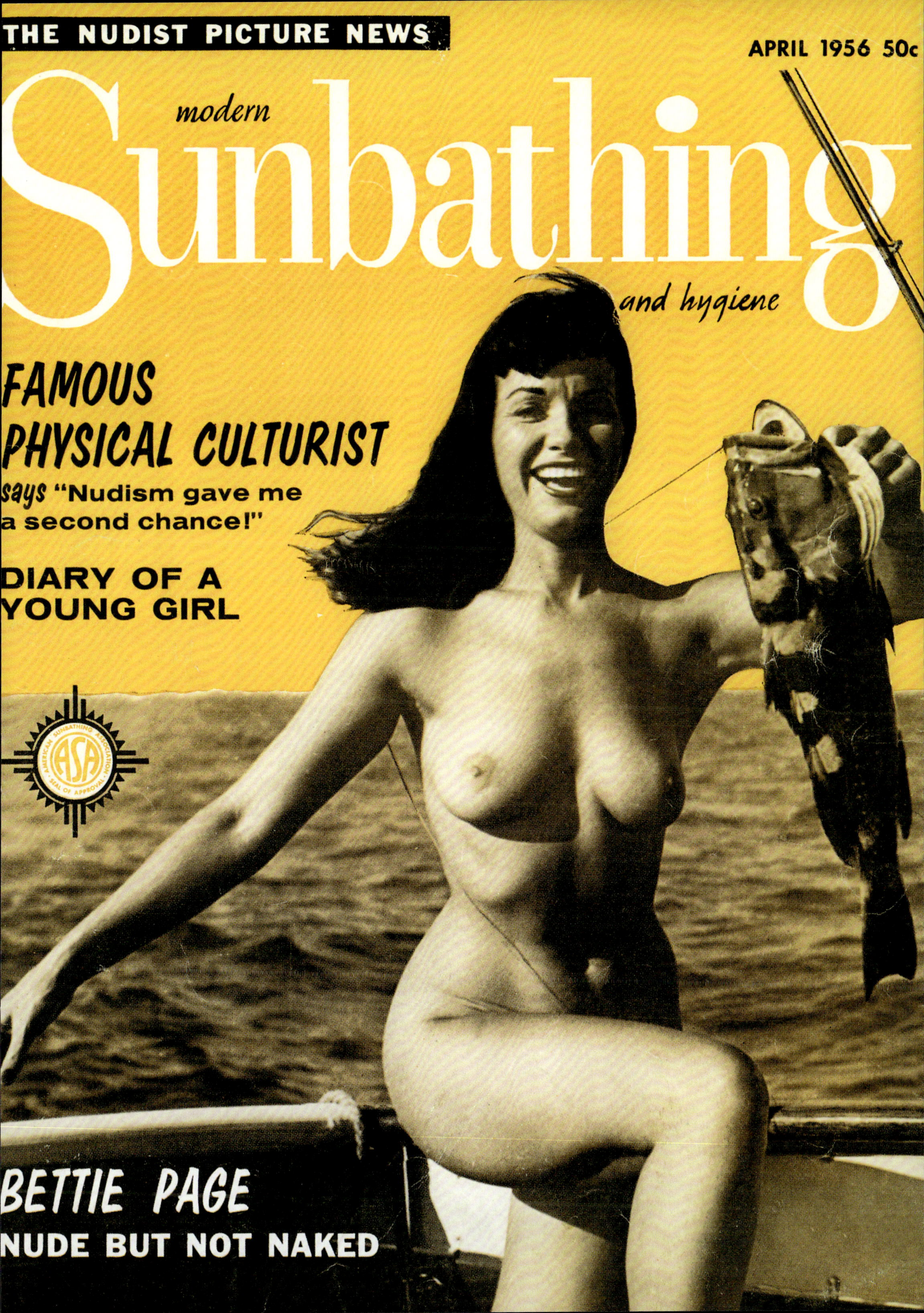
THE NUDIST PICTURE NEWS
APRIL 1956 50c
modern
Sunbathing
and hygiene
FAMOUS
PHYSICAL CULTURIST
says "Nudism gave me
a second chance!"
DIARY OF A
YOUNG GIRL
ASA
BETTIE PAGE
NUDE BUT NOT NAKED

SUNSHINE & HEALTH

Visits

Beaver Forest Club

Whether it's the warmth of summer or the snows of winter, members of this great Wisconsin club find life better the nudist way.

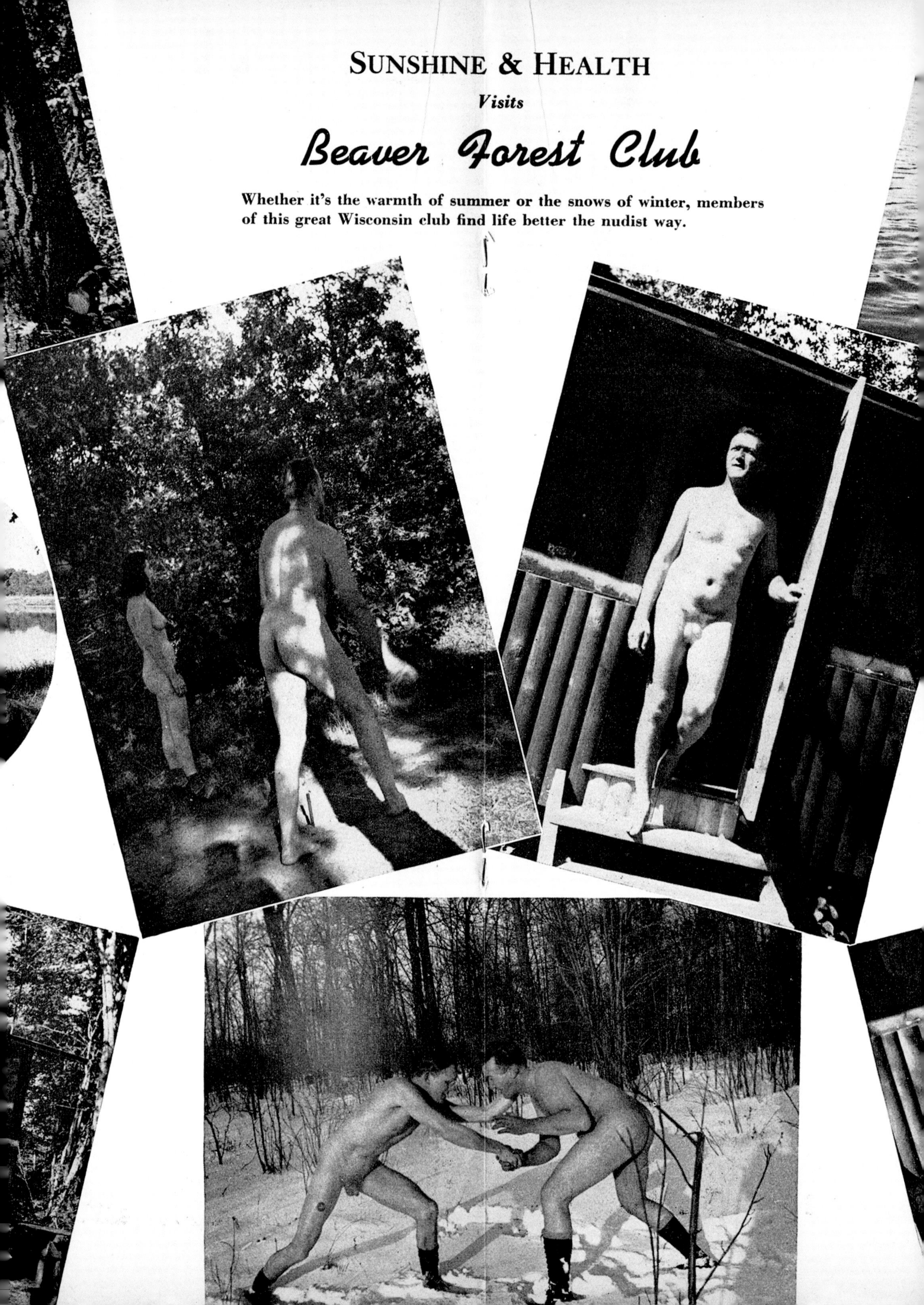

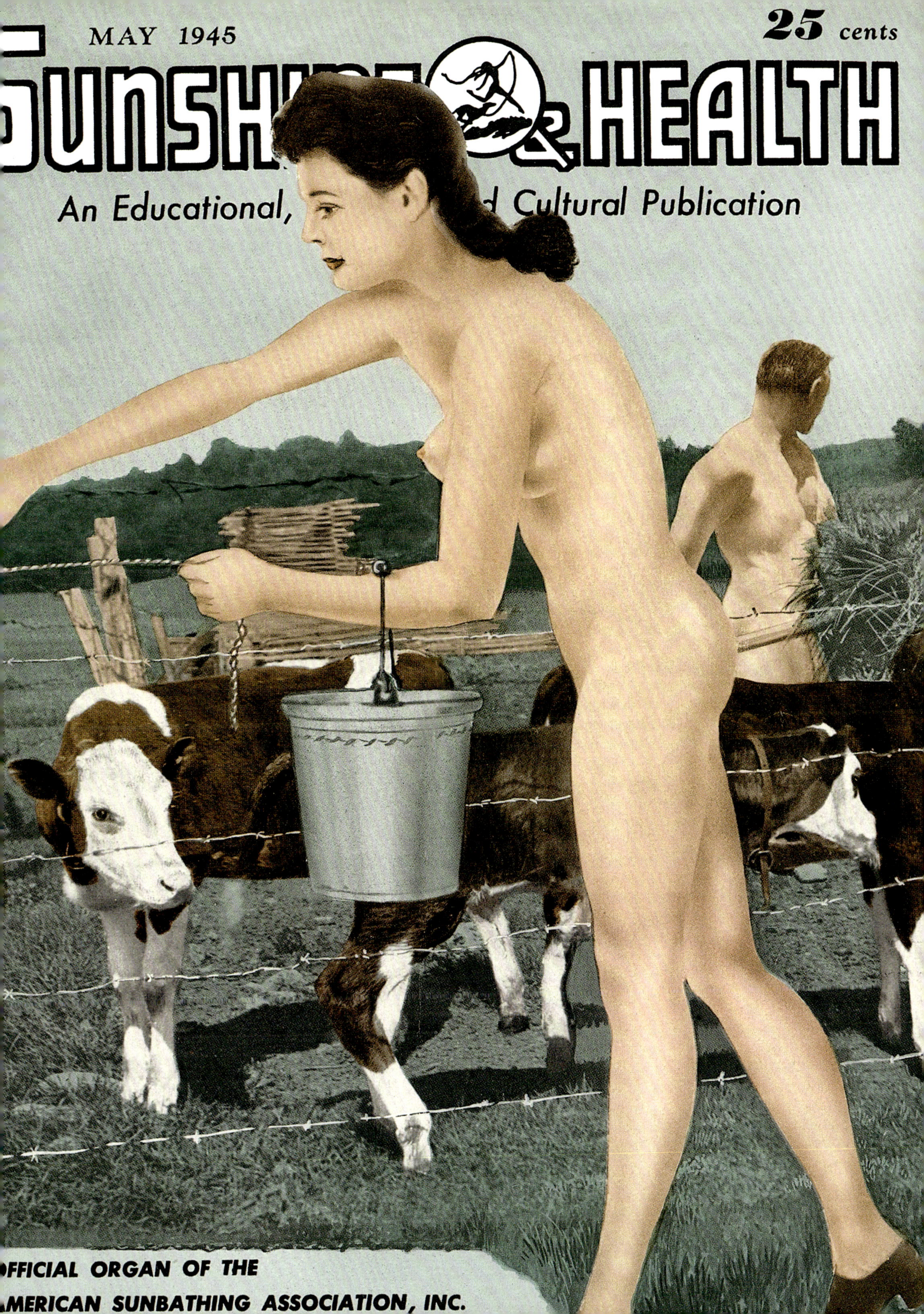
MAY 1945
25 cents
SUNSHI[…] & HEALTH
An Educational, […]d Cultural Publication
OFFICIAL ORGAN OF THE
AMERICAN SUNBATHING ASSOCIATION, INC.

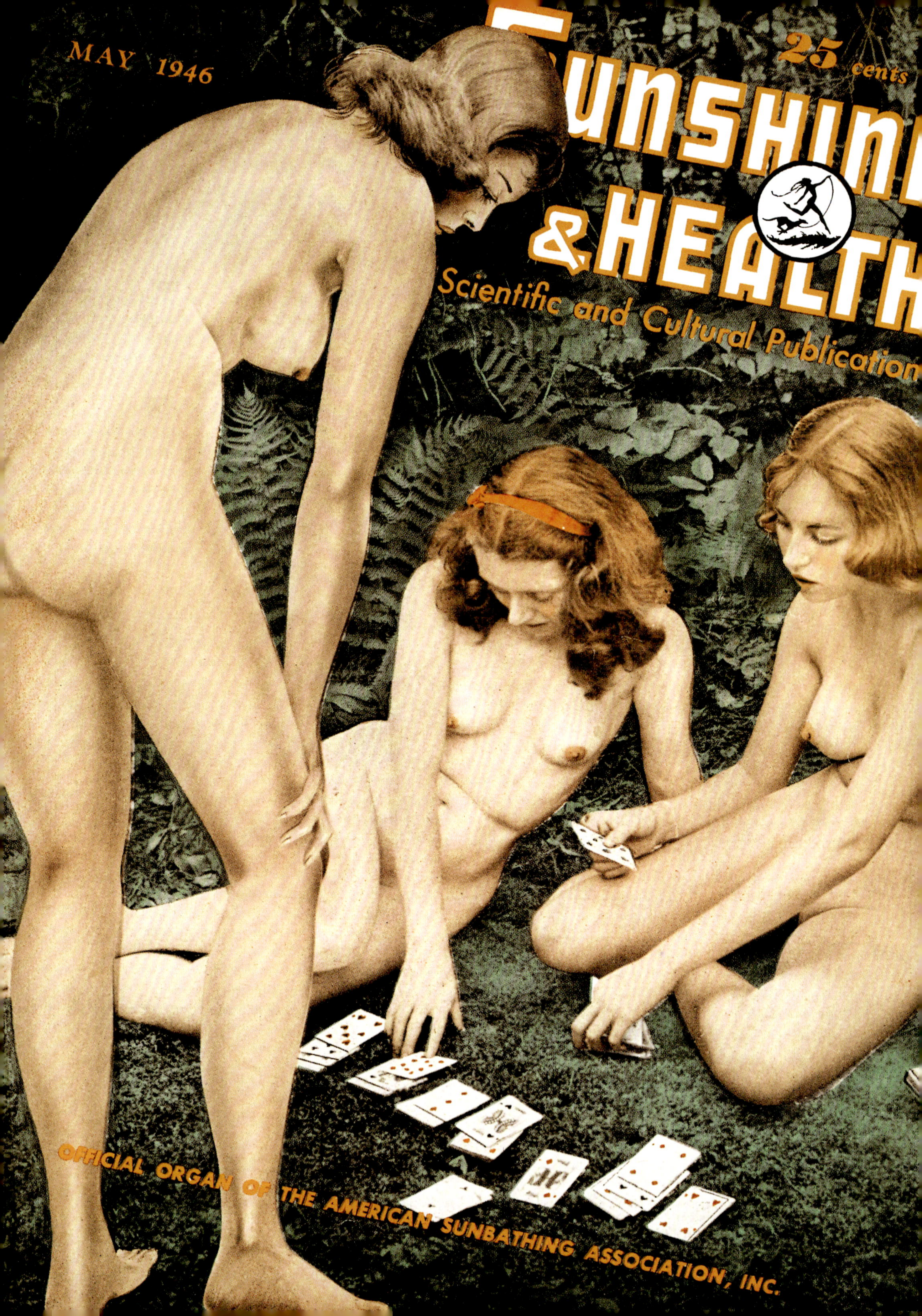
MAY 1946
25 cents
UNSHIN
&HEALTH
Scientific and Cultural Publication
OFFICIAL ORGAN OF THE AMERICAN SUNBATHING ASSOCIATION, INC.

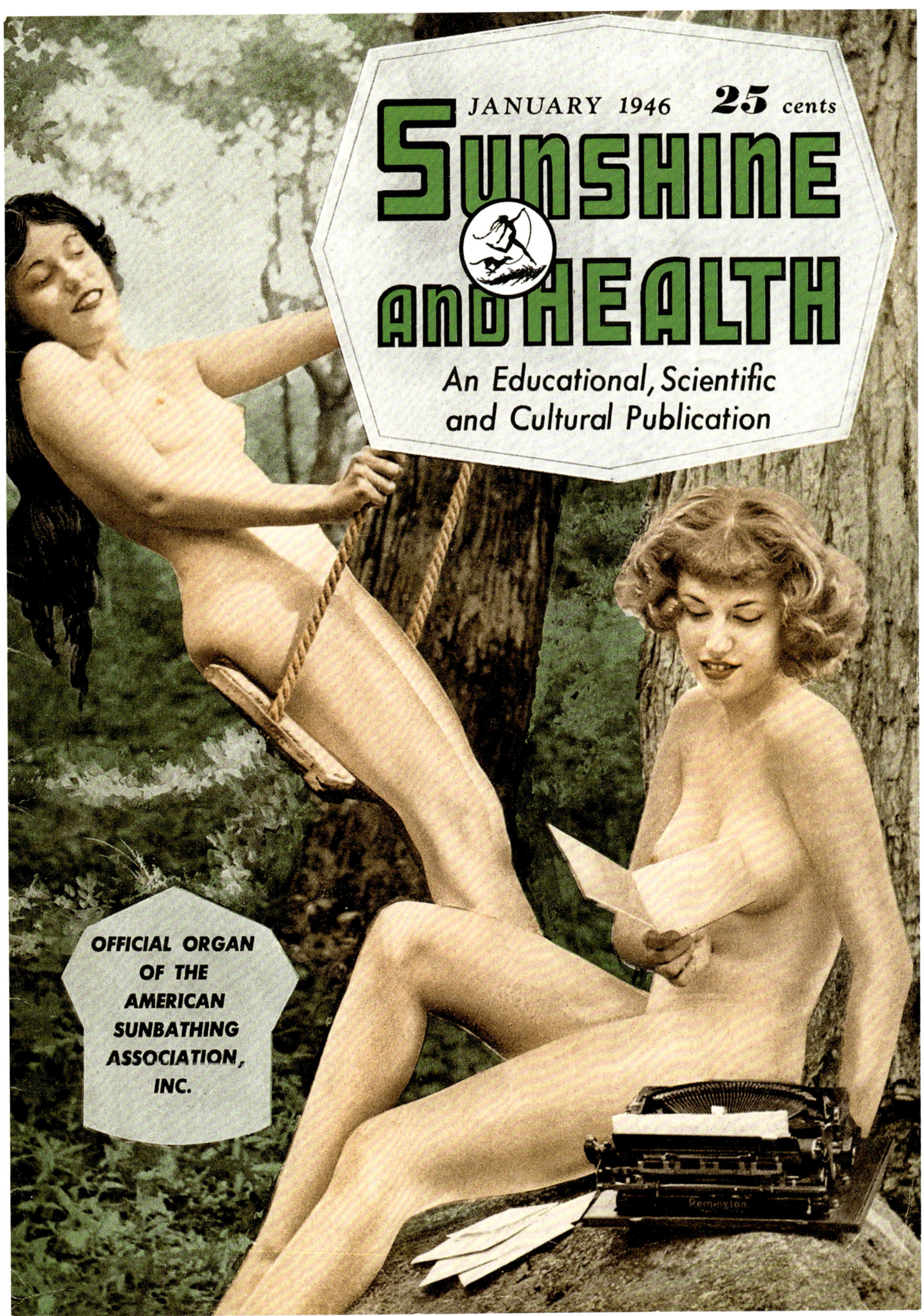

YEAR: **1946**. TITLE: **Sunshine & Health**. COUNTRY: **USA**.

YEAR: **1946**. TITLE: **Sunshine & Health**. COUNTRY: **USA**.

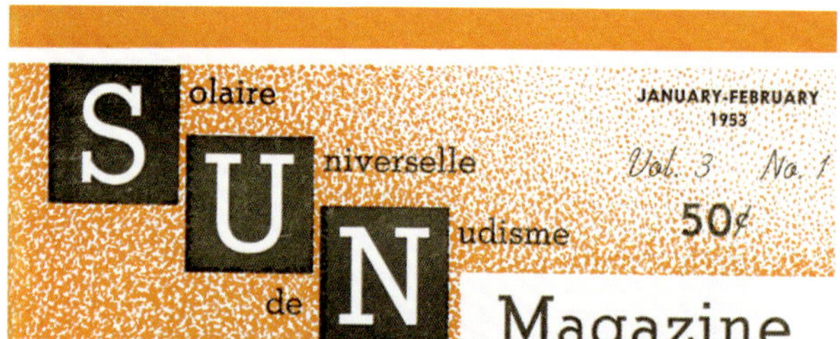

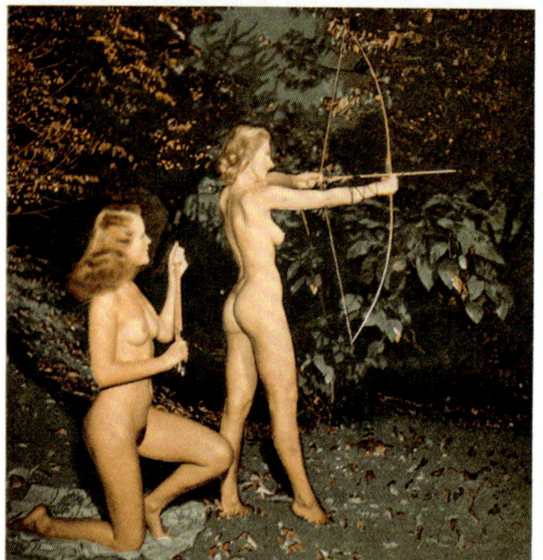

Year: **1953**. Title: **Sun Magazine**. Country: **USA**.

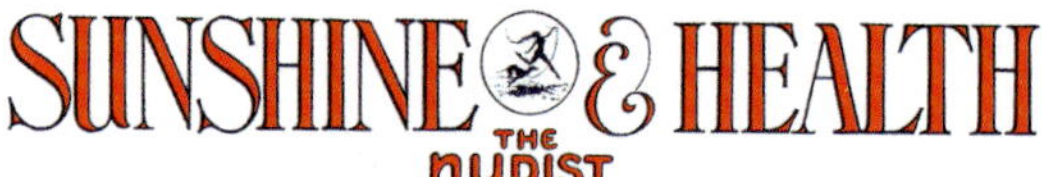

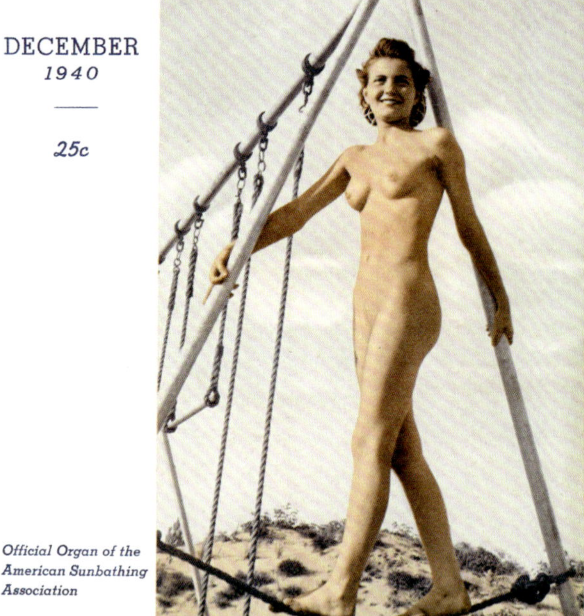

Year: **1940**. Title: **Sunshine & Health**. Country: **USA**.

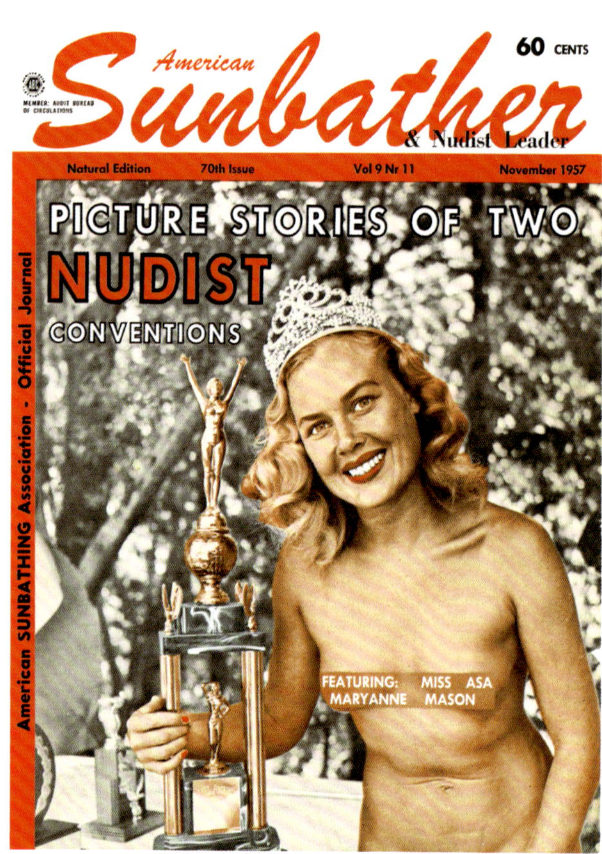

Year: **1957**. Title: **American Sunbather**. Country: **USA**.

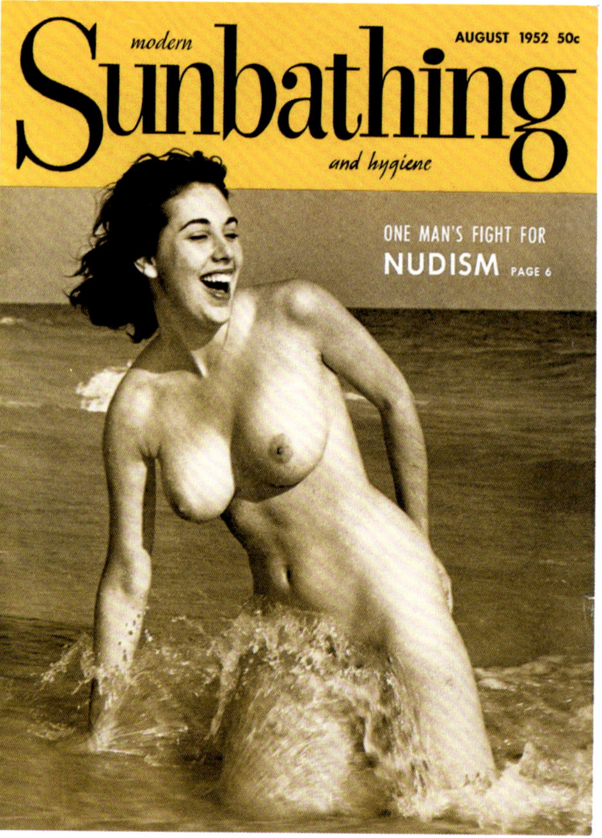

Year: **1952**. Title: **Modern Sunbathing and Hygiene**. Country: **USA**.

Year: **1955**. Title: **Sun and Health**. Country: **USA**.

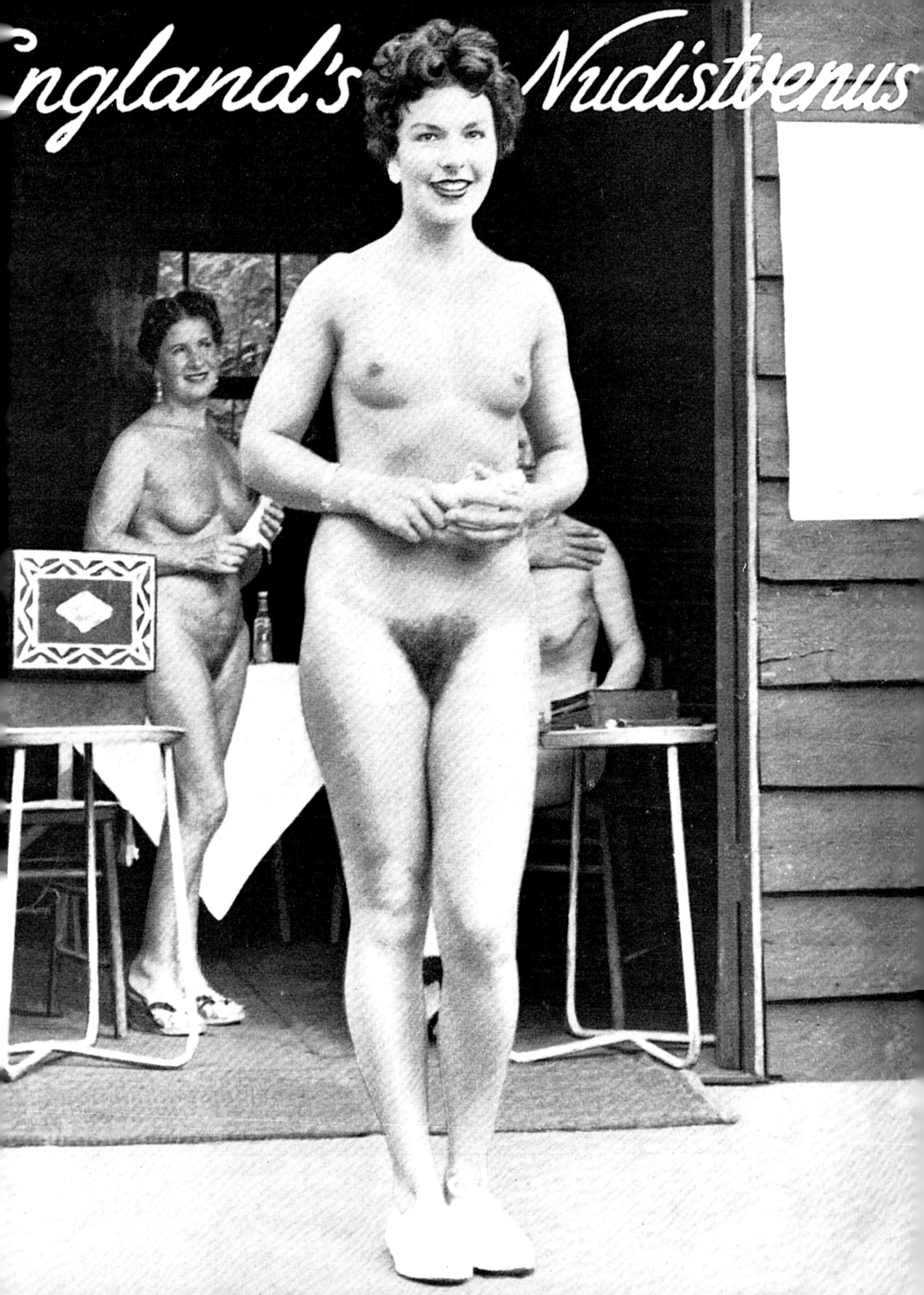
ngland's Nudistvenus

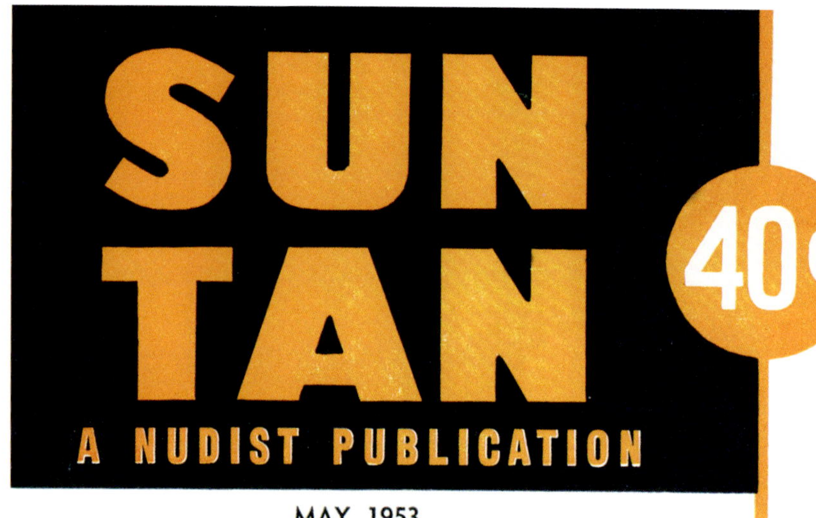

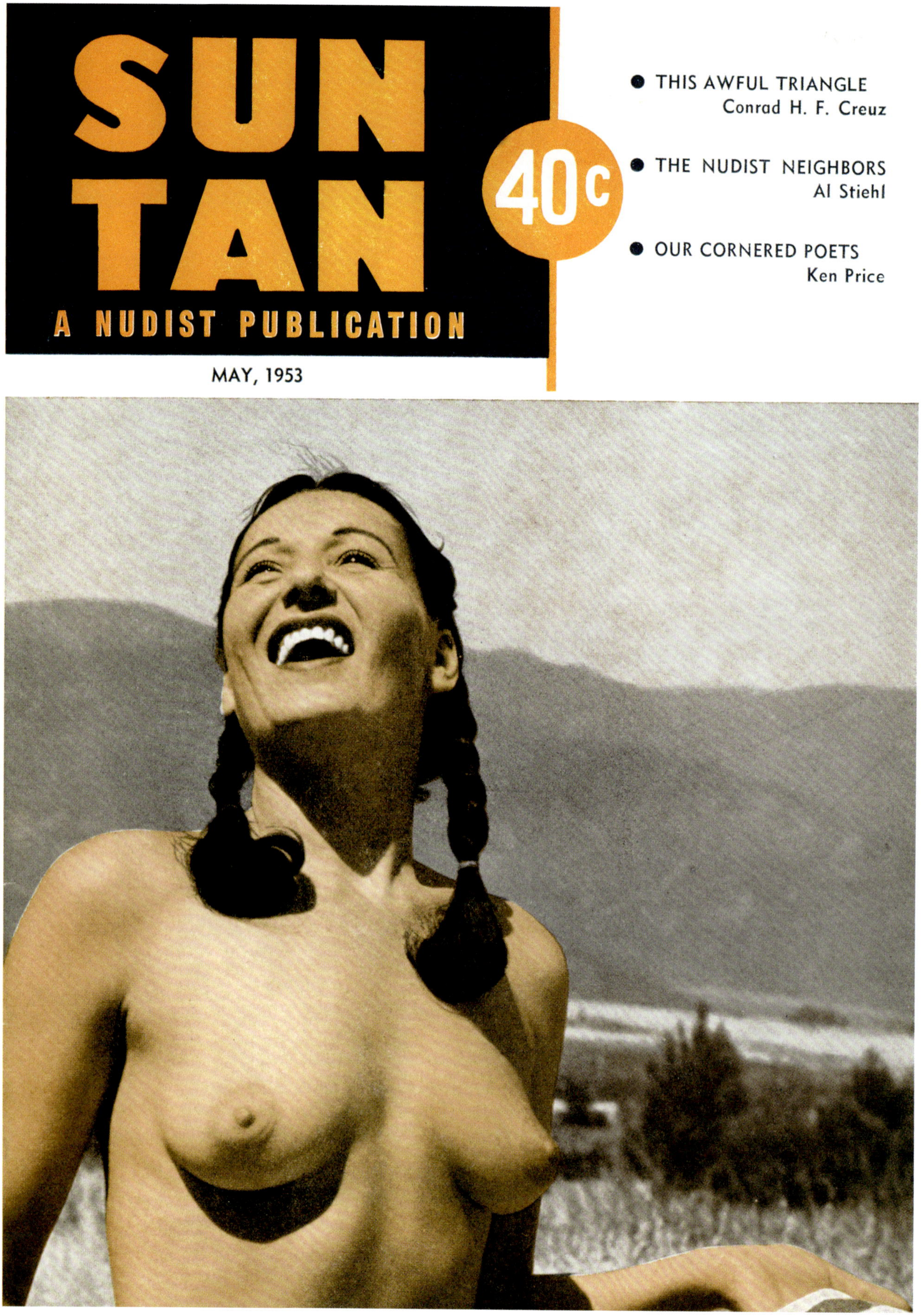

YEAR: **1953**. TITLE: **Sun Tan**. COUNTRY: **USA**.

YEAR: **1945**. TITLE: **The Sunbathing and Health Magazine**. COUNTRY: **USA**.

THE SUNBATHING AND HEALTH MAGAZINE

50

JULY

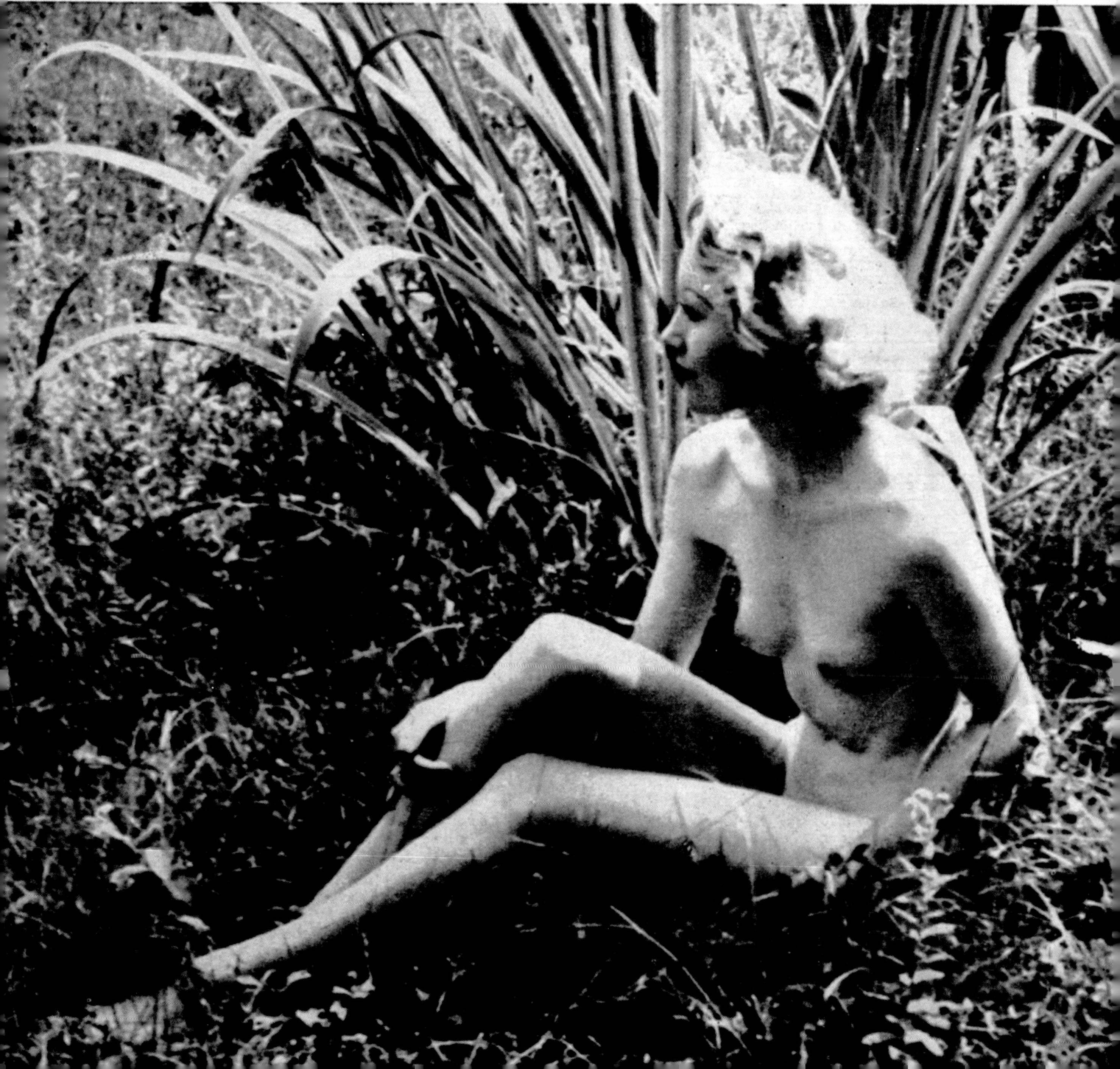

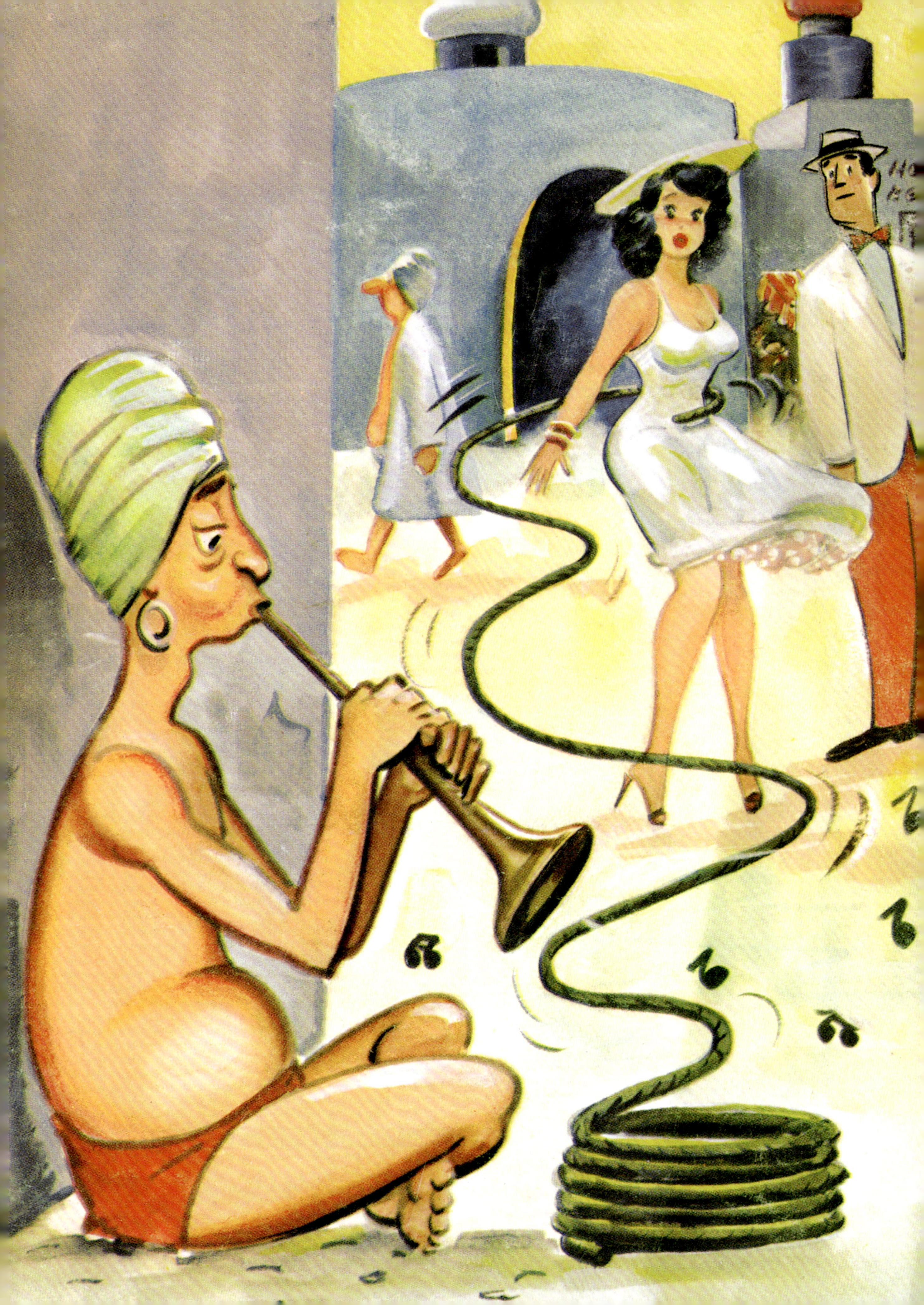

SEX AND HUMOR:

60 Years of Yuks

Sex und Humor: 60 Jahre Schenkelklopfen
Sexe et humour : 60 ans de gaillardise

Humor has always been a good cover for sex; people are much more comfortable joking about it than discussing it seriously. It's natural then that most countries that produced sex magazines also made risqué humor titles. Looking at how many and what kind of sex-humor magazines a country made is also a good barometer of humor's general value in a given society. The serious Scandinavians produced few; the English loved them both witty and Benny Hill slapstick; America just wanted their cartoon girls pneumatically endowed; and the Latin nations wanted lots of everything, with humor magazines outnumbering all others. In all countries, however, the humor declined sharply as purely sexual magazines became legal. The last sex humor magazine in America was the venerable *Sex To Sexty*, surviving into the 90s.

Sex-humor magazines are a good barometer of humor's general value in a given society.

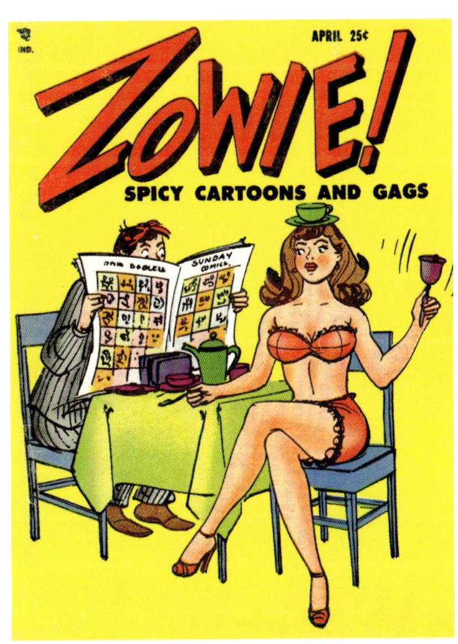

Year: **1954**. Title: **Zowie!** Country: **USA**.

Humor war schon immer eine gute Verpackung für Sex; die Menschen lachen viel lieber darüber, als ihn ernsthaft zu erörtern. Da ist es naheliegend, dass die meisten Länder, in denen Männermagazine hergestellt wurden, auch frivole Witzblätter produzierten. Wenn man sich anschaut, wie viele und welche Sex/Humor-Titel es in einem Land gibt, verrät es viel darüber, welchen Stellenwert der Humor generell in der bewussten Gesellschaft einnimmt. Die seriösen Skandinavier produzieren nur wenige solche Hefte, und die Engländer

L'humour a toujours été un bon prétexte pour aborder la sexualité, les gens étant beaucoup plus à l'aise en en riant qu'en en discutant sérieusement. Il est donc naturel que la plupart des pays qui produisaient des revues érotiques aient également publié des magazines d'humour grivois. Le nombre et le genre de grivoiseries que l'on réalisait dans un pays constituent également un bon baromètre de la valeur générale de l'humour dans une société donnée. Les Scandinaves, sérieux, en publiaient peu. Les Anglais appréciaient autant les mots d'esprit que la farce à la Benny Hill. Les Américains ne demandaient qu'une chose : que les héroïnes de leurs bandes dessinées aient de gros seins. Les Latins voulaient tout, étant ceux qui, de loin, avaient le plus grand nombre de magazines d'humour. Toutefois, dans tous les pays, l'humour déclina nettement dès que les publications purement sexuelles furent autorisées. Le dernier magazine d'érotisme et d'humour aux États-Unis était le vénérable *Sex to Sexty*, qui a perduré jusque dans les années quatre-vingt-dix.

Le premier magazine américain d'humour pour hommes à devenir très populaire fut *Capt. Billy's Whiz Bang*, lancé en 1919 par Wilford Fawcett, un « ancien combattant de la guerre hispano-américaine et de la Grande Guerre, dévoué aux forces combattantes des États-Unis

Year: **1956**. Title: **Smiles**. Country: **USA**.

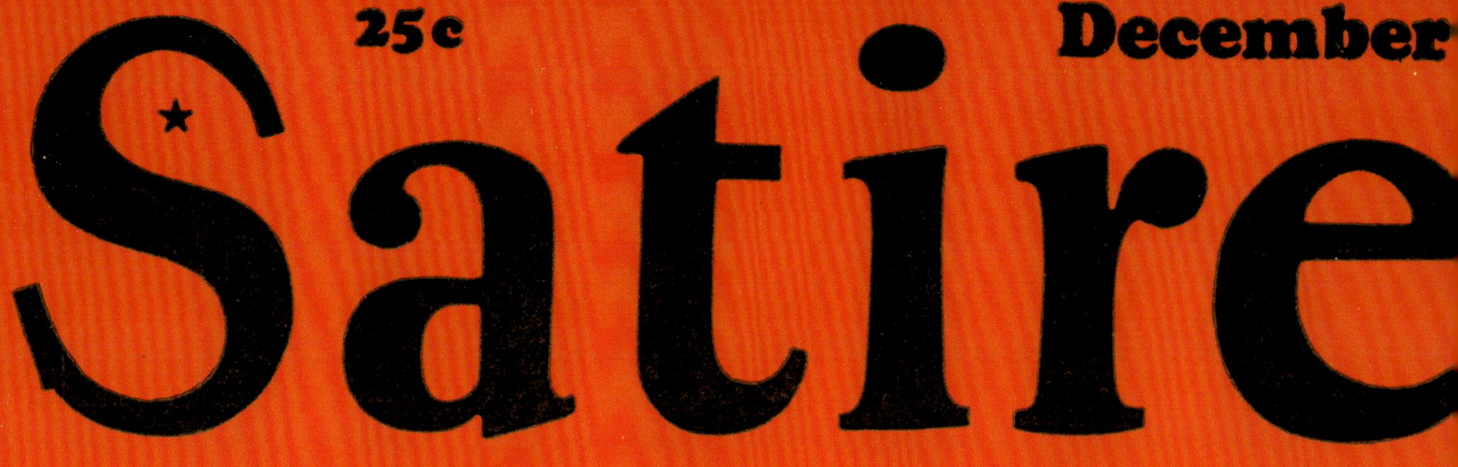

"The Funniest Book In The World"

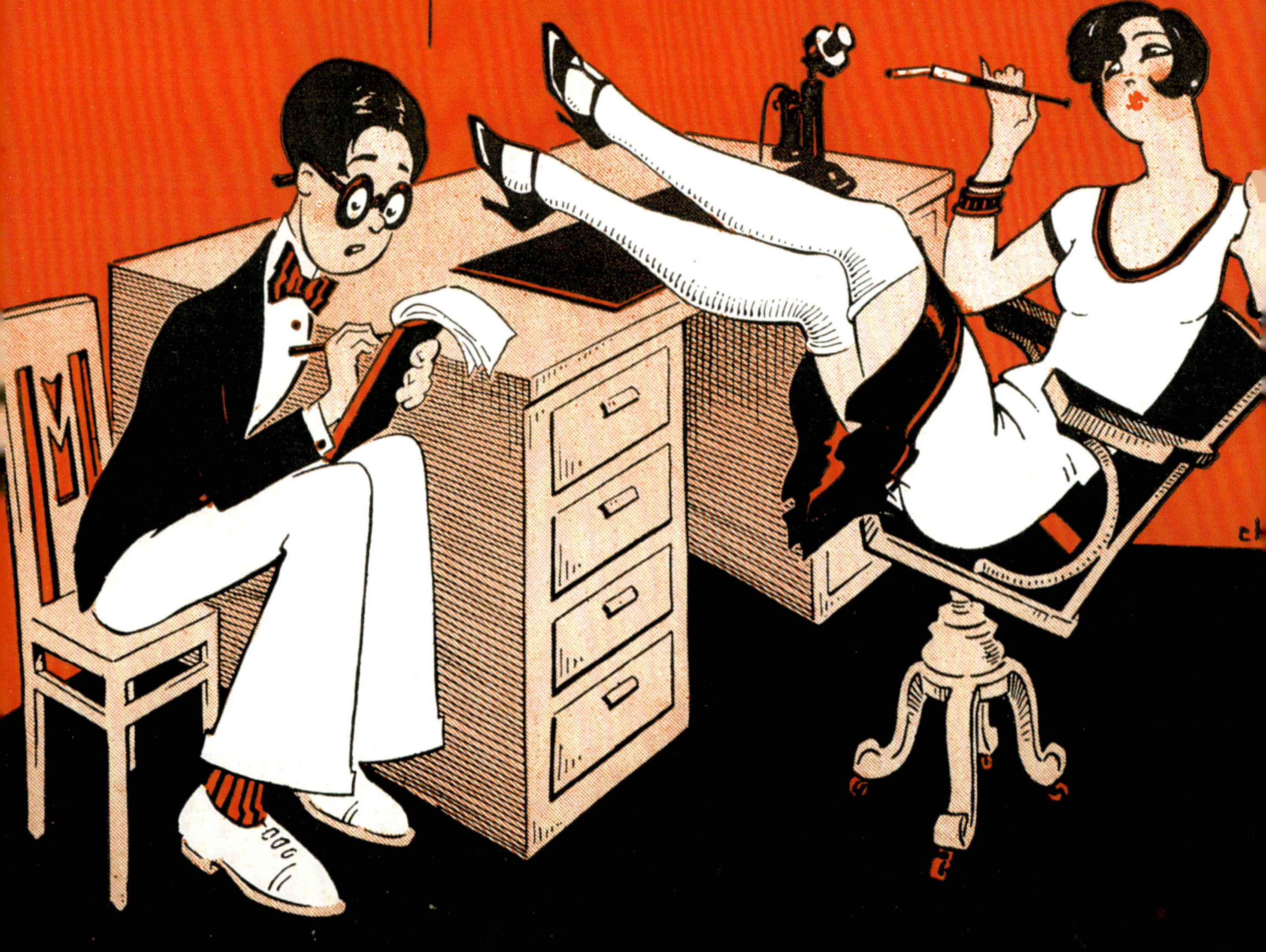

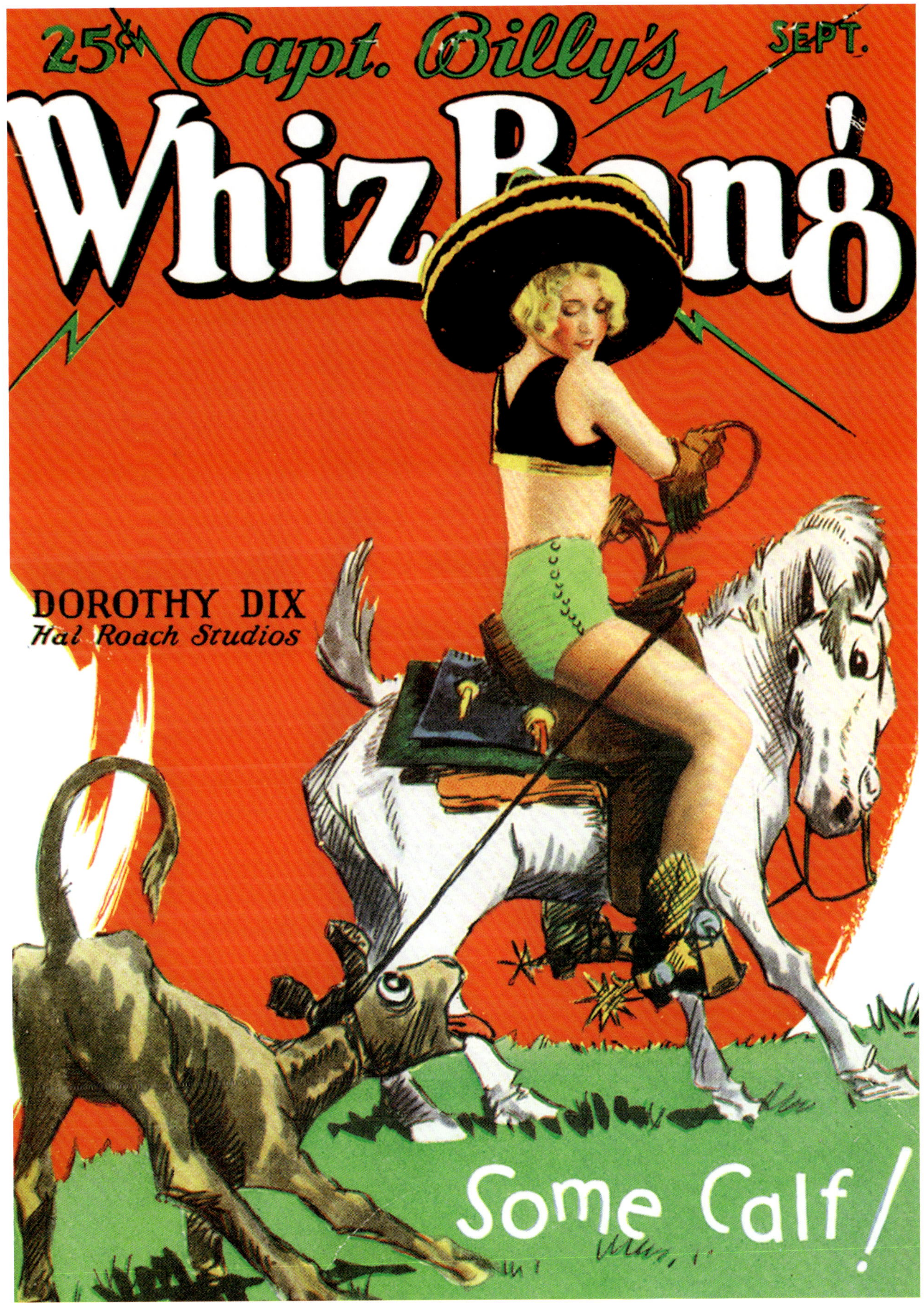

Year: **1928**. Title: **Capt. Billy's Whiz Bang**. Country: **USA**.

Year: **1927**. Title: **Satire**. Country: **USA**.

Capt. Billy was actually Wilford Fawcett, a Spanish American War vet who tried to raise his fellow soldiers' spirits with a homemade joke sheet. In 1919 this evolved into America's first adult humor magazine, though "adult" was as likely to mean racist as sexy back then.

Capt. Billy war in Wirklichkeit Wilford Fawcett, ein Veteran aus dem spanisch-amerikanischen Krieg, der versuchte, seine Kameraden mit einem selbst gemachten Witzblatt bei Laune zu halten. 1919 war daraus Amerikas erstes humoristisches Magazin für Erwachsene geworden, wobei dieser Zusatz damals ebenso Rassismus wie Sex im Inhalt signalisierte.

Capt. Billy s'appelait en fait Wilford Fawcett et était un ancien de la guerre hispano-américaine qui tenta de remonter le moral de ses camarades en publiant un petit journal de blagues. En 1919, celui-ci évolua pour devenir le premier magazine américain d'humour « pour adultes », ce qui à l'époque, pouvait signifier raciste comme sexy.

The first American men's humor magazine to gain widespread popularity was *Capt. Billy's Whiz Bang*, started in 1919 by "a Spanish-American and World War Veteran and dedicated to the fighting forces of the United States and Canada." The vet, Wilford Fawcett, would go on to produce a diverse range of magazines through his Fawcett Publications in the years to follow. Argentina beat America to sophisticated humor. In the 1930s *Caricatura* from Buenos Aires was mixing art nudes with high quality cartoons and slick design while Americans read Tijuana Bibles. World War II improved the American taste for risqué humor; soldiers needed levity as much as cheesecake. *Zippy*, *Screwball*, *Laff* and *Army Laughs* (changed to *Broadway Laughs* post-war) were all started in the early 40s for the boys at war. The pin-ups

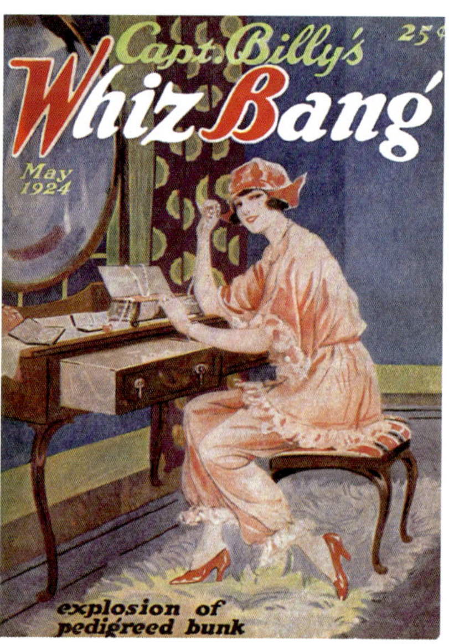

YEAR: **1924**. TITLE: **Capt. Billy's Whiz Bang**. COUNTRY: **USA**.

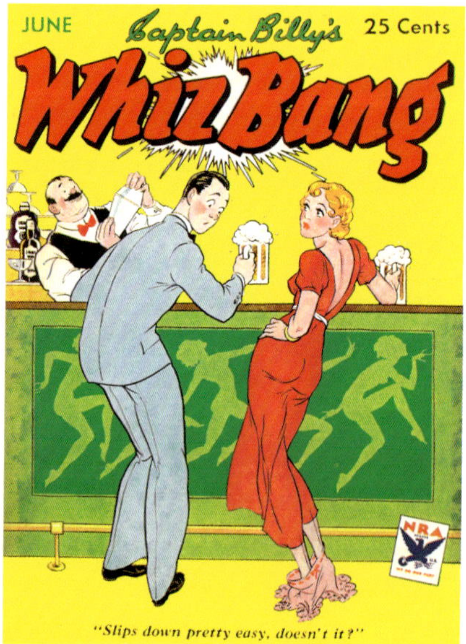

YEAR: **1934**. TITLE: **Capt. Billy's Whiz Bang**. COUNTRY: **USA**.

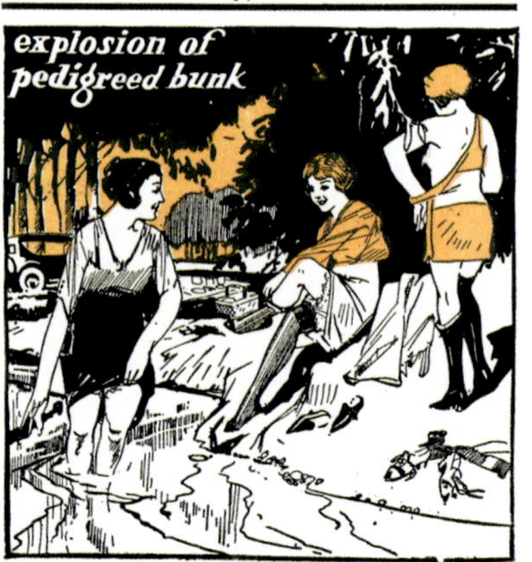

YEAR: **1921**. TITLE: **Capt. Billy's Whiz Bang**. COUNTRY: **USA**.

The first American men's humor magazine to gain widespread popularity was *Capt. Billy's Whiz Bang*, started in 1919.

mögen den geistreichen Witz genauso wie Slapstick à la Benny Hill. Die Amerikaner verlangen von ihren Cartoongirls in erster Linie Oberweite, und die Südländer wollen von allem jede Menge, dort gibt es mehr humoristische Männermagazine als sonst irgendwo. In allen Ländern nahm der Humoranteil allerdings rapide ab, als reine Sexhefte legalisiert wurden. Das letzte Sex/Humor-Magazin in den Vereinigten Staaten war das altehrwürdige *Sex To Sexty*, das immerhin bis in die neunziger Jahre durchhielt.

et du Canada ». Fawcett monta ensuite Fawcett Publications et publia tout un éventail d'autres magazines égrillards au cours des années suivantes. En matière d'humour sophistiqué, l'Argentine supplantait les États-Unis. Dans les années trente, *Caricatura*, une revue de Buenos Aires, conjuguait les nus artistiques avec des bandes dessinées de grande qualité et un graphisme soigné pendant que les Américains lisaient des bibles de Tijuana. La Seconde Guerre mondiale raffina le goût des Américains en matière d'humour salace, les soldats ayant

YEAR: **1943**. TITLE: **Fun Riot**. COUNTRY: **USA**.

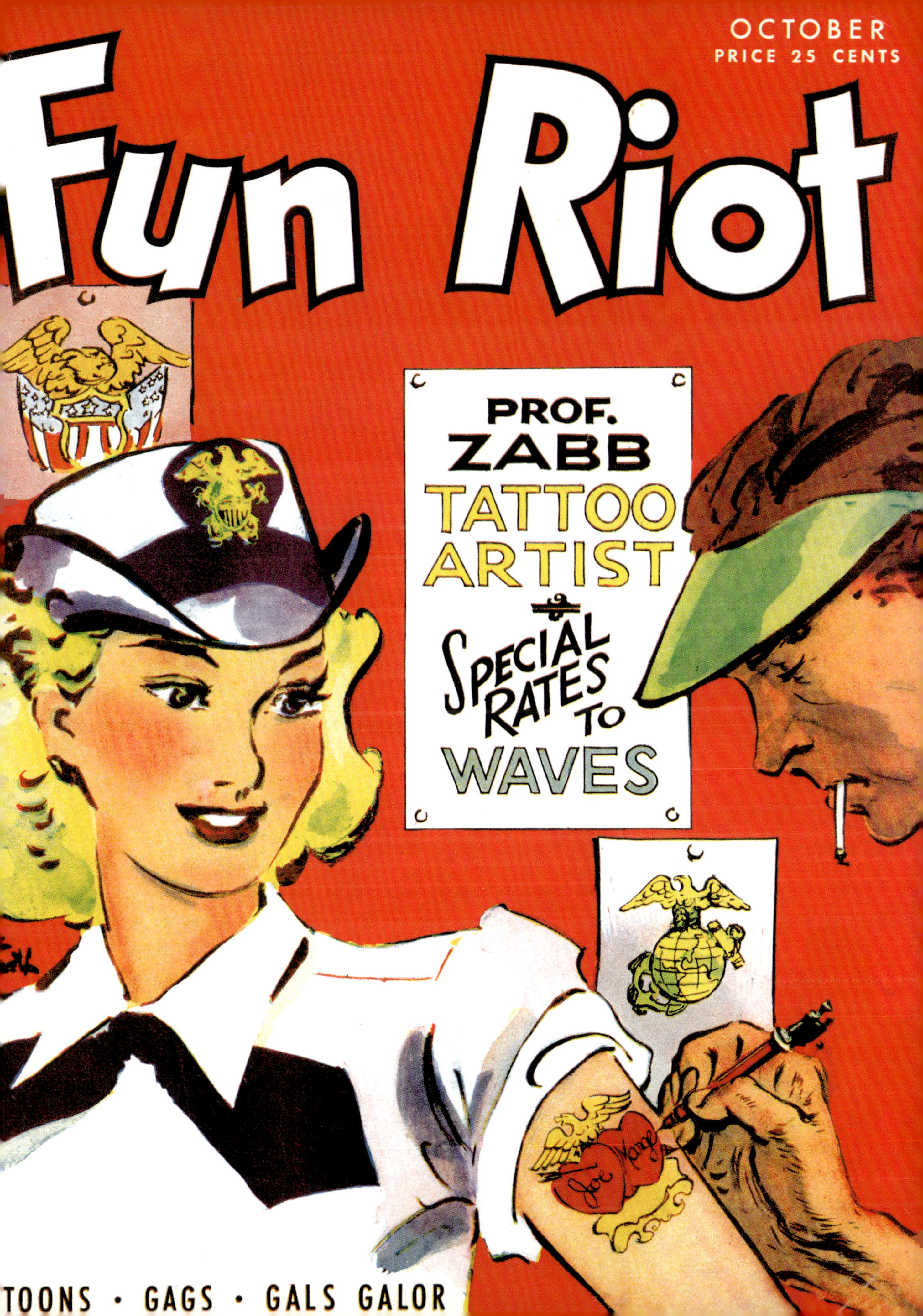
OCTOBER
PRICE 25 CENTS
Fun Riot
PROF. ZABB
TATTOO ARTIST
SPECIAL RATES TO WAVES
TOONS · GAGS · GALS GALOR

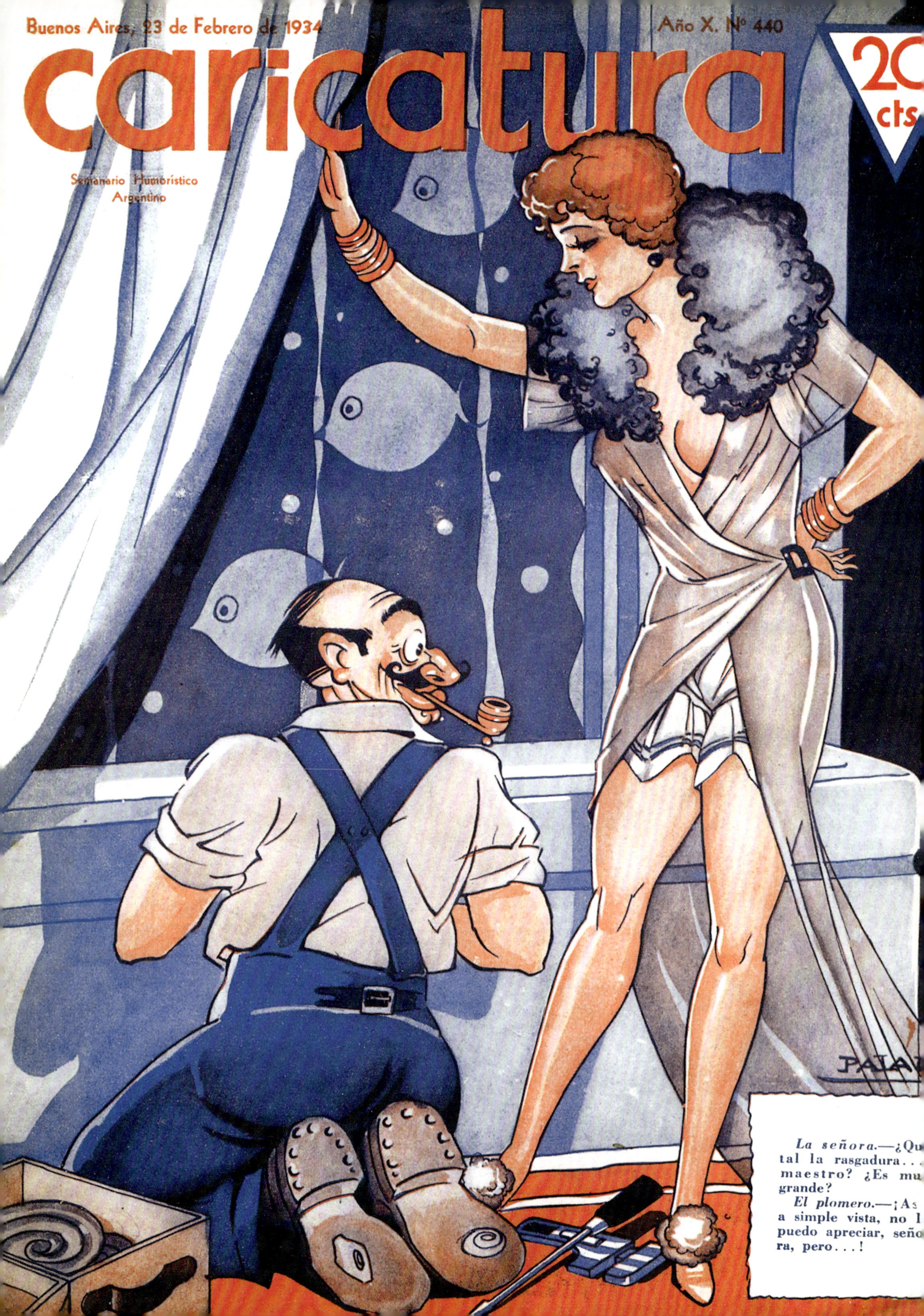
Buenos Aires, 23 de Febrero de 1934
Año X. Nº 440
caricatura
20 cts
Semanario Humorístico Argentino
La señora.—¿Qu tal la rasgadura... maestro? ¿Es mu grande?
El plomero.—¡As a simple vista, no l puedo apreciar, seño ra, pero...!

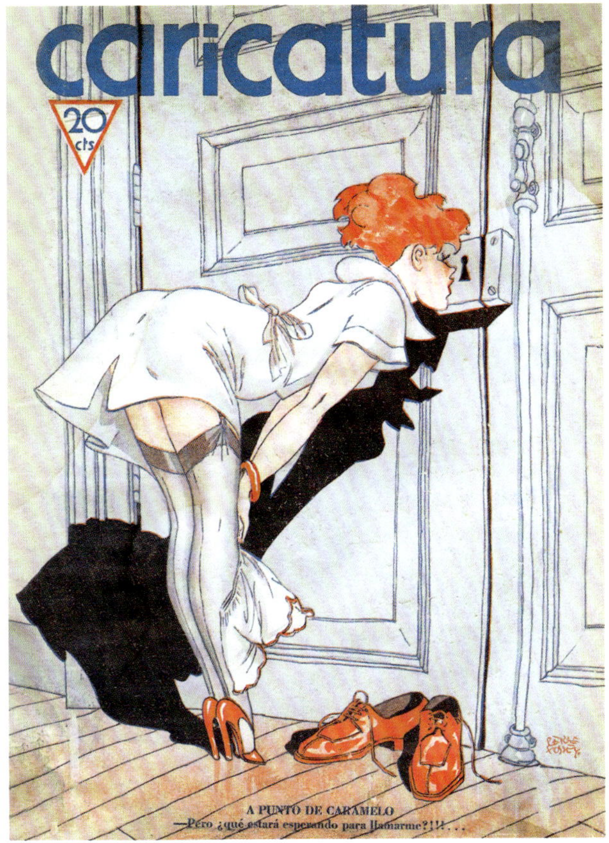

Year: **1936**. Title: **Caricatura**. Country: **Argentina**.

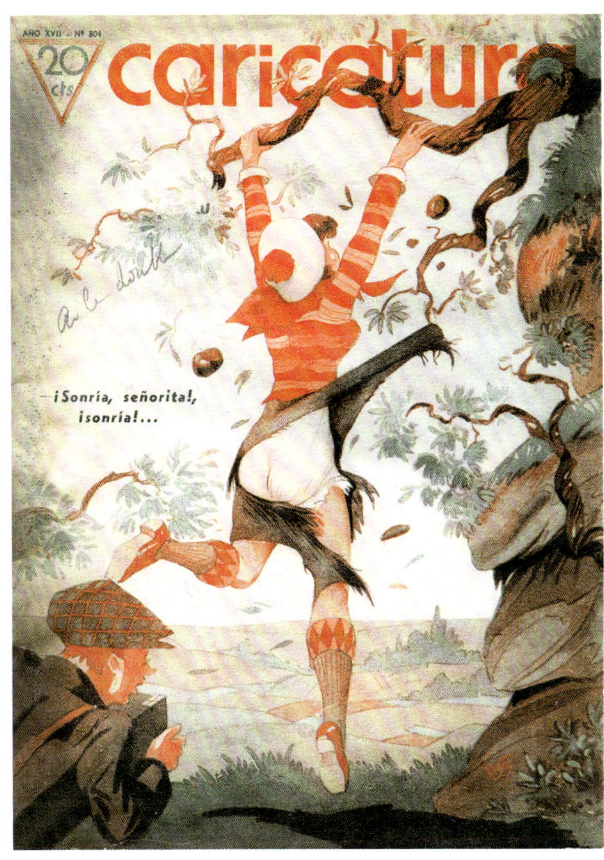

Year: **1941**. Title: **Caricatura**. Country: **Argentina**.

Left: Year: **1934**. Title: **Caricatura**. Artist: **Palau**. Country: **Argentina**.

Year: **1941**. Title: **Caricatura**. Country: **Argentina**.

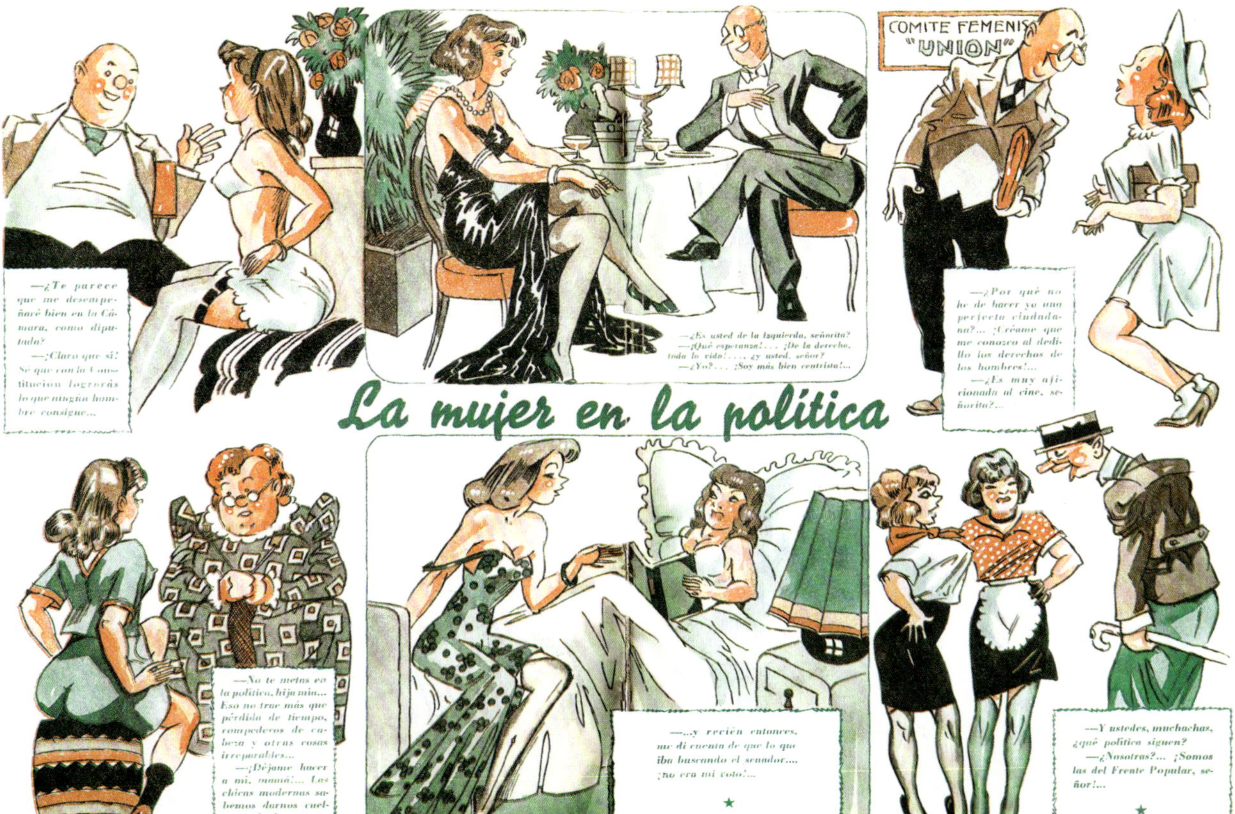

Argentina, and particularly the city of Buenos Aires, supported a large international middle class in the 1920s. Even during the economic instability of the 1930s high quality European style magazines flourished.

In den zwanziger Jahren war Argentinien, und insbesondere die Stadt Buenos Aires, zur zweiten Heimat einer großen internationalen Mittelschicht geworden. Sogar in den wirtschaftlich unruhigen Dreißigern blühten hier hochwertige Zeitschriften im europäischen Stil.

Dans les années 20, l'Argentine, surtout Buenos Aires, comptait une vaste classe moyenne cosmopolite. Même durant l'instabilité économique des années 30, les magazines de haute qualité à l'européenne florissaient.

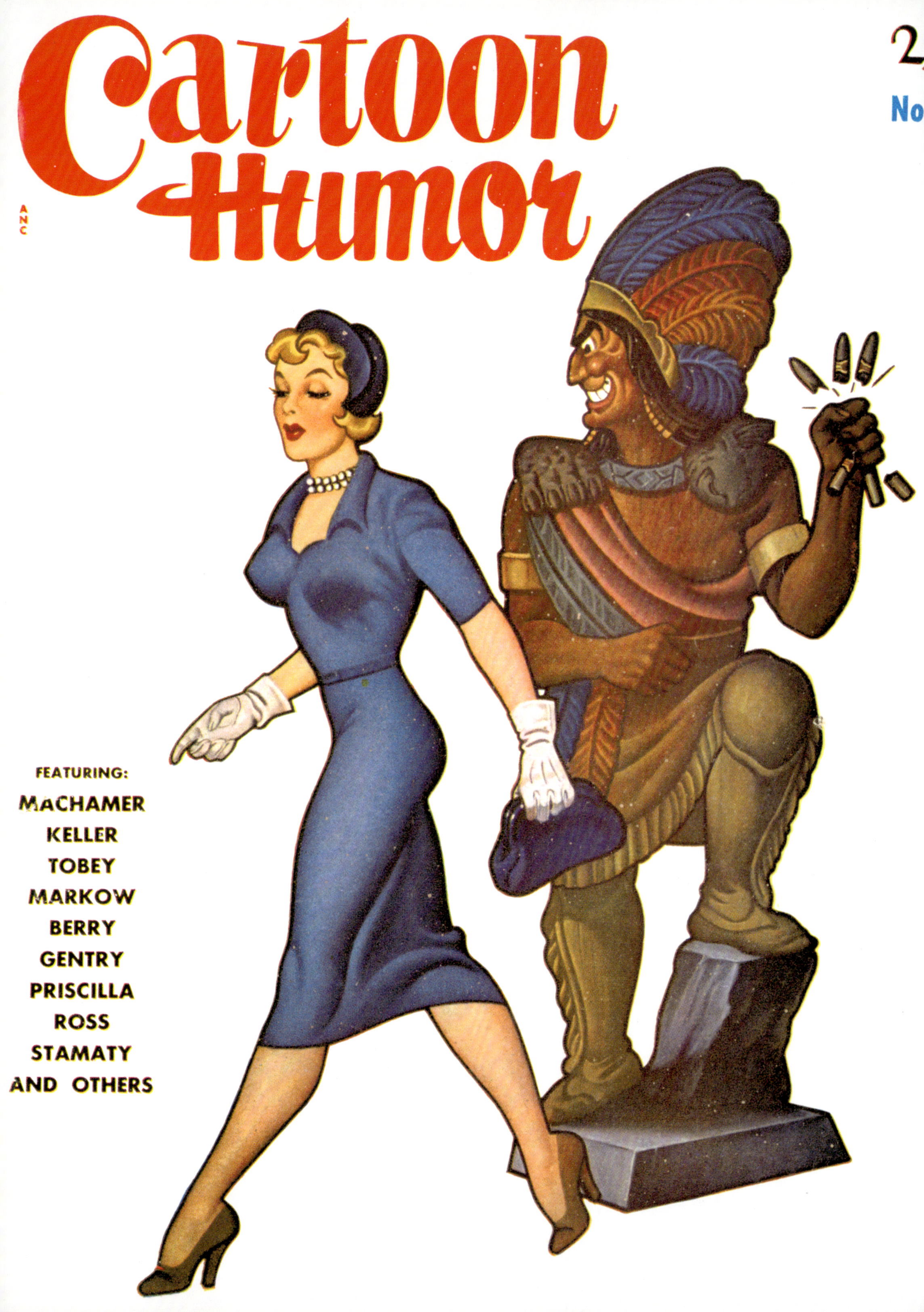
Cartoon Humor
2
No
ANC
FEATURING:
MACHAMER
KELLER
TOBEY
MARKOW
BERRY
GENTRY
PRISCILLA
ROSS
STAMATY
AND OTHERS

Year: **1952**. Title: **Cartoon Humor**. Country: **USA**.

What I wanted to get at is the value difference between pornographic playing-cards when you're a kid and pornographic playing-cards when you're older. It's that when you're a kid you use the cards as a substitute for a real experience, and when you're older you use real experience as a substitute for the fantasy.

—Albert Albee

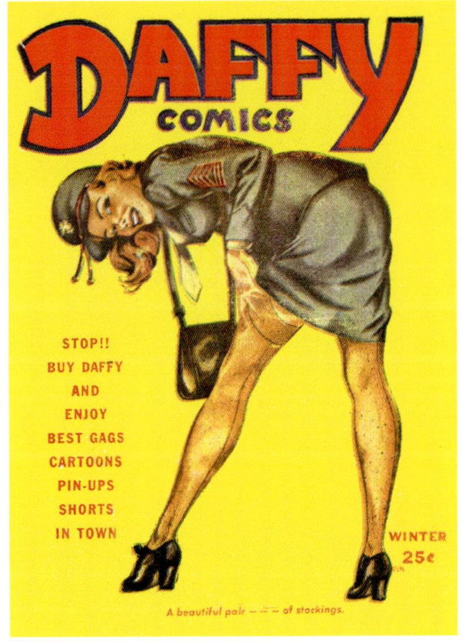

Year: **1944**. Title: **Daffy**. Country: **USA**.

weren't nude in these magazines; it was unseemly for red-blooded American fighting men to view vulgar material (they'd have to wait til they got to France for that). The cartoons were allowed more liberty. Impossibly voluptuous figures were the rule, riding atop yards of shapely stockinged leg that often made the women a good foot taller than their cartoon male counterparts. In England

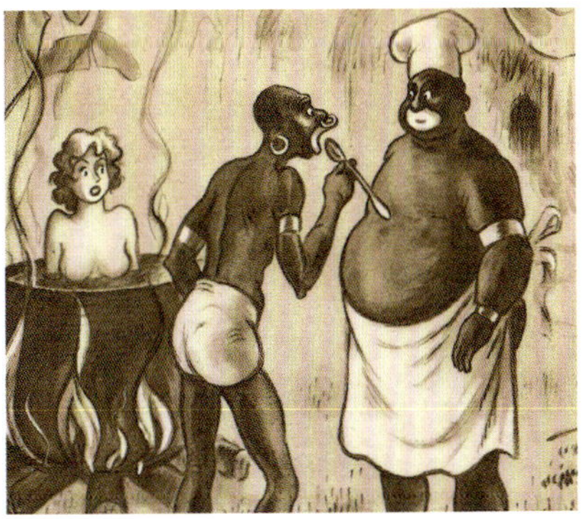

Year: **1939**. Title: **Hooey Annual**. Country: **USA**.

Das erste Magazin dieser Art, das es in den Staaten zu großer Popularität brachte, war *Capt. Billy's Whiz Bang*, das 1919 von einem „Veteranen des spanischamerikanischen Krieges und des Ersten Weltkriegs für die Truppen der Vereinigten Staaten und Kanada" gegründet wurde. Dieser Veteran, Willard Fawcett, sollte in den folgenden Jahren noch zahlreiche Zeitschriften herausbringen. Was den geistreichen Witz anbelangt, übertraf Argentinien die Staaten. In den Dreißigern kombinierte *Caricatura* aus Buenos Aires Aktstudien mit erstklassigen Cartoons und todschickem Layout, während die Amerikaner ihre Tijuana Bibles lasen. Der Zweite Weltkrieg verbesserte Amerikas Sinn für gewagten Humor, die Soldaten hatten ein befreiendes Lachen mindestens so nötig wie ihre Pinups. *Zippy*, *Screwball*, *Laff* und *Army Laughs* (nach dem Krieg: *Broadway Laughs*) erschienen alle in den frühen Vierzigern für die

tant besoin de légèreté que de pin-up. *Zippy*, *Screwball*, *Laff* et *Army Laughs* (rebaptisé *Broadway Laughs* après la guerre) furent tous conçus au début des années quarante pour les boys au combat. On n'y voyait pas de femmes nues car présenter ce genre de vulgarités aux vaillants soldats américains aurait été inconvenant (pour ça, ils n'avaient qu'à attendre d'être en France). Les auteurs de bandes dessinées bénéficiaient d'une plus grande liberté. Les silhouettes aux formes d'une volupté affolante étaient la norme. Perchées sur des jambes d'une longueur impossible, moulées dans des bas, les femmes dominaient souvent de quelques centimètres leurs partenaires masculins. En Angleterre, les soldats connaissaient les mêmes réjouissances dans *Bligthy*, mais sans les pin-up. Les G. I.'s de retour au bercail conservèrent leur sens de l'humour. *Bust Out Laffin'*, *Maybe You're Screwy Too!* et *Zowie!*

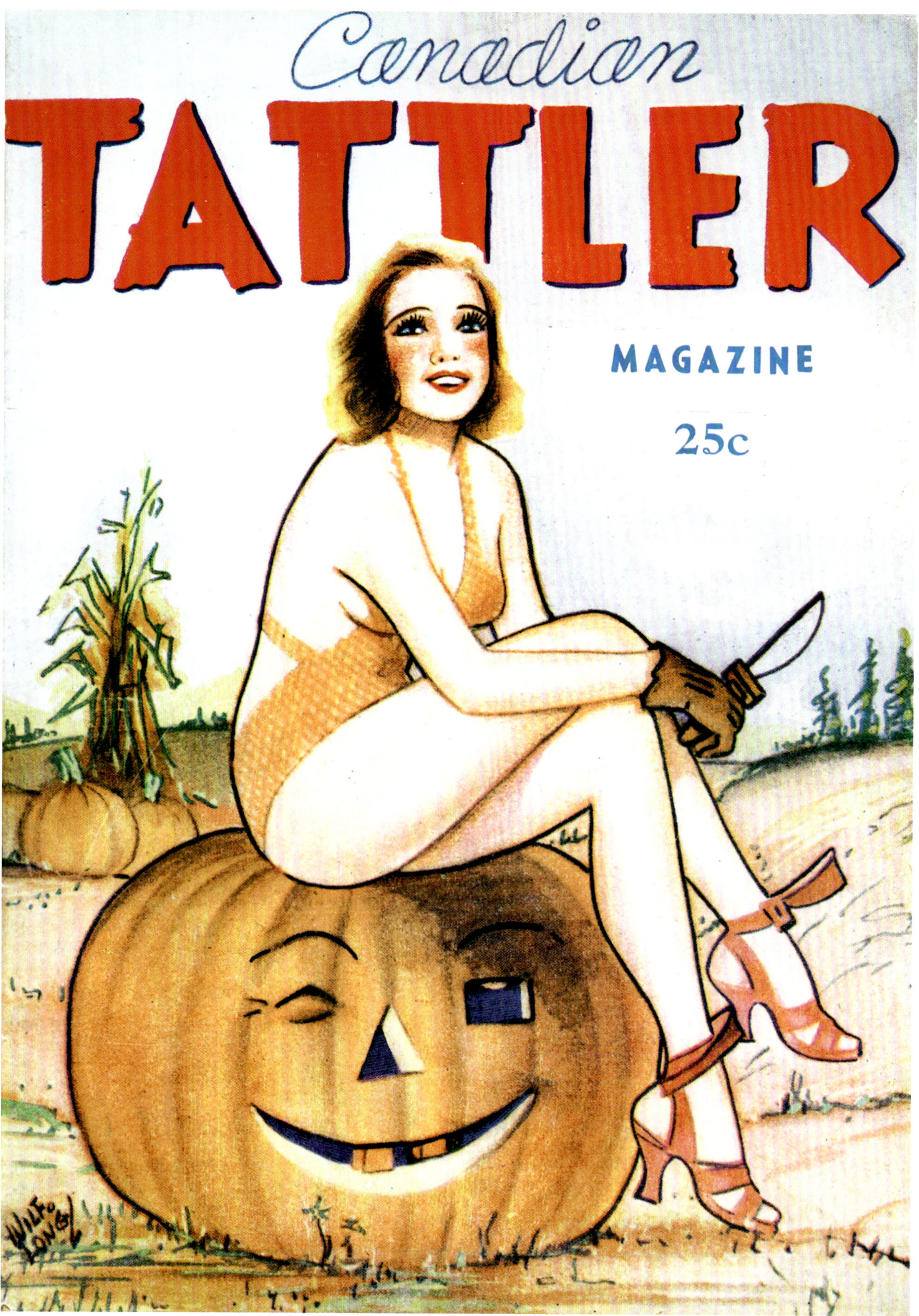

Year: **1939**. Title: **Canadian Tattler**. Country: **Canada**.

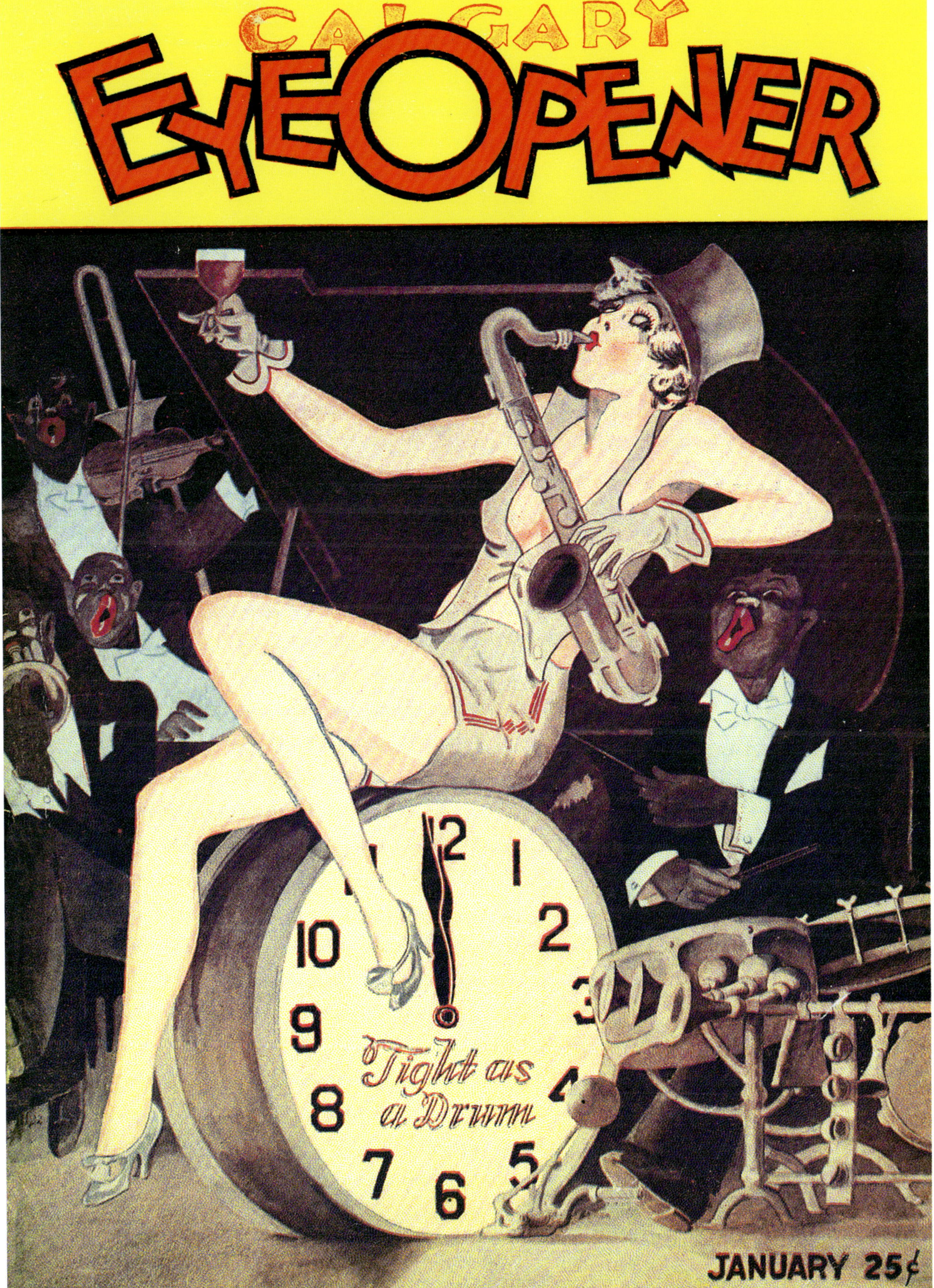

Year: **1939**. Title: **Calgary Eyeopener**. Country: **Canada**.

Year: **1947**. Title: **Smiles**. Country: **USA**.

the soldiers were enjoying similar fare in *Blighty*—without the pin-ups. Returning GIs retained their taste for humor. *Bust Out Laffin'*, *Maybe You're Screwy Too!*, and *Zowie!* kept them chuckling into the late 50s. By that time England had allowed pin-ups into *Blighty*, which was seeing competition from steamier digests like *Razzle* and the clumsily titled *A Basinful of Fun*.

America's Humorama Publishing started its distinctive digests around 1950. *Snappy*, *Jest*, *Gee-Whiz*, *Comedy*, and others were a mix of stripper pin-ups and Bill Ward cartoons that survived into the mid-70s with almost no change in format.

Ja-Já was Mexico's version, with jokes and photos stolen right out of the American magazines. Most of America's sex humor magazines disappeared by 1960, followed by a minor flare-up of new titles in the 70s. The famously lowbrow *Sex To Sexty* survived because it

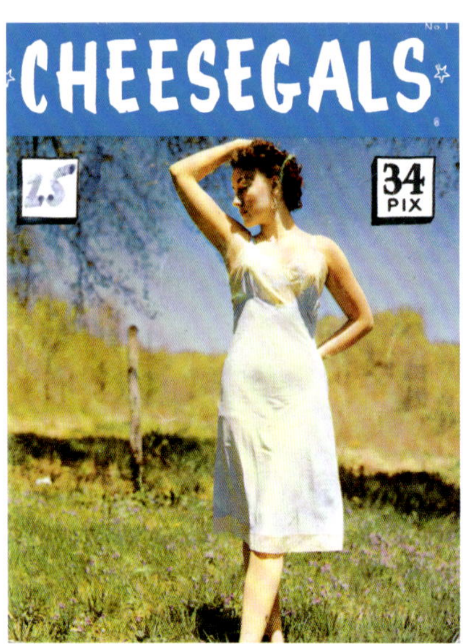

Year: **1950s**. Title: **Cheesegals**. Country: **USA**.

Jungs im Krieg. Die Pinups in diesen Heften waren allerdings nicht nackt; es gehörte sich nicht für einen amerikanischen Soldaten, vulgäre Bilder zu betrachten (damit musste er warten, bis er nach Frankreich kam). Bei den Witzzeichnungen hatte man größere Freiheiten. Unglaubliche Kurven waren die Regel, darunter endlos lange, wohlgeformte, bestrumpfte Beine, die die Frauen oft ein gutes Stück größer erscheinen ließen, als die dazugezeichneten Männer.

In England erfreute *Blighty* die Soldaten mit ähnlicher Ware – allerdings ohne die Pinups. Auch in die Heimat zurückgekehrt bewahrten sich die GIs ihren speziellen Humor. Über *Bust Out Laffin'*, *Maybe You're Screwy Too*! und *Zowie*! lachten sie bis in die späten Fünfziger.

Zu dieser Zeit durfte *Blighty* in England dann endlich auch Pinups bringen und bekam Konkurrenz von deftigeren Heften im Digest-Format wie *Razzle* oder dem etwas ungeschickt betitelten *A Basinful of Fun*.

Humorama Publishing in den USA startete seine unverwechselbaren Publikationen um 1950. *Snappy*, *Jest*, *Gee-Whiz*, *Comedy* und andere zeigten ein Potpourri aus Pinups von Stripperinnen und Cartoons von Bill Ward, das praktisch ohne Änderung bis Mitte der Siebziger überlebte.

In Mexiko erschien *Ja-Já* mit Witzen und schamlos aus amerikanischen Magazinen geklauten Fotos. Die meisten amerikanischen Magazine dieser Art waren 1960 vom Markt verschwunden, ein kleines Strohfeuer gab es nochmal in den Siebzigern. Das legendär geistlose Magazin *Sex To Sexty* überlebte, weil es sich damit zufrieden gab, ein Relikt zu sein und seine betagte Leserschaft mit den

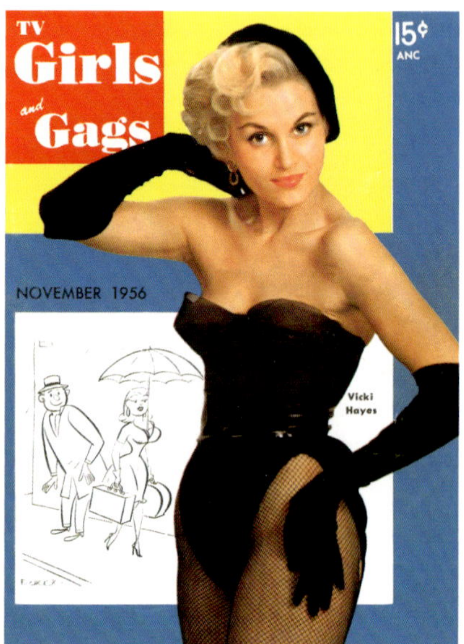

Year: **1956**. Title: **TV Girls and Gags**. Country: **USA**.

continuèrent à les faire s'esclaffer tout au long des années cinquante. Entre-temps, en Angleterre, les pin-up s'étaient frayé un chemin jusqu'à *Blighty*, qui devait rivaliser avec des digests plus osés tels que *Razzle* et le bizarrement nommé *A Basinful of Fun* (pouvant s'interpréter comme « une cuvette pleine de rire » ou « ras le bol de s'amuser »).

Aux États-Unis, Humorama Publishing commença à faire paraître ses digests vers 1950. *Snappy*, *Jest*, *Gee-Whiz*, *Comedy* et d'autres mêlaient les pin-up strip-teaseuses et les bandes dessinées de Bill Ward. Ils survécurent jusqu'au milieu des années soixante-dix sans avoir pratiquement changé de format. *Ja-Já* était la version mexicaine, avec des blagues et des photos directement puisées dans les magazines américains. En 1960, la plupart des magazines d'humour grivois américains avaient déjà disparu. Il y eut

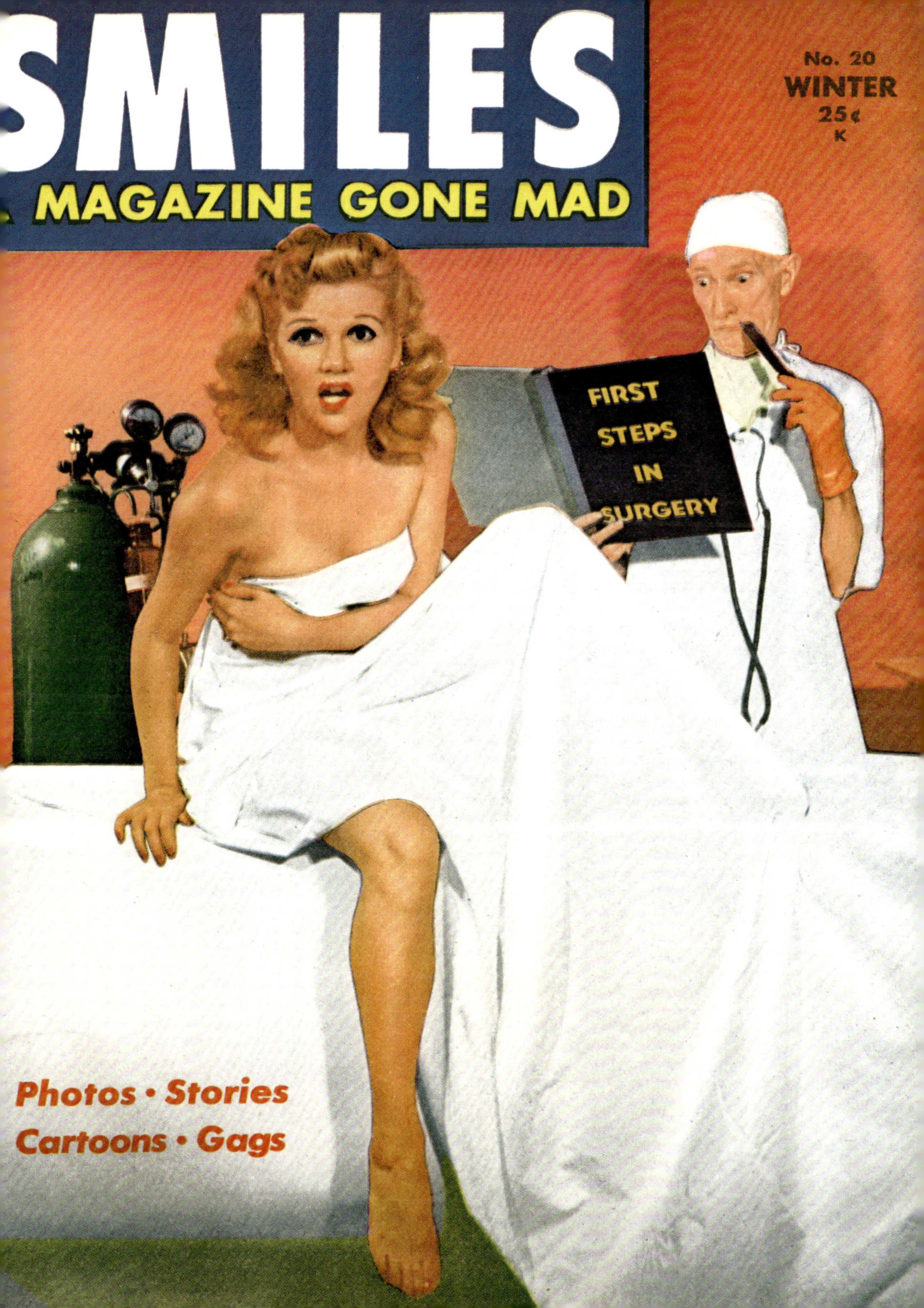
SMILES
MAGAZINE GONE MAD
No. 20
WINTER
25¢
K
FIRST
STEPS
IN
SURGERY
Photos • Stories
Cartoons • Gags

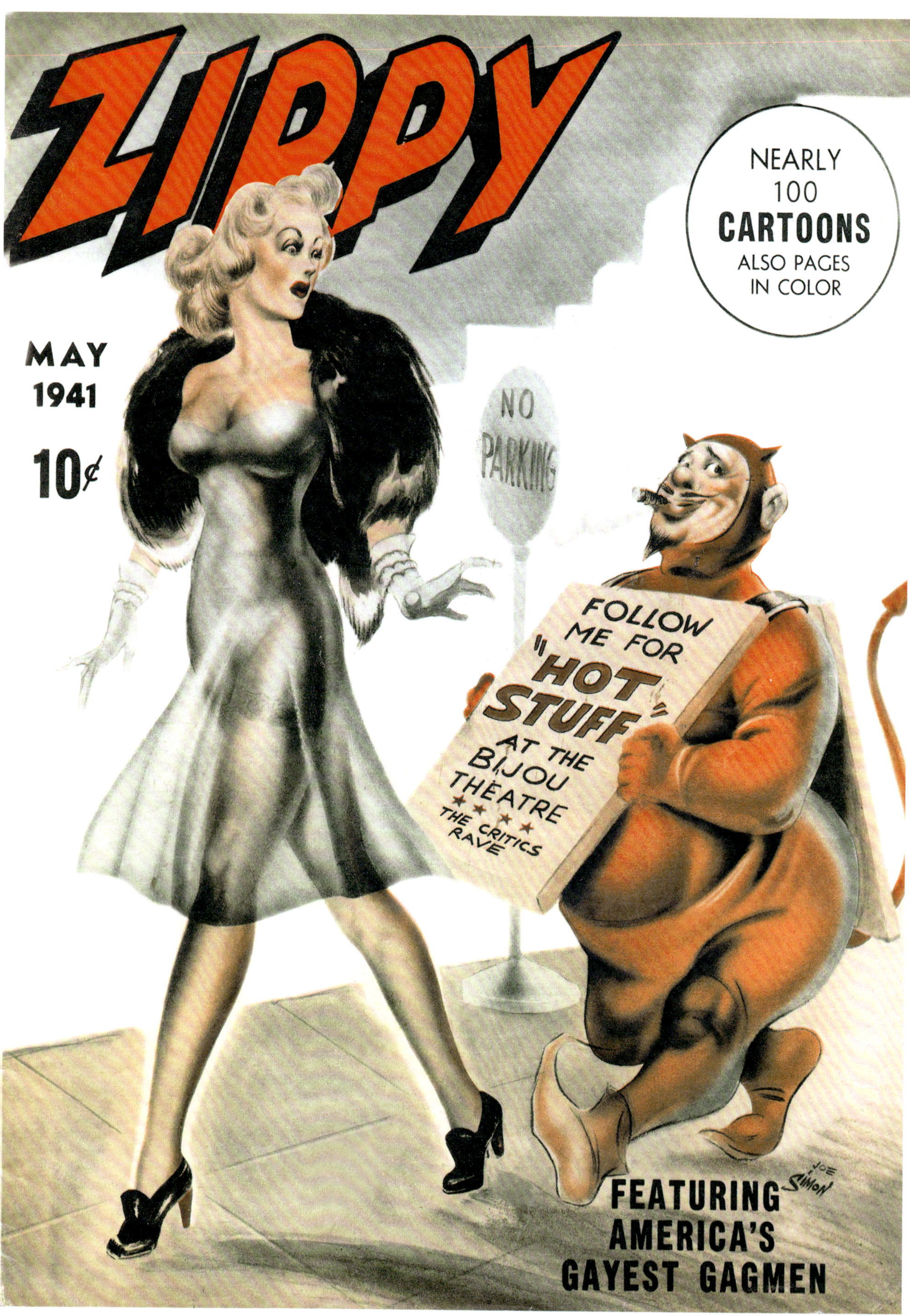

YEAR: **1941**. TITLE: **Zippy**. ARTIST: **Joe Simon**. COUNTRY: **USA**.

Risqué humor magazines such as the bedsheet format Zippy saw America through World War II.

Mit schlüpfrigen Witzblättern wie dem großformatigen Zippy schlug sich Amerika durch den Zweiten Weltkrieg.

Des magazines d'humour osé tels que ce Zippy grand format soutinrent le moral des Américains pendant la Seconde Guerre mondiale.

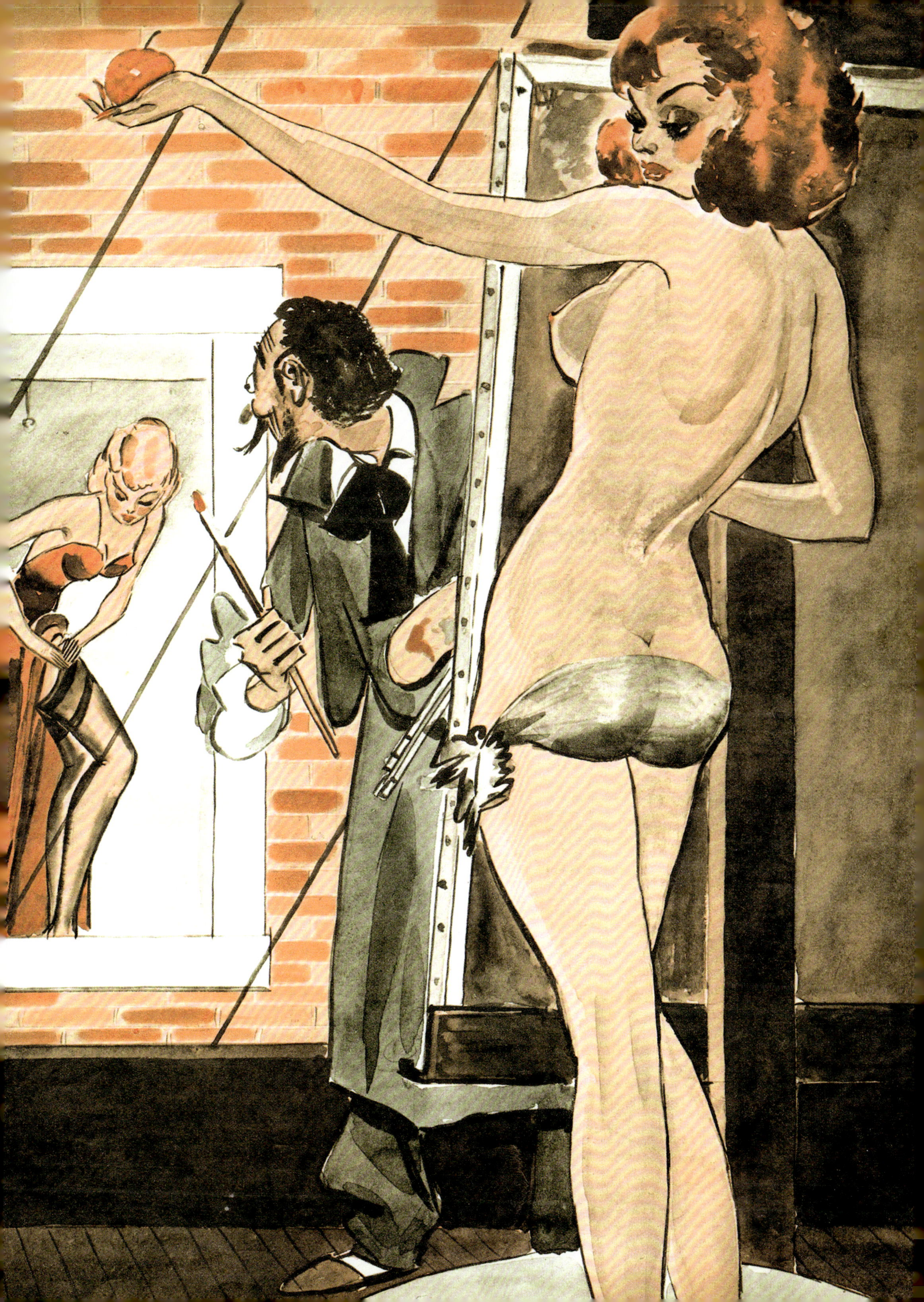

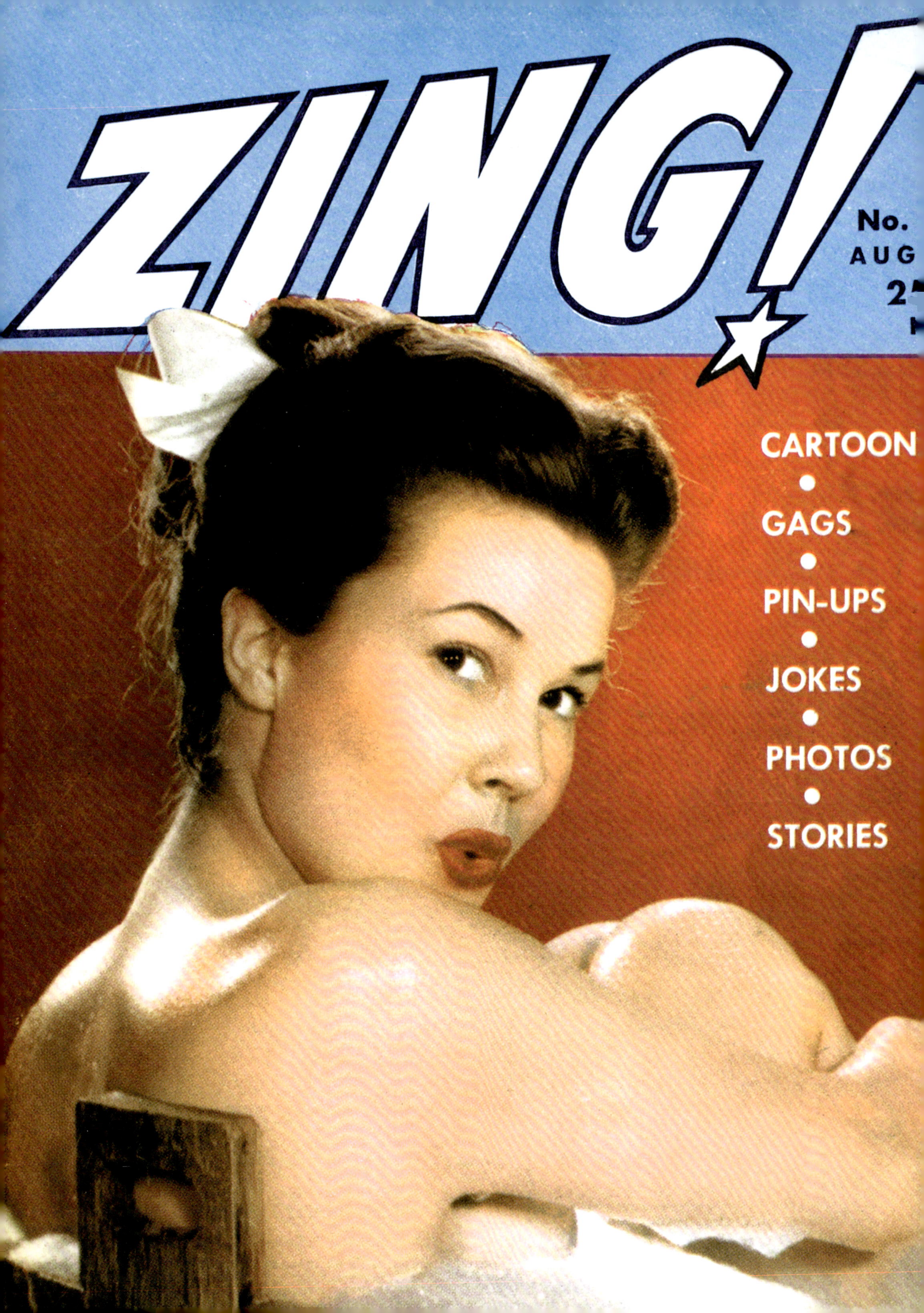
ZING!
No.
AUG
CARTOON
GAGS
PIN-UPS
JOKES
PHOTOS
STORIES

Page 255:
Year: **1941**. Title: **Zippy**. Country: **USA**.
Left:
Year: **1950s**. Title: **Zing!** Country: **USA**.

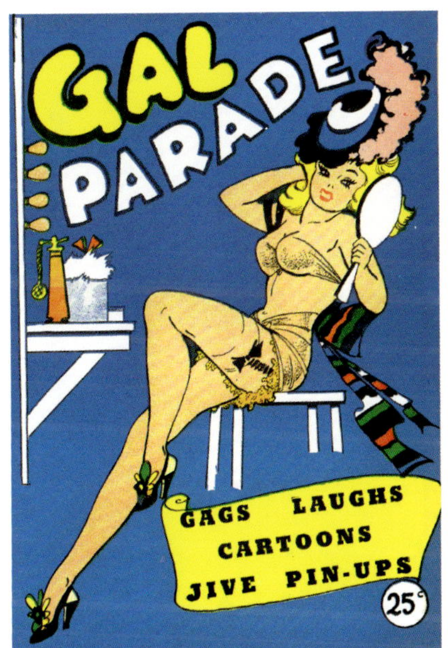

Year: **1950s**. Title: **Gal Parade**. Country: **USA**.

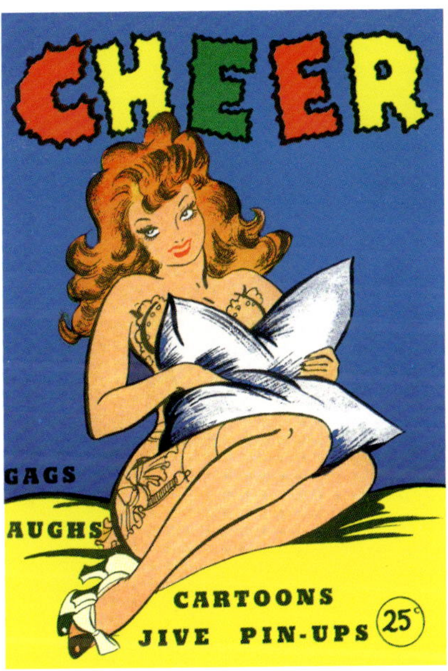

Year: **1950s**. Title: **Cheer**. Country: **USA**.

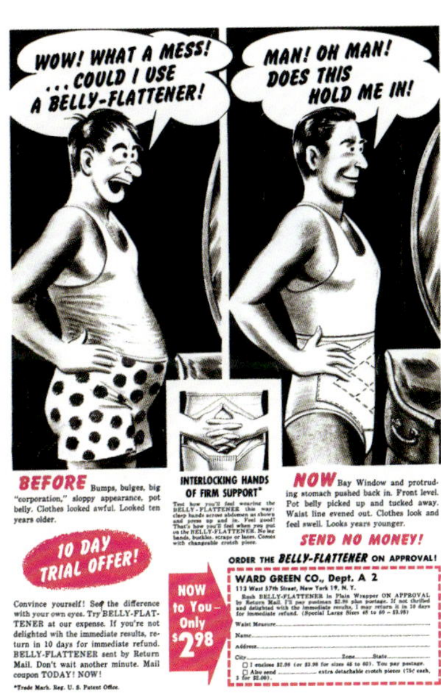

Year: **1950s**. Title: **Gal Parade**. Country: **USA**.

chose to remain a relic, pleasing an aging audience with the same gags and artists that had worked in the war years. When the artists and their audience began passing on to the great barracks in the sky, the magazine quickly followed.

immer gleichen Gags und Illustratoren zu beglücken, die auch in Kriegszeiten schon gut angekommen waren. Als sich Zeichner und Leserschaft in die großen himmlischen Armeebaracken verabschiedet hatten, folgte das Magazin ihnen auf dem Fuße.

Es sieht so aus, als hätten wir jetzt, wo wir es endlich wagen, Sex ernst zu nehmen, keinen Bedarf mehr für das Sexund-Humor-Genre.

une brève éclosion de nouveaux titres dans les années soixante-dix mais ce ne fut qu'un feu de paille. Le fameux *Sex to Sexty* survécut en cultivant son statut de relique, régalant un public vieillissant des mêmes gags et des mêmes artistes qui avaient assuré son succès pendant la guerre. Lorsque les artistes et les lecteurs s'en allèrent pour rejoindre le séjour des bienheureux, le magazine les y suivit rapidement.

World War II improved the American taste for risqué humor; soldiers needed levity as much as cheesecake.

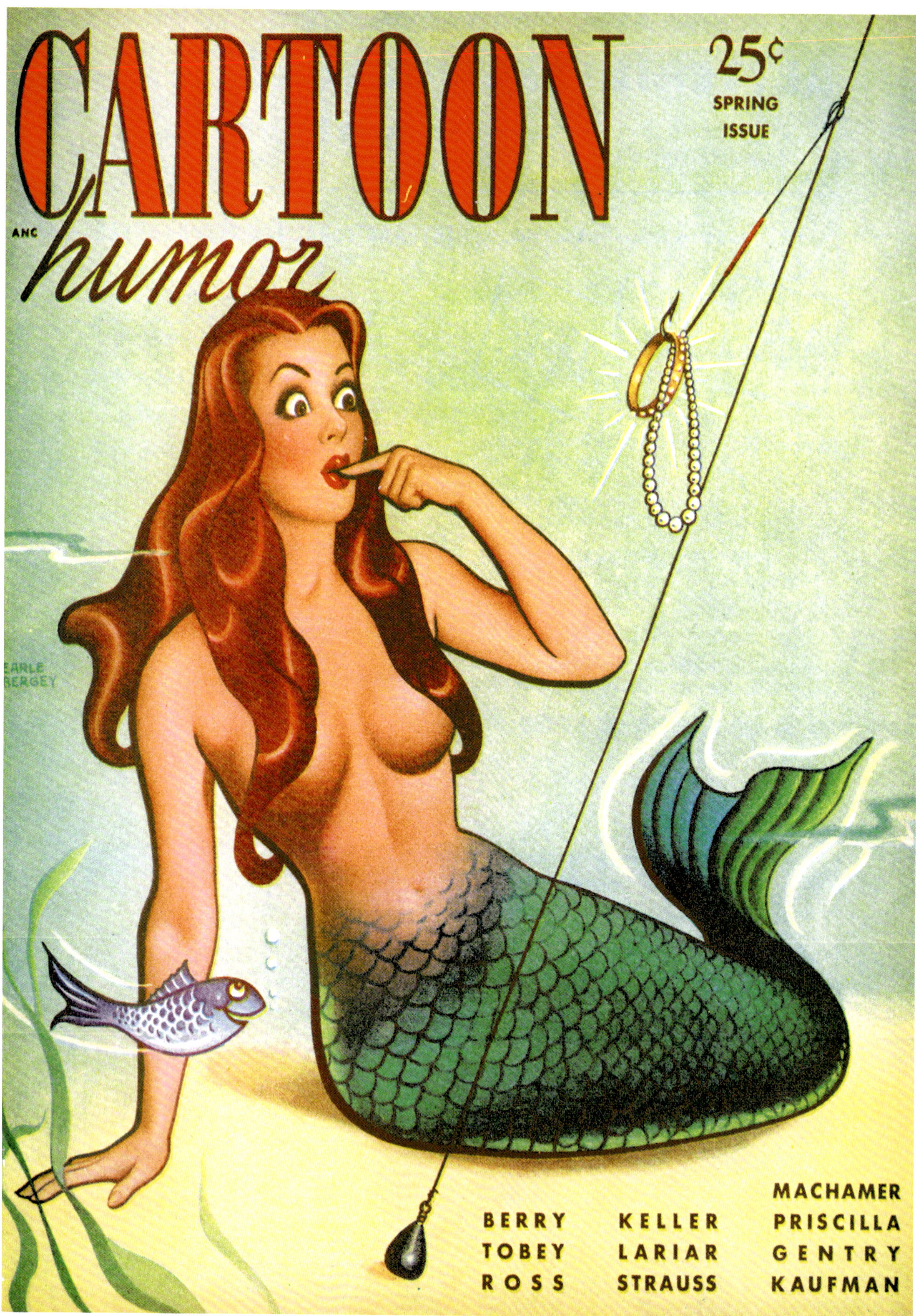

YEAR: **1949**. TITLE: **Cartoon Humor**. ARTIST: **Earle Bergley**. COUNTRY: **USA**.

YEAR: **1944**. TITLE: **Fun Riot**. COUNTRY: **USA**.

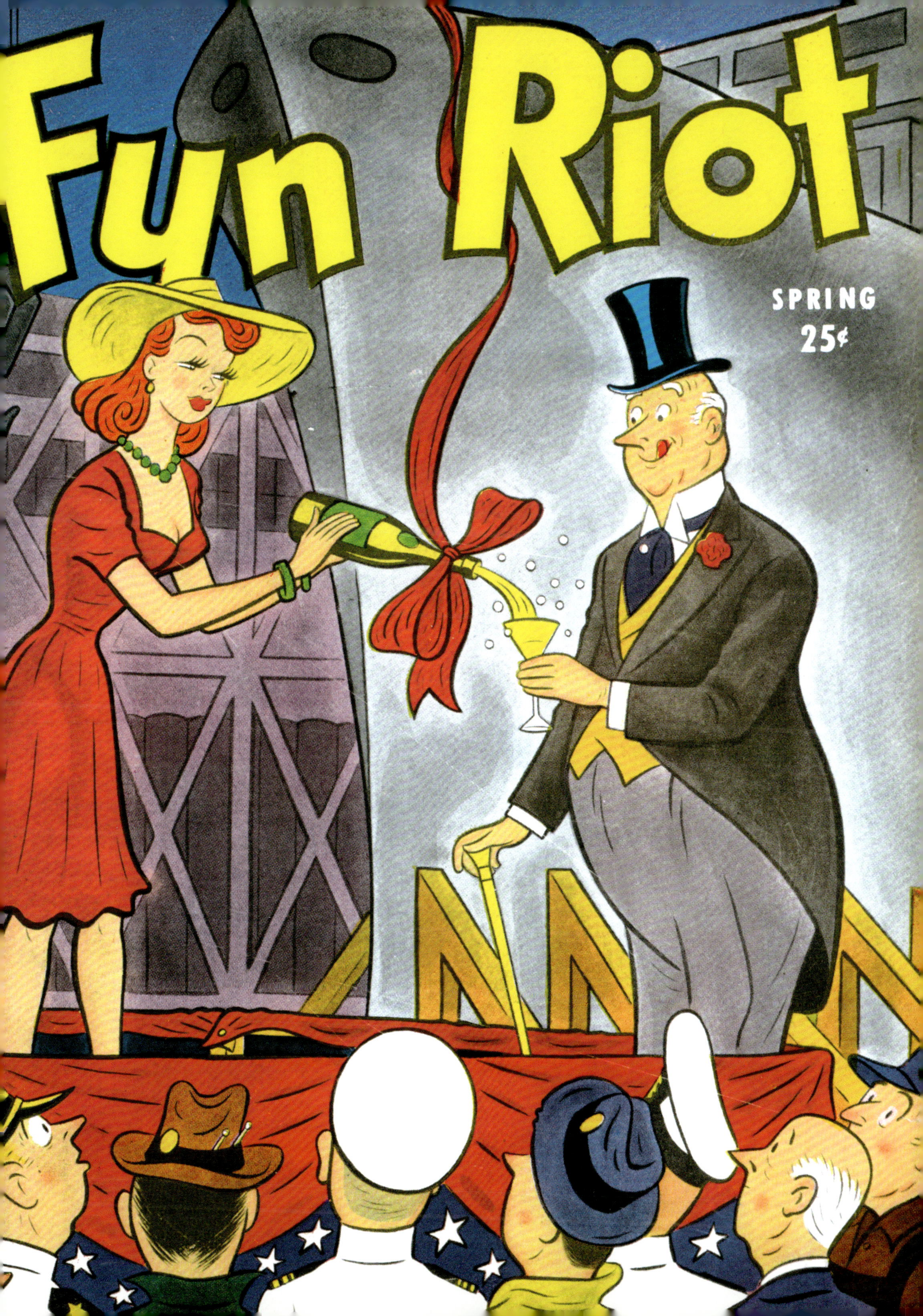
Fun Riot
SPRING
25¢

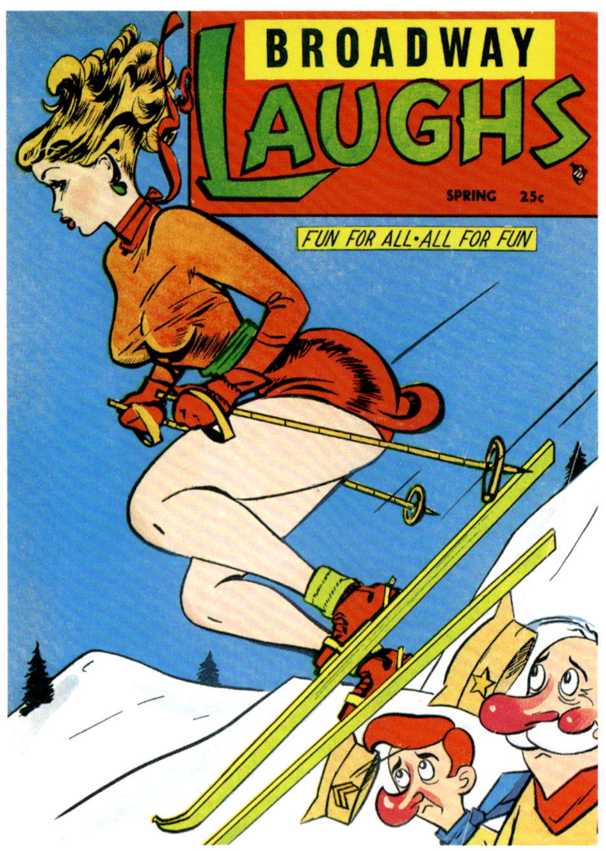

YEAR: **1950**. TITLE: **Broadway Laughs**. COUNTRY: **USA**.

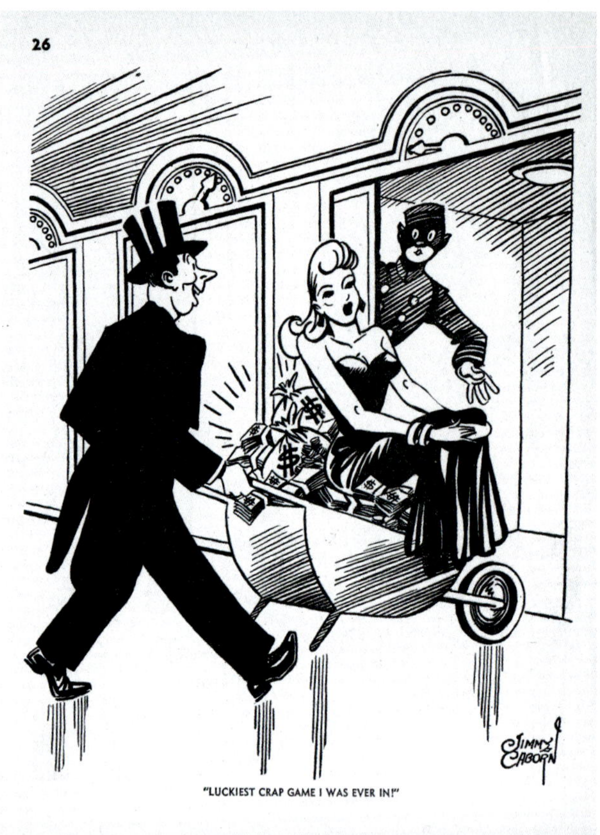

YEAR: **1950**. TITLE: **Broadway Laughs**. ARTIST: **Jimmy Caborn**. COUNTRY: **USA**.

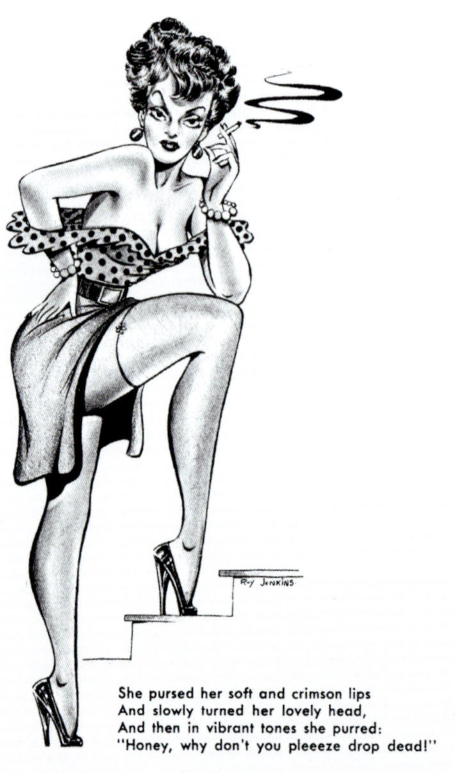

YEAR: **1959**. TITLE: **Zing!** ARTIST: **Roy Jenkins**. COUNTRY: **USA**.

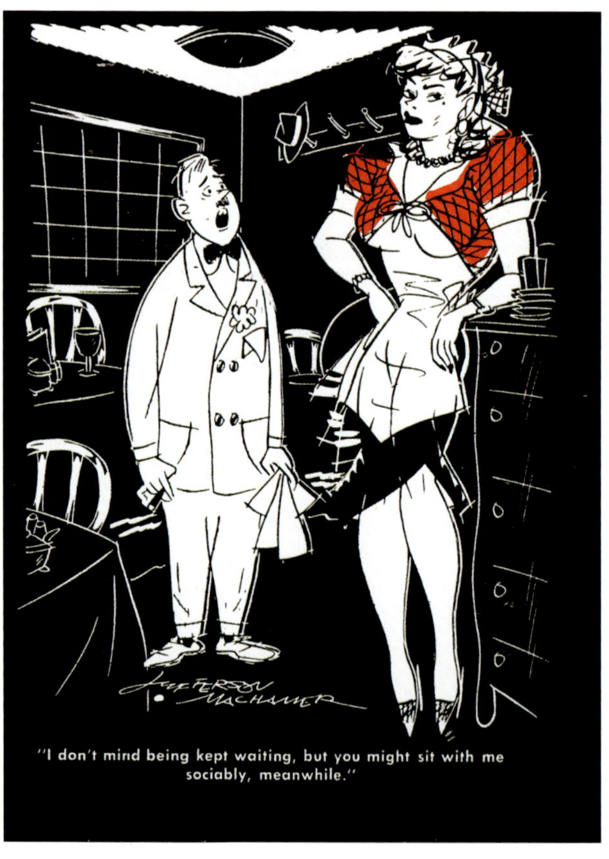

YEAR: **1956**. TITLE: **Chicks and Chuckles**. COUNTRY: **USA**.

YEAR: **1947**. TITLE: **Cartoon Comedy**. ARTIST: **Jefferson Machamer**. COUNTRY: **USA**.

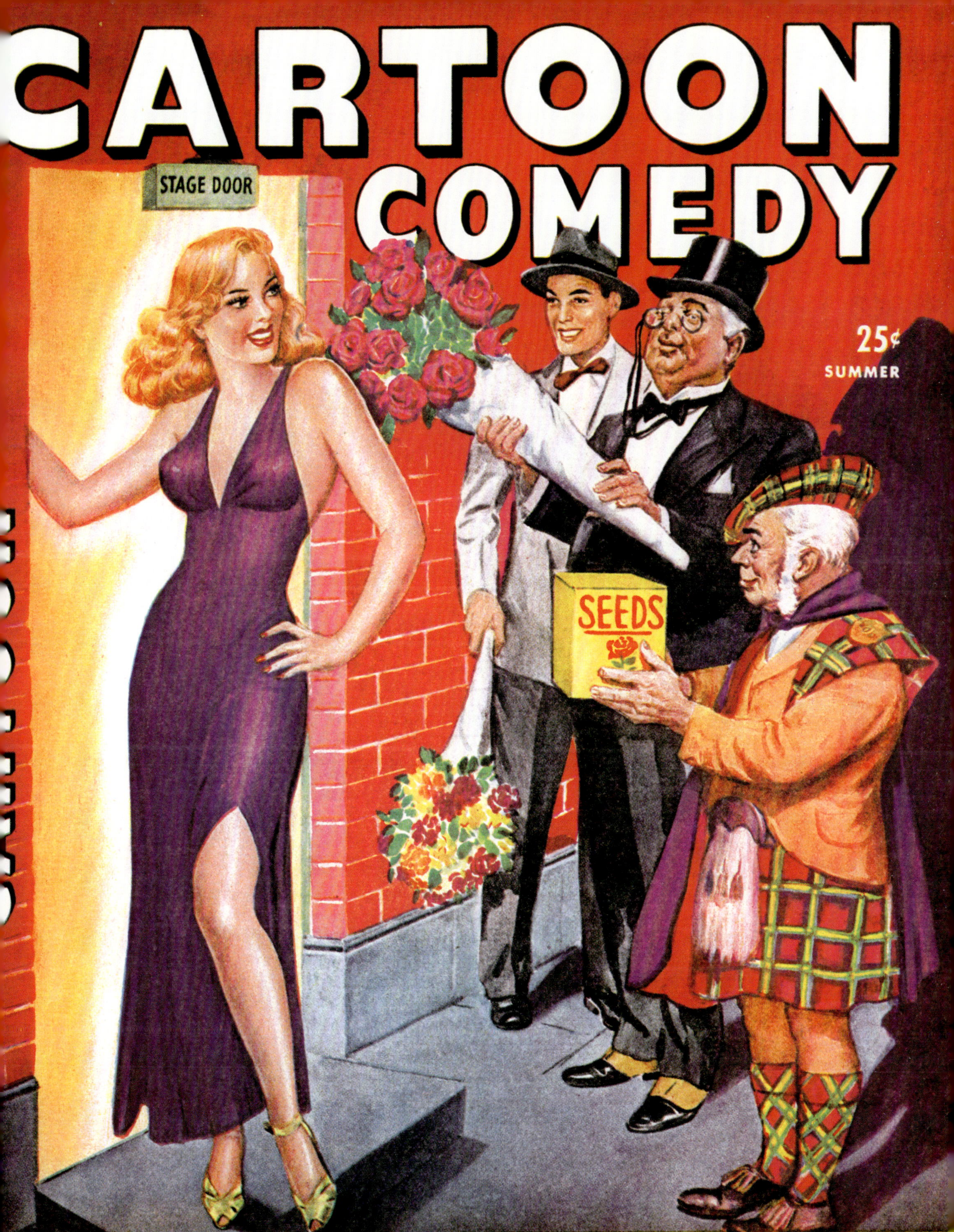

FRESH JAM-PACKED PAGES by AMERICA'S LEADING CARTOONISTS!

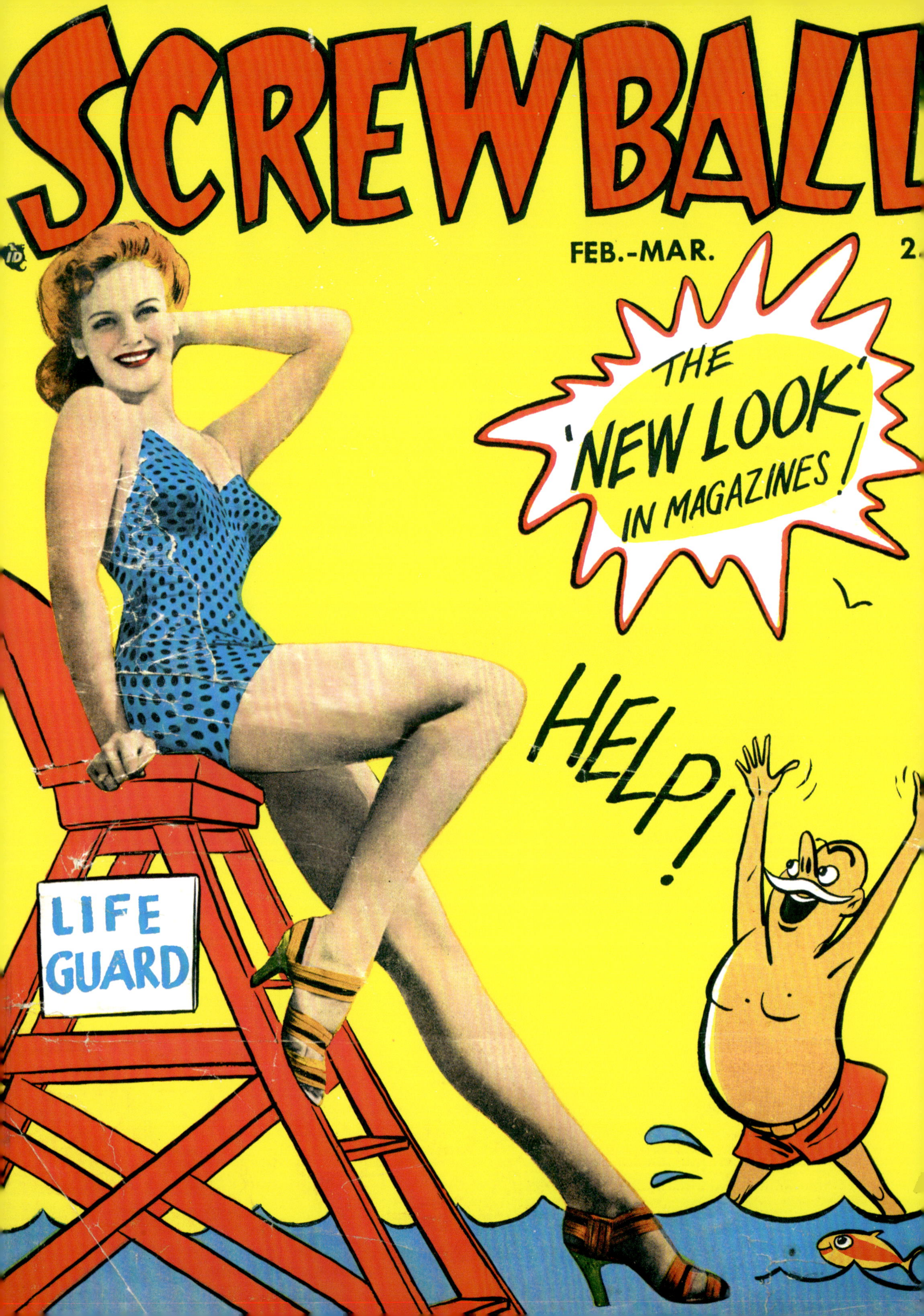
SCREWBALL
FEB.-MAR.
2
THE 'NEW LOOK' IN MAGAZINES!
HELP!
LIFE GUARD

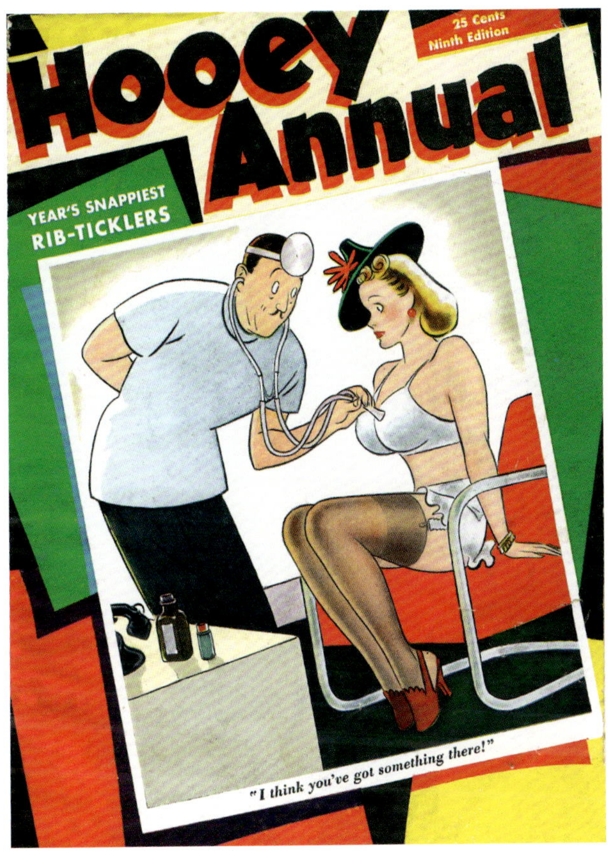

Year: **1939**. Title: **Hooey Annual**. Country: **USA**.

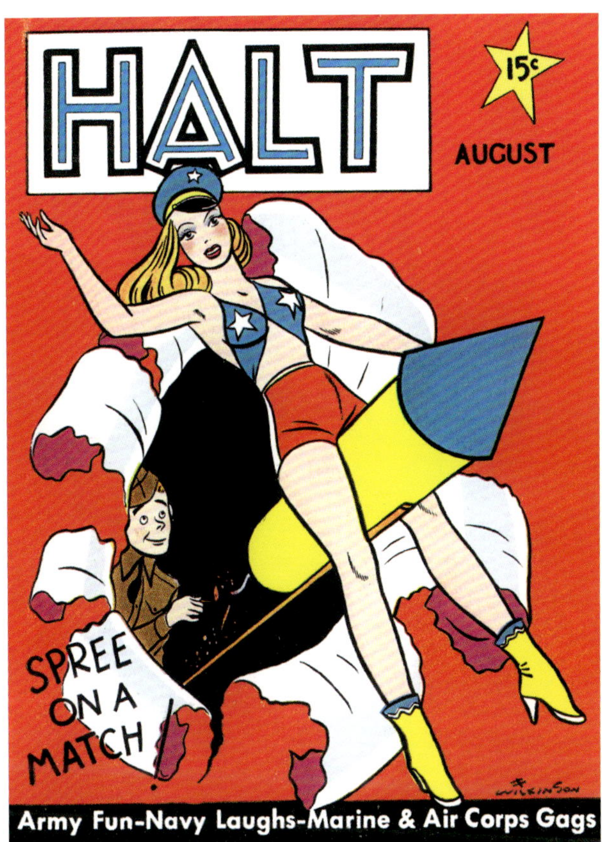

Year: **1942**. Title: **Halt**. Artist: **Wilkinson**. Country: **USA**.

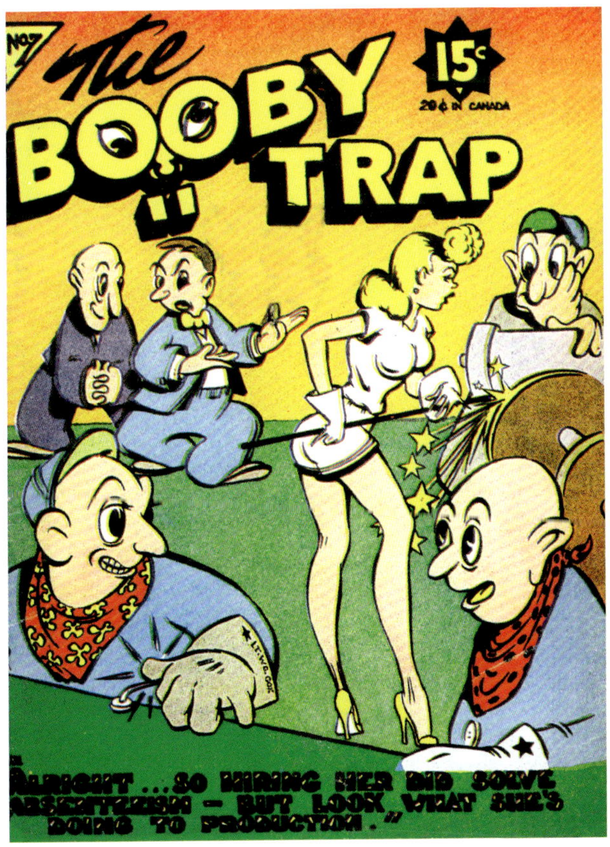

Year: **1945**. Title: **The Booby Trap**. Country: **USA**.

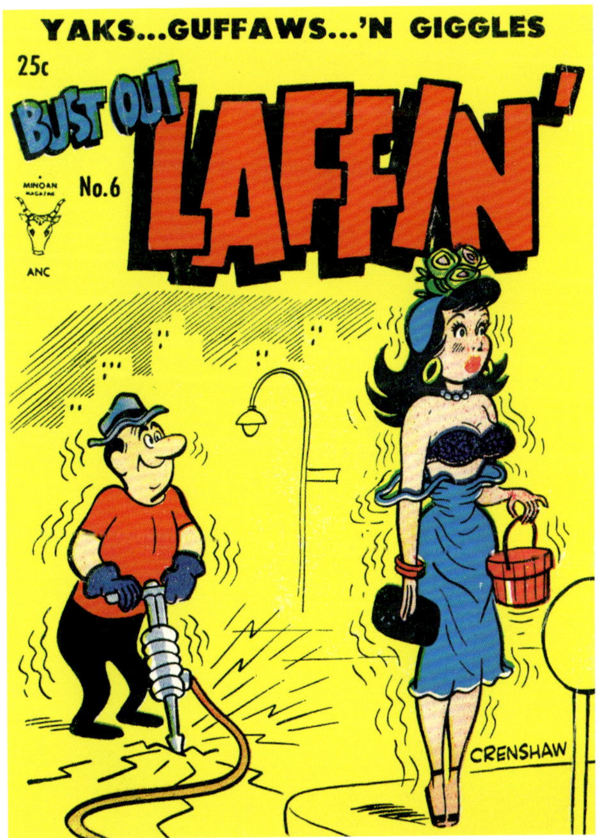

Year: **1950s**. Title: **Bust out Laffin'**. Artist: **Crenshaw**. Country: **USA**.

Year: **1949**. Title: **Screwball**. Country: **USA**.

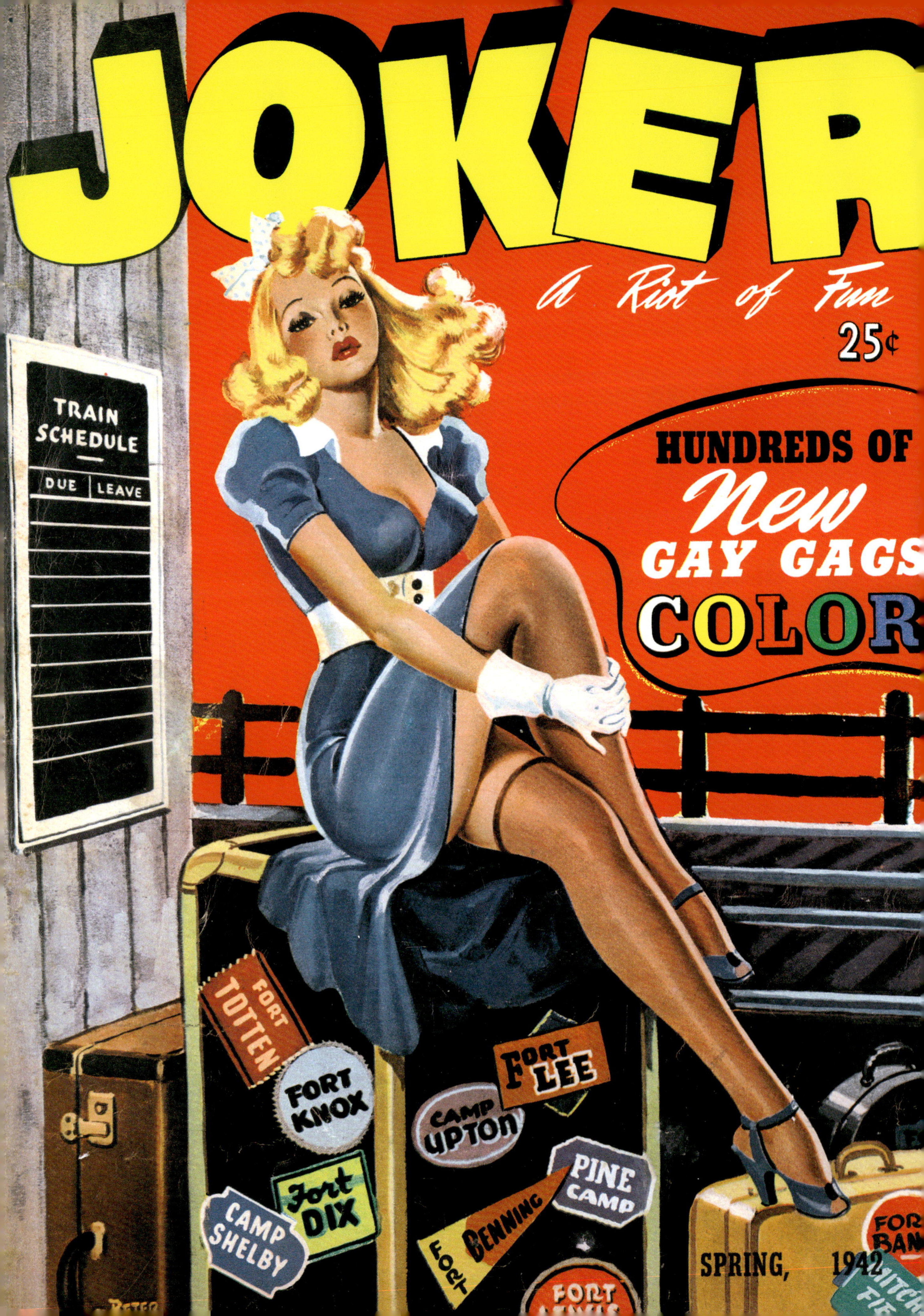
JOKER
A Riot of Fun
25¢
HUNDREDS OF
New
GAY GAGS
COLOR
TRAIN
SCHEDULE
DUE
LEAVE
FORT
TOTTEN
FORT
KNOX
Fort
DIX
CAMP
SHELBY
CAMP
UPTON
FORT
LEE
PINE
CAMP
FORT
BENNING
SPRING, 1942

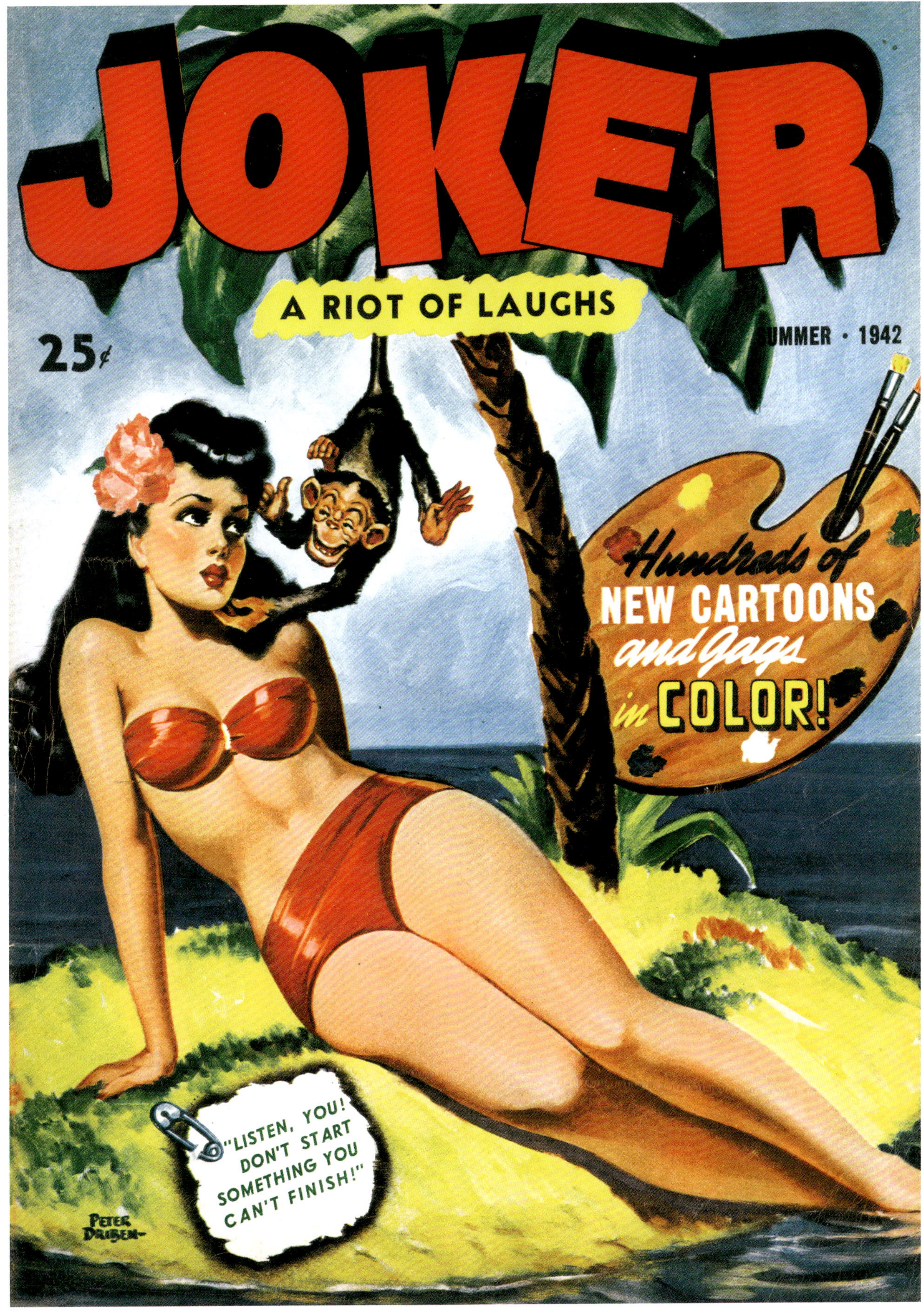

YEAR: **1942**. TITLE: **Joker**. ARTIST: **Peter Driben**. COUNTRY: **USA**.

YEAR: **1942**. TITLE: **Joker**. ARTIST: **Peter Driben**. COUNTRY: **USA**.

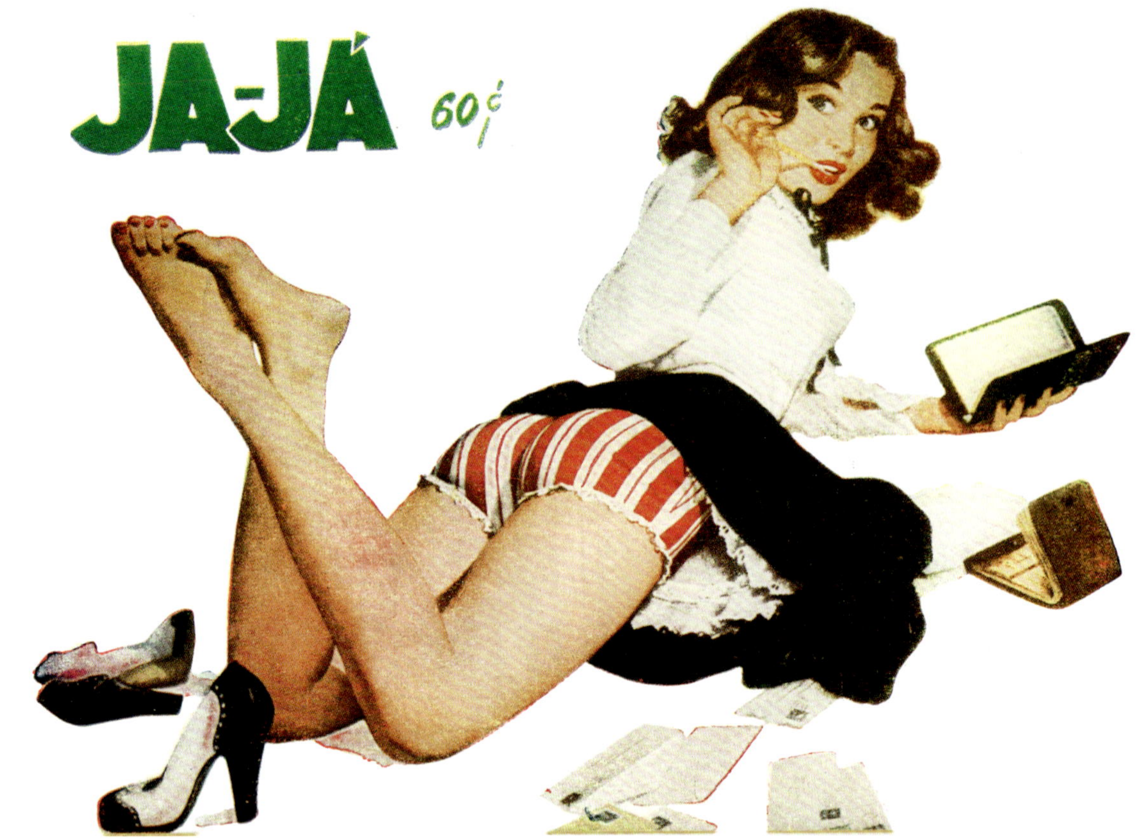

Year: **1952**. Title: **Ja-Já**. Country: **Mexico**.

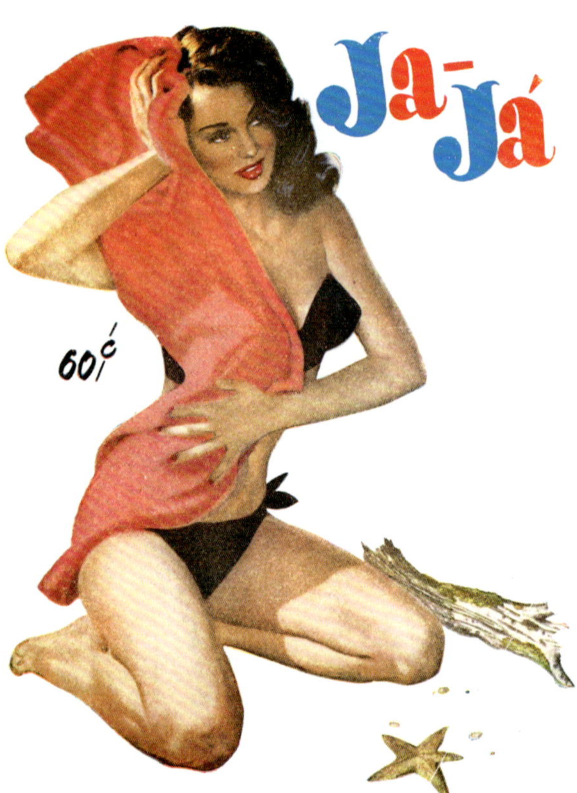

Year: **1952**. Title: **Ja-Já**. Country: **Mexico**.

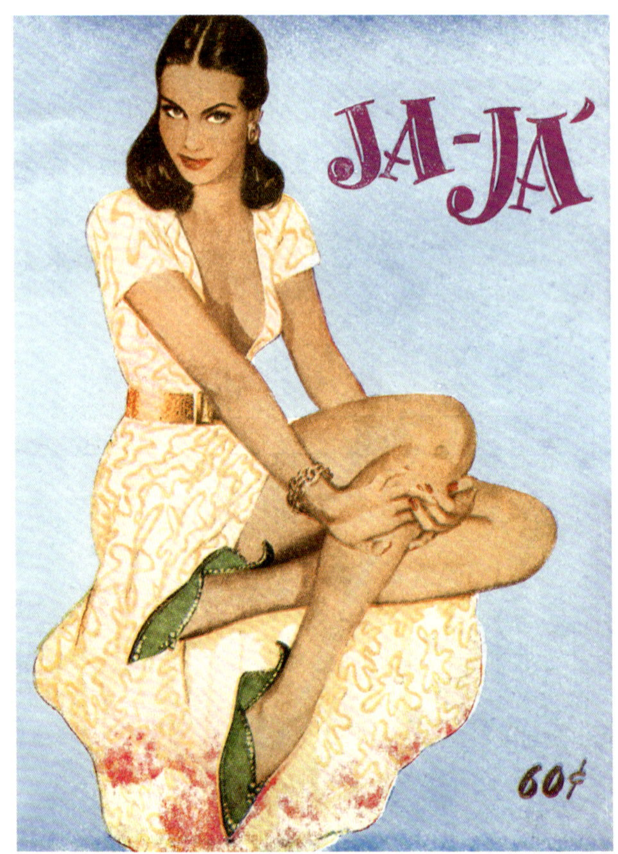

Year: **1952**. Title: **Ja-Já**. Country: **Mexico**.

Year: **1952**. Title: **Ja-Já**. Country: **Mexico**.

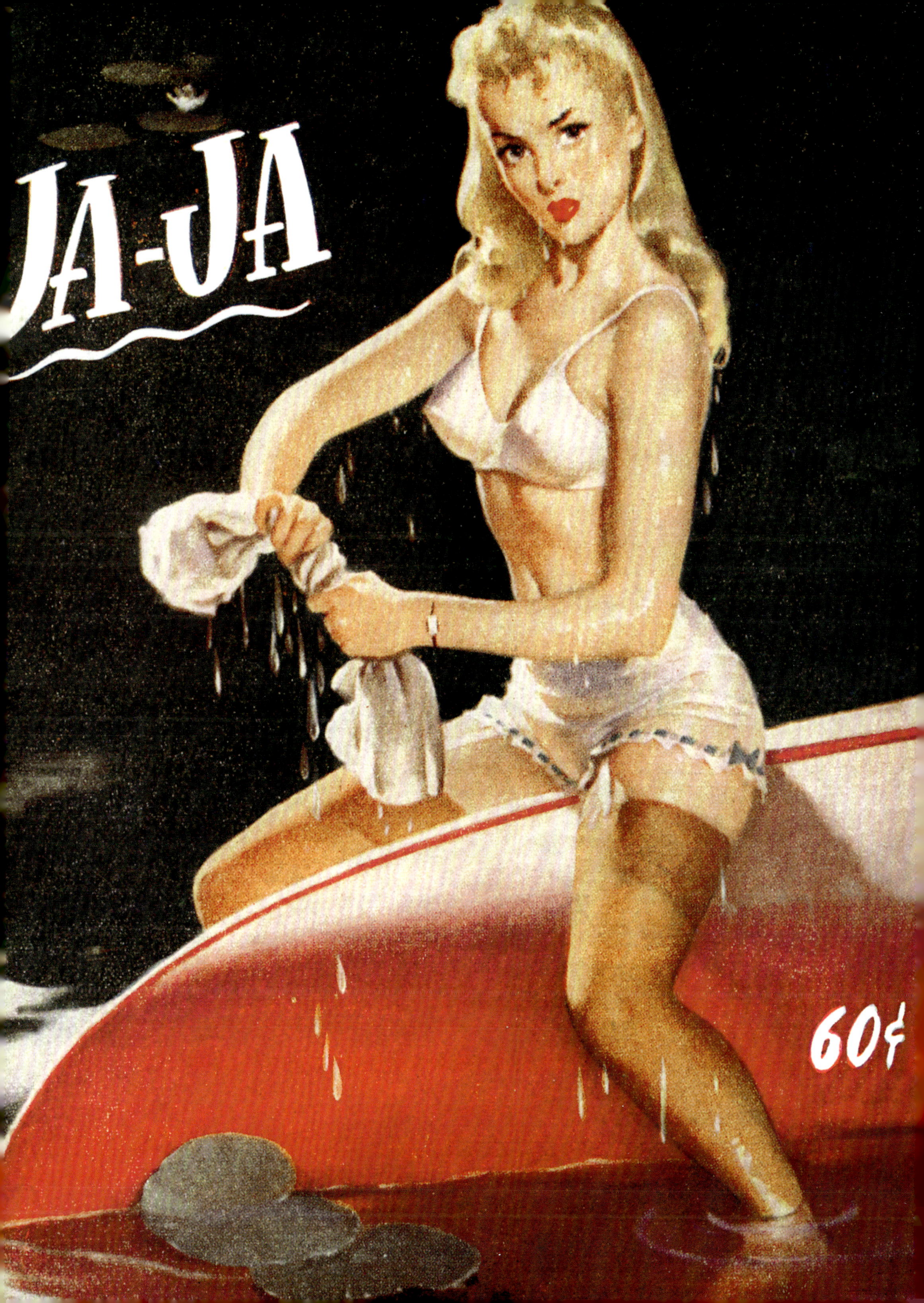
JA-JA
60¢

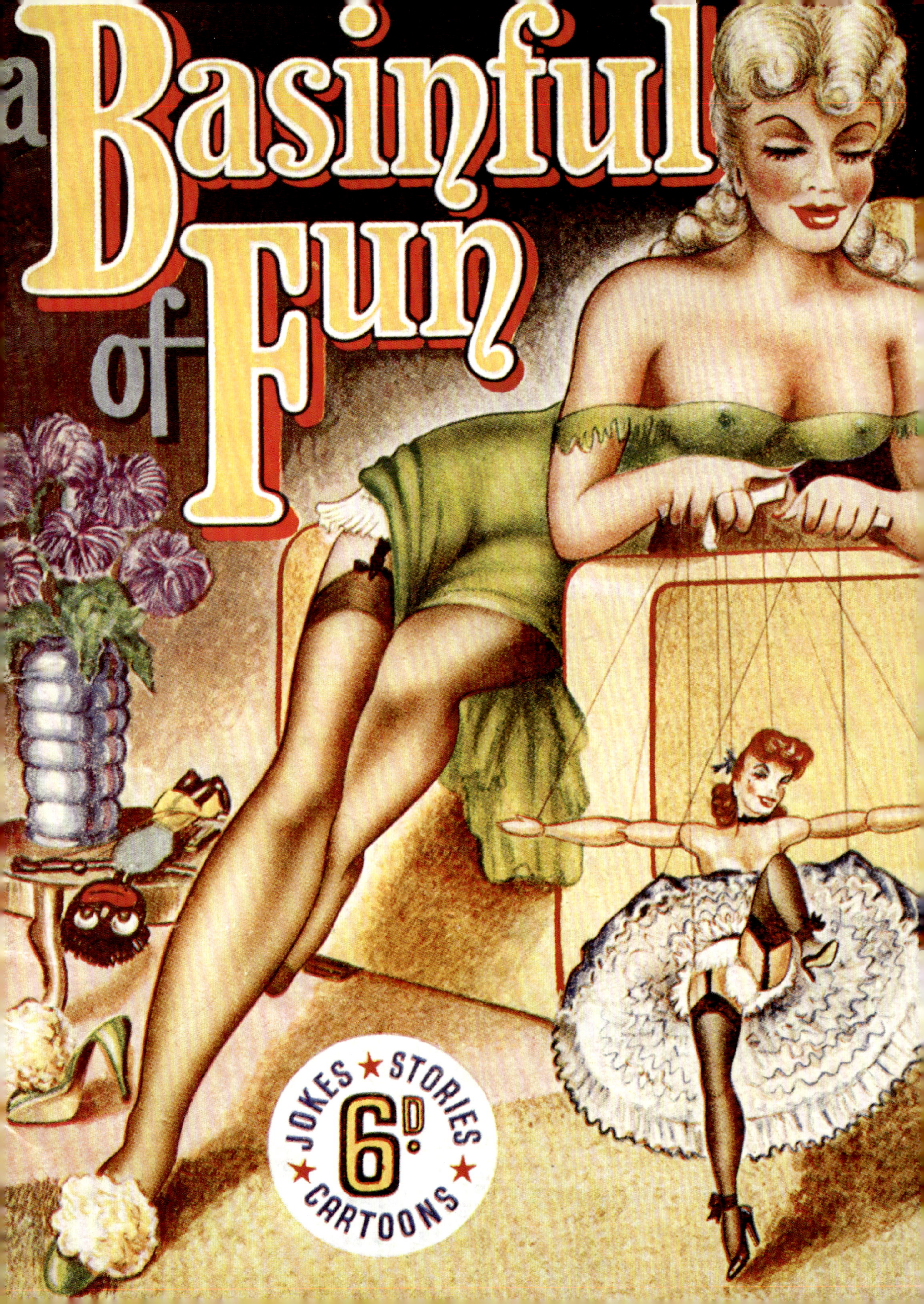
a Basinful of Fun
JOKES ★ STORIES
6D.
★ CARTOONS ★

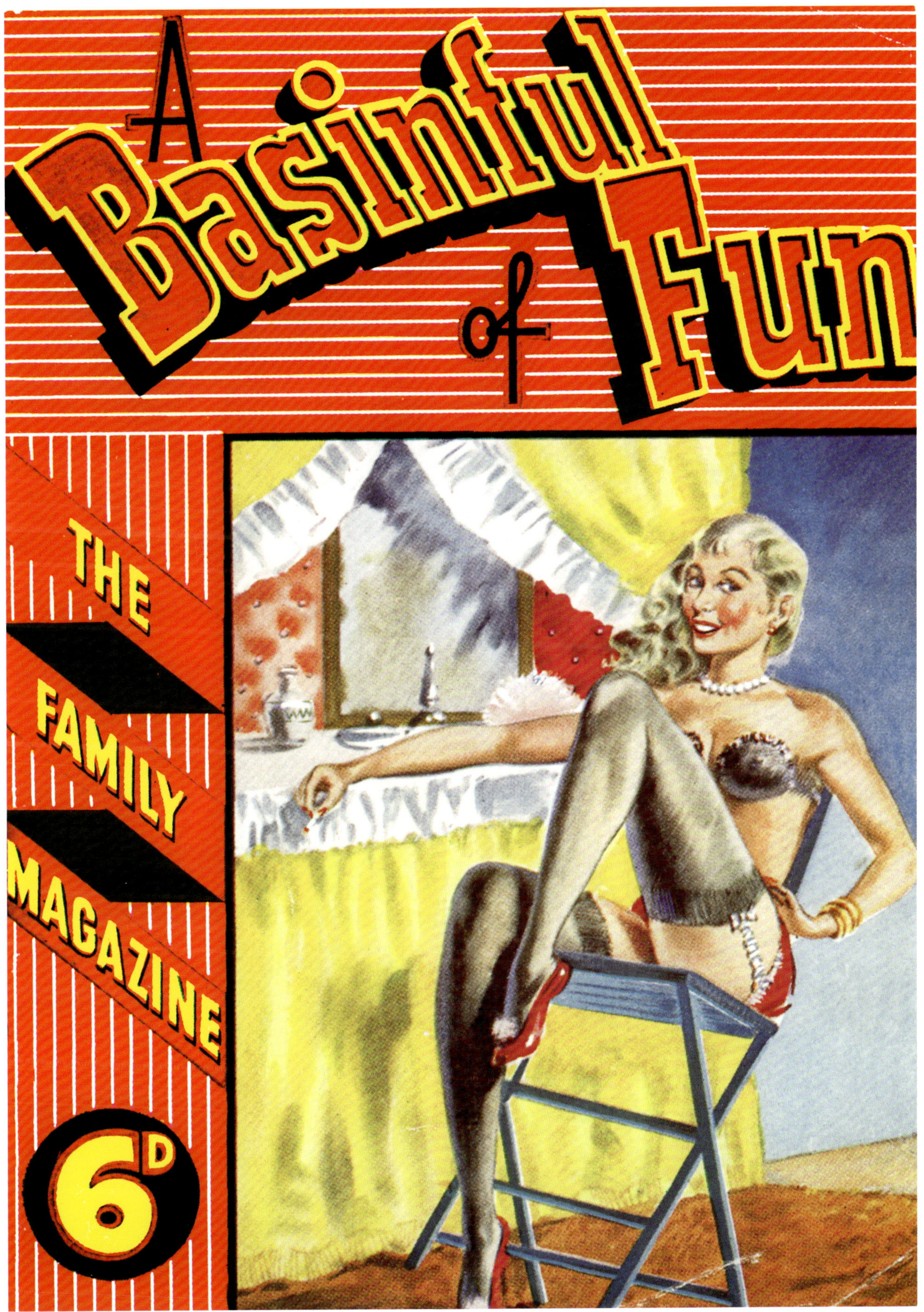

Year: **1953**. Title: **A Basinful of Fun**. Country: **England**.

Year: **1953**. Title: **A Basinful of Fun**. Country: **England**.

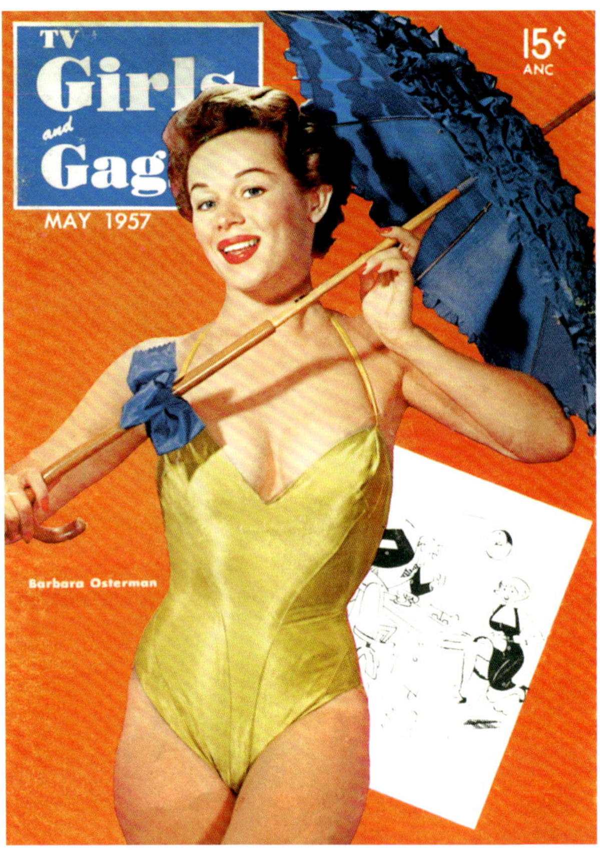

YEAR: **1957**. TITLE: **TV Girls and Gags**. COUNTRY: **USA**.

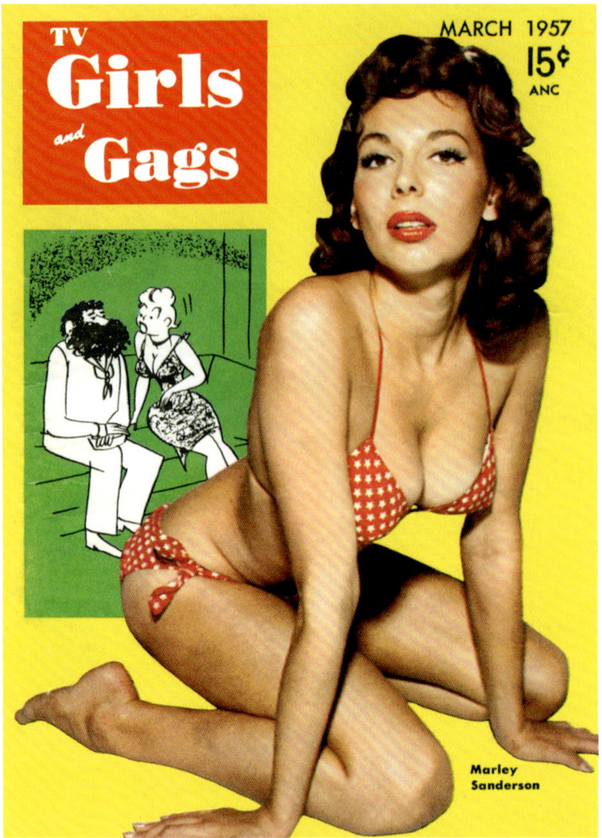

YEAR: **1957**. TITLE: **TV Girls and Gags**. COUNTRY: **USA**.

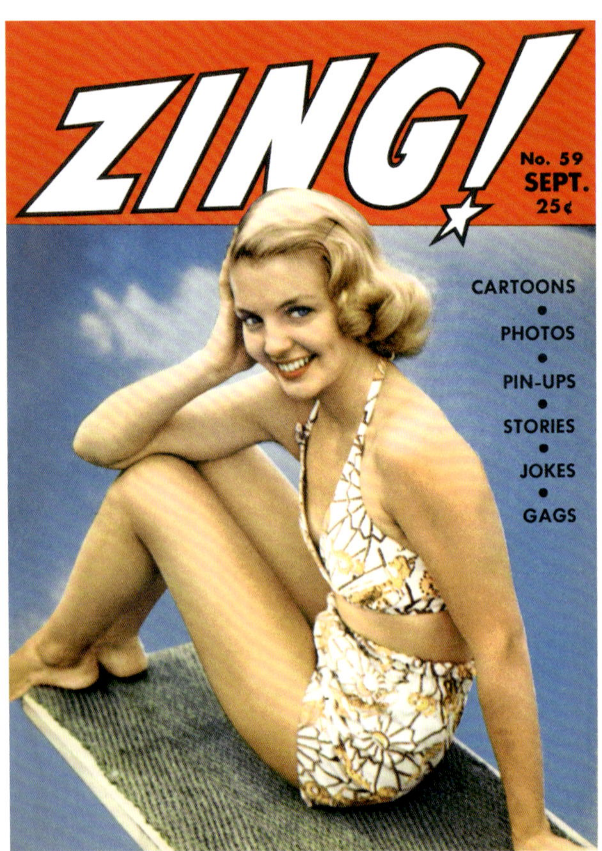

YEAR: **1950s**. TITLE: **Zing!** COUNTRY: **USA**.

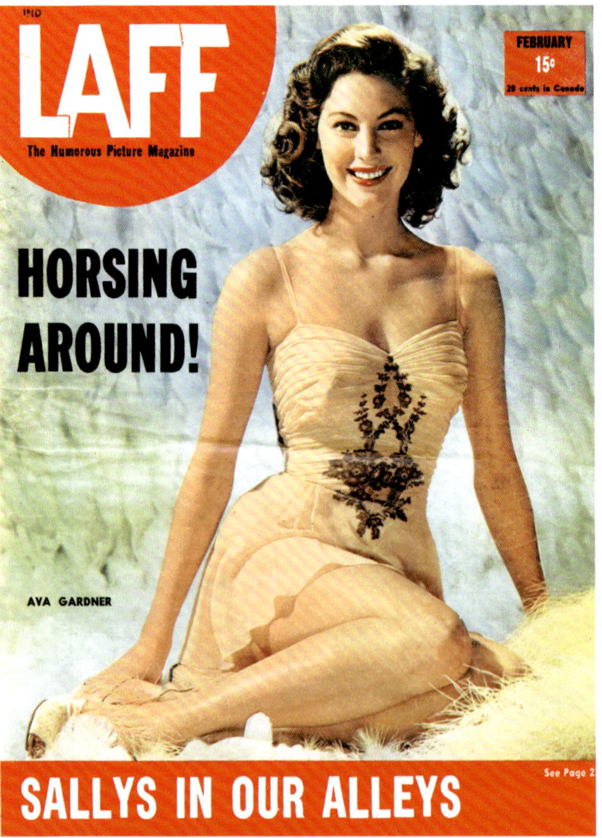

YEAR: **1952**. TITLE: **Laff**. COUNTRY: **USA**.

YEAR: **1956**. TITLE: **Chicks and Chuckles**. COUNTRY: **USA**.

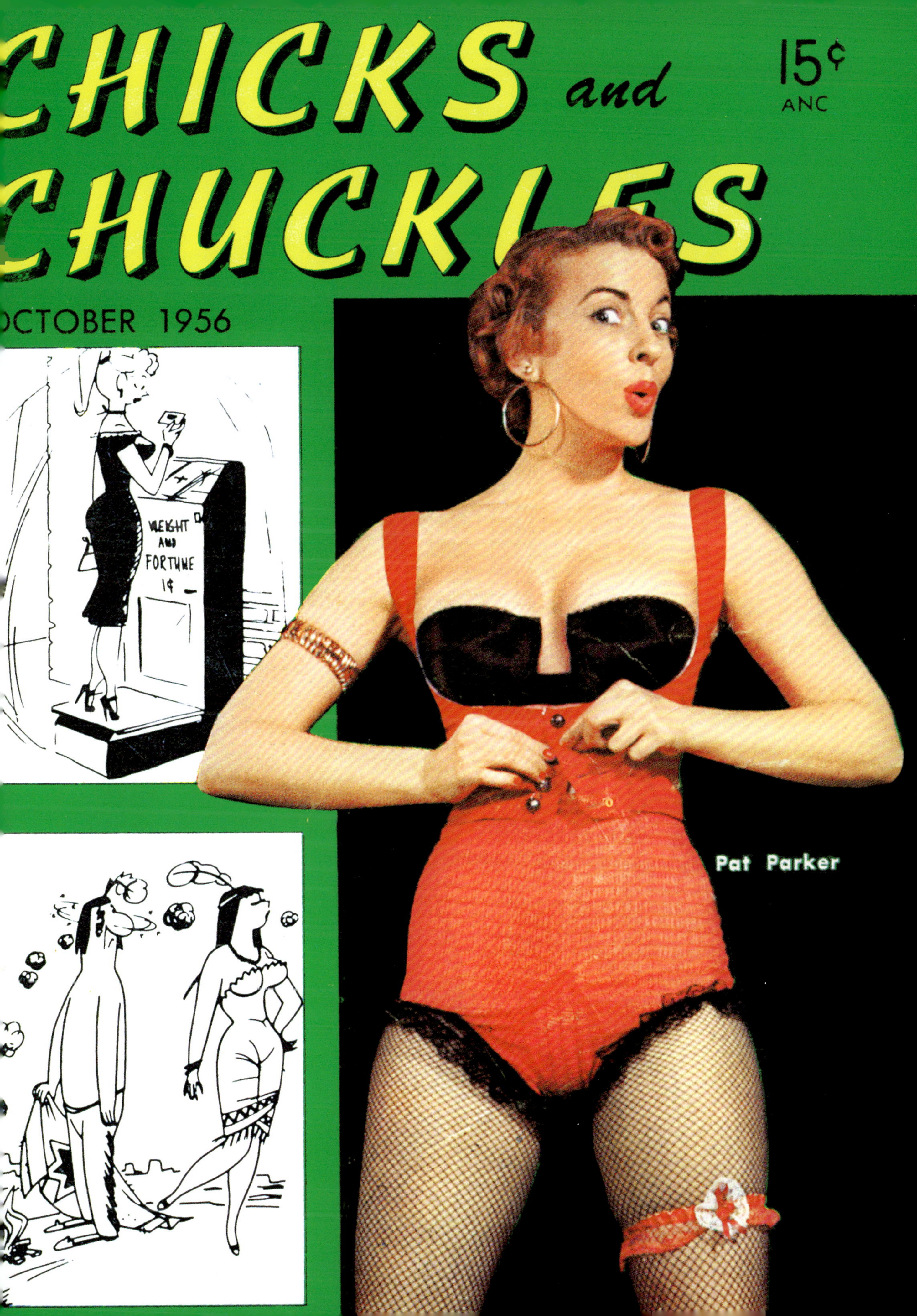
CHICKS and CHUCKLES
15¢
ANC
OCTOBER 1956
WEIGHT AND FORTUNE 1¢
Pat Parker

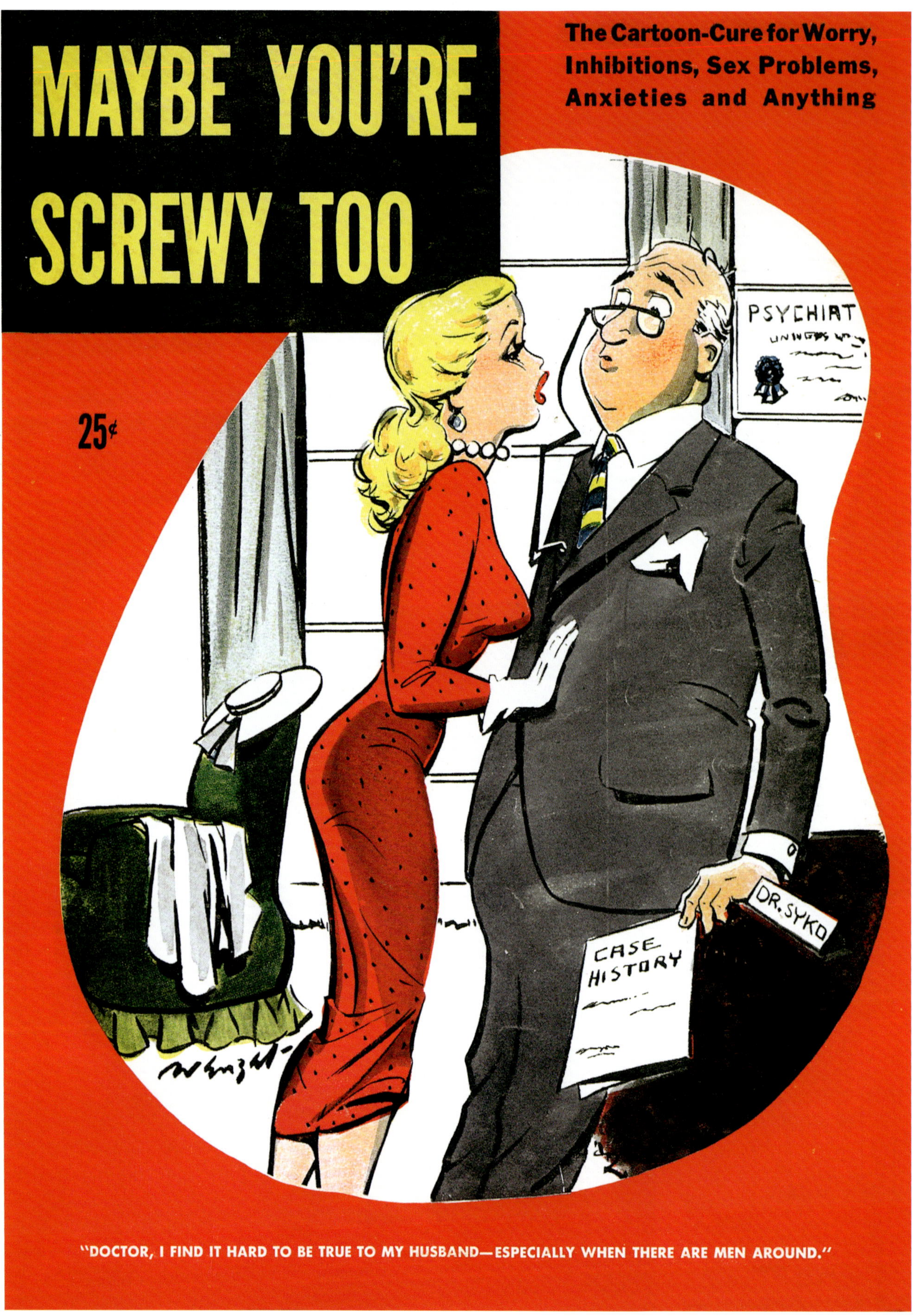

YEAR: **1950s**. TITLE: **Maybe You're Screwy Too**. COUNTRY: **USA**.

YEAR: **1956**. TITLE: **Smiles**. COUNTRY: **USA**.

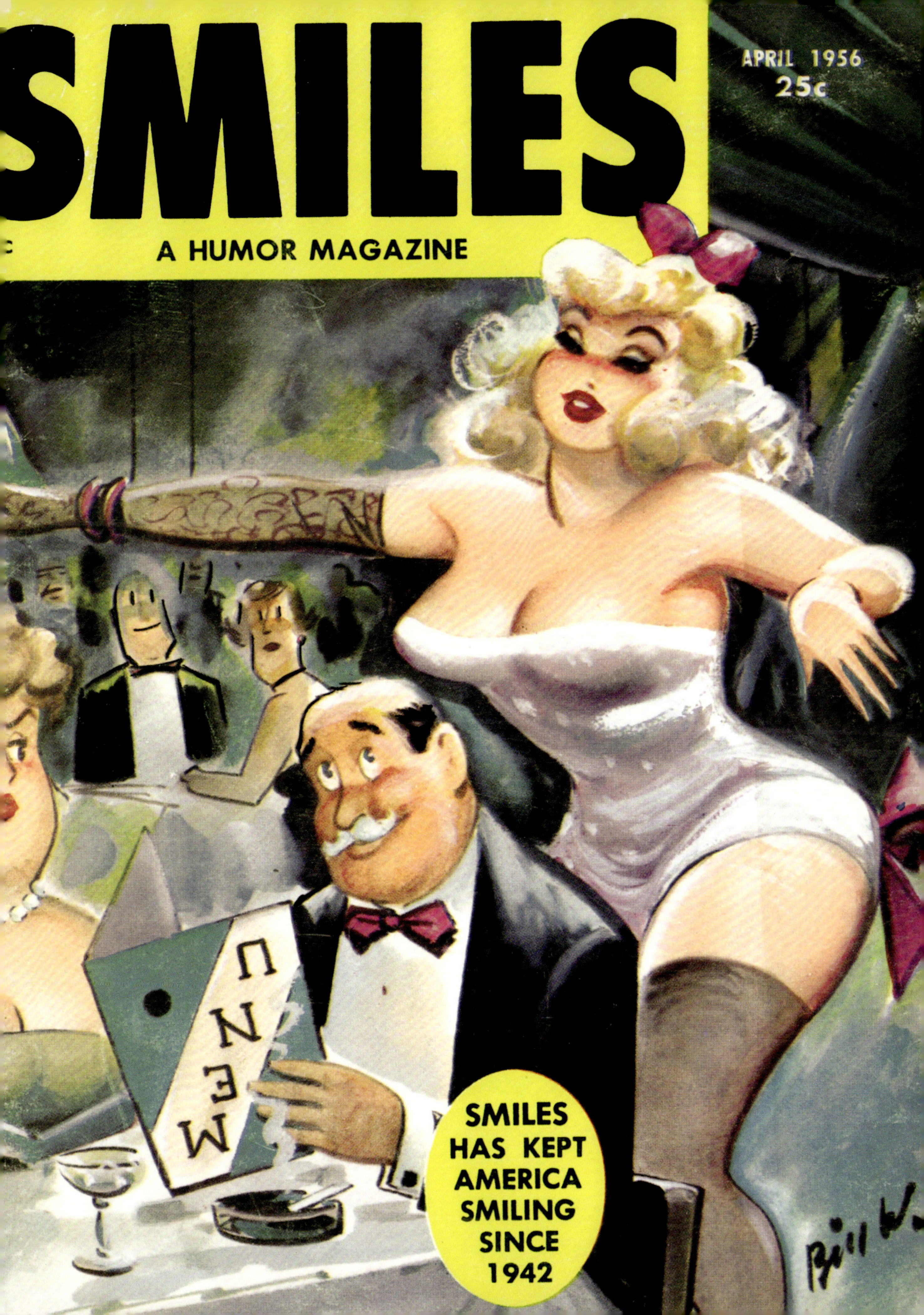
SMILES
APRIL 1956
25c
A HUMOR MAGAZINE
MENU
SMILES HAS KEPT AMERICA SMILING SINCE 1942
Bill W.

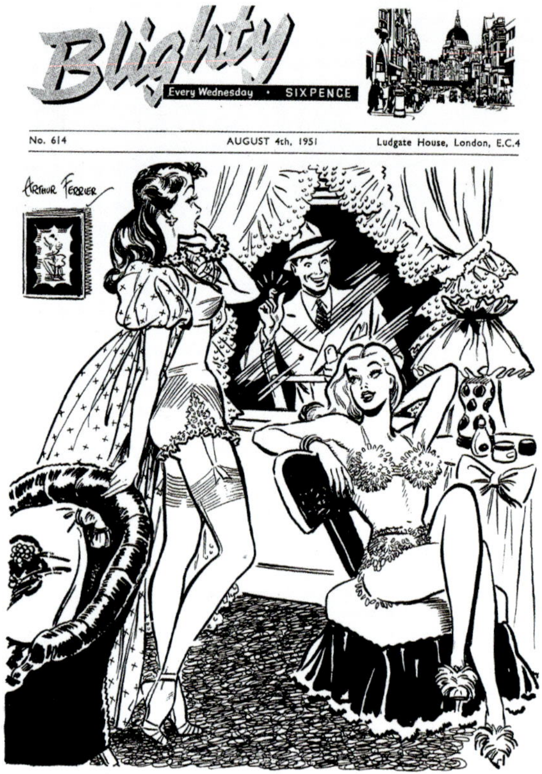

YEAR: **1951**. TITLE: **Blighty**. COUNTRY: **England**.

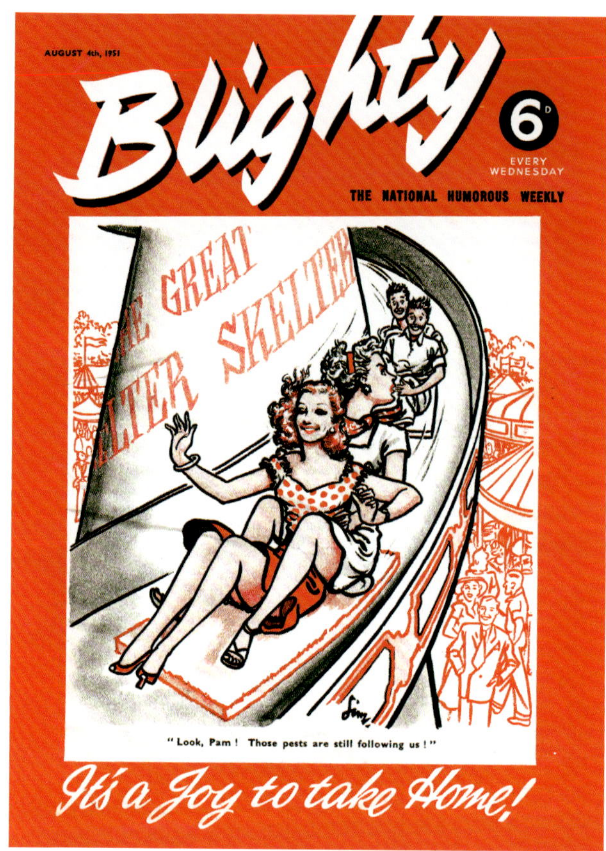

YEAR: **1951**. TITLE: **Blighty**. COUNTRY: **England**.

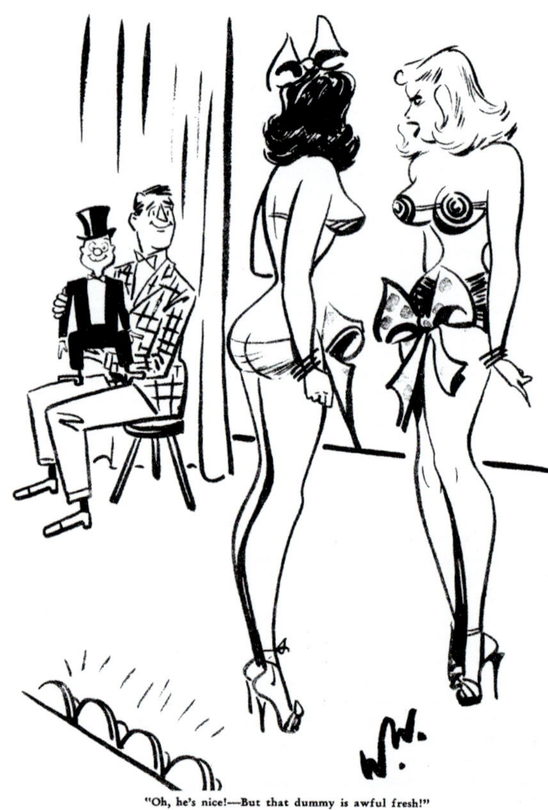

YEAR: **1952**. TITLE: **Laff**. COUNTRY: **USA**.

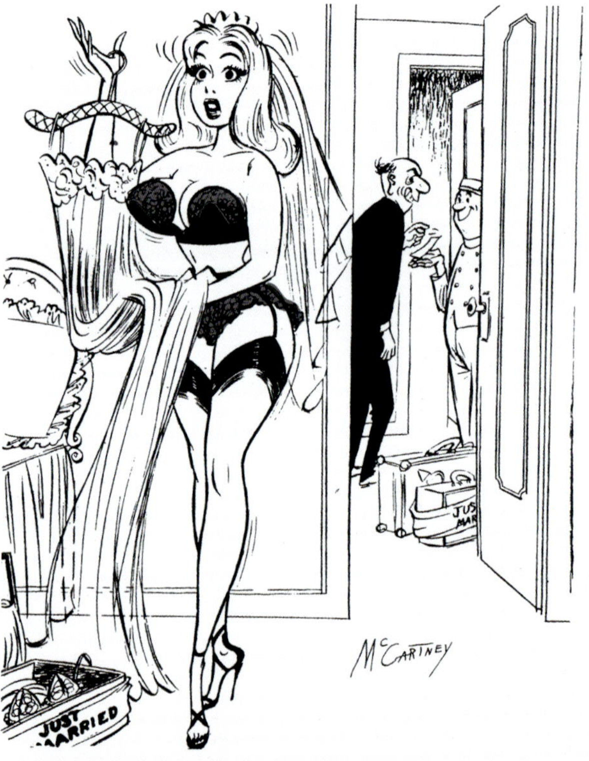

YEAR: **1957**. TITLE: **TV Girls and Gags**. COUNTRY: **USA**.

YEAR: **1942**. TITLE: **Jest**. COUNTRY: **USA**.

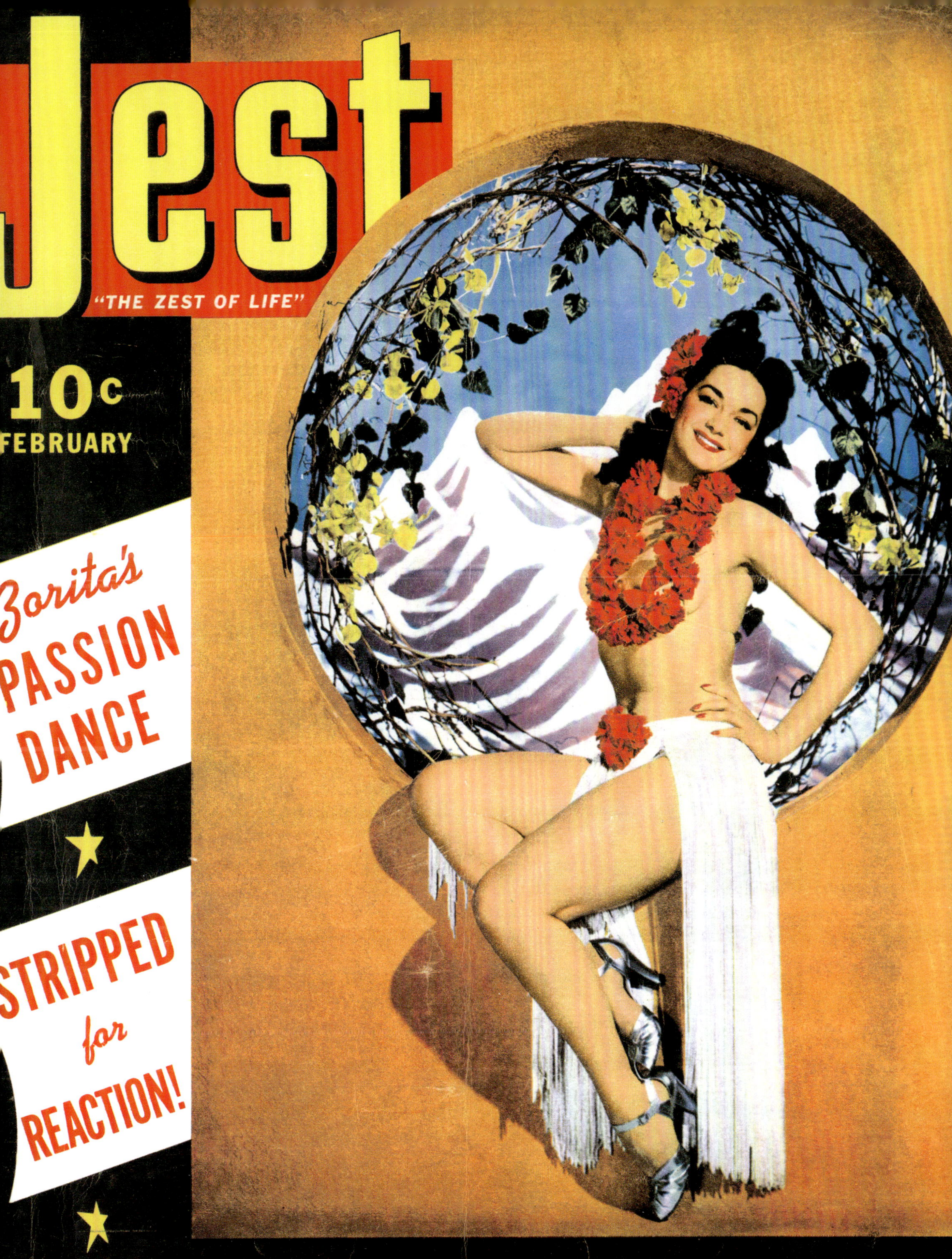
Jest
"THE ZEST OF LIFE"
10c
FEBRUARY
Zorita's
PASSION
DANCE
STRIPPED
for
REACTION!
Many SHOW GIRLS and CARTOONS

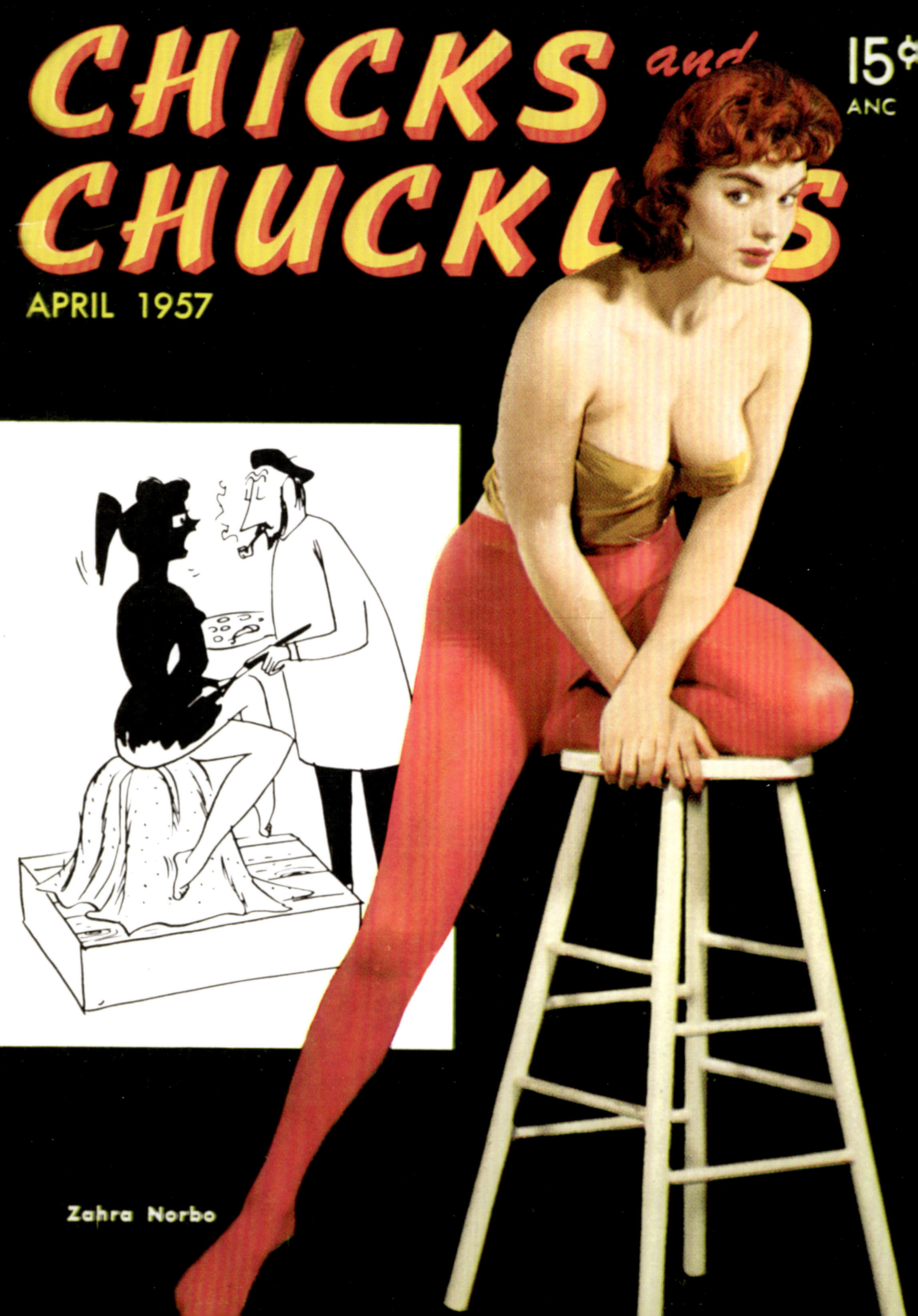
CHICKS and
CHUCKL S
15¢
ANC
APRIL 1957
Zahra Norbo

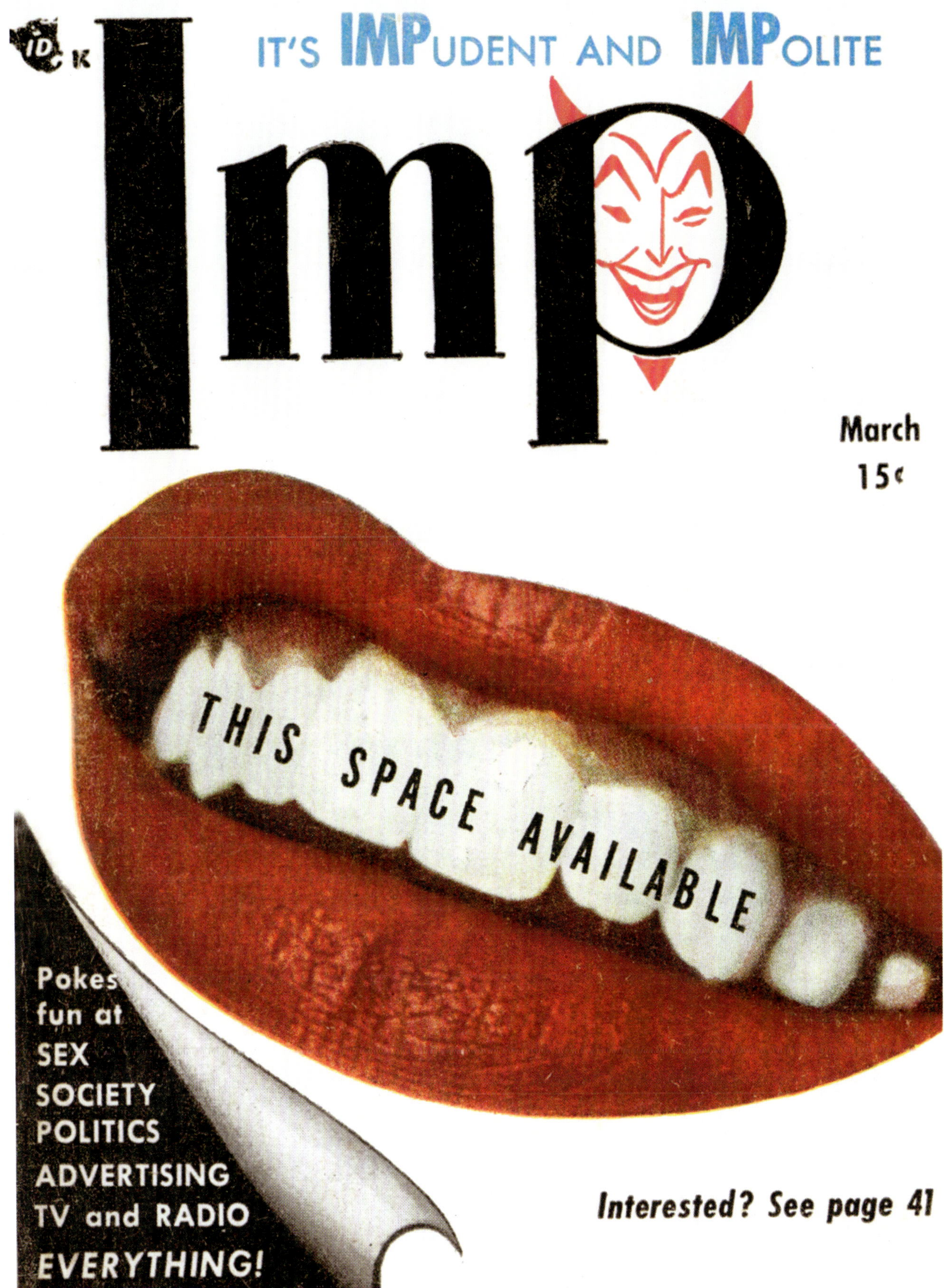

YEAR: **1950s**. TITLE: **Imp**. COUNTRY: **USA**.

YEAR: **1957**. TITLE: **Chicks and Chuckles**. COUNTRY: **USA**.

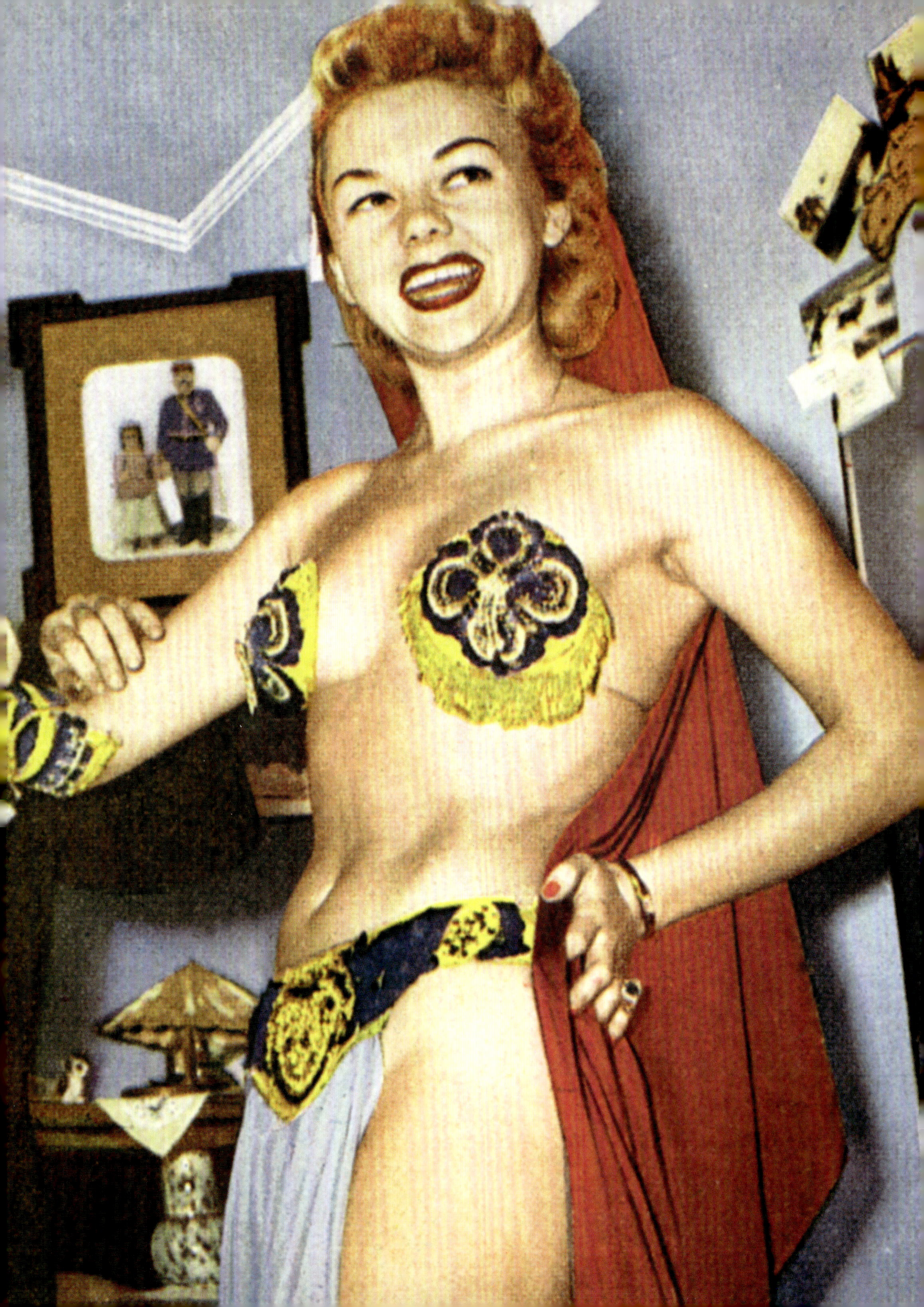

ATTABOY, ATATÜRK!:

The Turkish Anomaly

Schluss mit dem Fez!: Der türkische Sonderweg
Atatürk attaque ! : l'exception turque

The countries of the Middle East have a richly varied, ancient history. They have art, they have architecture, they have literature, music and cuisine. They do not, however, have men's magazines, with the single exception of Turkey. What makes this predominately Muslim nation different from its neighbors? Mustafa Kemal Atatürk.

It's said that Atatürk (which means Father of the Turks) was raised by a strong-willed mother. Following his father's death it was apparently she who infused young Mustafa with a love of Western culture and a burning desire to bring his countrymen into the modern age. He was no sissy, though. At the time of his birth in 1881 Turkey was part of the ancient Ottoman Empire. Mustafa was schooled at the national War Academy to serve the empire, and during World War I he served it with savage brilliance. It was

Under Atatürk women were granted the same rights as men and stopped wearing the veil.

YEAR: **1954**. TITLE: **Cennet Bahçesi**. COUNTRY: **Turkey**.

Die Länder des Nahen Ostens können auf eine lange, wechselhafte Geschichte zurückblicken. In Kunst, Architektur, Literatur, Musik und Kochkunst haben sie eine facettenreiche eigene Kultur entwickelt, doch Männermagazine sucht man bei ihnen vergebens, abgesehen von einer Ausnahme – der Türkei. Warum unterscheidet sich dieses vorwiegend muslimische Land in diesem Punkt von seinen Nachbarn? Verantwortlich dafür ist Mustafa Kemal Atatürk.

Es heißt, Atatürk („Vater der Türken") sei von einer eigensinnigen und willensstarken Mutter erzogen worden. Sie war es, die in dem jungen Mustafa nach dem Tode des Vaters die Liebe zur westlichen Kultur und den brennenden Wunsch weckte, seine Landsleute in die Moderne zu führen. Ein Muttersöhnchen war er jedoch nicht. 1881, zum Zeitpunkt seiner Geburt, war die Türkei noch Teil des alten osmanischen Reiches. Mustafa besuchte die staatliche Militärakademie und diente dem Reich im Ersten Weltkrieg mit militärischer Bravour. Unter seinem Kommando hielten die Türken die Halbinsel Gallipoli über acht blutige Monate, in denen an die 9000 australische Soldaten fielen. Mustafa soll es aber auch gewesen sein, der nach dem Krieg die ethnischen Säuberungen in der Türkei organisierte. Der Sultan war von ihm so angetan, dass er ihn zum General

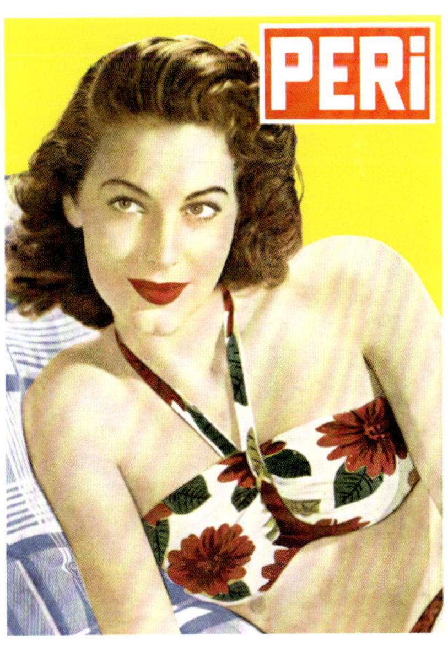

YEAR: **1950**. TITLE: **Peri**. COUNTRY: **Turkey**.

Les pays du Moyen Orient ont une histoire très ancienne, riche et variée. Ils ont l'art, l'architecture, la littérature, la musique, la gastronomie… En revanche, ils n'ont pas de magazines pour hommes, à l'exception de la Turquie. Qu'estce qui rend cette nation majoritairement musulmane différente de ses voisines ? Mustafa Kemal Atatürk.

On raconte qu'Atatürk (qui signifie «père des Turcs») fut élevé par une mère au caractère bien trempé. Après la mort de son père, c'est apparemment elle qui inculqua à son fils l'amour de la culture

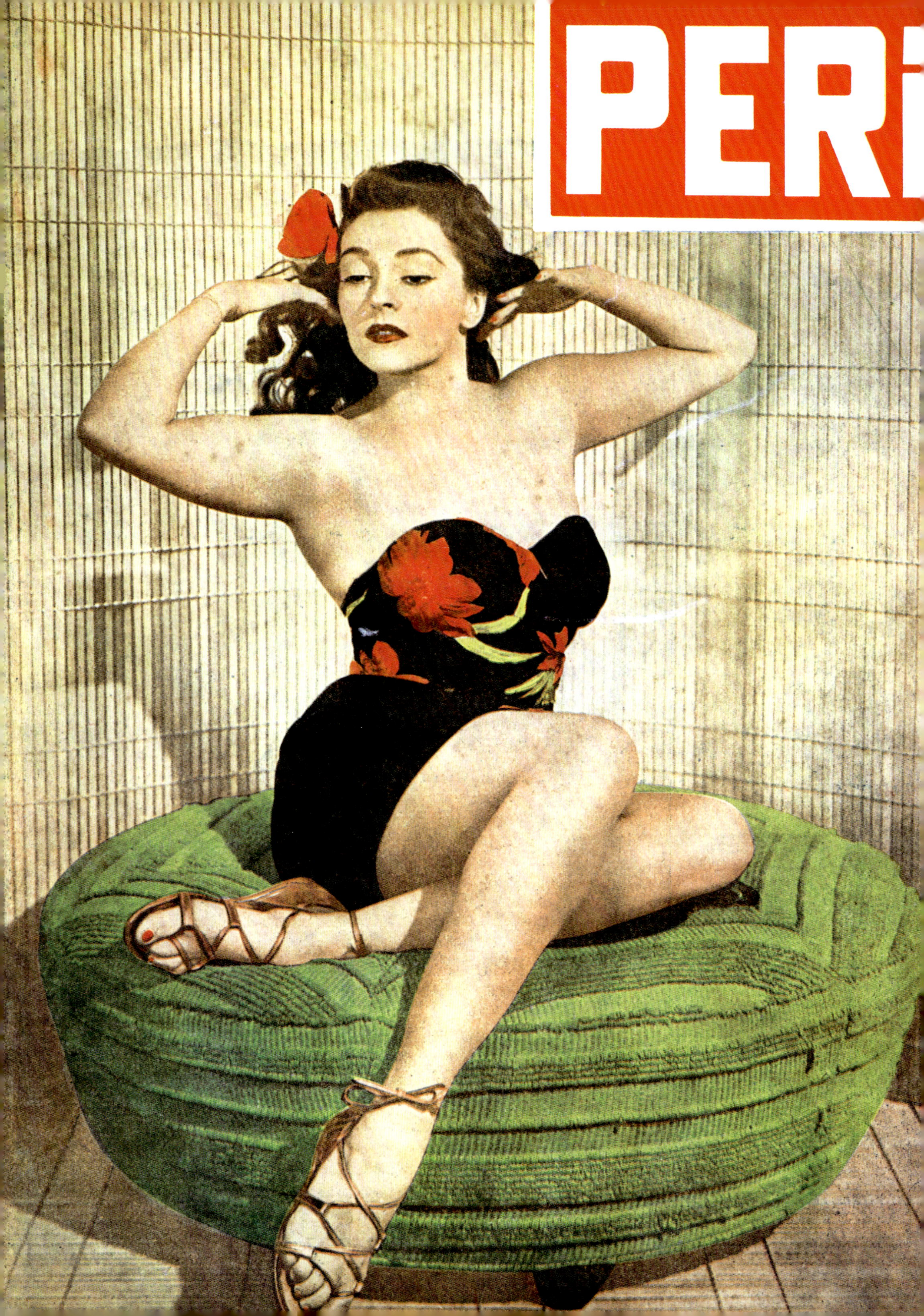
PER

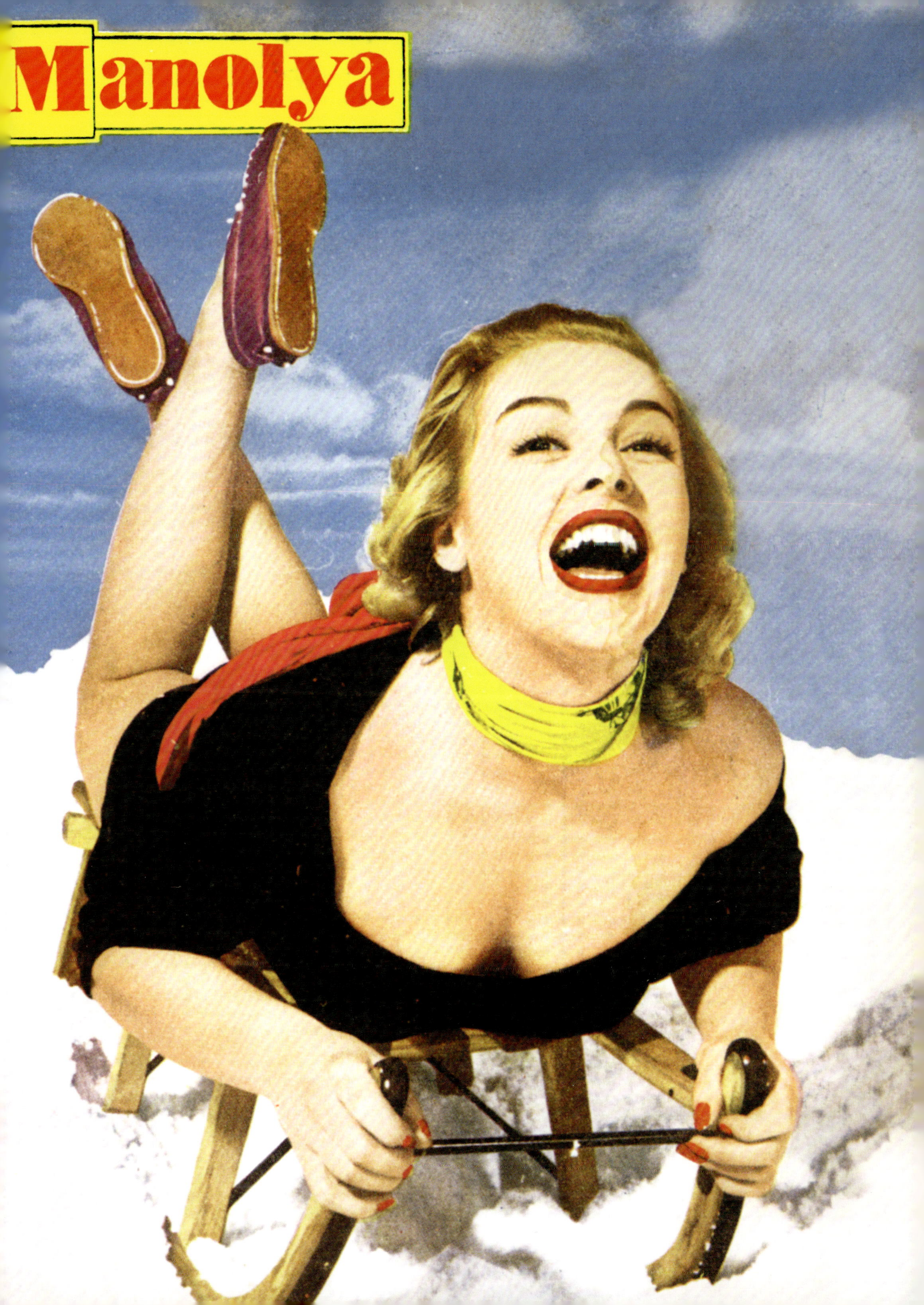
Manolya

Pages 280 & 281:
Year: **1949**. Title: **Peri**. Country: **Turkey**.
Year: **1955**. Title: **Manolya**. Country: **Turkey**.

Right:
Year: **1954**. Title: **Cennet**. Country: **Turkey**.

It is not good to live as a consumer. Let's be a producer.

—Mustafa Kemal Atatürk

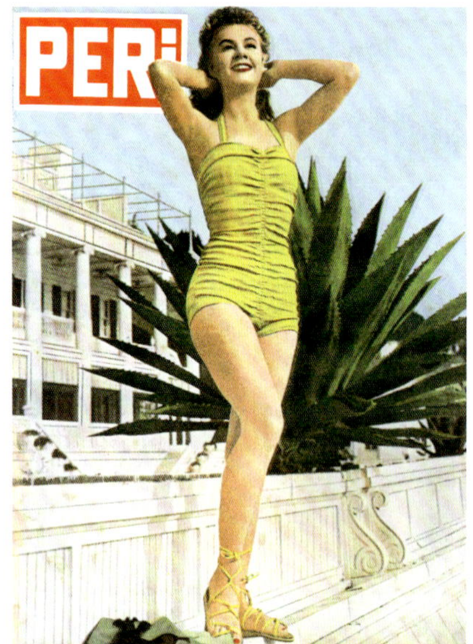

Year: **1950**. Title: **Peri**.
Country: **Turkey**.

he who successfully defended Gallipoli for eight bloody months, his troupes killing nearly nine thousand Australian soldiers before the end. It was also reputedly he who organized Turkey's ethnic cleansing after the war. The Sultan was so pleased he promoted Mustafa to the rank of General and declared him a national hero. Mustafa responded by gathering his own army and using everything he'd learned fighting for the Ottomans to defeat them. It took only four years for Mustafa Kemal to end seven centuries of Ottoman rule. On October 29th, 1923 Turkey was declared a sovereign republic, with Mustafa, now bearing the surname Atatürk, as its president.

From that day until his death in 1938 Atatürk pushed relentlessly to reform and modernize the new country. With all his battles won, he advocated peace. Religious laws were abolished; women

und Helden der Nation ernannte. Mustafa dankte es ihm, indem er seine eigene Armee aufstellte und seine im Dienste der Osmanen gesammelten Erfahrungen dazu einsetzte, ihre Herrschaft zu bekämpfen. Er brauchte nur vier Jahre, um sieben Jahrhunderte osmanischer Vorherrschaft zu beenden. Am 29. Oktober 1923 wurde die Türkei eine Republik, und Mustafa, nun mit dem Beinamen Atatürk, ihr erster Präsident.

Von diesem Tag bis zu seinem Tod 1938 betrieb Atatürk energisch die Reformierung und Modernisierung des neuen Staates. Als siegreicher Held trat er nun für Frieden ein, er trennte Staat und Religion, setzte die Gleichstellung der Frau durch, Arme erhielten die gleichen Rechte wie die Reichen, der Fez, die traditionelle Kopfbedeckung, wich westlicher Hutmode, der Schleierzwang für Frauen fiel, und der islamische Kalender wurde durch den westlichen ersetzt. Selbst die Sprache änderte Atatürk: Die lateinischen Buchstaben lösten die arabische Schrift ab.

Die darstellende Kunst, von den Osmanen, die die Abbildung des menschlichen Körpers für Gotteslästerung hielten, unterdrückt, wurde von Atatürk mit Nachdruck gefördert. Museen wurden eröffnet, neue Bauten in Auftrag gegeben, und man erfreute sich an westlicher Musik, Oper, Ballett und Theater. Mit der Übernahme der neuen Sprache erlebten auch die Printmedien einen Aufschwung. Besonders populär waren Filmzeitschriften, die neben den Stars des jungen türkischen Films auch exotische europäische und amerikanische Schauspielerinnen in vergleichsweise freizügiger westlicher Kleidung präsentierten. Wie in Deutschland, Frankreich

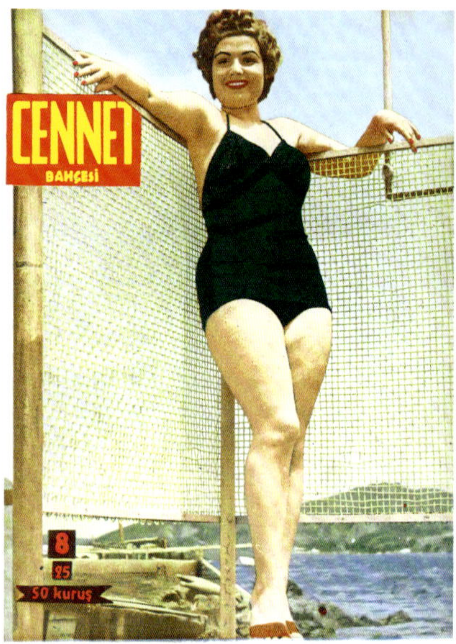

Year: **1954**. Title: **Cennet Bahçesi**.
Country: **Turkey**.

occidentale et le désir ardent d'entraîner ses concitoyens dans la modernité. Ne croyez pas pour autant qu'elle en fit un fils à Maman. À l'époque de sa naissance, en 1881, la Turquie faisait partie de l'Empire Ottoman. Mustafa fit ses études à l'académie militaire nationale afin de servir l'empire, qu'il défendit brillamment et farouchement au cours de la Première Guerre mondiale. Il défendit avec succès Gallipoli pendant huit mois sanglants, ses troupes tuant près de neuf mille soldats australiens. Il est également connu pour avoir organisé l'épuration ethnique de la Turquie après la guerre. Le sultan était tellement content de ses services qu'il le promut général et le déclara héros national. Mustafa le remercia en rassemblant sa propre armée et en utilisant tout ce que lui avaient appris les Ottomans pour les éliminer. Il ne lui fallut que quatre ans pour mettre fin

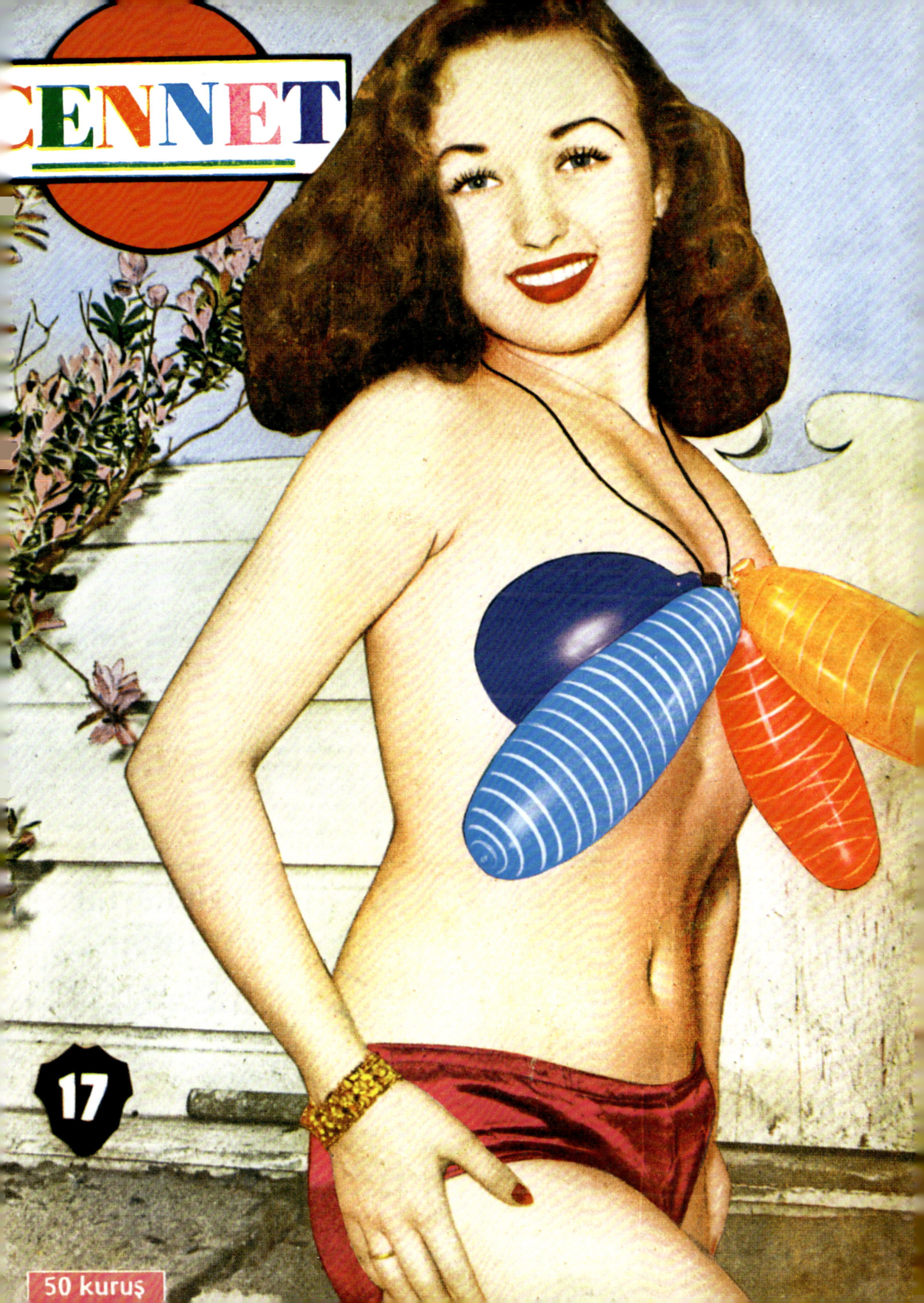
CENNET
17
50 kuruş

APAŞ SEVERDE DÖVERDE

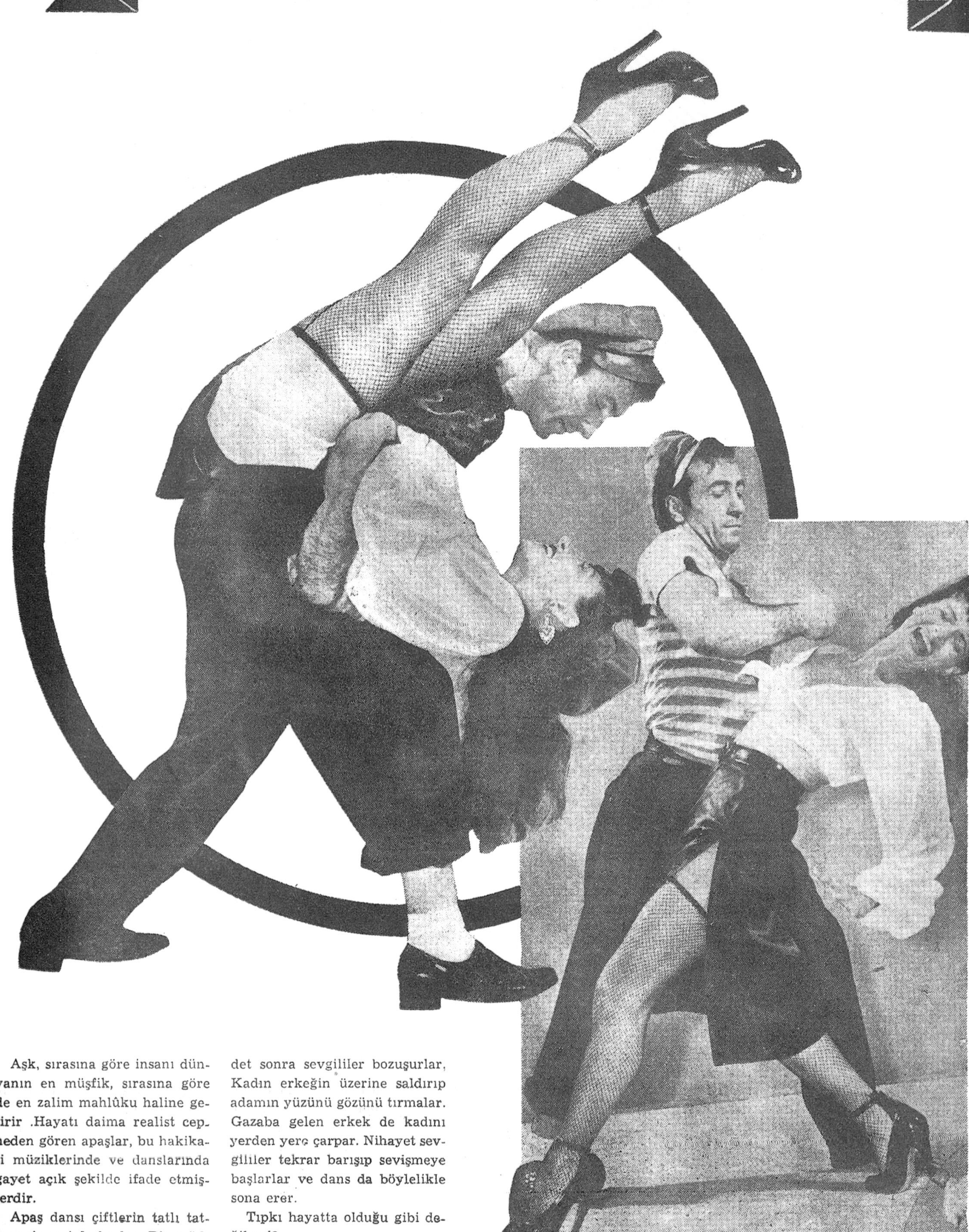

Aşk, sırasına göre insanı dünyanın en müşfik, sırasına göre de en zalim mahlûku haline getirir .Hayatı daima realist cepheden gören apaşlar, bu hakikati müziklerinde ve danslarında gayet açık şekilde ifade etmişlerdir.

Apaş dansı çiftlerin tatlı tatlı sevişmesiyle başlar. Bir müddet sonra sevgililer bozuşurlar, Kadın erkeğin üzerine saldırıp adamın yüzünü gözünü tırmalar. Gazaba gelen erkek de kadını yerden yere çarpar. Nihayet sevgililer tekrar barışıp sevişmeye başlarlar ve dans da böylelikle sona erer.

Tıpkı hayatta olduğu gibi değil mi?

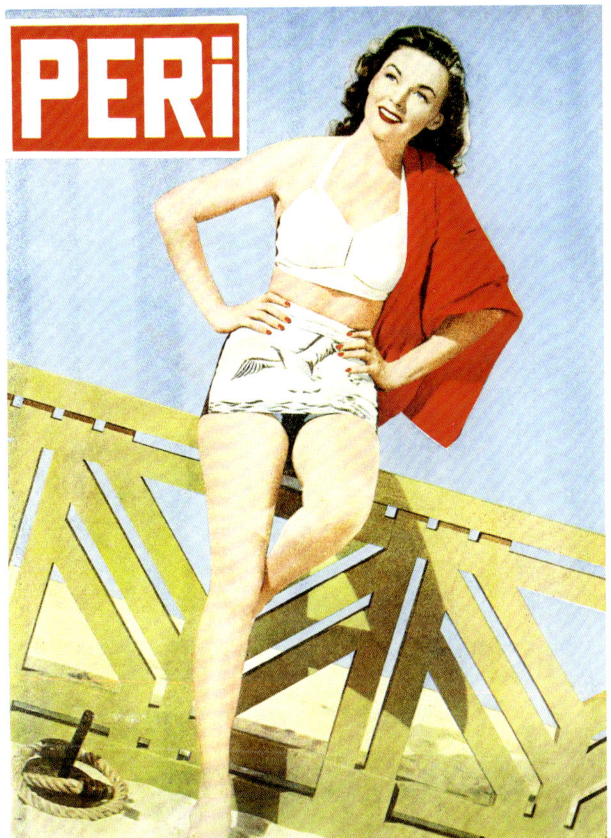

Year: **1950**. Title: **Peri**. Country: **Turkey**.

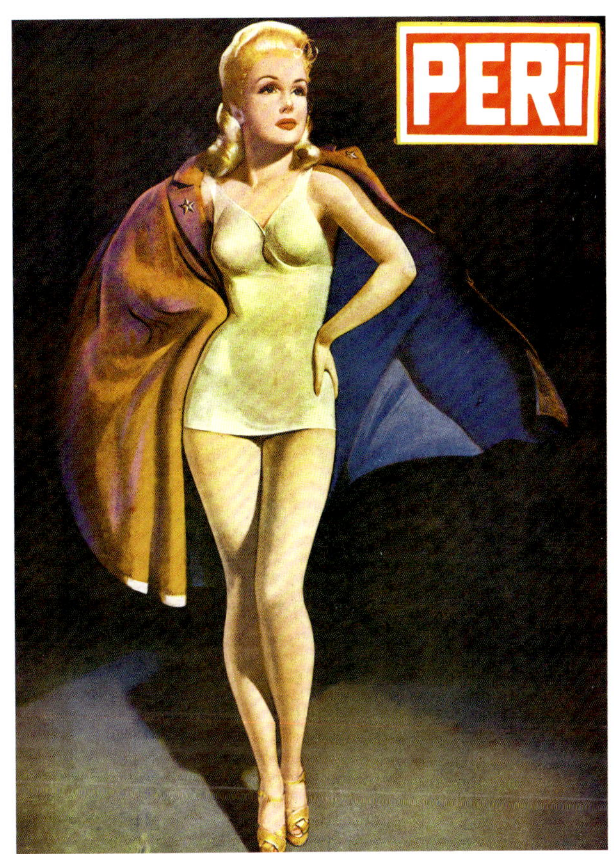

Year: **1951**. Title: **Peri**. Country: **Turkey**.

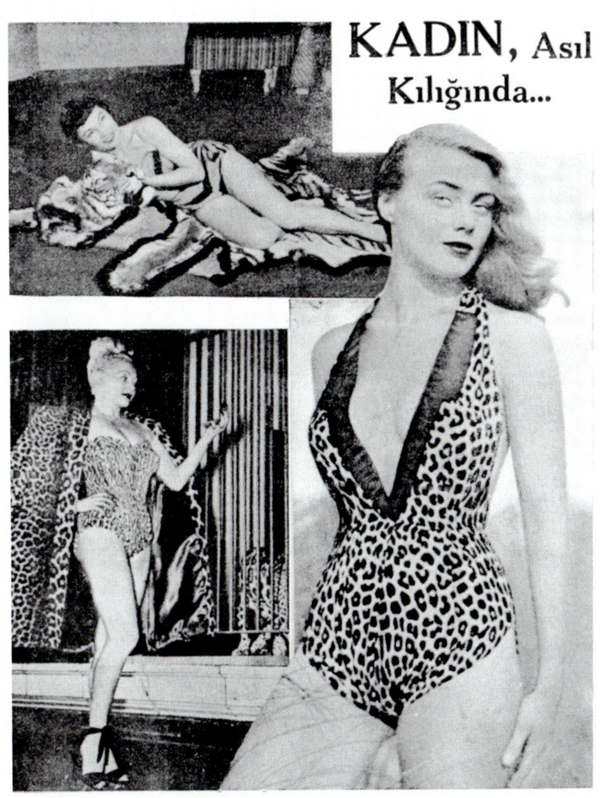

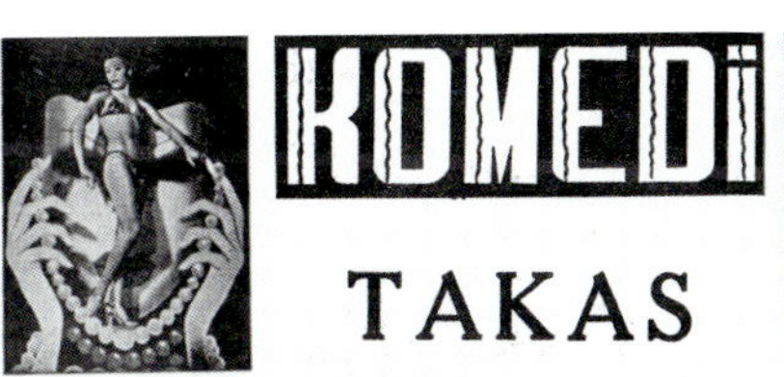

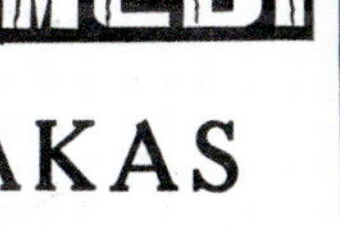

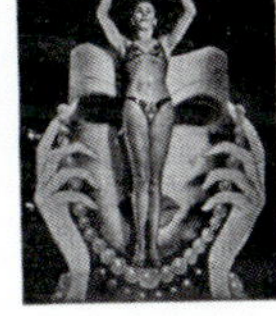

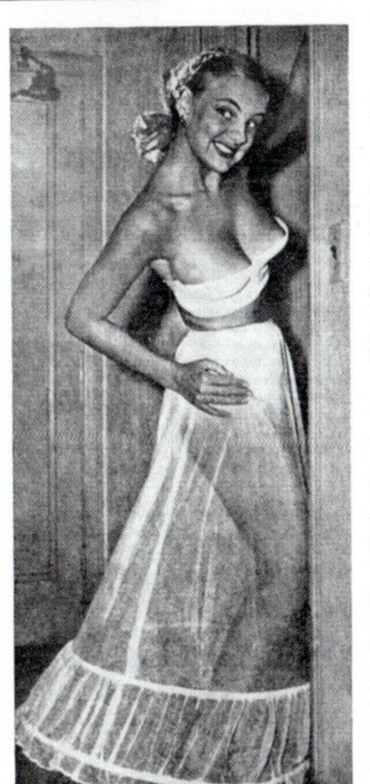

Odadan çıkarken, şöyle bir güldü.

Şahıslar:

Sarışın güzel kadın
Yakışıklı koca
Esmer güzel kadın
Esmer kadının kocası
(Vak'a meçhul bir zamanda ve meçhul bir diyarda geçer)

— Birinci perde —

Sarışın güzel — Bu akşam ne yapacaksın?

Yakışıklı koca — Hiiiç! Evde oturup dinleneceğim; çok yorgunum!

Sarışın güzel — Tabii münasebetsiz bir misafir gelmezse...

Yakışıklı koca — A... Ona ne şüphe. Traşçının biri damlarsa vallahi kaçarım!

Sarışın güzel — Ayol, ağzını hayra açsana, bak kapı çalınıyor!

— İkinci perde —

Yakışıklı koca — Bak kim geldi!

Esmer kadının kocası — Nasılsınız hanımefendi?

Sarışın güzel — (Soğuk) Teşekkür ederim. Hoş geldiniz, buyurun!

Yakışıklı koca — (Öbür odaya geçerken, karısına) Biraz gelsene! (Misafire) Kahve nasıl olsun?

— Üçüncü perde —

Yakışıklı koca — Nedir bu münasebetsizlik?

Sarışın güzel — Ayol, ben davet etmedim ya miskin herifi? Soğuk mendebur...

Yakışıklı koca — A... Vallahi giderim, billâhi giderim. Şimdi sözüm olduğu için çıkmak zorunda kaldığımı söyler, özür dilerim...

Sarışın güzel — Deli misin sen? Ben patlarım bu soğuk neva ile...

Yakışıklı koca — Fena mı? Oturmaz kerata, defolur, gider...

— Dördüncü perde —

Yakışıklı koca — Sakın kusura bakmayın... Geleceğinizi evvelden bilmediğim için verilmiş bir sözüm var, mutlaka gitmem lâzım...

Esmer kadının kocası — (Kalkarak) A, ben de gideyim öyleyse, beraber çıkarız...

Yakışıklı koca — Karım evde canım, biraz dinlenin, rica ederim...

Sarışın güzel — A, tabii, hemen gitmek olur mu?

— Beşinci perde —

Esmer kadının kocası — Canım...

Sarışın güzel — Şekerim...

Esmer kadının kocası — Nasıl becerdin ?Nasıl atlattın?

Sarışın güzel — Kadın ne ister de elde etmez? Senin aleyhinde attım tuttum, ne traşçılığın kaldı, ne soğuk nevalığın!

Esmer kadının kocası — Hah hah hay! Yamansın kâfir... Çabuk döner mi?

Sarışın güzel — Zannetmem. Ama ihtiyatlı olalım. Döndüğü zaman seni burada bulmamalı. Hadi gel...

— Altıncı perde —

Esmer güzeli — Sen misin canımın içi?

Yakışıklı koca — Tabii.

Esmer güzeli — Karını nasıl atlattın kuzum?

Yakışıklı koca — Traşçının biri geldi. Bahane ettim, kaçtım.

Esmer güzeli — Ama, bize iyiliği dokunmuş işte. Kim o sersem?

Yakışıklı koca — Kim olacak, kocan!

Esmer güzeli — Hah hah hay! Çabuk dönmese bari...

Yakışıklı koca — Merak etme. Erken dönmiyeceğimi bildiği için bizimki onu bir müddet oyalar. Nazik kadındır...

Esmer güzeli — Doğrusu becerikli adamsın! Hayatım benim!

(Kollarına atılırken perde iner)

Year: **1950**. Title: **Peri**. Country: **Turkey**.

Year: **1949**. Title: **Peri**. Country: **Turkey**.

Year: **1949**. Title: **Peri**. Country: **Turkey**.

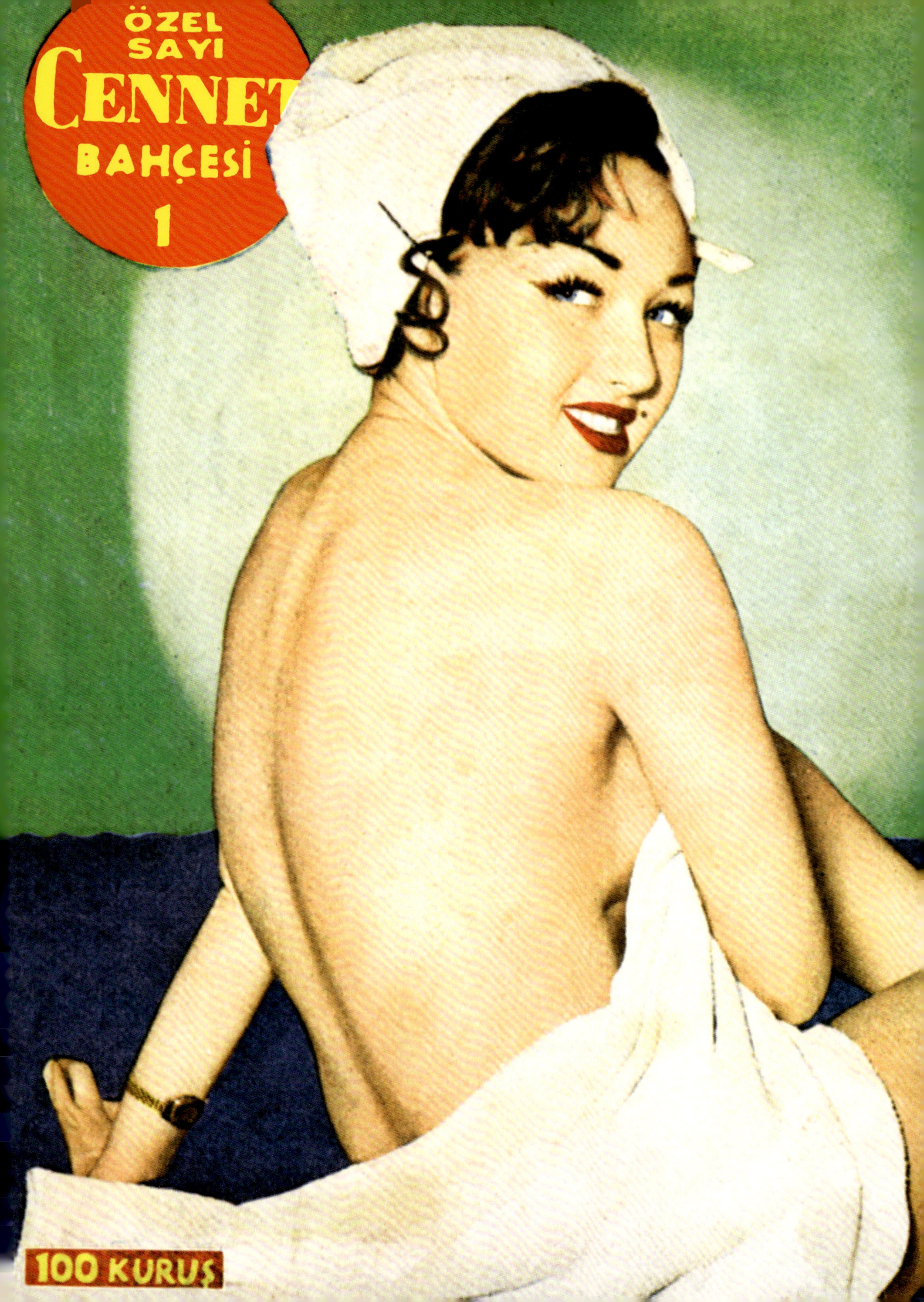
ÖZEL SAYI
CENNET BAHÇESİ
1
100 KURUŞ

Year: **1954**. Title: **Cennet Bahçesi**.
Country: **Turkey**.

Film magazines strayed, adding unknown starlets, chorus girls and models dressed even more provocatively than the foreign actresses.

were granted the same rights as men, peasants the same rights as the wealthy; European hats replaced the fez; women stopped wearing the veil; the Islamic calendar gave way to the Western calendar. Even the language was changed, with the Latin alphabet replacing Arabic script.

The visual arts, suppressed by the Ottomans who believed that depictions of the human form constituted idolatry, were strongly encouraged by Atatürk. Museums were opened, architecture commissioned, Western music, opera, ballet and theater enjoyed. And with the adoption of the new language, book and magazine production boomed. Movie magazines were especially popular, and featured not only the stars of the fledgling Turkish cinema, but exotic European and American actresses in comparatively skimpy Western dress. Then, as happened in Germany, France and the US, some film magazines strayed further, adding unknown starlets, chorus girls and models dressed even more provocatively than the foreign actresses. Step by careful step these magazines kept shifting the balance, until one day Turkey became the only country with a 99% Muslim population producing genuine men's magazines. Admittedly, what you see here are very tame men's magazines, but with the exception of *Pleypoy*, an unsanctioned *Playboy* knock-off from the seventies, all were made between 1949 and 1955 when men's magazines were pretty tame everywhere. *Pleypoy* shows how things progressed, kind of like Turkey's take on the sexual revolution. Basically, the publisher got hold of some American men's magazines, mimeographed the pages, then doodled in the necessary censorship—much the same

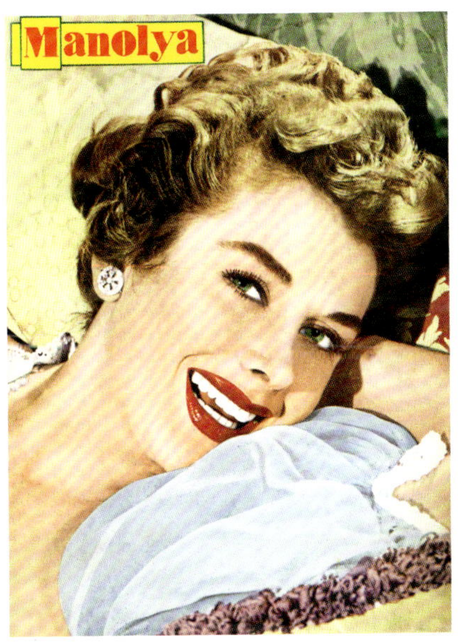

Year: **1955**. Title: **Manolya**. Country: **Turkey**.

und den USA wurden einige dieser Zeitschriften immer kesser und zeigten auch Starlets, Tänzerinnen und Models in noch gewagterer Garderobe. Peu à peu ließen diese Blätter die Hüllen fallen, bis die Türkei das einzige muslimische Land war, das eigene Männermagazine produzierte. Zugegeben, unsere Beispiele hier sind recht brav, aber mit Ausnahme des *Pleypoy*, einem *Playboy*-Plagiat aus den Siebzigern, stammen alle abgebildeten Hefte aus der Zeit zwischen 1949 und 1955, und zu dieser Zeit waren die Männermagazine überall auf der Welt sehr brav. *Pleypoy*, sozusagen die türkische Version der sexuellen Revolution, zeigt, wohin die Entwicklung ging. Im Grunde hat da ein Verleger ein paar amerikanische Männermagazine genommen, den Inhalt kopiert und dann die notwendigen Zensurbalken reingesetzt – ziemlich so wie es die amerikanischen Hippies Mitte der Siebziger bei ihren Magazinen

à sept siècles de domination ottomane. Le 29 octobre 1923, la Turquie fut déclarée république souveraine avec, comme président, Mustafa, désormais surnommé Atatürk.

De ce jour à sa mort en 1938, Atatürk ne cessa de réformer et de moderniser le nouveau pays. Après avoir remporté tant de batailles, il devint un chantre de la paix. Les lois religieuses furent abolies ; les femmes obtinrent les mêmes droits que les hommes ; les paysans les mêmes droits que les riches ; le fez céda la place aux chapeaux européens ; les femmes cessèrent de porter le voile ; le calendrier islamique fut remplacé par le calendrier occidental. Même la langue fut changée, l'alphabet latin se substituant à l'arabe.

Les arts visuels, étouffés par les Ottomans qui considéraient que la représentation de la forme humaine constituait une idolâtrie, furent fortement encouragés par Atatürk. On ouvrit des musées, on commanda des bâtiments publics, on se pressa aux concerts de musique occidentale, à l'opéra, au ballet et au théâtre. Avec l'adoption du nouveau langage, la production de livres et de magazines grimpa en flèche. Les revues de cinéma étaient particulièrement populaires et montraient, outre les vedettes de l'industrie cinématographique turque naissante, des actrices exotiques européennes et américaines dans des tenues comparativement plus légères. Puis, comme en Allemagne, en France et aux États-Unis, certains magazines de cinéma allèrent plus loin, ajoutant des starlettes inconnues, des girls de revue et des modèles vêtues de manière encore plus provocante que les actrices occidentales. Prudemment mais sûrement, ces publications commencèrent

What you see are very tame men's magazines, with the exception of *Pleypoy*, an unsanctioned *Playboy* knock-off from the seventies.

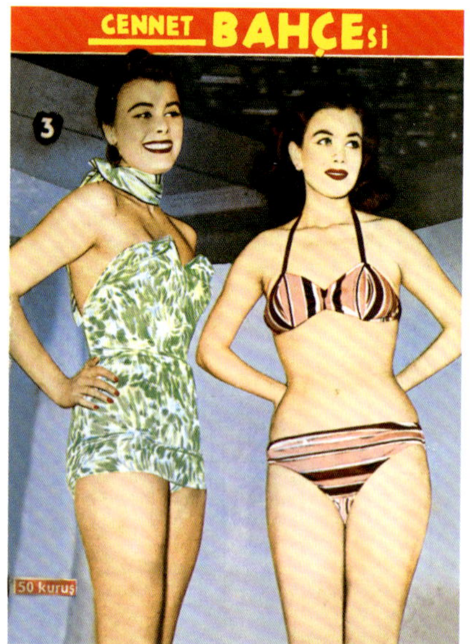

Year: **1954**. Title: **Cennet Bahçesi**. Country: **Turkey**.

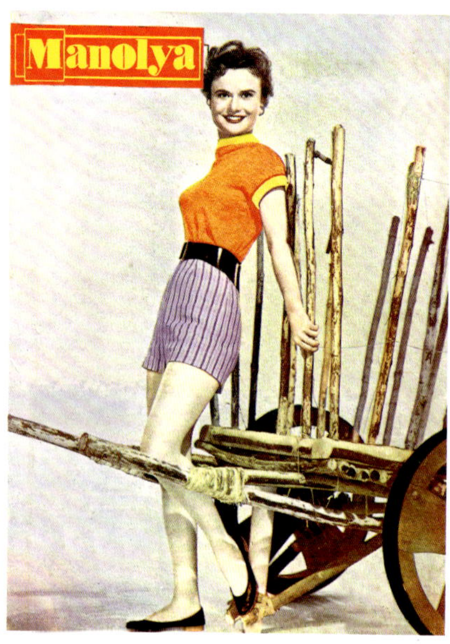

Year: **1955**. Title: **Manolya**. Country: **Turkey**.

technique used by American hippies to make their "reader written" pornography in the mid-seventies.

In postscript I wish to make it clear that there is no evidence personally linking Mustafa Kemal Atatürk to men's magazines, as a publisher, supporter or consumer. According to his biographers, Irfan and Margaret Orga, "He has never loved a woman. He was used to the camaraderie of the Mess, the craze for handsome young men, [and] fleeting contacts with prostitutes..." With all that going on, who needs tame pleasures like *Peri*?

mit „von Lesern eingesandter" Pornografie machten.

Abschließend möchte ich jedoch betonen, dass es keinerlei Anlass gibt, Mustafa Kemal Atatürk mit Männermagazinen in Verbindung zu bringen, sei es als ihr Verleger, Befürworter oder Konsument. Seinen Biografen Irfan und Margaret Orga zufolge, hat er nie eine Frau geliebt. „Er bevorzugte die Kameraderie des Offizierskasinos, hübsche junge Männer und flüchtige Kontakte zu Prostituierten ..." Wer braucht bei so viel Entertainment schon so biedere Reize, wie sie *Peri* bietet?

à inverser la balance, jusqu'à ce que la Turquie devienne le seul pays avec une population à 99% musulmane à produire de vrais magazines masculins. Certes, ce que vous voyez ici vous paraîtra bien sage mais, à l'exception de *Pleypoy*, un ersatz non autorisé de *Playboy* des années 70, ils furent tous réalisés entre 1949 et 1955, à une époque où les magazines pour hommes étaient assez chastes partout dans le monde. *Pleypoy* illustre bien l'évolution des mœurs, sorte de vision turque de la révolution sexuelle. En gros, son éditeur prenait des magazines pour hommes américains, polycopiait les images, puis gribouillait par-dessus la censure nécessaire, plus ou moins la même technique que celle utilisée par les hippies américains pour produire leur publications pornographiques « réalisés par les lecteurs » au milieu des années 70.

En guise de conclusion, je voudrais ajouter que rien n'indique que Mustafa Kemal Atatürk ait eu le moindre lien avec la presse masculine, que ce soit en tant qu'éditeur, promoteur ou consommateur. Selon ses biographes, Orfan et Margaret Orga : « Il n'a jamais aimé une femme. Il était habitué à la camaraderie du mess, à la proximité de beaux jeunes hommes (et) aux contacts éphémères avec des prostituées ». Dans un tel contexte, les pages de *Peri* devaient lui paraître bien fades !

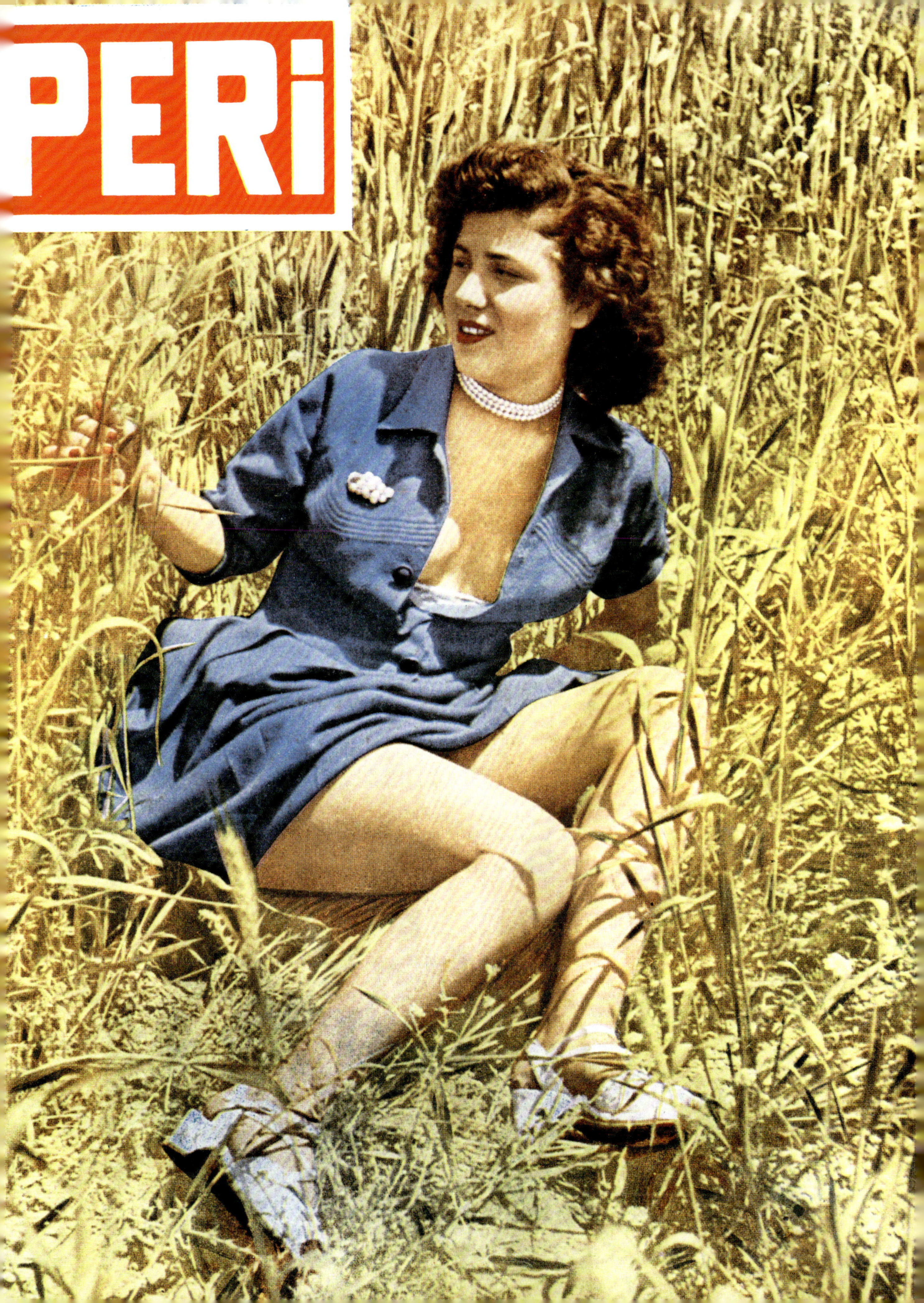
PERi

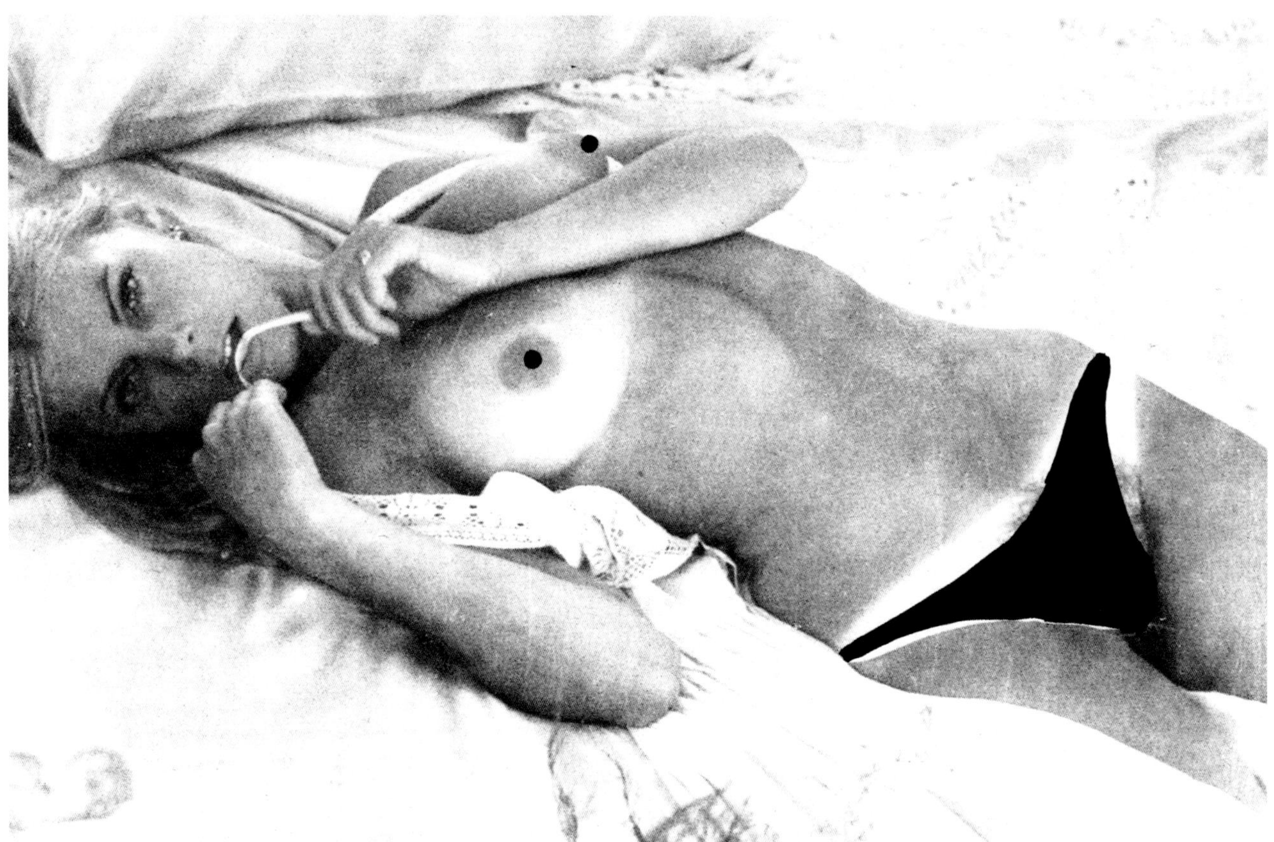

Year: **1970s**. Title: **Pleypoy**. Country: **Turkey**.

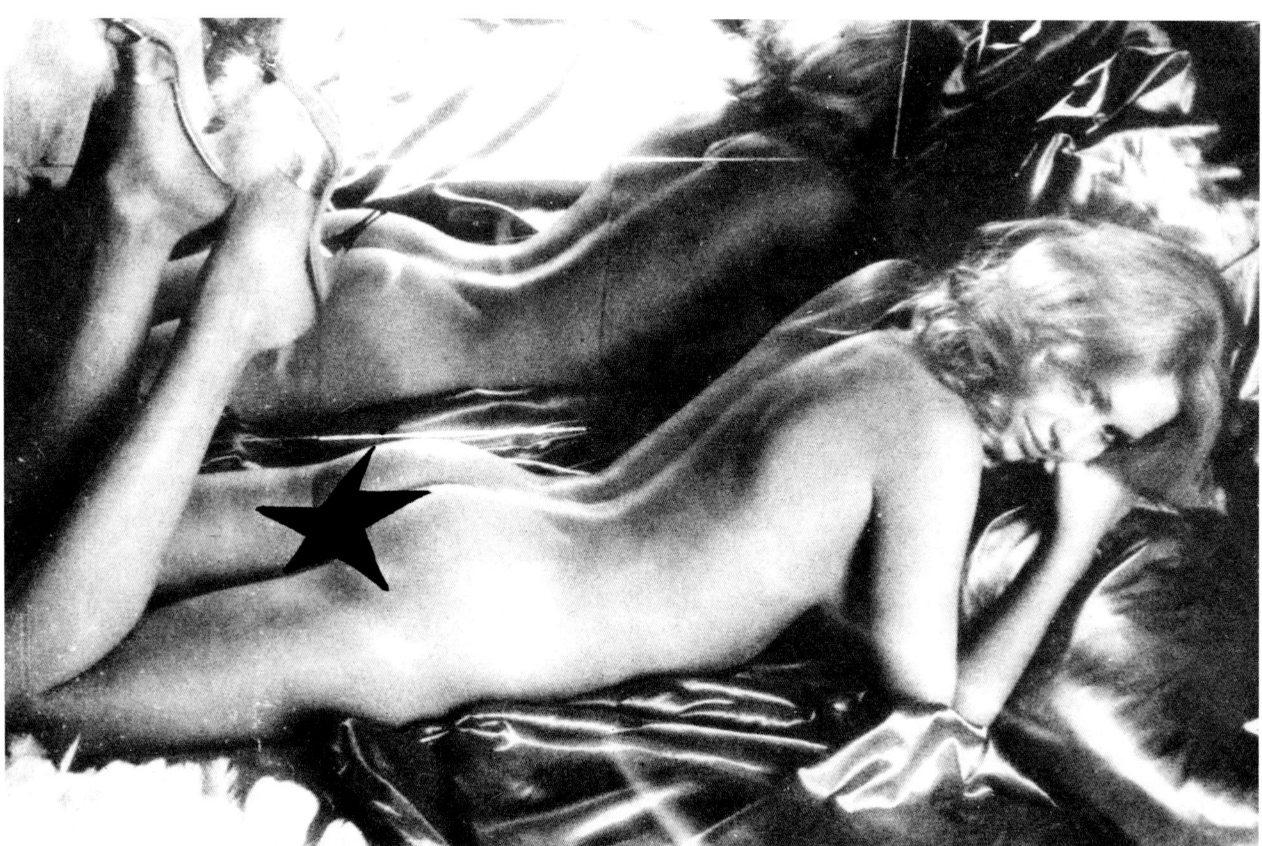

Year: **1970s**. Title: **Pleypoy**. Country: **Turkey**.

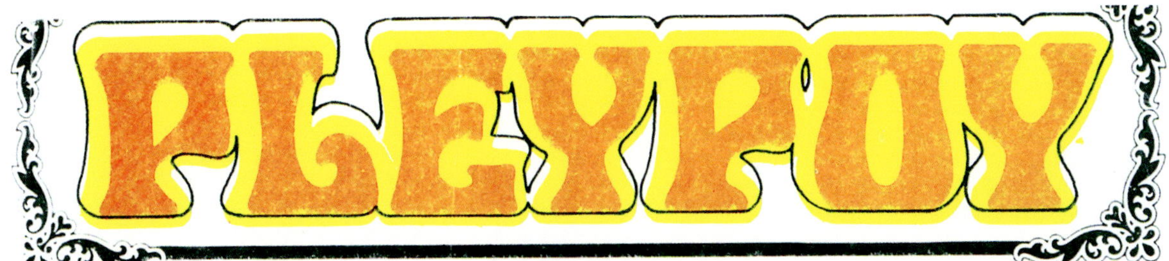

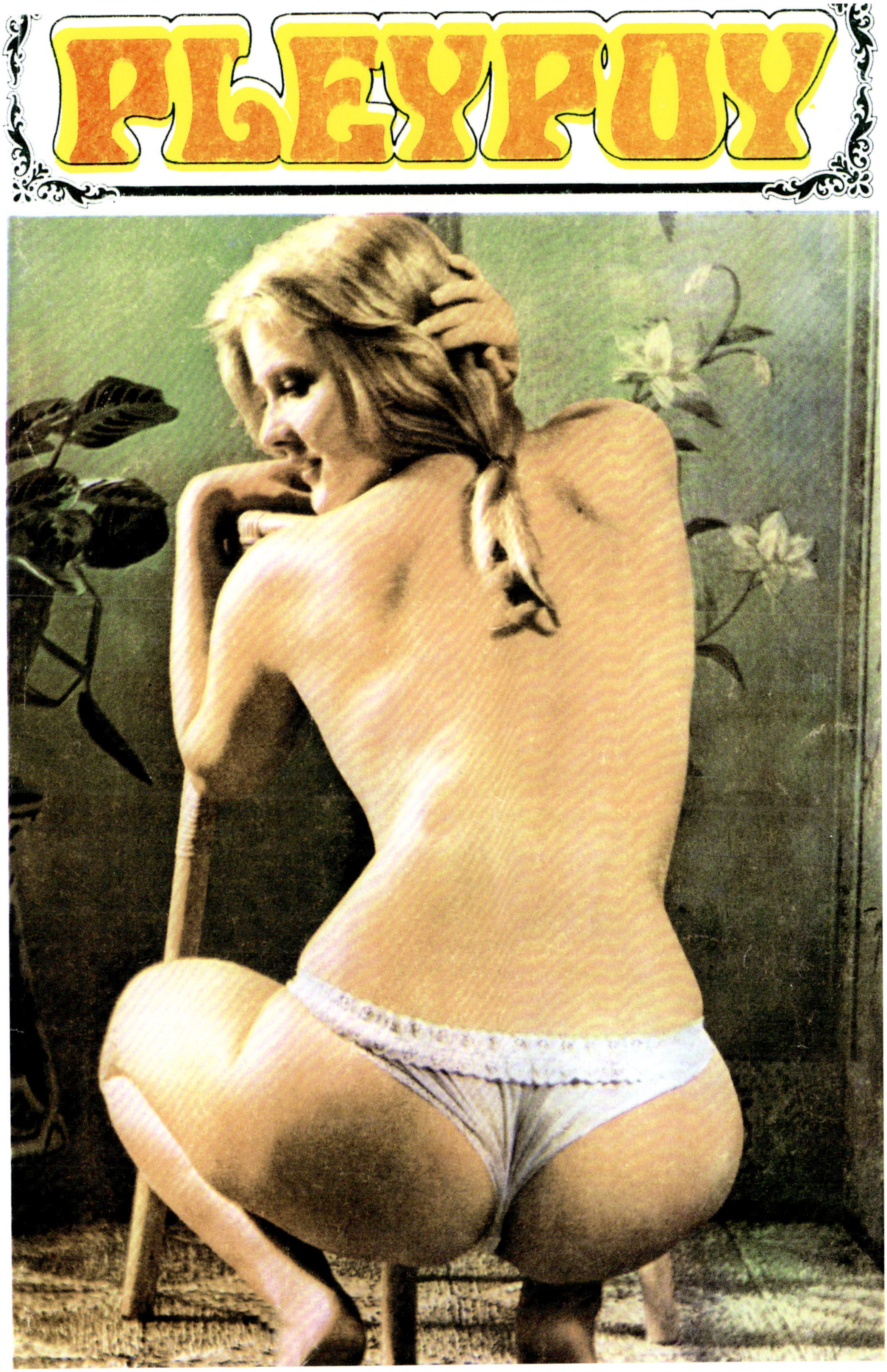

Year: **1970s**. Title: **Pleypoy**. Country: **Turkey**.

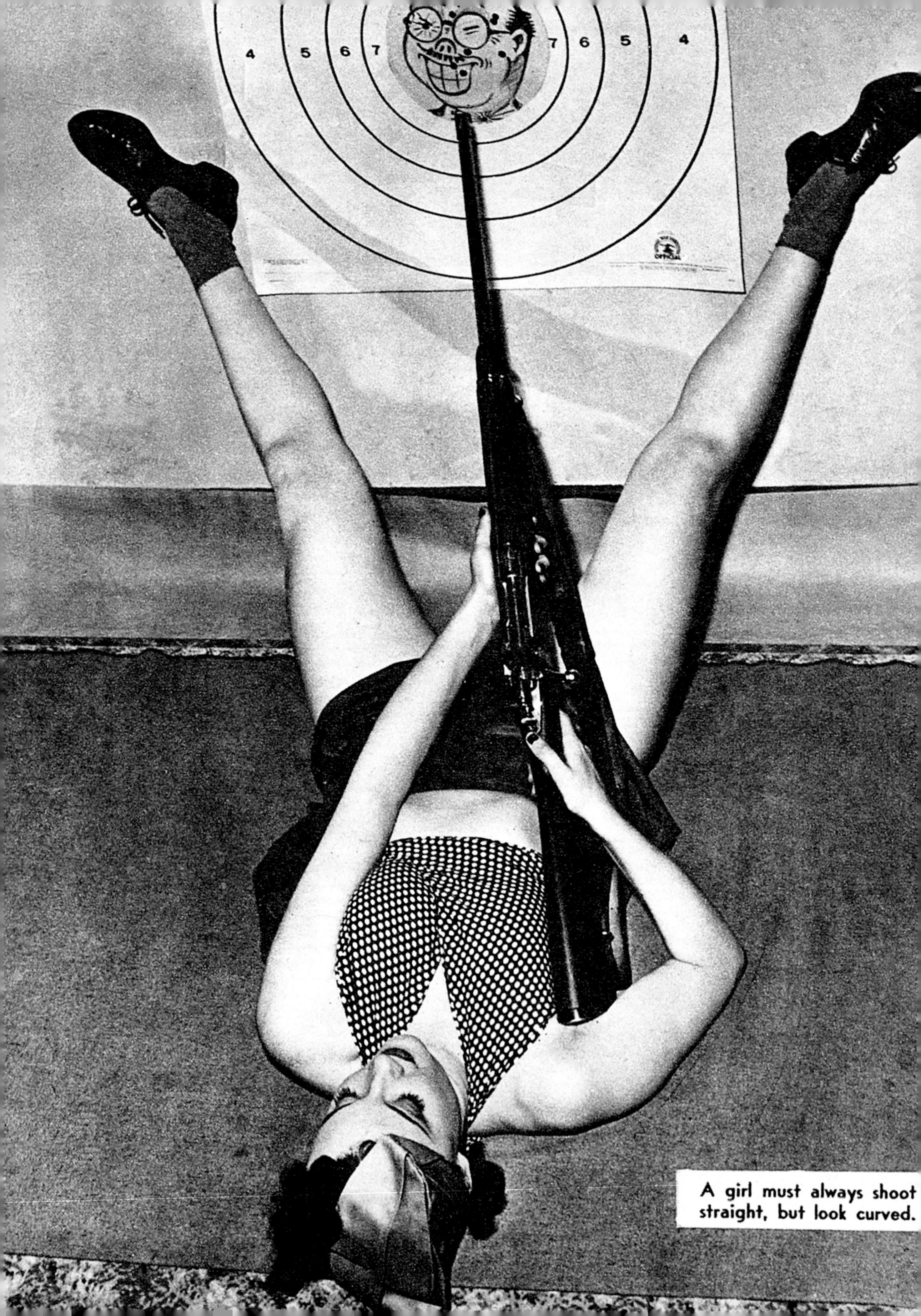

A girl must always shoot straight, but look curved.

PATRIOTICA:

Meeting the Needs of Men at War

Patriotika: Was der Mann im Felde braucht

L'érotisme patriote : Comment satisfaire les besoins des hommes en temps de guerre

Following liberal advances in the 20s and 30s American sex publishing took a giant leap backward in the 1940s. Gone were the artful nude starlets and eugenics' models, away went the *Spicy* stories and saucy French nudes; Patriotica was the wave of the 40s: apple-cheeked good girls in modest swimsuits a boy could be proud to hang over his army cot. Even *Gay Book,* with its sophisticated sheer lingerie shots and near naked breasts back in 1937, backed off to bathing suits by 1942. *Carnival* (combined with *Show*) was more daring, allowing nude backs with hints of breast, but for most magazines the formula was cartoons—often military-themed—and a new style of slapstick photo story predicated on the difficulties girls had doing simple tasks with their men away at war. The models were "showgirls" now instead of

Men needed sex, but didn't want any reminders that their wives and girlfriends back home might need the same.

Nach Liberalisierungen in den zwanziger und dreißiger Jahren erlebte das Geschäft mit Männermagazinen in den Vierzigern einen herben Rückschlag. Die kunstvoll ins Bild gesetzten nackten Starlets und die Eugenik-Models waren verschwunden, ebenso die schlüpfrigen Stories und gewagten Aktfotos aus Frankreich; in den Vierzigern gab man sich ganz patriotisch und präsentierte brave Mädchen mit roten Apfelbäckchen in sittsamen Badeanzügen, Bilder, die jeder Junge mit Stolz über sein Feldbett hängen konnte. Selbst *Gay Book*, das 1937 noch raffinierte Fotos von Mädchen in hauchdünnen Dessous und halbnackte Brüste gezeigte hat, machte einen Rückzieher und brachte nun brave Badeanzüge. *Carnival* (vereinigt mit *Show*) war da schon mutiger und wagte sich an Rückenakte mit dezent angedeutetem Busen heran, doch die meisten Magazine setzten auf Cartoons – oft mit militärischen Themen – und eine neue Sorte von Slapstick-Fotostories, in denen zu sehen war, welche Schwierigkeiten die Mädchen daheim selbst bei den einfachsten Aufgaben hatten, während ihre Männer fort waren. Die Models waren nun „Showgirls" und nicht mehr Stripperinnen, hübsche Brünette statt sexy Blondinen, und der Subtext war stets dazu angetan, die Moral „unserer Jungs" zu stärken. *Stocking Parade* vom April 1943

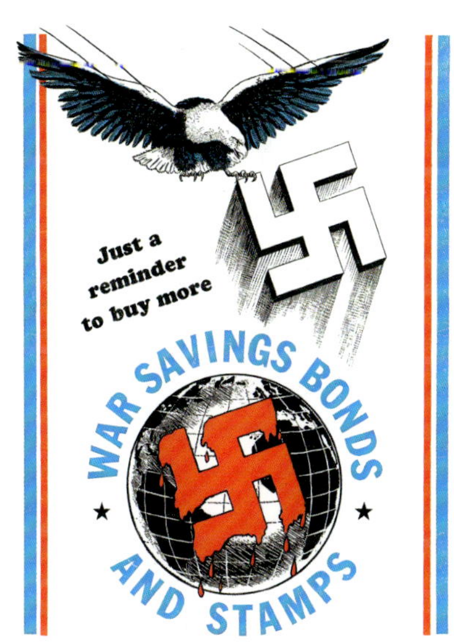

YEAR: **1942**. TITLE: **Male Home Companion**. COUNTRY: **USA**.

En dépit des progrès libéraux des années vingt et trente, l'édition érotique américaine fit un grand pas en arrière dans les années quarante. Adieu les nus artistiques de starlettes et les modèles eugéniques, fini les histoires *Spicy* et les impertinents nus français. Le style des années quarante était résolument patriotique : de braves filles joufflues au teint rose posant dans des maillots de bain pudiques et que les braves soldats pouvaient punaiser sans rougir au-dessus de leur lit dans les chambrées. Même *Gay Book* qui, en 1937, publiait des photos

YEAR: **1943**. TITLE: **Giggles**. COUNTRY: **USA**.

Year: **1940**. Title: **Spot**. Country: **USA**.

For just $1.98 you could read about the Fuehrer's "Secret Disease," his "Bestialism," and even his "Queer Behavior."

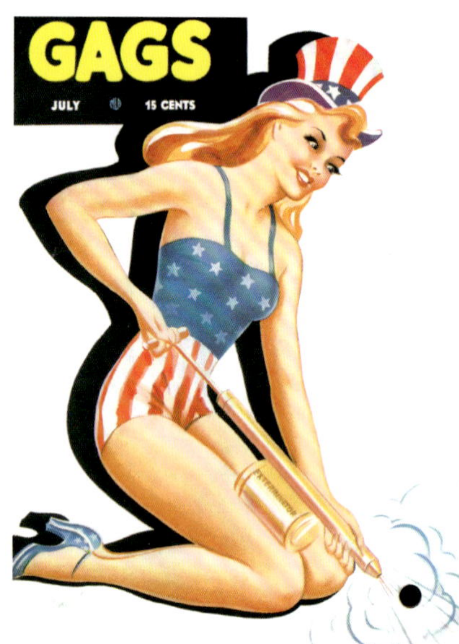

Year: **1942**. Title: **Gags**. Country: **USA**.

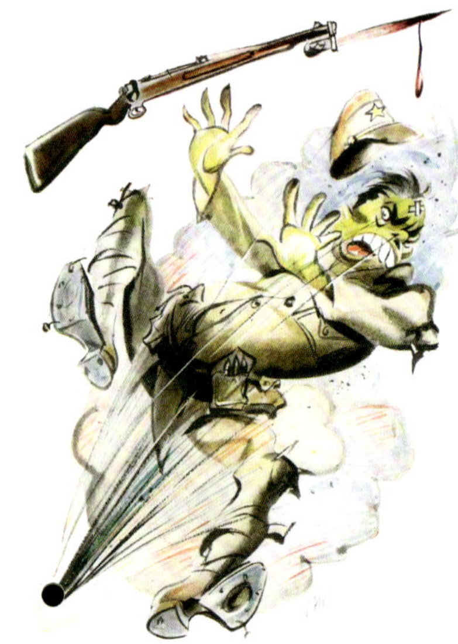

strippers, sweet brunettes instead of sexy blondes, and the subtext was always "supporting our boys." *Stocking Parade*, April 1943, covered a Victory Venus beauty contest for young women working in defense plants. When strippers did appear they were transformed by pseudo-military uniforms into nice girls, or shown stripping off their nylons to be recycled into parachutes—a photo concept recycled more often than the nylons themselves.

Sometimes the patriotism bordered on fetishism. A 1942 issue of *Burlesk* ran a sequence in which a gorgeous brunette in a tight military uniform toyed with an unconscious blonde. The photos supposedly demonstrated emergency medical techniques—as art-directed by John Willie. Even the ads reflected wartime anxiety. A book called *I Was Hitler's Doctor* got the back page on many magazines. For just $1.98 you could read

berichtete über einen Victory-Venus-Wettbewerb unter jungen Arbeiterinnen in den Waffenfabriken. Wenn überhaupt Stripperinnen auftauchten, wurden sie durch pseudomiltärische Uniformen in propere Mädchen verwandelt oder dabei gezeigt, wie sie ihre Nylons abstreiften, damit man daraus Fallschirme herstellen konnte – ein Einfall, der öfter recycelt wurde als die Nylons.

Manchmal grenzte der Patriotismus schon an Fetischismus. In einer Ausgabe von *Burlesk* aus dem Jahr 1942 konnte man eine Fotosequenz sehen, in der eine hinreißende Brünette in hautenger Uniform mit einer ohnmächtigen Blondine herumspielt. Die Bilder sollten vermutlich Erste-Hilfe-Maßnahmen illustrieren – da hatte wohl John Willie Regie geführt. Selbst die Anzeigen spiegelten die Kriegsängste wieder. In vielen Magazinen wurde auf dem Backcover ein Buch mit dem Titel *I Was Hitler's Doctor*

sophistiquées de belles en dessous transparents et aux seins presque nus, revint aux costumes de bain en 1942. *Carnival* (associé à *Show*) se montra plus audacieux, laissant poindre des nus dont on devinait les seins. Cependant, la plupart des magazines se rabattirent sur les bandes dessinées – souvent avec des thèmes militaires – et un nouveau style d'histoires drôles en photos montrant les malheurs des filles empêtrées dans des tâches simples pendant que leurs hommes étaient sur le front. Désormais les modèles étaient des « girls » au lieu de strip-teaseuses, de gentilles brunes plutôt que des blondes incendiaires, et le message implicite était toujours « elles soutiennent nos soldats ». En avril 1943, *Stocking Parade* couvrit le concours de beauté Victory Venus (« la vénus de la victoire »), ouvert aux jeunes ouvrières des usines d'armement. Lorsque des strip-teaseuses apparaissaient, elles étaient transformées en braves filles par des uniformes pseudo-militaires ou montrées ôtant leurs bas en nylon pour qu'ils soient recyclés en parachutes, un prétexte lui-même plus souvent recyclé que les bas en question.

Parfois, le patriotisme frisait le fétichisme. Dans un numéro de *Burlesk* datant de 1942 on peut voir une séquence où une superbe brune dans un uniforme militaire moulant s'affaire sur une blonde évanouie. Les photos étaient censées montrer des techniques de secourisme – artistiquement mises en scène par John Willie. Même les publicités reflétaient l'angoisse de la guerre. Un livre intitulé *J'étais le médecin d'Adolf Hitler* fit la quatrième de couverture de nombreux magazines. Pour $1,98, vous pouviez tout savoir sur « la maladie secrète »

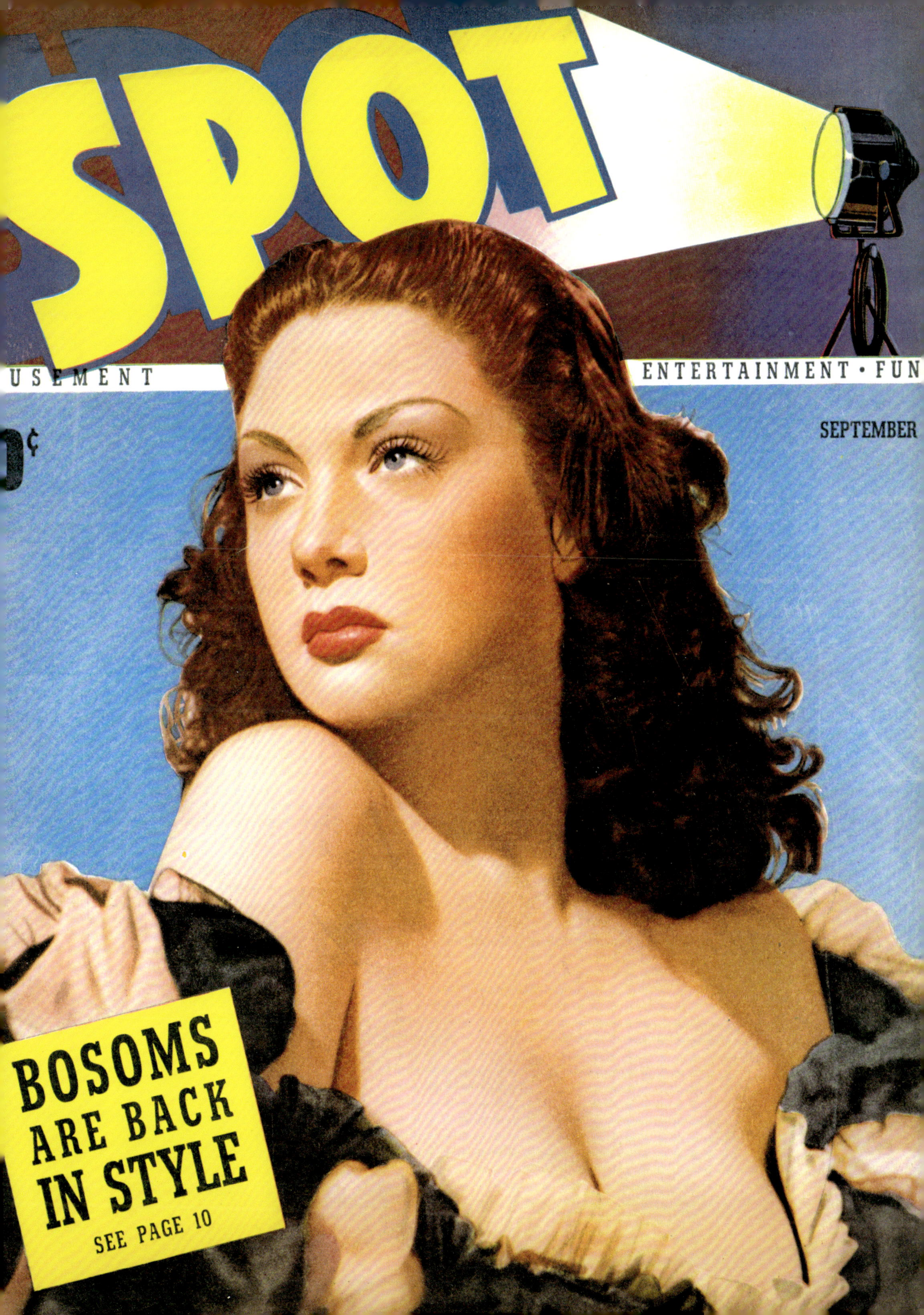
SPOT
USEMENT
ENTERTAINMENT • FUN
0¢
SEPTEMBER
BOSOMS ARE BACK IN STYLE
SEE PAGE 10

Right:
Year: **1943**. Title: **Gay Book**. Country: **USA**.

Pages 298 & 299:
Year: **1944**. Title: **"Pin Me Up"**. Country: **USA**.
Year: **1941**. Title: **"IT"**. Country: **USA**.

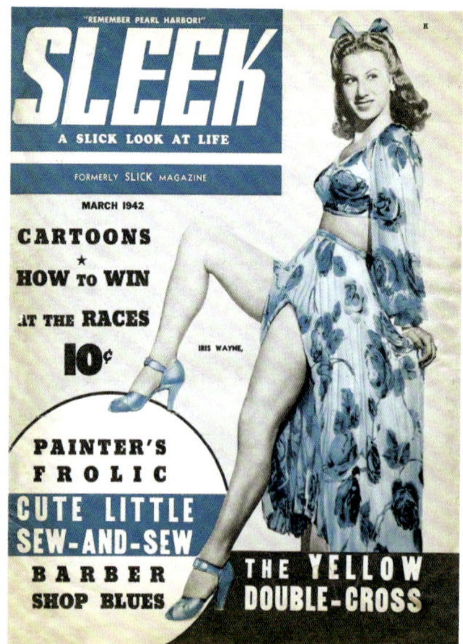

Year: **1942**. Title: **Sleek**. Country: **USA**.

about the Führer's "Secret Disease," his "Bestialism," his "Chorus Girl Fantasy" and even his "Queer Behavior." If that didn't appeal, a husband worried about his wife back home could buy *Sex And This War* to learn about "Sex Problems of Women Left Behind". Alternately he could get the *Guide To Intimate Letter Writing* and "Keep the flame of love burning high with living, throbbing, romantic letters." Men's magazines have always been a good place to flog books on marital problems, but the number and range of titles in the war-time publications exposes the anxieties of young men away at war. And explains why the magazine models looked like wholesome virgins. At that time men needed the escape and comfort of sex more than ever, but they wanted no reminders that their wives and girlfriends back home might need the same. Once they were safely home, all that changed.

beworben. Für nur 1,98 Dollar konnte man sich darin über die „geheime Krankheit" des Führers kundig machen, über seine „Bestialität", seine „Revuemädchenfantasien" und sogar sein „schwules Verhalten". Wenn ihn das nicht ansprach, konnte sich ein Mann, der sich Sorgen um seine Frau in der Heimat machte, *Sex And This War* zulegen, um sich über die „sexuellen Nöte der allein zurückgebliebenen Frau" zu informieren. Oder er besorgte sich den *Leitfaden für Liebesbriefe* um „das Feuer der Liebe durch lebendige, leidenschaftliche und romantische Briefe anzufachen." Männermagazine waren schon immer ein guter Platz, um Bücher über Eheprobleme zu verkaufen, doch die große Zahl und Vielfalt derartiger Titel während des Krieges enthüllte die Sorgen junger Männer, die in den Krieg mussten. Das erklärt auch, warum die Models in den Magazinen wie propere Jungfrauen aussahen. In jenen Tagen brauchten Männer mehr den je Ablenkung und Trost durch Sex, aber sie wollten nicht daran erinnert werden, dass ihre Frauen oder Freundinnen daheim möglicherweise die gleichen Bedürfnisse hatten. Sobald sie wieder sicher in der Heimat waren, war es damit vorbei.

du Führer, sa « bestialité », son « fantasme de girl de music-hall » et même son « comportement inverti ». Si cela ne lui convenait pas, le mari inquiet pour sa femme restée au pays pouvait acheter *La sexualité et cette guerre* pour tout apprendre sur « les problèmes sexuels des épouses délaissées ». En guise d'alternative, il pouvait se procurer *le Guide de la correspondance intime* et « entretenir la flamme ardente de l'amour par des lettres vivantes, palpitantes et romantiques ». Les magazines pour homme ont toujours été un bon support pour vendre des ouvrages sur les problèmes conjugaux, mais le nombre et la variété des titres que l'on trouve dans les publications de la période de guerre montre bien les angoisses des jeunes hommes envoyés sur le front. Cela explique aussi pourquoi les modèles avaient l'air de vierges débordantes de santé. Ces hommes avaient plus que jamais besoin de l'évasion et du réconfort du sexe, mais ils ne voulaient pas qu'on leur rappelle que leurs épouses et leurs petites amies esseulées avaient les mêmes besoins. Une fois rentrés sains et saufs à la maison, ce fut une toute autre histoire.

Never since Napoleon's expedition to Egypt had an army's sexual needs been so scientifically catered for. It was an abandonment of the principals on which sex-education had hither to been based.

—*A History of Sexual Customs*, Richard Lewinsohn, translated from the German in 1958

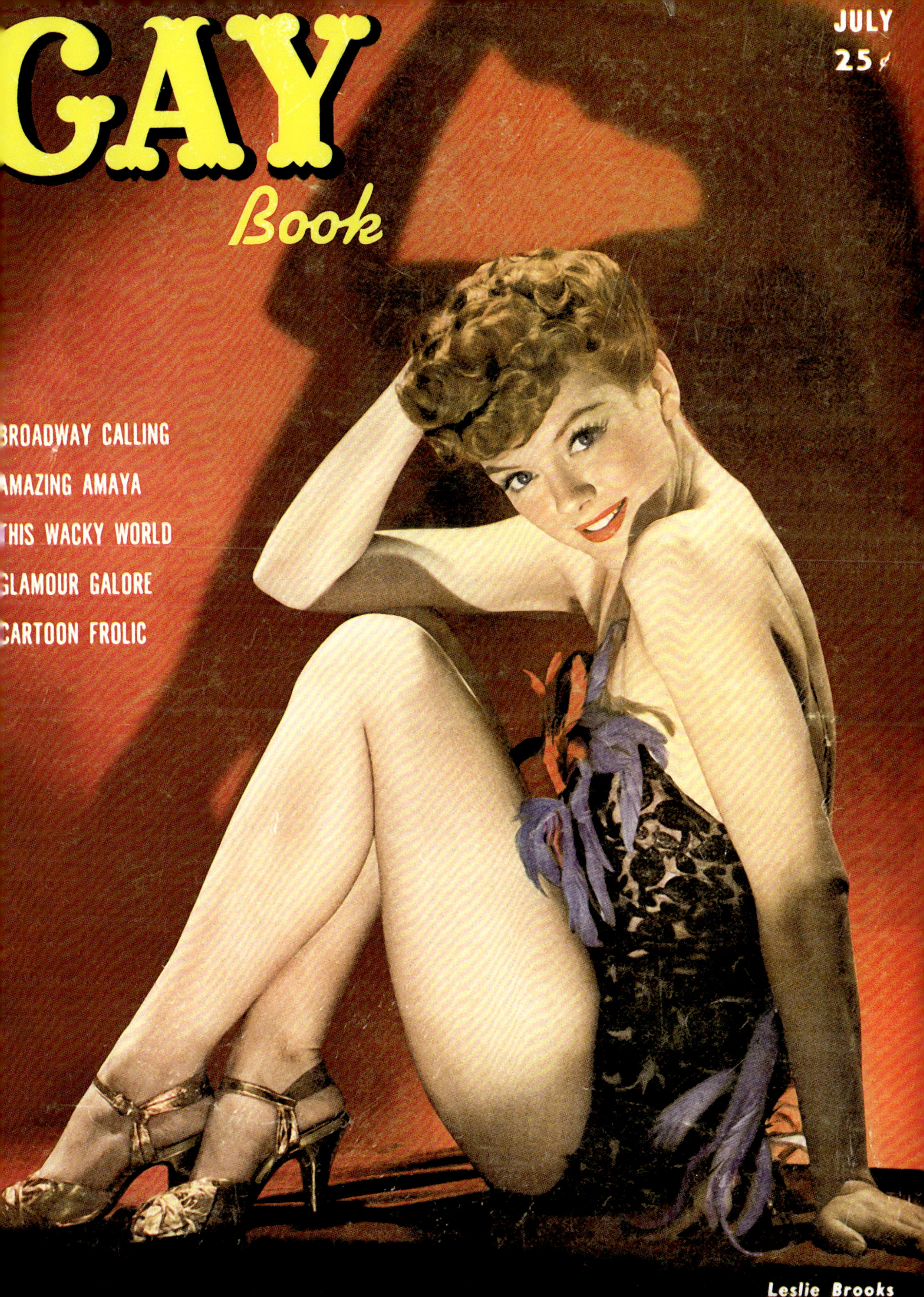
GAY
Book
JULY
25¢
BROADWAY CALLING
AMAZING AMAYA
THIS WACKY WORLD
GLAMOUR GALORE
CARTOON FROLIC
Leslie Brooks

"PIN ME UP

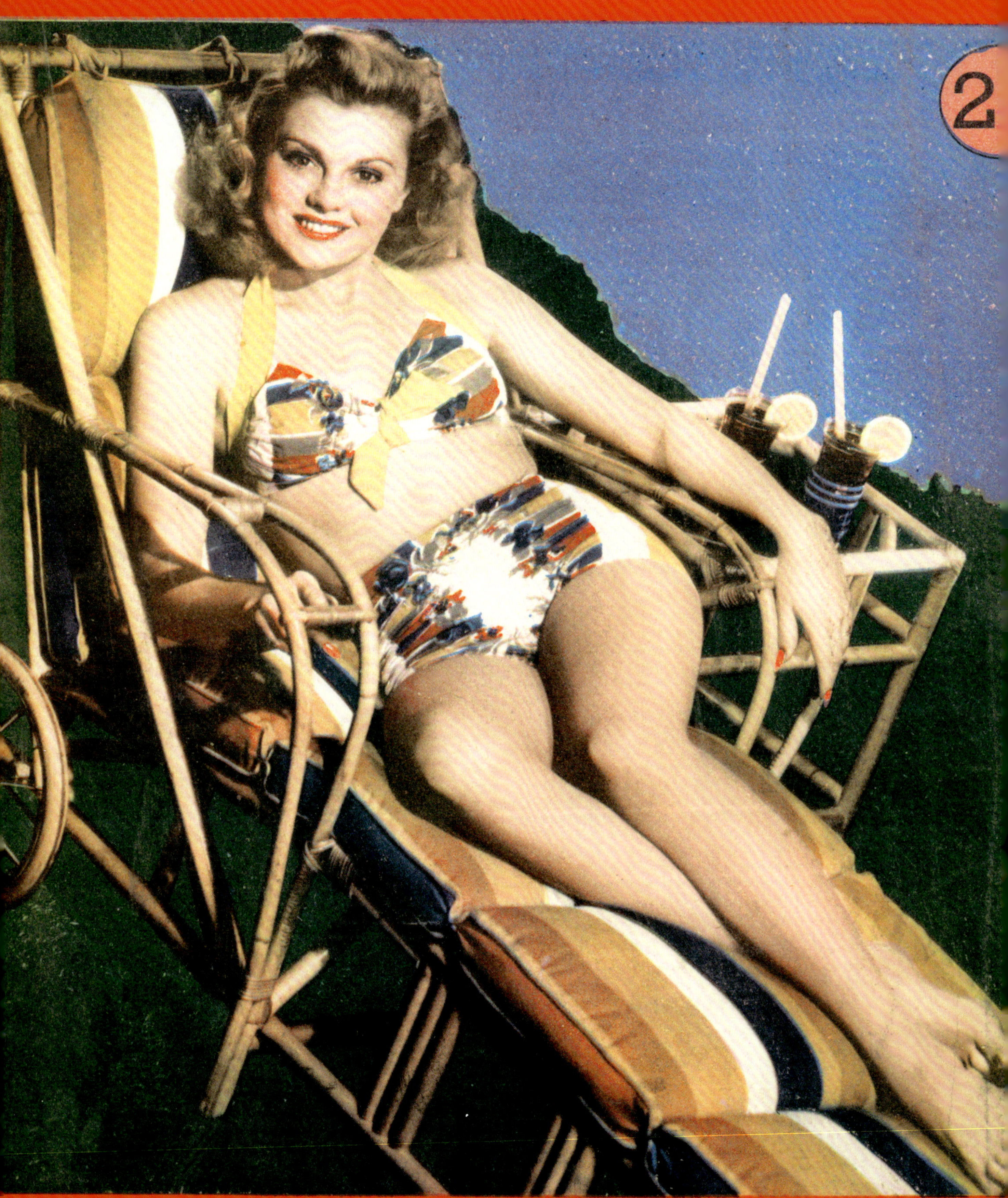

A BOOKFUL OF PIN-UP GIRLS

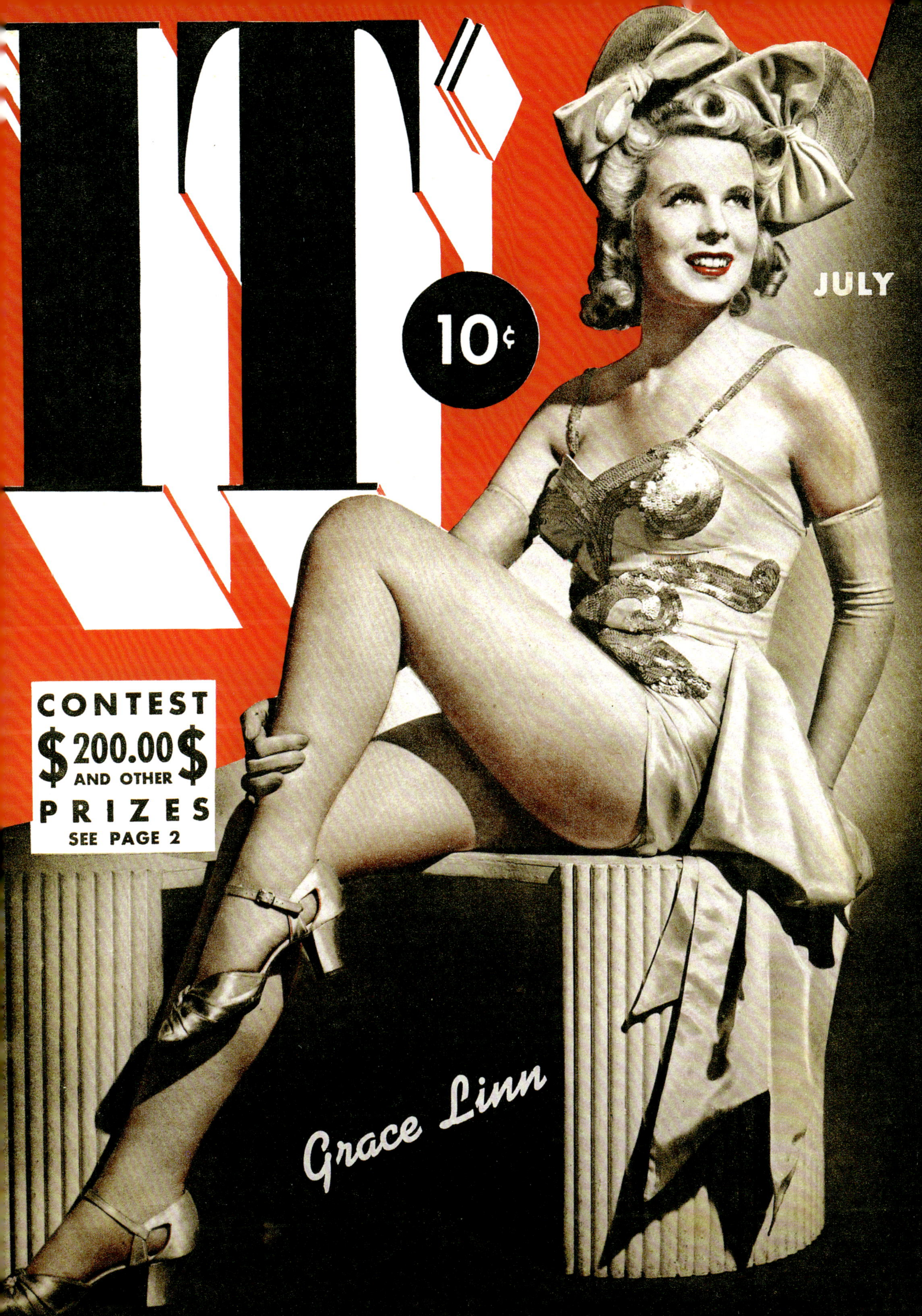
IT
10¢
JULY
CONTEST
200.00
AND OTHER
PRIZES
SEE PAGE 2
Grace Linn

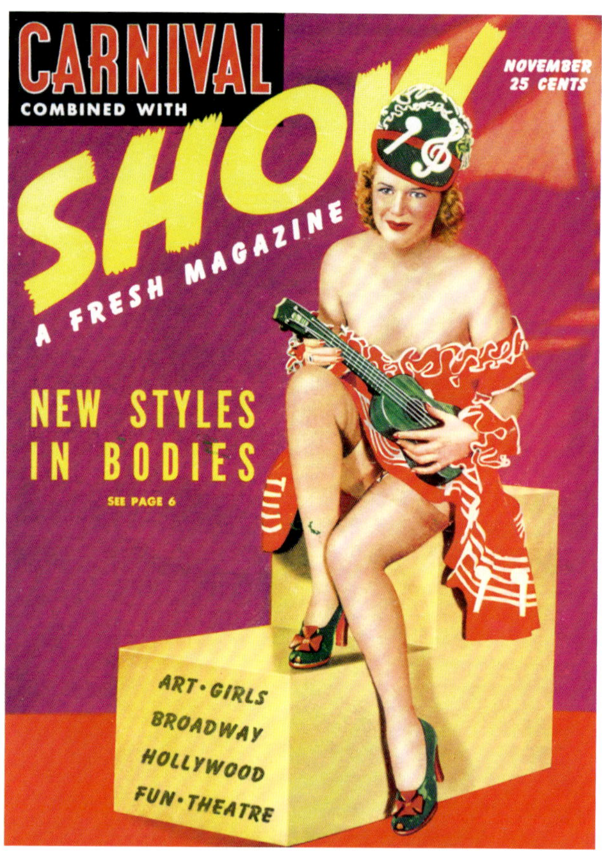

Year: **1940**. Title: **Carnival Combined with Show**. Country: **USA**.

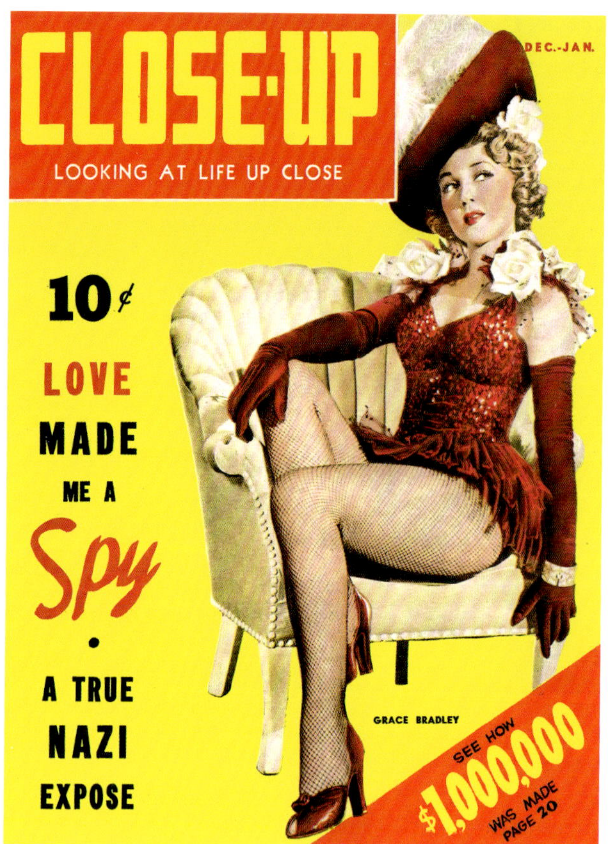

Year: **1942**. Title: **Close-up**. Country: **USA**.

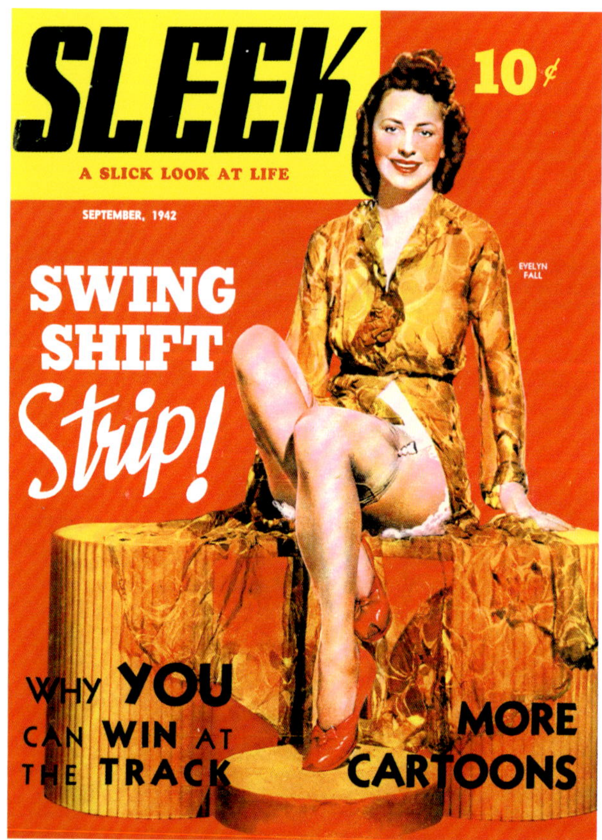

Year: **1942**. Title: **Sleek**. Country: **USA**.

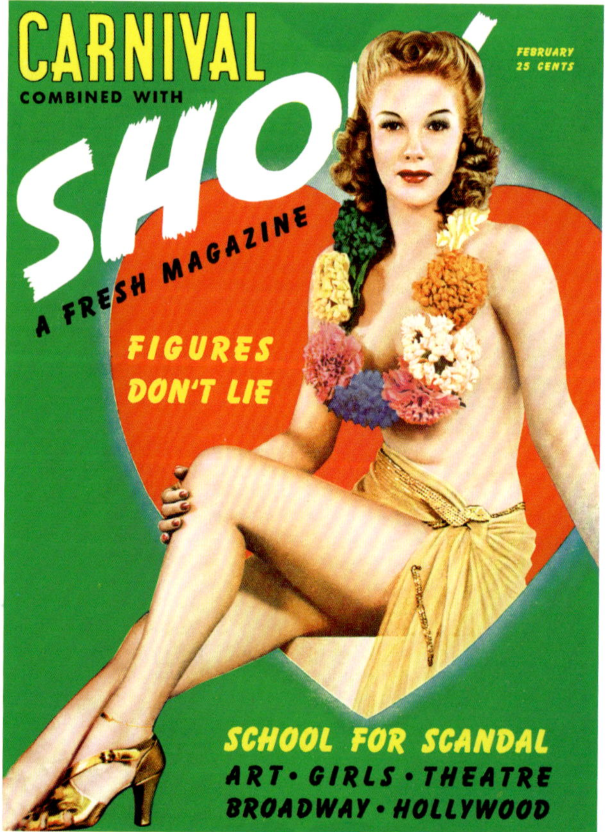

Year: **1941**. Title: **Carnival Combined with Show**. Country: **USA**.

Year: **1942**. Title: **Burlesk**. Country: **USA**.

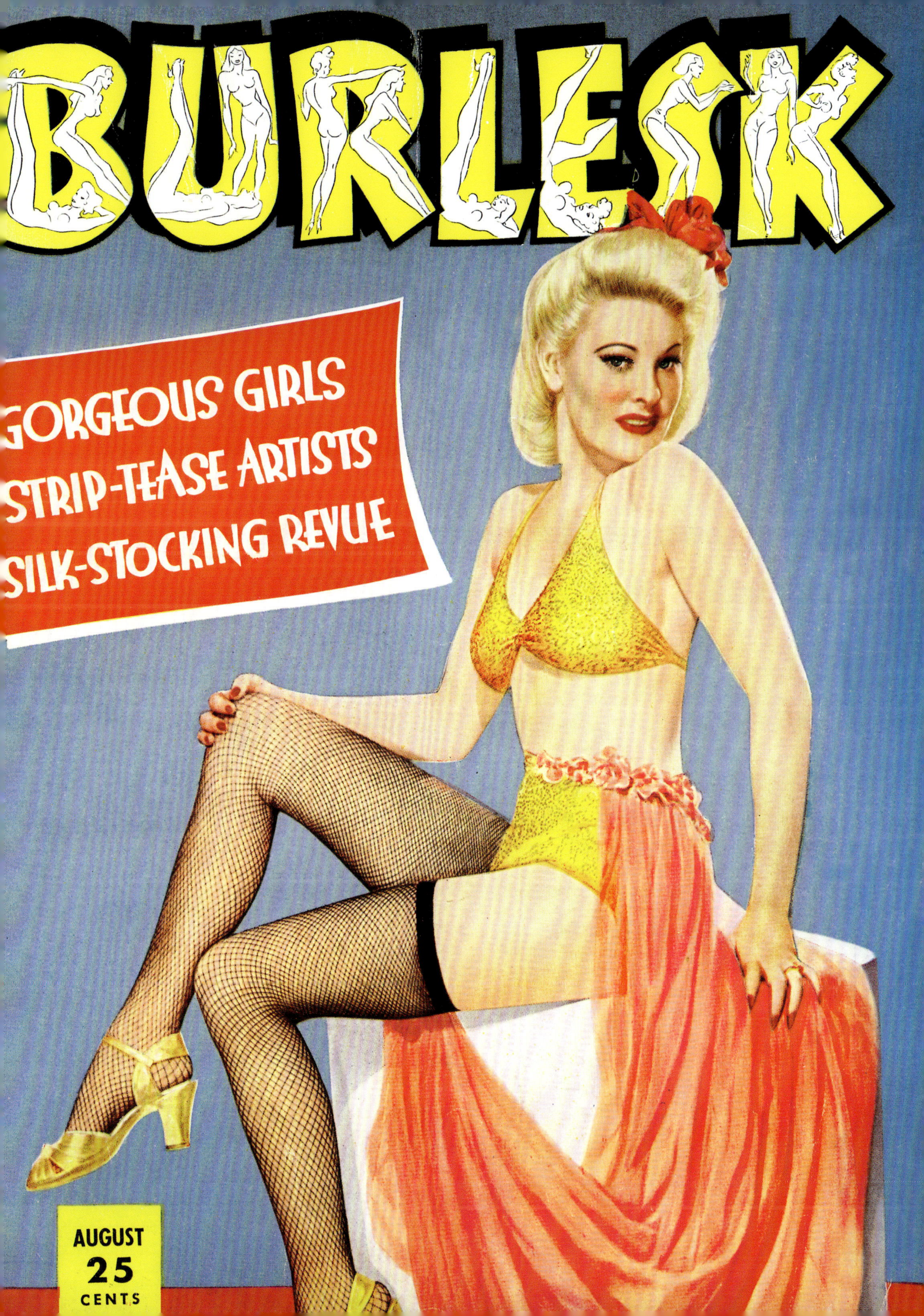
BURLESK
GORGEOUS GIRLS
STRIP-TEASE ARTISTS
SILK-STOCKING REVUE
AUGUST
25
CENTS

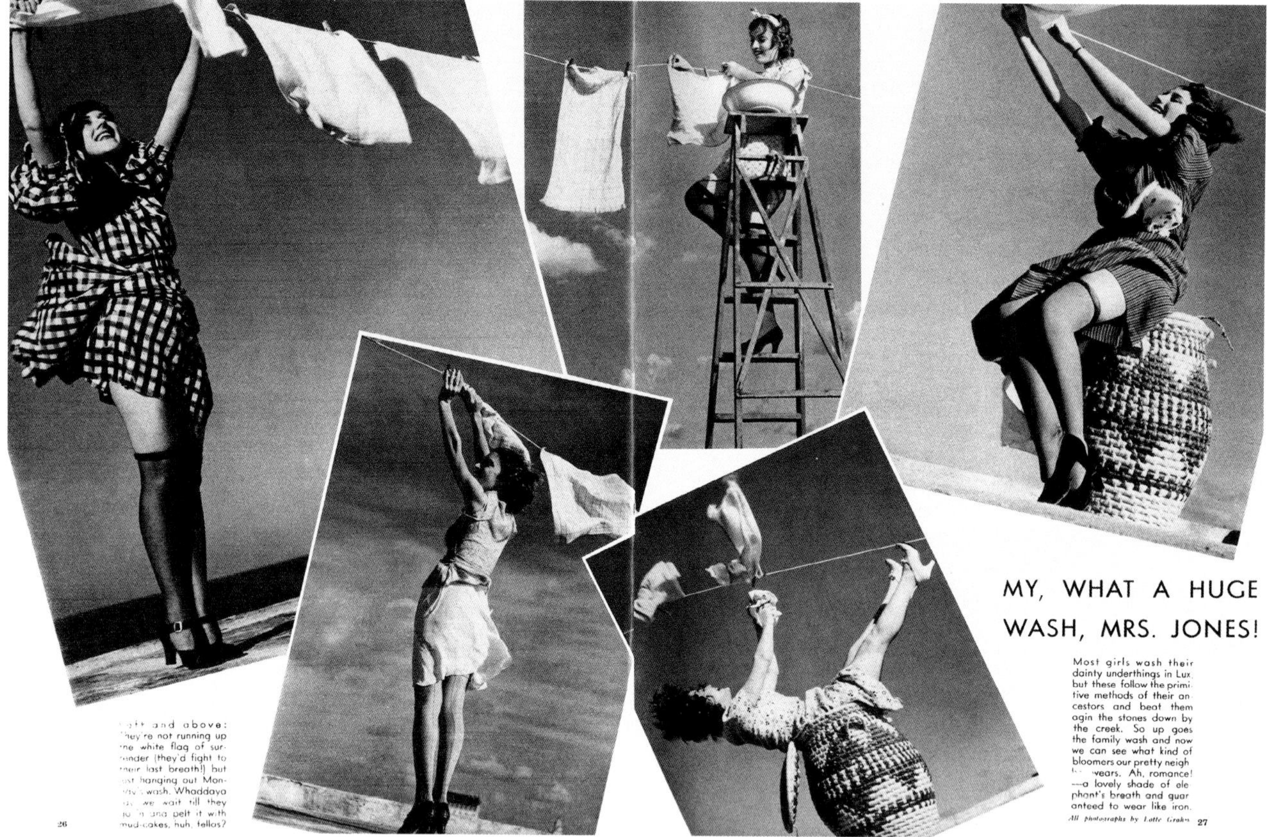

gft and above: hey're not running up ne white flag of sur-ender (they'd fight to their last breath!) but st hanging out Mon-ay's wash. Whaddaya we wait till they and pelt it with mud-cakes, huh, fellas?

26

MY, WHAT A HUGE WASH, MRS. JONES!

Most girls wash their dainty underthings in Lux, but these follow the primitive methods of their ancestors and beat them agin the stones down by the creek. So up goes the family wash and now we can see what kind of bloomers our pretty neigh wears. Ah, romance! —a lovely shade of elephant's breath and guaranteed to wear like iron.

All photographs by Lotte Grahn 27

YEAR: **1937**. TITLE: **Gay Book**. COUNTRY: **USA**.

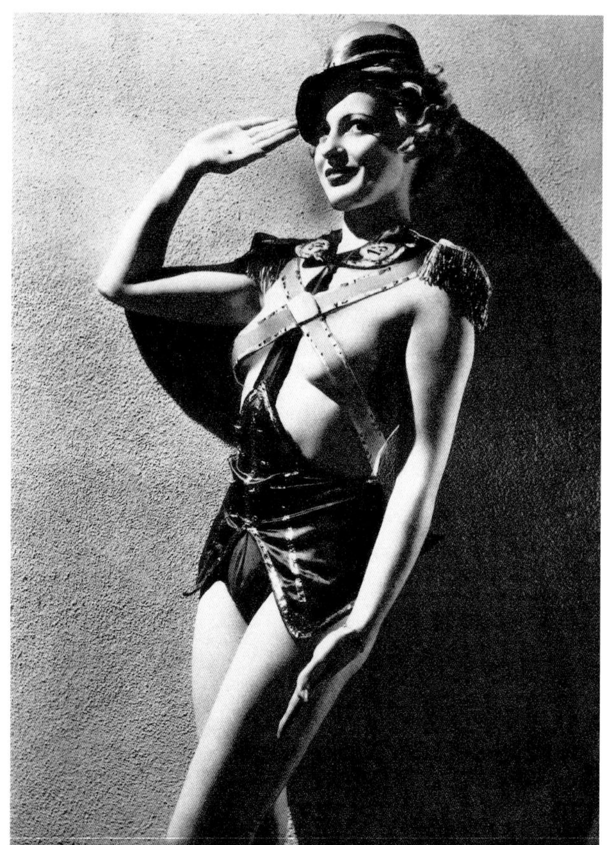

YEAR: **1937**. TITLE: **Gay Book**. COUNTRY: **USA**.

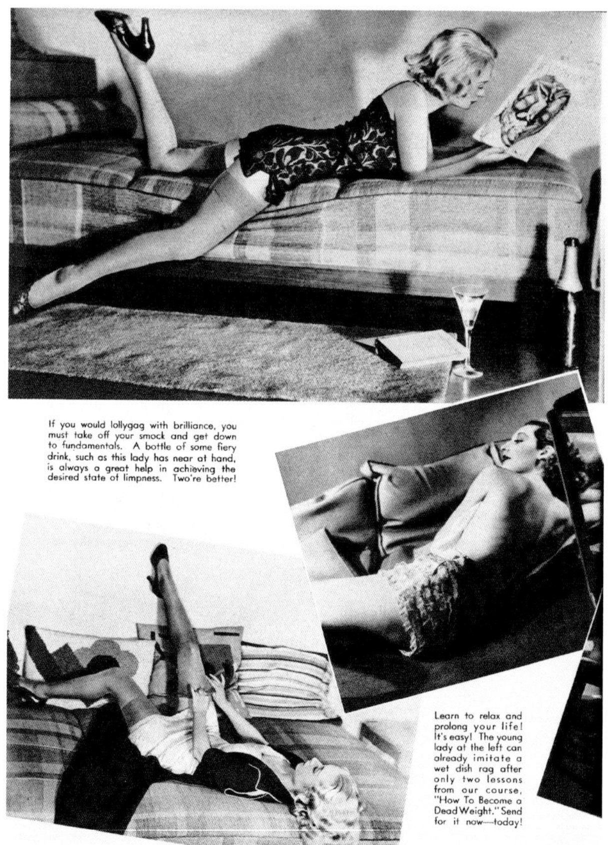

If you would lollygag with brilliance, you must take off your smock and get down to fundamentals. A bottle of some fiery drink, such as this lady has near at hand, is always a great help in achieving the desired state of limpness. Two're better!

Learn to relax and prolong your life! It's easy! The young lady at the left can already imitate a wet dish rag after only two lessons from our course, "How To Become a Dead Weight." Send for it now—today!

YEAR: **1937**. TITLE: **Gay Book**. COUNTRY: **USA**.

YEAR: **1937**. TITLE: **Gay Book**. COUNTRY: **USA**.

March, 1937

GAY BOOK

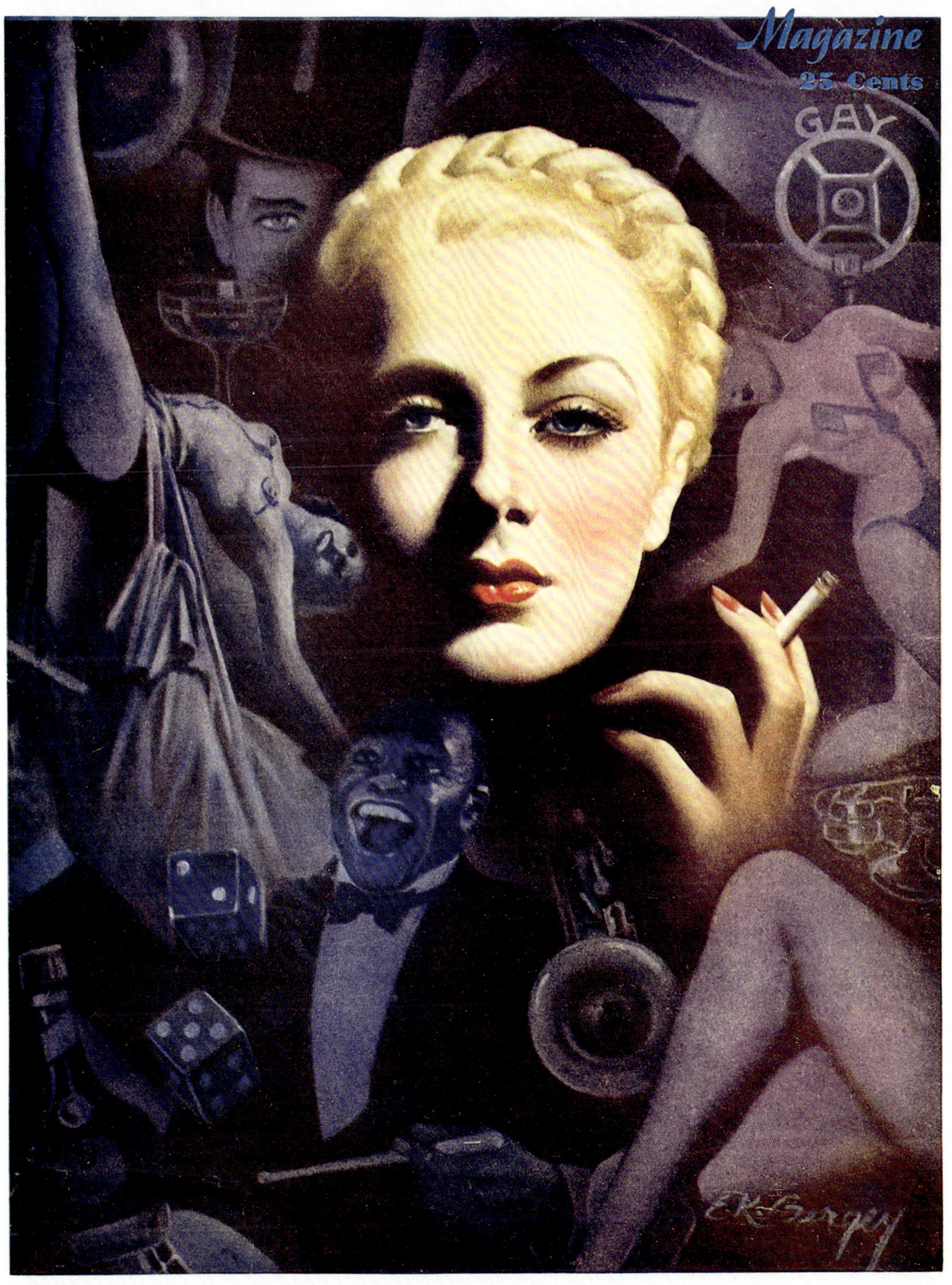

FICTION • PHOTOGRAPHS • CARTOONS • BOOKS • THEATRE • WHIMSY

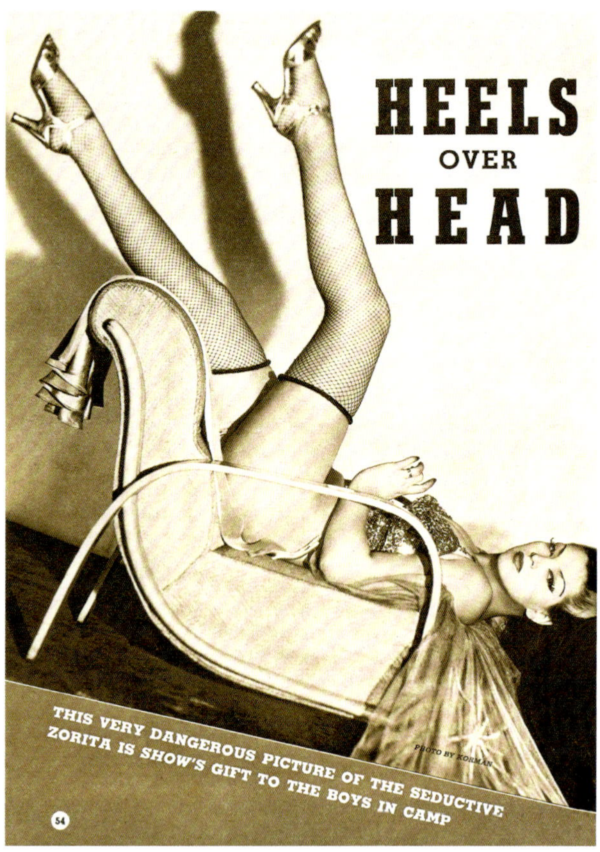

Year: **1941**. Title: **Carnival Combined with Show**. Country: **USA**.

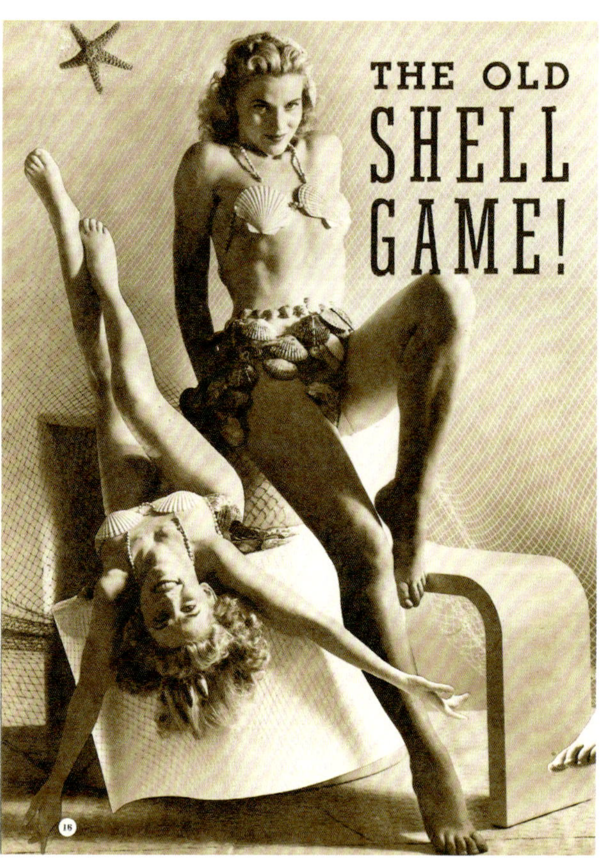

Year: **1941**. Title: **Carnival Combined with Show**. Country: **USA**.

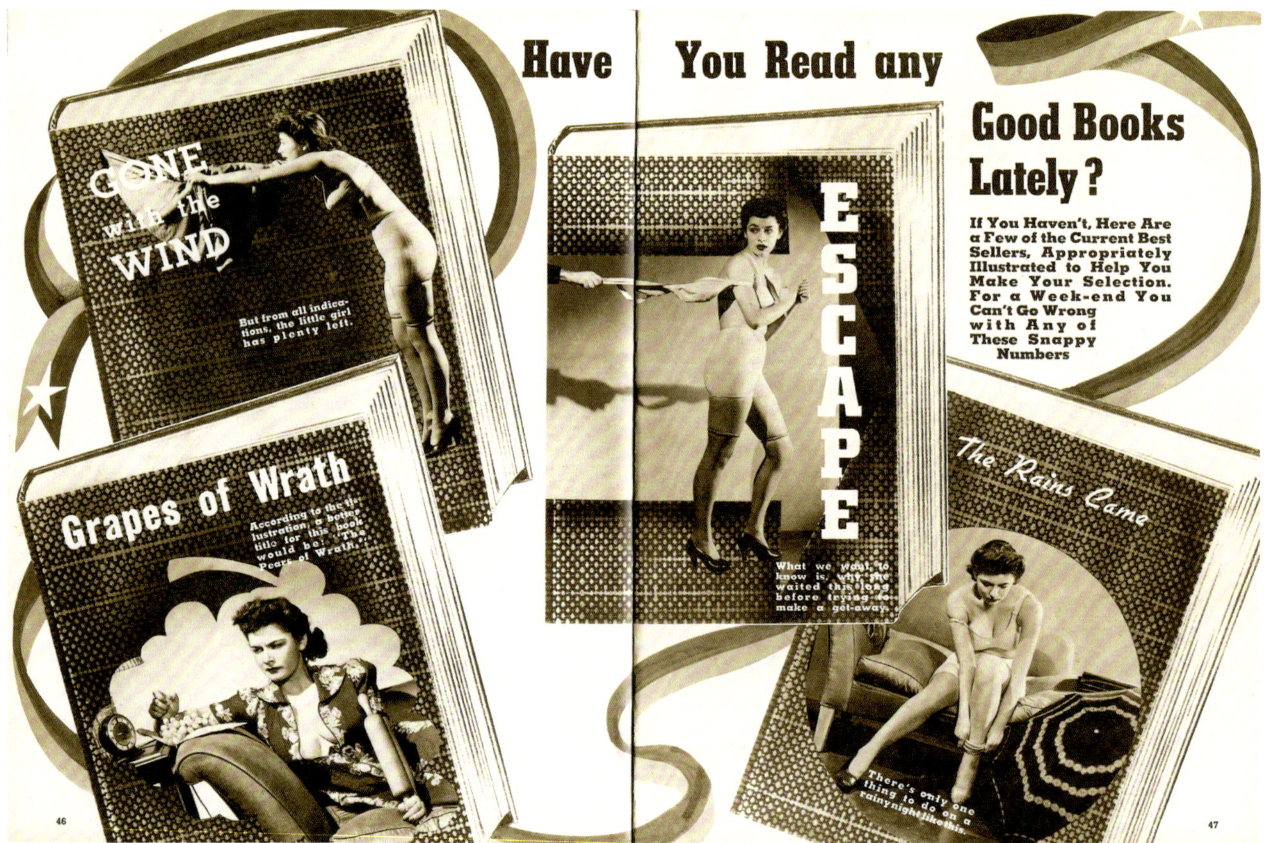

Year: **1941**. Title: **Carnival Combined with Show**. Country: **USA**.

Year: **1941**. Title: **Burlesk**. Country: **USA**.

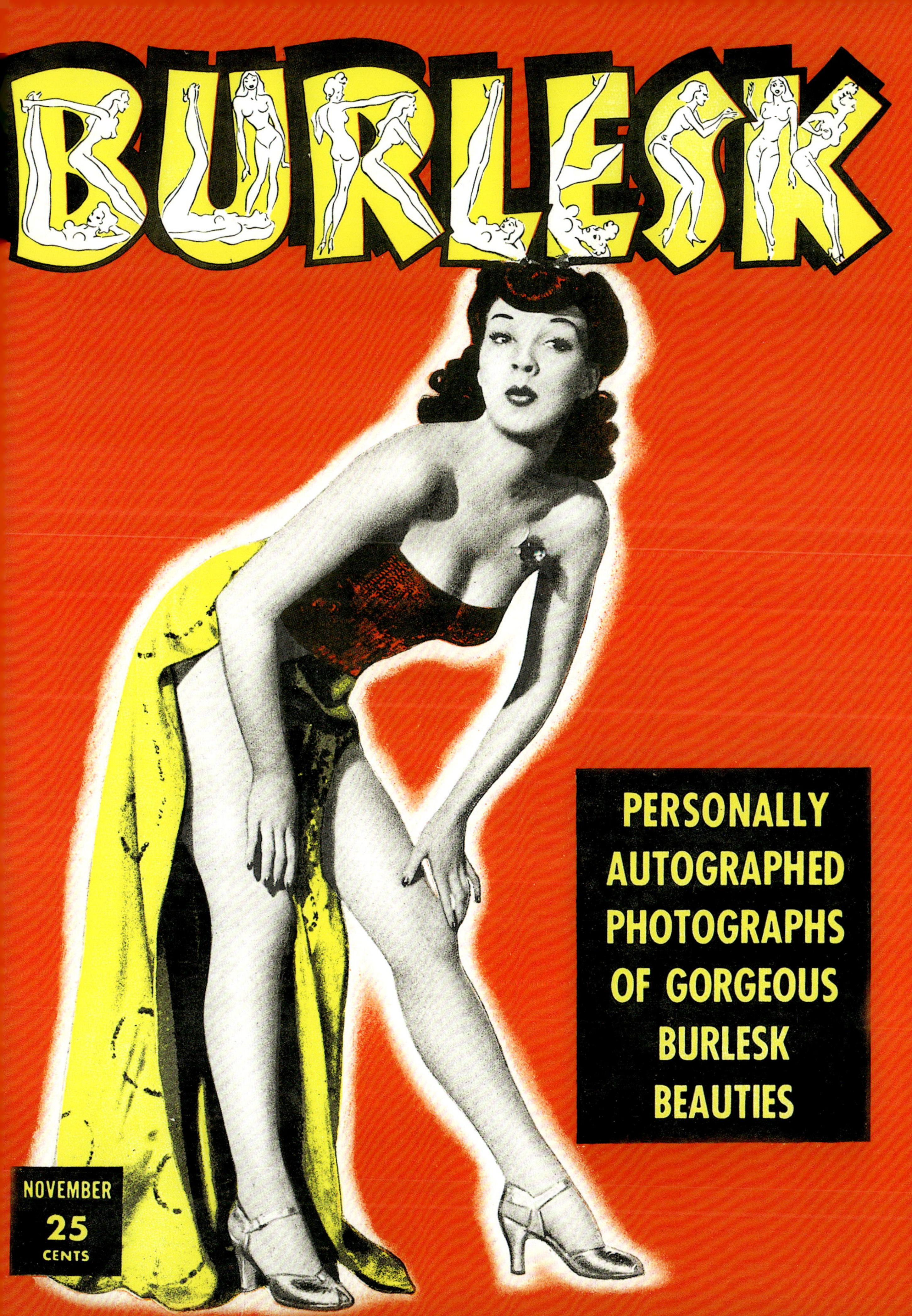
BURLESK
PERSONALLY AUTOGRAPHED PHOTOGRAPHS OF GORGEOUS BURLESK BEAUTIES
NOVEMBER
25
CENTS

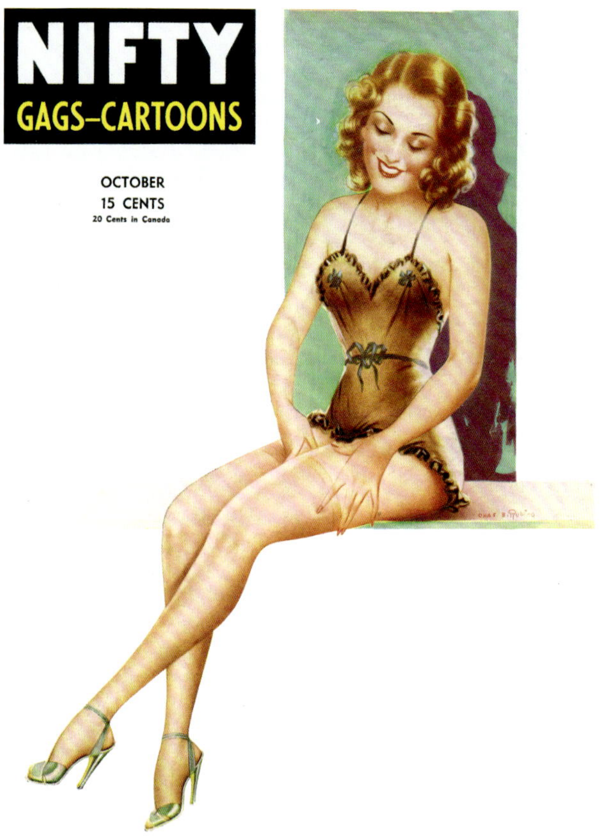

Year: **1943**. Title: **Nifty**. Country: **USA**.

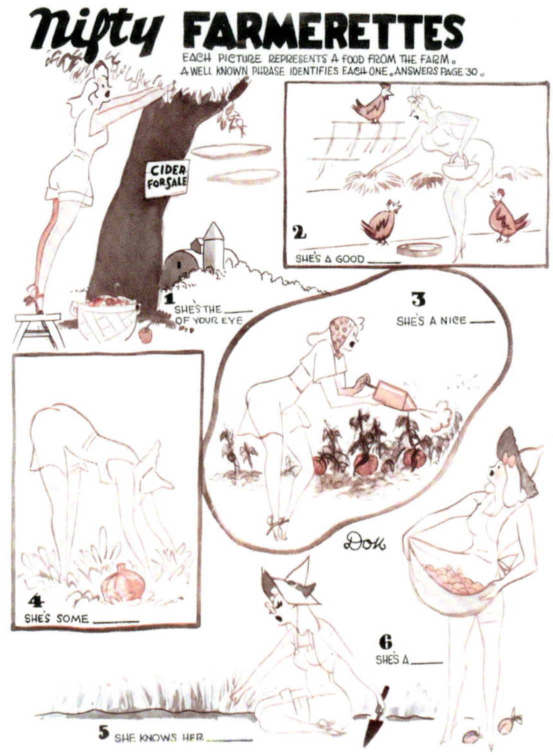

Year: **1943**. Title: **Nifty**. Country: **USA**.

Right:
Year: **1942**. Title: **Nifty**. Country: **USA**.

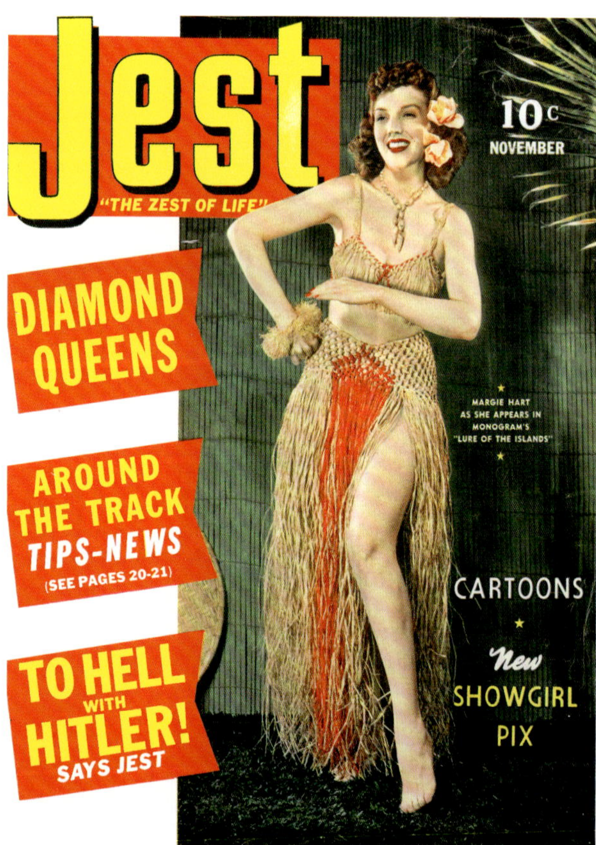

Year: **1942**. Title: **Jest**. Country: **USA**.

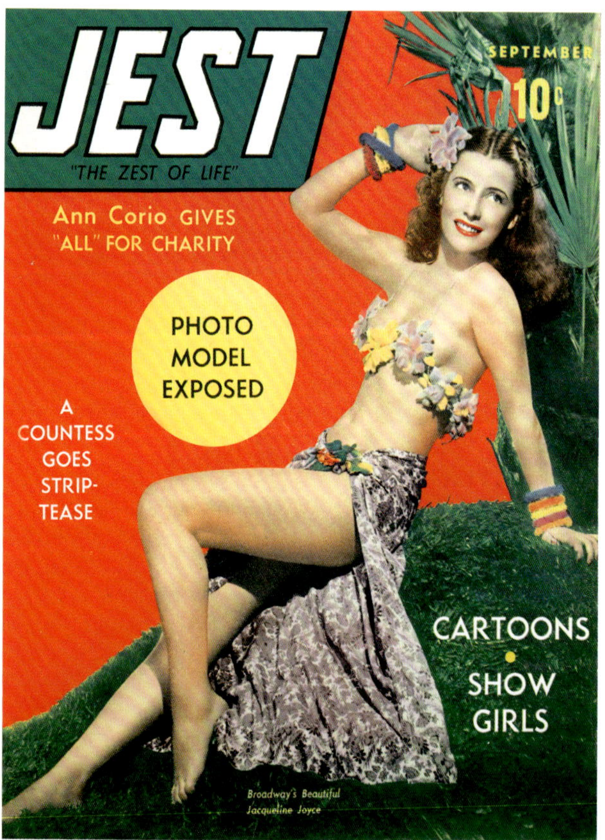

Year: **1941**. Title: **Jest**. Country: **USA**.

Pages 308 & 309:
Year: **1942**. Title: **Sleek**. Country: **USA**.

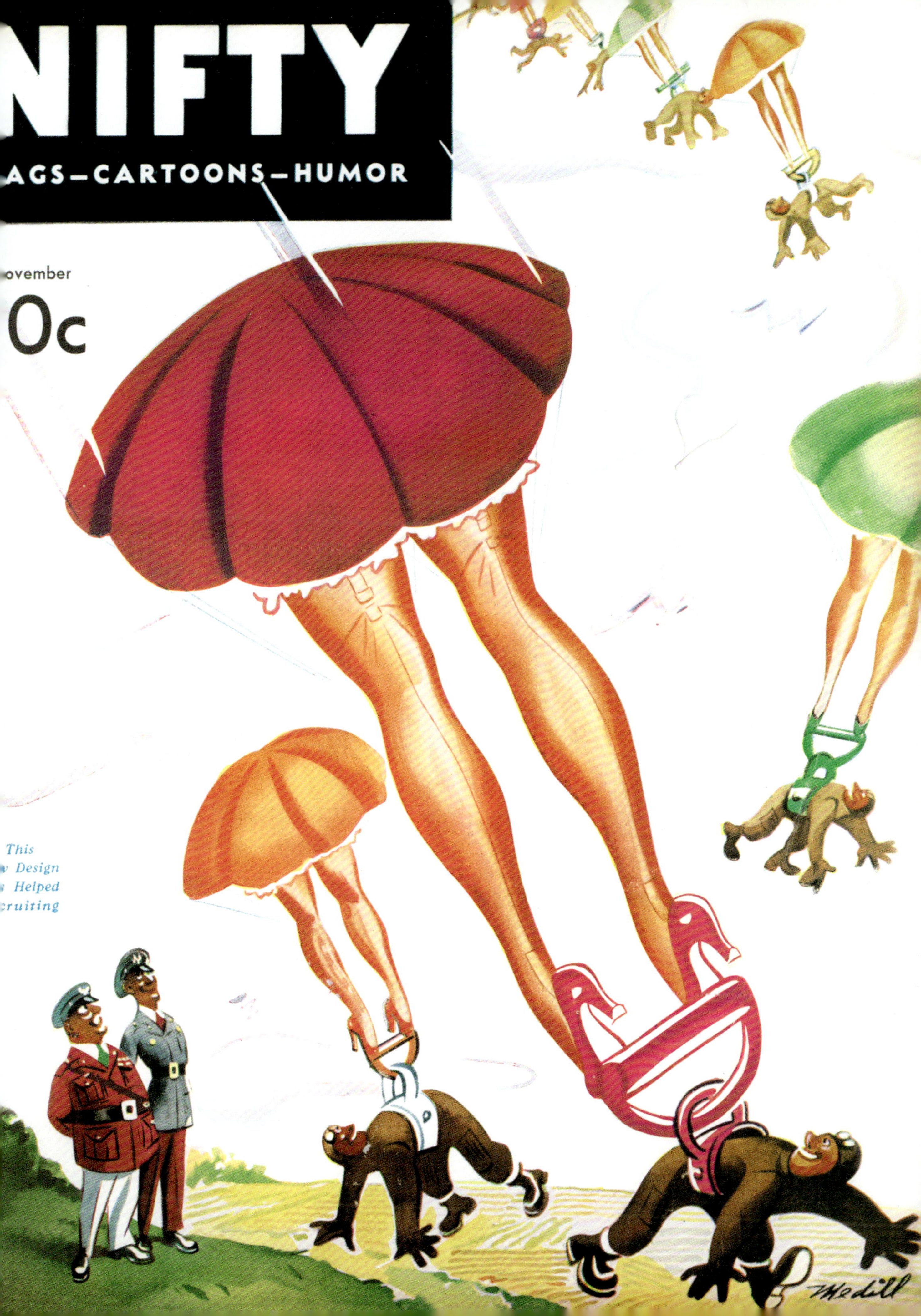
NIFTY
AGS—CARTOONS—HUMOR
ovember
0c
This
Design
Helped
cruiting
Medill

STOP THOSE HICCUPS!

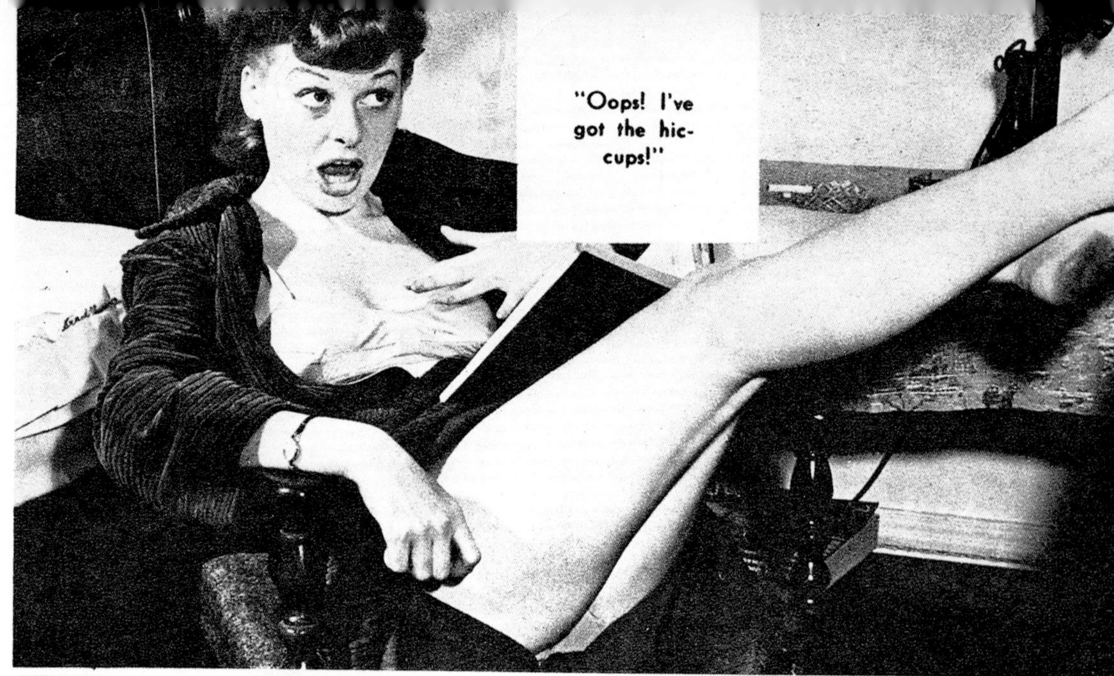

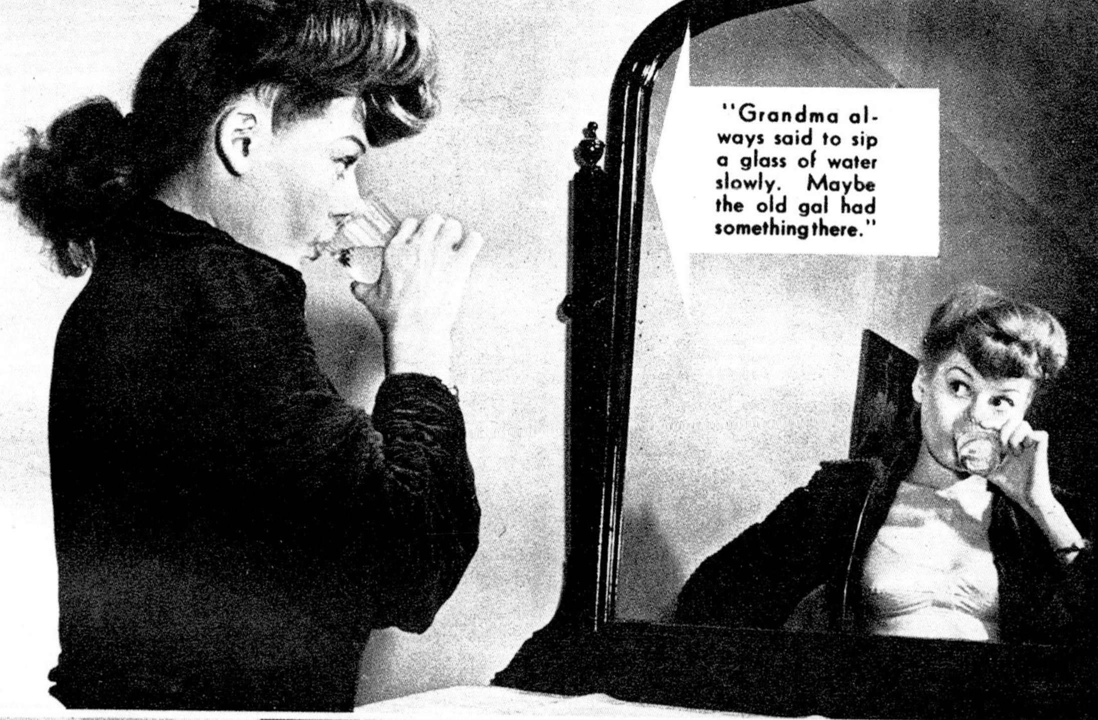

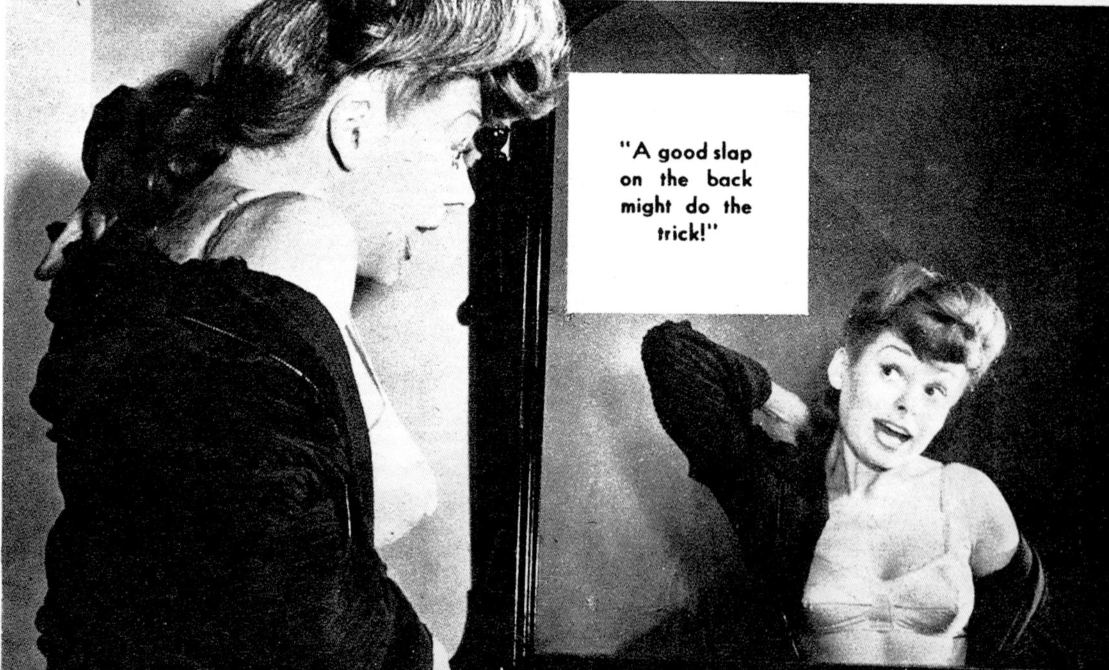

Home Life of a Contortionist

Posed by Donette de Lys, the "spineless" girl.

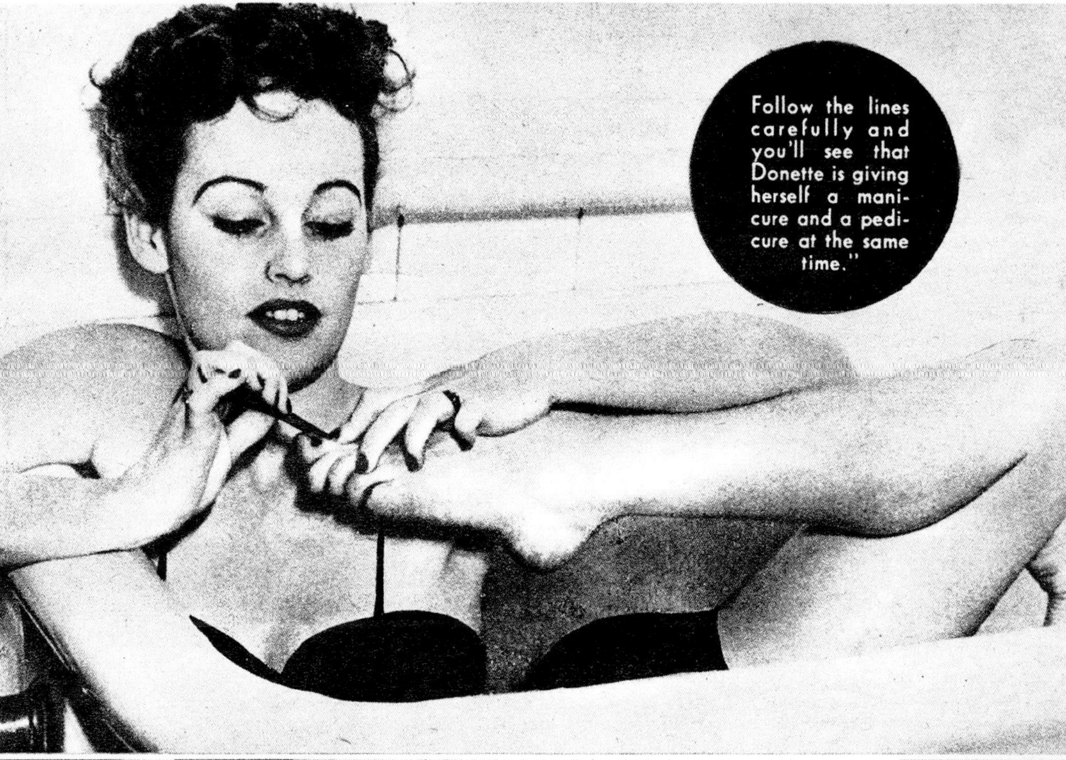

Follow the lines carefully and you'll see that Donette is giving herself a manicure and a pedicure at the same time."

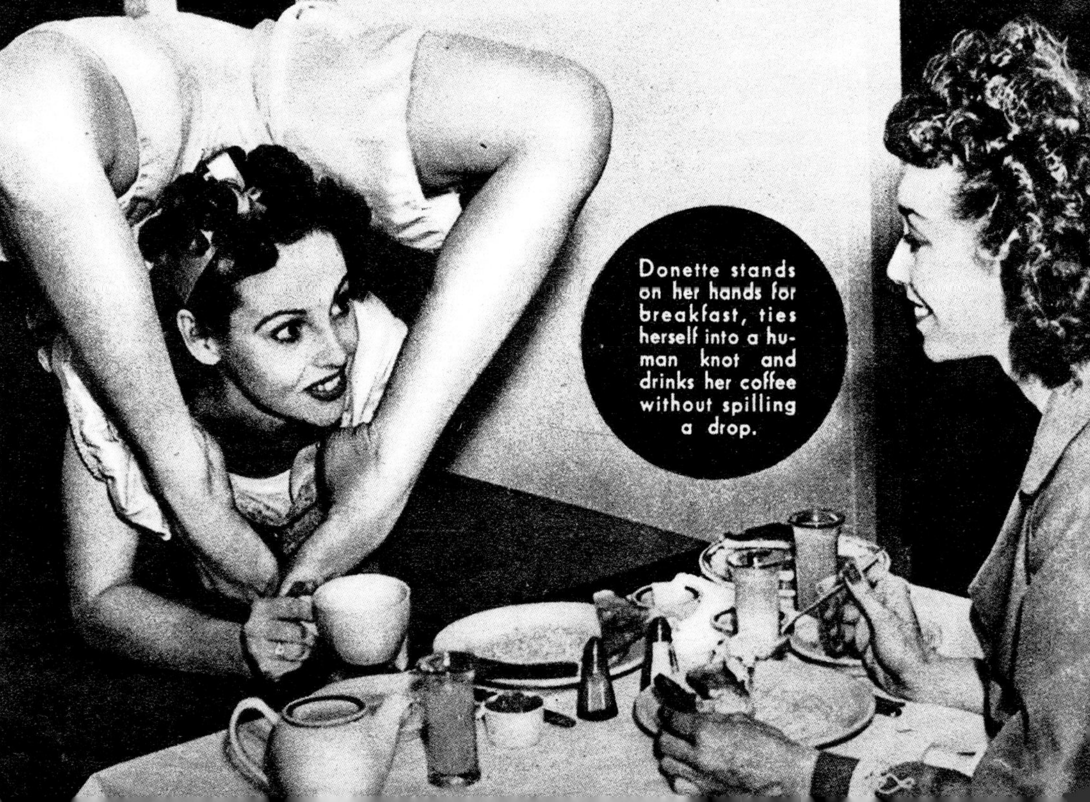

Donette stands on her hands for breakfast, ties herself into a human knot and drinks her coffee without spilling a drop.

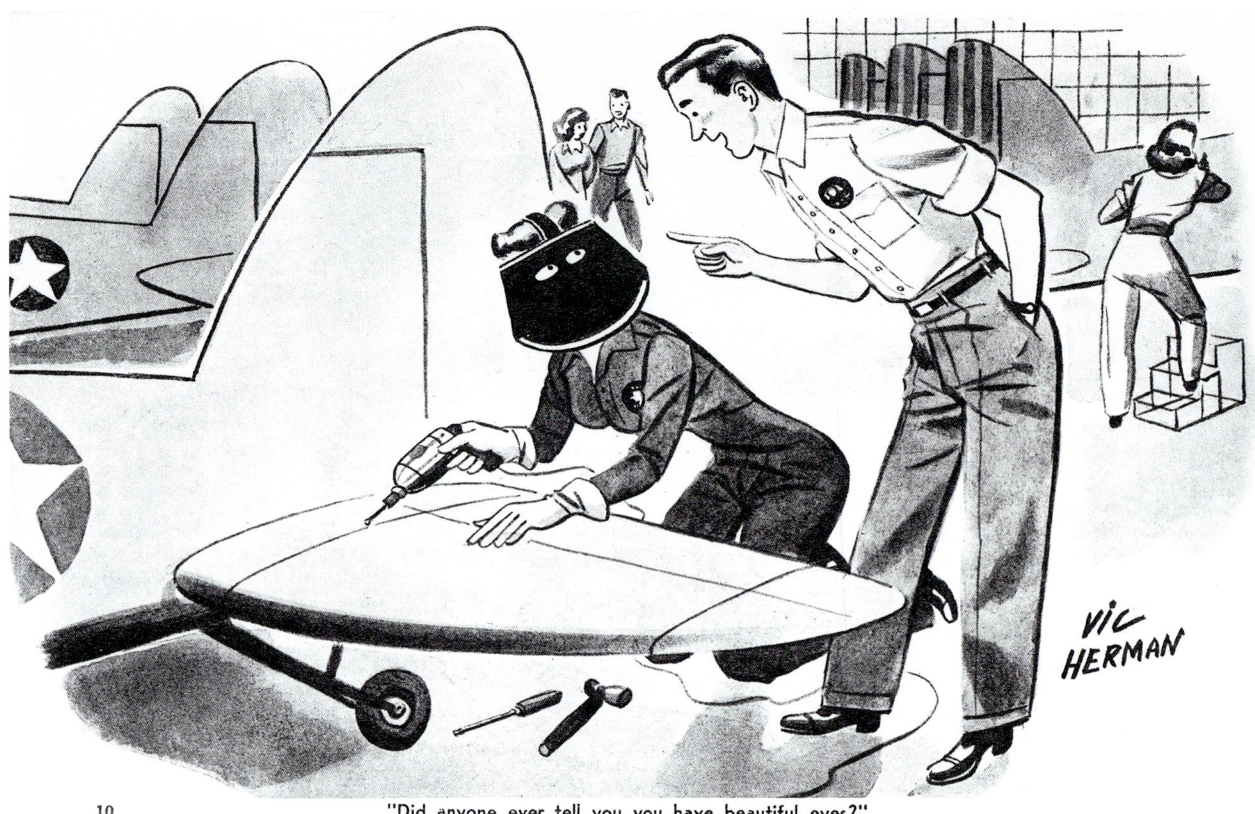

Year: **1945**. Title: **Giggles**. Artist: **Vic Herman**. Country: **USA**.

Right:
Year: **1943**. Title: **Gay Book**. Country: **USA**.

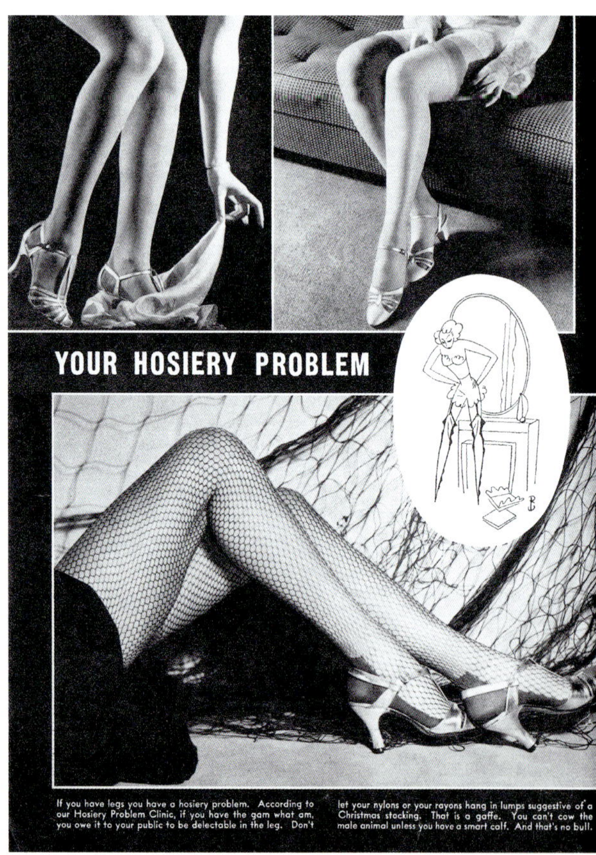

Year: **1943**. Title: **Gay Book**. Country: **USA**.

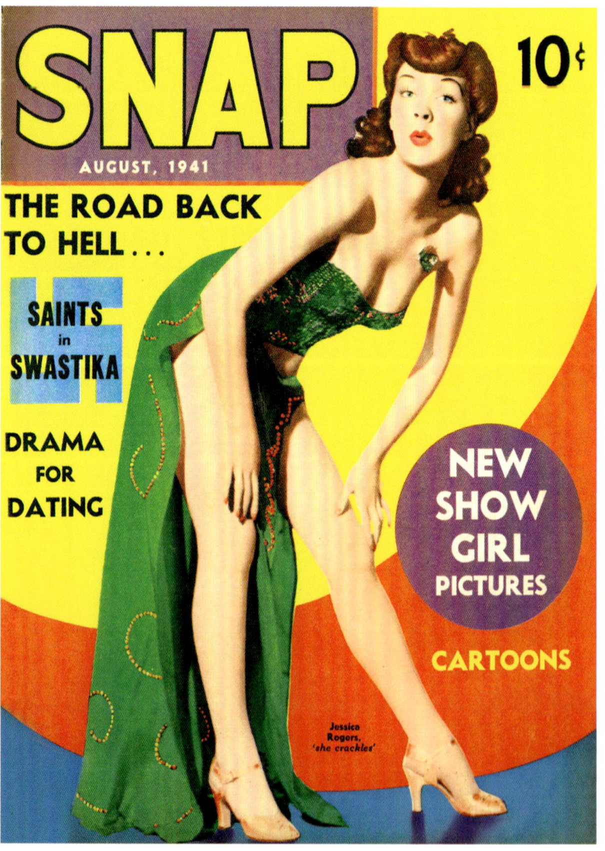

Year: **1941**. Title: **Snap**. Country: **USA**.

Pages 312 & 313:
Year: **1944**. Title: **Play**. Country: **USA**.

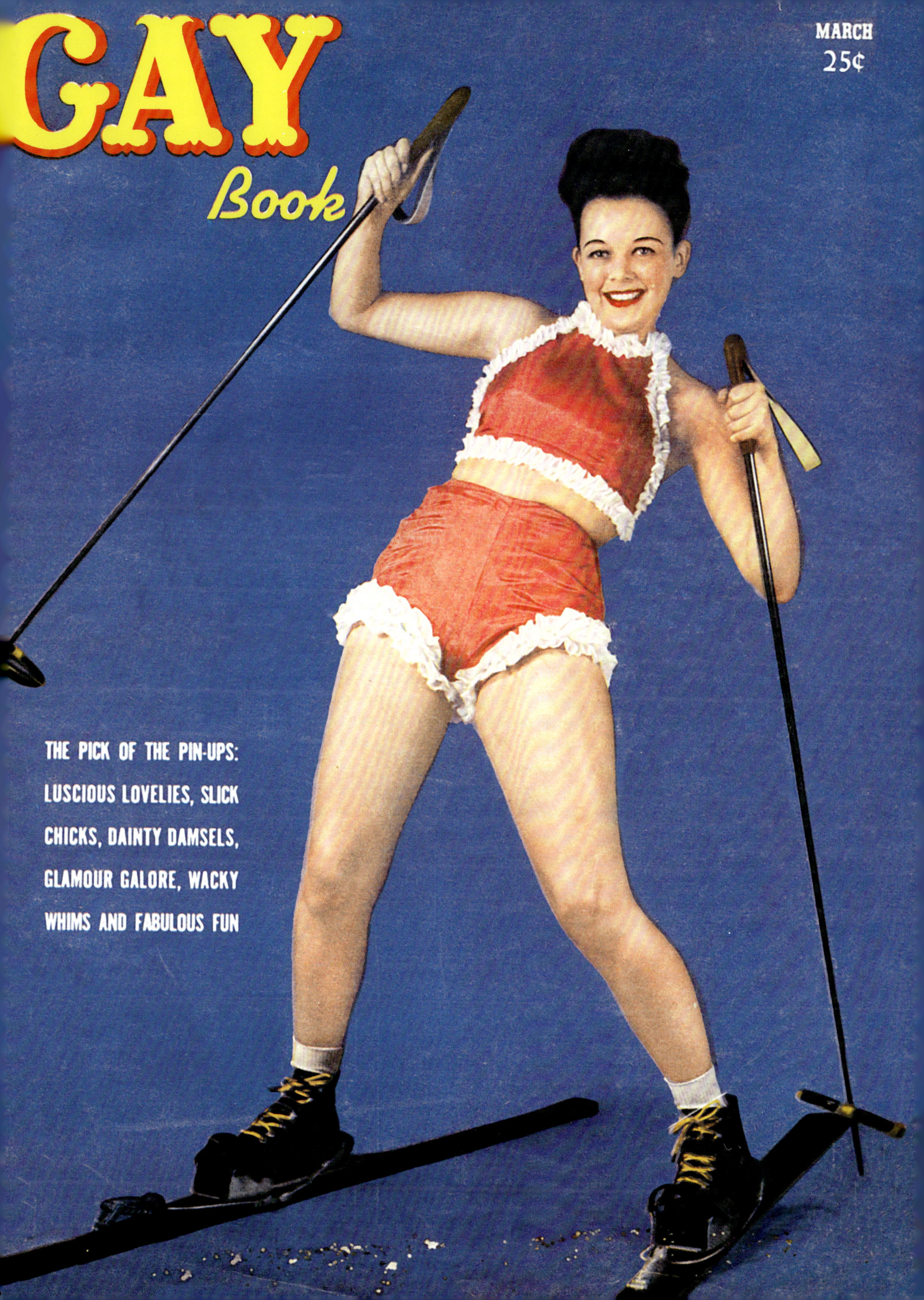
GAY
Book
MARCH
25¢
THE PICK OF THE PIN-UPS:
LUSCIOUS LOVELIES, SLICK
CHICKS, DAINTY DAMSELS,
GLAMOUR GALORE, WACKY
WHIMS AND FABULOUS FUN

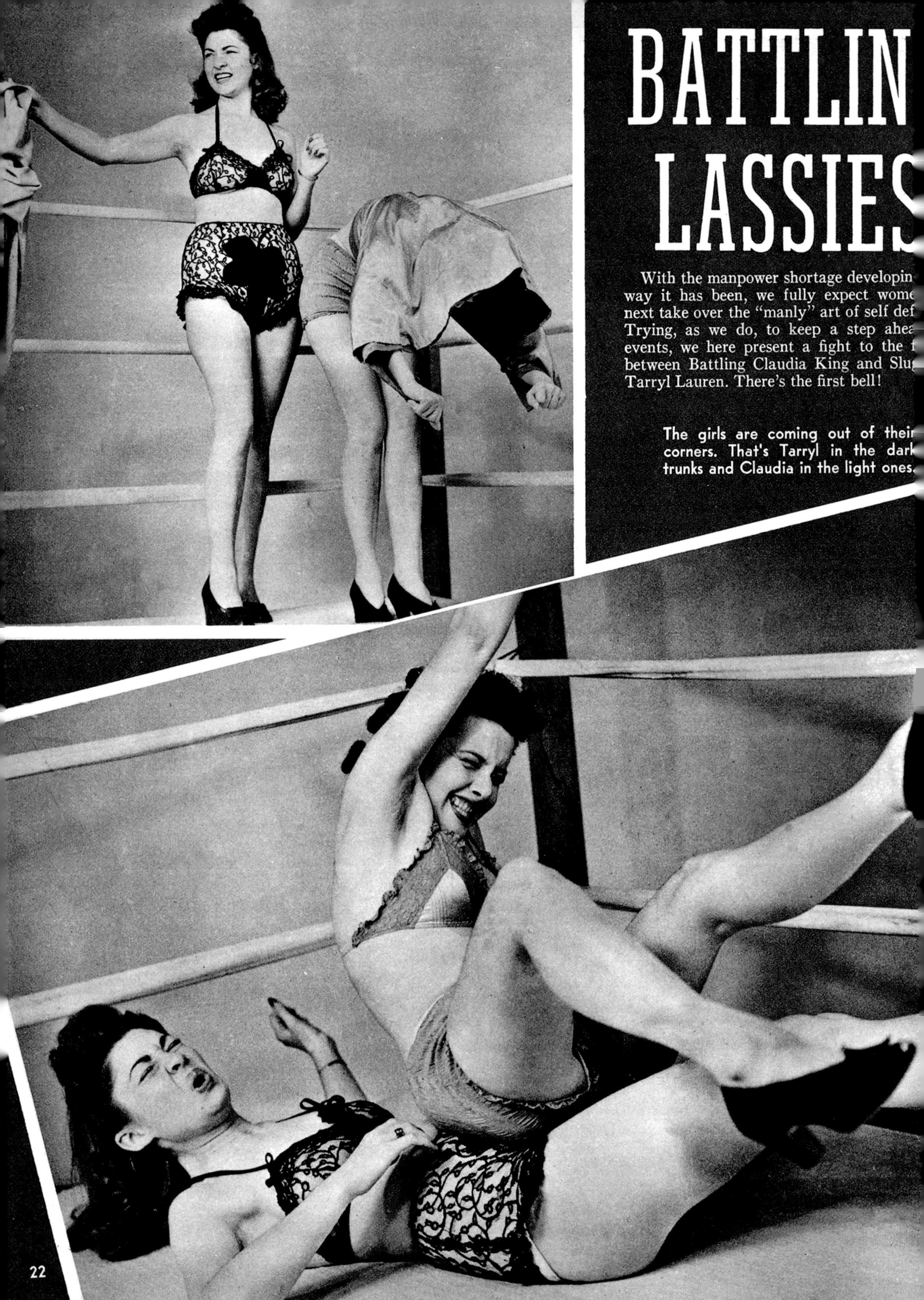

BATTLIN LASSIES

With the manpower shortage developin way it has been, we fully expect wome next take over the "manly" art of self def Trying, as we do, to keep a step ahea events, we here present a fight to the f between Battling Claudia King and Slug Tarryl Lauren. There's the first bell!

The girls are coming out of their corners. That's Tarryl in the dark trunks and Claudia in the light ones.

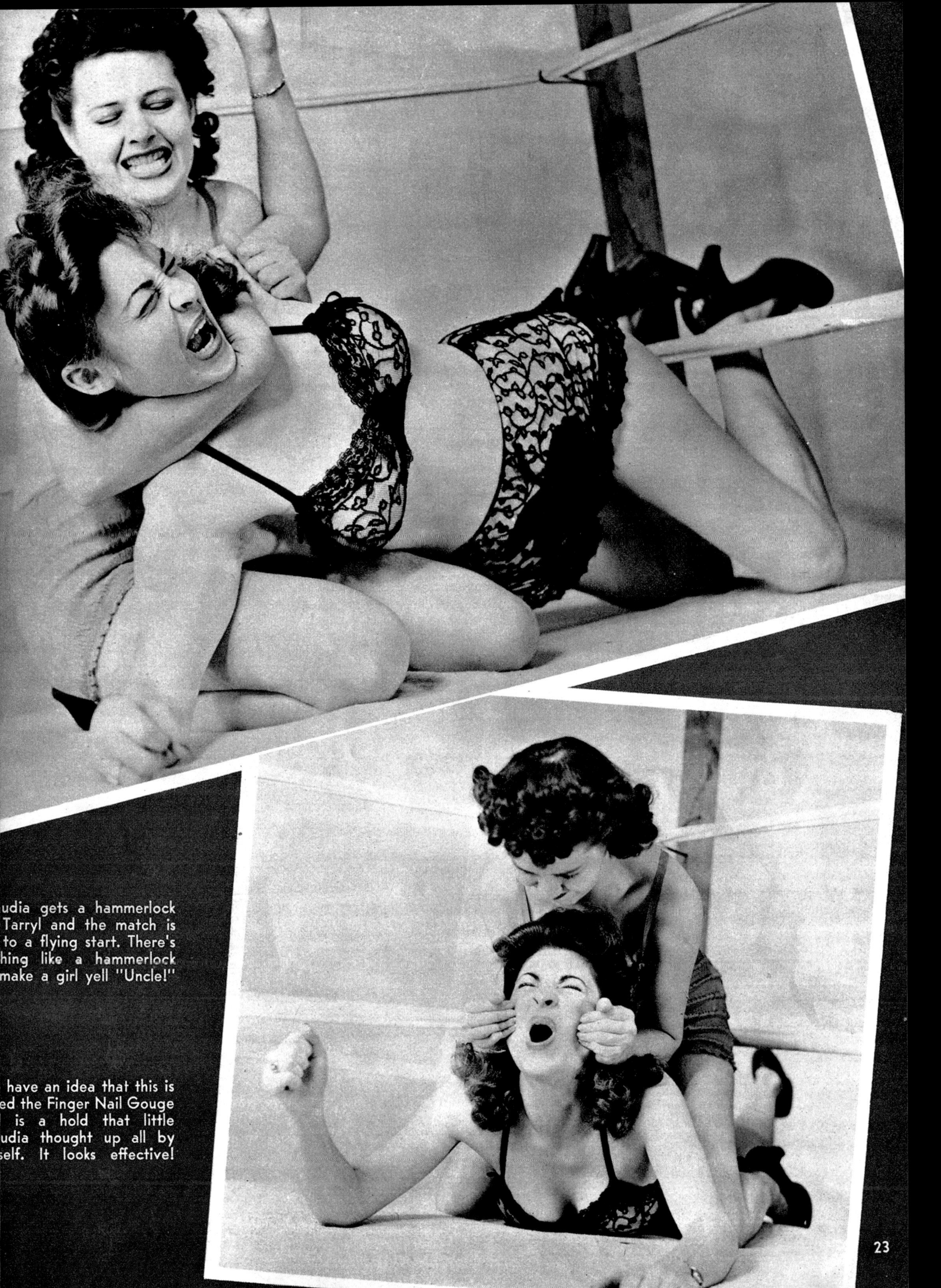

udia gets a hammerlock Tarryl and the match is to a flying start. There's hing like a hammerlock make a girl yell "Uncle!"

have an idea that this is ed the Finger Nail Gouge is a hold that little udia thought up all by self. It looks effective!

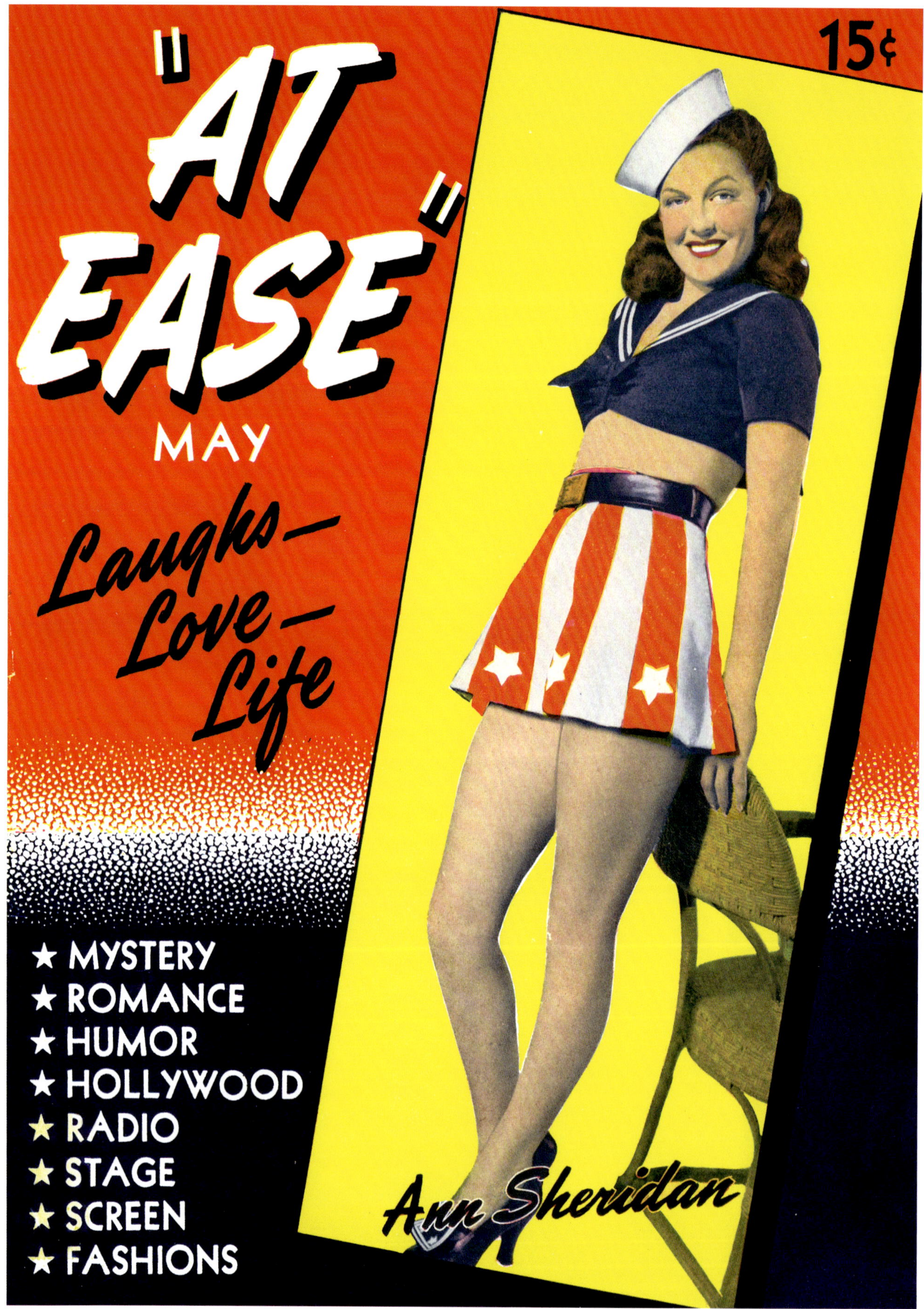

Year: **1942**. Title: **"At Ease"**. Country: **USA**.

Year: **1951**. Title: **G-Eyefuls**.
Country: **USA**.

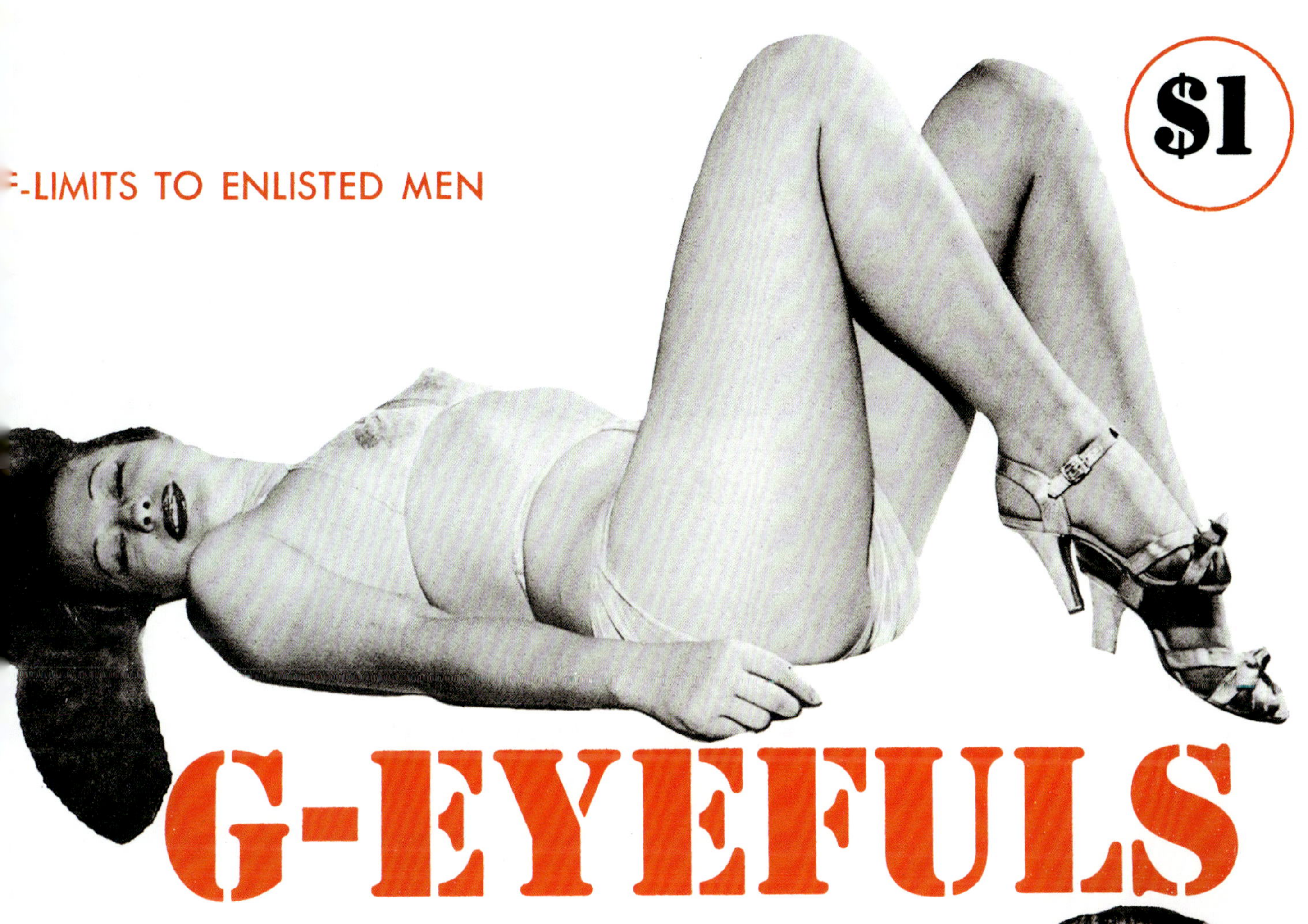

G-EYEFULS

A MANUAL OF ARMS . . .
AND LEGS

Bill Boltin

FIELD STRIP, Mmm-1

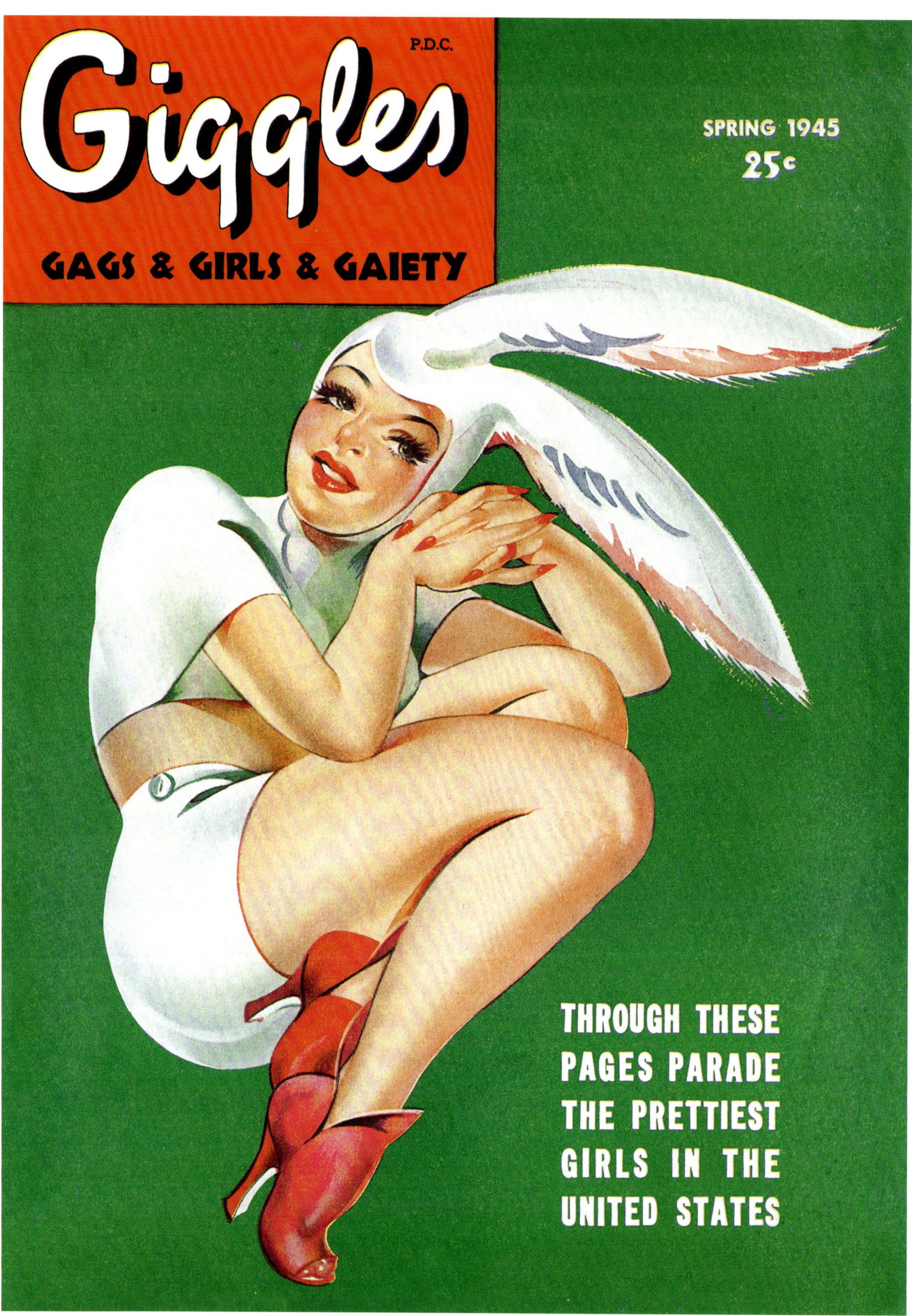

YEAR: **1945**. TITLE: **Giggles**. COUNTRY: **USA**.

YEAR: **1943**. TITLE: **Giggles**. COUNTRY: **USA**.

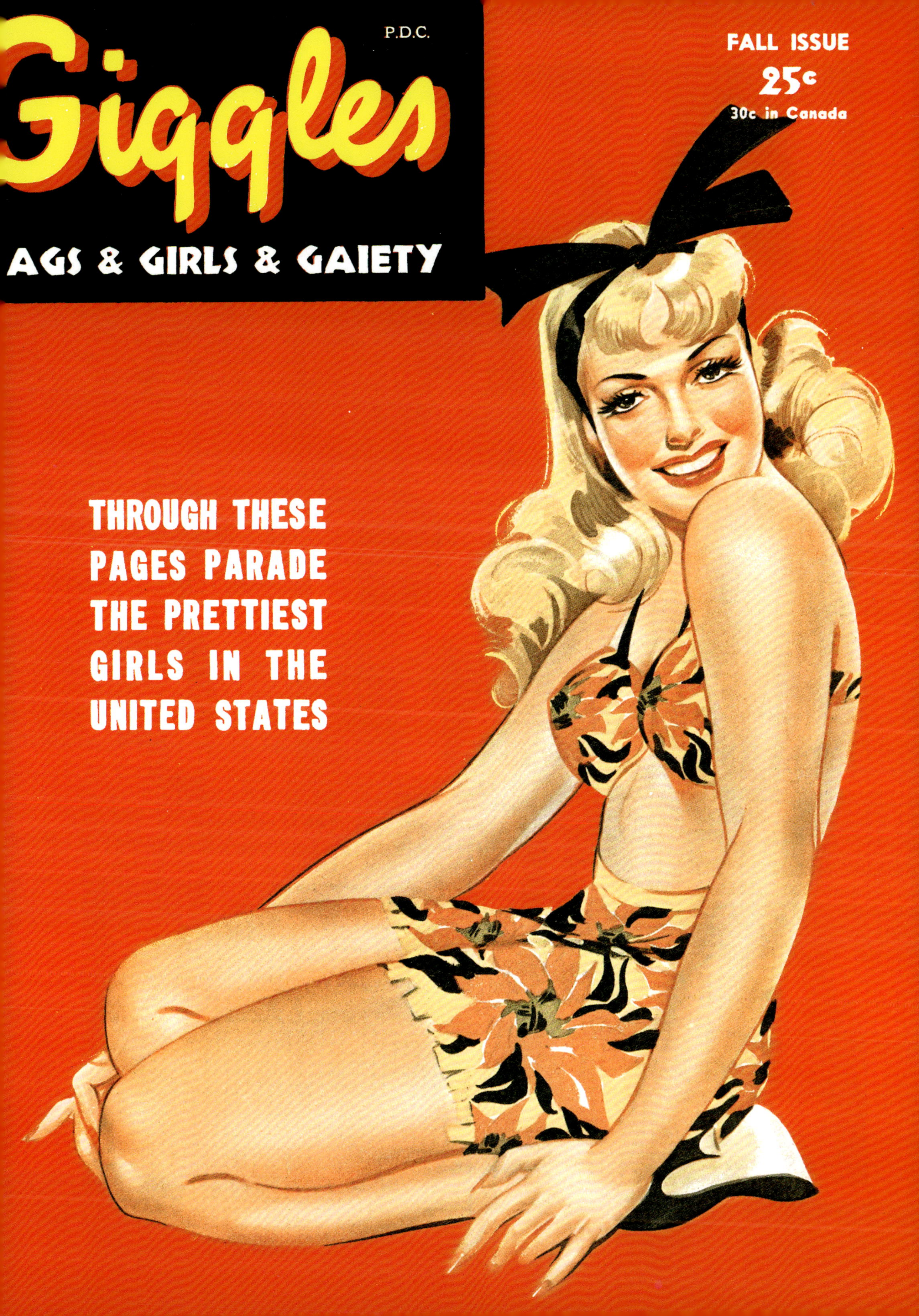
P.D.C.
Giggles
AGS & GIRLS & GAIETY
FALL ISSUE
25c
30c in Canada
THROUGH THESE
PAGES PARADE
THE PRETTIEST
GIRLS IN THE
UNITED STATES

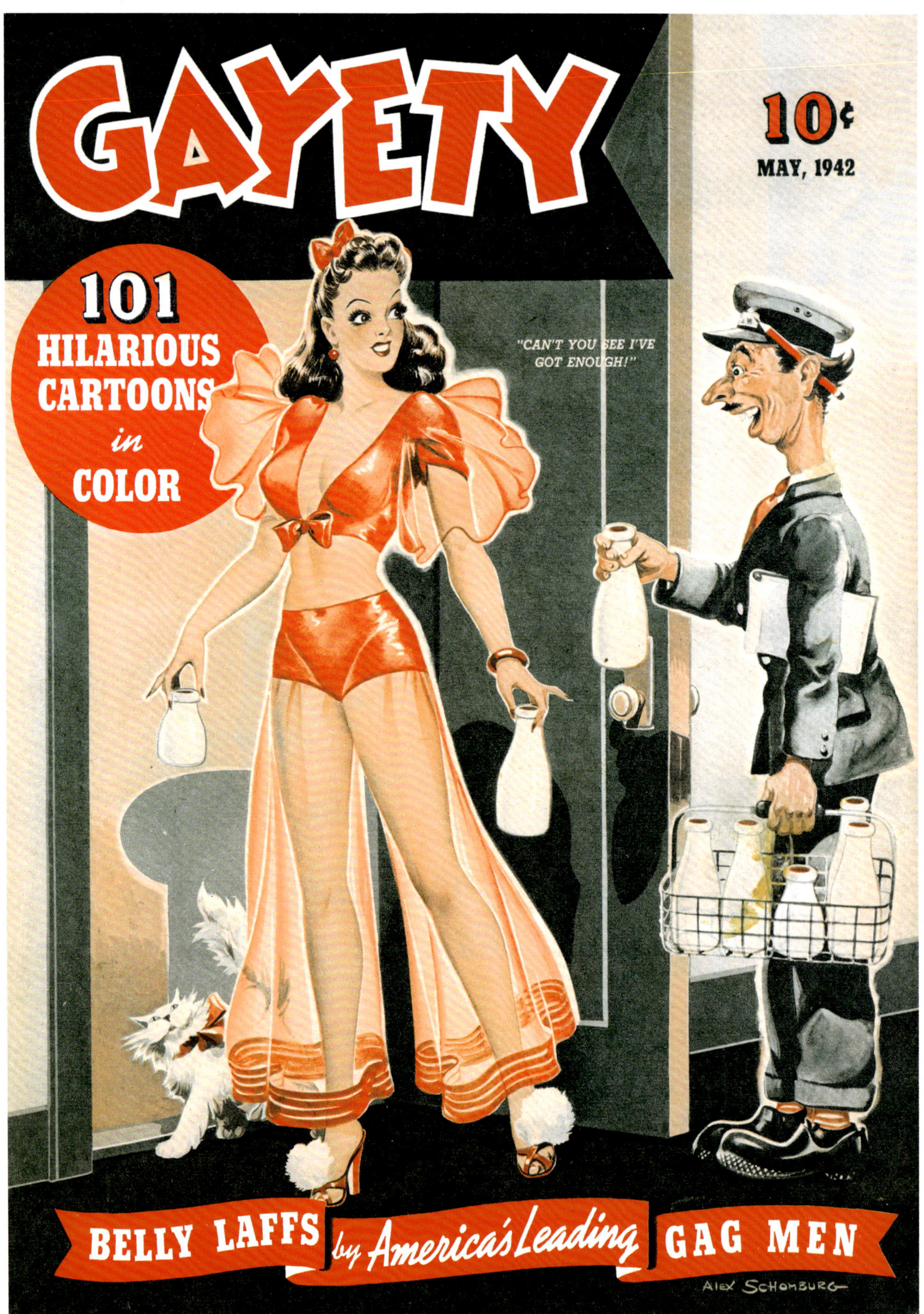

Year: **1942**. Title: **Gayety**. Artist: **Alex Schomburg**. Country: **USA**.

Year: **1941**. Title: **Gayety**.
Artist: **Alex Schomburg**. Country: **USA**.

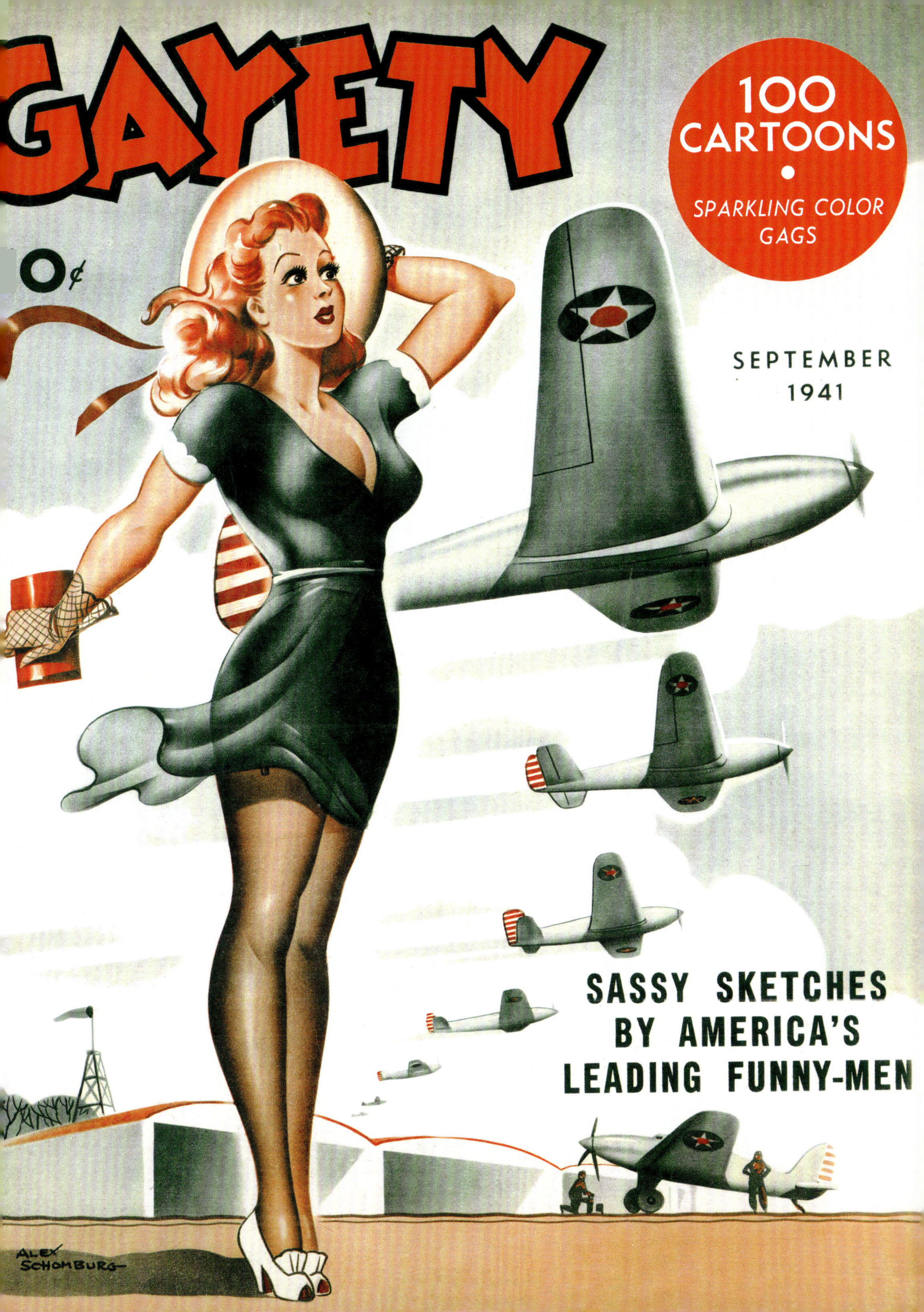
GAYETY
100 CARTOONS
SPARKLING COLOR GAGS
0¢
SEPTEMBER 1941
SASSY SKETCHES BY AMERICA'S LEADING FUNNY-MEN
ALEX SCHOMBURG

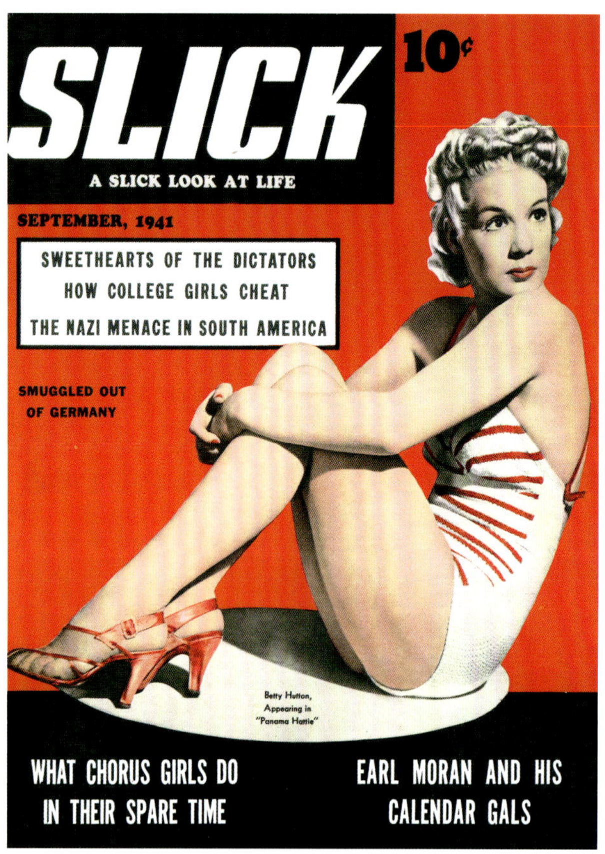

Year: **1941**. Title: **Slick**. Country: **USA**.

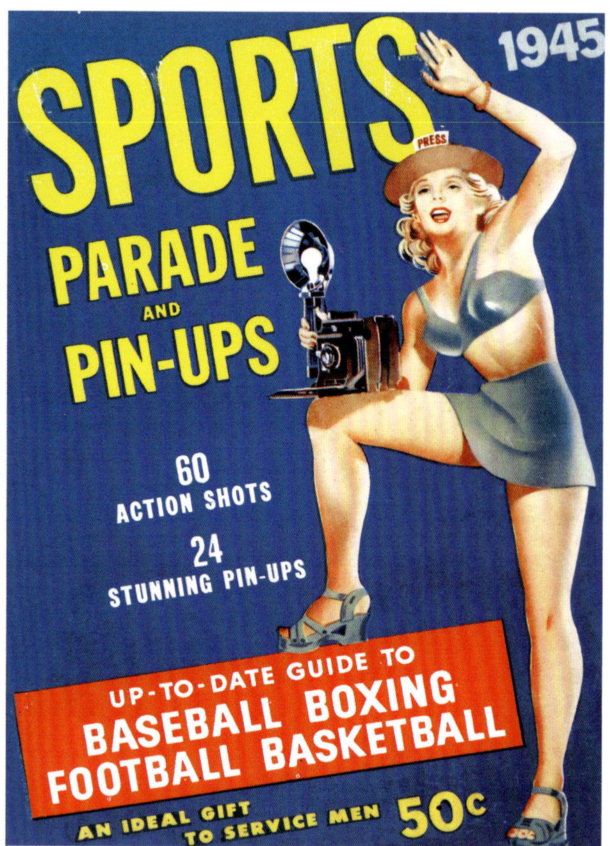

Year: **1945**. Title: **Sports Parade and Pin-ups**. Country: **USA**.

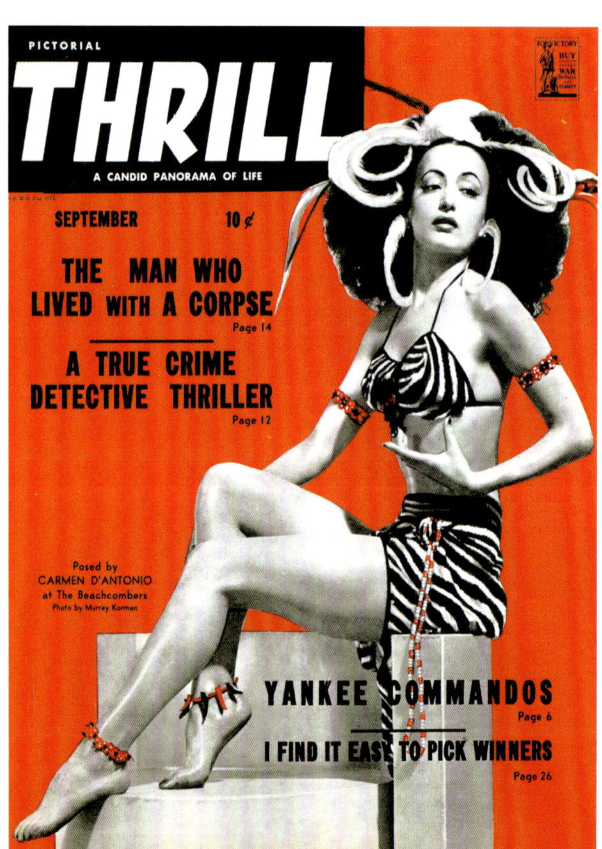

Year: **1942**. Title: **Pictorial Thrill**. Country: **USA**.

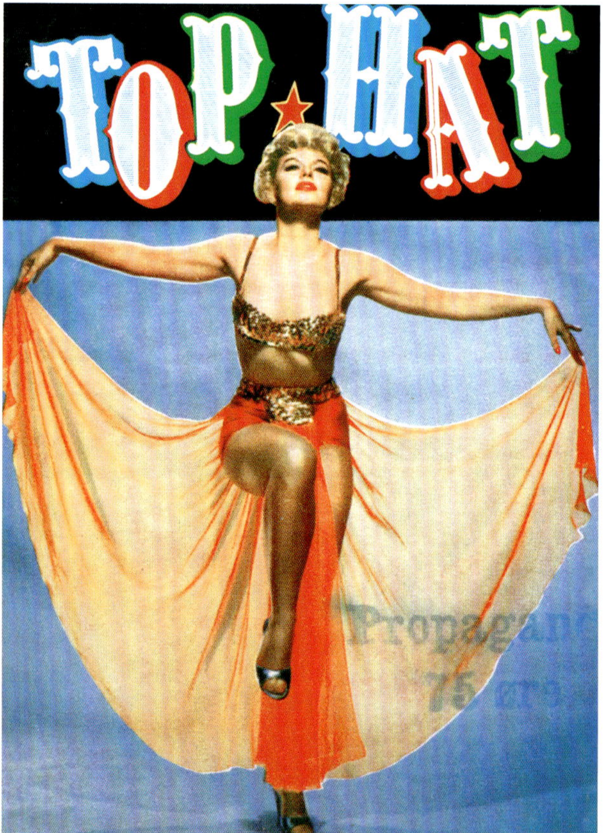

Year: **1940s**. Title: **Top Hat**. Country: **USA**.

Year: **1941**. Title: **TNT**. Country: **USA**.

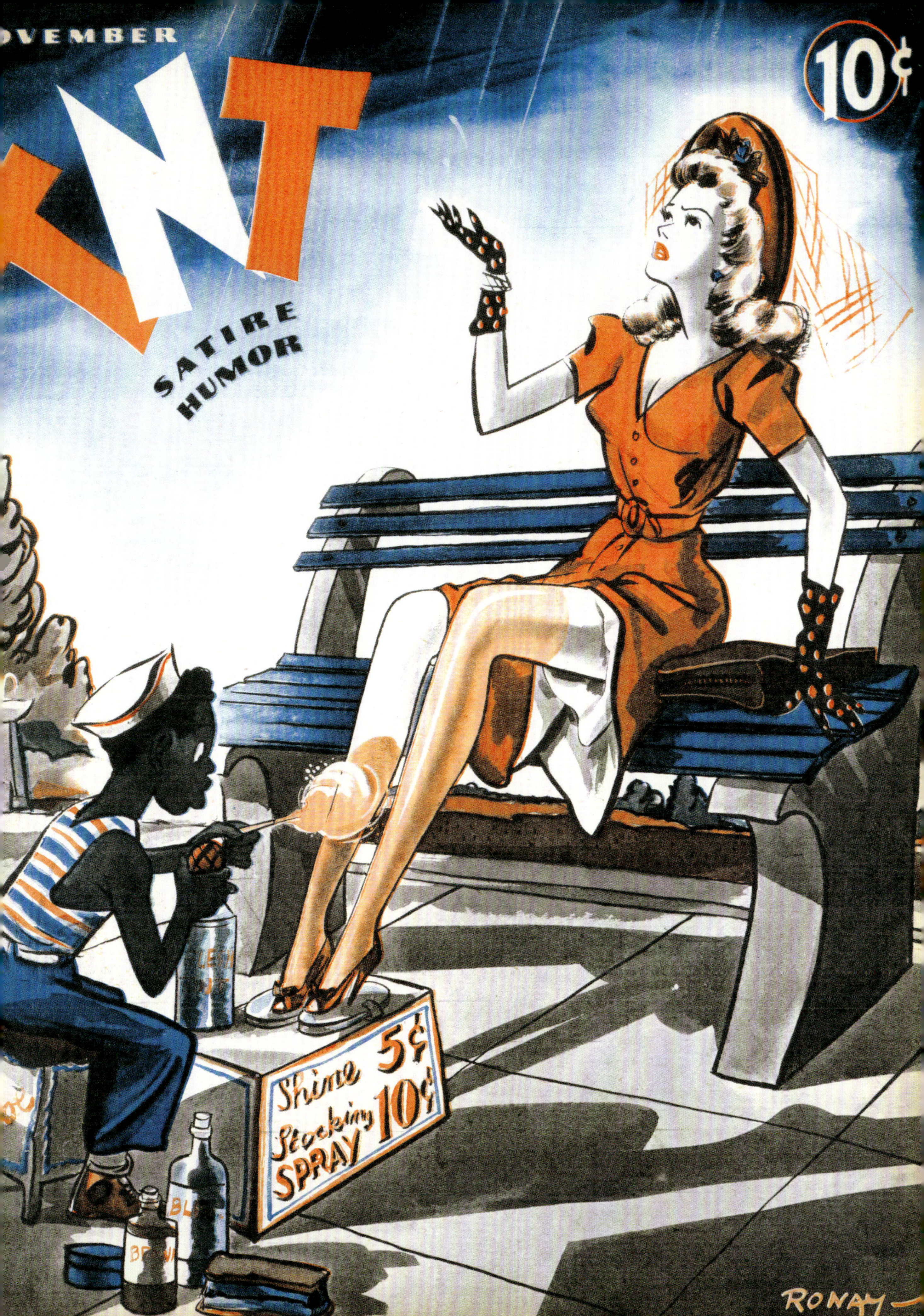
OVEMBER
10¢
SATIRE
HUMOR
Shine 5¢
Stocking 10¢
SPRAY
RONAY

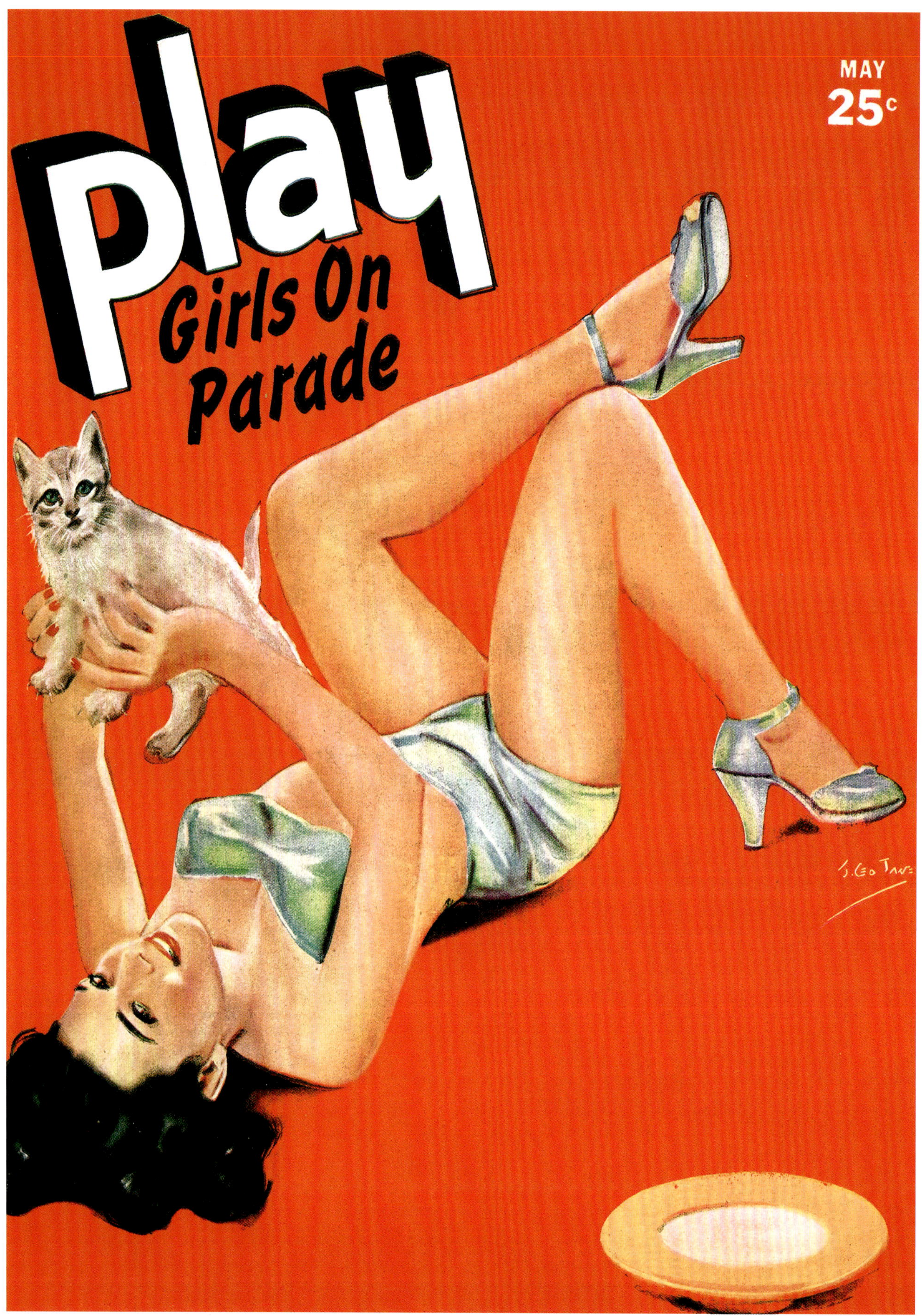

Year: **1944**. Title: **Play**. Artist: **J. George Janes**. Country: **USA**.

Right:
Year: **1943**. Title: **Play**. Artist: **J. George Janes**. Country: **USA**.

Pages 324 & 325:
Year: **1943**. Title: **Giggles**. Country: **USA**.

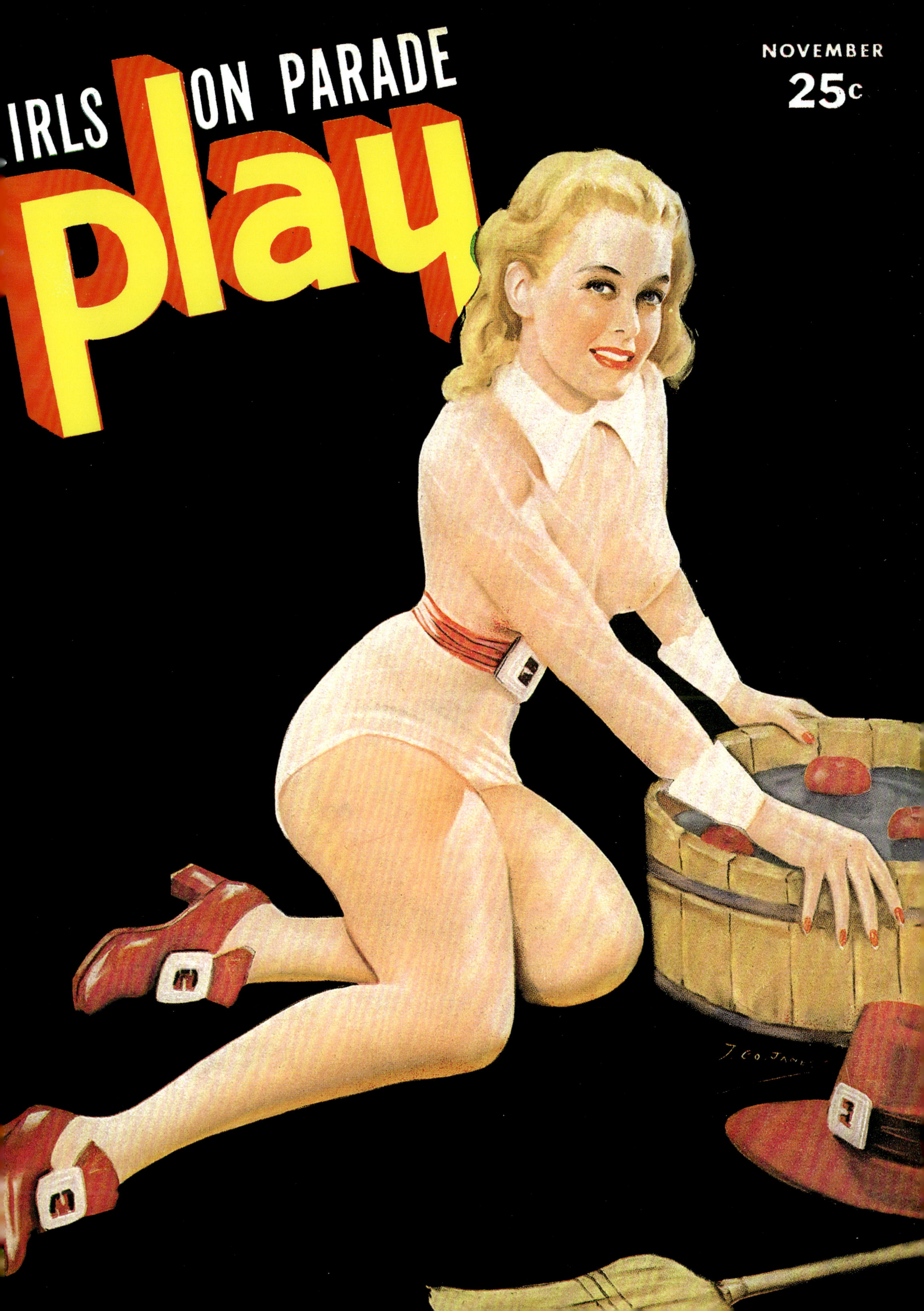
IRLS ON PARADE
play
NOVEMBER
25c

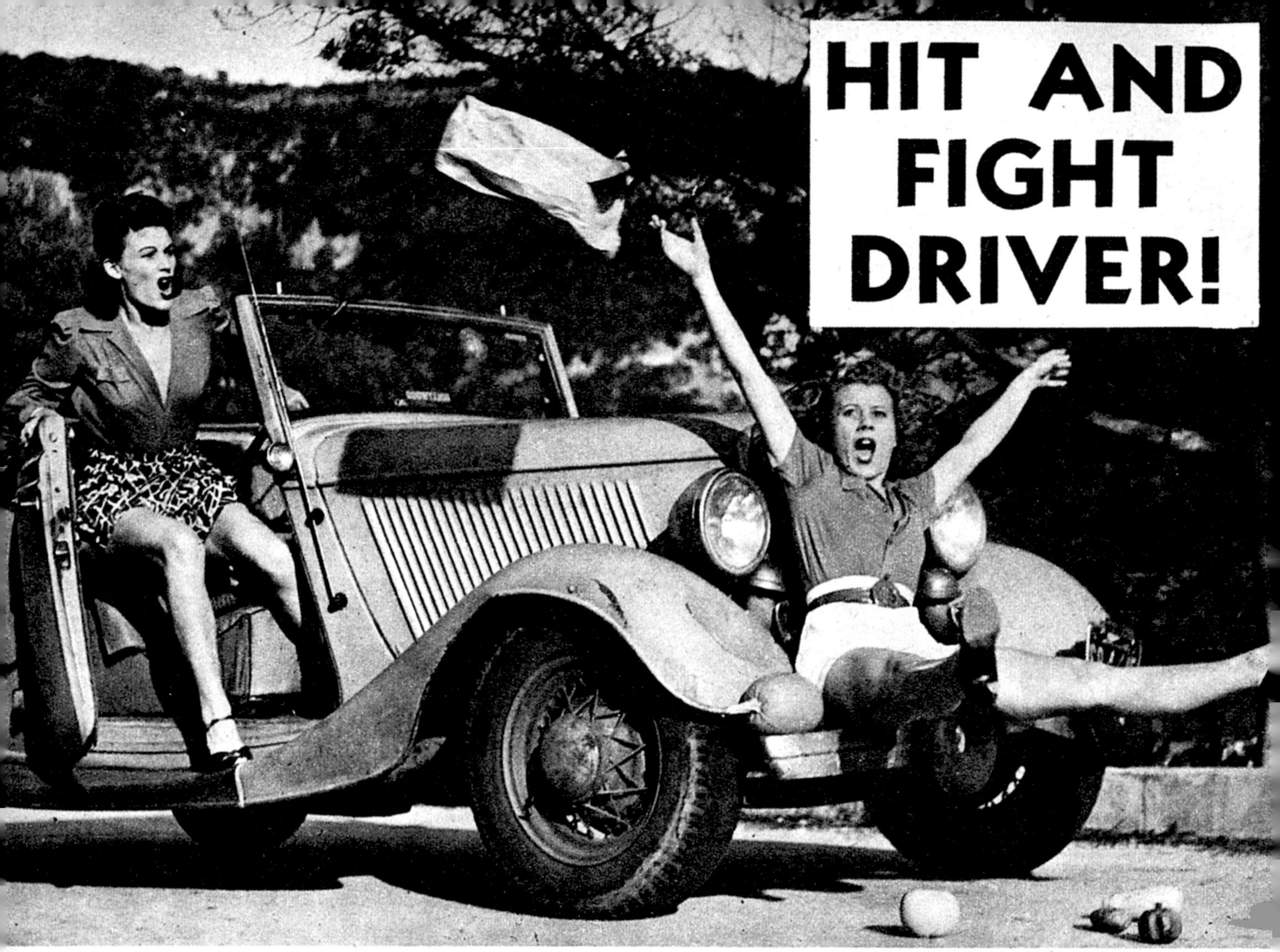

HIT AND FIGHT DRIVER!

(Above) "You've struck me! I'm killed! And besides my vegetables!"
(Below) "I'll teach you to ruin a bag of expensive vegetables!"

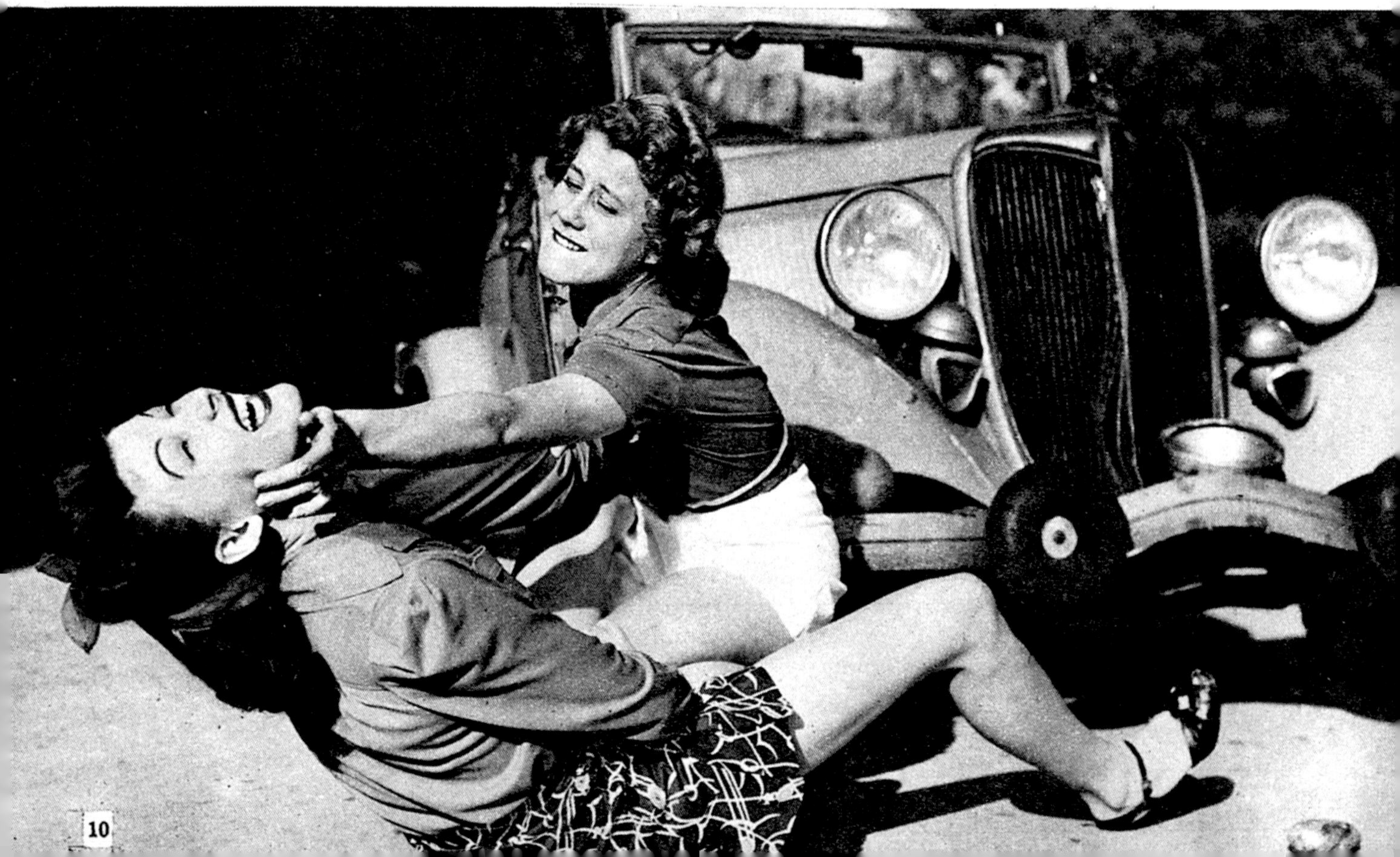

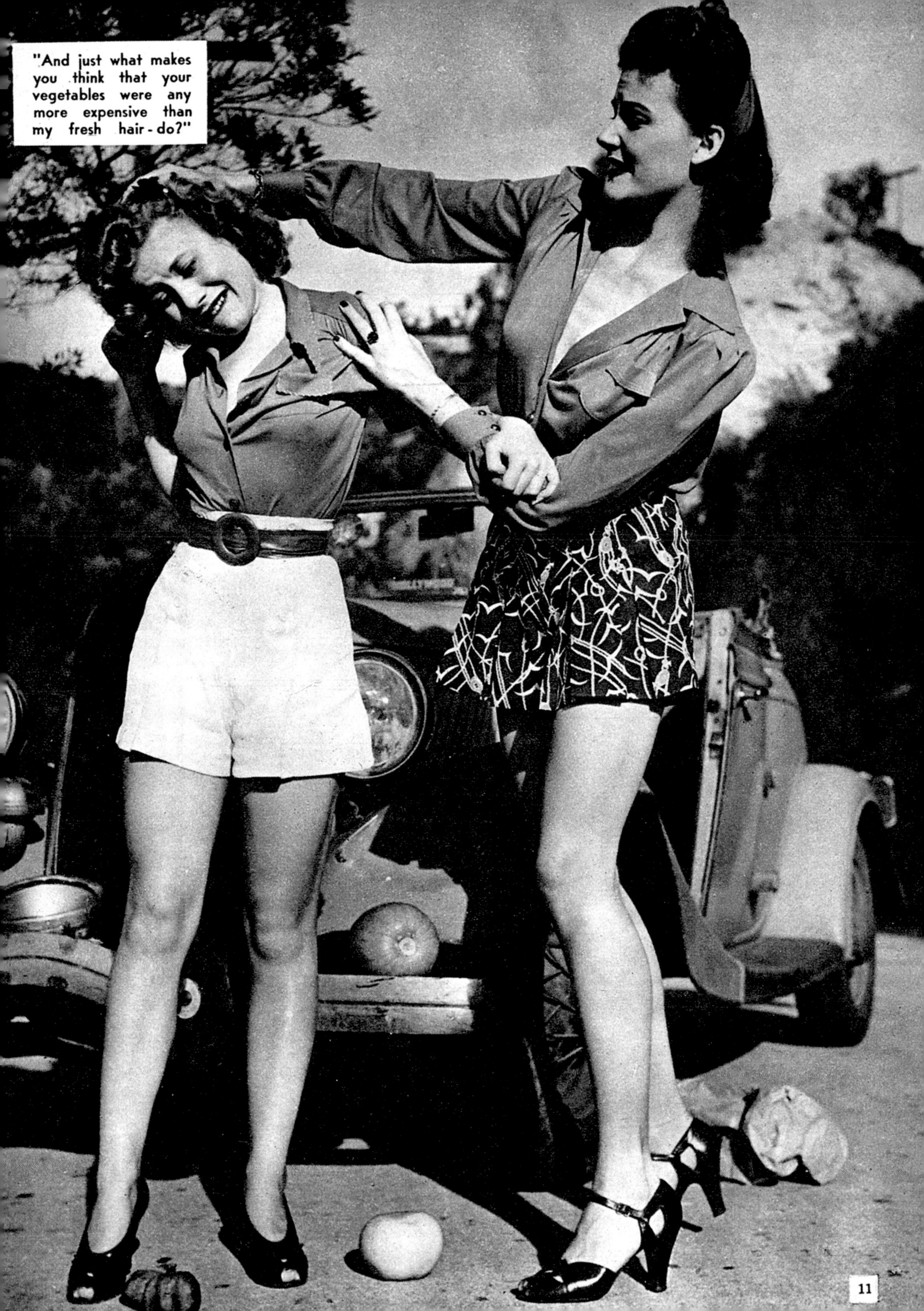

"And just what makes you think that your vegetables were any more expensive than my fresh hair-do?"

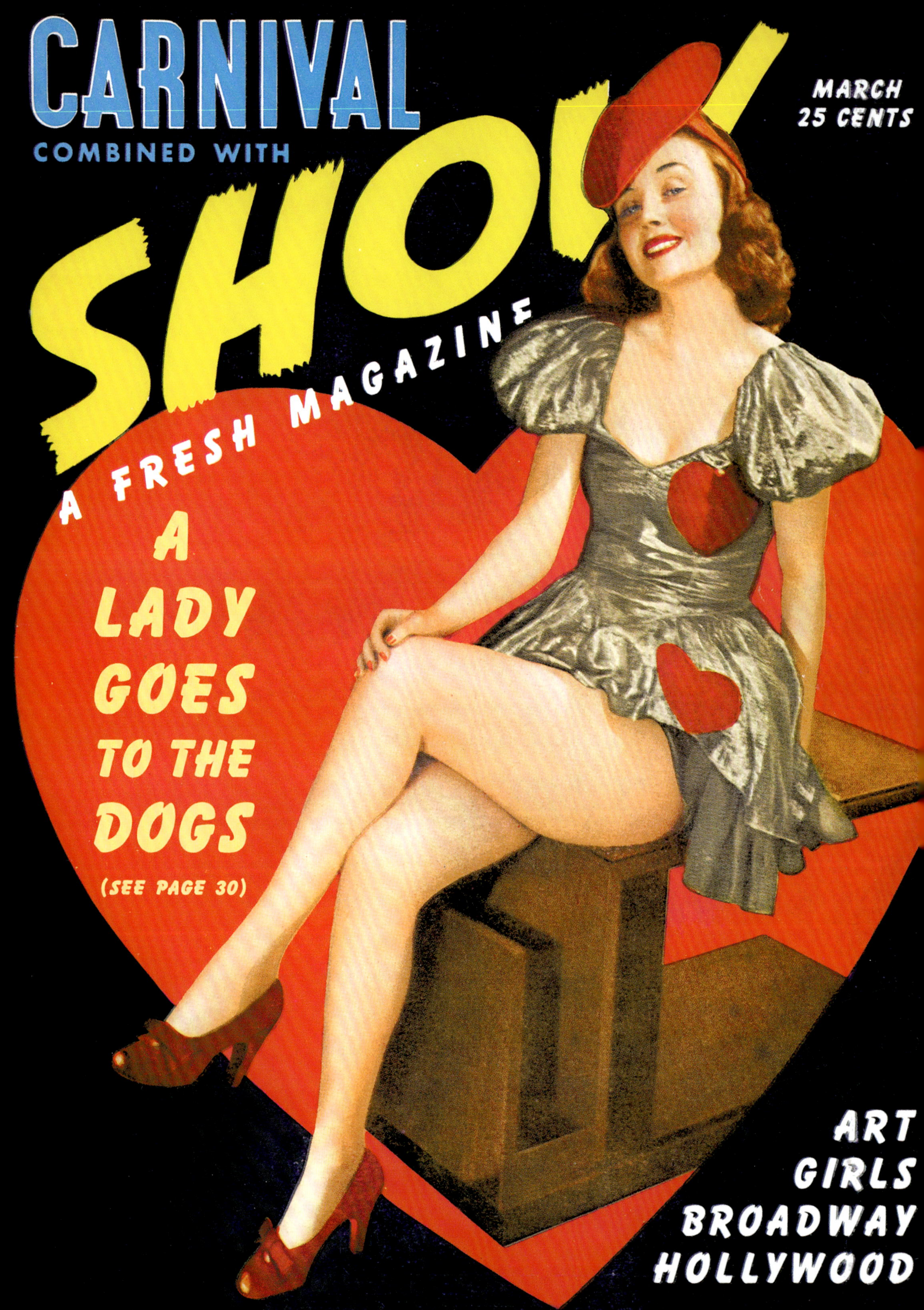

CARNIVAL
COMBINED WITH
SHOW
MARCH
25 CENTS
A FRESH MAGAZINE
A
LADY
GOES
TO THE
DOGS
(SEE PAGE 30)
ART
GIRLS
BROADWAY
HOLLYWOOD

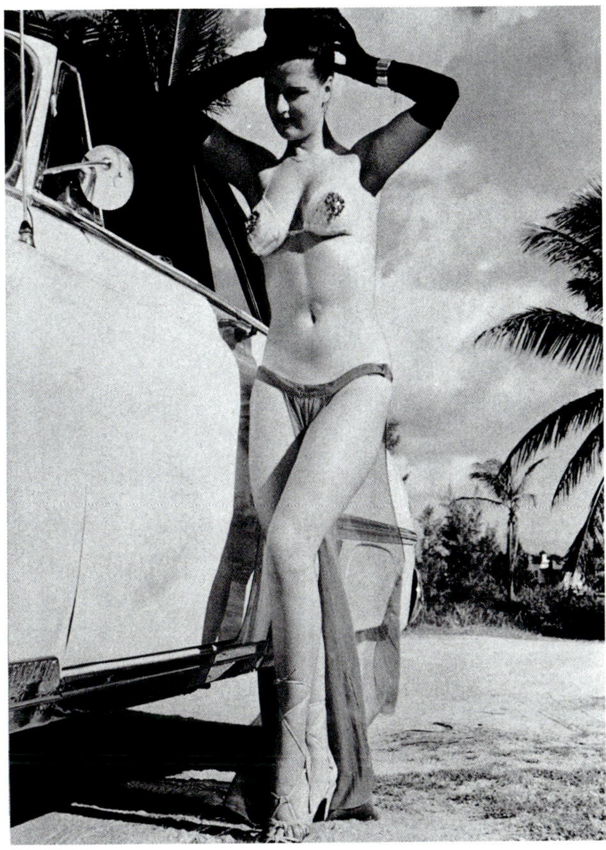

Year: **1951**. Title: **G-Eyefuls**. Country: **USA**.

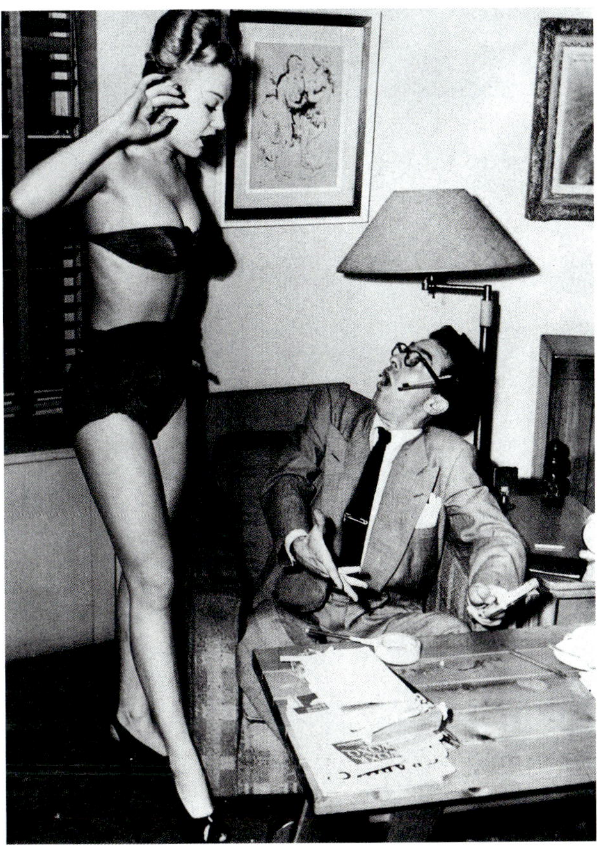

Year: **1951**. Title: **G-Eyefuls**. Country: **USA**.

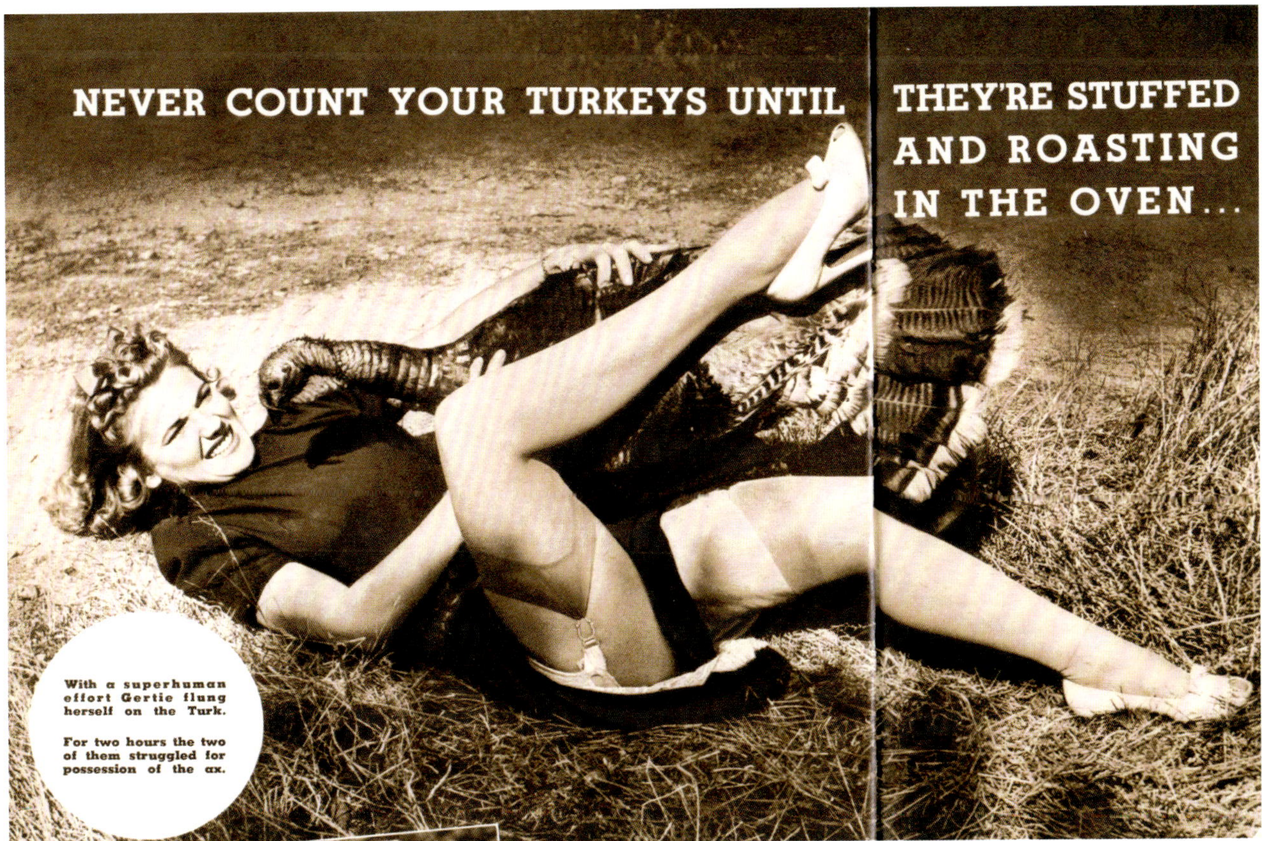

Year: **1940**. Title: **Show**. Country: **USA**.

Year: **1941**. Title: **Carnival Combined with Show**. Country: **USA**.

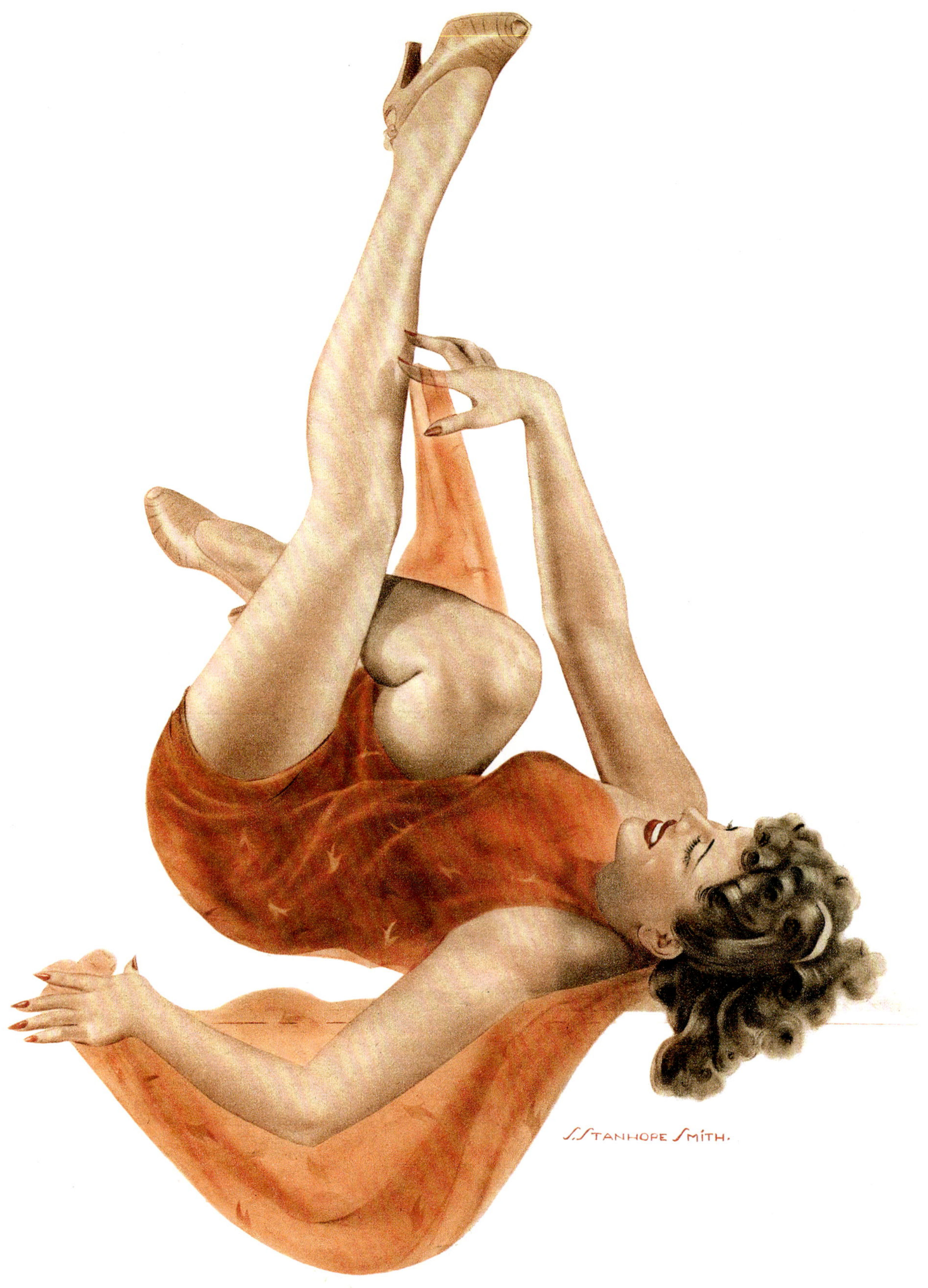

Year: **1942**. Title: **The Male Home Companion**.
Artist: **S. Stanhope Smith**. Country: **USA**.

Year: **1942**. Title: **The Male Home Companion**. Artist: **Cardwell Higgens**. Country: **USA**.

Pages 330 & 331:
Year: **1946**. Title: **Who is Your Pin-up Girl?** Country: **USA**.
Year: **1943**. Title: **War Laffs**. Country: **USA**.

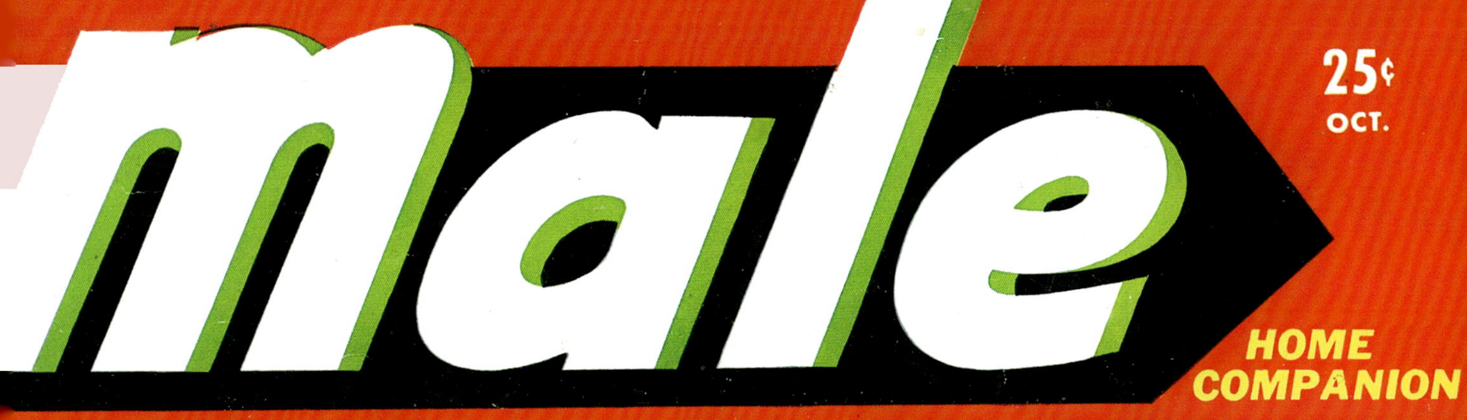

"Make a Wish!"

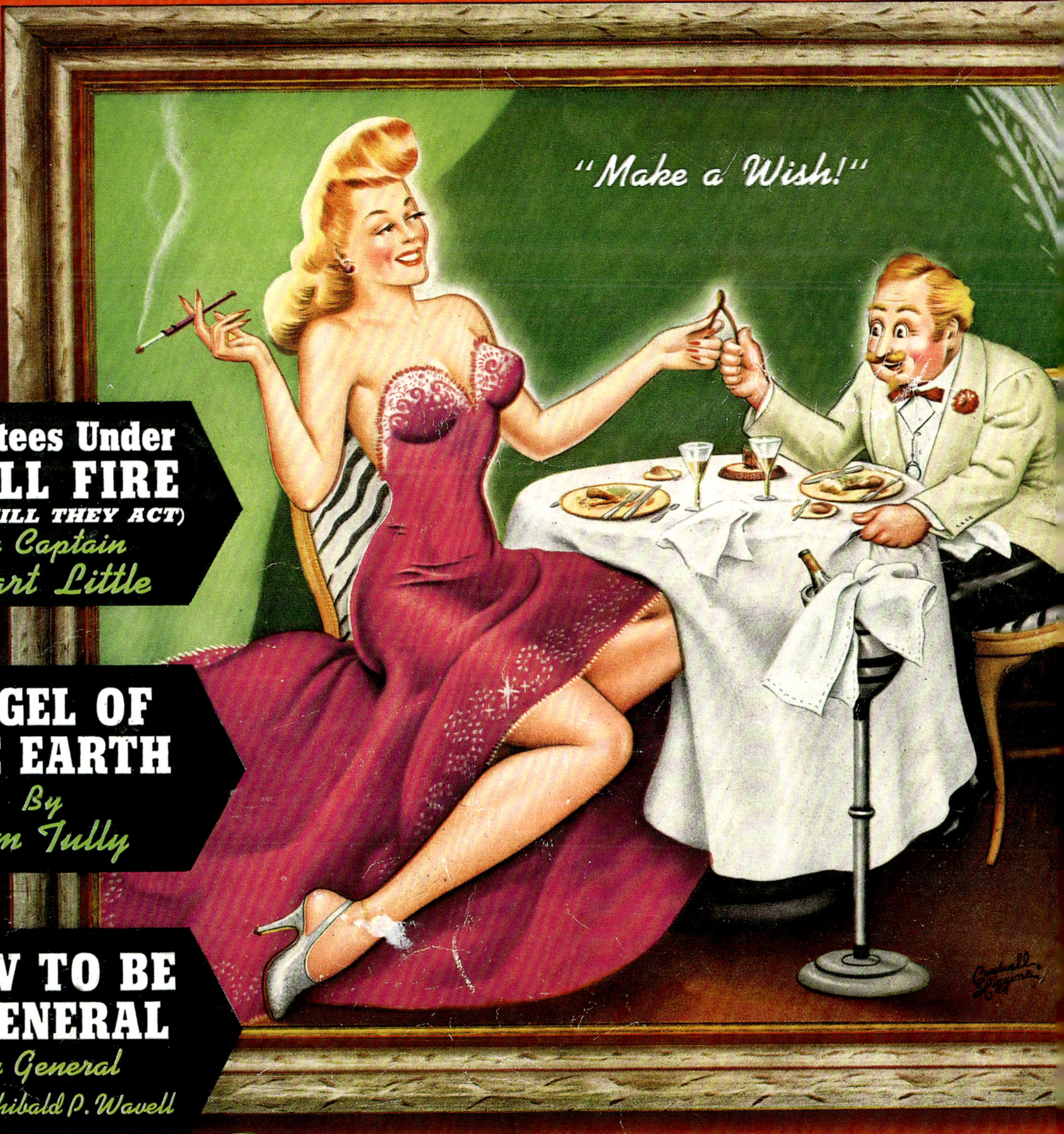

lectees Under
IELL FIRE
W WILL THEY ACT)
By Captain
tuart Little

NGEL OF
HE EARTH
By
Jim Tully

OW TO BE
GENERAL
By General
Archibald P. Wavell

℞ **WHO'S A JERK?**... *Jerome Weidman*

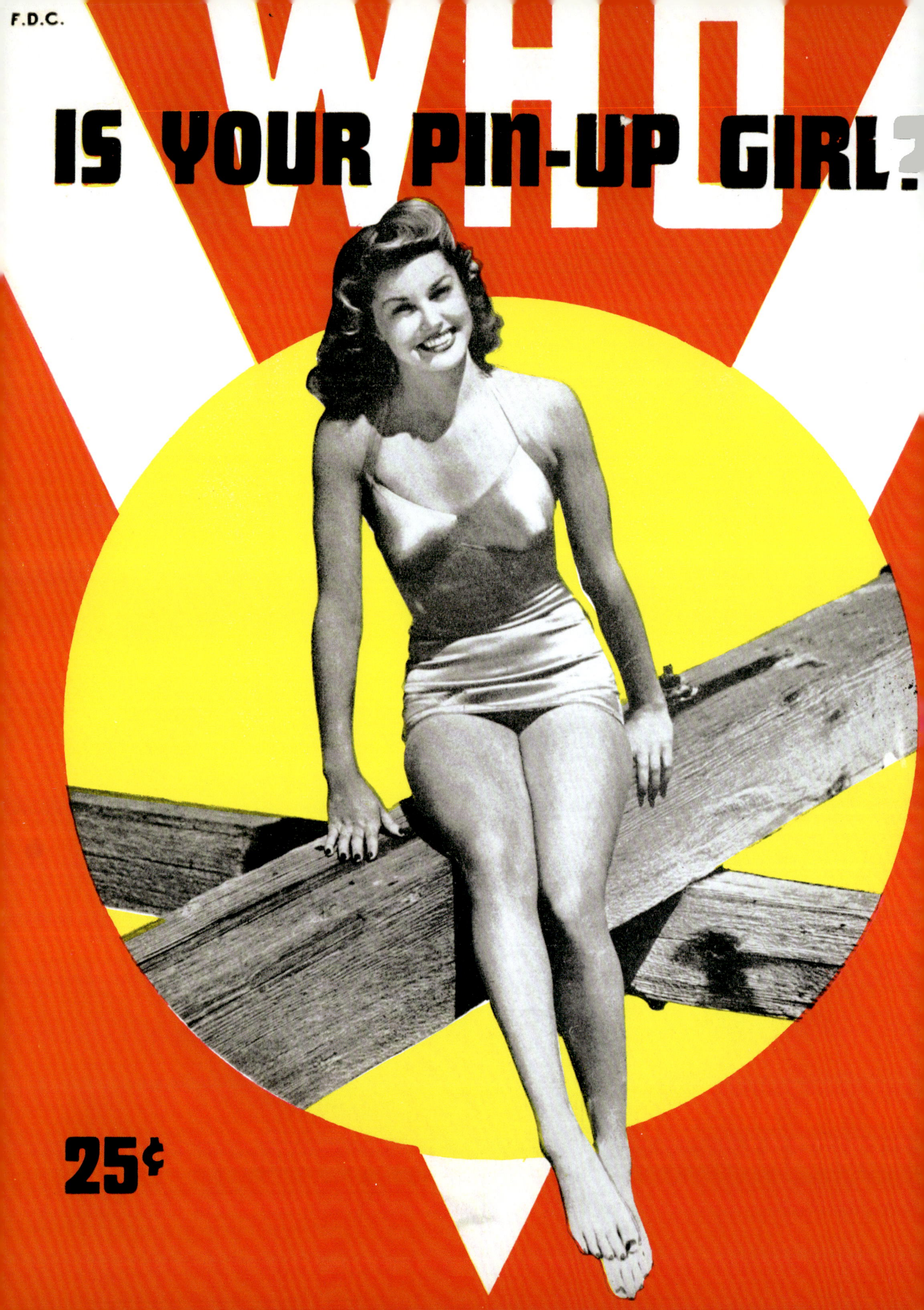
F.D.C.
WHO
IS YOUR PIN-UP GIRL?
25¢

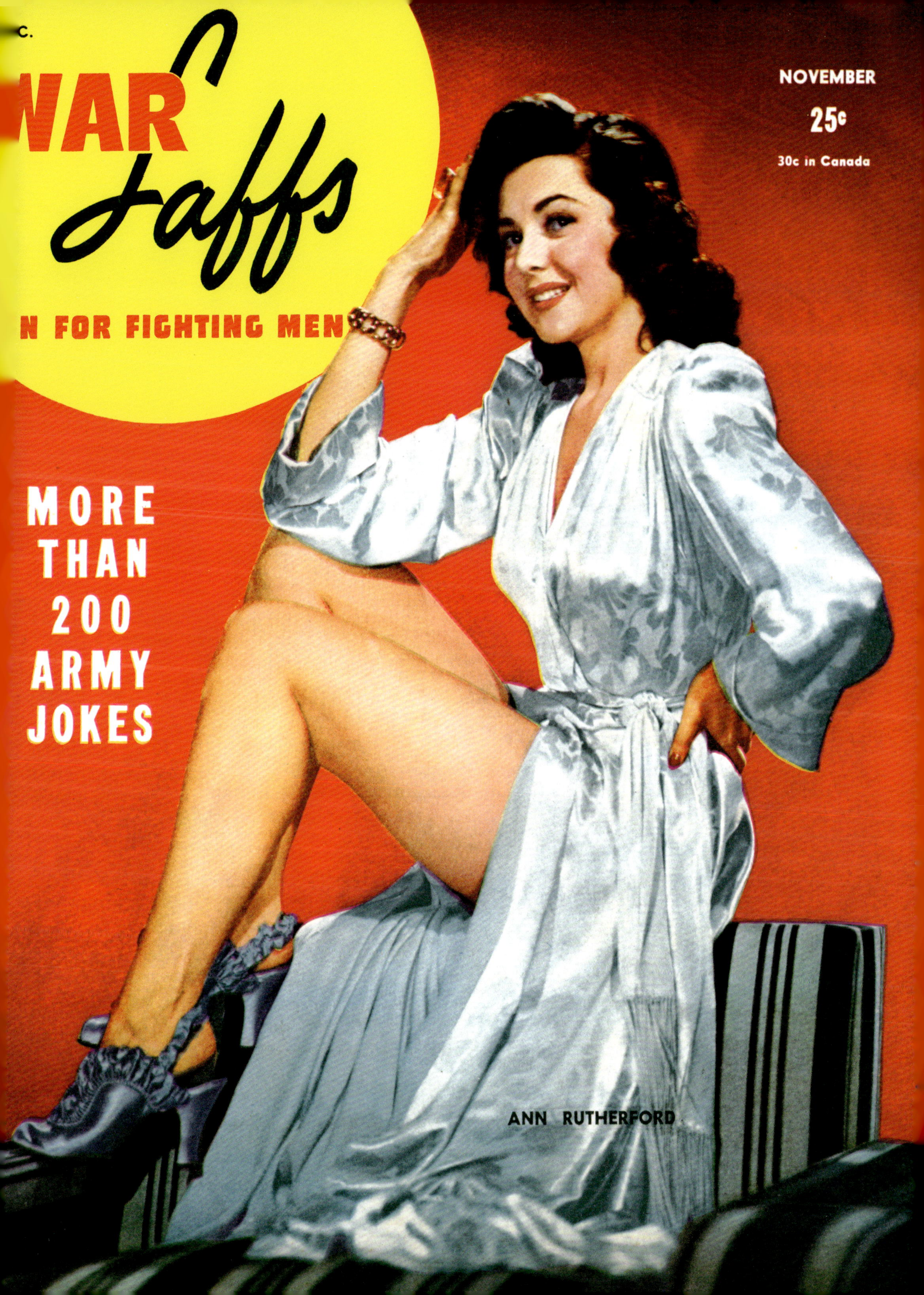
C.
WAR Jaffs
NOVEMBER
25¢
30c in Canada
N FOR FIGHTING MEN
MORE
THAN
200
ARMY
JOKES
ANN RUTHERFORD

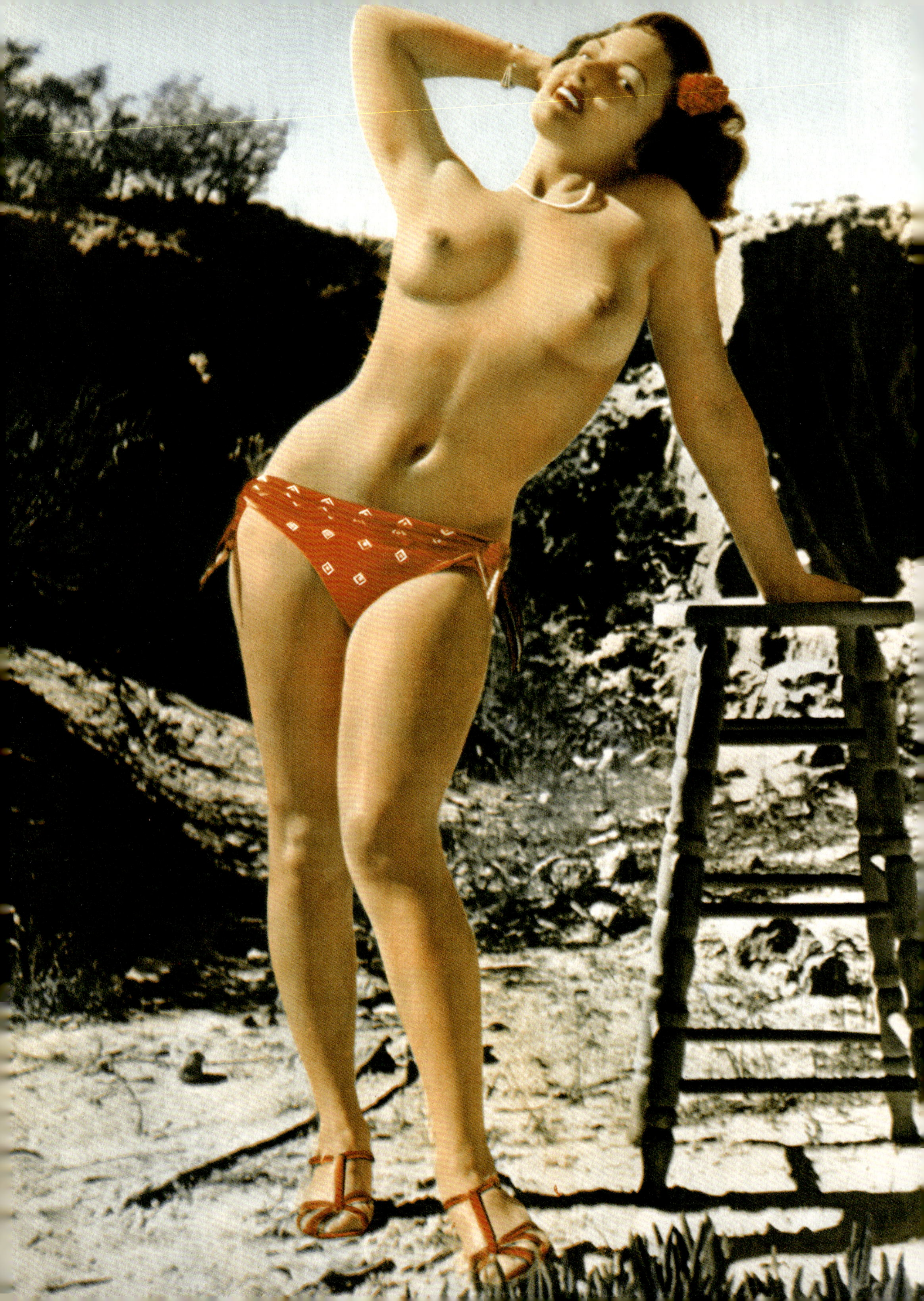

PARIS-HOLLYWOOD:

The French Post-War Recovery Effort

Paris-Hollywood: Der Wiederaufbau auf Französisch

Paris-Hollywood : l'effort de reconstruction français dans l'après-guerre

In the 1950s and 60s America had *Playboy* and France had *Paris-Hollywood*. World War II devastated Europe in ways Americans can never fully appreciate. The return of men's magazines was one step towards emotional recovery. Started right after World War II by a father/son team of surgeon/publishers named Mauclaire, the first *Paris-Hollywood* was large in format but small in page count. Post-war paper shortages were severe, but France being France, and especially Paris being Paris, no amount of rationing could keep them from their erotica. Thus the first issue of *Paris-Hollywood*, published in June 1946, had only 28 pages including covers. Compared with the glossy, sophisticated Parisian magazines of the 20s and 30s this sepia-tinted pulp looked anemic, but compared to anything else produced in Europe at the time it was a triumph.

From 1946 to 1948 *Paris-Hollywood* was essentially a film review magazine, maintaining the long tradition of disguising sex with seemingly innocent reportage of a sinful industry. *Paris-Hollywood* did have more serious credentials than many of its like, as the Mauclaire press group also published the famous *Cinémonde* and *Le Film Français* magazines. Maurice Bessy, future administrator of the Cannes Film Festival, was the first editor, and for a while the nudes were few and discreet and

In den Fünzigern und Sechzigern war *Paris-Hollywood* für Frankreich das, was für die USA der *Playboy* war. Der Zweite Weltkrieg hatte Europa stärker verwüstet, als Amerikaner sich je vorstellen können. Die Rückkehr der Männermagazine war ein Schritt zurück zur emotionalen Gesundung. Unmittelbar nach Kriegsende wurde von einem Vater/Sohn-Team namens Mauclaire das erste *Paris-Hollywood* herausgegeben – groß im Format, aber arm an Seiten. Papier war im Frankreich nach dem Krieg streng rationiert, aber Frankreich ist nun einmal Frankreich, daher ließen sich die Franzosen durch keine noch so drastische Rationierung von ihren Erotika abbringen. So hatte denn die erste Ausgabe vom Juni 1946 inklusive Cover nur 28 Seiten. Verglichen mit den niveauvollen Hochglanzmagazinen der Zwanziger und Dreißiger sah dieses sepiafarbene, billige Papier etwas blutarm aus, aber verglichen mit

World War II devastated Europe. The return of men's magazines was one step towards emotional recovery.

Dans les années cinquante et soixante, les États-Unis eurent leur *Playboy* et la France son *Paris-Hollywood*. La Seconde Guerre mondiale avait dévasté l'Europe d'une manière que les Américains n'ont jamais vraiment pu comprendre. Le retour des magazines pour hommes constitua une étape vers la guérison affective. Lancé juste après la guerre par les Mauclaire, un père chirurgien et son fils éditeur, le premier *Paris-Hollywood* était grand par son format mais petit par le nombre de ses pages. Les restrictions sur le papier étaient sévères mais la France étant la France et, surtout, Paris étant Paris, pas question de laisser une question de rationnement priver les gens de leur ration d'érotisme. Le premier numéro, publié en juin 1946, ne comptait donc que 28 pages, couvertures incluses. Comparé aux revues parisiennes sophistiquées sur papier glacé des années 1920 et 30, ce magazine imprimé sur de la pâte à papier sépia faisait anémique, mais par rapport à ce qui se faisait en Europe à la même époque, c'était un triomphe.

De 1946 à 1948, *Paris-Hollywood* fut essentiellement un magazine de critique de cinéma, entretenant la longue tradition consistant à déguiser le sexe sous des reportages apparemment innocents sur une industrie aux mœurs légères. *Paris-Hollywood* possédait de fait des références plus sérieuses que toute autre publication

YEAR: **1947**. TITLE: **Paris-Hollywood**.
COUNTRY: **France**.

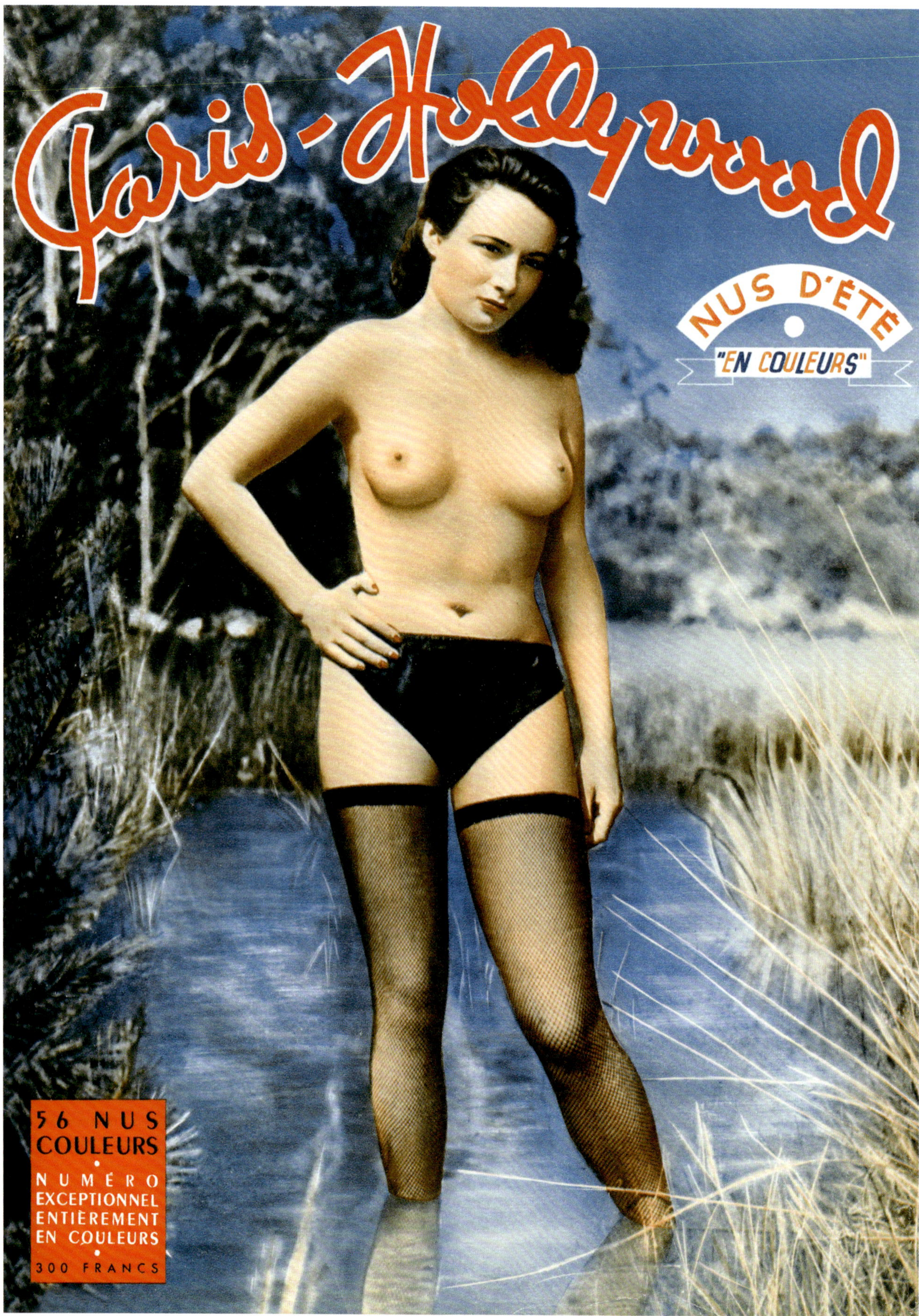

The original Paris-Hollywood *was a film review magazine concentrating on mildly risqué movies, plus a few cabaret photos.*

Ursprünglich war Paris-Hollywood *eine Zeitschrift, die sich auf Kritiken leicht anrüchiger Filme konzentrierte und daneben ein paar Cabaret-Fotos zeigte.*

À l'origine, Paris-Hollywood *était un magazine de critiques cinématographiques se concentrant sur les films vaguement osés, auxquels s'ajoutaient quelques photos de cabaret.*

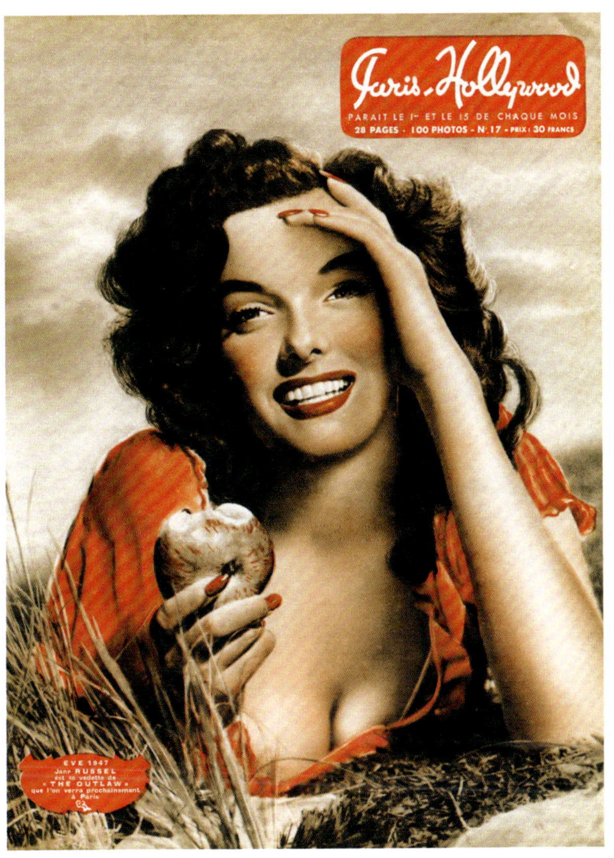

Year: **1946**. Title: **Paris-Hollywood**. Country: **France**.

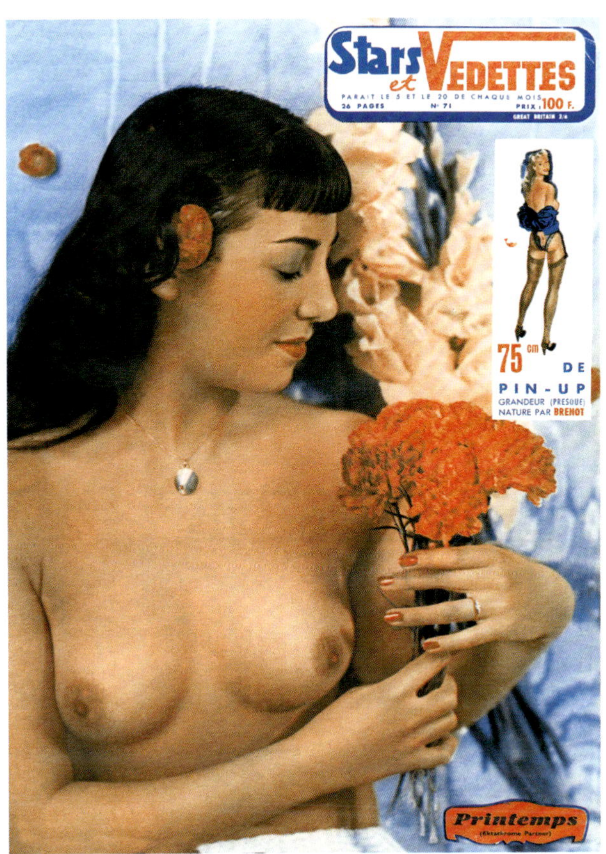

Year: **1950s**. Title: **Stars et Vedettes**. Country: **France**.

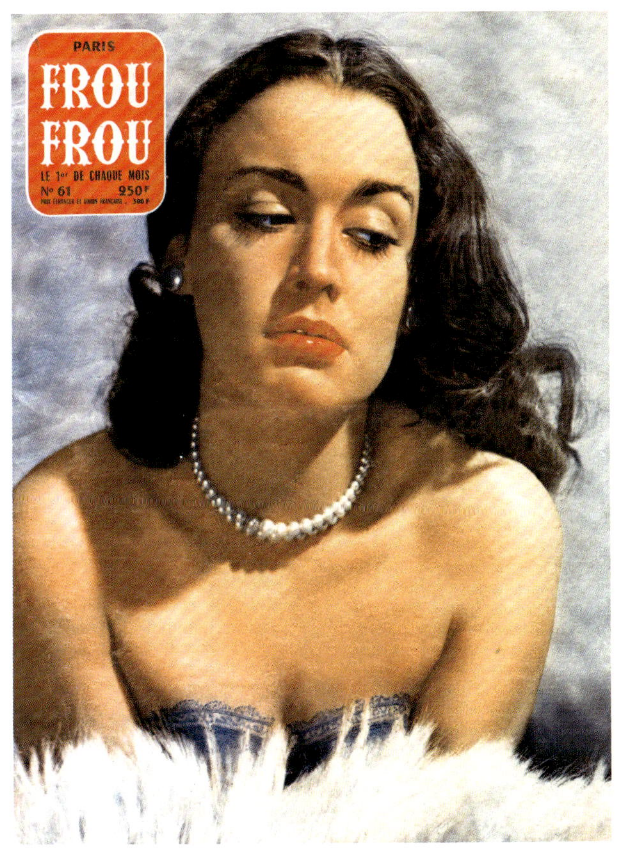

Year: **1958**. Title: **Paris Frou Frou**. Country: **France**.

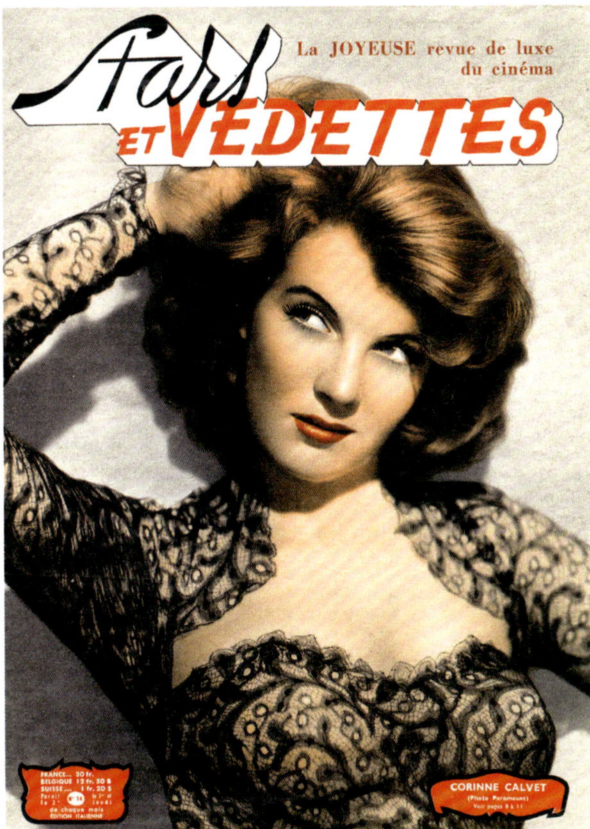

Year: **1950s**. Title: **Stars et Vedettes**. Country: **France**.

Left:
Year: **1947**. Title: **Paris-Hollywood**. Country: **France**.

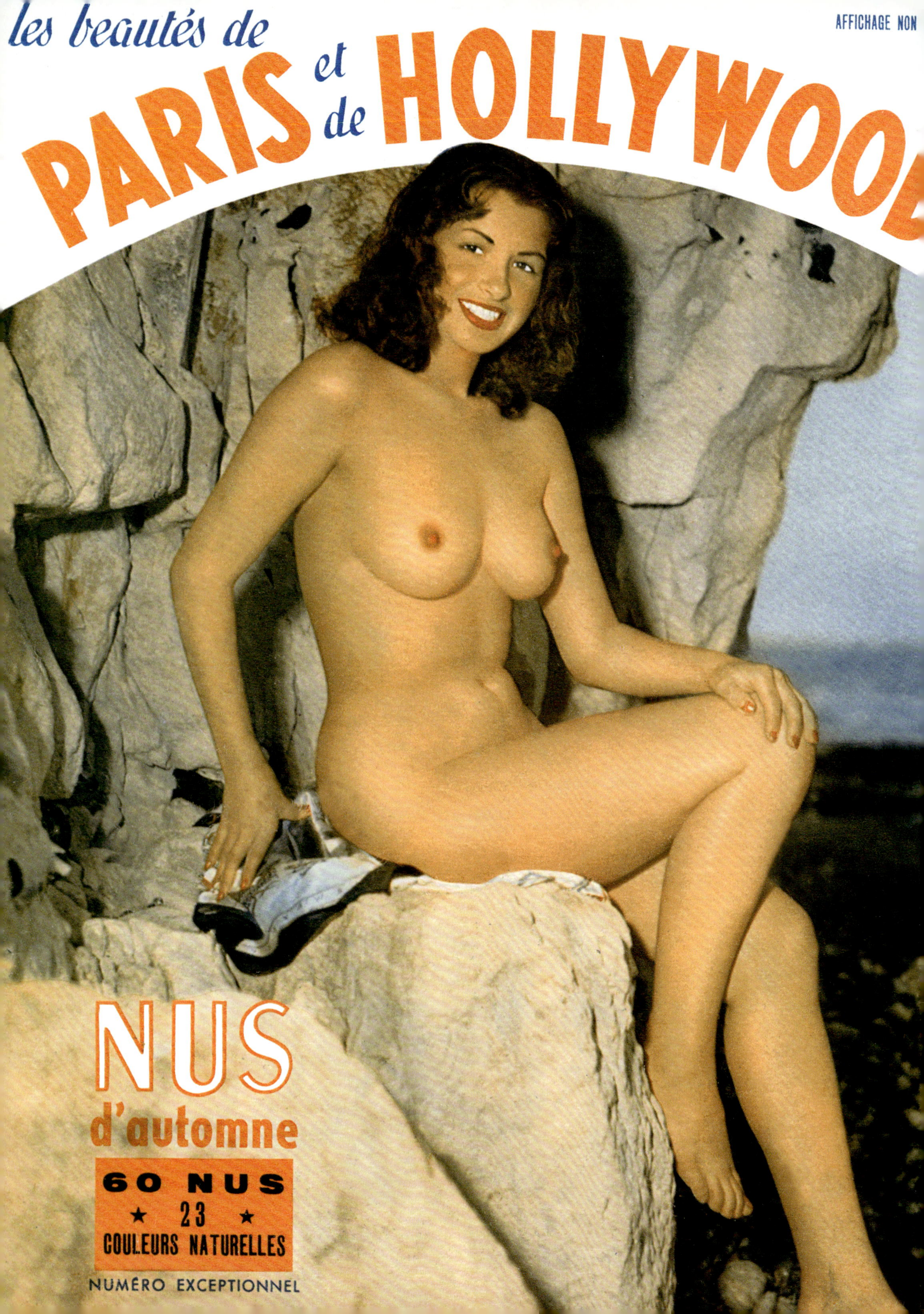
les beautés de
PARIS et de HOLLYWOOD
AFFICHAGE NON
NUS
d'automne
60 NUS
★ 23 ★
COULEURS NATURELLES
NUMÉRO EXCEPTIONNEL

Les Beautés de Paris et de Hollywood *emerged in 1949 as the nuder, sexier revamp of* Paris-Hollywood.

Im Jahre 1949 erschien Les Beautés de Paris et de Hollywood *als gewagtere, erotischere Version von* Paris-Hollywood.

Les Beautés de Paris et de Hollywood *parut en 1949 comme une version plus nue et plus sexy de* Paris-Hollywood.

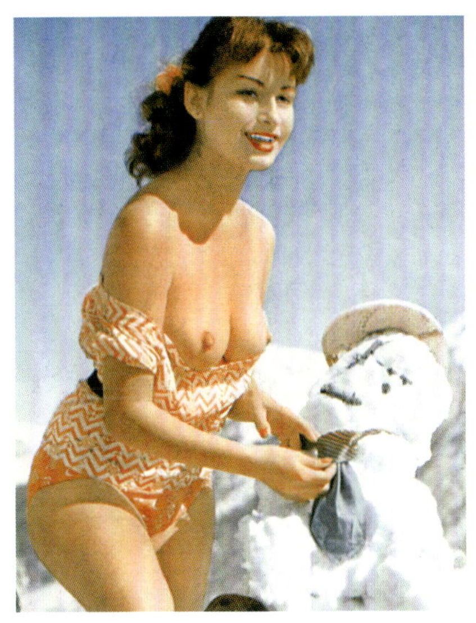

YEAR: **1950**. TITLE: **Les Beautés de Paris et de Hollywood**. COUNTRY: **France**.

taken exclusively from the Paris stage. This didn't last long. In late 1948 *Paris-Hollywood* was split into two magazines, a hard and a soft version. The soft one was called *Stars et Vedettes* and kept to the film theme, while *Paris-Hollywood* went stronger, and then became *Les Beautés de Paris et de Hollywood,* which was stronger still. In 1949 a signature feature debuted: undress-them-yourself pin-ups, where painted nudes were hidden under a sheet of tissue showing a dress, a car, an umbrella. Lift the sheet and Voila! There was your naked lady. These "Pin-up Deshabillables" became as popular as the photographs.

Paris-Hollywood disguised sex with seemingly innocent reportage of a sinful industry.

YEAR: **1950**. TITLE: **Les Beautés de Paris et de Hollywood**. COUNTRY: **France**.

allem anderen, was zu dieser Zeit in Europa erschien, war es großartig. Von 1946 bis 1948 war *Paris-Hollywood* in erster Linie eine Filmzeitschrift und pflegte die lange Tradition, Sex verpackt in vermeintlich unschuldige Reportagen über eine sündige Industrie zu verkaufen. Verglichen mit anderen Magazinen dieser Art hatte *Paris-Hollywood* jedoch seriösere Referenzen vorzuweisen, denn im selben Verlag erschienen auch die renommierten Filmzeitschriften *Cinémonde* und *Le Film Français*. Maurice Bessy, der zukünftige Leiter der Fimfestspiele von Cannes, war der erste Chefredakteur, und eine Zeit lang gab es nur wenige und dezente Aktaufnahmen zu sehen, die ausschließlich in den Pariser Varietés aufgenommen wurden. Doch dabei sollte es nicht lange bleiben. 1948 wurden aus *Paris-Hollywood* zwei Hefte, ein züchtigeres und ein unzüchtigeres: Das harmlose *Stars et Vedettes* beschäftigte sich weiter ausschließlich mit Film, *Paris-Hollywood* dagegen wurde frecher, benannte sich schließlich in *Les Beautés de Paris et de Hollywood* um und wagte sich noch weiter vor. 1949 erschien es erstmals mit einem neuen Markenzeichen – dem Auszieh-Pinup. Unter einem Bogen Seidenpapier, auf dem ein Kleid, ein Auto, ein Regenschirm zu sehen waren, verbarg sich eine Aktzeichnung. Man hob das Blatt an und, voilà, hatte man seine Nackte. Diese „Pinups Deshabillables" wurden so populär wie die Fotografien.

In Heft 85, 1950, gab das Magazin bekannt, dass es nicht länger an Kiosken zu haben war. Zahllose Stadtverwaltungen waren zu dem Schluss gekommen, das Magazin sei keine Filmzeitschrift und lediglich das Pinup auf dem Cover habe noch mit Film zu tun. Von nun an musste

de ce genre, le groupe de presse Mauclaire éditant également le célèbre *Cinémonde* et *Le Film Français*. Maurice Bessy, le future directeur du Festival de Cannes, en fut le premier rédacteur et, en un premier temps, les nus étaient peu nombreux, discrets et empruntés exclusivement aux planches parisiennes. Cela ne dura pas.

À la fin de 1948, *Paris-Hollywood* se scinda en deux magazines, une version tempérée et l'autre plus corsée. La tempérée s'intitulait *Stars et Vedettes* et s'en tenait au thème cinématographique, tandis que *Paris-Hollywood* mettait la barre de l'érotisme plus haut, puis encore plus haut en devenant un peu plus tard *Les Beautés de Paris et de Hollywood*. En 1949, le magazine lança une nouvelle rubrique qui devait devenir sa signature : « les pin-up déshabillables ». Des nus peints étaient cachés sous une feuille de papier de soie montrant une robe, une automobile, un

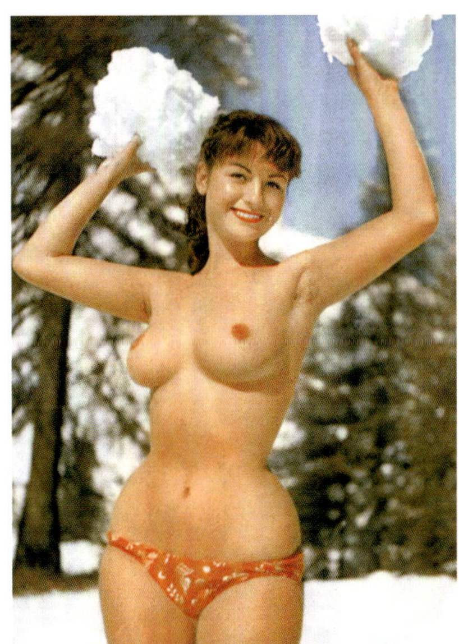

YEAR: **1950**. TITLE: **Les Beautés de Paris et de Hollywood**. COUNTRY: **France**.

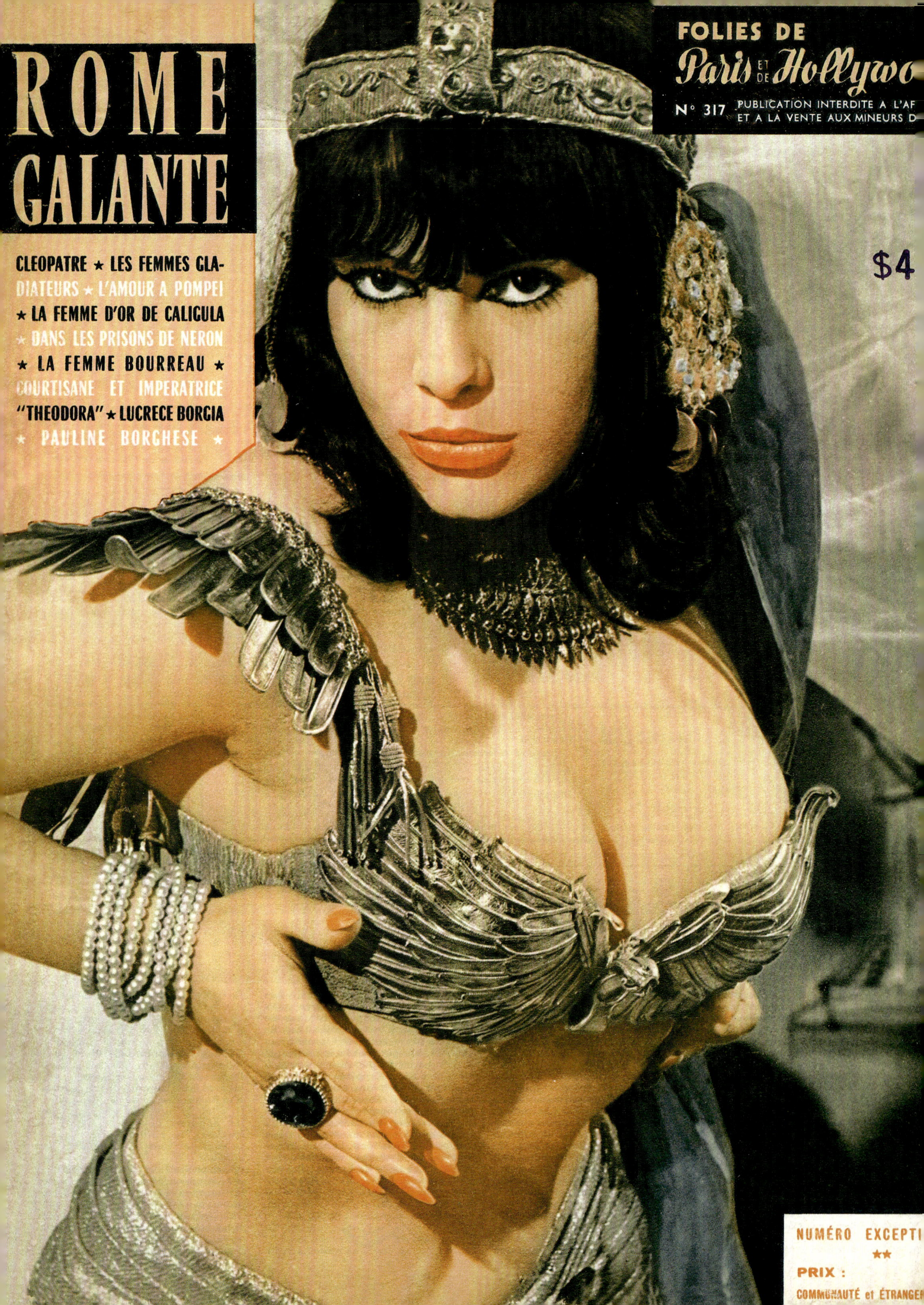
ROME
GALANTE
FOLIES DE
Paris et de Hollywo
N° 317 PUBLICATION INTERDITE A L'AF
ET A LA VENTE AUX MINEURS D
CLEOPATRE ★ LES FEMMES GLA-
DIATEURS ★ L'AMOUR A POMPEI
★ LA FEMME D'OR DE CALIGULA
★ DANS LES PRISONS DE NERON
★ LA FEMME BOURREAU ★
COURTISANE ET IMPERATRICE
"THEODORA" ★ LUCRECE BORGIA
★ PAULINE BORGHESE ★
$4
NUMÉRO EXCEPTI
★★
PRIX :
COMMUNAUTÉ et ÉTRANGER

Year: **1960s**. Title: **Folies de Paris et de Hollywood**. Country: **France**.

In 1950, with issue no 85, *Paris-Hollywood* announced it would no longer be sold on public newsstands. Numerous city councils had decided the magazines weren't film reviews, that indeed the only film left was that covering the pin-ups. From then on the big magazine joined its new digest competitors under the counter. This was a curse and a blessing. While it was harder to market a magazine that no one could see, once *Paris-Hollywood* was under the counter it was free to evolve. Some of the greatest French girlie photographers joined the magazine at this time. With the June 1950 issue both Serge Jacques and Roland Carre showed their first photos; André Belorgey joined them a year later. Between 1950 and 1957 these three built the magazine's reputation, and helped return France to its pre-war position of European erotic dominance. They built their personal reputations as well, so that by the late 50s all were shooting for American magazines, particularly the slick California titles. Serge Jacques, never one for costuming, even became the European stringer for American hippy nudist magazine called *Jaybird*, appearing naked alongside his models.

Paris being Paris, no amount of rationing could keep them from their erotica.

With his photographers increasingly busy Mauclaire brought in Russell Gay from England to bolster his ranks. Reports are that against French fashion Mauclaire

A special edition from the 1960s, when Paris-Hollywood *was falling into decline.*

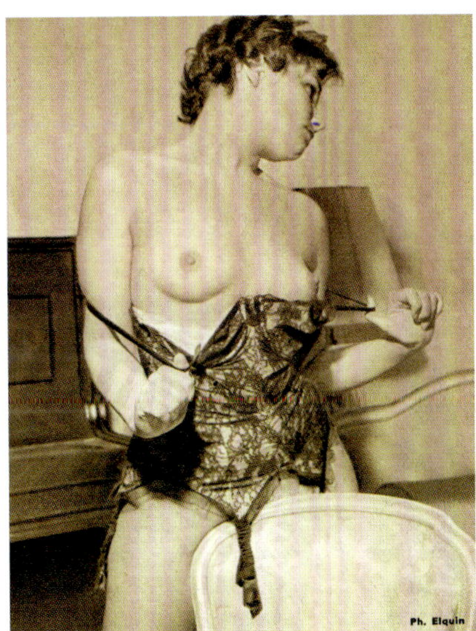

Year: **1960s**. Title: **Les Beautés de Paris et de Hollywood**. Country: **France**.

das Magazin unter der Ladentheke verkauft werden. Das war Fluch und Segen zugleich. Es war zwar zwar schwieriger, ein Magazin zu verkaufen, das aus dem Blickfeld verschwunden war, andererseits gewann *Paris-Hollywood*, als es erst einmal unter die Ladentheke verschwunden war, die Freiheit, sich zu entwickeln. Einige der berühmtesten französischen Girlie-Fotografen fanden in jener Zeit zu dem Magazin. Im Juni 1950 zeigten erstmals Serge Jacques und Roland Carre ihre Arbeiten, ein Jahr später schloss sich ihnen André Belorgey an. Diese drei begründeten zwischen 1950 und 1957 den Ruf des Magazins und trugen dazu bei, dass Frankreich in Eurpoa seine Vorkriegsdominanz auf dem Feld erotischer Printmedien wiedererlangte. Sie festigten auch ihren persönlichen Ruf, sodass sie alle Ende der Fünfziger auch für amerikanische Magazine fotografierten, vor allem für die erstklassig aufgemachten

Eine Sonderausgabe aus den sechziger Jahren, als es mit Paris-Hollywood *bergab ging.*

parapluie. On la soulevait et la demoiselle se retrouvait toute nue. Ces pin-up devinrent aussi populaires que les photos.

En 1950, le numéro 85 de *Paris-Hollywood* annonça que le magazine ne serait plus en vente dans les kiosques. De nombreux conseils municipaux avaient décidé que la revue n'avait plus rien à voir avec le cinéma et que les seules pellicules dont il y était question étaient celles qui recouvraient ses pin-up. Dès lors, le grand magazine rejoignit les digests, ses nouveaux concurrents, dans la clandestinité. Ce fut à la fois une malédiction et une bénédiction. S'il était plus difficile de commercialiser un magazine que personne ne pouvait voir, une fois sous le manteau, celui-ci put évoluer librement. Certains des plus grands photographes de charme français virent travailler pour la revue. Dans le numéro de juin 1950, Serge Jacques et Roland Carré présentèrent leurs premières photos ; André Belorgey les rejoignit un an plus tard. Entre 1950 et 1957, ils construisirent à eux trois la réputation du magazine et aidèrent à rendre à la France sa suprématie d'avantguerre en matière d'érotisme. Ils forgèrent également leur propre réputation, si bien qu'à la fin des années cinquante tous trois travaillaient également pour des magazines américains, notamment les titres luxueux de Californie. Serge Jacques, qui n'avait jamais été porté sur les costumes, devint même le correspondant européen de *Jaybird*, un magazine nudiste hippy, posant nu au côté de ses modèles.

Ses photographes étant de plus en plus accaparés ailleurs, Mauclaire fit venir Russell Gay d'Angleterre. D'après les témoignages, Mauclaire était grand amateur de poitrines, et Gay pouvait lui fournir les gros seins anglais réputés dans le

Un numéro spécial des années soixante, quand Paris-Hollywood *était en plein déclin.*

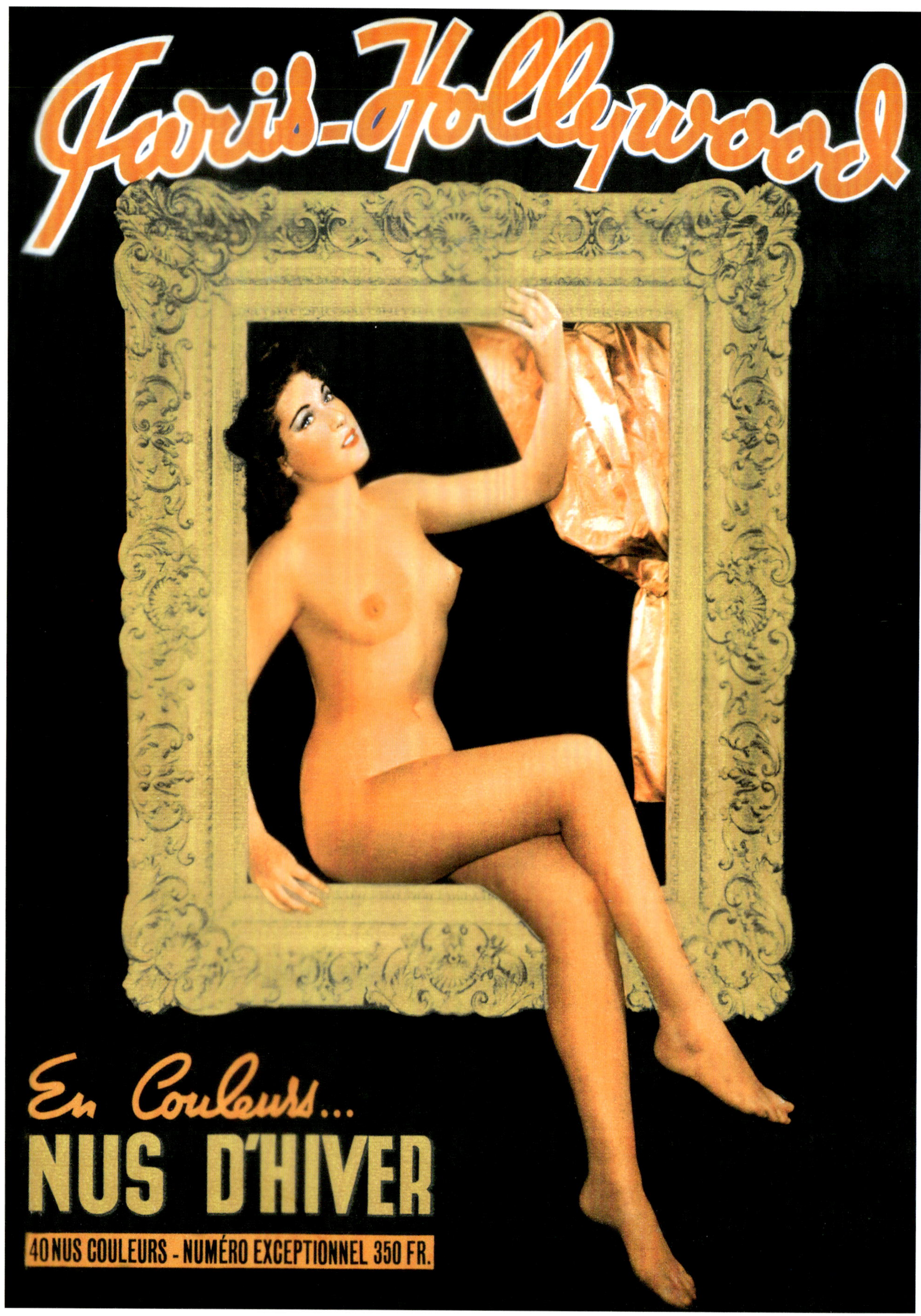

YEAR: **1950s**. TITLE: **Paris-Hollywood**. COUNTRY: **France**.

YEAR: **1950s**. TITLE: **Paris-Hollywood**.
COUNTRY: **France**.

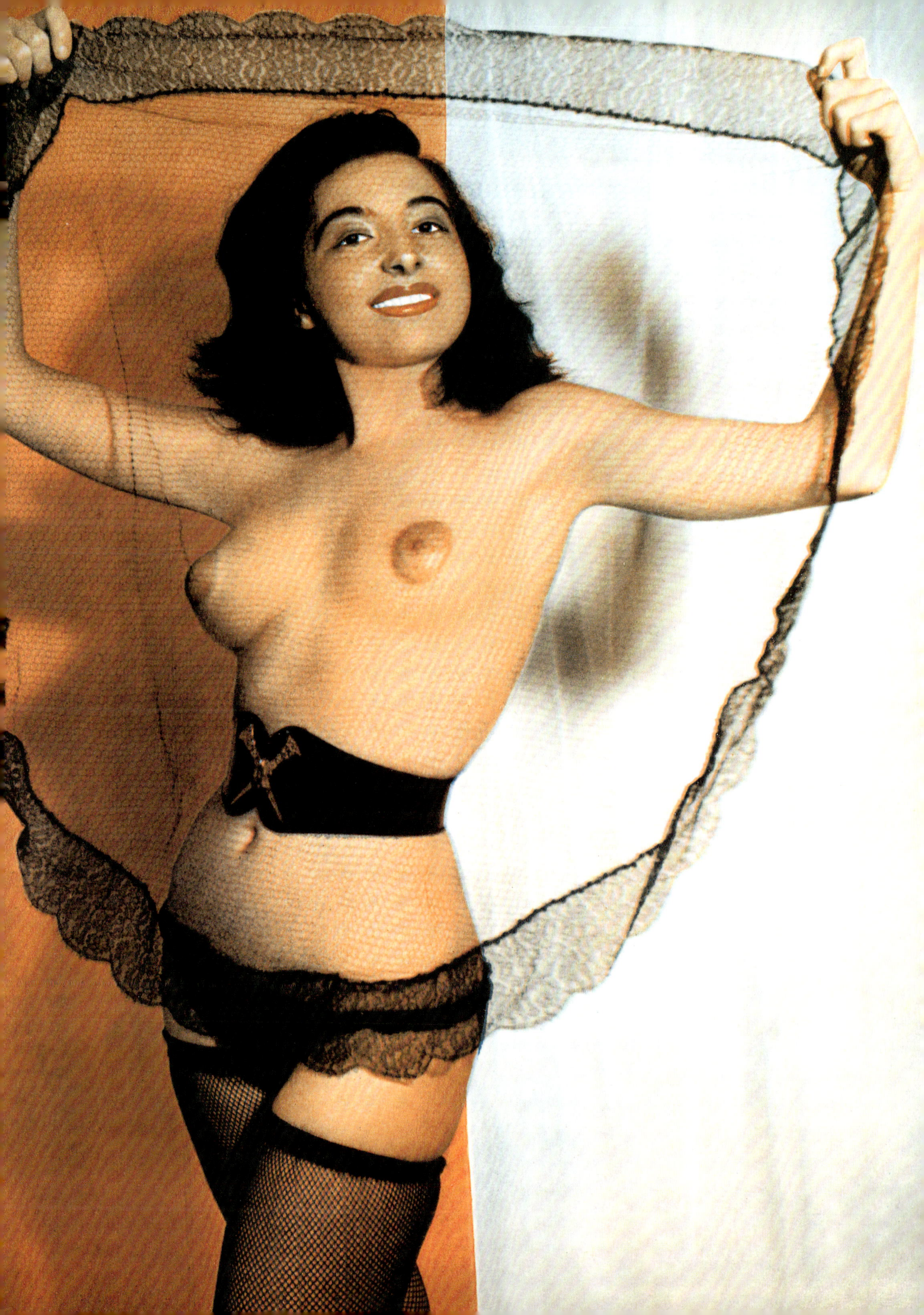

By 1960 Folies de Paris et de Hollywood *had replaced movie reviews with nude folies reviews.*

Im Jahre 1960 hatte Folies de Paris et de Hollywood *die Filmkritiken durch Kritiken von Nacktrevuen ersetzt.*

En 1960, Folies de Paris et de Hollywood *avait remplacé les critiques de films par des reportages sur les revues nues.*

was a big breast enthusiast and Gay could deliver the world-renowned English bosoms. *Paris-Hollywood* continued to dominate the French market for nearly three decades, at its height selling up to 250,000 copies of a single issue. Then, as with all magazines, times and tastes began to change. By 1970, tissue-overlaid pin-ups no longer titillated an audience with access to the explicit Swedish and Danish pornography. In 1974 *Paris-Hollywood* printed its last issue.

In 1999 *Paris-Hollywood's* title patents became obsolete. A fan of the magazines re-registered them and started the website *www.paris-hollywood.com*, where he displayed his complete collection of the magazines and their original, unretouched photos—which show just how hard the airbrush artists had to work on those flagrant French pudenda. So for a new audience, in a new medium, France's post-war salvation lives again.

(Original text. www.paris-hollywood.com is no longer functional.)

Maurice Bessy, future administrator of the Cannes Film Festival, was the first editor, and for a while the nudes were few and discreet.

Magazine aus Kalifornien. Serge Jacques, noch nie ein Freund überflüssiger Kleidung, wurde gar europäischer Repräsentant für das amerikanische Hippie-Nudistenmagazin *Jaybird* und posierte nackt neben seinen Models.

Da seine Fotografen zunehmend eingespannt waren, holte sich Mauclaire Russell Gay aus England zur Verstärkung. Es heißt, Mauclaire sei entgegen dem vorherrschenden französischen Geschmack ein großer Busen-Fan gewesen, Gay habe ihm die berühmten englischen Oberweiten liefern können. *Paris-Hollywood* sollte fast drei Jahrzehnte französischer Marktführer bleiben und zu seiner Glanzzeit bis zu 250 000 Hefte pro Ausgabe verkaufen. Und dann erging es dem Magazin, wie es allen Magazinen ergeht: die Zeiten und Geschmäcker änderten sich. 1970 törnte ein mit Seidenpapier verhülltes Pinup ein Publikum, das Zugang zu tabuloser skandinavischer Pornografie hatte, nicht mehr an. 1974 erschien die letzte Ausgabe von *Paris-Hollywood*.

1999 wurden die Rechte an *Paris-Hollywood* frei; ein leidenschaftlicher Fan erwarb sie und richtete die Website *www.parishollywood.com* ein, unter der er nicht nur seine komplette Sammlung ins Netz stellte, sondern auch die unretuschierten Originalfotos. So kann man sich anschauen, welche Mühen die Retuschierkünstler mit der schamlosen französischen Vulva hatten, und Frankreichs Nachkriegsfrivolitäten sind für ein neues Publikum in einem neuen Medium wieder zugänglich. Für ein neues Publikum, in einem neuen Medium lebte Frankreichs Nachkriegsrettung also wieder auf.

(Originaltext. www.paris-hollywood.com ist nicht mehr funktionsfähig.)

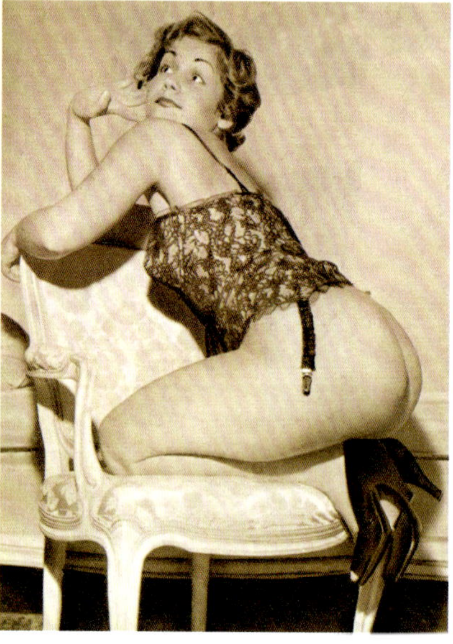

Year: **1940s**. Title: **Les Beautés de Paris et de Hollywood**. Country: **France**.

monde entier. *Paris-Hollywood* continua à dominer le marché français pendant près de trois décennies. Puis, comme c'est le cas avec tous les magazines, les temps et les goûts changèrent. En 1970, les pin-up cachées sous le papier de soie ne faisaient plus recette auprès d'un public qui avait accès à la pornographie explicite venant de Suède et du Danemark. Le dernier numéro de *Paris-Hollywood* parut en 1974.

En 1999, le titre *Paris-Hollywood* tomba dans le domaine public. Un grand admirateur le réenregistra et lança le site web *www.parishollywood.com* où il présenta sa collection complète de la revue et les photos originales intactes. Ainsi revit, pour un nouveau public, avec un nouveau médium, le titre qui a assuré le salut de la France dans l'après-guerre.

(Texte original. www.paris-hollywood.com ne fonctionne plus.)

Year: **1958**. Title: **Folies de Paris et de Hollywood**. Country: **France**.

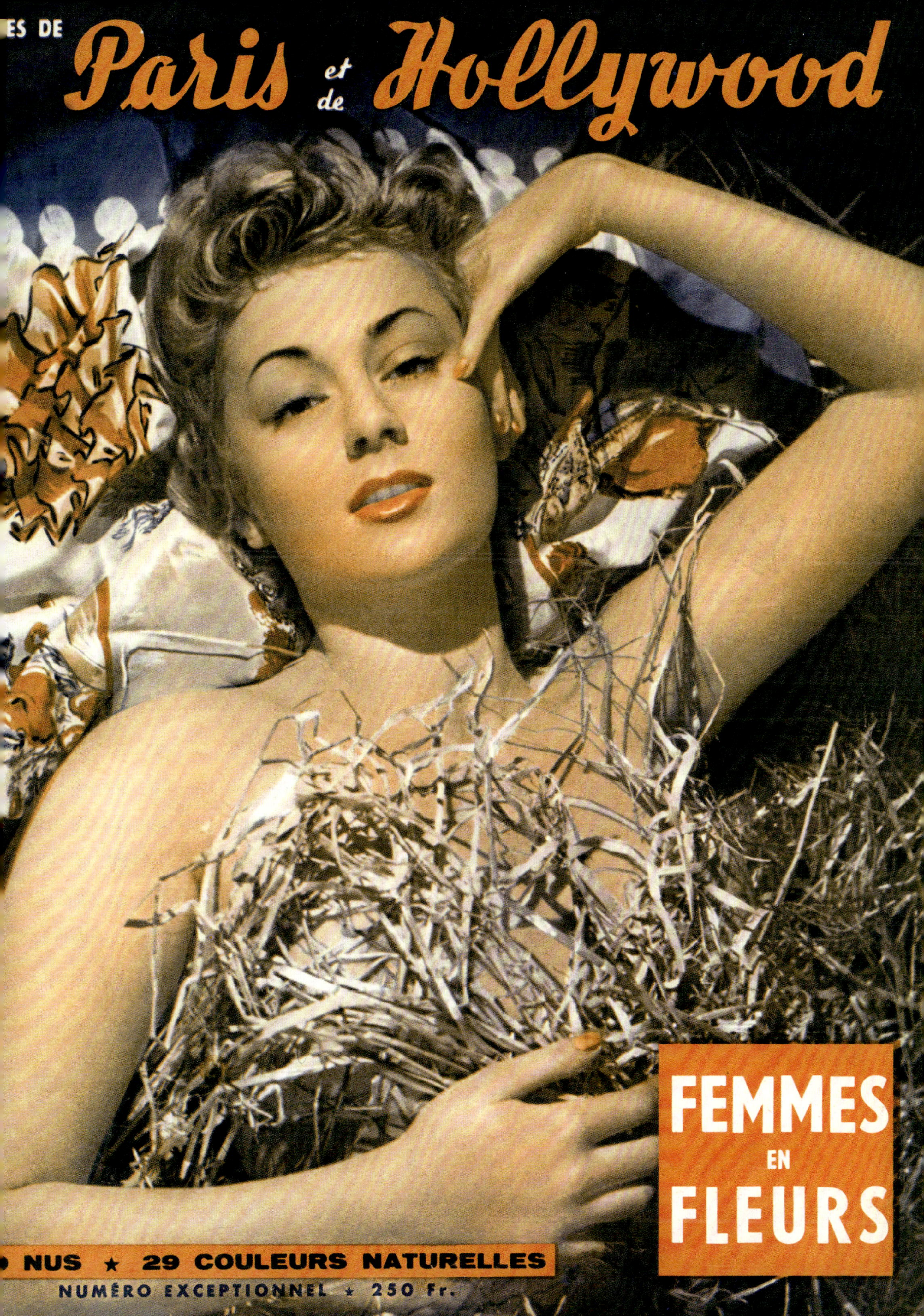

ES DE
Paris et de Hollywood
FEMMES EN FLEURS
NUS ★ 29 COULEURS NATURELLES
NUMÉRO EXCEPTIONNEL ★ 250 Fr.

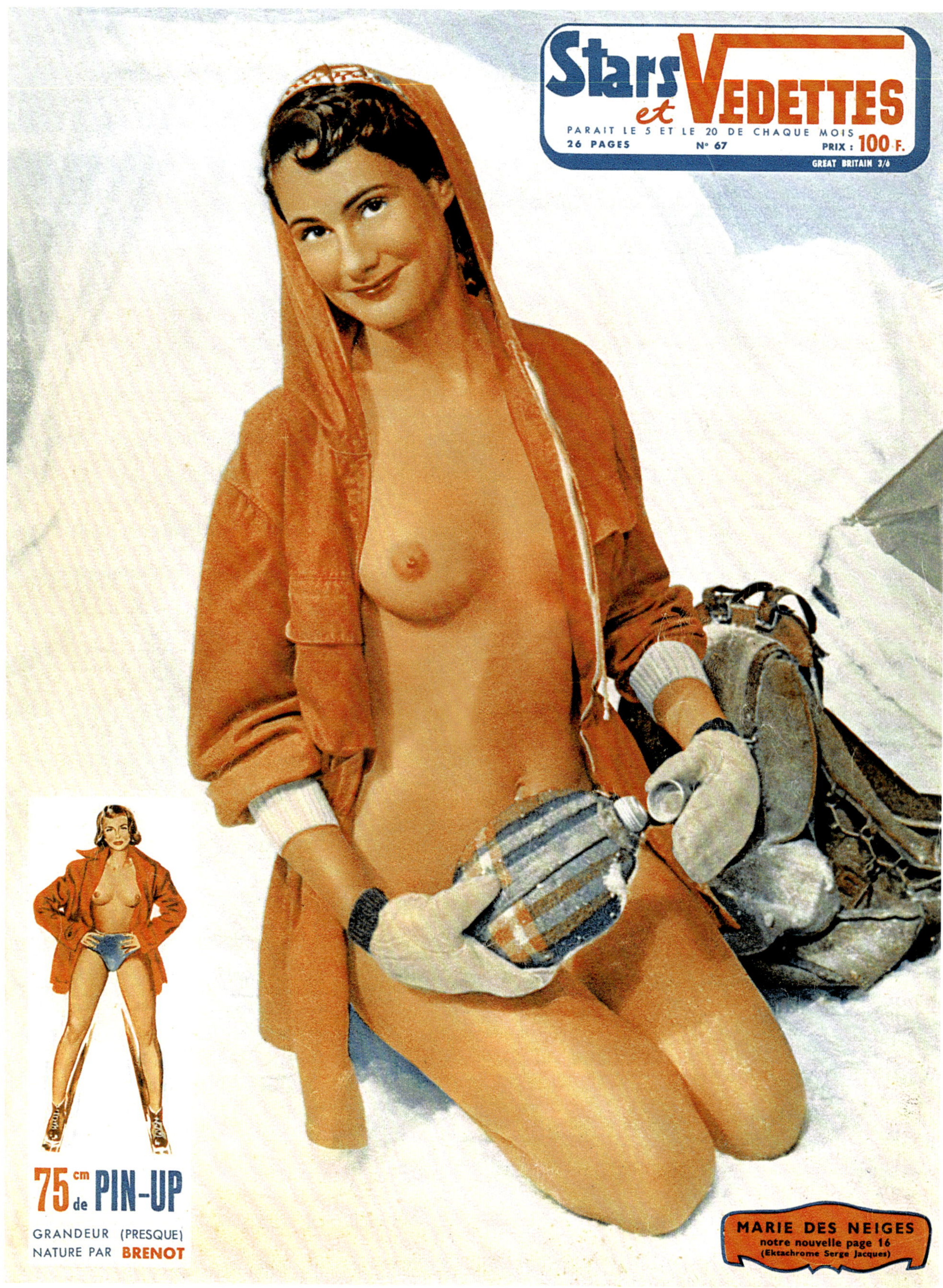

YEAR: **1948**. TITLE: **Stars et Vedettes**. COUNTRY: **France**.

YEAR: **1948**. TITLE: **Stars et Vedettes**. COUNTRY: **France**.

When Paris-Hollywood *adopted a stronger format in 1948 the publisher created* Stars et Vedettes *to satisfy readers who liked the softer film-oriented original.*

Als sich Paris-Hollywood *1948 härteren Stoffen zuwandte, brachte der Verleger für alle Leser, die das softere, filmorientierte Original bevorzugt hatten, das Magazin* Stars et Vedettes *heraus.*

Lorsque Paris-Hollywood *adopta un format plus choc en 1948, l'éditeur créa* Stars et Vedettes *pour satisfaire les lecteurs qui préféraient l'original plus cinématographique et moins osé.*

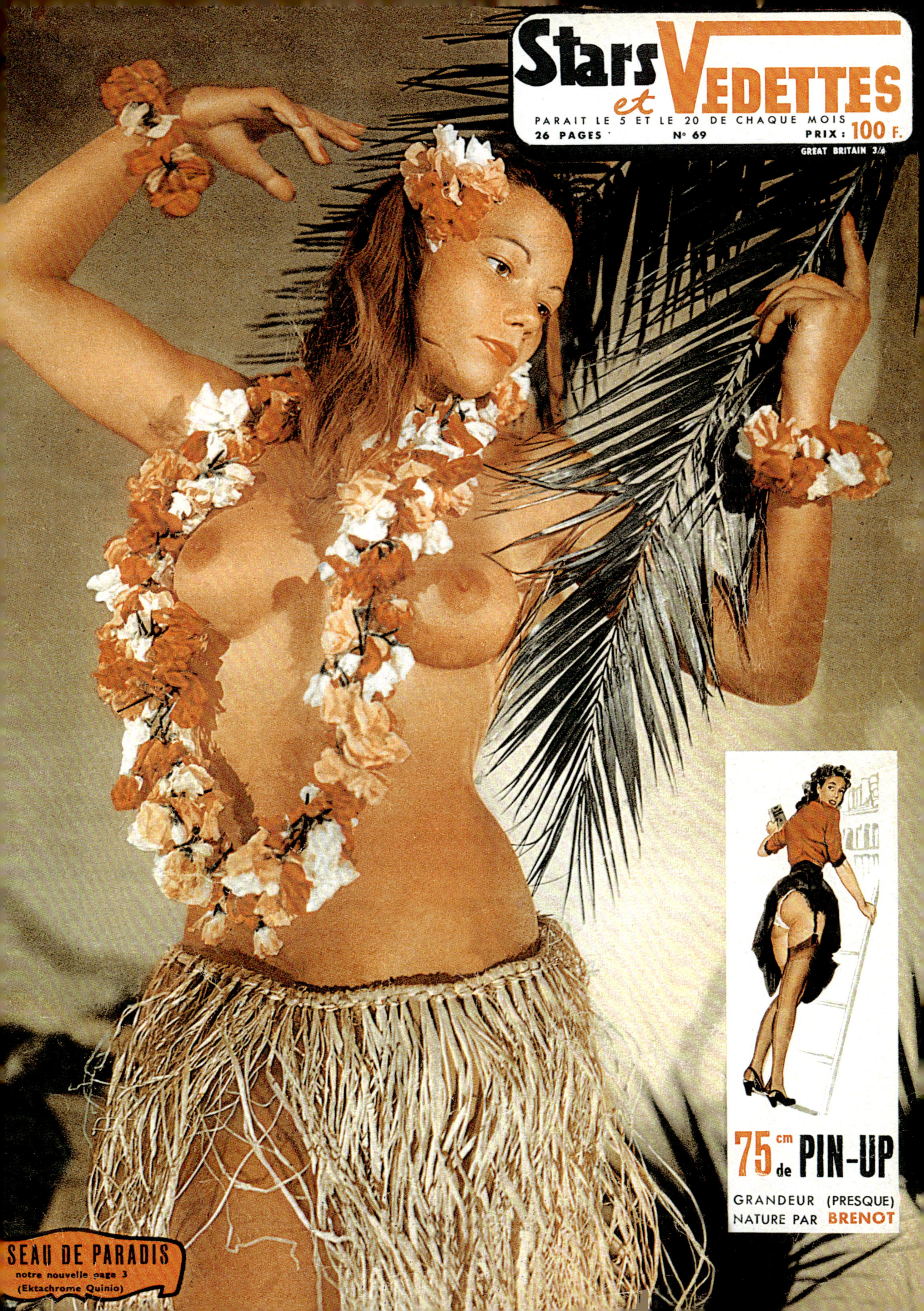
Stars et VEDETTES
PARAIT LE 5 ET LE 20 DE CHAQUE MOIS
26 PAGES
N° 69
PRIX : 100 F.
GREAT BRITAIN 3/6
75 cm de PIN-UP
GRANDEUR (PRESQUE) NATURE PAR BRENOT
SEAU DE PARADIS
notre nouvelle page 3
(Ektachrome Quinio)

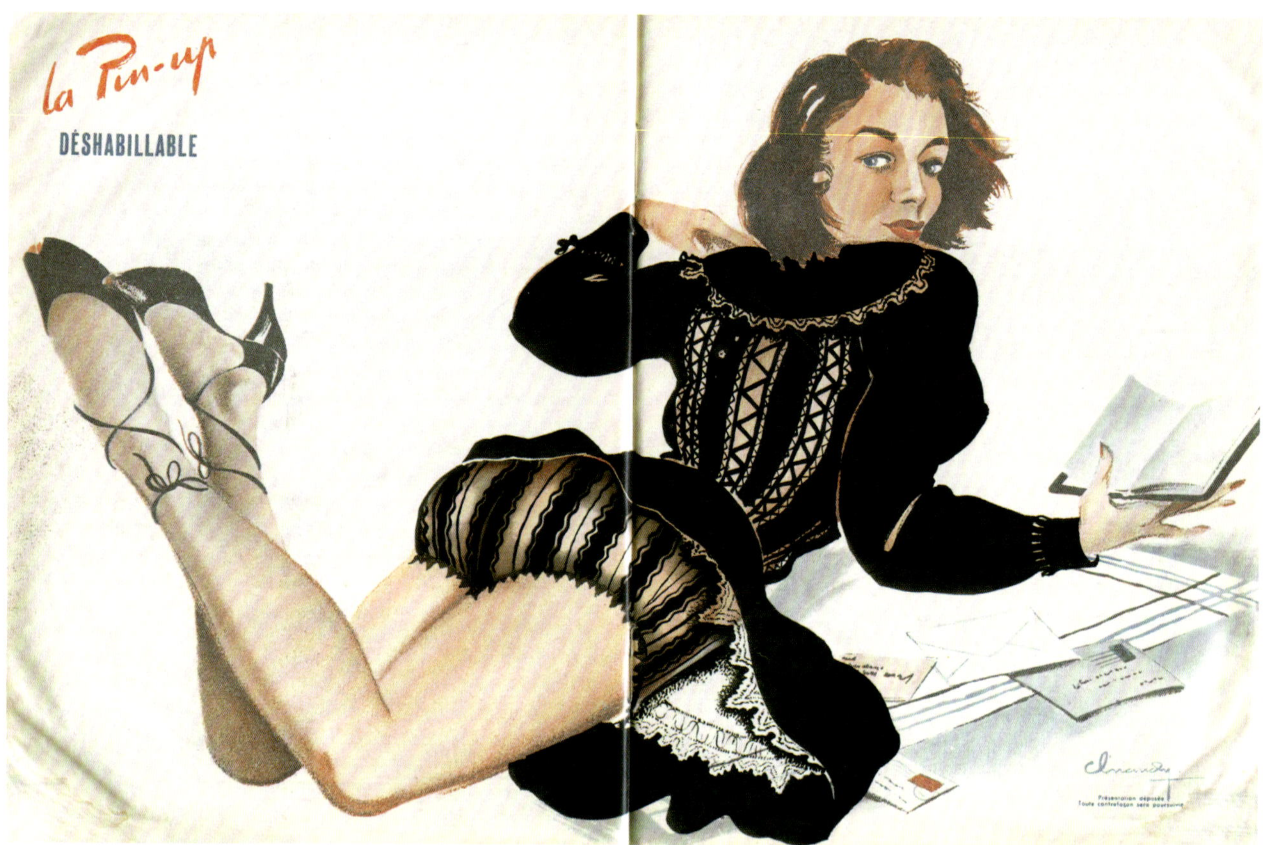

Above & Below: Year: **1940s**. Title: **Album Sélection de Pin-Up**. Country: **France**.

Right: Year: **1940s**. Title: **Album Sélection de Pin-Up**. Country: **France**.

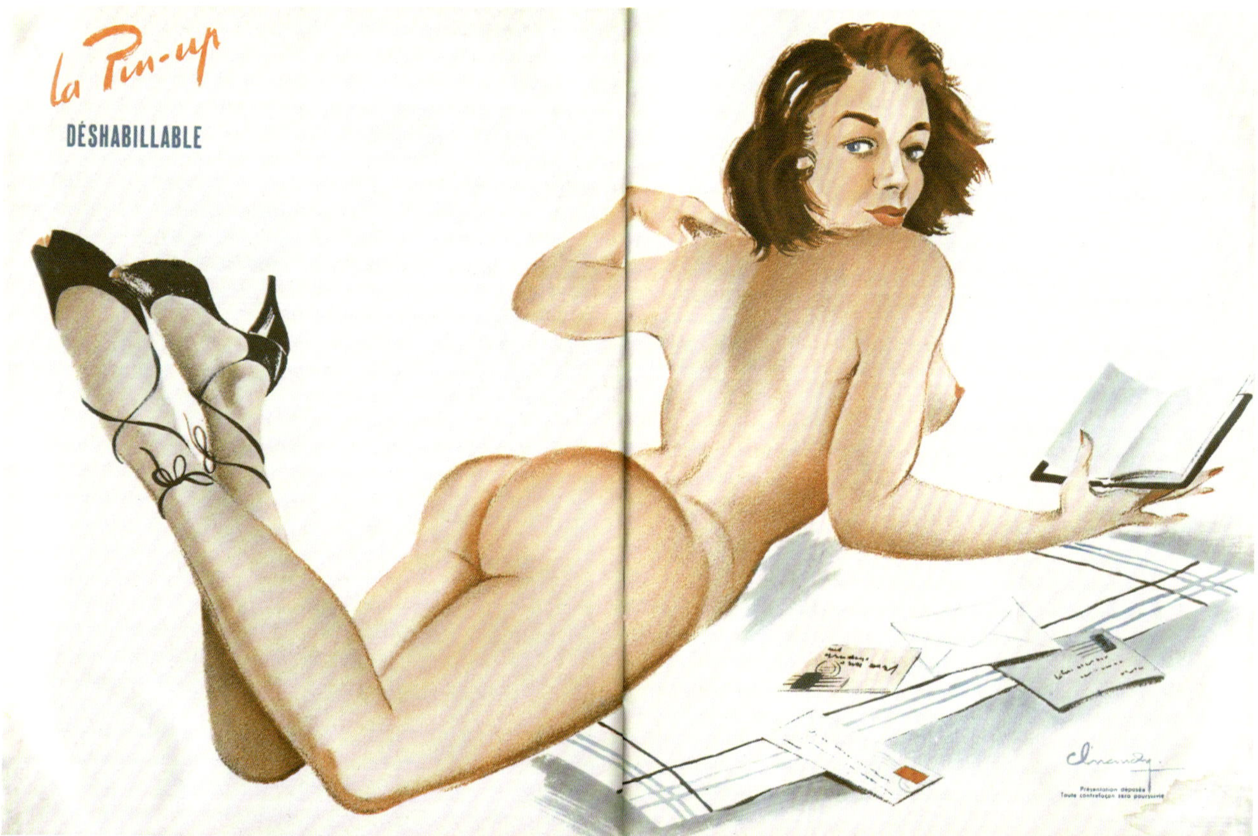

Painted tissue overlays covered Paris-Hollywood's *famous nude centerfolds, allowing the reader to "undress" the girls himself.*

Bemalte Stoffüberzüge bedeckten die berühmten nackten Centerfolds von Paris-Hollywood *und erlaubten es dem Leser somit, die Mädchen selbst zu „entkleiden".*

Des caches en tissus peints recouvraient les célèbres nus des posters centraux de Paris-Hollywood, *laissant au lecteur le plaisir de « déshabiller » lui-même les modèles.*

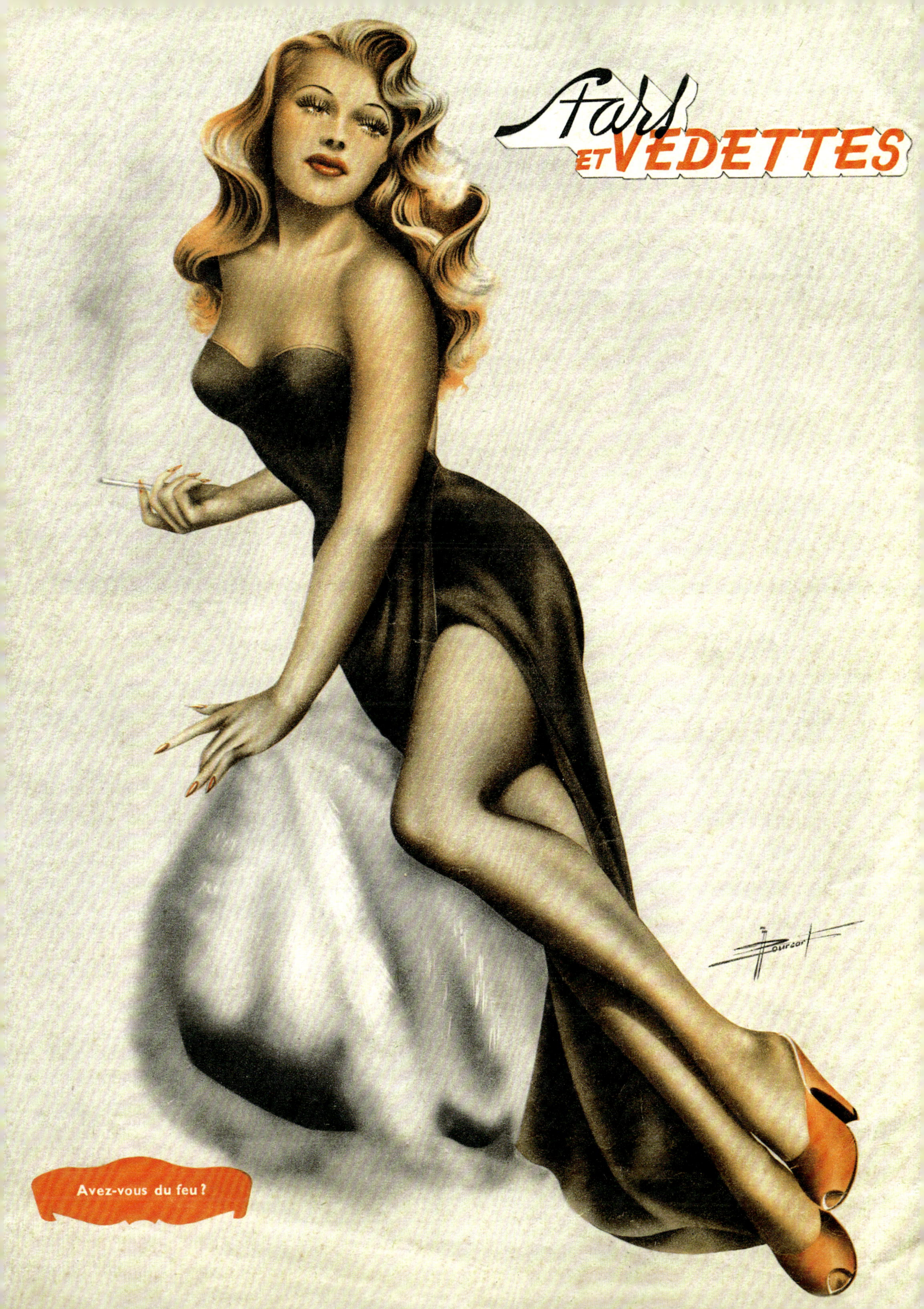
Stars
ET VEDETTES
Avez-vous du feu ?

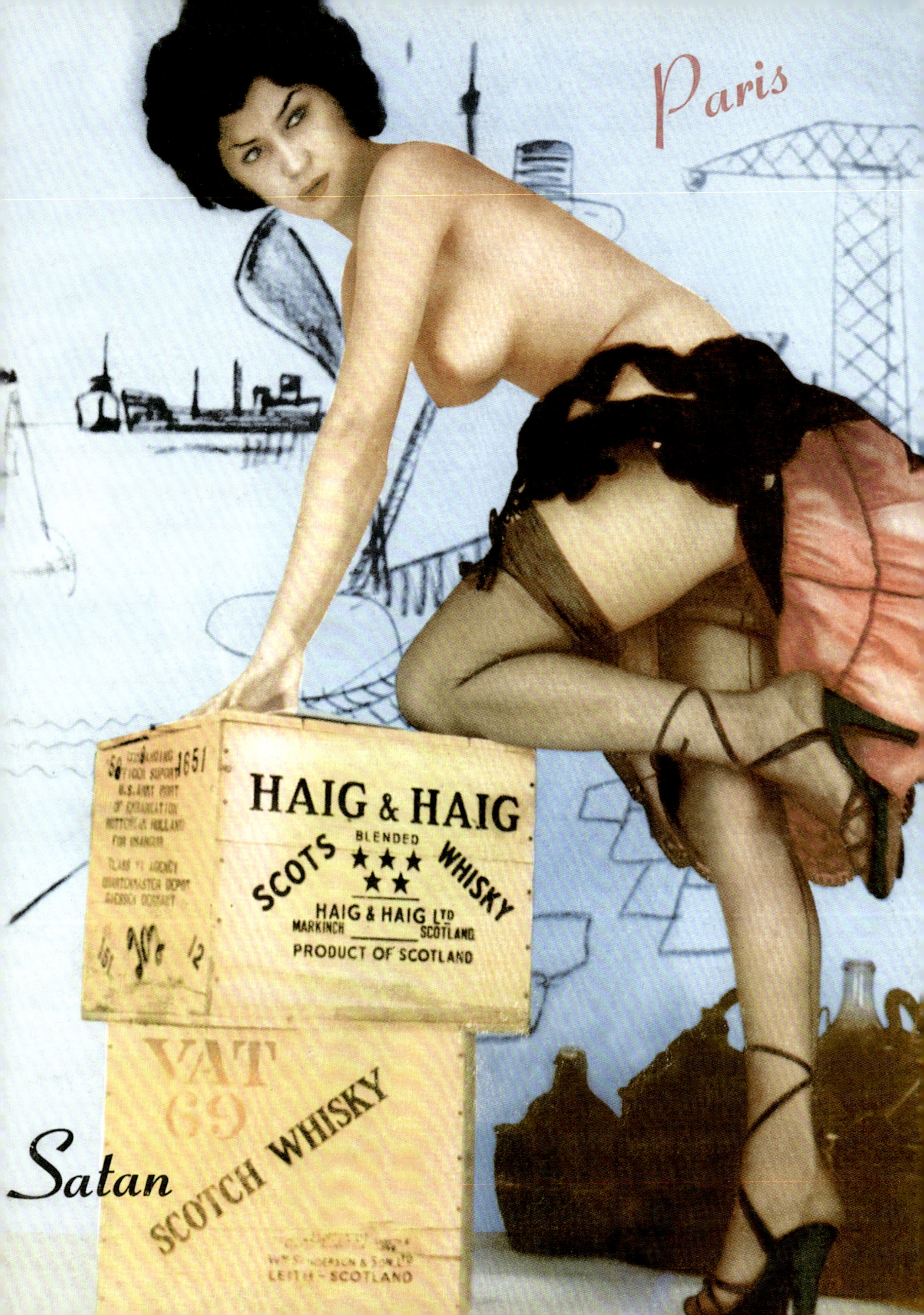
Paris
1651
HAIG & HAIG
BLENDED
SCOTS
WHISKY
HAIG & HAIG LTD
MARKINCH
SCOTLAND
PRODUCT OF SCOTLAND
VAT 69
SCOTCH WHISKY
LEITH - SCOTLAND
Satan

DIRTY LITTLE MAGAZINES:

The French Post-War Digest

Schmutzige kleine Hefte: Frankreich in der Nachkriegszeit
Petites revues cochonnes : les digests français de l'après-guerre

Paris-Hollywood opened the post-war publishing door—and a host of other French magazines followed. *La Vie Parisienne* and *Paris Sex-Appeal* had soldiered on right through the war, but other high quality magazines like *Beauté* and *Paris Plaisirs* had fallen to the paper, money and manpower shortages. American GIs stationed in France were thrilled by cheap sepia digests like *Paris-Folies* and *Paris-Frivole* that mixed recycled photos from the 20s and 30s with wartime humor, but to the French they were a depressing low point in a rich erotic history. When *Paris-Hollywood* debuted in the year 1946 it signaled a return to serious sex publishing, and when it became more explicit two years later a host of intriguing digests followed.

The most distinctive late 40s, early 50s digests came from Editions Extentia (*Régal*, *Sensations*, *Chiche*, *Rose et Noir* and *Paris Tabou*) and from rival R. M. Dupuy (*Paris Gai*, *Paris Sourire* and *Moi et Toi*). Both companies delivered high-quality black-and-white printing of sophisticated, *film noir* style photo features, and each had a signature artist for added distinction.

Italian Gino Boccasile created the humorous *Paris Tabou* covers for Extentia. All his paintings featured the company's mascot, a mischievous young boy, tor-

Year: **1950s**. Title: **Paris Satan**.
Country: **France**.

When *Paris-Hollywood* became more explicit in 1948 a host of intriguing digests followed.

Paris-Hollywood war nach dem Krieg der Vorreiter, und eine Vielzahl anderer Magazine folgte. *La Vie Parisienne*

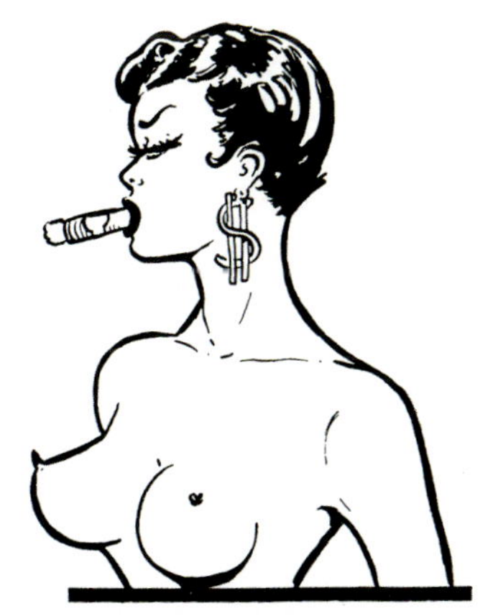

Year: **1950s**. Title: **Paris Satan**. Artist: **J. David**.
Country: **France**.

Dès la fin de la Seconde Guerre mondiale, *Paris-Hollywood* rouvrit la porte à la presse française et un tas d'autres publications lui emboîtèrent le pas. *La Vie Parisienne* et *Paris Sex-Appeal* avaient survécu mais d'autres revues de grande qualité tels que *Beauté* et *Paris Plaisirs* avaient succombé aux pénuries de papier, d'argent et de main d'œuvre. Les G. I.'s américains stationnés en France raffolaient de digests imprimés sur papier sépia comme *Paris-Folies* et *Paris-Frivole,* qui mêlaient des photos recyclées des années vingt et trente à l'humour de corps de garde. Mais pour les Français, ces magazines bon marché marquaient un creux déprimant dans leur riche histoire érotique. Lorsque *Paris-Hollywood* vit le jour en 1946, il annonçait le retour d'une vraie édition de charme. Quand il devint plus explicite en 1948, il entraîna dans son sillage toute une série de digests inattendus.

Les digests les plus singuliers des années quarante et cinquante furent publiés par les éditions Extentia (*Régal*, *Sensations*, *Chiche*, *Rose et Noir* et *Paris Tabou*) et leurs rivales, les éditions R. M. Dupuy (*Paris Gai*, *Paris Sourire* et *Moi et Toi*). Les deux maisons offraient des impressions noir et blanc de haute qualité de photos de style film noir. Chacune avait son artiste attitré qui lui apportait sa touche de distinction. L'Italien Gino

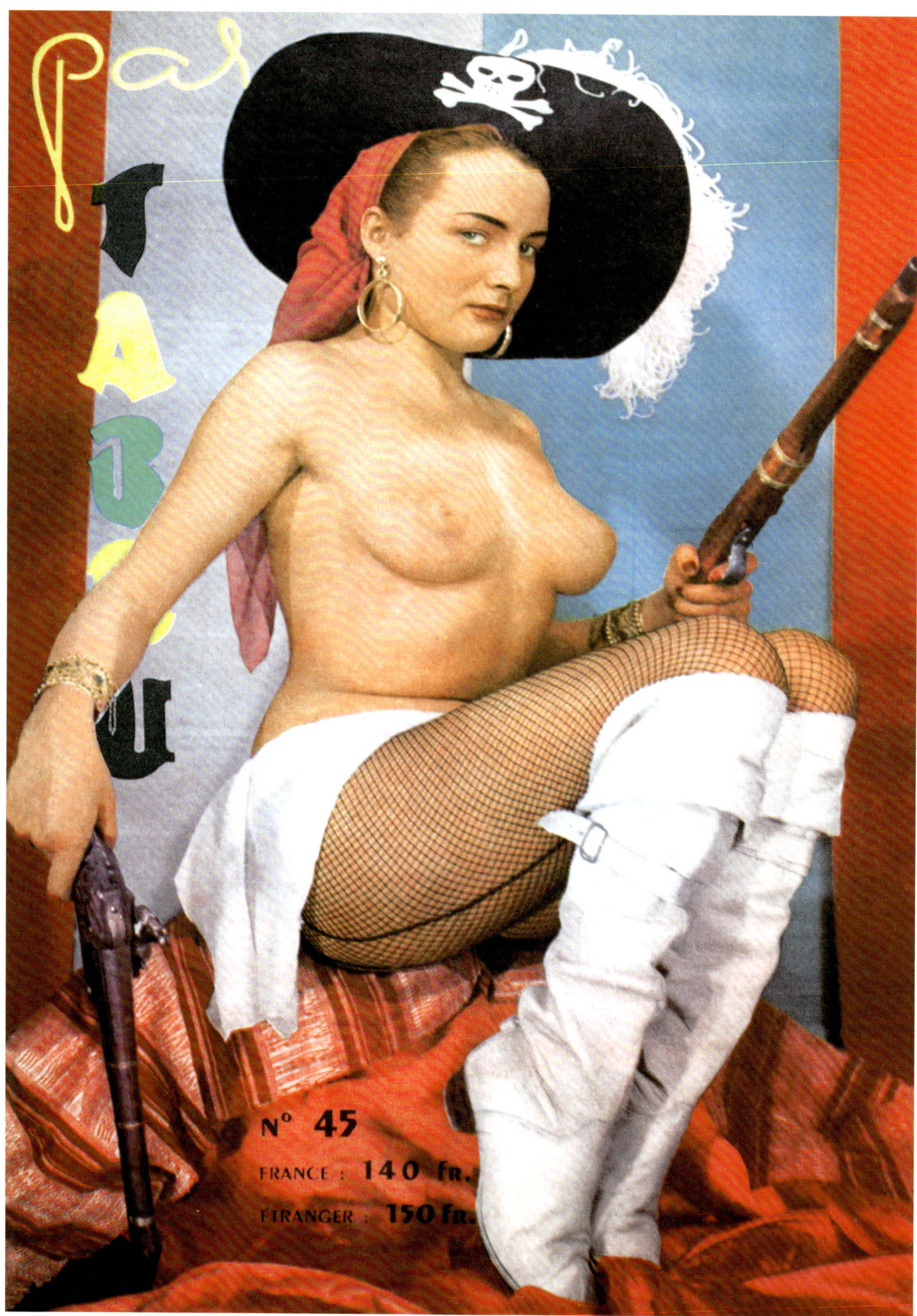

Gino Boccasile gradually phased out his illustrative work for Paris Tabou*. By the end of the 50s he gave up the girlies altogether for a career as a children's book illustrator.*

Nach und nach gab Gino Boccasile seine Arbeit als Illustrator für Paris Tabou *auf. Vom Ende der fünfziger Jahre an illustrierte er Kinderbücher.*

Gino Boccasile cessa progressivement de réaliser des illustrations pour Paris Tabou*. À la fin des années 50, il abandonna définitivement les jolies filles pour illustrer des livres d'enfants.*

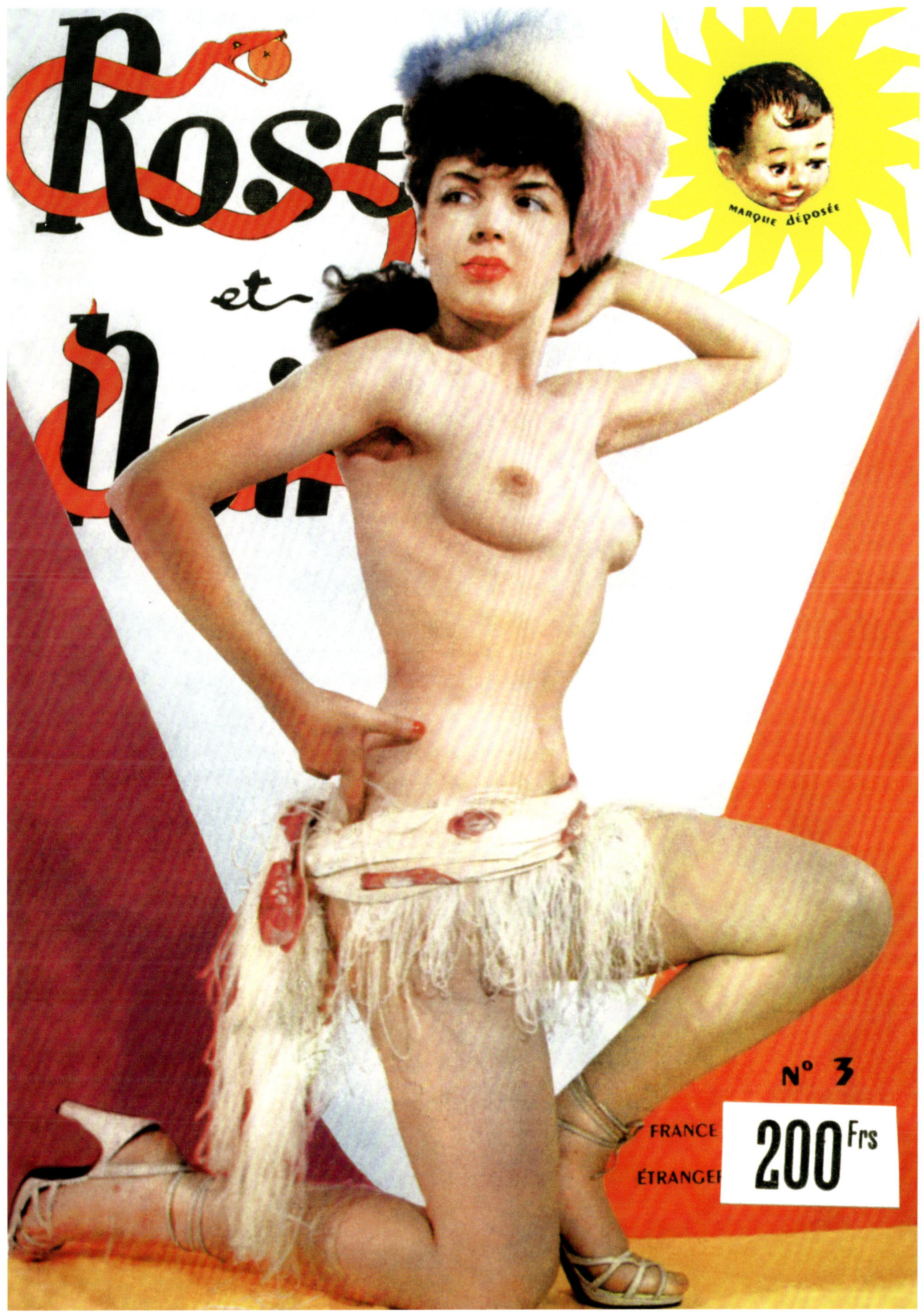

YEAR: **1950s**. TITLE: **Rose et Noir**. COUNTRY: **France**.

LEFT:
YEAR: **1953**. TITLE: **Paris Tabou**. COUNTRY: **France**.

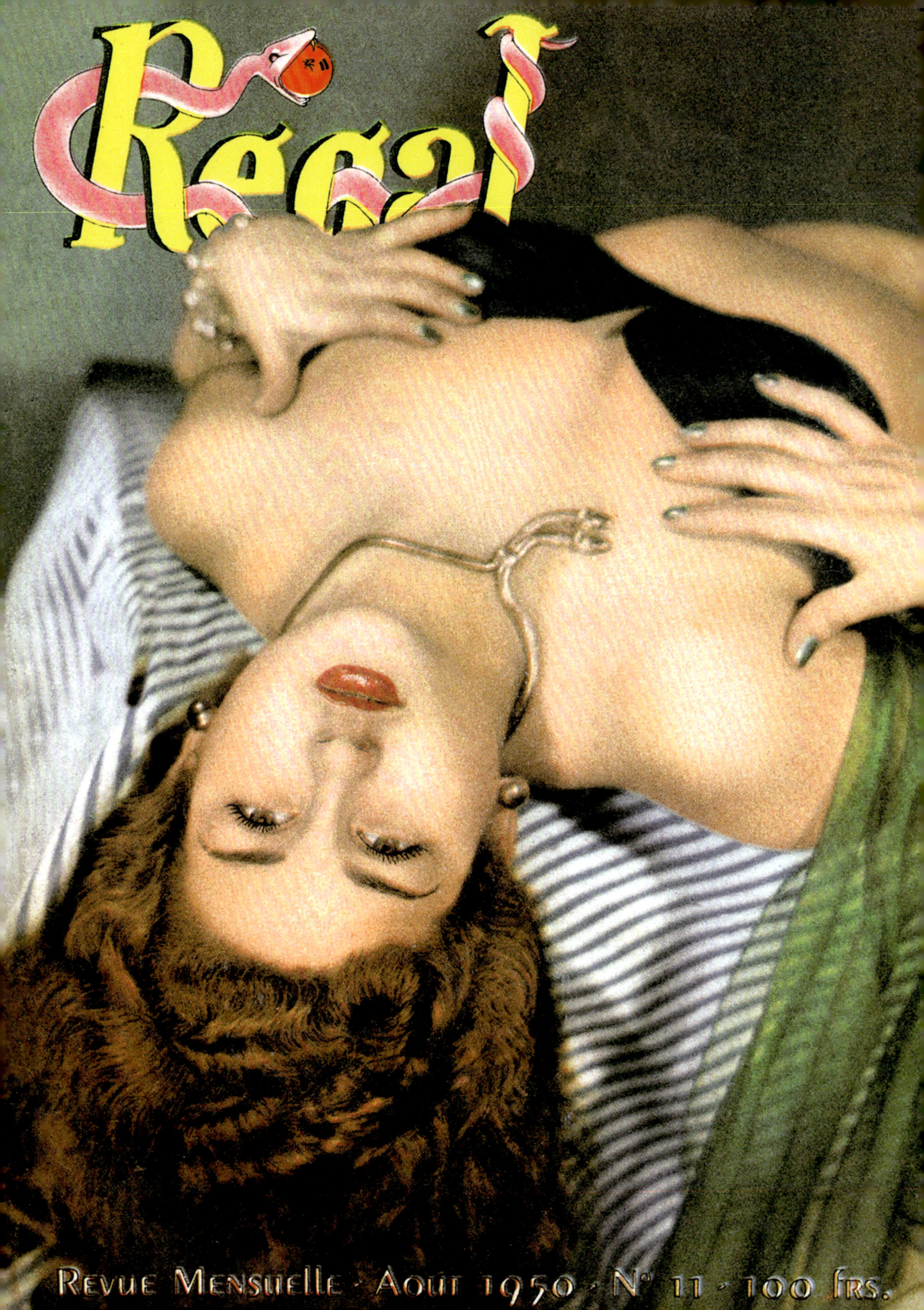
Regal
Revue Mensuelle · Aout 1950 · N° 11 · 100 frs.

The French may have given up their freedom when the Nazis marched on Paris in 1940, but they never surrendered their men's magazines.

Die Franzosen mögen ihre Freiheit eingebüßt haben, als die Nazis 1940 in Paris einmarschierten, aber ihre Männermagazine gaben sie nie auf.

Les Français avaient peut-être perdu leur liberté avec l'occupation nazie de Paris en 1940, mais ils ne renoncèrent jamais à leurs magazines pour hommes.

The most distinctive late 40s, early 50s digests came from Editions Extentia (*Régal, Sensations, Paris Tabou*) and from rival R.M. Dupuy.

menting a voluptuous covergirl. Boccasile honed his talents during the war painting propaganda posters for Mussolini's fascist regime. By the late 50s Extentia swapped its sex magazines for children's books—and Boccasile continued painting the imp without his sexy victims.

Dupuy's house artist was a cartoonist named J. David, who appeared to be channeling American Al Capp; his shapely heroines resembled Daisy Mae crossed with a Paris streetwalker.

The Golden Era for the French digest was 1949 to 1955, but once established the format maintained its popularity through the 70s. The content evolved in very much the same way as American magazine content, from stockings and lingerie, to complete nudity, to pubic emphasis, to spread shots, to simulated sex. As the magazines changed, their

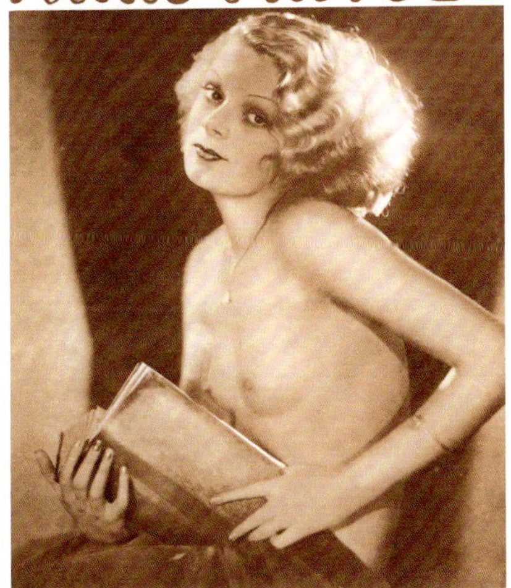

YEAR: **1940**. TITLE: **Paris-Frivole**.
COUNTRY: **France**.

und *Paris Sex-Appeal* hatten während des Krieges wacker durchgehalten, aber andere qualitativ hochwertige Magazine wie *Beauté* oder *Paris Plaisirs* waren dem Papier-, Geld- und Personalmangel zum Opfer gefallen. Die amerikanischen Soldaten, die in Frankreich stationiert waren, begeisterten sich an billigen, sepiafarbenen, kleinformatigen Heften wie *Paris-Folies* oder *Paris-Frivole*, die alte Fotos aus den Zwanzigern und Dreißigern wiederverwerteten und mit kriegstypischen Witzen anreicherten, doch für Franzosen war das der deprimierende Tiefpunkt einer langen Tradition erotischer Publikationen. Als 1946 die erste Ausgabe von *Paris-Hollywood* erschien, war das ein Signal, dass man nun bei den Männermagazinen wieder Nägel mit Köpfen machte, und als das Magazin 1948 noch gewagter wurde, fand es eine ganze Reihe faszinierender Nachahmer.

Die besten dieser Magazine im Taschenformat der vierziger und fünfziger Jahre stammten aus der Editions Extentia (*Régal*, *Sensations*, *Chiche*, *Rose et Noir* und *Paris Tabou*) und von der Konkurrenzfirma R. M. Dupuy (*Paris Gai*, *Paris Sourire* und *Moi et Toi*). Beide Firmen publizierten anspruchsvolle Schwarzweiß-Fotos im Film-Noir-Stil und gaben sich mit jeweils einem hauseigenen Pinup-Künstler zusätzliches Profil. Der Italiener Gino Boccasile war bei Extentia für die humoristischen Coverillustrationen von *Paris Tabou* verantwortlich. Auf all seinen Bildern sah man das Firmenmaskottchen, einen kleinen Lausbuben, der ein sinnliches Covergirl neckt. Boccasile hatte seine zeichnerischen Fähigkeiten während des Krieges an Propagandaplakaten für Mussolinis faschistisches Regime vervollkomnet.

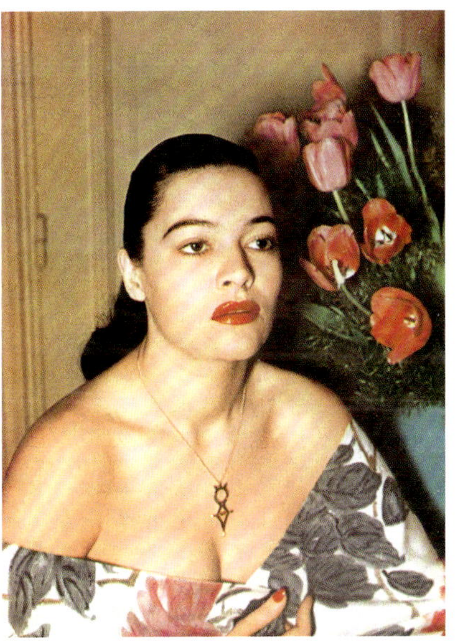

YEAR: **1952**. TITLE: **Paris Plaisirs**.
COUNTRY: **France**.

Boccasile créait les couvertures humoristiques de *Paris Tabou*. Toutes ses images incluaient la mascotte de la maison, un garçonnet espiègle tourmentant une beauté voluptueuse. Boccasile avait peaufiné ses talents pendant la guerre en peignant des affiches de propagande pour le régime fasciste de Mussolini. À la fin des années cinquante, Extentia abandonna ses revues de charme pour se reconvertir dans les livres pour enfants et Boccasile continua à peindre le chenapan sans ses victimes sexy. L'artiste maison de Dupuy était un illustrateur de bandes dessinées nommé J. David dont le style rappelait fortement celui de l'américain Al Capp. Ses plantureuses héroïnes étaient une sorte de croisement entre Daisy Mae et une péripatéticienne parisienne.

Les digests français connurent leur âge d'or entre 1949 et 1955 même si, une fois établi, le format resta populaire

YEAR: **1950**. TITLE: **Régal**. COUNTRY: **France**.

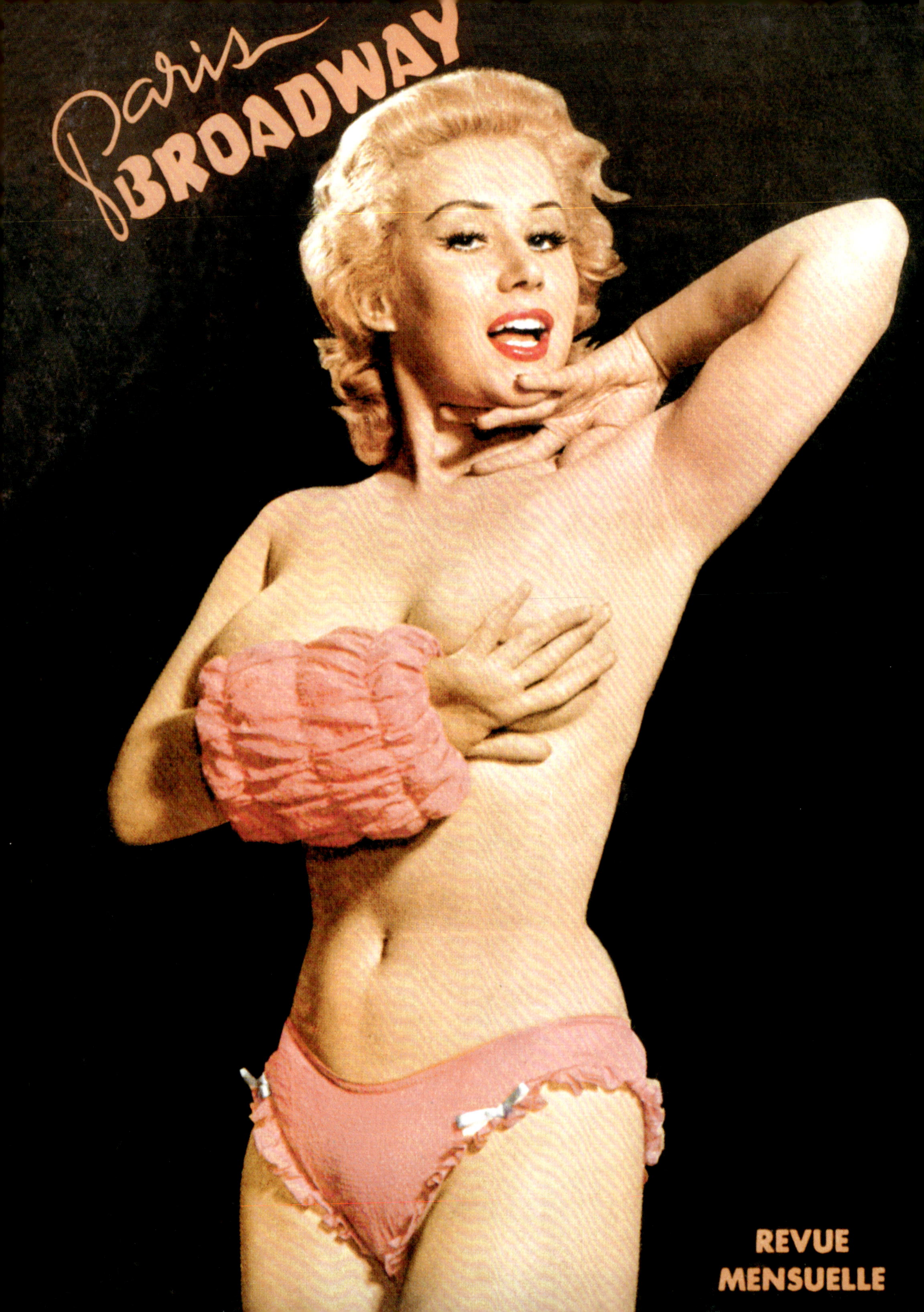
Paris
BROADWAY
REVUE
MENSUELLE

Year: **1950s**. Title: **Paris Broadway**.
Country: **France**.

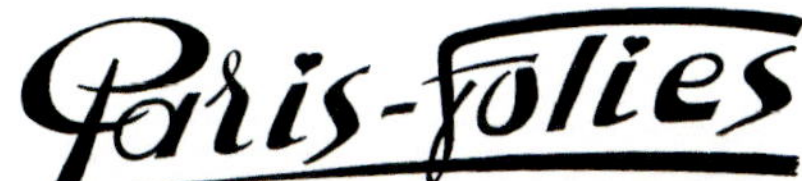

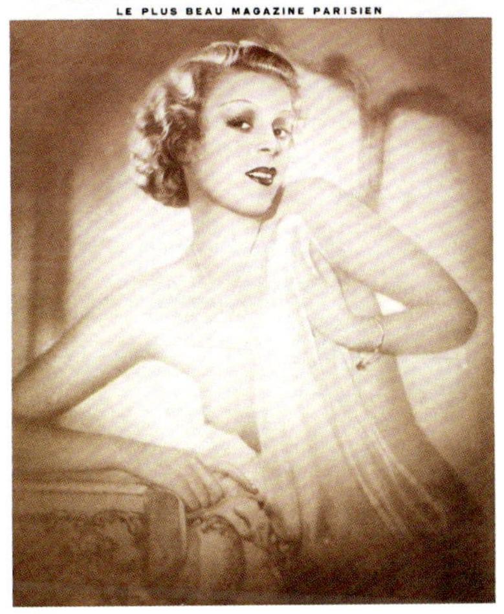

Year: **1940**. Title: **Paris-Folies**.
Country: **France**.

print quality and production values dropped until they were nearly indistinguishable from the cheapest Scandinavian digests. Perhaps, as happened elsewhere, publishers found their audiences grew less demanding as content grew more explicit.

Ende der Fünfziger gab Extentia seine Sextitel zugunsten eines Kinderbuchprogramms auf, und Boccasile zeichnete seinen kleinen Racker fortan ohne dessen berückendes Opfer. Dupuys Hausillustrator war J. David, der sich den Amerikaner Andy Capp zum Vorbild genommen zu haben schien: seine kurvigen Heldinnen erinnerten an eine Mischung aus Daisy Mae und einer französischen Bordsteinschwalbe.

Die Blütezeit für französische Magazine in diesem Format lag zwischen 1949 und 1955, aber nachdem das Format einmal eingeführt war, hielt es sich bis in die Siebziger. Inhaltlich entwickelten sie sich wie die amerikanischen Pendants: anfangs Strümpfe und Unterwäsche, dann völlige Nacktheit, dann Betonung der Scham und schließlich gespreizte Beine und simulierter Sexakt. Im Laufe der Zeit verschlechterten sich Druckqualität und Produktionsstandard so sehr, dass die Hefte sich kaum noch von den billigsten skandinavischen kleinformatigen Magazinen unterschieden. Vielleicht war es auch hier so, dass die Verleger feststellten, dass ihr Publikum mit zunehmend härterem Inhalt geringere Ansprüche an optische Präsentation stellten.

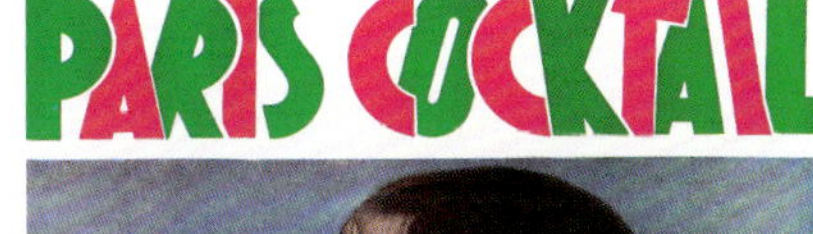

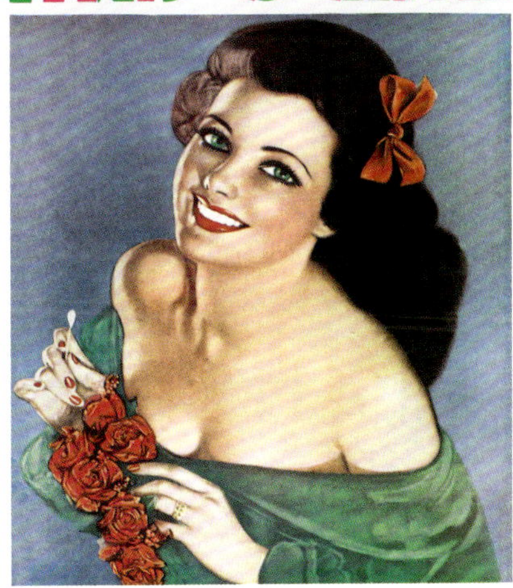

Year: **1940**. Title: **Paris Cocktail**.
Country: **France**.

jusque dans les années soixante-dix. Leur contenu évolua plus ou moins comme celui des digests américains, des bas et de la lingerie à la nudité intégrale, puis à l'accent sur les pubis, aux poses jambes écartées et enfin aux simulations de rapports sexuels. À mesure qu'ils changeaient, leur qualité d'impression et de production baissèrent jusqu'à ce que plus rien ne les distingue des digests scandinaves les plus bas de gamme. Sans doute, comme partout ailleurs, les éditeurs trouvaient-ils que leurs lecteurs étaient de moins en moins exigeants à mesure que les contenus devenaient de plus en plus explicites.

Taboo is the oldest human unwritten code of laws. It is generally supposed that taboo is older than gods and dates back to a period before any kind of religion existed.

—Wilhelm Wundt, 1906

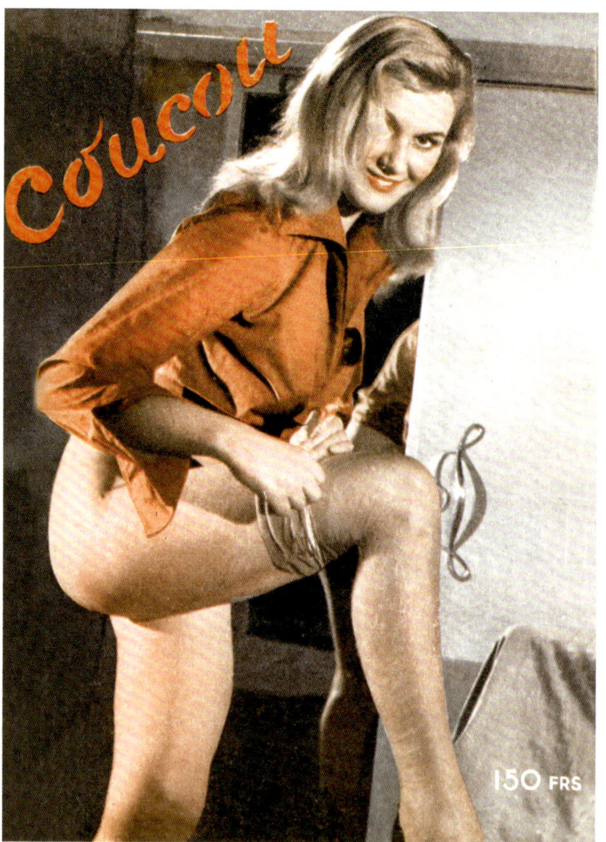

Year: **1952**. Title: **Coucou**. Country: **France**.

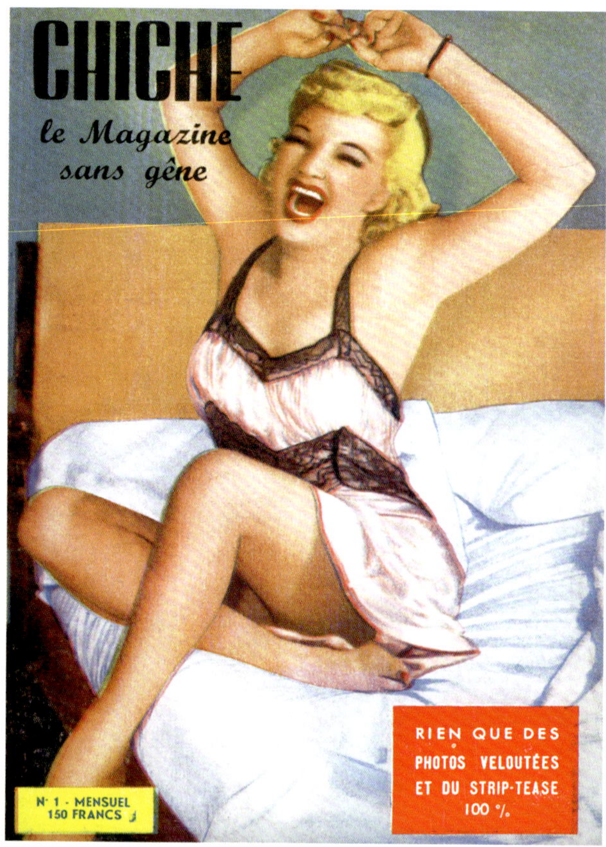

Year: **1950s**. Title: **Chiche**. Country: **France**.

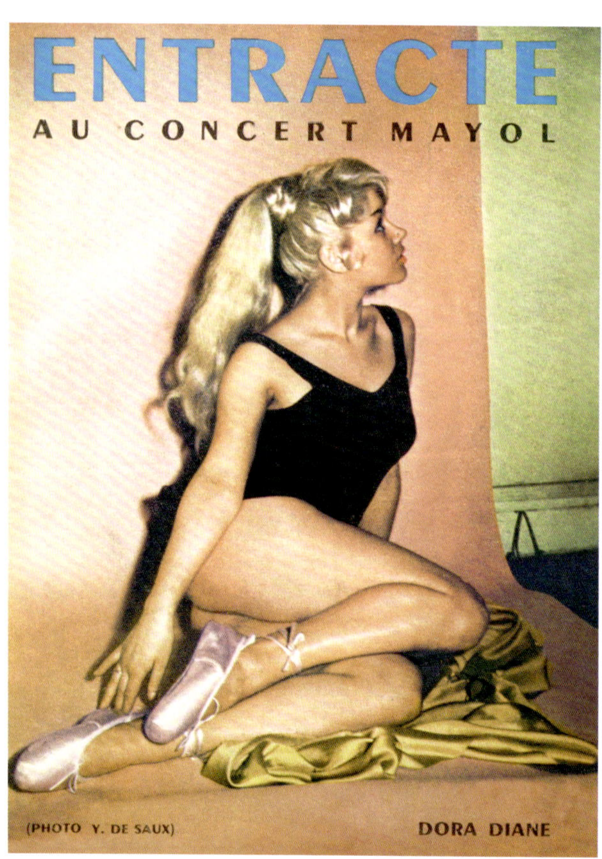

Year: **1950s**. Title: **Entracte**. Country: **France**.

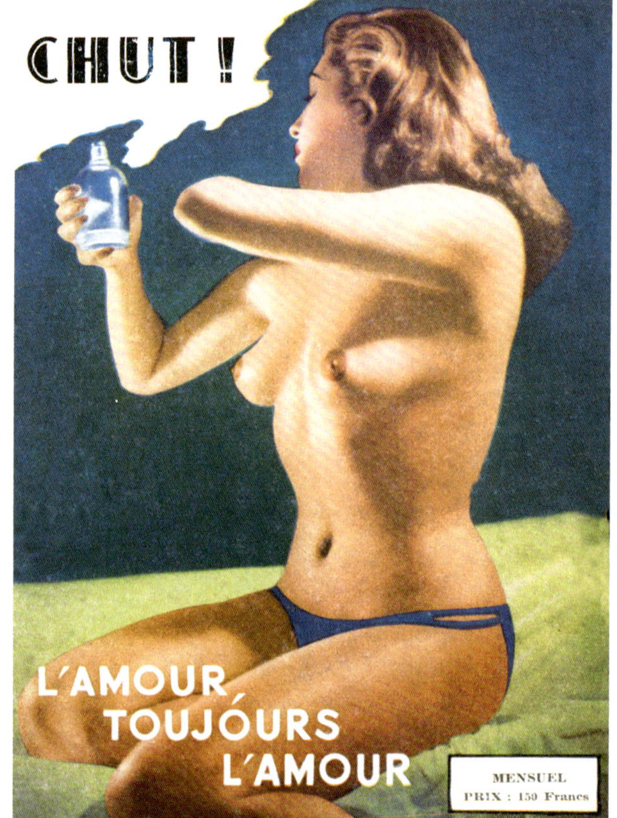

Year: **1950s**. Title: **Chut !** Country: **France**.

Right:
Year: **1950**. Title: **C'est Paris**. Country: **France**.
Pages 362 & 263:
Year: **1951**. Title: **Paris Cocktail**. Country: **France**.

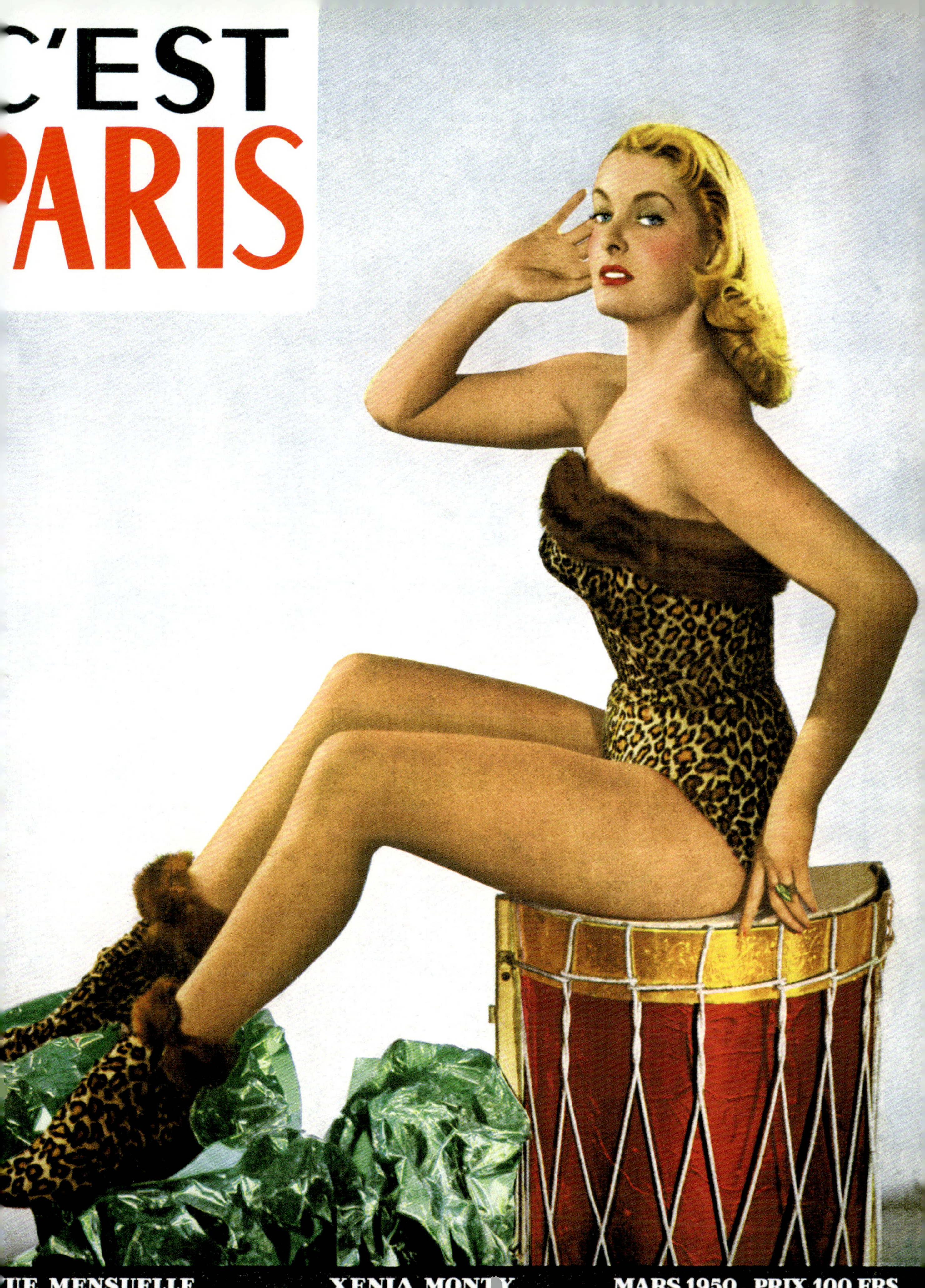
C'EST
PARIS
UE MENSUELLE
XENIA MONTY
MARS 1950 . PRIX 100 FRS

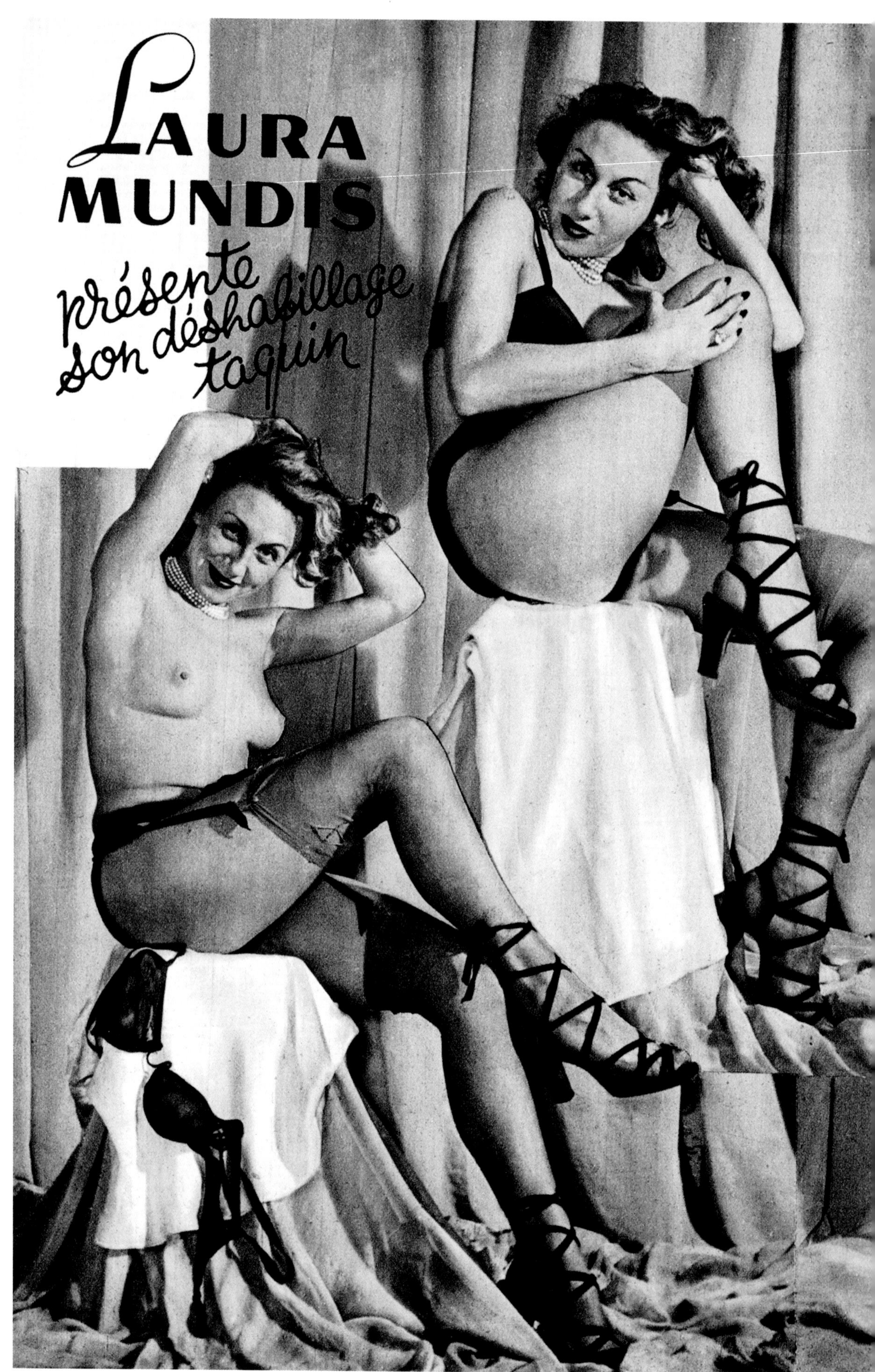
LAURA
MUNDIS
présente
son déshabillage
taquin

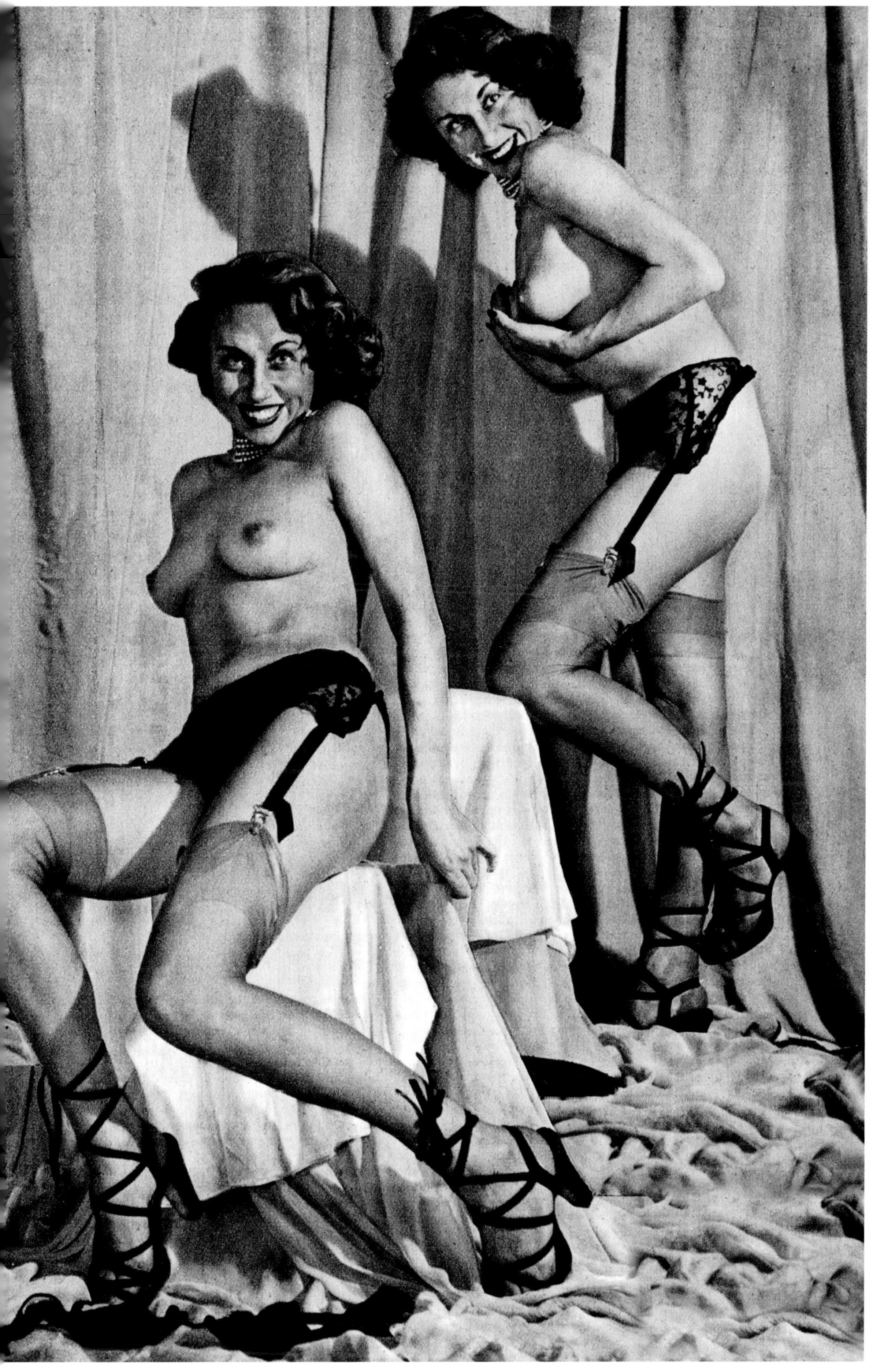

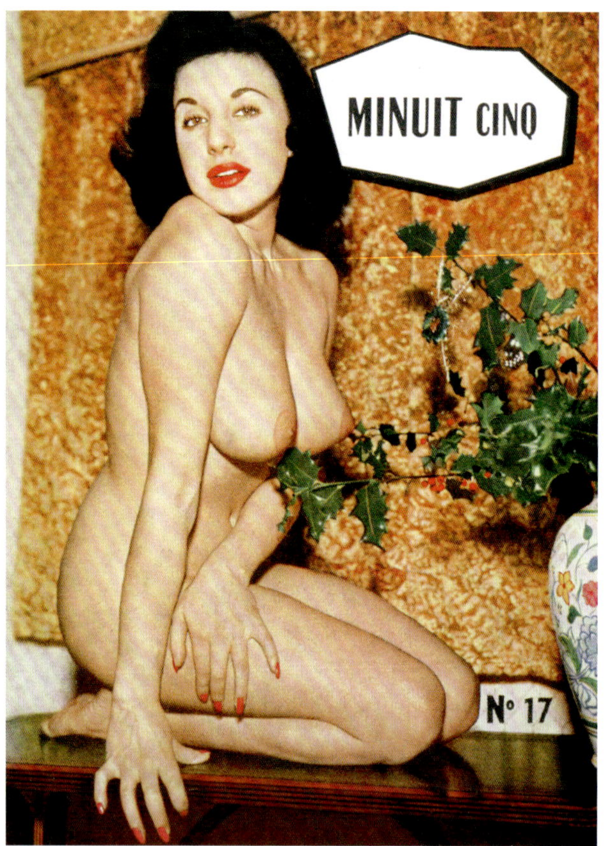

YEAR: **1950s**. TITLE: **Minuit Cinq**. COUNTRY: **France**.

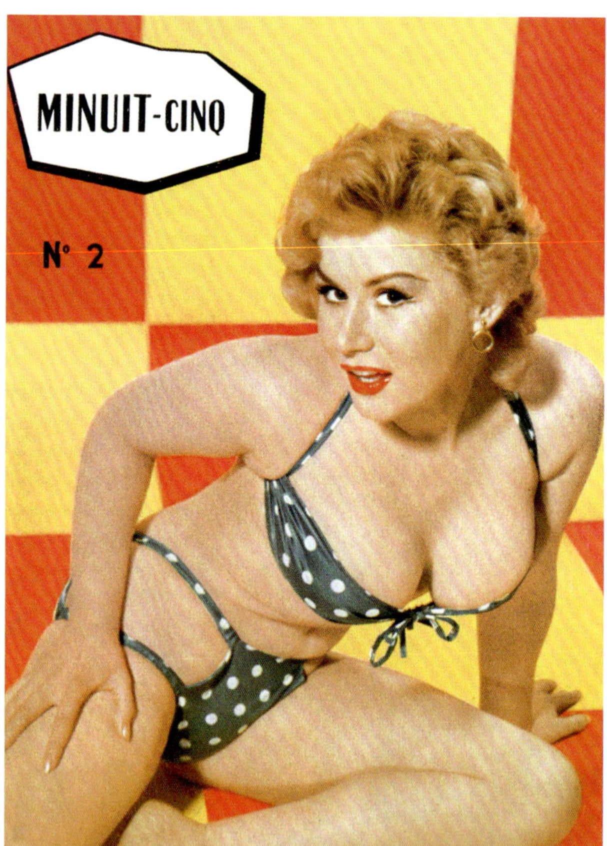

YEAR: **1950s**. TITLE: **Minuit Cinq**. COUNTRY: **France**.

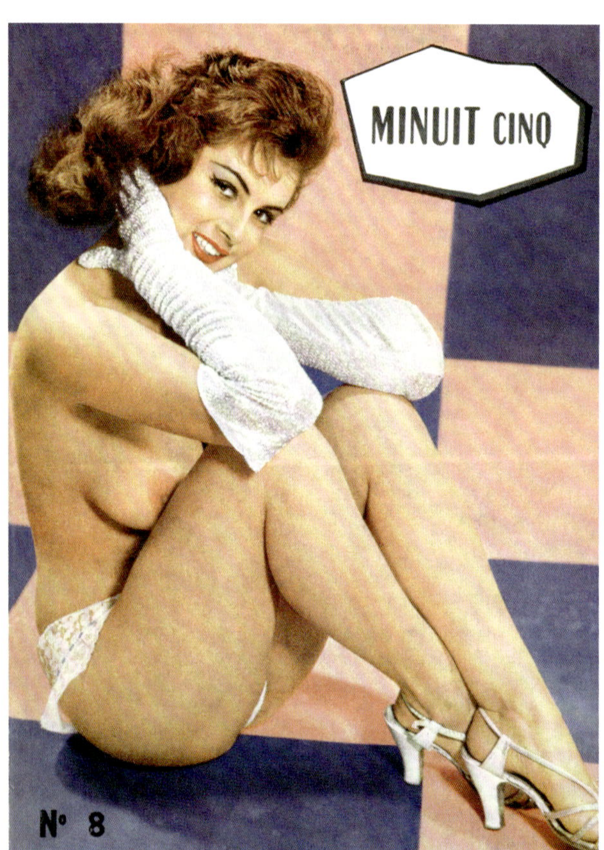

YEAR: **1950s**. TITLE: **Minuit Cinq**. COUNTRY: **France**.

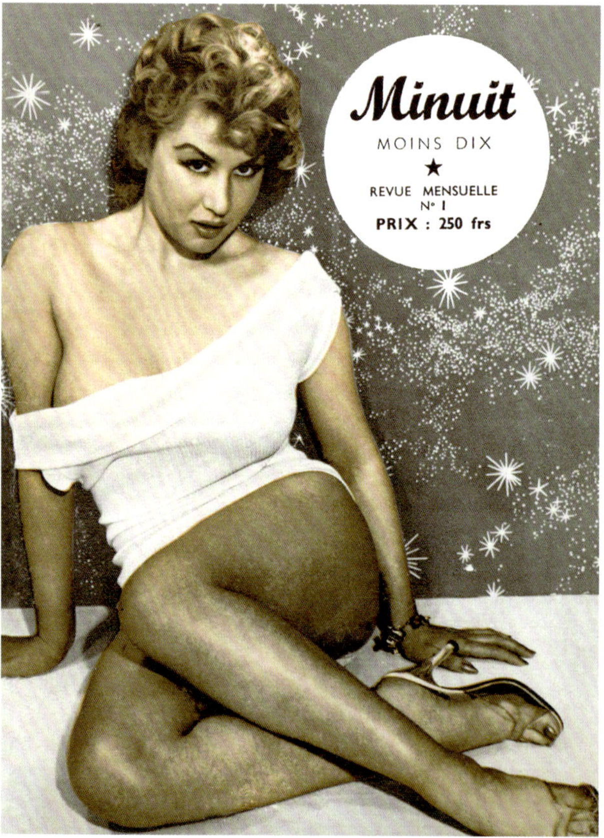

YEAR: **1950s**. TITLE: **Minuit**. COUNTRY: **France**.

YEAR: **1950s**. TITLE: **Minuit Cinq**. COUNTRY: **France**.

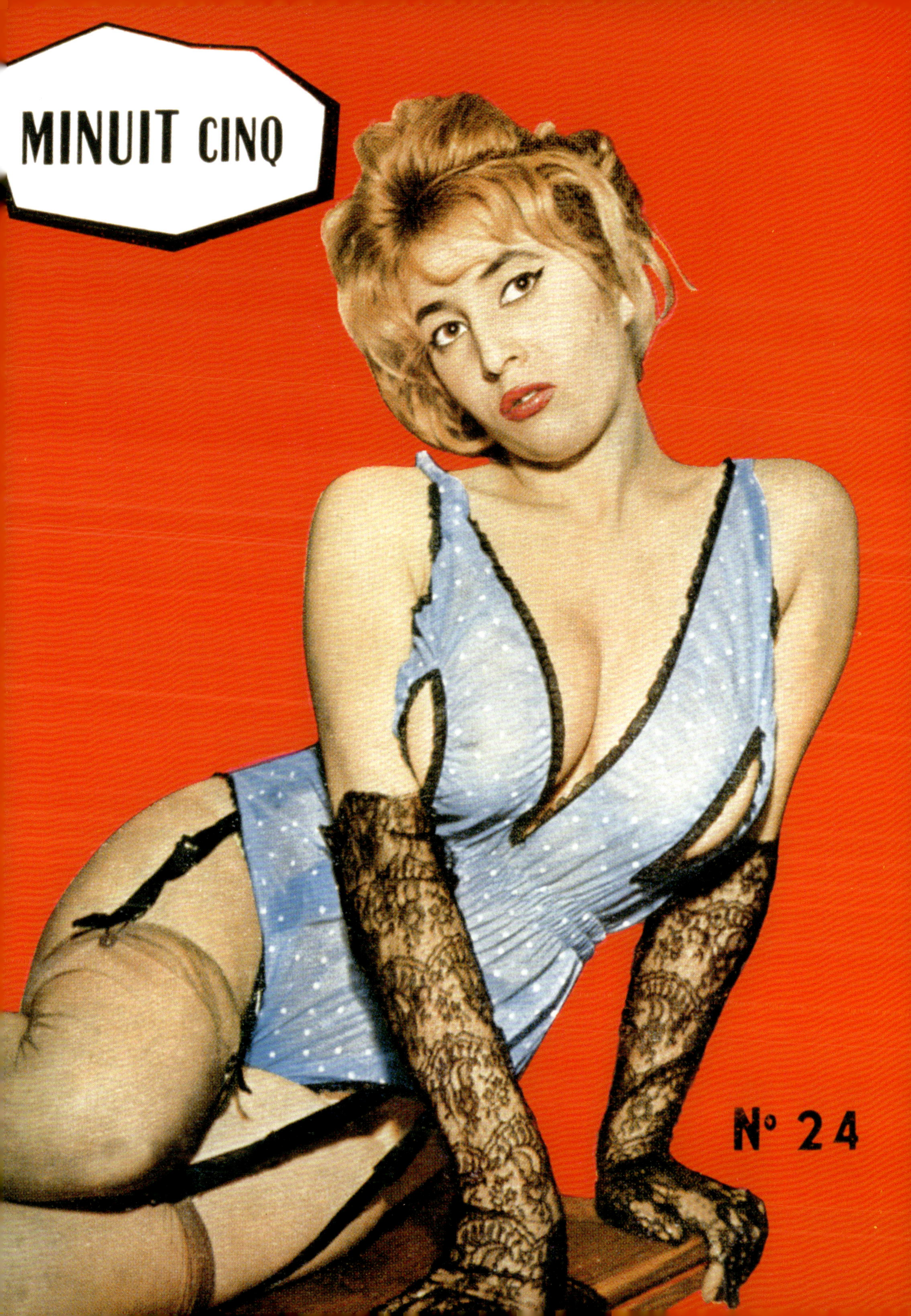
MINUIT CINQ
N° 24

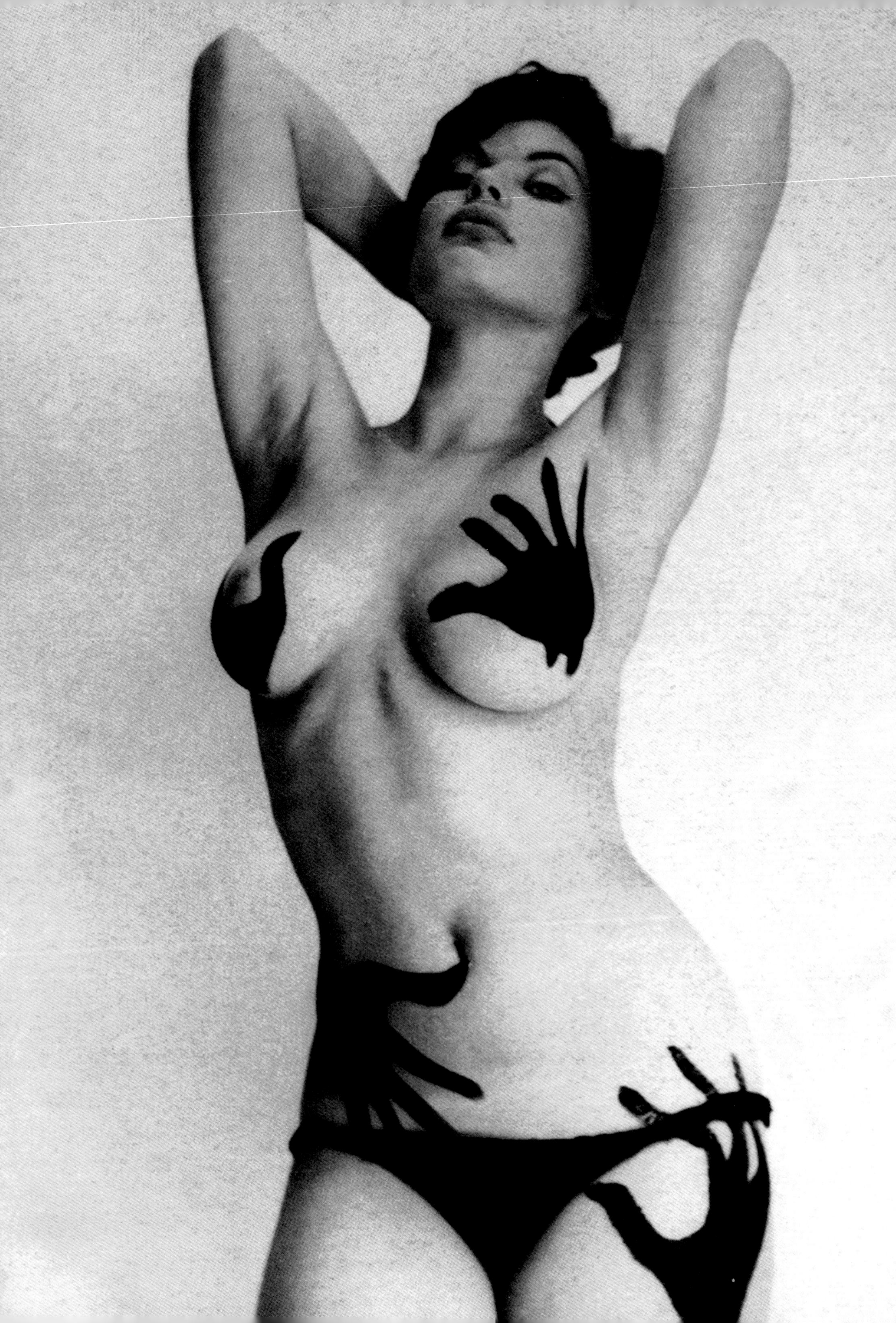

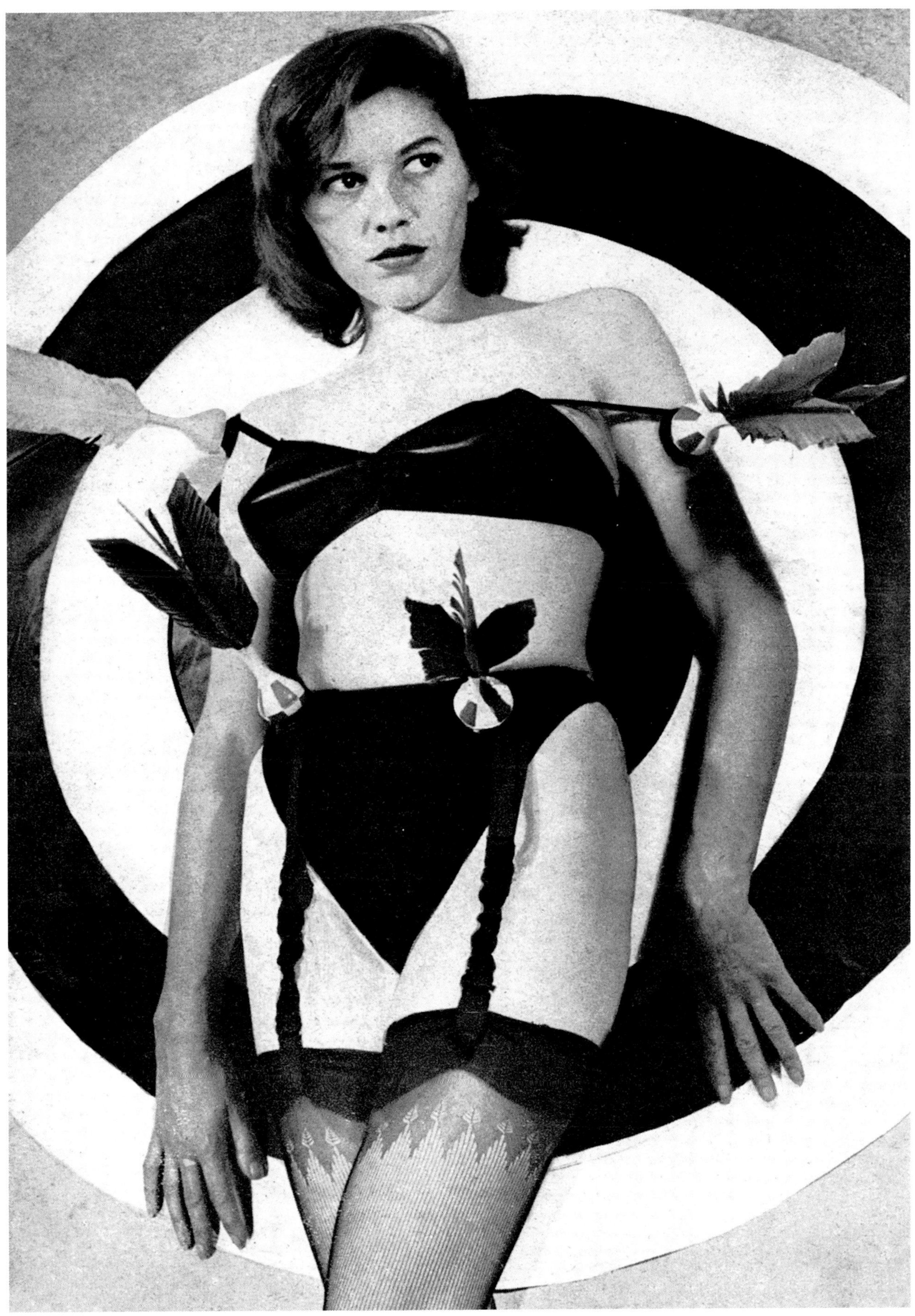

YEAR: **1950s**. TITLE: **Frin Gale**. COUNTRY: **France**.

YEAR: **1950s**. TITLE: **Paris Satan**. COUNTRY: **France**.

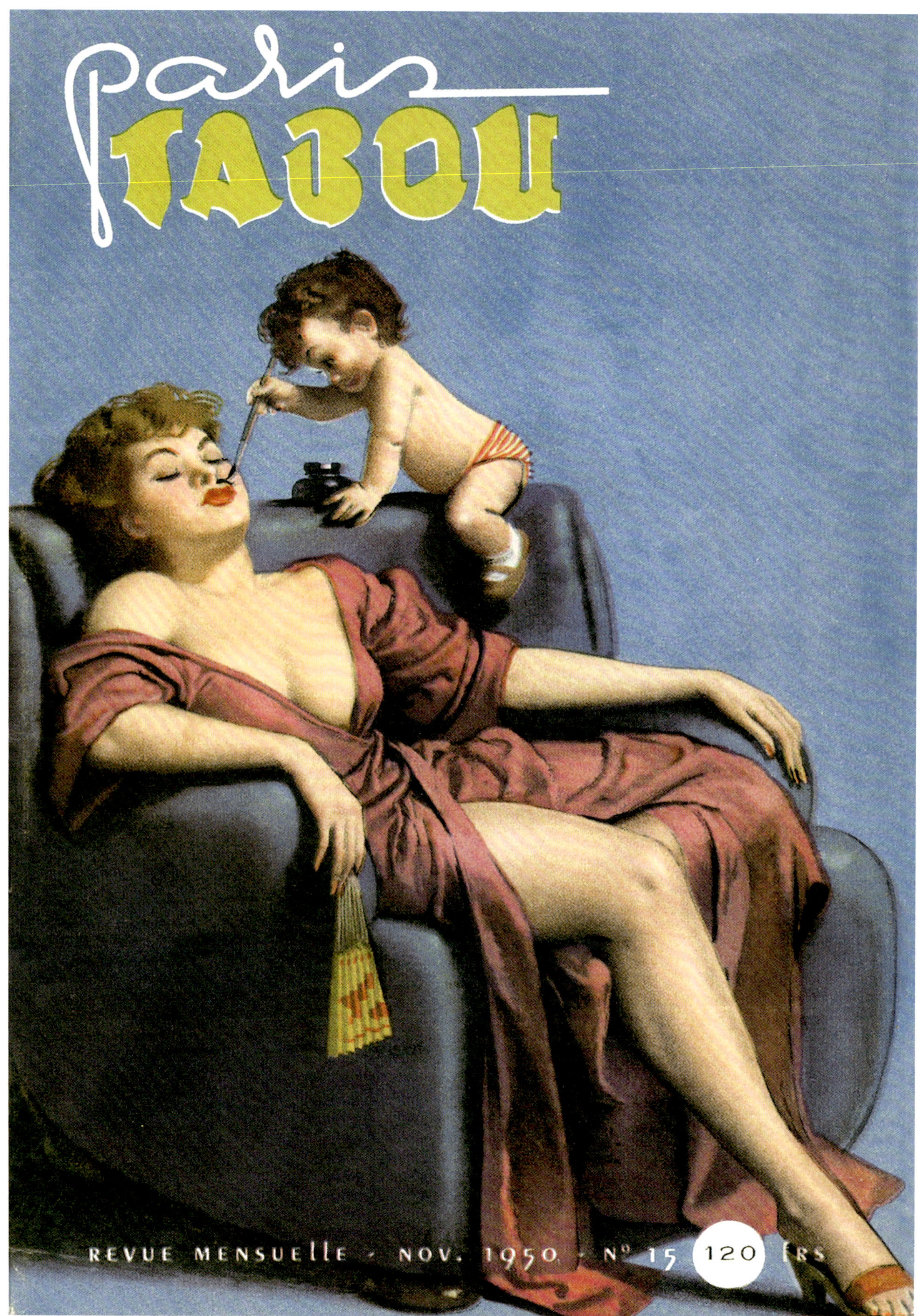

Every cover of this Editions Extentia publication from 1952 featured a little boy tormenting the voluptuous covergirl. The responsible artist was Gino Boccasile, one-time propaganda artist for Mussolini.

Jedes Titelbild dieses Magazins von Editions Extentia zeigte 1952 einen kleinen Jungen, der das sinnliche Covergirl peinigte. Die Bilder stammten von Gino Boccasile, einstmals Propagandakünstler Mussolinis.

Sur chaque couverture de cette publication des éditions Extentia de 1952, un garçonnet torturait la voluptueuse cover-girl. C'était une création de l'illustrateur Gino Boccasile, autrefois artiste de propagande de Mussolini.

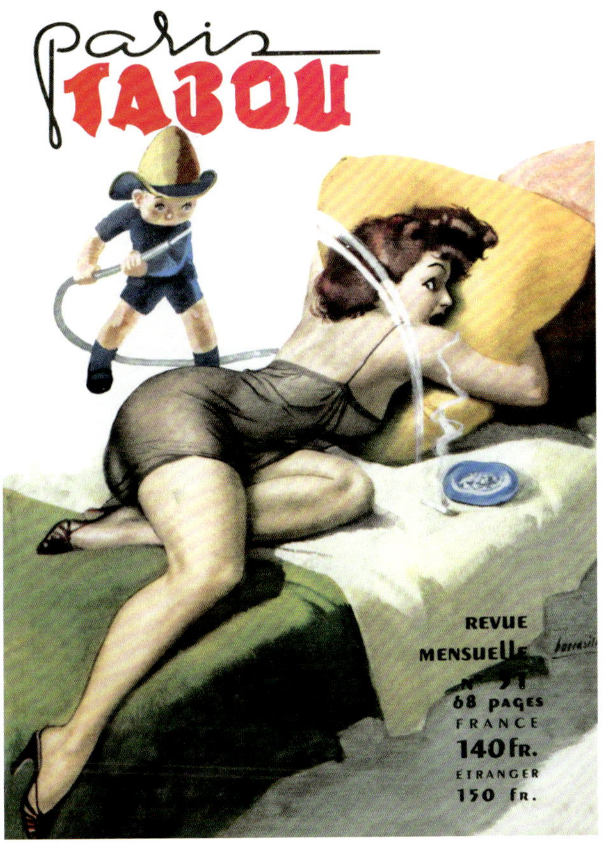

Year: **1952**. Title: **Paris Tabou**. Artist: **Gino Boccasile**. Country: **France**.

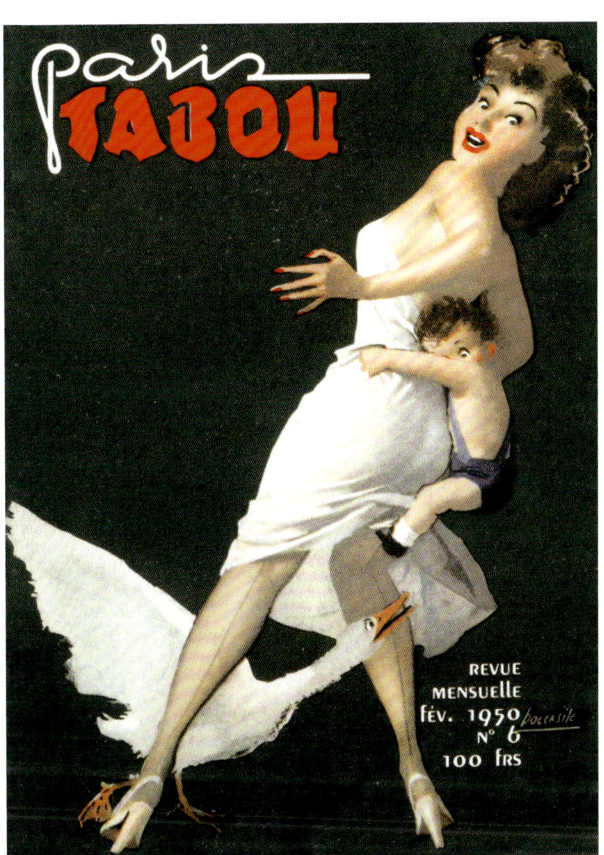

Year: **1950**. Title: **Paris Tabou**. Artist: **Gino Boccasile**. Country: **France**.

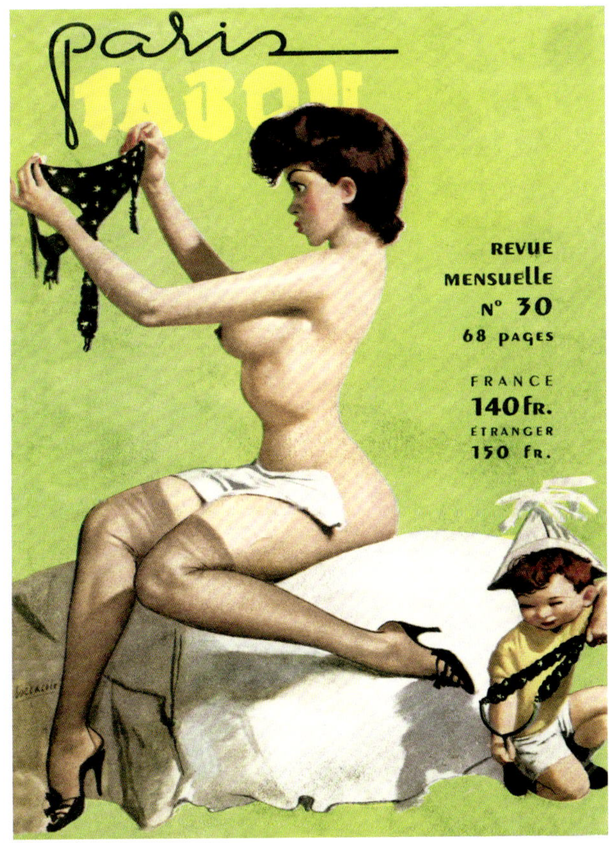

Year: **1952**. Title: **Paris Tabou**. Artist: **Gino Boccasile**. Country: **France**.

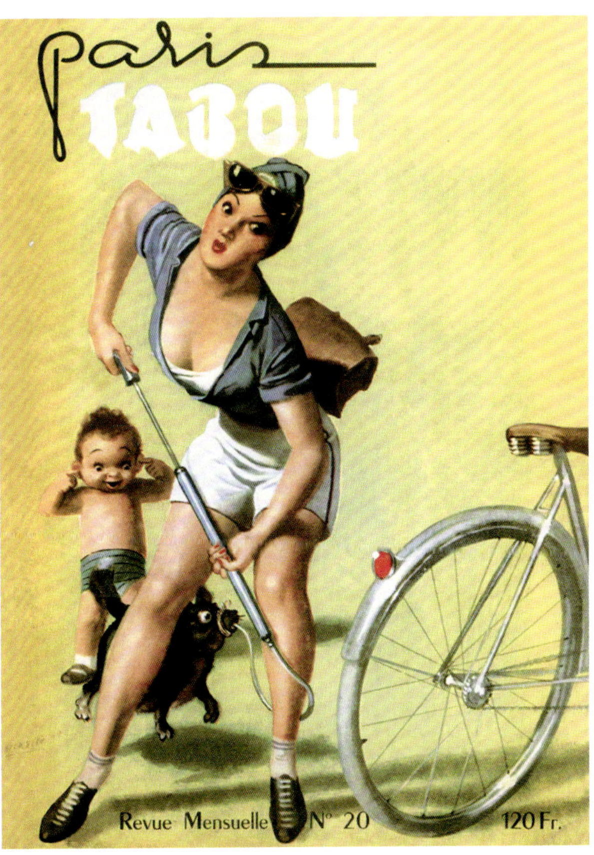

Year: **1950s**. Title: **Paris Tabou**. Artist: **Gino Boccasile**. Country: **France**.

Year: **1950**. Title: **Paris Tabou**. Artist: **Gino Boccasile**. Country: **France**.

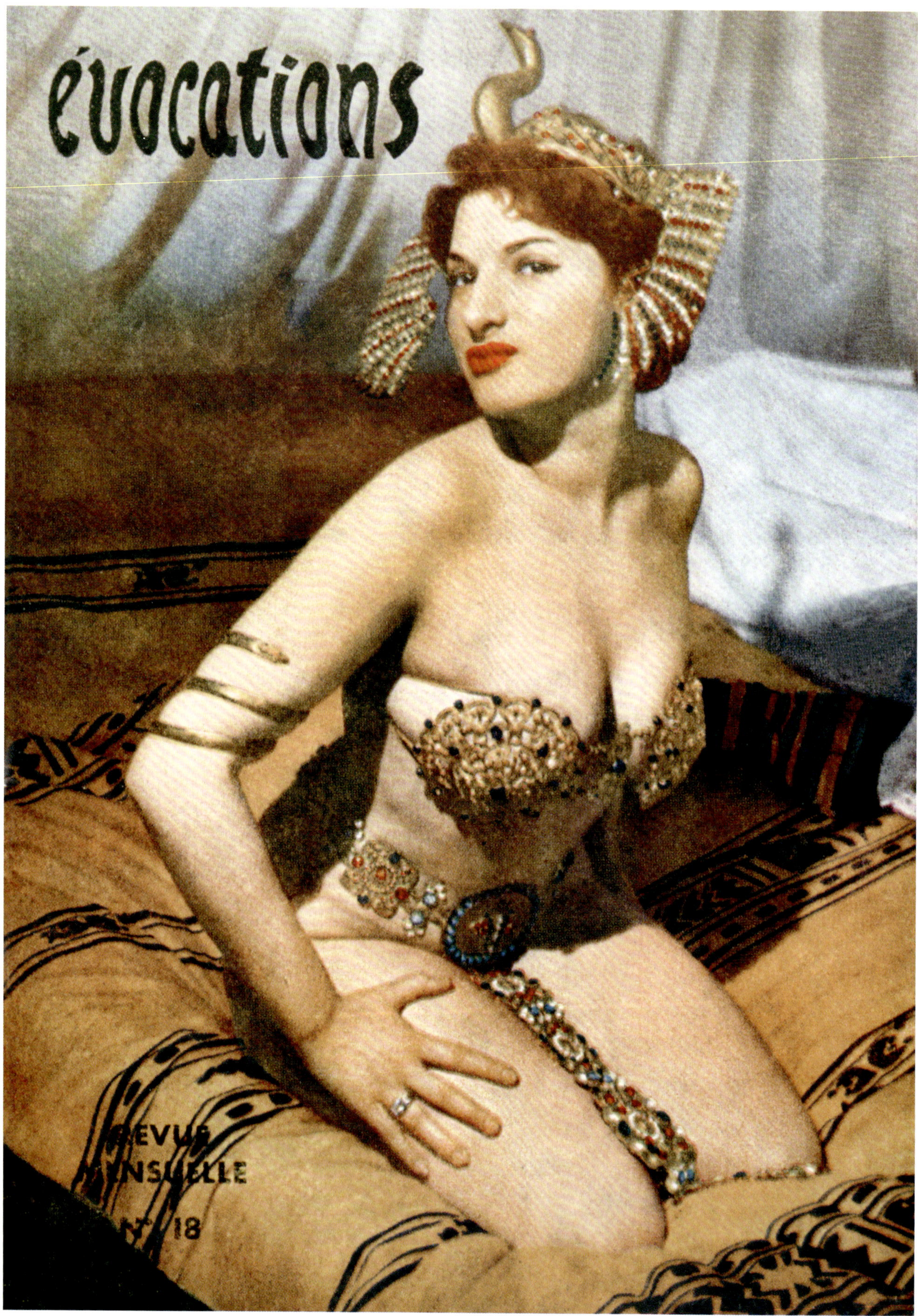

YEAR: **1950s**. TITLE: **Évocations**. COUNTRY: **France**.

YEAR: **1950s**. TITLE: **Fascination**. COUNTRY: **France**.

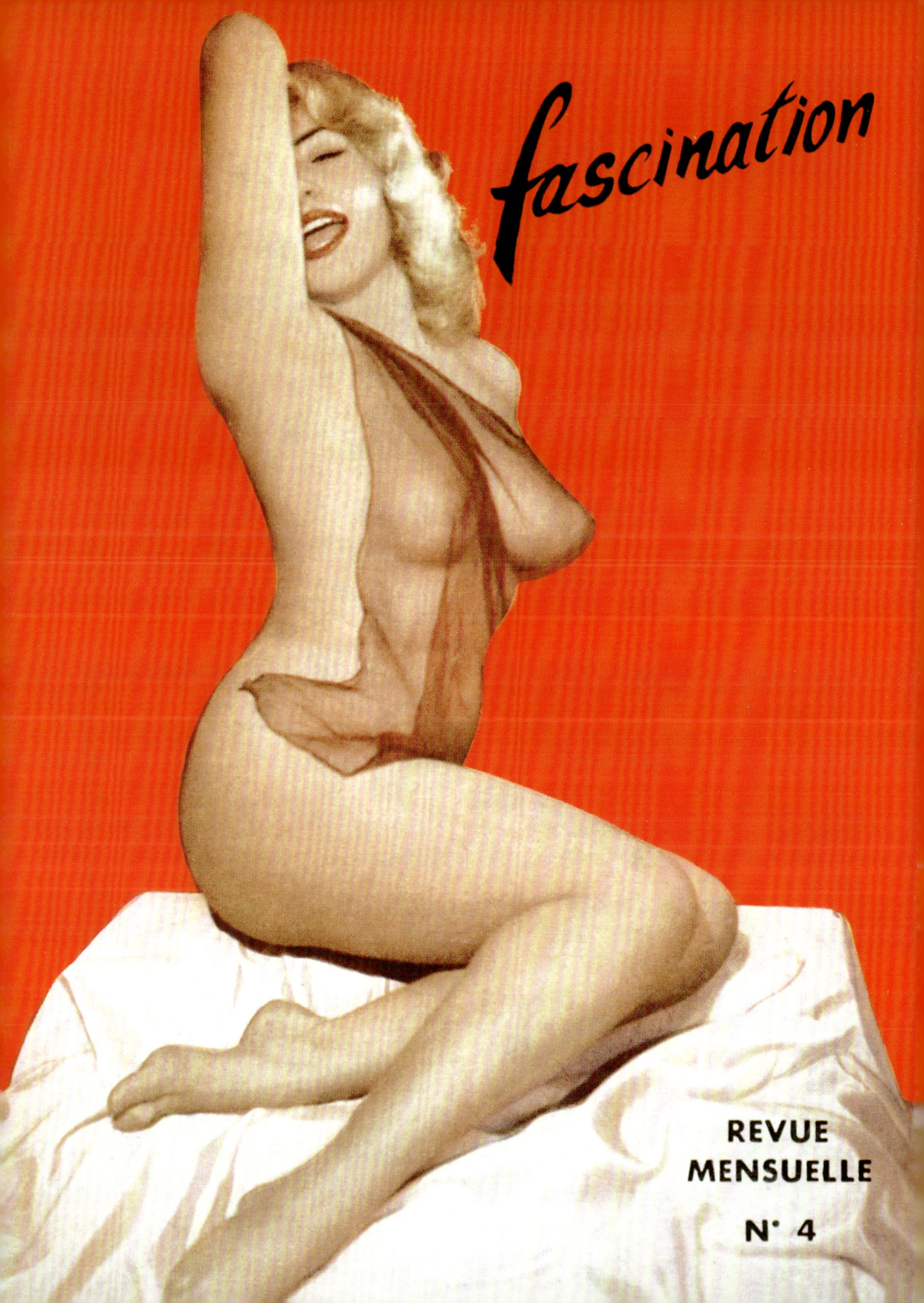
fascination
REVUE
MENSUELLE
N° 4

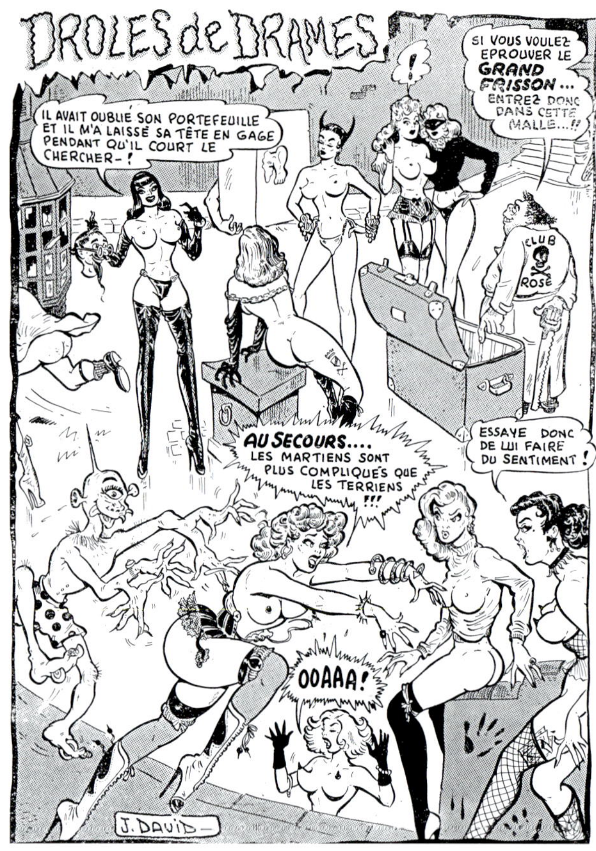

YEAR: **1950s**. TITLE: **Supervamps**. ARTIST: **J. David**. COUNTRY: **France**.

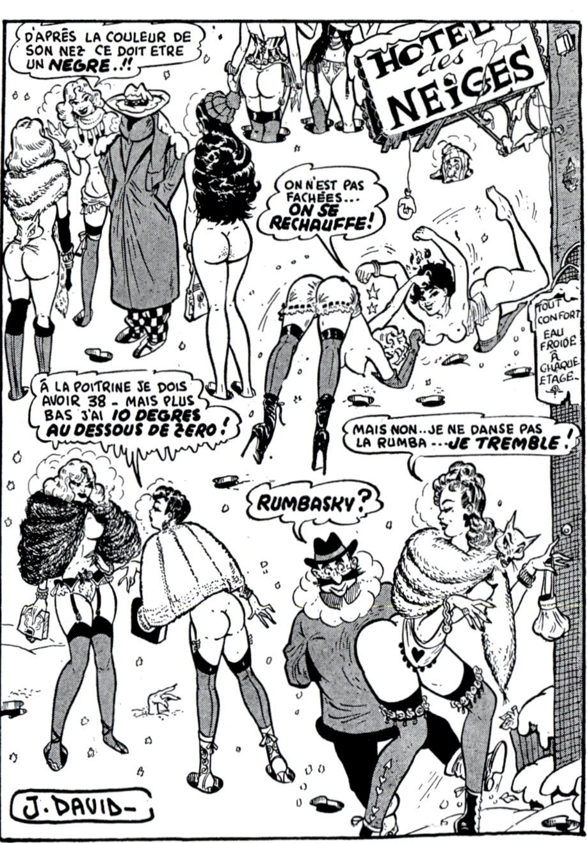

YEAR: **1950s**. TITLE: **Supervamps**. ARTIST: **J. David**. COUNTRY: **France**.

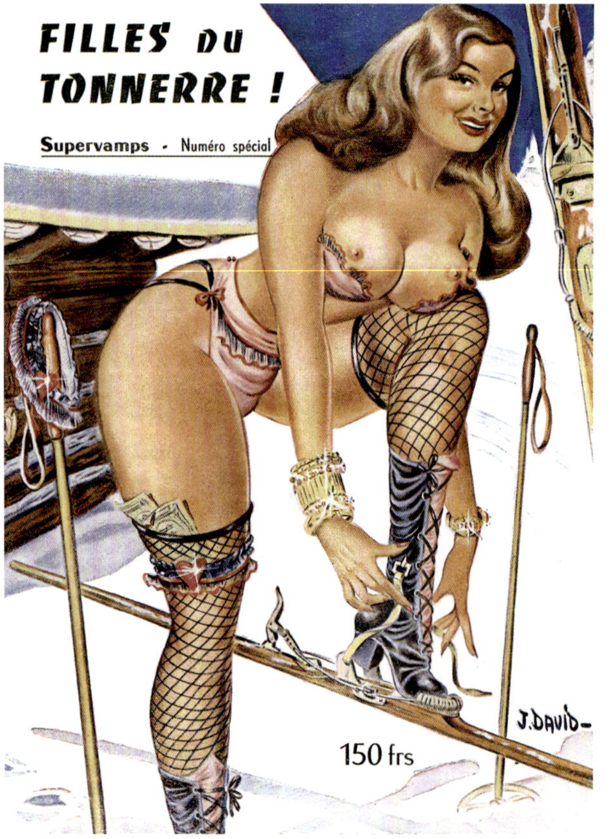

YEAR: **1950s**. TITLE: **Supervamps**. ARTIST: **J. David**. COUNTRY: **France**.

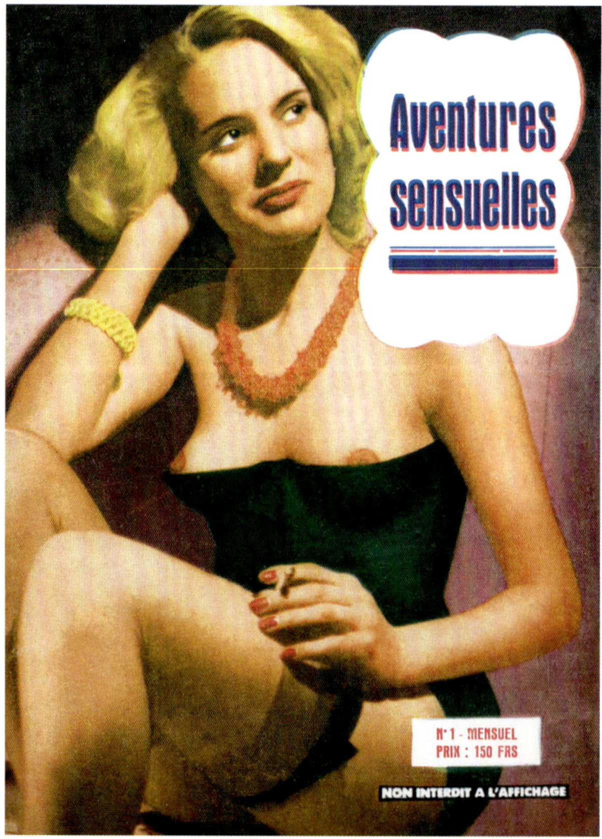

YEAR: **1950s**. TITLE: **Aventures sensuelles**. COUNTRY: **France**.

YEAR: **1950s**. TITLE: **Clins d'œil de Paris**. COUNTRY: **France**.

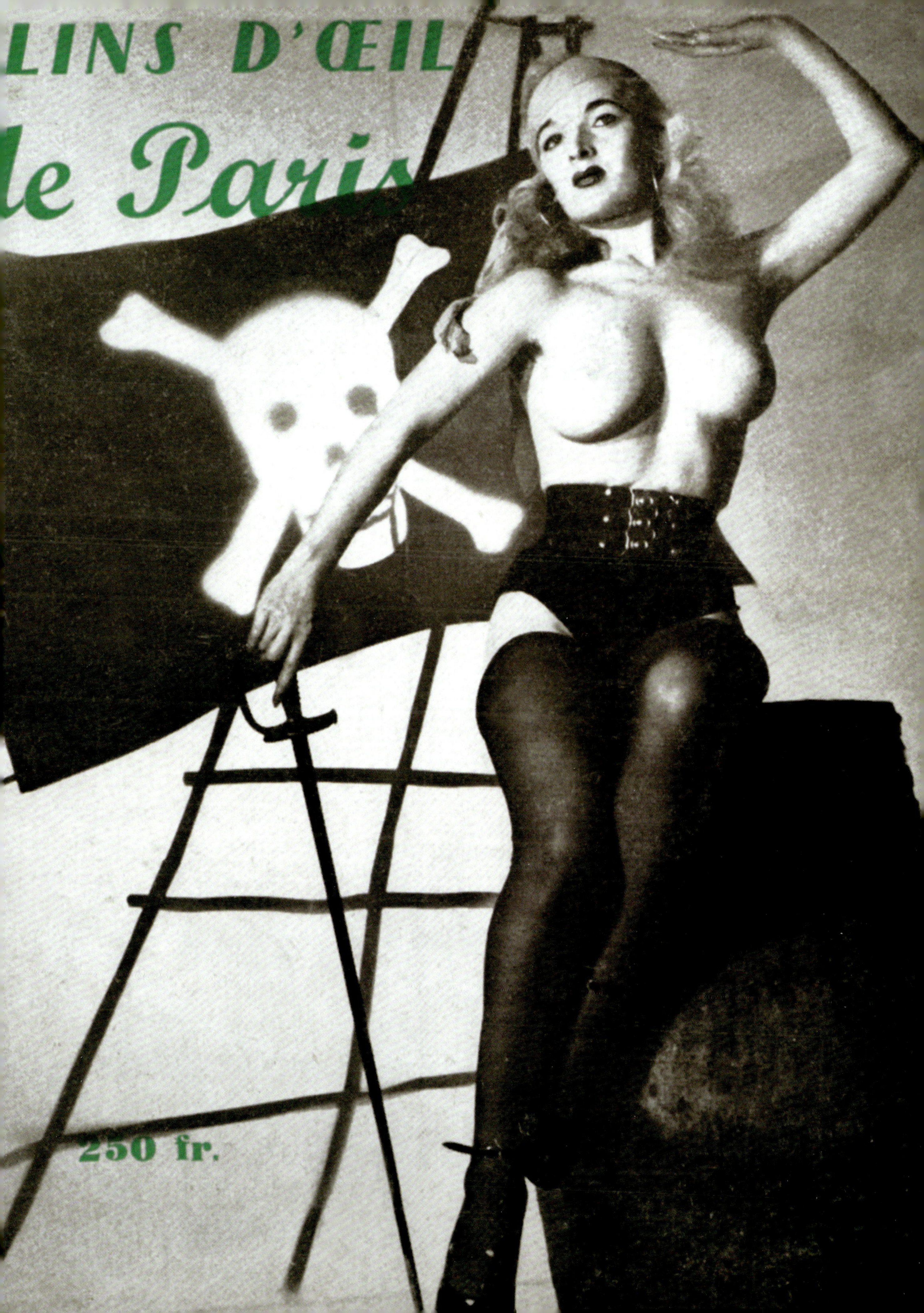
LINS D'ŒIL
le Paris
250 fr.

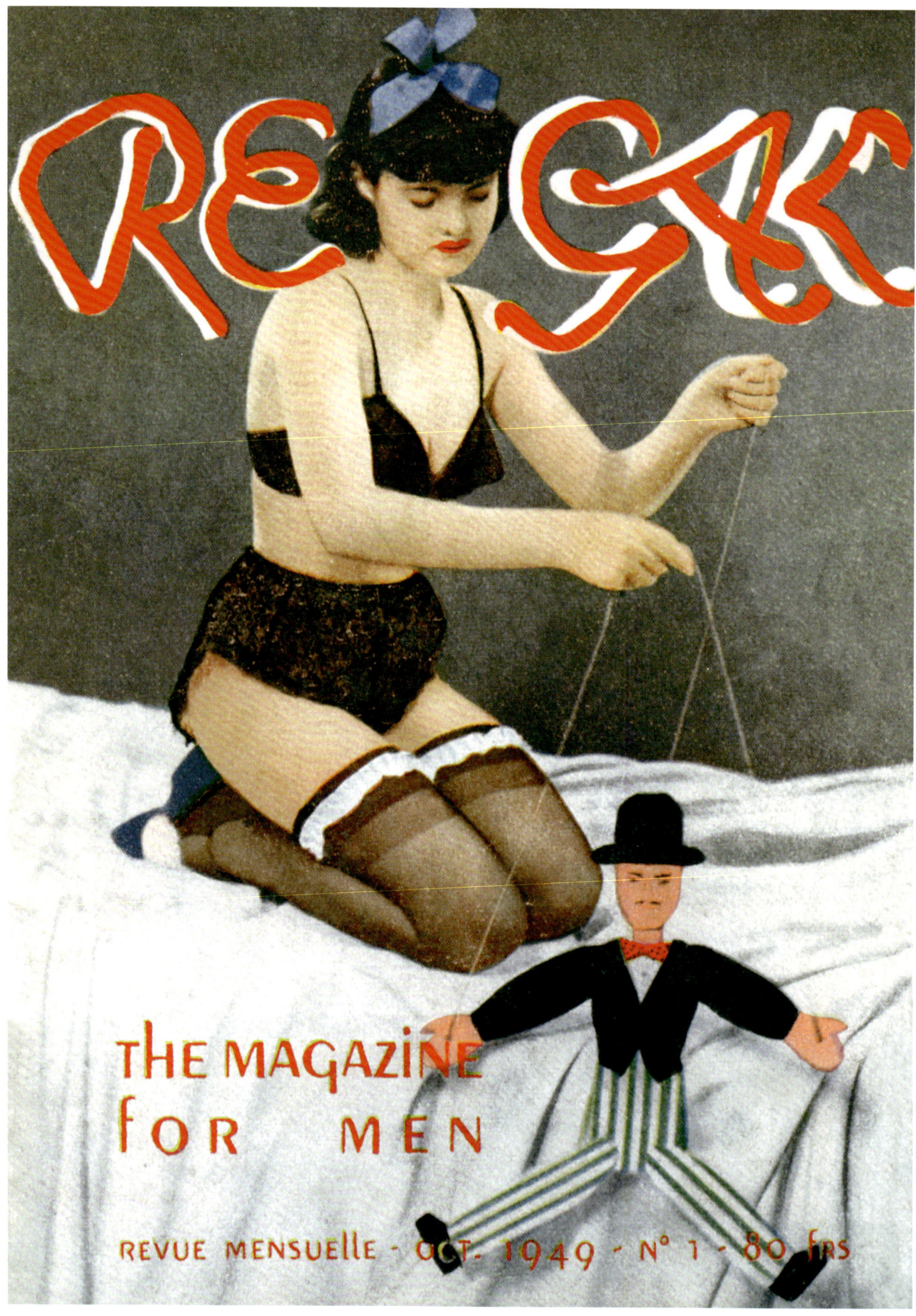

YEAR: **1949**. TITLE: **Régal**. COUNTRY: **France**.

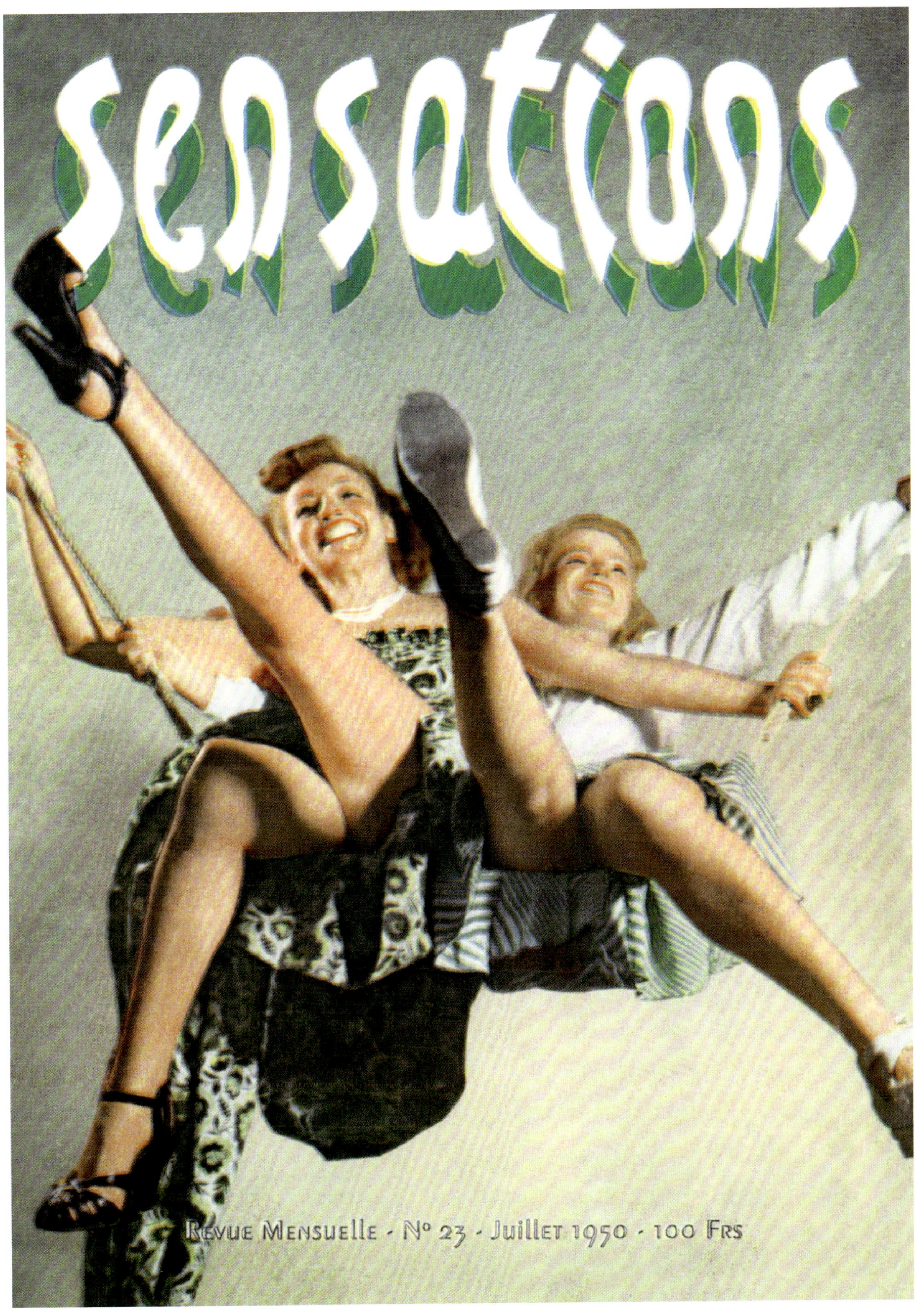

YEAR: **1950**. TITLE: **Sensations**. COUNTRY: **France**.

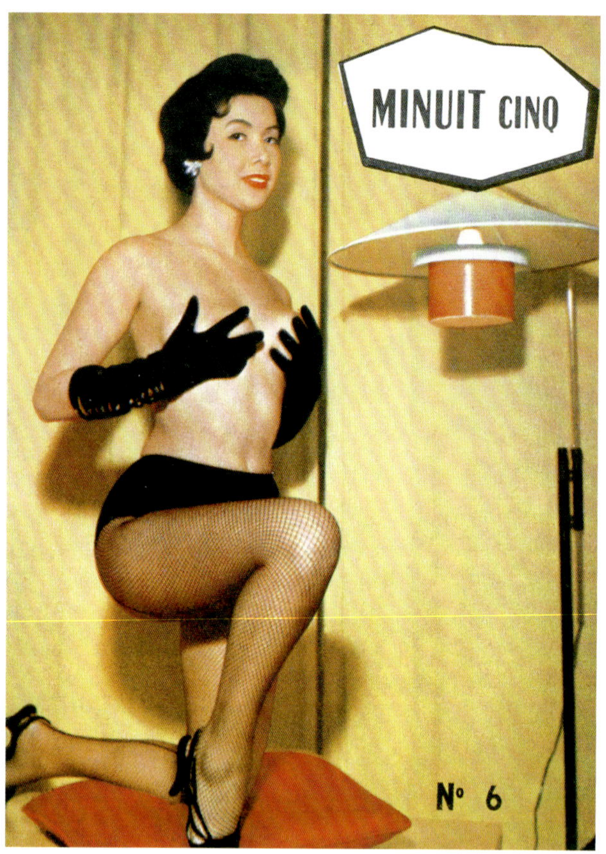

YEAR: **1950s**. TITLE: **Minuit Cinq**. COUNTRY: **France**.

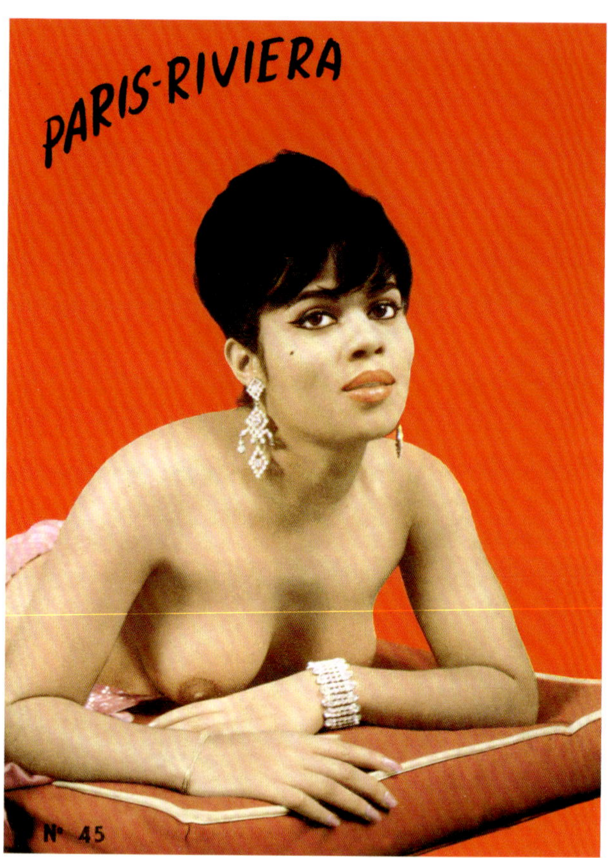

YEAR: **1950s**. TITLE: **Paris-Riviera**. COUNTRY: **France**.

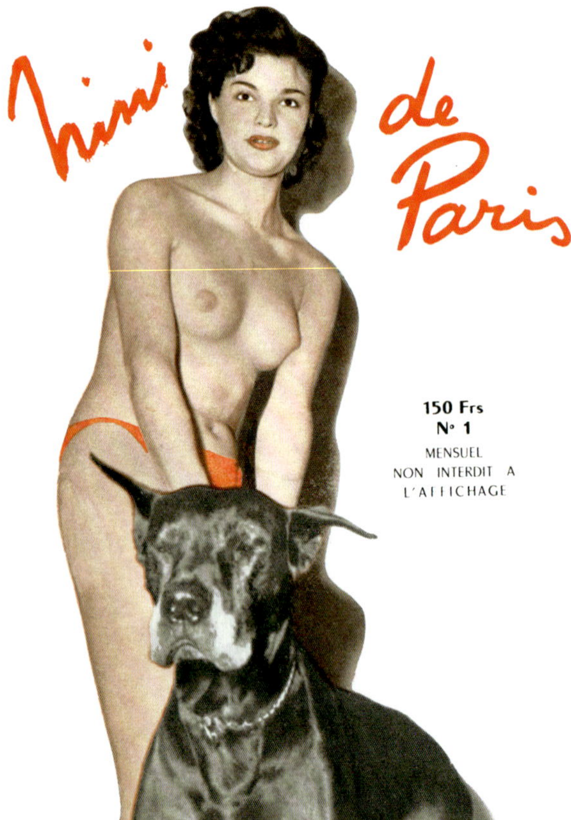

YEAR: **1950s**. TITLE: **Mini de Paris**. COUNTRY: **France**.

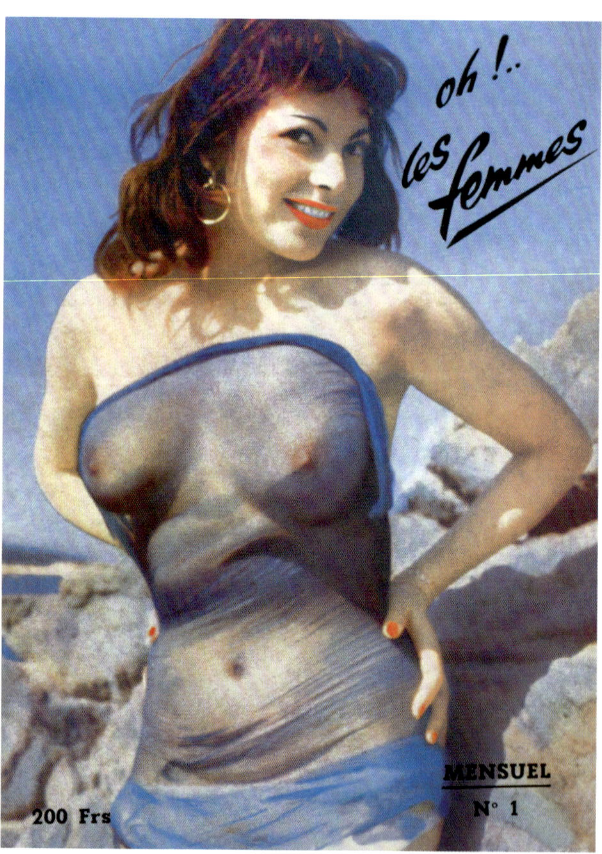

YEAR: **1950s**. TITLE: **Oh ! Les Femmes**. COUNTRY: **France**.

YEAR: **1950s**. TITLE: **Moi et Toi**. COUNTRY: **France**.

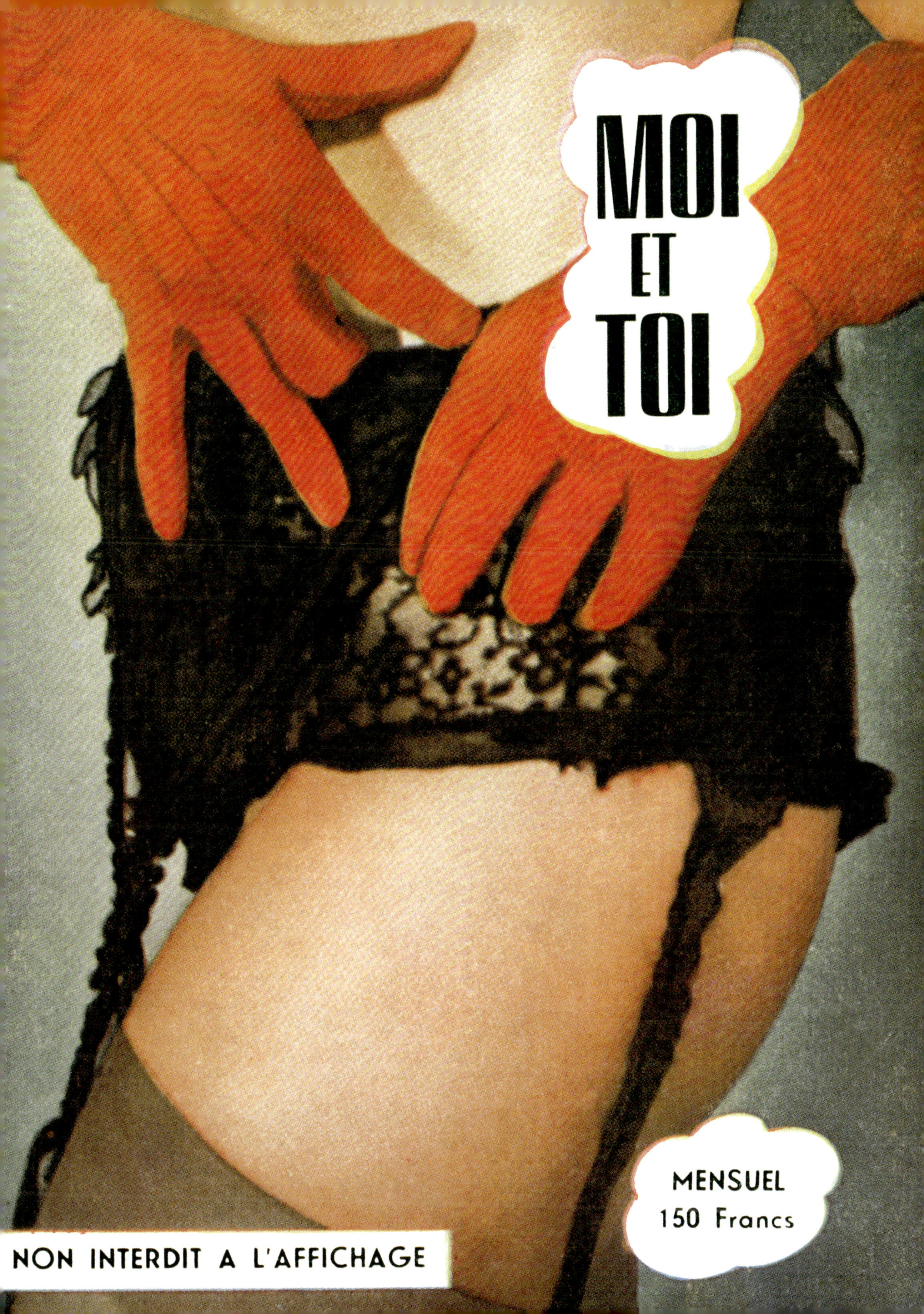
MOI
ET
TOI
MENSUEL
150 Francs
NON INTERDIT A L'AFFICHAGE

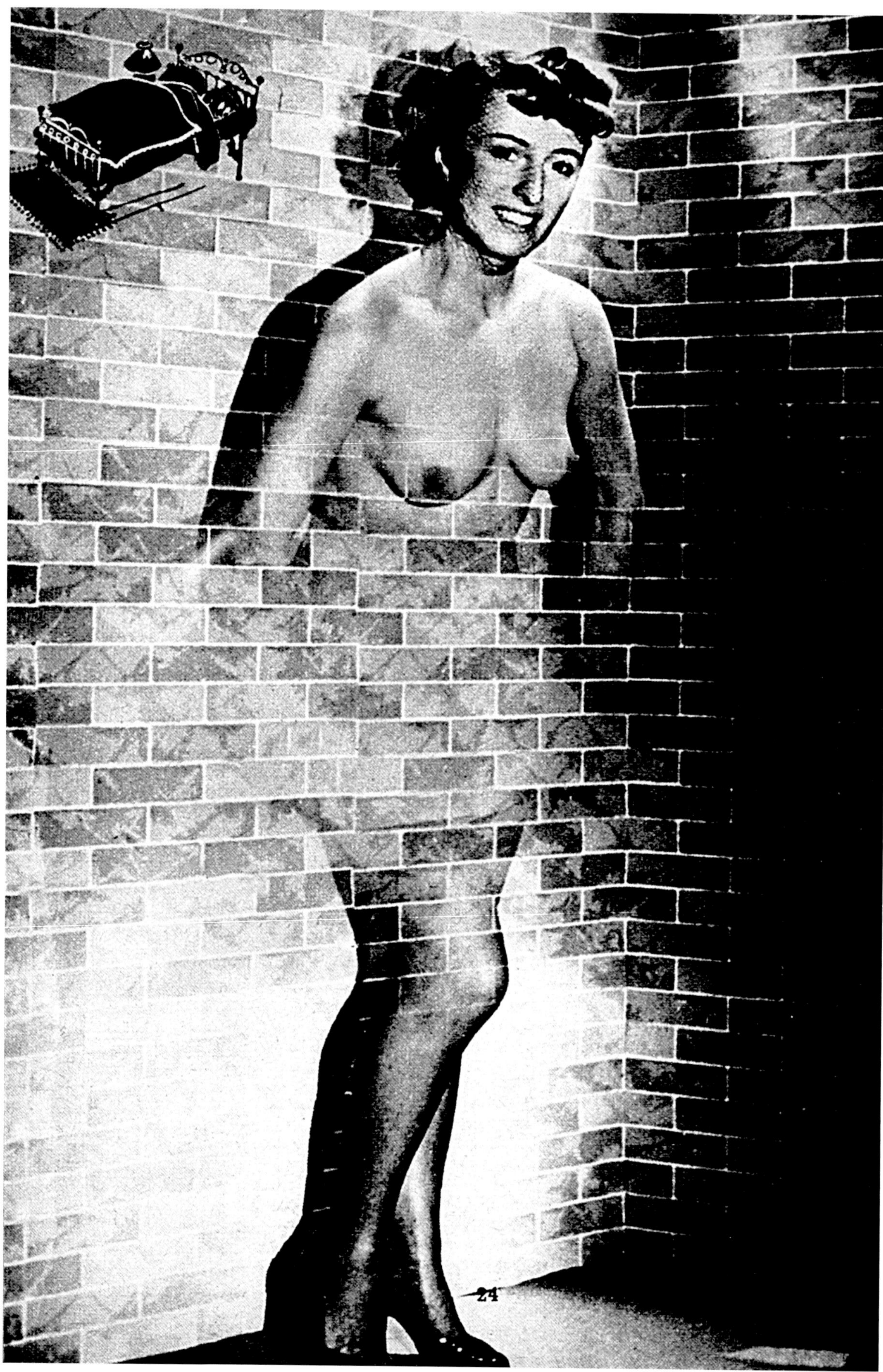

Year: **1953**. Title: **Enquêtes**. Country: **France**.

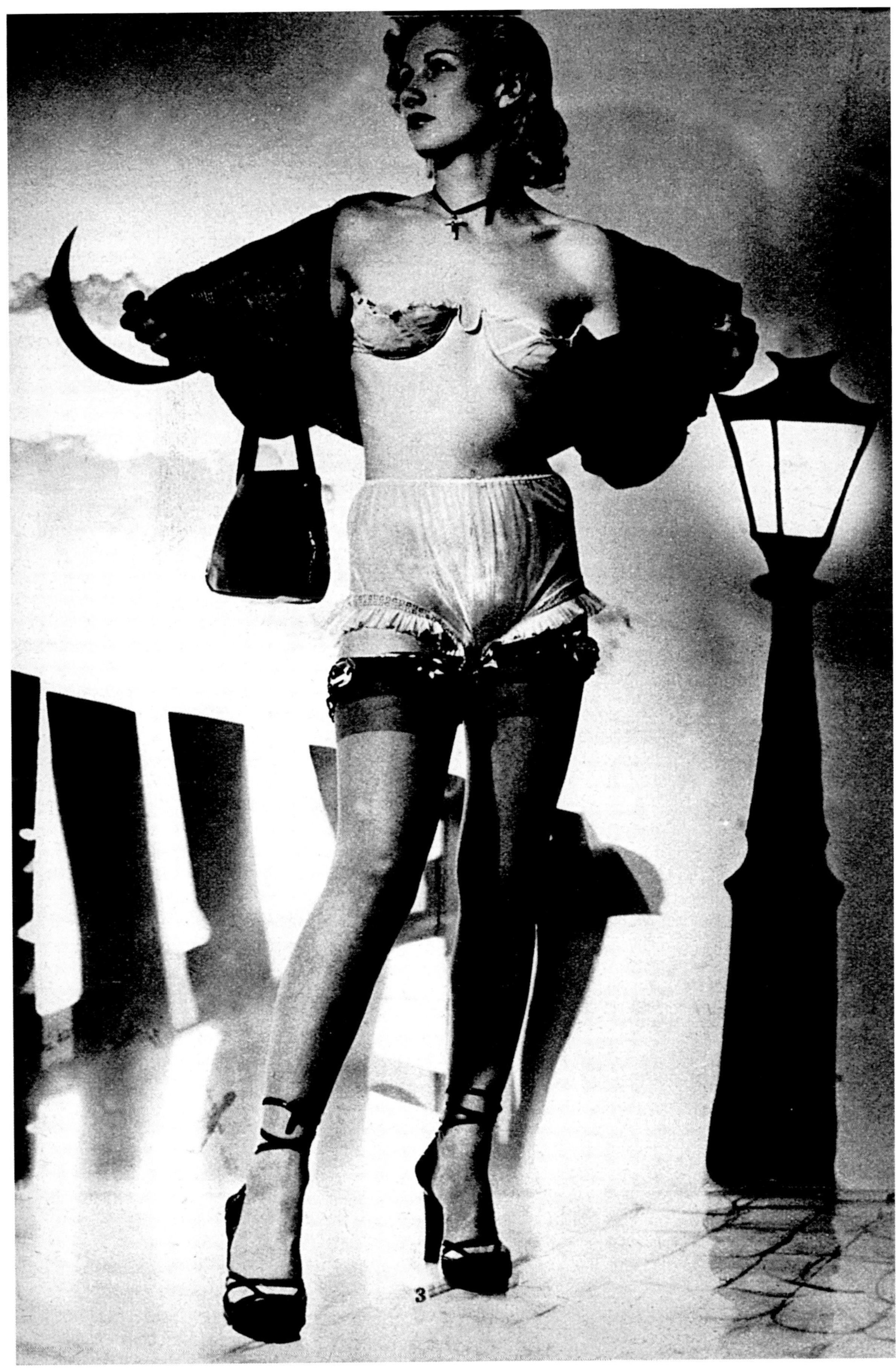

Year: **1953**. Title: **Enquêtes**. Country: **France**.

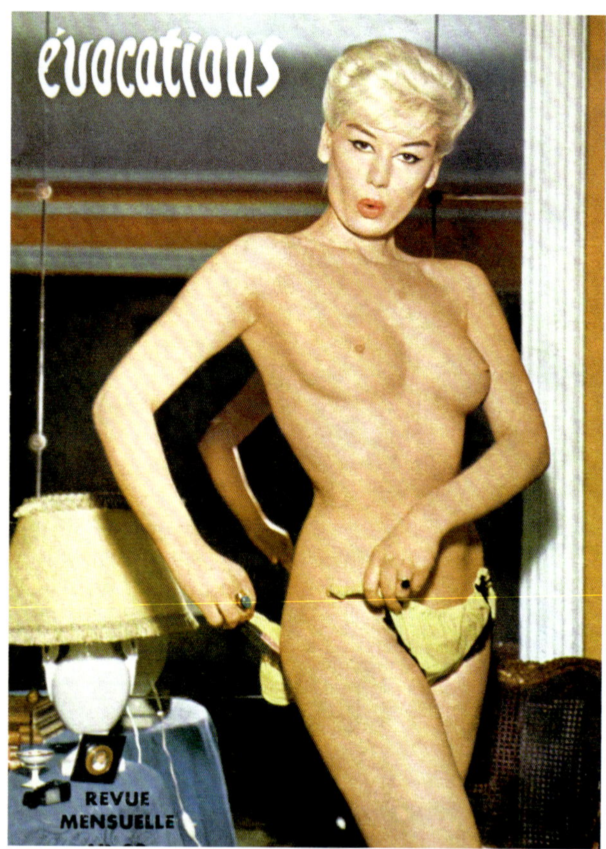

Year: **1953**. Title: **Évocations**. Country: **France**.

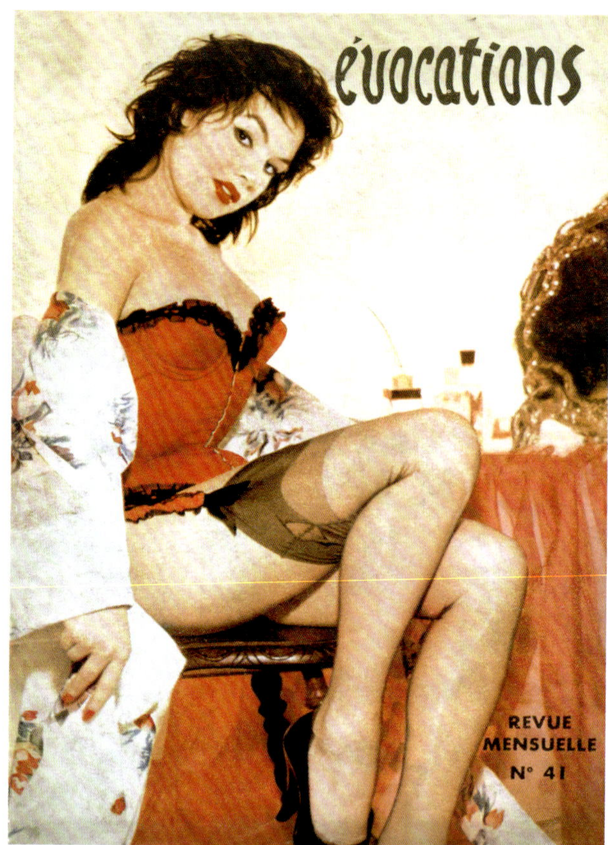

Year: **1950s**. Title: **Évocations**. Country: **France**.

Right: Year: **1953**. Title: **Enquêtes**.
Artist: **Serge de Sazo**. Country: **France**.

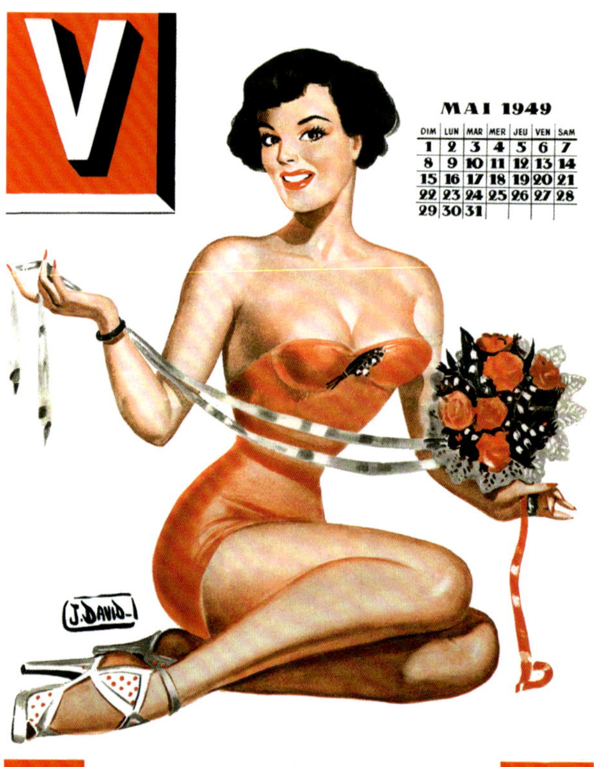

Year: **1949**. Title: **V**. Artist: **J. David**. Country: **France**.

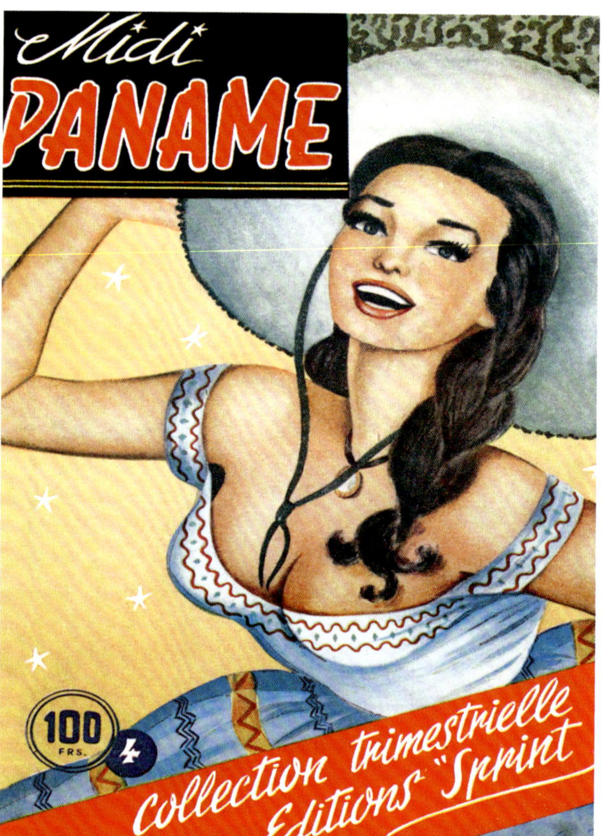

Year: **1950s**. Title: **Midi Paname**. Country: **France**.

1949's V *was a rare bedsheet-sized lifestyle magazine modeled on* La Vie Parisienne.

V *war 1949 eines der seltenen großformatigen Lifestyle-Magazine nach dem Vorbild von* La Vie Parisienne.

Original, V*, de 1949, était un magazine vie moderne grand format modelé sur* La Vie Parisienne.

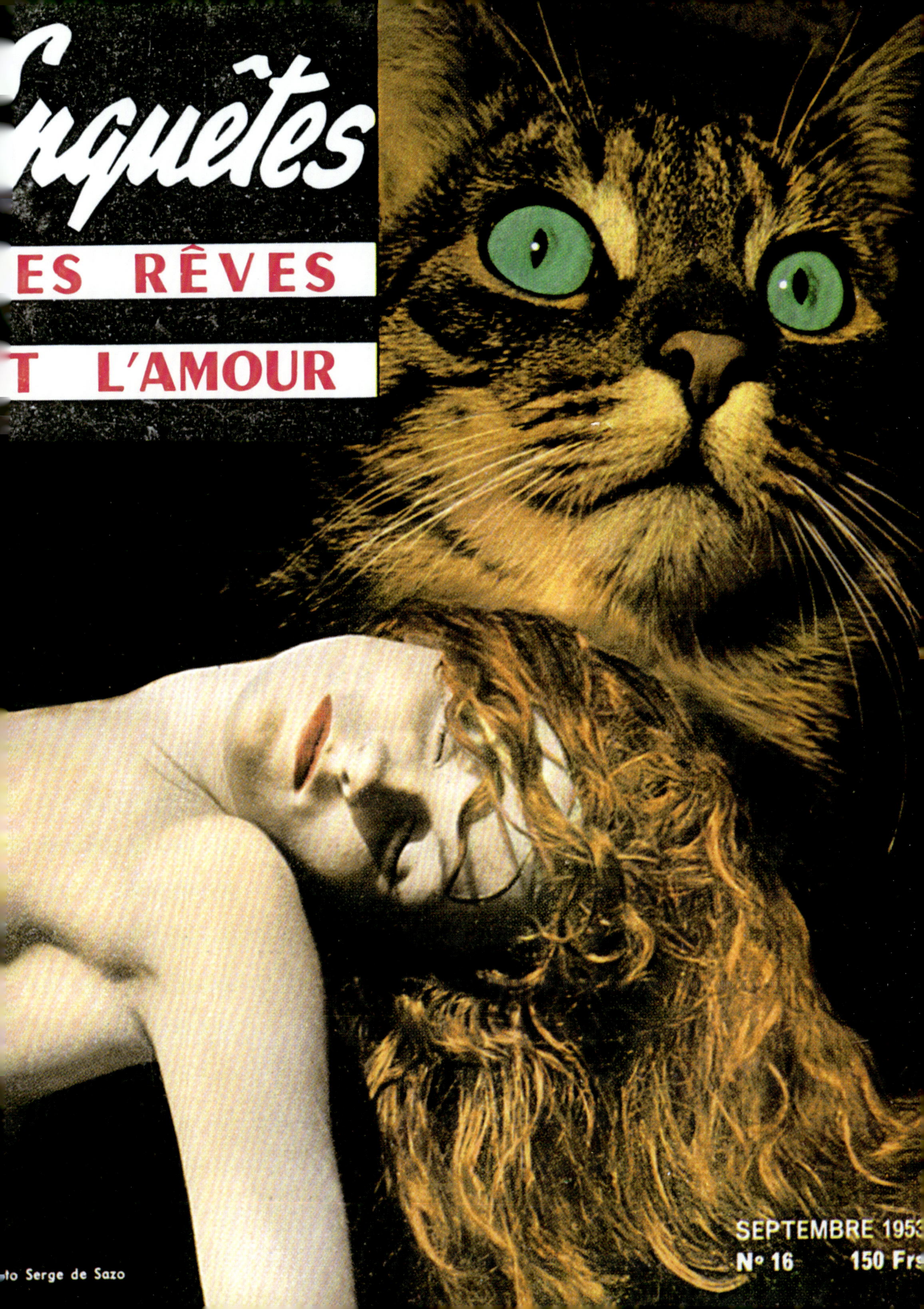
nquêtes
ES RÊVES
T L'AMOUR
SEPTEMBRE 1953
N° 16
150 Frs
oto Serge de Sazo

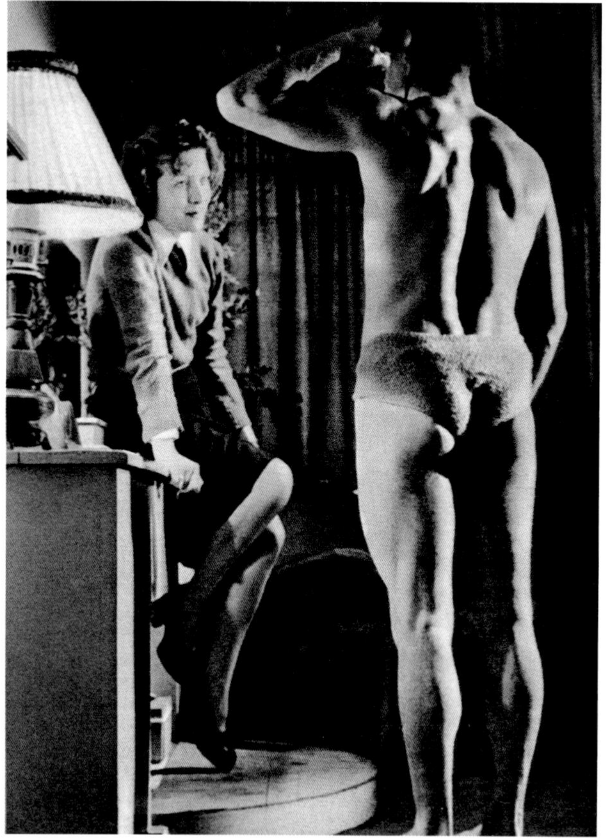

Year: **1950**. Title: **Régal**. Country: **France**.

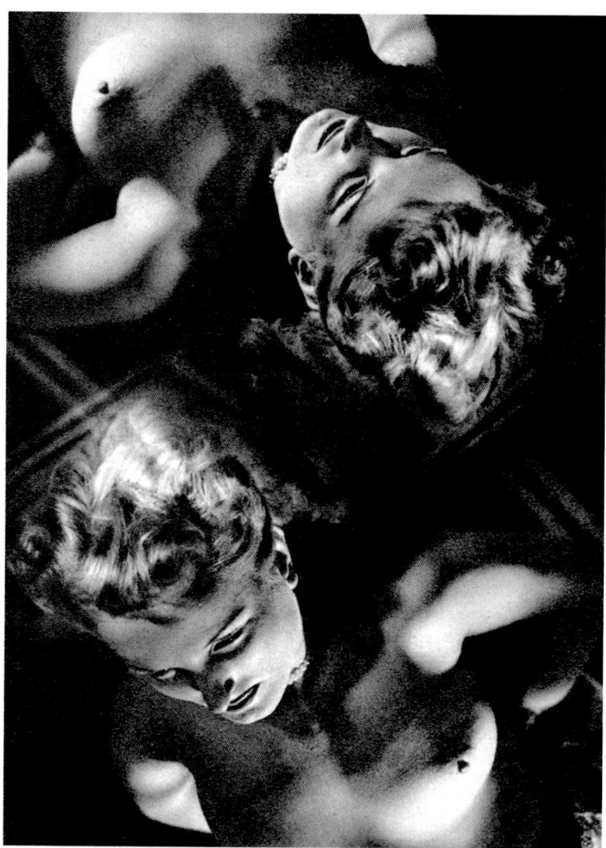

Year: **1950**. Title: **Régal**. Country: **France**.

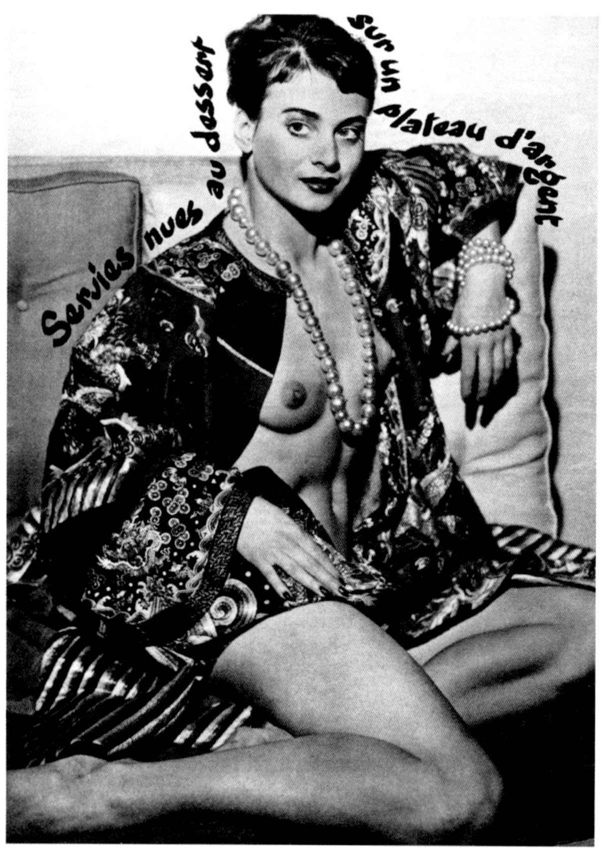

Year: **1950**. Title: **Sensations**. Country: **France**.

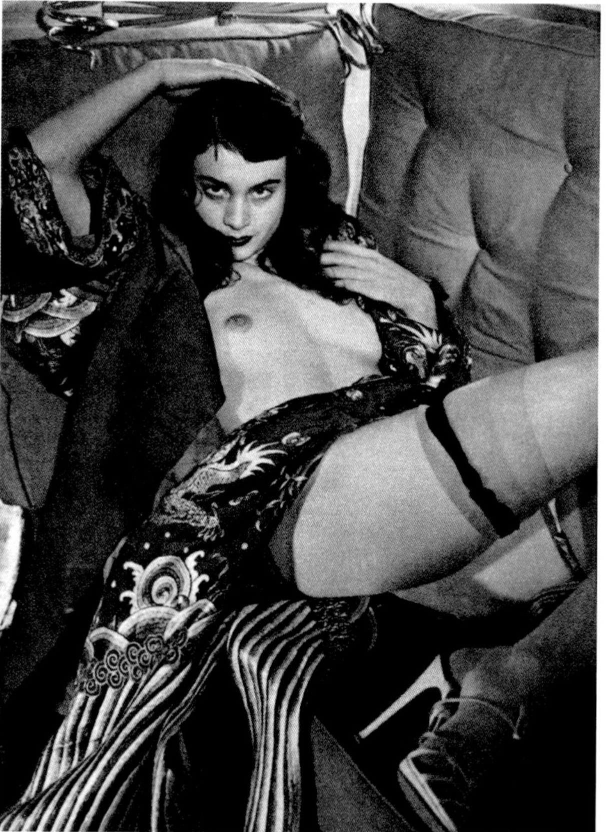

Year: **1950**. Title: **Sensations**. Country: **France**.

Right: Year: **1953**. Title: **Sensations**. Country: **France**.

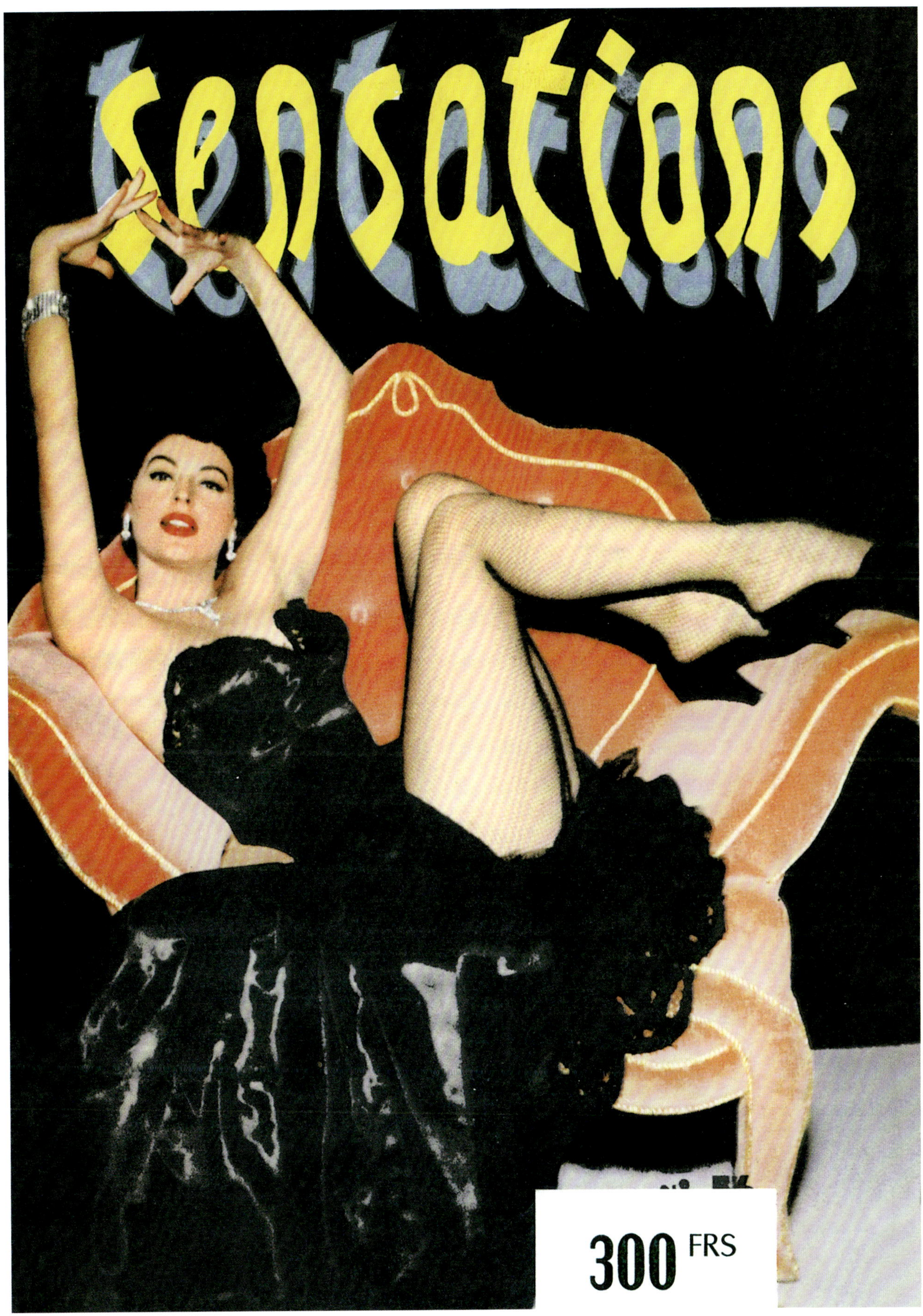

Sensations, *like* Régal *and* Paris Tabou, *came from Editions Extentia in Paris and featured surprisingly sophisticated content*

Sensations *kam, wie* Régal *und* Paris Tabou, *aus dem Hause Editions Extentia in Paris und war inhaltlich überraschend anspruchsvoll.*

À l'instar de Régal *et de* Paris Tabou, Sensations *était publié par les Éditions Extentia de Paris et offrait un contenu étonnamment sophistiqué.*

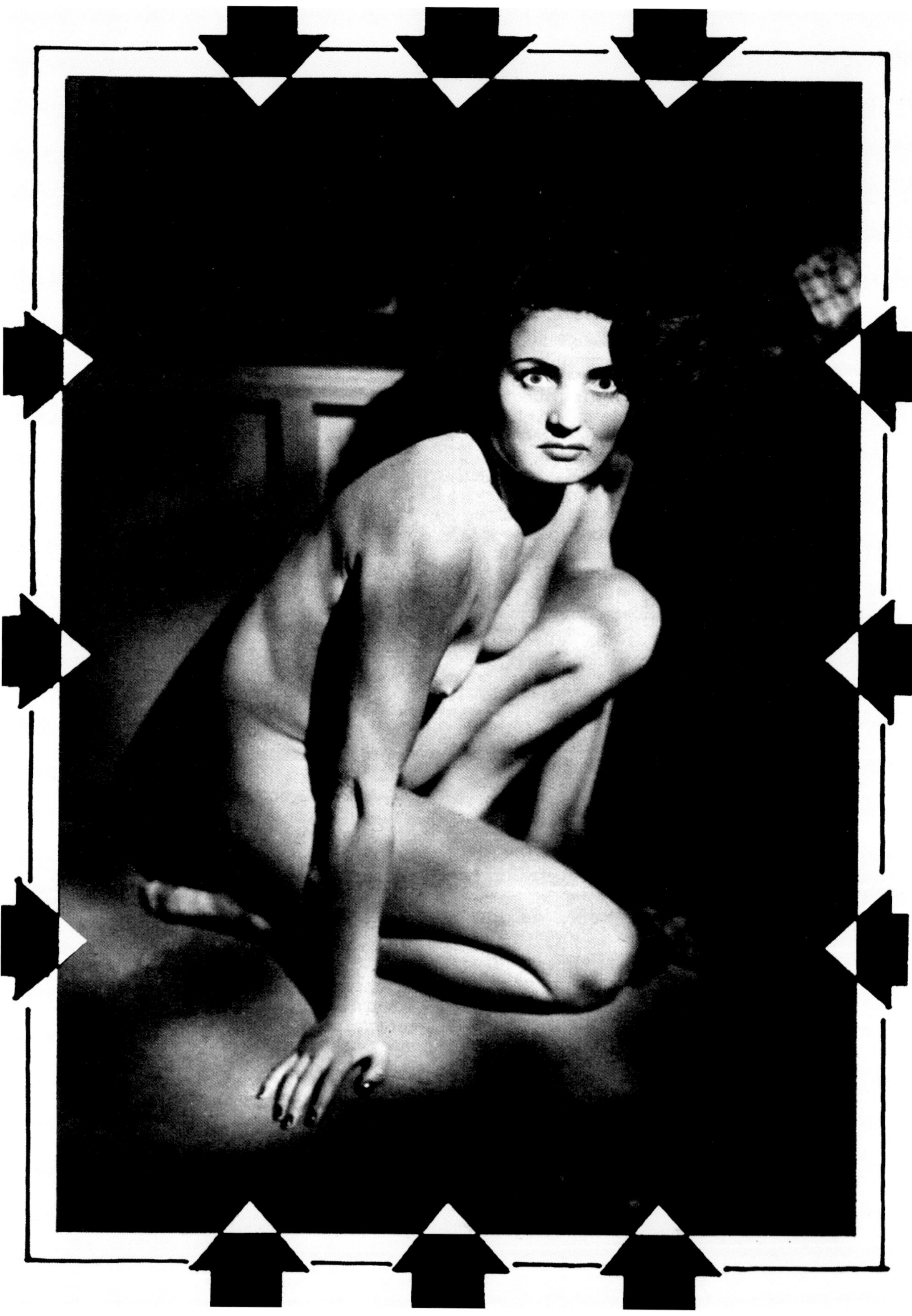

Year: **1950**. Title: **Paris Tabou**. Country: **France**.

Year: **1950**. Title: **Paris Sex-Appeal**. Country: **France**.

PARIS
SEX·APPEAL

VUE
SUELLE

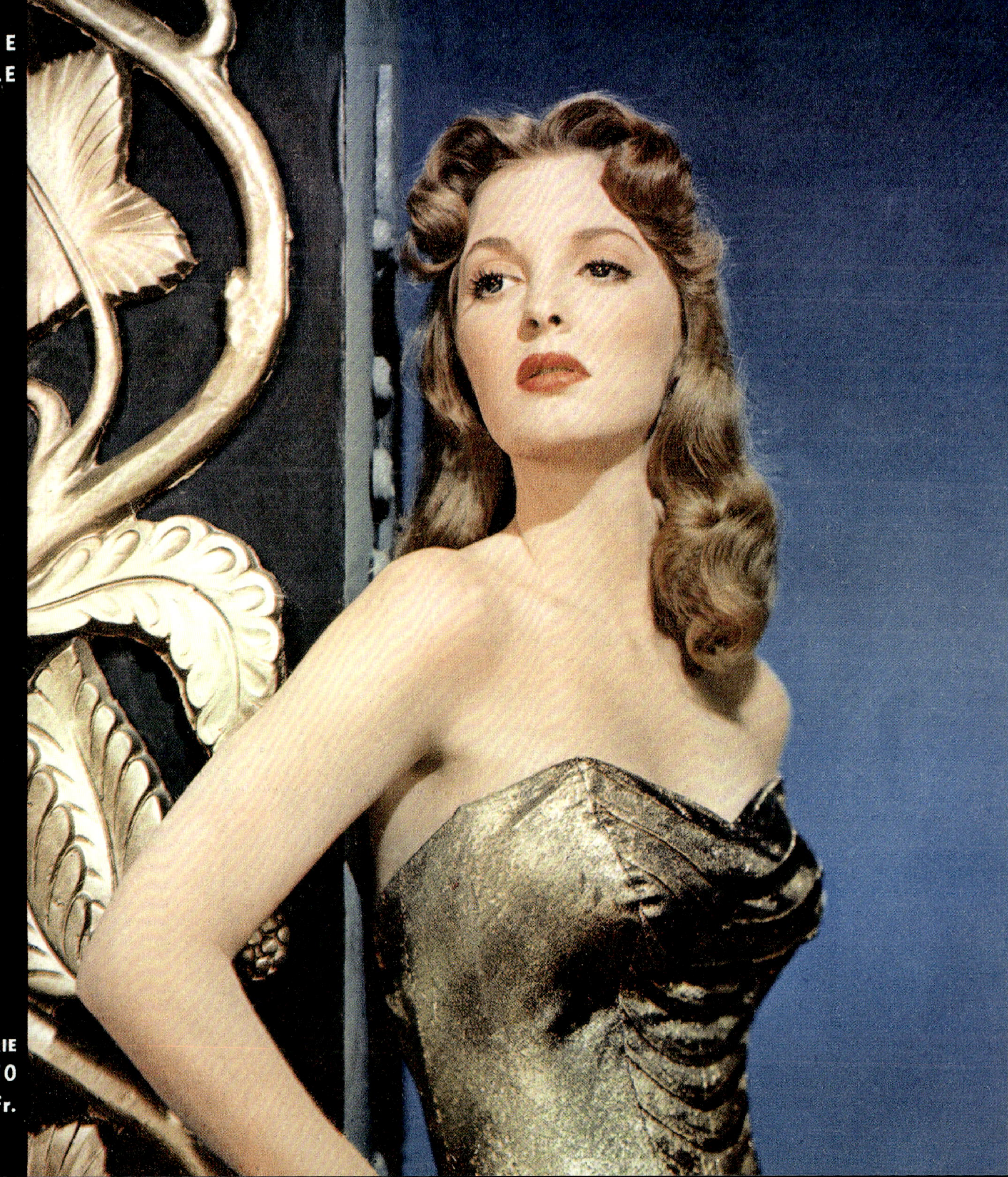

ELLE SERIE
ERO 10
: 100 Fr.

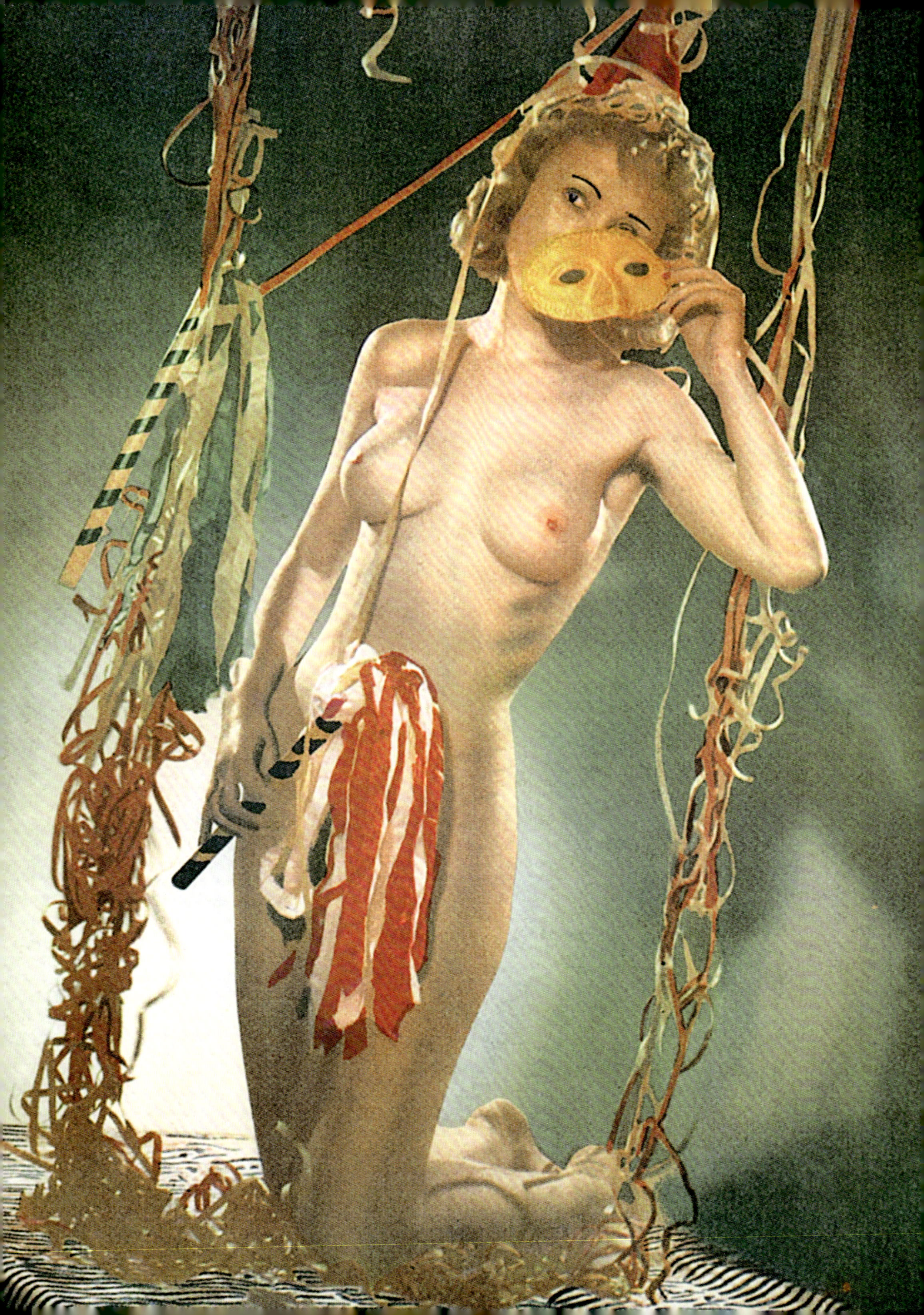

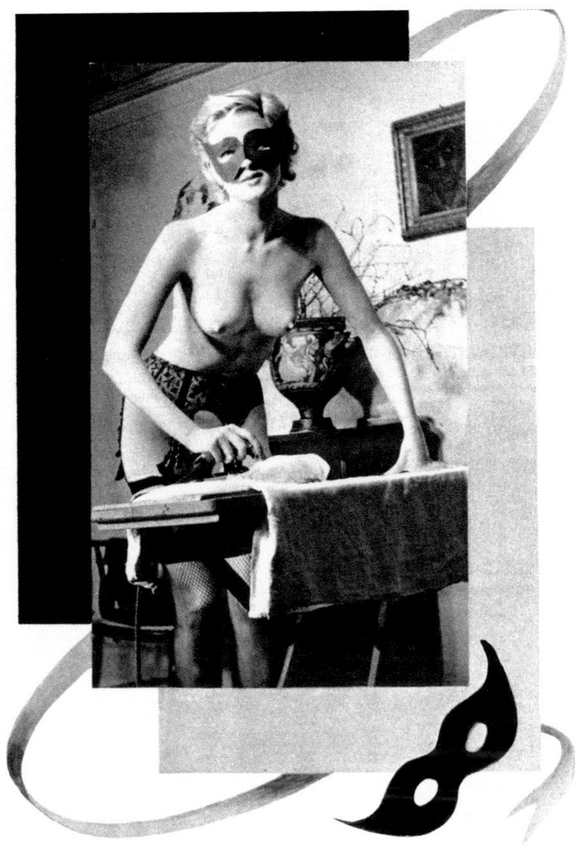

YEAR: **1951**. TITLE: **Collection Minuit Pigal**. COUNTRY: **France**.

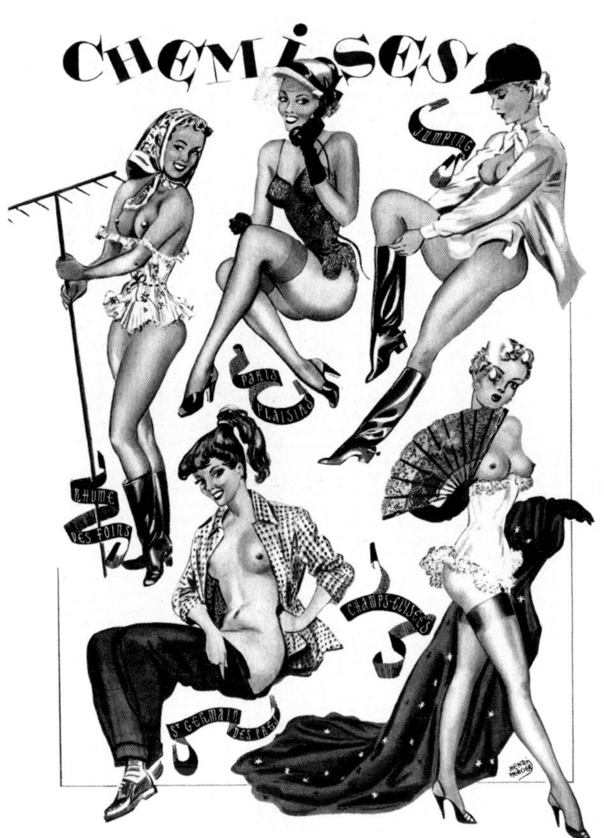

YEAR: **1951**. TITLE: **Collection Minuit Pigal**. COUNTRY: **France**.

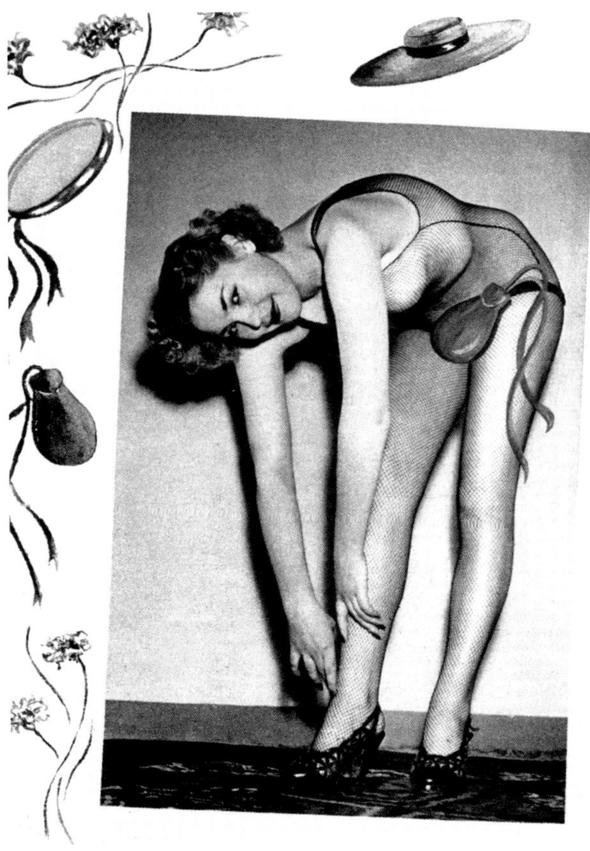

YEAR: **1951**. TITLE: **Collection Minuit Pigal**. COUNTRY: **France**.

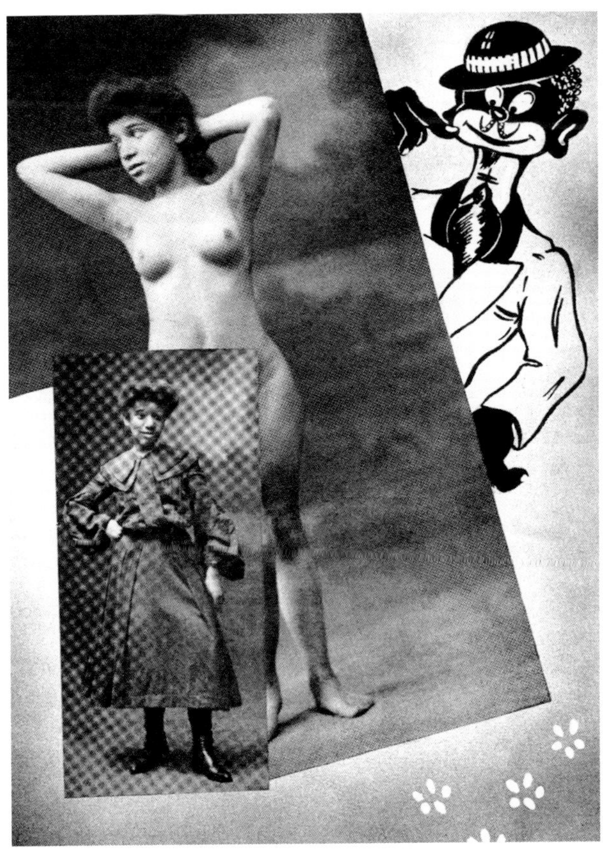

YEAR: **1951**. TITLE: **Collection Minuit Pigal**. COUNTRY: **France**.

YEAR: **1951**. TITLE: **Paris Cocktail**. COUNTRY: **France**.

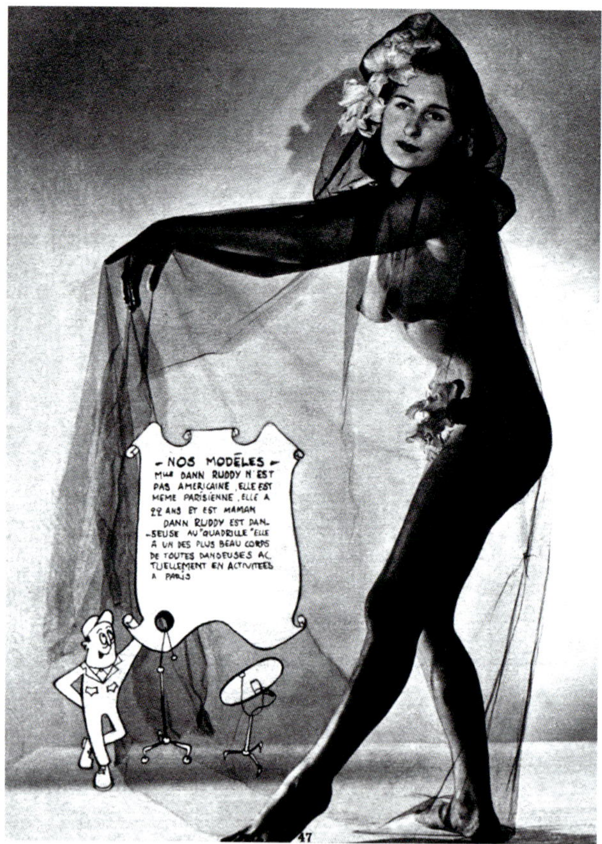

Year: **1952**. Title: **Paris Tabou**. Country: **France**.

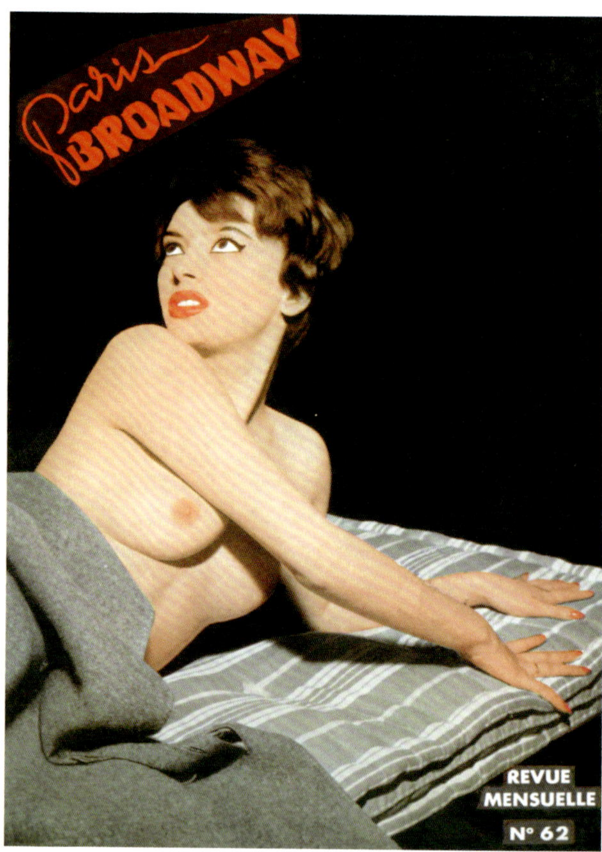

Year: **1950s**. Title: **Paris Broadway**. Country: **France**.

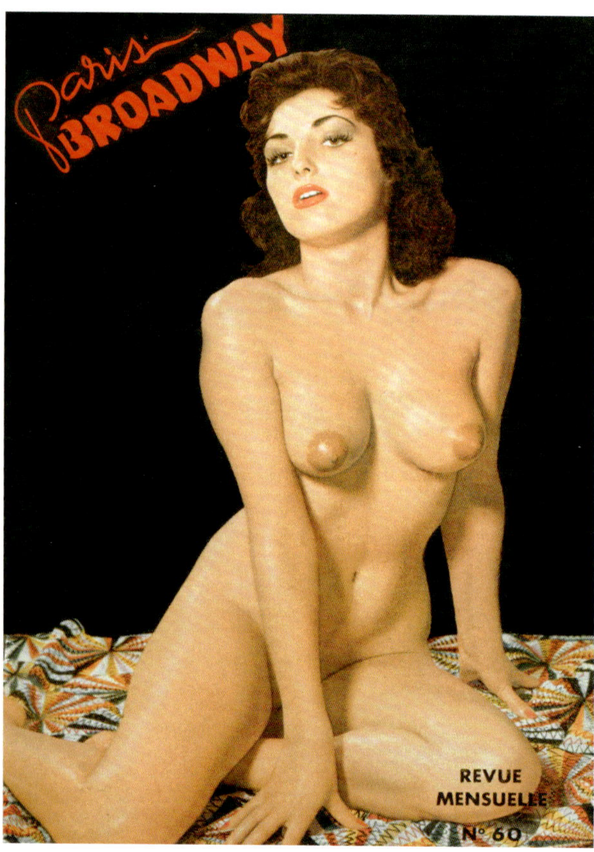

Year: **1950s**. Title: **Paris Broadway**. Country: **France**.

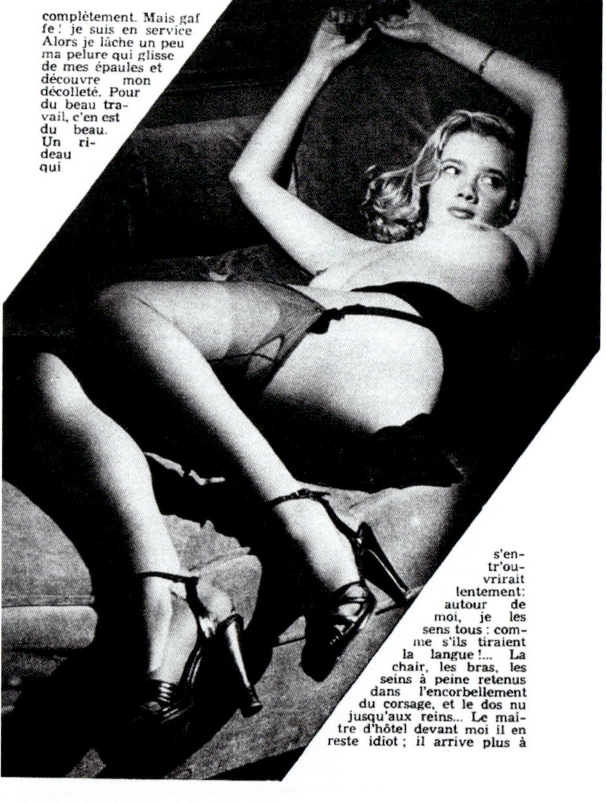

complètement. Mais gaffe ! je suis en service. Alors je lâche un peu ma pelure qui glisse de mes épaules et découvre mon décolleté. Pour du beau travail, c'en est du beau. Un rideau qui s'entr'ouvrirait lentement: autour de moi, je les sens tous : comme s'ils tiraient la langue !... La chair, les bras, les seins à peine retenus dans l'encorbellement du corsage, et le dos nu jusqu'aux reins... Le maître d'hôtel devant moi il en reste idiot ; il arrive plus à

44

Year: **1952**. Title: **Paris Tabou**. Country: **France**.

Year: **1952**. Title: **Paris-Zazou**. Country: **France**.

PARIS-ZAZOU

150 frs

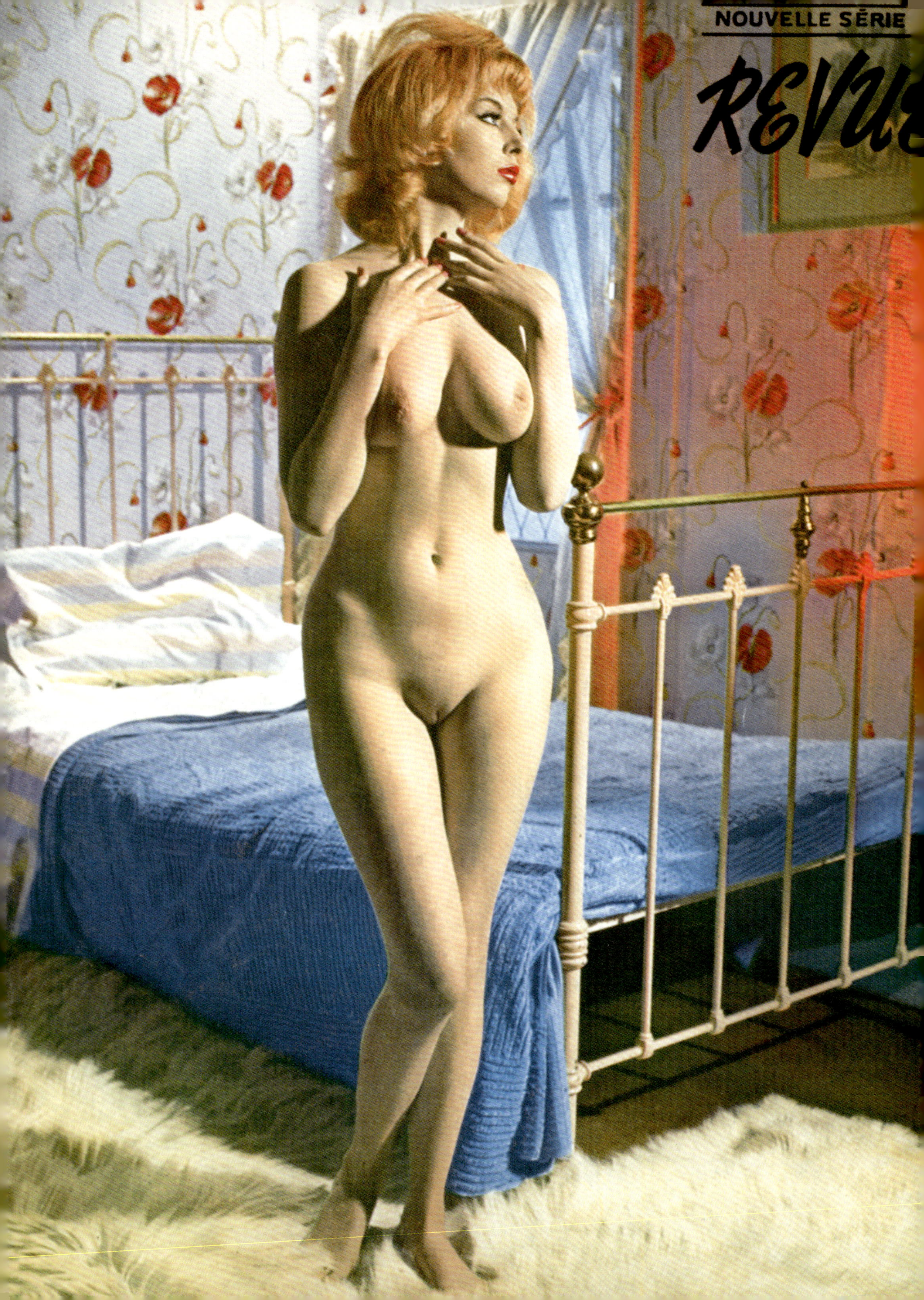
NOUVELLE SÉRIE
REVUE

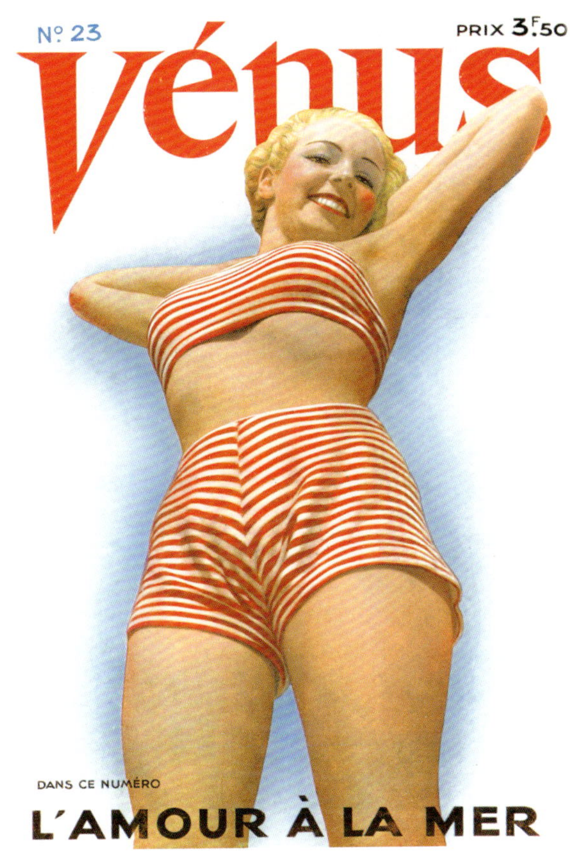

YEAR: **1950s**. TITLE: **Vénus**. COUNTRY: **France**.

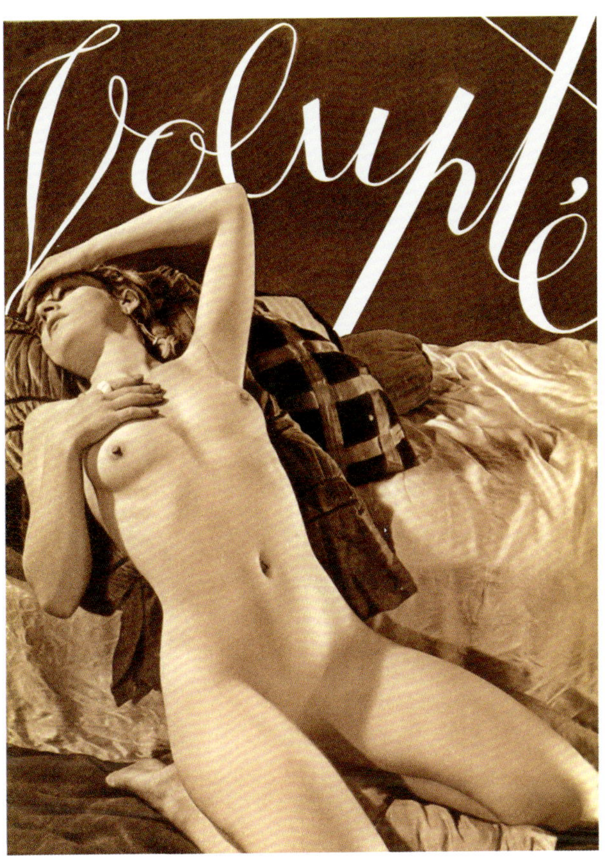

YEAR: **1950s**. TITLE: **Volupté**. COUNTRY: **France**.

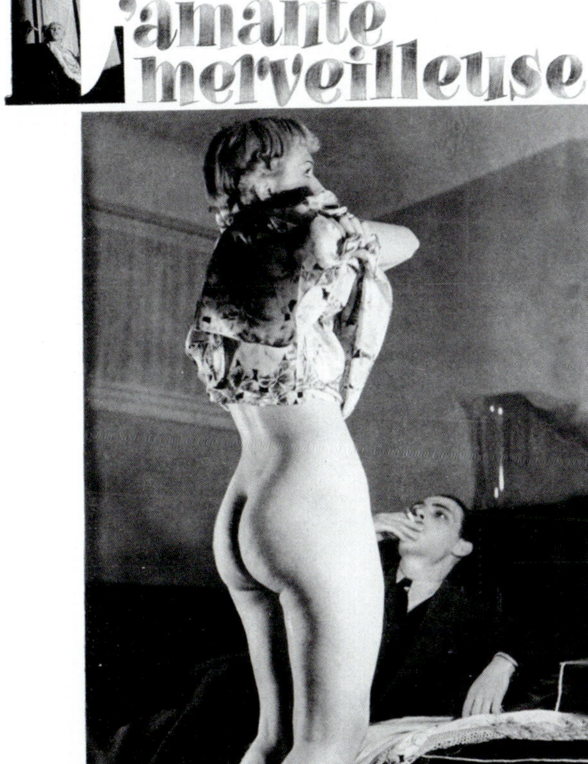

YEAR: **1950s**. TITLE: **Vénus**. COUNTRY: **France**.

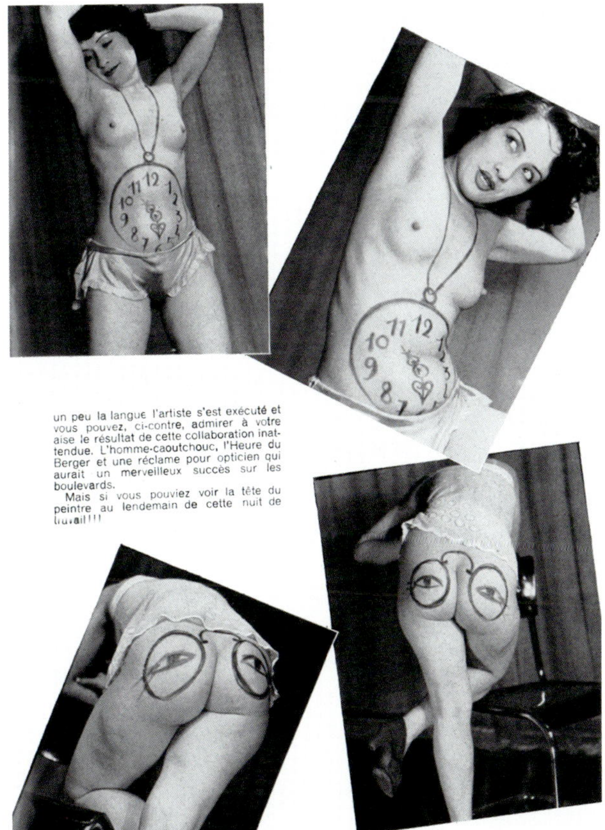

YEAR: **1950s**. TITLE: **Vénus**. COUNTRY: **France**.

YEAR: **1950s**. TITLE: **Revue**. COUNTRY: **France**.

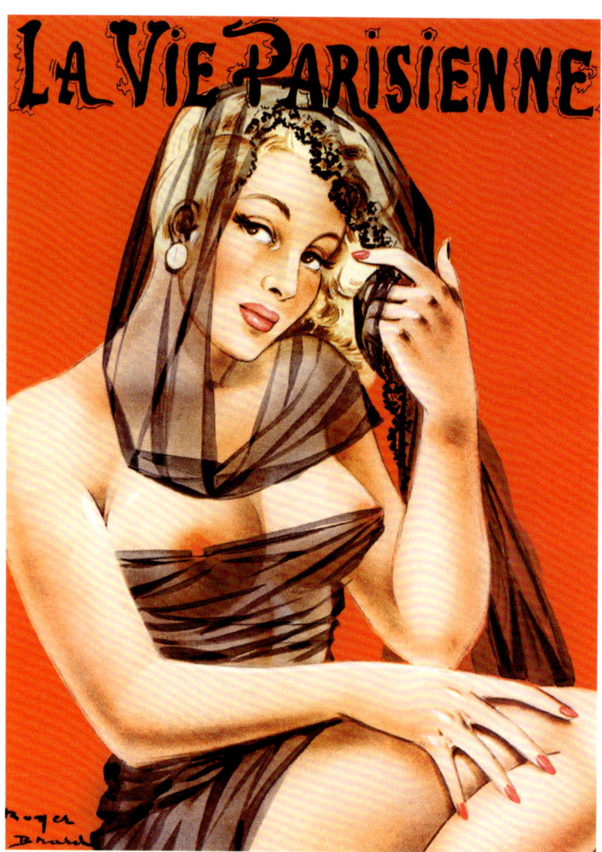

YEAR: **1957**. TITLE: **La Vie Parisienne**. COUNTRY: **France**.

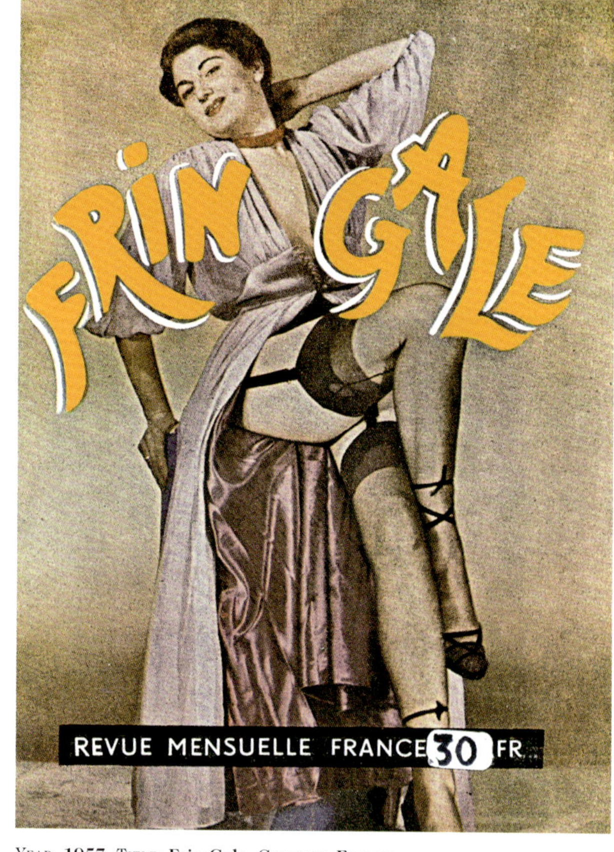

YEAR: **1957**. TITLE: **Frin Gale**. COUNTRY: **France**.

RIGHT: YEAR: **1950s**. TITLE: **Paris Etoiles**. COUNTRY: **France**.

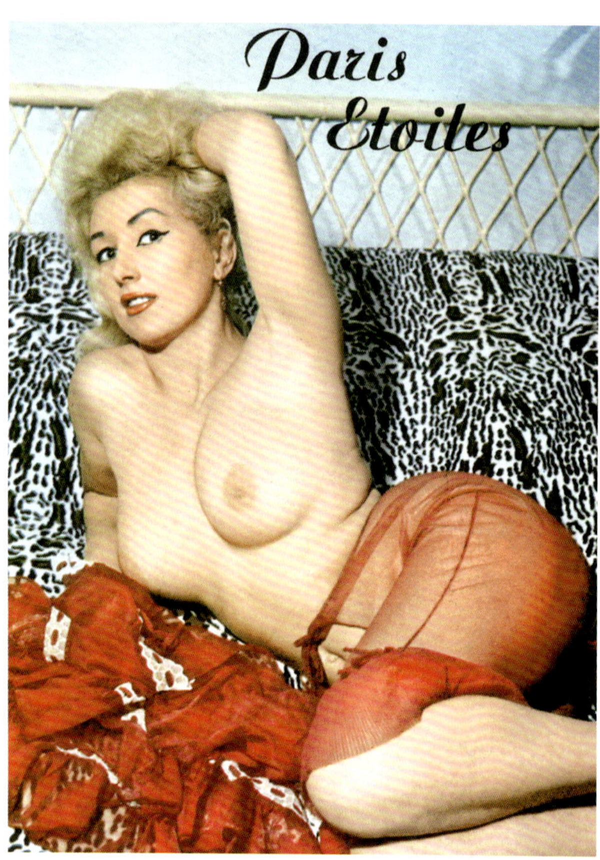

YEAR: **1950s**. TITLE: **Paris Etoiles**. COUNTRY: **France**.

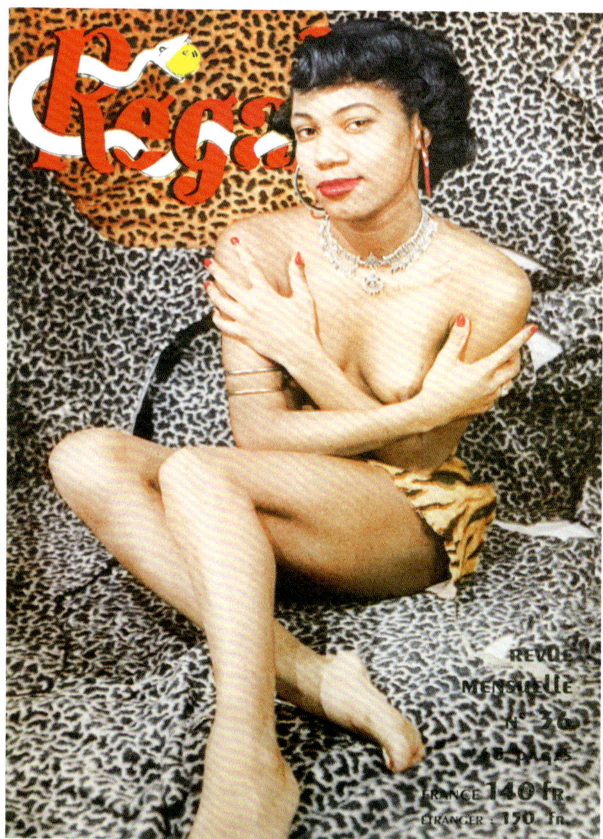

YEAR: **1950s**. TITLE: **Régal**. COUNTRY: **France**.

PAGES 394 & 395:
RIGHT: YEAR: **1954**. TITLE: **Enquêtes**. COUNTRY: **France**.
LEFT: YEAR: **1950s**. TITLE: **Paris Gai**. COUNTRY: **France**.

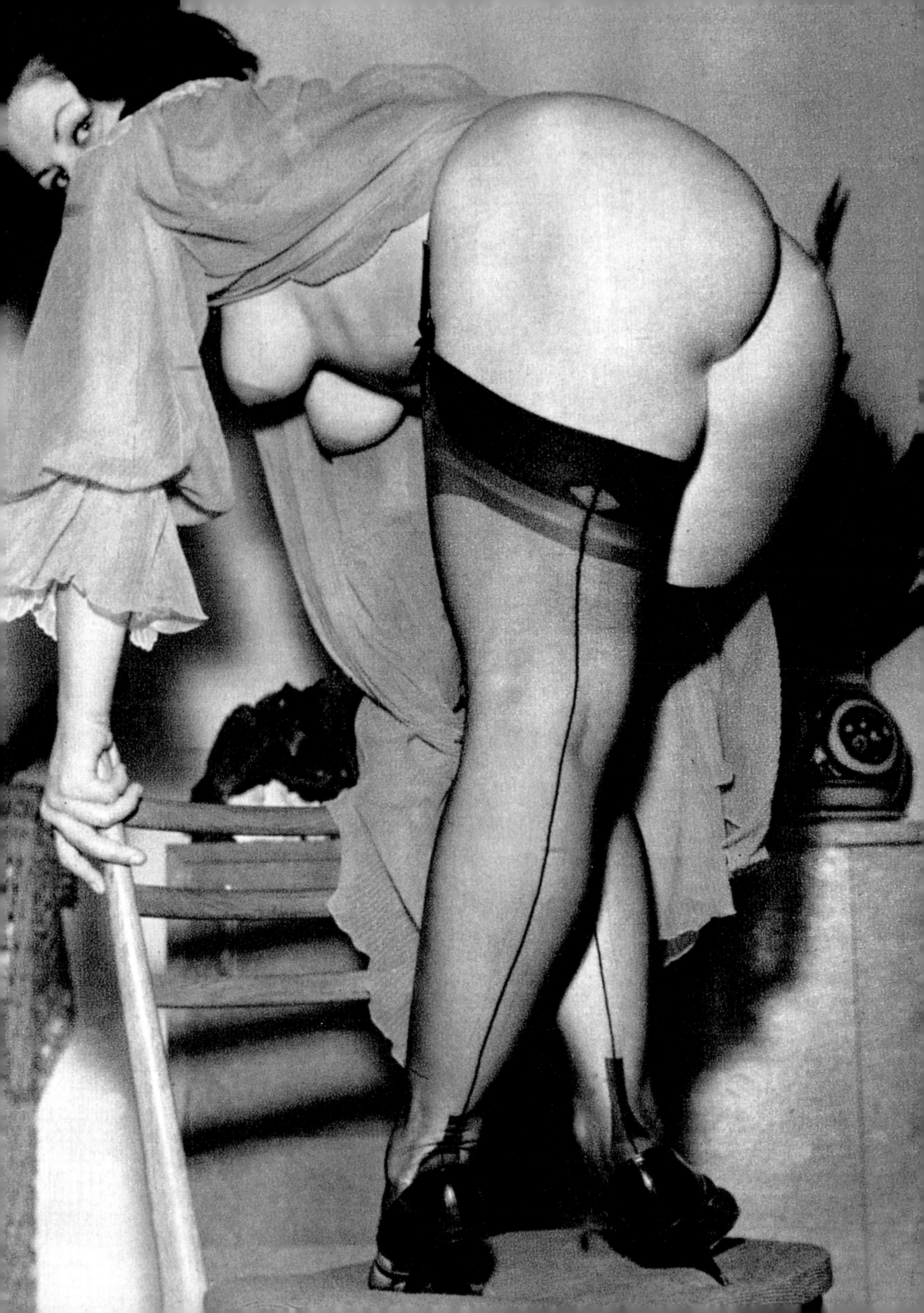

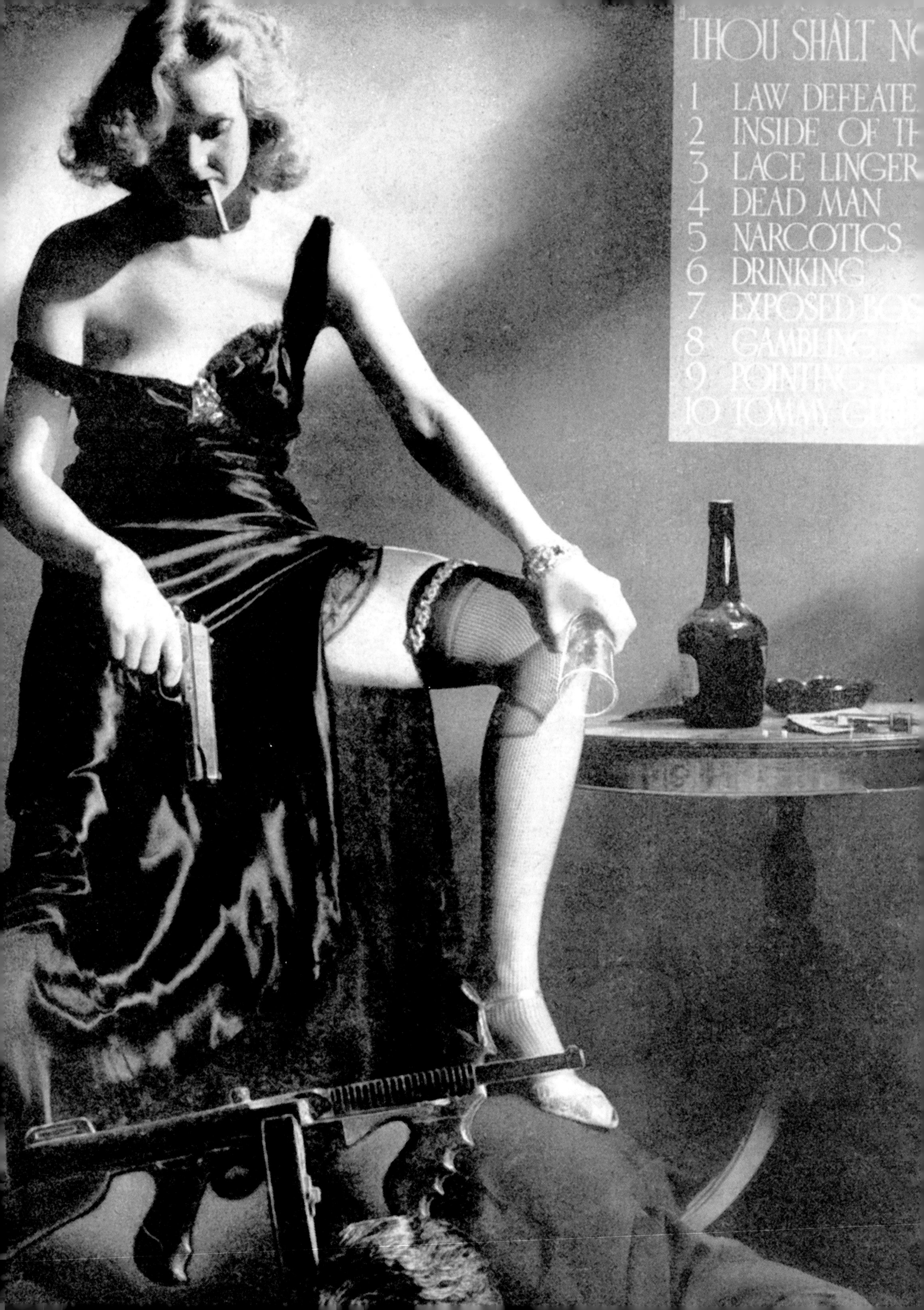
THOU SHALT NO
1 LAW DEFEATE
2 INSIDE OF TH
3 LACE LINGER
4 DEAD MAN
5 NARCOTICS
6 DRINKING
7 EXPOSED BOS

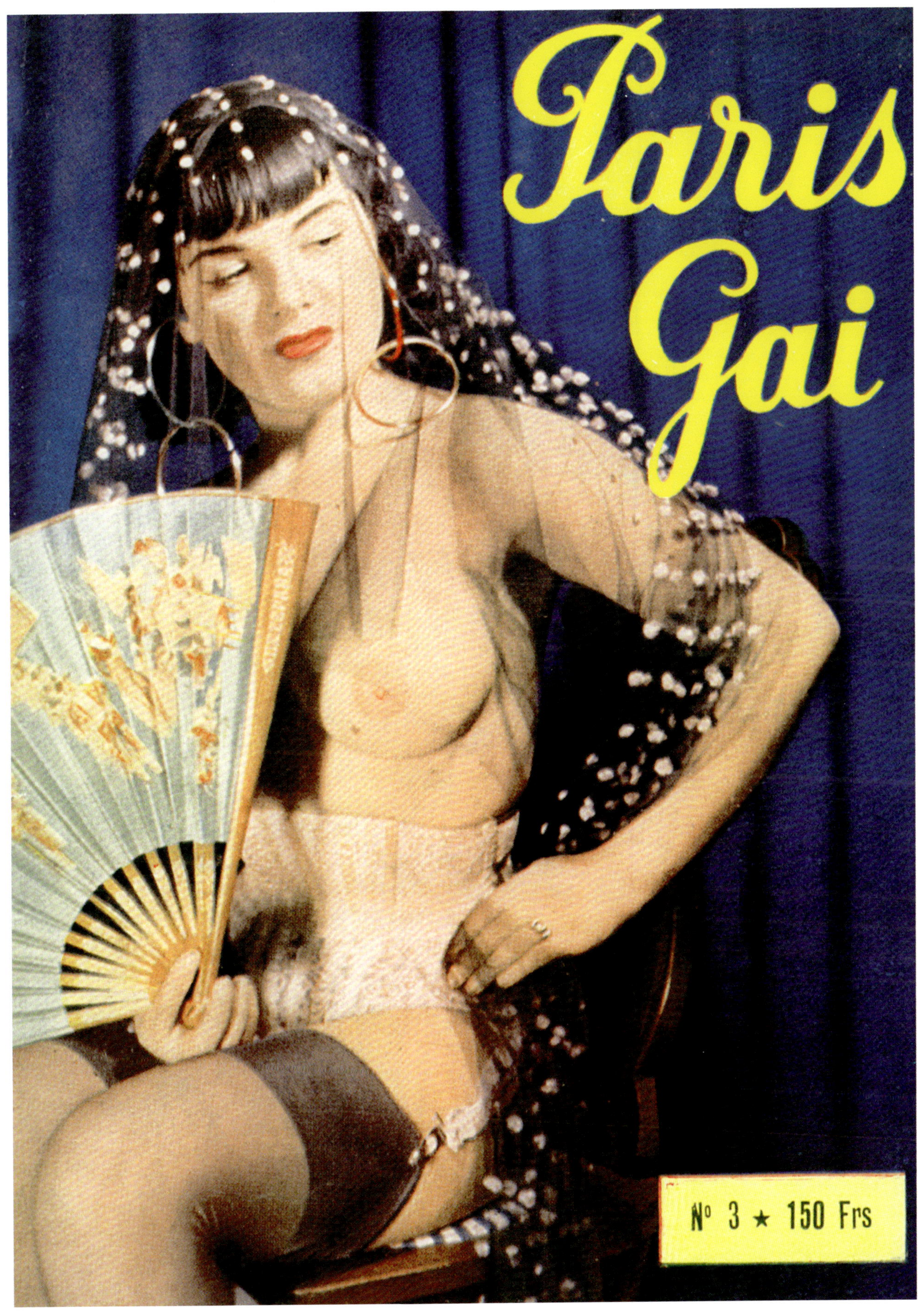

Left: This photo breaks all the rules laid down by the American Film Board, as listed on the wall.

Links: Dieses Foto bricht alle Vorschriften des American Film Board, die an der Wand angeschlagen sind.

À gauche : cette photographie rompt avec toutes les règles de l'American Film Board, affichées sur le mur.

PARIS COCKTAIL

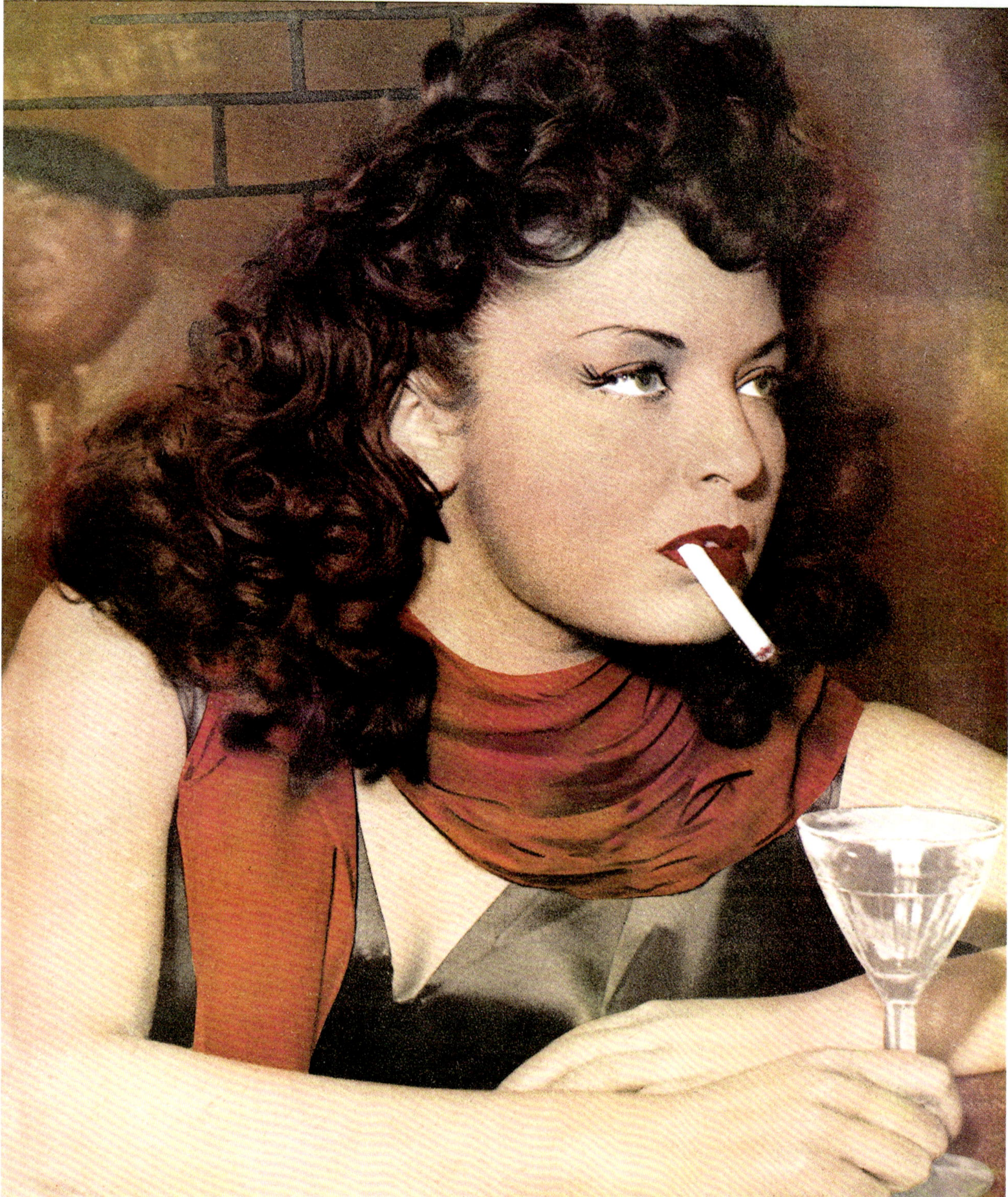

YEAR: **1951**. TITLE: **Paris Cocktail**. COUNTRY: **France**.

PARIS PIN-UP

R E V U E M E N S U E L L E

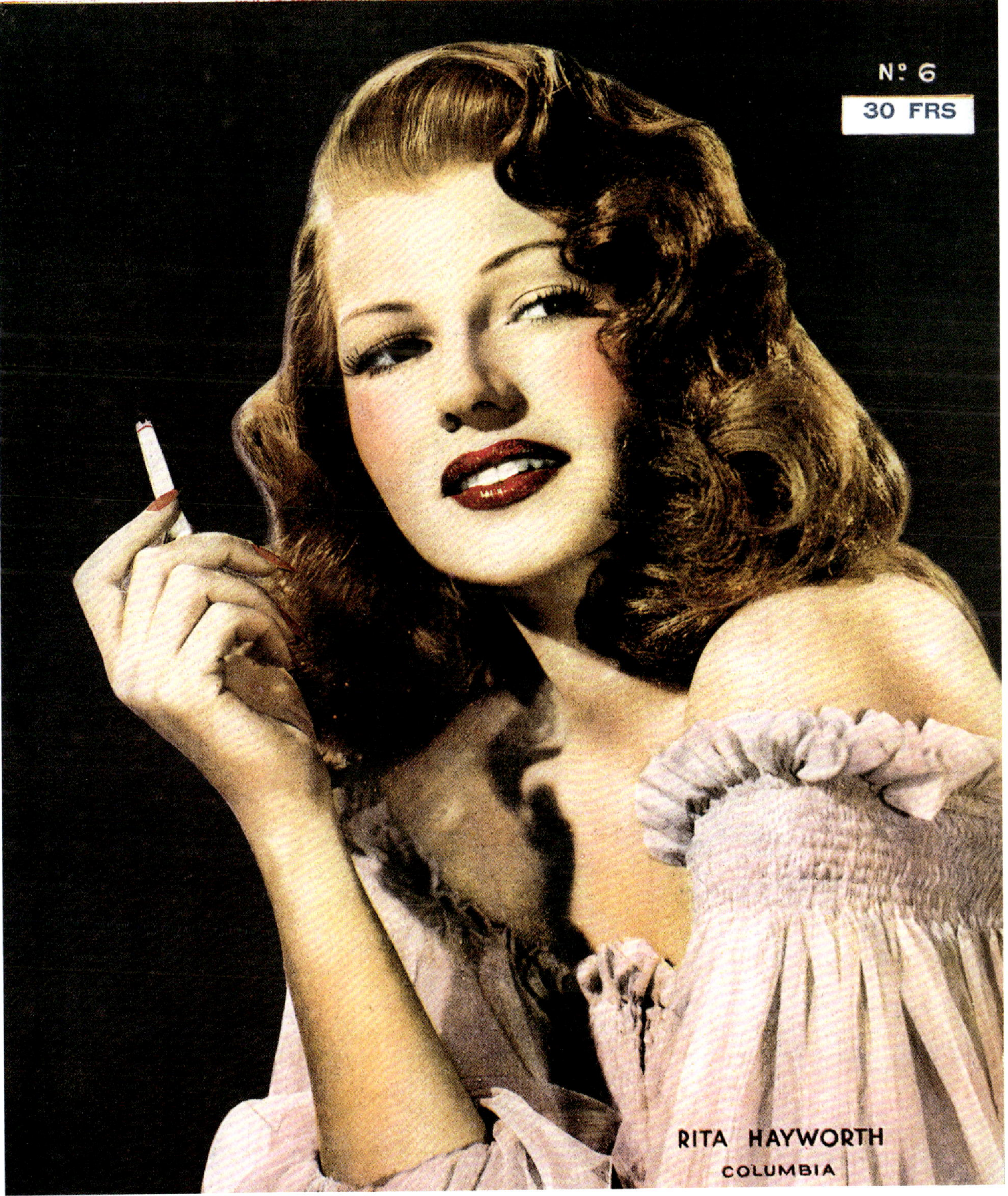

Year: **1950s**. Title: **Paris Pin-up**. Country: **France**.

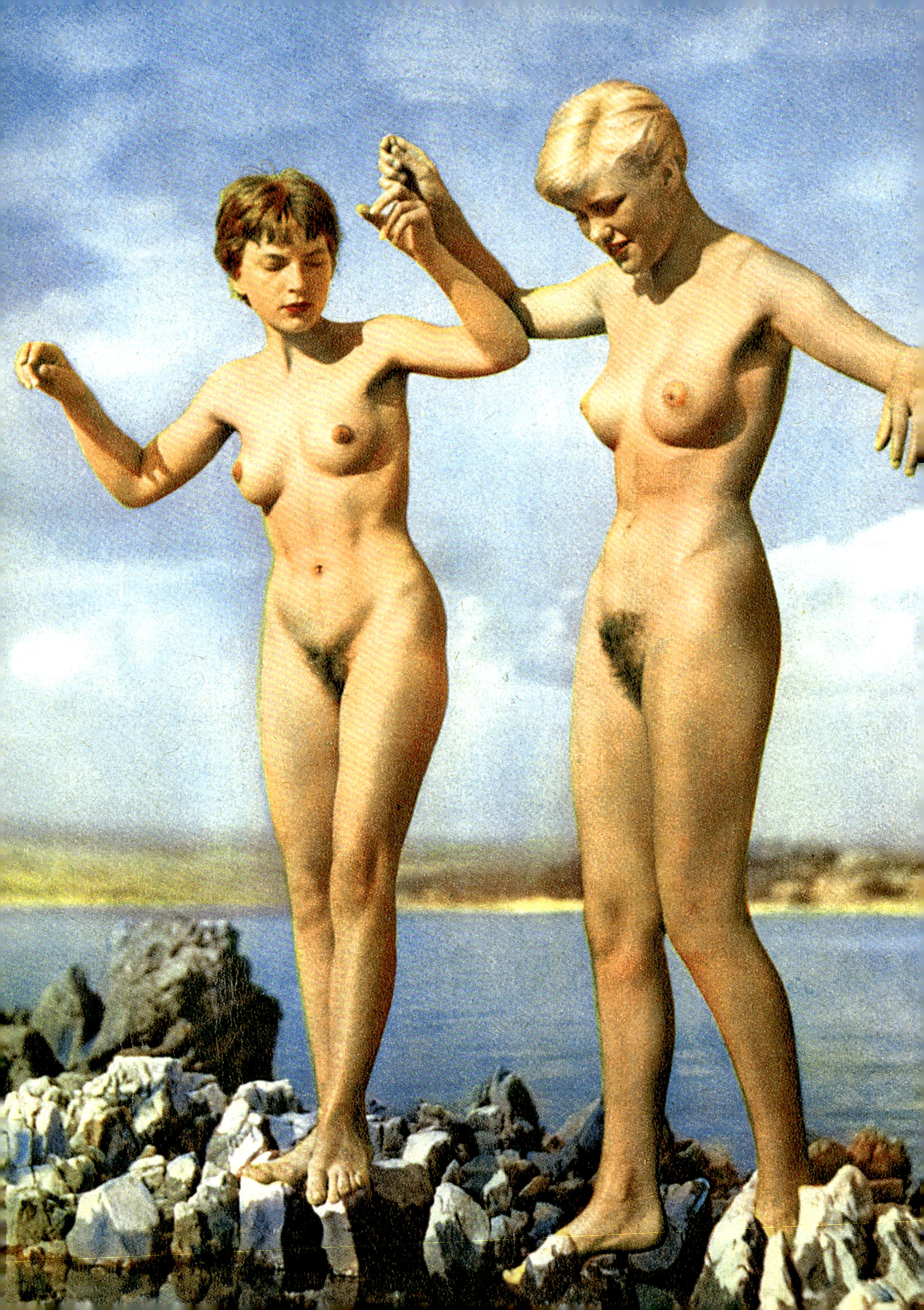

NORTHERN EUROPE REBUILDS ITS MEN'S MAGAZINES:

A Kinder, Gentler Nudism

Der Wiederaufbau der europäischen Männermagazine: Nudismus ohne erhobenen Zeigefinger

L'Europe du Nord se reconstruit : Un nudisme plus doux et modéré

Given the rich variety of nudist magazines in pre-war Germany, the post-war product was pale indeed. Gone were sex, politics, mysticism and eugenicist screeds. The new magazines, printed in a paper-conserving digest size, promoted only health, fun and youthful—mostly female—beauty. The cleansing was not confined to Germany; Sweden, Denmark, Holland, Austria, Switzerland and France all contributed to the post-war wave of feel-good nudism. No doubt it was another way to reaffirm life after the long and devastating war. The little magazines also spurred the post-war popularity of American nudism, as they were carried home by the GIs overseeing reconstruction. The leading late-40s and 50s titles were *Helios* (Denmark), *Sonnensport* (Switzerland), *Die Neue Zeit*, *Lebensfreude* and *Sonnenfreunde* (Germany), *Vivre d'Abord!* (France),

The new magazines promoted only health, fun and youthful—mostly female—beauty.

Wenn man die Vielfalt der Nudistenmagazine im Vorkriegsdeutschland bedenkt, sahen die Produkte nach dem Krieg wahrhaftig blass aus. Sex, Politik, Mystizismus und eugenische Tiraden waren verschwunden. Die neuen, im Papier sparenden Taschenformat gedruckten Magazine warben lediglich für Gesundheit, Vergnügen und jugendliche, meist weibliche Schönheit. Diese Säuberungen beschränkten sich nicht nur auf Deutschland; Schweden, Dänemark, Holland, Österreich, die Schweiz und Frankreich hatten ebenso großen Anteil an der Welle des Frisch-Fromm-Fröhlich-Frei-Nudismus nach dem Krieg. Zweifellos manifestierte sich darin auch der Wunsch, nach dem langen und verheerendem Krieg wieder Lebensmut zu schöpfen.

Von heimkehrenden Soldaten mitgebracht, verhalfen die kleinen Hefte auch in den USA dem Nudismus zu neuer Popularität. Die führenden Titel der späten Vierziger und der Fünfziger hießen *Helios* (Dänemark), *Sonnensport* (Schweiz), *Die Neue Zeit*, *Lebensfreude* und *Sonnenfreunde* (Deutschland), *Vivre d'Abord!* (Frankreich) und *Tidlösa* (Schweden). England ging wie immer einen eigenen Weg und blieb in dem traditionsreichen Blatt *Health & Efficiency* einer spartanischeren Art von Nudismus treu, hatte aber wohl

Comparées à la grande variété de magazines nudistes dans l'Allemagne d'avant-guerre, les publications d'après-guerre semblent effectivement bien pâles. Finis le sexe, la politique, le mysticisme et les laïus sur l'eugénisme. Les nouveaux magazines imprimés sous format digest pour économiser le papier ne défendaient plus que la santé, les loisirs et la beauté juvénile (principalement féminine !). Ce grand ménage n'était pas limité à l'Allemagne. La Suède, le Danemark, la Hollande, l'Autriche, la Suisse et la France contribuèrent tous à cette vague de nudisme sain et enjoué. C'était sans nul doute une manière de réaffirmer son goût pour la vie après une longue guerre dévastatrice.

Rapportés par les G. I.'s restés en Europe pour aider à la reconstruction, ces petits magazines alimentèrent également la popularité du nudisme aux États-Unis. Les principaux titres de la fin des années quarante et des années cinquante étaient *Helios* (Danemark), *Solis* et *Sonnensport* (Suisse), *Die Neue Zeit*, *Lebensfreude* et *Sonnenfreunde* (Allemagne), *Vivre d'abord !* et *Nature et Beauté* (France), *Tidlösa* (Suède). L'Angleterre, se distinguant comme toujours du continent, s'en tint à un concept plus spartiate du nudisme avec le pérenne *Health & Efficiency*, même si l'on peut supposer qu'on s'y amusait autant,

YEAR: **1956**. TITLE: **Das Waldriff im Meer**.
COUNTRY: **Germany**.

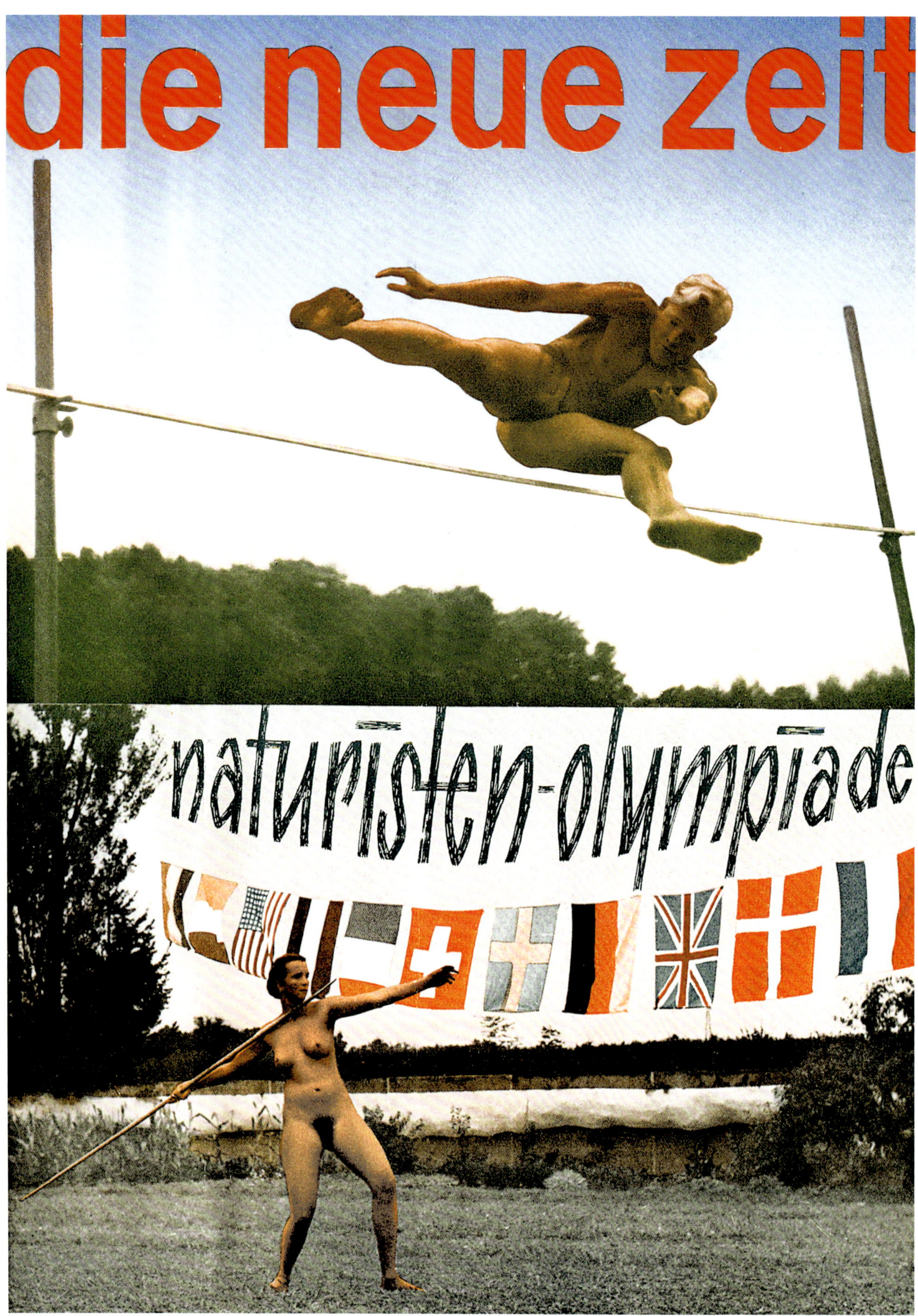

YEAR: **1952**. TITLE: **Die Neue Zeit**. COUNTRY: **Germany**.

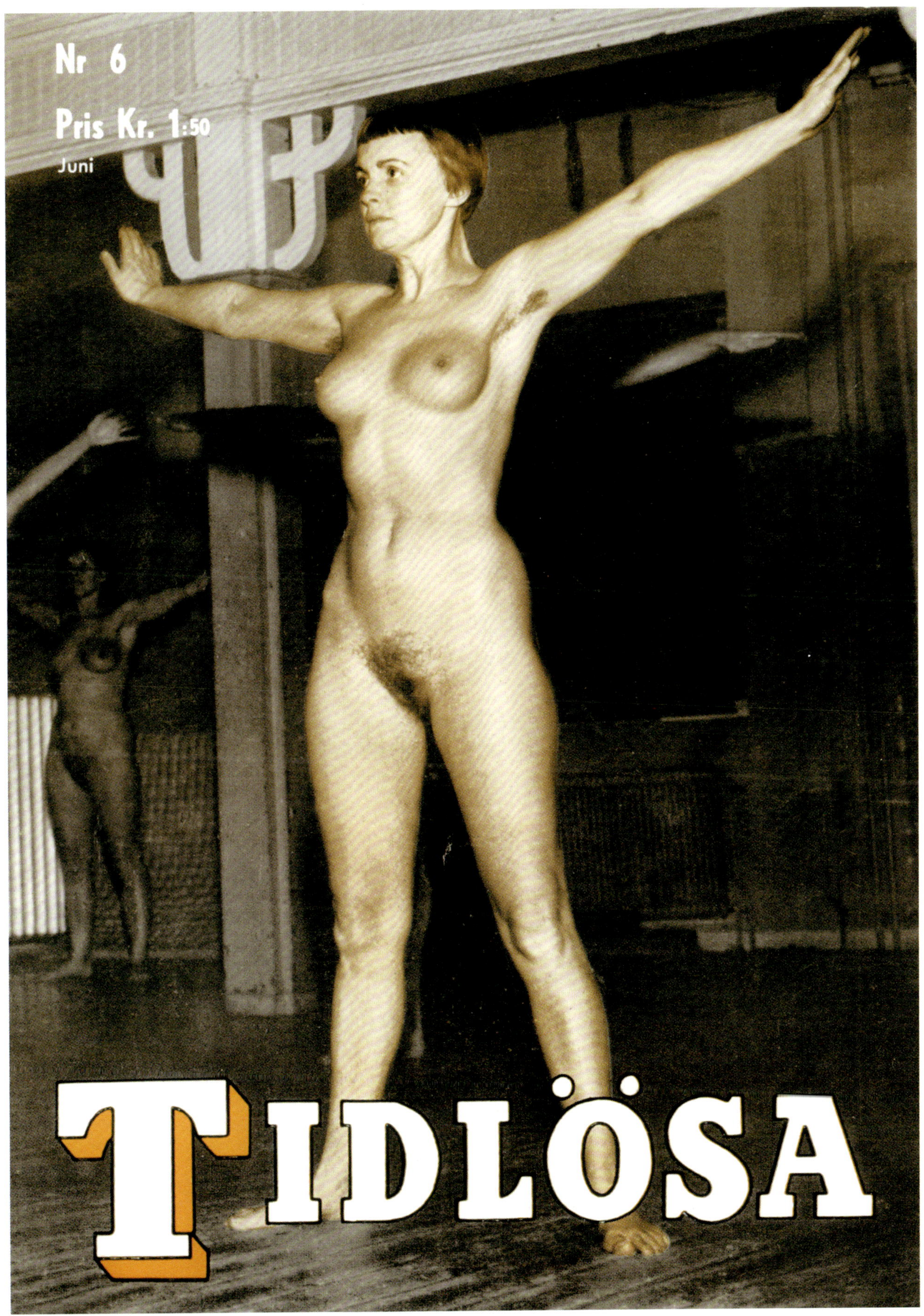

YEAR: **1957**. TITLE: **Tidlösa**. COUNTRY: **Sweden**.

N° 9 OCTOBRE 1956

LA REVUE NATURISTE INTERNATIONALE

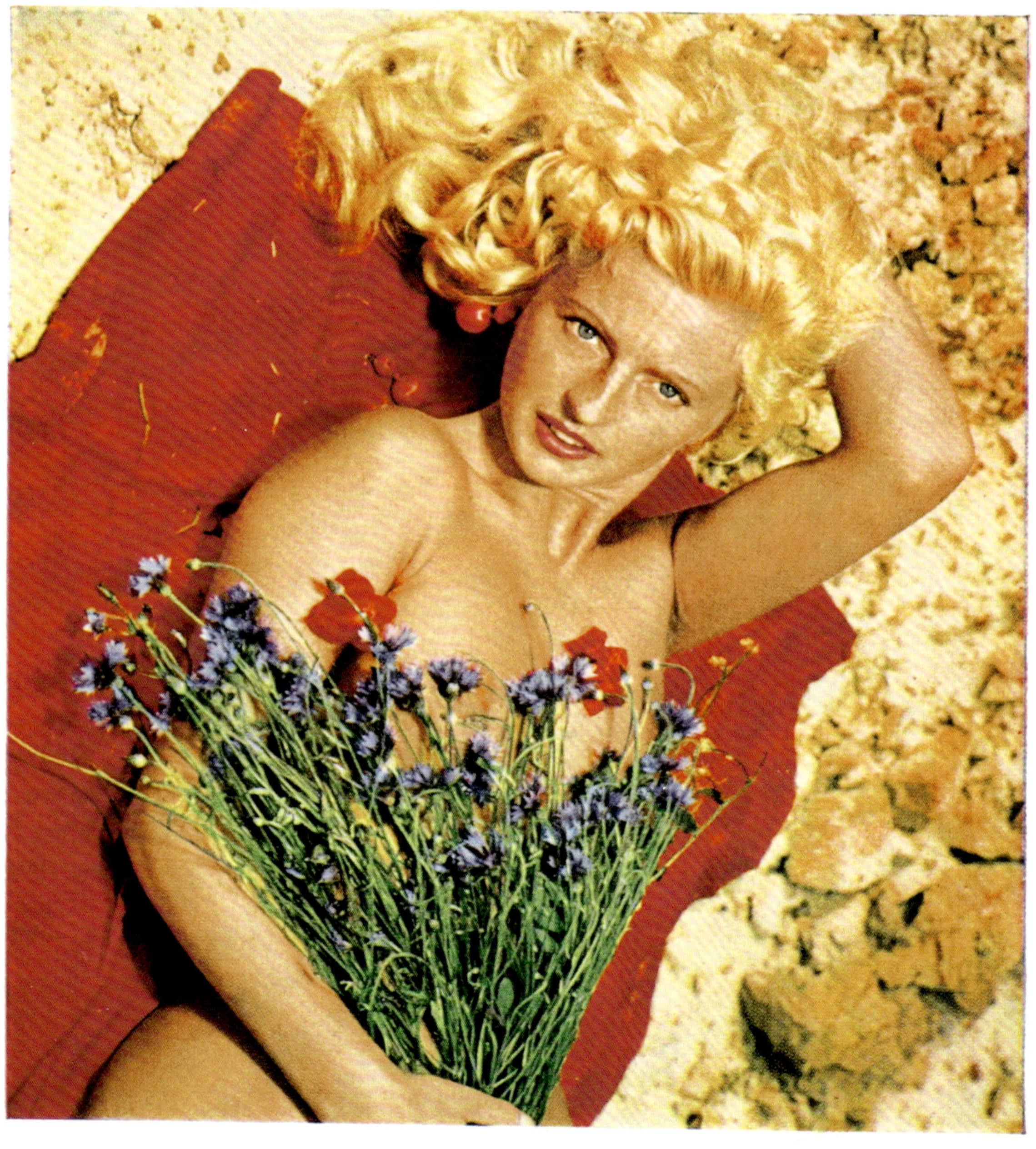

200 Frs

YEAR: **1956**. TITLE: **La Revue Naturiste Internationale**. COUNTRY: **France**.

Clothes... must be the insignia of the superiority of man over all other animals, for surely there could be no other reason for wearing the hideous things.

—*Tarzan of the Apes*, Edgar Rice Burroughs

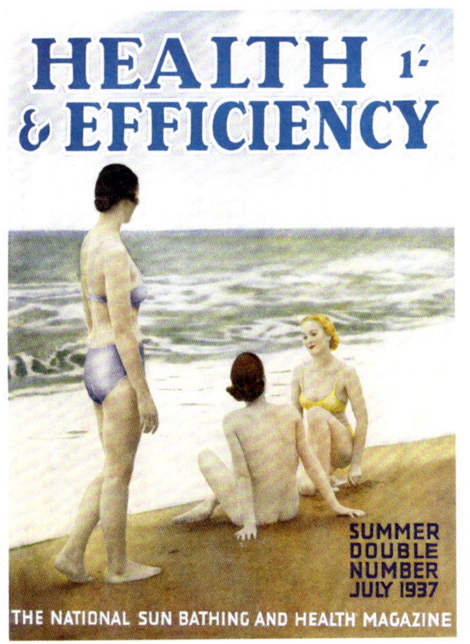

YEAR: **1937**. TITLE: **Health & Efficiency**.
COUNTRY: **England**.

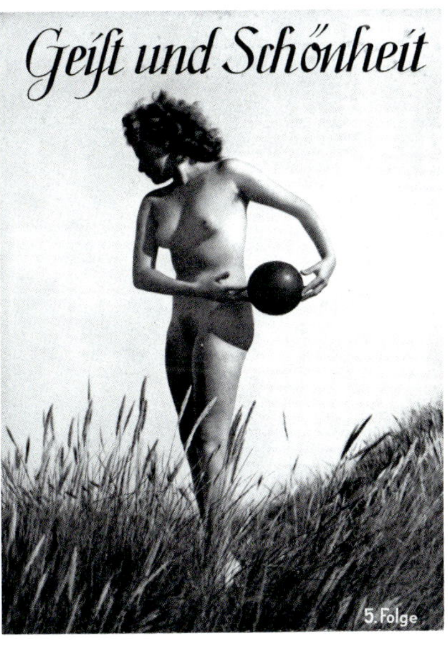

YEAR: **1940s**. TITLE: **Geist und Schönheit**.
COUNTRY: **Germany**.

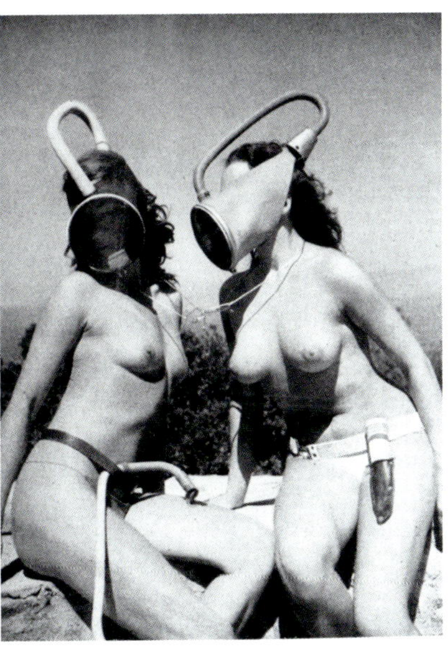

YEAR: **1954**. TITLE: **Naturisme**.
COUNTRY: **France**.

and *Tidlösa* (Sweden). England, never one with the Continent, stuck to a more Spartan concept of nudism in its long running *Health & Efficiency*, though one might assume they were having just as much fun, in a British sort of way. Maybe more, since *Health & Efficiency* was still in publication in 2002 after nearly 100 years. As happened in America, the European nudist magazines declined sharply when frankly sexual publications became available in the mid-60s. Unlike the American magazines they would never die out entirely, as nudism remains popular in Europe into the 21st century.

– auf seine britische Art und Weise – genauso viel Freude am Nudismus. Vielleicht sogar noch mehr, denn *Health & Efficiency* wird als Einziges der Magazine nach fast 100 Jahren immer noch verlegt. Wie in Amerika ging es auch in Europa mit den Nudistenmagazinen steil bergab, als Mitte der Sechziger richtige Sexhefte auf den Markt kamen. Aber anders als in den Staaten starben sie nicht gänzlich aus, denn in Europa ist der Nudismus auch im 21. Jahrhundert noch populär.

d'une manière toute britannique. Plus même, puisqu' *Health & Efficiency* est la seule publication de ce type existant encore après près d'un siècle de parution. Comme aux États-Unis, les magazines nudistes européens entamèrent une chute libre vers le milieu des années soixante quand les publications ouvertement sexuelles devinrent accessibles. Toutefois, contrairement aux publications américaines, ils ne devaient jamais disparaître complètement, le nudisme continuant d'être populaire en Europe à ce jour.

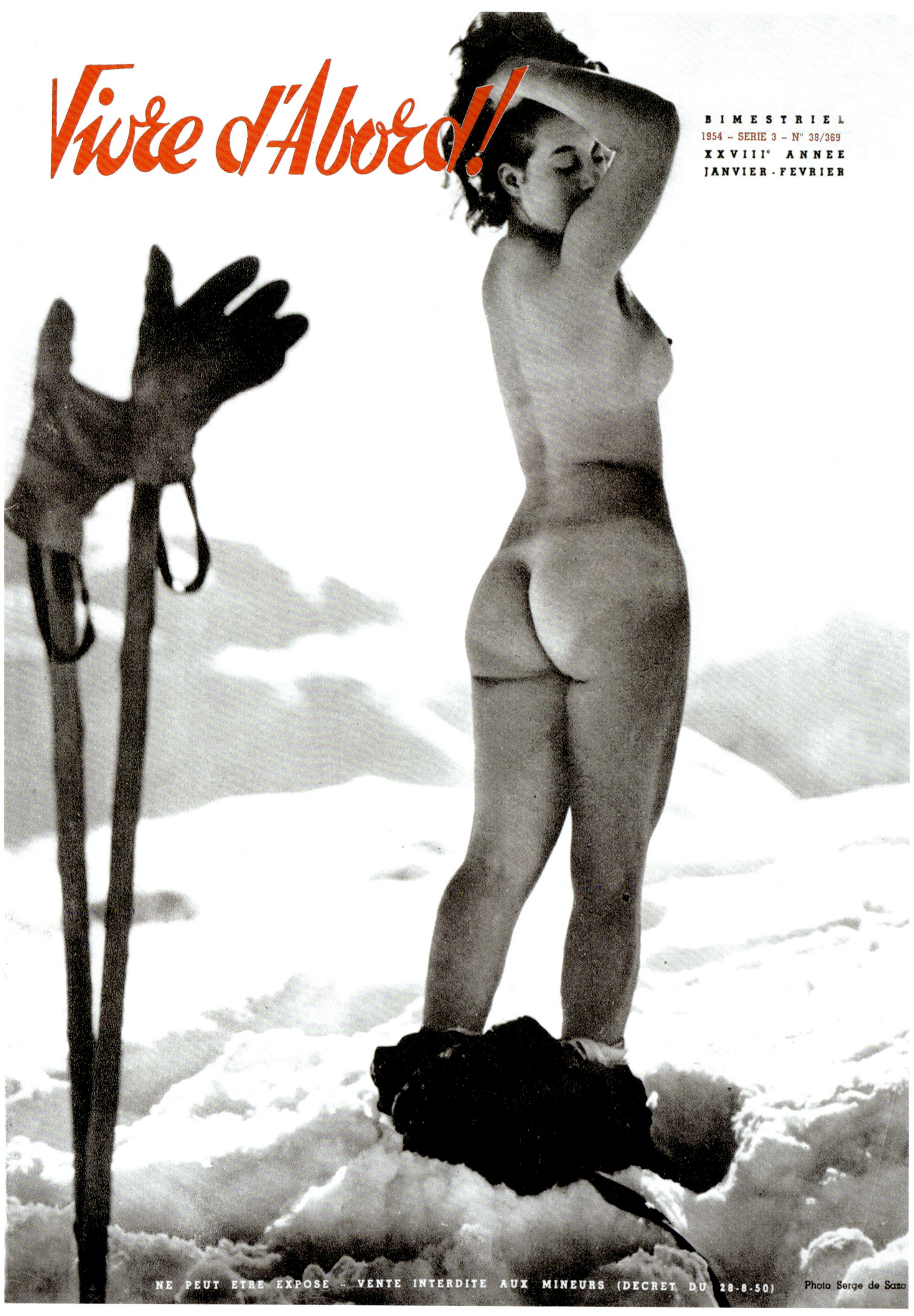

YEAR: **1954**. TITLE: **Vivre d'abord!** COUNTRY: **France**.

YEAR: **1952**. TITLE: **Vivre d'abord!** COUNTRY: **France**.

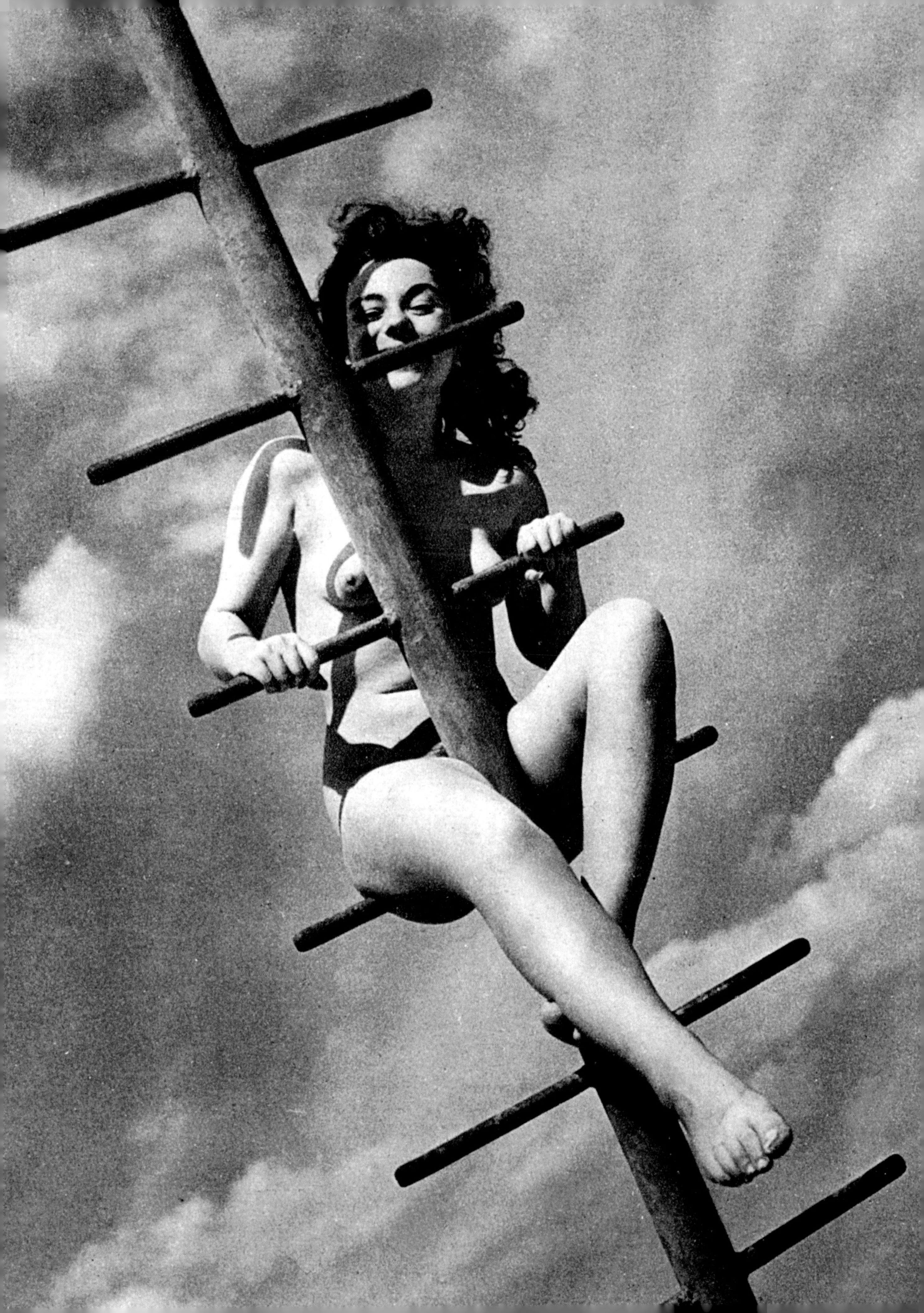

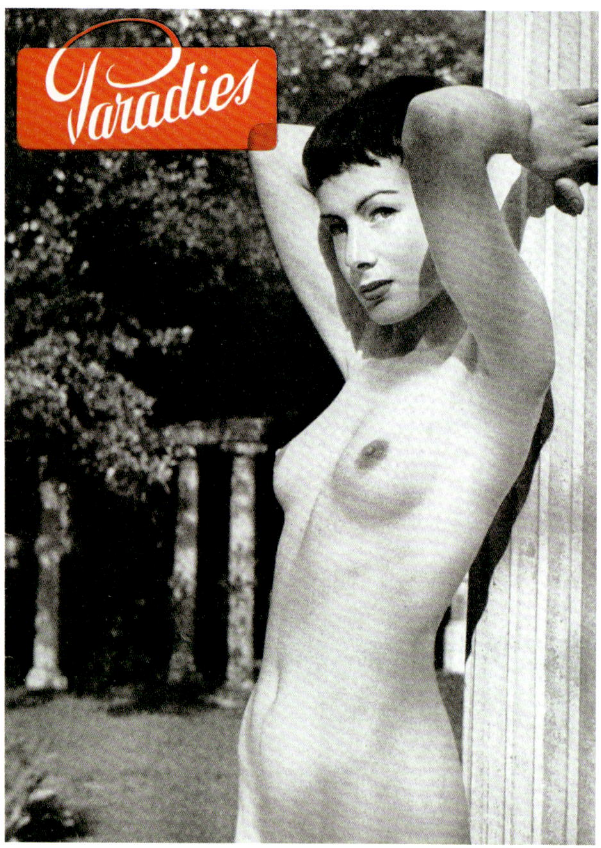

YEAR: **1950s**. TITLE: **Paradies**. COUNTRY: **Germany**.

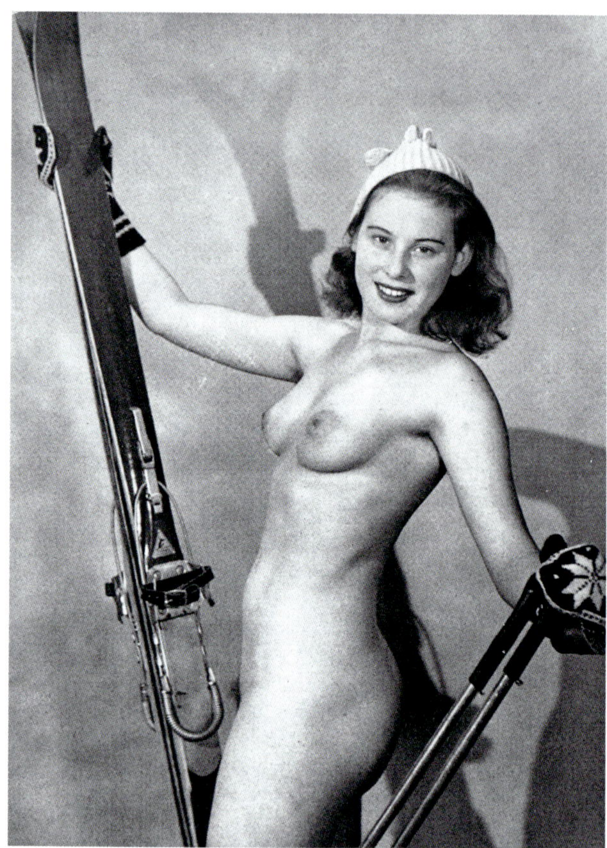

YEAR: **1950s**. TITLE: **Paradies**. COUNTRY: **Germany**.

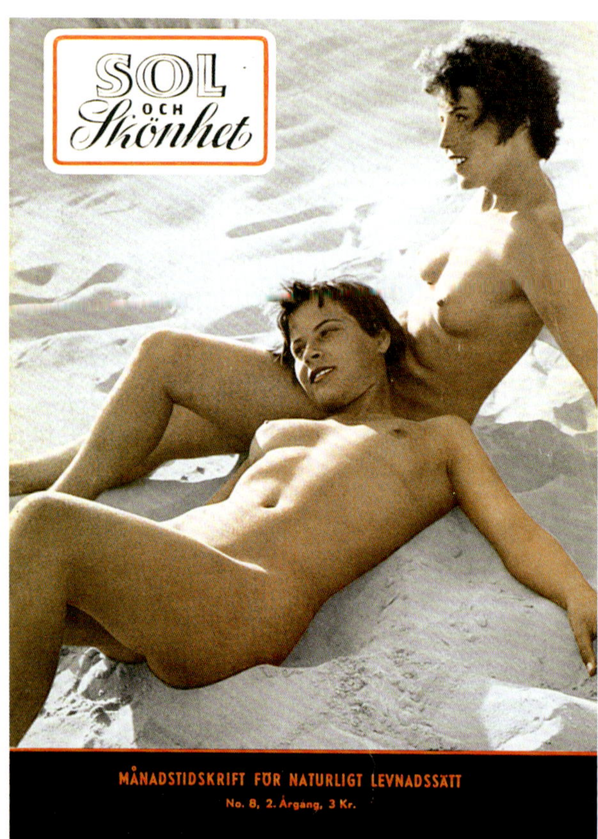

YEAR: **1954**. TITLE: **Sol Och Skönhet**. COUNTRY: **Denmark**.

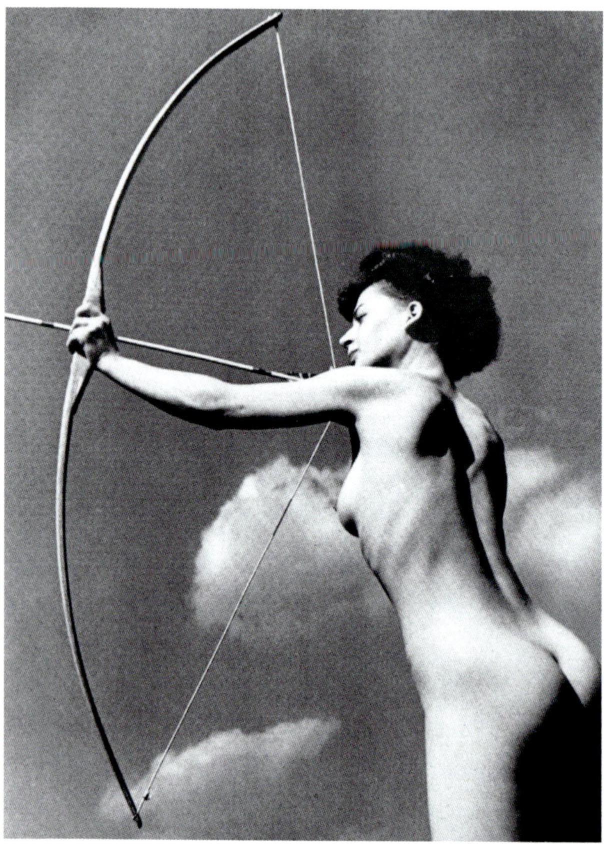

YEAR: **1954**. TITLE: **Sol Och Skönhet**. COUNTRY: **Denmark**.

PAGES 408 & 409:
YEAR: **undated**. TITLE: **L'île du Levant**.
COUNTRY: **France**.

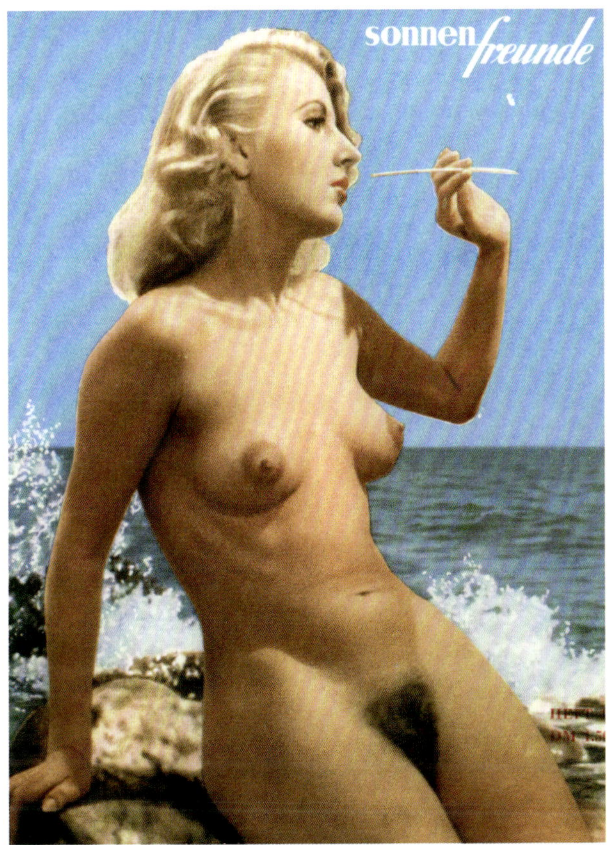

Year: **1957**. Title: **Sonnenfreunde**. Country: **Germany**.

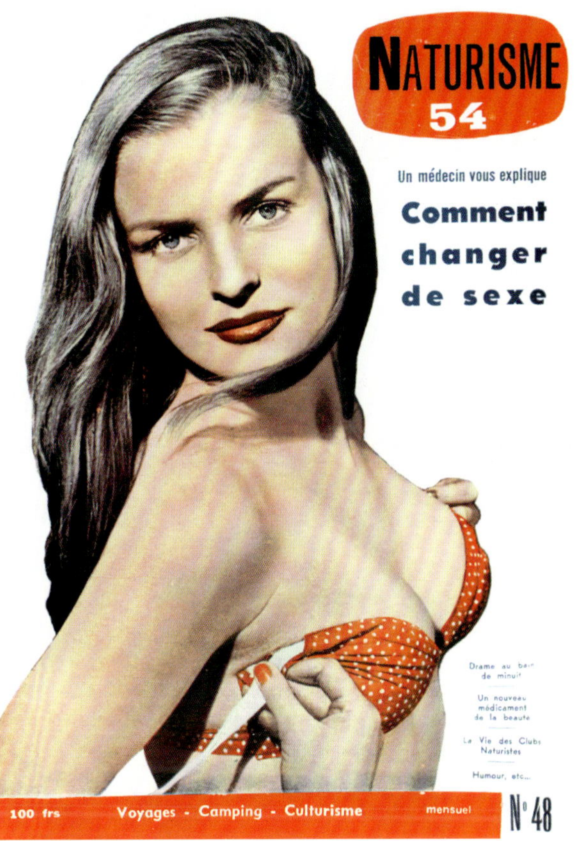

Year: **1954**. Title: **Naturisme**. Country: **France**.

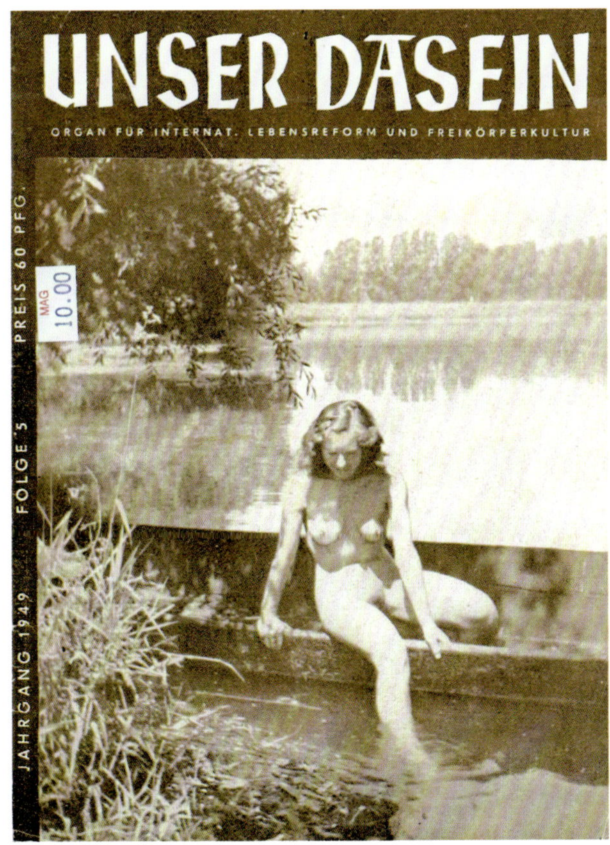

Year: **1949**. Title: **Unser Dasein**. Country: **Germany**.

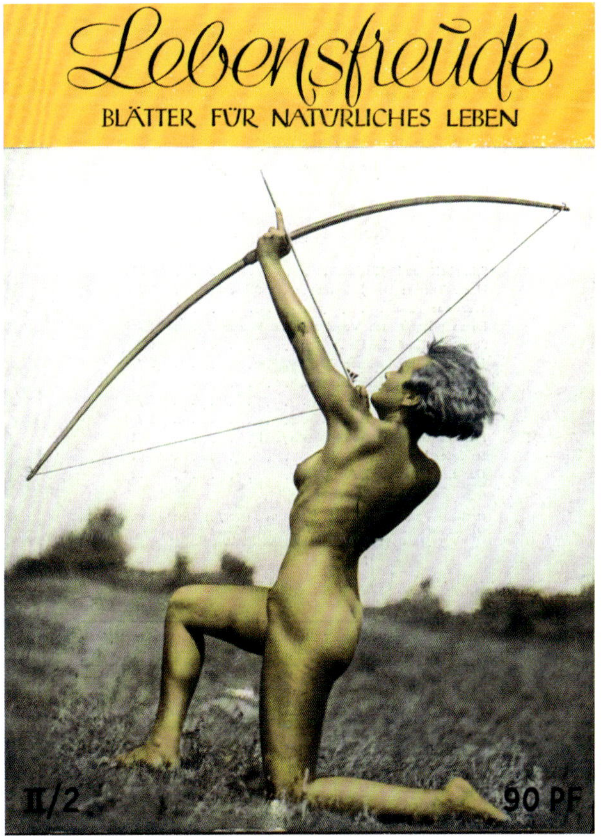

Year: **1950**. Title: **Lebensfreude**. Country: **Germany**.

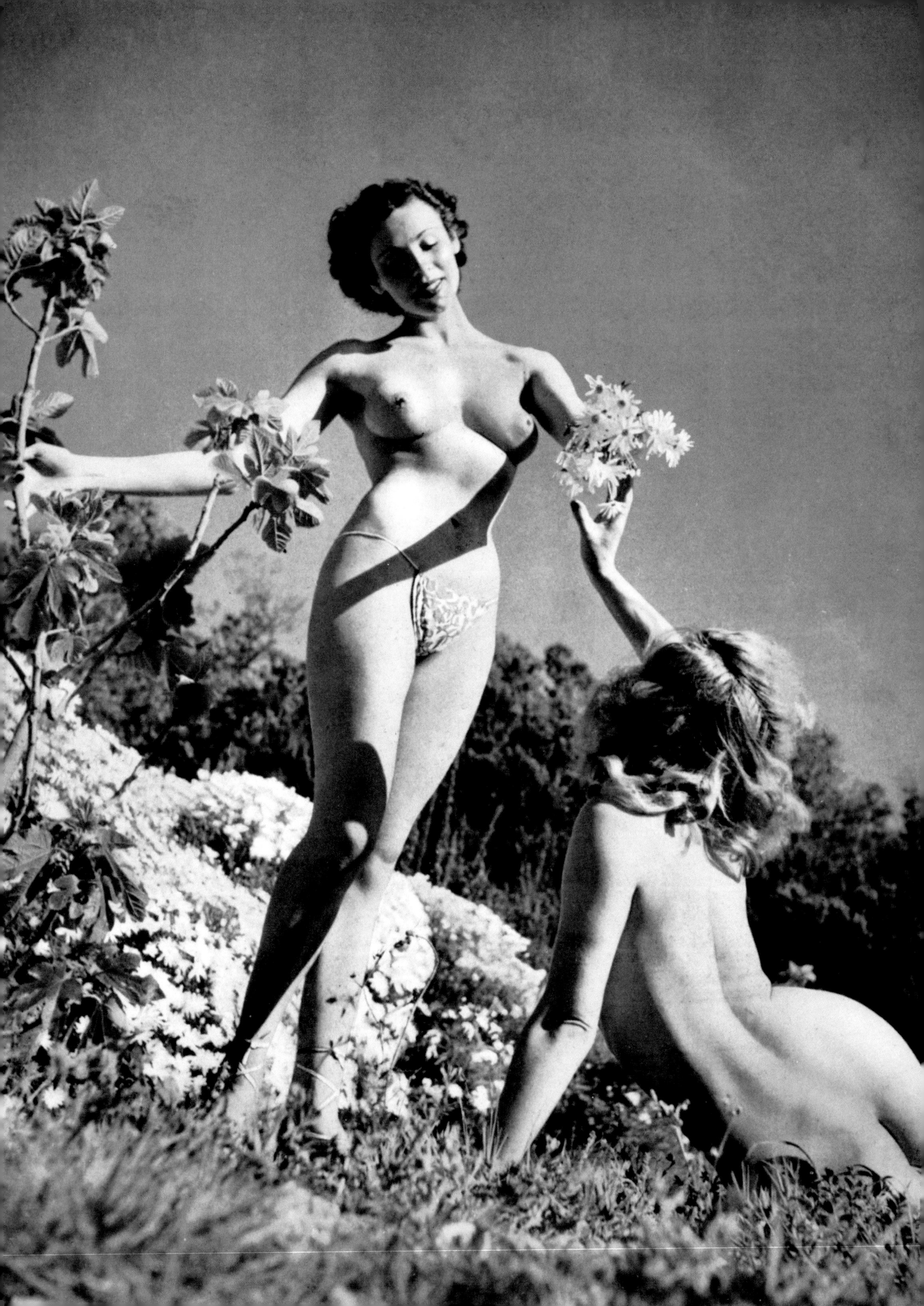

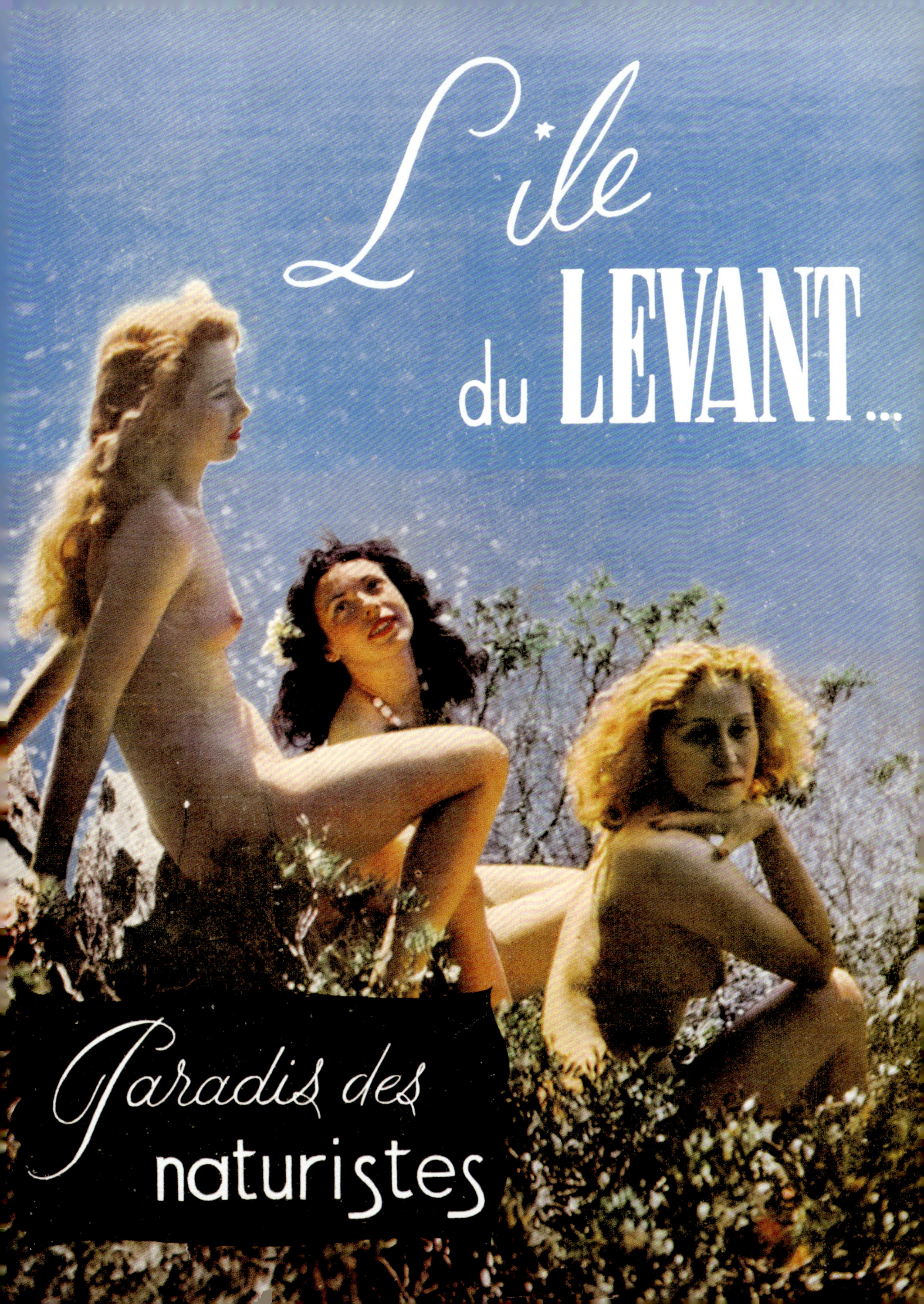
L'île
du LEVANT...
Paradis des
naturistes

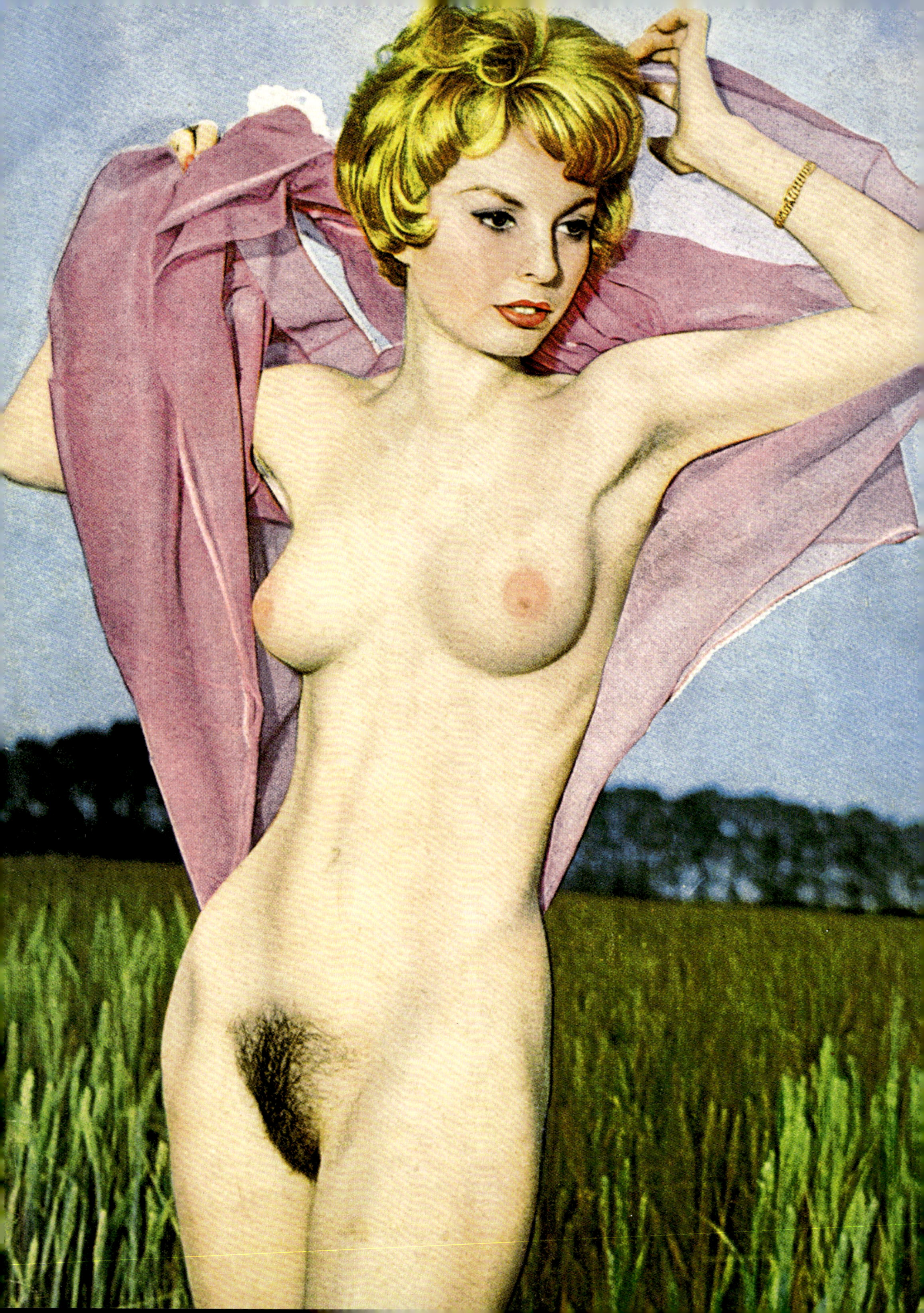

NO COMING BACK TO THE CABARET:

Germany Post-War

Das Cabaret bleibt geschlossen: Deutschland nach dem Krieg

Le cabaret est bien fini : L'Allemagne de l'après-guerre

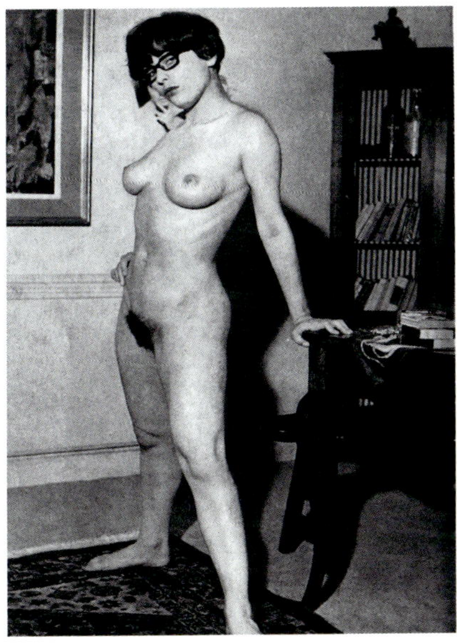

Year: **1950s**. Title: **Venus**. Country: **Germany**.

When German publishing resumed after World War II—and it did as quickly as in most of the European nations—what emerged was a far humbler product. The nudist magazines now concentrated on health and beauty and nothing more. The art nude magazines were indistinguishable from art nude magazines produced across northern Europe. *Reigen*, the *Playboy* of 1920s Berlin, was shrunken and stunted by paper shortages and forced to publish in Austria for the German audience. *Bolero*, nominally a film review magazine, mixed pin-ups

Die deutschen Männermagazine vor dem Zweiten Weltkrieg waren mondän, ungewöhnlich und in Inhalt und Aufmachung unverkennbar deutsch. Die zwischen 1925 und 1933 in und um Berlin produzierten zählten mit den französischen Magazinen zu den schönsten dieser Periode – und zu den originellsten überhaupt. Als nach dem Krieg wieder Zeitschriften verlegt wurden – ebenso bald wie in den anderen europäischen Ländern –, waren die Ergebnisse wesentlich bescheidener. Die Nudistenmagazine konzentrierten sich ausschließlich auf den Gesundheits- und Schönheitsaspekt. Die Zeitschriften mit künstlerischen Aktfotos unterschieden sich in nichts von anderen europäischen Magazinen dieser Art. *Reigen*, der *Playboy* des Berlins der zwanziger Jahre, durch die Papierrationierungen im Umfang geschrumpft, musste in Österreich für das deutsche Publikum verlegt werden. *Bolero*, nominell eine Filmzeitschrift, bot als blasse *Paris-Hollywood*-Imitation Pin-ups und Fotos von Filmstars. *Gondel* konnte mit wunderbaren Coverillustrationen beeindrucken, aber im Heft fand man eine vergleichbare Mischung von Fotos europäischer und amerikanischer Filmstars und unverfänglichen Artikeln, durchsetzt mit langweiligen Aktstudien. *Paprika* war eine Idee schärfer und eines der wenigen Hefte,

Les magazines de charme allemands d'avant la Seconde Guerre mondiale étaient sophistiqués, excentriques et typiquement teutoniques dans leur contenu et leur forme. Ceux produits à et autour de Berlin entre 1925 et 1933 étaient du même niveau que les français de la même époque : les plus beaux et les plus bizarres jamais réalisés. Lorsque l'édition allemande reprit après la guerre, ce qu'elle fit aussi rapidement que dans la plupart des autres pays d'Europe, ses publications étaient nettement plus humbles. Les magazines nudistes se concentraient désormais sur la santé et la beauté, rien de plus. Les magazines de nu artistique ne se distinguaient en rien de ceux produits dans toute l'Europe du Nord.

> When German publishing resumed after World War II —and it did as quickly as in most of Europe— what emerged was a far humbler product.

Year: **1950s**. Title: **Venus**. Country: **Germany**.

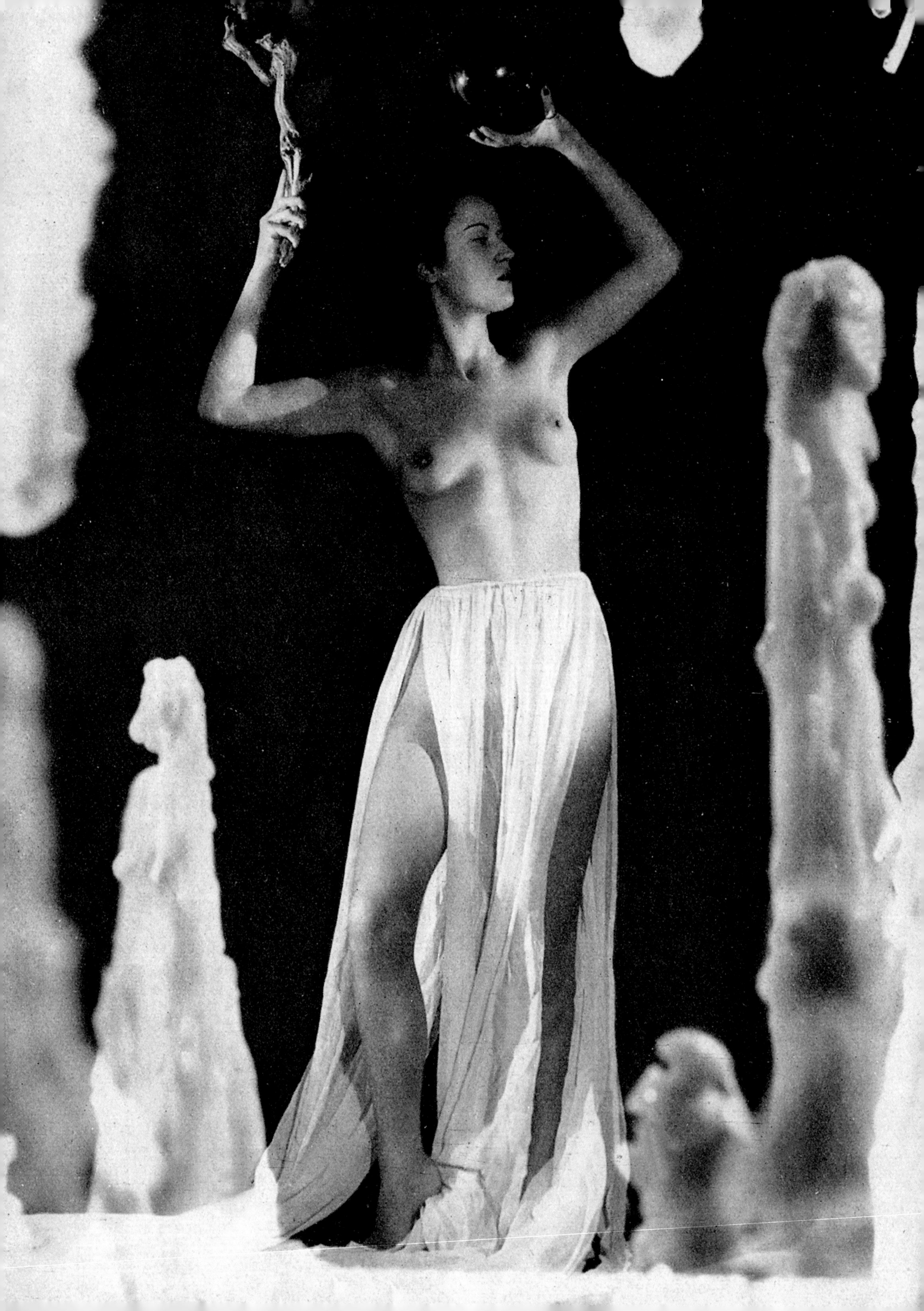

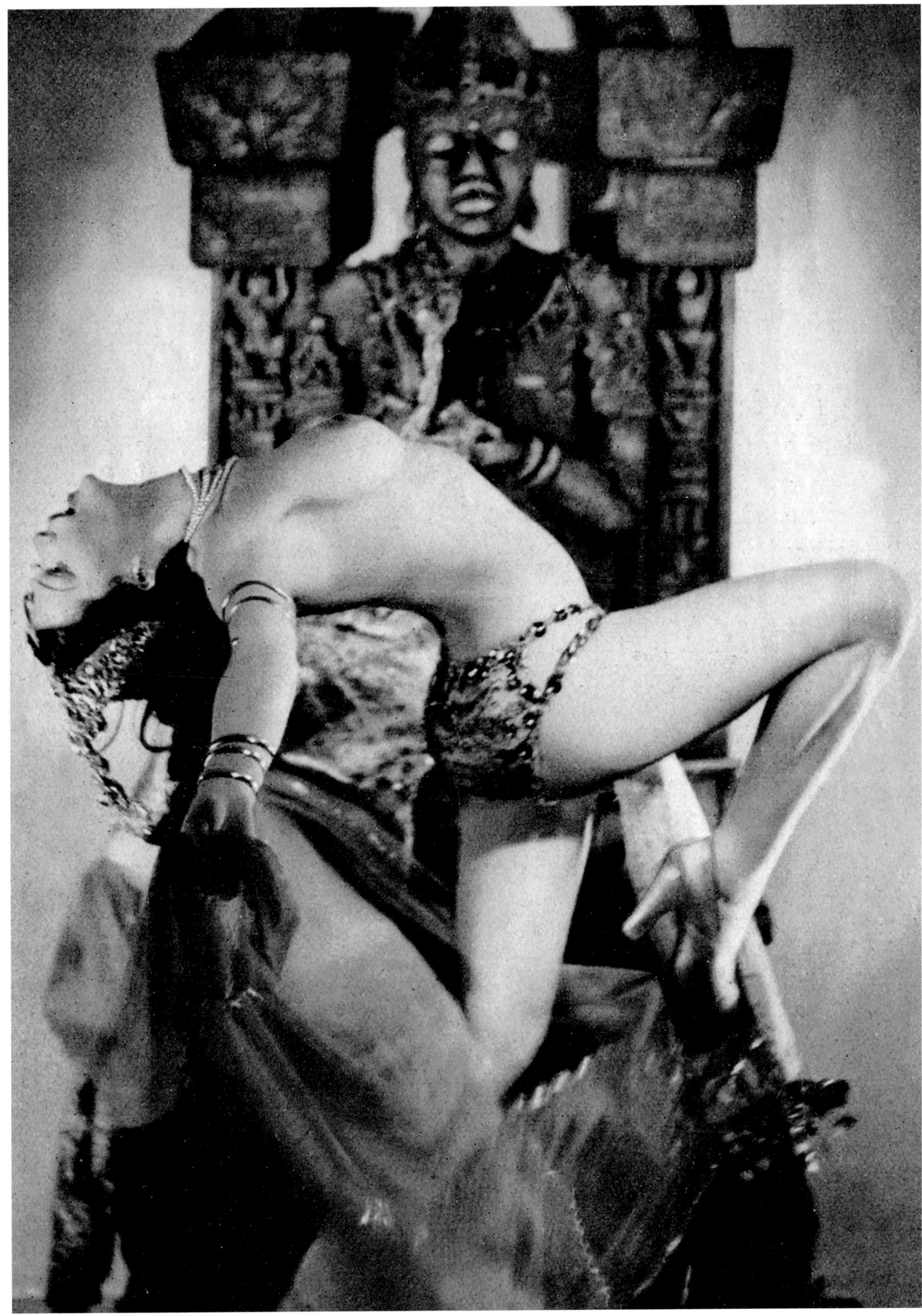

Left & Above: Year: **1950**. Title: **Tamburin**. Country: **Germany**.

A post-war version of the Weimar cabaret titles, the 1950's Tamburin *focused on modern dance.*

Als Nachkriegsversion der Cabaret-Titel aus der Weimarer Zeit konzentrierte sich Tamburin *1950 auf den modernen Tanz.*

Version d'après-guerre des titres de cabaret de la république de Weimar, Tamburin *(1950) se concentrait sur la danse moderne.*

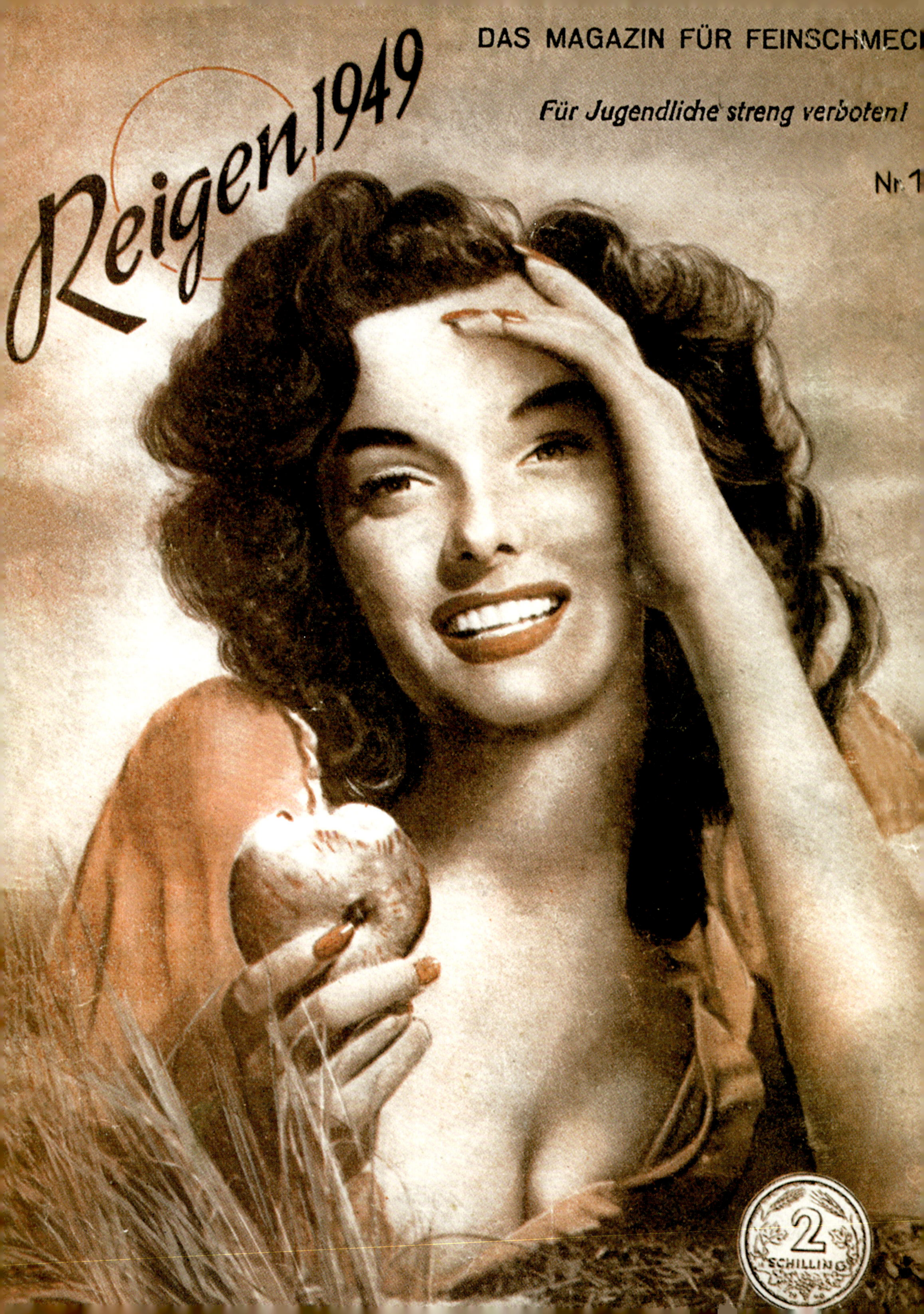
Reigen 1949
DAS MAGAZIN FÜR FEINSCHMEC
Für Jugendliche streng verboten!
Nr 1
2
SCHILLING

Sex is one of the nine reasons for reincarnation—the other eight are unimportant.

—Henry Miller

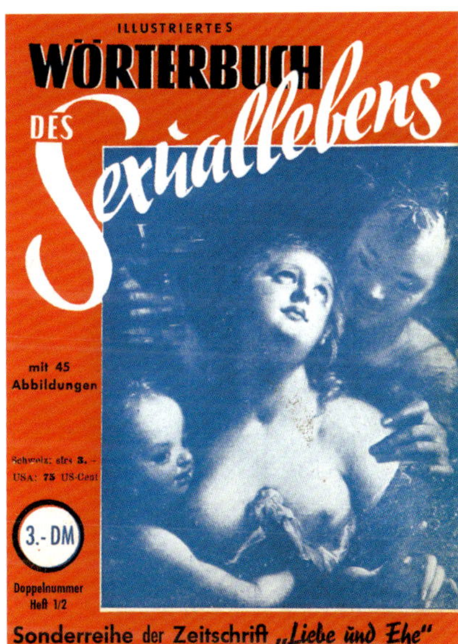

YEAR: **1950**. TITLE: **Wörterbuch des Sexuallebens**. COUNTRY: **Germany**.

with movie star photos in tepid imitation of *Paris-Hollywood*. *Paprika* was a bit spicier and one of the few that dared deal with post-war social issues under its banner "Das Magazin für Optimisten" (The Magazine of Optimists). *Mix*, *Neue Melange* and *Top Fit* copied the leggy French post-war digests.

Of the magazines I found from this period only a few resembled the finely crafted titles of the Weimar era. *Neues Kriminalmagazin,* from the mid-40s, is a dark mix of true crime and capering nudes, while *Venus* featured an exotic opium-eater centerfold and art deco design. The issue from 1949 seems to have been a last gasp of old Berlin; by the early 50s *Venus,* too, had been reconstructed.

das es wagte, unter seinem Untertitel „Das Magazin für Optimisten" Fragen der Nachkriegsgesellschaft zu erörtern. *Mix*, *Neue Melange* und *Top Fit* kopierten die viel Bein zeigenden französischen Nachkriegs-Digests.

Unter den Magazinen, die ich aus dieser Zeit gefunden habe, erinnerten nur wenige an die aufwändig gestalteten Titel der Weimarer Zeit. *Neues Kriminalmagazin* von Mitte der Vierziger war ein düsterer Mix aus wahren Verbrechen und herumtollenden Nackten, während *Venus* ein exotisches Centerfold mit einer Opiumesserin und ein Art-déco-Lettering zeigte. Allerdings muss diese Ausgabe von 1949 nur ein müder Abglanz des alten Berlin gewesen sein; Anfang der Fünfziger hatte man *Venus* ebenfalls ein neues Konzept verpasst.

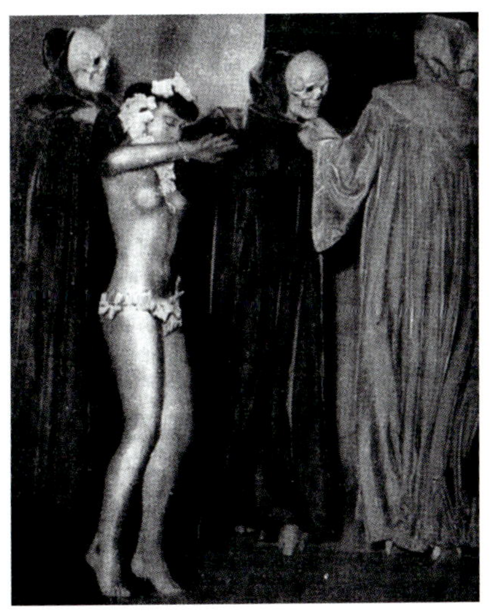

YEAR: **1945**. TITLE: **Neues Kriminalmagazin**. COUNTRY: **Germany**.

Reigen, le *Playboy* du Berlin des années vingt, rendu rachitique par les pénuries de papier, fut contraint de s'exiler en Autriche. *Bolero*, à l'origine un magazine de cinéma, mélangeait les pin-up et les photos de stars de cinéma dans une imitation pâlotte de *Paris-Hollywood*. *Gondel* possédait de magnifiques couvertures illustrées avec des pin-up, mais l'intérieur contenait un mélange similaire de vedettes de cinéma européennes et américaines et d'articles d'intérêt général saupoudrés de quelques nus artistiques insipides.

Paprika était légèrement plus pimenté et l'un des rares à oser aborder des questions sociales liées à l'après-guerre sous sa devise « Das Magazin für Optimisten » (« le magazine des optimistes »). *Mix*, *Neue Melange* et *Top Fit* copiaient les digests français axés sur les modèles aux longues jambes.

Parmi les magazines de la période que j'ai retrouvés, une poignée seulement rappelait les titres raffinés de la période de Weimar. *Neues Kriminalmagazin*, publié à partir du milieu des années quarante, mélangeait les faits divers et les nus faisant des cabrioles tandis que *Venus,* au graphisme Art Déco, proposait un poster central montrant une fumeuse d'opium. Toutefois, ce numéro datant de l'année 1949 semble plutôt avoir été un dernier sursaut du Berlin d'autrefois. Au début des années cinquante, *Venus* avait été, elle aussi, reconstruite.

YEAR: **1949**. TITLE: **Reigen**. COUNTRY: **Germany**.

"The Gourmet Magazine"

« Le magazine pour les amateurs du raffinement »

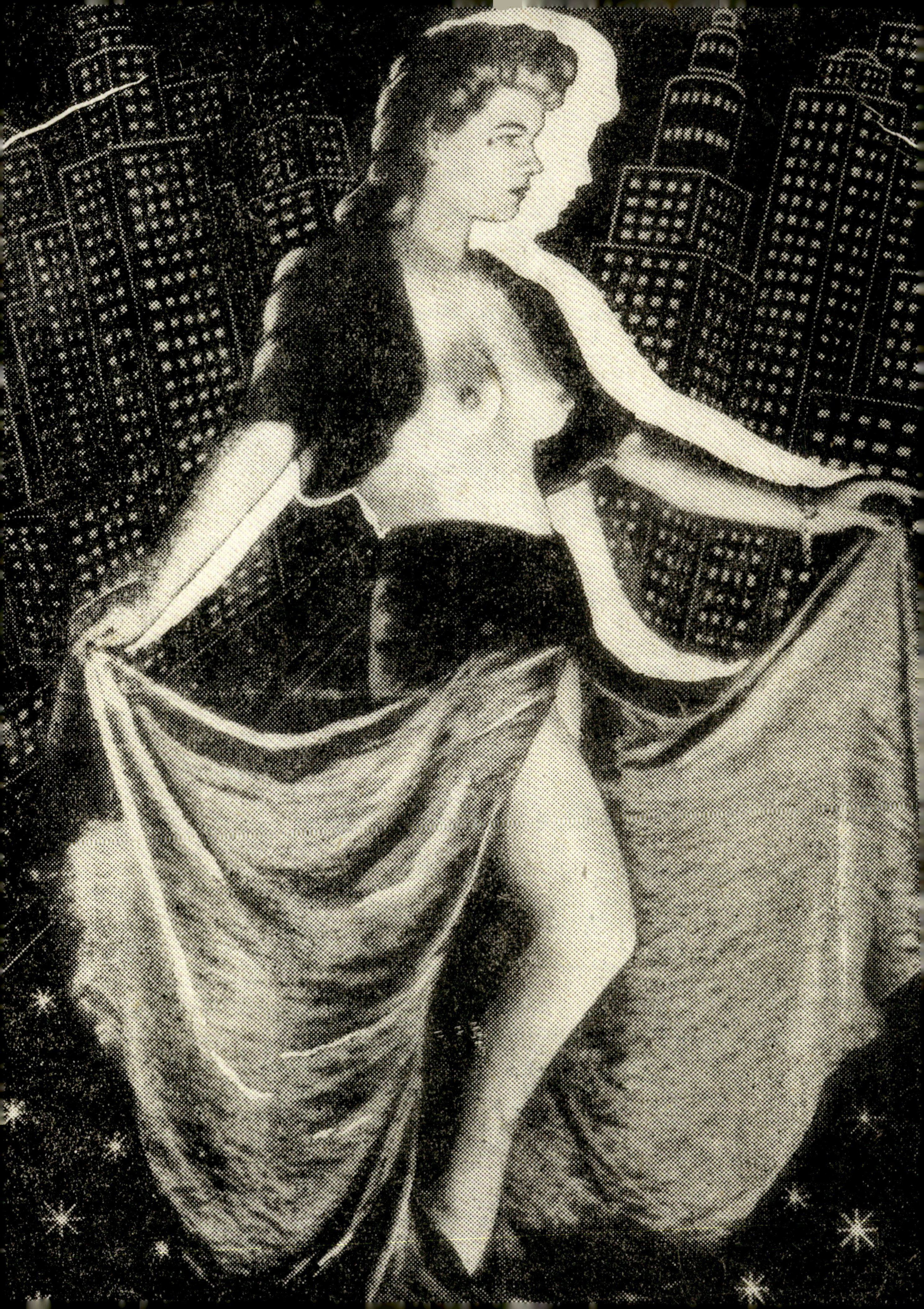

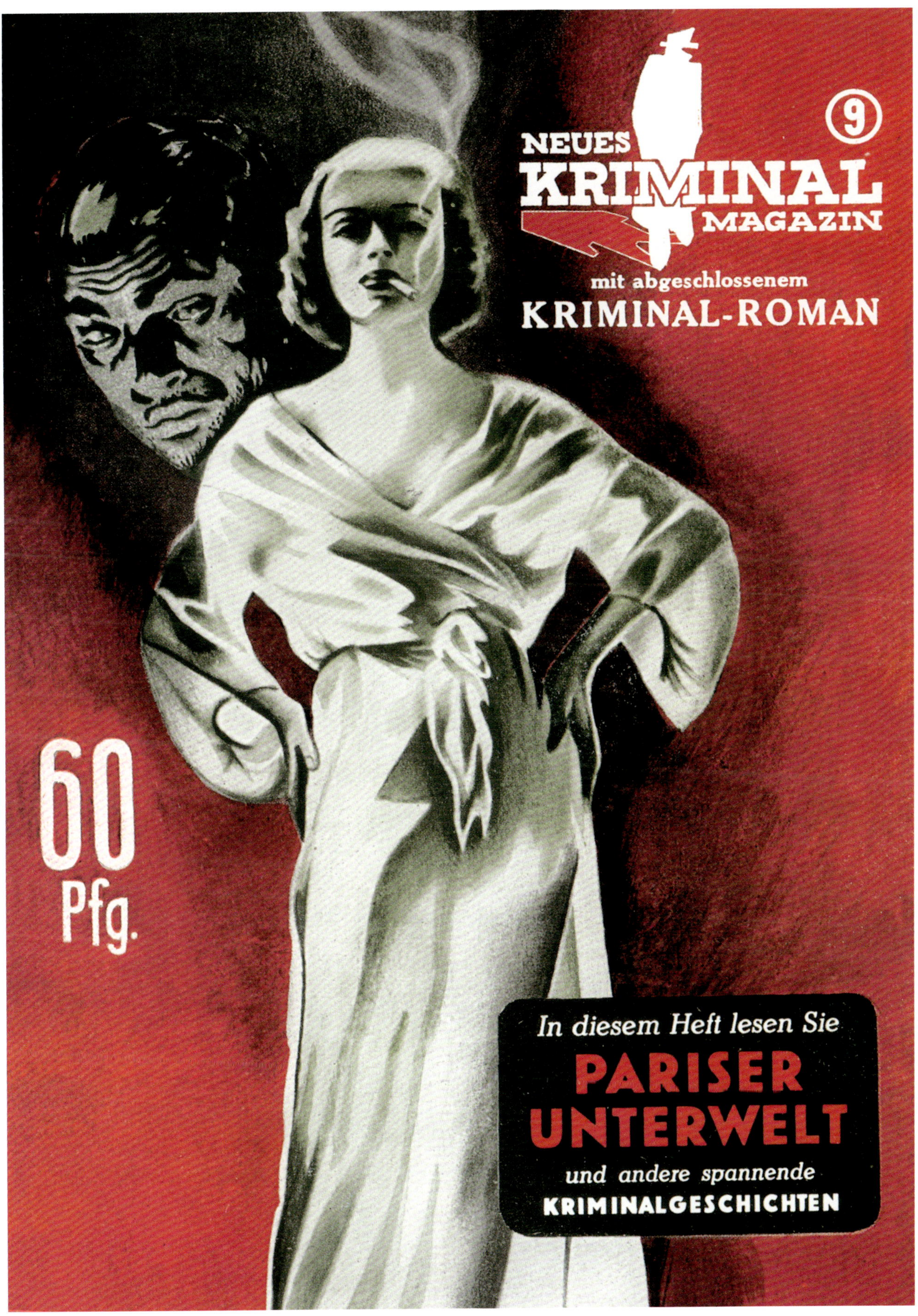

YEAR: **1945**. TITLE: **Neues Kriminalmagazin**.
COUNTRY: **Germany**.

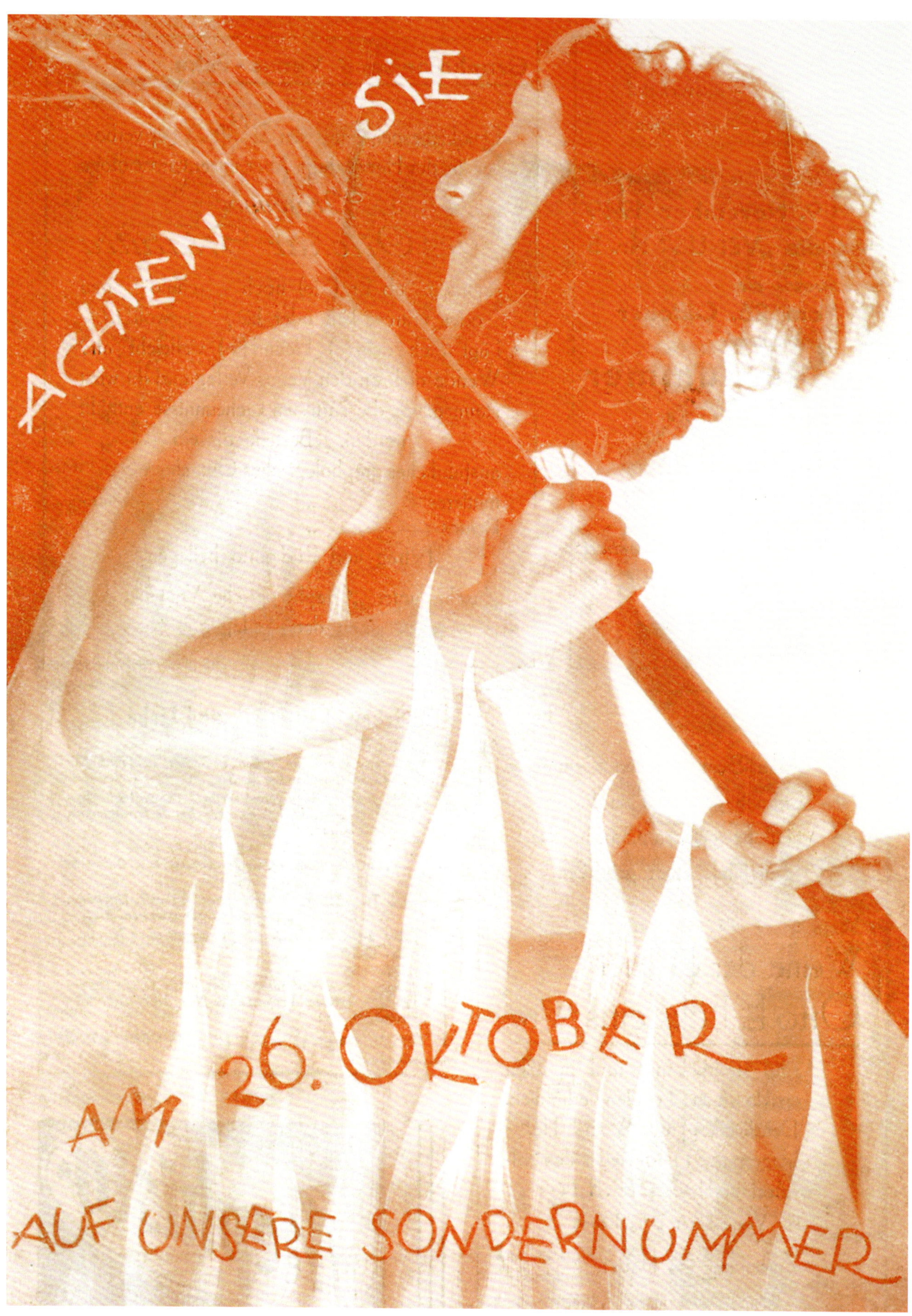

Year: **1949**. Title: **Venus**. Country: **Germany**.

"Watch out for our special issue on 26 October"

« Prêtez attention à notre numéro spécial du 25 octobre »

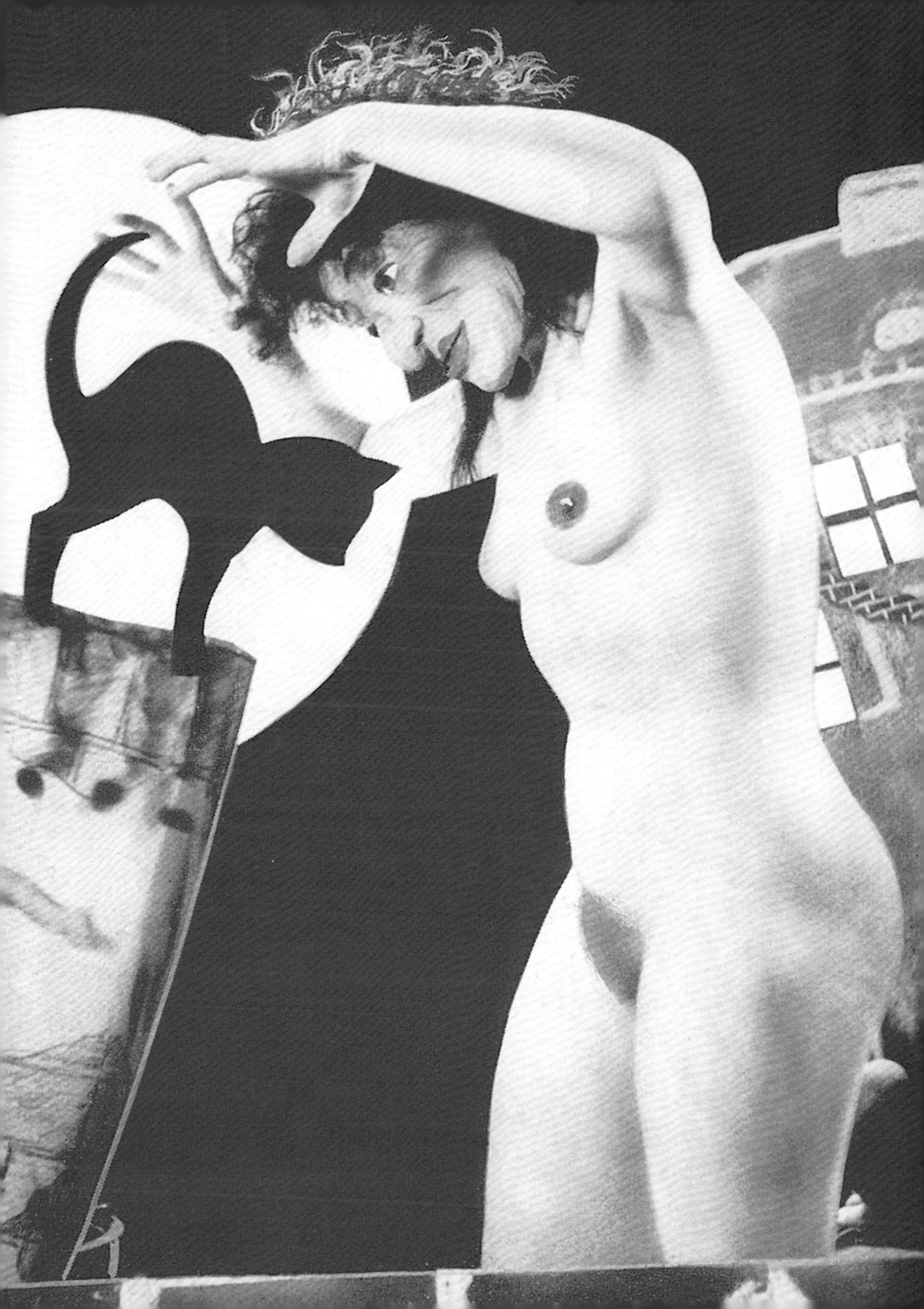

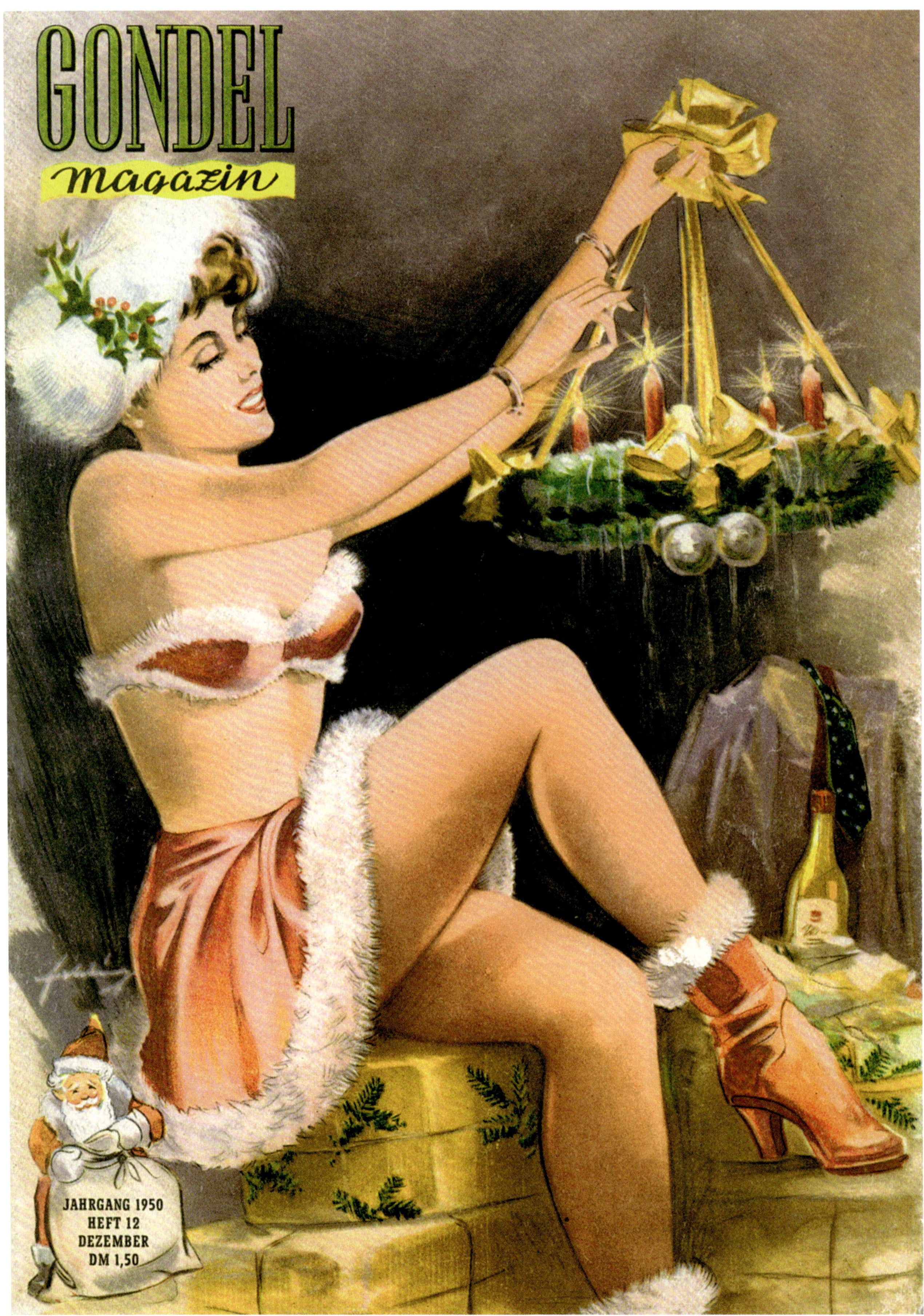

YEAR: **1950**. TITLE: **Gondel**. COUNTRY: **Germany**.

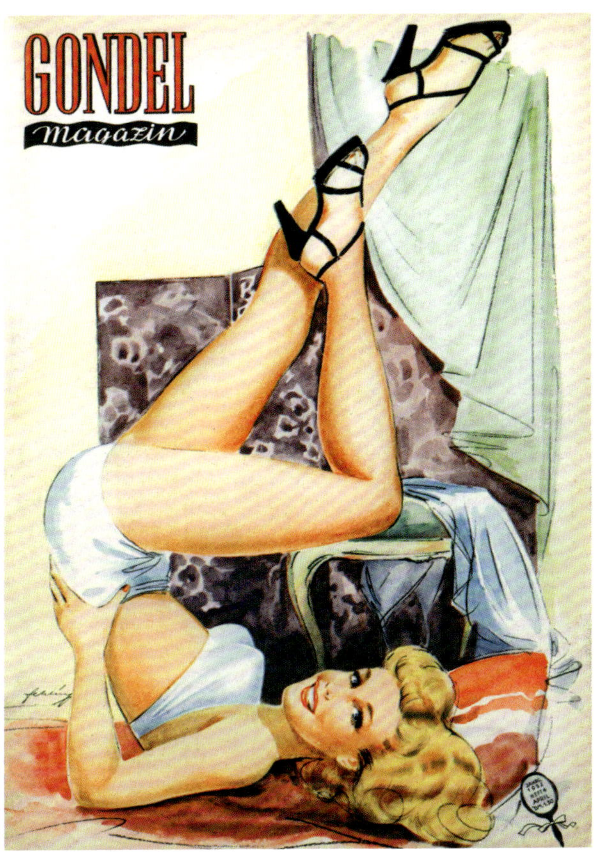

YEAR: **1952**. TITLE: **Gondel**. COUNTRY: **Germany**.

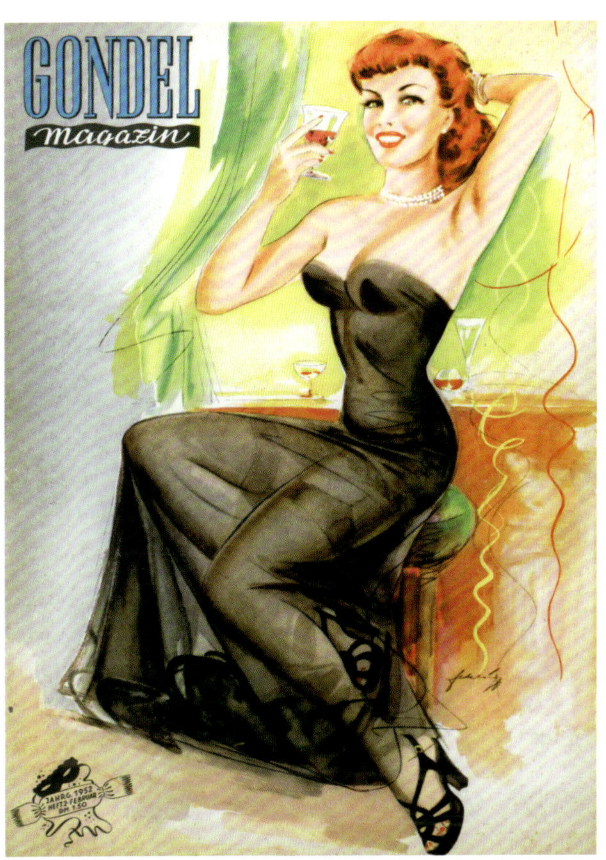

YEAR: **1952**. TITLE: **Gondel**. COUNTRY: **Germany**.

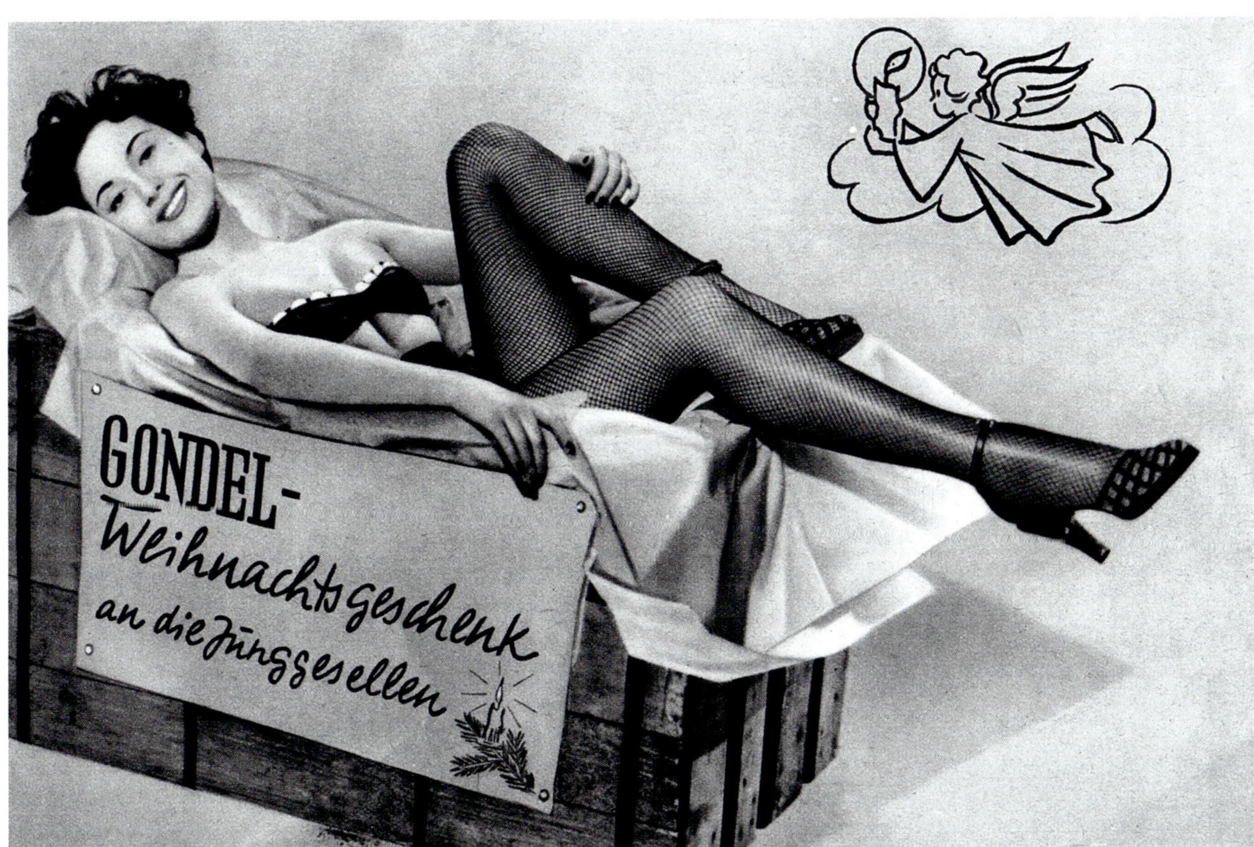

YEAR: **1950**. TITLE: **Gondel**. COUNTRY: **Germany**.

"Christmas present for bachelors"

« Cadeau de Noël aux célibataires »

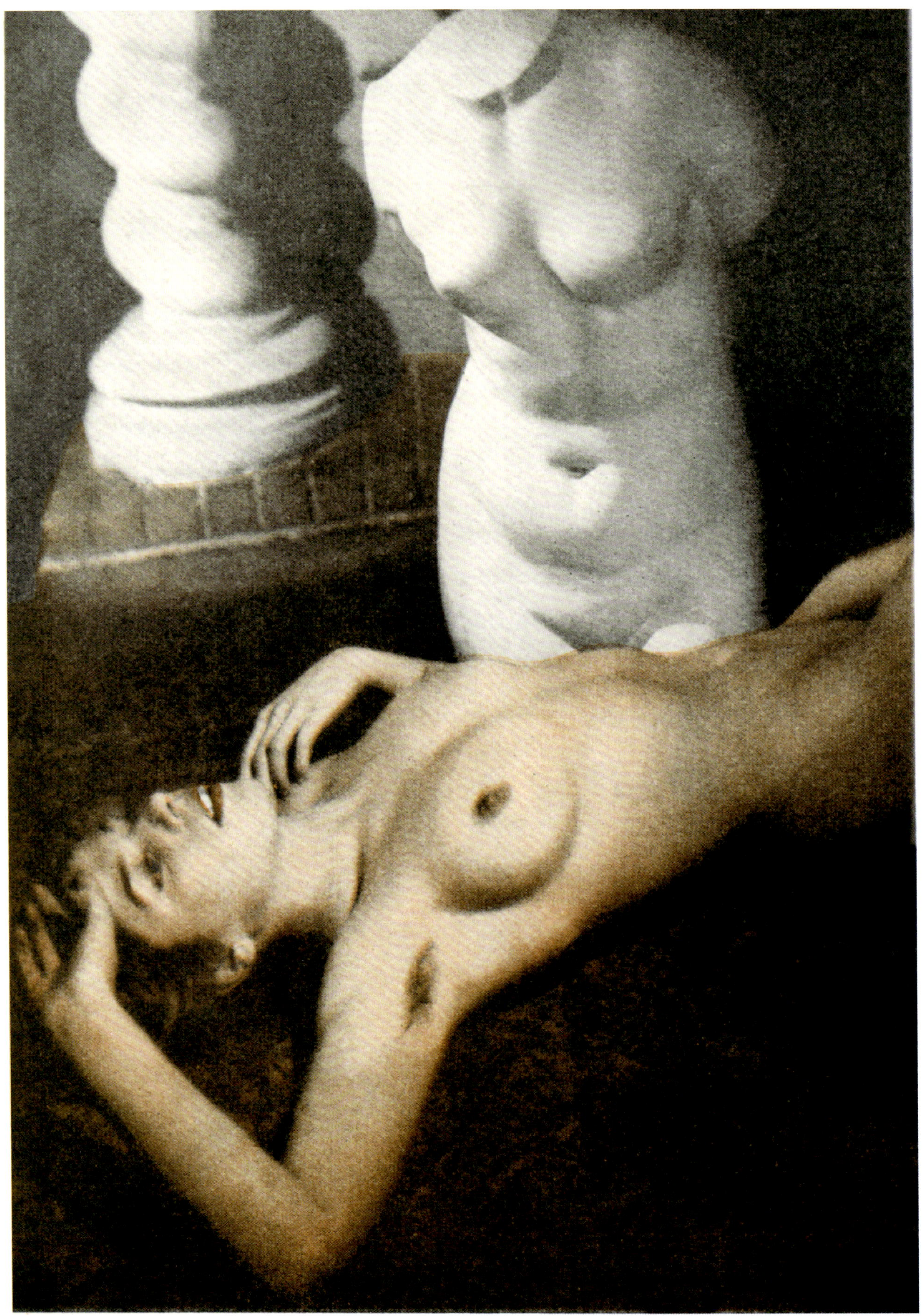

Year: **1950**. Title: **Corso**. Country: **Germany**.

Year: **1950**. Title: **Gondel**. Country: **Germany**.

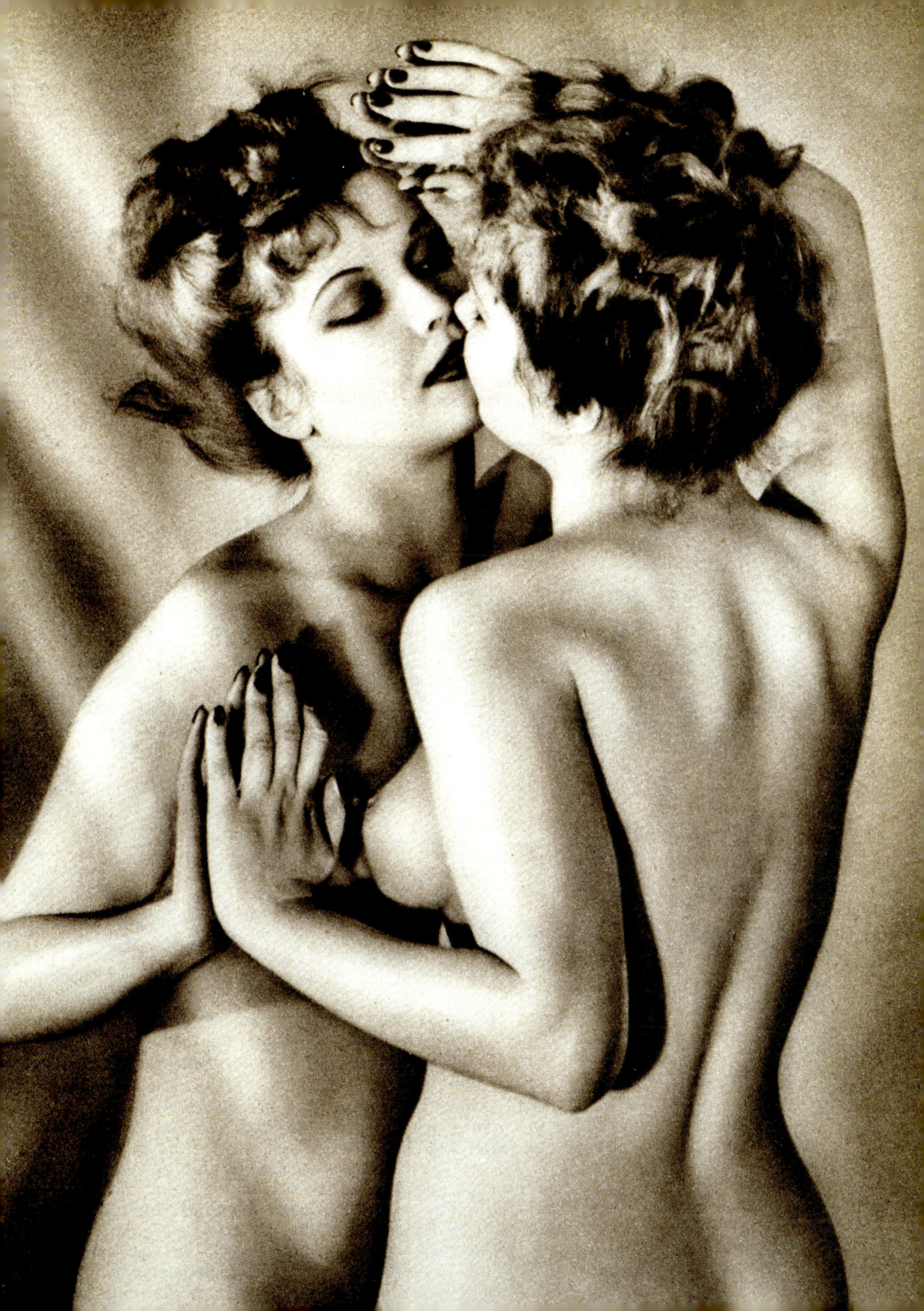

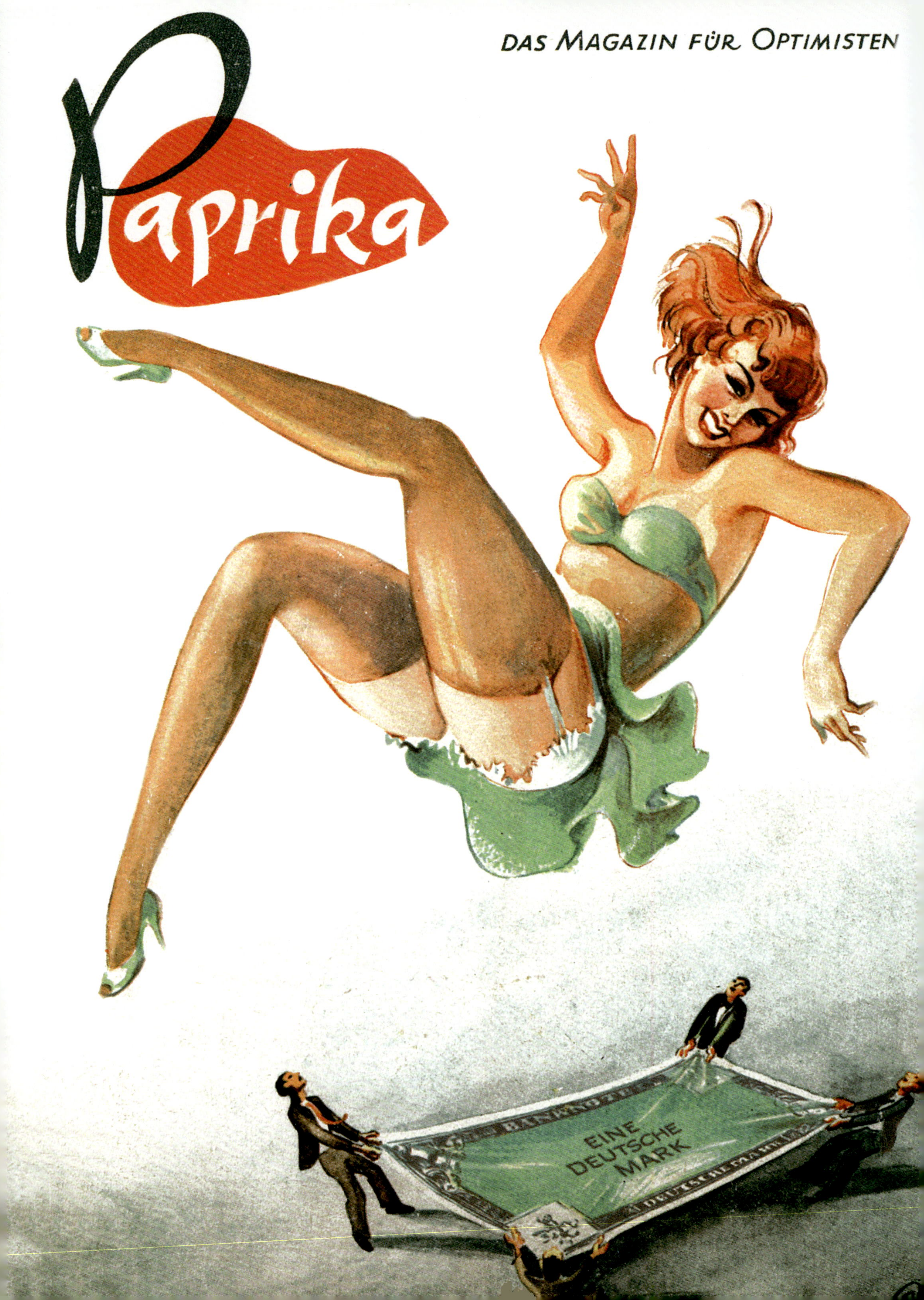
DAS MAGAZIN FÜR OPTIMISTEN
Paprika
EINE
DEUTSCHE
MARK

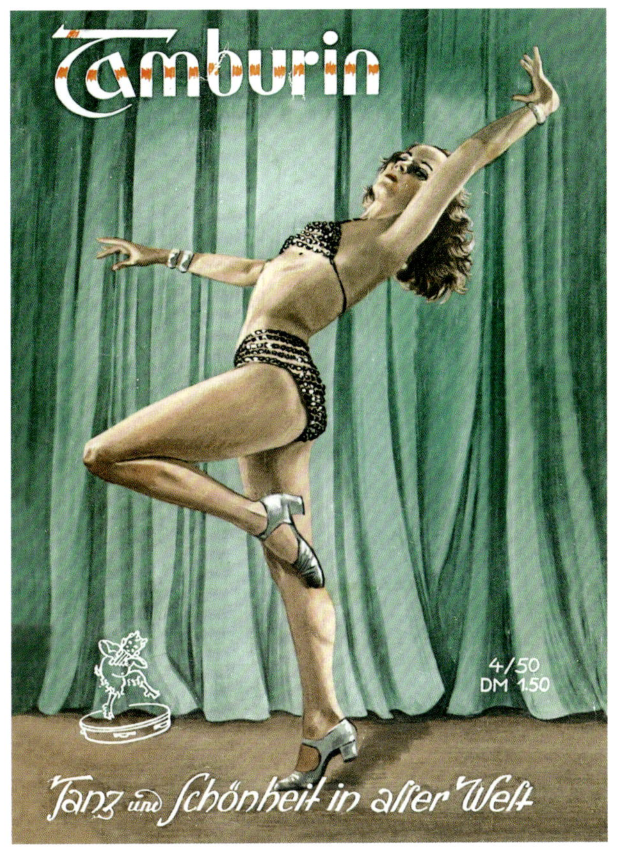

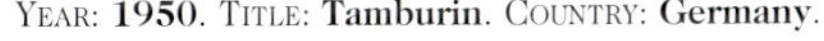

Year: **1950**. Title: **Tamburin**. Country: **Germany**.

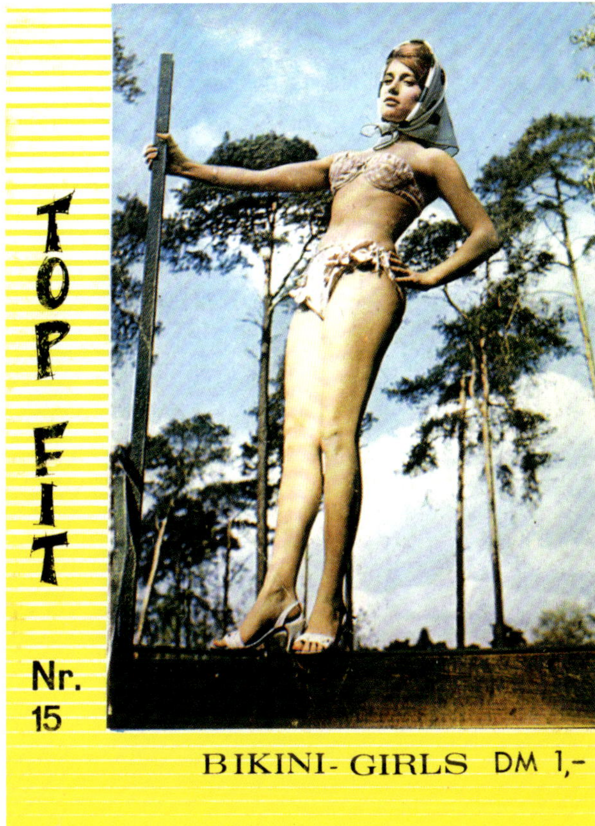

Year: **1950s**. Title: **Top Fit**. Country: **Germany**.

Left: Year: **1950s**. Title: **Paprika**. Country: **Germany**.
Below: Year: **1950**. Title: **Wörterbuch des Sexuallebens**. Country: **Germany**.

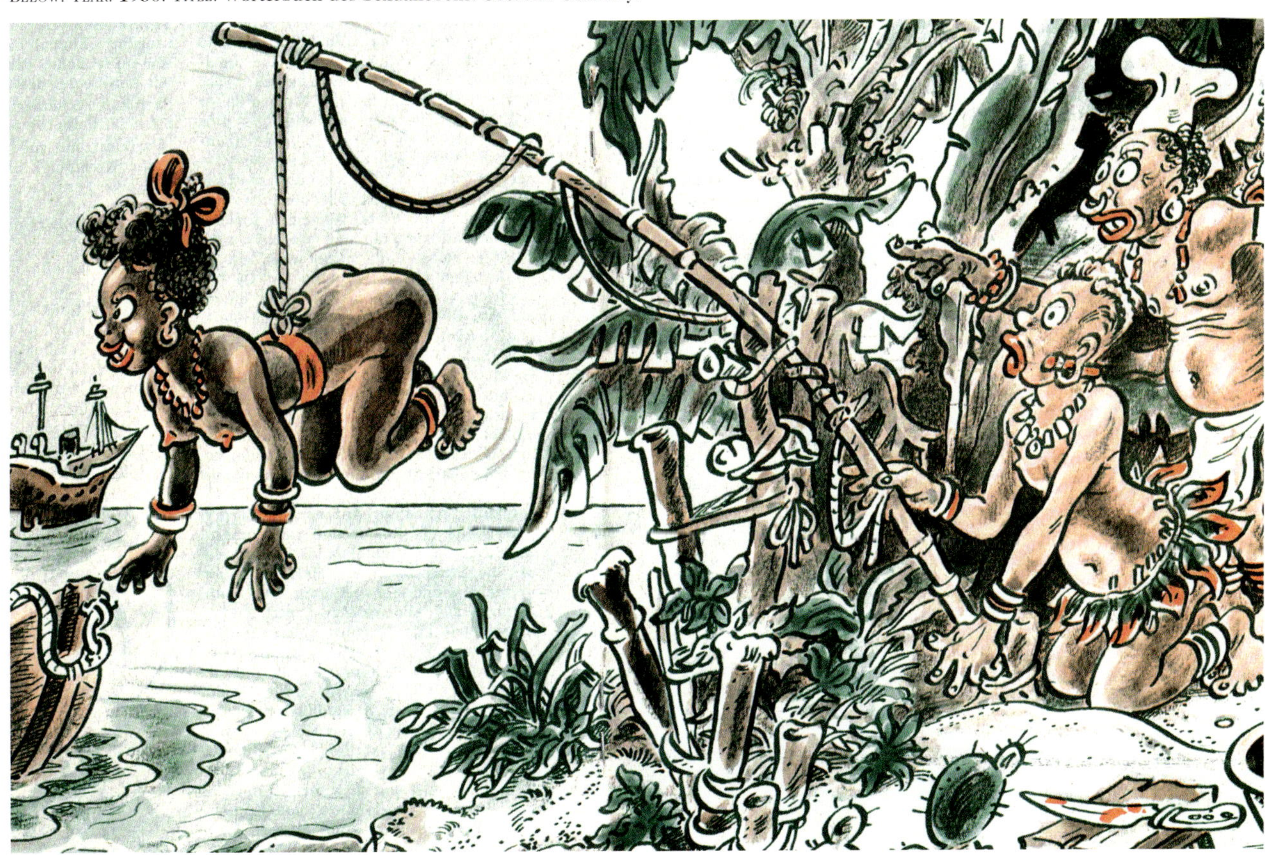

"The Magazine For Optimists" assumed the cure for Germany's post-war woes was humor and scantily clad frauleins.

Das Magazin für Optimisten *ging wohl davon aus, das deutsche Nachkriegselend ließe sich am ehesten mit Humor und leicht geschürzten Fräuleins verdrängen.*

« Le magazine des optimistes » soutenait que le remède aux malheurs de l'Allemagne d'après-guerre était l'humour et les fräuleins légèrement vêtues.

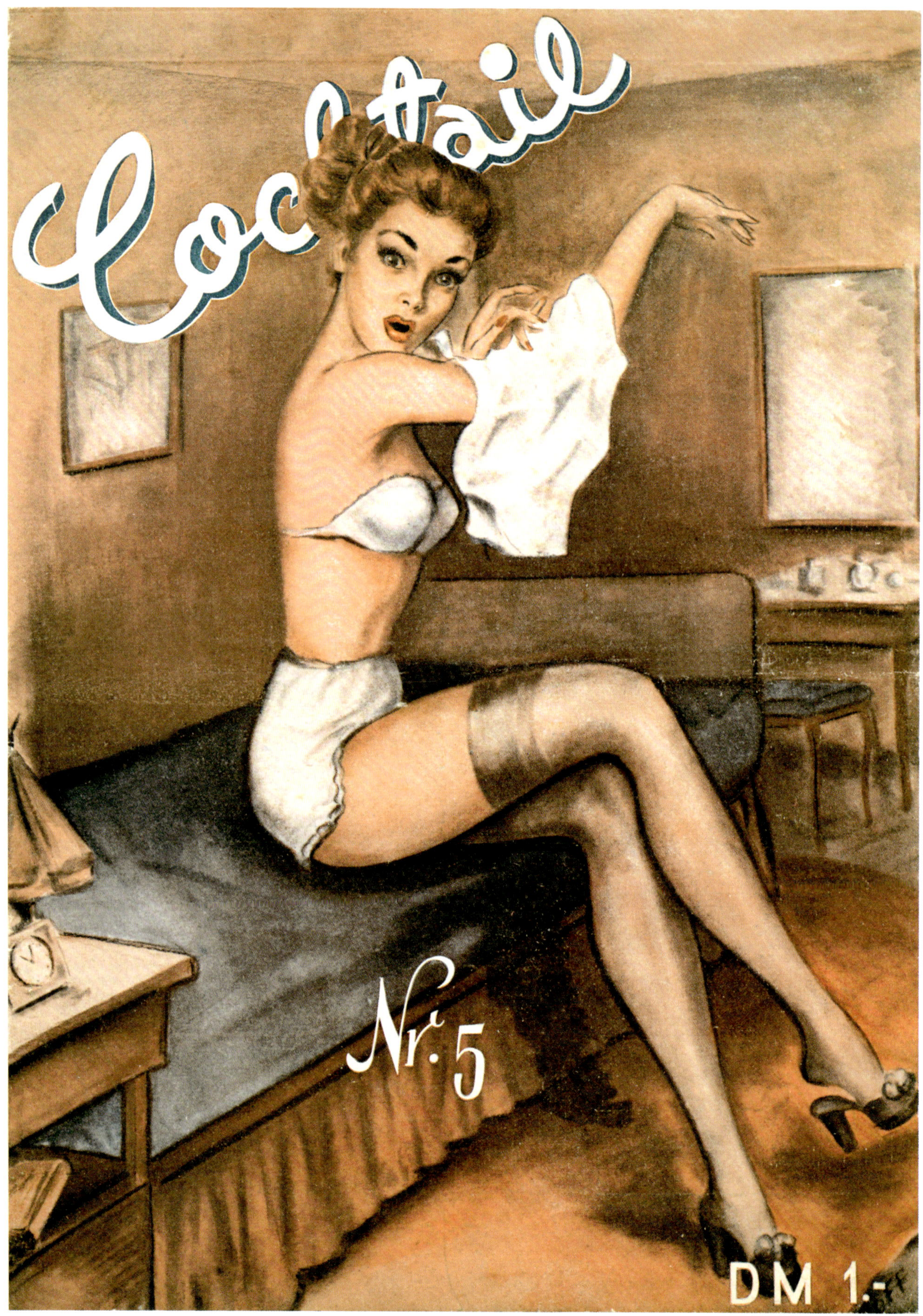

YEAR: **1951**. TITLE: **Cocktail**. COUNTRY: **Germany**.

YEAR: **1950**. TITLE: **Wörterbuch des Sexuallebens**.
ARTIST: **Manassé**. COUNTRY: **Germany**.

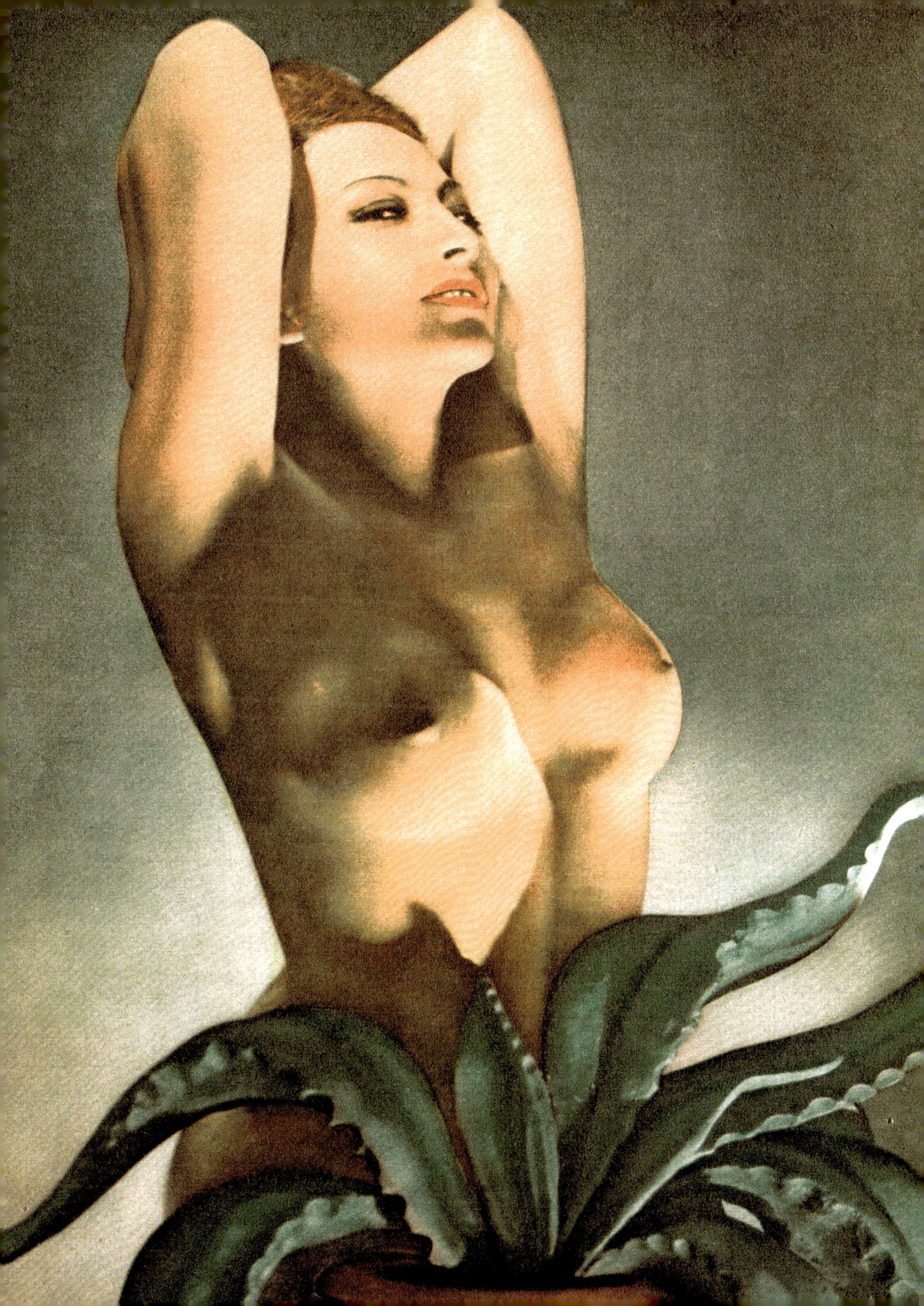

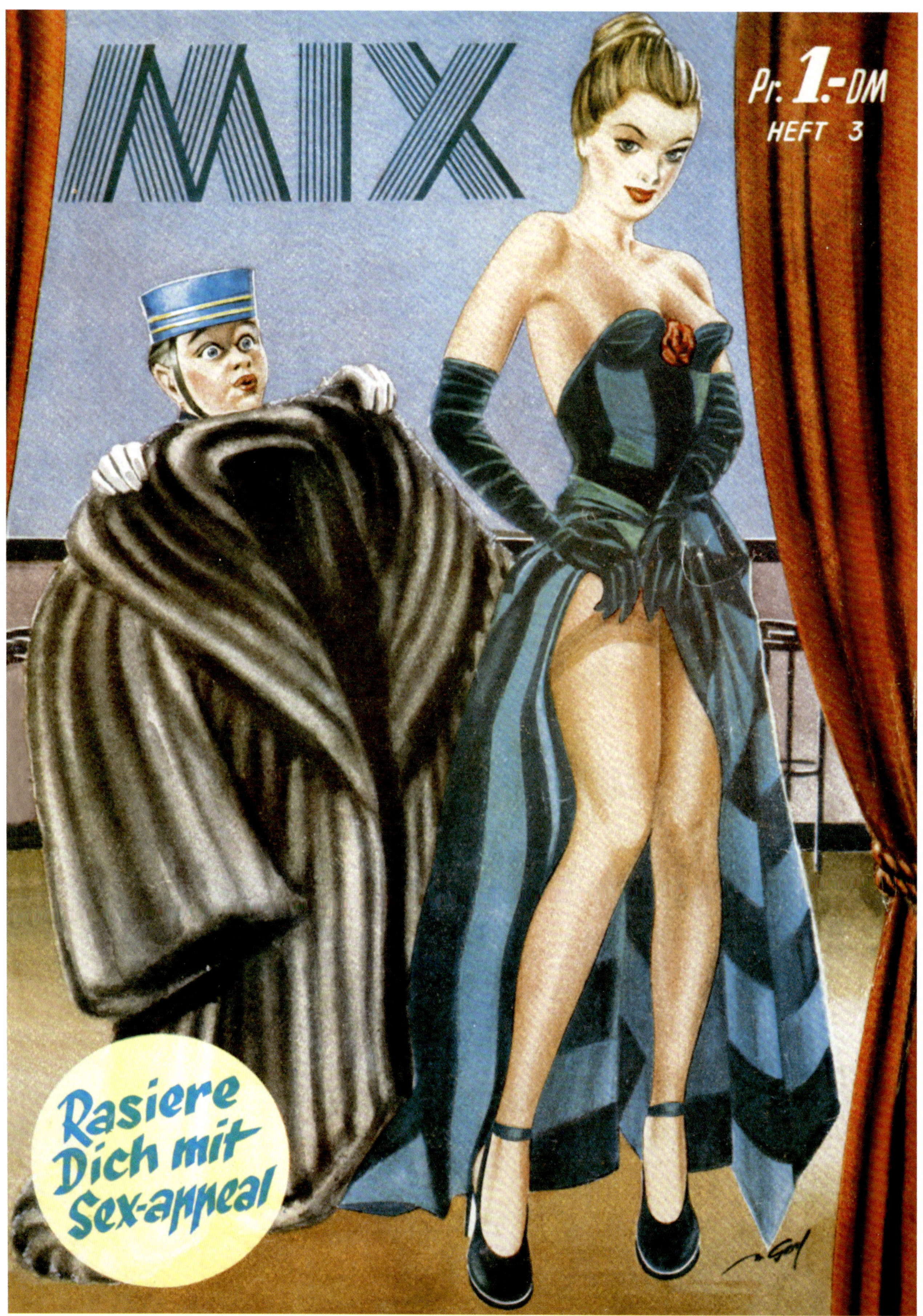

YEAR: **1950s**. TITLE: **Mix**. COUNTRY: **Germany**.

YEAR: **1952**. TITLE: **Neue Melange**. COUNTRY: **Germany**.

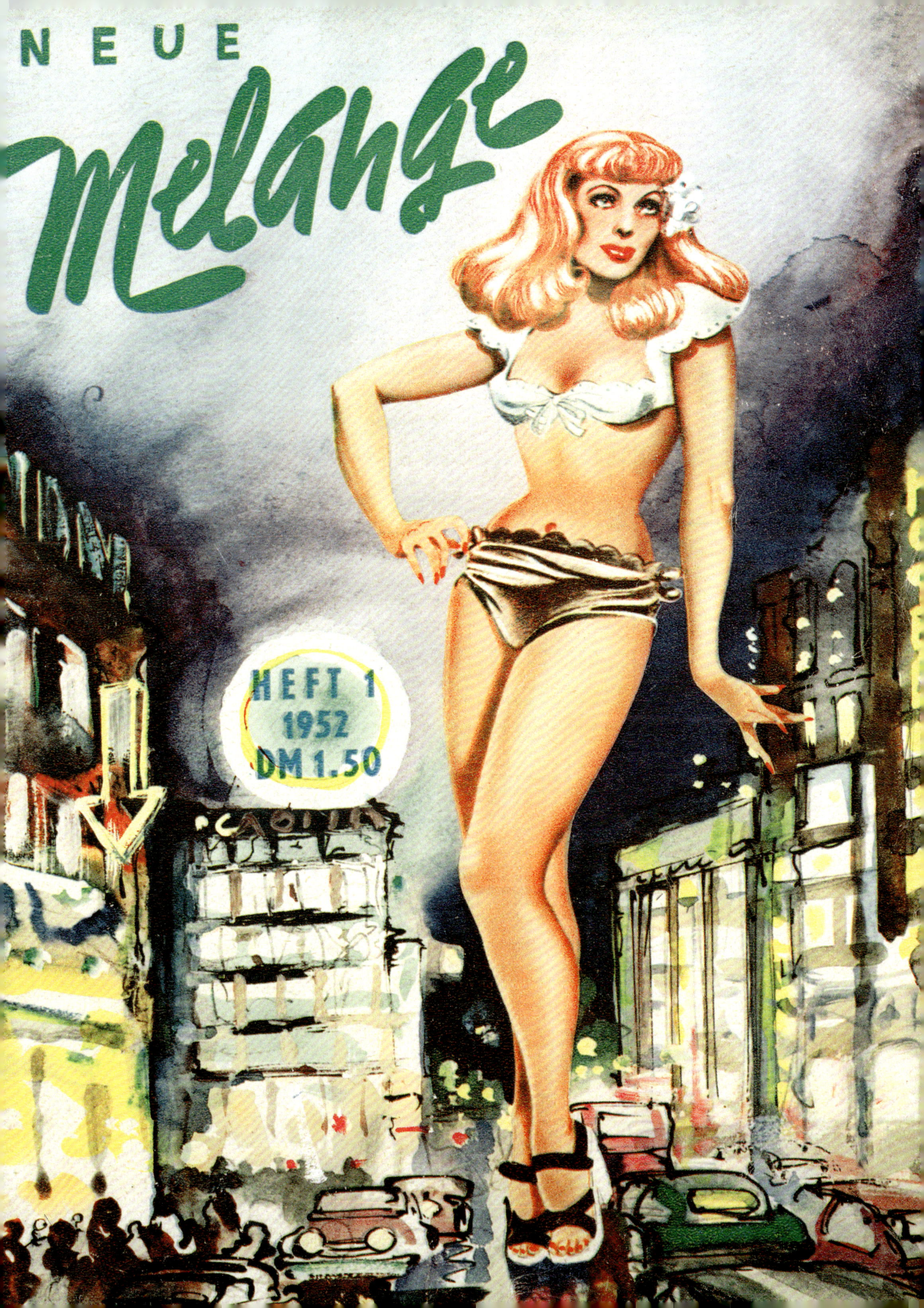
NEUE
Melange
HEFT 1
1952
DM 1.50

Venus

BARBARA PAYTON
Nr. 4
Strengstes
Verkaufsverbot an Jugendliche
FOTO: M.P.E.A.
S 3.—

YEAR: **1949**. TITLE: **Venus**. COUNTRY: **Germany**.

Corso

EIN NEUES MAGAZIN
DM 1.-
Nr. 1 1950
Postversandort München

YEAR: **1950**. TITLE: **Corso**. COUNTRY: **Germany**.

La Petite

Nr. 1
1,50 DM

Douze beautés nude à la nature
Zwölf mal Schönheit, Aesthetik, Freude

YEAR: **1950s**. TITLE: **La Petite**. COUNTRY: **Germany**.

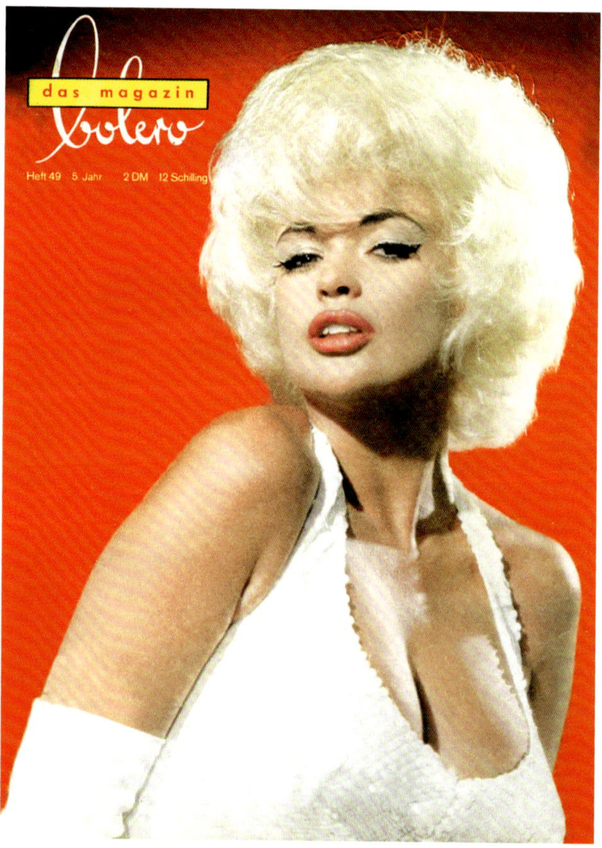

ABOVE & RIGHT: YEAR: **1950s**. TITLE: **Bolero**. COUNTRY: **Germany**.

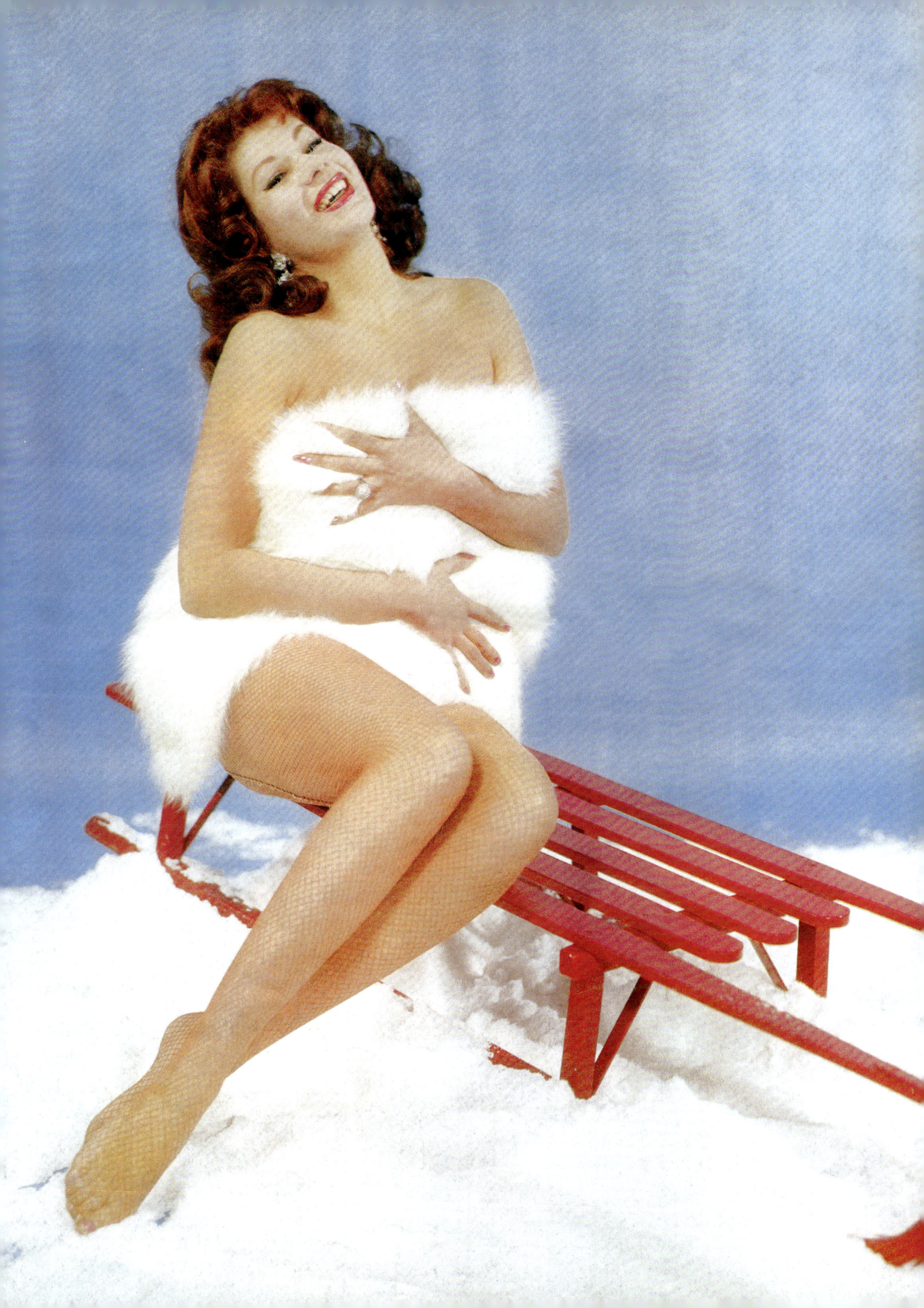

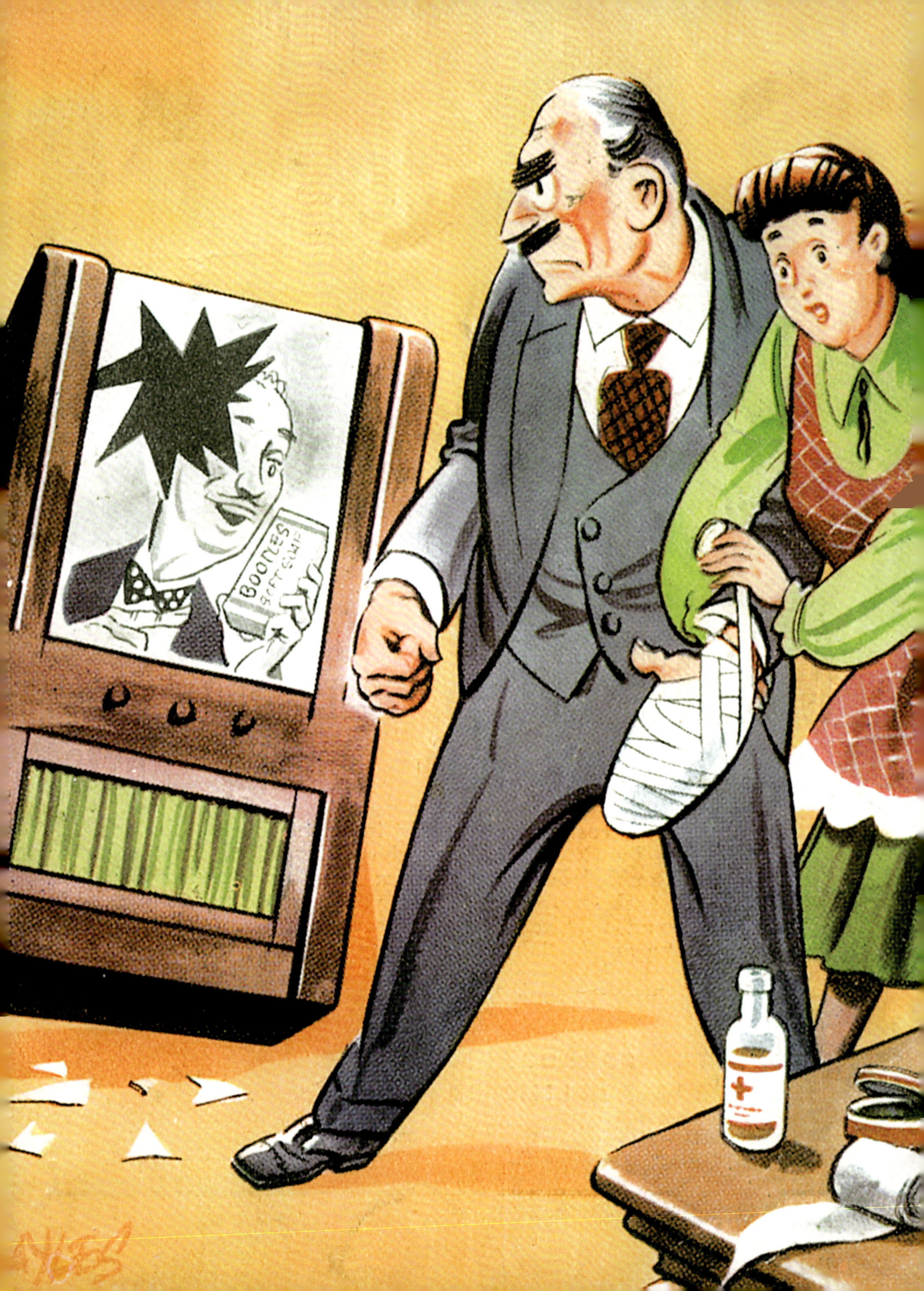
BOONES
SOFT SOAP

THE REST OF THE WORLD:

Obscure Titles from Expected Countries

Der Rest der Welt: Obskure Titel von den üblichen Verdächtigen
Le reste du monde : titres obscurs de nationalités inattendues

One might imagine that since every country contains men, every country would at some time produce some sort of men's magazine. One would be wrong. In many countries, notably the devoutly Islamic ones, the publishing and dissemination of sexual materials was and is a crime. Other countries were too poor to support the large-scale publishing industry required for men's magazines to exist. Sex publishers traditionally prowled the edges of the legitimate industry, relying on the unscrupulous photo processor or the printer in need of a fast buck. Only large-scale publishing could foster the competition needed to create desperate second-rate providers. Just as difficult as publishing was distributing men's magazines. A publisher might make his title out of personal passion, ideology or for financial gain, but the distributor was always a businessman, weighing the pluses and minuses. For this reason

Sex publishers prowled the edges of the legitimate industry, relying on the printer in need of a fast buck.

YEAR: **1949**. TITLE: **The Man**.
ARTIST: **Hayles**. COUNTRY: **Australia**.

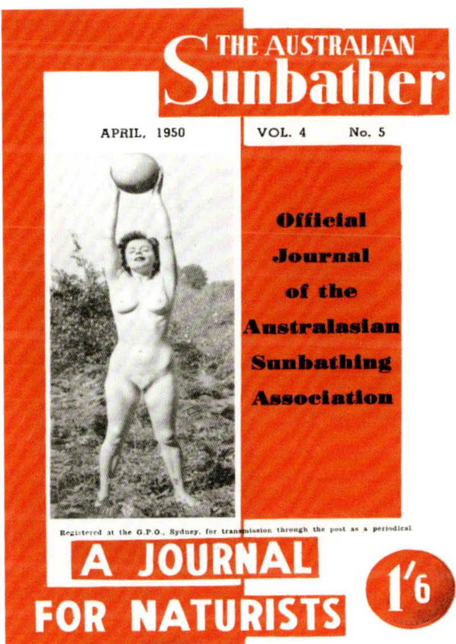

YEAR: **1950**. TITLE: **The Australian Sunbather**.
COUNTRY: **Australia**.

Da es in jedem Land Männer gibt, sollte man denken, dass in jedem Land irgendwann einmal irgendwelche Männermagazine auftauchen, doch dem ist nicht so. In vielen Ländern, insbesondere den streng islamischen, war und ist die Publikation und Verbreitung von allem, was mit Sex zu tun hat, ein Verbrechen. Andere Länder sind einfach zu arm, um die große Verlagslandschaft hervorzubringen, die Männermagazine zum Existieren benötigen. Sexverleger bewegen sich traditionell am Rande der legalen

Dans la mesure où il y existe des spécimens de la gent masculine dans tous les pays, on pourrait croire que tous les pays ont, à un moment ou un autre, produit un magazine pour hommes sous une forme ou sous une autre. Naturellement, on aurait tort. Dans de nombreux pays, notamment ceux pratiquant un islam rigoureux, la publication et la diffusion de documents érotiques étaient et restent un crime. D'autres pays étaient trop pauvres pour entretenir l'industrie éditoriale à grande échelle nécessaire pour qu'existe une presse pour hommes. Les éditeurs spécialisés dans l'érotisme se tenaient traditionnellement en marge de l'industrie légale, se reposant sur l'usage sans scrupules de l'appareil de traitement photo et de l'imprimante pour se faire de l'argent facile. Seule une édition à grande échelle pouvait nourrir une concurrence nécessaire pour créer des rivaux sans espoir de moindre qualité. La distribution de ces magazines était encore plus problématique. Les éditeurs travaillaient par passion, idéologie ou pour l'appât du gain mais le distributeur, lui, était toujours un homme d'affaires, calculant les avantages et les inconvénients. C'est pourquoi cette tâche était souvent confiée à des délinquants, qui l'abordaient comme une activité rentable à haut risque au même titre que le trafic de drogue et d'armes. Il ne servait

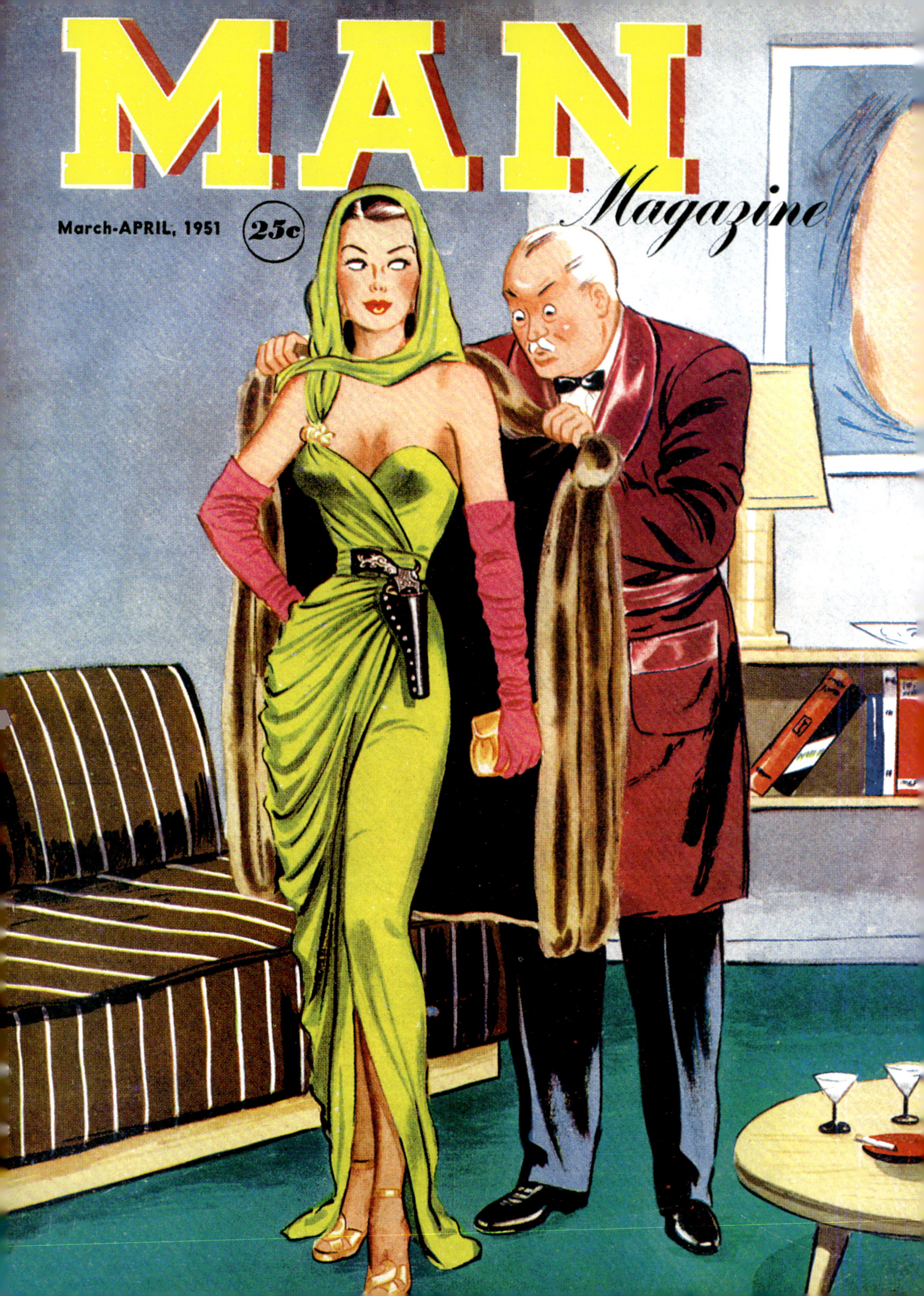
MAN
Magazine
March-APRIL, 1951
25c

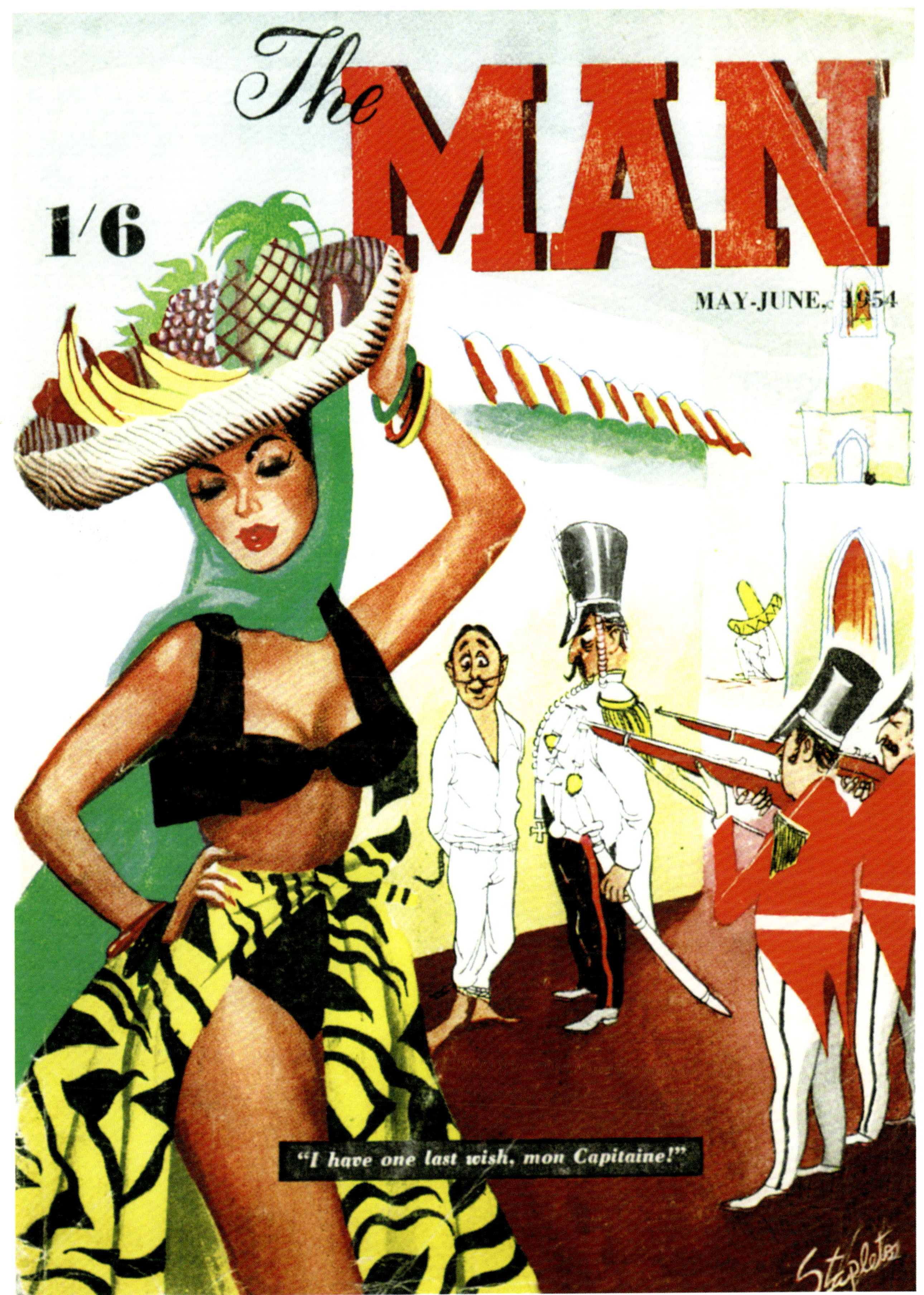

Year: **1954**. Title: **The Man**. Artist: **Stapleton**. Country: **Australia**.

Year: **1951**. Title: **Man Magazine**. Country: **Australia**.

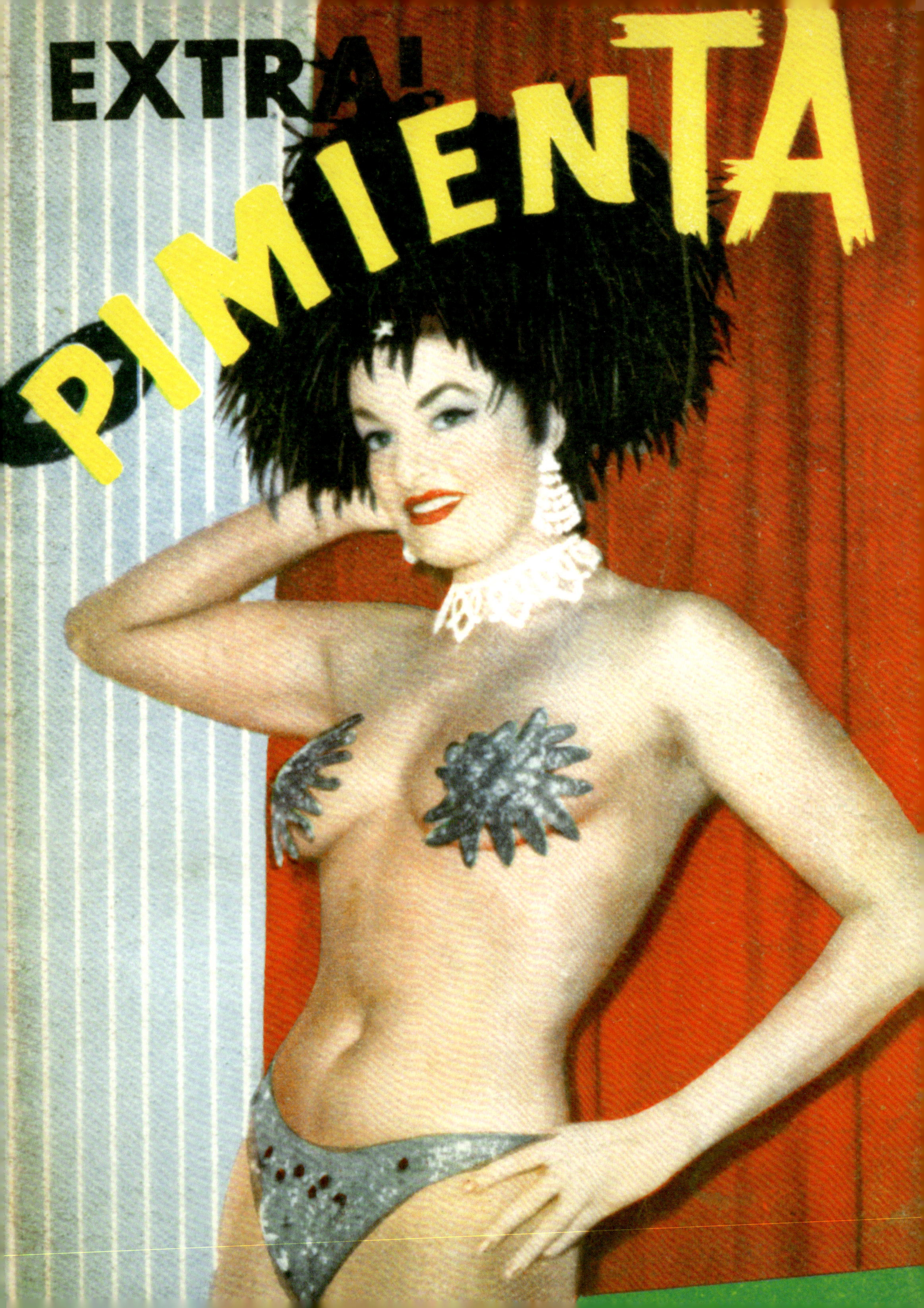
EXTRA!
PIMIENTA

Year: **1950s**. Title: **Pimienta**. Country: **Spain**.

In every modern language, the amount of deliberately pornographic material that has been produced is beyond ready calculation.

—*Sexual Behavior in the Human Female*, Alfred Kinsey, 1953

distribution was often accomplished through criminals, who approached it as a high risk/ high profit operation like drug dealing or gun running. If you couldn't feed the distributor enough magazines for his profits to outweigh his risks, publishing was futile. This is one of the reasons why even in countries that produced many sex magazines publishing was concentrated in one city where all could use the same distributor.

What this reduces to is, a country either made a lot of sex magazines or it made very few. We know the first major producers were France and Germany, followed by the US. Later came England, Mexico, Argentina and Hong Kong, then Sweden and Denmark, Japan and Italy. Other countries, notably Spain and the Netherlands, made magazines, but in my admittedly limited time to search I found only the few examples included here. Cuba, such an infamous center of sin in its time, must either have produced fewer artifacts of that sin than one would expect, or most were destroyed following Castro's take-over. *Show*, a guide to nightclubs and thick-hipped strippers, provides a peek at the pre-Communist fun. Italy, a country

Cuba either produced fewer magazines than one would expect, or most were destroyed following Castro's take-over.

Printlandschaft und sind von skrupellosen Fotolabors oder Druckern abhängig, die schnelles Geld brauchen. Nur eine ausgedehnte Verlagsszene kann den Konkurrenzdruck schaffen, der nötig ist, um verzweifelte Zulieferer der zweiten Garnitur hervorzubringen. Genauso schwierig wie das Verlegen von Männermagazinen ist deren Vertrieb. Ein Verleger mag sein Blatt noch aus persönlicher Leidenschaft, Überzeugung oder des Geldes wegen machen, ein Grossist jedoch ist immer Geschäftsmann, der Profitmöglichkeiten gegen Geschäftsrisiken abwägt. Aus diesem Grund wurde der Vertrieb oft durch Kriminelle abgewickelt, für die das auch kein riskanteres Geschäft als Drogen- oder Waffenhandel war. Wenn man dem Grossisten nicht so viele Hefte geben konnte, dass dessen Risiko dadurch ausgeglichen wurde, hatte es gar keinen Zweck, es zu verlegen. Aus diesem Grund konzentrierten sich häufig auch in Ländern, in denen viele Sexmagazine erschienen, die Verlage in einer Stadt, damit alle den gleichen Vertrieb nutzen konnten.

Letztlich läuft es darauf hinaus, dass ein Land entweder sehr viele oder nur sehr wenige Sexmagazine produziert. Wie wir wissen, waren Frankreich und Deutschland die ersten großen Produzenten, gefolgt von den USA. Später kamen England, Mexiko, Argentinien und Hong Kong hinzu, dann Schweden und Dänemark, Japan und Italien. Auch andere Länder wie Spanien und die Niederlande produzierten Männermagazine, aber in der begrenzten Zeit konnte ich nur die wenigen Beispiele zusammentragen, die hier abgebildet sind. Kuba, vor Castro ein berüchtigt sündiges Pflaster, produzierte entweder weniger Zeugnisse

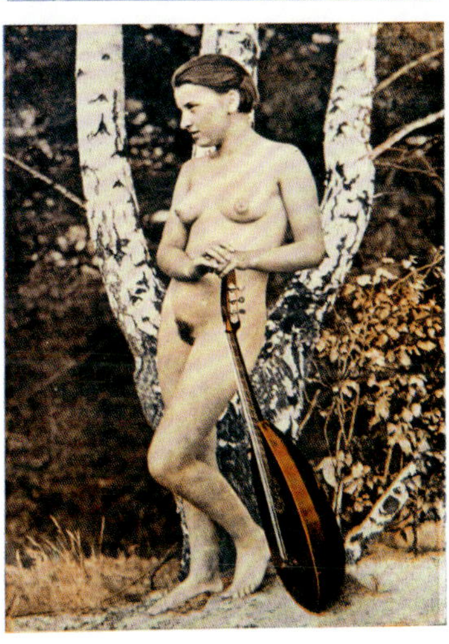

Year: **1935**. Title: **Almanaque Pentalta**. Country: **Spain**.

à rien d'éditer des magazines si vous ne pouviez pas en fournir suffisamment au distributeur pour que le risque en vaille la peine. Ce qui explique que, même dans les pays qui produisaient beaucoup de magazines érotiques, l'activité se limitait à une seule ville où tous les éditeurs pouvaient utiliser le même distributeur.

En résumé, un pays produisait soit beaucoup soit très peu de magazines de charme. Nous savons que les premiers producteurs furent la France et l'Allemagne, suivis par les États-Unis. Plus tard vinrent l'Angleterre, le Mexique et l'Argentine, puis la Suède, le Danemark, le Japon et l'Italie. D'autres pays, notamment l'Espagne et les Pays-Bas, en produisaient également mais, au cours de mes recherches (sur un temps limité, j'avoue), je n'ai trouvé que les quelques exemples présentés ici. Cuba, pourtant un lieu de débauche notoire en son

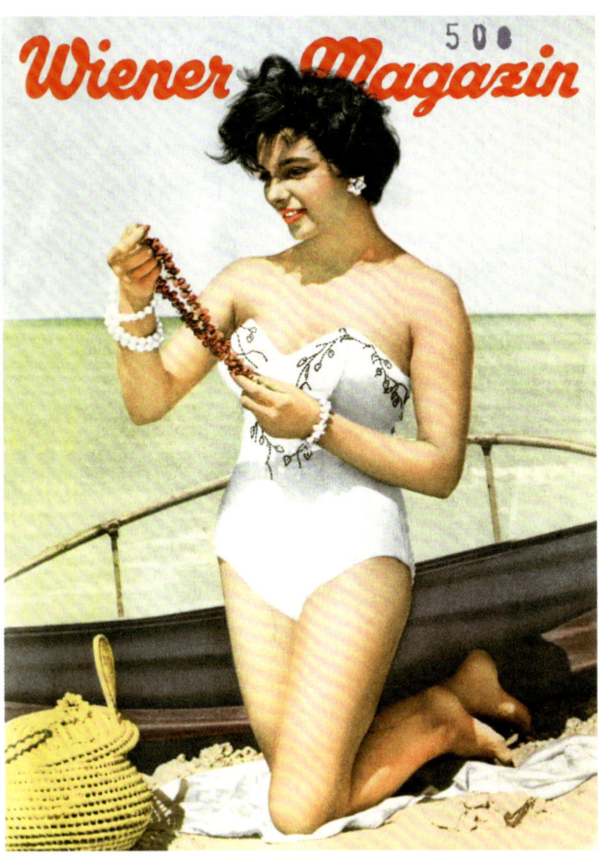

Year: **1957**. Title: **Wiener Magazin**. Country: **Austria**.

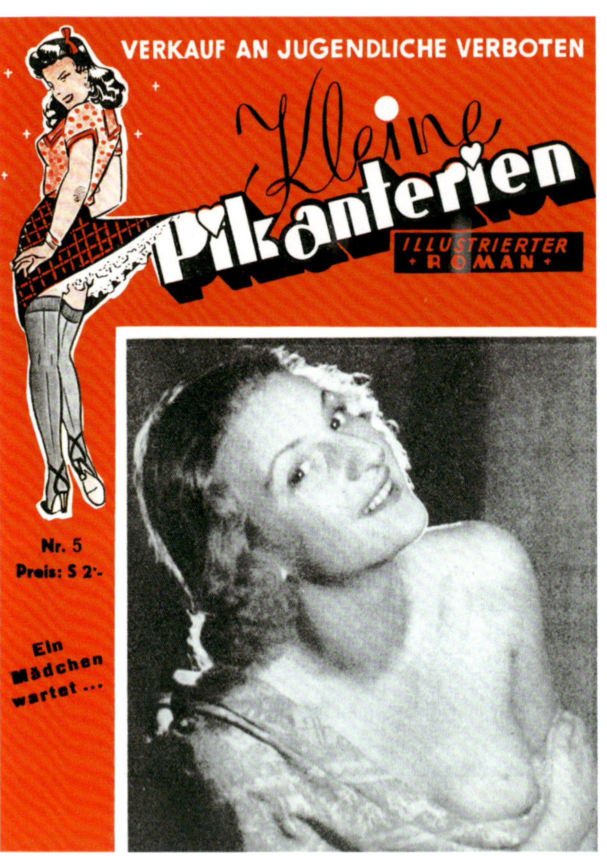

Year: **1946**. Title: **Kleine Pikanterien**. Country: **Austria**.

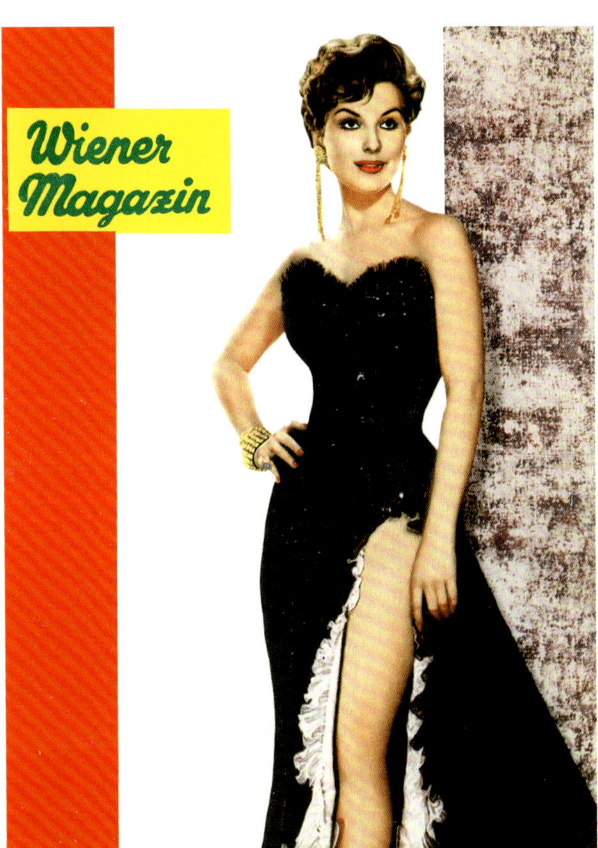

Year: **1958**. Title: **Wiener Magazin**. Country: **Austria**.

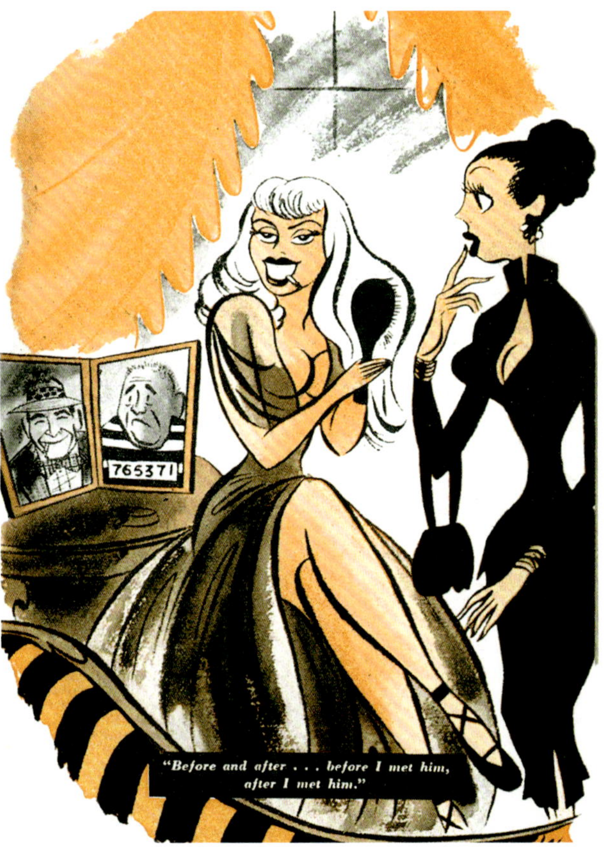

Year: **1949**. Title: **The Man**. Country: **Australia**.

Year: **1930s**. Title: **Mascotte**. Country: **The Netherlands**.

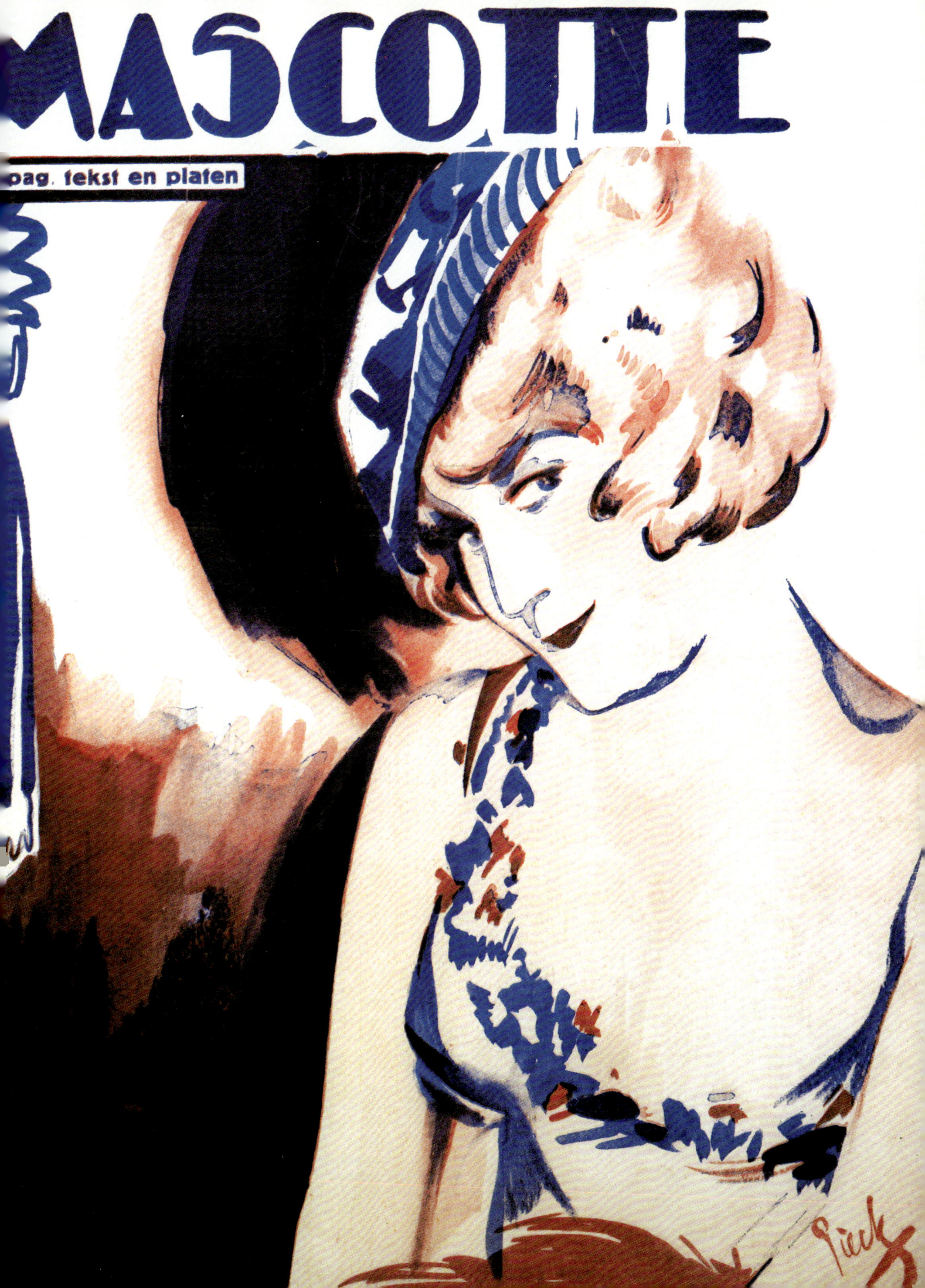
MASCOTTE
pag. tekst en platen
Pieck

Kleine Pikanterien announces its focus is sex rather than nudism by painting panties on its nudist photos.

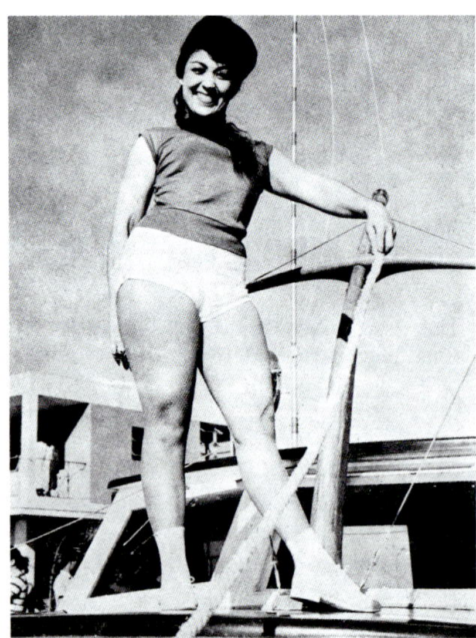

YEAR: **1960**. TITLE: **Show**. COUNTRY: **Cuba**.

that outlawed nudity until the late 1960s, produced a few photo-illustrated adult fiction magazines in the mid-40s. Perhaps such things were overlooked in the post-war chaos. Austria and Switzerland were responsible for several nudist magazines in the 40s and 50s but little true erotica, though I did find *Kleine Pikanterien*, a late-40s title from Vienna that announces its focus is sex rather than nudism by painting panties on its nudist photos.

The surprise for me among the minor producers was Australia. The Aussies have a thriving sex magazine industry today but I'd have thought they were too busy keeping the kangaroos down to publish *The Man* in 1954, a powerful, basic title perfectly in keeping with this rugged continent. I hope at some point to follow up this book (and its sister volumes) with one on the most obscure examples of sex magazines. By then I'm sure to have tracked down those rumored Turkish, Indian, Rumanian and South African titles.

der Sünde, als man erwartet hätte, oder die meisten wurden nach Castros Machtübernahme vernichtet. *Show*, ein Führer zu den Nachtklubs und Stripperinnen mit ausladenden Oberschenkeln, erlaubte einen kleinen Blick auf die vorkommunistische Zeit. In Italien, wo Nackte bis in die späten Sechziger ungesetzlich waren, gab es nach dem Krieg ein paar mit Fotos illustrierte Fiction-Magazine für Erwachsene. Vielleicht wurden sie in den Nachkriegswirren einfach übersehen. Österreich und die Schweiz haben in den Vierzigern und Fünfzigern verschiedene Nudistenmagazine produziert, aber wenige echte Erotika, obwohl ich *Kleine Pikanterien* entdecken konnte, ein in den späten Vierzigern in Wien verlegtes Heft, das die Tatsache, dass es ihm mehr um Sex als um Nudismus ging, dadurch kenntlich machte, dass man Höschen über Nudistenfotos malte!

Eine Überraschung unter den kleineren Produzenten war für mich Australien. Heute hat Australien eine blühende Sexmagazin-Industrie, aber ich hätte gedacht, dass man 1954 noch vollauf damit beschäftigt war, der Kängurus Herr zu werden, anstatt mit *The Man* ein kraftvolles, zupackendes Magazin zu gründen, das hervorragend zu diesem rauen Kontinent passte. Ich hoffe, dass ich einmal Gelegenheit haben werde, diesem Buch (und seinen Geschwistern) ein Buch mit den obskursten Sexmagazinen der Welt folgen zu lassen. Bis dahin werde ich hoffentlich die Hefte aus der Türkei, Indien, Rumänien und Südafrika aufgespürt haben, von denen gemunkelt wird.

temps, produisit beaucoup moins de représentations de cette débauche qu'on aurait pu le croire, à moins que presque tout ait été détruit après la révolution castriste. *Show*, un guide des night-clubs où se produisaient des strip-teaseuses aux hanches larges, nous offre un aperçu des réjouissances précommunistes. L'Italie, un pays où la nudité est restée proscrite jusqu'à la fin des années soixante, a vu naître au milieu des années quarante quelques magazines de nouvelles pour adultes illustrées de photos (les censeurs étaient sans doute moins regardants dans le chaos de l'après-guerre). L'Autriche et la Suisse éditèrent plusieurs titres nudistes mais rien de bien folichon. J'y ai néanmoins trouvé *Kleine Pikanterien*, un magazine viennois de la fin des années quarante présentant des photos nudistes sur lesquelles des culottes avaient été peintes, ce qui montre bien qu'il s'agissait de sexe plutôt que de nudisme.

Parmi les producteurs mineurs, c'est l'Australie qui m'a le plus surprise. Les Australiens possèdent aujourd'hui une presse érotique florissante mais j'aurais cru qu'en 1954 ils étaient trop occupés à maîtriser leur population de kangourous pour publier *The Man*, un magazine simple et puissant, parfaitement conforme à ce continent sauvage. J'espère pouvoir un jour donner une suite à cet ouvrage (et ses autres volumes) en me penchant sur les magazines érotiques les plus obscurs. D'ici là, j'aurais sans doute retrouvé la trace de ces fameuses et mystérieuses publications turques, indiennes, roumaines et sud-africaines.

YEAR: **1960**. TITLE: **Show**. COUNTRY: **Cuba**.

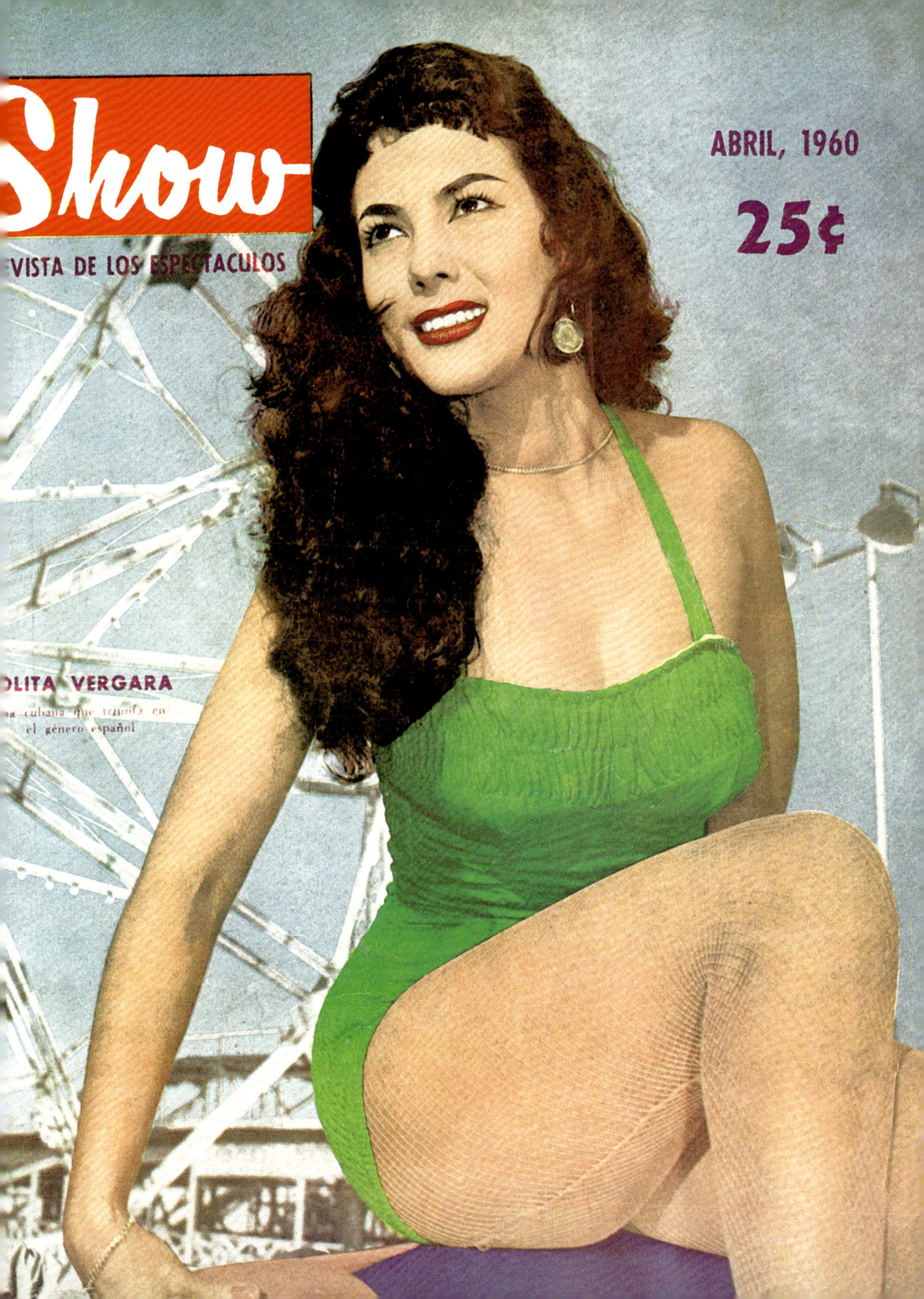
Show
EVISTA DE LOS ESPECTACULOS
ABRIL, 1960
25¢
OLITA VERGARA
a cubana que triunfa en
el género español

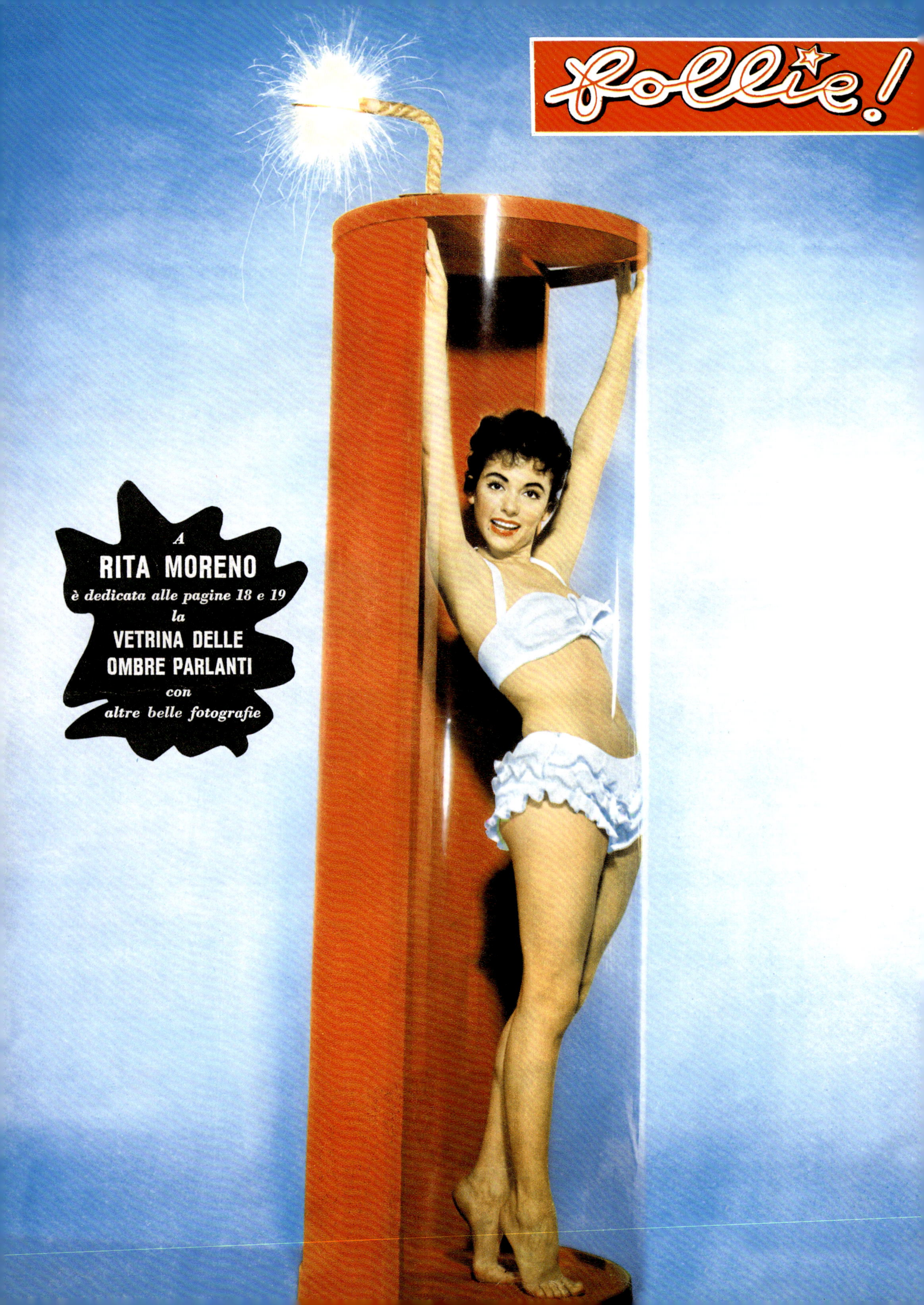

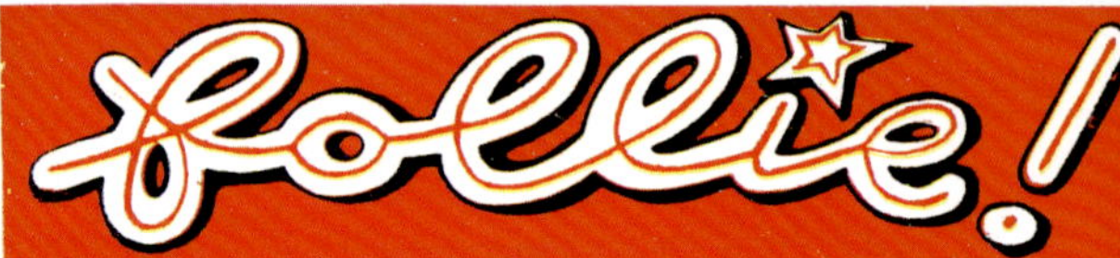

A
RITA MORENO
è dedicata alle pagine 18 e 19
la
VETRINA DELLE OMBRE PARLANTI
con
altre belle fotografie

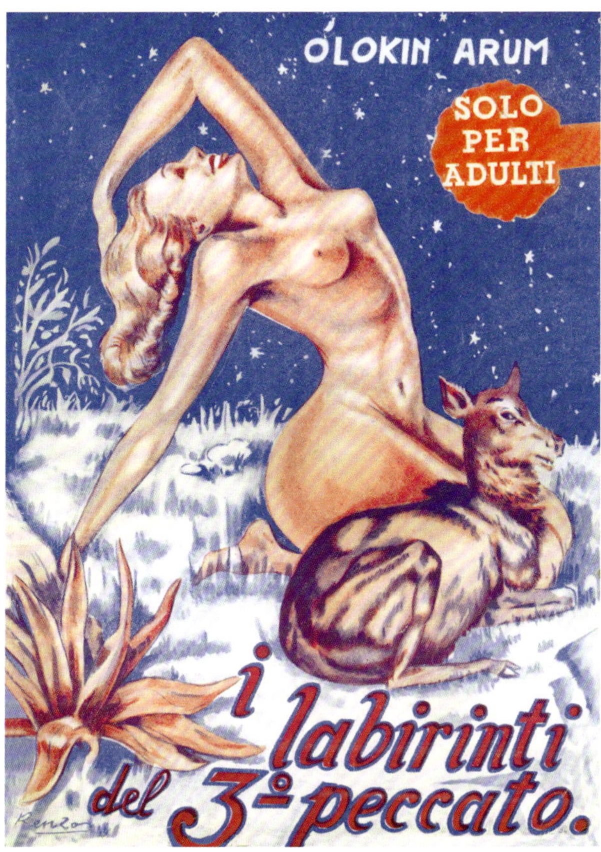

Year: **1946**. Title: **I labirinti del 3° peccato**. Artist: **Renzor**. Country: **Italy**.

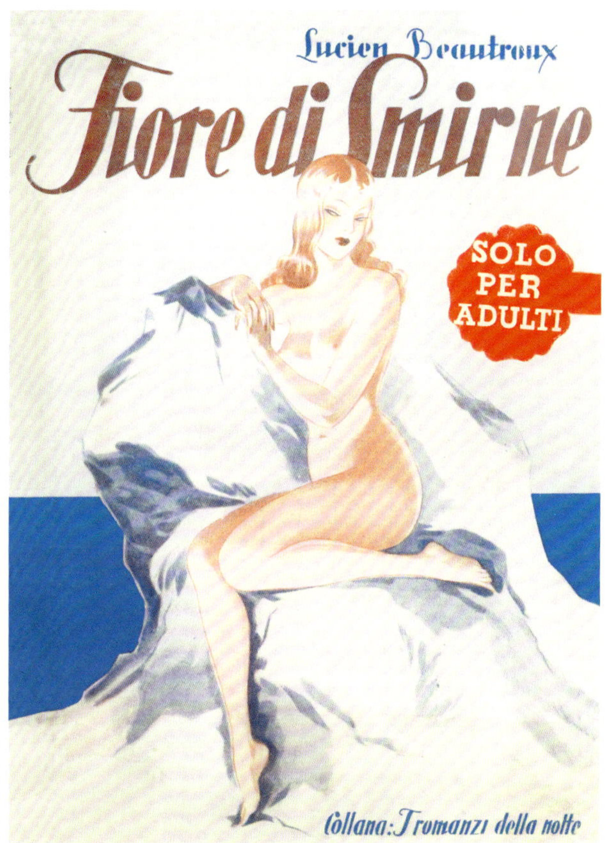

Year: **1946**. Title: **Fiore di Smirne**. Country: **Italy**.

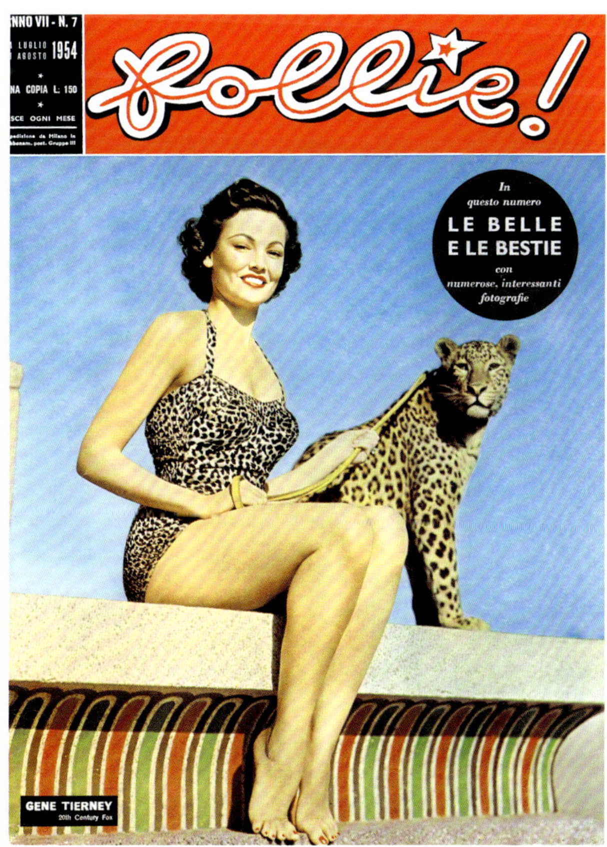

Year: **1954**. Title: **Follie!** Country: **Italy**.

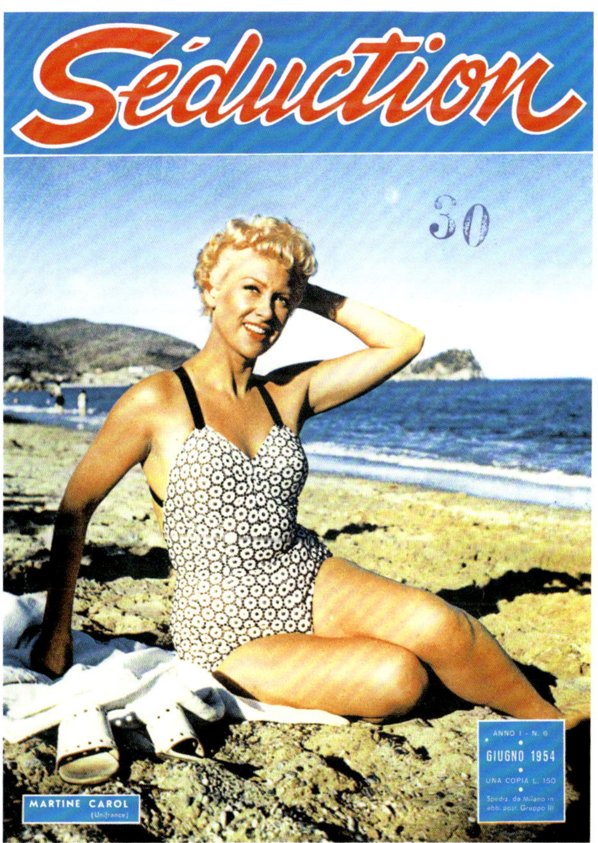

Year: **1954**. Title: **Séduction**. Country: **Italy**.

Year: **1954**. Title: **Follie!** Country: **Italy**.

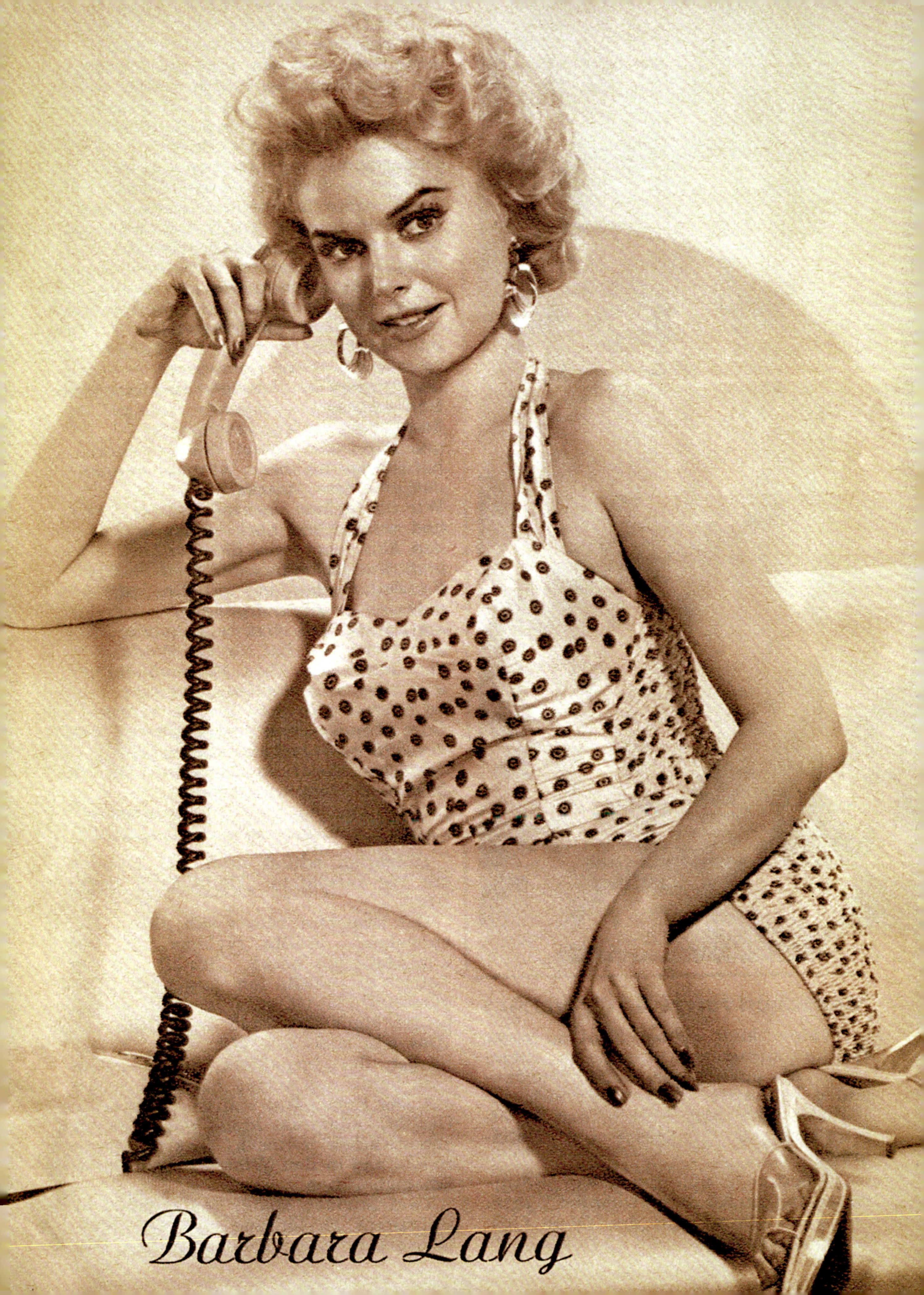
Barbara Lang

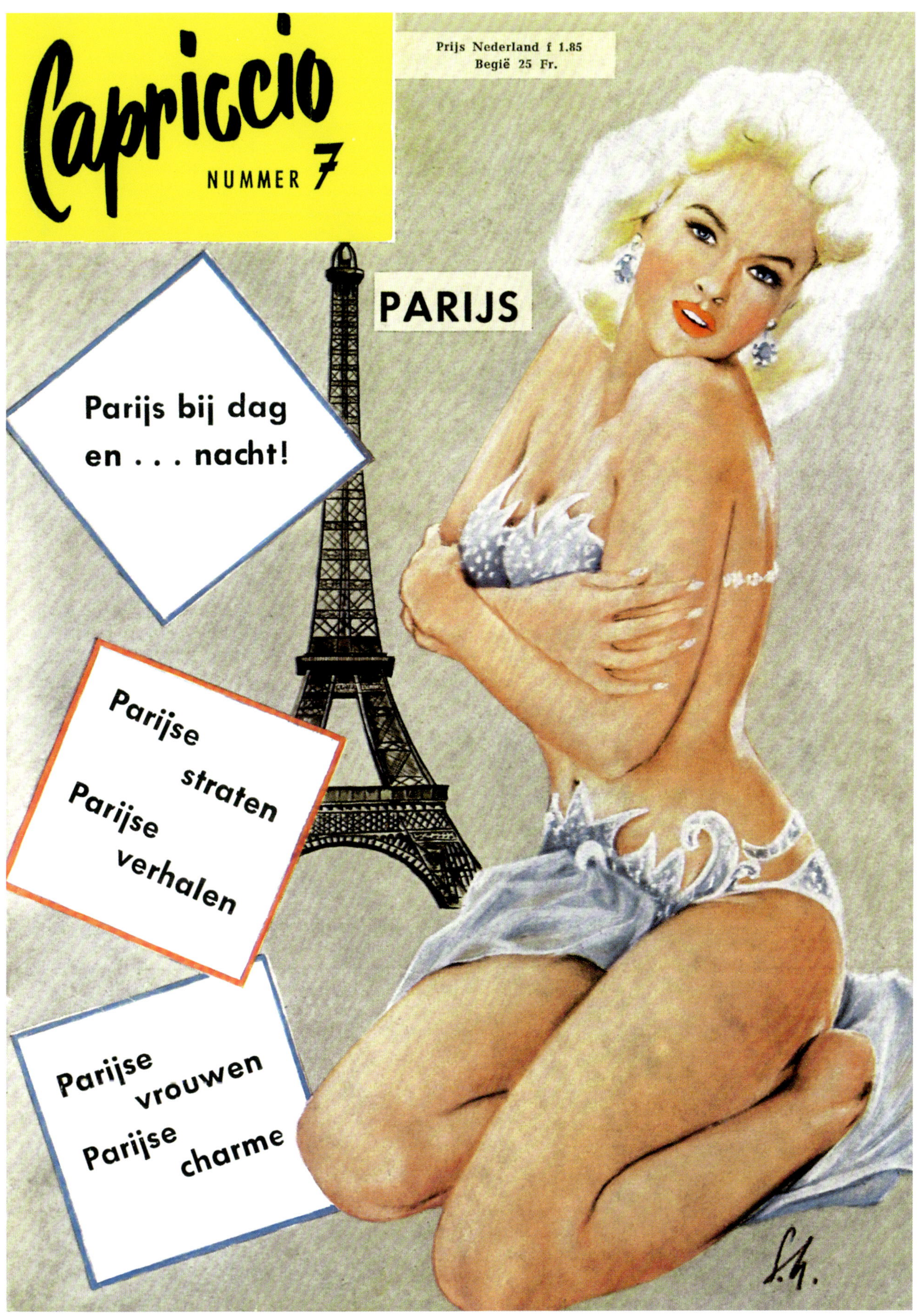

YEAR: **1950s**. TITLE: **Capriccio**. COUNTRY: **The Netherlands**.

YEAR: **1957**. TITLE: **Wiener Magazin**. COUNTRY: **Austria**.

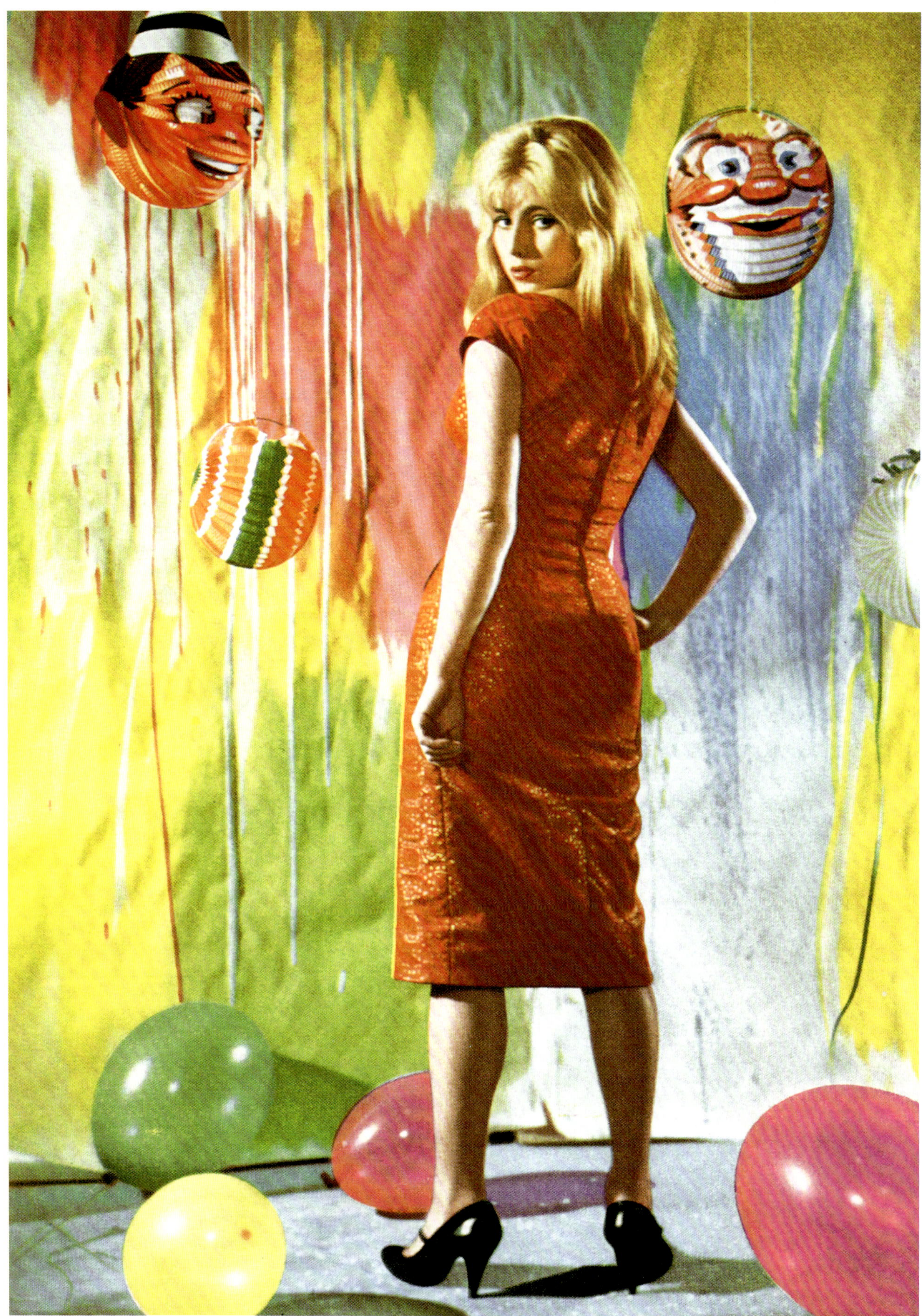

YEAR: **1950s**. TITLE: **Capriccio**. COUNTRY: **The Netherlands**.

YEAR: **1950s**. TITLE: **Capriccio**.
COUNTRY: **The Netherlands**.

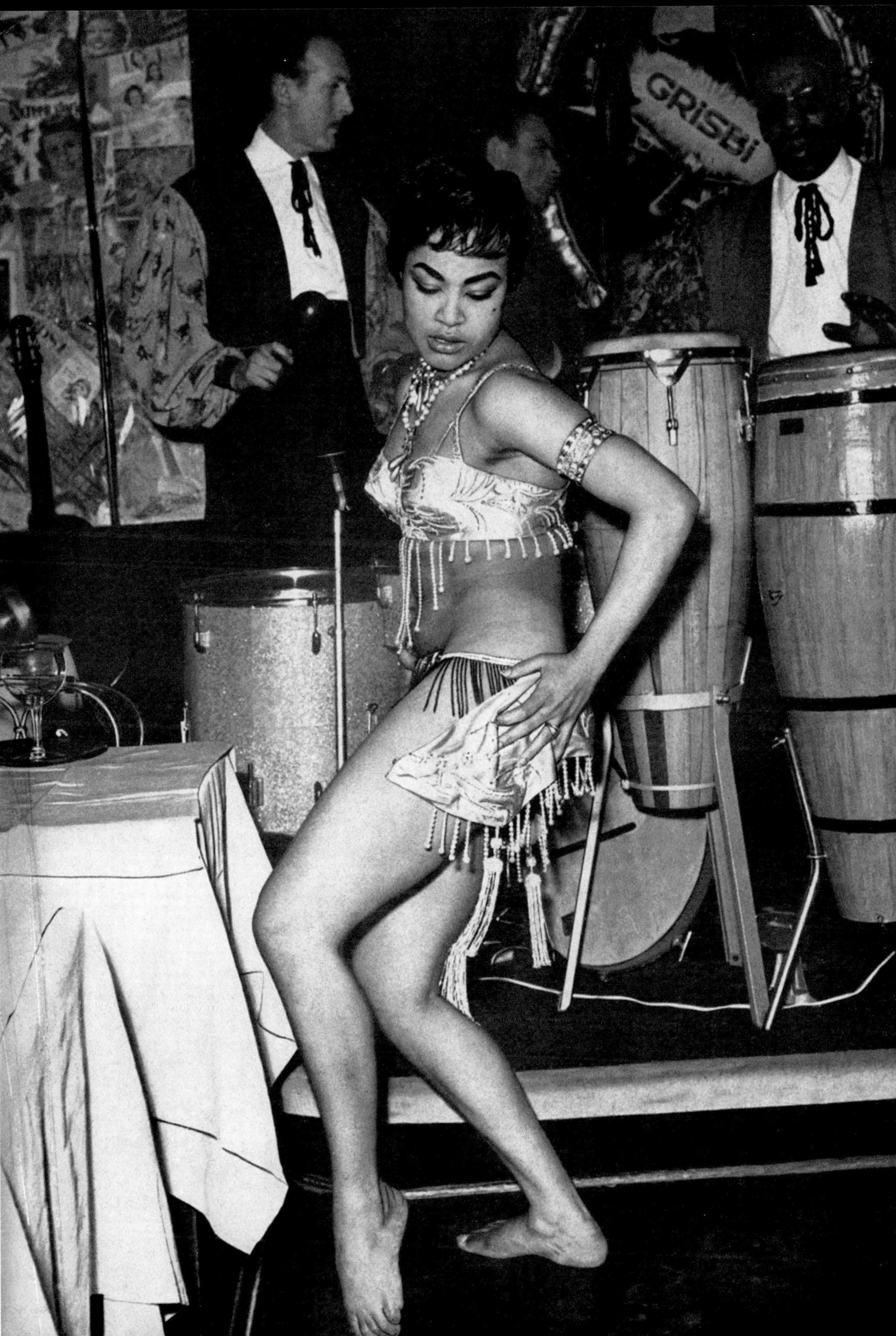
GRISBI

Bibliography

VOLUME I

A listing of every magazine in this volume by chapter, including month and year issued, volume (V), number (N), frequency, publishing company, country of origin and publisher/editor, where known. Note that many men's magazines included little or none of this information to protect the publisher from harassment or arrest, or simply because publishers didn't consider this information vital to its readership.

Introduction: Essence Über Alles

Sidebar: Distribution: How Men's Magazines Were Brought to The Masses

Bedtime Stories August 1933, V2N1, monthly, Nuregal Publishing, USA

Cap'n Joey's Gobs and Gals 1940s, V1N2, bi-monthly, Greenwich Feature Syndicate, USA. Editor—Cap'n Joey

Collection Minuit Pigalle June 1951, N6, Societes des Editions Sprint, France

Comedy Magazine Summer 1951, V2N7, quarterly, Stadium Publishing, USA

French Stories Fall 1933, quarterly, French Stories Publications, USA

Garter Girls 1930s, N7, monthly, Canada

Gay Book December 1944, V6N3, quarterly, Narrative Publishers, USA

Gayety December 1932, V1N2, Shade Publishing, USA

Girlie Gags February 1956, N3, bi-monthly, Arnold Magazines, USA. Editor—Alfred Grenet

Health & Efficiency July 1945, VXVN7, monthly, Link House, England

Hollywood Nights September 1931, V2N6, monthly, Follywood Publications, USA

Howl Fall 1944, Camp Comics, USA

Humor Digest 1939, V1N1, quarterly, Better Publications, USA

Jim Jam Jems September 1930, V20N1, monthly, Graphic Arts, USA

Joker Summer 1943, quarterly, Comedy Publications, USA

Khaki Wacky April 1942, N4, monthly, Comic Corp. of America, USA

L'Amour en Poche 1951, a ***Paris Tabou*** annual, Editions Extentia, France. Editor—Azarian

La Boheme Art Quarterly Winter 1920s, V1N1, Independent Magazine Dist., USA

La Paree Stories January 1931, V2N1, monthly, Irwin Publishing, USA

Le Frou-Frou March 1901, N24, France

Licht und Schönheit January 1952, Walter Lehning Verlag, Germany

Mirth May 1956, N43, bi-monthly, USA

Modellstudien 1950s, N27, Verlag Herbert Mattuschka, Germany

Modelstudier V22N82, quarterly, Forlaget Studia, Denmark. Editor—B. Hansen

Movie Humor October 1935, V2N3, Ultim Publications, USA. Editor—M.R. Reese

Movie Merry-Go-Round July 1937, V2N3, bi-monthly, Periodical House, USA. Editor—Frederick Gardener

Natura 1931, V6N3, Peru

Nifty Stories Aug/Sept 1930, V1N6, monthly, Crown Publishing, USA

Nouvelle Serie de Studio 1950s, N48, Nordisk Bladcentral, Denmark

Paris Music-Hall July 1 1931, N240, bi-weekly, France

Paris Plaisirs N40, France

Paris Studio N4, 1920s, Studio Manasse, Austria

Pep Stories August 1928, monthly, King Publishing, USA

Pep Stories June 1937, V7N6, monthly, D.M. Publishing, USA

Pin-Ups n' Puns Spring 1944, quarterly, Biltmore Publishing, USA

Play-Girl 1950s, N5, Sangko-Norden, Denmark

Pour Lire à Deux January 1935, N8, France

Real Screen Fun August 1938, V4N9, monthly, Tilsam Publications, USA

"Real Smart" Jan/Feb 1931, V2N4, monthly, Crown Publishing, USA

Schönheit 1949, Germany

Screen Humor January 1934, V1N1, monthly, Criterion Magazine Publishing, USA. Editor—Harold Hersey

Sex September 1926, monthly, Dawn Publishing, USA

Showgirls July 1957, N6, bi-monthly, Arnold Magazines, USA

Smiles July 1942, N2, quarterly, Comic Corp. of America, USA

Snap 1949, V1N9, quarterly, Skyline Publications, USA

Snappy May 1932, V2N5, monthly, Lowell Publications, USA. Editor—Virginia O'Day

Snappy Stories July 1936, USA

Squads Riot 1941, Country Press, USA

The Stocking Parade October 1937, V1N3, monthly, Arrow Publications, USA

Stolen Sweets March 1936, V2N3, monthly, Best Publishers, USA

Sun Tan May/Jun 1952, V2N1, bi-monthly, Suntan Publishing, USA. Editor—Donald Johnson

Tidlösa December 1956, N12, Sweden

Visuell 1950s, "sometimes monthly, sometimes quarterly", Amber Forlag, Sweden

Wow! April 1956, N1, bi-monthly, Starland Publications, USA

Zippy March 1939, V2N3, monthly, International Magazine Publishers, Canada. Editor—Howard G. Craig

Chapter 1

Paris 1900–1938: Cradle of Print Erotica

Beauté February 1933, N25, France

Beauté October 1933, N33, as above

Fantasio August 1935, N684, monthly, Societe Anonyme D-Editions Periodiques, France

Fantasio December 1935, as above

Fantasio March 1936, as above

French Frolics, La Vie Parisienne, February 1925, V1N2, monthly, French Frolics Publishing, USA. Editor—Daniel J. Walford

La Vie Parisienne August 29 1925, V63N35, France

Le Journal Amusant August 2 1924, N273, Le Journal Amusant, France. Editor--Jean Pascal

L'Étude Académique 1905 N38, Librairie D-art Technique, France

Le Sourire, 1917, weekly, France

Le Sourire, 1926, as above
Le Sourire June 23, 1927, as above
Le Sourire February 4 1932, as above
Pages Folles Nov/Dec 1934, N14, France
Pages Folles Jan/Feb 1935, N16, as above
Paris Music-Hall September 1 1930, N220, twice per month, France
Paris Music-Hall October 15 1931, N247, as above
Paris Plaisirs, no info
Paris Sex Appeal November 1936, N40, France
Paris Sex Appeal August 1937, N49, as above
Petite Amies 1920s, Les Editions de Paris, France

Chapter 2

American Morals Bifurcated: 1900–1930

10 Story Book March 1925, V24N1, 10 Story Book, USA
10 Story Book May 1928, V26N5, as above
10 Story Book November 1930, V29N5, as above
10 Story Book September 1935, V34N3, as above
Brevities October 17 1932, V8N1, New Broad Publishing, USA. Editor—Myron Hinsch
Burten's Follies February 1925, V3N3, quarterly, Bohemian Magazine, USA. Editor—Jo Burten
Cap'n Joey's Jazza-Ka-Jazza June/July 1922, V1N5, monthly, Jazza-Ka-Jazza Magazine, USA
Dawn Sept/Oct 1920s, Dawn Publishing, USA
Hot Dog March 1925, V4N6, monthly, Merit Publishing, USA
Hot Dog November 1925, V5N2, as above
Jim Jam Jems January 1930, V18N5, Graphic Arts, USA
The Live Wire April 1926, V5N11, Live Wire Magazine, USA
Night Life Stories 1920s, V2N4, monthly, Consolidated Magazine, USA
Old Bob Edwards' Calgary Eye Opener 1930 Year Book 1930, annual, Bob Edwards Publishing, USA
Paris Nights August 1929, V8N1, monthly, The Shade Publishing, USA
Parisienne Revue 1920s, V1N2, Eagle Magazine, USA
Pep Stories August 1928, V4N2, King Publishing, USA
Real French Capers 1920s, V1N24, USA
Sex December 1929, monthly, Dawn Publishing, USA
Shadowland March 1922, monthly, Brewster Publications, USA. Editor Eugene V. Brewster
Smokehouse Monthly May 1929, V3N17, monthly, Fawcett Publications, USA. Publisher/Editor—W.H. (Capt. Billy) Fawcett
Snappy Stories and Pictures April 1928, V107N1, New Fiction Publishing, USA
TNT September 1924, V1N11, monthly, TNT Publishing, USA. Editor—Tim N. Tut
Vanity Fair's May 30 1903, V27N719, weekly, Commonwealth Publishing, USA
Vanity Fair Bifurcated Girls June 6 1903, V27N720, as above

Chapter 3

German Life Reform and Weimar Vice

Berliner Leben 1924, V27N9, Germany, Editor—Egon Strassburger
Berliner Leben 1926, V29N9, as above
Das Freibad 1933, N2, Auffenberg Verlag, Germany
Das Herrenjournal April 1941, Germany
Das kleine Magazin 1938, N16, W. Stolle & Co, Germany
Der Individualist 1928, V1N1, Verlag Emil Wernitz, Germany
Der Leib 1920s, N1, Parthenon Verlag, Germany
Die Aufklärung April 1929, Das Institute fur Sexual-Wissenschaft, Germany. Publisher/Editor—Magnus Hirschfeld
Die Ehe June 1923, E. Ensle, Germany
Die Ehe November 1926, N6, as above
Die Ehe November 1933, Germany. Editor—Friedr. V. Zglinicki
Die Schönheit 1903, V1N10 Verlag der Schönheit, Germany
Die Schönheit 1926, V22N5, as above
Figaro January 1932, V9N1, Auffenberg Verlagsgesellschaft mbH., Germany
Ideal-Ehe March 1928, V2N3, F.R. Edgar Schulz, Germany
Ideal-Lebensbund July 1928, F.R. Edgar Schulz, Germany
Pelagius 1932, N1, Auffenberg-Verlagsgesellschaft mbH, Germany
Reigen 1923, V4N8, Verlag Wilhelm Borngraber, Germany
Reigen 1923, as above
Reigen 1927, as above
Wiener Magazin April 1930, V4N4, Neuzeitlicher Buchverlag, Germany

Chapter 4

For Serious Art Students only: The Rise and Fall of "Model Study" Magazines

Denmark:
Beaute 1950s, n9, Denmark
Modelstudier N13, Imberts Forlag, Denmark. Editor—Niels H. Imbert
Nouvelle Series de Charme, 1950s, Denmark
England:
Charm 1950s, England
Forme et Contour 1950s, Gaywood Press, England
Line and Form 1950s, N1, monthly, Gannet Press, England
France:
Bagatelles Gallantes 1940s, France
Nus Album 1950s, #6, France
Germany:
Atelier February 1958, N30, Germany
Atelier October 1958, N34, as above
Formen und Linien 1960s, German edition of Form and Line, from Edition et Diffusion de Livre Francais, France
L'art et le nu 1950s, Edition Speciale N11, Verlag Herbert Mattuschka, Germany
Sweden:
Foto-Studier 1958, N8, Firma Berwe, Sweden. Editor—I Svensson
Foto-Studier 1964, N11, as above
Swedish Croquis Models 1950s, Amber Forlag, Sweden
United States:
Amateur Art and Camera Winter 1950s, V9N3, quarterly, Camerarts Publishing, USA
Art and Camera September 1955, V6N1, bi-monthly, Camerarts Publishing, USA. Publisher/Editor—Joseph Sorren
Art Group Quarterly Fall 1920s, King Publishing, USA
Art Group Quarterly, Winter 1920s, as above
Artists' Notebook 1930, N6, Graphics Arts, USA
Art Photography February 1951, V2N8, monthly, Art Photography, USA
Brazen Beauty of Belle 1950s, USA
Fiery Flesh of Francine 1950s, USA
Figure Quarterly 1950s V13, apparently from the publisher of Cabaret magazine, USA
French Art 1920s, N7, USA
Girl Pageant 1940s, N3, semi-annual, Dow Periodicals, USA
Girl Pageant N5, as above
Girl Pageant N7, as above
Glamour Photography Summer 1957, N5, Glamour Photography, USA
Model Studies Annual 1950s, V10, an Amateur Art and Camera magazine special edition, USA
The New Models Beautiful 1950s, V9, Greenwich Art Syndicate, USA

Paris Models Artcraft January 1920s, monthly, Educational Art Press, USA
Peter Gowland's Photo Secrets 1958, N1, as above
Photo Arts August 1952, V2N4, Tel Publications, USA. Editor—Ben Peters
Photographer's Masterpieces—The Collection of Philip O. Stearns 1957, V1N1, quarterly, Skye Publishing, USA
Shape 1950s, n3, USA
Screen Art Studies December 1929, V1N2, monthly, Graphic Arts, USA
Torso Del Femme N1, Jaro Publishers, USA. Editor—G.W. Service

Chapter 5
Tijuana Bibles: The Big Boys' Comic Book

Bibles:
Andy Hardy Rides West
Baby Face Nelson in "Oh Yeah"
Burma in "A Dose of Yellow Fever"
Clark Gabel in "The Sheik"
Danielle Darrieux in "The French They Are a Funny Race"
Effie Wood presents Connie in "Oh Doctor!"
Flash Gordon In "Red Hot"
Foozy in "The Decoy"
The Frigidaire Salesman
Harold Teen
He Didn't Speak French
Joan Craford in "The Teaser"
John Dillinger in "A Hasty Exit"
Jungle Jim in "Lil Goes Straight"
Machine Gun Kelly In "The Kidnapper"
Maggie
Moon Mullins
Phil Fumble
The Professor Makes Jane An Honor Student
Remember Way Back When
A Scotchman's Hole In One
Sonja Henie and Tyrone Power in "Hot Stuff On The Ice"
Stella Clinker in "Too Weak"

Readers:
A Prick Has No Conscience, All Sport Fornications Press
Cora And Her Wants, M. Seuferin, Nice, France (actually USA)
A Father Eluded 1935, as above
Hot Shots N1, Noveltype Publishers, USA
The Mad Fuckers, Mod Mod Fornications Press, USA
Seven Whores, Paris, France (actually USA)
Tantalizing Tales, Requoit Publishing, Paris, France (actually USA)
This Was Their Love, Bibliotheque St. Germaine, Paris (actually USA)
Through a Door, USA
What a Wonderful Fucking World, Mod Mod Fornications Press, USA

Chapter 6
Spicy Pulps of the 1930s: Hot Words under Glossy Covers

Beauty Parade October 1941, V1N1, Beauty Parade, USA. Editor—Lee Mortimer
Breezy Stories April 1937, bi-monthly, Phil Painter Publications, USA
Broadway Nights July 1931, monthly, King Publishing, USA
Cupid's Capers December 1933, Nuregal Publishing Corp, USA
French Follies November 1930, V2N4, Follywood Publications, USA
French Follies, February 1930s, USA
Gay French Life January 1939, V1N1, monthly, Eagle Magazine, USA
Gay Parisienne July 1933, V4N7, monthly, Merwil Publishing, USA
Ginger Stories December 1928, V1N2, King Publishing, USA
High Heel Magazine April 1937, V1N1, monthly, Ultem Publications, USA
La Paree Stories July 1930, V1N4, monthly, Irwin Publishing, USA
La Paree Stories March 1934, V5N3, monthly, Merwil Publishing, USA
Modern Girl Book March 1939, V1N1, bi-monthly, Lex Publications, USA
Nifty Stories December 1930, V2N3, Crown Publishing, USA
Paris Nights February 1930, V8N7, monthly, Shade Publishing, USA
Paris Nights June 1930, V8N11, as above
Paris Nights, as above
"Real Smart" Aug/Sept 1930, V1N6, Crown Publishing, USA
Silk Stocking Stories January 1939, V3N6, monthly, Lex Publications, USA
Snappy February 1934, V13N2, monthly, Merwil Publishing, USA. Editor—Merle W. Hersey
Snappy June 1936, V15N6, monthly, D.M. Publishing, USA
Speed Detective June 1945, V4N1, bi-monthly, Trojan Publishing, USA
Speed Mystery March 1943, V1N3, as above
Spicy Detective June 1941, Culture Publications, USA
Spicy Stories June 1932, V7N7, monthly, Merwil Publishing, USA
Spicy Stories November 1936, V7N11, monthly, as above
Spicy Western Stories November 1941, V8N4, Culture Publications, USA
Spicy Western Stories December 1942, V8N4, as above
Stolen Sweets August 1935, V1N4, Nudeal Publishing, USA
Stolen Sweets December 1930s, as above
Studio Life 1930s, USA
Tid Bits of Beauty Summer 1943, quarterly, Personality Publications, USA

Chapter 7
Naughty Magazines about Naughty Films

Film Fun September 1933, V59N533, monthly, Dell Publishing, USA. Editor—Lester C. Grady
Film Fun February 1933, V58N526, as above
Film Fun January 1934, V61N537, as above
Film Fun February 1934, V61N538, as above
Film Fun October 1936, V58N570, as above
Film Fun November 1936, V58N571, as above
Film Fun January 1938, V68N585, as above
Film Fun November 1939, V71N607, as above
Film Fun May 1940, V71N613, as above
Film Fun April 1941, V71N624, as above, but Editor—Victor Bloom
Film Fun November 1941, V71N631, as above
Film Fun January 1942, V72N633, as above
Film Fun August 1942, V72N640, as above, but Editor—Charles Saxon
Film, Tanz, Exotik 1928, an EOS Special, Germany
French Peep Show 1952, one shot, P.A. DeCenzie, USA
Movie Fun September 1940, V1N1, monthly, Crestwood Publishing, USA
Movie Humor September 1934, V1N4, monthly, Norwood Publishing, USA
Movie Humor November 1934, V1N6, as above
Movie Humor January 1935, V4N6, as above
Movie Humor February 1936, V2N7, Ultim Publications, USA. Editor—M.R. Reese
Movie Humor March 1936, V2N8, as above
Movie Humor June 1936, V2N11, as above
Movie Humor July 1936, V2N12, as above
Movie Humor September 1936, V3N2, as above
Movie Humor January 1937, V3N6, as above
Movie Humor February 1937, V3N7, as above
Movie Humor April 1937, V3N9, as above
Movie Merry-Go-Round September 1937, V2N5, bi-monthly, Periodical House, USA. Editor—Frederick Gardener
Paris Magazine April 1933, N20, France

Paris Magazine May 1937, N69, France
Reel Humor February 1938, V1N4, bi-monthly, Periodical House, USA. Editor—Frederick Gardener
Reel Humor December 1938, V2N1, as above
Real Screen Fun May 1936, V2N8, monthly, Tilsam Publications, USA
Real Screen Fun September 1936, V2N12, as above
Real Screen Fun February 1938, V4N4, monthly, Tilsam Publications, USA
Real Screen Fun November 1938, V4N12, as above
Real Screen Fun February 1941, V5N9, as above
Real Screen Fun November 1941, V5N12, as above

Chapter 8
From American Hero to American Psycho: 80 Years of Detective Magazines

Amazing Detective Cases December 1940, V1N2, monthly, Crimes Files, USA. Editor—Robert Levee
Best True Fact Detective 1946, quarterly, Detective House, USA
Crime Detective April 1939, V1N5, monthly, Hillman Periodicals, USA. Editor—Lionel White
Crime Detective June 1941, V3N7, Crime Detective, USA. Editor—George Scullin
Daring Detective January 1938, Country Press, USA
Detective World November 1948, bi-monthly, World at War Publishing, USA
Dynamic Detective June 1937, as above
Dynamic Detective October 1938, as above
Famous Police Cases April 1953, V4N2, bi-monthly, Mr. Magazine, USA. Editor—Everett Meyers
Front Page Detective December 1937, V1N8, Exposed Publishing, USA
Front Page Detective September 1949, V13N5, monthly, Dell Publishing, USA
Manhunt Detective Story Monthly, May 1953, V1N5, Flying Eagle Publications, USA. Editor—John McCloud
Manhunt Detective Story Monthly, August 1953, V1N8, as above
Manhunt Detective Story Monthly, November 1953, V1N11, as above
Manhunt August 1956, V4N8, as above, but Editor—Walter R. Schmidt
Nick Carter Weekly April 12 1902, N276, USA
Photo Detective September 1937, V1N1, monthly, Emess Publishing, USA. Publisher/Editor—Adrian B. Lopez
Police Dragnet Cases March 1956, bi-monthly, Brookside Enterprises, USA
Real Detective September 1942, V9N3, monthly, Sensation Magazine, USA. Editor—Lionel White
Sensation 1942, quarterly, MacFadden Publishing, USA
Special Detective Feb 1954, V17N2, bi-monthly, Special Magazines, USA. Editor—Georgia H. Cooper
Startling Detective January 1955, V46N267, bi-monthly, Fawcett Publications, USA. Editor—Ralph Daigh
Startling Detective July 1958, V29N303, as above
True Police Yearbook 1956, V1N5, as above
True Cases of Women in Crime March 1950, bi-monthly, Detective House, USA
True Cases of Women in Crime January 1950, as above
True Cases of Women in Crime November 1951, as above
Uncensored Detective November 1952, V8N5, monthly, Uncensored Detective, USA

Chapter 9
Naked vs. Nude: American Naturist Magazines 1933 to 1958

American Sunbather November 1957, V9N11, monthly, Outdoor American, USA. Editor—Mervin Mounce
Modern Sunbathing and Hygiene August 1952, V22N63, monthly, USA. Editor—Lee Madison
Modern Sunbathing and Hygiene April 1956, V26N4-107, monthly, USA. Editor—Lee Madison
The Nudist January 1934, monthly, Outdoor Publishing, USA. Editor—Henry S. Huntington
The Nudist 1936, as above
SUN Magazine Jan/Feb 1953, V3N1, bi-monthly, USA. Editor—Ilsley Boone
Sun and Health 1955, V19N33, monthly, International Edition from International Bladforlag, Denmark. Editor—Erik Holm
Sunbathing And Health Magazine July 1945, V7N3, Health Publications Publishing, Canada
Sunbathing For Health Magazine April 1950s, USA
Sunshine & Health December 1940, V9N12, Outdoor Publishing, USA. Editor—Ilsley Boone
Sunshine & Health May 1945, V14N5, as above
Sunshine & Health January 1946, V15N1, as above
Sunshine & Health May 1946, V15N5, as above
Sunshine & Health September 1951, V20N10, as above
Sunshine & Health September 1953, V22N9, as above
Sun Tan May 1953, V2N4, Suntan Publishing, USA. Editor—June Poole

Chapter 10
Sex and Humor: 60 Years of Yuks

A Basinful of Fun, January 1953, N84, monthly, F. Youngman, England
A Basinful of Fun, November 1953, N94, as above
Blighty August 4 1951, N614, weekly, England
The Booby Trap, Aug/Sep 1945, V1N7, bi-monthly, Goodman Publishing, USA
Broadway Laughs (formerly ***Army Laughs***) Spring 1950, V9N2, quarterly, Crestwood Publishing, USA
Bust Out Laffin' 1954, N6, Minoan Publishing, USA
Calgary Eye Opener January 1939, V37N11, monthly, Bob Edwards Publishing, USA
Canadian Tattler November 1939, monthly, International Magazine Publishers, Canada
Capt. Billy's Whiz Bang July 1921, V2N22, Fawcett Publications, USA. Editor—Wilfred Fawcett
Capt. Billy's Whiz Bang May 1924, V5N59, as above
Capt. Billy's Whiz Bang September 1928, V10N116, as above
Capt. Billy's Whiz Bang June 1934, V16N188, Popular Magazines, USA. Editor—Wilfred Fawcett
Caricatura Feb 23 1934, weekly, Argentina
Caricatura Feb 7 1936, as above
Caricatura Feb 14, 1941, as above
Cartoon Comedy Summer 1947, V1N1, quarterly, Zenith Publishing, USA
Cartoon Humor Spring 1949, V13N3, quarterly, Better Publications, USA
Cartoon Humor 1952, V16N3, quarterly, as above
Cheer 1950s, USA
Cheesegals 1950s, Retail News, USA
Chicks and Chuckles October 1956, V2N3, bi-monthly, Enterprise Magazine Management, USA
Chicks and Chuckles April 1957, V3N2, Sports Report, USA
Daffy Comics Winter 1944, quarterly, Comic Art, USA. Editor—Jerry Allen
Fun Riot October 1943, V1N1, bi-monthly, Baffling Mysteries, USA
Fun Riot Spring 1944, V1N3, all as above
Gal Parade 1950s, Alto Publications, USA
Halt August 1942, V1N9, monthly, Crestwood Publishing, USA
Hooey Annual 1939, 9th Edition, Country Press, USA
Imp March 1954, bi-monthly, Beacon Enterprises, USA

Ja-Já Feb 13 1952, weekly, Mexico, Editor—O. Colmenares
Ja-Já Oct. 8 1952, as above
Ja-Já Oct 29 1952, as above
Ja-Já Nov. 5 1952, as above
Jest February1942, V1N2, bi-monthly, Jest Publishing, USA
Joker Summer 1942, USA
Joker Spring 1942, USA
Laff March 1952, V13N12, monthly, monthly, Volitant Publishing, USA. Publisher/Editor—Adrian B. Lopez
Maybe You're Screwy Too! 1950s, Farrell Publishing, USA. Editor—Theodore Irwin
Satire December 1927, V2N2, monthly, Merit Publishing, USA
Screwball Feb/Mar 1949, V8N2, bi-monthly, Crestwood Publishing, USA
Smiles Winter 1947, N20, quarterly, Fifty Crosswards, USA
Smiles April 1956, N76, USA
TV Girls and Gags November 1956, V3N3, bi-monthly, Enterprise Magazine Management, USA
TV Girls and Gags March 1957, V4N2, bi-monthly, Sports Report, USA
TV Girls and Gags May 1957, V4N3, as above
Zing! 1950s, USA
Zing! 1950s, USA
Zippy May 1941, V1N1, USA
Zowie! April 1954, monthly, Youthful Magazines, USA

Chapter 11
Attaboy, Attatürk!: The Turkish Anomaly

Cennet (Paradise) April 3 1954, V2N17, weekly, Hadise Yayinevi (publisher), Turkey
Cennet Bahcesi (Garden of Paradise) 1954, special issue N1, Hadis Publishing, Turkey. Editor—Munir Coskun
Cennet Bahçesi May 15 1954, V1N3, as above
Cennet Bahçesi 1954, V1N8, weekly, as above
Manolya (Magnolia) August 16 1955, V1N2, weekly, Huseyin Kavala (publisher), Turkey
Manolya August 30 1955, V1N4, as above
Manolya September 6 1955, V1N5, as above
Peri June 18 1949, N8, bi-weekly, Turkey, Publisher/Editor—Ahmet Kocer
Peri July 2 1949, N9, as above
Peri January 28 1950, N24, as above
Peri August 26 1950, N39, as above
Peri September 9 1950, N40, as above
Peri January 13 1951, N49, as above
Pleypoy 1970s, Turkey

Chapter 12
Patriotica: Meeting the Needs of Men at War

"At Ease" May 1942, USA
Burlesk August 1942, V1N1, monthly, Your Guide Publications, USA
Burlesk November 1942, as above
Carnival Combined with Show March 1941, monthly, Show Magazine, USA. Editor—Tony Field
Carnival Combined with Show, November 1940, V1N4, as above
Carnival Combined with Show, March 1941, as above
Carnival Combined with Show, February 1942, V2N7, as above
Close-Up Dec/Jan 1942, V1N10, bi-monthly, Close-Up, USA
Gags July 1942, V1N9, bi-monthly, USA. Editor—Charles E. Rubino
Gay Book March 1937, V3N1, monthly, Gay Book, USA. Editor—William H. Kofoed
Gay Book July 1943, V5N6, quarterly—Narrative Publishing, USA
Gay Book March 1945, V6N4, as above
Gayety, September 1941, USA
Gayety, May 1942, USA
G-Eyefuls 1951, Bill Boltin Production, USA
Giggles Fall 1943, Starlite Magazine, USA
Giggles Spring 1945, Volitant Publishing Co, USA
"It" July 1941, V2N4, monthly, Personality Publications, USA
Jest September 1941, V1N2, bi-monthly, Jest Publishing, USA
Jest November 1942, V1N8, as above
Male Home Companion October 1942, V1N1, Select Publications, USA. Editor—Robert L. Richards
Nifty December 1942, Par Publishing, USA. Editor—Charles E. Rubino
Nifty October 1943, Par Publishing, USA
Pictorial Thrill September 1942, V1N7, Crestwood Publishing, USA
"Pin Me Up" 1944, Milrose Publishing, USA
Play November 1943, V2N5, bi-monthly, Play Magazine, USA
Play May 1944, V3N1, bi-monthly, Play Magazine, USA
Sleek March 1942, V1N4, bi-monthly, Close Up, USA
Sleek Sept 1942, V1N7, as above
Slick September 1941, V1N1, as above
Snap August 1941,V1N7, Snap Publishing, USA
Sports Parade and Pin-Ups 1945, one shot, Graphic Enterprises, USA
Spot September 1940, Country Press, USA. Editor—Fred Feldkamp
TNT November 1941, USA
Top Hat 1940s, #3, USA
War Laffs, November 1943, USA
Who is Your Pin-Up Girl? Autumn 1944, V1N9, Gerard Publishing, USA

Chapter 13
Paris-Hollywood: The French Post-War Recovery Effort

Album Sélection de Pin-Up, Paris-Hollywood, Special edition, Paris, France
Les Beautes de Paris et de Hollywood 1940s, N10, bi-weekly, France. Publisher—J.P. Mauclaire
Les Beautes de Paris et de Hollywood Autumn, Imprint Sapho, France
Les Beautes de Paris et de Hollywood Summer, as above
Folies de Paris et de Hollywood April 1958, N132, as above
Folies de Paris et de Hollywood 1950s, Special edition, as above
Paris Frou Frou 1958, N61, as above
Paris-Hollywood 1946, N1, bi-weekly, France
Paris-Hollywood 1947, N5, bi-weekly, France
Paris-Hollywood 1940s, N7, English language edition, France
Paris-Hollywood 1940s, N32, as above
Paris-Hollywood Special edition, as above
Folies de Paris et de Hollywood 1960s, France. Editor—H.B. Giovannoni
Stars et Vedettes 1940s, N14, France
Stars et Vedettes 1950s, N67, as above
Stars et Vedettes 1950s, N69, as above
Stars et Vedettes 1950s, N71, as above

Chapter 14
Dirty Little Magazines: The French Post-War Digest

Adventures Sensuelles 1950s, N1, France
C'est Paris March 1950, France
Chiche 1950s, N1, Fance
Chut! 1950s, France
Clins d'oeil de Paris, 1950s, France
Coucou 1952, Editions du Beau Navire, France
Enquêtes September 1953, N16, France. Editor—V. de Valence
Entracte 1950s, Editions Mistral, Monaco
Évocations 1950s, N18, France
Évocations 1950s, N38, France

Évocations 1950s, N41, France
Fascination 1950s, N4, France
Frin Gale 1950s, France. Editor—Gerant Max Dupuy
La Vie Parisienne November 1957, N83, Publications Georges Ventillard, France
Midi Paname 1950s, N4, Societe des Editions Sprint, France
Mini de Paris 1950s, N1, France
Minuit 1950s, N1, des Editions des Mille et une Nuits, France
Minuit Cinq 1950s, N2, France
Minuit Cinq 1950s, N6, France
Minuit Cinq, 1950s, N8, France
Minuit Cinq 1950s, N17, France
Minuit Cinq 1950s, N24, France
Moi et Toi 1950s, N2, Edite par Secti, France. Editor—R.M. Dupuy
Oh!..les Femmes 1950s, N1, Edition Collection Laura, France
Nouvelle Serie de Revue, 1950s, France
Paris Broadway 1950s, N36, France
Paris Broadway 1950s, N60, France
Paris Broadway 1950s, N62, France
Paris Cocktail 1940, AS Editions, France. Editor—Pierre Ulysse
Paris Cocktail March 1951, N55, as above
Paris Etoiles 1950s, France
Paris-Folies 1940s, N2, Paris Editions, France
Paris-Frivole 1940s, N1, France
Paris Gai 1950s, N3, Edite par S.E.C.T.I., France. Publisher—R.M. Dupuy
Paris Pin-up 1950s, N6, "Document 47", France
Paris Plaisirs May 1952, AS Editions, France
Paris–Riviera 1950s, N45, France
Paris Satan 1950s, Imprimerie Speciale, Des Editions Vue, France. Editor—Maurice Du Moulin
Paris Sex-Appeal August 1950, as above
Paris Tabou March 1950, N6, Editions Extentia, France. Editor—Azarian
Paris Tabou November 1950, N15, as above
Paris Tabou 1951, N20, as above
Paris Tabou March 1952, N30, Editions du Siecle, France
Paris Tabou April 1952, N31, as above
Paris Tabou June 1953, N45, as above
Paris-Zazou 1952, Editions du Beau Navire, France
Regal October 1949, N1, France
Regal September 1950, Editions Extentia, France
Regal 1952, as above
Rose et Noir 1950s, N3, as above
Sensations July 1950, as above
Supervamps 1950s, N2, Edition S.E.C.T.I., France. Editor—R.M. Dupuy
Tentations Sensations 1953, N56, Les Petites Inprimeries, France
V April 1949, monthly, France
Vénus 1950s, N23, France
Volupté 1950s, N19, France

Chapter 15
Northern Europe Rebuilds its Men's Magazines: A Kinder, Gentler Nudism

Die Neue Zeit 1952, "Naturist Olympics" special edition, Germany
Geist und Schönheit 1940s, N5, Verlag "Geist und Schönheit", Germany
Hajo Ortil: Das Waldriff im Meer 1956, Rudolf Zitzmann Verlag, Germany
Health & Efficiency July 1937, V7N7, monthly, Link House, England
La Revue Naturiste Internationale October 1956, N9, West Germany
Lebensfreude February 1950, N2, Verlag Lebensfreude, Germany
Lile du Levant 1950s, France
Naturisme 1954, N43, France
Paradies 1950s, Paradies-Verlag, Germany
Sol Och Skönhet 1954, N8, Denmark
Sonnenfreunde 1950s, N17, Sonnenfreund Verlag, Germany
Tidlösa 1957, N6, Sweden
Unser Dasein January1949, N5, Germany
Vivre d'abord! 1952, Series 3, N31, France
Vivre d'abord! 1954 Series 3, N38, France

Chapter 16
No Coming Back to the Cabaret: Germany Post-War

Bolero 1950s, N49, Germany
Cocktail 1951, N5, Verlag Cocktail, Germany
Corso September 1950, V1N1, Verlag Kruger, Germany
Gondel Magazin December 1950, Germany. Editor—Wolfgang Janicke
Gondel Magazin February 1952, as above
Gondel Magazin April 1952, as above
La Petite 1950s, N1, USA
Mix 1950s, N3, USA
Neue Melange 1952, USA
Neues Kriminalmagazin 1945, V1N9, Münchener Verlagsbuchhandlung, Germany. Editor—Dr. R. Kauka
Paprika 1950s, Germany. Editor—Dr. Wolf Strache
Reigen 1949, N1, German Language, printed in Austria. Editor—Dr. Arthur Werner
Tamburin 1950, Karl Hofmann Verlag, Germany
Top Fit 1950s, N15, Druck-und Verlags-anstalt, Germany
Venus 1949, N4, Venus-Verlag, Germany
Venus 1950s, EDLF, 20 rue Serpente, German language, printed in France
Wörterbuch Sexuallebens 1950, N16, Germany

Chapter 17
The Rest of the World: Obscure Titles from Expected Countries

AUSTRIA
Kleine Pikanterien 1946, N5, Austria
Wiener Magazin 1957, N9, Azet Verlag, Austria
Wiener Magazin 1958, N12, as above
AUSTRALIA
The Australian Sunbather April 1950, V4N5, monthly, Ron Ashworth Publishing, Australia. Editor—Ron Ashworth
Man Magazine March/April 1951, V1N3, bi-monthly, K.G. Murray Publishing, Australia
The Man December 1949, 19N33, Kenmure Press, Australia. Publisher—Ken G. Murray
The Man May/Jun 1954, V28N1, as above
CUBA
Show April 1960, V7N74, Ramallo, Cuba.Editor—Dr. Carlos M. Palma
ITALY
Fiore di Smirne April 1946, Italy
I Labirinti Del III Peccato, 1940s, Italy
Follie! August 1954, V7N7, Italy
Séduction 1954, Italy
THE NETHERLANDS
Capriccio 1950s, N7, Heisterkamp N.V., The Netherlands
Mascotte 1930s, Mulder and Company, Holland
SPAIN
Almanaque Pentalta 1935, Spain
Pimienta, 1950s, N10, Spain

Index

VOLUME I

G

H

I

J

K

L

S

T

U

V

W

Y

Z

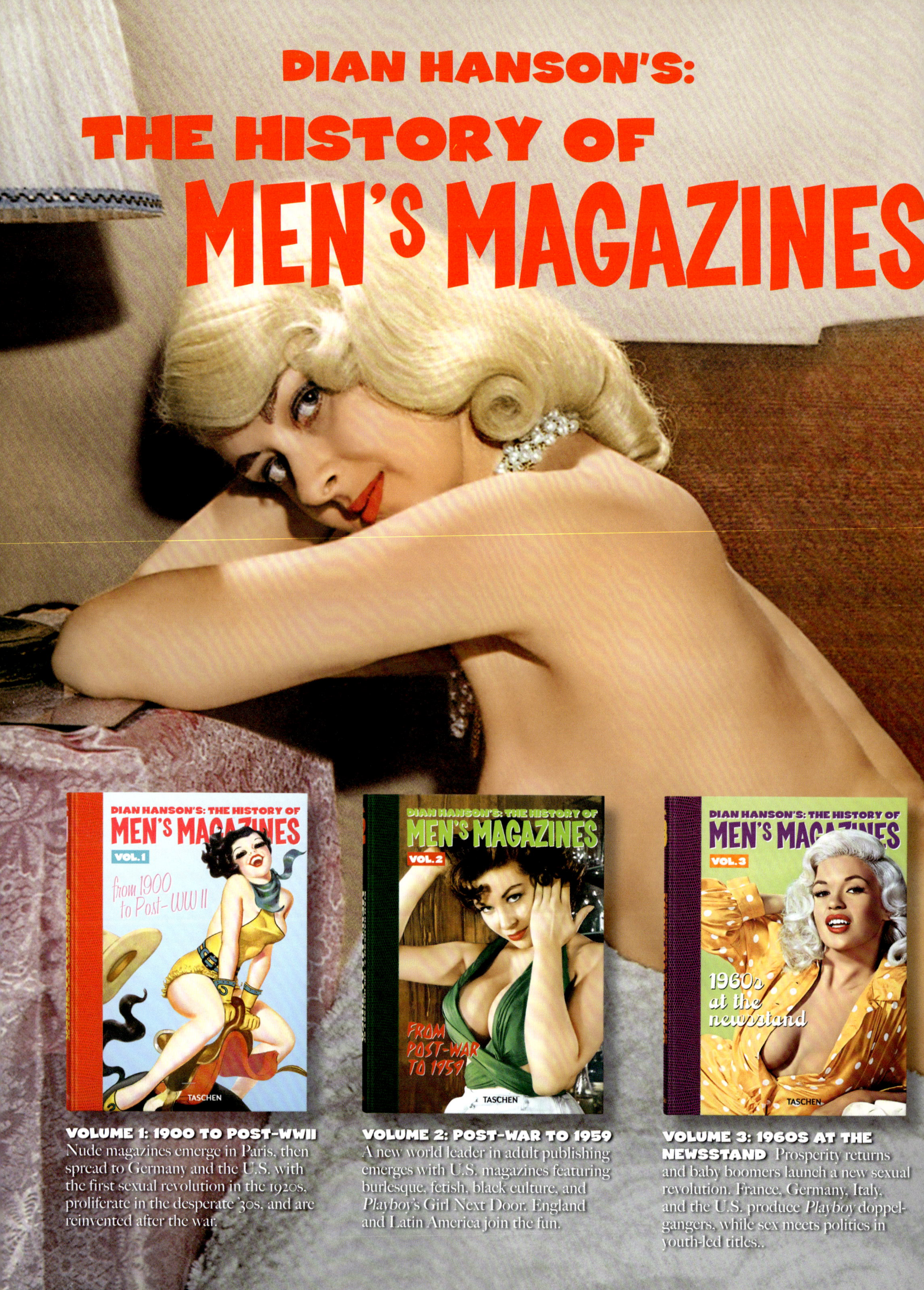
DIAN HANSON'S:
THE HISTORY OF
MEN'S MAGAZINES
DIAN HANSON'S: THE HISTORY OF
MEN'S MAGAZINES
VOL. 1
from 1900 to Post-WW II
TASCHEN
DIAN HANSON'S: THE HISTORY OF
MEN'S MAGAZINES
VOL. 2
FROM POST-WAR TO 1959
TASCHEN
DIAN HANSON'S: THE HISTORY OF
MEN'S MAGAZINES
VOL. 3
1960s at the newsstand
TASCHEN
VOLUME 1: 1900 TO POST-WWII Nude magazines emerge in Paris, then spread to Germany and the U.S. with the first sexual revolution in the 1920s, proliferate in the desperate '30s, and are reinvented after the war.
VOLUME 2: POST-WAR TO 1959 A new world leader in adult publishing emerges with U.S. magazines featuring burlesque, fetish, black culture, and Playboy's Girl Next Door. England and Latin America join the fun.
VOLUME 3: 1960S AT THE NEWSSTAND Prosperity returns and baby boomers launch a new sexual revolution. France, Germany, Italy, and the U.S. produce Playboy doppel-gangers, while sex meets politics in youth-led titles..

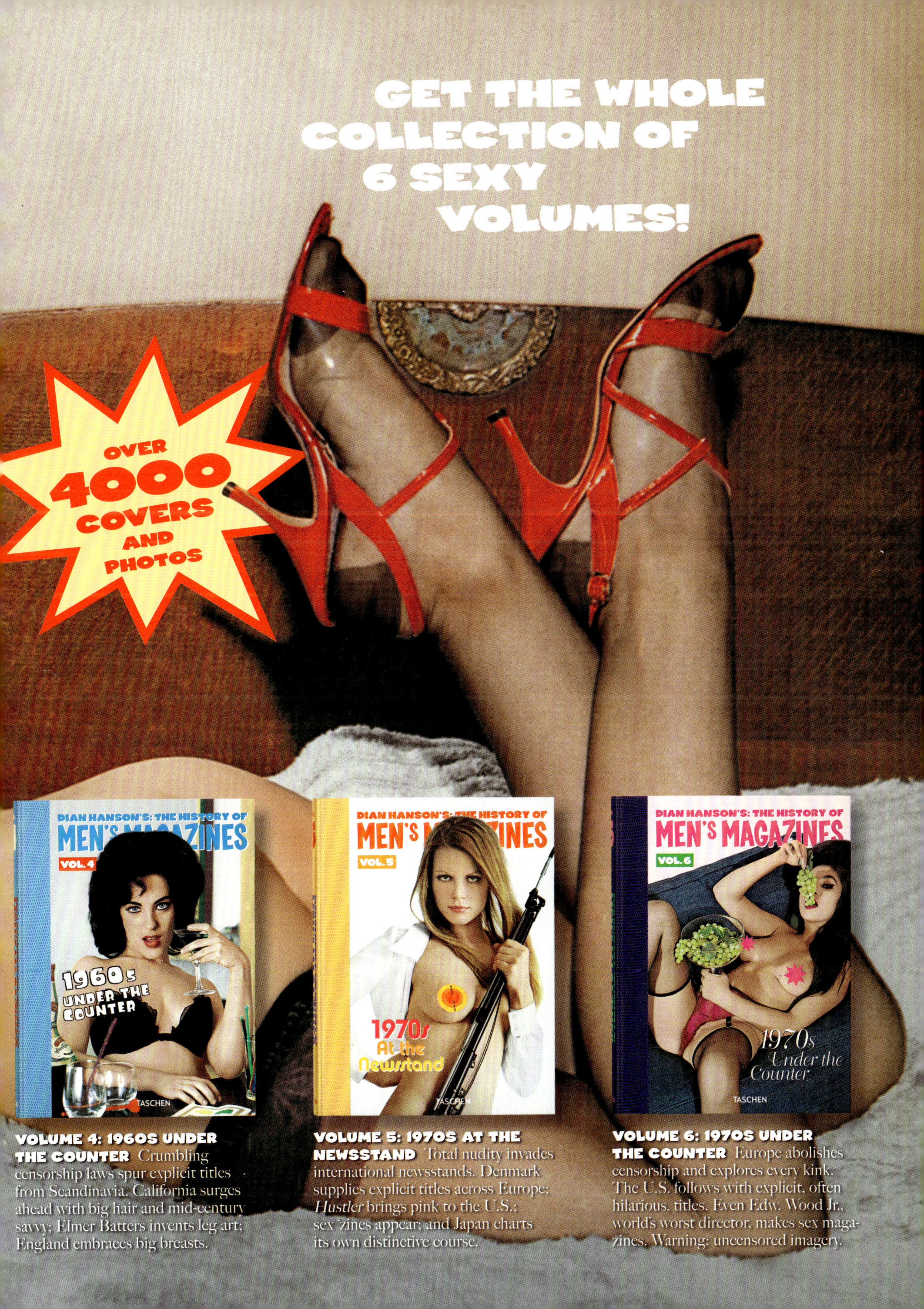

Acknowledgments

There are many people who made this huge project possible; I couldn't have done it without any one of you. If your name isn't here, please forgive my bad memory. Thanks to Michael Feldman, Joe Zinnato@erosarchive.com, Jay A. Gertzman, Robert Gluckson, Mel Gordon, Jutta Hendricks, Eberhard Kemmer, Stefan Klatte, Eric Kroll, Gilles Néret, Horst Neuzner, Yves Riquet, and Mark Rotenberg@vintagenudephotos.com.

Special thanks to Benedikt Taschen, Keith Kinsella, Marc Atlan, Geoff Nicholson, and especially Eric Godtland, collector extraordinaire.

Cover:
YEAR: **1937**. TITLE: **Movie Humor**.
ARTIST: **George Quintana**.COUNTRY: **USA**.

Back cover:
YEAR: **1945**. TITLE: **Giggles**.
COUNTRY: **USA**.